Contemporary
Literary Criticism

Guide to Gale Literary Criticism Series

When you need to review criticism of literary works, these are the Gale series to use:

If the author's death date is: **You should turn to:**

After Dec. 31, 1959
(or author is still living)

CONTEMPORARY LITERARY CRITICISM

for example: Jorge Luis Borges, Anthony Burgess,
William Faulkner, Mary Gordon,
Ernest Hemingway, Iris Murdoch

1900 through 1959

TWENTIETH-CENTURY LITERARY CRITICISM

for example: Willa Cather, F. Scott Fitzgerald,
Henry James, Mark Twain, Virginia Woolf

1800 through 1899

NINETEENTH-CENTURY LITERATURE CRITICISM

for example: Fedor Dostoevski, Nathaniel Hawthorne,
George Sand, William Wordsworth

1400 through 1799

LITERATURE CRITICISM FROM 1400 TO 1800
(excluding Shakespeare)

for example: Anne Bradstreet, Daniel Defoe,
Alexander Pope, François Rabelais,
Jonathan Swift, Phillis Wheatley

SHAKESPEAREAN CRITICISM

Shakespeare's plays and poetry

Antiquity through 1399

CLASSICAL AND MEDIEVAL LITERATURE CRITICISM

for example: Dante, Homer, Plato, Sophocles, Vergil,
the Beowulf Poet

Gale also publishes related criticism series:

CHILDREN'S LITERATURE REVIEW

This series covers authors of all eras who have written for the preschool through high school audience.

SHORT STORY CRITICISM

This series covers the major short fiction writers of all nationalities and periods of literary history.

ISSN 0091-3421

Volume 56

Contemporary Literary Criticism

Excerpts from Criticism of the
Works of Today's Novelists, Poets,
Playwrights, Short Story Writers, Scriptwriters,
and Other Creative Writers

Roger Matuz
EDITOR

Sean R. Pollock
David Segal
Thomas J. Votteler
Robyn V. Young
ASSOCIATE EDITORS

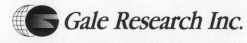 *Gale Research Inc.*

Detroit, New York, Fort Lauderdale, London

STAFF

Roger Matuz, *Editor*

Sean R. Pollock, David Segal, Thomas J. Votteler, Robyn V. Young, *Associate Editors*

Denise Broderick, Christina Cramer, Cathy Falk, Mary K. Gillis, Michael W. Jones,
Ronald S. Nixon, Anne Sharp, Bridget Travers, Debra A. Wells, *Assistant Editors*

Jeanne A. Gough, *Production & Permissions Manager*
Linda M. Pugliese, *Production Supervisor*
Jennifer Gale, Suzanne Powers, Maureen A. Puhl, Lee Ann Welsh, *Editorial Associates*
Donna Craft, Christine A. Galbraith, David G. Oblender, Linda M. Ross,
Editorial Assistants

Victoria B. Cariappa, *Research Supervisor*
Karen D. Kaus, Eric Priehs, Maureen R. Richards, Mary D. Wise, *Editorial Associates*
Heidi N. Fields, Judy L. Gale, Filomena Sgambati, *Editorial Assistants*

Sandra C. Davis, *Permissions Supervisor (Text)*
H. Diane Cooper, Kathy Grell, Josephine M. Keene, Kimberly F. Smilay,
Permissions Associates
Lisa M. Lantz, Camille P. Robinson, Shalice Shah, Denise M. Singleton,
Permissions Assistants

Patricia A. Seefelt, *Permissions Supervisor (Pictures)*
Margaret A. Chamberlain, *Permissions Associate*
Pamela A. Hayes, Lillian Quickley, *Permissions Assistants*

Mary Beth Trimper, *Production Manager*
Anthony J. Scolaro, *Production Assistant*

Arthur Chartow, *Art Director*
C. J. Jonik, *Keyliner*

Laura Bryant, *Production Supervisor*
Louise Gagné, *Internal Production Associate*
Sharana Wier, *Internal Production Assistant*

Contents

Preface   vii

Acknowledgments   xi

Authors Forthcoming in *CLC*   xvii

Preface

Literary criticism is, by definition, "the art of evaluating or analyzing with knowledge and propriety works of literature." The complexity and variety of contemporary literature makes the function of the critic especially important to today's reader. It is the critic who assists the reader in identifying significant new writers, recognizing trends, mastering new terminology, and monitoring scholarly and popular sources of critical opinion. Until the publication of the first volume of *Contemporary Literary Criticism (CLC)* in 1973, there existed no ongoing digest of current literary opinion. *CLC,* therefore, has fulfilled an essential need.

Scope of the Work

CLC presents significant passages from published criticism of works by today's creative writers. Each volume of *CLC* includes excerpted criticism on about thirty-five authors who are now living or who died after December 31, 1959. Nearly 2,000 authors have been included since the series began publication. Since many of the writers covered by *CLC* inspire continual critical commentary, authors frequently appear in more than one volume. There is, of course, no duplication of reprinted criticism.

Authors are selected for inclusion for a variety of reasons, among them the publication or dramatic production of a critically acclaimed new work, the reception of a major literary award, revival of interest in past writings, or the dramatization of a literary work as a film or television screenplay. For example, the present volume includes 1980 Nobel Laureate Czesław Miłosz; C. K. Williams, whose poetry collection *Flesh and Blood* won the National Book Critics Circle Award; and Georges Perec, whose novel *Life: A User's Manual* received much attention from critics and readers. Perhaps most importantly, works that frequently appear on the syllabuses of high school and college literature classes are represented by individual entries in *CLC; The Catcher in the Rye,* by J. D. Salinger, and *The Time of Your Life,* by William Saroyan, are examples of works of this stature covered in the present volume. Attention is also given to several other groups of writers—authors of considerable public interest—about whose work criticism is often difficult to locate. These include mystery and science fiction writers, literary and social critics, foreign writers, and authors who represent particular ethnic groups in the United States.

Format of the Book

Altogether there are about 600 individual excerpts in each volume—with approximately seventeen excerpts per author—taken from hundreds of book review periodicals, general magazines, scholarly journals, monographs, and books. Entries include critical evaluations spanning from the beginning of an author's career to the most current commentary. Interviews, feature articles, and other published writings that offer insight into the authors works are also presented. Emphasis has been placed on expanding the sources for criticism by including an increasing number of scholarly and specialized periodicals. Students, teachers, librarians, and researchers will find that the generous excerpts and supplementary material provided by *CLC* supply them with vital information needed to write a term paper, analyze a poem, or lead a book discussion group. In addition, complete bibliographical citations facilitate the location of the original source and provide all of the information necessary for a term paper footnote or bibliography.

A *CLC* author entry consists of the following elements:

- The **author heading** cites the author's full name, followed by birth date, and death date when applicable. The portion of the name outside parentheses denotes the form under which the author has most commonly published. If an author has written consistently under a pseudonym, the pseudonym will be listed in the author heading and the real name given on the first line of the biographical and critical introduction. Also located at the beginning of the introduction to the author entry are any important name variations under which an author has written. Uncertainty as to a birth or death date is indicated by question marks.

- A **portrait** of the author is included when available.

- A brief **biographical and critical introduction** to the author and his or her work precedes the excerpted criticism. However, *CLC* is not intended to be a definitive biographical source. Therefore, *cross-references* have been included to direct readers to these useful sources published by Gale Research: *Contemporary Authors,* which includes detailed biographical and bibliographical sketches of more than 92,000 authors; *Children's Literature Review,* which presents excerpted criticism on the works of authors of children's books; *Something about the Author,* which contains heavily illustrated biographical sketches of writers and illustrators who create books for children and young adults; *Dictionary of Literary Biography,* which provides original evaluations and detailed biographies of authors important to literary history; *Contemporary Authors Autobiography Series,* which offers autobiographical essays by prominent writers; and *Something about the Author Autobiography Series,* which presents autobiographical essays by authors of interest to young readers. Previous volumes of *CLC* in which the author has been featured are also listed in the introduction.

• The **excerpted criticism** represents various kinds of critical writing: a particular essay may be descriptive, interpretive, textual, appreciative, comparative, or generic. It may range in form from the brief review to the scholarly exegesis. Essays are selected by the editors to reflect the spectrum of opinion about a specific work or about an author's literary career in general. The excerpts are presented chronologically, adding a useful perspective to the entry. All titles by the author featured in the entry are printed in boldface type, which enables the reader to easily identify the works being discussed. Publication information (such as publisher names and book prices) and parenthetical numerical references (such as footnotes or page and line references to specific editions of a work) have been deleted at the editors' discretion to provide smoother reading of the text.

• A complete **bibliographical citation** designed to help the user find the original essay or book follows each excerpt.

Other Features

• A list of **Authors Forthcoming in *CLC*** previews the authors to be researched for future volumes.

• An **Acknowledgments** section lists the copyright holders who have granted permission to reprint material in this volume of *CLC*. It does not, however, list every book or periodical reprinted or consulted during the preparation of the volume.

• A **Cumulative Author Index** lists all the authors who have appeared in *CLC, Twentieth-Century Literary Criticism, Nineteenth-Century Literature Criticism, Literature Criticism from 1400 to 1800,* and *Classical and Medieval Literature Criticism,* with cross-references to these Gale series: *Short Story Criticism, Children's Literature Review, Contemporary Authors, Contemporary Authors Autobiography Series, Contemporary Authors Bibliographical Series, Dictionary of Literary Biography, Something about the Author, Something about the Author Autobiography Series, Yesterday's Authors of Books for Children,* and *Authors & Artists for Young Adults.* Readers will welcome this cumulated author index as a useful tool for locating an author within the various series. The index, which lists birth and death dates when available, will be particularly valuable for those authors who are identified with a certain period but whose death date causes them to be placed in another, or for those authors whose careers span two periods. For example, Ernest Hemingway is found in *CLC,* yet a writer often associated with him, F. Scott Fitzgerald, is found in *Twentieth-Century Literary Criticism.*

• A **Cumulative Nationality Index** alphabetically lists all authors featured in *CLC* by nationality, followed by numbers corresponding to the volumes in which they appear.

• A **Title Index** alphabetically lists all titles reviewed in the current volume of *CLC* followed by author's name and the corresponding page numbers where they are discussed. English translations of foreign titles and variations of titles are cross-referenced to the title under which a work was originally published. Titles of novels, novellas, dramas, films, record albums, and poetry, short story, and essay collections are printed in italics, while all individual poems, short stories, essays, and songs are printed in roman type within quotation marks; when published separately (e.g., T.S. Eliot's poem *The Waste Land*), the title will also be printed in italics.

• In response to numerous suggestions from librarians, Gale has also produced a **special paperbound edition** of the *CLC* title index. This annual cumulation, which alphabetically lists all titles reviewed in the series, is available to all customers and will be published with the first volume of *CLC* issued in each calendar year. Additional copies of the index are available upon request. Librarians and patrons will welcome this separate index: it saves shelf space, is easily disposable upon receipt of the following year's cumulation, and is more portable and thus easier to use than was previously possible.

Suggestions Are Welcome

The editors welcome the comments and suggestions of readers to expand the coverage and enhance the usefulness of the series. Please feel free to contact us by letter or by calling our toll-free number: 1-800-347-GALE.

Acknowledgments

The editors wish to thank the copyright holders of the excerpted criticism included in this volume, the permissions managers of many book and magazine publishing companies for assisting us in securing reprint rights, and Anthony Bogucki for assistance with copyright research. We are also grateful to the staffs of the Detroit Public Library, the Library of Congress, the University of Detroit Library, the University of Michigan Library, and the Wayne State University Library for making their resources available to us. Following is a list of the copyright holders who have granted us permission to reprint material in this volume of *CLC*. Every effort has been made to trace copyright, but if omissions have been made, please let us know.

COPYRIGHTED EXCERPTS IN *CLC*, VOLUME 56, WERE REPRINTED FROM THE FOLLOWING PERIODICALS:

America, v. 157, November 28, 1987 for " 'Red Noses' in Chicago" by Gary Seibert. © 1987. All rights reserved. Reprinted with permission of the author./ v. CIV, January 7, 1961. © 1961. All rights reserved. Reprinted with permission of America Press, Inc., 106 West 56th Street, New York, NY 10019.—*The American Book Review,* v. 2, February, 1980; v. 3, September-October, 1981; v. 7, March-April, 1985; v. 9, January-February, 1987; v. 10, May-June, 1988; v. 11, March-April, 1989. © 1980, 1981, 1985, 1987, 1988, 1989 by *The American Book Review.* All reprinted by permission of the publisher.—*American Quarterly,* v. XXIX, Winter, 1977 for "A Retrospective Look at 'The Catcher in the Rye' " by Gerald Rosen. Copyright 1977, American Studies Association. Reprinted by permission of the publisher and the author.—*American Speech,* v. XXXIV, October, 1959 for "The Language of 'The Catcher in the Rye' " by Donald P. Costello. Copyright 1959 by Columbia University Press. Renewed 1987 by The University of Alabama Press. Reprinted by permission of the author.—*The Antigonish Review,* n. 66-67, Summer-Autumn, 1986 for a review of "As Birds Bring Forth the Sun and Other Stories" by Janice Kulyk Keefer. Copyright 1986 by the author. Reprinted by permission of the publisher and the author.—*The Antioch Review,* v. XXXII, 1973. Copyright © 1973 by the Antioch Review Inc. Reprinted by permission of the Editors.—*Ariel: A Review of International English Fiction,* v. 15, April, 1984 for "The Fiction of Patricia Grace" by John B. Beston. Copyright © 1984 The Board of Governors, The University of Calgary. Reprinted by permission of the publisher and the author.—*The Atlantic Monthly,* v. 213, June, 1964 for "Talent in Search of a Subject" by William Barrett; v. 224, August, 1969 for "The London Show" by Yorick Blumenfeld. Copyright 1964, 1969 by The Atlantic Monthly Company, Boston, MA. Both reprinted by permission of the respective authors.—*Atlantic Provinces Book Review,* v. 9, December, 1982. © APBR Service. Reprinted by permission of the publisher.—*Belles Lettres: A Review of Books by Women,* v. 3, July-August, 1988. Reprinted by permission of the publisher.—*Best Sellers,* v. 33, October 15, 1973. Copyright 1973, by the University of Scranton. Reprinted by permission of the publisher./ v. 37, February, 1978. Copyright © 1978 Helen Dwight Reid Educational Foundation. Reprinted by permission of the publisher.—*Black World,* v. XXV, April, 1976 for a review of "What the Wine-Sellers Buy" by Xavier Nicholas. © 1976 Johnson Publishing Company, Inc. Reprinted by permission of *Black World* and the author.—*The Bloomsbury Review,* v. 8, March-April, 1988 for "Art & Artiface" by James Sallis. Copyright © by Owaissa Communications Company, Inc. 1988. Reprinted by permission of the author.—*Book World—The Sunday Herald Tribune,* January 31, 1965. © 1965, *The Washington Post.* Reprinted by permission of the publisher.—*Book Week—World Journal Tribune,* September 25, 1966. ©1966, *The Washington Post.* Reprinted by permission of the publisher.—*Book World—The Washington Post,* June 14, 1970 for "A Master's Farewell" by Denis Donoghue; September 13, 1970 for "An Anguish Worn with a Difference" by Daniel Stern. © 1970 Postrib Corp. Both reprinted by permission of *The Washington Post* and the respective authors./ June 12, 1977; August 17, 1980; January 12, 1986; December 20, 1987; June 12, 1988; June 19, 1988; September 18, 1988; January 8, 1989. © 1977, 1980, 1986, 1987, 1988, 1989, *The Washington Post.* All reprinted by permission of the publisher.—*Books,* New York, August 26, 1962; April 7, 1963. © 1962, 1963 I. H. T. Corporation. Both reprinted by permission of the publisher.—*Books Abroad,* v. 39, Summer, 1965; v. 40, Autumn, 1966; v. 45, Winter, 1971. Copyright 1965, 1966, 1971 by the University of Oklahoma Press. All reprinted by permission of the publisher.—*Books and Bookmen,* n. 345, June, 1984 for "Sex, Love and Marriage" by Jonathan Loake; n. 364, February, 1986 for a review of "A Piece of Mine" by Diana Hinds. © copyright the respective authors 1984, 1986.—*Books in Canada,* v. 14, March, 1985./ v. 15, August-September, 1986 for "Home Is the Haunter" by Jack Hodgins; v. 17, March, 1988 for "Breakdancing the Invisible" by Mary di Michele. Both reprinted by permission of the respective authors.—*Brick: A Journal of Reviews,* n. 27, Spring, 1986; n. 31, Fall, 1987. Both reprinted by permission of the publisher.—*The Canadian Forum,* v. LVI, June-July, 1976 for "Equivocal Victories" by Jon Kertzer; v. LX, May, 1980 for "Benediction and Babel" by Keith Garebian; v. LXIV, February, 1985 for "Thesen's Pose" by Bert Almon; v. LXVI, August-September, 1986 for "Modern Myths" by Fraser Sutherland. All reprinted by permission of the respective authors.—*Canadian Literature,* n. 76, Spring, 1978 for "Story and Teller" by Laurence Ricou; n. 107, Winter, 1985 for "Signatures of Time: Alistair MacLeod & His Short Stories" by Colin Nicholson; n. 112, Spring, 1987 for "Lowry's Mouths" by Ronald Binns. All reprinted by permission of the respective authors.—*The Christian Science*

'Kanthapura' to 'The Serpent and the Rope'," in *Indo-English Literature: A Collection of Critical Essays.* Edited by K. K. Sharma. Vimal Prakashan, 1977. © 1977, K. K. Sharma.—Riggan, William. From *Picaros, Madmen, Naïfs, and Clowns: The Unreliable First-Person Narrator.* University of Oklahoma Press, 1981. Copyright © 1981 by the University of Oklahoma Press, Norman, Publishing Division of the University. Reprinted by permission of the publisher.—Sarachchandra, Ediriwira. From "Illusion and Reality: Raja Rao as Novelist," in *Only Connect: Literary Perspectives East and West.* Edited by Guy Amirthanayagam and S. C. Harrex. Centre for Research in the New Literatures in English & East-West Center, 1981. Copyright © Guy Amirthanayagam & S. C. Harrex 1981. All rights reserved.—Schulz, Max F. From *Black Humor Fiction of the Sixties: A Pluralistic Definition of Man and His World.* Ohio University Press, 1973. © 1973 by Max F. Schulz. All rights reserved. Reprinted by permission of the publisher.—Simon, John. From *Uneasy Stages: A Chronicle of the New York Theater 1964-1973.* Random House, 1975. Copyright © 1975 by John Simon. Reprinted by permission of Random House, Inc.—Thorpe, Michael. From *The Poetry of Edmund Blunden.* Bridge Books, 1971. © Michael Thorpe 1971. Reprinted by permission of the author.—Thorslev, Peter L., Jr. From "The Poetry of Richard Eberhart," in *Poets in Progress: Critical Prefaces to Ten Contemporary Americans.* Edited by Edward Hungerford. Northwestern University Press, 1962. Copyright © 1962, 1967 Northwestern University Press. Reprinted by permission of the publisher.—Walker, Alice. From a foreword to *A Piece of Mine.* By J. California Cooper. Wild Trees Press, 1984. Copyright © 1984 Joan Cooper. Reprinted by permission of the author.—Wilson, Edmund. From *Classics and Commercials: A Literary Chronicle of the Forties.* Farrar, Straus and Company, 1950. Copyright 1950 by Edmund Wilson. Renewed 1977 by Elena Wilson. All rights reserved. Reprinted by permission of Farrar, Straus and Giroux, Inc.

PERMISSION TO REPRINT PHOTOGRAPHS APPEARING IN *CLC*, VOLUME 56, WAS RECEIVED FROM THE FOLLOWING SOURCES:

Photograph by Peter Bayliss. Courtesy of Peter Barnes: **p. 1;** Courtesy of Steven Berkoff: **p. 11;** Courtesy of Claire M. Blunden: **p. 24;** © Jerry Bauer: **pp. 54, 158, 202, 275, 283, 366;** Courtesy of Wild Trees Press: **p. 69;** © Nancy Crampton: **p. 73;** Photograph by Patricia J. O'Donohue. Reproduced by permission of Bruce Jay Friedman: **p. 92;** Photograph by Robert Cross. Courtesy of Patricia Grace: **p. 110;** Photograph by Robert Tragesser: **p. 124;** © 1988 by Fred McDarrah: **pp. 135, 146;** © Karel Kestner: **p. 162;** Courtesy of Rhoda Lerman: **p. 175;** Dayna Smith/*The Washington Post*: **p. 181;** Photograph by Wallace Ellison. Courtesy of McClelland & Stewart: **p. 191;** Sara Krulwich/NYT Pictures: **p. 220;** © Rollie McKenna: **p. 230;** Photograph by Anne de Brunhoff: **p. 252;** German Information Center: **p. 389;** Courtesy of William Heinemann: **p. 407;** Courtesy of Sharon Thesen: **p. 414;** © Jed M. Williams: **p. 424;** Courtesy of David Williamson: **p. 430.**

Authors Forthcoming in *CLC*

Isabel Allende (Chilean novelist)—In her novels *The House of Spirits, Of Love and Shadows,* and the recent *Eva Luna,* Allende combines elements of realism and fantasy to examine the tumultuous social and political history of South America.

Samuel Beckett (Irish-born dramatist and novelist)—A recipient of the Nobel Prize in Literature, Beckett often combines humor and tragedy in his works to create an existential view of the human condition in which life is regarded as meaningless. Beckett's entry will focus on his seminal absurdist drama, *Waiting for Godot.*

T. S. Eliot (English poet, critic, and dramatist)—A principal founder of modernism, Eliot greatly influenced modern letters with his innovative and distinctively erudite verse and criticism. Eliot's entry will focus on *The Waste Land,* an epic widely considered among the major works of twentieth-century poetry.

Percival Everett (American novelist and short story writer)—An author of tragicomic fiction, Everett often focuses upon characters who transcend destructive personal relationships to achieve a sense of self-worth. His novels include *Suder* and *Walk Me to the Distance.*

Richard Greenberg (American dramatist and scriptwriter)—In his plays *The Moderati,* a satire of self-absorbed literary society, and *Eastern Standard,* a critique of young middle-class professionals, Greenberg uses sympathy and humor to explore the American obsession with wealth and materialism.

Danilo Kiš (Yugoslavian novelist and short story writer)—Kiš first attracted critical acclaim in Western countries for his novels *Garden, Ashes* and *A Tomb for Boris Davidovich,* both of which focus upon the persecution of European Jews during World War II. Kiš's recently translated short story collection, *The Encyclopedia of the Dead,* has further enhanced his international reputation.

Peter Klappert (American poet)—Klappert garnered praise for the wit and technical innovations of his first poetry collection, *Lugging Vegetables to Nantucket,* for which he received the Yale Series of Younger Poets Award. His sequence *The Idiot Princess of the Last Dynasty* has been compared to such celebrated works as Ezra Pound's *Cantos* and John Berryman's *The Dream Songs.*

Cormac McCarthy (American novelist) —McCarthy is regarded as an important contributor to the Southern Gothic tradition as exemplified by such authors as William Faulkner, Carson McCullers, and Flannery O'Connor. McCarthy's novels, which are often set in his native Tennessee, are praised for their inventive dialect and powerful examinations of evil.

Mbongeni Ngema (South African dramatist)—Ngema's plays illustrate the consequences of apartheid and humanity's capacity for injustice. His recent musical drama *Sarafina!,* inspired by the Soweto uprising of 1976, chronicles the efforts of South African high school students to fashion a play from their country's tragic history.

Andrei Voznesensky (Russian poet)—A protégé of Boris Pasternak, Voznesensky is one of the Soviet Union's most prestigious contemporary poets. His complex experimental verse reveals a profound love for his country and often explores the alienation of youth in industrial society.

Fernando Arrabal (Moroccan dramatist and novelist)—Influenced by the Surrealist movement, Arrabal is best known for his macabre plays written in the tradition of the Theater of the Absurd. His works often examine human brutality and sexuality through the perspectives of children.

Cyrus Colter (American novelist and short story writer)—In his fiction, Colter attempts to bridge the gap he perceives between the experiences of black Americans and the ways in which they have been represented in literature. His deterministic plots emphasize the universality of his middle-class characters and their problems with loneliness, alienation, guilt, and communication.

Douglas Crase (American poet and critic)—A poet whose first collection, *The Revisionist*, earned high praise, Crase focuses upon the American landscape and such concerns as history and ecology. Critics often compare Crase's bold style to those of Wallace Stevens and Walt Whitman.

William Golding (English novelist and short story writer)—Winner of the 1983 Nobel Prize in literature, Golding is best known for his novel *The Lord of the Flies*. Commentary in his entry will focus on this allegorical work, which is widely regarded as a powerful psychological and sociological fable about the primal savagery underlying civilized behavior.

Chester Himes (American short story writer and novelist)—Perhaps best known for *Cotton Comes to Harlem*, one in a series of highly regarded detective novels set in New York that combine irony with biting humor, Himes is considered a valuable contributor to the American tradition of black protest fiction for his vehement portraits of racial oppression and black resistance.

Joyce Johnson (American novelist, short story writer, and autobiographer)—In her fiction, Johnson often relates her involvement with various members of the 1950s Beat generation, providing a rare female perspective on the era and movement. *Minor Characters*, a revealing, candid memoir of her romance with Jack Kerouac, won the National Book Critics Circle Award.

Maxine Hong Kingston (American autobiographer, short story writer, and novelist)—In her memoirs, Kingston blends myth, legend, and history to examine her dual heritage as a Chinese American. Kingston's entry will include commentary on *The Woman Warrior: Memoirs of a Girlhood among Ghosts*, a standard text in women's studies courses, as well as *Tripmaster Monkey*, her recent first novel.

Michael Moorcock (English novelist and editor)—Moorcock is associated with the British "New Wave" literary movement of the 1960s that introduced experimental techniques and a wider range of subject matter to fantasy and science fiction literature.

Christopher Nolan (Irish poet, short story writer, and autobiographer)—Nolan won wide acclaim for his first collection of poetry, *Dam Burst of Dreams*, and his autobiographical work, *Under the Eye of the Clock*. Nolan often describes his experiences as a paralyzed mute in an exhilarating prose style, which has been compared to that of James Joyce for its use of Celtic-styled alliteration and invented words.

Alice Walker (American novelist, poet, and essayist)—Regarded as an important chronicler of African-American life, Walker is best known for her novel *The Color Purple*, for which she received the Pulitzer Prize in fiction. Commentary in this entry will focus on Walker's recent novel *The Temple of My Familiar*, which concerns the multiple lives of a reincarnated woman.

Peter Barnes

1931-

English dramatist, scriptwriter, editor, and critic.

In his plays, Barnes combines farce and slapstick with witty dialogue to create social commentaries that often mock the British class system. Barnes integrates such diverse elements as opera, historical tragedy, musical comedy, modern slang, and literary allusions, adopting expansive settings and manic plots to evoke the vacuousness and absurdity that he believes are inherent in upper-class contemporary society. Bernard F. Dukore observed: "Barnes juggles the audience's moods and enables them to examine critically, detached and with a smile, the social values and attitudes he scrutinizes." While occasionally faulting Barnes's works as undisciplined and excessive, critics have commended his creative manipulation of language.

Barnes wrote several plays in the early 1960s, including *The Time of the Barracudas* (1963) and *Sclerosis* (1965), but first received significant critical attention for *The Ruling Class* (1968), a satire on the manners and customs of the British upper class. This work revolves around the fourteenth Earl of Gurney, a paranoid schizophrenic named Jack who believes he is Jesus Christ. Jack's pontifications on love, tolerance, and humility appall his elitist family, who attempt to cure him of his delusion. When they finally succeed, Jack reacts by adopting the persona of Jack the Ripper. Murdering lower-class women and exercising censorious justice, Jack becomes an accepted member of his family and the House of Lords. Although Barnes's swift comedic transitions puzzled several critics, many lauded his colorful imagery. Julius Novick asserted: "[Barnes] is a good hater. His work expresses a visceral loathing and disgust for the entrenchments of national feeling, such as no American playwright has been able to equal; and this loathing, expressed in vivid images of madness, gives his work an undeniable power."

Barnes's next two works, *Leonardo's Last Supper* (1969) and *Noonday Demons* (1969), are one-act plays that were originally presented as a joint production. These pieces were intended as allegories affirming the power of egoism over altruism. Set during the Italian Renaissance, *Leonardo's Last Supper* involves a middle-class family that yearns for the wealth and authority of the elite. To acquire these advantages, they kill Leonardo da Vinci and receive a tremendous burial commission. *Noonday Demons* concerns two fourth-century hermits who argue over the severity of their anguish, each insisting that he has suffered the most for God. *The Bewitched* (1974) chronicles the search for a successor to the throne of Spain at the beginning of the eighteenth century. Reiterating Barnes's vexation with the aristocracy, this farce focuses on Carlos II, the country's inept leader, whose many weaknesses precipitated the War of the Spanish Succession.

In *Laughter!* (1978), which examines malice, Barnes seeks to demonstrate that laughter merely evades life's disconcerting truths rather than alleviating human misery. The first act of *Laughter!* explores capricious cruelty through a darkly humorous account of Ivan the Terrible's reign in Russia during the sixteenth century, while the second act, set in a concen-

tration camp, illustrates how human brutality has evolved into deliberate, organized madness. Barnes's depiction of Auschwitz includes tap-dancing inmates who tell jokes while being gassed to death. Regarded as Barnes's most controversial work, *Laughter!* was condemned by critics who interpreted the play as a mockery of the Holocaust. *Red Noses,* written in 1978 but first performed in 1985, also questions the true purpose of laughter. To try to ease despair over the Black Plague, the ruling class of medieval Britain authorizes a monk to assemble a comedy troupe, the Red Noses, to amuse the dying populace. Their comedic success does not lessen the anguish, however, and the company eventually realizes that it has been used by the state to avoid vital issues and concerns of the ill-fated proletariat. Although English critics contended that Barnes's themes were becoming redundant, *Red Noses* garnered praise from American reviewers.

Besides writing his own plays, Barnes has adapted and edited the works of other authors, most notably those of the seventeenth-century Jacobean dramatist Ben Jonson. He has also contributed scripts to British radio and television and has written several screenplays, including the film version of *The Ruling Class.*

(See also *CLC,* Vol. 5; *Contemporary Authors,* Vols. 65-68; and *Dictionary of Literary Biography,* Vol. 13.)

IRVING WARDLE

Hanging judges, blood-sports enthusiasts and birch-wielding matrons are among the favorite targets of British satirists, but they have never prompted anything quite as wild as Peter Barnes's *The Ruling Class*. . . .

Although you might not notice it under the flood of extravagant fantasy, which takes in everything from Italian opera to melodramatic parody, the play is obsessively concerned with the tradition of British violence sanctioned by the upper class. Mr. Barnes illustrates it through the story of the 14th Earl of Gurney, released from a mental home to be married off and shut up again once he has produced an heir to the title.

The Earl, however, sees himself as Jesus Christ; and so scandalized is the family (particularly Bishop Gurney) at his priapic brand of worship that they confront him with a rival messiah. The trick seems to work: instead of preaching love, he now makes acceptable public speeches on discipline and punishment. In the setting of the Gurney mansion and the House of Lords no one notices that he has now changed into Jack the Ripper.

So loaded is this fable with vaudeville routines and fusillades of gags, that the audience is often left panting in the rear. But . . . Mr. Barnes has volcanic powers of comic invention and is one of God's gifts to actors.

Irving Wardle, " 'The Ruling Class', Satire on Violence, Staged in London," in The New York Times, *February 28, 1969, p. 31.*

YORICK BLUMENFELD

With Parliament bogged down much of this spring in an endless debate on the reform of the House of Lords, Peter Barnes hoped that his *The Ruling Class* might deliver the coup de grace. There is no denying that this comedy is a brilliant sequence of gibes at the Establishment. One would have to search far afield for anyone who could flog an old horse better than Mr. Barnes—but then the British are renowned as flagellists. In the program note to *The Ruling Class* Barnes condemns "the deadly servitude of naturalism." What he strives for is a dramatic reality of "opposites where everything is simultaneously tragic and ridiculous."

The Ruling Class opens as the thirteenth Earl of Gurney, a hanging judge, is taking his evening exercise dressed in a tutu. He climbs a stepladder over his ancestral bed and puts the hangman's noose around his neck. Usually this bit of eroticism is followed by a whiskey and soda. This time, however, he slips, and his butler finds him swiveling for real. He is succeeded by Jack, the fourteenth Earl of Gurney. . . . Jack is a certified lunatic who proclaims that he's the Trinity. When asked why he thinks he is God, Gurney answers: "When I pray to Him I find I am talking to myself." Indeed, while the card-carrying Communist butler pours tea, his nibs raves happily from a wooden cross preaching love, sex, and tolerance. The ruling class, according to Barnes, rejects Gurney's beatitudes as a cold, mean, greedy, and thoroughly self-absorbed group.

When confronted by another madman, a Scot who also believes himself to be God, the fourteenth Earl really goes mad. He remembers that there is also a God of wrath and transforms himself into Jack the Ripper, slashing away at the aristocratic Establishment. This time, however, he is regarded as eminently sane by society. Gurney, addressing the crutch- and earphone-filled debating chamber of a decrepit House of Lords, denounces fornication and homosexuality. Eulogizing the hangman, Gurney is applauded by the honorable assemblage.

But what is Barnes really saying? The cornerstone of English society is certainly not the public hangman. And contrary to his derogatory satire, the Lords have been in the very forefront of reform: abolishing the death penalty and liberalizing the laws on homosexuality which the popularly elected chamber of Parliament was loath to discuss. The implication is that conservatism, or the safeguarding of the traditions of the past, is madness. If this is indeed Barnes's message, then it is a grave oversimplification.

The critics hailed *The Ruling Class* as "uproariously funny." They hardly seemed perturbed by the savagery of its neo-Jacobean ridicule. However, if Barnes had been attacking only a heraldic Britain which exists solely in tourist brochures, would the audiences have found it so funny? It seems anomalous that the upper-class attendance at the theater should titter so nervously about its social standing when darts have been thrown at it for so many decades. The welfare state is now a generation old, the *Times* is no longer the stuffy representative of a wooden culture. And yet Peter Barnes writes as if nothing had happened. (pp. 99-100)

Yorick Blumenfeld, "The London Show," in The Atlantic Monthly, *Vol. 224, No. 2, August, 1969, pp. 99-101.*

JULIUS NOVICK

"Alienation," somebody has remarked, "is when your country's in a war and you want the other side to win." It is no secret that many Americans, including a particularly large number of artists and intellectuals, are becoming alienated in this sense. . . . Many people, inspired by a revulsion against the [Vietnam] war, are moving toward a deep and wide rejection of our country; if we have done *this,* they feel, we must be a corrupt and evil nation, and corruption and evil must be deeply rooted in our national past.

In the theater, the two most significant expressions of this feeling have been Howard Sackler's *The Great White Hope* and Arthur Kopit's *Indians.* . . . *The Ruling Class* expresses a similar revulsion toward the national traditions and patriotic attitudes of our allies and friends in Great Britain. As the title indicates, Barnes concentrates his scorn on the aristocracy, but he seems to feel that this class still retains its power, and that it has shaped the tradition of British nationhood.

The hero of *The Ruling Class* is "the Queen's trusty and right well-beloved cousin" Jack, the fourteenth Earl of Gurney, who is a paranoid schizophrenic. Jack is convinced that he is not Jack but God, and that God is love. He is a friendly, mellifluous, and harmless madman, but his family finds his madness intolerable. They try to effect a cure by confronting him, in a scene of genuine horror, with a ferocious Scots madman named McKyle, who insists that *he* is God. Clearly they can't both be God, and the Earl yields, apparently cured.

But he is only mad in a new way. They have insisted that he is not the God of Love, but Jack; very well, he will be "God Almighty, God the lawgiver, the judge," but at the same time he will be Jack—Jack the Ripper. He embarks upon a career of mouthing reactionary platitudes, with a heavy emphasis on sanguinary, retributive justice, and stabbing every woman who makes sexual advances to him. The ruling class accepts him joyfully as one of their own, and at the end of the play, resplendent in his coronation robes, he takes his rightful place in the House of Lords.

The Ruling Class begins as a fairly cheerful satirical comedy, scattered with some pretty cheap jokes. ("I don't mince words. I prefer them parboiled, fried, or scrambled." "Well, it's true, as God is my witness—no, you weren't there, JC." "For what I am about to receive, may I make Myself truly thankful.") Steadily it darkens, into scenes of the blackest irony and horror. But the transitions and contrasts are clumsily managed, and the cheerfulness and the horror tend to trip each other up. In fact, Barnes has written a distinctly messy play. I think it was Lillian Hellman who said that the scenes and moments that a playwright particularly loves are usually the ones he ought to cut; Barnes lacks that kind of discipline, and his play is too long and very uneven.

But he is a good hater. His work expresses a visceral loathing and disgust for the entrenchments of national feeling, such as no American playwright has been able to equal; and this loathing, expressed in vivid images of madness, gives his work an undeniable power. Barnes has done what no American playwright has done with anything like the same success (though some of the black playwrights have been working on it): he has connected the perversions of privilege with the perversions of sexual feeling, and this, for *The Ruling Class,* is an important source of both loathing and consequent power.

It is a wild nightmare vision, preposterous if taken literally—but the truths of nightmare are never literal truths. (pp. 16-17)

I'd think twice before sending any friend of mine to see *The Ruling Class.* Its secular blasphemies have less impact in this country than they must have had in England; its horrors are hard to take, and sometimes, perhaps, gratuitous; and I doubt if I have succeeded in conveying how *second-rate* much of the writing in it is. But it has a kind of mad stature. (p. 17)

*Julius Novick, "It's My Lord Jack the Ripper," in
The New York Times, January 31, 1971, pp. 16-17.*

T. E. KALEM

Encountering Barnes is somewhat like fencing in a Noel Coward drawing room while seething with the stomach-pit anger of the early John Osborne, and then leaving the room for a short session in the late Joe Orton's black-comic vomitorium. What remains as the distinguishing mark of Barnes himself? An exuberantly antic disposition, for one thing, plus schoolboy zest and schoolboy humor—which, in the British, seem to last for a lifetime. Perhaps a more significant trait is that he is a painter's playwright, a man with a gift for bringing images to vivid life on the stage.

Consider the prologue [of *The Ruling Class*]. After a hard gray day dispensing law from the bench, the 13th Earl of Gurney likes to indulge in a kinky pick-me-up. He has his valet bring him a step stool and orders him to slip a silk hang-

man's noose over a beam of his stately home. The valet departs. The earl strips down to his long underwear, dons a tricornered cocked hat, buckles on a sword, and struggles into a white ballet tutu. He mounts the stool, puts his head in the noose, and steps off. He twitches there, gasping hoarsely, neck muscles bulging red.

It is not the end. With a desperate little back jump, his feet regain the stool. The earl's face is bleary with ecstasy. He speaks in a kind of Nirvana rasp, and we get the full inebriant impact of Barnes' imagistic powers:

> Touched him, saw her, towers of death and silence, angels of fire and ice. Saw Alexander covered with honey and beeswax in his tomb and felt the flowers growing over me. A man must have his visions. How else could an English judge and peer of the realm take moonlight trips to Marrakesh and Ponders End? See six vestal virgins smoking cigars? Moses in bedroom slippers? Naked bosoms floating past Formosa? Desperate diseases need desperate remedies. Just time for a quick one. (Puts his head back in the noose.) Be of good cheer, Master Ridley, and play the man. There's plenty of time to win this game, and thrash the Spaniards too. (Draws his sword.) Form squares, men! Smash the Mahdi, and Binnie Barnes!

With a lustful gurgle, he steps off—and inadvertently knocks over the step stool. This time, it is the end for the 13th Earl of Gurney. Mind you, this has occurred in less than five minutes after the curtain has gone up, a sure sign of the revved-up authority of a born playwright. Understandably, Barnes cannot maintain this pace for the rest of the evening, but unlike many new playwrights, he does not suffer from plot anemia. (p. 60)

In barest outline, the play proper concerns itself with two themes. One is a lambasting of the British upper class. This is fast, funny, furious and unrelenting, but it is scarcely fresh, since Osborne began doing it 15 years ago in *Look Back in Anger.*

On a more intriguing level, the work deals with the God of the Old and New Testaments, that is, the ruling order of the universe as apart from, though sometimes ironically similar to Britain's ruling class. The young and appealing 14th Earl of Gurney . . . turns out to be far battier than the 13th earl. He believes that he is God. This irritates the bejesus out of his relatives. They trick him into a marriage to sire a 15th earl, after which they plan to commit the 14th earl to an asylum. But an officious psychiatrist insists that he can cure the 14th earl by confronting him with the "true" God, a mad Scot with his eyes and his rrrrrrr's in a fine frenzy rolling. The cure is splendid theater, and it is right out of Pirandello's *Henry IV,* where the madman-hero claims he is a medieval emperor and is similarly confronted with "reality."

What about reality, that eternal alter ego of drama? In the first act, dressed and behaving in hippie fashion, the 14th earl is the Jesus figure of the New Testament, the God of love and redemptive grace. He is figuratively crucified. His "cure" takes place on an actual cross. In the second act, he becomes the God of the Old Testament, who rules by law, by the book, by the doctrine of an eye for an eye, a life for a life. To Barnes, this is the law of the gibbet, in which the hangman is the cornerstone of a sound society. This is God as a wrathful Jack the Ripper, and acting as that dominion and that power, the 14th earl disembowels the two women who love him the most. Noose and knife, a circle of doom. Barnes has seamlessly linked his idea content—law, love, the ruling order and murder—with coruscating imagery. (pp. 60-1)

T. E. Kalem, "The Hangman God," in Time, *New York, Vol. 97, No. 7, February 15, 1971, pp. 60-1.*

JIM HILEY

Playwright Peter Barnes suggests that there is [a human need to laugh] and that it derives from unrespectable motives. Laughter is for losers, he says, and a means of groundless reassurance. 'Things can't be all that bad if we can still laugh' seems to be the general idea. But Barnes reckons things are indeed all that bad, and by laughing at them we're just kidding ourselves they're not. 'Laughter,' he says, 'is dangerous.'

Which is precisely why his latest play . . . is called **Laughter!** In it, Barnes says he is dealing with 'man's inhumanity to man'. The first act depicts the unpredictably despotic viciousness of Ivan the Terrible, and the second act is set in Auschwitz. He seeks to show that cruelty, having been a personal affair based on whim in feudal times, has progressed into something more systematic. 'It is now more widespread,' he says, 'because it is organised.'

The officials of the concentration camp first seem to be unaware of the horrors their pen-pushing is facilitating. We see them bogged down by the minutiae of form-filling and inter-office diplomacy. The appearance of a visiting superior, Gottleb, sets them manoeuvring through various situations that might be described as comic. It is only when Gottleb needs to pull rank that he unleashes on them, and us, a catalogue of the unspeakable realities of Auschwitz. This passage, based on painstaking research by Barnes, is so harrowing as to be difficult to sit through.

Quite simply, Barnes is trying to stop us laughing, and the implication is that we shouldn't have been laughing earlier in the play either. We are criticised for being seduced by the attitudes of the characters and the skills of performers and author. '**Laughter!** is an experiment in comedy,' says Barnes. 'As in all experiments, you have to take it to an extreme form. I'm asking, "Is comedy a help? Does it relieve the injustices of this world?" I do want to change the world—just a little, just a little. Great comedy has not had the effect it should. (p. 15)

Jim Hiley, "Liberating Laughter," in Plays and Players, *Vol. 25, No. 6, March, 1978, pp. 14-17.*

BERNARD F. DUKORE

In his Introduction to [the text of] Peter Barnes's **The Ruling Class,** Harold Hobson, then theatre critic of London's *Sunday Times,* declares, "The most exciting thing that can happen to a dramatic critic is when he is suddenly and unexpectedly faced with the explosive blaze of an entirely new talent of a very high order." Such an event, he adds, may "prove a turning point in the drama. . . ." In twenty years, only four playwrights unexpectedly excited him: Samuel Beckett, with *Waiting for Godot;* John Osborne, with *Look Back in Anger;* Harold Pinter, with *The Birthday Party;* and Peter Barnes, with **The Ruling Class.**

Time and critical consensus have confirmed Hobson's assessment of Beckett, who is Irish and more than a generation older than the rest, who are English and of the same generation: born 1929, 1930, and 1931, respectively. Today, Osborne's early promise seems largely unfulfilled and despite the historical importance of *Look Back in Anger,* he appears less prominent than he used to; but Hobson's judgment of Pinter and Barnes remains valid and both have grown in stature. In originality, distinctiveness, theatrical and intellectual power, they tower above all other contemporary English dramatists.

Yet how different they are. Whereas Pinter's drama is not politically orientated, class hatred and a loathing of social, economic, and religious bastions of Western society permeate Barnes's. While both are theatrical, their use of the stage differs. Pinter's art is intense and contractive, like that of Beckett, whom he reveres. Barnes's is full-blown and expansive, like that of Ben Jonson, whom he reveres. Pinter's proscenium-arch stage is an enclosed, confined space, often like a tomb. Barnes's is a show-place, evocative of the amusement-park atmosphere of the pier at the seaside resort Clacton-on-Sea, where he spent most of his youth. (p. 97)

[The titles of Barnes's plays] indicate their subject matter. **The Ruling Class** [1968] dramatizes the nature of that class, its values and viciousness, its perversions and pernicious charm. The existence of a privileged, ruling class depends upon the existence of unprivileged, ruled classes; authority requires submission and the maintenance of the status quo. Is not such a society lunatic? In the play, its leading exponent is insane. Does it not pervert humanity? The madman's father relaxes by wearing a tutu ballet skirt, a three-cornered hat, and a sword, then obtains sexual thrills by pretending to hang himself (he accidentally succeeds). Are the words it uses to impose upon the masses and bolster its own self-esteem gibberish? Barnes has members of the ruling class misquote Shakespeare and recite a popular nonsense song ("Mairzy Doats"). Does its perpetuation intimidate and kill members of the lower classes, and subdue possible revolt? The play's peers do so.

The Ruling Class revolves around the fourteenth Earl of Gurney, who on an August 25th (the birthday, Barnes knows, of mad Ludwig of Bavaria) received the revelation that he was God. As his psychiatrist, Dr. Herder, explains, he has delusions of grandeur, and since he belongs to England's ruling class, the only being he considers grander is God. Disliking his name, Jack, he substitutes such titles as "My lordship," "the Naz," and "J. C." Although the ruling class employs religion to maintain its powers, his relatives—including a bishop—fear he may take seriously the teachings of Jesus. "Pomp and riches, pride and property will have to be lopped off," says J. C. "All men are brothers. Love makes all equal. The mighty must bow down before the pricks of the louse-ridden rogues." Such a declaration upsets Sir Charles Gurney more than Jack's belief that he is God. To call for the destruction of property and the equality of all men is proof that "he's not only *mad,* he's *Bolshie!*" No matter that J. C. calls the lower classes "louse-ridden rogues," no matter that he continues to employ a butler, Tucker, who brings him tea while he meditates on a huge cross—both revelatory of his essentially aristocratic nature—to consider social equality is subversive.

Serving the interests of the ruling class, for he aims to make people adjust to society, Herder cures J. C.'s delusion that our world is based on the idea that God is love. Because two people cannot be God, Herder confronts him with a rival madman, McKyle, who considers himself to be the Old Testament God of vengeance. McKyle rids J. C. of the belief that he is God.

But Jack, a name he now accepts, substitutes one form of madness for another. When he jokingly remarks that a cousin who thought he was Christ would not be a political asset to Dinsdale, who hopes to win a seat in the House of Commons, Dinsdale—referring to Edward Heath—responds, "I don't know. The Tory Leader's the son of a carpenter, after all." Jack is surprised: "Lord Salisbury's a carpenter's son?" His reference to a Conservative Prime Minister of the previous century hints what he soon confirms, that he believes he lives in 1888, when the ruling class held great power. He thinks he is Jack the Ripper. Jack apostrophizes the class system, wins the admiration of those he appalled when he called for love, subdues subversion (he frames the secret radical Tucker for a crime he himself committed), inspires the devotion of the police who serve his interests, delivers a rousing speech in behalf of his class's values, and kills his lower-class wife, who had done her job (provided a male heir).

Although Jack is mad, he is not essentially different from the other peers. The play is named after his class, not him. His skirt-wearing father is also looney. As Tucker says, Jack is "a nut-case all right, but then so are most of these titled fleabags." While Jack's final speech—which calls for the restoration of flogging and hanging the lower classes when the social order requires such measures—is shocking, other lords express similar views and the basis of Dinsdale's electoral campaign is "the reintroduction of the death penalty." He and Jack, in the House of Lords, will "work as a team," for "We think alike on lots of things." The main concern of the former Etonian who certifies Jack's sanity is "property and its proper administration."

Whereas *The Ruling Class* provides a view of the top, *Leonardo's Last Supper* (1969) offers one further down. Property and authority concern not only the ruling class, which has them, but also the middle class, which wants them.

In *Leonardo,* the painter of "The Last Supper" has a last supper—though it occurs after, not before, his resurrection. Like Jesus, he is betrayed by his own people, fellow Florentines. Jesus's supper celebrated Passover, named to commemorate the night before the Israelites departed from slavery in Egypt into the promised land, when the Angel of Death slew first-born Egyptian children but passed over the Israelites' homes. In *Leonardo,* no Angel flies over the Ambois charnel house that is the play's set, but one resides within, *Angelo* Lasca, who with his wife and son kill Leonardo for money to return to Florence, which to them is a promised land and a deliverance from the poverty that enslaves them.

Commissioned to bury Leonardo, the Lascas delight at their fee and the prospect of increased trade once it becomes known whom they buried. When his death turns out to have been a mistaken diagnosis, they demand payment for both the burial and loss of trade. Lasca regards the gratitude of future generations as insufficient. Plunging Leonardo headfirst into a bucket of excrement, urine, and vomit, they drown him. (pp. 98-100)

Written as part of a double-bill with *Leonardo, Noonday Demons* (1969) takes place in the fourth century. "Still the Devil stirs at noon," says the hermit St. Eusebius. At that time of day, demonic powers are highest. To Eusebius, who has lived in a cave, chained, on a daily diet of seven olives and muddy

water, the demon arrives punctually. "It's Temptation Time, folks!" he announces, and projects onto a pile of excrement the lures of money, lust, and power. The play also suggests that saintliness and religion are themselves demonic. The devil is not a separate character but resides within the holy hermit, who changes his voice to tempt himself. When a rival saint, Pior, claims the cave as his own, each becomes convinced that the other is a demon sent to corrupt him. Wrapping their chains around their right fists, they fight and cry, "Kill, kill, kill for Christ!" Atop a mound of excrement, Eusebius strangles Pior and sings "Gloria in Excelsis." Murder results from extreme devotion to God. (p. 101)

Dramatized in earlier plays, such themes as a ruling class, profit, murder in the name of religion, and show biz reappear in new form in *The Bewitched* (1974). True to its title, it concerns people bewitched by secular and religious authority, which employs murder, torture, intimidation, and entertainment for the purpose of bewitchment. It even employs murder, torture, and intimidation *as* entertainment. Insidiously, those who bewitch are themselves bewitched.

The play revolves around Carlos II, seventeenth-century King of Spain, last of the Hapsburgs, whose failure to beget an heir resulted in the War of the Spanish Succession, which left millions dead and wounded. In this play, church and state join to help an exemplar of absolute authority procreate. What is the person who would reproduce himself? Reigning by divine right, he believes, his empire administered by churchmen and statesmen, the King is a stuttering, slobbering, vomiting, pants-wetting, impotent, spastic epileptic. This is authority. As Carlos's limbs jerk spastically, he cries, "III aaaaam Spain." Referring to Carlos's penis, a courtier genuflects: "Like Atlas, Sire, you balance our world on 'ts tip." So he does. For the future of Europe to depend on a grotesque lunatic's erection and potency is both symptom and symbol of authority's bewitchment.

The play's action consists of attempts to obtain a successor. Since Carlos cannot create one in the conventional manner, his wife and mother vie with each other to persuade him to name their choice. To stimulate his virility, and provide entertainment for the exploited populace, the church stages a massive auto-da-fé. Unwilling to believe the royal Carlos is naturally impotent, his confessor attributes the deficiency to diabolical influences. To cure his impotence, the Inquisition overcrowds dungeons with people suspected of witchcraft. Their torture and murder fail to give Spain a prince.

Yet the bewitched victims of authority reject neither the cause of their sufferings nor the established rituals which maintain them. Visiting the torture chamber, Carlos accidentally moves the rack handle. A prisoner screams in pain and gasps, "Twas a great honour, Your Majesty." A tortured nobleman appreciates that "E'en in the House o' Pain my rank and privileges were observed. My body's fire-wracked, my mouth blood-filled, but I cry out, 'God save the King!' "

One reason they submit is that authority relieves them of choice and provides certainty. In a moment of post-epileptic lucidity, Carlos perceives, "Authority's the Basilisk" and as long as one man commands and another obeys, it will ruin the world. But when he offers to renounce his crown, his subjects cry in terror and flee. Without authority, the bewitched believe, "Blind chance rules the world!"

However, it is authority which creates chaos, not its absence. At the play's end, Carlos acts upon the logic of authority and the status quo, not rational skepticism and humanity. Although he and his councillors recognize that to name Philip of France as his heir will plunge Europe into a ruinous, bloody war, he names him, for "Only France's strong enough t' hold our Empire together." When Carlos says he is Spain, he is right. This cretin's sole logical choice derives from and aims to maintain what he incarnates. Its logic "makes all that's gone afore meaningless."

Carlos is exemplary, not unique. According to the Queen's brother, "all the Catholic crowned heads o' Europe've been possessed f' years." The Epilogue shows Carlos's Bourbon successor to be *"another freak, with massive legs and arms, bloated stomach and a small elephant's trunk hanging down over his chest in place of a nose."* His face is that of a grinning imbecile. Although a voice calls Philip's ascension the hopeful light of the Age of Reason, the sight of a monstrosity even more grotesque than Carlos derides this assertion. As subjects cry, "God save the King," Barnes makes clear that the generations after Carlos's are as bewitched as his.

Laughter! (1978) gives major emphasis to a theme treated less prominently in earlier plays. In particular, it links to the torture scenes of **The Bewitched,** which draw laughs from suffering. In *Laughter!* Barnes also prods the audience into recognizing why they should not have laughed. *Laughter!* is about the nature of its title. Framing two one-act plays, **"Tsar"** and **"Auschwitz,"** is a Prologue—a comic attack on laughter by a character called the Author—and an Epilogue—the murder, both comic and horrifying, of two comedians who are concentration camp inmates.

According to the Author, laughter is "no remedy for evil. . . . It softens our hatred. An excuse to change nothing, for nothing needs changing when it's all a joke." He demands we "root out comedy." During his impassioned jeremiad, a custard pie hits his face and his pants fall down. The slapstick comedy demonstrates how laughter diverts us from ideas that should engage our attention. The Author's statement, less a thematic summary than a challenge based on a recognition of the limitations of the satirist's art, is more extreme than Barnes's own view. Through the Author, Barnes raises questions rather than provides answers.

Laughter! dramatizes themes of earlier plays in an entirely new manner. In **"Tsar,"** Ivan the Terrible embodies the authority of a ruling class. In **"Auschwitz,"** the Nazis do. The subjects of both are bewitched. Shibanov, whose foot Ivan has speared to the floor, tells why he worships him: "You're God's anointed. You've the authority o' blood, Sire, authority that rests on the past. It gi'es our world a permanence which men need. . . . You gi'e us certainty, Sire, which is better than goodness." As in **Demons** and **The Bewitched,** "Tsar" derides the value of suffering for God. (pp. 102-04)

Whereas **"Tsar"** derives comedy from individual despotism, **"Auschwitz"** focuses on impersonal slaughter. "In the coming years," Death tells Ivan in a transitional scene between the plays, "they'll institutionalize [death], take the passion out of killing, turn men into numbers and the slaughter'll be so vast no one mind'll grasp it, no heart'll break 'cause of it."

"Auschwitz" is the German concentration camp and also a symbol of how most people blind themselves to and thereby perpetuate other horrors. Audaciously, Barnes manipulates spectators' responses to make them recognize their kinship to functionaries at Auschwitz. A group of civil servants, who tell jokes to help them bear (not change) their lot, engage in

bureaucratic rivalry with Gottleb, the quintessential Nazi. As Gottleb goads his rival Cranach to tell an anti-Hitler joke, and tries to turn Cranach's co-workers against him, spectators sympathize with the functionaries, people like themselves, and become hostile to the ruthless Nazi zealot. At the start, they laugh at Cranach's bureaucratic jargon. . . . After Gottleb fails to enlist Cranach's co-workers, he makes them face the reality behind the jargon, which refers to the concrete chimneys of the crematoria. While he does so, spectators see what they have laughed at. In reality, the civil servants know: "Deaths and paragraph fifteen isn't any of our business." To close their minds to their knowledge, they replace descriptive language with neutral. Gottleb, our enemy as well as theirs, employs description to open their—and our—minds to Auschwitz's atrocities. The functionaries protest their inability to prevent them: "I can't fight 'em. . . . This isn't the time to say 'no.' I've just taken out a second mortgage!" "But what can I do? I'm only one woman." "You can't expect me to say 'no.' . . . I'm retiring next year." Having previously manipulated our sympathies toward ordinary people at the mercy of a Nazi beast, Barnes turns us against them. Fighting Gottleb with bureaucratese, which divorces meaning from words, they shut their minds to Auschwitz's horrors. . . . Those with whom we empathized are worse than the Nazi Gottleb, who does not blind himself to the truth about Auschwitz, as people "like . . . us" have done, as we "like them" still do.

In an Epilogue, two hollow-eyed concentration camp inmates do a dance and patter number, with such gags as: "According to the latest statistics, one man dies in this camp everytime I breathe." "Have you tried toothpaste?" Gassed during their act, they die while telling jokes. As they expire, one recalls the words of the Author in the Prologue: "In the face of . . . Ivan the Terrible . . . or Auschwitz, what good is laughter?!"

Red Noses, Black Death (written 1978)—to date, Barnes's greatest and most complex work—represents both the culmination of his previous original plays and a new direction, in that it suggests the basis of positive action to eliminate the social evils he satirizes. Chiefly, according to Barnes, it derives from the Prologue to its immediate predecessor, *Laughter!* "It dramatizes a situation in which people use laughter. Does it help to alleviate the suffering that goes on around them, or does it make it worse?" In *Red Noses, Black Death,* Barnes makes theatre people his central figures. Although one should be careful not to identify a dramatist too closely with a character, even—as in *Laughter!*—a character called the Author, Father Flote, the protagonist of *Red Noses,* comes by the end of the play to a realization similar to that of Barnes, who admits, "A lot of what he goes through is a progress I have undergone in writing comedy. I've theorized about it, but he lives it as a created character."

The fourteenth century was a time of death on a vast scale. "One-third of Christendom lies under sod," says Flote well before the plague ends. It was a time of chaos and anarchy, for death struck randomly. Goodness, wealth, and trappings of power were no proof against it. From Pope to peasant, everyone was terrified. (pp. 104-05)

Three groups contend to influence the populace. Although each is necessary, each is insufficient as a force for social improvement.

Lamenting that "Men can't live in this misery, die in this despair," Flote forms the Red Noses, a religious "brotherhood of joy, Christ's Clowns, God's zanies," designed to "cheer the hearts of men with gibs, jibes, and jabber jinks; masques and other merriments." Each member wears a symbol of the order, a clown's red nose. Trying to lighten the dying moments of a plague-stricken woman, the red-nosed priest jokes, "Old Dubois told the marriage broker he wouldn't marry the girl without a sample of her sexual powers. 'No samples,' said the girl, 'but references he can have!' The woman smiles and dies. Believing that laughter is more apt to discourage than encourage rebellion, Pope Clement VI blesses the order.

The Red Noses' compassionate mirth diverts people from such facts as "Ten percent of the population of Auxerre dies of starvation every year without plague help" and "Free men're made bondsmen, dress in tatters, whilst [their] fields're enclosed and stolen by landlords." Thus, the Red Noses perpetuate social conditions which constitute a plague comparable to the Black Death.

Opposing them are the Black Ravens, former galley slaves freed to bury corpses, whose possessions they loot. Nihilistic, they seek destruction of the existing order and ask the poor to join them in killing the rich, but they understand only hatred, not how to implement their egalitarian vision. As one of them later confesses, "I broke the eggs but I didn't know how to make the omelette."

The Flagellants, who seek salvation through suffering, are evangelical proto-Protestants. Calling the Pope "a sucking dog-leech" who sells religion for profit, they aim to "appeal to God direct. We need no mitred prelates to intercede for us. No man needs to go to Avignon [where the papal seat has moved] nor Hell to find Pope or Devil. Both lodge in his own breast!" But its leader afterward recognizes, "We Flagellants embraced pain when we should've been trying to eliminate it."

Individually, each has something of value: the Red Noses, the joy and laughter that should be cornerstones of a new world, in contrast to the misery and pain of the old, and the ability to influence the masses; the Black Ravens, the conception that the populace should overthrow the ruling classes and seize power; the Flagellants, the idea that within each human being is divinity. In a climactic scene, they recognize that only together can they hope to create a better world, and they join in fraternal communion.

But they act too late. At the scene's end comes the announcement that the plague is over. The Black Ravens' egalitarian ideas threaten authority and the Flagellants endanger the church's revenue: "what's to become of the most profitable function of the Holy Office—selling salvation, if men can cleanse themselves of sin by self-inflicted penances?" With the normal order restored, church and state join to isolate and crush them. Still, Clement VI sanctions Flote's Red Noses. "He's helped keep unrest down to a minimum, made men more readily accept their miserable lot. . . . A revolution never returns." But the laughter of the radicalized Flote now serves revolution, not the status quo. He creates an acronym for social reform through moderation: "Slow, Lawful, Orthodox Progress: S-L-O-P, SLOP." The Pope has the Red Noses killed. (pp. 106-07)

"Every play is a problem of language," says Barnes in his Introduction to **Leonardo** and **Demons.** For them, he sought "a live theatrical language," an "artificial vernacular" with "historical weight yet . . . flexible enough to incorporate modern songs and jokes. For such deliberate anachronisms can only

work fully if they spring out of an acceptable period texture. So I pillaged; everything from Elizabethan argot to the Bible." . . . Barnes's language is invented, different for each play and character. The "gotch-gutted curs" of Lasca would be as inappropriate in the mouth of Pior as his "grimliche" would be in Lasca's, or as either would be in anyone's in **Red Noses.** There, he pillages such period sources as a traditional flagellant's hymn, "Pain, pain, pain," Chaucer's *Canterbury Tales,* "a very perfect gentle knight," and mystery plays, as when Mary says of the infant Jesus, "Lookee, look how he merrys, my sweeting laughs. Oh, he's a prince, divine." (p. 108)

Into his period texture, as he says, he inserts modern jokes. In **Demons,** the tempter says Eusebius has "B. O." In **The Bewitched,** a parrot screeches, "Jesus saves but Moses invests." In **Red Noses,** an actor punningly calms an actress with stage fright, "you'll get a warm hand on your opening." (p. 109)

Barnes's linguistic thefts conform to his themes and situations. Largely because of the apt and original use to which he puts his plunder, of both literature and pop culture, he transforms it into his own property. First, his literary allusions.

At the start of **The Ruling Class,** he parodies, misquotes, jumbles the order, and thereby transforms John of Gaunt's famous praise of England (*Richard II*) into a condemnation—unintended by the speaker—of the basis of English society: a "teeming womb of privilege" (not "of royal kings"), still "a feudal state," beating back "foreign anarchy" (not "envious siege")—no doubt the revolutions of 1789 and 1917. Important too, these lines derive from Gaunt's *dying* words, since the entire Prologue—which ends in death—is a compendium of allusions associated with death, including the last words of Sidney Carton in Dickens's *A Tale of Two Cities* ("It is a far, far better thing," etc.), a paraphrase of Claudius after he discovers Hamlet has killed Polonius ("Desperate diseases need desperate remedies"), and the last words of Viscount Palmerston in 1865 ("Die my dear doctor? That's the last thing I shall do"). Even if one recognizes none of these sources, the archaic mode of some passages suggests moribund tradition (Gaunt); death is sometimes implicit (Claudius), sometimes explicit (the Viscount), sometimes visualized (the speaker climbs steps to a noose before he quotes Dickens).

Literary and Biblical allusions pepper **The Bewitched.** Diseased and dying, Philip IV tries to engender a legitimate heir. In order to achieve an erection, he conjures in his imagination a beautiful, young, scantily clad former mistress, who erotically stimulates him. Soon, he observes, "*It quivers.* 'Tis not as hard as a ram's horn, nor as stout as Hercules but 'twill serve." Whether or not one recognizes the allusion to *Romeo and Juliet* (Mercutio's comment on his death wound, " 'tis not so deep as a well, nor so wide as a church-door; but 'tis enough, 'twill serve"), the statement is funny. Also, it is both ironic and appropriate. Romeo and Juliet are young, romantic lovers, whereas Philip is decrepit and unromantic; and by the end of the scene—which begins with a funeral bell—Philip will be, in Mercutio's words, "a grave man." The Queen's parrot cries, "O impotence, where is thy sting? which parodies "O death," etc. (I *Corinthians,* 15:55). Though ironic—the parrot addresses the absence of *le petit mort* in words evocative of *le grand mort*—the allusion becomes apt at the close of the scene, when the Queen Mother strangles the parrot.

In "The Second Coming," Yeats writes, "Things fall apart; the center cannot hold." In *Red Noses,* a character observes that with the plague more than the center cannot hold: "The rim and centre's breaking." During the Black Death, prostitutes raised prices, for money was valueless to those who might die and death decreased supply while it increased demand. When the plague ends, prostitutes—about to marry and give what they once sold—lament, "we've dwindled to wives." The allusion is to Congreve's *The Way of the World,* where Millamant, having set forth conditions under which she would marry Mirabell, says, "I may by degrees dwindle into a wife." In one respect, the reference is ironic. Whereas Millamant will retain her independence, the prostitutes will lose theirs. As they recognize, they are rushing to their chains. In another respect, the allusion is apt. *This,* Barnes hints, and not Millamant's contract, is the way of the world.

While most of Barnes's references to pop culture are anachronistic—only *The Ruling Class* is set in the present—they are what Bernard Shaw, in his notes to *Caesar and Cleopatra,* calls *apparent* anachronisms, for they mock the notion that mankind has progressed since the play's historical period.

In *Demons,* fourth-century hermits sing "Monks," a parody of "Kids," from the musical *Bye Bye Birdie.* Barnes's changes are appropriate to the saints, each of whom believes the other is less worthy than himself, and to the play's anti-religious theme. Whereas the musical's father complains that no one can *understand* anything kids say, the hermits sing that no one can *believe* anything monks say. Whereas kids "do just what they want to do," monks "say anything—even if it isn't true!" In the Epilogue to *Laughter!* the song to which the dying Auschwitz inmates dance, as they tell jokes, is "The Sunny Side of the Street," which is more apt than might first appear. In death, these victims of Nazism will leave their worries on the doorstep, and conditions will be sweeter on the other side of life's street. In *Red Noses,* Flote sings "Life Is Just a Bowl of Cherries" to people dying of the plague. True to the Red Noses' job, to take people's minds off serious matters, it urges them not to take life seriously and it tells the poor that they cannot lose what they never owned. (pp. 109-10)

Language is only part of the extravagant theatricality of Barnes's plays. As Ivan unsuccessfully tries to persuade Semeon to remain Tsar, an invisible force pulls Semeon backward, until he is spreadeagled against an upstage wall, which sucks him in and swallows him. In the first-act climax of *The Bewitched,* sounds of whipping and moans accompany an onstage strangulation and red-lighted stakes; while the red wax of an effigy bubbles and flows like blood, a choir sings a hymn, an immense phallus sprouts from between Carlos's legs, grows eight feet, and—carried by a priest—impales the Queen. A superbly theatrical tour-de-force in *Red Noses* combines language, sounds, song, banners, and the movement of objects. Rather than kill each other, the Black Ravens, Flagellants, and Red Noses let God determine the victor. The Ravens unfold their banner, a black raven against a red background; the Flagellants theirs, a crucified Christ; the Noses theirs, an angel and St. Genesius, patron saint of actors. Releasing a black balloon, a Raven cries *"Caw-caw-caw"* and enunciates his creed. Releasing a red one, a Flagellant cries *"Ahhh-ahhh-ahhh"* and declares his. Releasing a blue one, Flote laughs *"Haaa-haaa-haaa"* and states his. Boos from the flies follow each speech. Then, Flote recognizes that jokes should be revolutionary and that the three

groups should join to create a better world. As the leaders link hands, the black, red, and blue balloons—now tied together—descend, accompanied by applause from the flies. Everyone sings, "Join together, that's the plan. It's the secret. Man helps man. . . . Join together. Go, go, go. Change conditions. Here below."

Expressionism is among Barnes's theatricalist devices. Instead of explaining that the ruling class is outmoded and monstrous, Barnes shows members of the House of Lords to be skull-faced, cobweb-covered, bloated-bellied, goitered people smothered in dust, seated beside a skeleton. In *The Bewitched,* to express that Ana is not pregnant, he has a patriarch, during her account of a dream about her baptised child, pour blood over her and a baby in christening clothes. (p. 111)

Barnes's most distinctive artistic signature . . . consists of disorientating transformations from one theatrical mode to another. Swiftly and lightly, actors switch from intellectual discourse, to period argot, to poetry, to modern slang, to rhetoric, to musical comedy, to ritual, to dance, to opera, to slapstick. Entertainingly, Barnes juggles the audience's moods and enables them to examine critically, detached and with a smile, the social values and attitudes he scrutinizes. Perhaps in homage to Ben Jonson, he refers to this style not as Barnesian but as "Barnesonian."

In *Leonardo,* the revived da Vinci goes within seconds from today's slang ("The verdict is in. I'm alive."), to prayer ("Jesu, I'm alive."), to a jig and a whoop of joy, to intellectual discourse ("The evidence proves I'm in the land of the living in the bosom of a natural family. I recognize the species: genus homo sapiens. Bipedal primate mammals. Erect bodies, short arms, large thumbs, developed brains with a capacity for articulate speech and abstract reasoning."), to a parody of "Molly Malone" ("Alive-alive O, alive-alive O, singing pasta and pizza alive-alive O.") In **"Tsar,"** Ivan—within three pages—dances Cossack-style, jumping and écarting with joyful cries; speaks in archaic diction ("My leming lufsom boy. I leif you more than life"); hears the screams of a skeleton of a man he tortured and killed, and cracks a joke in modern diction ("They don't write songs like that anymore"); goes into convulsions as he tries to strangle himself; delivers a running joke to the audience ("Root it out!"); murders his son by repeatedly spearing him; employs inarticulate sounds to convey emotion; and sings two arias from Gluck's opera *Orfeo and Eurydice.*

A major reason for the success of so daring a mixture of modes is their analogical appropriateness. Since rational discourse is insufficient to express Leonardo's delight at being alive, he bursts into song, whose lyrics celebrate life. Ivan derives pleasure from the "songs" or cries of his victims, and the world he creates is a hell, perhaps worse than the one into which Orfeo descends in search of Eurydice.

Barnes' transformations reflect our fragmented world, which encompasses and accommodates Rembrandt and Magritte, Vivaldi and Frank Loesser, Seneca and tap dancing. They succeed on stage partly because one is accustomed to them in daily life. Is it unusual to play a record of a Mozart quartet, then of a Broadway musical, on one's own player? Is it unusual to read the comic section of a newspaper during morning coffee, then the *Oresteia?* On TV, a gripping scene in a concentration camp might suddenly shift to an animated tuna fish who recites Shakespeare and is told that the manufacturer wants tunas who taste good, not tunas with good taste. The difference between Barnosonian transformations and diurnal transformations is that the Barnesonians are purposeful and unified, not merely random. In brief, they are art. (pp. 113-14)

Bernard F. Dukore, "Peter Barnes," in Essays on Contemporary British Drama, *edited by Hedwig Bock and Albert Wertheim, Max Hueber Verlag, 1981, pp. 97-116.*

BENEDICT NIGHTINGALE

One can't see *The Duchess of Malfi* in revival, or many another Jacobean play, without being burningly aware that over the past 350 years our drama has lost much in the way of size, savagery and gaudy spectacle. That's Peter Barnes's strongly held belief, and doubtless also the reason for his lonely mission, which is to restore to the theatre some of its old ebullience and attack. Hence his *Bewitched,* a garish entertainment about inquisition, auto-da-fé, massacre and other such Iberian diversions, and hence his more recent *Laughter!,* which somehow managed to enlist both Ivan the Terrible and Eichmann's grey-suited apparatchiks in an argument about the purpose of humour.

And hence what, when it was penned in 1978, was called *Red Noses, Black Death:* not the most alluring of titles, but one which aptly summed up Barnes's style as well as his subject, his mix of grand guignol and big top as well as his fascination with things horrendous and hilarious in periods of ignorance.

Why hasn't *Red Noses,* as it's been rechristened, been performed before? Perhaps because 40-plus characters are dauntingly many. . . . Perhaps because others share the doubts I've more than once professed about Barnes himself. Has he a sense of horror to match Webster's, or a sense of humour as rich and scathing as that of his beloved Jonson? Is he as Jacobean as he superficially seems, or, indeed as provocatively modern as he would also like to be? Is his content as interesting as his style is arresting, his mind as sharp and his sensibility as fine as his imagination is ambitious? Or not?

On to the big Barbican stage, all jagged crosses and crimson haze, comes representative after representative of 14th-century Christian society in frightened disarray. The archbishop's reaction to seemingly unstoppable plague is to run away, the Pope's to cocoon himself in what . . . looks like a huge condom with giant toes.

Others are less gingerly and feeble. The merchants, who don't see much future for themselves, lavish their energies and fortunes on the prostitutes, who do. A band of cowled flagellants, led by a grinning fanatic who has borrowed his greenish hue as well as his crown of thorns from some Duccio Christ, roams the countryside and the cities, ostentatiously atoning for the sins of both. A group calling itself the Ravens, ex-galley slaves turned wandering morticians, preaches violent revolution and does what it can to bring it into being, mainly by smearing bits of infected corpse on the doors of the rich. And one Father Flote . . ., a blend of Holy Fool, Simple Simon and Walt Disney's Happy, assembles a sort of mediaeval ENSA troupe with which to amuse the stricken masses. These oddly assorted mummers are Barnes's 'red noses', the motley evidence in another debate about power, laughter and (more precisely) the power of laughter.

When they're jollying people along, distracting them from the miseries of the plague and the Church's failure to cure it, they're officially tolerated and even encouraged. When they become less anodyne and actually start performing mildly subversive nativity plays, they're promptly destroyed. The authorities of their day, Barnes would suggest, are not so very different from those of our own. Ours too prefer 'meringues' to 'meat', in art, in politics. They too rapidly turn ruthless at socially volatile times. Occasionally something happens to create the possibility of change—a Black Death, a war, whatever—but the result is usually more and worse oppression. Disasters come, disasters go, and then 'a greater darkness falls, for we return to normal'.

These gloomy musings are mostly unexceptionable, but also unexceptional. After all, what has Barnes added to the more intellectually sophisticated and no less passionate study of the politics of humour that Trevor Griffiths made in his *Comedians?* The answer is, nothing very essential. A good deal of verbal play, and some rather forced puns; Puck's 'Lord, what fools these mortals be' appears, strenuously recycled into 'ah, what food these morsels be'. An occasional weakness for whimsy: Barnes becomes embarrassingly enamoured of a dumb jester named Bells, at whose sweetly-sad death a single balloon is released, to carry his spirit up to the flies. Much droll swagger and technicolour show: Flote's trip to see the Pope in Avignon kept reminding me of Dorothy's quest for the Wizard of Oz, though I don't think she met any swamp monsters, still less a bearded transvestite cooing 'hello, sailor'. And a certain moral sententiousness, examples of which I cannot bring myself to quote. If all these elements . . . add up to a Jacobean tragi-comedy, then that's what *Red Noses* anachronistically is. My own feeling, though, is that what Barnes has pumped into the veins of our theatre is not good 17th-century gore, but a red-coloured amalgam of patent medicine, stage make-up and cherryade. (pp. 32-3)

Benedict Nightingale, "Stage Blood," in *New Statesman, Vol. 110, No. 2834, July 12, 1985, pp. 32-3.*

GARY SEIBERT

"Root it out!" The world grows hard, harder. . . . Laughter's too feeble a weapon against the barbarities of life. A balm for battles lost, standard equipment for the losing side; the powerful have no need of it. Wit's no answer to a homicidal maniac. So, in the face of Attila the Hun, Ivan the Terrible, or Auschwitz, what good is laughter?

So speaks the character of Author in the prologue of Peter Barnes's 1978 play, *Laughter!*—which, though it deals with Auschwitz, is very funny. *Red Noses,* . . . likewise probes the reality below the surfaces of both comedy and tragedy. The sacred subject matter, this time treated as comedy, vaudeville show and play with music: the 14th century's bubonic plague that struck Europe and eventually wiped out, by some estimates, two-thirds of the populace—in some areas more.

Indeed, Barnes's earlier Author would object to treating such a serious catastrophe through laughter. But Barnes is a playwright who understands the common roots of tears and laughter, who understands that there are many ways to investigate dramatically the horrors of the 20th century. He has a clear vision of evil and dramatizes what preachers preach and historians fret about: Greed, bureaucratic power games and lack of imagination and faith are morally evil because they immobilize moral goodness, vision and spirit. A playwright as shrewd as he is angry knows that audiences like to laugh in spite of themselves, and he intelligently uses the theater, as did George Bernard Shaw, to dramatize political and spiritual ideas through character.

A political satire, *Red Noses* savagely, wittily and joyfully denounces the hypocrisy of all establishments, most clearly those institutionalized in the corrupt papal court of Clement VI of Avignon. Barnes mercilessly lampoons Pope Clement and his court, who hide from the plague, and the flagellants who whip themselves in the hope that God will take the incomprehensible pestilence away. Parallel to these evil forces, however, is the dramatic life of the simple, good-willed and faithful monk, Father Flote. In him and his crazy band of misfits, Christ's vigorous and joyful message takes on the cowardice and greed of medieval Europe. . . .

Red Noses is a dramatic attack on the cataclysmic aftermath of a possible nuclear disaster that in the middle 1970's seemed more and more probable due to the proliferation of warheads stockpiled in Europe. *Red Noses* speaks as directly, if unwittingly, to the current AIDS pandemic. The differences between the epidemics are outweighed by the playwright's uncanny insights into the common responses each elicits: paralyzing terror, panic and desperate scape-goating of handy victims.

Red Noses is typically British (and so plays more delightedly in Chicago) in that it unashamedly crackles with political de-bate, attacks hypocritical bureaucracies, and still manages to provide ample room for solo vaudeville turns, personal comic shtick and word play. . . .

Barnes has concocted a masterpiece of farce, comedy, vaudeville piece and morality play. The medieval church, embodied in the corrupt Pope Clement VI and his Avignon court, takes it roundly on the chin, back, legs and any available sore spot. The playwright's biting anger is aimed at the dissolute church, symbol of institutions that perpetuate themselves at their members' immortal expense. Amoral greed and the built-in tendency of those in power to prolong their administrations at the cost of human lives are his real targets.

As hard as the plague is to live through, the second act of *Red Noses* reveals that life after the plague has its own pitfalls. It profoundly examines what happens to humor and joy when the crisis is over. There is, of course, no way this joyful group can outwit the powers-that-be. The ramshackle group faces martyrdom with nobility and humor. As they meet the Christ they so joyfully served in the poorest of the poor in Act I, their faces light up with joy, and they are finally appreciated not for their talent, limited as it is, but for the beautiful persons they have always been in the eyes of God. . . .

Not only is [*Red Noses*] good theater, it is one of the best homilies I have ever seen. I recommend it to anyone who has doubts about the validity of Jesus' message in a time of plague.

Gary Seibert, "'Red Noses' in Chicago," in America, Vol. 157, No. 16, November 28, 1987, p. 411.

Steven Berkoff

1937-

English dramatist, short story writer, and travel writer.

One of contemporary Britain's most flamboyant dramatists, Berkoff combines satire, black humor, and social commentary to create brazen psychological comedies that confront modern prejudices and anxieties. Berkoff worked in repertory companies until 1973, when his dissatisfaction with conventional British realism led him to establish the highly acclaimed London Theatre Group. An innovative troupe that allowed Berkoff the freedom to write, direct, and act in his own plays, the London Theatre Group sought to fully utilize the skills of its actors through such elements as pantomime, dance, and music. Contending that theater "should deal with the profane and the unmentionable," Berkoff challenges complacent attitudes by centering on such discomfiting topics as incest, class struggle, and human cruelty. Jack Kroll commented: "[Berkoff is] a one-man avant-garde who . . . has raised eyebrows and hackles with angry, scabrous and satirical plays that paint a withering picture of corruption and despair in modern Britain."

Berkoff made his debut as a director and writer with *In the Penal Colony* (1968), a work about organized bureaucracy and torture adapted from Franz Kafka's short story of the same title. Acknowledging affection for the surreal elements in Kafka's fiction and admiration for the author's ability to present ordinary events in an unusual manner, Berkoff also adapted such Kafka works as *The Metamorphosis* and *The Trial*. *The Metamorphosis* (1969), an expressionistic psychological drama that has enjoyed several revivals, revolves around Gregor Samsa, a salesman who awakens one morning to find he has turned into an insect. Although Samsa is still mentally human, his physical change repulses his family, and he is made a prisoner in his own apartment. In Berkoff's rendering, Samsa's apartment is a simple cage, actors are outfitted solely in black costumes and whiteface, and the performer who portrays Samsa scuttles about the stage on extended limbs to suggest the movements of an insect. Bruce Elder observed: "In many ways, [*The Metamorphosis*] is the finest flowering and most perfect articulation of Berkoff's notions of theatre."

Berkoff's first original drama, *East: Elegy for the East End and Its Energetic Waste* (1975), is a ribald comedy set in the working-class region of East London where he was raised. Comprised of nineteen sketches, this work combines modern argot and Shakespearean idiom to explore the stymied fantasies of a bourgeois family. While Mum and Dad live in the past, their two sons compete in sexual exploits and regard their sister Sylv as the ultimate conquest. Sylv, however, perceives her sexual urges as a weakness. In an acclaimed soliloquy, she expresses her desire to have been born male and thus achieve complete emotional control over herself and others. The play's conclusion offers no sense of catharsis, suggesting that the family's resignation will continue. Dave Robins asserted: "*East* shows the East End as it is—a city of violent, comic, deeply frustrated people, a hard place to grow up and develop in."

In *Greek* (1983), Berkoff attacks the compliant attitudes of the British working class through a modern retelling of Sophocles' *Oedipus Rex*. Relocating the play from ancient Greece to the East End of contemporary London, Berkoff transforms the character of Oedipus into a vulgar, rebellious youth named Eddy who is overwhelmed by his passion for power and money. Eddy's struggle to join the British upper class causes him to lose perspective of his true identity and, as in the classical myth, he succumbs to fate. In *Sink the Belgrano!* (1986), Berkoff examines values and manners exposed by the English during the Falklands War of 1982. The Yiddish title of Berkoff's next play, *Kvetch* (1987), is defined in English as "to fret or fuss." Set almost exclusively in the dining room of a Jewish-American family, *Kvetch* centers on five characters who exchange verbal pleasantries while revealing their true feelings in asides to the audience. This play achieved neither commercial nor critical success, due at least partially to what many perceived as offensive racial and ethnic humor.

Berkoff recently directed *Coriolanus* (1988), his controversial adaptation of Shakespeare's tragedy of the same title. Set in ancient Rome, this story of corrosive politics features one of Shakespeare's most disagreeable protagonists. As a reward for conquering the Volscians of Corioli, Caius Marcius is awarded the surname "Coriolanus" and hailed as a hero by the Roman populace. He is prompted to lead the Volscian armies in an attack on his own city, however, after being banished from Rome for defying tradition by refusing to exhibit his wounds for the masses. In his version of *Coriolanus,* Berkoff modernizes the play by using expressionistic settings and contemporary costumes that reflect twentieth century historical events. For example, the Roman tribunes are dressed in pinstripes and fedoras to suggest gangsters, while the Volscians march in black shirts, reminiscent of Fascists. Although several critics contended that Berkoff's extensive editing of Shakespeare's original text resulted in one-dimensional characters and that such modern touches as lewd jokes and bicycle messengers in unitards only served to trivialize the play's tragic content, most considered *Coriolanus* insightful and compelling. David Sterritt commented: "[Berkoff's] *Coriolanus* preserves the essence of its classic text while giving it an urgency—and an irony—rooted deeply in our own time."

(See also *Contemporary Authors,* Vol. 104.)

JAMES F. GAINES

Few enterprises in experimental drama illustrate the achievements of "total theatre" as vividly as the productions of Steven Berkoff. . . . These two plays [*East* and *Agamemnon*] are a striking example of a single methodology of drama, applied and adapted to very different environments ("settings" would certainly be an incorrect term, for Argos and East London are incidental locales). The difference between *East* and *Agamemnon* is the difference between a persistent illusion of escape and a recurrent nightmare.

As *East* begins, a pair of late-adolescent siblings, Mick and Les, greet each other and immediately invite the audience to take an active role by saying: "Now you know our names." The rest of their "family" consists of Sylv, both little sister and bitch-goddess, and Mum and Dad, menopause and hernias in a rented flat. Berkoff eschews any kind of linear plot in order to investigate the inner yearnings of these lumpen-proletarians in a series of disjointed scenes. For Mick and Les, eroticism and power are inextricably linked: they dream of swaggering along at the head of a gang, fighting for the precious turf of Whitechapel and Bethnal Green, and copulating furiously with the voluptuous Sylv. The object of their naive lust, however, sees her own desires as a weakness and, in a marvelous soliloquy on penis envy, she expresses her craving to manipulate others rather than allowing herself to be callously used by them. She is enchanted when rivals Mick and Les almost kill each other in an alleyway duel. Dad spews clouds of crumbs at the dinner table as he expostulates on the virtuous days of pounds, shillings, and pence, while Mum, although neutered by years of subservience, has her own secret dreams of escape.

Berkoff allows his five characters to form their own chorus, and they move with startling fluidity from the personal to the anonymous and back again, on a usually bare stage with stark black walls. To one side sits a piano player who accompanies the family's adventures. With the earthy East London dialect as a source, Berkoff's interest in developing a new dramatic poetry results in some outstanding verbal rhapsodies. When Les suggests, for example, that he "try using words," Mick launches a last-ditch effort to seduce a reluctant Sylv, resulting in an extravagant commercial for lust. Berkoff also excels in mime. One memorable scene represents Dad's obsessive memory-fantasy, a family trip to the seaside complete with the scramble for Italian ices and the rides of the Fun Fair. In another, near the end of the play, Mick transforms Les into a human motorcycle, a monster machine that will leave a wake of contempt across the landscape of English Civilization.

East is essentially a psychological comedy with relatively few topical jokes. The rather dark humor consists in the frustration of each character's individual fantasy. . . . [For example], Mick intends to soar on a cloud of machismo above the cheapened world, but he is constantly brought back to earth by the knock on his door of an irate black neighbor who is transformed in Mick's mind into a King Kong, threatening to crush his shell of self-delusion. The fact that Mick and his family are trapped in the coils of their own psychological fabrications is reinforced by the last line, which echoes the beginning: "Now you know our names."

Even more boldly theatrical than *East, Agamemnon* begins with the Feast of Atreus and dramatizes the Sacrifice of Iphigenia and the Trojan War. Thyestes' account of the feast, at which he discovers his own son's finger in the stew, sets the tone of horror for the entire production. His efforts to preserve decorum by concealing his vomit prefigure the later attempts of other humans to resist the curse. The cycle of violence nevertheless continues to rise and fall, claiming victim after victim: the children, Iphigenia, Greek and Trojan troops, Cassandra, finally Agamemnon himself.

Brilliant mime sequences, performed by a chorus of nine bare-chested men, help to preserve the theme of the unbreakable circle. In the battle scenes, dance is combined with martial arts to create friezes of intertwined warriors. In one sequence, bamboo poles are poised geometrically in a mobile sculpture that ends with an unknown soldier impaled on a forest of weapons. The Run of the Herald turns every strained muscle into a study in pain and an omen of impending death. The thundering arrival of Agamemnon and his cavalry in Argos is a much more effective expression of the brute force of war than the oral account of Troy being blown to pieces by automatic weapons and napalm bombs.

Music once again complements the other theatrical effects, as eerie pipes and piercing percussion respond to the shrieks and barks of the actors' voices. Lines are sometimes delivered in staccato bursts of words, while, after the battles, language disintegrates into subhuman grunts, trills, and mangled syllables.

The central theme of Berkoff's *Agamemnon* is that the curse illustrates the cycle of karma, where every action is evil and unavoidably propagates evil consequences. Thus, the writer-director deliberately undercuts the traditional tragic elevation of the king and queen. Agamemnon, wearing aviator glasses and a cartridge belt, speaks in broad tones that recall Teddy Roosevelt and LBJ. Clytemnestra is reduced to quarreling like a fishwife before she gains her revenge while slowly casting her net over the naked and utterly vulnerable Agamemnon.

As examples of total theatre, both *Agamemnon* and *East* show Steven Berkoff's ability to blend mime and music with heightened dramatic language. Neither the cycle of delusion in *East* nor the cycle of karma in *Agamemnon* is "entertaining." Instead, they may leave the spectator with the bitter taste of frustration and vomit. They seek to question and to probe rather than to soothe, and the spectator who boldly accepts the invitation to Dad's dinner table or to the Feast of Atreus will share in Berkoff's electrifying experimentation. (pp. 110-11)

> *James F. Gaines, in a review of "East" and "Agamemnon," in* Educational Theatre Journal, *Vol. 29, No. 1, March, 1977, pp. 110-11.*

DAVE ROBINS

Faces projected on a screen; faces of dockworkers, pensioners, market women—all scarred by hard experience. So begins Steven Berkoff's *East.* The stage is dark and bare. The only scenery is a wall covered with graffiti. 'Fuck'. 'Cunt'. 'Denis Law Is King'. 'Mike And Les Rule OK'. Crude, black-humoured messages of teenagers struggling to survive in a tough neighbourhood. Next, silhouetted against the light, the faces of the five actors. . . . Slowly they embark on a cacophonous medley of Cockney tunes and cheery chatter. 'Any old Iron', 'evening all', 'cuppa tea love?'—a biting put down of all those horribly sentimental showbiz versions of the East End. . . . (p. 28)

East shows the East End as it is—a city of violent, comic, deeply frustrated people, a hard place to grow up and develop in. Its form is impressionistic semi-biographical, and Berkoff mobilises all the elements of theatre—including pantomime, movement, music and speech—to bring his themes to life. . . . It certainly tears holes in our accepted stage versions of the East End, from Wesker's earnest social realism to Joan Littlewood's political romanticism, through to the slushy sentimentality of Lionel Bart and Max Bygraves.

The action starts with two likely lads Mike and Les, preparing to 'fancy each other round the back' with bottles, knives and the rest. Crop-headed, with big boots, cutaway jeans and heavy bracelets, they look like 60s skinheads (whose dress was an unconscious parody of the belt-and-braces work culture of their dads). At the same time, there is about their dress a hint of David Bowie-style teenage 'camp', while their blank stares suggest the amoral nihilism of Clockwork Orangemen, and even—the latest convulsion of youth culture—the degeneracy of today's punk rockers.

The nub of Mike and Les's little argument concerns Sylv, 'of legendary knockers'. An untouchable disco sexolet, Sylv arouses the lads to fiery passions worthy of an Elizabethan revenge drama. Their language in fact moves, hilariously, from the rhythmic power of Shakesperian blank verse to straight Cockney slang. 'So I said to him, "fuck off, thou discharge from thy mother's womb before with honed and sweetened razor I do trouble to remove thy balls from thee".'

Such passionate outpourings are accompanied by a lot of vacant 'screwing', macho swaggers, and tightening of stomach muscles. Growing up in the East End involves mastering a whole repertoire of these techniques of bodily control, techniques that will later define the key social concepts of '*hard man*', '*soft as a girl*' and so on. Berkoff and his company's controlled physical expression brilliantly captures the precise grammar of this working-class body language. (pp. 28-9)

One of the most effective weapons in Berkoff's impressive dramatic armoury is the Joycean stream of consciousness soliloquoy. Sylv, for example, fed up with the 'whip it in, whip it out, wipe it off' mentality of the blokes in this male-dominated culture, whines 'I for once would like to be a fella, unwholesome both in deed and word'. Les fantasises about the upper-class crumpet he espies on the number 38 bus as it snakes its way out of Hackney down the Essex Road, into posh Bloomsbury. 'I could have breakfasted on her knickers, so sweetly pure she was.' Mum's solo spot consists largely of an inane list of popular tv shows. Interspersed with memories of *Opportunity Knocks* and *The Golden Shot,* however, are cultural double-take lines, such as memories of lunch with Hemingway at the Brasserie Lip in Paris! . . .

[The] heavy sexism and 'macho' violence of *East,* together with the fact that it avoids any overt political commitment, will provoke allegations that Berkoff is a reactionary. Certainly, his youthful protagonists are left at the end with little more than the desire to escape into organised crime, like the Kray twins. The rest is blind frustration. 'We will not end our days like this, waiting, while ma and pa make little noughts and crosses upon coupons called hope-or-death.'

East may lack any further commitment to positive social change, yet it shows the way things are in the East End with considerable accuracy. . . . It shows how concrete high rise ghettoes breed pessimism and despair. It shows how the more locked the kids are into the grim realities of their *local* life, the more narrow-minded, the more miserable, the more dehumanised, they become.

East is also a very funny comedy, by the way. Truly, to borrow a line from the play, Steven Berkoff doth bestride Commercial Road like a colossus. (p. 29)

> *Dave Robins, in a review of "East," in* Plays and Players, *Vol. 24, No. 12, September, 1977, pp. 28-9.*

BRUCE ELDER

[*The essay excerpted below incorporates commentary by Bruce Elder with an interview between Elder and Berkoff. Berkoff's remarks appear in indented form.*]

The actor stands black waistcoated, denim jeaned legs spread in a posture of alienation, bovver boots anchoring him to the unfriendly world, delighting, flavouring, wallowing in the image of an unattainable girl glimpsed on a bus. His arms float and sway in expressive parabolas; his face, always animated and excited, shifts and alters its expression to catch every nuance of his fantasy; his body moves—glides, leaps, bounces, weaves—as it strains to make the experience complete.

This is Steven Berkoff's *East*—one of the most interesting, experimental, and worthwhile plays to grace the London stage in the last few years. (p. 37)

East is total theatre, gut reaction theatre, call it what you will. Subtitled 'Elegy for the East End and its Energetic Waste', it is a great theatrical scream of pain and resentment, a kaleidoscope of images of life in the East End. Like all of Berkoff's productions (he scripts, directs, produces, and acts in all his own plays) it deploys every aspect of stagecraft—mime, dance, song, text, improvisation, lighting, makeup, but no set—into a compelling piece of theatre. Berkoff has written of the play:

> *East* takes place within my personal memory and

experience and is less a biographical text than an outburst of revolt against the sloth of my youth and a desire to turn a welter of undirected passion and frustration into a positive form. I wanted to liberate that time squandered and sometimes enjoyed into a testament of youth and energy. It is a scream or a shout of pain. It is revolt. There is no holding back or reserve in the East End of youth as I remember . . . you said what you thought and did what you felt.

Like his plays, Steven Berkoff is super-charged with energy. He is a self-confessed enthusiast whose conversation tumbles and cascades in a great torrent of fact, opinion, and anecdote, tender and tendentious, abusive and abrasive, delivered in a bewildering number of voices. . . . All the while his face alive with his own excitement and enthusiasm for the subject, his broad mouth describing a myriad of shapes as he pouts, looks down his nose and enunciates his distaste, smiles at his own sardonic wit, grimaces with mock horror at the thought of one more bad review. (pp. 37-8)

Like Mike, the hero of *East,* Berkoff is himself an East Ender. A teen product of the restlessness and pointlessness of the postwar years, he is 39 this year. The son of a Stepney tailor whose parents had fled from Russia, he first went to school in Stepney, then to Hackney Downs Grammar where Harold Pinter had been a pupil seven or eight years before.

Coming from such a background he has a healthy distaste for the arty, toffee-nosed approach to contemporary theatre. He believes in himself and what he is doing. It is in this sense of committed zeal, and readiness to take on the whole theatrical establishment, that Berkoff's strength really resides. He is not a person happy to fit into other people's grand designs.

In 1973, after years and years of being a lackey to other people's creative whims, he set up the London Theatre Group. Its credo was clear and unequivocal: 'To express drama in the most vital way imaginable; to perform at the height of one's powers with all available means. That is, through the spoken word, gesture, mime and music. Sometimes the emphasis on one, sometimes on the other.'

It was Berkoff giving notice that he was rejecting British realism. Why?

> Because it's very, very boring. You come to the theatre and people are totally fucking bored out of their minds. The really sad thing is that people start to accept the boredom and get corrupted by the boredom and eventually they start to think that boredom is okay.
>
> When actors leave drama school they all want to work in really exciting theatre. They want to do exciting parts. They all start out like this. They all look out for this holy grail that is in their systems. Then they come face to face with mundane West End theatre and they say, 'I'm a bit disappointed. I hate this', and yet they keep doing it.
>
> (p. 39)

The trouble is that the people who own and run and work for the West End theatres are pathologically limited. They've seen realism as an easy way for the amateur. When realism came in everybody thought they could be a director. You'd get the charlady from the street and say, 'Move around here, luv', and people would say, 'Is that a charlady or an actress pretending to be a charlady?' Somehow real-

ism lets people off the hook. Theatre used to be a tremendous world of soloists, acrobats, harlequins—every actor had to sing, dance, mime; every man to be a Shakespearian actor had to do juggling, sword fighting, lots of things. Now suddenly, in this age of realism, that's all gone. The last stylization you had in England was the Elizabethan era. Shakespeare was an experimental writer, so were the Jacobeans. They wrote in iambic pentameters. Those playwrights were writing with five stresses and rhyming couplets—that's stylization.

(pp. 39-40)

After six years of slogging, working in repertory in Nottingham, Liverpool, and Coventry as well as the highly regarded Citizen's Theatre in Glasgow, Berkoff made his directorial debut in 1968 with [*In the Penal Colony*], a version of Franz Kafka's [short story of the same title]. . . . It was the beginning of a ten year obsession with Kafka. A year later he created his first version of *Metamorphosis,* a play he subsequently revived . . . , and in 1971 he brought *The Trial* to the stage. Today Berkoff still describes . . . *The Trial,* which he directed, in German, for the Dusseldorf Playhouse, as his 'seminal work', and, commenting on Berkoff's production, the *Frankfurter Allgemeine* described it as 'unquestionably the best theatrical interpretation of Kafka ever seen in the world'. Not surprisingly, Berkoff is humbled, still, by the accolades.

> I'm just Steve from Islington and here were people acclaiming me over great men like Peter Weiss and Barrault and Orson Welles. Of course when I got it back to London the critics dismissed it. Said we were just a bunch of automatons because we were trying to capture the mechanistic qualities of the bureaucracy. They couldn't deal with it. It was pathetic.

Recently *The Trial* has slipped from the London Theatre Group's repertoire, but *Metamorphosis* is still being performed, and appeared in no less than three London theatres last year. In many ways it is the finest flowering and most perfect articulation of Berkoff's notions of theatre.

Played on a stage bare except for simple scaffolding, the play breathes life into Kafka's world with terrifying effectiveness. Actors dressed in black with faces made up in flat, emotionless, china white—echoing gothic nightmares and Kabuki artifice all at once—retell the strange tale of Gregor Samsa, the salesman who awoke one morning to find that he'd been metamorphosed into a beetle. It is an ideal vehicle for Berkoff's talents. He always seems to relish the psychological parable and *Metamorphosis,* with its resonances of human cruelty, of prejudice, of familial cruelty and insensitivity, stretches his imaginative powers to their limit. . . .

Ask Berkoff about Kafka and he replies enthusiastically:

> I think Kafka had an immense imagination which dealt with the unconscious side of ourselves or the dreamlike side of ourselves. He dealt with the everyday in a very macabre, very interesting, and almost satiric way. He brilliantly described the everyday in uncommon terms. What theatre is all about is the ability to describe the everyday in uncommon terms. So you don't always have to choose fantastic subjects. You can choose an ordinary subject and do it fantastically. That's the main thing about Kafka.
>
> What we are trying to do is express something

which is inexpressible and do what is inexpressible uncommonly well or in a unique way. I like to take on the impossible because then it makes a demand upon the imagination. So how would you stage a beetle? How would you create an insect? How would you create a house with no props or scenery? How would you do these things?

(p. 40)

The actor's body is the environment of the stage rather than a set. The actor is the set. Like Barrault would say, 'The actor is his environment.' Barrault invented the term total theatre because he said the actor should be totally used. You should know that he didn't always do it, but his theories are very fine. He occasionally had big lumbering sets but to put a set on the stage, I think, is already halfway to giving up. In some of the conventional theatres they put a big set on the stage and then all the actors are gathered at the first rehearsal and look at the set and say, 'You'll come down the stairs here', 'You'll come in over there', 'You have a piss over there'. Then they make little figures to represent the actors and the director sits at home saying, 'He'll go down there', 'She'll come in over here'.

That's all very nice, but supposing you can't have a set? Supposing you didn't have a sofa to stick your big fat arse on? Supposing you had no chair? Supposing you have no armchair and the actress says, 'Oooh, darling, what am I going to sit on?' You get some really farty English actress who's been subsidized by the West End and agents and television for years, when she should have been doing some proper work like gardening or something.

I've seen hundreds of them at auditions, and they're really broken wrecks because their arses are all shaped into chairs. They come on stage and say, 'Where will the chair be?' So suppose you say, 'There's no chair you silly fat bitch, but express a chair. Feel it. Talk about it. This is your house. Let this man become the house. Use your voice. Sing him a scaffolding. Change your environment.'

What I'm basically saying in my insulting smears is that it's not so much another way as a way away from laziness, away from the ordinary, because in laziness we tend to accept gross crimes of the mind.

While Berkoff has directed scripted drama—*Macbeth,* Strindberg's *Miss Julie,* and Albee's *Zoo Story*—he feels that the finished play is simply 'a mass of dialogue with no resonances of inner life', and is happier working from short stories which give the whole situation 'the inner and outer life and subjective thought of the characters'.

This, combined with a fascination for the grotesque, the surreal and the paranoic, led him, quite naturally, to Kafka. And from Kafka it was but a step to the strange dream-world of Edgar Allen Poe.

With Poe, Berkoff was free to deal with gothic horror without Kafka's oppressive bureaucracy to stifle the primal screams and fears. The work he chose was "The Fall of the House of Usher"—a horrifying study of energy turned in upon itself. Its resonances of incest and fratricide were, once again, perfect vehicles for Berkoff's imagination.

He took as his inspiration one of the key textual lines from Poe's short story, 'The House of Usher—an appelation which seemed to include, in the minds of the peasantry who used

it, both the family and the family mansion', and so accepted the unenviable task of playing both Roderick Usher and the ancient, craggy house. (pp. 40, 42)

In his own short essay **"Introduction to Poe and Performance,"** Berkoff gives both an insight into the play and to his whole approach to drama:

> The tale of the impossible. . . . A house with its own soul. A death. A resurrection. A moor's pestilential environment. A house that outwardly manifests the crumbling nature of Roderick's inner decay. A febrile fantastical story that served as an occult tale for our voices and senses, to find their expression through. The actors must be the house and its decaying fabric, must speak as stones and the memories of the house that are seared into its walls . . . must be the death rattle and atmosphere, must be the environment, and since humans are born of the environment they must reflect it.
>
> Our bodies link, break away, dance, flow to each other passing these valuable segments of information. . . . [They] must be stretched plastic, communicative. Mime demands exactness as any ritual must since it is mutually shared with the audience whose imaginative participation is required to make it live.

The Fall of the House of Usher is, almost unquestionably, the most stylized and ritualized work to emerge from contemporary British theatre. From its opening scene of Madeline lying contorted by rigor mortis, through Roderick's dramatic portrayal of the actual house of Usher, to Madeline's horrific attempts to escape her coffin and her final emergence in full ritualized Kabuki attire (white face, flowing robes, and tatters of red ribbons symbolizing blood) it is built on traditions and rituals which are both alien and familiar. It seems to touch the essence of our dramatic being, penetrating deep into our myths and psyche. . . .

Berkoff has created a theatrical form that is uniquely his. He is out on a limb, but he enjoys being there. Ask him what is the possibility of anybody else producing his work and he is unequivocal:

> No way. Impossible for anyone to do it anywhere in the world because it's unique to me. I invented it like Picasso paints Picasso, Renoir paints Renoir, Kafka writes Kafka. I think there can be impersonators, but it would be very hard because I think it comes from an innate sense of performance. You can copy the style a bit but it's a way of thinking which has taken years: thinking in terms of mime and metaphysically knowing how to get a desired result.
>
> This is the age of the mundane, and I just stand out in it because I don't like the mundanity. I'd rather stand out with the great poets and the painters and the French impressionists and the German expressionists. That's why people come to see me.

(p. 42)

Bruce Elder, " 'Doing the Inexpressible Uncommonly Well': The Theatre of Steven Berkoff," in Theatre Quarterly, *Vol. VIII, No. 31, Autumn, 1978, pp. 37-43.*

CHARLES EDELMAN

Steven Berkoff's *East* is a violently funny evocation of the hard life in London's East End, where, within one family at least, the name of British Nazi Oswald Mosley still strikes a responsive chord, and the only meaningful recreations are having "charver" (sex) or a "bundle" (fight). Berkoff . . . has combined East End slang, Yiddish, and Elizabethan poetic speech, including some fractured quotations from Shakespeare, into an argot of iambic pentameter to create what might be described as a series of explosions in this working class family. There is Dad, Mum (played not incongruously by a man), the voluptuous Sylv, and the two boys Les and Mike, replete with hobnail boots and chains.

More a series of sketches than a play, *East* depicts the family's day-to-day life—a night at the movies that turns into a ridiculous case of mistaken identity and mutual masturbation, a holiday at the seashore, and dinner with the family that includes Dad's side-splitting reminiscence of the day he marched with Mosley, in which he goes quite insane while spraying the rest of the cast with baked beans. These sketches, which except for the splendidly obscene language have something of the feel of a t.v. situation comedy, are alternated with lengthy monologues, in which each character addresses the audience and delivers a scathing description of his or her life. The most effective of these is Sylv's lament, "I, for once, would like to be a fella," as she bemoans her existence as a mere plaything for men to prove their virility. Music Hall, vaudeville, Shakespearean declamation, stand-up night club comedy, and a silent film parody are all part of the play's nineteen scenes. (p. 547)

My one cavil about what was overall a highly competent production of a good play was a tendency for the cast to plant their feet too firmly on the night club stage—Les ad libbing and Mike telling the audience "Don't laugh. You'll only encourage him." Had the entire play been performed as a piece of cabaret theatre, which would be most appropriate, these moments might have been less jarring. Still, what Berkoff says about Mike is true of himself: "He doth bestride Commercial Road like a colossus." (p. 548)

Charles Edelman, in a review of "East," in Educational Theatre Journal, *Vol. 30, No. 4, December, 1978, pp. 547-48.*

MICHAEL BIRTWISTLE

In the fall of 1982, Steven Berkoff came to Los Angeles to mount productions of two of his previously staged adaptations; both stimulated technical and thematic interest and discussion. Although it would be pointless to imply that they surpassed the works on which they are based, neither *Metamorphosis* nor *Greek* in any way trivialized their sources.

Berkoff, a theatre-maker in the Edward Gordon Craig tradition, is both author and director of *Metamorphosis* and *Greek.* In *Metamorphosis* he is also the original performer of the central role. His hand is unmistakably present in the scenic, costume, and lighting designs, and it is hard to imagine a theatre experience more completely controlled by one person.

Berkoff is remarkably faithful to Kafka's "Metamorphosis:" Gregor awakes one morning to find that he has turned into a dungbeetle. But rather than fill out the scenic world of Kafka's cluttered apartment, Berkoff calls for a spare setting with a single small platform which serves as the base for the dominant scenic motif—a large iron cage, shaped like a megaphone. On this angular space, the Samsa family tells Gregor's story, using only their vocal and physical resources.

The production style is even more blunt. Often using Kafka's words, the actors playing Gregor and his family speak directly to the audience in a choral mode; they enact critical moments from the family history; they transform family encounters into memories. Berkoff has plundered techniques from the recent history of theatrical practice, but his assembly of Story Theatre, mime and expressionism presents a unified surface. (p. 241)

[*Greek*], unlikely as it may seem, is the Oedipus legend transferred to contemporary East End London. *Greek* gives us Eddie, his Mum and Dad, his Wife, a Fortune Teller, and even the Sphinx, but Berkoff does not follow Sophocles's organization or use his late point of attack. He shows us Eddie murdering his father, for example, and gives us an ending which lacks the traditional self-mutilation. Particularly challenging, in contrast to Sophocles's great leader, is Berkoff's creation of Eddie as a rebellious, foul-mouthed punk. Both have a great drive to get ahead, and both lose sight of their place in the social and cosmic scheme of things.

Metamorphosis is cool and reflective whereas *Greek* is hot and aggressive, but they share the same theatrical conventions. If anything, *Greek* is presented even more bluntly, and the audience's close proximity to the action . . . increases the impact. We see again the storytelling structure, the flashbacks, the small company of actors playing several roles, and the entire drama centered on the protagonist. (p. 242)

Metamorphosis and *Greek* are the work of an assured, exciting theatrical storyteller. "We make theatre as if there had never been theatre before," Berkoff has said. Although many of his adaptations are in print, his unique vision is difficult to catch as it comes off the printed page. . . . (pp. 242-43)

Michael Birtwistle, in a review of "Metamorphosis" and "Greek," in Theatre Journal, *Vol. 35, No. 2, May, 1983, pp. 241-43.*

TONY DUNN

[Berkoff's *Metamorphosis*] extracts a complicated psychodrama from the famous story. Everyone remembers that the hero, Gregor, wakes up one morning to find he has been transformed into a giant beetle. Mentally he is still human, physically he is an insect. The event is so horrific, and its symbolism so rich, that the rest of the story, Gregor's relations with his family, tends to be forgotten. Berkoff's stage-set gives equal prominence to Gregor and his relatives. A cage of tubular bars, with the audience-wall removed, gradually expands out from a hutch at the back, Gregor's lair, to a fan-like structure within which father, mother and daughter enact their play of attraction and repulsion. The 'fine flat' that Gregor was so proud of providing for his parents from his hard work becomes an enclosure for domestic hell. The family tries to get in a lodger to replace Gregor's lost income, but he exits in horror when Gregor scuttles out of his backroom. The father becomes the pivotal figure. It is he who gets a job and throws the apple that embeds itself in Gregor's back and causes his eventual death; but it is also the father who lifts Gregor back into his room, the only person who actually touches him. The daughter is sympathetic but terrified, the mother is repelled. It's therefore a very Oedipal story that Berkoff has uncovered within Kafka's text. . . . (p. 32)

[*Sink the Belgrano!*] is completely contemporary, and this is its weakness. The walls of the foyer are covered in press-cuttings, statements and photographs about the events leading up to the Belgrano's sinking on May 2, 1982. A video at one end plays tapes from British and Argentine TV, and the programme contains a chronology of the important dates from April to June, flanked by columns which balance the official version of events with opposing interpretations. This then is the history, one which everyone in Argentina and Britain lived through four years ago, and one about which everyone has a definite view. What can the theatre add? Berkoff's 90 minute piece indicts the chauvinism of the British working-class, reduces the War Cabinet to a comic three-some of Maggot, Pimp and Nit, and choreographs the drilling and disciplining of a submarine crew. All good agit-prop stuff, and very pleasing to the Argentines, who've boosted the production in Buenos Aires and helped to pack out the audience in East London. But Berkoff makes the fatal mistake of trying to rise above the humdrum of documentary realism by having all his characters speak in blank-verse. Not only is modern verse-drama entirely the territory of the Christian Right, but also, to any educated theatre-goer, the achievements of the four- and five-beat lines begin and end with Shakespeare, Marlowe, Jonson and Webster. And what makes them still bearable is the continuous movement of inventive image and thought against the monotonous beat. Within 50 years the medium had died. Otway's *Venice Preserv'd* is deadly dull because the images are entirely predictable. *Sink the Belgrano!* has the same effect. Expectations raised by the beat of the first half of the line are, on every occasion, disappointed by the metaphor in the second. 'Like giant whales of death'; 'stomachs loaded full like gorged beasts'; 'as we cling to mastheads in the freezing sea'. The play is full of deliberate plagiarisms from *Henry V* and Macbeth, and to set up Maggot as a kind of demonic chauvinist, shouting 'Bring forth men-soldiers only' and stirring up a witch's cauldron of Argie entrails, is a promising idea. Shakespeare, however, is weighty competition. Trigger off the famous passages from *Henry V's* Chorus or Lady Macbeth, and you need either very distinguished writing or a very clever structure to stop that poetry from the past overwhelming your own efforts.

There is just one moment when Berkoff might have broken free. The attention is downstage, with the crew lying on the floor in their submarine-space. Their commander tries to evoke their psychological state as they wait for their first engagement. The beauty of the marine depths is twinned with the beauty of precision killing. It is a very twentieth century site—the aesthetics of fascism—already explored by Marinetti, Céline and Coppola's *Apocalypse Now.* But Berkoff's language can't pull it off. The images are banal, the rhythmic movement gets hopelessly snarled up, and we move back to the cartoon-comedy of the War Cabinet. (pp. 32-3)

> *Tony Dunn, in a review of "Metamorphosis" and "Sink the Belgrano!" in* Plays & Players, *No. 398, November, 1986, pp. 32-3.*

JEREMY GERARD

To kvetch, Leo Rosten wrote in his dictionary-cum-cosmology, *The Joys of Yiddish,* is, literally, to squeeze ("Don't kvetch the peaches"); in its verb form it can mean to fuss, to fret, to delay or to shrug, though it has entered the American lexicon as the more generic to complain or gripe.

Improvising only slightly on all of those definitions, the British playwright Steven Berkoff defines a kvetch—at least in its noun form—as a pinch, something that bites at the consciousness of the insecure, which is to say, at all of us, in times of stress or indecision. Paradise for Mr. Berkoff is a place without a kvetch, and that place, he suggests, surely is one not to be found on earth.

The phrase most often invoked by the five characters in *Kvetch,* Mr. Berkoff's absurdist comedy of Jewish-American mismanners . . . is "I'm afraid"—indeed, it is the play's opening line. Subtitled "An American play about anxiety," *Kvetch,* which Mr. Berkoff is also directing, is dedicated to "the afraid," from those afraid of not getting to work on time to those afraid of muggers, women, men, dying, parking tickets, unemployment, blacks, whites, spiders and others too numerous to mention.

"A kvetch has a lot to do with indecision," Mr. Berkoff said, during a recent conversation after rehearsal. "A kvetch is something that starts to gnaw at you. That doesn't happen when you're sure of something."

Kvetch might best be described as a situation comedy in which the characters seem to have no superego to mediate between their conscious and unconscious selves. The audience hears everything the characters think as well as say, and there are no balloons above their heads to indicate the difference between circumspect conversation ("You want some coffee, everybody?") and raw fear ("What are they looking at? Do I look funny?"). It is worth noting that the two comments quoted above may be the only two in the play eligible for retelling in polite society.

The play opens with its five characters—a salesman, his wife and mother-in-law, a friend and a business associate—sitting at a table, facing the audience and going through a catalogue of exaggerated facial expressions. They begin slowly, against a cacophony of music rising in the background, and then come on stronger, faster, more grotesquely. From that startling opening, *Kvetch* does not let up. . . .

Some theatergoers at *Kvetch* are bound to think they've died and gone to family hell, as Mr. Berkoff's characters dredge up deep-seated feelings about sex, identity and race.

"These are things that aren't supposed to happen on a stage, in public," he said. "Theater is like therapy to me. I wanted to exorcise all those irrational fears that I have, that everybody has."

Part theatrical triple-threat (he has won critical praise for his work as director and actor in works of his own and others' devising), part unashamed snake-oil salesman, Mr. Berkoff writes plays that compel an audience to face without mercy contemporary stereotypes and prejudices. In the 1983 *Greek,* Mr. Berkoff reinvented the Oedipus myth as a no-holds-barred vision of contemporary urban disintegration. That play had successful runs in London and Los Angeles before being practically run out of New York on a rail. . . .

"I try to get to the ultimate experience of whatever I'm writing about," Mr. Berkoff said. "*Greek* is a vital, modern expression of London society in the grip of a plague called apathy, violence and sickness. In New York it was received with a mixture of hysteria and disbelief." . . .

Finding himself on an extended stay in Los Angeles, Mr. Berkoff . . . came up with the idea for *Kvetch.* "I suffer from various obsessive anxieties which I accepted as part of the wear-and-tear of living as a playwright, as an actor," he said.

"I began writing sketches about those irrational fears. Not about big questions—'What is the meaning of life?' I was concerned with the everyday fears that obsess me. Do I look funny? Will I be able to act?

"I grew up in a Jewish family in the East End of London, played in the street a lot, it was very much like [New York's] Lower East Side. *Kvetch* is what I grew up with."

Though *Kvetch* seemed, in Los Angeles, to derive much of its energy from the freeway culture around it, Mr. Berkoff insisted that it is a Jewish-American play that could take place in any city. It combines, he said, his identity as a Jewish writer with the influence of those itinerant, politically oriented American troupes he saw as a young man in London, like the Living Theater, the Open Theater and La Mama.

What he'd learned from them, Mr. Berkoff said, was respect for a theater that deals straight-on with contemporary problems, leaving gentility to others. "Theater should deal with the profane and the unmentionable," he said. "*Kvetch* is about fear. 'I'm afraid.' The confession of angst can heal, but it needs full, frontal attack, not subtlety."

Jeremy Gerard, " 'Kvetch' Asks 'Why Complain?' and Replies 'Why Not?' " in The New York Times, *February 15, 1987, p. H3.*

HOWARD KISSEL

If *Kvetch* were not written, directed and, as nearly as one can tell, performed by Jews, it would be denounced as anti-Semitic. It is a collection of sex jokes, mother-in-law jokes and ethnic jokes tied together by a plot so primitive it would be dishonest even to call it a play.

The intention of Steven Berkoff, who wrote and directed *Kvetch,* seems less to tell a story or describe characters than to take material that is coarse to begin with and inflate it until it becomes stupefyingly vulgar.

In 1968 this might have been regarded as politically and socially daring, a gesture of defiance at middle-class conventions. When Lenny Bruce performed gross material, it was highly neurotic but it had the shock of truth. Bruce attacked hypocrisy with sharp observation of how people behaved.

Nothing about Berkoff's work suggests observation. He fills the stage with jokes and stereotypes. In *Kvetch,* grossness is an end in itself. . . .

The lines are not delivered. They are shouted, belched, groaned or whined. (*Kvetch* is a must for students of whining, since Berkoff and his cast exploit the grating capacity of every known nasal cavity.)

But what can you do with a line like, "What is a breast? A little piece of tissue with a cork on the end?" What can you do with a character whose most interesting moments are pantomiming flatulence.

In some ways, one sympathizes with Berkoff. His "art" consists of shocking the audience. What can he do when the audience is too jaded, too blase to be shocked?

The night I saw *Kvetch* the audience consisted largely of middle-class Jews, who, far from seeming shocked or disgusted, responded heartily. A young man in a skullcap told me he found it "cute and amusing."

Would it be less or more disturbing to discover he was a backer?

Howard Kissel, "Please, Don't 'Kvetch'," in Daily News, *New York, February 19, 1987.*

MARILYN STASIO

With a vengeance, Steven Berkoff crosses the line from comedy to cruelty in *Kvetch,* a black comedy about the secret, obsessive anxieties that make monsters of us all—sometimes. By rejecting the very notion of "sometimes," human nature itself becomes monstrous, in Berkoff's book.

The Jewish family he dissects here is positively riddled with irrational fears of social, sexual, professional, economic and personal inadequacy. A simple family dinner that brings a stranger to the table drives them all into paroxysms of neurotic terror. In true monster fashion, they project their own anxieties into seething hatred and contempt for each other.

And that's only the first act.

The unusual theatrical style of the play, which Berkoff himself has directed, makes it clear that the playwright believes he is slicing the jugular to let truth flow out.

Almost all the action takes place at a long table where the characters interact on a public level, in which they babble social inanities and look exceedingly foolish and a private level, in which they freely vent their deep, raging hysteria. . . .

[Despite the] incisive writing and bravura theatrical style of the piece, *Kvetch* lacks a comic soul. It conveys plenty of contempt, but no compassion for its characters, depriving them of all vestiges of humanity.

If this is truth, I'll take a pastrami on rye.

Marilyn Stasio, " 'Kvetch' Seethes with Contempt," in New York Post, *February 19, 1987.*

MEL GUSSOW

"Kvetch," as in the title of Steven Berkoff's new comedy [*Kvetch*], is a complaint, which, if allowed to fester, can become an anxiety attack. As the play begins, we hear Mr. Berkoff's voice offstage, intoning an introduction to his tale of comic woe. As an actor, the playwright specializes in villainy, and his doom-filled narration starts the evening on a properly prophetic note.

Around a table are five characters, each compartmentalized by his individual kvetch. The principals are a husband, wife and the wife's mother. Outwardly they seem relatively compatible, but beneath the surface are tremors of resentment. Each character reveals his kvetch as a confession, rising in chorus until everyone is kvetching on a grand scale.

As in [Eugene O'Neill's] *Strange Interlude,* the audience hears the other, blacker half of the story. Husband and wife despise everything about one another, and the mother-in-law is a noisome creature. The husband brings a business friend home for dinner, and though he is mannerly in public, he is miserable in private—and tells us about it. As a light strikes the speaker, the others freeze, and the caterwauling rises in intensity.

For a time, *Kvetch* is amusing, provoking the audience to nervous laughter of recognition as the author assails the complacency in an American Jewish family. Then Mr. Berkoff reaches for a plot. What could have been a brief sketch, followed by other sketches on related themes, tries—and fails—to become a full play. An older man woos the hapless wife, almost against his will. The unhappy husband, gloomy about his marriage, discovers within himself an unconvincing passion for his business friend, a relationship that, predictably, is destined to repeat the trauma of marriage.

The comedy hovers and then settles in sitcom-land. The bite becomes blunt rather than ferocious. As the show winds down, it is apparent that for all Mr. Berkoff's bark, his play is like a guest who is offended by the company but is reluctant to speak his mind out loud and receive a direct response. This was not the case with his play *Greek,* a far less enjoyable work of graphic excess.

While the characters in *Strange Interlude* spoke in asides to the audience—with, admittedly, far less malice than is exhibited in *Kvetch*—later playwrights, such as Edward Albee, Jules Feiffer and Wallace Shawn, have been forthright in their truth-telling.

Mr. Shawn's *Marie and Bruce* is, in fact, an excellent counter to *Kvetch.* In it, a wife says what she thinks without self-censorship—and her husband blithely accepts the abuse. In television there is, among other shows, *Fawlty Towers,* in which John Cleese hilariously attacks everyone—wife, waiter and guests in his hotel. With these precedents and with all the insults endured in everyday life, Mr. Berkoff's indictment seems somehow covert.

*Mel Gussow, "'Kvetch': Steven Berkoff Comedy,"
in* The New York Times, *February 19, 1987, p. C26.*

ALLAN WALLACH

Steven Berkoff, who has written plays based on such intellectual sources as Kafka and Greek tragedy, is after smaller game this time.

His target is the anxiety of daily living, and his method is to have the polite things people say contradicted by the dark thoughts they dare not utter. The premise might serve nicely for a *Saturday Night Live* sketch lasting 10 minutes or so. In Berkoff's *Kvetch,* it goes on and on for two acts. My own dark thought was that the actors should stop kvetching already. . . .

Kvetch goes on long after its single comic device—not all that original—has stopped paying dividends. (To be fair, the audience at the performance I caught laughed, most often at obscenities, Yiddish expressions and references to bodily functions.)

Kvetch is essentially a succession of sketches, all falling into the same pattern: Someone says something, then thinks the opposite. For variety, someone thinks something, then says the opposite. Unlike the other people onstage, the privileged members of the audience get to hear the hidden thoughts.

The pattern is established early, when Frank invites Hal home to dinner but thinks, "Oh, God, I hope he says no." Hal smilingly accepts, although he really wants to turn down the invitation, fearful that he won't be able to carry his share of the conversation.

This sort of thing goes on all through dinner, which makes the meal seem as long as a banquet. [Frank's] wife, Donna, is anxious that she'll say or do something embarrassing, while her old Jewish mother *does* do something embarrassing.

Not satisfied with ruining dinner, Berkoff pursues the anxieties into bed and business. Donna finds Frank sexually inadequate and is aroused only by a fantasy involving virile garbage men. He thinks smugly, "I excite her like mad." His smugness doesn't last long: His own sex fantasy involves Hal, which makes him worry that he's gay.

Frank is just as worried in his job as salesman, when he must swallow his rage at a contemptuous clothing manufacturer. In his turn, the manufacturer is fearful of rejection when he tries to seduce Frank's wife, who, of course, has her own set of secret fears. And so it goes. . . .

Although *Kvetch* is subtitled "an uncommon comedy," it resembles old-fashioned common comedies in one important respect: It relies on recognition humor. We all know those fears that can turn social discourse into discord. Berkoff keeps reminding us of them, knowing that some people find discomfort funny—as long as it's someone else's.

Allan Wallach, "Kvetch after Kvetch, Sketch after Sketch," in Newsday, *February 19, 1987.*

BETTY CAPLAN

[In *Greek,* Berkoff] takes his three companions on a wild, anarchic journey through Freud's favourite bedtime story. Our "septic isle" is the target for Berkoff's spluttering rage—in particular, the passivity of a working class that has allowed the Thatcherite plague to happen. Combining political satire with a treatise on sexual repression, Berkoff's play comes to a splenetic climax in Eddy's (Eddy-pus) encounter with the Sphinx. But the terms of her argument are almost as debased as its object—woman's superiority is to be measured by her greater potential for orgasm, ten to every one of his. Her reward for this wisdom is to have her head chopped off upon which Eddy heads straight back to his ma. The play's message is a curious one: Cleveland needn't have worried—incest apparently is OK.

Berkoff's prodigious talent as actor, director, mime artist and writer seem to me totally misdirected in this piece. Having taken more than a few liberties with the original, he might have been more courageous still and taken another one by allowing the Sphinx her head. As it is, the conclusion simply reinforces Eddy's irksome habit of making those around him into objects.

Betty Caplan, "Family Fortunes," in New Statesman & Society, *Vol. 1, No. 5, July 8, 1988, p. 48.*

CHRISTOPHER EDWARDS

Steven Berkoff directs and acts in a revival of . . . *Greek.* The Oedipus myth is lifted out of Thebes and put down in a council flat in Tufnell Park. Eddy is thrown out of home by his parents after a fortune-teller predicts that he will do his dad in and have it off with his mum. Eddy walks into a caff, verbals the owner to death and marries the widow. Soon, Eddy has made it big in the fast food industry. He invites his stereotype working-class parents (pub, telly and the Royal Family) to see his splendid new life only to learn that they pulled him out of the Thames after an accident in which his new wife also lost a son.

Greek is full of Berkoff's usual relish for bodily functions, obscenity and jeering abuse. He has his targets: working-class inertia, false consumer values and, most importantly, violence. He launches his attacks through a mix of pseudo-blank verse ('this septic isle') and puncturing blows of crude vulgarity which is awash with scatological imagery.

The ancient myth and Berkoff's attack on violence meet at the point where Eddy rejects the taboo about incest ('bollocks to all that') and rushes back to his mother's bed. The message is 'make love not war'. Unexceptionable in its way, only Berkoff reveals a frail sentimentality when he actually tries to celebrate erotic love in terms other than vomit, shit, pus and stink. The flights of passion between Eddy and his wife are trite and quite without the raw liberating energy that characterises Berkoff's writing at its best. With its celebratory message failing to take flight, we are left with maudlin yobbo ranting. (pp. 72-3)

Christopher Edwards, "Comic Distortion," in The Spectator, *Vol. 261, No. 8348, July 9, 1988, pp. 72-3.*

CLIVE BARNES

Coriolanus—hero or villain? Soldier or politician? Vain or proud, simpleton or fool? Obvious questions that do not always deserve obvious answers. Beethoven knew the answer—just listen to his overture. But do we?

Joseph Papp's complete Shakespeare canon got an unusual salvo . . . last night, with the opening of an unexpectedly revisionist version of *Coriolanus.*

The staging [of the new *Coriolanus*] is by the British director and playwright Steven Berkoff (the first time a Brit has been invited to run in this hitherto all-Yankee marathon), who is not particularly accustomed to Shakespeare but is certainly no stranger to controversy.

What he has done to Shakespeare is partly to cut it down to his own size—he felt the play was padded and proceeded to destuff it.

Bertolt Brecht—who once commented on how much easier it was to stage Shakespeare when you were able to re-translate him for the purpose—also once had his way with *Coriolanus.*

Talking of a new *Coriolanus,* he wrote: "I believe he [Shakespeare] would have taken the spirit of our time into account much as we have done, with less conviction no doubt, but more talent." That was nicely humble.

Brecht's adaptation of *Coriolanus* was politically geared—the Roman patrician, much concerned with the economics of grain prices, is out to fool and rule the deserving mob of plebeians.

Oddly enough, Brecht's recension of the story and remodeling of the hero has had some subliminal effect on almost every post-war production of *Coriolanus.*

No one now quite sees him as a Rambo-style hero humming stirring Beethoven tunes as he is misunderstood by the ungrateful populace. At best—for the pendulum has surely gone too far—he is now envisaged as a vain, hubristic bullyboy who gets no more than he deserves.

Like Brecht, Berkoff also sees *Coriolanus* in political terms, but terms less dialectically ordained than party lines. With Berkoff the theme is still the vain hero versus the masses, but the masses now come from Little Italy rather than Rome, and indeed it is more the loner versus the Mob.

These people are gangsters as well as politicians—it is as if Brecht's Coriolanus has met up with Brecht's Arturo Ui for an ideological showdown.

Berkoff has played hell with the play—cutting it (quite savagely at times, especially with the roles of Menenius and Cominius), omitting some roles (notably young Marcius, Coriolanus' son), and condensing many of the others into a Greek chorus taking a Roman holiday.

When the text does not suit his purpose he even adds to it, so we have the Volscian general Aufidius (Coriolanus' heroic antagonist) carousing with his soldiers, and we catch the tagline of some Berkoffian dirty joke that runs: "So, I said, for 50 ducats I want to see her naked!"

Let it be said that respect for the text is not the production's strong suit. Berkoff even has Aufidius delivering a coup de grace to Coriolanus' dying body—another telling touch that Shakespeare unaccountably omitted.

On the other hand, these choric gangland shenanigans—they are mostly choreographed in a jerkily balletic, expressionist style not unlike Kurt Jooss' *The Green Table*—do not run against at least the Brechtian spirit of the play, which pits this vainglorious boy-general against the people.

What [Berkoff's *Coriolanus*] misses is Shakespeare's sense of Coriolanus as a loner, as a spiritual outcast; here he is merely a spoilt gangland brat who don't get no respect.

Berkoff has imposed a skillful physicality on the production, which most remarkably uses a fascinating percussion score as a veritable trampoline for the action. . . .

[*Coriolanus*] is no waste of time. At the end, you feel that you have really seen something—your attention has been engaged, your interest sparked—but that Berkoff has not achieved the modern synthesis that he meant to achieve.

Clive Barnes, "The Bard without Stuffing," in New York Post, *November 23, 1988.*

FRANK RICH

Politics is a dirty business, yet, in a democracy, someone has got to do it. But who? To many Americans, the answer was hardly satisfactory in 1988, a year in which the handlers the pollsters and the advertising men often seemed to have more say than either the candidates or the voters. The national disenchantment that was registered on Nov. 8, when a low turnout produced a mandate of dubious import, could hardly find more articulate or sorrowing expression than it does in *Coriolanus,* Shakespeare's corrosive view of Roman democracy in the fifth century B.C. *Coriolanus* is a tragedy in which the political process proves every bit as chaotic and poisonous as war.

The point is brought home with blazing, bitter irony in Steven Berkoff's striking production [*Coriolanus*]. . . . Mr. Berkoff is an idiosyncratic English playwright, director and actor . . . whose view of Shakespeare will infuriate purists. His *Coriolanus* is performed in more-or-less-modern dress, nearly all of it black, with the star . . . outfitted in the hip, double-breasted jackets worn by aging pop royalty. The play's pulse has been quickened to a rock beat by textual slashing and fiddling, sharply choreographed movement (alternately martial and MTV), and an inventive all-percussion score that echoes Shakespeare's own percussive imagery even as it recalls Philip Glass's thematically related music for the film *Mishima.*

Those who have seen Mr. Berkoff's stage work—most specifically, *West,* a neo-*West Side Story* about London's disaffected working-class young—will recognize his blueprint for *Coriolanus.* One would hate to see the high-pitched Berkoff brand of stylization imposed upon most classics, but *Coriolanus* is one (*Arturo Ui* might be another) that is enriched by his colloquial approach. . . .

[The] exact place and time of this *Coriolanus* remain vague; it's the intellectual point of view that's firm. Usually in concert with the author, Mr. Berkoff takes a cynical stand on nearly everyone in the play. The Roman plebeians are black-shirted rabble, virtually indistinguishable from their enemy, the fascistic Volscian army commanded by a vulgar Aufidius. The people's tribunes are conniving, street-corner gangsters in pin stripes, while the generals are steely bureaucrats. . . . Coriolanus's hard-driving mother, Volumnia, is the quintessential political manipulator, always masking her lust for power as maternal affection. . . .

It's no wonder that . . . Caius Marcius, who is awarded the surname Coriolanus after conquering the Volscian city of Corioli, detests being a candidate for the consulship. Given the populace and its leaders, the campaign can only soil a brave military man of his patrician standing and egotistical pride. When [he] refuses to surrender his "own truth" to electoral expediency—choosing to be an enemy of the people rather than a toady to them—our sympathies are with him. In this production, Coriolanus's arrogant refusal to pander to the popular will, though ultimately carried to destructive extremes, is clearly the principled response of an honest man to a system that would warp him into an instrument of demagoguery. . . .

It can't be happenstance that while Mr. Berkoff dispenses with all actual weapons in his *Coriolanus,* he pointedly does emphasize one realistic prop: a gray diplomatic envelope containing a peace treaty. The evening ends with a chilling sequence in which that document, so frail a symbol of a citizenry's best hopes, is abruptly doomed to the oblivion of a government briefcase. The brutal political caravan, meanwhile, inexorably marches on.

> *Frank Rich, "Jagged, Percussive 'Coriolanus' from*
> *Steven Berkoff," in* The New York Times, *November 23, 1988, p. C9.*

LINDA WINER

The words "entertaining" and *Coriolanus* are not often said in the same breath. But here they are—bizarrely right together—in Steven Berkoff's updated and truncated, impertinent, overboard but overwhelmingly beautiful production ***Coriolanus.*** . . .

Shakespeare called his dense exploration of mass vs. state power a tragedy. Shaw decided it was a comedy. Kenneth Tynan called it "more a public meeting than a play."

Now Berkoff, the British actor-director seen as Hitler in *War and Remembrance,* has turned it into a kind of macabre fascist-chic dance that could have been performed in a store window of Charivari. Of course, this is hardly the only *Coriolanus* one ever needs to see. But the production . . . is powered by a sweep and vision that . . . seem truer to the life of Shakespeare than a dozen earnestly faithful readings of the text. . . .

[Berkoff] seems to revel in finding the pleasures of evil and the darkness of pleasure.

He has updated *Coriolanus* to the 20th Century, suggesting everything from late '20s workers revolution to late '80s messenger-service bikers. Music is a vital character, mostly percussion . . . , with different drum rolls and motifs for different characters, often underscoring the speeches, which Berkoff sometimes condenses effectively and sometimes turns into unfortunate colloquial clinkers.

The stage is black slate with white squares and a dozen high-back black chairs. Fashions—and fashion is the operative word here—tend toward black shirts and shades, with a long leather coat for our hero. Berkoff has cleverly turned all the ensembles—the people's mob, the Roman and Volscian senators—into a tight nine-man performance group that can goof off with mob-scene ignorance, pass judgments with officious menace, dash around and halt, poetically, in ravishing freezes.

The conspiring Roman tribunes plot in trench coats, delightfully *noir,* somewhere between CIA operatives and the wicked cat and fox in *Pinocchio.* Scenes change with cinematic dissolves and telling overlaps. Battles are slow-motion choreography. You can almost see the blood drain from the faces—like Sam Peckinpah in mime. . . .

Berkoff, unfortunately, seems unable to judge when to let Shakespeare alone.

Thus, genuine innovation gets soiled with blots of juvenile behavior, a vaudevillian ditty here, an unlikeable line there. But then Berkoff redeems himself with scenes like the final one—in which, Coriolanus and hope dead, a character slowly and deliberately puts the peace document back into his briefcase. You see, Berkoff taketh away, yes, but he also giveth.

> *Linda Winer, " 'Coriolanus': Tragedy in Trench*
> *Coats," in* Newsday, *November 23, 1988.*

SYLVIANE GOLD

Whether you see in it vindication for the tactics of the Republicans or sympathy for the Democratic debacle, [the issues of *Coriolanus*] are the stuff of our current politics. Here is a public official placating a hungry, rebellious mob with Shakespeare's elegant version of the trickle-down theory. Here are restless militarists greeting an imminent war as a welcome break in the monotony of peace. Here are common folk who expect to be flattered and lied to in exchange for their votes. Here is a candidate who stubbornly believes that his record speaks for itself and doesn't need defending.

This last, of course, is Coriolanus, the patrician general who returns to Rome after heroically defeating the Volsces only to offend the plebeians by not displaying his wounds in the marketplace. They refuse to support his bid to become consul, an honor he knows he has earned. When he angrily rails against the people's hard-won power, they banish him as a traitor. Joining the Volsces, Coriolanus leads an army to the gates of Rome—but is stopped short of destroying it by the pleas of his wife and mother.

Although Coriolanus cannot look to us as he did to the Elizabethans, who took for granted the divine right of the nobility to manage the state for the masses, he remains one of Shakespeare's most fascinating heroes. His contempt for the plebeians is balanced for us by his complete honesty. He is incapable of flattery or subterfuge. And his pride is equaled by his disdain for ceremony and the trappings of power. He doesn't want to grovel in the marketplace, but he also can't sit through the Senate's recitation of his glorious deeds.

With so much contemporary resonance, *Coriolanus* should work perfectly in modern dress. And Steven Berkoff's production [*Coriolanus*] . . . outfits the Roman mob with torn suit-jackets and baseball bats; Coriolanus wears a long leather trenchcoat; the Volscian general, Aufidius, sports guerrilla gear; and both armies march around in sinister black shirts. . . . [The] set design, a stark black-and-white checkerboard decked out with shiny molded chairs, reinforces the modern feel. Yet somehow, this *Coriolanus* seems less relevant than one in togas and sandals might have been.

Mr. Berkoff's intricate, stylized staging has much to do with this. Propelled by . . . [a] pulsing percussion score, the actors move in stiff, ritualized patterns. . . . [Coriolanus] adopts a deliberate swagger that calls to mind not an American politician but some Kabuki potentate, elbows thrust out and shoulders rocking with every step. The scheming tribunes of the people . . . become a pair of mobster song-and-dance men. The Roman Senate lines up like a drill team, while the Roman mob moves in a threatening cluster reminiscent of the Jets and the Sharks in *West Side Story*. The choreography gives the production a visual punch it would not otherwise achieve; but it also distances the play's plot and characters. They seem less important than the stage effects.

Another unfortunate result of Mr. Berkoff's approach is the laughter that erupts at some inappropriate moments. Mr. Berkoff is not, I think, reaching for lightheartedness. But who can blame an audience for tittering when a breathless messenger runs onstage in a bicycle-racing unitard? It's just the kind of modern touch that should, in theory, bring contemporary audiences closer to Shakespeare's play. In practice, the audience doesn't need the costume to figure out that the actor is playing a messenger—his message is sufficient—and so the costume is seen as an impertinence, a joke. . . .

Coriolanus glares and bristles with splendid power. But he often sounds like a street tough. If the character is deprived of his nobility, the play loses much of its meaning. This performance, though, is consistent with Mr. Berkoff's conception. He doesn't really see Coriolanus as a hero. Among the lines he has cut, presumably to allow time for all that choreography, are the ones in which Coriolanus requests clemency for an enemy who has shown him kindness. It's Shakespeare's way of letting us know that Coriolanus's low opinion of the rabble doesn't prevent him from behaving like a gentleman when one of them has deserved it. But Mr. Berkoff's production has no room for such mitigating factors. His characters must match the set: either black or white.

You don't have to buy this view of the play, however, to concede that Mr. Berkoff has nonetheless mounted a forceful, compelling piece of theater. And this makes it a welcome change from several recent, wan offerings. . . . Better a Shakespeare production with a mistaken point of view than one with none at all.

Sylviane Gold, "Shakespeare and Modern Politics,"
in The Wall Street Journal, *November 29, 1988.*

MIMI KRAMER

Coriolanus is Shakespeare's play about Caius Marcius, the Roman general who, having won a glorious victory over the Volscians at Corioli, and feeling misprized by the Senate and the people of Rome, turned his back on them and led the Volscians in an attack against his own city. It shares with *Richard II* and *King Lear* the dubious distinction of having been adapted by Nahum Tate, who became Poet Laureate in 1692. Tate's *Coriolanus* was called *The Ingratitude of a Commonwealth,* but Tate (whose version of *Lear* restored the old King to his throne) was notoriously bad at understanding Shakespeare. *Coriolanus* isn't about the ingratitude of a commonwealth any more than *King Lear* is about the ingratitude of a youngest daughter. Both plays raise the question of exactly what is due the virtuous man, and they use the figure of the disgruntled autocrat to explore it. (p. 139)

A sulker, a turncoat, a despiser of the common people, [Coriolanus] is one of the most immediately objectionable of Shakespeare's heroes—not least because he is first and last a soldier. True, we have been taught to accept valor as a manifest sign of moral virtue. But what appeals to us in Henry V is his ability to talk to the common man; in Othello, his ability to tell stories. We are drawn to Macbeth for his habit of metaphor and to Richard III for his Machiavellian wit. In each case, Shakespeare gives us some *theatrical* reason for valuing the hero. Coriolanus isn't a showman with words; that's the whole point. He really *is* the character that Richard pretends to be: a man who "cannot flatter and look fair," to whom pretense—whether for social or political ends—would be as insupportable as cowardly flight. So when the monster mother who created Coriolanus entreats him to speak politically to the people, she is asking him to go against his own nature—just as surely as she is when later she begs him to spare Rome.

If Shakespeare's challenge in *Coriolanus* is to make us care about an unsympathetic character, [Mr. Berkoff's *Coriolanus*] hardly gives him a chance to prove himself. Steven Berkoff . . . has his own agenda. In general, Mr. Berkoff's view of the play is similar to that of Kenneth Tynan, who had little use for either *Coriolanus* or its hero. . . . Mr. Berkoff sees nothing good in Coriolanus, and he makes certain that nobody else will, either. Every scene or speech or line that might possibly serve to redeem Coriolanus in our eyes is either dropped or else edited and staged in such a way as to alter its meaning. Every value is distorted and every device that might lead us to care about Coriolanus dismantled. The two corrupt tribunes, Sicinius Velutus and Junius Brutus, become genuine populist reformers. (This is achieved by trimming or obfuscating with comic business all the scenes that establish the demagogues' lack of scruples.) The silly, empty-headed Valeria, there to serve as a foil for Coriolanus' sober, Penelope-like wife, Virgilia, is made to seem Virgilia's equal in grace and wisdom. (This is achieved by the simple expedient of cutting all the lines that effect a contrast between the two women.) Mr. Berkoff reduces all aspects of Coriolanus' character to a Rambo-like arrogance and machismo; everything he does or says is made to seem laughable or disingenuous.

As a result, this *Coriolanus* bears about as much resemblance to Shakespeare's play as most Disney animations bear to the works they're based on. All the same, the production is seductive. . . . Part of its interest lies in its very Englishness. Mr. Berkoff, trained in the modern British/European tradition of Shakespeare production, which is highly stylized and conceptual, uses mime, music, multiple casting, and nonrealistic staging to hammer home his point. (A chorus of nine men performs all the soldier-citizen-messenger roles.) The production is clad almost entirely in blacks, whites, and grays, with a minimalist set that proves hospitable to props and clothing from different periods. . . . [The] costumes are eclectic and ambiguously timeless: the double-breasted jackets, pin-striped suits, fedoras, and oversize raglan coats seem as fashionably "retro" as they are reminiscent of the eras they evoke. There are instances of historical specificity: Aufidius wears an urban-guerrilla outfit, Menenius a coat with a twenties-style fur collar (perhaps, like Mr. Berkoff's expressionist lighting, an allusion to the rise of Fascism). Mostly, though, the production seeks to bridge the gap, visually, between now and forever.

This is, in itself, a European idea. That Shakespeare's plays need not be exclusively either "modern dress" or costume drama—need not adhere to any one time—goes without saying in London, where stagecraft and theatrical design are more strongly influenced by Brecht and his precursors than by the realism of Belasco and Stanislavsky. To us, accustomed to Public Theatre Shakespeare, it comes as a surprise that actors in a single scene can speak or move or be dressed with varying degrees of realism or stylization. . . . At its best, nonrealistic staging can expand and embellish our reading of a play. Berkoff uses it to reduce the play to one notion. (pp. 139-40)

Mimi Kramer, "Director's Tragedy," in The New Yorker, *Vol. LXIV, No. 43, December 12, 1988, pp. 139-40.*

WILLIAM A. HENRY, III

In a Broadway season when eight of the eleven new plays have been comedies, three of them sex farces, and the cheapest of four new musicals cost $5 million to stage, it is heartening to see work as simple, spare and serious as *Metamorphosis.* One just wishes it were better. . . . [The] most ballyhooed highbrow event in the theater so far this year is all but bereft of emotional force. At the finale, two actresses stand rigid, their cheeks glazed with tears, yet much of the audience reacts only with uneasy titters. Director Steven Berkoff's highly stylized script and direction circle around the story, adding layer upon layer of ornament, when what is needed is a clean, quick cut to the emotional core of an incident as simple as it is mysterious.

Nothing is wrong with the source material, which has inspired countless other stage adaptations. Franz Kafka's story of a man who one day wakes up as a giant insect has provided one of the 20th century's hallmark nightmare images. The essence of the horror is that there is no explanation for it, no deeper meaning, no instructive or redemptive metaphor: the suffering just *is.* In the transmutation of Gregor Samsa, the world ceases to be predictable or rational; natural and moral order disappear. Critics have found in Kafka's vision hints of everything from the Holocaust to AIDS. But to burden the story with greater weight is in fact to lessen it. The thump in the gut comes from the literal details. The man who used to hurry to work now scuttles beneath the bed; the fastidious fellow who loved milk now detests "the fresher foods" and slurps deafeningly over anything decayed. When he agonizes with wounds inflicted by members of his family, they cannot bear to touch him to help heal him.

Berkoff manages to convey the essence of the dilemma for Gregor's parents and sister, albeit without the least sympathy for their natural anxiety and revulsion. He is far more interested in portraying them as grasping and money mad, in a Marxist gloss on the plight of the worker. They are so coarse and reprehensible—more animalistic when eating than the bug in the back bedroom—that there is no point of connection for the audience, certainly no creative tension between expecting the family to take a noble course and knowing why it succumbs to a selfish one.

William A. Henry, III, "A Nightmare without Force," in Time, *New York, Vol. 133, No. 12, March 20, 1989, p. 90.*

Edmund (Charles) Blunden

1896-1974

English poet, critic, biographer, memoirist, editor, translator, novelist, travel writer, and nonfiction writer.

A leading authority on the Romantic movement of the late eighteenth and early nineteenth centuries, Blunden drew upon the British pastoral tradition exemplified by such poets as William Wordsworth and John Keats to evoke the tranquility of nature and the English countryside in his own verse. Although widely recognized as a member of the Georgian poets, a group of stylistically diverse writers who rejected modernist literary tendencies while describing the idyllic qualities of rural Britain, Blunden was also praised for both his war poetry and his light verse. While critics initially commended his picturesque representations of rustic life, many commentators from the 1930s era of social reform dismissed Blunden's work as derivative and superficial, asserting that his preference for outmoded literary techniques often reflects a lack of concern for modern social, psychological, or philosophical issues. Later critics, however, have praised Blunden for his subtle variations on traditional poetic forms. A reviewer for *The Times Literary Supplement* commented: "[Blunden] has been pigeon-holed in his time as a pastoral poet, as a war poet, as a 'literary' poet, yet it is impossible to pin his variety into such narrow limits. . . . Like Hardy he can take the accepted cadences of classical English verse, and bend them to his purpose with beautiful dexterity. . . . But in general Mr. Blunden commands his own music as he wants it."

Blunden's appreciation of provincial Britain and its poetic tradition stemmed from his childhood in the Kentish countryside and at Christ's Hospital, a prestigious school for boys previously attended by such authors as Charles Lamb and Samuel Taylor Coleridge. A dedicated student, Blunden received a scholarship to Oxford University but abandoned his studies at the outset of World War I to enlist in the army. A lieutenant with the Royal Sussex Regiment in France and Belgium from 1916 to 1918, Blunden survived the third battle of Ypres, a failed British offensive that resulted in the estimated deaths of more than 300,000 soldiers. Although he received the Military Cross as an Intelligence and Field Works officer, Blunden was declared unfit for further overseas duty due to repeated exposure to poisonous gas and was sent back to England in 1918. He soon returned to Oxford but felt alienated from his fellow students due to his war experiences and withdrew from the university in 1919.

In 1920, Blunden traveled to London, where he became a regular contributor of essays and literary reviews to the British periodical *The Athenaeum* under the tutelage of critic John Middleton Murry. Although he had published several chapbooks of verse prior to World War I, Blunden initially attracted critical attention for *The Waggoner and Other Poems* (1920) and *The Shepherd and Other Poems of Peace and War* (1922). Several critics compared the simplicity of the pieces in these collections to the work of nineteenth-century English pastoral poet John Clare and favorably likened Blunden to his older contemporary Thomas Hardy for his detached portrayal of authentic aspects of rural existence. Only a few

poems in *The Waggoner* and *The Shepherd* overtly describe Blunden's experiences during World War I, yet many critics concur that these volumes reflect his awareness of war in their violent imagery and resigned tone. While combat destroyed his youthful belief in the invulnerability of nature, Blunden continued to draw inspiration from the pastoral world. F. R. Leavis commented: "[Out] of the traditional life of the English countryside, especially as relived in memories of childhood, Mr. Blunden was creating a world—a world in which to find refuge from adult distresses; above all, one guessed, from memories of the war."

After leaving Great Britain to regain his health in South America, Blunden completed the travelogue *The Bonadventure: A Random Journal of an Atlantic Holiday* (1922) prior to accepting a professorship in 1924 at Tokyo University and moving to Japan. During the late 1920s and 1930s, Blunden's evocations of natural tranquility and beauty as well as his apparent lack of modernist disillusionment prompted some reviewers to fault his preference for seemingly dated traditional forms and values. Later critics, however, have asserted that Blunden's pastoral poetry possesses a psychological and imagistic complexity often lacking in the verse of the Georgian poets with whom he is commonly grouped. Many also suggest that his experiences as a British army officer during

World War I often serve to temper the pacifistic elements of his verse and to convey a sense of both the mutability of human existence and the permanence of death. Philip Gardner asserted: "The very precariousness of nature and human life, which war taught him, only increased his appreciation of their beauty and value; and as they helped to maintain a sense of perspective in wartime, so wartime itself, recalled in peace, prevented complacency, and brought to Blunden's poetry a bracing tension." In such collections as *English Poems* (1925) and *Masks of Time: A New Collection of Poems, Principally Meditative* (1925), Blunden makes use of the four seasons to explore such concerns as time, death, and the durability of art.

Although memories of World War I continued to haunt him, the cultural differences between Japan and postwar Europe allowed Blunden to objectively confront his experiences in *Undertones of War* (1928), one of his most popular and acclaimed works. Described by H. M. Tomlinson as a book "by a ghost for other ghosts," this volume combines older war poems, previously unpublished verse, and memoirs to chronicle the disorientation, fear, and disenchantment that characterized trench warfare during World War I. Comparing *Undertones of War* to the autobiographical works of Robert Graves and Siegfried Sassoon, critics lauded Blunden's eloquence, objectivity, and tone of moderation. Alec M. Hardie asserted: "[*Undertones of War*] is the outstanding example of an author creating in retrospect the moment of human waste, emphasizing war as man's greatest error, not by uncontrolled savage shocks and crudities, but by quietness, restraint, by understatement."

Blunden returned to England in 1928. The controversy that greeted his collected verse in the volumes *The Poems of Edmund Blunden* (1930) and *Poems, 1914-1930* (1930) foreshadowed future debate regarding his work. While some critics faulted Blunden for his lack of modernistic innovation and preservation of archaic styles, others claimed that he intelligently explored such timeless themes as the existence of God and the manifestation of good and evil in nature. In 1931, Blunden became a fellow and tutor of Merton College at Oxford University. His ensuing collections, including *To Themis: Poems on Famous Trials, with Other Pieces* (1931), *Halfway House: A Miscellany of New Poems* (1932), *Choice or Chance* (1934), *An Elegy and Other Poems* (1937), and *Poems, 1930-1940* (1940), often reflect his academic sensibility in their classical and metaphysical concerns.

In his poetry of the World War II era, Blunden's fears of imminent catastrophe became intensified. *Shells by a Stream* (1944) and *After the Bombing and Other Short Poems* (1949), which many critics consider among his most penetrating and mature works, express Blunden's apprehensions of again witnessing the devastation of the earth by global warfare as well as his disappointment with society for repeating past mistakes. Blunden returned to Japan in 1948 as a cultural liaison officer and in 1953 became a professor of English literature at Hong Kong University. He received wide praise for his sincerity and meticulous attention to formal concerns in *Poems of Many Years* (1957), a volume that combines representative pieces from his career with new poetry. Blunden's later collections, *A Hong Kong House: Poems, 1951-1961* (1962) and *Eleven Poems* (1965), generally received favorable notices.

Blunden also composed several highly respected biographies of figures from the British Romantic movement. These works include *Leigh Hunt: A Biography* (1930; published in the United States as *Leigh Hunt and His Circle*), *Keats's Publisher: A Memoir of John Taylor (1781-1864)* (1936), and *Shelley: A Life Story* (1946). In addition, Blunden wrote several acclaimed critical works, including *Leigh Hunt's "Examiner" Examined* (1928), *Votive Tablets: Studies Chiefly Appreciative of English Authors and Books* (1931), and *Three Young Poets: Critical Sketches of Byron, Shelley, and Keats* (1959).

(See also *CLC*, Vol. 2: *Contemporary Authors*, Vols. 17-18, Vols. 45-48 [obituary]; *Contemporary Authors Permanent Series*, Vol. 2; and *Dictionary of Literary Biography*, Vol. 20.)

MARK VAN DOREN

[In Edmund Blunden's *The Waggoner*], England drops out of the world, forgets the war, and returns or departs to pastoral poetry. It is an infinite distance from the shell-holes and the bloody, stumbling men of Wilfrid Owen's poems to the secret coppices where Mr. Blunden watches green and silver fish slip through black weir-water. *The Waggoner* is as cool to the touch as a rock at the bottom of a spring, and it is as brightly incrusted with bubbles. It basks under no warm sun and scans no friendly fields. It does not belong to the enameled-green, the high-lawn, the billiard-table tradition of pastoral verse. It creates another landscape of its own, a landscape darkly thicketed and withdrawn, a country underrun with shadowed streams, a private wilderness significant with fatal birds. Mr. Blunden has chosen his language with no less care than he has chosen his scene, which is to say, one eventually must admit, with overcare. He has been passionately local in his diction, crowding his stanzas . . . with primitive Anglo-Saxon monosyllables that singly are fresh but by accumulation become thick and throaty to the degree of Lewis Carroll at his merriest. . . . There is scarcely a passage which it would be fair to Mr. Blunden to quote by way of commendation, for on every page his atmosphere is richer than either art or nature demands. But it is clear what new thing he has tried to do, and it is certain that if he does it henceforth with restraint he will write astonishingly beautiful poetry.

Mark Van Doren, "War and Peace," in The Nation, *New York, Vol. CXII, No. 2916, May 25, 1921, p. 747.*

THE TIMES LITERARY SUPPLEMENT

The Shepherd more than fulfills the rich promise of *The Waggoner* and is itself still a book which, great in its accomplishment, is even greater in its promise. Mr. Blunden, as he touches the deeper veins of his experience, develops a clearer and more musical tone. There are passages in his new volume which make much of his earlier work sound like the artist's exercises and which lead us to divine, in almost all that he has written hitherto, some flavour of the craftsman's deliberate practice, the craftsman jealously guarding and reserving the poet to be. . . .

Mr. Blunden's craftsmanship is so distinguished, the leaves of his tree are themselves so beautiful, that we could gladly accept it and rest in it and ask no more. His prevailing theme is the English countryside, and it has seldom been studied by a mind possessed so fully as is his of the power to see both parts and whole, and to express a pervading atmosphere in terms of characteristic detail. Readers of poetry are apt to forget that in his choice of detail the poet has to satisfy a double claim and often to reconcile claims that conflict. His poem has its own atmosphere, and it also recreates the atmosphere of a natural moment, scene, or process. A thousand characteristics of the one are for various reasons, for merely technical reasons it may be, unavailable for the other; the characteristics of which the poet can make use are the few which at the same time express his theme and construct his verse. The more individual his manner, the likelier is he, as his poem develops, to find a contest arising between truth and style. . . .

That Mr. Blunden is deeply occupied with the technical problem can be seen from the adroitness with which he applies his acutely personal phrases to disparate ends. **"The Giant Puff Ball"** is studied with the same sympathetic intensity as **"The Poor Man's Pig,"** and is placed in its surroundings with the same happy gift of vivid and concise description. Mr. Blunden does not seem to have observed that, while the feelings of a pig are authentic and very near to our own, those of a puff-ball are remote, hypothetic, and improbable. This is a little disconcerting. As we have been required to pass from the puff-ball to the pig, so we pass on inevitably to the mole catcher and the shepherd and ask ourselves whether the objects have not been found for the style rather than the style for the objects. If we turn from Mr. Blunden's studies of rustic life to those of Wordsworth, we shall be apt to answer the question more abruptly than would be fair; there is in Mr. Blunden, obviously, so much less discrimination between the elements of pictorial and of human interest, that it might almost seem as if his shepherd interested him only in so far as he was picturesque. Probably it is true that the source of his inspiration, his impulsion to poetry, has been the countryside in an undifferentiated unity, and how much nearer, after all, is man to the plants and animals than he was in Wordsworth's time! Then his countryside—as was Wordsworth's also for that matter—is that of one who watches rather than shares in its activities—the countryside viewed from a retirement and therefore predominating over the lives of the men and women whose lot is cast in it. Yet if we are inclined to suspect superficiality or heartlessness in such an attitude of universal contemplation, our prejudice is corrected as we perceive how genuine, whatever the object treated, is the appreciation of its inner being. . . .

A leading quality of Mr. Blunden's style is its closeness of texture, and this, again, marks him a little as the artist practising his craft. Every line is full, every word is an observation. But is it certain that the greatest number of observations, however thoughtfully entwined, will produce the most convincing and distinctive vision? Nothing is more beautiful in the wood than its rides and clearings. Packed sentences weary us like interlacing boughs if they are the rule instead of the exception. We mention the point chiefly because Mr. Blunden himself seems to have an eye for it and to be readier than in earlier days to feel the beauty of thinking one thought at a time. Yet he still gives us poems of which the general tenor is hard to catch, and now and then sentences which resist analysis and even defy the subtler powers of intuition. We are glad that he has mitigated his predilection for dialect words; he seems already to have reached the secret of a happy compromise, never dragging us to the dictionary, and yet giving romance and character to his descriptions by an occasional localism of which we divine or think that we divine the meaning. And

as he goes to the miller or the shepherd and borrows from their vocabulary, so he goes also to the poets, his predecessors, and puts himself with equal freedom and independence in their debt. In some of his loveliest things, some that are most completely his own, there are whole passages which might have been written a hundred or two hundred years ago:—

> By the white damson then I took
>   The tallest osier wand
> And thrice upon the window strook,
>   And she so fair, so fond,
> Looked out and saw in wild delight
>   And tiptoed down to me,
> And cried in silent joy that night
>   Beside the bullace tree.

What is this but the note of piercing-sweet romantic simplicity which is so often heard in the *Lyrical Ballads*? . . . Lines like these entitle us to look to Mr. Blunden for the very best things a poet has to give; and perhaps their confident traditionalism is their chief sign of strength. Mr. Blunden has realized that the poet we are expecting, and for whom our love is reserved, is not the poet who will be different from his predecessors. The great past has decided for us what English poetry must be. The poet of our dreams is the poet who will be content to continue doing what Spenser or Keats or Coleridge has done before him, and who, remaining himself, a modern product of our modern world, will shine a new yet a familiar star in the fixed and splendid firmament.

We have treated Mr. Blunden's work mainly from the point of view of its craftsmanship. But we must not leave this volume without remarking that its chief distinction lies, to our mind, in its distinct avowal of personal experience as the core of living poetry. Of his power of detached observation, of the readiness and fullness with which he lends his interpretative sympathy to all that he sees and pecks, so to say, with the sparrow in the gravel, Mr. Blunden has given us the amplest evidence. And now, a little shyly it may be, he allows that the poet is of more value than many sparrows, and admits us by degrees into immediate intercourse with himself. The poems in which he thus deals with us directly seem, moreover, to be his best. . . .

Mr. Blunden has suffered the war and survived it. There was little about war in his first volume, written almost entirely under the more or less immediate impact of its stupendous and irreducible experiences. There is much more in his second, enough to show that we have in him a man capable of relating the peace of the woods and the desolation of that unending mortal struggle to one paramount vision of reconciling love and beauty. Whatever else he may have to say, we can be confident that Mr. Blunden will derogate nothing from the outrage, nor soften the affliction, nor erase one item of the waste and loss. He will find means to tell us faithfully— as others have in their own time and their own way already told us—how these things go with the beauty of flowers and sky and the singing of birds. Wordsworth saw the Revolution in France and could not bear it. Mr. Blunden has seen Ypres; the iron has been driven into his soul, and its weight and heat have neither crushed nor scared him. We can understand why his instinct as a poet was to reserve his experience and perfect his craft.

A review of "The Shepherd and Other Poems," in The Times Literary Supplement, *No. 1060, May 11, 1922, p. 305.*

J. C. SQUIRE

Mr. Blunden was, is, and probably always will be, a poet mainly of the countryside. "Landscape poet" is a misnomer. Landscape poets are very often townsmen, with an eye for colour and shape and a feeling for nature in general, but not necessarily a knowledge of the characters or even the names of any but the commonest and most conspicuous country things, who have never shared in the occupations of a farm or the sports of a village. Lark and nightingale are well enough; Jones's Warbler is another matter; there is no reason to expect that poets should be expert ornithologists; nor do they necessarily suffer by the defect. We have a very great wealth of "landscape poetry" in English, but not much has been done from the habitual countryman's angle. Mr. Blunden's work is so done. It has affinities with certain parts of Wordsworth; but the poets nearest him are Edward Thomas, and still more John Clare, whom he has enthusiastically edited, and he often reminds us of Richard Jefferies, the essayist. The life of the country is his own life, and he finds the beautiful where a transient passenger would fail to find the picturesque. He does not, as a rule, wait for the remarkable natural conformation, or the remarkable natural effect; and he does not usually wait for a great emotional moment in himself. But he has a steady love of the South English rural scene in all its changes and in all its details: barns with sagging roofs, cornfields, oast-houses, clay pastures, mills, small rivers, fish pools, grass, nettles and the wild flowers of the downs. Anything in that world may give him a poem. . . . A complete example is **"The Poor Man's Pig"**:

> Already fallen plum-bloom stars the green
>   And apple-boughs as knarred as old toads'
>   backs,
> Wear their small roses ere a rose is seen;
>   The building thrush watches old Job who stacks
> The bright-peeled osiers on the sunny fence,
>   The pent sow grunts to hear him stumping by,
> And tries to push the bolt and scamper thence,
>   But her ringed snout still keeps her to the sty.
> Then out he lets her run; away she snorts
>   In bundling gallop for the cottage door,
> With hungry hubbub begging crusts and orts;
>   Then like the whirlwind bumping round once
>   more;
> Nuzzling the dog, making the pullets run,
>   And sulky as a child when her play's done.

This is not landscape, though there are fragments of landscape in it; it is a reproduction of a part of rusticity, of rural life. (pp. 171-74)

[Mr. Blunden's writing] springs from daily familiarity. But it also springs from daily delight. It is not "mere description," as some modern writing is. Feeling is implicit everywhere; it is explicit in . . . [phrases such] as "sulky as a child," . . . ; a pervading sentiment and awareness of the goodness of it all, a relish of the quality in everything seen, all these perennial trifles, all these day-to-day occurrences. . . . [There] are many poems in which the poet makes himself much more clearly evident, and some in which the life he reflects is a background for emotions externally derived by himself or other persons. But it is almost always there. When you have read his books there have been recalled to you innumerable sounds, sights, and scents which you have experienced in the English countryside, and many which you never consciously recorded or recalled: the smells of the farmyard, the ways of poultry and cattle, the dim and stealthy movements of fish,

black weeds hanging on sun-dried sluices, the texture of stone drinking-troughs. . . . I huddle them together without order; so, sometimes, does Mr. Blunden; but he delights in them all, and he makes the reader delight too. He might say of ten thousand things what he says of the not conventionally musical practice of the woodpecker:

> From all these happy folk I find
> Life's radiance kindle in my mind,
> And even when homeward last I turn,
> How bright the hawthorn berries burn,
> How steady in the old elm still
> The great woodpecker strikes his bill;
> Whose labour oft in vain is given,
> Yet never he upbraids high heaven:
> Such trust is his. O I have heard
> No sweeter from a singing bird
> Than his tap-tapping there this day,
> That said what words will never say.

The last line echoes the accents of a hundred poets; but Mr. Blunden differs from most of them in that he never attempts to say this inexpressible thing. He speculates and reasons hardly at all; his philosophy or his search for a philosophy is to be guessed; he does not even incite to the guessing. He is content to recount his loves and leave the argument to someone else.

For Poetry is an expression of gratitude for things enjoyed. The elements of Life in which the spirit takes most intense delight and on which the memory broods most fondly, vary from poet to poet. . . . [Mr. Blunden's favorite] is rural Nature; not Nature the personification, or Nature the instrument of the Almighty; the manifestations, not the power behind, though it may be the instinctive perception of that power that gives wonder and beauty to those manifestations. Mr. Blunden is not entirely concentrated on this one aspect of Life. He has written some powerful war-poems, some exquisite love poems, a touching elegy on a child. Yet war he sees most clearly as a cruel disturbance of rural peace, and he is continually driven to exhibit its vileness by contrasting it with pictures of the natural beauty which it destroys and from which it drags its victims. The loves he felt (his poems are all dated) in 1914 had become intensified when he returned after his years in France, to watch the lightest gossamer and the hungriest pike with a renewed and deepened affection. A country parish will serve as a symbol for all he deals with; and he writes of war as something inimical to the country parish. And his recollections of human relations are always thickly intertwined with wildwood flowers and mingled with the racing of mill streams and the noises of birds and beasts. There is merit in the rather Wordsworthian story of **"The Silver Bird of Herndyke Mill."** There are some admirably sympathetic portraits of rural characters: in **"The Shepherd"** for example, and in the Arcadian **"Almswomen,"** a poem about two old women in a cottage with a flower-garden. They and their small possessions are described quietly and affectionately. . . . Yet if there be no strong force diverting him he will always return to the contemplation of country life. Not landscape in the ordinary sense. He does occasionally make a generalised picture, a few large lines and a few selected details. But, as a rule, he does not "compose" in that way. He sees every detail with acute clearness, but they are all of equal importance to him. They are important in themselves, not merely as contributions to a picture. He loves every sound and scent, every form of animal and plant and insect; each thing that lives has character to him, and he discriminates very little between people and beasts and flowers. They all live, ploughman and whistling boy, heifer and fish; they all have pleasure in their lives, and suffer; they all are beautiful and die. Even timbers and stones, bells, carts, and tools seem animated to him; so intense is the quality of each, so characteristic its function, so like its progress from newness to decay to that of all things that live.

Varied as [*The Shepherd and Other Poems of Peace and War*] is, he showed a sound instinct when he placed at the end of it **"The Last of Autumn,"** a poem in which his most prevalent mood and most habitual joy are expressed as it were in a summary. The sun is gilding autumnal oaks. The fields are shorn of the harvest, sheep "dapple the broad pale green, nabbing or resting," haystacks and hurdles gleam, and the heart, conscious of transience,

> Cannot let a bird
> Chance by but counts him into memory's tribe.
>
> (pp. 174-78)

[Mr. Blunden] is one of the least sorrowful of poets; when he is sad there is a specific reason for it. He communicates a steady joy, "the harvest of a quiet eye." His work had the marks of permanence from the start; apart from the general merits of his early poems, they showed an unmistakable and rare gift for the timeless phrase. "All things they have in common, being so poor," he wrote, with classic inevitability, of his two old Almswomen [in **"Almswomen"**]; and, lying at leisure in an autumn landscape, he idly watched

> The feather's fall, the doomed red leaf delaying,
> And all the tiny circumstance of peace.

Those last lines, with their touch of Keats, anticipate, by the way, one of the loveliest passages in [*The Shepherd*], a stanza beginning:

> Here joy shall muse what melancholy tells,
> And melancholy smile because of joy,
> Whether the poppy breathe Arabian spells,
> To make them friends, or whistling gipsy-boy
> Sound them a truce that nothing comes to cloy.

But the second book [*The Shepherd*] is very much more impressive than the first [*The Waggoner*], and the third will probably be better still. A tendency to overdo dialect words and neologisms—for coining which Mr. Blunden has an extraordinary talent—has disappeared (though "slats the weazen bine" may defeat some readers); but he has still to make some sacrifices to euphony. Some of his lines are so crowded with consonants as to be almost unpronounceable (he lacks that strange power of Mr. Hardy's which fuses the most intractable material into music), and he still inclines to crowd his epithets and his images so that one cannot see the wood for the trees. The crowding comes from his very eagerness, the variety of his affections: everything reminds him of something else, and everything he thinks of is a thing he has seen and noted and savoured, distinguishing its character. Nevertheless the music of the verse is growing more certain and more varied; and the shape of the poems is better. There is still room for development, I think, in this last regard. The defects of Mr. Blunden's qualities are obvious and not easy to fight. A man whose eyes are on the near thing and not on the far horizon, will naturally be tempted to crowd his admirable details too much together; a man so acutely sensitive to those details will sometimes dispense with a theme, and will sometimes be drawn from one to another regardless of begin-

ning, middle, and end. One may still say of some of his poems that each line taken separately is perfect, but that the poems are not perfect. But there is no writer against whom something—usually much—cannot be said. (pp. 179-81)

J. C. Squire, "Mr. Edmund Blunden," in his Essays on Poetry, *Hodder and Stoughton, 1923, pp. 171-81.*

THE TIMES LITERARY SUPPLEMENT

Readers of Mr. Blunden's poems know how sharply scenes of the War are etched upon his memory, and may have guessed how often he trod

> those memory ways
> Where by the dripping alien farms,
> Starved orchards with their shrivelled arms,
> The bitter mouldering wind would whine
> At the brisk mules clattering towards the Line.

Two years with infantry, from the spring of 1916 to that of 1918, prove to have been the source of these memories—enough, heaven knows, for many memories and keen. It now appears that the War poems in his various volumes were but a selection, for he has added a whole sheaf of verses to this account in prose of those two years. [*Undertones of War*] is, in the first place, a very able record of the infantryman's existence in France and Flanders: faithful, observant and precise. But that is only its exterior merit. There is a great deal more to be found in it by the imaginative, a sort of essence of the battlefields. . . .

For a long time Mr. Blunden was attached to battalion headquarters as works or signalling officer. That is all to the advantage of his record; for it frequently happened that company officers saw very little beyond the actual trenches they held, up to which and down from which they were led by a guide in the dark. In his position he had to roam, and his roamings were over fields well suited to his extraordinary powers of observation. He brings back many little phases which those who fought in the War have forgotten and of which others have never been told. There was, for example, his trench maintenance party, lodged with the tools of its trade in Hamel village.

> They made themselves comfortable in cellars, and went to and fro in the exact and ordinary manner of the British working man. One, by turns, stayed at home to cook; the others kept the line tidy, and left no staircase, recess nor buttress unbeautified. They enjoyed this form of active service with pathetic delight—and what men were they?—willing, shy, mostly rather like invalids, thinking of their families.

We suspect Mr. Blunden went for something in this "pathetic delight." The British soldier was in general a poor trench-keeper compared with "Jerry" over the way, unless his enthusiasm was aroused; then, it is not too much to say that he came to treat the results of his handiwork, such as a traverse buttressed with expanded metal held in place by iron pickets and wire, with pride and affection. Or there is the Potijze road, just behind the line, which he had to examine for reinforcing routes, where "your East Anglian huckster might have made a fortune with a pony and van" out of mahogany beds, bassinettes and sewing-machines. Scattered through these pages are like instances of the melancholy but very strong fascination which the spectacle of civilization sudden- ly cut off, in a fashion not untypical of the War as a whole, had for many of us. . . . Of the War itself there is hearty loathing, which, however, never degenerates into what may be called a "defeatist" attitude—as cannot be said of all the recent books of haters of war.

We are glad indeed that Mr. Blunden has included his "Sup- plement of poetical interpretations and variations," which contains thirty hitherto unpublished poems and the remark- able **"Third Ypres"** already published in *The Shepherd.* We do not say that more than five or six of them equal the war- poems already known; yet all deserve to be known, and the best are splendid. The lightest of them, **"The Prophet,"** a sur- vey of a hundred-year-old guide-book to the Netherlands, has particular charm, because in it there gleams an impish hu- mour of a kind which the author has hitherto in general re- served for prose. But there is one of elegiac type, **"Their Very Memory,"** which in its beautiful simplicity and power seems to evoke in the noblest fashion the feelings we have for the lost friends with whom we served.

A review of "Undertones of War," in The Times Lit- erary Supplement, *No. 1401, December 6, 1928, p. 949.*

MARGARET WILLY

> Others in London sigh with equal force
> For Sussex downs and whiffs of Kentish gorse,
> And though the trains puff out from noon to eve,
> Vastly prefer to stay at home and grieve.

Thus Roy Campbell . . . neatly pinpointed in *The Georgiad* the romantic nostalgia of the Georgian poets for the joys of an impossibly idyllic English countryside. The majority of the contributors to Edward Marsh's anthology *Georgian Poetry* . . . adopted the sentimental attitude of the country- cottage week-ender towards a rural life of which they were in a position to know little at first hand.

There were, of course, notable exceptions at the time to this rule of rustic rhapsodizing by town poets. . . .

Today, more than forty years since he published his first book, Blunden's work continues to command the respect of discerning critics and readers of poetry. It has again been offi- cially honoured, . . . and a handsome new selection of his work was published last June. Chronologically arranged, [*Poems of Many Years*] includes poems from all Blunden's earlier books of verse, from *The Waggoner* to the 1949 *After the Bombing,* and concludes with a section of new poems not so far collected in book form. (p. 213)

Edmund Blunden was never the mere week-end visitor cele- brating unfamiliar pastoral delights: he had studied and—in his own phrase—'caught the country's meaning' from boy- hood up. In his long autobiographical poem **"A Summer's Fancy"** he tells us that his 'father and grandfather shared these joys'; and his own chronicling of them has the quiet verisimilitude, a precision of eye and listening alertness of ear, belonging to one who habitually apprehends more than the mere prettily picturesque aspects of Nature. He writes with love of 'trees of slow limbs, tough rinds'; finding solace for a black mood in the simple act of touching the bark of a 'chance-planted, many-centuried tree', and knowing 'temper- ate sense' recur amid

> Twilight societies, twig, fungus, root,
> Soundless, and speaking well.

His pages abound in authentically recognizable country folk: gipsies, hop-pickers, gleaners, mole-catcher and farm bailiff, waggoner and shepherd; the 'ploughman whistling out his spells' and the shade of a rural parson of former days hover- ing beside his barn, distilling 'sky-wisdom'. . . . The wild creatures of the landscape are observed with a closeness equally satisfying: cattle drinking in lily-pools, the cat 'more rapid than a gypsy's knife', down to the urbane toad taking his twilight walk. . . . (pp. 213-14)

It is perhaps in the water-world that Blunden is more than anywhere at home. As a boy, he tells us, he would lie by the river imagining that he was

> a reed that whispered here, a stone
> To make the water talk.

("A Summer's Fancy")

Streams flanked by forget-me-not, flag and rush, guarded by sentinel osier, pollard, alder, and 'goblin willows', and haunt- ed by 'kingfishers like flames'; the old Chaucerian mill, win- dowless, 'mountain-roofed, wry-angled'; the cool waterfall and the 'rock-browed, shag-haired weir', the 'moat where roach make rings', the 'tunnelled verge where red fins lay'— all these felicitously move the poet's imagination to verse which itself seems to flow with the effortless limpidity of water. **"Shells by a Stream"**, **"Watching Running Water"**, **"The River House"**, **"The Pasture Pond"**, **"The Hurrying Brook"**, **"A Waterpiece"**, **"Voices by a River"**, **"The Name- less Stream"**, and the magnificent **"The Pike"** ('murderous patriarch' of the pool, poised for slaughter), are only a few of the poems which express this writer's constant delight in aquatic creation, in such haunting lines as 'Where fallen oak- leaves and pale bubbles glide', or

> the polished lessening ripple
> Shaped by the angler's gentle oar.

Notice in both these quotations the skilful onomatopoeic use of the cool, liquid 'l'.

It is mainly the memorable impact of many of his images— the wind 'with its starved white mouth', 'the mumbling trains with eyes of flame', winter 'blowing on his nails, / Leading long jingling teams from black-barned farms'—which sets the work of Blunden apart from so much that was tame and tepid in Georgian versifying. Largely abandoning the convention- ally 'poetic' diction of his contemporaries, he turned to what often seems a deliberately prosaic tone: in his chronicling, for instance, of the village scene—church, inn, forge, and cot- tages clustered round the duckpond and cricket green, and the 'clink of work and bell of time / And stroke of bat and ball'; of the market town ('a piece of stubborn antiquity') with its stalls, horsy little men, bawling hucksters, and hens peer- ing out of crates. . . . None of this could justly be called in- spired, and no doubt was not intended to be. It is straight de- scription rather than evocation; yet description which brings the apparently ordinary, commonplace sight vivid and con- crete before the inward eye. . . . Amid the vague lyricism, vapid sentiment, and devitalized poeticisms which character- ized so much contemporary writing about the country scene, Blunden's matter-of-fact exactitude had a refreshing vital- ity. . . . (pp. 214-15)

[If] Blunden walks at a leisurely, ruminative pace more often than he runs, sings, or dances to lyric measures, he is nevertheless constantly aware of the wonder and exaltation of living which are inextricably bound up with, and spring from, its very ordinariness. His perception that every soaring flight must begin from earth is well epitomized in the little poem **"Lark Descending"**:

> A singing firework; the sun's darling;
> Hark how creation pleads!
> Then silence: see, a small, grey bird
> That runs among the weeds.

Travelling from youth to maturity, he himself finds new rewards

> where now no more
> My early angels walk and call and fly,
> But the mouse stays his nibbling, to explore
> My eye with his bright eye.

In his note on the selection of Blunden's work which he has included in *The Penguin Book of Contemporary Verse* (1950), Kenneth Allott remarks how subtly 'human unease is hinted at in much verse which at first would appear to be purely descriptive'. We may observe this trait very clearly in a poem like the much (and justly) anthologized **"The Midnight Skaters"**—where those who disport themselves above 'the pond's black bed' defy 'death at watch' / Within those secret waters'. . . . In **"October Comes"** there is a vivid evocation of the hushed tranquillity of autumn, seemingly timeless; yet the final image left on the mind is one of foreboding—a sense of peace encircled and threatened—in the leaves which, though not falling, glowed 'To warn that even this calm was not perpetual'. Constantly there recurs throughout Blunden's work a wry awareness that things are not always as they seem. Words are not adequate ('Praise is not safe, description will not do') to communicate the rarest and subtlest shades of feeling; and that what is said to be, or should be, is not always so, is conveyed with a peculiarly pungent disenchantment in **"Report on Experience"**. . . . (p. 215)

It was inevitable that, beginning to write poetry at the time he did, so much of Blunden's work should either deal directly with, or be implicitly permeated by, his experience of trench warfare. He himself affirmed, in the Preface to his *Poems 1914-30*, that 'war became a part of [his] experience at a date so early . . . as to mould and colour [his] poetry'. Many of his poems show the familiar post-war disillusion of the '20s—that era ironically termed 'the Peace', where nevertheless

> we live in doubt
> Whether her sins or War's more misery show.
> **("Some Talk of Peace")**

In **"About these Germans"** he wonders what would happen

> If war were fought by those who frame
> The hideous goblins due to be destroyed;

and bitterly observes in **"War Cemetery"**, of poets who glorify war,

> Thus lyric genius ever stooped to cheer
> The march that ends in billets under clay.

There is something of the savagery of a Sassoon in his remark, in the same poem, that

> No one can say they are not buried well,
> At least as much of them as could be found.

The note of disenchantment sounds again in **"The Memorial, 1914-18"**, where the poet ironically demands of the dead why they do not feel duly honoured by the monolith raised to their memory by the living. . . . And the poem immediately following this in *Poems 1930-40*—that entitled **"Inscribed in War-Books"**—sadly comments on just how short a time man's memory does preserve names already half-forgotten under a new shadow 'of battles dark and worse presage'.

Long afterwards the poet is still haunted by inescapable memories—enshrined in such poems as " 'Can You Remember?' ", **"Nights Before Battle"**, **"A House in Festubert"**, **"Into the Salient"**, **"Third Ypres"**, **"Nearing the Ancre Battlefield,"** or **"1916 seen from 1921"**. . . . **"On a Picture by Dürer"** sees in the artist's drawing the mutilated pines of his own doomed generation—'Our sign, our shape, our dumb but eloquent trees'; while **"At Rugmer"** embodies a melancholy autumnal sense of men falling like leaves:

> We have lived this landscape,
> And have an understanding with these shades.
> (pp. 215-16)

So compelled was Blunden's imagination by his experiences of 1914-18 that his imagery echoes with those reverberations even when he is writing on totally different themes. A tower, for instance, 'bombards' the night with bells; for the verb 'outwitted' we find in another poem the more arresting 'outsoldiered'; a mood of spiritual restlessness is communicated through the image of being 'always on the bivouac'. An adjuration to his beloved to come out in spring is phrased in military jargon: 'You deserve compassionate leave / As wise campaigners called it.' Writing of winter stars, he sees them 'ready to strike . . . ready to roar / Their sparkling deathway down'. . . .

Yet if, for Blunden, Nature in certain moods awakens memories or mirrors images of war, more often the innocence of the natural world stands in triumphant contrast to all the horrors man can contrive against man. An orchard brook in 1916, flowing

> Westward in blossoming waywardness,
> Such beauty neighbouring so much slaughter,

is a symbol of peace. . . . (p. 216)

Despite the large proportion of war poems in the body of his work, however, it is not finally to Edmund Blunden but to Sassoon and Owen that we turn for the most memorable and enduring utterances about the 'pity of war, the pity war distilled'. It is first as the faithful chronicler of the English countryside that Blunden remains in the mind of his readers. Nature to him has been a perpetual healing for all the hurts of life—from the dark mood of a private despair (**"The Recovery"**) to the newspapers' public 'auguries of tomorrow's peace or war' (**"Present Discontents"**). Rook, peewit, and heron, the lark 'crying to the sun' or 'some coral-berried tree' can bring to this poet news of far greater and more significant worth. To one who loves her with a passion, not man-made struggles but 'Nature's war is news'. Walking through the lanes and reviewing 'the country troops, heifer and steer and ewe', such a man is

> deeper struck with the victory of the grass
> Than all [he] view[s] elsewhere of steel-sharp might:

From

> Machines which even change men to ma-
>   chines . . .
> The televisionary world to come,
> The petrol-driven world already made
>   **("Minority Report")**

he will find refuge and tranquillity in 'Mere moonlight in the last green loneliness'.

Celebrating country things, from 'Earth's kindest loves, farms, inns and cottages', down to such small miracles as 'the wasp-nest in the bank', 'the silk wheel / The yellow spider has wrought', the work of Edmund Blunden is far more than the 'pastoral archaism' (his own phrase) for which some critics have dismissed it with that of many of his contemporaries. Kenneth Allott . . . makes a point of differentiating him from his fellow Georgians by observing his 'niceness of obser-vation' and 'how the attempt to "compose" a pastoral world . . . and the exquisite delicacy and formality of move-ment in many poems imply a criticism of a merely naïve di-rect approach to the writing of nature-poetry'. That meticu-lous precision of observation is born of the poet's realization that

> An empire pulses in a hollow tree
> If you will share with mite and moth and mouse.
>   **("In Childhood")**

In his close familiarity with and pictorial exactitude in re-cording this empire of the natural world, Edmund Blunden is . . . firmly planted in the sturdy pastoral tradition of En-glish poetry. (p. 217)

> Margaret Willy, *"The Poetry of Edmund Blunden,"*
> in English, *Vol. XI, No. 65, Summer, 1957, pp. 213-
> 18.*

ALEC M. HARDIE

Early in 1914 the young schoolboy, Edmund Blunden, inter-viewed an unworldly bookseller and printer in Horsham. His purpose was to discover the cost of publishing two slight 'vol-umes' of poems at his own expense. One contained transla-tions from French poets, and the other a collection of English verses that imaged more than a schoolboy's dream of the countryside. It is to the credit of the printer that he agreed. . . .

Other slim volumes followed, and it was not without signifi-cance that one was dedicated to Leigh Hunt, another to John Clare. Blunden showed an original trend of thought, now seen as very much his own, in **"The Silver Bird of Herndyke Mill"**. He was richly concerned with the 'Spirit of this sweet land' and the 'mist of magic'. (p. 5)

[But in 1914], he joined the Royal Sussex Regiment and was thrown into the life of an army training camp, a fierce peripe-ty for a young man who had been sheltered in the security of his native countryside and the continuity of an ancient school. The effect of the years of war on his nervous sensitivi-ty he has told himself in *Undertones of War,* the echoes of which continue.

He wisely did not attempt to make that record until years after, in 1928, when artistic detachment had guided his emo-tions. It is the outstanding example of an author creating in retrospect the moment of human waste, emphasizing war as

man's greatest error, not by uncontrolled savage shocks and crudities, but by quietness, restraint, by understatement.

Something more is needed to explain why this true personal statement should remain equally significant after another war and rumours of war. Artistically it is an integrated work that avoids the episodic; instead, it flows along in a quick stream of continuous and connected thought in which the prose-writer is identified with the poet. But that would be insuffi-cient to indicate why in Britain *Undertones of War* has ap-peared in many editions and is now set among the World's Classics. . . .

Perhaps one of the most reasoned prophetic considerations of *Undertones of War* was given by H. M. Tomlinson in 1930. After reflecting upon several other war records Mr. Tomlin-son declared:

> As you read deeply . . . your uneasiness grows.
> This poet's eye is not in a fine frenzy rolling. There
> is a steely glitter in it. . . . Blunden's book, in fact,
> is by a ghost for other ghosts; some readers will not
> know what it is all about . . . Yet it is a humorous
> book, though its fun is wan; through pale fun you
> can see the tangibilities of today solid in their ap-
> propriate places . . . His cheerful voice is ad-
> dressed over your shoulder, and your amusement
> fades when that fancy chills it. You turn round; and
> nothing is there!

This 'uneasiness' is more than the 'atmosphere' of the book; it is Blunden's method of disturbing his readers into under-standing his undertones. Mr. Tomlinson continues:

> The men are the best of Blunden's book; and that
> is right. That at least we were sure to get from a
> poet. This story of war stirs and proceeds with liv-
> ing figures, and its scenes are authentic . . . Some-
> thing aeolian breathes through its lines. You may
> hear echoing, as one used to hear desolation mur-
> muring when the night was suspect and the flares
> above the trenches were few before dawn, the won-
> der and awe of the sacrificed who did not know why
> this had come to them; for Blunden's is a tribute to
> the unknown soldier more lasting than the pomps
> about a cenotaph.

It is the ghost of the 'unknown soldier' that makes the whole narrative universal and exact. The author tries to stay in the background; the reader hears comparatively little of his own reactions. His comrades, in the strong bond which can link strangers together under uncertainties and dangers, are the central figures, figures of humanity split by an unknown force into allies and foes. The very 'uneasiness' and the friendships are symbols of the poet trying to depict allies and foes togeth-er in the name of man; of so dramatizing common feelings that horror and revulsion result. (pp. 7-8)

[Blunden's] poems written during the war . . . reveal the swift maturity, only half-comprehended, which war forces upon youth. Through *Undertones of War* the soldier seizing every moment to be a poet is clear enough. Equally clear—and significant—is his awareness of the French and Belgian countryside. . . .

[Blunden's] irony is rarely cynical, his anger rarely outra-geous. The memory of his youth is mingled with the horror of his experience; a flower takes on a new meaning when set beside a gun; and he feels bewildered. . . . (p. 10)

It was after his discharge in 1919 that the real impact slowly and insidiously made itself felt. The world, and England in particular, had irrevocably changed. For older men more experienced and saddened by life the return to peace was not easy; for one so young and sensitive the imprint of the experience could not be eradicated, and was almost the standard by which the rest of life was to be judged. With many others he joined in trying to explain his disillusionment, not with self-pity but with an urgent desire to prevent another such disaster to the dignity of man. (pp. 10-11)

The ghosts have never left him, and, as with so many of his generation, have haunted him ever since:

> The struggling Ancre had no part
>   In these new hours of mine,
> And yet its stream ran through my heart;
>   I heard it grieve and pine,
> As if its rainy tortured blood
>   Had swirled into my own,
> When by its battered bank I stood
>   And shared its wounded moan.

Such memories have shaped his mind to the purpose of life, and even appear as he paints his own countryside. If Sussex were to be found in France, France he sees no less in Wiltshire. . . . (p. 11)

[Returning to England as a] civilian with military decorations, a man who had been a boy when last out of uniform, he decided to take up his Scholarship and return to Oxford. More important than studying for classical honours, however, was the task of coming to terms with himself. He recorded, soon after, the dilemma of this personal aftermath:

> The eyes that had been strength so long
> Gone, or blind, or lapt in clay,
> And war grown twenty times as strong
> As when I held him first at bay;
>
> Then down and down I sunk from joy
> To shrivelled age, though scarce a boy,
> And knew for all my fear to die
> That I with those lost friends should lie.

He presently surmised that Oxford was not for him; it was hardly likely that undergraduate life would be sympathetic to prematurely 'shrivelled age'. Restless, he moved out of College to a small cottage on Boar's Hill, where many of the young literary group often made their way. (pp. 11-12)

In the London of 1919 many had a happy belief in literature; whatever else might change in post-war England literature and the arts would always be needed, always encouraged. Many tried hard to do their part in fostering talent. Their zest and their experience delighted Blunden; when offered the opportunity, he quitted Oxford for London literary life. In 1920 he joined *The Athenaeum* magazine as assistant to his schoolfellow, Middleton Murry. The beliefs that such men held were hardly shared by the general public; in 1921 *The Athenaeum* was amalgamated with *The Nation* under the illustrious editorship of H. W. Massingham. Blunden remained as a regular contributor. (p. 13)

[At the same time that Blunden began] proving himself a masterly writer of reviews and essays for periodicals, able to condense in one short paragraph a wealth of understanding and appreciation, he devoted his poetic energy to the manners and scenes of English country life. His youth, background, education, and experience had all prepared him for this moment, and the volumes that appeared during the war

of 1914-18 had strengthened his technical mastery and perception. Throughout the years in the trenches he had carried a volume of Edward Young's *Night Thoughts,* and John Clare's poems were usually with him. Thomson's *Seasons* and de la Mare's works were often handled. Now to his knowledge of Kent and Sussex countryside he added the very different landscape of Suffolk, where he spent his leisure hours.

During these early post-war years his reputation and fame rapidly grew as the volume of *The Waggoner* (1920) was succeeded by *The Shepherd* (1922), which brought him the Hawthornden Prize. He had a great descriptive power which allowed him to develop his individual rural poetry, but he was never just the 'pastoral' poet; he knew too well the harshness of country life. He was not didactic or moralizing; 'He approaches Reality by another, the artist's road'. Few have looked so closely and found so much in the minutest detail; he not only delighted in words and their music but he brought a sharpness to small moments that easily escape the less watchful. . . . (pp. 15-16)

He was writing from too full an experience and too practical a knowledge to fall into the trap of sentimentality. He turns to a humour, not droll but briefly spoken as by a countryman himself. (p. 16)

One line will hint the sly humour, as in **"Forefathers"** he describes the long generations of the unknown, the unread countrymen, and in the last line of the stanza sharply brings the reader back to the extent of their worth.

> Names are vanished, save the few
>   In the old brown Bible scrawled;
> These were men of pith and thew,
>   Whom the city never called;
> Scarce could read, or hold a quill,
> Built the barn, the forge, the mill.

In most of these poems lingers a sense of the sorrow that a keen contemplation of Nature indulges; a vivid melancholy mixed with wonder and mystery. **"The Pike"**, by the very freedom of its construction, hints at more than a river scene, but the reader is hardly prepared for the shock of the final stanza:

> Sudden the gray pike changes, and quivering
>   poises for slaughter.
> Intense terror wakens around him, the shoals
>   scud awry, but there chances
> A chub unsuspecting; the prowling fins quicken,
>   in fury he lances;
> And the miller that opens the hatch stands amazed
>   at the whirl in the water.

The complete beauty of **"Almswomen"**, with its strong pathos, changes its tone from the brightness of a summer's day to the fearfulness of loneliness at night. When the world is well we can forget 'Death's shadow at the door', but in darkness we have to face ourselves. . . . (pp. 16-17)

"The Shepherd" with its delineations echoes a similar sense of foreboding, timelessness, the curious reality of all nature:

> The hounded leaf has found a tongue to warn
> How fierce the fang of winter, the lead rain
> Brings him old pictures of the drowning plain,
> When even his dog sulks loath to face the morn.
> The sun drops cold in a watery cloud, the briars
> Like starved arms still snatch at his withered fires.

(p. 17)

Blunden followed no school or fashion. The post-war disillusion hit hard at the literary world, old gods apparently had feet of clay, and newness, originality and revolt were the catchwords. To believe in the immediate past was to believe in sterility and decadence. Edmund Blunden was labelled a 'Georgian' by many of the rebels, and that term was taken to unify a group of poets quite diverse in age, temperament, environment and writing, who frequently had not even met each other.

Very early in his career it was seen that his mastery of language, imagery and technique was unusually strong. He enjoyed words and found music in the conversation of the countryman. He lingered over their possibilities, and added a virility to many of his verses by the skilful use of dialect. Robert Bridges was among the first to realize this art and after the publication of *The Waggoner* in 1920 wrote a detailed analysis of the dialectal diction in the poems:

> Since a young poet, Mr. Edmund Blunden, has lately published a volume in which this particular element of dialectal and obsolescent words is very prominent, it will be suitable to our general purpose to consider it as a practical experiment and examine the results. The poetic diction and high standard of his best work give sufficient importance to this procedure; and though he may seem to be somewhat extravagant in his predilection for unusual terms, yet his poetry cannot be imagined without them.

His country poetry continued to increase his reputation, and as he experimented widely in ballads, lyrics, songs and love poems a more profound note was struck. The effect of the war would not allow him to pursue any other course; through his mind the themes were mixed—war, waste, nature, man's experience and man's relation to God. He struggled to connect all he knew, rather than give way to bitterness, a despairing negative creed. His imagination, more delicately poised over reality, went with a haunting dream-like quality. In **"The Midnight Skaters"**, for example, who are these figures, and what is the pond on which they move? (pp. 18-19)

Water, streams and rivers have always fascinated [Blunden]. Earlier, life had been a gentle flowing stream, attractively clear and shallow, but now the stream had turned into a river with unknown depths that were hazardous and yet had to be explored. He looks again at one of his boyhood streams, and writes:

> And do you then, gentle stream,
> Assume your wintriest wild extreme,
> And (as I have known amazed) pour down
> Among your goblin willows brown
> Deep-dooming floods and foaming flocks
> Of whirlwaves till the midnight rocks
> With what you say to those who dare
> Affront you with some coarse affair.

From his own 'wintriest wild extreme' he was given some relief. His health had never been good since the war, and in the hope of making a recovery he crossed to South America in a cargo boat, and the travel-book *The Bonadventure* was the result, a volume that showed a man of letters with a keen awareness of new experiences. It was the evidence of imaginative travelling much farther than from Sussex to Flanders.

Soon after his journey to South America a suggestion was made by his friend Ralph Hodgson that seemed unlikely and impossible; it was that he should go to Japan for a period. Hodgson was himself about to go to Tohoku University. Blunden hesitated, but when Professor Takeshi Saito made a direct personal request, he agreed, and so became Professor of English Literature at Tokyo University for three years. (p. 20)

The poet who found a bond between Belgium and Wiltshire, between Sussex and France instinctively found that, with all the great differences of another civilization, there was beneath a common essence:

> We moved . . .
> Into a most familiar air,
> And like spring showers received it from the hills
> That stood from our old hills ten thousand miles—
> Or none; we paused along the yellow plains
> And kissed the child that ran from shyer friends
> To take our hand.

He pays poetical tribute to the Japanese scene, and respects it with a modesty that is his main quality as man and poet. (pp. 21-2)

In 1928 Blunden returned to England and to the office of *The Nation*. He was able also to return to Kent and to live at Yalding in the rambling Elizabethan house, Cleave's, that he had admired since childhood when it was the home of his Grammar School master. An interim followed while he resumed old ties and settled some of his questionings. By writing *Undertones of War* in Japan he had rid himself of many of his haunting fears.

It was almost inevitable that he should be needed by Oxford again, and he was elected a Fellow and Tutor of Merton College in 1930. (p. 23)

By the time he returned to Oxford a calmer and quieter mood pervaded his work. A more certain note of belief is evident; **"Report on Experience"** tells something:

> Say what you will, our God sees how they run.
> These disillusions are his curious proving
> That he loves humanity and will go on loving;
>   Over there are faith, life, virtue in the sun.

These lines were not the end but the beginning of a deeper searching into the relationship between nature, 'the mysterious Mother', and the human and spiritual mind. In **"Values"** he asks himself and his reader to combine intellect and emotion and find the basic essence of man, using language and imagery that are Shakespearian in their tensity and vastness. . . . An awesome note alternates with his peace, more intense than many acclaimed voices of the mystical. Throughout the thirties he wrote in this way, and as his works were more highly metaphysical, he exercised more emotional control over the undercurrent. These were years in which the very climate of the world—and he had never shut out the world—made the task more than usually difficult.

Over much of his work of the period lingers the academic atmosphere of Oxford; the number of set literary pieces, of verses addressed to past authors and unknown divines, together with the humour of such as **"Incident in Hyde Park 1803"**, increases. Lyrics and ballads, sketches from the country are mingled with more memories of the war. Often he permits himself to grow angry, as the years bring nearer a repetition of what he hoped, standing apart from politics and full of mankind's faith, could never happen again. . . . (pp. 26-8)

It was as though some foreboding allowed him no peace; this was the one period where often his works contain many 'half-ideas, verges of shadows and misty brightness'. In many diverse pieces he asserts, defiantly, 'calm in calm atmosphere', or how 'the safe paths curve through unexalted fields'. He writes anxiously, and in his best moments the searching emotional tone makes his readers think carefully. Oddly, it was in 1940, just after the war began, that he freed himself and, as though his personal and intellectual ideas were clarified, wrote **"The Sum of All"**:

> Crossing the artillery ranges whose fierce signs
> Mean nothing now; whose gougings look like
> Bird-baths now; and last, the frontier farm
> And guard-house made of bracken.
> Rising to this old eyrie, quietly forsaken,
> You bear me on, and not me only.
> All difference sheds away,
> All shrivelling of the sense, anxious prolepsis,
> Injury, staring suspicion,
> Fades into pure and wide advance.
> So rise; so let me pass.

His fears and anxiety had been concentrated on hoping that the disaster of another world war would be prevented, but once it happened, he could not persist in backward lamentations. He retained the poet's vision that this second outbreak would be more devastating; the power of destruction had become so much greater and the ability to control the machine correspondingly weaker. However, basically he reasserted his confidence in the faith of the past, that the best spirit of man, almost the divine spark of man, would survive. . . . (pp. 28-9)

Once again he put on uniform and found himself instructing among others some of the young war poets, until he left Oxford in 1943. He returned to a war-scarred London and joined the staff of *The Times Literary Supplement.* Despite the war these were active years when his studies of Thomas Hardy and Shelley were written. And he paid his tribute to his favourite sport that had started in boyhood at Yalding, cricket. He is the first poet to write verses for a Test Match captain! *Cricket Country* was not only an affectionate book reflecting the game, it was a timely affirmation that the philosophy of cricket would outlast temporary setbacks. Philip Tomlinson likened it in its sphere to Walton's *Compleat Angler* as it roams in gentle and reminiscent thought over the game and the world around.

As a poet Blunden began what may be considered his third period. Such divisions are arbitrary and often misleading, but the two volumes, *Shells by a Stream* and *After the Bombing,* published between 1940 and 1950, offer a change of mind and technique. His voice became, as though to counter the confusion of the period, more distinct; its simplicity was still subtlety, because the thought was increasingly metaphysical as the language grew less involved.

Sometimes he suggests that he is not quite the source of this confident note:

> It is not mine to choose; the deeper call
> Is master yet. The child is that they made him.

And though death is brought nearer to the world, yet, because of that, life has a lighter, subtly happier cause:

> O living love in whose great birth
>   Death counts for nothing, proved a lie,
> Still blaze and blossom through old earth,
>   And sea and sky.

Any imaginative poet, such as Blunden, justifies the theory of 'unacknowledged legislator', not in the simple sense of the term but in the ability to foresee the temper of the future; he pierces the coming mind of man, and is always some years ahead of the moment of writing. Many of his poems written in the thirties gave warning of the trials of war, [while] the poems written during or just after the war went further forward beyond the years. . . . Hope and security can come to man through a plain faith of understanding the pattern of creation, and he avers it with delicate imagery in **"The Blueprint"**:

> Will you too fashion a church that's awake to the
>   April showers
> Where the merry angels are ready to wing
> In the painted roof with praise and prayer
> To one who being heaven's King
> Is splendour enthroned over earth's dim air?
> A church where the altar lilies appear as the soul's
>   new flowers?

The range is as wide as ever; memories of the countryside are clearer, and the light notes as **"The Blackthorn Bush in Spring"** are more simply lyrical. One of the clearest poems of this kind is a tribute to his wife, **"Serena"**, in which the calmness of his mind is reflected in the language. . . . (pp. 29-31)

Of considerable poetical importance were his thoughts on time, change, ghosts and God which had been a source of power for him since his early days. They were all interlinked, and the first war, and the ways of the countryside had played a part in this interest and speculation. The years had intensified his preoccupation and now, as with his other subjects, a purity of inspiration is frequently apparent. . . . (p. 31)

Several poems dealing with timelessness and ghosts stand out, but two are great achievements, and have the simplicity of the mysterious tale where reality and imagination touch only to fly apart again. The two poems are **"When the Statue Fell"** and **"Thomasine"**. The former tells of the Statue of the Virgin and Child on a church-tower in Picardy. The church was almost totally destroyed; the statue remained:

> The Queen of heaven and votaress of the place;
> Only, she bowed, she stooped as she would kiss
> The ground and turn its misery into bliss—
> Even so she hovered in hell-haunted space;
> It looked that every moment she must drop,
> She and her Baby, from the jagged tower's top.

The story is easy and its whole atmosphere is created by the contrast of ordinary devotional images and the 'mad plague murderous' of devastation's 'airy devils'. When the statue falls the war will end; in God's time an end will be put to war, 'worse than a ghoul'.

"Thomasine", the earlier of the two poems, has a more involved story of a dream, and the figure of Thomasine enchants her lover and the reader; but who is this figure of youth, of life or imagination—'That call in the reeds was all her theme'?

> I dare not screen
> My thought from the chance that just this one
> Reed-note from beyond the world else known

> Woke a new song in sauntering Thomasine.

Reality is suspended, Thomasine emerges as a symbol of hope in universal love; the poem ends quietly and with imaginative delicacy. . . . (pp. 32-3)

[*Shells by a Stream* and *After the Bombing*] maintain without exception a high level of poetic power. They were composed during restless years, and the next volume will be awaited with great expectation. (p. 33)

Concluding a critique of Blunden's poetry in 1926 E. G. Twitchett wrote:

> It seems that there is little now that he cannot describe, and less that he dares not attempt. But to succumb to the glamour of prophecy . . . would be an impertinence in this merely interim estate—would be indeed to march against the omens. Mr. Blunden is thirty and he has not yet finished growing.
>
> (pp. 33-4)

It is a rare attribute in a well-known man of letters that he can inspire such sensations, that he is free of labels, and that his genius is not already set and controlled by strong trends of thought and ideas. Since the 'Georgian' title has been found worthless, Blunden has continued to be isolated and the product of himself. That readers can pick up a book by a poet, who established a high reputation some thirty-six years ago, still confident that he is 'growing', is a fine proof of his freshness, his poetic youth and spring-like energy.

The danger, however, of this expectancy is that it is easy to fail to appreciate how much has already been achieved. Cecil Day Lewis wrote in a notable poem to Blunden on his 50th birthday that he

> never has burned or bowed
> To popular gods, and when fame beckons
> Modestly melts in the crowd.

For too long verse anthologists have scarcely looked beyond a few of his early perfect pieces, deservedly popular, but not adequate to represent his scope.

The *corpus* of his work both in verse and prose is formidable and comprehensive. English literature owes much to him for his biographical discoveries, critical originality and perspicuity. . . . (p. 34)

To this animation and criticism belong the many verse tributes to past authors in which a portrait is painted of the spirit and mind of the subject, which only with great difficulty and less emotion could be contained in prose. His prose is closely linked to his verse; it has the same nervous accuracy and rhythm. (p. 35)

Another field in which he shows himself the inheritor of good literary traditions is that of ceremonial or occasional verses. Such pieces, since the days of classical Greece, have been the amusement of poets, and only modern iconoclasts have objected. The occasional poet has to be able to write for the moment, to unite craftsmanship with a touch of personality to sympathetic propriety. Blunden has provided a profusion of such moments and given his own standard whether writing verses on the death of King George V or a madrigal for the Queen's Coronation, a birthday greeting, a prologue to a play or a compliment to the citizens of a Japanese town.

On another and higher plane his poetic range is extensive and enviable; the country poems cover a wide area of experience and observation in which landscape, tree or stream not only reveal their natural essence and beauty but signify a larger connection with the world. And here the strange and the mysterious, the divine purpose and revelation, appear stealthily; he never fills in all the scene. The detail is minute, but something more could be told. The scenes may be taken from Kent or Sussex, but they can never be just 'Blunden country'. The imaginative feeling and conception are too great, despite the sensitive choice of rhythmic and dialect words.

This is apparent, no less, in the war-poems and the later memories that haunt him. Neither bitter or cynical, their effect is slower and so more sure; in any factual moment he envisages a larger terror that makes the reader feel a blush of guilt. The Sussex characters and the Flanders soldiers are ghostly symbols of man endowed with a life larger than the naked mind would understand. Few poets have looked upon the world so tolerantly and yet without compromising their basic belief in the essential dignity given to man by God.

His 'personal' poems represent the pilgrimage of a poet often bewildered and in doubt, but rarely in despair, and it is hardly to be wondered at that his imagination and thought have explored more widely the metaphysical realms in ever-increasing persistence. In his earlier days the truths he told were hard-won and learnt only through personal experience. The 'growing' aspect was in the revelations that had to come after such beginnings. A similar atmosphere pervades his purely imaginative poems; he opens his wings in the clouds of mystery, the kingdom of "The Ancient Mariner" and "Christabel". The riddle of man's power and mind are challenged.

'Blunden's country' cannot be confined. He has found a common link between England and France, England and Japan. Imaginative and poetic reasoning is his country.

He seems the legitimate inheritor of the legacy of English literature, and has increased the value of his inheritance, not least by his modesty, tolerance and artistic sincerity. (pp. 35-6)

> *Alec M. Hardie, in his* Edmund Blunden, *Longmans, Green & Co., 1958, 43 p.*

THE TIMES LITERARY SUPPLEMENT

[Mr. Blunden] has been unwilling to lend himself to any muse but his own. We do not associate him with shared attitudes, with group loyalties or passionate manifestos. For much of the time he has not even been physically present in the rival powerhouses of modern literature. . . . Poetry lies on him like dew on a leaf; it is the natural condensation of the atmosphere he breathes, so that all his verse is, in the best sense, occasional. It arises from a direct response to life.

This latest collection [*A Hong Kong House: Poems, 1951-1961*], covering ten years mainly spent as Professor of English at Hong Kong University, makes it easier to assess the rare contribution which Mr. Blunden is still making to the literature of his time. He makes it after his own fashion, and at times so demurely that close attention is needed before his originality is perceived. The casual reader will note that he is not afraid of the second person singular, [and] that he uses obsolete and "poetic" words, like "agone" and "nigh." . . .

In brief it is possible to accuse him of turning away from the new freedoms which have conditioned poetry during his lifetime, in an effort to graft his own thought to the traditional stem of verse-making, even at the expense of sounding at times either whimsical or archaic.

This will not hold, however. It is essential to Mr. Blunden's art that he is a scholar as well as a maker. He perceives that in a time of general flux it would be absurd for a poet whose theme is the human spirit to show himself too painfully aware of the contesting voices which surround him. He has his own points of reference—they include Henry Stephens, ink-maker and friend of Keats, Gerald Finzi, musician, and a vast anonymous tribe of those who have given his native Kent its special tone, as well as familiar ghosts from the First World War, from a variety of countrysides, and from all literature, in echo or amusing parody. Part of the pleasure of reading Mr. Blunden is therefore to spot his hidden connexions. His mind is so richly stored that each smallest disturbance throws out great rings of fancy, yet at the same time so personal that it is reliably himself who speaks. What in others might sound like an echo is always a timbre.

He has been pigeon-holed in his time as a pastoral poet, as a war poet, as a "literary" poet, yet it is impossible to pin his variety into such narrow limits. Then, his metrical invention has been insufficiently praised. Like Hardy he can take the accepted cadences of classical English verse, and bend them to his purpose with beautiful dexterity. Sometimes, it is true, the mould grips a poem too tightly; the reader is conscious of a certain strain, which manifests itself in gnarled rhyme or syntax. But in general Mr. Blunden commands his own music as he wants it, and *A Hong Kong House* shows that he is always ready to extend his range. . . . And on every page there is a felicity of experience translated into the right words.

"A Felicity of Experience," in The Times Literary Supplement, *No. 3168, November 16, 1962, p. 874.*

MICHAEL THORPE

'A true poet in the great English tradition' runs the blurb on the jacket of Blunden's *Poems of Many Years.* As this is the kind of phrase we tend to accept unthinkingly, it may be useful to begin by trying to give it some constructive meaning in relation to Blunden's poetry. 'English tradition' may be interpreted restrictively, as referring to the local, or regional folklorist tradition inspired directly by rural life; this is largely anonymous, but includes such 'peasant' poets as Bloomfield and Clare. Alternatively, the 'tradition' may be the distinctive current of nature poetry which runs, now strongly, now quietly and unobtrusively, throughout the centuries, irrespective of the dominance of other themes. At times, this current carries the stronger impulses, as in the mystics Traherne and Vaughn and in the poetry of most of the great Romantics and Hardy; sometimes the less powerful, as in the eighteenth-century poetry of rural retirement, and the nostalgia of some Victorians and the lesser Georgians. One of the complexities—and curiosities—of Blunden's poetry is that it embraces examples of all these more sophisticated modes of feeling, yet takes its origin and essential strength from the (once) unchanging soil ploughed by the regional poets.

In *The Darkling Plain,* an excellent survey of the fluctuating fortunes of English Romanticism from Darley to Yeats, John Heath-Stubbs devotes a sympathetic chapter to the regional poets of the nineteenth century who wrote in a folk tradition that ran parallel to and, perhaps, Mr Heath-Stubbs thinks, deeper than that travelled by their famous but 'more polite' contemporaries. The poets in this tradition whom he chiefly distinguishes are John Clare, William Barnes, Robert Stephen Hawker and, at a more intellectualized level, Thomas Hardy. (p. 13)

Certainly, as Mr Heath-Stubbs says, the world into which they were born has passed away and they themselves, Hardy preeminently, were already its elegists. Edmund Blunden, late-comer though he is, nevertheless belongs by right to their tradition and their descent. Yet he is the last of the line, for he began to write just within the period that saw the utter dissolution of the old rustic order and fought (sad irony) in the First World War which precipitated its end. He was born just early enough (in 1896) to have known a 'brighter morning' in quiet and prosperous Kent where—despite the decay Hardy's novels of a near-by rustic environment had revealed and foreshadowed—the way of life could still seem immemorial. The impress of those early years was deep enough to enable him to begin writing strongly and confidently in the possession of a Wordsworthian relationship with nature and ample human material supplied by his daily life in a settled community. Thus, he could prolong into our century the tradition Mr Heath-Stubbs describes, that of the essentially rooted writer. . . . [In] no other poet of the period is the impression of local and intensely known rural life so strong as in Blunden's early poetry—in the volumes entitled *The Waggoner* (1920), *The Shepherd* (1922) and *English Poems* (1925), partly written before the Great War but chiefly later, in passionate recollection of what the deluge obliterated.

His strongest ancestral affinities in the regional tradition are perhaps Clare and Hardy—both of whom he has appraised with great insight—but he has his own unique quality. On the one hand, he shares with Clare simplicity of expression and detailed and faithful observation—providing what he himself calls Clare's 'multitudinous delight'—combined with an acceptance of the ordering of the universe (sustained by faith); on the other, he has something of Hardy's detachment and even a tempering scepticism, which derives from his intellectualized attitude. (pp. 14-15)

Blunden's range is not confined to the pastoral, nor is his pastoralism a figment of the fancy, two strong reasons why he must be thoroughly detached from the general Georgian run, whose cardinal weaknesses he himself defined when singling out Ivor Gurney for praise: 'neither easy sentiment nor an indifferent "eye on the object" can be imputed to him, nor yet languor nor studied homeliness of expression'. This is true also of Blunden's own best work, not only in his most widely praised early period, but throughout poetry extending over fifty years. (p. 15)

'Of all the poets who have emerged since the war Mr Blunden is the one whose position is most secure.' So wrote J. C. Squire in January 1920, then as editor of the *London Mercury* preparing to inherit Edward Marsh's role as patron and 'shepherd' of the Georgian poets; amongst whom Blunden, unfortunately for his later reputation, was belatedly numbered. When Squire made his large predication, Blunden was only 24—but the Georgian revolution had spent its impetus. By 1932 F. R. Leavis, whilst canonizing Eliot and Pound, set aside a few typically judicial pages of *New Bearings* to show Blunden and his kind the door; Blunden was pigeon-holed as that unhappiest of souls, the poet of unfulfilled promise.

Certainly, for one whose position early seemed to many beside Squire 'secure', Blunden has received remarkably little close appreciation; to discover why this should be so it is worth while to begin with a consideration of Leavis's acute criticisms, since their adverse influence doubtless remains strong. The promise, Leavis thought, had been in the early volumes, **The Waggoner** and **The Shepherd.** In these he saw that Blunden had created a richly particularized rural world which served equally as a 'refuge' from the harshness of the Great War and as a means of conveying, through an inclusive vision of the 'tooth and claw' as well as the idyllic element of that world, an imaginative symbol of man's self-torn world and of the poet's painful awareness of it.

Though Leavis offered no concrete examples of this, one can readily support his interpretation. If there were the 'golden-age beckonings' and the 'loving-kindness' (Hardy's valued word) of the richly Keatsian 'Leisure' and ideal Wordsworthian projections of man at one with his natural environment (**"Shepherd"** and **"The Veteran"**), there were also the murderous energy of **"The Pike"**, the disenchanted autumnal vision of **"The Sighing Time"** and **"A Country God"**—which, though written in Armistice Year, contains no promise of spring not 'far behind'—the devilish visitation of **"The Barn"** and the sullen, solitary figure of **"The Waggoner"**. In later volumes (from **English Poems,** 1925, onwards) Leavis found this quality of stress diminished and outweighed by an inferior 'literariness', 'which takes the form of frank eighteenth-century echoes, imitations, and reminiscences'. . . . Leavis concluded that the 'visionary gleam' had faded, leaving behind at best 'the poetry of simple pieties'—a 'notable' achievement, but limited, evidently because it belonged to what we must now consider one of the backwaters of literature.

One can see the force of Leavis's comment, yet, without going so far as some of Blunden's most ardent devotees, feel that the first hectic flush of the Eliot Age having faded, it is time to look at Blunden more for what he is than what he is not. Leavis, as usual, was concerned to 'place' writers in the first or second eleven—or nowhere. *Professor* Blunden, on the other hand, to think of him for a moment in his critical role, has consistently sought the best in the mixed company of poets he has, as it were, lived with, and to convey that to others without affixing arbitrary labels. Kirke White and Keats, Collins and Coleridge, have been, in the first place, men to him and their subject-matter *what it is to be a man*. If Leavis's judgements rest upon the dictum that 'Poetry matters because of the kind of poet who is more alive than other people, more alive in his own age', Blunden would lay greater emphasis than he upon the first part of this statement; the second part is not so urgently relevant for him as it was for such as Eliot and Yeats, since, though he does not think the concerns of the 'age' should be disregarded, he has never felt the need to involve himself in the contemporary search for a new scheme of values to replace beliefs, which are not, for him, outmoded.

Leavis's complaint of conscious 'literariness' is the least damaging. 'Literary' poems obtrude far less in the great bulk of Blunden's work than Leavis implies. These derive quite naturally from his feeling of being intimately related to the poets or artists of the past who, like himself, have worked in the rural tradition. Such poems are either direct celebrations of this kinship—**"The Wartons"**, **"Nature Displayed"**, or the two poems inspired by admired landscape artists, **"A Favou-**

rite Scene (Recalled on Looking at Birket Foster's Landscape)"** and **"Family Discourse (Or, John Constable's Painting 'The Valley Farm')"**—or else they are, by imitation, an implicit acknowledgement of his lineal tradition: **"Old Homes"**, which memorializes his native Yalding, recalls Goldsmith's *The Deserted Village* in both manner and sentiment, whilst **"Gleaning"** is reminiscent, in the diligent and loving accumulation of observed detail and its acceptance of the rightness of the rustic dispensation, of numerous pastoral poets of the eighteenth century. Blunden is so steeped in the poetry of the past—especially that of the late eighteenth and early nineteenth centuries—that such echoes naturally recur, but they are a part only, and not the most distinctive part, of his variously toned poetic voice.

Much of Blunden's work is, in a good sense, 'occasional'. Bulk may be, as Kenneth Hopkins suggests, an 'essential quality of an important poet', but it renders the task of disentangling his best work difficult and may, on a cursory view, obscure what is best. . . . [Blunden] himself reasonably considers that much poetry—or 'verse', as he too often modestly describes his own efforts—should be occasional. . . . Like Hardy, Shelley and Wordsworth before him, he puts into verse much that will entertain, divert or instruct more effectively in this form—yet without absolutely demanding it. So he has celebrated in verse both a Test Match captain (**"Hammond, England"**) and a village cricketing 'giant' of his boyhood days (**"Pride of the Village"**); elsewhere he rhymes forty whimsical lines **"To a British Jar Containing Stephen's Ink"**. One can easily imagine how such diversions offend the devotees of 'poetry', and it is indeed disconcerting when they nudge the more serious writing familiarly on facing pages, sometimes unsettling one's response to it. But this element in his writing gives 'verse' its due meaning and place, no more—and if he has little company in this respect today he has excellent company amongst earlier poets, among them his admired Coleridge and Shelley, whose reputation is diminished by this no more than his own deserves to be.

The 'verse' and the 'conscious literariness' are not the essential Blunden, merely elements in his highly inclusive subject-matter. An inclusiveness of a more serious and moving kind is what he has always aimed at: to touch, in Wordsworth's words, 'the general passions and thoughts and feelings of men', which are connected 'with our moral sentiments and animal sensations, and with the causes which excite these; with the operations of the elements, and the appearances of the visible universe; with storm and sunshine, with the revolutions of the seasons, with cold and heat, with loss of friends and kindred, with injuries and resentments, gratitude and hope, with fear and sorrow'. In his early poetry, like Wordsworth, he drew upon ample material for these essential themes supplied by an intimately known local rural life. The early work paints the whole body of rustic life, complete—as Leavis noted—with its blemishes: the charm and innocent beauty of **"The Flower-Gatherers"** are complemented by the laborious harshness of **"The Waggoner"**; there are the necessary murder of **"The Mole-Catcher"**, the gentle fidelity of **"The Shepherd"**, and in a quiet corner the pathos of **"Almswomen"**—all his people are fully placed in community.

The stylistic affinity with Wordsworth is less marked—though in the words of 'an aged woman . . . not fair' in the **"The Silver Bird of Herndyke Mill"** one recognizes the accent and mood of *Lyrical Ballads*. . . . (pp. 15-19)

Generally, however, [Blunden's] poems have a denser descriptive texture than Wordsworth's and he relies more upon his own voice, but it is a voice nourished upon muscular dialect words. . . . In his capacity for re-animating the ordinary language by recruiting fresh reserves from a vocabulary born of local perception he is more akin to Hardy or Clare than to Wordsworth. Significantly, this feature is most marked in the first decade of his poetry, 1914-24, during which he was in closest physical touch with English country life.

Introducing Blunden's *The Face of England* (1932), J. C. Squire wrote, 'no English poet . . . has so extensively enshrined typical English scenes and typical English characters in verse'. This is a just estimate, but a dangerously limiting one: limiting in its implicit invitation to consider him solely as a pastoral poet of the picturesque and because one might infer that Blunden's attitude toward his subject-matter is partial and narrow.

Blunden's valuation of nature and rustic life is neither simple nor simple-minded. He has often in prose, besides arguing the merits of the old rural order, frankly granted its shortcomings—the sometimes degraded condition of the farm labourer, the brutishness of the untutored man, the lack of hygiene—and such things have their place in his realistic poems. But his positive claims for the old rural life as *he knew it* (a necessary emphasis) should not, any more than those of Leavis's 'discovery', George Sturt, be lightly brushed aside. They derive from the full and firmly based experience of his early years in the Kent village of Yalding, where he found 'a relationship of various talents and masteries, and courteous differences, which composed a serene, just kind of life'. What, above all, has been lost is the highly articulated life of a local community: 'The loss is not only one of a picturesque spectacle, but of a social idea'. . . . [Blunden had] the good fortune to have been reared in one of those fruitful pockets of rural England where a creative community life survived till near our own time. It stands for him as no fanciful ideal against which to measure what succeeded it. Inevitably, he well knows, it has become 'the lifetime in the picture' (**"A Family Discourse"**), but looking back to recall its values is not escapism. . . . (pp. 19-21)

Blunden is an honest poet; he is clear-sighted enough to look upon that former landscape with an artist's eye, as a country of the mind now. An obliterating shadow was cast over that dead Arcadia by the terrible struggles of our century—first and most deeply by the Great War, 'the difficult dumb-show of my generation', which exploded not only humanitarian visions but also 'the pastoral fairy-tale'. In his war poems, as in **"The Dynasts"**, the fair face of nature is ravaged and scarred.

Drafted as a (not altogether metaphorically) 'harmless young shepherd in a soldier's coat', he was, in one sense, closer than any of the major English war poets to those inarticulate battalions pitchforked roughly from the ordered furrow to the incomprehensible fields of France. It is as if in him their bewildered, outraged minds and sense found a voice. . . . All the notable First World War poets portray war as an abomination, a breach of nature's balance of forces. But in none is the theme of warring man's devastation so pervasive as in Blunden's war poems, most of which form "A Supplement of Poetical Interpretations and Variations" to *Undertones of War* (1928). One of their unique qualities is that it seems time and again as if, like the countrymen who can only think in terms of nature (his inevitable correlative), he were striving to *naturalize* the scenes and weapons of war. Thus, bullets become 'steel-born bees' invading the flowered garden, to sting not build (**"A House in Festubert"**); the foul trenches seem 'earthy lanes' in the moonlight (**"Illusions"**). . . . Such images, because of the unbridgeable gap between the two elements of the metaphors, painfully reveal the poet's inability to unify his terrible experience: they are indeed 'yoked by violence together'. The sense of strain is most intense when the infantryman in a 'subnatural' assault becomes a twisted plant with 'hands which twine / On grotesque iron' (**"Come on, my lucky lads"**). The man is natural in that he kills, subnatural in that he is a mere *uncreating* killer, the tool of some demonic force. Blunden speaks of 'uncreation' in **"Third Ypres"**, his most sustained poetic attempt to convey the feel of action. This poem has an emotionally climactic moment when, driven almost insane by the spectacle of his mangled companions, the poet is calmed by the appearance of nature's mildest creatures:

> Look, from the wreck a score of field mice nimble,
> And tame and curious look about them; (these
> Calmed me, on these depended my salvation).

Nature can calm, not cure—'thou must give, else never canst receive'. Blunden could give enough to survive and, like nature herself, accept the devastation without crying out. He is almost nature's voice—an effect which is more marked in the accumulation of prose descriptions in *Undertones of War*. . . . At the end of the book he sounds a deeply disturbing note that has remained with him ever since; looking upon the freshly ripened fields around the so recently devastated Albert, he wonders: 'The mercy of nature advances. Is it true?' The pastoral is permanently flawed. . . . (pp. 21-3)

Blunden's outraged sense of man's negligence of his trust as companion and guardian, not only of man (Owen's strongest theme) but of the nature he breathes, is his distinctive contribution to the poetry of the First World War. (p. 23)

Upon Blunden the war—a prototype of what one day the whole human race may suffer—left an ineradicable scar. The sense of the best prematurely blighted has never left him. . . . Over forty years later, this feeling returns, but without bitterness, as he reflects wistfully 'how we went / At once much farther than the slow extent / Of life since then'. In his *Poems 1914-30* the section containing war poems is headed significantly, **"War: Impacts and Delayed Actions"**. At first, as most powerfully in **"A Country God"**, nature's language runs wholly dark,

> But now the sower's hand is writhed
> In livid death, the bright rhythm stolen

this anti-pastoral ends 'With all my murmurous pipes flung by / And summer not to come again'. In **"1916 Seen from 1921"**, also in *The Shepherd,* 'the charred stub outspeaks the living tree'. . . . The war provided [Blunden] most concretely with a vision of evil which forms the counterpart in his poetry to the Waste Land imagery of Eliot. At the same time his darker-toned nature poetry deepens his affinity with Hardy.

This extremely dark vision is, naturally, not sustained, but its hold is never completely broken. In the later volumes of the twenties, he turns through all the degrees of feeling: in **"Harvest"** he asserts confidently 'Earth accuses none that goes among her stooks', but in **"The Deeper Friendship"** this stales into the morbid, . . . or he may yearn for the vanished diurnal vision of a less tainted age [as in **"The Age of Herbert and Vaughan"**]. (pp. 24-5)

But in poems later than these he refuses to shun the darker side of truth, yet paints his dilemma with a forceful clarity. . . . **"The Kiss"** (1932) begins,

> I am for the woods against the world,
> But are the woods for me?

It does end affirmatively, but only after an open-eyed recognition and inclusion of the ominous 'swollen river', 'the hurling seas of brown'. In **"Nature's Beauty"** (1949), written during a crisis in the Second World War, he discerns some consolation, but it is hard-won, fleeting, known to be no anodyne:

> I passed as he who bears
> But a brief-dated leave, and in this age
> Scarcely to be acquired. The radiant page
> So gently shown, so firmly turned, might seem
> Of earth's and man's book once; this day, a dream.
> So shown, so turned, the fairy writ was gone,
> And only a pretty mist, unmeaning, lingered on

—his detractors would endorse the meaning of the last line, but they cannot deny that it is Blunden's own. If not the antithesis of escapism, these firm lines are at least a case of setting the ideal to the whetstone of truth. As elsewhere in the volume *After the Bombing* (1949) and the earlier *Shells by a Stream* (1944), this poem recognizes harsh truth yet consoles; for a less qualified, but valuable, consolation in Blunden's human vein there is **"The Boy on the Waggon"** which celebrates a small joyful human drama, developing the spirit in which Hardy ended his "In Time of 'The Breaking of Nations' ".

At this point we should note where Blunden, like another of that great poet's disciples, Sassoon, parts company with Hardy: he has always—as, for example, the early **"The Pasture Pond"** clearly shows—been able to say, with Herrick

> I sing (and ever shall)
> Of Heaven, and hope to have it after all.

Though this has not (as has been suggested already) blinded him to the darker side of things, it does give much of his poetry a hopeful, even sometimes a devotional tone which is rare in modern poetry—even modern religious poetry, which expresses rather, as in Eliot and Edwin Muir, a painful step-by-step struggle towards belief. Blunden's note (like Sassoon's) often echoes that of Vaughan, whom he invokes in **"A Psalm"**—yet prays with revealing anxiety,

> O God that Abraham and our Vaughan knew,
> Hide not thyself, let first love prove not wrong.

He ranges from the serene piety of **"At a Cathedral Service"**—surely, to faithful eyes, one of the most beautiful of poems about the reflection of divine love in the human—and the exalted, exultant,

> Clean flows the wind as from its grand source flow-
> ing
> At once to man, clean flows the eternal God:
> The clouds dance with that splendid presence glow-
> ing,
> Earth's silver brilliance flashes from that flood.

—to the perturbed meditations upon life's disillusions, **"Report on Experience"** and **"The Sum of All"**, where 'Unity; now discerned beyond / Fear, obscureness, casualty, / Ex-

haustion, shame and wreck,' is proclaimed in the ominous days of 1939 'As what was best, / As what was deeply well designed.' Deeply, obscurely—acceptance of the necessity of the struggle between good and evil is sustained by a thread of passionate confidence that good will triumph that runs through forty years. But it is a thread, hardly to be disentangled from the disenchantments, doubts, the awareness of evil's immediate power and the limits of our consolations. Most hopefully, this is epitomized in the sonnet **"Values"**, whose involved shifts of metaphor produce an intensity that justifies the epithet 'Shakespearian'. Another poem, **"The Memorial 1914-18"**, expresses an attitude which, far from being faithful overmuch, is rather a chill Hardyesque resignation (it recalls Hardy's "The Souls of the Slain"). . . . [**"The Memorial 1914-18"**] is not a consoling poem; Blunden's religious urge, seen in its wholeness, is neither mechanical nor complacent. . . . Man's suffering solitude may be imaged, as he thinks, in nature, but his consolation is not to be found there; whatever else he may depend upon, it cannot be a nature into which he has injected his own feelings.

The most moving example of how the harshness of the truth may, momentarily, overpower the larger hope is given by **"To Joy"**, an elegy for a baby daughter. Here, the desolate feeling (as in **"The Memorial"**) finds no relief in faith. . . . Elsewhere—he often returns to this subject—there is the pantheistic consolation, as in **"The Child's Grave"**, where he feels 'Joy's spirit shone then in each flower I went by', but still it is hard won, for,

> It seemed but as yesterday she lay by my side,
> And now my dog ate of the grass on her grave.

A similarly clear-eyed vision distinguishes **"Achronos"**, **"In a Country Churchyard"** and **"A 'First Impression' (Tokyo)"**. . . . In the latest of this group, **"But At Last"**, he still probes undying memories with painful candour. Its involved shifts of feeling allow no simple interpretation and the reader, like the poet, can rest complacently nowhere. It is remarkable that in so late a poem Blunden can remind one (*pace* Dr Leavis) of a quality he shares with Edward Thomas at his best, of letting the poem follow the feeling—despite what at first may deceive, the rhyming facility, the surface neatness of composition.

As these elegies best reveal, Blunden is pre-eminently a poet of the affections. This is his strong ground—and, in poetry's broad province, it is not the marginal thing Leavis's phrase 'simple pieties' seems to imply. Poetry may never harmonize the world, but it has always for many made it more bearable. In **"A Calm Rain"**, a tranquil meditation upon poetry's value—the value, that is, of his kind of poetry—Blunden suggests its nature in the image of 'a shy and dream-like rain' that falls gently to comfort and console. . . . In the margin this poetry may be, but it is not marginal; for Blunden, poetry has always been a compassionate resource.

His poetry of the affections ranges widely. Another notable group is formed by the limpid love poems to Claire (his wife) in *Shells by a Stream.* These restored a buoyancy to his poetry which had been rare in the volumes published during the gloomy 1930s; their taut language and alliterative rhythm give the sense of passionate life revived. The situation differs of course, but their freshness rediscovered is reminiscent of the brighter retrospects in Hardy's "Veteris vestigia flammae".

His affection extends strongly not only to those actually

known—outstanding are **"Lascelles Abercrombie"** and the elegies for his father, **"To C. E. B."** and **"An Empty Chair"**, where he excels in dignified yet homely remembrance—but also to those among the dead with whom he feels a kinship as near as if he had known them in the flesh; he is drawn, as his literary researches show, to the obscure, forgotten dead, and this is feelingly expressed in **"Dead Letters"**, **"Writing a Sketch of a Forgotten Poet"** and **"Lonely Love"**. He has sought, irrespective of age or fame, 'the native thought, / The character, the self, the singular gift.' It is typical that, at the beginning of the Second World War, he should have found space for **"In the Margin"**, a plea for the common Japanese whom he had known and loved. An earlier Japanese poem, **"The Author's Last Words to his Students"**, has all the grace and humility of one who has discerned that 'it is not uncommon for English natures to be gracious and intimate in verse'—yet today it seems to be.

The themes I have touched upon illustrate his many-sided concern with 'the general passions and thoughts and feelings of men'. Though he is not, one readily grants Leavis, amongst those who (in Arnold's phrase) 'apply modern ideas to life', it is time to affirm, as did Arnold of the similarly 'limited' Wordsworth and Keats, that he has 'left admirable works'. As time passes he will not be set aside as '*simple* pietist' but praised rather as a rarer being of the kind who, at his best, handles these permanent themes with a tact and truth to feeling few can match (his early Romantic hero, Coleridge, is amongst these few). *At his best*—for he is too often 'weak-sided': we now admire, now in reaction deplore, as when faced with the dangerous facility of Shelley, or the lapses of triteness of sentiment and weary diction and imagery of Wordsworth and Hardy. Had he revised more and published less, and laboured to load every rift with ore, many would estimate him more highly than they do—he would also, perhaps, have lost some devotees. Some of these latter have served him ill, as he may himself have thought when in the Preface of *Poems 1914-30* he felt compelled to plead 'that those who take up this book will not altogether skip those pages which are non-rural. They are derived from unstrained, general feelings'. These last words now deserve more emphasis and value than Blunden perhaps intended. (pp. 25-30)

Michael Thorpe, in his The Poetry of Edmund Blunden, *Bridge Books, 1971, 52 p.*

PHILIP GARDNER

Among the "New Poems" included at the end of *Poems of Many Years,* the now standard selection of Edmund Blunden's poetry published in 1957, was one entitled **"Frank Worley, D.C.M., July 1954."** It is a short graceful requiem for a man whom Blunden had first met almost forty years earlier, when both were fighting in northern France, Worley as a corporal (later a sergeant), Blunden as a young lieutenant. Worley's combination of bravery and gentleness endeared him immediately to Blunden. . . . In 1954 Blunden paid tribute to his now dead comrade . . . as one whose especial gift it was 'To share, to give, to make privation / No trouble at all.' When Blunden published *A Hong Kong House* in 1962, Worley was again remembered [in a second poem], along with others about whom the poet enquired 'Where are the sergeants, passed beyond?' . . . In these two late poems Blunden is remembering, primarily, people; but the people exist in a context, and what the poems show is simply that, for Blun-

den, the context has never been forgotten. The context was the First World War. (p. 218)

[Blunden] entered the army virtually straight from school early in 1915, and a year later was posted to France as a sub-altern in the 11th Royal Sussex Regiment. His war service was passed in three distinct sectors of the Western Front. From April to August 1916 he was variously stationed between Béthune and La Bassée, doing trench-duty at Festubert, Richebourg, Givenchy, Cuinchy, and Auchy. The next four months were spent in the area unpleasantly summed up as 'the Somme.' . . . The greater part of Blunden's war however, consisted of just over a year, from November 1916 to January 1918, spent in the salient around Ypres, a landscape 'knocked silly' by the German bombardments of 1914. Here, in due course, Blunden took part in the Third Ypres (or Passchendaele) offensive launched on 3 July 1917. . . . (pp. 218-19)

Early in 1918 Blunden's battalion moved south again, and in March he himself was transferred, from the village of Gouzeaucourt near Cambrai, to a training centre in England. At some point in his long active service Blunden had been gassed and was therefore pronounced unfit for further duty overseas, though he tried twice to go (thus risking the same fate as Wilfred Owen, tragically killed only a week before the Armistice). After a short period with the postwar occupation forces, Blunden was finally demobilized in 1919. As well as being gassed in the war, Blunden also won the Military Cross, though with characteristic modesty he leaves no clues in his work as to when, where, or how. J. H. Johnston, almost the only critic who has written about Blunden's war poetry, has called him 'a miraculous survivor of nearly two years of extremely hazardous trench fighting.' Considering the average life-expectation of a subaltern in France—about three weeks—Johnston's description by no means exaggerates: Blunden was lucky.

To escape the war in body, however, was one thing; to escape it in memory was quite another, and hardly to be expected. I have particularized the locations of Blunden's war experience not simply as a biographical preliminary, but because the names of these locations (and many others) recur in his poetry for many years after. From *The Waggoner* (1920) to *A Hong Kong House* (1962), poems more or less related to the First World War are rarely absent from Blunden's many volumes: they diminish, but never disappear, and their total, even at a conservative estimate, exceeds one hundred.

In view, therefore, of such a quantity of poems, the almost total critical neglect of Blunden as a war poet is unaccountable; in view of their quality, which I hope if only in small part to display here, it is little short of outrageous. (pp. 219-20)

There has always been a tendency to type Blunden as a 'pastoral' poet. His earliest volumes of poetry, published in 1914 and 1916, deal with country scenes, and one of them is even entitled *Pastorals.* There would be no point in trying to deny this important aspect of his work, it being always understood that 'pastoral' is not of itself a pejorative label. The conviction, however, that such a term does not sum up Blunden's work is supported not only by the work itself but also by Blunden's own words in the preface to *Poems 1914-1930,* a collection which contains many poems of a different sort:

The titles and contents of my books *The Waggoner* and *The Shepherd* have, I apprehend, done me a slight injustice; that is, they have labelled me among poets of the time as a useful rustic. . . . Great as is the power of country life over me, and of that stately march of the seasons above, around, below it, yet I have always suspected myself of some inclination to explore other subjects.

As if to protect himself against the risks attendant on such understatement, Blunden becomes quite explicit a few paragraphs later:

> . . . War became part of the author's experience at a date so early as to mould and colour the poetry almost throughout this book.

It was not only up to 1930 that Blunden's poetry was so moulded and coloured. Even in his volume of 1949, *After the Bombing,* his reaction to such an apparently small death as that of **"The Hedgehog Killed on the Road"** gains force from helpless and not dissimilar deaths many years before, and the remembrance helps both to bring control to what might otherwise seem sentimental, and to reveal a more human significance and poignancy in it. . . . In the poems recalling Sergeant Worley and his fellow 'sergeants of other days' one can discern the workings of a conscious memory; here it is more latent memories which revive, stirred by an incident which might otherwise have been ignored or treated by itself. Throughout Blunden's poetry two impulses are intermittently at work: one from the poet, harking back to the war, and one from the war itself, haunting the mind and rising to its surface when it contemplates later, and apparently different, scenes and events.

Of the poems by Blunden which survived the war, a number were not published until 1930, in the collection *Poems 1914-1930.* Some of these, like **"Les Halles d'Ypres,"** are descriptive and of no great significance; others, like **"The Festubert Shrine"** and **"Festubert: The Old German Line"** (both dating from May 1916), are too derivative in manner to involve the reader completely. Some, however, reveal by a certain tension in their expression a deeper and more personal response to the war.

It is not surprising to find a poet like Blunden, brought up in the English countryside, recalling its beauties even in the distorting mirror of the Ypres salient; thus in **"Zillebeke Brook"** (April 1917) his fancy can recognize 'a glassy burn / Ribanded through a brake of Kentish fern.' But the illusion cannot be sustained, and later lines suggest that the impact of war is felt through its capacity, by poisoning the present, to make even memories painful. . . . War becomes progressively harder to ignore, and even where, as in **"Bleue Maison"** (1917), the landscape is not itself distorted, the poet's enjoyment of it involves conscious escapism:

> Now to attune my dull soul, if I can,
> To the contentment of this countryside
> Where man is not for ever killing man
> But quiet days like these calm waters glide.
> And I will praise the blue flax in the rye . . .

It would be naive to take this 'contentment' as one which completely possesses the poet; the implications of 'if I can' and the effort of 'I will praise' register themselves all too clearly.

The most poignant early poem of this type, **"In Festubert,"** written in 1916, was published in *The Waggoner,* Blunden's first post-war volume, in 1920. Here Blunden recalls the land-

scapes and sights of peace, but instead of bringing calm they 'peer' at him 'with bedlam eyes.' The poem's language suggests a mind close to the edge of its control, a mind that feels itself, irrationally but inescapably, cast out by nature. Far from strengthening him in his wartime circumstances, Blunden's memories only make them harder to endure, and the poem's last lines are desperate with the need to forget a past that cannot help the present and has, indeed, been distorted by association with it. . . . (pp. 220-22)

Blunden's **"War Autobiography,"** published in 1922 in *The Shepherd,* traces the waning of nature's power to sustain him. At first

> War might make his worst grimace
> And still my mind in armour good
> Turned aside in every place
> And saw bright day through the black wood.

But though this might have been so, few early poems exemplify such confidence; certainly **"In Festubert"** describes an 'armour' worn dangerously thin. . . . In 1917, in such a poem as **"The Unchangeable,"** Blunden was able intermittently to recollect the rivers and the 'primrose lags and brakes' of Sussex, but it was a recollection indulged 'spite of' the landscape of France and Belgium 'stamped into sloughs of death with battering fire.' When he returned to England in 1918 he exchanged the precarious memories of England-in-France for the indelible memories of France-in-England, and it was to be many years before he could enjoy the 'pastoral fairy-tale' without too quickly seeing it as a 'lie,' even a 'kindly meant lie.'

The bitterness of return was powerfully embodied in **"A Country God,"** one of his best early poems, written in 1918 and published in *The Waggoner* (1920). Here he remembers his earlier self, a pastoral poet at one with all the activities of rural life, which he celebrated with 'melodious pipes.' Now he feels no more than a ghost in a landscape whose pattern has been thrown out of true not only by his own traumatic recollections of natural disfigurement elsewhere but, less subjectively, by the deaths away from home of so many of its former inhabitants, the farmers, hedgers, and scythesmen of Sussex in whose regiment he had served. The violence of alteration is enacted both in Blunden's imagery and in the metrical disruption of lines four and five:

> But now the sower's hand is writhed
> In livid death, the bright rhythm stolen,
> The gold grain flatted and unscythed,
> The boars in the vineyard, gnarled and sullen,
> Havocking the grapes; and the pouncing wind
> Spins the spattered leaves of the glen
> In a mockery dance, death's hue-and-cry;
> With all my murmurous pipes flung by
> And summer not to come again.

It was unlikely that the hold of an experience which had such power to dispossess the past would be soon shaken off. **"The Estrangement"** (1919) continues to picture Blunden as a 'soul grown strange in France,' moving like a sleepwalker in a 'grim No Man's Land.' Though his next volume, *The Shepherd,* published in 1922, contains a number of nature poems many of them are uneasy, and the first poem in the volume, **"11th R.S.R.,"** is an attempt to fall back on memories of his regimental comrades as talismans against a disquiet nakedly expressed in its second stanza:

> What mercy is it, that I live and move,

> If haunted ever by war's agony?
>
> (pp. 222-24)

[F. R. Leavis dealt] summarily with Blunden's work in 1932; though ignoring the obvious 'war' poems, he saw clearly the effects of war on Blunden's other poetry:

> . . . out of the traditional life of the English countryside . . . Mr Blunden was creating a world—a world in which to find refuge from adult distresses; above all, one guessed, from memories of the war.

The truth of this observation is illustrated by **"The Veteran,"** written in 1919 and published in *The Waggoner.* It is a portrait, not of Blunden himself, but of his former colonel, G. H. Harrison, for whom his affection approached hero-worship. The poem is rich in its language, full, at first view, of the secure delight in a country farm retirement of one for whom 'the long misery of the Line is dead':

> Mellow between the leafy maze smiles down
> September's sun, swelling his multitude
> Of gold and red and green and russet-brown
> Lavished in plenty's lusty-handed mood
>   For this old man who goes
> Reckoning ripeness, shoring the lolling sprays,
> And fruits which early gusts made castaways
> From the deep grasses thriftily rescuing those.

Yet the slightly eccentric turn of syntax in the last line alerts the reader to look more closely; it suggests a quirky carefulness, an absorption in small tasks which seems almost a kind of therapy. The veteran 'stumbles' and 'babbles' and 'steeps himself in nature's opulence'; he seems to have returned, not unscathed, to a world whose 'ripeness' and 'opulence' exist in welcome contrast to something else. He may now be able to 'rescue' the windfall apples, but the image has overtones of a time when 'early gusts' of a different kind 'made castaways' who could not be rescued. When the setting sun lights his 'oaken-raftered room' it picks out not only 'the blue delft ranged along the wall' but also his gun, however rusty and cobwebbed it now is. The ambiguous final lines of the poem are pregnant with an uneasiness they overtly deny:

> And if sleep seem unsound,
> And set old bugles pealing through the dark,
> Waked on the instant, he but wakes to hark
> His bellman cockerel crying the first round.

To read **"The Veteran"** just as a description of someone else would be to neglect the dense suggestiveness of its language; it seems rather the careful building-up of a vicarious security. The richness of the poem's imagery reinforces the desirability for Blunden of the state which it attempts to present, but the fact that, even vicariously, he was unable to make that security impregnable indicates how far he still was from attaining it for himself. The point is not so much whether Colonel Harrison's sleep is 'unsound' as that Blunden's sleep was. (pp. 224-25)

Up to about 1920 Blunden's poems are reflections of war-experience; in **"Third Ypres"** (published in 1922 in *The Shepherd*) he makes what seems to be his earliest, and longest, attempt to confront that experience by reliving it.

The so-called "Third Battle of Ypres," launched on 31 July 1917, was intended to clear Ypres by driving back the Germans from their uncomfortably-close vantage-points. . . . Blunden's poem does not deal with the whole campaign—the

attempt would have been merely tautological. Instead he presents a microcosm of it: that section lasting from the early morning of 31 July to midnight on 2 August, in which his own battalion was involved. . . . During that short time the battalion suffered about two hundred and seventy-five casualties.

The method of the poem may perhaps be loosely called cinematic. In keeping with the apparent success of the first assault, the scope of its beginning is broad, a wide-screen view of general optimism:

> Here stood we trampling down the ancient tyrant.
> So shouting dug we among the monstrous pits . . .
> The War would end, the Line was on the move,
> And at a bound the impassable was passed.
> We lay and waited with extravagant joy.

But the word 'extravagant' is shadowed with the irony of 'too good to be true'; soon waiting becomes uneasy, rain 'shuts in our world,' and the poem's focus narrows to depict only the sharp anguish of individual death and hopelessness. The breadth of heroic sentences is replaced by the staccato phrases of distracted compassion. . . . (pp. 225-26)

The poem's middle section shows the battalion 'moving to the relief' of the 14th Hampshire Regiment, at least those of them 'whom no shell / Has charred into black carcasses.' Here again the action is shown in close-up, as Blunden and three others endure shell-fire in a pillbox and one of them is killed by a direct hit through the roof. The shock of this is transmitted to the reader by a semi-lunatic incoherence of language suddenly replaced by a detailed focussing on the incongruous normality of nature—'a score of field-mice' escaped from the ruins: '(These / Calmed me, on these depended my salvation).'

The last section restores a wider perspective to the poem only by means of a far greater disaster, one which gives scale to the events experienced at first hand but also magnifies the horror they have already inspired. By field telephone comes an appeal for help from the 13th Royal Sussex battalion headquarters, pulverized by an enormous shell and now 'all splashed with arms and legs' of forty men killed. The ending of the poem expands to a vision of cosmic destruction expressed in language of almost Shakespearean intensity, and contracts to lay bare with no less intensity the inside of the poet's mind, overwhelmed by the events he has set down but not yet exorcized. . . . The largest single collection of Blunden's war poems appeared in 1928 as a supplement to *Undertones of War,* the first to be published of the three classic war autobiographies in prose [that includes Robert Graves's *Good-Bye to All That* and Siegfried Sassoon's *Memoirs of an Infantry Officer*]. The prose account itself was written in Japan, where Blunden had gone in 1924 to teach English literature at the then Tokyo Imperial University. That war experience haunted him on the other side of the world is evidence of its continued power, which is further confirmed by a poem, **"The Author's Last Words to his Students,"** written on his departure from Japan in 1927: in it he apologizes for a state of 'eyeless lethargy' and for seeing literature 'through a gloomed perspective in strange mood.' (pp. 226-27)

Like **"Third Ypres,"** which Blunden reprinted in the volume (as perhaps being their larger-scale ancestor), a number of the thirty-two poems in *Undertones* are re-creations of war experience. The impression of 'total recall' which they give, whether by density of language or vividness of detail, suggests their origin in the irresistible urgings of involuntary memory. The penultimate line of **"Recognition,"** a poem which otherwise celebrates returning daytime sanity, makes it clear that Blunden was long haunted by nightmares of war: 'Tonight I, too, must face the world's mad end—.' The sinister last stanza of **"Two Voices"** acts as prolegomenon to the poems grouped after it:

> Now far withdraws the roaring night
> Which wrecked our flower after the first
> Of those two voices; misty light
> Shrouds Thiepval Wood and all its worst;
> But still 'There's something in the air' I hear,
> And still 'We're going South, man,' deadly near.

Of these relivings of the war (which include **"Preparations for Victory," "Come on, My Lucky Lads,"** and the more wryly painful **"Pillbox"** and **"The Welcome"**) two only must serve as illustration. **"Escape"** is a fragment of Blunden's experience on the Somme, and is unusual in being presented dramatically. **"A Colonel"** reads a message telling of the death of four officers 'at the foot / Of Jacob's Ladder,' a dangerous communication trench running from Mesnil to Hamel; someone must identify the bodies. Blunden's mind hastily intervenes with a tense, almost gabbled, prayer not to be chosen: 'Now God befriend me / The next word not send me / To view those ravished trunks / And hips and blackened hunks,' The contrast between this (almost a charm against ill-luck) and the colonel's documentary brevity economically conveys the mixture of personal horror and military routine in the life of any young officer. The colonel's reply, an intuitive acknowledgement of the poet's mute appeal, brings relief to poet and reader alike, though this relief, which rushes in to fill the gap in the metrically-incomplete last line, is touched with forebodings on behalf of the unlucky officer who is yet to be informed:

> No, not you, Bunny, you've just now come down.
> I've something else for you.
>   Orderly!
>   (Sir!)
> Find Mr Wrestman.

The irony of his name is noticeable, and the whole 'simple' poem is as sharp-edged as a piece of shrapnel.

"The Zonnebeke Road" is a re-experiencing of the physical and emotional fears, exacerbated by a winter of 'scarcely tolerable cold,' of a trench-tour in the Ypres salient early in 1917. The tensions felt by the soldiers, in whom 'agony stares from each grey face,' are only mastered by a tremendous effort of will: 'men clench their chattering teeth / And freeze you back with that one hope, disdain.' The extremity of their circumstances, in frosty trenches which 'the minenwerfers have . . . to the inch,' is matched by the straining of the poem's language, which has much of the nightmarish grandeur of **"Third Ypres."** . . . (pp. 228-29)

Blunden's war memories persisted not only of themselves but also because the enormous sacrifice of life seemed to have brought no compensating improvement to the post-war world. No 'land fit for heroes' had been built, and still, in the words of Herbert Read's "To a Conscript of 1940," 'Power was retained where power had been misused.' This feeling of futility is strongly present in Blunden's poem **"II Peter, ii, 22,"** 'written in despondency in a Suffolk village,' in the New Year of 1921. Blunden echoes the Bible's use of proverbs from the farmyard ('The dog is turned to his own vomit

again; and the sow that was washed to her wallowing in the mire') in pastoral imagery sharp with disgust:

> And Quarrel with her hissing tongue
> And hen's eye gobbles gross along
>   To snap that prey
>   That marched away
> To save her carcass, better hung.

In such circumstances another view of the war reveals itself: while haunted by war's horror Blunden nostalgically calls back the human virtues which stood out against it—'the heights which crowned a deadlier year.'

Thus it is not surprising that some of the poems in *Undertones of War* exemplify another category of 'remembering,' already illustrated for Blunden's readers by **"11th R.S.R.,"** published in *The Shepherd* in 1922: his conscious and grateful celebration of a companionship shared with his fellow-officers and fellow-men. Post-war gloom is lightened by **"Their Very Memory"** (its echo of Vaughan beautifully appropriate), just as the gloom of war itself was lightened by the friendship summarized in this perfect lyric, whose inherent poignancy is only increased by the poet's fear that his tribute is inadequate. . . . (pp. 229-30)

Blunden's deep sense of comradeship informs the whole of the long ode **"On Reading that the Rebuilding of Ypres approached Completion"**; but this difficult, yet ultimately very moving poem, with its slow, complex rhythm and baroque language, requires more scrutiny than can be attempted here. It is also found, however, in shorter, simpler poems which recall brief interludes of peace in villages behind the front line. . . . (p. 230)

From Blunden's re-creations, both of war's anarchic horror and of the human comradeship and the precarious restfulness of nature that alone palliated it, the reader infers him to be a man haunted by the past. The haunting is explicitly admitted, however, when Blunden recalls the landscapes which war disrupted and when, as in **"Another Journey from Béthune to Cuinchy,"** his past and present selves engage in an intricate dialogue in which they are constantly exchanging roles. . . . In **"The Ancre at Hamel: Afterwards,"** Blunden's present is disoriented by the phantom of a river whose desecration by war had so shocked him that he had become identified with it. . . . (p. 231)

Such memories of landscapes lay on Blunden's mind well after the landscapes themselves had returned to normal . . . but the sensitive mind could less easily grow scar-tissue. Whatever secondhand facts might say, Blunden's reflex response to **"La Quinque Rue"** still sent him on a nightmare journey among 'forlorn effigies of farms,' 'trees bitterly bare,' and 'collapsed skeletons.' . . . (pp. 231-32)

In the summer of 1929, two years after his return from Japan, Blunden revisited Ypres, and recorded what he found there in **"Return of the Native,"** a poem whose near-tranquillity suggests the laying at last of war's ghosts. Though the red puffing of a steam-train, in the restored cutting below the once-infamous Hill Sixty, is confused for a moment with remembered shell-fire, Blunden cannot fail to recognize the oblivious peacefulness of the landscape. . . . Soothed by the 'consonance / Of boughs and airs and earthy purities,' Blunden is thankful, yet a trace of bewilderment shadows him. The absence of any visible evidence of war makes it seem impossible, now, that the 'ordinance of eternity' could have been 'reversed'; but the memory of man—'We only, watching, seemed / The relics'—outlasts the memory of nature. The war did happen. Though the poem's beautiful last lines tend toward a calm conclusiveness, they do not quite reach it. . . . Throughout Blunden's poems of the later nineteen-twenties runs a strong undercurrent of alienation caused by the war. It is obvious in a title like **"Old Pleasures Deserted"**; it darkens the tripping 'prettiness' of **"The Brook"** with 'shadowing piteous chronicles'; it brings, to the picture of an ordered and harmonious landscape, the resigned comment: 'This was my country, and it may be yet, / But something flew between me and the sun.' Though Blunden was grateful for the consolations of nature, and for the beauty of appearances, he could no longer trust them.

"The Sunlit Vale," in which the intrusion of memory is nicely translated by the breakdown of archaic rhythm and diction, sums up these effects of the war:

> Nymph of the upland song and the sparkling leaf-
>   age young,
> For your merciful desire with these charms to be-
>   guile,
> For ever be adored; muses yield you rich reward;
>   But you fail, though you smile—
>   That other does not smile.

The last page of **Undertones of War,** describing the 'innocent greenwood' of Buire-sur-Ancre when Blunden, little suspecting its destruction a few weeks later, left it in 1918, is evidence enough that he had cause for distrust. And an essay, published in 1931, which mentions an early-recognized resemblance between the River Ancre and the rivers of his childhood village of Yalding, suggests just what it was that Blunden must have feared. If one landscape (however it recovered later) could be marred, would any other remain safe? . . . (pp. 232-33)

His election, in 1931, to a Fellowship of Merton College, Oxford, did nothing to steady Blunden's feelings of disorientation. A poem written in that year reveals how far he still was, more than a decade after the war, from being planted four-square in his immediate surroundings; instead he was

> Here and elsewhere, for ever changing ground,
> Finding and straightway losing what I found,
> Baffled in time, fumbling each sequent date,
> Mistaking Magdalen for the Menin Gate.
> This much I saw, without transmortal talk,
> That war had quite changed my sublunar walk—
> Forgive me, dear, honoured and saintly friends;
> Ingratitude suspect not; this transcends.

The painfulness of this 'transcendence' is made clear in **"Fancy and Memory,"** a poem of the same period. 'Fancy' is discarded in favour of the various pleasures represented by 'Memory,' but 'memory' includes the memories of war, which spring as if from ambush (the idea is cleverly suggested by the patterning of phrases) to take the poet unawares and cause him to break off with shocked reproach. . . . (pp. 233-34)

In **"The Memorial, 1914-1918,"** however, the haunting of the past brings something more than personal pain. A new element enters Blunden's memories of the First World War—the fear that the dead are being forgotten by the world. His resistance to this springs not only from his own loyalty (though that is movingly clear in a later poem, **"In My Time"**), but also from the strong suspicion that such forget-

fulness may be dangerous to an age which has not learnt the lessons of war. In **"The Memorial,"** first published in **Halfway House** in 1932, Blunden's sorrow for the dead takes the unusually ironic form of a recommendation that they should accept, in lieu of true *pietas,* the monuments erected 'in their honour.' Though Blunden's method is far subtler, his purpose is little different from that of Siegfried Sassoon in his scathing poem "On Passing the New Menin Gate." . . . In picturing the dead, with an abrupt, piercing compassion, as forgotten and homeless, Blunden implies a harsh judgement on those whose 'tribute' is no more than a contribution to a memorial fund. . . . (p. 234)

That the past still spoke directly to Blunden is clear from sixteen poems (with titles like **"In May 1916: Near Richebourg St Vaast"** and **"Rhymes on Béthune, 1916"**) which he included at the end of **Poems 1930-1940** under the general title **"Echoes from the Great War."** These echoes were becoming, if not fainter, at least less dissonant, and their embodiment lacks the immediacy of the poems in **Undertones of War.** **"Farm behind Battle Zone"** is sad, but without the bereaved grief of **"A House in Festubert"**, and **"The Camp in the Wood (Somme Battle, 1916)"** can even be called mellow. . . . Some time in the later nineteen-thirties it would seem that Blunden again revisited the scenes of his past, and in the poem **"In West Flanders"** (first published in 1939) he recorded impressions of a lake whose peace was scarcely disturbed by the voices of contemporary visitors. His image of a 'deep flood' applies equally to the lake and to his own well of memories; but though the latter has not dried up, the poem's conclusion suggests, strongly enough, that it is no longer so dizzily fallen into. . . . (pp. 234-35)

Unfortunately, however, Blunden was a traveller on the increasingly turbid stream of history; the irony of his situation in the nineteen-thirties was that, whatever separate peace he was beginning to make with his own memories, events beyond his control were shaping up to substitute for them the realities of a new war. The 'Doomsday' of Martinsart Wood was approaching sooner than it was looked for. Two of Blunden's poems published in **Choice and Chance** in 1934 seem to mark the recognition of a turning-point: to memories of the past less gentle than those paradoxically-later ones found in **"Echoes of the Great War"** and **"In West Flanders"** are joined forebodings of the future.

"At Rugmer" shows Blunden identifying his own past self with 'kex and thorn and shifting leaf' of an English autumn landscape, prompted by them to remember

> . . . a dim time when we were kex and thorn,
> Sere leaf, ready to hear a hissing wind
> Whip down and wipe us out; our season seemed
> At any second closing.
> So, we were wrong. But we have lived this land-
>   scape,
> And have an understanding with these shades.

There is an ominous ring to this, a feeling that 'we were wrong' by only a very narrow margin, which belies the assumption that all is over. And in **"The Branch Line"** the sight of a small train somewhere in Kent calls up, with an urgency transmitted by the quickening rhythm,

> . . . another picture: of war's warped face
> Where still the sun and the leaf and the lark praised
>   Nature,
> But no little engine bustled from place to place.

The flashback to 'the terrible telegraph-posts' and 'the shattered local train' ends with a glance forward to the possible return of such scenes, a glance so sharply broken off as to convey the sense of a horror too great for the poet to contemplate. . . . (pp. 235-36)

As the menace of war grew steadily greater, so did Blunden's denials of its possibility. It could not, it must not, return. But the certainties of **"War Cemetery"** seem over-strenuously maintained, and the comradely hopefulness of **"To the Southdowns,"** written for the annual reunion of Blunden's battalion in 1939, gibes oddly with the mass-oblivion of the First World War postulated by **"The Memorial"** in 1932. . . . Blunden's response to the results of the 'settlement of Munich' in September 1938, expressed in his poem **"Exorcised,"** reveals the strength of the 'stubborn and total fear' which, along with his memories, had haunted his mind for twenty years: the fear of a second war. The laureate-like promptitude and rhetorical loudness of the poem, with its pathetic trust in appeasement and its tragically inaccurate inclusion of Hitler and Mussolini among 'the generous, selfless, wise,' only emphasize the desperate desire to avoid a second war of one who had so long and so deeply remembered the first. . . . (p. 236)

The irony of entitling the poem **"Exorcised"** was only too quickly revealed. Within a year, Blunden's poem **"By the Belgian Frontier"** had to retract all that he had hoped for, and thought he had seen, in the spring of 1939. . . . The few volumes which Blunden has published since the Second World War are gentle, ruminative, and accomplished. War, by implication or direct reference, enters such poems of **Shells by a Stream** (1944) as **"October Comes," "The Ornamental Water,"** and **"A Prospect of Swans,"** but not in the form of Blunden's memories of first-hand experience, rather as a contemporary, shared, awareness. In **"The Halted Battalion,"** however, a poem published in **After the Bombing** (1949), he was again able to report that 'one hour from far returns,' and his comment on this memory of a peaceful moment snatched from an earlier war indicates that the link with the past still held. . . . The poems mentioned at the beginning of this essay are further evidence of the link, as are the recollections, muted by distance, of **"Over the Valley"** [published in 1962 in **A Hong Kong House**]. . . . (pp. 236-37)

It is thus very surprising that J. H. Johnston, in his book *English Poetry of the First World War* (1964), should say that 'Among the soldier poets who survived the war—Nichols, Graves, Sassoon, and Blunden—not one returned to his battle experiences as the source of further poetic inspiration.' Certainly this is not true of Blunden: as I hope has been shown, not only has he returned himself but the war has frequently returned to him, an intruder—sometimes an old friend—demanding accommodation. (p. 237)

Though he has been other kinds of poet as well, Blunden has, in fact, never ceased to be a war poet, and this 'war element' in his poetry is all-important. This is not simply because his direct experience of war is expressed with a moving eloquence and immediacy for which he has received little critical credit. These harsh realities also deepened and enlarged his compassion and his awareness of the human virtues of kindness, friendship, loyalty, and sacrifice. War sharpened his entire perception in such a way that he once wondered 'whether ordinary life without the fierce electricity of an overwhelming tempest of forces and emotions could project such deeplighted detail.' The very precariousness of nature and human

life, which war taught him, only increased his appreciation of their beauty and value; and as they helped to maintain a sense of perspective in wartime, so wartime itself, recalled in peace, prevented complacency, and brought to Blunden's poetry a bracing tension. It is a warlike 'fury' which 'lances' the pastoral calm of **"The Pike,"** and the memory of war which lurks under the thin ice of **"The Midnight Skaters."**

Finally, even when Blunden's poetry bears no marks whatever of war, when it is gentle, ruminative, 'literary' in subject, working at low pressure in an old-fashioned idiom—when it is, in short, 'verse'—it is made acceptable not just by its well-turned accomplishment but by the reader's knowledge that it proceeds from a mind which contains, and has expressed, far more unpleasant themes. The 'ease' of such verse has not been easily won, and its place in Blunden's poetry as a whole may aptly be suggested in the words of E. M. Forster, as he concludes his description, in *Howards End,* of the diversity of Beethoven's Fifth Symphony: 'But the goblins were there. They could return. He had said so bravely, and that is why one can trust Beethoven when he says other things.' (p. 238)

Philip Gardner, "Edmund Blunden: War Poet," in University of Toronto Quarterly, *Vol. XLII, No. 3, Spring, 1973, pp. 218-40.*

THOMAS MALLON

Critical categorization of Blunden's poetry has been restricted largely to the terms "pastoralism" and "war poetry." His name is not usually associated with what might be called the poetry of ideas, even though his large body of work contains as many essentially "philosophic" poems as nature or war pieces, indeed probably more. But he was singled out for his talents in describing nature and war early in his career, accumulating much praise before he was thirty, and the labels stuck. . . . It was above all the precision of Blunden's portraiture that was noticed, almost wholly to the neglect of his more abstract work. When he collected his poems in 1930 he expressed pride that he had been recognized as part of the pastoral tradition, but also "the desire that those who take up this book will not altogether skip those pages which are non-rural. They were derived from unstrained, general feelings."

The few times he essayed definitions of poetry itself produced results which probably, by their breadth, surprised many of his readers: "Poetry in general is an attempt to pass beyond or else to peep beyond the outward and seemingly solid structure of our physical being, and therefore some of its exponents have thought that it might replace religion and philosophy." The verb "to peep" is the most important one here. He was always dubious about the possibility of achieving orderly philosophical systems and realized that it was the province of "[c]ountless English poets, not of the order of Dante or Milton, [to] have told of some flash of that beauty beyond all beauty, wisdom beyond all wisdom, which Dante 'stedfastly pored upon.' " "Flashes," moments better given expression in the lyric than in the longer poem, is a good word to use in characterizing his philosophical insights and poems.

He was a poet of plain things, but many critics have failed to notice that these plain things were often springboards toward more complex reflections. He should in fact be seen as an example of those imaginative people who, he said, "first discern their large world in and through something very simple." He could look deeply into his rural world, and had a right to resent such remarks as T. Earle Welby's that his poetry usually consisted of "loving or surprised inventory" of nature's gifts without reflection upon their relation to each other or to man. Kenneth Allott was much closer to the mark when he noted that " 'human unease is hinted at in much [of Blunden's] verse which at first would appear to be purely descriptive.' "

It is the apparent tranquillity of the subject matter which provoked Blunden's larger reflections that sometimes deceives a reader into looking at no more than the skillful portraiture mentioned earlier. Blunden never deprecated a poet's attempts to probe the secrets of the universe. . . . (pp. 71-2)

Blunden devoted large parts of his poetry to expressions of his ideas about death, time, love, religion, and what might be called life itself. These poems are almost invariably lyric expressions, flashes of thought conveyed in an orderly style. Basic "positions" emerge from a survey of fifty years of his writing on each of these questions, but there are shifts of mood and feeling. What might be called not too neatly a "consistent inconsistency" is the pattern of his lyrics in each of these areas. His intellectual poetry is marked by the often searched for and debated quality of poetic sincerity; a personal voice and tone, rarely transferred to any persona, are almost always detectable. The earnest, sometimes desperate, quality of his search for firm answers and values may come as a surprise to those who have viewed him as a pastoralist, but it should not be surprising to those who remember the persistence of his attempts to make sense of the war which opened a nearly unbridgeable fault between his adolescence and manhood.

The war forced Blunden to look at death repeatedly and in its most brutal and sudden forms, but even before he went into battle he had sensed death's part in the particular rhythm of village life. In many of his poems death is viewed as a presence lurking, perpetually, undramatically, in nature or the hamlet. Margaret Willy has remarked on Blunden's frequent use of war imagery in poems not specifically about the war, something Blunden himself noted in the preface to his collection of 1930, but he rarely gives death a martial, screaming air. More often it is simply an ominous, brooding thing, frequently resting in the water. In **"The Midnight Skaters"** it lies beneath the surface of the pond; in **"The Subtle Calm"** it is below the deceptively calm surface of the sea. In **"What Is Winter?"** the poet tries to convince himself that winter is merely a word, that the spirit continues to live; but even so, death "is no more dead than this / Flower-haunted haze." It is an evergreen part of the landscape. (pp. 72-3)

Blunden noted in *Votive Tablets* that as early as the writing of Gray's "Elegy" the old ballad-maker's terrible images of death were being replaced by more misty and romantic ones; and the twentieth century had turned to the scientific and rational view: "The grinning Monster with his arresting finger-bones is gone, and a chemical law or evolutionary confidence is our usual substitute." But Blunden himself could still find an arresting recognition of death's presence, often and forcefully, in stark country circumstance.

After leaving the battlefields of the Great War, Blunden married Mary Daines and began to raise a family. But death suddenly entered his life once more: his baby daughter Joy died in the summer of 1919 when she was little more than a month old. . . . Joy's father was not yet twenty-three. For forty years Blunden tried in his poetry to understand and reconcile

himself to this death, just as he continued to speak of and to the ghosts of his fellow soldiers. The peace he made with her passing was every bit as uneasy as his tenuous reconciliation to the losses of war.

In an early one of these poems, which are too nearly completely concerned with the survivor's state of mind to be called conventional elegies, the poet refuses to be weighted with sorrow as he makes his way to his daughter's grave on a beautiful April day. . . . But he cannot, particularly in this Easter season, refrain from wanting to hear from her spirit: "But the grave held no answer, though long I should stay; / How strange that this clay should mingle with hers!" A few years later, alone in Japan, he took **"A 'First Impression' (Tokyo)"** and delighted in the sounds of the playing children, realizing there were millions of them in the world, "so kind in this / Is nature. . . ." But at last he still "saw a ghost, and lacked one child."

Michael Thorpe is correct when he remarks that **"For There Is No Help In Them,"** in *Retreat,* is "emotionally satisfying . . . finely balanced between feelings of loss and acceptance." "Finely" in the sense of tentatively, precariously. This is the mood of most of these poems. The balance is indeed so "fine" that Blunden must write the same poem again and again, as he must write his war verses over and over, to be sure that he can cope with changes in mood, be honest about them, resist the temptations toward easy solution, mere palinode. During the Second World War, he takes a **"Winter Walk"** and thinks of someone else who died too soon. Love and nature console him, but this peace cannot remain whole. (pp. 73-4)

It was Blunden's great fortune to raise a new family when he was well into middle age. A new daughter, Margaret, is introduced to his memory of Joy in a poem written a quarter-century after the latter's death:

> we bring
> A second self with whom your span
> May round, with Margaret now you can
> Make fun of things, feed, call and sing,
> Tease, tantalize, adore, bewitch.

Heartfelt as these final lines of the poem may be, their nature, one realizes, is tentative, nearly desperate. The opening lines of the poem have a force the final ones lack:

> My darling, what power is yours
> To make me weep, after such years;
> For twenty-seven years at least
> Are gone since your brief coming ceased,—
> And still you force my hopeless tears
> And still your fate dwarfs all my wars.

The reference to "all my wars" makes the reader familiar with Blunden's other verse conclude that this is the essential feeling, the one that has endured and will continue to do so, and to be skeptical of the final lines, whose catalog of verbs is weak, an attempt by the poet to impose his will on a situation that he cannot control for long. Any one of the Joy poems, or, indeed, almost any of Blunden's poems on death, time, love, or religion, will evoke substantially different feelings from a reader if it is read in the context of Blunden's other work rather than as a single lyric. The individual poems frequently end with a kind of resolution; the corpus presents a tentativeness that more accurately represents the poet's vision. Thorpe, in discussing **"Joy and Margaret,"** says that "poetry often obeys mood and the mood [here] is true enough." But a reading of **"Children Passing,"** which follows **"Joy and Margaret"** in *After the Bombing,* sheds light on Blunden's awareness of the need to *manipulate* his moods in order to keep distress from becoming too great. Its light verse rhythm and diction almost belie the central idea that the growth of children makes for an infinite series of deaths. (pp. 75-6)

Blunden's most constant attitude toward death was a kind of quiet defiance—the sort he learned in the war. In his most famous poem of all, **"The Midnight Skaters,"** he urges "Earth's heedless sons and daughters" to defy the death that lies beneath the ice." . . . The kind of self-imposed illusion described in **"Children Passing,"** realized for what it is, must sometimes be employed as a survival tactic, much as the "respite" of nature in the war had to be imposed even when its falseness seemed all too demonstrable. **"Winter Stars"** is almost a cosmographical inversion of **"The Midnight Skaters"**: death comes at man not from below, but from the stars "ready to roar / Their sparkling death-way down. . . ." Men must fight the universe, and they sometimes, but only briefly, do well. . . . (p. 76)

Death was indeed a constant part of Blunden's vision, a grim presence in his poems on the progress and origin of life itself. But he was able to see beyond it; he supported what he understood to be Coleridge's feeling that "if the human being simply stops at death, then we are just nonsense and the universe is meaningless." Death itself does not provide the master key to this universe—or to a better one. (pp. 76-7)

[Few critics have noted] the importance of time in Blunden's poetry. . . . What Chloe asks herself about Duncan in *We'll Shift Our Ground* is a question Blunden had to ask himself: "What was this Time, that had crowded an inexhaustibly terrible drama into the brief dates of such as this enthusiast?" In that same novel Blunden and Miss Norman put the serious issue of much of Blunden's philosophical verse in whimsical terms: "Those who have seen the recluse-like figure of Professor Einstein passing with the grace of the Romantic Movement over the speed-maddened street of a modern town will have felt, as from an object lesson, the fact that periods coexist, that you cannot cut off time in blocks, that the expression 'one damn thing after another' is unscientific."

Blunden's initial awareness of time was benign; it came through his youthful observance of the seasons. An understanding of time as a series of renewals was inculcated early and remained with him as a hedge against the darker view to which he later fell prey. Continuing harvests, he saw, give labor meaning and reward. . . . Time, in the field, reveals nature's inexhaustibility. The innocent love and festivity celebrated in **"The May Day Garland"** make the wish to rein time seem almost possible of fulfillment. . . . (p. 77)

But far more often it is the savage effects of time that Blunden notes; the cyclical aspect of nature is time's sop, cruel and tantalizing. Time usually checks rather than enhances man's joy of nature: this is the theme of a number of poems in what is perhaps Blunden's darkest volume, *English Poems,* published in 1925, while he still mourned the death of Joy, was lonely in Japan, and was particularly troubled by war memories. . . . In **"A Fading Phantom,"** "chilly [runs his] summer blood / To know Time's fluttering sign." The poet wishes to be "untimed by the stern sun," but knows that his chief solace must be the realization of the even distribution of time's doom. One can attempt aphoristic comfort, answer

rhetorical questions by conventional wisdom, but time will have its will; comfort must be sought in the knowledge that however horrible Joy's fate was, it is the universal one. . . . (p. 78)

Blunden's pleas for preservation of the countryside were excited by impulses as much metaphysical as environmental. Time was an idea he apprehended not just as feeling, but as a living presence. The poem **"A Connoisseur"** is a remarkable exercise in extended personification: Time is seen as a magpie and a miser, not "a mere insensate mill of hours." He is a crazy acquisitor who never ceases to "swell the mad collection of his loves."

Time's rapacity can be so subtle, however, that many of its effects go almost unnoticed; they are recognized after the fact. Time kills the "lyrical impulse" in such youths as **"The Lost Leader"**—a kind of working-class Chatterton of the army kitchen memorialized by Blunden in prose shortly after the war. Age, experience, and practical affairs do their coarsening. So certain is time's victory that Blunden, a skillful practitioner of the sonnet and longer lyric in octosyllabic couplets, can rarely summon enough confidence to deliver even the *carpe diem* theme often expressed in those Renaissance forms. (p. 79)

[Blunden's] concern with time became, in his later years, more specifically a concern with his own aging. In *A Hong Kong House,* which shows the greatest Japanese influence in style of all Blunden's books, although still not as profound a one as one might expect, he tries to be optimistic in the face of decline, but is often forced to retreat into happy childhood memories in a new strategic movement against time. The poem **"Once on a Hill"** faces the fact that "nothing shall placate the will of time," but realizes nevertheless the simple mitigating wonder of recollection: "But a hill there was, and on that hill was I." Even so, time reigns with little challenge; age and death cannot be dismissed. . . . (p. 80)

When Blunden was in mid-career, Richard Church sent him a letter praising *An Elegy* and declaring that he heard in that collection "an increasing terseness, a 'dryness,' and soon, when you are even more venerable, we shall have to christen you Old Ironic. For that will be your general tone in the years to come." There is only a small element of truth in this comment. One might regard some of the collections of the 1930s as more self-assured than the particularly dark work of *English Poems* from a decade before, and one might see a more quiet resignation still in *A Hong Kong House* in spots, but the constant shiftings of mood in the face of such forces as time, the inability to reach any final assurance, stand out more than any steady development of attitude or style. Blunden surely did not end his days as an ironist—particularly when it came to time. He strove, as he believed Shelley had, for an appreciation of its grandeur. . . . His own poems tried to search out some pleasure in a terrible truth. **"An Ancient Goddess: Two Pictures"** attempts an even-handed dealing with Time, first pessimistically, then otherwise. There was **"The Excellent Irony"** to note that it was after all Time who sent him love. . . . (pp. 80-1)

Time, personified more than any other idea in Blunden's verse, remains defiant and alive. . . . Like any enemy of some duration, it becomes something of a friend. All of Blunden's darker preoccupations call on him casually, constantly, and the results are poems that show an odd familiarity between the poet and his grave themes. . . . (p. 81)

In the light love poem **"An Aside,"** in *Halfway House* (1932), Blunden, attempting to show how aesthetic theorizing in the face of love is folly, minted an octosyllabic couplet worthy of the best of Herrick and Marvell: "About the stern defining phrase / A gay indefinition plays. . . ." Love in his poetry is a powerful transformer of experience, a joy, a solace, and something whose gifts may be mangled by his own dark moods; it is, in short, more like nature for him than anything else. His ideas of it were shaped in much the same way as his other important feelings and beliefs: by having his early country experience disastrously modified by the Great War.

His youthful reading and acquaintance with natural surroundings prepared him to compose such early love monologes as **"The Covert,"** spoken by a boy and filled with archaic diction and mythological reference. But Blunden's intelligence was always as critical as lyrical, and he could never long avoid the questioning personal voice. Even in **"The Covert"** the speaker shifts in the last stanza from being the boy to the poet himself, in a dying fall that attempts to put distance between the poet and the attitudes expressed just before with such lyric confidence:

> —Thus murmured to himself the boy
>   Where all the spinneys ring
> With as rich syllables of joy
>   As ever hailed the spring.

This is an ominous distancing; the boy is made vulnerable by the dash which separates him from the wiser poet—a poet made mature in love, as in all else, by war wisdom; one who had to hold love in his heart when "lost in tortured days of France!"

Just as the war made nature more desperately beautiful, and time more powerful in its swellings and shrinkings, it intensified Blunden's perceptions of love and friendship: "on shipboard, they say, people soon fall in love; in war, you fall in friendship, and know your neighbour as you probably will never do otherwise." (p. 82)

Blunden's celebrations of love are stylistically varied, showing the influence of his enthusiasm for different poets and literary periods. There are the longer narrative poems such as **"The Nun at Court"** and **"Thomasine"**: the first is in the sturdy manner of Browning, and the latter, from the Second World War, plants an expression of faith in love's ability to overcome the ugliness of the world and "the tangles of chance and time" in a story that has the exciting power of anticipation one finds in Keats's "Eve" poems. (pp. 82-3)

Most satisfying of all, and the best showcases for Blunden's talents, are his celebrations of homely, enduring country love, such as **"Village Song"** and **"Lonely Love."** The latter is an exquisite lyric which honors love among the plain and no longer young, and manages to remain unsentimental: this humble love sustains the poet as well as the lovers; they share with him "the strangest happiness." The poem is a worthy companion piece to the earlier **"Almswomen."** (p. 83)

[Blunden] is predictably concerned with expressing the ties that bind love and the land. The poet in love will have a heightened sense of nature's beauty and power. This relationship is expressed in a number of poems, among them **"Lovelight," "Fulfilment,"** and **"Among All These,"** in *Shells by a Stream,* composed in the early 1940s when Blunden despite and in defiance of the war, was in love with Claire Poynting, whom he married in 1945. Love brings unity to the landscape riven by the war: "her young face / Charmed into one all else he knew. . . ." In the same period, in *Cricket Country,* Blunden confessed: "Never was there a poorer naturalist than I, but I have loved nature and am able to be as pleased with her characteristic looks and preoccupations and voices as with those (almost) of my true love." He frequently addresses nature in his poetry as a lover might; here was an emotional phenomenon and technique he saw carried to extremes in the poetry of John Clare, whose thwarted love made "a great part of his verse . . . a history of the transference of love in him from woman to Nature."

Love's pleasures are also much like the land's in their vulnerability. They can be given and taken away capriciously by the "south-west wind of the soul," and are dependent on one's relative freedom from the war and war memories. (pp. 83-4)

But if love's solace is imperfect, and if, like nature, it is a sometimes illusory respite from horror, it must be sought and reverenced: one must impose upon oneself a belief in its healing power. It is most often this quality in his beloved which Blunden selects to hymn. . . . After love's early ardor dims, a "daily sustenance" remains; Blunden returns often to this quality usually neglected or sentimentalized in lyric poetry. (p. 84)

When love is finest, it makes the former soldier's having "[d]odged many deaths" worthwhile; in the Second World War it is able, sometimes, to make death count "for nothing, proved a lie," and give a poet a "sense of wide free ways, so free / And wide that I count nothing of time and space, / But think these present gifts will ever be. . . ." On 20 February 1940, Blunden rejoiced in the love of the young woman who was later to become his wife; it is again the healing power of love, love as a hedge against destruction and time, that is singled out for commemoration in his diary, as it is in his most successful love poems. . . .

He had to remain open to love's power, which was sometimes strong enough to let him defy time and darkness openly: "shatter me quite," he exclaims to them at the end of the sonnet **"Millstream Memories."** His gratitude for such moments was such that he could often, in return, restrain himself from darkening those he loved any further with his own woes. Or even from imposing on them his particular joys. . . . (p. 85)

One must sometimes, in order to survive, force belief further than it can naturally go—this is the basis of many of Blunden's love poems. It is also the unifying idea among his many religious verses. In them most explicitly emerges the intellectual and emotional virtue he prizes above others—aspiration.

Blunden's religious poems can best be explored by beginning with the relationship he sees between God and nature: a relationship so close as to be a source of both happiness and jealousy for man. . . . It is to nature that Blunden goes to find evidence of God and to experience His power. (pp. 85-6)

[In] ecstatic moments the poet mingles with "shades that lived before Stonehenge stood." There is in Blunden's moods of wildest nature appreciation a pantheistic element, a worship of **"The Gods of the Earth Beneath."** In that early poem from *The Waggoner,* the Traveller hears "the god of things that burrow and creep" tell of six gods of the earth who sense "one greater" God. This sense of the presence of many gods is stronger in the most rustic poems of that first major collection of Blunden's verse than in later volumes, but it remained part of his theological and poetic makeup. (p. 86)

Once taken into account, however, it would be unwise to exaggerate this element in Blunden's religious thought and work, for he remained primarily interested in the "greater" God, the "Sun of Suns." Nature was first and foremost good *evidence* of a supreme existence. . . . God does not really emanate from nature so much as shine downward on it, animating its individual elements. But the location of God's presence shifted in Blunden's perception according to mood and purpose, and he would have regarded doctrinal neatness in this to be an expensive waste of his particular emotions and intellect. An emotional perception of God, in or above nature, was the highest goal of his religious experience.

The local tradition of religious observance he grew up in was simple and firm. . . . As a child he experienced easy familiarity with God: in the sketch **"Bells on the Breeze,"** he tells how he and his young friends bargained with the Deity for some runs at cricket, or a roach or a chub on the ends of their fishing lines: "If Heaven granted the boon, we undertook not to break into the plantation on the way home; if not, we were free, and willing, to take our cherries or apples. I am not sure whether even this was the final state of that theory of prayer." If not quite noble, here surely was a simple and direct relationship with God! And that is the kind of arrangement Blunden most admired. In **"Hardham,"** in the early *Pastorals,* he shows his preference for rustic low-church ritual as a more direct link with God than any more elaborate worship would be. . . . (p. 87)

Many of these poems of simple faith are monologues delivered by characters possessed of country diction and rhythm. Blunden does not sentimentalize or satirize these figures; he envies them their direct expressions of faith in the face of the twentieth century. They say what the poet sometimes cannot bring himself to say in his own voice. God Himself is sometimes imagined as a man of the country. . . . The English church meant community to Blunden, and the common aspiration of a congregation was often, in his poetry, taken as being itself evidence of the existence of a God and a heaven. (p. 88)

Blunden's beliefs and doubts are emotional and often not particularly modern ones. His common sense tells him there is a heaven; it also tells him that this knowledge is sometimes precious little comfort to the men below it. . . . The nature of God forces one to reconcile His good and evil; this is the central issue of several poems. . . . The natural world offers abundant examples of the troubling coexistence of Blake's tiger and lamb. It is easy to know that the "young moon" comes "from some calm triunion's brow," but what of the storms that follow?

More often than not the opposing elements resolve themselves into an endurable whole. In *Near and Far* (1929) the poet gives his **"Report on Experience,"** acknowledging that it was "peculiar grace" to live to see the war's devastation and then the destruction of what he thought had been a perfect love. But:

> Say what you will, our God sees how they run.
> These disillusions are His curious proving
> That He loves humanity and will go on loving;
> Over there are faith, life, virtue in the sun.

God remains, like love and nature, another source of solace. The poet's direct, Donne-like addresses to Him in verse are rare, but he sometimes calls on Him, "[u]nasking what Thy form or mind may be," to sustain his faith in the face of sorrow.

Blunden's poetry does not inquire deeply into the exact form of God or the origins of the universe. Like old Japhet he is largely untroubled by such questions. He can leave the debate over the godly or accidental origins of a **"Running Stream"** to "sage, saint, seer. . . ." The streams have never "revealed if a spirit indwelt their bubbling adown." He enjoys these questions of origin; they do not bedevil him. They provide him with musings, and, in this case, merely add to the pleasure he takes in the stream. (pp. 88-9)

Commentators have wondered whether Blunden's religious poetry is insufficiently rigorous in a post-Darwinian world. (p. 90)

[Blunden] was not unaware of the scientific revelations of his own century and the one before, but he chose optimism and aspiration, reminding us that Darwin himself felt his science would "open new and unsuspected regions of truth for man's discovery and thus, in the end, . . . make man's consciousness and sense of the rights of nature more distinct, more alert." Having experienced the **"Death of Childhood Beliefs"** with the arrival of the Great War, Blunden nevertheless came home from the front to deplore the modern soul's insistence that it is "[e]nough for us to lantern our own night." On a **"Stormy Night"** he wishes to hear the bells of the faithful ring; the particular discoveries and horrors of the twentieth century are no excuse for a silence into which earlier troubled centuries did not retreat. . . . (p. 91)

There was in this man of what so often appears a calm devotion a mystical streak as well—one he appreciated in his literary subjects. He preferred Vaughan's spiritual leaps to Herbert's methodical journey; he would rather wait for sudden religious experience in an attitude of receptivity than seek it through structured meditational exercise. (p. 92)

At the end of his address on **"Religion and the Romantics,"** Blunden appended representative textual selections for a Japanese audience. One was "A Defence of Elia Against the Charge of Want of Religious Feeling," in which Lamb wrote: "The shapings of our heavens are the modifications of our constitution; and Mr. Feeble Mind, or Mr. Great Heart, is born in every one of us." Blunden's religious poetry springs from the temporary dominance of any one of these temperamental qualities inside himself; in that poetry he shows the same persistent shiftings that mark his poems on other ideas. In **"From the Flying-Boat"** he may wonder of God: "Why hides He His face?" But at other times his heart will be greater; **"Cathedrals"** are the real "starships," and man has only to allow his spirit to be moved by forces not from within. . . . (pp. 92-3)

He was a man at peace with both his born institutional affiliation and new religious influences. He playfully wrote Edward Marsh from Japan in 1925: "In spite of the lotus I remain C. of E., and don't go to church." He was a doctrinally casual poet, and this has proved infuriating enough to men like Eliot and Fairchild. But the simplicity of his poems of aspiration, in the face of his century and his own grim experience, gives him, in the eyes of others, an assured place in the modern writing of religious poetry.

Blunden always held the Arnoldian view that poetry should be a "criticism of life" in the largest sense, and he was troubled more by the increasingly political nature of the poetry

of the mid-twentieth century than by any formal innovations. . . . Life itself, he felt, should be poetry's province;
guesses, unsystematic ones, should be made at its meaning.

For that meaning he went first to the land, for its appearance,
with all its changes and constancies, could be equated with
the movement of a human life. . . . The natural world, he
felt, was the best-equipped philosophical laboratory; those
poets who knew it well had the most to tell us of life. . . .
The English countryside, with all its variation, was for Blunden the richest in meaning of all. Scholars like John P. Mills
are correct to note that Japan had less of an impact on Blunden's view of life than one might expect, and the reason for
this lies probably in the way the Japanese landscape struck
him. In *A Wanderer in Japan* (1950) he conjectured

> that the enchantment of Japanese scenery had been
> a reason for the comparative dearth of a clear phi-
> losophy and natural history in the annals of the
> country, at least until the modernisation and the
> excitation of untried abilities. The charm was too
> great. Why should men pursue something which
> would never be so beautiful and complete as the
> picture?

Despite his attraction to philosophical verse, Blunden was
uncomfortable about placing a final interpretive stamp upon
any phenomenon, and he was reluctant to have any experience overwhelmed by analysis. (pp. 93-4)

In the poems of *A Hong Kong House,* his last major collection, he continued to search for **"A Life's Unity,"** indirectly
expressing the wish that his own final utterances would be full
of the "Mercy and peace met together" that he found in
Shakespeare's last plays. But in **"Summer Storm in Japanese
Hills"** he recognized the insoluble difficulty of knowing anything for certain in "the wan-hued tempest world / Where
rock and tree like spindrift hurled / Will know as much as
we at last." And yet it was still the function of poetry to try
to "peep" beyond. (pp. 94-5)

The poet should be a thinker and a dreamer, but he must not
force his instants of revelation into ordered philosophy:
"Mastery in poetry consists largely in the instinct for not ruining or smothering or tinkering with moments of vision."
The immediacy of the idea should be preserved even as the
poem is, as it must be, shaped.

In his address "Experience and Record," Blunden said: "We
cannot hope to bring all experience into the same diagram.
This ocean of life is too vast to be represented in one kind of
blue, grey, green or golden." Blunden's poetic corpus is appropriately multi-colored, but it does not constitute a case of
trying to "have" things both or many ways. What a
critic . . . perceives as a lack of rigor might more properly
be called, in Blunden, lyric sincerity. This brings one back to
the nature of his war writings: there too he was unable and
unwilling to erect the coherent intellectual scaffolding that
might support epic treatment of that experience at the expense of accuracy in portraying the vagaries of a half-century
of feelings. Nearing his seventieth year, Blunden was lucid in
his refusal to express more than guarded optimism—but un-
afraid to express that much: "The world seems, on the face
of it, so darkened with crime and idiocy at the moment that
the other faction, the angels, are working hard too, and I
think in the end they will probably get ahead." (p. 95)

Thomas Mallon, in his Edmund Blunden, *Twayne
Publishers, 1983, 139 p.*

PAUL FUSSELL

"There are few mental exertions more instructive," says
Coleridge, "than the attempt to establish and exemplify the
distinct meaning of terms often confounded in common use
and considered as mere synonyms." He proceeds to instance
words like *Agreeable, Beautiful, Picturesque, Grand,* and
Sublime. If he were here now, I think he might enjoy de-
synonymizing a couple of latter-day critical terms. I am
thinking of the word *Modernist* as distinguished from the
word *Modern.* If Coleridge could be present and rapidly
brought up to date, he might approve a distinction between
those two terms that would go like this. A *Modernist* is a late-
nineteenth- or twentieth-century artist or artistic theorist
who has decided to declare war on the received, the philistine,
the bourgeois, the sentimental, and the democratic. (p. 583)

Having exemplified one meaning of the term *Modernist,* our
up-to-date Coleridge would proceed to suggest the way an
artist or critic fit to be called a *Modern* differs. A Modern, he
might conclude, is capable of incorporating into his work
contemporary currents of thought and emotion without any
irritable need to quarrel with the past—intellectually, psychologically, or technically. A Modern can embrace the past
and not just feel but enjoy its continuity with the present. (p.
584)

[Following World War I], a twenty-nine-year old British
poet, gentle, shy, generous, enthusiastic, was living in Tokyo
and trying to use art, and thought as well, as therapeutic procedures for regaining his humanity. He had been badly battered by the Great War—gassed, traumatized, brought near
to total disillusion and despair. He confessed some difficulty
understanding the apparent cosmic pessimism of both Eliot
and Joyce since neither had experienced the trenches at first
hand. He had, and much of his later life he spent trying to
make some sense of that appalling business. Indeed from
1918 to the end of his life he preserved a view of actuality that
can be called the gentle infantryman's (*gentle* to distinguish
it from Robert Graves's very different, angrily adversary
view). After his experience of the war Blunden knew that
being scared to death most of the time is undignified and ultimately unmanning, that bullets and shell fragments hurt, that
absurdity and unreason—in literary criticism and artistic rationalization as well as in life—will get you if you don't watch
out, and that living in an adversary environment was something he'd had quite enough of.

Edmund Blunden was born in London in 1896. His parents
were schoolteachers. They soon moved to a school in Yalding, Kent, where Edmund grew up in an atmosphere of literary high-mindedness and laid in a lifetime's images of hop-
gardens, oasthouses, and benign brooks and streams. There
would ultimately be nine children in the family and little
money, but being from boyhood a most assiduous reader and
writer, Edmund won a scholarship to Christ's Hospital. . . .
His Greek and Latin grew impressive enough to secure him
a scholarship at Queen's College, Oxford, and at this point
he could look forward to a lovely life of lettered repose.

But before he could install himself in his Oxford college, Britain declared war on the Central Powers, and soon this quiet
young poet and literary scholar found himself commissioned
in the Royal Sussex Regiment, where his shyness won him
the nickname Bunny but his bravery won him the Military
Cross. Miraculously he survived two years at the front, perhaps because he was sent home a gas casualty before he could

be killed. After the war he joined the writers living at Boar's Hill, Oxford, where in proximity to Robert Bridges, such young poet-veterans assembled as Graves, Edgell Rickword, and Robert Nichols. By 1920 Blunden had abandoned Oxford for London and a life of high journalism, assisting J. Middleton Murry on the *Athenaeum* and producing countless literary essays and reviews. In 1922, that Modernist *annus mirabilis,* Blunden made his own gentle bid for fame, a volume of poems entitled **The Shepherd,** which won the Hawthornden prize and brought its author a good deal of notice. In a poem like **"The Pasture Pond"** the careful reader could detect a sophisticated pastoralism comparable to Andrew Marvell's lurking behind a mock-simple surface comparable to Robert Frost's. The scene of Blunden's pasture pond differs markedly from the world of literary dispute, for

> Here's no malice that could wither
> Joy's blown flower, nor dare come hither;
> No hot hurry such as drives
> Men through their unsolaced lives;
> Here like bees I cannot fare
> A span but find some honey there.

And birds of different species and sizes find

> No cause . . . to grudge or brawl,
> For nature gives enough for all.

But as Blunden indicates in a poem like **"1916 Seen from 1921,"** his pastoralism is war-haunted, stained by remembered horror, and that is why it is complicated and unpatronizable, even, as we might say, *Modern.* In the midst of the Forest of Arden it is impossible to forget Mametz Wood, or as Blunden puts it, "The charred stub outspeaks the living tree." And in another poem (**"Third Ypres"**), which seems only ironically present in a volume called **The Shepherd,** Blunden revisits the worst experience of his life—the hours during the Battle of Passchendaele when the pillboxes sheltering his battalion were pierced by German shells and very many men were wounded or killed, their bloody parts strewn about inside the concrete rooms. His desire to get away from that terrible scene made the word *relief* an obsession then, but now, as he says, "who with what command can now relieve / The dead men from that chaos, or my soul?" Blunden proved so unable to put the war decently behind him that his colleagues on the *Athenaeum* feared for his sanity, and they encouraged him to take a restful voyage to South America, which he wrote up charmingly in **The Bonadventure: A Random Journal of an Atlantic Holiday**. . . . He took off for Japan and spent the years from 1924 to 1927 teaching English at the Imperial University of Tokyo. It was there, in a setting of modest beauty and order, ceremony and delicacy, that he recalled his wartime experiences for **Undertones of War,** his classic memoir published in 1928.

Back in England he wrote for the *Nation* for a time, but finding he needed a more stable profession than literary journalism, he became a fellow and tutor of Merton College, Oxford. . . . After the second world war he quit England again for Japan, this time as cultural liaison officer with the British Mission. In two years he traveled all over the country and gave some 600 lectures on English literature. And for eleven years, from 1953 to 1964, he served as professor of English at the University of Hong Kong, retiring finally to Suffolk to a well-earned rest disturbed only in 1966 by the small, uninvited controversy between Ancients and Moderns culminating in his defeat of Robert Lowell for the position of professor of poetry at Oxford. He died in 1974 in the quiet En-

glish countryside he loved, but the flowers that covered his coffin were not English pastoral flowers—they were Flanders poppies.

One thing apparent throughout Blunden's life was his disinclination to engage in adversary utterance or persuasion, either to advance his critical views, to object publicly to those advanced by others, or to aggrandize his particular kind of poetry. (pp. 589-92)

If a way to establish one's identity as a Modernist is to quarrel with one's predecessors, as if to suggest that the new or current literary mode has finally located for all time the permanent forms of verbal validity, Blunden is only a Modern. His feeling of indebtedness to the literary past is as lively as his feeling for the social-historical past, as he develops it in a poem like **"Forefathers."** In his sonnet **"Victorians"** he quietly advises the current enemies of the preceding generation to read them first, and then to "Devise some creed, and live it, beyond theirs, / Or I shall think you but their spendthrift heirs." The reviler of the past should keep in mind, as Blunden suggests in some characteristic lines entitled **"On Tearing Up a Cynical Poem,"** that he himself will be, in his turn, revilable. . . . [Blunden believed that] literature should be rather inclusive than divisive, and, as Thomas Mallon writes, Blunden's literary-historical ideal is "a quiet community of poet, reader, *and past poet*"—that is, the other poet present in every poem by allusion, or present in a way (to the fully literate reader) even by absence. (pp. 593-94)

Thus a context for Blunden. Now one should ask: What kind of a writer is he? What is the worth of his work? Is he really Modern, and does it matter?

To begin with the bad news first. Some of his odd and self-indulgent rhetorical habits may suggest that he has become stuck somewhere back in the middle of the nineteenth century. Like his fondness for beginning a poem with an earnest apostrophe, often accompanied by the interjection *O!* Or his adhesion to the subjunctive mode when most other poets gave it up generations ago. Or his weakness for inverted word-order. Or his addiction to quaint or archaic diction, like *whence* and *thence,* not to mention his calling poetry *verses,* prosody *verse-music,* and a book of poems a *poetry-book,* as well as referring to writers as *scribes*—sometimes *quillmen*—and calling writing itself, on one occasion, *pencraft.* And what about his genteel expletives like "Bless me!" or "As I live"? If those things can be overlooked, how about his use of exclamation marks in his poems, or his ripe and chummy way of referring to the Great of the past with the word *old,* as in Old Chaucer or Old Camden?

And there are other characteristics, of theme and focus as well as style, that may put off the devotee of Modernist—and sometimes even of Modern—writing. Like Blunden's unabashed patriotism, for example. Or his not scrupling to produce poems for specific occasions. Or his speaking right out in his own undisguised person, his "I" not for a moment pretending to stand for J. Alfred Prufrock or Sextus Propertius, and speaking out personally to memorialize some moment in his own life. All such behavior is likely to offend the reader nurtured on the Modernist classics and tempt him to dismiss Blunden as a mere late-Romantic pastoral-minded reactionary.

But wait. When we read his poems carefully, we notice something unexpected, and then we may want to agree with what H. M. Tomlinson says of **Undertones of War:** "The poet's eye," he notes, "is not in a fine frenzy rolling," and he continues: "There is a steely glitter in it." The steely glitter is often there in Blunden's poems too, and it arises from their frequent enactment of an ironic dynamics—we are soothingly led to expect mere "charm" and are brought, instead, to scandal. His poems have the effect of shaking us out of the complacency to which they seem to invite us. For example a standard kind of poem from the Great War is one that finds an odd beauty in the trench scene. This poem deploys an optimistic or romance "plot": it first projects the normal materials of ugliness and seems to invite the normal response, and then it pretends to read them more intensely and contemplate them more sensitively and thus discover the beauty that was there all the time. . . . Blunden's way, on the contrary, is quietly to astonish the reader by reversing the normal procedure, as he does in his fourteen-line poem **"Illusions."** The beauty comes first, then the destruction, or rather the complication, of that illusion. But there are really three phases in the poem through which the understanding passes: first the illusion of beauty; then the illusion of menace, generated by corpse-rags fluttering on the barbed wire; then finally the dissipation of the illusion of menace into an illusion of quiet ironic horror. . . . ["**Illusions**" is] a characteristic Blunden poem: we think we know where we are, and we become comfortable with the tone and the movement, and then we learn that we've not known all the time what we might have known. The structure of **"Illusions"** is like that of **"Concert Party: Busseboom,"** where the first half of the poem conducts us into the delight of a soldier show behind the lines, full of laughter and singing, but the second half, depicting the audience leaving, dispels the illusion that in such a world escape from horror is possible, for now

> We heard another matinee,
> We heard the maniac blast
>
> Of barrage south by Saint Eloi . . .
>
> To this new concert, white we stood;
> Cold certainty held our breath;
> While men in the tunnels below Larch Wood
> Were kicking men to death.

The effect is that of discovering in the midst of a pastoral field a snake in the grass, and that effect is possible only if you know how to entice the reader joyfully into the pastoral field in the first place. Or into a scene of homely recreation—ice-skating this time—as in **"The Midnight Skaters,"** where it is precisely the fun that betrays the presence of the menace.

> Can malice live in natural forms,
> As tree, or stone, or winding lane?

he asks in the poem **"The Ballast-Hole,"** which goes on to answer the question:

> Beside this winding lane of ours
> The fangy roots of trees contain
> A pond that seems to feed the powers
> Of ugly passion. Thunder-storms
>
> No blacker look. If forth it shook
> Blue snarling flashes lightning-like
> I scarce should marvel; may it strike
> When I'm not by its sullen dyke!

That is like Frost's "Design," or his "Tree at My Window," or his "Desert Places," which it resembles by shrewdly couching its highly pessimistic, hence "Modern," attitude in a mode which is not at all Modernist.

A similar complicated and not-at-all complacent poem of Blunden's is **"Sheet Lightning,"** a poem that seems not very well known or often anthologized because presumably untypical of the sweet and pastoral Edmund Blunden. Here a group of men returning from a village game feel themselves sobered to an unaccustomed solemnity by a sudden outbreak of sheet lightning, whereupon "each man felt the grim / Destiny of the hour speaking through him." But by the time they reach a wayside pub, fright and seriousness are forgotten, and the ribaldry resumes—and the petty abuse and cruelty and "anger's balefire." And as the group finally boards the brake again to leave,

> The waiting driver stooped with oath to find
> A young jack rabbit in the roadway, blind
> Or dazzled by the lamps, as stiff as steel
> With fear. Joe beat its brain out on the wheel.

That could be proposed as an eminently Modern poem, but probably it can't qualify as a Modernist one, for it renders the complicated modern scene in such a way as to engage human sympathy. Indeed it would seem to be his fondness for people, with all their frailties and deformities, that finally helps Blunden not become a Modernist.

If the Modernist dehumanization of art has required the severe demotion if not the total disappearance of the portrait as a serious genre of painting, Blunden's art engages boldly the kind of poem analogous to that sort of painting. I am thinking not just of his portraits of Colonel Harrison and Sergeant Worley but also of the poem **"Almswomen."** There it is the George Crabbe of *The Borough* who is invited to join poet and reader in understanding and valuing the "two old dames" who live together in the village almshouse, proud of the show their garden makes from the road, praying amid tears "That both be summoned in the selfsame day." Imagine an Eliot or a Pound, not to mention a Wyndham Lewis, giving a damn about such people. Or about the couple of unprepossessing unfortunates Blunden depicts in **"Lonely Love"**:

> Two walking—from what cruel show escaped?
> Deformity, defect of mind their portion,

and yet clearly in love, "She with her arm in his," causing Blunden to pray,

> let her never have cause
> To live outside her dream, nor unadore
> This underling in body, mind and type.

To try imagining such a topic as material for a confirmed Modernist is to realize how deeply the Modernist movement has been based on a satiric perception of contemporary actuality, where positive human values enter works of art only by ironic negatives, like the exposure of modern love as only rape or perversion in *The Waste Land.* (pp. 595-600)

Artistic Modernism has enjoyed such a favorable press for the past eighty years or so that perhaps we've not sufficiently noticed what we sense when we focus on a writer like Blunden—namely Modernism's limitations, its rejections and refusals, its narrowness and exclusions, its emotional chill, its dogmatisms refuted hourly by our own honest feelings. (pp. 600-01)

Edmund Blunden remains one of the neglected—an irony if we consider how much of his effort he devoted to resuscitating the neglected figures of the past: Lamb, Leigh Hunt, Clare, Smart, Collins, Kirke White, as well as the more recent neglected like Ivor Gurney. But to revisit Blunden is to realize how much life there is in even the neglected. To revisit Blunden is also to be reminded of the basis of literary criticism and literary response in humanity rather than in any form of science, or pseudoscience. As Blunden says when writing of Kirke White, "In almost all our critical performances the affections play some part, and I do not see that anything can be done to keep them out." The only way they can be kept out is for critics to turn from the humane and the empirical and the difficult to the doctrinaire and the facile. (p. 601)

Paul Fussell, "Modernism, Adversary Culture, and Edmund Blunden," in The Sewanee Review, *Vol. XCIV, No. 4, Fall, 1986, pp. 583-601.*

Harold Brodkey

1930-

(Born Aaron Roy Weintraub) American short story writer, essayist, novelist, and poet.

Brodkey is acknowledged as a formidable stylist whose prose is characterized by grandiose metaphor, intense lyricism, and minute descriptions of emotions and events. In his fiction, Brodkey generally eschews plot and linear time, preferring instead to produce accumulations of insights and feelings about small but important incidents in the lives of his characters. Most of his writing is concerned with reconciling personal tragedy through reminiscences of his childhood and adolescence, during which Brodkey endured the death of his mother and his adoptive parents. A major theme in Brodkey's fiction involves the loss of innocence and the struggle to regain grace. Michiko Kakutani observed: "Besides making us reconsider the possibilities of fiction and the shifting equations it draws between memory, imagination and language, [Brodkey's] family portraits possess the potential to move us."

The nine stories in Brodkey's initial collection, *First Love and Other Sorrows* (1958), which won the Prix de Rome, are composed in the slick, realistic manner characteristic of fiction published in the *New Yorker*, where eight of these pieces first appeared. Brodkey employs lean, meticulous prose and draws on events from his own life to depict familiar experiences of Midwestern childhood, college romance, marriage, and parenthood. William Goyen commented: "Mr. Brodkey shows an uncommon eye for recording the lackluster, the dulled ordinary—and sometimes an uncommon perception of the secret glow within the trivialities of our poor human majesty." Brodkey's next work, *Women and Angels* (1985), consists of fragments from *A Party of Animals,* a novel-in-progress that has been compared by some critics to Marcel Proust's *Remembrance of Things Past.* All of the pieces in *Women and Angels* focus upon the emerging consciousness and imagination of Wiley Silenowicz, a sensitive prodigy who serves as Brodkey's persona. The first story, "Ceil," details Wiley's attempt to visualize his mother, who died when he was two years old, through conversations with his adoptive mother, Lila, and others who knew her. The second section, "Lila," concerns the difficult but ultimately sympathetic relationship between Wiley and Lila, who is slowly dying of cancer. The last story, "Angel," praised by Leon Wieseltier as "one of the most astonishing pieces of prose I have been blessed to discover," describes Wiley's supernatural encounter with an angel. Wieseltier added: "The story is about the reception of revelation, about which it is startlingly convincing, and perfectly in place in a significant strain of mystical literature."

Brodkey's recent volume of short fiction, *Stories in an Almost Classical Mode* (1988), which contains twenty-five years of previously published work, exhibits radical changes in his writing, from carefully crafted tales of middle-class Jewish life to highly metaphorical, visionary stories that attempt to recreate the sensations of childhood and adolescence. According to many critics, Brodkey's transitional story is "Innocence," originally published in the *American Review* in

1973. A stylistic tour de force, "Innocence" is an explicit account of a college student endeavoring to help his beautiful girlfriend overcome her sexual unresponsiveness. Twelve of the book's eighteen stories involve Wiley Silenowicz, the protagonist of *A Party of Animals,* exploring in exacting detail his progress from infancy to Harvard University student and his turbulent relationship with his adoptive family. Although some critics faulted Brodkey for inadequate plot and character development and a narrow range of subject matter, others lauded his ability to render nuances of perception and complex psychological and moral states. In addition to his fiction, Brodkey has published essays and verse in such magazines as *Esquire, Partisan Review,* and *Antaeus.*

(See also *Contemporary Authors,* Vol. 111.)

COLEMAN ROSENBERGER

The short stories which make up *First Love and Other Sorrows* have an individual distinction and vitality, a wit and perception, a rightness and sureness of tone, which are unmistakably [Brodkey's] own and unmistakably uncommon. . . .

The first three stories provide a sort of autobiographical sequence, with what appears to be a fairly specific correlation between the "I" of the narrative and the author. (It is possible that the author did not grow up in St. Louis, did not attend Harvard, and did not spend an undergraduate year travelling in Europe, but that the framework of these stories is so wholly imaginative seems improbable.)

In the first of them, **"The State of Grace,"** the narrator (adult now in the telling) is a boy of fifteen, living with his mother and older sister, with his father, remote, dying in a hospital. The story achieves an almost total evocation of the sense of "loneliness and the queer, self-pitying wonder that children whose families are having catastrophes feel" and of its corroding effect, with the reader made to share the "terrible desire to suddenly turn and run shouting back through the corridors of time" to erase the corrosion and alter the old withholding of affection.

In the second story, [**"First Love and Other Sorrows"**], the "I" is sixteen, and his sister, twenty-two, will soon be married. The longest single sequence here, it is, equally, the study of each of them, and it is a superb and sustained display of the author's sure mixture of humor and pathos. It is a story of growing up and parting, of a mother's concern for a proper marriage for her daughter, and of the brother's concern with his own affairs.

With the third, **"The Quarrel,"** the humor wins out, although the author's sharp evocation of scene and personality is in no way lessened. . . .

The "I" gives way to "Elgin Smith" in **"Sentimental Education,"** perhaps for greater inventive license, perhaps merely to avoid the possible embarrassment of a first person narrative. For this is the chronicle of "the combustibility of the emotions" of Elgin and Caroline, traced in some detail, intimate and wholly convincing, from their first encounter on the steps of Widener to their final parting.

Five briefer stories constitute a second cycle, or what one may hope is only the beginning of a second cycle of stories. In these the central figure is Laura Andrews, seen at intervals as a girl, a wife, and a young mother. It may well be that these, with their insights into Laura's world, represent an even more remarkable feat of the creative imagination.

In any event, there is abundant evidence here, alike in the more sustained stories and in the slighter ones, of a richly gifted and disciplined new writing talent.

> *Coleman Rosenberger, "Nine Stories by a Newcomer with a Gift Already Mature," in* New York Herald Tribune Book Review, *January 12, 1958, p. 5.*

WILLIAM GOYEN

Here [in *First Love and Other Sorrows*] are some tender and witty pieces, most of them in the form of autobiographical narrative—and, where they are not, seem still to be within the framework of personal history. . . .

First Love and Other Sorrows constitutes the writer's progress from boyhood in St. Louis through young manhood at Harvard to fatherhood in upstate New York. They raise a question—which might be in order, considering that the pieces themselves are in the category of subjective revelation: What is the point at which a writer's sensibility (which he presumes to be urbane) reveals, against all his purpose, a provincial and bourgeois world?

Larger values have suddenly vanished, or are effaced, and they are replaced by the sturdy, small and everlasting ordinary affections of life. There seems a sadness—the sadness of disappointment—over these pieces as they move with the chronology of the author's own history, as though another confessional revelation had fallen over the pages, like an overtone. Is this the author's intention or is it that addition of accident that tells another thing?

In **"The State of Grace"** the author rues with guilt and self-blame his inability or refusal to show tenderness, when he was 13, toward a boy of 7 whose sitter he was. . . .

Mr. Brodkey shows an uncommon eye for recording the lackluster, the dulled ordinary—and sometimes an uncommon perception of the secret glow within the trivialities of our poor human majesty. Sometimes he is a shade too glib as he urges us to love one another while getting his collegiate and commuter jokes in at the same time. There is little honest involvement—except in the title story [**"First Love and Other Sorrows"**].

This piece, set in St. Louis, is a subtly revealing, gentle story about a mother, son and daughter on the night of the daughter's engagement to be married. Some of the other stories show momentarily the quality of this tale: an untampered with, courageous letting-alone of what is given whole and outright by human life. Those moments hold the promise of the author's future.

> *William Goyen, "Young Man's Memory Lane," in* The New York Times Book Review, *January 12, 1958, p. 29.*

WILLIAM PEDEN

The chief virtue, perhaps, of *First Love and Other Sorrows* is Mr. Brodkey's quietly perceptive approach to nonexceptional human beings in customary or nonexceptional situations: the St. Louis boyhood of a pleasant, moderately sensitive boy only mildly disturbed by "being Jewish" ("it meant I could never be one of the golden people—the blond athletes with their easy charm"); the adolescent years of the same boy, going out for track, discussing philosophy and sex with his friends, and "falling in love."

In other stories, Mr. Brodkey's major character is a young woman, Laurie or Laura, whom we see in successive stories as an attractive and vivacious Wellesley junior dressing for a date; and as a young wife and mother nursing her first baby, having minor difficulties with her husband, and finally dozing happily while contemplating the advent of her second child. These are pleasant stories reaffirming the fact that human relationships are more important than philosophical speculation or that love is more vital than nuclear physics. But I wish, somehow, that before too long Mr. Brodkey would transfer his affections elsewhere. In spite of Laurie's obvious charm, she is likely, after a few more stories at any rate, to become pretty much of a bore.

The surface simplicity of Mr. Brodkey's stories is disarming; it is, of course, the result of real ability and hard work. Mr.

Brodkey writes well, in a clear, uncomplicated, unaffected prose. He sees well, too; more important, he thinks about what he sees, and understands its meanings and implications. He is warmhearted without being a sentimentalist. As well as any of the younger writers of our times he has succeeded in capturing the essence of one segment of American youth in the post-World War II era. (p. 18)

William Peden, "Short Fiction vs. Long," in The Saturday Review, *New York, Vol. XLI, No. 4, January 25, 1958, pp. 17-18, 31-2.*

MARY SHIRAS

[*First Love and Other Sorrows*] adds to the pile of accurate, real-life fiction that has been steadily accumulating in the past few years. The technique is to reproduce situations rather than invent plots, characters or simple narratives. At their worst they read like human interest items in a newspaper; at their best they report situations or describe people of more than usual interest. But as stories they are never finished products. (p. 493)

The first few stories, **"The State of Grace," "First Love and Other Sorrows," "The Quarrel,"** and **"Sentimental Education,"** are concerned with early and late adolescence. . . . Brodkey's hero bears a superficial resemblance to Fitzgerald's tender-hearted, midwestern young men who, with dreaming eyes directed to the east coast, turn their backs on life without glamour. Brodkey's nameless hero is also misplaced: he is sensitive, lonely and intelligent; ashamed of his neighborhood in St. Louis; wistful for popularity and good looks. Early in life he attaches himself to a dream:

> I could always console myself by thinking my brains would make me famous (brains were good for something, weren't they?) but then my children would have good childhoods—not me. I was irrevocably deprived, and it was the irrevocableness that hurt, that finally drove me away from any sensible adjustment with life to the position that dreams had to come true or there was no point in living at all. If dreams came true, then I would have my childhood in one form or another, some day.

Some hundred pages later, the same young man, now in college, affirms with some self-satisfaction, "I knew I would survive my youth and be forgiven." In the meantime, first love (and it wasn't so very sorrowful) has come and gone; Harvard has awarded him a scholarship; his grandmother wills him $5,000; he buys himself some new clothes; in the summer he departs for Europe with his best friend. The irrevocably deprived child is showered with one gift of fortune after another. He has come away from unlovely St. Louis; people like him, even find him charming.

So the dream passes, or is fulfilled; there is no disenchantment at any rate. But then, why should there have been?—it was such an accessible dream—his wish for love and social recognition. Hence the Brodkey hero's *superficial* resemblance to Fitzgerald: the latter's heroes do not simply long for popularity; they are possessed by passionate and extravagant visions of wealth, beautiful women, and fashionable society, and the city in New York is the fabulous place of their dreams. Or, to cite another example of true-blue, uncompromising adolescent hunger, Thomas Wolfe's young men want to possess the earth: they are "torn apart with ecstasy, and cry out in their threats with joy. . . ." They "believe in love and victory and

think that they can never die." Compared with these wholehearted romantic illusions, Brodkey's childish dream appears as a simple, realistic desire for objects that are well within reach. (pp. 493-94)

There isn't much to be said for this fiction, except that it reads easily. If you should go through the whole volume, you will begin to feel a powerful craving for well-made and consciously developed stories that reflect the passions and decisions of an adult world. (p. 494)

Mary Shiras, "Accessible Dreams," in The Commonweal, *Vol. LXVII, No. 19, February 7, 1958, pp. 493-94.*

MARVIN MUDRICK

Harold Brodkey's collection [*First Love and Other Sorrows*] is simply dumbfounding, not fiction but a cosmetic application of the limberest and most knowing *faux-naïf* manner to the most elementary preoccupations of women's-magazine maudlin—rather like the roué who, having exhausted every other sensation, has a try at what he regards as innocence:

> All I know is that Edward needed my love and I wouldn't give it to him. I was only thirteen. There isn't much you can blame a boy of thirteen for, but I'm not thinking of the blame; I'm thinking of all the years that might have been—if I'd only known then what I know now. The waste, the God-awful waste.
> Really, that's all there is to this story. The boy I was, the child Edward was. That and the terrible desire to suddenly turn and run shouting back through the corridors of time, screaming at the boy I was, searching him out, and pounding on his chest: Love him, you damn fool, love him.

Really, that's all there is to this racket: all you have to do, to conclude a story, is race back shouting "Love!" through those dependable corridors of time which are pretty well worn by now but can still yield up the echo of a choked sob. Anyway Frank O'Connor, bland old sentimentalist, is so impressed that he waxes simultaneously banal and incoherent: "Harold Brodkey is a master of narrative prose—prose that does not merely describe an artistic experience, but conveys it as poetry does."

Mr. Brodkey is not unskilful: his grasp of the tricks of the trade is in fact very depressing. **"Sentimental Education,"** for instance, tells of a shy Harvard undergraduate who falls in love with a beautiful Radcliffe girl, signs up in Professor Bush's class on Metaphysical Poets to be near her, eventually has an idyllic coltish affair with her (they of course scrub their faces vigorously like good little children after each session in bed; they're really awfully sweet, and one can't help but enjoy watching them), and sees her leave for summer vacation with considerable sadness: " 'God!' he said to himself. 'I love her'." The style behaves with a tender, awkward, confused, almost disarming inanity: "After that they took to kissing each other a great deal"; "The truth of the matter is, they were caught up in a fever of their senses";

> "Listen, Caroline, we haven't done the right thing. You want to have children?"
> A pink, piteous flush covered Caroline's face.
> "Oh," she said.
> "We ought to get married," he said doggedly.

If you go for chromium melancholy and like to think of life and art as essentially uncomplicated by anything more than the need to turn a phrase, Mr. Brodkey is your man. . . . (pp. 294-95)

Marvin Mudrick, "Is Fiction Human?" in The Hudson Review, *Vol. XI, No. 2, Summer, 1958, pp. 294-301.*

LEON WIESELTIER

[*Women and Angels*] is comprised of three chapters, fragments of the tarrying novel [*A Party of Animals*], preceded by an ignorant and insufferably self-important introduction on the subject of the author's Jewishness. Two of the fragments, **"Ceil"** and **"Lila,"** have already appeared in *The New Yorker*. They constitute a series of nasty revisions of the most platitudinous of all premises of American Jewish fiction, the son's trouble with the mother (in this instance, with the foster mother, too).

They are not especially impressive, except to establish Brodkey as an unpleasant man immensely alive. Their subject, most fully developed in **"Lila,"** is the tyranny of need. The author is for it, and not against it. These are some of the ugliest construals of human relationship that I have ever seen. The controlling assumption of the bond between the foster mother Lila and the adopted son Wiley Silenowicz (Brodkey's embarrassingly exact representative) seems to be that dependence is the secret of love. The only commitment of which the heart may be certain, Brodkey seems to be saying, is a commitment founded on the weakness of the other. Extorting love, as Lila thinks of it.

"Lila" is the sad and sadistic tale of Wiley's watch over Lila's degeneration, while making a study of himself as "a bad person." It describes the adolescence of the son and the aging of the foster mother as the mutual manipulation of each other's pain. There is some relief near the end. Wiley undergoes in his imagination a vivid (and brilliantly written) metamorphosis into middle-aged womanhood, and extracts from it an uncharacteristic sensation of sympathy, a sudden grasp of the utility of "unselfishness" in a generally hard life. As Lila lies dying, there occurs their only conversation without cruelty. The scene is deeply touching. . . . But really the effect is owed only to the remission of the aggression. When the author concludes the story with the exhortation to "make what use of this you like," the reader is returned to his world without mercy.

The first two chapters of Brodkey's book leave you thinking many things, but not a thing that prepares you for the third. It is called **"Angel,"** and it is one of the most astonishing pieces of prose I have been blessed to discover. It begins like this: "Today The Angel of Silence and of Inspiration (toward Truth) appeared to a number of us passing by on the walk in front of Harvard Hall—this was a little after three o'clock—today is October twenty-fifth, nineteen-hundred-and-fifty-one." It proceeds to describe in detail the appearance of this illumination ("The shadow came first . . ." followed by a "facedness, a prow of knowing making Itself known"), and then the permutations of Wiley's psyche in its presence. Since the story is so strange, and for the purpose of conveying both the strictness of its conception and the sloppiness of its execution, both of which are typical of mystical texts, I must give a representative page:

It existed in front of me, It had only to exist in my sight and as the major sweetness and crisply, almost burning center of the field of my attention, It had only to be There in Its Very Real Presence *in front of me,* for Its Literal Existence, Its True Presence to precipitate in me a changeable and varying conviction about many things and a Great Love for It, and This Conviction and This Love, this immense burden of meaning and awe loosened my self-control violently every few seconds, so that my inner state was one of varied heats of pieties, madnesses, catatonias, bits of peace, of grace, the varying convictions of Final or Real Meaning and of my struggles of will not to expect further moments and a return to silliness and doubt and emptiness—that is, my will still struggled to be a Will That Mattered and to be The Will that dominated my conscious existence—this even in the presence of So Awesome a Will as that of The Seraph, or The Minds Behind The Seraph—and this came and went, these opposed heats and states of the soul, or states of mind, burningly and varyingly, like a flame, like one's heartbeat without seeming to have any nature of a paradox any more than one's usual heartbeat does—I mean one's own heartbeat, that variable and many parted, confers, with a reason, a rhythm, that a kind of invariable or unvarying meaning exists so long as my heart beats.

I know of nothing like this in the literature of the day. It takes courage to write about God (much more courage than it takes to write about religion). If *this* is what Brodkey is up to, he may be up to a lot.

The duration of the vision is not long, only an hour and some minutes, though by the standards of mystical experience that is rather a substantial helping of holiness. . . . Brodkey's attempts to describe the numinous object of the vision, and to name it, are awkward and frantic, which is fitting for a work written under the shock of such a communication. Sometimes the writing is awful, but it seems genuinely overwhelmed. In any case, it is not as an essay in theosophical description that **"Angel"** is unforgettable. It is a report not of the deity, but of the disturbances in the author's very sentient soul, of the commotions of identity that result from its access to the godhead. Brodkey is not rapt, or lost in absorption; he remains, even in the presence of this "steady and unparticled fire," a monster of consciousness. The story is about the reception of revelation, about which it is startlingly convincing, and perfectly in place in a significant strain of mystical literature.

Brodkey's subject is a classical one—the pressure on the self of the apocalyptic longing. What is the condition of one whom revelation has failed to redeem? That is what happens (or rather, does not happen) to Wiley Silenowicz in Harvard Yard. He sees God and survives. The profound puzzlement over the continuity of his self is his great theme. For he had expected discontinuity, as befits the appearance of an angel on a Cambridge afternoon.

Final rightness would explode you—The Angel's was not final. . . . The Angel did not end my life. . . . No finality—such as the rising up of the dead—occurred to make this clearly the ultimate moment. . . . Perhaps it is impossible to give up one's nature at first or perhaps ever. . . . What we had was enough even for someone greedy of spiritual glory but it was not the ultimate.

Brodkey, in short, is a disappointed apocalyptic. The extinction, or at least the transformation, that promised to be an essential part of such an experience failed to come.

The perdurability of the self in the presence of the divine has the consequence for Brodkey of its spectacular aggrandizement. This is an ego that even God could not destroy. And here Brodkey's massive vanity coincides with one of the characteristic spiritual motions of modernity. "If the truth is not final, then it is not greater than me beyond all endurance. . . ." He writes wildly, later, of a "universal disrespect in us—because the power—love or force—was never in fact absolute—irresistible—final," of "the possible *universal reality of rebellion—disrespect as making itself into a truth,*" of "Impiety. Self-defense. Rebellion. Whatever." This is grand and familiar. It is the secular man's last resort in his refusal to relinquish completely the spiritual scale of sacred life: the religious inflation of the self.

Writing recently in *The New York Review of Books,* Harold Bloom briefly mentioned Brodkey as an heir of Whitman. For the magnitude of his identity, he is; but Whitman was *too* secular. It is Emerson, rather, who was America's true pioneer in the salvaging of God by the swelling of the self. It was he who recognized that there may be no other alternative to the disenchantment of the world. For such minds rebellion is only the most drastic form of reverence; divinity is protected by the memory of its disappearance.

Whitman, Emerson—these are, again, big claims. (Denis Donoghue has compared Brodkey to Proust, and in an uncharacteristically juridical manner pronounced the work-in-progress "a work of genius.") Is Brodkey really one of them? The literary and spiritual authenticity of **"Angel"** makes you think so. And yet, and yet. Even in **"Angel"** there are traces of something smaller, signs that suggest an immaturity unworthy of the material. There is the occasional eruption of an incomprehensible vulgarity—in a moment of doubt, for example, "I knew The Seraph was bullshit." And there is the systematic introduction into this story of sublimity of an embarrassing sexual insistence of the rankest form of masculine confidence. Brodkey writes of "the sloppy Armageddons of fucking girls"; of the Seraph speaking "homosexually"; of flirting with the angel "as in any romantic situation"; of experiencing "toward the end of the manifestation . . . a headache and considerable nausea and an erection"; and so on.

Now there is no contradiction, obviously, between mystical illumination and carnal intensity; Brodkey has an ancient tradition that he can invoke. But his version of sacred sex is a long, long way from the Song of Songs, to put it mildly. It is, rather, the sort of crudity and erotic unloveliness that some of Brodkey's earlier writings (**"Innocence"** in particular) have led you to expect. This is not mysticism; it is machismo. And it is the tritest kind of literary wickedness, as further evidenced by a strange attack on "our being Middle Class, our training in *Respectability,* in self-willed conformity," and so on. Before God's glory, you would have thought, sociology would fall away. (pp. 30-3)

Leon Wieseltier, "A Revelation," in The New Republic, *Vol. 192, No. 20, May 20, 1985, pp. 30-3.*

D. J. ENRIGHT

Harold Brodkey surmises that Jewish sacredness is "the highest level of transcendence yet reached," and *Women and Angels* is published in a series of books "planned to stimulate the definition and growth of Jewish culture in America." To what extent he is representative of Jewishness is a question beyond my capacity.

But not, I would venture, beyond Leon Wieseltier's. In a sensitive essay printed in *The New Republic* [see excerpt above] he comments that the first two of these "parts of a larger work nearing completion" are "nasty revisions of the most platitudinous of all premises of American Jewish fiction, the son's trouble with the mother (in this instance, with the foster mother, too)." While agreeing that the pieces are chiefly impressive in establishing Brodkey as "an unpleasant man immensely alive"—though isn't "immensely" too big a word?—I would think that they are more boring than nasty. In **"Ceil"** the narrator, Wiley (because it recalls his original name, Isaac) Silenowicz, talks about his real mother, a Russian Jew who died when he was two. With the help of his adoptive mother, Lila, and other witnesses, he draws a picture of her which, for all its heaped-on concrete details, remains abstract. . . .

Actions speak louder than statements, and enactments more forcefully than descriptions. There is little evidence here of a specifically novelistic gift; much of it reads like an extended obituary produced by a team of more than usually fanciful computers. "Oh, you don't have any grip on what she was like," Lila tells Wiley. But it is not his fault that his real mother died before he could know her. The second piece suggests that it was his adoptive mother's fault that she went on living throughout Wiley's adolescence. Neither she nor S. L., his adoptive father, was kind to him in "the essential ways"; at times he didn't think they were so bad, at times he did; at least S. L. had the grace to go away and die without fuss. Poor Wiley could never do right in Lila's eyes. . . . Lila demands the love she is too ugly and sick (and too demanding) to inspire. When Wiley tells her that unselfishness and generosity and concern for others will ease her pain, it is no great wonder that she should scream and throw an ashtray at him. "Her temper astounded me. Where did she get the strength for such temper when she was so ill?" In a moment of what resembles self-understanding, he concludes that "the *I* is what in you most hurts other people—it makes them lonely"; but he doesn't take the thought to heart, it is merely "an untrained exercise of intellect."

Toward the end Wiley changes tack and assures Lila of her kindness, bravery, and selflessness, of the many sacrifices she has made on his behalf. "Of course it was a swindle all the way," yet it worked: she became patient, even-tempered, almost gentle. This affords some relief, however ambiguous. Otherwise it seems to me chiefly the syntax that might almost persuade us, rightly or wrongly, of the writing's profundity. . . . I don't find the tale as sadistic as does Wieseltier; it is the grinding egotism of the narrator that is hard to take. It reads like another of those books about people's mothers, by no means exclusively Jewish ones, in which old grudges are worked off in new bouts of self-pity. . . . (p. 20)

The third piece turns to the **"Angel"** of the book's title. "Today The Angel of Silence and of Inspiration (toward Truth) appeared to a number of us passing by on the walk in front of Harvard Hall—this was a little after three o'clock— today is October twenty-fifth, nineteen-hundred-and-fifty-one." Wieseltier is correct in saying that it takes courage to write about God, if that is what Brodkey is doing. But I am not convinced he is right when he says that nothing in the first two pieces prepares us for this third. Much has prepared us. The Angel is subjected to the same cool and simultaneously overheated inspection, from this angle and from that, as were Ceil and Lila. And it is still the beholder who counts for more than the beheld.

And yet there are things to admire in **"Angel."** An impressive passage—"The New Figure was white indeed, but the white of all the colors, as if it were dressed in prisms"—ushers in a long string of ponderous capitals—"The Figure had no Great Light or Clarity at first or Clear Dimension or Knowable Perspective"—in the archaic manner of William Blake, who also saw an angel. . . . The style is often what the first pieces prepared us for. Not being a Christian, Wiley feels no right of immediate access to the Divine as it took human form and suffered accordingly:

> Nor do I think prayer is answered by Figures who just as a man being hanged or a woman in childbirth or being fucked is so entirely available to our usages of eyes and thoughts and physical action if we so desire, if we are not prevented, so was Divinity on the cross and is still as Suffering Mother or Father or Son or Wisdom.

But elsewhere there occur truly epiphanic moments: "It was dressed in nothing but indefinability," and "It was glumly radiant inside a spreading bell of altered light, not the light of a dream, the light of thought." The style can rise to a new sinewiness and sinuousness as multi-branching sentences interweave with one another to progressive and good effect. That the account is highly abstract is, we take it, inevitable, in the nature of angelic things. The witness cannot well be blamed if he is preoccupied with his responses, his own state of mind, and "I wanted suddenly to be like It" is a licit, decent desire. But in "God in this form faced me" we sense the stress waiting for the final word; and it needs a saint to stand very much of the self-indulgent playfulness, the self-regarding exegesis in Brodkey's narrative.

> I was given nothing and I was given everything, I was not tested, I was too much tested. . . . I was not the most just or good or the most obstinate or the most sly (or sly at all in Its eyes, Its view) among those who were present or was but *it was not known.*

"Sheer Otherness" though it may be, the Angel is "Very Sexual," and toward the end of the manifestation, which lasts for about one hour, Wiley has an erection. (His ego was erect throughout.) I suppose we could read this as a conventional metaphor of mystics, the carnal standing for the divine, but in our time it seems unaccountably otiose in an angel to induce erections. The magazine racks can do that for us.

Yet these touches of what Wieseltier calls "incomprehensible vulgarity" are almost endearing. Finally—and even though we should be hard pressed to know what the Angel could or ought to have said or done—the disappointment is that It said and did nothing. "It was just flattery to believe The Superhuman would bother with us"—but never mind such unaccustomed modesty, It had bothered to show Itself, or someone had bothered to show It. Yet the apparition is no more than gazed at and drunk in, as a painting is scrutinized by a connoisseur in a gallery.

Wieseltier interprets **Women and Angels** as a sign and a portent in that here at last is a contemporary American writer who "insists on metaphysics, on the possibility of spiritual incident in the city." However, Wieseltier's answer to the question posed earlier is that Jewishness matters little to Brodkey's literature and Brodkey's literature matters little to Jewishness. [Amos] Oz's Jewishness, Israeliness rather, seems to me genuine and natural, conscientious but as little self-conscious as these things can be in this highly conscious world of ours, as unarguable as the landscapes he pictures with such intimacy. In comparison, Brodkey's Jewishness, if that is what it is, strikes me as operatic, staged, a matter deliberately chosen rather than enforced. (pp. 20, 22-3)

D. J. Enright, "Jews, Have Pity!" in The New York Review of Books, *Vol. XXXII, No. 14, September 26, 1985, pp. 19-20, 22-3.*

BONNIE LYONS

All three stories [in **Women and Angels**] focus on the developing consciousness and imagination of the protagonist, Wiley Silenowicz. **"Ceil,"** the first story, traces Wiley's attempt to imagine and thus feel his deceased mother's life. **"Lila,"** the second, is about the profound, deeply painful, and finally loving relationship between Wiley and his stepmother, Lila. **"Angel,"** the third, is about Wiley's mystical experience of an angel.

At their best these stories capture moments of consciousness with remarkable fullness and convincingness. They give the impression of rendering the most delicate nuances of consciousness, both the simultaneity of multiple feelings and thoughts and the fleetingness with which they flicker through the mind. The sixty pages of **"Angel"** about Wiley's encounter with a supernatural being is a *tour de force* in the way it paradoxically describes the indescribable angel and traces the varied responses that Wiley experiences including awe, humor, delight, suspicion, disbelief, mockery and exaltation. But for me the most memorable and totally successful story in the collection is **"Lila,"** in which the dramatic focus is Wiley's self-transcending moment of empathy with his tortured and torturing step-mother. Unable to bear Lila's violent and abusive demands, Wiley recognizes that he must try to empathize but asks himself, "How could I be a dying, middle-aged woman walking around in a housedress?" Then he manages to do just that. . . . This act of total empathetic imagination allows Wiley to experience and thus to understand his step-mother's fury and cruelty and later to help lessen her pain.

The two most remarkable aspects of this extraordinary book are Brodkey's convincing explorations of consciousness—the motion and emotions of the mind—and his ability to find language to embody the most transitory, complex, intense feelings and thoughts. (pp. 456-57)

Bonnie Lyons, in a review of "Women and Angels," in Studies in Short Fiction, *Vol. 23, No. 4, Fall, 1986, pp. 456-57.*

MICHIKO KAKUTANI

As in [*First Love and Other Sorrows*], the theme of innocence is central to nearly every tale in *Stories in an Almost Classical Mode* from the intertwined portraits of family life to **"Innocence,"** a highly acclaimed and highly graphic account of a man's attempt to bring his frigid girlfriend to orgasm. To these Brodkey characters, innocence is not only a natural attribute of youth, its loss is also a necessary condition of maturity, signifying initiation into the duplicities and responsibilities of the real world.

In other respects, the tales in this volume fall sharply into two categories. The first group is made up largely of stories written during the 1960's—fairly conventional stories, with beginnings, middles and ends. The language here is straightforward with occasional dips into Fitzgerald-like metaphor, the relationship between the author and his characters sympathetic but cordially removed.

In **"The Shooting Range,"** a Communist named Ann falls in love with a married laborer, leaves him and then, almost haphazardly, marries a young lawyer and settles down to a middle-class life. In **"Hofstedt and Jean—and Others,"** a middle-aged professor takes up with one of his former students, a young woman who reminds him of his best friend's wife. And in **"Bookkeeping,"** a man by the name of Avram finds himself torn between his obligation to some dinner guests and a friend's request for help, unable to make a commitment he invites the friend, who's having a bad acid trip, to join his dinner party—with predictably unpleasant results.

The heroes in Mr. Brodkey's later stories share Avram's ambivalence, his self-consciousness, his tendency to think too much. But these later stories are as unwieldy, raucous and urgent as the earlier ones are tidy and well-mannered. Told in the first person, **"Largely an Oral History of My Mother," "His Son in His Arms, in Light, Aloft," "Ceil"** and **"S.L."** are obsessive meditations on a familial past in which a narrator tries to recapture and communicate his childhood to the reader through a flood of facts, reminiscences and highly emotional interpretations of those facts and reminiscences. . . .

[In **"A Story in an Almost Classical Mode"**], the narrator bluntly refers to himself as Harold Brodkey, and while the names change in the other tales, the author's close identification with his narrator remains the same, as does the basic cast of characters. Indeed, the reader can only assume that these overlapping stories are fragments of Mr. Brodkey's much awaited novel. In each case, the setting is the Midwest, the time, the 1930's or early 40's. And in each case, the narrator is a sensitive and intellectually gifted child, torn between the love and anger he feels for both his real and adoptive parents. . . .

The narrator's real mother, a ghostly figure who died when he was an infant, emerges as a proud Jewish immigrant who came to the United States, made a poor marriage to a ne'er-do-well and died an early, stupid death. In contrast, his adoptive mother—named, variously, Leah or Leila or Lila—comes across vividly as a hectoring, melodramatic woman, vain about her fading looks, intolerant of others' shortcomings, a woman capable of shocking verbal cruelty and startling moments of vulnerability. Her husband, usually referred to as S. L., seems a slightly more elusive figure, prone to dispensing conditional love, a charming, faintly disreputable fellow, he cherishes his young son's innocence while at the same time wanting to undermine this reminder of his own corruptibility.

In each of these tales there is an acute awareness of the distortions wrought by time, language and point of view. Some of them take the form of a pseudodocumentary in which quotations from other characters are juxtaposed with the narrator's reminiscences; others simply underscore the compres-

sion and reinvention involved in any attempt to conjure up the past. . . .

Besides making us reconsider the possibilities of fiction and the shifting equations it draws between memory, imagination and language, these family portraits possess the potential to move us. There is something heroic about their narrators' ardent, nearly desperate efforts to piece together the fragments of their youth, something touching about their inability ever to fully do so.

Too often, however, these later stories sound like transcripts of a stranger's analysis sessions. The smallest incident (pedaling a bicycle up a hill or being carried in father's arms) tends to generate long, windy self-assessments and tired existential musings; the tiniest observation is footnoted and annotated by further musings. The prose can be forceful and lucid, but it can also be irritatingly vague and pretentious. . . .

As a result, the reader finishes this volume exhausted and convinced that Mr. Brodkey needs an editor, a Maxwell Perkins who might not only goad him into finishing his novel but who might also shape and refine his stories.

> *Michiko Kakutani, "First-Person Stories, Tidy and Not," in* The New York Times, *September 14, 1988, p. C25.*

WILLIAM McPHERSON

Stories in an Almost Classical Mode is a huge collection of a quarter-century's work: 18 stories, some as long as novellas, some of them apparently pieces of the novel that has been in the works for a very long time and, according to *The New York Times,* was once delivered to his publisher in 2,000 manuscript pages. But that was 11 years ago. *Party of Animals* never appeared. . . .

Beginning with **"Innocence"**—a brilliantly achieved, 30-page study of a woman so stunning that "to see her in sunlight was to see Marxism die," and of the narrator's dogged struggle to bring this distant, reluctant beauty finally to earth, to orgasm—twelve of the stories are written in the various first-person voices of the novel's protagonist, Wiley (Ulysses) Silenowicz, free man. "Good or bad," he says in **"The Boys on Their Bikes,"** "I am a free man."

The Wiley stories concern the parents who adopted him at the age of two, his nurse, his older sister Nonie, his biological parents, a couple of boyhood friends, various others. And of course they concern Wiley himself, a difficult, questing, tormented, tormenting, altogether vain, wretched, funny and, at bottom, admirable guy. Also handsome and good at sports. They take him from his tenuous middle-class beginnings near St. Louis, through puberty and the death of his adoptive parents, to a kind of rickety freedom at Harvard. The narrative, however, within each story and in the collection as a whole, does not flow consecutively; it loops and turns as memory does, in a kind of dreamlike mind-time roaming in, playing against, and being carried along by the spin of the world in actual time: encompassing it, mastering it insofar as it can be mastered, surrendering to it.

In **"Largely an Oral History of My Mother,"** he writes:

> Sometimes, then, there is a room; and the room is
> a conglomerate of rooms I saw her in; memory fills
> it, but with stuff from different years, different eras,

different times of day, so that the light is different where she stands from the light that surrounds me, the observer, the one who has returned to this room that never existed in this form, to this compendium of rooms. Sometimes one's own inner voice speaks. . . . And he sometimes speaks for the gray-lit figure who is saying things inaudibly—he speaks for her as she once spoke for me when I was an infant; he will say something like *'One thing I'll say for myself—'* which was one of her phrases at a certain stage in her life; and then maybe something like a flashbulb goes off, and all the grayness turns swiftly to color—maybe a little washed out by glare but close to actuality; and I may grasp, or almost grasp, the sound of my mother's voice . . .

This is how the mind works, and how these stories work as they move, backing and filling, toward what I can only call a kind of slowly unfolding of (yet incomplete) freedom. Let us call it the moving toward the achievement of a voice, of a self, of consciousness. This—the motion or the achievement—is not a small thing. The narrative *I*, the sentient *I* in this work, goes far beyond solipsism, in fact, is the agent of the struggle against it, the means of awareness of something other than the self. It is the powerful *I* of the creating artist.

The dominant narrative voice is Wiley's, but his is not the only one; other voices rise and fall, surface and submerge like the voices in a fugue. Wiley is the medium, rather than the ventriloquist. He comes from "a long line of magic-working rabbis, men supposedly able to impose and lift curses . . . known for their inflexible contempt for humanity and their conceit; they pursued an accumulation of knowledge of the Unspeakable—that is to say, of God." Shamans, in other words, of which the narrator is at least an apprentice (and the writer, Brodkey, a master). One of the many motifs in this collection is that of the magical child, the foundling who "from now on will run this history, this oral history; I will order it, arrange it." The actual world, of course, is less tractable than that—as the astonishing final story, **"Angel,"** testifies. . . .

Brodkey's theme—if such a simplistic statement can be made about so complex a book—is Miltonic: fallen man, and the intimation of grace. "I believe in freedom even if it's only the posture one takes for the fall," Wiley says in **"The Boys on Their Bikes."**

In an essay published last spring in *The Threepenny Review,* Brodkey says that although liars may make the best friends because truth is so often cruel, they do not make the best novelists. "The novel is an enterprise having truth as its starting point and with truth as its ending; and in between it is a truthful journey. It is a study in truth about people, about moments, actions, feelings, and ideas and ideals." That is why it is so hard, and why Brodkey's achievement in these stories is so great. Even so, as he writes in **"Angel"**: "I suppose part of me had always known that a sense of Failure must accompany any attempt at Truth." Wiley settles for something more modest: his story ends, "Only after many years were there convincing but frail and as if whispered attempts at honesty, of which this is one." And so does Brodkey: the book ends there too.

Writing at this level of intensity, of seriousness, of risk: that is the work of a master. Its truths are difficult, and not amenable to translation. Primary confrontations with reality and consciousness, with love and terror, magic and death—the

"almost classical mode" of the title—never are. . . . He has published a heroic book. I believe it is a great one.

William McPherson, "Harold Brodkey's Intimations of Grace," in Book World—The Washington Post, *September 18, 1988, p. 5.*

FRANK KERMODE

Mr. Brodkey's most striking characteristic [in ***Stories in an Almost Classical Mode***] is his passion for what I can only call protraction. One of the more appalling of these stories is called **"The Pain Continuum."** About 10,000 words long, it is a fantastically detailed account by a little boy of the tortures inflicted on him by his stepsister. Juvenile torture comes up elsewhere in the book from time to time, but more or less intermittently. In this tale the torment is apparently endless. The awfulness of the child's situation is reflected in Mr. Brodkey's prose. He likes (though that hardly seems the right word) to write virtually interminable sentences—as if a period would bring the reader unearned relief from the mimetic pain he ought to be suffering. I have just picked a sentence at random and counted 130 words, a sentence as reluctant to stop as the boy's sister, and, like her, not so much ending as collapsing. . . .

The prose, then, is a prose of painful abundance. Perhaps it is inevitable that from time to time it should degenerate into bombast, as defined by Coleridge: "thoughts and images too great for the subject." . . .

When the stories concern a child's vision of the world and its people—and that is the dominant theme of the whole book—the effort is palpable and tremendous. To assess the high temperatures produced by the friction of Mr. Brodkey's language, one might simply recall the opening pages of Proust or of *A Portrait of the Artist as a Young Man.* Recollection in tranquillity is of no interest to Mr. Brodkey; he recollects in a sort of poetic fury, nothing is too strained or too bizarre. . . .

Several of the stories have the same central and perceiving character, often called Wiley, but once tentatively named Harold Brodkey ("I am only equivocally Harold Brodkey," he says, because in truth he is neither Harold nor Brodkey, but Aaron, "the name I'd had with my real mother," and Bezborodko, the Russian name of which Brodkey is a corruption). Whatever the name, the consciousness is always that of an adopted child. There is some family romancing here—not surprisingly, since few of the adoptive parents in this book would be anybody's first choice. The mothers, ranting on about their pains, their misfortunes, their lost looks, are in general self-centered though gutsy scolds. In the worst case the mother has breast cancer and the father is bedridden. Fathers tend on the whole to vague and insensitive masculine amiability, needing to feel they feel rather than feeling.

The longest story, **"Largely an Oral History of My Mother,"** is typical. The mother talks torrentially, the father is clumsy, the sister malevolent. Succor comes from an Alsatian maid, who later gets a remarkable short story to herself—she sings to the sick child as, contemplating the food he cannot digest, he tries not to vomit. In one story the child is only on probation—he may get adopted, but if unsatisfactory he may be returned to sender. In other stories he may be incredibly popular or prodigiously clever. Having been adopted precisely because of his good looks, he may seek his revenge by growing fat. Always he has a keen sense of himself as well as of his elders. . . . (p. 3)

He also listens carefully. In the dialogue there are repeated attempts to render sociolects and idiolects—class or individual inflections, accents—with an effect sometimes of sharpness and accuracy, sometimes of hardly tolerable strain.

It may be that the true cause of the habitual surface agitation is a kind of horrified pity at the shapes and straits imposed simply by living. A story called **"The Shooting Range"** gives us an account of one woman's life—early membership in the Communist Party, a working-class lover, bourgeois marriage, psychotherapy—and does so without much comment; yet the life is pitied, there is a feeling that lives ought not to be like this, that the artist should do something to make up for their being like this, should strive turbulently to do so.

The last story in the book, **"Angel,"** is a surprisingly gentle apocalypse, almost as if all passion were spent: a seraph appears over Harvard Yard, somewhat in the manner of Hawthorne. It seems right to end a book that tries to make sense of a frantic world with a sober tale of the frantic world's end.

The quiet of that last story is uncharacteristic; mostly the world of *Stories in an Almost Classical Mode* is that of the child, a bafflingly complex and various world, lacking beginnings and endings, a world he never made. It is interesting that in the earliest of these stories, **"The Abundant Dreamer,"** which was published in 1963, the prevailing pattern of adoption and childhood perception is already present. This story is a disciplined affair, carefully written, with a well-judged series of flashbacks. A movie director is making a film in Rome when he learns of the death of his grandmother. His mother had consigned him at an early age to this grandmother's care—it is what Mr. Brodkey's mothers tend to do, whether from death, necessity or choice. This mother had an "amusement-hungry, warm, and depthless face"; when amused, "she let slide a glass tray of laughter." The grandmother, on the other hand, was rich, responsible, deep. The two worlds, of the child and the mature artist who finally achieves grief, are rendered with all the density and strangeness of this writer at his best. Like the artist at the center of his story, he works to make a world, full of specificities and structures, out of the world perceived. (pp. 3, 51)

A transient character in one of the stories says, "I wish I were a poet. What is a poet? A poet is a man whose words ring—noncounterfeit." Mr. Brodkey wishes to be and is a poet, never counterfeit, though not always current coin. "I know no simple stories," says one of his narrators, and anything that happens to look simple here is really part of something complex. In the jungle of these immense sentences, amid the mixtures of times and tenses, in the dimmer passages of Mr. Brodkey's large lexicon, the reader certainly needs not only to keep his wits about him, but to be prepared to undergo some vicarious suffering. All that protraction is damnably hard on the nerves. (p. 51)

Frank Kermode, " 'I Am Only Equivocally Harold Brodkey',' in The New York Times Book Review, *September 18, 1988, pp. 3, 51.*

ROBERT ALTER

Since the publication of *First Love and Other Sorrows* in 1958, Brodkey has been known to be engaged in a large novel called *Party of Animals,* and roughly the last two-thirds of *Stories in an Almost Classical Mode* are pieces that would appear to be fragments or spin-offs of that project. . . .

Now that all of Brodkey's production since the '50s is available for inspection between hard covers, it is clear that his fictional enterprise has gone through three distinct phases. *First Love* is made up of nine rather slight stories, some of them brief sketches of only a few pages, all of them pastel renderings of familiar scenes of growing up and of bourgeois domestic life: acquiring a first girlfriend, a quarrel between college buddies on a European bicycle trip, a young mother anxiously nursing her first baby, the daunting appearance of an unexpectedly authoritative new baby sitter. All these situations are handled with an efficient precision of notation and dialogue that must have pleased many of the readers of the *New Yorker* in giving back to them the circumstances of their lives in clarified prose. The big problem with these early stories is that there is scarcely anything in them that transcends the banality of their subject matter, providing real insight into it or transforming it into the occasion for a distinctive aesthetic experience.

Brodkey himself must have sensed something of this limitation. The half-dozen stories he published between 1963 and 1973 are more expansive, richer in detail, some of them reaching novella proportions. All are concerned in one way or another with character and destiny, and all offer a good deal to engage one's attention. Their central flaw, it seems to me, is that they work with plots and characters that cry out for patient novelistic elaboration through hundreds of pages of accumulated details, and instead we get summary, flat assertion, and a verbal gesturing toward a concreteness of experience that is largely absent from the stories. At times Brodkey tries to compensate for this sketchiness with mannered metaphor. . . . (p. 30)

The one wholly successful story in this phase is **"Innocence,"** which appeared in 1973 in *American Review.* It is also, perhaps instructively, the only piece by Brodkey that treats sex with a high degree of explicitness. The first-person narrator announces early on, "I distrust summaries, any kind of gliding through time," and professes to "admire the authority of being on one's knees in front of the event." The full presence of the event is precisely what is too often lacking in Brodkey's incipiently novelistic stories, all in the third person, of the ten previous years. . . .

Brodkey has been trying, since 1973, to reach that authority of kneeling before the event through the unstable medium of memory. All of the stories are now retrospective first-person narrations, almost all of them going back to childhood and adolescence in a suburb of St. Louis in the '30s and '40s. One assumes that the stories are essentially autobiographical. A few details vary from piece to piece. . . . The family setting of this autobiographical fiction is second-generation American Jewish, but the ethnic identity is, in most respects, an irrelevancy. For Brodkey offers a microscopic vision of an imploded nuclear family in which all that really matters are the looming personalities of mother, father, and sister, with social contacts accorded no more than intermittent glimpses.

In the most recent of these stories, the narrator wonders about the "necessity I feel and have for the impossible return, the approximate recurrence, of certain smokey moments, images that arise only in this person's or that person's company," and construes that necessity to be "what I mean by love." This statement nicely defines the radical nature of Brodkey's undertaking over the last decade and a half, but it also intimates what is problematic about it. Other aspects of fiction—above all, plot and progressive time—have been drastically subordinated to the pursuit of the impossible return, the evocation of those smokey moments. The prose becomes densely lyric and the stories themselves terrifically static. Characteristically, present-tense narration often displaces the past tense as the narrator tries to get back to the actuality of the remembered moment, sometimes turning the story into an achronological shuffling of related experiences.

Because all this is anchored in the remembering consciousness of the narrator, what we get, for the most part through an elaboration of metaphor, is the feel and look and affective impingement of the experience, object, or person on the remembering subject. One might call this procedure lyric sensationism. (p. 31)

Such transcriptions of affective sensation and perception tend to run on for long, cumulative paragraphs. Let me offer a suggestion of their cumulative movement by quoting two full sentences from a smokey moment of the boy's father speaking to him:

> Mostly, if I hear him well, the fog-chambered street vanishes, the silver and brown spaces, some of which are bright silver off and on as the clouds and the sky shift in meaning and in luminescence. Instead, I see what he says, blinkingly, a squinched, knotted, vertiginously knotted picture, knotted on itself and yet clear, too, a sort of active picture, mysterious and lucid, as a dream is, but with his direct authority.

There is something remarkable about such writing. But to put the question bluntly, is it, when sustained to the length of a whole story, good writing?

There are no doubt some critics who will hasten to acclaim Brodkey as an American Proust, but the crucial respect in which he falls far below Proust is his being confined within the narrow limits of lyric sensationism. Proust was also an addict of the impossible return, but implicated in that imaginative effort was a large and complex vision of society, culture, moral life, aesthetic value, and the kaleidoscopic intricacies of individual character. By contrast, what the reader of the later Brodkey is likely to experience is merely a constant, restless fine-tuning of language to catch the delicate edge of sensation remembered.

There is, in the end, something that seems excessively personal in Brodkey's pursuit of the evanescent past. If the meaning of that pursuit, as he says, is love, then it is too much his own unconditional love for the voice of his father, the perplexing narcissism of his mother, the intensity of sibling rivalry, the look and smell of a Midwestern street a half century ago. However sensitively his language may limn those objects of recollection, not enough goes on in the fiction to build bridges from the island of private experience into that larger world that imaginative writing at its best can engage with depth and illumination. (pp. 31-2)

> *Robert Alter, "Almost Classic," in* The New Republic, *Vol. 199, No. 17, October 24, 1988, pp. 30-2.*

BRUCE BAWER

To examine the stories in *First Love and Other Sorrows*—an exercise which can provide a highly instructive prolegomenon to a perusal of *Stories in an Almost Classical Mode*—is to be surprised that its author's unpublished work could be the focus of so much feverish speculation. For *First Love* is a decidedly unspectacular item—an assemblage of quiet, innocuous little fictions about Midwestern boyhood, campus romance, and young marrieds. Since eight of the nine stories appeared originally in *The New Yorker,* it should not be surprising that the campus is invariably that of Harvard University, that the young marrieds are invariably fainter, more plastic versions of John Cheever's vaguely discontented New York suburbanites, and that the style is invariably spare, precise, graceful, and passionless. In most of these stories, every detail seems shamelessly tailored to the requirements of 1950s *New Yorker* fiction. (p. 59)

Yet not all the stories in *First Love* are equally contrived. The first three stories in the book—**"The State of Grace," "First Love and Other Sorrows,"** and **"The Quarrel"**—are all told in the first person (the others are in the third person), and each of them manifestly derives from the author's own youth. They have a touch of genuine feeling and originality that the remaining stories in the book don't have; their boy protagonists are the only characters in *First Love* who come alive. Perhaps the most memorable of these three stories is **"The State of Grace,"** whose protagonist is a thirteen-year-old resident of St. Louis; as in Brodkey's later, more blatantly autobiographical stories of boyhood, the narrator makes a point of how tall he was, how attractive, how brilliant . . . and how "remarkable". . . . The story concerns the thirteen-year-old's relationship to one of these "other boys"—a "precocious and delicate" seven-year-old neighbor for whom our protagonist baby-sits and with whom he identifies, since he feels that both he and the child are unloved and unappreciated by their parents. Yet he doesn't give the boy his love because the boy, like everyone else, doesn't love *him*: "I was fierce and solitary and acrid . . . and there was no one who loved me first. I could see a hundred cravennesses in the people I knew, a thousand flaws, a million weaknesses. If I had to love first, I would love only perfection." The story ends with a rather touching paragraph, the last sentence of which is, in its modest way, probably the most emotionally unrestrained in a very restrained book:

> Really, that's all there was to this story. The boy I was, the child Edward was. That and the terrible desire to suddenly turn and run shouting back through the corridors of time, screaming at the boy I was, searching him out, and pounding on his chest: Love him, you damn fool, love him.

Of the nine stories in *First Love,* it is the three stories of boyhood that prefigure the direction Brodkey was to follow in his later work; and of all the sentences in the book, it is perhaps the closing sentence of **"The State of Grace"** that comes closest to the passionate, oracular prose for which Brodkey would become famous. To read Brodkey's debut volume is to recognize that it wasn't necessarily a bad idea for him to pursue the Midwestern-boyhood material that his later stories would obsess over; on the contrary, any reader who looked at *First Love* in 1958 would have had to conclude—from the strength of **"The State of Grace," "First Love and Other Sorrows,"** and **"The Quarrel,"** relative to the other stories—that if Brodkey wanted to produce fresh and lyrical fiction, he would stand a better chance of doing so if he abandoned the college-romance and young-suburbanite material and concentrated instead on the imaginative treatment of themes drawn from his boyhood. Yet those three stories also contain intimations of some of the cardinal failings of Brodkey's later fiction—namely, his egocentrism, his indifference to plot, and even (in that closing sentence of **"The State of Grace"**) his addiction to sentimental, self-pitying, and overheated prose.

To be sure, the first five stories in Brodkey's new book do not exhibit these failings in profusion. Published in *The New Yorker* between 1963 and 1969, they are, like the majority of stories in *First Love,* typical *New Yorker* stories, if with a few significant differences from those Fifties narratives: longer, darker, more adventurous, they represent the *New Yorker* story at a somewhat later stage in its development, the mid-to-late-Sixties era of, say, Cheever's "The Swimmer." The earliest and longest of them, **"The Abundant Dreamer,"** makes use of a present-tense narrative and a generous number of flashbacks to tell the story of Marcus Weill, a highly regarded Jewish-American film director who reacts with apparent indifference when told, on the set of his movie in Rome, that his grandmother has just died. Gradually, the flashbacks reveal to us the intricate set of circumstances and feelings behind that reaction, and what ultimately emerges is a rather affecting evocation of the emotionally fragile boy that stands behind, and to an extent still exists within, this egocentric and seemingly self-sufficient man of consequence. Perhaps it is needless to say that there are strong similarities between Weill and Brodkey, both abundant dreamers: like Brodkey, Weill is a "genius" with a complex relationship to his Jewishness and his past; as Brodkey was raised by relatives after his mother's death, so Weill was raised after his parents' divorce by his grandmother. What's more, when Brodkey writes about Weill that "a movie is to him primarily an arrangement of recognitions, an *allée* laid out so that at every step what is being seen alters the sense of what has been seen," Brodkey appears to be offering as well, by implication, his own definition of fiction. Yet **"The Abundant Dreamer"** is not merely a document in self-absorption or a meditation on memory; it is an objective short story in which Brodkey does not confuse himself with Weill, does not place Weill on a pedestal, does not treat Weill's thoughts on art and Judaism and death as holy writ. Though deeply felt and abundantly human, the story steers clear of rhetorical excess; in terms of style and structure, it is as elegant as anything else Brodkey has ever published.

In nearly the same league is **"Bookkeeping"** (1968), the story of an evening on which Avram Olensky, a thirtyish New York Jew, finds himself caught in the crossfire between his self-destructive Dutch friend Annetje—whose parents both perished in World War Two and who is experiencing the aftereffects of an LSD "experiment"—and his dinner guests, a well-to-do New England WASP and her German husband, neither of whom sympathizes with Annetje's predicament. Inevitably, the conversation turns to the Holocaust, to questions of collective guilt and individual responsibility. As in **"State of Grace"** and **"The Abundant Dreamer,"** the nature of love and friendship figures importantly here; Avram must weigh compassion against gratitude, must determine the extent of his various obligations to his friends. Here, too, as in **"The Abundant Dreamer"** (though not quite so fully as in **"The State of Grace"**), the protagonist can be identified with Brodkey himself; as in both **"The Abundant Dreamer"** and **"The State of Grace,"** furthermore, the protagonist's love

and compassion seem to be regarded by both protagonist and author as favors, as gifts to be bestowed or withheld, often for strategic reasons. As the boy in **"The State of Grace"** refuses to confer his love upon his seven-year-old charge, and as the director in **"The Abundant Dreamer"** decides that he doesn't have time to "fend off death" for his grandmother, so **"Bookkeeping"** ends with Avram contemplating not the tragedy of Annetje's life but his own virtue in being so kind to her. Is Brodkey out to make a point about human self-centeredness? It doesn't seem so. He doesn't even appear to be aware that these characters are self-centered; to his mind, this is simply the way people think about things. In the world according to Brodkey, true selflessness doesn't exist.

By far the slightest of these five Sixties stories is the short, facile **"On the Waves"** (1965), which depicts the unspoken rapprochement—in a Venetian gondola, of course, this being a *New Yorker* story—between a divorced ex-tennis player and his less-than-believable seven-year-old daughter (who finds Venice "insincere"). The remaining Sixties stories are somewhat more impressive, though not without crucial weaknesses. **"Hofstedt and Jean—and Others"** (1969) is about a forty-five-year-old English professor's romance with a student less than half his age; despite certain merits, the story is rather too long and diffuse, crowded with extraneous and redundant details in what comes across as an amateurish attempt to capture its characters completely and definitively. The ultimate point seems to be that Jean's attraction, for Hofstedt, resides less in her inherent charms than in the fact that she reminds his old college buddy of the buddy's wife when she was young. Hofstedt's affair, in short, is essentially a consequence of the two men's puerile competitiveness, which dates back to their days at Harvard (where they were, naturally, the top two students in their class). Though Hofstedt never tires of analyzing his own thoughts and feelings, he pays little heed to Jean's; indeed, he hardly makes an effort to know what they are. His commentary upon her is confined chiefly to expressions of admiration for her body, cruel ridicule of her use of slang, and a superior, dismissive attitude toward her deepest expressions of affection. Essentially, his take on the relationship amounts to: *I'm too good for her, of course, but being as vulnerable as the next man to human folly I find her youth and beauty irresistible.* Is Brodkey's purpose here to satirize Hofstedt for this self-absorption? Decidedly not. There's no ironic distance at all between this author and his obnoxious protagonist; in fact, Brodkey seems not to realize for a moment just how obnoxious Hofstedt is. At one point in the story a friend tells Hofstedt that he "occup[ies] a private world," and this story is unquestionably set in that world. It is Hofstedt's emotions and observations, and no one else's, which we are supposed to take seriously.

Only the last of Brodkey's Sixties narratives has a female protagonist. **"The Shooting Range"** (1969) chronicles the life of a middle-class woman named Ann Kampfel from the time of her romance, at age twenty, with a factory foreman in a small Illinois town, to her long, not particularly happy marriage to a Washington bureaucrat. Bouncing along from one period of Ann's life to the next, the story doesn't pause often to render Ann's thoughts in any depth, but instead concentrates upon capturing the shifting currents of her romantic life over the years. The picture of Ann never quite comes together: though she is a believable character, one feels as if one knows her only from a distance, like a neighbor glimpsed every so often from across the street. When Brodkey tells us that "Ann never contemplated infidelity [because] it would make

Fennie [her husband] unhappy," we accept the explanation, but we don't feel as if we know Ann well enough to be certain that she would actually think this way. We don't know why she leaves the foreman (whom she loves) or why she marries the bureaucrat (whom she doesn't) or why she doesn't pursue the career for which she prepared in college. What we do know about her is not very endearing: she's grim and humorless and fatalistic, and in her whole life, as Brodkey gives it to us, there is hardly a moment of real joy or even lightheartedness; she derives no apparent pleasure from her husband, her children, or the privileges of her life in Washington. Brodkey's point, however, is not that this is an exceedingly dour woman, but that life can be an exceedingly dour affair.

He seems also to want to make a point about class. At the beginning of this extremely long story, Ann has been talked by a college boyfriend into being a Communist, a believer in "the brotherhood of man and the release of men from economic pressures that distorted them and their lives" (the year is 1934); the foreman persuades her easily enough to leave the Party, and she goes on to lead the life of a typical bureaucrat's wife. Yet it is not until the end of the story that she, now the mother of two grown daughters, complains she's "turning middle-class. . . . Why is that, Fennie?" It's a disappointing conclusion; one feels cheated that we have come all this way for so feeble a fare-thee-well. It isn't even clear whether we're expected to mourn with Ann over her middle-class metamorphosis or laugh at her for not realizing that she's been middle-class all her life. Perhaps we're supposed to recognize Ann's seemingly automatic and self-defeating life choices as having been a consequence of her middle-class mentality; if so, however, the first forty-one of the story's forty-two pages must be considered extremely ineffective—for there is little justification in these pages for blaming Ann's confusing behavior on the class into which she was born. Even discounting the class-mentality theme, the story is a weak one. In its shape and tone, and of course in its attempt to present an entire unremarkable life in unadorned fashion, it much resembles Flaubert's "Un coeur simple"; but any reader who recognizes this similarity must be struck at once by everything that Flaubert has and that Brodkey lacks: not only poignancy and moral rigor, but also a humility before life, an affection for one's characters, and an instinctive awareness that one is addressing an audience.

Brodkey's four substantial Sixties stories, then, have their failings. To be sure, they are all highly readable, even compelling, and are blessed with poise and grace; unlike most of the stories in *First Love,* they have the texture of real life, and their characters convince. But to read through them in chronological order is to feel increasingly that they are the work of an author who is eager to render an extremely complicated vision of life, but who either has not yet brought that vision into focus or has not yet arrived at a satisfactory means of communicating it. To put it another way, Brodkey wants us to climb inside his skin—or a skin that is very much like his own—and to experience what it is like there, but he is incapable of giving us our bearings; he speaks to us in a language of the heart, but it is a language that is not quite our own, and is one for which he has failed to provide a lexicon. So it is that the protagonists of these four sizable Sixties stories—Marcus Weill, Avram Olensky, Leo Hofstedt, and Ann Kampfel—are alive enough to make one believe in them and to make one angry at them, but they never grow quite familiar enough to make one understand them or care about them.

It was, of course, not these Sixties stories but those of the Seventies and Eighties that catapulted Harold Brodkey into a position of eminence enjoyed by few writers in our time. Thirteen in number, these stories occupy more than two-thirds of *Stories in an Almost Classical Mode.* Turning the page after the end of **"The Shooting Range"** and beginning the first of these stories—**"Innocence"**. . . . one crosses a boundary into an utterly different world. Suddenly Brodkey's prose is loose, talky, even offhand. The sense of control that is evident throughout his earlier work has disappeared. Brodkey makes little attempt to disguise the fact that he and his protagonist—here, as in most of these later stories, called Wiley Silenowicz—are essentially the same person. He makes little attempt, indeed, to pretend that what he is giving us is fiction and not autobiography. Toward the beginning of **"Innocence,"** Brodkey unleashes what is, in view of his previous output, a remarkable manifesto:

> I distrust summaries, any kind of gliding through time, any too great a claim that one is in control of what one recounts; I think someone who claims to understand but who is obviously calm, someone who claims to write with emotion recollected in tranquillity, is a fool and a liar. To understand is to tremble. To recollect is to reenter and be riven. An acrobat after spinning through the air in a mockery of flight stands erect on his perch and mockingly takes his bow as if what he is being applauded for was easy for him and cost him nothing, although meanwhile he is covered with sweat and his smile is edged with a relief chilling to think about; he is indulging in a show-business style; he is pretending to be superhuman. I am bored with that and with where it has brought us. I admire the authority of being on one's knees in front of the event.

At the time of its original publication, a reader of **"Innocence"** might not have made much of this passage, but to read it where it appears in *Stories in an Almost Classical Mode* is to recognize it as a veritable declaration of independence on Brodkey's part—independence, that is, from the obligation to transfigure his obsessions into fiction, from the obligation to rein in his *Angst* and to surmount his morbid self-obsession and to edit his rambling ruminations into something well-crafted and coherent. If in his stories of the Sixties he sought an effective means of rendering his authorial vision in fictional terms, in **"Innocence"** he abandons that attempt, essentially renouncing, in his manifesto, the very concept of fiction. His true interest, after all, lies not in imagined lives—or, for that matter, in the real lives of other people—but in the tormented history of his own soul; with **"Innocence"** he announces his unwillingness to persist in pretending otherwise: his refusal to continue hiding behind some fictional characters and feigning curiosity about others, his impatience to serve up reams of vatic, well-nigh stream-of-consciousness prose in place of the taut, polished sentences he'd produced for two decades. Just as another *New Yorker* writer, J.D. Salinger, had turned from the compact, civilized prose of his *Nine Stories* to manic, effusive excursions into the eccentric world of the Glass family, so Brodkey now put his *New Yorker* stories of the Fifties and Sixties behind him and embarked upon a frenzied, fanatical voyage into himself.

To read **"Innocence"** and most of the stories that follow, then—the majority of which have been identified, at one time or another, as sections of *A Party of Animals*—is to find oneself trapped within the extraordinarily arrogant and self-obsessed soul of Harold Brodkey, a.k.a. Wiley Silenowicz, and condemned again and again to relive his agonizing childhood and youth. Brodkey's is, to be sure, a genuinely tragic personal history. He was born in 1930 in Staunton, Illinois, with the name of Aaron Roy Weintraub. His mother died when he was an infant, whereupon his father, an illiterate junk man, allowed him to be adopted by relatives named Doris and Joseph Brodkey; these new parents renamed him Harold Roy Brodkey, and raised him in a St. Louis suburb named University City. When Brodkey was nine, his adoptive father had a stroke or heart attack and became an invalid, finally passing away when the boy was fourteen; when he was thirteen, his adoptive mother came down with cancer, and lingered on for years in pain and bitterness, finally dying while Brodkey was an undergraduate at Harvard. Wiley shares every bit of this personal history with Brodkey, the chief differences being that Wiley's adoptive parents are named not Doris and Joseph but Lila and S.L.

Life with Lila and S.L., as recounted in these stories, is hardly *Life with Father.* In **"A Story in an Almost Classical Mode"** (1973), Brodkey/Wiley describes a typical day of his youth: "I would come home from school to the shadowy house, the curtains drawn and no lights on, or perhaps one, and she [Lila] would be roaming barefooted with wisps of hair sticking out and her robe lopsided and coming open." If he said hello, she would scream: "Is that all you can say? I'm in *pain.* Don't you care? My God, my God, what kind of selfish person are you? I can't stand it." If he said, "Hello, Momma, how is your pain?" she would scream: "You fool, I don't want to think about it! It was all right for a moment! Look what you've done—you've brought it back. . . . *I don't want to be reminded of my pain all the time!* " In either case, she would end up yelling: "Do you think it's easy to die? . . . Do something for me! Put yourself in my place! Help me! Why don't you help me?" One cannot read this sort of thing without feeling profound sympathy for Harold Brodkey and for the boy he was; if even a fraction of his anecdotes about his childhood and youth are true—and taking into account, as well, the distinct possibility that Brodkey is giving us a very one-sided view of things—then it is certainly a great credit to him that he survived and prospered. To criticize him for his continued fixation upon such memories would be not only unfair but heartless.

Yet a critic who is faced with the task of passing judgment on these stories—and of evaluating, as well, the legitimacy of the reputation that they have gained—cannot, alas, do anything other than criticize most of them. For the fact is that Brodkey is so fixated upon the tragic memories of his childhood and youth that he has virtually no sense of proportion about them. In one story after another, he offers up pages of gratuitous detail, straining, it seems, to squeeze every last drop of significance out of every last inane particular. Whole paragraphs are devoted to such matters as his adoptive mother's pet phrases, her opinions on a multitude of subjects, the way she dressed, the way she walked. Though these stories contain a number of affecting—and even emotionally draining—passages, the adversities and tensions and interrelationships and tastes and daily routines of the family in which Brodkey grew up are described so extensively and repeatedly that the ultimate effect of these stories is almost invariably one of numbing monotony. As a rule, not only is there no plot—there's no movement whatsoever. What power the stories do have is primarily not aesthetic but documentary in nature; the young Brodkey's diary, if he'd kept one, would

doubtless be just as powerful, and in precisely the same way. Indeed, to all intents and purposes these stories do amount to a diary, the record of a man talking to himself about himself. (pp. 59-65)

Brodkey is baldly, brutally, shamelessly confessional, speculating about his boyhood state of mind in the tireless, self-absorbed manner of a patient on a psychiatrist's couch: ". . . perhaps I was not a very loving person. Perhaps I was self-concerned and a hypocrite. . . . Perhaps I just wanted to get out with a whole skin." That such narcissistic maunderings fail to get us anywhere doesn't appear to matter to Brodkey; he seems to think that they are in themselves somehow equivalent to self-knowledge. If there is a reason for his obsessive, seemingly pointless accumulation of remembered details, it appears to be that he believes the more details he sets down, the more satisfactory a catharsis he will achieve. As for the rest of us, he seems to be suggesting, we can bloody well sit back and watch. (pp. 65-6)

To Brodkey, nothing seems to mean anything unless it means just about everything. Even the ordinary little tussles between a boy and his sister can't be described on their own terms, but must instead be magnified beyond recognition into something cosmic and Wagnerian. . . . Orgasms, the arrivals of angels, the thrill children feel when they are hoisted in the air by their fathers: when in his later stories Brodkey attempts to describe these phenomena, they all somehow seem to come out to the same thing—a fact which doubtless goes a long way toward accounting for the stories' monotony. (pp. 67-8)

Brodkey's stories of the Seventies and Eighties have developed a truly towering reputation; and yet the most cursory inspection is enough to establish that they contain some of the very worst prose of our time. Brodkey writes not only like a man who is certain that his every fleeting thought and trivial act is fascinating and pregnant with meaning; he writes also like a man who is convinced that his every word, comma, and ampersand is divinely inspired. He mistakes bombast for profundity, lexical flatulence for the divine afflatus. Some of his sentences are so wordy and abstract (not to mention pretentious) that they read like examples of bad writing in a freshman composition textbook. . . . (p. 68)

There is always the possibility, of course, that Brodkey will redeem himself—that he will publish *A Party of Animals* and that it will be everything his champions say it is. But if the stories of boyhood which he has collected in the present book are any indication, readers who have been led to expect a work of genius are in for a major disappointment. One particularly odd phenomenon is that even those commentators who admit their dissatisfaction with Brodkey's work have a way of turning their criticism to his advantage. When James Wolcott writes that the lesson of Brodkey's career is that "genius can be both too much and not enough," he is taking a familiar line. But the truth is in fact quite different: the lesson of Brodkey's career is that one should not be surprised when an egocentric writer who is preoccupied with his own supposed genius—and who is mesmerized by the image of himself as a suffering prodigy—produces hundreds of pages of jagged, vainglorious, even infantile prose. The Brodkey of the Eighties may be bearable in small doses but is insufferable at lengths of thirty and forty pages; one can only imagine what he might be like at novel length. Then again, ***Stories in an Almost Classical Mode*** may be all we will ever see of *A Party of Animals.* (p. 69)

Bruce Bawer, *"A Genius for Publicity,"* in The New Criterion, *Vol. VII, No. 4, December, 1988, pp. 58-69.*

ADAM BEGLEY

Besides offering a preview of coming attractions [for Brodkey's unfinished novel, *A Party of Animals*], *Stories in an Almost Classical Mode,* which includes stories written over a twenty-five-year span, charts the evolution of Brodkey's fiction. His unexceptional subject-matter (the difficult intimate relations of middle and upper-middle-class white Americans, many of them Jews) hasn't changed at all: but his voice, and his whole approach to this material, has changed greatly.

In the stories from the Sixties, as in *First Love and Other Sorrows,* Brodkey marks off a comfortable distance between his readers and his fictional world—a distance maintained, in part, by irony. His characters struggle with emotions too powerful to control: some hope to embrace them, some to avoid them, some merely to understand them. . . .

Brodkey's stories don't have elaborate plots, but the narrative scope and frame of reference of most of the early work from this collection is broad—plenty of action stretched over long periods of time. In **"The Abundant Dreamer"** a prominent director shooting a film in Rome learns of the death of his grandmother, the cold, domineering woman who raised him, with whom he eventually quarreled. He thinks back on their quarrel, on the break-up of his first love affair—a record of past failures. The play of his memory is set against the day's filming (he manipulates his actors with a skill born of hard experience), and the result is a richly textured, complex story that seems to encompass a character's entire life.

The turning-point in Brodkey's fiction comes with the infamous **"Innocence"**, originally published in 1973. This is the first of the many stories narrated by Wiley Silenowicz, who at this stage in his life is a Harvard undergraduate intent on providing for his girlfriend, Orra, her first orgasm. Orra is no virgin: famous for her beauty, she has been the 'trophy' of a number of men before Wiley—but as she realises, belatedly, 'they were doing it wrong.' Some twenty pages of **"Innocence"** are devoted to an exhaustive description of Wiley finally doing it right. Oddly enough, the scene isn't particularly erotic: Wiley's account veers between the clinical dissection of sexual mechanics and self-conscious, inflated prose. . . .

As if to explain the obsessively narrow focus of the story, Wiley proclaims that he distrusts controlled, detached summaries: 'I think someone who claims to understand but who is obviously calm, someone who claims to write with emotion recollected in tranquillity, is a fool and a liar. To understand is to tremble. To recollect is to re-enter and be riven.' Whether or not this defiant manifesto is in fact also Brodkey's, the rest of the stories in the collection (all of which have first-person narrators) are written from Wiley's recommended posture: 'I admire the authority of being on one's knees in front of the event.' Brodkey often adopts the perspective of a very young child, and writes of a small, circumscribed world ruled by fumbling, sometimes terrifying giants. The irony has not entirely vanished, but the reader, drawn to the child's side, no longer enjoys the spectacle at a comfortable remove: in the best of these stories, to recollect is indeed to re-enter and be riven. . . .

Nearly all of Brodkey's recent fiction is a single-minded ex-ploration of one unhappy family. The names change (inexplicably), but the characters remain the same: mother, father, older sister, immigrant nursemaid—and the narrator, Wiley, who also appears as Alan Cohn and Harold 'Buddy' Brodkey. Adopted at two, Wiley/Alan/Buddy goes through several distinct phases: damaged infant, beautiful child, ugly and precocious young boy, ungainly, brooding adolescent. His point of view, therefore, shifts subtly—sometimes in the course of a single story—as he grows older.

Occasionally Brodkey lets him get up off his knees so that he can comment, either on the action or on the process of recollection, in a mature (if not quite tranquil) voice. But his point of view is so personal as to exclude everything but the family itself. A brief attempt at placing the parents in a wider social context (this from **"A Story in an Almost Classical Mode"**) ends in meek retreat: 'They were good-looking small-town people, provincially glamorous, vaudeville-and-movie in-structed, to some extent stunned, liberated ghetto Jews loose and unprotected in the various American decades and milieus in which they lived at one time or another—I don't know that I know enough to say these things about them.' Within the compass of his certain knowledge, Brodkey recognises no such constraint: his narrator observes everything, tells everything.

"Largely an Oral History of my Mother", by far the longest of these stories, displays all the characteristic virtues and flaws of Brodkey's more recent work. An ambitious story, its themes are love and fear and memory and the bond between parent and (adopted) child—in this case Alan Cohn. Leila Cohn adopted him only to lure back her husband, S. L., who had left her; she is too busy worrying about aging gracefully to give Alan a mother's attention. S. L., a weak sentimentalist, wants an adoring son and has no use for the complexities of a flesh-and-blood child. Nonie (whose name never changes) is (as always) the jealous and sadistic sister. When a battery of scientists discover that young Alan has a phenomenal IQ and suggest that he needs special treatment, the Cohns, seeing their chance to rid themselves of a suddenly unwanted child, try unsuccessfully to return him to his natural father, an illiterate junk man. Alan adopts a variety of childish strategies to secure his place, but only in memory, or looking back as narrator, can he control his adoptive family, fix them in a constellation around the bright sun of a child's ego: 'I will run this history, this oral history; I will order it, arrange it.'

Parts of the story are extraordinary, especially where Brodkey concentrates on what the child perceives and feels. Accurate detail is essential to the enterprise: it grounds more daring excursions into the hazy area of an infant's mental processes. Smells, the play of light, voices, and especially textures—these are Brodkey's building-blocks. . . .

But the story is (largely) a portrait of Leila Cohn in her early thirties, a complex, unhappy woman, interesting enough to hold the reader's attention for a while, but not for 90 pages, through an endless boring catalogue of her character traits and typical phrases, sprinkled with unaffixed musings. Leila is inconsistent, and so, doggedly, is Alan's account, which comes to resemble a thick Cubist tangle: 'She's not too honourable. So her feelings for me are amusing, unreliable; she is not without a kind of honour; and so, although I do not trust her, there is some way in which I trust her more than I do anyone else—which is maybe sad, maybe not sad.' Part of the problem is that Brodkey doesn't give Leila anything to do, as though action, incident or sustained dialogue might compromise the purity of the portrait. **"S. L."** (largely an oral history of Wiley's father) succeeds as a portrait of an adult because S. L. is described almost exclusively in terms of his overtures to the two-year-old Wiley as they take a rainy walk to a nearby park. Brodkey has a superb ear for the mindless chatter directed towards a child thought too young to understand, and S. L.'s babble works like a stream of consciousness, an intimate record of half-formed thoughts and associations. But Leila is entombed in her history; she comes to life only on those rare occasions when, as part of a larger action, she is allowed a completed gesture. . . .

"Angel", the last story in the collection, is a daring, in some ways admirable piece of writing—and also a monument to Brodkey's chief failing. Once again we find Wiley on his knees before the event: an angel appears before him (and many others) on an otherwise unremarkable afternoon in 1951. The real subject of Brodkey's typically intense scrutiny is not the Seraph but the workings of Wiley's all too adult mind. His testimony turns into an investigation of the meaning of the apparition and drags on far too long. As for The Angel (who, predictably, *does* nothing), Wiley confesses to being unable to describe it in any except vague, awestruck terms. This admission, which sums up the difficulty of writing with so narrow a focus on matters so abstract, carries with it a warning: 'It is sad to know by how much a written account, removed from physical presence, fails.'

Adam Begley, " 'I Am Going to Make a Scene When Momma Comes Home'," in London Review of Books, *Vol. 11, No. 6, March 16, 1989, p. 22.*

J. California Cooper

19??-

American short story writer and dramatist.

Cooper's short story collections, *A Piece of Mine* (1984), *Homemade Love* (1986), and *Some Soul to Keep* (1987), consist of portraits of rural black females seeking affection and respect from indifferent lovers and husbands. While suffering many disappointments in their lives, these women manage to sustain optimism, courage, and sense of humor. Most of Cooper's stories are monologues in which a woman tells of a crisis in the life of a close friend, relative, or acquaintance through informal language and homespun observations. While faulting Cooper's subject matter as limited and contending that occasional didacticism curtails the dramatic urgency of her writing, reviewers have generally praised her strong characterizations, attention to detail, and authentic rendering of the African American oral tradition. Alice Walker commented: "In its strong folk flavor, Cooper's work reminds us of Langston Hughes and Zora Neale Hurston. Like theirs, her style is deceptively simple and direct, and the vale of tears in which some of her characters reside is never so deep that a rich chuckle at a foolish person's foolishness can not be heard. It is a delight to read her stories."

ALICE WALKER

It is with both pleasure and pride that I introduce the wise and exhilarating stories of Joan California Cooper's *A Piece of Mine.* Pleasure because I know others will now have the opportunity to enjoy Cooper's talent, humor, and insight into character, and pride because her book is the first to be published by Wild Trees Press, started in 1984 by my partner, Robert Allen, and me. (p. vii)

Recently, while conversing with a friend about the importance of stories and storytellers, our talk turned to Hurston's 1937 classic, *Their Eyes Were Watching God.* My friend said she regretted that Pheoby, Janie Crawford's "kissing friend," to whom Janie told the story of her adventurous life, had not had more, herself, to say. My friend was annoyed that Pheoby, after hearing Janie's saga of romance, danger and death, said only that she now intended to make her husband, Sam, take her with him fishing next time he went. This conversation started me thinking of the role of She-Who-Listens-to-Other-Women in literature and life and about what that listening means.

In Cooper's work it is primarily the "Pheobys" of the world who *tell* the story, and it is invariably the story of a best friend, occasionally that of a sister—but still a best friend—and it is the friend, or main character, who remains silent, known only through the observations of the anonymous "Pheoby" whose own name is rarely, if ever, mentioned. Cooper creates vividly the voice of the sister-witness that all of us, if we are lucky, and if we are loved, have in our lives. She is the woman you trust with your story *as it is happening to you;* she is the woman from whom you hide nothing. She is on your side. If you fall, she is the one to take the message to your mother and your children. It will be the right one. (pp. vii-viii)

This bonding between women comes partly through a natural affinity two women may feel for each other, but beyond their mutual liking is a sense of the oppressed role of woman in society (an oppression that also victimizes men who love women) and an awareness of the psychic and physical brutality by which women, all women, are forced to conform. Bearing witness, even in a mode as seemingly innocuous as listening, is a form of resistance to this role. It is even further resistance when the listener finally speaks. For what we eventually come to appreciate in life no less than in art is that the divulging of confidences is easy compared to the keeping of them, and that while the telling of one's own story to anyone, even a trusted friend, requires skill, the retelling of it by another, to still another, requires both skill and craft. And I mean craft, as in craftiness. For the aim of the re-teller (another name for storyteller and artist) is to make a disinterested third party see the originator of the tale in the same light of understanding in which the originator saw her or himself. This requires knowledge not only of the teller and the tale, but of the limitations of the third party, the listener, as well.

If the question is, "Can we trust another woman to tell our story for us?" or, "Is Pheoby as good a storyteller as Janie?" the answer provided by Cooper's stories and by Cooper herself is "Yes."

In its strong folk flavor, Cooper's work reminds us of Langston Hughes and Zora Neale Hurston. Like theirs, her style is deceptively simple and direct, and the vale of tears in which some of her characters reside is never so deep that a rich chuckle at a foolish person's foolishness can not be heard. It is a delight to read her stories, to come upon a saying like "There ain't no sense beatin round the bush with the fellow who planted it," and to know it will be with you perhaps forever.

Recently my partner and I were talking to a woman in Florida (a poet and college teacher) about sexual fantasies and she said that what turned her on was sitting on the porch with her lover, after a real good day, eating fish. No whips, no chains, no funny underwear. No special lighting or perfume or nothing. Just—sittin' on the porch with her lover, after a real good day, eatin' fish. There is a knowledge of that kind of uncontrived intimacy, a longing for it between all kinds of people, in this book. That is one of its pleasures and its strengths. I know that some of you will ask, "Well, could it have been the fish?" But many of you will not. (pp. viii-ix)

> *Alice Walker, in a forward to* A Piece of Mine, *by J. California Cooper, Wild Trees Press, 1984, pp. vii-ix.*

KIRKUS REVIEWS

[J. California Cooper's *A Piece of Mine* contains twelve] stories of man/woman troubles in a black, small-town setting—nearly all of them narrated, in a folksy/anecdotal style, by older-and-wiser black women. Most of the men are abusive, most of the women are victims . . . at least at first. In **"$100 and Nothing!"** an under-appreciated wife takes posthumous revenge on her no-good husband. Other rotten men get their comeuppance in assorted ways: a jealous (but philandering) husband tries to kill his unfaithful wife, accidentally killing his tacky mistress instead; another leech of a man dies by hanging . . . ; middle-aged men are abandoned by their newly liberated spouses. In a few cases the women never get revenge or better men or freedom: **"Loved to Death"** is a mawkish lament for a woman driven to fatal alcoholism by cruel men; **"Sins Leave Scars"** chronicles the life of an abused girl who grows up unable to love. And the didactic, platitudinous strain that runs through almost all of Cooper's stories is especially emphatic in **"Color Me Real"**—about a part-black woman who suffers from the prejudices of both white and black men . . . until she finds true love with a childhood playmate. ("She was neither white nor black now. She was a woman, his woman. It lasted til death did them part, leaving beautiful brown children on the beautiful brown earth.") Still, if there's little variety in this collection, and little shape or depth to Cooper's monologues, there's plenty of energy, personality, and humor—all of which (along with the sponsorship of Alice Walker) should help to attract a black/feminist audience.

> *A review of "A Piece of Mine," in* Kirkus Reviews, *Vol. LII, No. 22, November 15, 1984, p. 1056.*

DIANA HINDS

J. California Cooper possesses the ability to win the reader's trust and establish a rare intimacy as soon as she begins a story. She writes often as the best friend, sometimes the sister, of the woman whose story she tells; and we believe her. Her tone [in *A Piece of Mine*] is relaxed, colloquial; she admits to her own curiosity in her friends' lives, even confessing at one point 'I shouldn't be tellin this secret'. She writes with a robustness that can express both anger, when women (and men) are abused . . . as well as a generous love for those around her, in their successes and their sufferings: 'But I felt so bad for her I loved her. I know whatever was killing her was started by a heavy sad heart, shaking hands, a sore spirit, hot tears, deep heavy sighs, hurtful swallows, and oh you know, all them kinda things.'

She is clear-eyed and takes a sturdy, commonsensical view: 'Anything good is hard to find and if you got any sense you don't want nobody else's', or 'I know you don't need nothin "forever" just so you get close to love sometime'. This, however, sometimes verges on moralising—as in **"Sins Leave Scars,"** when the narrator's summing up seems to be that misfortune comes on those who are beautiful, so 'thank God, ugly as I may be, I am who I am'.

Cooper can be funny. **"The Free and the Caged"** is a charming knockabout between Vilma who thinks she wants to run away and Jacob who wants to keep her. Their playful use of the phrase 'So what?' finally enables them both to live happily ever after, and the phrase runs through the story as a motif binding it all together. An example of how colloquial storytelling can also be beautifully crafted.

> *Diana Hinds, in a review of "A Piece of Mine," in* Books and Bookmen, *No. 364, February, 1986, p. 18.*

KIRKUS REVIEWS

[*Homemade Love* consists of] funny/sad cautionary tales—modern folk-tales, really—about small-town blacks, by the author of 17 plays and a previous collection of short stories, *A Piece of Mine.*

The narrators of these 13 pieces (different narrators, though their voices are nearly interchangeable) speak of the common wisdom of everyday life in glowing terms: "All I know is there ain't nothin like love. Love and happiness! That's a fact, and you can blive that," but many of the characters never get close to realizing that happiness lies (as the title indicates) at home. "You've got to have some kind of good sense. Common sense," cries the narrator of **"The Magic Strength of Need."** She's telling the story of her friend Burlee, an ugly girl who grows up swearing she's going to marry a rich man. She becomes a success in business, but keeps spurning the advances of Winston, the man who really loves her, just because he's not rich. But a one-night stand with a truly wealthy man (who nearly rapes her) brings her back to Winston—and home. Home is also the subject of **"Without Love,"** where Geneva, a proper lady who worked hard all her life for a family and a lovely house, tells the story of her wild friend Totsy, who drank and slept around all *her* life and now has nowhere to go in her old age. There's a kind of Aesopian simplicity here that transcends the basic cliché. And the young narrator of **"Happiness Does Not Come In Colors"** watches an older woman she's admired marry a white man, and she herself decides that a so-called "square" who's been wooing her isn't half-bad.

Cooper is humorous, wise, self-deprecating, and always *expressive,* right down to her cheerful overuse of exclamation points. The ordinariness of her subject matter works well for her; her stories are about simple truths told with a great energy that makes them shine.

A review of "Homemade Love," in Kirkus Reviews, *Vol. LIV, No. 13, July 1, 1986, p. 955.*

PUBLISHERS WEEKLY

The stories in [*Homemade Love*] from the author of *A Piece of Mine* are all about love. About sex and family too, and life when it is lived with wonder and relish. Told in first-person, in a lively, unobtrusive black dialect, these tales, set in both country and city, are lit with wisdom and high-spirited humor. . . . **"Spooks"** is a sexual comedy in which two men enjoy the favors of a recent widow whose "husband" returns to her each night. Cooper is overfond of aphoristic commentary and exclamation marks, and her narrators may have similar-sounding voices, but she tells stories that move and dance, about people who pop off the page to lodge themselves firmly in the reader's affection.

A review of "Homemade Love," in Publishers Weekly, *Vol. 230, No. 2, July 11, 1986, p. 53.*

JANET BOYARIN BLUNDELL

[*Homemade Love*] concerns black women and men, parents and children, as they struggle and love. Told in a folksy first-person voice, these stories nearly all have happy endings. Contrasts abound: In **"Living,"** a middle-aged man leaves his wife and piece of land to try city life, and after three days and four hospitalizations crawls gratefully back home. **"The Watcher"** is the neighborhood snoop, so intent on everyone else's business that she does not see that her own son is on smack. The overabundance of exclamation points and the sameness of style do get a little tiresome, but the stories are saved from preachiness by the wry and somewhat ingenuous tone.

Janet Boyarin Blundell, in a review of "Homemade Love," in School Library Journal, *Vol. 111, No. 13, August, 1986, p. 168.*

JEANETTE WINTERSON

J. California Cooper (so called because someone compared her work to Tennessee Williams's) has produced a collection of stories [*A Piece of Mine*] in which the connecting thread is the ordinary lives and hopes of black women and their men in the small-town southern states of America—people trying to get by, struggling with poverty, jealousy and prejudice; women breaking out and making something of themselves. These are familiar areas to anyone not protected by class or wealth or colour, but Cooper knows how to make her readers think and feel as if they were new; she restores dignity and importance to the everyday.

Cooper's sentences brim with life ("always thought he had a mouth full of 'gimme' and a hand full of 'reach' " and "ain't no sense beatin' round the bush with the fellow who planted

it" are typical). In her hands language refuses to be self-conscious, drab or deliberately shocking. She has great control of her vivid tones and while the characters are all different, the narrative voice running through the book is the same; a continuity that improves each story and gives the whole the depth of a novel.

Jeanette Winterson, "Lightning and Loss," in The Times Literary Supplement, *No. 4351, August 22, 1986, p. 921.*

MICHAEL SCHUMACHER

I want to start out by making a confession: I rarely read short fiction to be entertained, and on those occasions when I do read for enjoyment, I still insist that the experience be memorable in some way. Graham Greene drew a distinction between the books he wrote as serious literature and those he wrote as entertainment, and for my dollar, I'd like to be entertained the Graham Greene way.

I have little patience for fluff. I want to read fiction that cuts and grinds, challenges or blows away the mind, presents a vision I'd never (by dare or design) seen, expounds through a voice speaking almost a different language. . . .

It seems to me that good short fiction is a lot like a magical illusion: the trick appears to be physically impossible, and it is performed with a smoothness and ease that only further astounds the audience; yet, the principles behind the illusion are relatively simple. Both storytellers and magicians are aided by their commitment to knowledge, skill, practice and hard work.

For example, read J. California Cooper's exquisite collection of stories, **Homemade Love.** The 13 stories read as if they had been spoken for the benefit of a tape recorder hidden on the front porch of any home in any small Southern town. These are contemporary folk tales, laced with down-home flavor and Southern dialect. Cooper's dialogue runs as smooth as honey off a wooden spoon. Her stories, however, pack a tremendous power that belies the simplicity in which they are told, a force that must be countered by the storyteller with the proper emotional balance. . . .

Anyone who has had the pleasure to see Cooper read her work knows that her stories are virtual performance pieces, wonderfully paced and written with an ear for the music in colloquial language. The trick—the magic—springs from her ability to write prose that seems as informal as talk in the local diner, yet from which not a word can be cut without upsetting the balance of the story.

Michael Schumacher, in a review of "Homemade Love," in Writer's Digest, *Vol. 67, No. 2, February, 1987, p. 21.*

KIRKUS REVIEWS

As in **Homemade Love,** the message [in **Some Soul to Keep**] is homey and simple: goodness wins out in the end, and love conquers all. The abandoned little orphan girl in **"Sisters of the Rain,"** the blind unwed mother in **"Feeling for Life"** (whose social worker says she is "blind, black, and broke!"), the former maid turned landlady in **"About Love and Money,"** and the middle-aged, deserted wife in **"The Life You Live (May Not Be Your Own)"** all overcome hostile environments, uncaring relations, and personal disabilities because they are hard-working, determined people whose capacity for love turns conditions in their favor. "Sometimes you got to have the rain in order to get to the rainbow," says the narrator of **"Sisters of the Rain,"** who's telling the story of Superior, a quiet girl who works as a maid while her friend Jewel gallivants around with other women's husbands, wears fine clothes, and has fun. Nevertheless, it is Superior who has the last laugh—despite a crippled, cheating husband, four children to raise, and a manic-depressive employer, she is the one who ends up with successful, loving children, a beautiful house filled with things her children buy for her, and lots of love, while Jewel dies embittered and alone.

Cooper is interested in the simple truths of simple people, and the pithy insights, energetic colloquial language, and sheer good nature expressed in these stories carry the reader willingly with her.

A review of "Some Soul to Keep," in Kirkus Reviews, *Vol. LV, No. 16, August 15, 1987, p. 1178.*

PUBLISHERS WEEKLY

The five long stories in [*Some Soul to Keep*] radiate the same energy that readers of Cooper's *A Piece of Mine* and *Homemade Love* will expect. Love between parents and children, between sisters, friends, women and men, are all illuminated in the author's sprightly vernacular prose. . . . Cooper has a sharp eye for detail and her characters are distinct in their circumstances—some had loving families, some cruel, one is blind and abandoned—but all follow the same path to happiness and satisfaction, gamely choosing love over security, revenge or dependence. Ultimately, no matter how admirable and lively these stories are individually, the sameness of their tone and structure (the tales are all retrospective and chronological) defuses the impact of the volume as a whole.

A review of "Some Soul to Keep," in Publishers Weekly, *Vol. 232, No. 11, September 11, 1987, p. 79.*

TERRY McMILLAN

Fiction writers are always told that wherever possible they should show, not tell. But in J. California Cooper's third collection of stories, *Some Soul to Keep,* she rejects this notion entirely. The five tales here are all told in the first person; they give you the feeling that you're sitting on the front porch with the narrator, somewhere in the South; it's hot and humid, she's snapping beans, you're holding the bowl and she's giving you the inside scoop on everybody. You listen, pass her back the bowl and don't know whether to believe her. In their

own gossipy, circuitous, roundabout way, the stories enchant you because they are not stories; they are the truth reconstructed. . . .

"The Life You Live (May Not Be Your Own)" is the most successful of the five tales. Two women, Isobel and Molly, have lived next door to each other for 12 years and never spoken. They discover that Isobel's husband, Tolly, started the lie that they couldn't stand each other. It's not until Tolly dies, and Molly's husband, Gravy, leaves her for a younger woman, that they learn the truth and become real friends. At middle age, the two women bury their heavy past, buy some land by a lake and accept their aloneness. They tackle the fear many women face after the loss of someone they've grown accustomed to, and they make a new life for themselves.

In **"Red-Winged Blackbirds"** a 12-year-old girl, Birdie, is almost raped by the son of her father's employer, "who we all knew was a KKK." Birdie's father confronts her attacker. This is a mistake; a group of white men come to the house, and Birdie's mother orders her to run. She does, but watches her parents burn to death. For 46 years Birdie remains a virgin; she shares an apartment with various women who entertain male visitors; before she even realizes it has turned into a "business." Yearning for a child, she vicariously "adopts" the daughter of a woman who knows nothing about being a mother. While the woman is dying, Birdie stands over her and says, "You lived a lie when you called yourself Mother, you old evil bitch. Now . . . do something right! DIE!" The woman, Birdie reports, "did what I told her." . . .

The major problem with these tales is that each is somewhat didactic. One also has to adjust to Ms. Cooper's no-nonsense style, told in the oral tradition, but with a fablelike quality, often with the moral waiting for you at the end. The narrators can be intrusive, the voice doesn't alter from one story to the next and the excessive use of exclamation points is enough to get on your nerves.

What is present in all of Ms. Cooper's stories is the value, dearness, survival and loss of mothers; the children always have to learn to do without them. Also apparent here are her own beliefs that black people should own their own land and get an education, and that women in particular—no matter what their age—have to learn to deal with being alone. After reading *Some Soul to Keep,* you feel lucky to have entered the worlds of a few poor black women and their families who don't cry or whine about their condition, but are set on figuring out how to get on with their lives.

Terry McMillan, "Life Goes on, and Don't You Forget It!" in The New York Times Book Review, *November 8, 1987, p. 23.*

Richard (Ghormley) Eberhart

1904-

American poet, dramatist, critic, editor, and memoirist.

Eberhart is a highly regarded lyric poet whose verse examines fundamental questions about the nature of existence. His poems typically evoke quotidian images that illuminate conflicts between emotion and intellect, innocence and experience, chaos and order, and the spiritual and physical realms. Attracted to the ideals of such Romantic poets as William Blake and Walt Whitman, Eberhart celebrates the revitalizing effects of nature, affirming humanity's potential for spiritual transcendence while frequently exhibiting a melancholy fascination with death. Eberhart usually composes his verse spontaneously, with minimal revision. This method, which often produces ecstatic language and irregular syntax, has resulted in mixed reviews of Eberhart's poetry. Arthur Mizener observed: "[Eberhart] reads exactly like the poet who writes in the elation of 'inspiration' and then does not revise enough to get rid of inspiration's sloppiness, its clichés, its unconscious borrowings, its superficially imposing and hollow verbal exuberances." Mizener continued: "When Mr. Eberhart succeeds he achieves a kind of direct rightness of feeling toward central experiences which is about the rarest thing there is in contemporary verse; and he does it in language as simple and perfect for its purpose as you could ask."

Eberhart was born into an affluent Minnesota family, and his early years were characterized by academic and social success. At age eighteen, however, Eberhart's idyllic youth was tragically disrupted by the death of his mother, an event often cited as crucial in his development as a poet. In 1926, after receiving a Bachelor of Arts degree from Dartmouth College, Eberhart worked at a variety of odd jobs and wrote poetry in his spare time. During this period, editor Harriet Monroe accepted several of Eberhart's poems for publication in *Poetry: A Magazine of Verse*. In 1927, Eberhart began a journey around the world that eventually brought him to St. John's College, Cambridge, England, where his literary aspirations were encouraged.

Shortly after returning to the United States in 1929, Eberhart published his first book, *A Bravery of Earth* (1930). A single, long poem divided into four sections, this work is a pastoral meditation reminiscent of William Wordsworth's *Prelude* that metaphorically explores the theme of death as the passing of innocence. In this piece, as in much of his work, Eberhart found inspiration in the events of his own life. In his widely anthologized and perhaps best-known poem, "The Groundhog," which was initially collected in *Reading the Spirit* (1936), Eberhart draws upon personal experience to convey a young man's reactions to the decomposing carcass of a groundhog he notices during a series of walks through a field. In the opening lines, the stillness of the corpse is contrasted with the activity of the parasites swarming over it. The poem concludes as the speaker recognizes his own remains in those of the groundhog, as well as civilization's mortality. Eberhart's next volume, *Song and Idea* (1940), contains the famous poem "If I Could Only Live at the Pitch That Is Near Madness." In its depiction of the breach between youth and maturity, this piece embodies a Romantic

yearning toward both natural and spiritual experience. The poem's title alludes to Eberhart's compositional methods, which favor writing through inspired moments that such Romantic poets as Percy Bysshe Shelley and Samuel Taylor Coleridge likened to fits of madness. In his essay "Notes on Poetry," collected in John Ciardi's *Mid-Century American Poets,* Eberhart wrote: "In the rigors of composition it seems to me that the poet's mind is a filament informed with the irrational vitality of energy as it was discovered in our time in quantum mechanics. The quanta may shoot off any way. (You breathe in maybe God.)"

Throughout most of World War II, Eberhart taught aerial gunnery at various United States naval training-camps, and his postwar collections, *Poems, New and Selected* (1945), *Burr Oaks* (1947), and *Selected Poems* (1951), contain many pieces inspired by his wartime experiences. Among the most acclaimed of these is "The Fury of Aerial Bombardment," which grieves over the destruction and cruelty of war and questions the nature of a deity who allows such occurrences. Critics have observed that while much of the literature written by others during this time reflects the influence of existential philosophy, this poem, and much of Eberhart's work, operates within an unequivocally Christian framework.

Following the war, Eberhart worked at his wife's family business in Boston. During these years, he continued publishing poetry and began associating with such writers as Wallace Stevens, T. S. Eliot, William Carlos Williams, and Robert Frost. In 1950, Eberhart co-founded the Poets' Theatre in Cambridge, Massachusetts, where his verse plays *The Visionary Farms* (1952) and *Angels and Devils* (1956) were produced. Another of Eberhart's works published during this time, the poetry volume *Undercliff* (1953), has been viewed as transitional in the evolution of his artistic interests. James Hall remarked: "The unifying quality of [*Undercliff*] is its tentativeness. There are poems in the earlier modes, many poems about the problems of the poet, an effort to use urban settings, and a definite [Wallace] Stevens influence." In his subsequent volumes, *Great Praises* (1957) and *Shifts of Being* (1968), Eberhart continues to move away from strictly lyrical patterns of rhyme and meter toward more experimental types of poetic constructs. The verse collected in *The Quarry: New Poems* (1964) emphasizes Christian elements, and *Fields of Grace* (1972) illustrates Eberhart's abiding concern for both the natural and the spiritual facets of life. "Am I My Brother's Keeper?," one of Eberhart's most accomplished poems from this period, is a sonnet written in sprung-rhythm that exhibits his characteristic impulse to examine opposing sides of a fundamental question and to moralize upon the answer.

In the decades since the 1950s, Eberhart has received a variety of appointments to teach poetry and creative writing at universities throughout the United States. His many honors include the 1966 Pulitzer Prize for *Selected Poems: 1930-1965* (1965) and the National Book Award for *Collected Poems: 1930-1976* (1976). Other collections of his verse include *Collected Poems: 1930-1960* (1960), *Thirty-One Sonnets* (1967), *Ways of Light: Poems, 1972-1980* (1980), and *The Long Reach: New and Uncollected Poems, 1948-1984* (1984). In addition, Eberhart has published *Collected Verse Plays* (1962) and *Of Poetry and Poets* (1979), a volume of memoirs and interviews.

(See also *CLC*, Vols. 3, 11, 19; *Contemporary Authors,* Vols. 1-4, rev. ed.; *Contemporary Authors New Revision Series,* Vol. 2; *Dictionary of Literary Biography,* Vol. 48; and *Concise Dictionary of American Literary Biography, 1941-1968.*)

EDITH H. WALTON

First ventures into verse are apt to take the form of thin volumes of fragile lyrics, derivative and carefully whittled. One is somewhat startled, therefore, by the audacity of Richard Eberhart, whose long poem, *A Bravery of Earth,* is a kind of spiritual autobiography, a chronicle not wholly personal of the progressive states of being through which maturity is achieved. To quote one of Mr. Eberhart's happier phrases, it is a song "from the shocked throat of youth." It records youth's first fierce joy in the mere magic of living, before the "ache of the mind" destroys delighted awareness of sensuous beauty. Then follows disillusionment, perception of the chaos and cruelty of the world. . . . Chilled and driven back to earth and men, he finally comes by deep contact with reality to understand mankind's desire and destiny:

> Youth lies buried and man stands up
> In a bravery of earth.

In many ways this poem is groping, immature and confused. There are long abstract passages in which the concrete quickening image is lacking. There are frequent roughnesses of rhythm which seem quite wanton, considering the pure music of some of the lyric interludes. Nevertheless, Mr. Eberhart is master of a priceless secret. He touches ecstasy more closely and more often than do most of the poets of this century. There is a fresh, rapt quality of emotion in the earlier half of the poem which reminds one of the singing passages in Wordsworth's "Prelude" and particularly of those lines, "Bliss was it in that dawn to be alive." In the last section, moreover—an account of his trip to the Orient on a tramp freighter—there is an unleashed vigor, a crude power, which needs only discipline to direct it into unusually fruitful channels. Confessedly, Mr. Eberhart has buried his adolescence. From now on his work should be worth watching.

> Edith H. Walton, in a review of "A Bravery of Earth," in The New Republic, *Vol. LXIII, No. 814, July 9, 1930, p. 214.*

HARRIET MONROE

[*A Bravery of Earth*] should be read rapidly, as one explores a field large in sweep and contour; with appreciation of the general effect and some attention to rich growths here and there, and with a swift step over rank patches of weeds. Manifestly there is a big scheme here, and good soil for planting; and if the young poet is too careless and hasty in details of his work, we must still recognize the powerful imagination that sweeps him along the large curves of his landscape, and we must pause beside bright areas of flowers.

The scheme is youth's progression toward acceptance and understanding of his world. The first stage is sensory delight:

> Were ever flowers so burning-bright?
> Was ever grass so green and new?
> We pushed our bark along the bank,
> The lake upbuoyed us on the blue.
>
> (pp. 343-44)

Then comes the mind's gradual awakening to suspicion and despair, to the consciousness of change and death:

> Step slowly. Be still, be brave as you walk,
> As you step to the end of all man knows
> And stand on the verge of nothing. Dare
> Here the severest thought that grows
> Lost in the living mind, a flare
> Like lightning cleaving the sullen ground.
> But hold only one thought of earth—
> How this white portion of the ground
> Was sculptured out of the dust of earth
> To be a pillar of marble; flower
> Of the flowering soil; a poise of power
> That could not live, nor linger, long.
>
> (pp. 344-45)

The third phase is youth's effort to climb "the wilderness hill of art," to create

> Poems that are serene and free,
> Pictures calm and passionless,
> Or dissonant music, terrible forms
> That groan in marble . . .

And at last, as the fourth phase, we find the poet, in a dollar-less vagabond voyage around the world, getting acquainted with cowboys, sailors, longshoremen, coolies, and giving us some vivid sketches of these and other very human types.

There is plenty—a too great plenty—of bad writing in this one-hundred-and-twenty-page poem. It would be easy to complain of tiresome or even absurd passages—the "O wild Chaos" one, for example—in which the scheme of the poem over-reaches itself and collapses. But I prefer to credit this young poet, not only with sincerity and enthusiasm in his effort at a genuine interpretation of life, but also with an outreaching imagination, and an authentic talent which, we may hope, will develop a surer technique as time goes on.

Already we find strong figurative phrases—"fisted sea," "spears of music shearing his face." And there are vivid lines:

> He makes a trumpet of his hands,
> He pours his throat on the wind. . . .
> But night smothers his voice
> With the rough gloved hand of silence.
>
> (pp. 345-46)

Or this bit, which epitomizes the aspiration in the poet's mind:

> Man will never forget.
> What is not yet, not yet.
> This dust of stars must sing
> Some tremulous perfect thing
> More patient than the breath
> That blows it into death.

We may hope that Mr. Eberhart will succeed in disciplining his muse without beating the life out of her.

(p. 346)

Harriet Monroe, "Brave Youth," in Poetry, *Vol. XXXVI, No. VI, September, 1930, pp. 343-46.*

R. P. BLACKMUR

Mr. Eberhart is not an easy poet; he is too energetic, which he luckily cannot help, and he fails at critical points to complete his poems on the page either as examples of perception or as examples of craft, which is a failure that, luckily, he can help. It is his predicament, and ours, that his talent has seldom in the particular poem either found a satisfactory medium or discovered its governing limits. We feel him keep sensibility on the stretch in the struggle to get out of the predicament, and we see him in the rashness of poetic desperation resort to the overt modes—to what can be formularised of the rhythms, idioms, and typographical notations—of his chosen ancestors. What matters is that in this struggle and even in this resort a great number of images, insights, and vitalising observations are struck off; rich material of everyman's dilemma is exposed; and the general body of his work has the look, the feel, the twist, of poetry. . . .(pp. 52-3)

Mr. Eberhart is philosophical only in a vague all-round way. He has no system, his intellect does not operate in his verse as a mature instrument, he falls back on but does not really use, except emotionally, some of the conventions of the problem of knowledge. He is, however, concerned with the struggle to actualise his individual experience of good and evil, the true and inadequate, the beautiful and flat. This is the business of a poet, not of a philosopher; and it is a very ambitious sort of poet to be.

This ambition is the seed of the positive side of Mr. Eberhart's talent; it is the drive, or habit, or trope of his imagination, that keeps him at the poet's business of making something which can be appreciated *primarily* apart from its accidental inspiration—that is to say, something as near the actual or the objective as words can come. The whole matter may be managed for our present purpose by recalling T. S. Eliot's comment on Matthew Arnold's remark that "no one can deny that it is of advantage to a poet to deal with a beautiful world." Mr. Eliot thought a beautiful world an advantage to mankind in general. "But," he went on, "the essential advantage for a poet is not to have a beautiful world with which to deal: it is to be able to see beneath both beauty and ugliness; to see the boredom, and the horror, and the glory." Now that is a good deal to be able to see; it involves an inviolate sensibility, requires a visitation of the Muse, and demands a pretty continuous mastery of craft. Yet it is just some such profession that Mr. Eberhart's poetry wants to make; just as it is some formula of *escape* from this profession that your poetry of negative talent hints at, and your pure poetastry even promises to provide.

That Mr. Eberhart comes short is not surprising; and the reason, facilely thought of, is obvious: he so far lacks a theme adequate to his ambition as he sees it, or perhaps it would be more accurate to put it that he has never so felt a theme as to require his consistent utmost in craft. At any rate, the facts are that his poems show unevenness in execution, strain of sensibility amounting sometimes to falsified emotion, inconsistency in the modes of language in single poems, relapse into the banal when the banal is not wanted, and verbal or typographical experiment out of control. Most of these faults are at their worst when the poems present the problem of imitation in acute form; or put the other way round the faults tend to minimise themselves when his sensibility is not deracinated by using other men's modes conspicuously. It is the difference between gross imitation and genuine imitation. Michael Roberts, in his introduction to [*Reading the Spirit*], finds the influence of Blake in **"In a Hard Intellectual Light,"** and we may perhaps distinguish a sort of Yeats-Hopkins influence in **"Cynic Song"**; these are imitation digested and genuine, and it is flattery to point them out. Gross imitation is something else again.

One of the most interesting, and certainly one of the most ambitious poems in the book is **"Four Lakes' Days,"** in which the poet walks four different landscapes in four different weathers. The sense of landscape is fresh and stirring and intense; in its best passages, which are often inseparable from the worst, it revitalises and redirects the sensibility. Here is the best.

> In air-shiver against white wall
> A flower, blue, incandescent
> Does dance on the eye-ball;
> It makes beauty effervescent.
> At Fell Foot (charm) farm. Rob
> This, clover-over-the-dales;
> Smells of cows; good hob-
> Nail, spike my ear! and kissing pails.
>
> Till the twilight folds and all's
> As blue as the bluewashed walls.

The image in the first four lines is creative observation: it adds to the ability of the eye to see; and the last two lines carry besides possible observation their own ominous secret symbolism. As for the other lines (charm) is inexcusable, and together they form a complex trick which defeats its own solution by being unreadable.

On the next page, a little apart, I find these two contrasted passages.

> Not the woundedness of the soul;
> Of desire, the joy. And, soaked all day,
> Sky, earth make each other whole,
> You between, cold mote in the gray.
>
> . . . . . .
>
> So he, I go, we
> Slow to the pelt-rain-drum's rally-
> Of-loneliness in rained-on weather.

Of which the first forces an apposition which may or may not be, however strained, an excellent image, but is at least readable verse, with metrical joints and a common speed; and of which the second is not verse at all, but at most a kind of shrieking notation, from which we gather that at this point some emotion, not present, was needed.

I think all the faults listed above, including the banal (charm), are exemplified in these passages from what I repeat is the most interesting poem in the book. The whole poem is I think an imitation of Hopkins, the good passages genuine imitation because Mr. Eberhart had a subject, and the bad passages gross imitation because Mr. Eberhart lacked his subject. Hopkins' extraordinary and almost physical grasp of landscape in words, came, one supposes, from the struggle of an intensely detailed love to express, not itself, but what was loved; and this in turn came out of Hopkins' convicted faith that God might best be glorified in the knowledge of his created things. I do not know what Mr. Eberhart's motive may be; but I am sure that he does not naturally suffer from the disability of language of which Hopkins complained and which he tried to improve. Mr. Eberhart goes the whole hog, disability and all, of Hopkins on purpose, using as an expressive means to substitute for subject matter what was in Hopkins an expressive obstruction. In Hopkins even at his worst things forced themselves together and struck in the impact an inner light. When Mr. Eberhart imitates Hopkins to get out of his own necessity, his elements hinder each other and fall apart at the centre; only necessity could have driven them together. Gross imitation is its own punishment.

I do not charge Mr. Eberhart with insincerity; it would be nearer home to charge him with insufficient insincerity—for the best of poetry is Jesuits' trade, once the end is in view. It may rather be put that Mr. Eberhart wants to put more into his verse than he has got ready in imaginative form, and that he also employs imaginative devices beyond the scope of the material he actually does have. If he *himself* wrote the passages complained of above, and others in other poems drawn from Hopkins and Eliot, not only would the source of complaint disappear but the poems would be far more objective. That he could do this is demonstrated by what he has done; that he wants to do it is either obvious, or I am wrong entirely about what I feel as his sense of his profession: which for the practitioner must be above all the obligation of craft. (pp. 53-6)

R. P. Blackmur, in a review of "Reading the Spirit,"

in Partisan Review, *Vol. IV, No. 3, February, 1938, pp. 52-6.*

MURIEL RUKEYSER

Sometimes words drop away, and a clean intellectual meaning is left to startle the mind. When Richard Eberhart's poems invite that climax, they are first rate, and this happens often enough to give **Reading the Spirit** distinction. Straightforward and brilliant, his best poems, like **"The Groundhog,"** **"My bones flew apart,"** and **"New Year's Eve,"** stand up for themselves among the best poetic writing produced now.

[Eberhart's] influences are, for the great part, English and seventeenth century, a good part Blake, much Donne, some Herrick. He was printed in *New Signatures* with Auden, Day Lewis, and Spender; there the connection ends. Michael Roberts, who writes the preface to **Reading the Spirit,** does not help the poetry by attributing to it "a ghostly creative beauty," or by praising the nature poems, which are not good; Mr. Eberhart's work has its strength in its lack of "gostliness" or Poetick beauty. It is personal, philosophic, and internal work; it has a clear and enjoying feeling for life that is sensual even at its most disembodied, that has pleasure in flesh even during death, in any life. . . .

Technically he is stimulating, particularly in the mental poems, which have a strong developing line of music; again, he is flat in the nature and love pieces, which push their emotions hard and less originally with some heaviness and false conceits. But all the high places are excellent, and his level is rising (cf. the poems, written since this book, in *New Letters in America*); moments like these introduce actual poetry:

> My bones flew apart. They flew to the sky,
> And as great knockers knocked the air.
> The bone God said, Come in.
> My soul flew in small and dry . . .

or the admired ending of **"Caravan of Silence,"** sounding a long music:

> . . .The oldness
> Of sun and man he knew, earth's
> Coldness and goldenness.
> Night aged and pearled
> To a dawn; yet the philosopher
> Turned the globed world
> Colder and goldener.

Or [**"The Groundhog"**], the "anthology piece" of the book, sustained and fine, a striking poem of the steps of death. Here the groundhog is seen seething and maggotty, and later, a dry body, and later, down to the bone, and three years later, with poem and image whipped up to the top, there is no sign of the animal left on the ground, and the poem ends, in Richard Eberhart's full promise and height, recommending his present and future work. . . .

Muriel Rukeyser, "Straight Through to Life," in New York Herald Tribune Books, *February 27, 1938, p. 17.*

W. H. MELLERS

[There are] poems in the manner of the Blakean squib [in **Song and Idea**] (cf. **"I went to see Irving Babbitt"**); there are many passages such as

And from this I saw grow
Although my sense shook with fear
A crystal Tear
Whose centre is spiritual love,

complete with capitalized abstractions; and there are several poems in Blake's simple 'visionary' stanza. This overt statement of the Blakean tenet—

If I could only live at a pitch that is near madness
When everything is as it was in my childhood
Violent, vivid, and of infinite possibility;
That the sun and moon broke over my head . . .

I gave the moral answer and I died
And into a realm of complexity came
Where nothing is possible but necessity
And the truth wailing there like a red babe,

is continually reinforced by phrases such as 'Then I arose in holy love like a child'; and we all know that Blake is a very dangerous model. But it would be hasty to assume that there is, for Mr. Eberhart's interest in Blake, inadequate justification, since although he has not the visionary gleam, and probably could not have it (for 'Where have gone the grace and stately carriage, The thick perfections of a kind society . . . What can naked man do? What poems? Against disastrous wars of actuality?'), there is nonetheless a quality in his verse that may properly be called terrifying. It is not the terrifyingness of great poetry because it is too exclusively personal: but it is fiercely and passionately sincere and it gives to his verse its distinctive movement.

To say that an extreme, even excessive, sensitiveness, to nervous experience is the distinguishing mark of Mr. Eberhart's verse may not seem to be saying much: yet it does, I think, serve to differentiate him from the other poets (with the possible exception of the Auden of *Paid on Both Sides*) who were his contemporaries, for, apart from a certain dim relation to the sensuous aspects of the seventeenth century that Eliot probably orientated, his verse is, in its personal manner, singularly free of the representative contemporary influences.

The full of joy do not know; they need not
Know. Nothing is reconciled.
They flash the light of Heaven indeed.
Let them have it, let them have it, it is mild.

Those who suffer see the truth; it has
Murderous edges. They never avert
The gaze of calculation one degree,
But they are hurt, they are hurt, they are hurt.

Like the verses about the innocent eye of the child already quoted, this is perhaps too explicit, even the incantatory repetition, the painful catch-in-the-breath, of the last line: but something comparable with this anguish seems to me to be the impetus behind all Mr. Eberhart's best verse. In all of it there is a quality of suffering—nerves exposed and jangling, agitated by contact with the outside world—which is communicated in the queer nervous rhythms and in the characteristic verbal juxtapositions. . . . Similarly the 'surprising' verbal juxtapositions ('under the copeless skyscrapers just and queer,' 'the dark threat of being born,' 'The pupil in the eye is tight As a sprout in the air') have little in common with seventeenth century wit and nothing at all with early Eliot where the intention is to administer an audacious intellectual jolt: the effect here is never cerebral but almost physical, a sensuous quiver, a trembling in the nervous response.

This, then, is the essence of Mr. Eberhart's gift, and it is a remarkable one. But what made his early poems peculiarly interesting was that he possessed in addition what very few contemporary poets have—the faculty of using these vivid impressions to define an attitude, to create a poem as a whole. In a rather patent fashion one can see this in **"The Groundhog"** where some characteristic reflections on death and decay are woven into more complex and far-reaching emotions; more subtly it is manifested in the comparatively balanced movement—a tranquillity as it were poised over the most agile and alert conflict of feelings—in poems like **"Caravan of Silence"** and **"Necessity"**. It is in this respect of 'wholeness' that Mr. Eberhart's recent poems seem to me deficient. The delicate appreciation of the moment of sensuous response remains: but the ability—or perhaps the desire—to relate these moments to the complexity of adult interests is less marked. Significantly, it is the least pretentious poems in [*Song and Idea*] that are the most successful; and these poems repeatedly return to the recollection of childhood experience. The little poem called **"The Child"** supports the contention that the terrifying quality we have noticed in all Mr. Eberhart's verse has now become specifically associated with the child's fear and apprehension of the adult universe. . . . The incompleteness and fragmentariness of sensuous experience—the experience of the child—would seem, now, apart from one or two partial exceptions such as **"The Scarf of June"** and **"Two Loves"**, to be an end, rather than a means.

Certainly in the more pretentious of the recent poems we find that Mr. Eberhart is inclined to use Blake as an artificial prop to his wavering grasp of his experience, whereas in **"Maze"** or **"Request for Offering"** his distinction could be defined rather in terms of his difference from Blake than in terms of his likeness to him: and certainly we find that that obsession with decay (the eyeballs and the skeleton) which is the inevitable corollary of his sensuous impressionism, his intimate tactile seismography, is prone, when he writes from a less precise pressure, to degenerate into a species of lurid emotional melodrama ('my mind beats lively as a disease'). 'I must think; I have felt overmuch' remarks Mr. Eberhart in one poem; yet now it seems more and more that as soon as he tries to go beyond the 'fragment' of experience, to create some pattern out of the fragments, nothing much happens except that the fragments themselves lose precision and contour, dissipate into a series of vague gestures, into (say) the Whitmanesque urge

I flung myself down on the earth,
Full length on the great earth, full length,
I wept out the great load of human love

or into a rather literary preoccupation with the seventeenth-century death-sense—

I try something new, I break my skull,
Death, I try to get into you.

"Realm" and **"The Humanist"** might be said to suggest a comparison with the disorganization that afflicted such poems of Blake as "The Mental Traveller" and "The Crystal Cabinet", were it not that the dissipation of Mr. Eberhart's poetic energy does not necessarily tend to obscurity.

Not all the longer and later poems are without interest. Even in **"The Soul Longs to Return Whence it Came"** there are, at the beginning, passages of the attractive personal movement, and the odd poem **"Orchard"**, though it isn't altogether satisfactory because of a tendency to statement where the realization should be most sharp, gives tentative indication of a new manner—soberer, less nervous, but still sensuously rich. In [*Song and Idea*] the signs of a genuine talent take on the whole a less mature form, but they are still unmistakable; Mr. Eberhart remains one of the few poets whose future work may still be worth reading. (pp. 293-97)

W. H. Mellers, "Cats in Air-Pumps (or Poets in 1940)," in Scrutiny, Vol. IX, No. 3, December, 1940, pp. 289-300.

JOHN CROWE RANSOM

I think Dick Eberhart's best lyrics are quite important; they are unusual because really and positively poetic. The man's fundamental attitudes and strategies are right. There is no defeated mawkishness about him, and no self-conscious melancholy; these infections are for other younger poets. There is no sentimentality, either; and by sentimentality I mean the unthinking affirmation, the stereotype of a fixation that no longer looks at its objects. Eberhart's poems are full of tangible brilliant things and furious thinking. It is impossible to say of him that he "captures an emotion" or "communicates a feeling-tone," which is a disparaging thing to say of any poet, but sometimes is all that can be said. Extreme energy is his mark. Sometimes it is riotous and tasteless, but the man has, every time, a comprehensive poetic experience. The poems pour out easily but they are not relaxed, and they may be difficult but they are not labored. (pp. 68-9)

I will quote one fine poem, [**"Experience Evoked"** from *Song and Idea*], taking the liberty of spacing between the stanzas as I have seen the spacing done in his own manuscript (if I am not mistaken), though his printer now runs the stanzas together:

> Now come to me all men
> With savagery and innocence,
> With axe to chop the fir tree,
> Or seed, small, for the immense
> Sewing of earth with old Rose.
>
> Now come all men, arrayed
> With the colours of the garden
> Around them where they stayed
> Till bone began to harden
> Under the thinning of the nose.
>
> Come all men, unto whom
> Wind was a snarling wire whip
> In the contusions of a doom
> And with red flecks on their lip
> They leaped up, danced, grew tall.
>
> Come all, the babe bound
> In terror and panic cry;
> Or an old man found
> With a skylark in his eye.
> Come, harsh shroud over all.

We may register some little and local resistances against this, but on the whole would embrace it as true poetry. The final *harsh shroud over all* is logically odd—the characters are summoned out of memory, and it is at the end, not at the beginning, that the general qualification is conceded: they are all gone now, under the ground. This is astringent, anti-romantic, but in its order arbitrary and surprising. It is not a conclusion so much as a parenthesis placed at the end. The poet does not bother to turn his corners comfortably.

Of course I may not be construing this poem according to the author's intention. But against that possibility I should suggest that any reader having complete good will is going to construe the poem as best he can, and then to feel a little aggrieved if his poet, by intending what is not actually said, has let him down.

There are many poems of interest, and against some of them, and perhaps every one at some point, I have to make a painful reservation. The poetic quality is there, but the workmanship is rude. It shows in the meters, which have to struggle for existence; and in the broken and patchy logic of discourse. The poetry is not fine technically.

The climax of discontinuity is reached in a poem which is obscure but beautiful, if that collocation is possible, to the point of beguiling me a great deal:

> In prisons of established craze
> Hear the sane tread without noise
> Whose songs no iron walls will raze
> Though hearts are as of girls and boys.
>
> By the waters burning clear
> Where sheds of men are only seen,
> Accept eloquent time, and revere
> The silence of the great machine.
>
> On the sweet earth green and moist
> When vainglorious cities magnify,
> The senseless dissonance will foist
> As witless on the shining sky.
>
> There is some stealth in rhythm yet
> Albeit an even breath is not.
> In the mind is a gauge set,
> Lest the blood spill, and blot.

Responding to this verse one reader will say, Blake, and another will say, Stevens, while a third will say it is just nonsense verse. But so many of the images and ideas make a connection with categories in my own mind that I am reluctant to give it up as does this third reader. Roughly, but substantially, I "make it mean" something for me, and other readers will do the same.

John Crowe Ransom, "Lyrics Important, Sometimes Rude," in Furioso, Vol. 1, No. 4, Summer, 1941, pp. 68-70.

DAVID DAICHES

Mr. Eberhart is a sensitive and accomplished poet whose impressions and intuitions tend to be a little too subtle for his technique. Reading his poems one never has any doubt that here is a poet at work; but one does sometimes note a certain disparity between language and insight, as though he had not quite beaten out his words and rhythms to the fineness of his perceptions. It is not that he fails to mould the stanza to the content—his poetry is notable for flexibility of technique—but rather that he shapes his lines and stanzas too readily and superficially to the changing turns of thought so that an immediate effect is gained only at the expense of a certain lack of reverberation. The stanza as a stanza, as a rising and falling pattern of words, has no echoing enrichment to add to the words as words with each reading. Consider for example:

> They drop with periodic regularity
> From the summit of their goodness, young, to
>   death.

They leap to the blue
And it is out of the blue
Comes Death the Enemy.

The effect of slinging "young" between "goodness" and "death" does not illuminate the relation between these three concepts to the degree that one thinks it does at first reading, nor does the repetition of "blue" at the end of the third and fourth lines enrich the stanza's meaning. Yet, one feels, there is a subtlety here beyond what the technique is organized to convey. In the second stanza there is a switch from the plural to the singular:

Some young flier
When he least expected it slips,
Before he ever got into combat, in a training plane,
Before a backdrop of high-puffed, idealistic clouds,
Towering, still, complete, high, like all his dreams,
In luminous heat of sweaty Pensacola.

This is in many ways a fine stanza, yet the change of point of view in it is not as eloquent as the superficial reader thinks, while the use of the phrase "like all his dreams" deprives the "*idealistic* clouds" of the previous line of their infinitely subtle implications by making the point too specific—too opaque, as it were.

In true Eberhart fashion, the poem then swings from the fact to the commentary:

Closeness to machines going fast gives man brazen-
   ness,
Lags him back to brute-heart: who should be
Full of moral imperatives does what he is told,
Is cheerful, counts not the cost, gets in his licks.

This stanza (which is modeled on early Auden) is wholly different in style and tempo from either of the preceding stanzas. Here the change is justified, ideologically; but again the reader feels the insight is more delicate than the medium.

This is perhaps pushing a point too far. Yet the point is important, for it is central in Eberhart's poetry, explaining both his faults and his virtues. Sometimes he will start with a fine germinal observation and, because he intends to grow things from it later on in the poem, leaves it too solidly stated in its original expression, so that if it is printed as prose (without changing a word) it is seen simply as good prose: "Anti-aircraft seen from a certain distance on a steely blue night, say a mile away, flowers on the air absolutely dream-like; the vision has no relation to the reality." (The first stanza of **"Dam Neck, Virginia".**) What we have here, once again, is a technique less sensitive than what it is endeavoring to express.

But in several poems in [*Poems, New and Selected*] Eberhart has succeeded in aërating his language, in breaking down something of its oversolidity, so that each line and stanza responds more delicately to the idea which prompted it and which in turn is prompted by it. **"Triptych"**, an interesting and in many ways a striking piece, contains a passage (on the decomposition of the groundhog) which is a re-writing of an earlier poem, **"The Groundhog"**, printed later in this volume. The passage in **"Triptych"** shows a remarkable aëration of technique when compared with the earlier version, together with a more perfect objectivity which greatly adds to the effect:

          . . .I once saw a
Groundhog stick his fat corpse

Into the very light of July.
It blistered, broke loose, and you've never seen
So merry a sight. Soon he was aswim
In his own oils, hot as a lecher,
And then he was dancing with maggots. . . .

                                        (pp. 92-4)

There is a mature Jacobean technique here which shows what Eberhart can do if he tries. And the reader must look, too, at **"Retrospective Forelook"**, a wholly admirable poem except for the horrid first line.

In the manufacture of malt whisky the barley is soaked, then dried, and then the malt thus obtained is brewed into a beer-like liquid. This liquid, when distilled, produces the raw whisky. It has to lie mellowing a long time in sherry casks. Mr. Eberhart is always a good brewer but he does not always bother with the further processes of distilling and maturing—or rather, he often matures without distilling. Let him distil his poetry more often: the finer, subtler, stronger and more profound flavor of pot-stilled malt whisky (now almost unobtainable, alas) is more exciting to the discriminating palate than the pleasantest of beers. A good brewer makes good prose; true poetry comes from the distillery. There is a place for both. (pp. 94-5)

David Daiches, "Towards the Proper Spirit," in Poetry, *Vol. LXVI, No. 11, May, 1945, pp. 92-5.*

ARTHUR MIZENER

[Mr. Eberhart's] trouble has always been that his faults are very obvious and easy to feel superior to, because they are as unmodish as it is possible for faults to be; they are Victorian faults. That Mr. Eberhart also has the Victorian virtues is easy to overlook when we find him, for instance, earnestly urging us to consider that maybe God's existence is authenticated by elation. "The heart stood up and answered, 'I have felt,' " says [Tennyson's] *In Memoriam* with all that devastating lack of finality so characteristic of Victorian assertions on this subject. Mr. Eberhart's way of putting it [in his collection **Burr Oaks**] is:

But comes elation unto me
And blows God all through me

—not a very good way, certainly, with its Cecil de Mille inversion and its orotund "unto" (alas for Doctor Johnson who pronounced this word obsolete in the eighteenth century). Mr. Eberhart can be equally embarrassing to wellwishers about

The draft and depth of the poet's impossible desire
To fight for the truth, whether in glory or sordor,

about the dessication of scholars, the wickedness of restraining inspired poets, the philosophy in the eye of the cow, and how "though all turn to worm and dust, to death and ashes" (no less), spring returns. And he can be very uncertain about style; he reads exactly like the poet who writes in the elation of "inspiration" and then does not revise enough to get rid of inspiration's sloppiness, its clichés, its unconscious borrowings, its superficially imposing and hollow verbal exuberances. It is not easy to enjoy a description of the moment of mystery which says:

And it is to be non-mooned to morality
As it is to be bubbly-renunciatory,

or to believe in the resurrection of constructive appetance."

Yet these are mostly the faults of a remarkable honesty. It would obviously be easy for Mr. Eberhart to be smart about them: writers come a dime a dozen that way. It is not so easy to be honest and genuine; you are not so likely to see when what you honestly feel is second-hand, or horribly commonplace, or awkward, when your whole mind is on getting the thing just as it is. When Mr. Eberhart succeeds he achieves a kind of direct rightness of feeling toward central experiences which is about the rarest thing there is in contemporary verse; and he does it in a language as simple and perfect for its purpose as you could ask:

> Anti-aircraft seen from a certain distance
> On a steely blue night say a mile away
> Flowers on the air absolutely dream-like,
> The vision has no relation to the reality.

With the perfect, colloquial simplicity of its diction and rhythm, this gets the full force of the discontinuity Mr. Eberhart, like all of us, has felt, and really localizes it in the particular occasion. If he has to work up to this by telling us (because you'd never guess) that "the men are firing tracers, practicing at night," and conclude, with his almost comic earnestness, that he has been talking about "the beautiful disrelation of the spiritual," nevertheless, he does get there. This kind of writing brings him finally (I quote the whole poem) to:

> When I can hold a stone within my hand
> And feel time make it sand and soil, and see
> The roots of living things grow in this land,
> Pushing between my fingers flower and tree,
> Then I shall be as wise as death,
> For death has done this and he will
> Do this to me, and blow his breath
> To fire my clay, when I am still.

A writer does not earn that kind of simplicity, as Mr. Eberhart has obviously earned it, easily.

Once you have taken account of passages of this kind and begun to feel how genuine Mr. Eberhart's verse is, you may think that, for all the view's inadequacy, and for all the faults and foolishnesses it lets him in for, perhaps he is right that

> The force as odd as any
> After all is said
> Has more sense in it
> Than hounding the dead.
> And the bond of the obvious
> Blood in beauty
> Controls more, is not moral,
> Simply is.

(pp. 226-28)

Arthur Mizener, "The Earnest Victorian," in Poetry, Vol. LXXIII, No. 4, January, 1949, pp. 226-28.

HOWARD NEMEROV

Richard Eberhart too [along with Randall Jarrell] works toward freedom and increased possibility, but by another means; in their metrical practice, for example, he and Mr. Jarrell compare somewhat as do Yeats and Eliot, the one roughening and straining the formality of verse until he works with a great freedom that is yet in technical relations to the quatrain or other stanza, the other beginning in the ut-

most freedom and developing dramatically his own rituals of restraint. Mr. Eberhart's cadences, his combinations of sound, often wrenched and twisted to a deliberate awkwardness, remain attached to the artificial part of poetry by the minimum means, and produce from the old forms a special and new energy.

In this strict selection from his work [*Selected Poems*] I admire most a number of brief lyrics; the longer, discursive poetry seems to me very often diffuse and turgid, operating either by too many particulars too little imagined (**"The Brotherhood of Man"**) or by a rhetoric too enlarged for the feeling (**"The Soul Longs to Return Whence it Came"**). But there remains such a great deal that is fine, **"New Hampshire, February," "The Moment of Vision," "Four Lakes' Days," "Dissertation by Wax Light," "This Fevers Me."** And there is, of course, **"The Groundhog"** . . . , but the celebrated beauty of that poem ought not to obscure for us one that is in my opinion far better, the one called **"In a Hard Intellectual Light."** . . . [This] is very nearly absolute, this poem, and the only thing proper to be said is that you must read it.

Altogether [Eberhart's *Selected Poems*] has been a source of great pleasure to me; a difficult, unfashionable poetry which is above all things alive and intelligent. (p. 328)

Howard Nemerov, "The Careful Poets and the Reckless Ones," in The Sewanee Review, Vol. LX, No. 2, Spring, 1952, pp. 318-29.

JAMES HALL

The service one reader can hope to perform for another with a poet at Eberhart's stage is to sort out the consistent direction. The flexibility which gets together the contradictions and accommodations of his moral world is hard to define, but in the best poems up to 1950—half the work in *Selected Poems,* six or eight poems not included there—he has four analyzables working together: a sociable world of common experience, almost fixed states of mind represented by the abstract language; "moments of vision", when the fixed states shift a little and are seen in images opened up by some revealing experience; a strong strain of pastoral, often hovering just beyond the poem itself; and a warm-and-ironic feeling for the cliché.

The abstract language and the *in medias res* beginnings assume a sociability of spiritual contradiction. All self-conscious people, at least, will understand and need no long evocation of the common moods if the "moment of vision" has given this mood a genuine perspective. Eberhart undoubtedly has an instinctive preference for the abstracting over the evocative word, even for the Latinate sounds. But the effect is not, as it ought theoretically to be, of experience held at a distance, but of experience immediately and naturally translated into its perspectives. The abstractions name his preoccupations: rational, spiritual, intimacy, action, human, science, passion, eternity, effulgence, essence, ethereal, mathema, involvement, evanescence, the ineffable. But his talent is to include everyone generously in the state of mind being represented. There is no need, this language says, "to make you see, to make you feel" because everyone understands. The sense of ease which is one of Eberhart's main accomplishments comes from a confidence in the commonness of the states of mind he deals with and in the usefulness of names in representing them for conversational purposes. Further images will be necessary, but the poetry is in the wrestling with the emotion, not in identifying it.

But while this area of common experience is being established, the revealing personal tension is between the insight, often intense, with which the poem habitually begins and the near-cliché to which this insight has to be reconciled. Eberhart is a poet of moments of vision, but not of Rimbaud "illuminations." He is the most moral of poets—tempted by both exaltation and the desire for rest, but regularly accommodating these moments to the life of the platitude, which half-ironically, half-seriously jogs the spiritual elbow. (pp. 315-16)

The poems begin with intensely perceived facts, but move quickly toward understanding, acceptance, irony. Sometimes they all but rush toward the recognition of limitation and the human condition. At other times the recognition becomes an ironic but serious polemic against perfectionism—against Auden's in **"I Walked Over the Grave of Henry James"** and Yeats' in

> I walked out to the graveyard to see the dead
> The iron gates were locked, I couldn't get in,
> A golden pheasant on the dark fir boughs
> Looked with fearful method at the sunset,
> Said I, Sir bird, wink no more at me
> I have had enough of my dark eye-smarting,
> I cannot adore you, nor do I praise you,
> But assign you to the rafters of Montaigne.
> Who talks with the Absolute salutes a Shadow,
> Who seeks himself shall lose himself;
> And the golden pheasants are no help
> And action must be learned from love of man.

Poetry of this sort runs a risk, of course, but because there is always a struggle, a continuing argument with the self, Eberhart does not, like Frost in his lesser work, set up ready victories for the ordinary over a turbulent world. The cracker barrel does not vanquish a human world so diminished as to have little meaning in the contest. It would be easy to compile Eberhart's Book of Useful Quotations about action, faith, love, ordinariness; but the difference between these lines in context and out is the difference between plain moralizing and dramatic moralizing. The poems do not develop from tension to answer, but show an interruptible argument never won or lost, taken at the moment which focuses it.

The moments of insight, abstractions, and platitudes are anchored to a varied pastoralism which is usually suggested in the best poems, but developed elsewhere. Eberhart's first volume, the long poem *A Bravery of Earth,* has an extended celebration of vitality and harmony—the sensitivity and energy of youth reflected in a responsive outer world of apple orchards, sunlight, and fields. The title conveys the slight defiance of experience, but in the best parts of the poem the spirit, though highly conscious of its separateness, derives strength from a vital and sympathetic natural world. These images occur throughout Eberhart's work, but so do poems using nature as symbol of death and return. **"Rumination"** has an almost Tennysonian pantheism:

> When I can hold a stone within my hand
> And feel time make it sand and soil, and see
> The roots of living things grow in this land,
> Pushing between my fingers flower and tree,
> Then I shall be as wise as death,
> For death has done this and he will
> Do this to me, and blow his breath
> To fire my clay, when I am still.

(pp. 316-17)

In his best poems Eberhart's use of nature is equivocal, allegorical, egocentric. Nature becomes the place where one ought to feel at home. Some of the makings of a world of vitality, ease, and harmony—the love-and-death world—are there. A genial sympathetic outer nature ought to be in tune with the friendly abstractions. The naive moralities ought to fit in with and take care of their subjects—human limitation, the importance of loving the human world. But Eberhart at his most individual is the complex man arguing for these moralities and sympathies, involved strongly in wanting them and of course having difficulty with them. The poetry is in the combining of these tensions.

By the time he published *Selected Poems* Eberhart had established an individuality which fitted in with the times, but had its own unmistakableness. He had built up a large enough body of work that, even with the discards which a succeeding decade always makes, he could be reasonably sure of an important place. In the last four years he has been facing the problem of suiting his growth to new forms and techniques.

The greatest departure is his experiment with poetic drama. The best of the plays, *The Visionary Farms,* has wit, verve, lightness, and a dramatic opposition close enough to the theme of the poetry to fit his tone. In the poetry, significantly, there are almost no characters, and the dramatic form gives personality to the contradictions which he has hitherto dealt with in other ways. An aggressive and trusted employee who has helped to build the manufacturing company on which a small midwestern town depends is suddenly discovered to be an embezzler. The discovery sends him to jail—which he promptly organizes—and ruins the family of the company's general manager. The passive sympathy of the play is with the family who have slowly achieved all they have planned for and live in an Eberhart apple orchard world of family unity. But the active interest—and all the playfulness—is in "Hurricane" Ransom, whose urge for activity and promotion leads him to his hobby of the visionary, but real, model chicken farm. The action plays between Ransom's essential innocence of motive—he is following his bent—and the disastrous consequences to others.

The character of Ransom is done with lightness and imagination. He bounces with picaresque humor and poise through a caricatured, but recognizable, world of choices. The main weakness of the play is in the pastoralism which has been partly responsible for the poetic success. When Eberhart tries to show in the family scenes a realistic picture of harmony-in-dissonance, the characters fail to emerge from their peaceful background. What reality they have is so universal and quiet that the tableaux showing their lives do not give a real dramatic opposition to Hurricane's urgencies. But in spite of this pseudo-antagonism—it is not easy, after all, to make peaceful achievement measure up to anxiety—the dramatic form gives Eberhart a chance to work openly on the conflict which is in much of the poetry.

In *Undercliff* . . . the problems of the established poet appear in their multiplicity. The unifying quality of the book is its tentativeness. There are poems in the earlier modes, many poems about the problems of the poet, an effort to use urban settings, and a definite Stevens influence. The least successful poems are those which turn back on themselves to create a moral justification of the imagination. Eberhart is less successful, understandably, in glorifying inspiration than he has been in trying to resolve his dilemma of aspiration and limitation. Also, the poems which test an idea in his earlier manner do not seem to engage his lyric interest in the same way. He sees more frequently a plural rather than a dual world, and seems searching for ways of expressing the complexity of his perception. In this situation, again understandably though surprisingly, the Stevens influence leads to the best results: **"The Verbalist of Summer"** is one of Eberhart's best poems.

The difference from Stevens is more than the difference between color and grayness, tropic seas and plain ocean. Both Eberhart and Stevens are businessmen and intellectuals, but Eberhart is more of both as a poet. Each asks unanswerable questions which resist even formulation. But Stevens asks his question and "searches for music of the paladins/ To make oblation fit." He looks for an exotic answer from a vacation world of Havana or Key West. But when Eberhart asks questions by the sea he wants an answer that can be entered in the books. (He abandoned exoticism after his first volume.) The questions will be equivocal and shifting, but they will be relevant by all the sociable checks—experience, science, Berkeleyan philosophy, the prejudices of the age. Eberhart's language tries to see better than everybody what everybody sees. (pp. 318-20)

So the paradox of Eberhart's development is that its best possibilities lie in what might be, but is not, an imitative direction. He has always had the ability to learn from other poets and use them to increase his range. The poems in *Undercliff* which have no immediate connection with Stevens' reflect a world that has much in common with Stevens'—complex, certain and uncertain at once, self-aware. If, on one side, Eberhart has tried to deal with this world by overpositive assertion about the power of the imagination, on another he has dealt directly with its complexities in a way that he had not been able to do before. For the simpler conflicts which made the earlier poetry, the plays may now offer the best opportunity. Drama provides a framework for the antagonists, and the weakness of the Fahnstock family is probably not an insoluble difficulty. (pp. 320-21).

> *James Hall, "Richard Eberhart: The Sociable Naturalist," in* The Western Review, *Vol. 18, Summer, 1954, pp. 315-21.*

REUEL DENNEY

The attractions of the dramatically brusque in diction began to influence modern English and American poetry very strongly after Browning. He liked the prosy, the antimellifluous and the play-by-ear idiomatic. Some of that affection for the bang as opposed to the murmur was picked up in Imagism and associated movements. There, pictorial reference in verse was dramatized by showing unashamedly in certain lines the musical price that had to be paid for visual and intellectual integrity of communication. In Richard Eberhart's poetry, especially in the "suppressed dialogue" quality of the early work, we hear a controlled development of this style, development along lines of a different sort from the lines followed, in a related manner, by Pound, Bottrall, and Empson. This tone is evident, implicitly and explicitly, in Eberhart's portrait of the poetic artist in **"Letter One"**, from *Undercliff:*

> The artist is his own butcher or baker.
> Actually, he is a kept lighthouse keeper
> Who will offer his light to the tall voyeur . . .

Eberhart's poetry seems to me to be best appreciated as a combination of this quasi-dramatic brusqueness with still another tradition. This is the tradition about material and manner called the "metaphysical," meaning by this not only the seventeenth-century forebears, but those who have learned from them in the twentieth century. Developing this line, Eberhart's lyric gives us almost always the diction of a single speaker who is arguing a relation between appearance and reality. The language differs from the seventeenth-century poet chiefly in its determination to avoid the elaborate or extended figure of speech, or conceit. During his career, Eberhart has developed through, and out of, some aspects of this influence partly through a progression of subjects—from an early concern with mortality, through an intermediate concern with the problem of human knowledge, into a later concern with God and nature. This statement is an oversimplification, of course. He has developed through and out of the metaphysical even more noticeably in terms of form. From that point of view his direction has been from the sharply lyrical toward the more free-handed narrative and satiric forms and from them, by a leap, into verse dialogue and drama.

In its earlier stages, his work seemed in some sense to be a voice of pietist dissent blended with worldliness. If that seems a constricting definition, it may help to suggest that the same description could be applied to aspects of the work of Emerson. Like Emerson, Eberhart shows that he has learned from the conventions of language and feeling we associate with poets like Vaughan, Donne, and Herbert—none of them being "dissenters," of course, but all of them being marked to some degree by the Platonism that helped to reorganize sensibility after the Reformation. While the "metaphysical" influence was noted in many poets during the 1920's and 1930's, the only user of the style who incorporates an individualistic mysticism into his work, and controls it as contemporary reality, is Eberhart. Swedenborgian, existentialist, whatever this mysticism is, it makes the seventeenth and twentieth centuries akin. . . . (pp. 102-03)

Within the ways of his chosen and developed style, an intellectual style, Eberhart is a modern sort of idealist or, if you will, philosophical realist, and an unabashed reporter of how experience looks when it is understood in that way. His work abounds in reference to mystics such as Saint Theresa and Jacob Böhme, and it is understandable why it calls to mind, for Conrad Aiken, the spirit of William Blake. Many literal statements in Eberhart ask to be followed and understood in the way one might understand the more-than-literal propositions of a parable—they have that emblematic air about them. This is an important kind of distinction between Eberhart's lyrics and those of many another writer in the twentieth century. Many modern poems, pursuing the symbolist manner to the point of diminishing return, seem to their readers to dissolve in metaphor too much of their reference to things outside the poem. The emblems put forward by Eberhart occasionally present equally difficult problems of ascription of reference but they are always presented as if they were—and indeed they prove to be—pointing toward some undissolved core of literal meaning. He aims to use language in such a way that it reveals, given a reader's attention, beliefs that are unambiguously beliefs. . . . (p. 104)

Probably it was by consciously turning away from the somewhat overcondensed manner of many of the early poems in the *Selected Poems* of 1951 that Eberhart freed himself to write such more recent pieces as **"The Ode to a Chinese**

Paper Snake". This is a prime example of a later vein in which he developed a richly informal grace and effortless compunction. The **"Ode"**, among other things, is a tolerant re-examination of primitivism and anthropologism and priapism. Poems like this, in the later work, seem to represent a rapid comic transcendence of the gisty gloom of many of the earlier ones. (It is a disappointment that *Selected Poems* seems to contain not a section nor a line from the narrative poem about the freighter's voyage, from the early 1930's work.)

The conquest of the idiomatic kingdom has many fronts ranging from the lexical to the prosodic. One feels in Eberhart's work an unhurried search for the best qualities of daily speech. Especially in the later work, not so much in the lexical sense as in the sense of living grammar and flow of speech, a conversational elegance quite his own is one of the rewards of his skill. A logic of growth seems involved here, especially when we think of Eberhart's work as it has come to be known outside these volumes, more recently. It was by some practiced but impulsive move toward the looser and more discursive forms that Eberhart learned how "to throw his lines away" in dialogue and drama. In a discriminating way, he has dissociated from each other some of the plural voices that were present, unnamed, in his lyrics, and he has deployed them as the *personae* of drama, each one with diction of his own. (pp. 104-05)

> *Reuel Denney, "The Idiomatic Kingdom," in* Poetry, *Vol. LXXXV, No. 2, November, 1954, pp. 102-05.*

BYRON VAZAKAS

Richard Eberhart has achieved, after many years, the status of an authentic North American Primitive, a paesan of poetry. In a parallel with the graphic arts, he is closer in practice, however, to the Douanier Rousseau than to Grandma Moses.

But where Blake had visions, Henri Rousseau, who also versified, was inspired by apparitions of his first wife, Clemence. Eberhart is still searching "For the lost poem of vision and control." When a primitive becomes aware of the picturesque in his estate, it is detrimental to his development. Naïveté, like innocence, can be carried too far. On the other hand, it is doubtful whether Eberhart is that self-conscious. With him, the ingenuous seems to be merely a habit of letting go with words and ideas, a fortuitous hit-or-miss technique, relying heavily on the muse: "Mysterious seizure is what it is."

Perhaps the most moving quality of the primitive approach lies in the intimate character of any handicraft. From pottery to painting to poetry, practically everything homespun has its warmth, implicit in the personal touch. This warmth in Eberhart's poetry has often been pointed out. Like harmony, it is one of the rewards of surrender, a therapeutic consequence. (p. 106)

Coming so soon after the many virtues of his *Selected Poems,* published in 1951, [*Undercliff*], comprising poems published from 1946 to 1953, is something of an anticlimax. The reproach is sometimes made that certain poets publish too much. Actually, that is a charitable rationalization for what they publish. Perhaps Eberhart's next volume will prove more reassuring.

Psychoanalysis terms the rhythmic, verbal repetitions and babblings of primitives, children, psychotics, and poets, "Echolalia." As Eberhart describes it,

> Repetition is represented to be
> Myopia of an estuary.

Such Olympian rhythmic and verbal compulsions can even reverberate from poet to poet. For example, if Stevens' Crispin in "The Comedian as the Letter C" is "that mountain minded Hoon," then Eberhart's **"Verbalist of Summer"** is surely his yodeled echo. . . . (pp. 106-07)

Beyond echo, out of earshot, Eberhart has something of a poor ear. Even in some of the formal lyrics, his metrics lumber along to a breakdown. Too often, the sentiments share the ride. [In *Undercliff*] Eberhart, referring to rhythm, calls a spade a spade: "And prose is prose and prose is slow." And [then] he demonstrates it:

> The musician is endeared to mankind because
> By the ironic nature of his medium
> He has bottled up words with all their fuzz
> And given us a madman's immediacy.

As to the content of his poems, Eberhart persistently undermines his own reason, not to mention the instruments of any rationale:

> If it seems that I minimize the brain
> It is in deference to mind, most to spirit.

Going a step farther, he then disposes of the mind, also, under the extraordinarily apt title, **"On the Fragility of the Mind"**: "I think there is no mind at all." That leaves the spirit, in the quantity of X the unknown.

The problem of poetry, like most problems, is one of the intellect as well as of the emotions. Intelligence determines the form, and experience the content. Flights of fancy may be poetic; they are not necessarily poetry, which, as an art, is a discipline of the imagination. It might be argued that, after all, there remains the residue, "poetry." That is probably the "spirit" Eberhart eulogizes. Such disembodiment, such dissociation from the responsibilities of content and form suggests a reversal to primitive mumbo-jumbo, or the inspirations of a gaseous oracle less in the Greek than in the Victorian "tradition." As Eberhart puts it, "He reflects in his own art his state of grace." As such, sincerity pervades his work. The pity and the paradox is that he tries to juggle too many contradictions. (pp. 107-08)

> *Byron Vazakas, "Eberhart: A Negative Report," in* Poetry, *Vol. LXXXV, No. 2, November, 1954, pp. 106-08.*

KENNETH REXROTH

The years in which Richard Eberhart came to maturity as a poet were not good ones for American literature. They were very bad ones indeed for poets. Few survive from those days. Where is Herman Spector, Sol Funaroff, Edwin Rolfe? Many do not survive personally; many more, all but a handful, do not survive as literature. Economic crisis, political terror, the growing threat and final presence of worldwide war—the theory was, at the time, that these would all prove stimulating to the poet; out of the riots of the unemployed or the doomed battalions on the Ebro would come new Homers and Shakespeares. The terrible tragedy, considering all the expense of spirit, is that almost nothing came, almost nothing at all.

Muriel Rukeyser, Kenneth Patchen, Kenneth Fearing, Louis Zukofsky, the degree of their survival is the measure of their independence.

Richard Eberhart, in some mysterious way, remained close to totally independent, and survives intact. Today he is obviously the finest poet of his generation, the most lost generation of all the twentieth century, that century of lost generations. Hundreds perished, in an impenetrable moral fog, others slowly decayed. Eberhart is still here, totally alive. What saved him?

Innocence. Wisdom. A pure heart. He was foolish enough to concern himself primarily with the only subjects of poetry, the great platitudes, the facts of life. Hitler and Chamberlain, Trotsky and Stalin, even Franklin Roosevelt, who seemed immortal, all are dead. In their day Eberhart wrote a poem, now in all the anthologies, about a groundhog, telling them that was precisely what was going to happen to them. The information seemed trivial then, but it is what happened, and it turned out to be most important. In the days when art was a weapon and poetry purveyed spurious salvations, Eberhart ran the changes on **"Go, Lovely Rose,"** beauty perishes, value wastes away in the world of fact. How silly that seemed in the days when all Macdougall Alley spoke up with one voice for the proletariat. . . . He turned a jaded eye on the Savior State, so jaded that many people think he is a sort of Christian anarchist. In his own eyes at least, he is nothing of the sort, but just a rather conventional American, trying to get along. . . . Today he seems the most profound poet of his time.

And he has always spoken so simply. There were other forces abroad in the days of Eberhart's forming. This is the time of the Reactionary Generation, of Seven Types of Ambiguity in every cornbelt English seminar, of Classicism and Order, of Back to the English Tradition, of Neo-Metaphysical Verse, the days when Paul Valery's instrumentalism was quoted to justify good advertising copy on Madison Avenue and bad sonnets in Ashtabula. None of this seemed to touch Eberhart. He spoke as simply as Blake's "Songs of Innocence," or Burns or Landor, and he always spoke *about* something. (I will never forget a famous poetry festival at Bard College when everybody was so embarrassed by a long poem Dick read about the experiences of a prisoner of war. As a leading writress said, "After all, the subject is a bit obvious.") He escaped from the workers and peasants of the Village cafeterias, how did he escape from the gentlemen and scholars, the Southern colonels, the aristocrats of ambiguity?

It is very simple. Eberhart really was what they pretended and longed to be. He really had gone to Cambridge (both England and Mass.). He had not only seen William Empson plain, he knew him well. In fact, in the so-called Empson circle he was generally acknowledged the better poet.

Most English people are unaware he is an American. Just imagine the ecstatic vertigo that would anesthetize several Americans we might mention if they were ever mistaken for genuine English poets, educated in Cambridge, England! Mercy! Not only that, but Eberhart had the temerity of the actually cultured: he dared to disagree with fashion. While Mr. Eliot and Mr. Empson were holding up as models the cloying hysteria of Richard Crashaw and the crossword puzzles to be found in Saintsbury's "Minor Caroline Poets," Dick, with cool effrontery, turned away to the simplest voices in the language. People who are anxious to put up a good ap-

pearance at cocktail parties and in outland English departments simply do not do things like that. Culture came naturally to him; he didn't find it in "The Sacred Wood." So he is still here, coming on strong, and the Reactionary Generation is very much on the way out, even in Iowa and Minnesota, let alone Cambridge (England or Mass.).

In the final upshot this all does come to resemble Donne, but Donne approached as peer, not as a lesson. "Aire and Angels" or Blake's "Crystal Cabinet," these are the exemplars that always spring to mind with Eberhart's best poems. Perfect clarity of vision, perfect clarity of utterance, perfect control of the material means. Presentational immediacy—poetry at its best is always completely colloquial. It may be the conversation of saints or philosophers or devils or even angels, but it is a kind of glorified talk, not a specially complicated kind of reading matter. It has taken me a lifetime to learn to write like I talk. Dick seems to have been born that way, sublimely unaware of his extraordinary gift.

What is there to say about [*Great Praises*] as such, having said so much about Eberhart himself and generally? Not much. It is new, it is older, it is wiser, it is more profound and more confident than some things in some of the earlier books, but what is important is that it is more Eberhart. (pp. 15-16)

Kenneth Rexroth, "Finest of the Lost," in The Saturday Review, *New York, Vol. XL, No. 52, December 28, 1957, pp. 15-16.*

HAYDEN CARRUTH

It is good to have Richard Eberhart's work brought together in [*Collected Poems: 1930-1960*]. The *Selected Poems* [published in 1951] contained his famous poems, but has been out of print for some time. Besides, one can see now that some of Eberhart's finest writing occurs in poems that are less well-known. Some poems have been omitted, of course, since poets reserve the right to leave out of their "collected" editions the things they no longer care for. But I have looked up some of those missing, and we can rest, for the time being at least, on Eberhart's judgment. Some day, if his work is as good as I think, we shall need a scholarly edition of all that he has done.

Eberhart's best is very fine indeed. A dozen or so poems in this book are the equal of anything ever produced in America. Young writers who read this, those who have come along in the past ten years, will be astonished and skeptical, because Eberhart's recent poems have often been stony and too technical. His reputation is in danger of slipping. Young writers no longer know that he was the most exciting poet to come out of America during the thirties (they find it hard to believe that the thirties in America could have been exciting at all). Eberhart spent much time abroad, and is sometimes classified with the English poets of that period. But his language is American, his manner is Yankee. And the evidence of his genuine gifts is here in this book for young writers to study and the rest of us to enjoy again.

The really astonishing thing about Eberhart's poetry is not that it should be so good—his talent is obvious—but that so much of it should come so close to triteness. Eberhart has always approached experience with a conventional view. He is really a misplaced eighteenth-century sentimentalist; many of his poems are virtually "night pieces" and "graveyard poems" of the worst sort, with more than a hint of Thomson or the young Bryant. His themes are death, human frailty, the sad beauty of natural things, the acceptance of reality through a religiously motivated immolation in necessity, etc. These have not changed much in the course of his work, though his response has become more complex. He has written few political poems, few poems that attest the era of Freud, Fraser, Durkheim. Yet he has surmounted the familiarity of his attitudes by bringing to them a tough, original enthusiasm.

It is difficult to find Eberhart's affinities. Often the mystical strain in his work and the common metrical patterns have reminded critics of Blake or Emily Dickinson, but in rereading his poems this time I have found more of Gray, Wordsworth, even the Longfellow of the sonnets. The moderns are here too; in some poems Auden, in others Stevens, and in a few a strong anticipatory touch of Dylan Thomas. One concludes that Eberhart's style is really the central or common poetic style of the twentieth century. A theme for a future dissertation is the extent to which Eberhart created or helped to create it, and the extent to which he merely took from it.

Again the astonishing point is that he found a personal style within the commonplace, for there can never be any doubt that an Eberhart poem is an Eberhart poem. The individuality is a quality of feeling, an appealing awkwardness of metaphor, a brilliant, erratic play with common rhyme and meter. Eberhart has not been rigorous enough in his recent poems; he has often let them fall too easily into patterns learned earlier, not taking the trouble to choose words well. But there is more than enough fine work in this book to prove him a major lyric talent. (pp. 63-4)

> Hayden Carruth, "The Errors of Excellence," in The Nation, *New York, Vol. 192, No. 3, January 21, 1961, pp. 63-4.*

PETER L. THORSLEV, JR.

> It is absurd to wince at being called a romantic
>   poet.
> Unless one is that, one is not a poet at all.
>   Wallace Stevens, in *Opus Posthumous*
>   (p. 73)

From the first [Eberhart's] reviews have been "mixed"; their general tenor could be summarized in the nursery rhyme: "When he is good, he is very, very good; / And when he is bad, he is horrid." Such a reaction on the part of critics is not in itself remarkable, I suppose; a poet who writes such lines as these: "My being being being's essence, a mathema" (**"The Magical"**), or "Will will will him his own, a fabled ease" (**"Sestina"**), certainly risks offending the sensitive ears of his critics. Such verbal pyrotechnics perhaps distract more than they convey. (Admittedly much of Eberhart's verse reads like a poetry of inclusion, rather than of selection or exclusion. In his criticism and casual pronouncements he has not expressed much respect for the care-filled revision, for the serious second thoughts which would perhaps excise such lines as these.) But what is more remarkable in these reviews is the tone which Eberhart's critics assume. In the face of his successes they remain curiously inarticulate, almost in awe; with his "failures," on the other hand, they are never condescending, or merely disappointed: they become petulant, exasperated, almost infuriated. It is as if somehow they were personally involved, and personally betrayed. To put it another way:

with much contemporary poetry one is pleased or annoyed, surprised by an unexpected felicity or a clever image, or mildly irritated because so much cerebration seems to yield so little; and just below the level of consciousness hovers the question: But does it all really matter? With Eberhart's poetry this question never occurs; the reader is immediately aware that what is being said, with whatever success, does indeed matter, both to himself and to the poet. One may sometimes question the felicity of the expression, but one is never tempted to question the validity of the experience.

The qualities just indicated—the reliance on first thoughts or on "inspiration," the emotional intensity, the earnestness, and the assertive moral and personal sincerity—are, I think, enough in themselves to suggest what I believe to be Eberhart's first most distinctive characteristic: he is in a way a twentieth-century Romantic. Now "Romantic" is a nebulous and dubious epithet, not less so because in the last forty years it has been more often used as a pejorative than as a neutral descriptive term. (pp. 74-5)

But Eberhart is a Romantic, I believe, in an even more definite sense than Stevens implies in the assertion I have used as an epigraph. First, Eberhart is a nature poet, and what is more, he is a nature poet who would not object to being called one. Furthermore, he has allied himself with no twentieth-century (and therefore almost *ipso facto* anti-Romantic) school of poetry, and the poets who most obviously influenced him, especially in his earlier years, are three of the greatest Romantics: Blake, Wordsworth, and Whitman. Finally, and most important, the themes of his poetry, the problems which have concerned him most vitally from his first volume to his last, are problems posed first in their modern form by the great Romantic poets, and when Eberhart offers solutions to these problems they are often modified and modernized Romantic solutions.

Like all nature poets Eberhart frequently takes some object of everyday nature—a beast, a bird, an insect, or a flower: any sharply-defined natural phenomenon—as the central image around which to organize a poem meant to illustrate some facet of human or social experience. Nature poetry of this sort is at least as old as medieval bestiaries, or as those "emblem-books" of the earlier days of printing, whose major attraction was allegorical and moral illustrations, with short verses below to amplify the pictured text. And nature poetry of this sort is still popular in American letters: Marianne Moore draws lessons from seagulls or fishes; Richard Wilbur has compiled a modern *Bestiary;* and of course Robert Frost images forth truths of man and nature from birches, or butterflies, or cows in apple-time.

Some of Eberhart's poems of this sort resemble Frost's even in their ironic or whimsical conclusions: two wasps found wintering on a New Hampshire tree, brought into the kitchen, and breathed upon by the poet (like God on Adam's dust), come quivering to life. One wasp dares to attempt to fly, but dazed, it falls and is crushed accidentally by the poet's boot. The other, safer and sager, remains to become a pet; and Eberhart concludes:

> The moral of this is plain.
> But I will shirk it.
> You will not like it. And
> God does not live to explain.

>   (**"New Hampshire, February"**)

In another poem of the same period the poet finds wisdom in contemplating the "large soft cows" in a warm barn. The cow has "learned the lesson of the pacifist," that of passive sufferance. Eberhart concludes ironically:

> If acceptance after the storms of decades
> Is the ounce of wisdom in electrified flesh,
> Philosophy can end in the eye of a cow.
>
> **("Burr Oaks: The Barn")**

Others of these "emblem" poems seem to come closer, in theme and in spirit, to the poems of Blake. The dry husk of the sloughed skin of a cicada leads the poet to consider life, change, and perfect death-like form, and to question "What eternal hovers in / Him?" **("The Largess")**; and the sight of a "tight lizard on a wall" leads him to ask ultimate questions—"What the protection, who the protector?"—like Blake's in "The Tiger." Even cancer cells under a microscope, in their "spiky shapes," become an image of the poetic imagination, of the "fixed form in the massive fluxion." (pp. 75-7)

But Eberhart is by no means alone among contemporary poets in his use of animal or floral "emblems"; he is more particularly the nature poet in his celebration of the sheer sensuous and sensual pleasures in the physical world around him. In this he comes close, in spirit, at least, to Wordsworth, or to the Whitman of "Song of Myself." Eberhart's first volume of poetry, *A Bravery of Earth* (1930), opens and closes with the lines:

> This fevers me, this sun on green,
> On grass glowing, this young spring.

The whole volume is really one long poem in four parts, and it forms something unique in twentieth-century American verse, I believe: it is a spiritual autobiography of a poet, and its obvious model is Wordsworth's *Prelude.* Not in style or diction, certainly; Eberhart's short lyric lines, with their irregular rhymes and rhythms, are very much his own. But the stages in the poet's spiritual growth are remarkably like those Wordsworth describes in the *Prelude.* The "first awareness" is of life as will, as sensual force, the "fever" of the sun and of the world of energy and sub-intellectual life: much the same as the feeling for nature which Wordsworth describes in his youthful climbing over the Cumberland hills, or along the banks of the Wye. The "second awareness," however, is an intellectual disillusionment caused by analytic reason, which makes the world seem a dull and deadly mechanism, drained of will or purpose (Wordsworth describes a similar experience in his student life at Cambridge). Gradually, however, the poet grows into the light of a new manhood, "a bravery of earth," and this "third awareness" brings a new understanding not only of nature, but of man in nature—a vision of purpose and of human "destiny" which owes much, I think, to Whitman.

The elemental joy in physical nature is admittedly more characteristic of Eberhart's early poetry; still, enough of it remains to add a special poignancy to such later poems as **"Recollection of Childhood"** or **"If I could only live at the Pitch that is near Madness."** In the latter poem he laments the fact that in taking on manhood he has come "into the realm of complexity." . . . But sometimes even in his mature poetry he can achieve a pure nature lyric such as **"Now is the Air made of Chiming Bells,"** in which the delight in all of the senses is unclouded by analytic reason or moral second thoughts, as he sees that "The stormcloud, wizened, has rolled its rind away"; that "seeds, assuaged, peep from the nested spray," and "the sun"

> Begins to dress with warmth again every thing.
> The lettuce in pale burn, the burdock tightening;
> And naked necks of craning fledglings.

An even later poem, **"Summer Landscape,"** with its delicate observation and its richly sensuous imagery and sleepy rhythms, reminds one somehow of Keats' ode "To Autumn"—perhaps because of the swallows, although here, with their quick movements, their "playing / About the barn like brightest minds," they contrast sharply with the placid life around them: the algae on a stagnant pool, which become a "green mantle, a spreading tone," or even the snake, which "will hold his poise, then glide away." And, as the "waves of clover-ether triumph," the poet promises that "The moonlight will be as good as the hot day."

Nevertheless, such joy in uncomplicated nature is relatively rare in Eberhart's latest poetry; he moves on to consider themes and problems more complex and tragic. The "second awareness" comes for him as it came for the first Romantics; and nature and man, which seem simple and unified in childhood, break into the complexities of adult life. In Blake's terms, we move from innocence to experience, and the new "awareness" becomes painful and intense. The Romantics did not, after all, come by their mature "single visions" easily (in Blake's terms again): at first the old certainties of the Enlightenment broke into polar opposites, and what they found was rather a painful duality in man—between blood and mind, between passion and analysis, between imagination and reason; and a corresponding duality in the world of things—between nature as life and organism, and nature as mechanical necessity. When the Romantics arrived at a new unity, a new vision of the world as one (and the Romantics were, generally speaking, the last who dared a monist metaphysics), it was usually through a higher and dialectic synthesis in the realm of spirit, a new mystic vision which transcended both blood and the mind, both organism and mechanism. Wordsworth found his new unified vision in a Nature in which all things were transformed into spirit, but a spirit which seems often rather bloodless and passionless. Blake's synthesis is perhaps more modern in that he refused to relinquish the world of the flesh in the realm of the spirit: his God created both the tiger and the lamb. In this respect, Eberhart is closer to Blake, I think, than to Wordsworth.

For these Romantic themes (Romantic in their origins, at least) form the subject-matter of many of Eberhart's best poems. In some of these he laments the disillusionment, the loss of wonder, which comes when life is probed by analytic reason. . . . [In a] later "animal" poem, **"Seals, Terns, Time,"** the poet illustrates man's dual nature by picturing himself balanced in a boat on the surface of the sea, drawn between the seals, those "blurred kind forms / That rise and peer from elemental waters," and the terns, wheeling gracefully in the free blue of the sky.

In his earlier poetry Eberhart does sometimes discover a unity in organic nature, at the heart of things, but when he does, it is not the moral and personal Nature of Wordsworth. One of his longer poems, describing a walking trip through Wordsworth's lake country, appeals in turn to all of the senses, and the hurried, short, and irregular lines seem even to catch something of the breathlessness of mountain-climbing. The poem culminates in a mountain-top experience on Helvellyn, perhaps parallel to Wordsworth's on Snowdon, but Eberhart does not see Wordsworth's "emblem of a mind . . . that broods over the dark abyss"; he feels instead that

> A surge of demonic energy unites
> Blood and the bitter world-vitality
> As the flaying and flayed being ignites
> In elemental passion intensity
> Satanic, angelic, one harmony
> Of immense glory like fire clinging
> A blaze of terrible immediacy
> The wild blood of freedom singing . . .
>
> ("Four Lakes' Days")

In later poems, this transcendent unity is often more quiet, if no less terrible—a white hardness, like what he sees in the eye of a "Sea-Hawk," a "piercing, inhuman perfection / . . . A blaze of grandeur, permanence of the impersonal."

But in a very few of his latest poems Eberhart comes close to that vision of a unity in organic nature which is so peculiarly Blakean—in that vein which Middleton Murry, speaking of Keats and Blake (and, perhaps more appositely, of D. H. Lawrence) called an inverted "this-worldly" mysticism, because, paradoxically, it sees a "transcendent" unity not by denying the flesh, the senses, and things of the earth, but by reaching through the senses to the blood. Such a poem is **"Thrush Song at Dawn,"** the concluding poem in *Great Praises* (1957), a poem which seems to me entirely successful. The fourth stanza echoes the Immortality Ode, and the idea of a "lost purity" is perhaps also Wordsworthian, but the substance of the poem has more of D. H. Lawrence, and the image with which the poem closes carries the same tenor as that poet-as-Aeolian-harp image so popular with all of the Romantics. . . . (pp. 78-83)

Another way to face the central issue of the duality in man and nature is to approach it obliquely, by probing the ultimate mystery of death; and this theme was also a favorite of the Romantics. A realization of the evanescence of sensuous beauty in the face of death is the central agony of Keats' greatest odes; his solution was esthetic, in an eternal beauty which transcends time and death, but which also, unfortunately, transcends life. The life-long development of Shelley's thought can be traced in his changing attitudes toward death, and when he found his peace, it was in the concept of an impersonal immortality, in returning cycles of nature as in the "Ode to the West Wind," or in the more fully developed neo-Platonism of "Adonais." But it was for a belated minor Romantic, Thomas Lovell Beddoes, that death as an insoluble mystery became almost an obsession; and when he could no longer make a cosmic Jacobean joke of it (as in *Death's Jest-Book*), he twice attempted suicide, and at last succeeded.

I don't mean to imply that Eberhart has been influenced by Beddoes, nor that he shares the earlier poet's pessimism; but still Eberhart is the first poet since Beddoes, I think, for whom death has become such a persistent theme. His concern is not merely with death as a concept, or as a mystic attraction (although in such a poem as **"The Soul Longs to Return Whence It Came"** death is an attraction), but with death and decay as a brutal physical fact. . . . Sometimes this preoccupation with death seems only a defiant attempt to see "some

beauty even at the guts of things" (**"When Golden Flies upon My Carcass Come"**); sometimes Eberhart seems to take a Shelleyan consolation in the fact that death and decay are after all only a return to nature: nothing alive is ever wholly lost. This seems to be the conclusion of **"For a Lamb,"** a description of a dead lamb on a hillside, "propped with daises," which has returned to the wind and the flowers; or of the beautiful and quiet **"Rumination,"** in which the poet concludes that Death will "blow his breath / To fire my clay, when I am still."

But the poet cannot always find such solace in the thought of death as a return to living earth. From a strictly human point of view, the tragedy remains, and this is the theme of Eberhart's most famous and most often anthologized poem, **"The Groundhog."** It is another animal-emblem poem, but in this case the picture is of a dead body in a summer field, and a dead body paradoxically alive with decay. Changing attitudes toward death, in a series of visits to the tiny body in the fields, give the poem its structure. On the first visit, the poet is filled with an intense love and an intense loathing at the sight of fierce nature at work in the decaying flesh, the "immense energy of the sun." The second visit is made in the "strict eye" of Autumn, and an intellectual wisdom has controlled the fierce energy but has also left the earth and the body a "sodden hulk," bereft of meaning (as in the poet's earlier "second awareness"). On the third visit the poet sees only a bit of hair and bleached bones, "beautiful as architecture," as he achieves at last the indifference of spirit. But still the pathos remains, and when three years later there is no sign of the groundhog, the poet stands and thinks of the evanescence of all human life. . . . Still, even in this vision of death, a kind of fierce mystic joy is possible, an impassioned acceptance of the impersonal, of death and decay. This attitude is more than mere resignation: it is the affirmation which comes to the heart of tragedy. One of Eberhart's lyrics which illustrates this mystic experience also shows his poetry at its most intense, and I think perhaps at its best. The diction [of **"Imagining How It Would Be To Be Dead"**] is simple and the imagery is disciplined, but this seems only to heighten by contrast the intensity of the feeling. . . . In the nature of things, however, such intensely subjective mystical experiences [as in this poem] are necessarily brief and infrequent, and they don't provide moral truths to live by. Eberhart's final message is closer to a quiet humanism, an acceptance of the mystery of things, and a faith in the ultimate spiritual perseverance of man's love for man. In one of his latest poems (**"What Gives,"** first printed in *Collected Poems*), as a child of the twentieth century who has lived through two world wars and what has come between and after, Eberhart writes of the "absolute" which he has "tortured out in fifty years." He is tentative, to be sure—"I do not know, but think will show the same"—but this is what he concludes:

> Strength grows and throws around us holy love.
> It is this I count on to the end of time.
> Love is the end of knowledge, and sublime.

More frequently his optimism is tempered to a wry stoicism, as in the last stanza of **"Anima":**

> It is the perdurable toughness of the soul
> God and nature make us want to keep;
> The struggle of the part against the whole.
> Each time we take a breath it must be deep.

There could be a danger in too much emphasis on Eberhart's neo-Romanticism, I suppose. In the first place, such an emphasis may seem to imply that his verse is derivative in style and idiom, when this is not at all the case. Then, too, although those of his poems which I think are most likely to survive are concerned with personal themes—themes which are Romantic, in the best and broadest sense of the term—he has also upon occasion written on topical subjects, especially in some war poems and in his recent experiments in verse drama.

However much his poems share common themes with other Romantic poets, Eberhart's style and idiom are nevertheless always his own. His lines are short, his rhymes oblique or infrequent, and his rhythms intentionally irregular, but within these limits he shows a quite extraordinary range. Some of his lyrics are fluent, with simple unaffected diction, and in almost regular metric stanzas. The beauty of these poems, I think, as is the case with many of Blake's short stanzas or with Wordsworth's "Lucy" poems, lies in the reader's appreciation of restraint, of the tension between the apparently artless simplicity of the verse and the intensity of the controlled emotion. A few isolated lines which stick in my mind will perhaps illustrate the point: "And music a broken Ilium"; or, "Calm is but the end of a poem"; or, when the poet speaks of himself and of his art as

> Locked in this lone discipline
> Against the world's decay.

At the other extreme of his range, Eberhart writes many poems which, like the lyrics of Gerard Manley Hopkins, are crowded with stressed monosyllables and often almost choked with alliterative consonants, in which the effect seems to be to compress into each line as much poetry as possible. An extreme example is the youthful and experimental **"Four Lakes' Days,"** which, in spite of some striking images, is perhaps a little too Hopkins-like, with its compressed and distorted grammar and syntax and its strings of adjectives and nouns made adjectives.

References to current events of our time—political, economic, or social—were comparatively rare in his poetry all through the thirties, but the Second World War and his involvement in it did break into his poetry in the forties. He also began to collect war poems by other poets, and in 1948 he edited, together with his friend Selden Rodman, an anthology of these entitled *War and the Poet.* One of the poems anthologized was Tennyson's translation of the Old English "Battle of Brunanburh," and it may have been this poem which inspired the style of Eberhart's longest war poem, **"Brotherhood of Men."** The poem is an attempt to write a brief epic account of the death march of Bataan, and it is written in the style of Old English verse, in which the principle of coherence is not rhyme or quantitative meter, but recurring patterns of stressed alliterative syllables. Of his other less ambitious war poems few reach the level of his personal and "Romantic" lyrics, I think, but some of them, including the often anthologized **"Fury of Aerial Bombardment"** and the later **"A Young Greek, Killed in the Wars,"** achieve a considerable force of compassion, restrained by the irony of understatement and of prosaic diction and detail.

Eberhart's more recent incursions into the field of verse drama also demonstrate both his interest in poetic experimentation and his concern with topical themes. . . . [The fruits of this new interest are two verse dramas, **The Apparition** and **The Visionary Farms.**] Both of these are experimental "discussion" dramas, in which the play within the play is watched and commented upon by "Spectators" on the stage. The first is really a short "mood" play, the only action being a brief encounter between a salesman in a hotel and a bewildered young girl who wanders into his room on a caprice, talks with him for a while over a few drinks, and then disappears again into the hallway. The second play, **The Visionary Farms,** is more ambitious. . . . On one level, this drama is an incisive and sometimes humorous satire on hucksterism in the person of "Hurricane" Ransome, the recklessly ambitious manager of a midwestern firm, who, it turns out, has embezzled somewhat more than a million dollars from the company, and thus left Fahnstock, the half-owner of the company and the protagonist of the drama, on the verge of financial ruin. Read on another level, the play becomes a broad indictment of our American "ad-man" civilization, which perverts the ideals and the very personalities of all of the characters in the play. The drama is intentionally episodic and undramatic; as one of the choric "spectators" puts it, the purpose of the play is rather to "keep vile actions off, and bring on thoughts / To estimate these matters to a standstill."

These verse dramas, however, remain interesting experiments, and any summary estimate of Eberhart's achievement so far must stand on the basis of the considerable quantity of lyric poetry which he has published since 1930. His faults, in my opinion, lie at his extremes. In a very few poems, his verse seems to me not to rise above the prosaic. In one long poem entitled **"The Kite,"** for instance, he spends many introductory stanzas versifying instructions for the assembly of his kite "emblem"; and however these lines are read, they seem to me to remain something less than poetry (this poem was pointedly omitted from **Collected Poems**). More frequently, Eberhart's stanzas are crammed with figures and images which go off in the reader's mind like Roman candles; but, like all such fireworks, they sometimes leave no very lasting impression on the darkness. Fortunately, most of Eberhart's lyrics stand between these extremes. Some of the quieter ones are centered on a single image, or are unified by a tightly-controlled line of logical or psychological argument; in others, the very intensity of the expressed thought or emotion seems to fuse the varied images into a single vivid impression.

Among contemporary American poets who often seem either academic and a little tired, or else full of fire and wildly anti-intellectual, it is a pleasure to read a poet like Eberhart, who has, I think, something of the virtues of both camps: a keen intelligence, but also a warm humanity and a genuine inspiration. (pp. 84-91)

Peter L. Thorslev, Jr., "The Poetry of Richard Eberhart," in Poets in Progress: Critical Prefaces to Thirteen Modern American Poets, *edited by Edward Hungerford, Northwestern University Press, 1967, pp. 73-91.*

CLEANTH BROOKS

[*The essay excerpted below was delivered as a lecture on April 4, 1984, at the Writer's Festival, University of Florida, in honor of Richard Eberhart's eightieth birthday.*]

The immemorial themes of poetry have been love and death. It is proper that this should be so, for poetry ultimately deals with reality, and love and death are the great portals for our entrance into—and exit from—reality. (p. 21)

It will be no surprise, therefore, that I observe love and death to be the dominant themes, separate or conjoined, in Richard Eberhart's poetry. They are certainly, in my opinion, the themes of many of his best poems. I do not pretend that my judgment of what is his best is necessarily accurate. Certainly in what I shall say it is not my intention to present a list of his best poems. It will be more accurate, and certainly more modest, for me simply to say that many of his poems that most appeal to me are poems of which love and death are the themes.

Love and death are not, of course, Eberhart's only themes. Nature comes into some of his finest poems, for nature is the backdrop against which the human drama takes place, and to human eyes nature seems everlasting as compared with the brevity of human life. Eberhart has his favorite aspects of nature, the Maine coast in particular, and he writes about its grave beauty with admiration and love.

I want to mention also his poems in which certain typical New England characters figure—characters that obviously fascinate him. It is easy to see why. These characters are themselves grave, restrained, not in the least delicate or over-refined, but rugged and even stoical in their appraisal of life. Like region, like people, one might say, and such is what Eberhart's poems about his New England characters seem to imply. (pp. 21-2)

To get back to one of his finest handlings of the theme of death, refer to **"The Fury of Aerial Bombardment."** It is an early poem and deservedly well known. But good poems do not age and they can stand a lot of critical wear and tear without wearing out. . . . (pp. 22-3)

The speaker in the poem, shocked at what man is doing to man in modern war, wonders how God could ever have created such a ruthless creature. The implication is that God could have and so should have built gentleness and mercy into the human constitution. In view of the present carnage, surely you would think that God would "relent" and would now amend what was his earlier and obviously malign purpose, and "give man to repent." But clearly God has not repented of the mistake—or worse, was it his evil purpose in creating man? Cain had only a crude weapon with which to murder his brother. But now Cain's descendants have the horrifyingly sophisticated weapons with which to express the "ancient furies" that seem to inhabit them.

Finally, the outraged speaker has to confront the possibility that "the eternal truth" is that man's true soul is invincibly that of a fighting animal and that nothing whatever can be done about it. The implication is that God has never meant to do anything about it or else is now impotent to do so.

So much for a paraphrase of the first three stanzas. The tone deserves some special comment. The voice we hear is that of a man speaking out of shocked incomprehension. How can God allow such things to be? Is God indifferent to what is going on? Is it possible that he is an accomplice to the outrage, having actually planned it to come about?

It is the kind of almost irrational outburst that one might expect to issue from one of "the shock-pried faces" that the poet refers to in line 3. So, dramatically the tone is right, but the note sounded is too strident, too shrill for the poem to end upon. Apparently the poet himself had misgivings. At any rate, as he has told us, he left the poem at this point unfinished and put it aside. To quote his own words: "Sometime later . . . with an analytical mind, quite removed from the passionate one of the first three stanzas, I composed the last four lines" **("How I Write").**

The poet had cooled off, and so had the character who speaks the poem; and it is this change of tone and changed velocity that "makes" the poem what it is. Notice that it is the last stanza that brings the young dead soldiers back to life. They suddenly live before us as schoolboys, their names in all their variety are legible yet on the class roll which records their dutifully attending classes, learning what a "belt holding pawl" is and what it does, and the other working parts of the machine gun. We are struck with the fact that they were so young, who now are so thoroughly and untimely dead. This last stanza also humanizes their instructor. There was nothing malign in his teaching them the workings of a machine gun. It was an almost routine job. Now, like an instructor in freshman English looking over last year's class lists, he notices that he cannot call up the faces of the young men who were briefly in his crowded classroom.

In the first twelve lines of the poem, it was this very same man who, in his indignation, feels that God himself had a hand in bringing these young men to death. Now he seems to sense his own complicity. If those who take the sword die by the sword, he himself had taught them how to use a weapon far more deadly than the sword.

Note that I am not saying that the first three stanzas are "bad" because they are highly emotional and the voice strident, whereas the last four lines are "good" because they are cool and collected. If the first three stanzas need the last stanza, so does the last stanza need the first three. Imagine the first three written in the style of the last. Sixteen lines of chatter about levers and pawls would amount to just nothing. In poetry, contrast, change of pace, shift of tone are almost everything.

Another fine poem on death—on the impact and meaning of death—is that entitled **"Orchard."** (pp. 23-5)

Among the fruit trees an automobile is parked in which a family is gathered together: the father and mother and their three children, two boys and one little girl. As the poem unfolds, we learn what this family has evidently been told: that the mother has been stricken with some malignant disease. We hear none of the actual conversation that passes between the father and mother, and the children say nothing at all. They are caught up in a benumbing shock. Evidently the father talks to the rest of them, and so does the mother. But we hear none of their actual words.

It is as if we, hearing no words, had to infer the details of the colloquy largely from the expression on the faces of the adults which the poet describes in some detail. Thus, the father "with indomitable will / Strove . . . with a powerful complete contempt of defeat . . . and not a mark of fear." The mother "wonderfully mild, / Poured forth her love divinely magnified." The children make no reply, but the brothers put their arms around the "trembling sister."

The scene is evidently being described by one of the two brothers and, because he uses the diction of an adult, he is apparently remembering it years later. The poet's careful suppression of the actual words spoken by the father and mother accomplishes something positive, for we readers are required to use our imaginations, and the properly stimulated imagination can be a very powerful force. Every great poet knows how and when to use this device.

Editors have supplied the information that the poem reflects an actual experience in Eberhart's early life. His mother died of cancer, and the poem **"Orchard"** comes out of the reactions of the family sitting in a car parked in the orchard as they absorb the dread news. The knowledge of the fact that Eberhart actually went through this experience may for some readers account for the power of the poem. But this is too simple an explanation of the poem's impact on the reader. Not that the experience was not important to Eberhart himself in providing, not only the occasion for the poem but probably also an urgent need to express it—a compulsion to express what had shaken him so deeply. Rather, I am referring to the emotion of those readers who have never met Eberhart, including those who might assume that the scene described was merely the creation of Eberhart's imagination.

A person who entirely lacked a poet's eye and ear might suffer an experience just as grievous to him as what happened to the Eberhart family that day in the orchard, and yet not be able to express it for others—or at least express it so movingly and poignantly. The nonpoet may have had the experience, but be unable to put it into adequate words. After all, we who are assembled here to celebrate a poet's career must not forget that the poet proves himself a poet not merely by feeling deeply but in being able to turn such feelings into poetry.

One of Eberhart's first early achievements in poetry also makes use of the theme of death. I refer to the well-known poem, **"The Groundhog,"**—the fact that the poem is well-known is a good reason for discussing it here. The way it is constructed is worthy of comment, for it is the structure finally that brings the whole poem to life. The poem obviously does not bring the little dead animal to life, but it does bring the theme of death to intense life—a life that involves us who are human beings.

If you think that I am making too much of the verbal structure, just think what most of us, you and I, would make of seeing a dead animal lying by the side of the path. In the poem, the groundhog is dead, dead, dead, but around him the summer fields in June are almost fiercely alive. The observer cannot help noticing that if nature is vigorously alive in the vegetation, it is also alive in the groundhog's carcass, which the maggots have turned into "a seething cauldron" of activity. The life of nature expresses itself just as fully in the furious activity of the maggots as it does in the burgeoning summer fields. No wonder the poet uses phrases like "vigorous summer" and "senseless change," or that he refers to nature as "ferocious."

No wonder either that the man who speaks is shaken by what he has seen, that through his own body's frame there arises a trembling, and that he has to try "for control, to be still, / To quell the passion of the blood." For what is happening to the woodchuck foretells what will happen to his own body as being that of another natural creature. Looking at the disintegrating woodchuck, he does not say something like "there but for the grace of God go I." Rather, what this observer says to himself is something like: Nature cares no more for me than for this little animal. It will do to every living creature what comes "naturally," for everything that nature does is natural. The poet does not spell these things out for us. Far better, he provides the inciting incident, the images, and the human reactions which will clothe the thought in sensuous expression.

The poem might very well end here, but it does not. The speaker continues to take that same path throughout the changing seasons and so witnesses the changes that occur in the woodchuck's frame. For instance, next autumn, he notices that the carcass has become dry, but what the poem actually says is that "[t]he sap [had] gone out of the groundhog."

The vegetation too had lost its sap. The growing season is past. But the poet has put matters with a grim humor. In apparent synchronization with the plants, the groundhog has lost its sap too. The dry humor is not without point. If nature is expressing itself in the brown and dying plants, it continues to express itself in the groundhog also. Later still we are told: "Another summer took the fields again / Massive and burning, full of life." But the groundhog has by now been reduced to "bones bleaching in the sunlight." They are, the poet says crisply, "Beautiful as architecture."

Coming back to the spot three years after he had first noticed the dead animal, he sees that the bones themselves have disappeared. And so the poem ends, as many will remember, with the following powerful lines:

> I stood there in the whirling summer,
> My hand capped a withered heart,
> And thought of China and of Greece,
> Of Alexander in his tent;
> Of Montaigne in his tower,
> Of Saint Theresa in her wild lament.

What do these lines mean? Why did the experience "wither" his heart? And why did he think of the countries and the famous individuals that he tells us came to his mind? I have no license to answer these questions. I have not asked Dick Eberhart to tell me the answers. But even if my explanation is faulty, I hope it will demonstrate the rich suggestiveness of the passage and perhaps why it sounds somehow "right" to all of us at our very first reading.

China and Greece are both ancient and majestic cultures, and they are prime representatives of Eastern and Western thought. Both were the products, over thousands of years, of the work, cogitation, and experience of generations of mortal creatures, who, in Yeats's magnificent terms, were "Begotten, born and died." The great thinkers of those civilizations had to cope with the problem of death, and all of them, thinkers and non-thinkers, eventually experienced death. Like the lowly woodchuck whose rotting carcass has prompted the observer's thoughts, they who were once in life are here no more.

What of the historical figures mentioned in the last three lines of the poem? Alexander the Great is clearly the man of action, the great world conqueror. The phrase "in his tent" portrays him as a soldier on campaign. But he too had to cope with the general limitations of mankind and, as we know, died young. Montaigne is the typical man of thought, a seminal figure of the Renaissance. In "his tower" in southern France he meditated on the inevitability of death and its meaning. The record of those meditations is to be found in his famous *Essais*. St. Theresa of Avila is a kind of counterpart to Montaigne. If he is the rationalist and so representative of the skeptical mind, she is the mystic who, in terms of her religious beliefs, saw death in a very different way. But even she shared with the woodchuck an animal body and the same vulnerable biological mechanism. Though an early poem, **"The Groundhog"** remains one of Eberhart's finest poems on the subject of death.

Yet I must not in my praise of our poet's great themes give the impression that death is all that he writes about, or suggest that he probably keeps a skull on his writing table. Consider, for example, Eberhart's **"A Legend of Viable Women."** The title is, of course, a take-off on the title of Chaucer's "A Legend of Good Women." Chaucer was using "good" in a rather special sense. The dictionary (including the ponderous Oxford) will not provide much help. The original meaning is "capable of maintaining its own existence," and "viable" was generally used as a technical term to designate babies born prematurely, but not born so early that they could not survive. But the women of Eberhart's poem—"Betty the vigorous," who was "at home in Tanganyika," shooting wild elephants, and "Maxine, a woman of fire and malice," and "savage Catherine," and all the rest of them are clearly women tough enough to fend for themselves under practically any circumstances. Maybe this is just what Eberhart meant by his adjective *viable:* women independent as all hell, thoroughly capable of survival almost anywhere. Whatever the meaning of the title, the poem itself is the thing; and this one is delightful in its inventiveness, its exuberance, its audacious phrasings, and its occasional parodies of phrases in Chaucer's "Legend of Good Women."

I have already suggested that Chaucer is very inclusive of the types and kinds of women whom he deems "good," and so is Eberhart in the women that he is willing to call "viable." They range from self-acknowledged fluff-heads to formidable intellectuals; from modest nuns to women "without tenderness or pity." The following sample stanza puts their variety far better than I can:

> There were prideful women; women of blood and
>   lust;
> Patient women who rouged with scholarship's
>   dust;
> There were women who touched the soul of the
>   piano;
> Women as cat to mouse with their psychoanalyst.

It would be fun to read off more pithy characterizations: "Helen the blonde Iowan," "sultry Emma of West Virginia," "Kimiko the alabaster girl of Tokyo." But it is a longish poem. There are a lot of women included. One will simply have to read the poem for himself or herself. In fact, that is the point of this whole lecture: to incite the reader to appropriate Eberhart's poems for himself or herself.

Eberhart applies his power for hitting off characters of men also. I particularly admire his **"A New England Bachelor."** . . . (pp. 26-30)

[Eberhart's appraisal in this poem] is genuinely witty, and the Bachelor, in summing up his life, does not lack a sense of humor—even though the humor is at his own expense. He is the reserved man, close-lipped by nature. He never really speaks out, and his New England personality lies somewhere between that of E. A. Robinson's Richard Cory and T. S. Eliot's J. Alfred Prufrock. But Eberhart's character derives neither from Robinson's or Eliot's: he is very much Eberhart's own creation.

Eberhart does pay some homage to psychological theory—its account of what is likely to happen to the son whose father is weak and ineffectual and whose mother is strong and dominant. As he puts it in the poem:

> I was killed by my father
> And married to my mother
> But born too early to know what happened to me.

Very neatly put, but the poem does not reek of psychology. Moreover, this quiet, unfulfilled, and frustrated man has his virtues. He does not whine, he does not indulge in self-pity, and he has a saving sense of humor. Such humor is revealed in the opening lines of the poem that were cited above. The first line might in an earlier day have been spoken by an old-fashioned New England Calvinist, and spoken with a straight face. But the line that follows could scarcely be so spoken. For if he accomplished so little in his lifetime that in his small town no more than ten neighbors even noticed his death, then surely there had been in heaven much ado about nothing—or almost nothing. Our Bachelor is, as he tells us at the end of the poem, a cynic, yet he is able to "blow you all a kiss from the tomb." It is a brilliant poem. Much is accomplished in that scant thirty-four lines.

I expect my favorite of all Eberhart's poems is **"Aesthetics After War."** Like **"The Fury of Aerial Bombardment,"** it is a war poem, but it is constructed on quite another plan. It is an extended poem in which all sorts of philosophical problems—though they are intensely human problems—are treated. What makes it a very fine poem, however, is not merely the quality of the thought, though that is high, but the power of the imagery and the incisiveness of the phrasing, phrasing which is often arresting, even shocking, pregnant with meaning and gnomic in its concentration, but never merely mystifying.

The meditation finds its focus in the experience of a bombardier on a war plane, and a dominant image is the Mark 18 Bomb Sight and other such precision instruments. The poem is finally, I suppose, about man and God, death and life, and the function and nature of poetry itself. It is too long, too rich, and too intricate for detailed examination on this occasion, but there is sufficient space to quote at least the last twelve lines. They will give the flavor of the poem:

> The poet is a man of sense
> Who handles the brightness of the air,
> The viewless tittles he dandles,
> Timelessness is his everywhere.
>
> His blood is in the rose he contemplates
> The blood of the rose reddens in his mind,
> The poet is master of presences,
> He is the insight of the blind.
>
> Poetry is so mad and so kind
> It is so majestic an inventive surprise,
> Is it any wonder that in it
> The spirit of man arise?

It is a beautiful summary of what the best poetry aims at and accomplishes. It is the kind of success for which I want to pay special tribute to Dick Eberhart. (pp. 31-2)

Cleanth Brooks, "A Tribute to Richard Eberhart," in South Atlantic Review, *Vol. 50, No. 4, November, 1985, pp. 21-33.*

Bruce Jay Friedman

1930-

American novelist, short story writer, scriptwriter, dramatist, and editor.

Friedman is often linked with the black humorists of the 1960s, a category in which critics place novelists and dramatists who use irreverent or grotesque humor to emphasize the absurdities of existence. Objecting to the limits this classification places upon his fiction, however, Friedman refers to himself as "a very serious writer" whose paradoxical perspective evokes life's comic aspects. Employing visceral prose and deadpan humor, Friedman focuses upon the anxieties of middle-class Jews and the pretensions of mainstream society. Often set in New York City or its suburbs, Friedman's fiction features timid protagonists who are alienated and searching for acceptance and strength. Daniel Stern commented: "If ours is the Age of Anxiety, then Bruce Jay Friedman is the man of the age. . . . [His] prose aches with the tensions of his characters, people who don't so much lead lives as run away from them. In them, all our subterranean terrors surface: brazen with desperate humor."

Friedman's highly successful first novel, *Stern* (1962), chronicles the problems encountered by its eponymous hero, an urban Jew who relocates to a suburban Gentile neighborhood. His real and imagined experiences with anti-Semitism provoke paranoid fantasies, an ulcer, and a nervous breakdown. Stern's determination to justify his religion leads to the story's climax: a fistfight with his primary antagonist. Stern's innate impulse to defend a cultural heritage somewhat alien to him illustrates a pervasive dilemma among contemporary American Jews. Alfred Chester remarked: "Stern is a marvelous comic figure, created with just enough exaggeration to make him typify the cringing, cowardly dreamer without ever obscuring his own singular reality." Stern's meek personality manifests itself in many of Friedman's ensuing protagonists. The picaresque work *A Mother's Kisses* (1964) recounts the tumultuous seventeenth summer of Joseph, focusing on his efforts to break away from his domineering mother, Meg. After Joseph is rejected from numerous colleges, Meg uses her persuasive powers to get him accepted into Kansas Land Grant Agricultural and accompanies him there, intending to stay. Only through strong-willed determination does Joseph finally force Meg to leave. Friedman symbolically illustrates that their oppressive relationship will continue, however, for the true hostile thoughts Joseph shouts as Meg boards the departing train are drowned out by the train's whistle. Although several critics condemned Meg as cartoonish, most lauded Friedman's satirical portrait of a stereotypical Jewish Mother.

The Dick (1970) concerns the allure of violence for the browbeaten individual. Ken LePeters is a depressed public relations employee for the New York Police Department whose dismal personal life leads him to transfer to detective duty to obtain the power and authority of a police officer. Friedman presents LePeters' struggles to resolve his disordered life through fragmented anecdotes, a technique he similarly employs in his next book, *About Harry Towns* (1974), which revolves around a middle-aged screenwriter whose carefree

image is a facade for his bleak lifestyle. After the synchronous deaths of his parents and a bout with a blood disease, Harry reevaluates his life, but remains powerless to cope with disappointments. *Tokyo Woes* (1985) is one of Friedman's few works not set in New York City. A farcical commentary on modern Japan, the novel is related from the viewpoint of Mike Halsey, an erratic young man who travels to the Orient on a whim. On the airplane flight he meets Bill Atenabe, who invites him to stay with his family. Mike's visit with the eccentric Atenabe clan serves to illuminate and dispel American notions of Oriental culture. From encounters with the young and elderly, Mike discerns the resentment and friction caused by the clash between Japan's modern and traditional values. While critics commented that *Tokyo Woes* lacked the compassion of Friedman's earlier works, they applauded the author's use of slapstick humor and ironic dialogue.

Friedman's short stories share many of the themes of his novels. The pieces in his first collection, *Far From the City of Class and Other Stories* (1963), are characterized by startling conclusions. The critically acclaimed work "23 Pat O'Brien Movies," for example, concerns a police officer who, after successfully talking a man out of suicide, jumps off the building's ledge himself. Several of the pieces, including the volume's title story, contain characters and scenes later revised and included in *A Mother's Kisses.* Unexpected developments also occur in the stories in *Black Angels* (1966). Unlike Friedman's novels, this volume does not develop themes relating to Judaism, but perpetual feelings of alienation and repression unite the stories' successful yet unfulfilled protagonists. While many of the stories in this collection contain surrealistic elements, critics generally consider the best pieces to be clever treatments of reality, particularly "Black Angels," the tale of a suburban dweller who hires several black handymen to remodel his home. After requesting an extremely low fee for their work, the men charge the suburbanite four hundred dollars an hour for the casual psychiatric advice they have given him.

The sketches and essays in *The Lonely Guy's Book of Life* (1978; republished as *The Lonely Guy,* 1984), which originally appeared in such periodicals as *New York* and *Esquire,* parody the style of "how-to" manuals. Intended to guide forlorn single and divorced men through their urban lives, the book discusses such aspects of single life as eating alone, cooking, and going to the beach. Friedman was commended for his wry, empathetic treatment of contemporary bachelorhood. The pieces in *Let's Hear It for a Beautiful Guy and Other Stories* (1984) portray Manhattan residents as creative and neurotic. Throughout the collection Friedman sets the characters in alien environments to comment on their reactions. In "The Mourner," for example, a man impulsively attends the funeral of a stranger, then becomes incensed at the rabbi's deficient eulogy and offers his own. William Peden observed: "There's a manic quality about the best of Friedman's stories, a sometimes perverse humor, and the presence—never obtrusive but always there—of a really individual consciousness at work."

Friedman is also the author of several dramas. His first play, *Scuba-Duba: A Tense Comedy* (1967), confronts white society's phobias and misconceptions about black people. Harold Wonder, a neurotic Jewish copywriter vacationing on the French Riviera with his family, fears his wife has run off with a black scuba-diver. His masculinity intimidated, he vents his anxiety to all who will listen. In reality, his wife's lover is a sophisticated black poet who threatens Harold's intellect. Although Friedman's treatment of miscegenation and the play's abundance of ribald, ethnic humor provoked controversy, many critics were impressed with *Scuba-Duba's* innovative sociological statements. *Steambath* (1970) is set in Purgatory, which Friedman envisions as a steambath whose Puerto Rican janitor is God. The production is loosely centered on Tandy, a young man who bargains with God for another chance at life until he attains the self-realization that he is actually a shallow, undeserving soul.

Friedman has also written the screenplays *The Owl and the Pussycat* (1971), an adaptation of William Manhof's play of the same title, *Stir Crazy* (1980), *Doctor Detroit* (1983), which is based on his short story, "Detroit Abe," and *Splash!* (1984), on which he collaborated with Lowell Ganz and Babaloo Mandel.

(See also *CLC,* Vols. 3, 5; *Contemporary Authors,* Vols. 9-12, rev. ed.; *Contemporary Authors New Revision Series,* Vol. 25, and *Dictionary of Literary Biography,* Vols. 2, 28.)

EUGENE GOODHEART

The note about Bruce Jay Friedman on the jacket of *Stern* tells us that he attended DeWitt Clinton High School, where he was voted second funniest fellow in the senior class. After reading the book, I can imagine myself as having cast a vote with the majority of the class. The novel is an odd, whimsical descant, complicated by pathos, on the old theme of anti-Semitism. There is certainly enough wit and charm to make us attend to the story, but it leaves us smiling uncertainly at the joke. Contemporary literature has accustomed us to that vaguely defined zone between pathos and comedy, the zone of the absurd. Friedman, however, has not made himself master of the territory, and the result is a little trying. He is elusive without sufficiently inviting our curiosity.

The hero is a complicated fellow both in character and circumstance, with "pale wide hips," a wife who is called a kike and struck by an anti-Semite, a "flowering" ulcer, a lonely son who sucks blankets, an alcoholic mother, and a motley assortment of fears and vibrations. Since Stern is incapable of action, the novel is mostly about his fantasies, which are generally violent with Stern as victimizer or victim. Friedman tries hard to avoid solemnity (though he can't resist sentimentality on several occasions), and the fantasies frequently turn into jokes of the erotic, intestinal, or anal variety. The characterization is often incisive:

> Stern, who felt he'd married prematurely, now prowled tormentedly after women on his tours about the globe, keeping mental track of every loveless caress, every conversation, every female contact, as though only when he'd grabbed a certain number of breasts, stroked a certain number of thighs, racked up a magic number of sleepings would he be able to relax and be married. . . .

Friedman's trouble, I think, is that his attitude and manner immediately arouse expectation of continuous wit and wildness, both in fantasy and in expression, But, despite some extraordinary situations, the execution is strangely timid and thin. Nor has Friedman avoided conventionality in his treatment of Jewish life and "Jewishness" in the evocation of Stern's childhood.

Having said all these hard things, I would make for Friedman the claim that one makes for interesting novelists—that something is happening in his imagination, something still subterranean and secret. If and when it comes to the surface, the result may be quite impressive.

> *Eugene Goodheart, in a review of "Stern," in* Saturday Review, *Vol. XLV, No. 41, October 13, 1962, p. 38.*

JEREMY LARNER

Stern is less a novel in the conventional sense than simply a record of a particular mentality. The protagonist is a certain kind of Jew not unfamiliar in Yiddish literature, a *shlimazl,* the wise, tender fool, who operates on principles of imagination and humor in a world whose blunt force scares him out of his pants. The brutality of the world scares him so deeply because he has the sensitivity to imagine what could happen next—usually someone slamming him in the stomach, raping his wife, torturing his child, ruthlessly severing the fragile emotional threads on which he has so carefully hung his existence.

The most tenuous of all these threads is the respect he must maintain for himself as a man—in terms of the world's own definition of manliness. The peculiar pressure that inflates this book to the bursting point is created by the author's relentless juxtaposition of the inadequacy of the common notion of manliness with the unavoidable compulsion of the hero to judge himself by it. The texture of the book is essentially poetic; it is the poetry of the feminine, accepting, creative personality challenged from without and within by the necessity to be a man and defend one's home and family against forces which are probably insuperable. Particularly, the conflict is expressed in a mild incident of anti-Semitism: a neighbor calls Stern's wife a kike, pushes her so that she trips and (since the lady is not wearing panties) gains an unexpected glimpse into her privacy. The situation is ridiculous, and ostensibly could be dissipated by a harmless fist fight; but to the wide-hipped, soft-bellied Stern the complications are endless: for he sees beyond the immediate conflict to a hatred and cruelty that his loving nature can never solve by acceptance. In his fantasies, the anti-Semitic neighbor is only a representative of a vast and unbeatable mechanism of blind, unappeasable male viciousness against which he is eternally helpless.

The terrible thing about Stern's fantasies—the quality which makes them grip and hurt—is that they have a large foundation in fact. Could Stern use the history of this century to soothe away his nightmares? The fact of the pogrom shadows every page of the book. But of course Stern's Jewishness is just a special instance of a general fear and trembling that is the lot not only of Negroes in the South of South Africa, not only of Angolese and Algerians, but of every individual man who can be drafted by the aggressions of huge groups into situations where he must display his manhood and/or perish. (pp. 380-81)

In his terror, Stern looks for allies, but instead gets only good advice, as when he appeals to a Negro artist acquaintance: "You have got to abstract yourself so that you present a faceless picture to society." Or later, when he stops people on the street and tells them he's going out of his mind: "Never give more'n half a loaf." "You got to stop lookin' for things." "Don't let any person get hold of you." But the trouble with this advice, as with most sound practical advice, is that the nightmare is real.

Stern must go to a sanitarium, where he confronts others who have been grotesquely twisted and debilitated by their failure to meet the threat that they prove themselves. And even at the sanitarium, Stern must cope with his inner demand to act out what is commonly accepted as masculine sexuality. . . .

Even in his beautiful creative playing with his son, the fantasies of violence and helplessness intrude:

> "I'm down here on the floor trapped and the only thing that can get me up is if someone touches a secret place on my ear three times and then taps me with a banana." The boy followed instructions delightedly, and Stern leaped up to shake his hand, saying, "Thank you for saving your daddy. I now owe you one hundred giraffe tails."

If only imaginary giraffe tails could save, Stern at least would be able to pay the price, which is one of the reasons he's so lovable. The rest of the men in his world never think of giraffes and magic bananas, and Bruce Jay Friedman has a devastating ear for all the nasty little sayings they think are funny. Friedman is nervously alive to every bit of brutality that men grab to get through their lives untouched; he is wide open to the comedy and sadness that attend a man who will be touched. **Stern** is an exceptional first novel. The plot will rupture a purist's sense of novelistic completeness, but the emotional impact accumulates, is steady and of a piece—and that's what counts. (p. 381)

> *Jeremy Larner, "Compulsion to Toughness," in* The Nation, *New York, Vol. 195, No. 18, December 1, 1962, pp. 380-81.*

NAT HENTOFF

The circumstances which begin [*Stern*]—a splattering act of anti-Semitism against Stern's wife and child just after the family has moved into a strange suburb—will, of course, make the novel's gradual excavation of Stern's layers of fear acutely relevant to Jewish readers. All but the most diligently assimilated of Reform and disaffiliated Jews are still aware of being outsiders, to a smaller or larger extent, in a country in which "brotherhood" usually ceases after office hours. In my own case, although I have never seen a pogrom and have lived for thirty-seven years with only one beating for my Jewishness, the sudden announcement of a nationwide pogrom would somehow not be a total surprise. Certainly, this latent expectation of immolation because of lineage is irrational here and now, but it is shared by many more American Jews than will admit it—to others or to themselves.

Stern, however, is not only about Jews. It transcends that kind of "problem" novel by making its unhero bring more and more to the surface the tangled tensions and fragmentized self-delusions of the citizenry at large. Friedman, moreover, in a major stylistic achievement, fuses achingly realistic detail with enflamed fantasies to make Stern loomingly alive. Stern has a presence, almost a palpability of flesh and gait, that is exceedingly rare in current fiction and that ultimately makes Stern's struggle to stay in contact with reality, any kind of reality, a startlingly personal self-exposure while also reflecting . . . our common condition.

Stern is Everyman, who wonders whether he will spend all his life in a maze; and he is also only Stern, whom we leave with his ulcer temporarily at rest and holding his wife and child "a fraction longer than he'd intended."

The plot is both simple and bottomless. Stern's brooding and fantasizing about the insult to his family gradually disintegrates his barriers of self-protection against boss, strangers, his family, and ultimately, himself. The poisons of clenched rage, fear and self-contempt bring forth the ulcer. Stern is "cured" in a Home whose rotting patients are undressed by Friedman with a tartly affecting combination of compassion and gothic wonder at how misshapen a human being can become and still twist himself into yet another posture of survival.

Stern returns home, finally confronts the anti-Semite who started his ulcer blooming, and fails in his rite of exorcism by fists. He has been split into too many pieces for too long a time, and it is very doubtful that all the king's horses and all the king's men could possibly put him together again.

The novel does not so much end, as flow into "real life." It is entirely conceivable that some who read this book will look into the mirror and see Stern. Friedman, incidentally, offers neither solution nor catharsis. But he does take some of the bandages off our wounds. (pp. 294-95)

Nat Hentoff, "Anxiety and Paranoia," in The Commonweal, *Vol. LXXVII, No. 11, December 7, 1962, pp. 294-95.*

HASKEL FRANKEL

When Bruce Jay Friedman's first novel, *Stern,* appeared, reviewers in their desperation to convey what made the book such fun to read, came up with references to Chagall, Walter Mitty, Leopold Bloom, Charlie Chaplin, Hieronymous Bosch, Nathanael West, *Catch-22,* and Peter De Vries. While it may seem impossible that one novel and one author could encompass so many qualities, there isn't one I could cross from the list.

In fact, now that Mr. Friedman's second novel (a collection of short stories, *Far From the City of Class,* was published in 1963) has appeared, the only way I can begin to describe it is to take the above list and add to it *The Skin of Our Teeth, Ah Wilderness, Auntie Mame, The Goldbergs,* George Price's cartoons, *Gypsy* and a pinch of *Moll Flanders.* Put them all together and they may spell mother, but I doubt if they will convey the impact of this author's prose.

In *Stern,* Mr. Friedman was concerned with the emotional spiraling of a thirtyish neurotic, a man more at home on Madison Avenue than in a synagogue, who encounters anti-Semitism when he tries suburban living. In *A Mother's Kisses,* he details the key months that see a 17-year-old boy become an independent man. (Readers of *Stern* will easily recognize the ulcer-ridden hero of the first novel as the mother-ridden hero of the second.) *Stern* revealed a wild comic gift, but the zaniness came poking through an essentially somber story. In *A Mother's Kisses,* the amalgam is reversed. Pain lurks in the wings while the pig bladder and the baggy pants move downstage. Both novels suggest a world ordained by Freud but populated by the Keystone Kops.

Synopsizing a Friedman plot is like making a tracing of the Mona Lisa. You can reproduce the shape and dimensions perfectly but nothing that reveals the work's unique quality. To wit: *A Mother's Kisses* is a picaresque novel that tells of the summer that Joseph hung around Brooklyn brooding about the fact that he had no college waiting for him. His mother takes over and puts him in a summer camp, then rescues him from it, establishes him on a campus called Kansas Land Grant Agricultural, follows him out there and eventually goes home alone.

So what have you got? A Jewish boy breaks free of mama. So what's that? "Auntie Mame Goes to a Bar Mitzvah"? "Catcher in the Sour Rye"? Not in a million years. What you've got is a world where 14-year-old campers have "the faces of middle-aged manufacturers"; . . . where a father-son day of communing produces such shared intimacies as "I buy a paper here" at a newsstand and "I usually stand at this end and hold on to a strap" in the subway; where a sister's football-playing boy-friend wears an overcoat in summer and offers free coaching in "how to play dirty."

Most of all, you've got the most unforgettable mother since Medea. Meg is heaven and hell jammed into a hammock-sized bra and a too-tight girdle. She is a Bensonhurst Mae West, a Jocasta with no intention of telling Oedipus who he really is. She is Theda Bara with a henna rinse, and Molly Goldberg with a plunging neckline. . . .

"Did your mother ever let you down? Will you please learn to put your last buck on this baby?" Meg tells Joseph, and she is not just whistling "Yiddishe Mama."

Come to think of it, Meg's advice is good for readers, too. Run, push, play dirty. But get a copy of *A Mother's Kisses* immediately.

Haskel Frankel, "Oedipus Schmoedipus," in The New York Times Book Review, *August 16, 1964, p. 5.*

NELSON ALGREN

Although *Time* magazine described Bruce Jay Friedman's *Stern* as a novel "in the tradition of the Jewish *schlemiel* story and the Charlie Chaplin movie," and its author as a Jewish protagonist, *Stern* was a satire too angry, a farce too anguished, ever to reach the American screen; Stern himself has precisely nothing to do with the legendary ghetto chump; and Friedman is not a Jewish protagonist. . . .

Friedman has nothing of the cleverness of Roth; he lacks Bellow's intellectualism altogether. Unlike Malamud, his people don't even have connections to a life of the past. Their severance is demonstrated by Stern's own hallucinatory progress. For he embodies not tradition but disorder, the disorder of the great city. And Stern's way marks the end of a time, for American multitudes, when each man belonged to the company of men. "Plunged in torment plunged in fire"— Friedman's sources, if he must be categorized, are nearer to those of Beckett than to his New York colleagues. His people were weak in the head when they came into the world. It is Stern who drags along at the end of Pozzo's rope. And when Stern enters the Grove Rest Home for the cure of an ulcer ("a hairy coarse-tufted little animal that squawked for nourishment) we are truly among those whose birth was astride a grave. . . .

The difference between Friedman and Beckett is that while Beckett assigns a separate ash can to each of his characters, Friedman uses no props: his people simply live ash-can lives. Grove Rest itself is such a can, electrified and provided with cots, through which time alternates not between day and night but between Pill-and-Bandage Time and Milk-and-Cookie Time. (p. 142)

Stern has nothing to do with *The Rise of David Levinsky* and everything to do with the fall of Jack Ruby. His history puts the reader between Dostoevsky and Goldwater: between the Underground Man's warning that "We don't even know what living is now" and a summons "to come to the defense of Western Civilisation, that noblest creation of the mind and heart of man."

The devastation of human values, adumbrated by Dostoevsky, is embodied at Grove Rest. When it's Pill-and-Bandage Time among the Porch People, we realize what the mind and heart of man has created. And this is accomplished in a comedy of such depth, in a farce of such savagery, that dramatization of Grove Rest would require the services of Bert Lahr and Dorothy Loudon. Yet Friedman employs the findings of modern analysis without making the reader feel he is in Group Therapy.

The satire is sustained in Friedman's second volume, *Far from the City of Class.* In one of these stories, **"A Foot in the Door,"** the author has adapted the Faustian legend to the burlesque stage, in a take-off of the values that propel The Young Man on the Way Up. Here the ambitious *petit-bourgeois,* Gordon, is seduced by his insurance man, Merz, into giving up his hair in return for Merz's word that Gordon's rival, in a race for office promotion, will be put out of the running. Gordon's hair falls out within a month, and the rival is shipped to Dubuque. As Gordon's gains in money and prestige increase, his emotional life is diminished until he has no love left in his life. Here Friedman has put the Biblical wisdom, that he who gains his life must lose it, into fresh phrasing: "Beware of what you ask for—you may get it."

The same sense of loss, and of longing to belong, invests his current novel, *A Mother's Kisses.* "Wait till you have to say hello to life," the 17-year-old Joseph's mother warns him, "have you got surprises coming. Take a look over your shoulder and see what's really coming."

Meg herself provides most of the surprises; and Joseph's greatest hope is to look over her shoulder and not see *her* coming. When she gets him accepted as a freshman at something called Kansas Land U., the boy thinks he's going to get away from her. But Meg puts colleges in the same category as sold-out musicals and jammed restaurants. She had gotten him into hit shows by having the management set up a kitchen chair in the aisle. She had broken lines waiting at restaurants by saying to the headwaiter, "I've got a hungry kid. Do you think you could do a little something, doll?" And, magically, a table would appear and Joseph would have to eat under the indignant view of standees. Now, when she starts packing perfumes into a valise, he asks, "Why are you packing? You're not going anywhere." (pp. 142-43)

She can't leave him at all. And the boy himself lacks the strength to cut the cord. Under his need to gain his manhood runs a current of fear of living without Meg near. Friedman's craft is in provoking laughter at the same time that the air grows murderous. Meg is simply a mother of such personal force that she is an affliction.

In his desperation to rid himself of her hold, Joseph reminds her of the uses to which she put him as a child. He brings up all the times she had snatched him from deep midnight sleeps to sing "Prisoner of Love" for living room company.

"Who were those people that they were so important?" he wants to know now. "How do you think I felt singing at those hours, a little boy?"

And of how, the winter he had had chicken pox, she had whisked him along on her St. Petersburg vacation, hiding him in lower berths and telling conductors all he had was hives.

"I'll kill myself," is Meg's answer to that now, "and the son of a bitch remembered. Who knew it would develop such a month?" . . .

What makes Friedman more interesting than most of Malamud, Roth and Bellow is the sense he affords of possibilities larger than the doings and undoings of the Jewish urban bourgeois, which, after all, comprises but an infinitesimal aspect of American life. What makes him more important is that he writes out of the viscera instead of the cerebrum. What makes him more dangerous is that while they distribute

prose designed by careful planning for careful living, Friedman really doesn't know what he's doing. "I can remember being inside Mommy," Stern's infant son tells him, "I knew about the Three Stooges in there."

Bruce Jay Friedman is that rarity, a compulsive writer whose innocence makes his flaws of greater value, ultimately, than the perfections of skilled mechanics. (p. 143)

Nelson Algren, "The Radical Innocent," in The Nation, *New York, Vol. 199, No. 7, September 21, 1964, pp. 142-43.*

DAVID SEGAL

Ordinarily it is only good manners to judge a book on its own merits. However, when the book in question follows a brilliant first novel, comparisons become inevitable. Bruce Friedman's first novel, **Stern,** was deservedly a great critical success. Stern himself was a considerable achievement. Faced with a great range of disequilibrium, from crabgrass to anti-Semitism, from an ulcer to a dog that led him by the wrist the long way home, Stern never quite coped, but he never completely lost his balance. Friedman was hailed as the creator of a Jewish Everyman, but he had accomplished more than that. He had created a Jewish individual, whose implications reached far beyond the usual novel of Jewish life. The book is funny, and tender, and perceptive. Unfortunately. *A Mother's Kisses* is only funny. (pp. 302-03)

[If] *Stern* is funny in the direction of Chaplin, this book is funny in the direction of Bob Hope. Everything depends on timing, and turn of phrase, nothing on characterization or story. There is no movement of plot—the two main characters remain frozen in the same relation to each other from the first page to the last. These two are a son—gawky, adolescent, sensitive, dreaming—and a mother—shrill, brisk, vulgar, cocky, sexy, and a sure-fire laugh getter. She controls Joseph's life by an artful combination of self-pity, bull-headedness and boast, and she controls the rest of the world the same way. The trouble is, she does not exist at all; she is all rhetoric and cartoon.

She is Ma Goldberg blown up and done funny. . . . But that is all she is. Friedman takes his conception from the music hall and the soap opera, and he leaves her there. His comic imagination is marvelous for the broad stroke, but is not up to the distortion that illuminates.

There is only one scene in the book in which his conceptual ability is working at the same level as his verbal facility, and that deals with Joseph and his father. This is odd, because as in all versions of this myth of Jewish life, the father is dim to the point of non-existence. The father takes Joseph to work one day. . . . In the shop he introduces Joseph to his boss, then says, " 'The fellow I'm going to bring over now, I'm the boss of him.' The fellow comes over and says, 'Hi, kid. I work for your dad.' " In the subway, going home, the father says, " 'Now is when I read my paper.' " It is very terrible, and very true.

The trouble with Joseph's relationship with his mother is that it is not terrible enough, or true enough. They circle each other, but nothing happens. They play out a sexual pantomime but the final explosion does not occur. If they had been permitted to move from caricature to humanity the book could have had a culmination that would justify it. Some symbolic way should have been found for them to devour each other, or go to bed with each other, or both. Instead, having got Joseph into college, and gone with him, his mother finally goes home. Joseph yells to the receding train, "You're not great at all. I never enjoyed one second with you." But of course the mother can't hear, and the reader no longer cares. (pp. 303-04)

David Segal, "Only Funny," in The Commonweal, *Vol. LXXXI, No. 9, November 20, 1964, pp. 302-04.*

ROBIE MACAULEY

Mr. Friedman's worst tendency [in *Black Angels*] is to reach out for the neatly-packaged plot, the nifty magazine invention that can be forgotten almost before it is over. The kind of thing I mean is apparent in such stories as **"The Investor,"** **"Show Biz Connections,"** and **"The Mission,"** which sound like imitations of John Collier as re-told by an imitator of Bernard Malamud. In the first of these, a doctor discovers that a hospital patient's temperature rises and falls in exact and mysterious correspondence with the fluctuations of a certain stock on the market. In **"Show Biz Connections,"** a magic stranger gives the hero a chance to be teleported to various places where a beautiful woman is faced with disaster—and thus will fall into his arms. **"The Mission"** is an extended joke, worthy of Bob Hope or, perhaps more accurately, Eddie Cantor. A man who overcomes all kinds of obstacles to go into darkest Africa and obtain the tongue of an extremely rare animal and to have it cooked by a great French chef turns out to be an American prison officer providing the condemned man's last dinner.

Unfortunately, this kind of cartoon cleverness invades and diminishes a number of the more seriously-meant stories—such as **"The Punch"** and **"The Humiliation."** What strength there is in them (and in others such as **"The Neighbors"** and **"Black Angels"**) comes largely from the ghostly presence of the hero of Mr. Friedman's excellent first novel, **Stern.** Good as that book is, I was relieved to get rid of Stern with all his toppling load of guilt and paranoia. It is disappointing to find that his spirit, briefly and dimly recalled, is one of the few relatively-convincing things in this volume.

Robie Macauley, "Cartoons and Arabesques," in Book Week—World Journal Tribune, *September 25, 1966, p. 4.*

WEBSTER SCHOTT

Black humor goes places on gutbusters and shockers because it chooses to compete imaginatively with a factual world beyond "reality." . . . "A new Jack Rubyesque chord of absurdity has been struck in the land," Friedman said last summer, and it "can only be dealt with by a new one-foot-in-the-asylum style of fiction."

He runs this mutative new reality to a dead heat [in *Black Angels*]. In his title story, Negro workers swarm over a suburbanite's house and—for peanuts—turn it into a showplace. Complete paint job: $58. A fantastic network of drainage pipes for $12.50. Floors shellacked for $2.80. One evening Stefano, the owner, heart heavy as lead, invites one of the handymen in for a beer and talks about his runaway wife and lousy childhood. It helps.

"This is going to sound crazy," he says, "but what if we just talked this way, couple of times a week . . . for fun. What would you charge me? An hour?"

"Fo' hunnid," said the Negro.

"Four hundred. That's really a laugh. You must be out of your head. Don't you know I was just kidding around?"

The Negro took a sip of beer and rose to leave.

"All right, wait a second," said Stefano. "Let's just finish up this hour, then we'll see about other times. This one doesn't count, does it?"

"It do," said the Negro, sinking into the couch and snapping out a pad and pencil.

In **"The Neighbors"** a middle-class property owner goes on and on about the boorish loudmouth who has just moved in next door. Eventually we discover they are both dead, interred in adjacent plots. . . . In **"The Hero"** a high-school football player gets knocked in the head, turns into a human bulldog, and dies with his jaws clamped around the ankle of a would-be Presidential assassin. It's the Oswald story in reverse: the pseudo-mother gets $20,000 in beer money and a crack at the U.S. Senate.

Friedman invents as if he were taking a creative aptitude test for employment in a corporate nut house. . . . A professional dance critic enters erotic paradise—his recompense for extracting a thorn from a Broadway producer's foot—and goes up in flames. A job interviewer learns nothing about applicants because he can't think of anything except their secret sex lives. A young businessman attends a boxing match in commemoration of his dead Uncle Roger, who said fighters love one another. He sees one boxer's head literally knocked off: "It sailed out rather swiftly, in the style of a baseball hit . . . out into the sixth row ringside, where it was caught by a gentleman in the haberdashery business."

"In its essence," said Joseph Conrad "my work . . . is action, nothing but action," But he added, "action of human beings that will bleed to a prick." Like most black humorists, Friedman has the action but not the bleeding characters. He creates few authentic individuals: a lonely hot-pants entrepreneur in the Caribbean, a young Jew struggling to understand his family through his crazy uncle, an ex-army lieutenant who will never even an old score because it is with himself. His characters merge into a composite disturbed Everyman.

What Friedman and his colleagues are up to has an equivalent in junk sculpture. Using the materials at hand—our epidemic dislocation, conditioning to insanity, reality beyond explication and the sure finality awaiting us—he is trying to make our new intrinsic fiction. To disarm death, erotic disloyalty, matrimonial doom, to laugh at them. To discover the truth of our situation and expand it billboard-size.

Friedman succeeds. He's a very funny guy. Like poetry, his black humor leads us to infer personal truths from his ambiguous stories. (pp. 4-5)

Webster Schott, "Shockers and Gutbusters," in The New York Times Book Review, *October 2, 1966, pp. 4-5.*

TIME, NEW YORK

Stage humor is in transition. The old humor of the gag and the wisecrack was confident, benign, a pick-me-up rather than a put-down. The new humor, which draws its tone from play-wrights such as Albee and Pinter, is cruel, taut-nerved, and speaks the lingo of the obscene and the absurd, not funny-ha-ha but funny-peculiar. The new humor reigns in off-Broadway's *Scuba Duba*, a flagellatingly funny first play by Novelist Bruce Jay Friedman. . . .

The opening curtain finds *Scuba Duba's* hero holding a huge scythe in the middle of a Riviera château drawing room. Harold Wonder has an albatross complex and a symbolic knife at his throat. While his two children lie asleep upstairs, his wife is out cuckolding him with a Negro skindiver, or so he thinks. Harold, in a skull-popping panic, half-dials phones, swigs champagne from a bottle, runs to the door with his scythe and roars out bloody maledictions on "the Goddamn spade frogman." . . .

Perhaps a call back to Mom in the New York City Borough of Queens, "where I had defenses," might help. Cold comfort there. "Is that why you called, Harold?" bleats his *Yiddisha* Mama. "You thought your mother needed a little filth thrown in her face all the way from France?" More cheer is shed by a sexy sylph in a mauve postage-stamp bikini. Miss Janus has a Proust-like remembrance of flings past and an impish vein of insecurity: "I wish I could get to the state where I truly believed my behind was beautiful."

Throughout the play Friedman lances pet hates with an ardor so indiscriminate as to seem bracingly honest. The air is unfogged by any pious cant about brotherly love as he tongue-twits Jews, Negroes, Babbitts, Frenchmen, Chinese, Yugoslavs, white liberals, black militants, wives, husbands, thieves and psychiatrists. (p. 82)

Early and logically Friedman says: "There's just no right way to *be* about Negroes." In Act II, Harold's wife shows up with two Negroes, the skindiver and the man she really loves, a Brooks Brothers type who recites poetry and cherishes her femininity. Harold is more deeply nonplussed than he was by the notion of his wife's surrender to a typical minstrel man who is also a switchblade artist and a sexual athlete. Playgoers may be equally nonplussed by the belated stab at seriousness, especially after Friedman's nightlong skill at making race a laughing matter. (pp. 82-3)

"Cuckold in a Panic," in Time, *New York, Vol. 90, No. 16, October 20, 1967, pp. 82, 84.*

EDITH OLIVER

The setting for Bruce Jay Friedman's *Scuba Duba,* is the living room of a château in the south of France. There is a staircase leading to a balcony that runs partway around the room; white moonlight pours through enormous French windows, bleaching everything to pale and shadowy grays. Nothing could be more exquisite or romantic . . . and nothing could be more purposely misleading. For *Scuba Duba* is a *Hellz-a-Poppin* of black comedy-full of the roughhouse and the raw sight gags of burlesque, in which almost every traditional comic routine or attitude you can think of is exposed and given a new, curdled edge, and in which a number of non-comic attitudes, noble and ignoble, are changed in the course

of the action. I think I should report right off, though, that I was more galled than entertained by it.

The action takes place during a single night. The hero is an American advertising man—he writes copy for billboards—and a veteran of several civil-rights marches. He has rented the château for himself and his family for a month or two in summer, and now his wife has just run off with (he thinks) a Negro scuba diver, leaving him alone and in striped pajamas, with a couple of sleeping children upstairs. He is not alone for long. He is shortly joined by a footloose, kookie girl who has wandered in to play the piano and who decides to keep him company, telling him in a gentle, faraway voice one hair-raising, if pointless, anecdote after another. . . . The hero has put in a transatlantic call to his Jewish mother, and a life-size cartoon cutout of her slides onto the stage and off as her voice is heard over a microphone. There are also sliding cutouts of a psychiatrist and of the scuba diver, both of whom appear later on, the psychiatrist with a Louis Vuitton overnight case and a middle-aged Cockney lady (who at one point walks bare-breasted into the living room), and the scuba diver, in a helmet and a black rubber suit, with the missing wife and a Negro poet. Also among the intruders are an elderly, kittenish landlady, a Babbitty American tourist, a burglar, and a French policeman, the last two straight out of Mack Sennett. So much that takes place Off Broadway pretends to be wild yet is really conventional or milk-and-water underneath, but *Scuba Duba* is wild in conception. . . . Through the pandemonium as one stuffed target after another is not so much hit as slashed away at, there is a play, with a plot that is carried by dialogue even more than by business. (pp. 82, 84, 86)

Scuba Duba accomplishes whatever it sets out to do, I guess. The gutter talk that prevails is shocking (the shocks weaken as time goes by) and appropriate. The script, though too long by at least half an hour, is stylish and full of comic surprises and odd turns of speech, although some of the small throwaway lines seemed funnier than the big, important gags, sight and sound. I just wish it were not so disagreeable. Perhaps the humor is too know-it-all and indecent and self-indulgent for me, and, in its lip-smacking glee, perhaps it comes too close to showing off. (p. 86)

Edith Oliver, "Funny but too Funny," in The New Yorker, *Vol. XLIII, No. 35, October 21, 1967, pp. 82, 84, 86.*

EDITH OLIVER

Actually, [Bruce Jay Friedman's *Steambath*] does not work, but there is more fun in it, once it gets off the ground, than there is in any number of shows that do. The steam bath, where all the action takes place, is Purgatory—a metaphor that Mr. Friedman doesn't bother to pursue, which is just as well. His line of thought, while novel, is unimpressive, but it does give him room for jokes and routines that pay off. All the characters, except for the Puerto Rican attendant, who is God, and his assistant, are dead and on their way. The raffish crew includes an old-timer, who reports in one funny monologue after another all that he has seen and done in the course of a remarkably well-packed life; a couple of feathery chorus boys; a brash and tiresome Jew; a stockbroker; and, finally, a pretty blonde and a handsome young man. What plot there is concerns the young man's attempts to persuade, or needle, God into letting him return to life. All ends in a standoff. Only the two of them are left on the stage; the others have gone through the door that opens on Heaven or Hell. As the young man continues to plead, God, half noticing him, continues to play solitaire as the curtain comes down. That actual curtain coming down, for the first time in years Off Broadway, turns out to be the most exciting, though not the most entertaining, effect in the show. The most entertaining is one in which God dictates to a machine his specific instructions for running the world: "Clean bath towels in every room at the Tel Aviv Hilton;" "Give that girl on the bus a run in her body stocking."

Mr. Friedman's notion of making God a Puerto Rican steambath attendant, full of ethnic pride and ethnic touchiness—sometimes offhand, sometimes tough, and sometimes a downright showoff, as when he tries to affirm his identity by doing card tricks—is wild and original and entirely appropriate to the show. . . . As for *Steambath* as a whole, there are many slack or messy or dull lines along with the good ones. Mr. Friedman is a gifted comedy writer much of the time. What he could have used, I think, is a stretch on the staff of the late Fred Allen, a man who never made a mistake about humor and who could have told him to take that out or leave that alone or, most important, "That's enough." And I hope Mr. Allen would have advised him to cut all those swatches of feverish chatter sprinkled with the names of actors in old movies on television. They have grown so stale that even the audience doesn't laugh at them anymore.

Edith Oliver, "Outward Bound in a Cloud of Steam," in The New Yorker, *Vol. XLVI, No. 21, July 11, 1970, p. 48.*

ALEX KENEAS

God knows, life can be absurd. Jean-Paul Sartre knew it. And so does Bruce Jay Friedman. But while Sartre's *No Exit* tried to illuminate our spiritual nakedness with philosophy, Friedman in his second play, *Steambath,* snaps a wet towel at our vulnerably bare-bottomed psyches. And Friedman, author of *Scuba Duba* as well as such brilliantly biting novels as *A Mother's Kisses,* has the comic genius to bring off the idea that absurdity is its own best anodyne—and perhaps the only one.

As in Sartre, the characters are dead, trapped in the nowhere of a steam bath. There's a door to the Beyond. Heaven or hell? We don't know, but it can't be all bad—John Hodiak is there.

Simmering in slight discomfort are a motley lot, each with his story to tell. There is little overt plot except for the vain attempt of Tandy to return to the living. What moves the play along are the individual revelations, the baggage and debris and despair of urban life that each has carried into this way station: the unpaid bill at Bloomingdale's, the unfinished historical novel on Charlemagne, the charity work with brain-damaged welders.

It's all borne buoyantly on the billowing Friedman humor. "I've had some wonderful sweats in my time," says the Old Timer, relishing the steam room. The sexy blonde confesses that she thought death meant being condemned to spend each night in a different Holiday Inn. Another character cherishes nostalgic memories of a generation rich enough to produce two such stalwarts as Dane Clark and Norman Podhoretz.

Friedman's most elaborate joke is God—who is not only alive and well but a Guess What? The steam bath's Puerto Rican attendant is God. When He orders a sandwich, He says, "You burn the toas' I smite you with my terrible sweeft sword." . . .

Of course Friedman's steam bath is life not death. And though it makes you laugh rather than sweat, the dark vapors of living linger—the private hangups, the unfulfilled longings. They may not be much but they are quintessentially human. Besides, Friedman tells us, they're all we have.

Alex Keneas, "Sweating It Out," in Newsweek, *Vol. LXXVI, No. 2, July 13, 1970, p. 101.*

DANIEL STERN

In his new novel **The Dick** Friedman chooses to work with the horrors—and seductions—of violence that are surfacing in our lives. It is, in many ways, his most ambitious work. Less glued to autobiography than either *Stern* or *A Mother's Kisses, The Dick* creates a metaphor for our ambivalence towards violence. Actually, the dick is not a dick at all. He is, as described in the unusually witty jacket copy, a demi-dick. He wears not a badge but a badgette. And he doesn't beat up or gun down crooks like the real dicks in the homicide bureau where he pursues his uncertain career. He is a public relations man for a "large, violent but somehow conscience-stricken homicide bureau in the East that needed a public-relations team to repair its grim and tawdry image."

The dick's name was originally Kenneth Sussman. While in the Army he had, on impulse, changed his name to Ken LePeters.

> Immediately after tacking on the new name, LePeters could have sworn there had been a global Sussman breakthrough. Each time he picked up a newspaper, it seemed a Sussman had rocketed to the top of an international cartel, smashed a record at Grand Prix, become a leading fashion photographer. . . .

Still "loosely sutured" to his new name, LePeters lives a split life (a little too clearly embodied in a face divided by a long, wandering scar). He has come from the vague and bland Midwest to the East. Though not a real cop he lives on Detective's Hill, a suburb favored by retired police chiefs, and hence the only completely safe neighborhood in fiction or life. He is a fearful (and semi-admiring) observer of the violent detectives with whom he works. His daughter's enrollment in an almost entirely black school throws him into a panicky attempt to get her out—panic is the natural state of the Friedman hero and LePeters is no exception. By coming East he hopes to put his life more in touch with some undefined reality. But it is utterly out of reach. When he makes love to his wife he can, somehow, never find her lips, and settles for a lifetime of lipless sex. In spite of all his efforts his daughter remains in the all-black school—the only results of his extrication attempts being the first psychosomatic hernia in modern fiction.

Towards the end of the somewhat rambling tale LePeters's wife Claire has an affair with an ex-dick named Chico—formerly the holder of the highest kill-count at police headquarters. It is not a conventional climax, though it serves as a lever for movement. Friedman does not rely on narrative tension to hold his people in place or the reader to the page. If anything, his novels are a series of mad anecdotes piled one on the other, tied together by obsessions, anxieties, and by language more full of surprises than any new American writer I can think of (as in Céline, a writer who has greatly influenced Friedman). What is new in *The Dick* and, I'm told, in his new play *Steambath,* is the use of poetic metaphor and emblems for the conduct of his hero. These, like the title, the facial scar, the genital mess and the west-to-east movement, are all on the obvious side. Yet they work. Perhaps this is because the language is so strong, the laughter so wild and the imagination that informs both prose and incident so unique.

At any one time there are never more than a few writers of whom it can be said that any new book of theirs *has* to be worth reading, give or take a few faults of intention or execution. For some time now I've felt this to be true of Bruce Jay Friedman. With *The Dick* he proves it is still so. His urban Jewish Everyman wears his anguish with a difference, skating on the edge of sexual and parental failure (and occasional success), beset by racial fears and violent fantasies. In the present book he almost breaks out of that terror-enclosed circle by choosing to be the rat instead of the cheese. LePeters trains to become a *real* dick. Surprisingly, he makes it. But still another surprise follows which I will not spoil by revealing. Not that one can spoil a book like this—all tone and wild wit. Read it for yourself. If you believe in reading, then when a book by Friedman comes along you have to read it. It's as simple as that. (pp. 4-5)

> *Daniel Stern, "An Anguish Worn with a Difference," in* Book World—The Washington Post, *September 13, 1970, pp. 4-5.*

DENIS DONOGHUE

Mr. Friedman writes with American verve, he drives his style as if it were a fast car. His common talk is fast, the book offers lots of chuckles. (pp. 23-4)

The trouble with *The Dick* is that it has no subject, no content, it is about nothing. The book is all margin, no text. The fragments fly past, but they do not cohere at any point. It is significant that Mr. Friedman tells us everything about Ken's vacancy, but nothing about his job; plenty of sex life, but no life. The paragraphs are lively while they last, but it is easy to forget them. The only character for whose fate it would be possible to care is the daughter, Jamie, and it is clear that she will come to no permanent harm. Once that is established, the history of Mr. and Mrs. LePeters is something I can contemplate with indifference; whether she returns to Ken's nest, or goes off permanently with Chico, is a matter of literary indifference, whatever a moralist chooses to make of it.

"What am I supposed to do?" the erring wife asks her husband.

"I can't help you on that," Ken says, and he guns the car away. A few minutes before, the wife had put up a fight to save the home.

"You don't see it at all, do you? That all of this was just for us. So I could be a better wife." I would not take her back after that line: adultery is bad enough, but a woman emitting those lines deserves hanging. (p. 24)

> *Denis Donoghue, "Ghosts and Others," in* The New York Review of Books, *Vol. XV, No. 8, November 5, 1970, pp. 22-4.*

GILBERT SORRENTINO

One of the great problems of "black humor," of which Mr. Friedman is a practitioner, is that it hovers uneasily between satire, which it is not, and camp, which it sometimes is. Satire, in Wyndham Lewis' phrase, is "the great Heaven of Ideas," and its intent is to destroy; on the other hand, in that most gutless of genres, camp, large servings of the decayed are proffered with the tacit suggestion that the author knows their nature and is therefore not to be indicted for stupidity.

I have read several reviews of *The Dick,* all of which point apologetically to the tattered symbolism of the book as a kind of flaw: the title; the bisected face of the hero, Kenneth LePeters; his psychosomatic groin injury—and on and on. It seems to me, however, that Mr. Friedman is perfectly well aware of the bathos of such symbolism, that it is folded into the book in a shamelessly disingenuous way, that it is, absolutely, an instance of camp. It is impossible in these times for a professional writer not to know how ineffective such lumpy and intransigent symbols are. On the contrary, the author has placed them in the book in so obvious a way that only a numskull could take them at face value. Mr. Friedman *means* for you to see the triteness of such weary machinery, and to applaud its clanking.

The narrative line of *The Dick* is secondary and merely conventional—which is by no means a fault: the plotted novel has been finished off by masters, and the modern writer must use it simply as a structural device or eschew it completely. Doing away with the story line forces the writer to concentrate on his language—which is what finally determines the quality of all writing, good or bad. The difference between this novel as published and this novel as the short story it might have been lies in the padding Friedman has applied to it. Somewhere in this morass of hip Myron Cohen stories, there is the possibility of a short story: it grew as the jokes grew, and ended as the novel now before us.

The Dick is composed of block-like paragraphs, most of them sufficient unto themselves, laced with gags, and ending with one-liners. The jokes are at the expense of everybody—another difference between black humor and satire, since satire aims point-blank at something the author means to kill. The laughter in *The Dick* is human laughter, very different from the laughter one hears thinly in the pages of *Gulliver's Travels* or *The Apes of God* or, for that matter, *Naked Lunch.* I bring up this point not to belabor *The Dick* for what it is not but to call into question the entire genre of literature loosely labeled black humor. For the satiric scourge it substitutes a gentle nudge, a gesture that passes current with the literate elite who have accounts at the First National Bank of Hip Ideas. If it is fashionable to be gently anti-Semitic, it is equally fashionable to be gently anti-black. This sort of humor is without focus; it gives equal time to everybody; it operates off the *Zeitgeist,* confident that it will be recognized as sophisticated. In a word, it pleases.

One "knows" that *The Dick* is not anti-Semitic, though it is; nor is it anti-black, nor even anti-cop—though it is. All these things, it is assumed, are equally absurd to those who make steady withdrawals from the First National, so all these things may be ribbed. But nothing is flayed alive and nothing is destroyed, and here we are in camp.

There is not much to say about Friedman's prose. It is thick, has a dead weight to it, and is spiced with vulgarisms and sudden intrusions of "surprise" words that work to give it a life that its cadences deny it. Yet this prose serves the purposes of the novel perfectly. It is a sort of sham prose, smoothly engineered to chew up everything. It is a prose that seems to grin knowingly at the reader, and mutter, "We all know what I'm talking about, right?" It does not define, it skates over; it does not discriminate, it lumps together; most important, it does not deal with things but with sophisticated notions about things. (pp. 536-37)

The Dick is successful on its own terms, but I am against it. However, I recognize that this novel, and all black humor, give a voice to confused liberals. No doubt the genre will have a long run as a palatable substitute for satire, for which the absurd is not a bedfellow but a target. (p. 537)

Gilbert Sorrentino, "Shooting Blanks," in The Nation, New York, Vol. 211, No. 17, November 23, 1970, pp. 536-37.

SANFORD PINSKER

We are hardly surprised when a contemporary novelist declines rather than develops. By now the pattern—of novel after novel building on the substructure of an impressive, initial effort—is all too familiar. *Stern* is such a novel, the sort that is likely to be resurrected when the furor about Black Humor is over and Salinger no longer seems to be the alpha and omega of the Fifties. It's all there in *Stern:* the uneasy Jewishness, the ulcers, the suburban situation. But the sense of terror about it all is actualized, located in a compactness which never quite appears again in Friedman's fiction.

Some fifteen years earlier Hollywood had imagined what the complications of the pastoral homeowner might be like and they called it *Mr. Blandings Builds His Dream House.* Predictably enough, the results were full of good cheer, even when nightmares gained on dreams and Cary Grant seemed, almost, to lose his cool. *Stern* shares much of the scenerio, but, this time, it is Kafka who looms just beyond the klieg lights.

Stern is an angst-ridden apartment dweller, nose pressed against suburbia while visions of extra rooms dance in his head: "As a child he had graded the wealth of people by the number of rooms in which they lived. He himself had been brought up in three in the city and fancied people who lived in four were so much more splendid than himself."

But as Stern quickly discovers, he is not one of the Chosen People who can make the exodus from the bondage of crowded apartments to the Promised Land of suburban living. He is, at best, a reluctant pioneer, a man who misses the cop on the beat, the delicatessan at the corner. (p. 16)

[Beseiged] by problems on all sides—caterpillars devour his garden; dogs attack him on a nightly basis—Stern prefers to substitute an ever-growing number of self-generated (and, thereby, controllable fears) for the one who lives just down the street. He pictures the police as "large, neutral-faced men with rimless glasses who would accuse him of being a newcomer making vague troublemaking charges." Especially if he complains about the threatening dogs. "They would take him into a room and hit him in his large, white, soft stomach." And so he swallows his impulse, only then to imagine himself "fighting silently in the night with the two gray dogs, lasting eight minutes and then being found a week later with open throat by small Negro children."

Some of the best sections in *Stern* are flashbacks, designed to deal with the problem of being called a "kike." In J. D. Salinger's "Down By Dinghy," Boo Boo Glass defused the epithet by skillfully changing it to "kite," something her assimilated son can understand. But Stern knows all too well that the word is *supposed* to hurt. And, yet, it is hard for him to make a viable connection between a Judaic tradition and his individual experiences. The vignettes which results are filled with poignant alienation. And in the best of them Friedman is able to strike a balance between the humor and the pathos of his material:

> As a boy, Stern had been taken to holiday services, where he stood in ignorance among bowing, groaning men who wore brilliantly embroidered shawls. Stern would do some bows and occasionally let fly a complicated imitative groan, but when he sounded out he was certain one of the old genuine groaners had spotted him and knew he was issuing a phony. Stern thought it was marvelous that the old men knew exactly when to bow and knew the groans and chants and melodies by heart. He wondered if he would ever get to be one of their number. He went to Hebrew School, and there seemed to be no time at all devoted to theatrical bows and groans, and even with three years of Hebrew School under his belt Stern still felt a loner among the chanting sufferers at synagogues. After a while he began to think you could never get to be one of the groaners through mere attendence at Hebrew School. You probably had to pick it all up in Europe.

But, alas, black humor is often a study in excess and Friedman has a nasty habit of overplaying his cards until the returns are diminishing ones indeed. Stern's father, for example, contributes puns on "orange Jews" or "prune Jews," while his college roommates coin the term "Geeyoo." But none of this banter has much to do with Stern, to say nothing of his long-postponed confrontation with the "kike man."

In fact, the "kike man"—Stern discovers he is named De Luccio—remains more a fixation than character, the focus of Stern's ever-widening projections:

> Stern took note of every detail of the man's house, a new one registering each night as he drove by. A television aerial. This was good. It meant the communications industry was getting through to the man, subtly driving home messages of Brotherhood. But he imagined the man watching only Westerns, contemptuously flicking off all shows that spoke of tolerance. Stern saw himself writing and producing a show about fair play, getting it shown one night on every channel, and forcing the man to watch it since the networks would be bare of Westerns.

With all this we are scarcely surprised when Stern's x-rays unearth a duodenal ulcer. After all, he is riddled by equal doses of repression and anxiety—and to clinch the cliche, he works for a Madison Avenue ad agency! Of course, Stern's ulcer is the "kike man" internalized, but, somehow, knowing that doesn't help. The same is true of Stern's breakdown. It may be physically inevitable, but that hardly makes it aesthetically earned. In fact, only his periodic fantasies about cuckoldry manage to keep the threat of Friedman's novel alive. . . . As Stern's *extension ad absurdem* argument would have it, DeLuccio stands—symbolically if you will—for all that he despises: DeLuccio's veteran's jacket dredges up visions of militaristic might, while his softball playing, beer drinking style of Gentile life is hostile to all the vague Judaic traditions Stern holds dear. (pp. 19-21)

In *Stern* Friedman concentrated on such middle-aged phenomena as cuckoldry and the problems of Gentile suburbia. In *A Mother's Kisses,* the psychodynamics of Black Humor shrink to Momism and the difficulties of getting into college. But, more importantly, the aesthetics of Black Humor give *A Mother's Kisses* that same touch of the grotesque Milo Minderbinder brings to the art of war profiteering. Excess is the heart of the matter. Realistic elements are stretched until the resulting fabric has that curiously elongated look we associate with fun house mirrors. Unfortunately a great many contemporary writers who enjoy being lost in the funhouse lack John Barth's talent for getting out. All too often Black Humor becomes a blank check issued to the unbridled imagination. For example, Sophie Portnoy may be the apotheosis of the Jewish mother, but Friedman's is only a push or two away. Portnoy's mother *kvetches;* Joseph's mother drools, but a paperback Freud covers them both. (p. 22)

The literature of the sixties is filled with whiners, some serious (and likely to be found in novels of Saul Bellow), others comfortably comic. Joseph belongs to the latter league. His fantasies are a strategy of control, rather than a method of confrontion. And herein lies the difference between the darkly comic visions of, say, a Melville or Faulkner and the pale copy that is *A Mother's Kisses.* It has become fashionable to blame the whole thing on affluence, as if the shoddy culture of the last twenty years has made genuine art impossible. But the real issue is courage. *A Mother's Kisses* is a superficial novel because it refuses to face its own implications or deal adequately with the enigmatic. Friedman relies, instead, on the intellect, preferring a fantasy of his own design to an encounter with the stuff of fiction already there. (p. 23)

Friedman would have us believe that the only alternative for the contemporary satirist lies in outdoing the headlines, no matter what the aesthetic cost. The result is a curious sort of escalation; life forces the novelist from the outrageous to the zany and, ultimately, exhausts him. The mechanics of Black Humor become predictable, which is to say, tedious. And, ironically enough, we quickly learn how to be comfortable with the most grotesque and/or irreverent news such an aesthetic has to offer.

Joseph's mother begins as a vulgar cliche; Friedman's touch merely raises it to the second *power.* For example, she follows her son to camp one day—and then the next, setting up a base of sexual activity just across the lake. When Joseph is finally accepted to Kansas Land Grant Agricultural—where courses like "the history and principles of agriculture" and "feed chemistry" comprise the curriculum—Mom insists on coming too. Add a handful of zany minor characters and the self-parody is complete.

Still, there are moments in *A Mother's Kisses* when the terrors of modern life are rendered with sharp, even metaphorical, precision:

> A long line had formed in the men's room, leading to a single urinal, which was perched atop a dais. When a fellow took too long, there were hoots and catcalls such as 'What's the matter, fella, can't you find it?' As his turn came nearer, Joseph began to get nervous. He stepped before the urinal finally, feeling as though he had marched out onto a stage.

> He stood there a few seconds, then zipped himself up and walked off. The man in back of him caught his arm in a vise and said, 'You didn't go. I watched.'

Very little of Kafka's flavor is lost in the translation. And the hand which descends to unmask our smallest deception strikes us as real, all too real.

In *A Mother's Kisses* Black Humor meets the Oedipus complex, but the results are hardly decisive. Friedman's irreverance is matched by his self-consciousness and the long shadows of puerile comedy fall everywhere. With his latest novel, *The Dick,* the focus centers on the world of law-and-order. Friedman means to draw a parallel between sexuality and crime fighting, as the title of the novel and the name of his protagonist—LePeters—suggest. Nor do the bad jokes stop there. When LePeters has his psychological interview, the conversation goes something like this:

> "What do you think all these guns around here represent?" he asked LePeters in a lightning change of subject.

> "Oh, I don't know," said LePeters. "Phalluses, I guess." Actually, he had dipped into a textbook or two and was taking a not-so-wild shot.

> "Not bad," said Worthway, lifting one crafty finger in the Heidelberg style and making ready to leave. "But some of them are pussies, too."

Outraging the already outrageous is a full-time, which is to say, desperate, activity in *The Dick.* And, yet, there are spots when Friedman's satire is right on target. . . .

LePeters is a study in ballooning ambivalence. His face is divided by a childhood scar, one side suggesting the Jewishness of his Sussman past, while the other speaks to his LePeters' present. He vacillates between the sentiments of a liberal and those of a dick. Part of him had "read Moby Dick in one sitting . . . Hadn't he thought of death and infinity, wrestling with the precise structure of time until his teeth ached and his eyeballs, like tiny runaway planets, did backward loops in his head." Surely *that* is not the sensibility of a dick. And, yet, LePeters/Sussman is plagued by another part of his nature, one which suggests empathy (rather than revulsion) with everything dickdom stands for. . . . The result is a comic war, one LePeters wages with decidedly mixed feelings. All the traditional themes are there—paranoia, fantasy, cuckoldry and diluted Jewishness—but *The Dick* never rises above sophomoric snicker. (pp. 24-7)

> *Sanford Pinsker, "The Graying of Black Humor," in* Studies in the Twentieth Century, *Vol. 9, Spring, 1972, pp. 15-33.*

MAX F. SCHULZ

The pace of a scientific and technical society has fallen out of phase with man's traditional time sense. His inner time clock as well as the ticking of his cultural time table no longer coincide with social change. One consequence has been the increased tension of urban existence and of twentieth-century life. Friedman's fiction faithfully renders the bewildered impulse of the modern consciousness. His prose has a brash bounciness and nervous tempo, which catches faithfully the "near hysterical new beat in the air" that is the mid-century idiom of our culture, with its stereoscopic and stereophonic dance halls, amplified discotheques, scheduled love-ins, bare-bosomed waitresses, and neon-lit nights—what Friedman in the Foreword to *Black Humor* calls the "punishing isolation and loneliness of a strange, frenzied new kind." His language . . . is bare of pretense, recklessly vulnerable to the sneer of sophistication. Its nakedness, its impetuous innocence, underscores the morbid anxiety that the conformist hero imbibes daily with his morning coffee. (p. 105)

His fiction underscores in its structural conception the *non sequitur* of current human actions. For him, events are ultimately motiveless, the line between fantasy and reality, thought and occasion, impression and object, continually wavering and blurring. That they happen, not why, becomes central. Hence Friedman concentrates on the rich texture of surface details. His individuals . . . lack the inward complexity, the self-consciousness, which could relate the events of their lives to a larger frame of social reference. Instead they are at any given moment the two-dimensional embodiment of circumstance and accident. Thus they are fixed in being, yet constantly in motion. In adolescent echo of his father's feeble thrust for awareness, Joseph is inclined much of the time to conceive of his life in terms of arrested stills of great cinema moments. The fixed narrative continuity of the movies represents for him the ultimate achievement or order in his worried effort to give meaning to his inchoate experience. Thus he nervously wonders, after learning that Columbia University has turned down his application for admission, "why he could react to tragedy only with movie routines. Now he was the high school hero caught stealing exam answers on the eve of the big game, waiting outside the principal's office to see whether he would be allowed to compete against State." Seeing a "slender blond woman, whose body seemed all pressed out beneath her slacks," he decides that she has that "whimpering look to her face as though a young, handsome rogue had just run out of her starved and loveless mansion . . . a whipped Barbara Stanwyck style" that he knew "he was going to find attractive later in life." (pp. 106-07)

Stern and *A Mother's Kisses* consist of incidents that either end inconclusively or lack coherence between person and event, thought and action. Stern's ulcer and nervous breakdown wax out of all proportion to the insult his wife receives from a neighbor. At the conclusion, by way of avenging his wife's dishonor, he sustains a beating by the man; so his anxiety flourishes as usual. Similarly, nothing is meaningfully concluded in Joseph's world, whether it is his aborted stay as a waiter at a summer camp, his affliction with a mysteriously infected arm, or his fantastic "temporary" lodgement in a hotel room as prerequisite to his registering for college classes. The absurd disjunction between the archaic human timetable and the juggernaut of civilization's calendar is dramatized in Stern's inability to synchronize his recognition of the need to paint his house and to spray his shrubbery against insects with the "printed" instructions about when the chemical products must be used for maximum effectiveness. Consequently his house remains unpainted and his shrubs are decimated by caterpillars.

Friedman's world is ominously dependent on chance, a world of inconsequential meetings and partings. The future ceases to exist as an estimable series of actions. The categories of time and space fail to define the limits of perception, leaving Stern and Joseph forever vulnerable to the indefinites of unfolding experience. . . . [In] would-be conformist worlds of

Stern and *A Mother's Kisses* discontinuity and simultaneity have displaced uniformity and consecutiveness. Hence the absence in Friedman's stories of family history, of sense of place, of names (what is Stern's first name? Joseph's last? Joseph's father's?), of anything other than the rudiments of narrative succession; and contrariwise an emphasis on the terrifying involutions of the moment. Under the circumstances not to feel anxiety is not to be human. (pp. 107-08)

Ironically in this century the conformist lives in a Kafkan nightmare, incurring apprehension from those same institutions that he turns to for succor. By limiting himself to their bureaucratic order, he hopes to impose a rationale upon his existence. Instead he finds himself paralyzingly isolated, bereft of individuality, a faceless integer who counts simply as a population statistic. If he happens to be like Stern he fails to convince even his wife that he is a person distinguishable from other human beings. When they go up to their second-floor bedroom, she has him go first because she does not "like to go upstairs in front of *people*"(my italics). (pp. 110-11)

Underlying Stern's obsession with the "kike man's" hostility is clearly the larger question of his place in society. Stern is afflicted not only with an ulcer but also with the more psychically virulent American malady of wanting to be liked, of wanting to be accepted as a full-fledged, paid-up member of a group. When he checks out of the Rest Home, he feels "as though by getting healthy he had violated a rotted, fading charter" of the other sicker inmates. "He had come into their sick club under false pretenses, enjoying the decayed rituals, and all the while his body wasn't ruined at all. He was secretly healthy, masquerading as a shattered man so that he could milk the benefits of their crumbling society. And now he felt bad about not being torn up as they were." (p. 111)

[Not] differentness but sameness is Stern's social goal. In the novel he realizes this ambition only once, on the night he does the town with a local girl and two other inmates of the Rest Home; and his reaction to their togetherness indicates its prime importance for his psychic well-being. They have a fracas in a bar and leave hurriedly before the police arrive. As they jog down the street Stern thinks happily that "they were comrades of a sort and he was glad to be with them, to be doing things with them, to be running and bellowing to the sky at their sides; he was glad their lives were tangled up together. It was so much better than being a lone Jew stranded on a far-off street, your exit blocked by a heavy-armed kike hater in a veteran's jacket."

So urgent is Stern's desire for communal acceptance that it takes precedence over his need to compensate for sexual inferiorities. Even though he makes love to the Puerto Rican girl and is excited to try it again, he joins forces with the other two boys when they begin to toss her into the air straddled on a broomstick. "Ooh, you really hurt me . . . you cruddy bastards," she cries.

> Stern felt good that she had addressed all three of them, not excluding him, and it thrilled him to be flying out of her apartment with his new friends, all three howling and smacking each other with laughter at the pole episode. He wanted to be with them, not with her. He needed buddies, not a terrible Puerto Rican girl. He needed close friends to stand around a piano with and sing the Whiffenpoof song, arms around each other, perhaps before shipping out somewhere to war. If his dad got sick, he needed friends to stand in hospital corridors with him

and grip his arm. He needed guys to stand back to
back with him in bars and take on drunks. These
were tattered, broken boys, one in a wheelchair, but
they were buddies.

A man's sense of identity depends in part on his relationship
to the conventional age-groups of his society. Friedman captures the peculiar non-existence of today's Everyman,
trapped in an impersonal round of homogenized activities, by
portraying him as an American Jew, alienated from Judaic
values but as yet unassimilated by American traditions. Thus
Stern belongs at least in this respect in the company of the
many Jewish fictional heroes of the fifties and sixties. He
shares with Bellow's protagonists the disinheritance of the
American Jew. At the same time he partakes of the dissociation of the Black Humor protagonist of the sixties. He is both
physically part of and mentally apart from the collective
community. He lives in it but does not belong to it. He is a
non-person, vividly dramatized by his lack of involvement
with people. With neither wife, parents, co-worker, employer, friend, nor acquaintances does he successfully communicate. (pp. 111-12)

Friedman's nervous prose is highly suggestive of violence.
The frequency of active verbs has the fictional characters
twitching as energetically and erratically as high-speed, ma-
chine-driven marionettes. Henry James's people *swim* into
rooms, Friedman's *fly* through them.

No character in modern fiction leads a mental existence more
violent than Stern. At every turn of his humdrum round of
affairs, he moves like one besieged by superior forces, wary
of sudden attacks and skillful murderous incursions into the
citadel of his puny defenses. Clenched fists, military chants,
body bursting blows—every kind of mayhem perfected in this
century of violence runs riot through Stern's impressionable
imagination. No one walks, enters, or exits in Stern's world.
He plunges, flies, erupts, bursts. His movements imitate the
explosive disruptive forces of violence. Not since the nineteenth century and the heyday of the Darwinian fever has
man been conceived of as so tremblingly naked before the
murderous onslaughts of a hostile environment. Stern must
be the most frightened figure in American fiction, his panic
more profound than the stagey terrors of Brockton Brown's
and Poe's heroes, because ultimately more commonplace and
everyday. Perched on the front steps of his house in the evening, his son on his lap and his great soft body pressed against
his wife's hips for security, Stern feels jittery and isolated, a
disturbing, ill-defined menace surrounding him. Lost is the
paradisal pleasure that was once rural America's of sitting
peacefully on the door stoop to watch the day darken. In the
foreword to his anthology of Black Humor, Friedman comments on the extremes of today's life. The effect of the bi-
zarre-as-norm on the man in the street is polarizing: he becomes a frantic Stern or his antidotal contrary, a representative of "the surprise-proof generation." **Stern** is Friedman's
embodiment of this askew world from the harrassed point of
view of one of its reluctant draftees.

Tactics of march and counter-march have filled Stern's mind
since boyhood. As a child he had lived in terror of an orphan
boy whom he imagined would someday "appear suddenly in
an alley with a great laugh, fling Stern against a wall, lift him
high, and drop him down, steal his jacket in the cold, and run
away with it, come back and punch Stern's eyes to slits." His
grandmother was jokingly supposed to have "a whole mob"
of other old ladies "organized." His uncles would sing the

prayers at Passover as if they were "militant chants." His
Uncle Mackie, with "bronzed, military-trim body" would do
"a series of heroic-sounding but clashing chants" with "great
clangor" as if to "enlist a faction to his banner and start a split
Seder."

As an adult he cowers in abject fear at imaginary reprisals of
the "kike man." He avoids driving past the "kike man's"
house, "afraid that the man would pull him out of the car and
break his stomach." In retaliation Stern dreams of crushing
the "kike man" with a blow "battering his head through his
living-room window." or of catching the "kike man's" little
boy on the bumpers of his car and then driving the mile to
his own house in seconds, disappearing undetected into his
garage. But the thought of the "kike man's" counterattack
paralyzes him. . . . The "kike man" is named De Luccio.
Checking in the telephone book, Stern discovers that there
are eighteen other De Luccios in town. Immediately he concedes to himself that even "if he were to defeat the man, an
army of relatives stood by to take his place." (pp. 114-16)

Apart from the contretemps with the "kike man," the normal
round of Stern's life is an endless fantasy of cringing self-
defense. His assistant at the office, an effeminate young man,
always appears to Stern to be darting menacingly, body
coiled "with vicious ballet grace," toward his desk. Fearful
of being reported to a Board of Good Taste for having an
ulcer—a "dirty, Jewish, unsophisticated" malady—Stern
longs instead for "dueling scars and broken legs suffered
while skiing. He hesitates to admonish a baby sitter for teaching his son about God, "afraid she would come after him one
night with a torch-bearing army of gentiles and tie him to a
church."

The same fantasy of punitive constraint pursues Stern like a
Fury when he goes to the Grove Rest Home. The somber
New England air of the place makes Stern-the-good-citizen
self-conscious of his Semitic genesis, certain that the founders
would veto him "with clenched fists" in spite of his desire to
be a loyal American. Informed that milk and cookies are
served at five, with only one tardiness allowed, Stern reflects
that "even were he to flee to the Netherlands after a milk and
cookie infraction, getting a fifteen-hour start," the crippled
Negro attendant, with "great jaw muscles," "would go after
him Porgy-like and catch him eventually." (pp. 116-17)

There is no escape for Stern, no place to hide. Neither conva-
lescence nor work nor home life offers him a haven. He
crouches in his office, locks himself in the toilet stall—hiding
in uncontrollable panic from the confident steps of his boss
in the morning. The phone ring slices at him like a knife. His
house awaits him, "an enemy that sucked oil and money and
posted a kike-hating sentry down the street." Even in the refuge of his bed, his thoughts are invaded by "numb and choking fear."

Stern lives in a "stifled, desperate" world that knows no primal cause and effect, a world ruled over by a Mosaic dispensation run amok, the Judaic law of an eye for an eye swollen
to horrifying, bizarre proportions. Stern dreams of his Negro
friend Battleby flinging off his horn-rimmed glasses and filling "an open-cab truck with twenty bat-carrying Negro mid-
dle-weights, bare to the waist and glistening with perfect
musculature," to do battle with the "kike man." The usual
scale of values is tipped into frightening ratios. Man trembles
before the accusing eye of a traffic cop, but indulges complacently the excesses and enormities of the Mafia. All the time

that he is decrying mass racial extermination, individual cruelty is losing significance.

Stern reacts to the real and imagined dangers of every day with a mental life of sexual aggression and finally in the climactic stages of his nervous breakdown with violent actions. He is the little man on the street, one of the *vox populi* of this century, through whose eyes and ears has been refracted too much violence and pretence. Hollywood and Madison Avenue's exploitation of love as a commodity to be hucksted has left Stern obsessed with sexual nightmares of his wife engaged in "endless, exhausting, intricately choreographed, lovemaking" with her dance instructor. He runs "with teeth clenched through a crowded train station, as though he were a quarterback going downfield, lashing out at people with his elbows, bulling along with his shoulders." To outraged complaints, he hollers, "I didn't see you. You're insignificant-looking." He sasses a traffic cop, lecturing him when stopped for a traffic violation, "Is this your idea of a crime? With what's going on in this country—rape and everything?"

Significantly, Stern's fantasies of fright often revert atavistically to the bare fists of savage reprisal. The friendly handshake has metamorphosed in his daily nightmare into a ubiquitous fist that threatens his existence in crescending multiples. Stern refrains from contradicting a Negro taxi driver, fearful of being backed "against a fender, and cut . . . to ribbons with lethal combinations" of fisticraft. The gentlemanly rules of pugilistic defense do not apply in Stern's imagined world. The Gangland law and senseless rumbles of big city ghettos prevail. Stern's father carries a jagged scar on the ridge of his nose, given to him one day "by two soccer players in a strange neighborhood who had suddenly lashed out and knocked him unconscious." Friends of his father had gone looking for the men with steel piping. A recurrent hallucination of Stern's depicts him as the victim of ordinary people—drugstore countermen, for example, who suddenly mobilize according to an attack plan and trap Stern in a store against the paperback books, insanely "hitting him in the stomach a few times and then holding him for a paid-off patrolman."

The symbolic action of such hallucinations is obvious. Friedman conceives of man ironically as having regressed to a lawless state in response to an overstructured civilization. The monolithic impersonality of a technocracy communicates to man no sense of his belonging to a group. He has become an outsider, groping in terror for signs that will relate him to his world. Out of a desperate will to survive he slips into a new savagery—a vivid but cruel Alice-in-Wonderland where sadistic Red Queens and Mad Hatters force him, like Alice, continually to reformulate his assumptions about people and manners. The actual has been abandoned for a mental world that more accurately reflects reality. Illogic and mystery have succeeded reason and clarity. "Were you ever a magician before you became my father?" the sexually incompetent Stern is asked by his son. "Right before," Stern answers with the starkness of things seen through the looking-glass.

In *Stern* Friedman portrays the end product of this century's assault on the human sensibility. Man's private and public lives run on separate treadmills these days. A bland noncommittal exterior masks a ferocious fantasy life. Outward acquiescence in a dehumanized society reduces the inner life to catatonic silence or jangling disconnected protest. Stern's affliction is mainly the latter. (pp. 117-19)

Max F. Schulz, "The Aesthetics of Anxiety; and,

The Conformist Heroes of Bruce Jay Friedman and Charles Wright," in his Black Humor Fiction of the Sixties: A Pluralistic Definition of Man and His World, *Ohio University Press, 1973, pp. 91-123.*

PETER LaSALLE

Over the past few years, novelist Bruce Jay Friedman has been writing humorous pieces for *Esquire, Signature* and *New York* magazines to advise the not-so-young, divorced male—who often can be classified as a "Lonely Guy"—how to survive in the urban world today. Now he has collected them in *The Lonely Guy's Book of Life.*

On one level, this is sound entertainment, a take-off on those personal guides currently cluttering supermarket paperback racks, with each piece addressing a particular topic. Examples: **"The Lonely Guy's Apartment," "The Lonely Guy's Cookbook," "Eating Alone in Restaurants," "How to Take a Successful Nap," "At the Beach,"** etc. Friedman surely is as adept at fast gags as the best of the supposed pros—the rare goofs who occasionally trot out from behind the rainbow-striped curtains on "The Tonight Show" and surprise you by actually being funny. Examples again: on defining Lonely Guys, "They tend to be a little bald and look as if they have been badly shaken up in a bus accident." And, "Women can be Lonely Guys, too. . . . She's not going to be throwing any eggs in the pan at four in the morning, but Jacqueline Onassis may be a Lonely Guy. On nights when she has been escorted to the ballet by the wrong Iranian." And, "All of Canada may be a Lonely Guy."

On another level, Friedman appears to be getting at soberer matters here. Without getting into an extended theory of humor (whether black, satiric or otherwise), I think that what makes this writing more than just the strutting of a stand-up comic is the pain whispering behind the gags. For instance, in the section **"Eating Alone in Restaurants,"** Friedman suggests several ways for the Lonely Guy to feign doing something other than dining solo (he might bring a walkie-talkie, so he will be taken for an undercover cop" about to bust the salad man as an international dope dealer"); at the same time, Friedman is implying that the embarrassment of loneliness is worse than the loneliness itself, especially in a society where everything from television sweat sock commercials onward seemingly commands that Thou Shalt Not Be Lonely. Meanwhile, of course, it is a society where loneliness is epidemic, despite all the new personal freedom.

The humor doesn't always effervesce, and in some stock situations (on the psychiatrist's couch or sick with the flu), it stumbles. But Friedman's novelist's eye for detail . . . usually sustains even the weaker stretches.

Overall, a book to make you laugh out loud—and to make you see. (pp. 29-30)

Peter LaSalle, in a review of "The Lonely Guy's Book of Life," in The New Republic, *Vol. 179, No. 25, December 16, 1978, pp. 29-30.*

HERBERT GOLD

[*The Lonely Guy's Book of Life*] is a funny tract, on the surface a parody of the how-to genre. Within this form, which enabled pieces of the book to be published as sparkling interludes in *Esquire* and *New York* magazine, novels, poems, essays, chronicles of the time are squirming to get out. Much of my joy in the book comes of the fact that they succeed in poking their heads up in miserable, sly, engrossing maneuvers before their author crams them back into the form again.

I recall meeting Bruce Friedman some years ago; we were both then in Chicago, traveling in the company of interesting wives; the evidence seems to be that we are both now husbands emeritus, and therefore my fellow feeling for this work might be qualified by the fact that I too must arrange meals, apartment, Sunday afternoons and national holidays with that melancholic dignity of the lonely guy. Ordinarily your true lonely guy hardly has the strength to realize that everyone else is at times a lonely guy. This book may not be universal, but it is more universal than the title suggests. Some former wives might find, with small translations and a few adjustments for child custody and slipcover skills, that they are really lonely guys, too.

Yet it takes a certain flow of cash and time—and perhaps not too pressing conditions of child care, be it admitted—to become a champ of lonely-guyness like the implied hero of this non-novel. It's a big-city book. It is even, forgive him, a somewhat hip book. But none of that means it isn't both winsome and true. Even middle-aged bachelors get the blues. . . .

Mr. Friedman offers plenty of useful tips on lonely-guy life, such as when to find a fashion model beginning to act like a decent human being (possibly at age 29) and where to put the furniture (wherever the moving men drop it; they know best); how to avoid writing if you're a writer (visit the Chinese laundry in case some of your shirts came back early); how to take naps, enjoy sex (or at least not be made extra-miserable by it), cook, deal with dogs, restaurants, grooming, money. One of his brilliant insights on erotic interior decoration points to the dangers of mirrors over the bed. They may be O.K. if you happen to find an *au pair* girl slipping under the covers, but what about the nights when you find yourself there alone, staring up at your own middle-aged hips? (p. 10)

Mr. Friedman's novels, plays and stories have been mostly about lumbering Jewish lummoxes, dimly intelligent, speaking and thinking a stylized urban language out of media clichés. He was one of the more brilliant practitioners of what used to be called—remember the literary movements of the 1960's?—black humor. *About Harry Towns,* his most recent novel, a loosely connected series of stories, is a chilling expression of the isolation of the natural-born black humorist leaving his youth behind. A certain unpleasantness in the subject, or at least a lack of niceness and upbeatness, brought it the chilly reception it did not deserve. I recall with a singular chill the orphaned Harry Towns describing how he had lost both his parents "back to back." That phrase "back to back" is a good miniature example of how Bruce Jay Friedman takes painful emotion, diminishes it abruptly, and then allows a little shock of perception to renew it.

A combination of subtle chisel and naked need is what makes the lonely guy book work so well. This is not exactly laugh-clown-laugh time; it's time for the clowns to look at themselves. I can imagine no book that would be more appropriate reading, propped up against the Blue Plate Special in a cafeteria on Father's Day. (pp. 10-11)

> *Herbert Gold, "Even Bachelors Get the Blues," in* The New York Times Book Review, *February 11, 1979, pp. 10-11.*

DAPHNE MERKIN

[In *The Lonely Guy's Book of Life*], Friedman has included running as one of the paramount symptoms: "Running is basically a Lonely Guy activity. If you doubt it, go out and run and start waving to people running toward you and see what happens. No one will wave back. The only ones to respond at all will be people who are curious about everything that moves." Friedman himself concedes that the dividing-lines are flexible: "Warren Beatty gets you mixed up because of all his dating. He may be a secret Lonely Guy. Why else would he have made *Shampoo*, which winds up with him on a hill, albeit a Beverly Hill, puzzling over the folly of the human condition? . . . Horses are Lonely Guys, unless they are the spoiled favorites of girls named Wendy in Darien. All of Canada may be a Lonely Guy. . . ."

Playful cataloguing aside, this book is a study of forlornness and the measures of solace one can take to ameliorate it. Friedman is a wily scout, brimming with helpful hints on how to handle the uneasy situations that strew the Lonely Guy's path like hidden mines. On Eating Alone in Restaurants: "After each bite of food, lift your head, smack your lips thoughtfully, swallow and make a notation in a pad. Diners will assume you are a restaurant critic." On Cooking: "Veal is the quintessential Lonely Guy meat. There is something pale and lonely about it, especially if it doesn't have any veins. It's so wan and Kierkegaardian. You must know it's not going to hurt you. So eat a lot of veal." On Coping with Psychotherapy: "As a general rule, the Lonely Guy who tells the doctor too much risks losing his mystery and allure. No longer under his spell, the psychiatrist may turn his attention to other patients."

Friedman's self-parodying manual contains some of the funniest writing I've read in a long time. Although permeated with a painfully accurate consciousness of the embarrassments that nip at the heels of the unwary, it is not averse to modest redemptive possibilities: "Bacon cheeseburgers, Cheryl Ladd posters, Ibsen revivals, pine tar room fresheners, the scent of wisteria on another guy's terrace—they're all out there for the Lonely Guy with red blood in his veins and the courage to say: 'I can have these things, too, even though I happen to be living alone for the moment.' " Should you be one of those fated to wander lonely as a cloud, give yourself a head start and take this guide with you. (p. 13)

> *Daphne Merkin, "Writers & Writing: Jewish Jokesters," in* The New Leader, *Vol. LXI, No. 7, March 26, 1979, pp. 12-13.*

ANATOLE BROYARD

"Let's Hear It For A Beautiful Guy," the title story of Bruce Jay Friedman's latest collection, is inspired by an item from Earl Wilson's gossip column. "Sammy Davis," according to Mr. Wilson, "is trying to get a few months off for a complete rest." This is the kind of thing Mr. Friedman does best: exploiting the pretensions and incongruities of a culture that takes itself too seriously.

The anonymous narrator imagines himself helping Sammy Davis to get a complete rest. He owes it to him, he says, for "the pleasure he's given me over the years, dancing and clowning around and wrenching those songs out of that wiry little body." "None of us," he observes, "will ever be able to calculate what it took out of him each time he had a falling out with Frank." "And does anyone," he asks, "ever stop to consider the spiritual torment he must have suffered when he made the switch to Judaism?"

The narrator says he will hide Mr. Davis in his studio apartment, take him to his sister and brother-in-law in Jersey, to a borrowed cabin in Vermont, where they'll talk about "the mystery of existence," a subject Mr. Davis has frequently explored on panel shows.

This is Mr. Friedman in his manic phase, sputtering with invention, as he was in *Stern* and *A Mother's Kisses* more than 20 years ago. After that, he seemed to go into a depressive phase with *The Dick* and *About Harry Towns.* When he's manic, Mr. Friedman is often a fine comic writer; when he's depressive, he offers us what seem like interminable jokes without punch lines. We wade through all the monotonous development, the symptoms, as it were, only to find that the joke is that there is no joke. Mr. Friedman indulges in what might be called the metaphysical feint or philosophical pratfall, the story that refuses to break into a "false" surprise.

Some of Mr. Friedman's most successful pieces consist of a character's suddenly pulling up to examine one of everyday life's unexamined premises. In **"The Mourner,"** for example, Martin Gans drives out to the Long Island funeral of Norbert Mandel, a total stranger whose death is announced in the paper. When he finds that the rabbi giving the funeral address didn't know the deceased very well. Gans becomes indignant.

After listening to a series of polite generalizations, Gans jumps up and says "You haven't told anything about him," and goes on to evoke the heartbreaking minutiae that probably made up Mandel's life. "Do you know anything about his disappointments?" Gans asks. "How he wanted to be taller?"

In **"Detroit Abe,"** a character named Abrahamowitz, who teaches irony in a "heavily ethnic" city university, meets a young pimp named Smooth who asks him to take over his "birds" while he serves a short jail term. This illustrates another of Mr. Friedman's methods he introduces a random element into a structured or closed situation and then observes its effect. In **"Detroit Abe,"** this works very well, but it doesn't always. Sometimes the random element appears to be merely a labor-saving device, a lazy author's way of forcing movement. . . .

Mr. Friedman has a soft spot in his heart for the romance of failure. Many of his characters are losers simply because it provides the author with a voice he likes, a rejection-dejection rhetoric right out of Malamud and Roth. A few of these stories are about peculiar psychoanalysts, which makes *Let's Hear It for a Beautiful Guy,* seem dated. And some of the book *is* dated. Mr. Friedman tells us in an introduction that he found one of these stories, **"Business Is Business,"** in a trunk. He wrote it, he says, when he was 26 years old, and we wonder why he unpacked this particular trunk.

What Mr. Friedman does all too often is to *flirt* with the real. This leaves him in a limbo between the deliberately contrived pieces of a humorist like Woody Allen and the contemporary short story. If you read these pieces as stories, their randomness may derail them. If you read them as straight humor, they suffer from an embarrassment of sentimental human data.

In **"Detroit Abe,"** Abrahamowitz explains irony to Smooth. "A way to spot irony," he says, "is when you can't quite

make out the intentions of the author and when the hero ends up in puzzled defeat." This definition leaves something to be desired, and so, for all their occasional felicities, do the majority of these 18 stories.

Anatole Broyard, in a review of "Let's Hear It for a Beautiful Guy," in The New York Times, *August 29, 1984, p. C21.*

DOROTHY H. ROCHMIS

"Sammy Davis is trying to get a few months off for a complete rest.—Earl Wilson, Feb. 7, 1974". That's the head on the final story, **"Let's Hear It for a Beautiful Guy"**, in Friedman's new tome. . . . Friedman has a quirky comedic sense which contains all the foibles of "the human condition" and his collection of stories is quite delightful. There are in all some 18 stories here, plus an introduction and all of them are evidence of Friedman's fecund mind. He is indeed a chronicler of modern day angst as well as love in all its guises and disguises.

Friedman, in his introduction, asserts that as a youngster at camp, he heard the quixotic tales of the Wise Men of Chelm who were really very, very foolish and who always were vindicated by twists of fate or trepidationless faith. Most of Friedman's stories have a smidgeon of the Chelm flavor: they are brief, revelatory and even surprising. Most of the stories were written in the '60s and '70s and while they are not especially revelatory of those times, they are ever deliciously entertaining.

Dorothy H. Rochmis, in a review of "Let's Hear It for a Beautiful Guy," in West Coast Review of Books, *Vol. 10, No. 5, September-October, 1984, pp. 44-5.*

D. G. MYERS

Bruce Jay Friedman's third story collection [*Let's Hear It for a Beautiful Guy*]—his first in nearly two decades—brings together 17 standard magazine pieces, most of them fairly short and quick hitting. The world is the Upper East Side, and it is populated by screenwriters who have never quite managed to get a screen credit ("the story of my life"), drama critics, freelance writers, playwrights and anyone else who might be mistaken for an artist—"a designer of low-cost copying machines," for instance, who had "always enjoyed a small cult following." As is usually the case in Mr. Friedman's writing, the characters are mostly Jews, with a black man thrown in here and there as a pimp or a friend from civil rights days. The women are submissive, devoted. For the most part, the stories take the form of fantasies—daydreams of adventure or success, imaginary sexual intrigues. A college teacher is asked to take over a prostitution ring. A successful director imagines surprising the girl who jilted him in college. The author of a hit play escapes to Florida, meets gangsters, beds a female bartender and is arrested trying to carry cocaine back to New York. Reading the tales consecutively is like listening to a man boasting without pause—one is left feeling pity and exhaustion. In the finest story in the collection, **"The Mourner,"** a Manhattan businessman attends the funeral of a stranger whose obituary he read in The Times. He interrupts the rabbi's eulogy. "How can you just toss him in the ground? That was a man there. He cut himself a lot shaving. He had pains in his stomach." A promising notion, but Mr.

Friedman's tale ends in a thin gruel of sentimentality: "I guess I just didn't think enough of a fuss was being made," the businessman says.

> *D. G. Myers, in a review of "Let's Hear It for a Beautiful Guy," in* The New York Times Book Review, *November 18, 1984, p. 32.*

KIRKUS REVIEWS

[In *Tokyo Woes*], Mike Halsey is an impulsive, loose, semi-vacant, very California sort of guy. He gave up 16 years of middle management security to go off "to restore houses with a short gay guy named Rick." He and live-in love Pam are held together by palship, sex, and a shared love of gossip columns. And then one morning, en route to buy the daily papers, Mike gets a major zap of his old wanderlust, blood pumping and legs springing. . . . So, next thing you know, wild-and-crazy Mike is on a plane to Japan—for reasons he can't quite explain: he doesn't even like sushi that much, he doesn't know a soul there. Luckily, however, Mike finds a great new chum on the flight to Tokyo: Bill Atenabe, a corporate type and "swell guy" who invites Mike to become the Atenabes' house-guest. And the rest of this brief vaudeville consists of sight gags, geisha/bowing jokes, one-liners, non sequiturs, stray bits of satire and farce—as Mike gets some up-close-and-personal glimpses of modern Japan. . . . But things get a little downbeat when moody host Bill, burdened with heavy sports-gambling debts, decides to commit *seppuku*—and asks Mike to be his *kaishaku*: "After I run the dagger through my belly, you chop my head off." (There's no rush, however: "I have to buy a new loincloth and get my white kimono over to the dry cleaners.") A few strong laughs, lots of little ones—but, with a jerky hero and a series of uncoordinated, often-visual short takes, this is more like a screenplay (first draft) for Steve Martin than a full-fledged comic novel.

> *A review of "Tokyo Woes," in* Kirkus Reviews, *Vol. LIII, No. 6, March 15, 1985, p. 235.*

PAUL GRAY

You might think that a guy who hadn't published a novel in eleven years would show a few signs of nervousness, make a false move here and there, when he gave it another try. But Bruce Jay Friedman, who was almost certainly, pound for pound, the peppiest black humorist of the whole 1960s (Remember *Stern*? *A Mother's Kisses*?), hasn't exactly been idle during his long layoff. He wrote *The Lonely Guy's Book of Life,* which not only advised single fellas how to cope but became a motion picture vehicle for Steve Martin. He did the screenplay for *Stir Crazy* and pitched in on the scenarios of *Doctor Detroit* and *Splash.* So it should come as no surprise to anyone that Bruce hasn't lost a step in the dialogue department. And the way he spins yarns is enough to make even nonreaders feel right at home. In fact, if the truth be told, after a couple of pages of "guys" and "fellas," and clichés strung together so you know he's kind of kidding them, but not in a serious way, most readers may even start thinking and talking like Bruce.

So here's the deal on *Tokyo Woes.* A "big strapping fellow" named Mike Halsey suddenly gets it into his head to go to Japan. Why? That's just Mike for you. On the flight over he meets a returning native, "William (call me Bill) Atenabe," who has managed to blow $100,000 betting on U.S. high school basketball games. Before they land, Bill has invited Mike to stay with the Atenabes, whose home sprawls over one-eighth of an acre in Tokyo. Mike is not one for making snap judgments, but the Atenabe clan is certainly unusual. Take Poppa Kobe, for example. He is being forced into retirement by a giant conglomerate, but not before an attractive female deprogrammer has been sent to squeeze everything he learned on the job out of his head. Then he can open a noodle shop, like all the other Japanese oldsters.

In fact, Mike picks up a lot of friction under the surface of this peculiar foreign place, and wonders, "Had he come to a nation of moody guys?" . . . Bill also lets on that Japan has been building a huge offensive army in secret all these years, and advises, "Don't mess with us, Mike. We're not just a bunch of little cassette guys."

By the time Mike gets safely back to the good old U.S. of A., a few soreheads may complain that Bruce hasn't really got the hang of Japan and that what we have here is sort of a dumb parody of a caricature. Or you might hear that the language is not actually ironic and incisive and all the rest, but more like a transcript of lonely guy bar talk, right there at the pitch it reaches when happy hours are ending. Don't listen to the gloom and doom. But if you do and decide not to give *Tokyo Woes* a good shot, you can always wait and catch the video on MTV. (pp. 70, 75)

> *Paul Gray, "Cassette Guys," in* Time, *New York, Vol. 125, No. 16, April 22, 1985, pp. 70, 75.*

MICHIKO KAKUTANI

Such British masters of comedy as Evelyn Waugh, of course, always liked the genre of novel as travelogue because it gave them a chance to take their characters abroad, gawk at all the funny foreigners and reconfirm their own superiority. But in *Tokyo Woes,* Mr. Friedman turns this convention on its side, showing us that it's just as hard to get a handle on things abroad as it is at home. The whole contemporary world—domestic and foreign, private and public—tends to strike Mr. Friedman as astonishing, incongruous, absurd. And to mirror, perhaps compete with, this ludicrous reality he uses his inventiveness, his gifts for verbal pratfalls and deadpan humor, to create an even more manic fictional world.

By sending his hero off to Japan to resolve an incipient identity crisis, Mr. Friedman also provides himself with some perfect setups for favorite comic routines. As an innocent abroad, Mike gets plenty of chances to feel a little nervous, paranoid and generally out of it—he even comes down with psychosomatic flu—and at the same time, function as a sort of wild card among the Japanese, popping up, at random, to disturb his hosts' seemingly ordered routines. He's forced to question assumptions he used to take for granted (trying to decide what to do about a friend who's determined to commit *seppuku,* he muses that "shrinks in this strange country would probably tell you to go ahead and kill yourself if it made you feel better"), and he unwittingly engages in a lot of inappropriate social behavior (he innocently gives a new acquaintance a "curt and formal bow of the type that generally terminated an acrimonious meeting," instead of one of the "light and friendly variety").

Diverting as *Tokyo Woes* can be, however, it lacks the depth of compassion and seriousness that distinguishes the best of Mr. Friedman's work. For all their outrageous routines and flip, infectious language, *Stern, About Harry Towns* and *Scuba Duba* were actually about guys in precarious, even scary situations—guys trying to deal with divorce, racial prejudice, abandonment and death—and a visceral sense of what one Friedman character called "the bile and sweetness of life" emerged from behind the jokes and jive. For some reason, *Tokyo Woes* lacks both the anger and tenderness of such earlier works.

No doubt the character of Mike Halsey himself contributes to the reader's feeling of detachment. He's a nice enough guy, Mike—good-natured, earnest, maybe a little muddled—but his emotional dilemma and his resolution of it are never made very clear. If his trip to Japan is supposed to represent his desire for adventure, for freedom from the circumscribed routines of domestic life, we never experience the urgency of his need to escape. Nor do we ever wonder about the eventual outcome of his sojourn abroad.

In a sense, the person most beset with difficulties in *Tokyo Woes* is not Mike, but his friend Bill Atenabe: Bill's wife is leaving him for a teak dealer; his son is giving up a brilliant scholastic career to become a talent scout for a modeling agency; his father's being forced into retirement, and his maid is considering a high-paying job with an orthodontist. Bill himself owes a local thug thousands of dollars, which he lost betting on a high school basketball game.

The thing is, Bill—like the rest of the supporting cast in *Tokyo Woes*—remains little more than a paperdoll figure, a bunch of odd traits tentatively stuck together with glue; and we fail to care whether Mike helps him solve his problems or not. As a result, the novel, too, has a patchwork flavor—it devolves into a haphazard collection of slapstick routines starring Bill and Mike. Still, many of those routines are amusing; a few are very funny, and they make for tangy, if unfilling, reading.

Michiko Kakutani, "Mike on the Ginza," in The New York Times, *April 27, 1985, p. 13.*

Patricia Grace

1937-

New Zealand short story writer, novelist, and author of children's books.

A member of the Maori tribe of New Zealand, Grace illustrates the traditional familial values of her native people by composing fiction that focuses on themes of humanity and cultural pride. Writing in an unusual prose style based on Maori speech patterns, Grace addresses such universal topics as birth, sexual maturation, marriage, and death. To avoid offending New Zealand's white European majority, or *pakehas,* Grace rarely makes direct mention of the complex subjects of racial tension and discrimination, and her stories usually end with an acceptance of the prevailing Maori situation. Although faulted for a limited artistic range, Grace has been praised for her distinctive narrative voices and attention to detail.

In her early works, Grace illuminates tribal customs by contrasting the simplistic Maori people with the industrialized, individualistic *pakehas. Waiariki* (1975), Grace's first collection of short stories, chronicles ordinary events that reveal the continuing importance of Maori values in contemporary New Zealand society. In "Parade," a Maori girl who returns home from a *pakeha* college is embarrassed by her people's customs and questions her heritage until a ride on the tribal float in the town parade reaffirms her ethnic pride. The novel *Mutuwhenua: The Moon Sleeps* (1978) centers on the marriage of Ripeka, a Maori woman, and Graeme, a British schoolteacher. When adjusting to her marriage and new urban *pakeha* lifestyle proves difficult, Ripeka begins to rely on her Maori upbringing and the compassion of her relatives. This familial love, or *aroha,* a basic Maori value, allows Ripeka to find happiness in her new life. Alex Raksin commented: "[Grace has] the character depth of contemporary American novelists, the sensitivity of feminist writers and a hope for the harmonious co-existence of tradition and change that has few antecedents."

Grace's succeeding works focus on the Maori respect for tradition and strong attachment to their ancestral lands. While *The Dream Sleepers and Other Stories* (1980) garnered mixed reviews, critics applauded the strong character portraits contained in many of the stories. In one of these pieces, "Letters from Whetu," a Maori student about to graduate from a *pakeha* high school combats classroom boredom by writing letters to friends. Rather than assimilate into the *pakeha* community, Whetu vicariously experiences *aroha* with his Maori friends through his writing. In "Journey," Grace indirectly condemns *pakeha* society by relating a Maori man's unhappy memories of his confrontation with indifferent European bureaucrats who purchased his land. Grace further develops this theme in *Potiki* (1986), a novel that revolves around the clash between *pakeha* land developers and Maori natives who desire to preserve their territory. As the threats of the developers become more menacing, the Maori unite, strengthened by *aroha* and tribal legends that intimidate the *pakehas.* Michael Owen Jones asserted: "With great sensitivity Grace portrays the vicissitudes faced by her people, weaving together Maori legends and beliefs with some of the white

man's own myths. Her style captures the rhythms of the finest oral poetry. Her imagery is memorable and her observations are penetrating."

Grace's recent collection, *Electric City and Other Stories* (1988), features pieces that concentrate on the darker side of human nature. Several of these tales contrast the innocence of children with the innate cruelty of which they are capable. In addition to her novels and short stories, Grace has also written several books for children, including *The Kuia and the Spider* (1983) and *Watercress Tuna and the Children of Champion Street* (1986).

NORMAN SIMMS

To a certain extent the small number of Maori writers now beginning to publish in English have set themselves the task of doing more than being Maori writers who publish in English, such as one might find among Negro or Jewish writers in America. The development of New Zealand society, and especially the increased prestige and strength of Maoritanga—Maori culture as a spiritual and social integrity, rather than as an ambience imposed on the general *pakeha* ("European") culture of New Zealand—means that such writers feel that what they write, although in English, must be distinct from the English tradition itself in terms of generic and conceptual categories. Above all, it is probably the existence of another kind of Maori novel—written by Europeans—which motivates the Maori writers to seek out more distinctive modes of literary expression.

Even when sympathetic to the Maori, this former kind of regional novel written by *pakehas* does not offer a sense of Maori consciousness satisfying to the sensitivities of articulate Maori writers themselves. (pp. 186-87)

[Patricia Grace's] anthology of stories under the name of *Waiariki* is a breakthrough in Maori publishing in English for more reasons than the editorial puffing as "the first collection of stories by a Maori woman to be published". For these twelve tales are vital experiments in language and form which, even if they do not all succeed, show a self-conscious sensibility in the process of seeking a proper vehicle of literary expression. The two poles of the exercise are signalled by the opening and closing stories, their very titles proclaiming this polarity of verbal and experiential custom is search of form: **"A Way of Talking"** and **"Parade"**.

I would like to divide the tales into three types and then show Patricia Grace modulating between them as well as asserting each formally. Three of the twelve fall clearly into what I call the "Maori Tales", that is, those written with English words, but following Maori syntax and thought patterns; two others are modified versions of this type. The second category contains one distinct and two modified versions of what I call the "Macaronic tales"; these are stories which either in the narrative line and/or the dialogue contain a high frequency of Maori words and suggest in their syntax an impression of Maori thought-patterns. The last type are the "English tales", and these four show a more integrated approach, in which there is no sense of disturbing English syntax beyond its normal bounds and the experience of Maoriness is made to flow through the narrative shape of a European story.

It is, of course, in these four stories of the last kind that Patricia Grace will ultimately be judged and I think we may say in advance that her success is partial and admirable, but that much more remains to be done before the boundaries of the short-story as evolved for the European experience are adjusted fully to accommodate the Maori experience.

The three clearly Maori stories are: **"Toki"**, **"At the River"**, and **"Huria's Rock"**. Aside from all other considerations, this form of tale has very limited prescriptive value and is interesting only from a technical point of view. A single paragraph from **"At the River"** will show the liberties taken with normal English syntax and thought patterns—

> To the tent to rest after they had gone to the river, and while asleep the dream came. A dream of death. He came to me in the dream, not sadly but smiling, with hand on heart and said, "I go but do not weep. No weeping, it is my time".

The cumulative effect is, I think, mere annoyance—one feels one is simply reading a poor translation, not an original English tale. The task for the Maori writer, however, must be, once the choice of writing in English is made—or made for her by history and politics—to find a way of making English accommodate new modes of thinking and feeling, new patterns of organizing narrative, description, and meditation; so that, on the one hand, the logic of English as it has evolved— and by logic I mean its syntactic organizing core, rather than any mere vocabulary register or stylistic devices—remains effective, while, on the other, there is a new dimension, that of *whatever* it is that distinguishes Maori experience from European.

In the three Maori stories there is, of course, more than this playing with language. The patterning of the tales is also significant, as is the content. In each a distinguishing trait seems to be timelessness—not timeless in the sense that there is not felt the movement of human time, the ebb and flow of generations and the passing of the old ways, but timeless in the sense that there is no one particular time for the story. In **"Toki"**, for instance, it would be hard to say whether this story of a boastful fisherman from the north and the trick played upon him happened today, yesterday, or a hundred years ago. While some of the details pretty well fix the setting in the post-European period, the impression is not at all of events set within the space-time continuum of modern European sensibility, but rather of that more general period of human life, a life bounded by family and tribe, life and death.

"At the River" and, especially as its title suggests **"Transition"** are concerned with the passing of time, but again, the emphasis is on human time, a time bounded emotionally by family on one side and death on the other; and yet, also, there is the hint of another time—the time of the European, a more artificial, arbitrary, and regular concept of time. As these lines from **"The Transition"** show, this Maori sense of time is intimately connected with the land, with a sense of place, and it is the insecurity of place which the European historical time imposes that is felt so acutely. The grandmother, fearful of moving away, of losing her family and her place, concludes, with a sad resignation—

> This old one awaits that time, which is not long away, Not long. Then this old body goes to this old ground, and the two shall be one, with no more to be given by one or the other to those who weep.

She then offers a sense of hope to the next generation, a hope that the timelessness of the land, of place, will give a security to the fearful transition—

> And from the two—the land, the woman—these ones have sprung. And by the land and by the woman held and strengthened. Now, from knowing this the old one in turn draws strength as the old light dims, as the time of passing comes.

The sadness of this passing by the older generation is more poignant in a tale like **"Huria's Rock"** for there the security of the next generation is questioned. The grandfather who thinks too much about his long-dead wife, who drowned at sea while collecting agar, does not have a clear place like his wife's rock. His daughter speaks to him.

> "You sit too much in the sun, Grandpa," she says. "And you think too much of Huria. It was wrong to come to this place for agar. It was bad to bring you here."

But the story turns on the old man's revelation—he has seen Huria, and she has warned him that the spider, *Katipo*, may kill his grandchild. While this affirms the truth of the archaic vision—the world large enough for more than visible, physical realities—that old way of life is passing. The old man knows Huria will soon be back for him, to take him to the otherside of life. (pp. 189-91)

While the important Maori themes of place, time, and the other come through in these tales, and while there are very sensitive character sketches of old men and women, the whole effect of the mode is superficial and even approaching the sentimental; for the relevation of character comes from without, and the inner feelings or dialogue cannot capture any distinct tones, in that the totality of expression is flattened by the belaboured syntax. While it may be true that such flattening is appropriate to the oral style of Maori oratory and story-telling, the transference into a European mode means that the nuances of the host language and the expectations of the new genre must first be met and then surpassed. Above all, it is evident that whatever is said in the forced prose could be said with no loss of sense in more conventional prose. (pp. 191-92)

The macaronic tales may also be seen as genre pieces, and aside from the frequent trips to the glossary they force on the reader, pose a tricky aesthetic problem. If, in reality, the Maori of today thinks and speaks partly in English and partly in his own language, should the literary language, even when "echoing" real thoughts and real conversation, reproduce the mixed language? (p. 192)

One story, **"The Ocean"**, is clearly macaronic, and two, **"Holiday"** and **"Waiariki"**, are English tales with a great number of Maori words. If the intrusion of one language into another merely on the lexical level does no more than add local colour, the story must be strong enough to sustain the intrusion; but if character or theme can be shown to depend upon the intrusion, and if such character and theme can be shown to have more than local interest, then the macaronic or near-macaronic mode does have aesthetic validity. (pp. 192-93)

"Holiday", told by a young girl, captures the small child's innocence in describing grown-up innuendo and worry in a language that is childish, colloquial in the Maori way, and sprinkled with Maori words and phrases. The little girl is describing her several weeks of summer holiday with Nanny Retimana, a holiday framed by her childish concern with change—fear that Nanny and Uncle might be changed before she gets there, and that Mum and Daddy might be changed when she gets back, and even that she herself might have changed beyond their recognition.

In a way, the story is full of local colour and sentimental details about their domestic life, capturing images and fleeting phrases of conversation that give a realistic picture of the love and the teasing that go on in a Maori community. But there is just enough of something more profound to sustain the story as more than a hook to hang Maori phrases on.

This is hinted at in the little girl's fear of changes. Her name is Lynette, but her aunt renames her Atareta for her visit.

> My name's Lynette. But Nanny says I look just like my Auntie Atareta who lives way down the South Island and who I've never seen. And when my Auntie Atareta was little she used to sit on her legs with her feet sticking out at the sides the same as I do. Well that's what Nanny Retimana says, and Nanny Retimana, she calls me Atareta all the time.

There is behind the worries about change of the child not only the reality that eventually she will change and be grown-

up, but the equivocal nature of the Maoriness she loves in Aunty Retimana's house. It is at once a place of peace and security, created by love and attention, and it is confirmed even when Lynette's own parents squeeze her between them in the car in the same way as her country relatives did; and also a deceptive and vulnerable quality, perhaps partly revealed in the little girl's *Pakeha* name, Lynette, and partly in the shabbiness of the houses she visits. The human warmth is real and the security of the family, enunciated in their Maori-English phrases and teasing macaronics, comforting, but occasionally automobiles turn over, train-rides separate families, and people *do* change.

In this story the Maori words seem appropriate to the characters and the situation, but mostly as local colour, and can be justified mainly on the grounds of the child's unsophisticated reproduction of the surface situation around her.

The title story of the collection, **"Waiariki"**, is the recollection of a grown man of a youthful adventure on the beach and a present return with his family to the lagoons, especially the one named after himself, Waiariki. As he says,

> The other place, Waiariki, is very special to me. Special because it carries my name which is a very old name, and belonged to my grandfather and to others before him as well.

This story [is] about nostalgia for youth, but even more so about the sad realization and resignation to the fact that the old days of Maori tradition have passed. The narrator, a man who knows the *pakeha* ways and lives in a world of "scientific" reasons, feels deep regret that his boys must miss out on the rich emotional life he enjoyed as a boy. (pp. 193-95)

But the story works neither on the assertion of nostalgia nor on the argument for environmental protection. The contrast of the present and the past is more complicated, too, than that of the narrator's youth at the heart of the story—the several anecdotes he tells of fishing in the lagoons; it contrasts the traditional past, which hardly changed, and the past of a generation ago when change was still essentially superficial, though movies, radio, and World War II were meshed with Maori customs and myths.

Here, then, the Maori phrases and words belong to the past, while the present is narrated in standard English. The near-macaronic style functions to set off then from now, and its use is minimal enough not to be intrusive, and usually explained in the text, so that the English reader need not be turning to the glossary constantly.

Turning now to the four tales I have called English, that is, those which do not seem to be predicated on special effects with language, we shall see if Patricia Grace has made any significant expansions on to the conception of character, events, or structure.

The opening story, **"A Way of Talking"**, alerts the reader of the book to the focus on language. **"Valley"** is a longer tale, full of interesting realistic detail, but almost sentimental in its lyrical structure. **"Parade"**, the concluding narrative is stronger in concept, and points to the power of the new Maori-English synthesis, turning the emphasis off language as a key area of aesthetic experimentation onto gesture, and so to the inner dynamic of fiction itself.

In **"A Way of Talking"**, the central character, Sara/Hera, a Maori living with her family in a small rural town, observes the return of her sister Rose/Rohe, a university student on holiday from Auckland. The characteristic quality of Rose is her talking, and it is the narrator's changed attitude towards her sister's language that motivates the tale. Rose is introduced as unchanged—

> She's just the same as ever Rose. Talks all the time flat out and makes us laugh with her way of talking.

But Rose is more than just the articulate, intellectual member of the family. "Rose is the hard-case one in the family, the kama-kama one, and the one with the brains". She is often cynical, excitable, and witty.

The main incident occurs on a visit to a Mrs Jane Frazer, a pakeha dressmaker, who has prepared a gown so Rose can attend a wedding. Warning Rose not to "say anything funny when we go up there", because their Mother knows that Sara is the one with commonsense, the narrator knows that "Jane often says the wrong thing without knowing". At first all goes well; Rose's kamakama ways impress Mrs Frazer. But then as Mr Frazer arrives in the truck,

> Jane said "That's Allan. He's been down the road getting the Maoris for scrub-cutting."

With a cool voice, Rose begins to get at Jane Frazer, showing that she should know the names of the workers, should see them as individuals not as some amorphous mass, the Maoris.

At home, embarrassed, Hera says, "Rose, you're a stink thing." But Rose eases Hera's fears and tears; she mimics Jane Frazer's liberal palaver, and glides back into the banter and teasing of Maori friendliness with her sister, her mother and father.

There are two points at the beginning and at the conclusion of the story which open it to more than a tale of how Maoris live and interact with Pakehas. At the very end, the narrator says—

> I'll find some way of letting Rose know I understand and I know it will be difficult for me because I'm not clever the way she is. I can't say the same and I've never learnt to stick up for myself.
>
> By my sister won't have to be alone again. I'll let her know that.

Here Hera shows that she is clever in another way than Rose. She has had an insight into her sister's kamakama ways; the isolation and bitterness that comes from being intellectual, from having the ability to articulate the feeling of insult she shares with her sister and all her fellow Maoris. But in that articulation seeming to be alienated from Hera, from the very heart of Maoriness itself. Realizing this weakness and loneliness in her sister, Hera wishes for a way to let Rose know.

The other point indicates the means, though this story cannot bring the diverse qualities together. On their first evening together, before the episode at the Frazer home, the girls' grandmother leaves the room.

> At last Nanny got out of her chair and said, "Time for sleeping. The mouths steal the time of the eyes." That's the lovely way she has of talking, Nanny, when she speaks in English.

This would seem a passing trivial bit of local colour in the story if the title did not alert us to its significance. The old

woman's proverbial expression opens the language to the richness of Maori experience; it contrasts with the clever manipulation of Rose's kamakama intellectualism and with the halting immature speech of Hera. The problem set out in this story—and in the collection as a whole, insofar as it is focused on language—is to find a bridge between English, and its distant, impersonal range of tones (as the Maoris only partly integrated into the cultural mentality of the language and partly cut off from their own cultural mentality hear and speak English), and Maori, and its rich treasury of expression and nuances of human relationship. The love between Rose and Sara, within the context of a warm family, hints at a resolution—but Rose is only home on a short visit and it is likely that Hera will become more distant from her educated urbane sister.

The four-part structure of **"Valley"** is more lyrical than convincing in its depiction of a country school in a Maori district, following the seasons formally, and implicitly a cycle of youth and age, life and death, a movement from strangeness to acceptance in the community. Focusing on the infant class, the teacher-narrator describes her efforts to make the children more sensitive to the details of their life; while at the same time she becomes aware and more sensitive to the human details of the community, its customs and rituals. That the text should often break into poetry is fitting, as this is more idyll than short story; and yet it integrates Maori words and Maori insights into the fabric of English narration.

Unresolved, however, are the problems which arise in the area of character and social conflict among adults and in more urban settings, the area of serious fictional prose. The last story in *Waiariki* begins this resolution at a higher level than the idyll.

"Parade" is told by an intelligent, sensitive girl who has left her small town for education in the city. She returns home for the local carnival and agrees to dress in Maori costume and to perform on a float along with her relatives and friends in a dance party. As she does so, she feels disgraced—she realizes that the Pakeha community is staring at the Maoris at best as museum curios and at worst as circus freaks. She finds it difficult to understand why her relatives go on with the farce, accepting the gratuitous and condescending remarks of European officials. Her Granny Rita tells her—"You grow older, you understand more," but—

> Then old Hohepa, who is bent and sometimes crabby, said, "It's your job, this. To show others who we are."

Yet on the ride home the narrator begins to understand, her maturity coming not with age, as she sees that what is done not so much to show others—the Pakeha—who she is, but for her to express her true, her real self as a Maori. From within the Maori community, in its personal concerns and its sensitivity to the human feelings within the landscape—history, ancestors, work, meaning—arise the songs, the dances, the customs, the old stories. To dance and sing with the other Maoris is to affirm her identity in that community. And the story concludes with two stanzas of the song about the arrival of the various canoes—the text completely in Maori, with no translation.

Here is the world of the Maori framed by that of the pakeha, but now seen from within, so that the voices of the mayor and the prissy ladies seem grotesque and unreal, while the Maori tradition feels warm and real. Yet the story also shows lines of interaction—once again, the main character comes from without, from the city, is articulate in English, feels cut off from an aging rural community, and she will return to the city with new understanding though how she will make the resolutions of her new feeling with that of European life remains unworked out. What is important, however, is that the Maori language crystallizes as a full text, not as occasional words or false locutions in English; the well-written, structurally-sound English tale sustains the insights as well as the other language. The problem is not linguistic any longer, but structural—how to make the English well-made tale fit with the insights of Maori tradition and feeling. Part of the answer, of course, lies in the fact that the English tradition at its best, so opposed to the sloppy day-to-day reality of New Zealand life, is sensitive and warm, is already available to the rich expressions of Maori and the bantering nuances of its human relationships. The other part of the answer lies in the skill of the Maori writers who attempt more sustained efforts to fuse the two cultures in imaginative fiction. (pp. 195-99)

Norman Simms, "A Maori Literature in English, Part I: Prose Fiction—Patricia Grace," in Pacific Quarterly Moana, Vol. III, No. 2, April, 1978, pp. 186-99.

PAT EVANS

Patricia Grace is someone who seems never to have doubted who she is or what her culture ought to give her; her writing is sure and deft, unpretentious and integrated, simple and (I'm sorry) graceful. As a short story writer she seems simply to make up her own rules, producing in **Waiariki** charming, intimate stories in which innocent folk and unpretentious incidents often indicate very much more than their size would seem to allow. We would expect pretty much the same in her first novel, **Mutuwhenua**; and we get the same strength and charm in a story of a young country girl's love for and marriage to a city European—a story which is also about the country and the town, the Maori and the European, a father and his daughter, and above all, the botched heritage which we all share.

Novels, however, need more 'stiffening' than stories as a rule, and it is here that Patricia Grace seems to have been persuaded briefly to follow other people's rules, using recurrent symbols to give a sense of form to her work. Because the novel is not long these techniques do not require to be very substantial; but the reader may find them a little inappropriate: not so much a ngaio mentioned on the first page (its placid exterior versus tangled interior suggests a symbolism that seems to me not fully consummated by the book) as a rather obstrusive hunk of greenstone that is discovered by a European boy and retrieved from his profit-hungry father to be bulldozed back into its rightful Maori land. Symbols like this have the sense of being imposed in any fiction; in Patricia Grace's fiction imposition has no real place, for her strength as a writer is based on close, vivid observations of small things . . . and tiny, particular habits. . . . From this level of particularity Patricia Grace's meanings grow, giving her work that resonance we have learned in such a brief time to associate with her writing.

In fact the real form of **Mutuwhenua** derives from this organic kind of growth; the novel opens out from its first chapter like a flower unfolding. That chapter mentions both the greenstone and a macrocarpa; the stone's significance is explored in the second chapter, and then the macrocarpa sud-

denly becomes for the time being an important index of the girl's growth in the third. The brief apotheosis of the macrocarpa makes an interesting contrast to the nagging references to the stone, too: for humans seize on symbols in their environment as they seem relevant to them at the time, and as summarily discard them. Once the girl has grown enough to reach its lowest branch and swing on it, the macrocarpa has done its work, and the writer proceeds to explore the wider processes of growing up that no simple hedge can account for—processes that will take her from the plant and the familiar ground it stands on.

That process of growth is initiated when Linda (she has rejected her Maori name) falls in love with a young schoolteacher called Graeme, and persuades her father to permit the marriage. The novel movingly describes the price of such a decision, in a way that makes the reader feel not guilty but sad—in my case, sad that we have not allowed ourselves to know the richness of a life lived among trees that have names as humans have names, among ancestors who have not been turned into the euphemistic roses of suburban cemeteries but are still very much about; and with myths that still have everyday meanings, on soil that is somehow alive. The real culture shock in this novel comes not from the cheery stench of cooking food in the girl's home but from the cheerless stench of culture rotting in the city in which the girl must live as a married woman. In the first, there is the happy effluvia people make when they are genuinely and earthily alive; in the other—more dominant, alas—the reek of death. Related to these two different kinds of smell is a subtle contrast between the concept of *home* in the first half of the novel—warmth, love, spontaneity, caring—and the concept of *house* in the second, when the girl finds herself unable to adjust to living in a perfectly ordinary rented city dwelling haunted by the births and deaths of complete strangers. It is a risky contrast, of course, for the reader who thinks that all Linda needs to pull through is a Conray heater or a Kenwood Chef has missed the point of the contrast.

In underlining such contrasts I have probably made the novel sound rather more polemical than it is—a Maori woman's *Maori Woman*, perhaps. But Patricia Grace's compassion and wisdom ensure that she emphasizes the common ground that all forms of life have in this country. The young couple meet at a tennis club which does not have rules about colour other than those which apply to sporting attire; they are equally decent and chaste; ashamed of her mother's bottling of beetroot Linda visits Graeme's home to find his mother—bottling beetroot. The stereotypes we always import into novels are skilfully flicked aside: Linda's father, not Graeme's, is the sternly puritanical force in the novel; she works as a typist in an office, not as a waitress in a hotel; the young couple do *not* have wild, liberating sex under a heaving canopy of stars, nor does any sick holidaying accountant tumble dead to the sand on seeing pakeha and Maori together.

For there are no goodies and baddies in this novel; there is simply that botched, impersonal heritage I mentioned before which for all its impersonality deeply affects the lives of all the people Patricia Grace writes about. It is all the more powerful for being so inferentially, even casually, shown—in the failure of Linda's cousin, a cheery oaf called Toki, to keep his job; in the failure of some young Maoris to respect or understand the superstitions of their elders which have become so real and important a part of the novel's world. It is chiefly present in the misgivings of Linda's father, whom she initially sees as a cantankerous middle-aged man unable to acknowledge the inevitability of change but who, she realizes, once he has died near the end of the novel, has always seen the fecklessness of what we happily call Progress, but also the impossibility of simply retreating into Maori life as if the urban European world did not exist. His decision to allow his daughter to marry the young European, Graeme, is the novel's most calculated attempt to make a compromise that will endure; the birth of a grandson at the moment of his death implies the possibility of its eventual success. Yet Patricia Grace knows that nothing is quite that easy, and the novel concludes with no simple solutions to the young couple's problems; indeed, with a strong sense that the real problem may be that there are no solutions.

Patricia Grace is an honest, original, intelligent writer; and her first novel will please and impress anyone who cares about the development of New Zealand writing. (pp. 372-75)

> *Pat Evans, in a review of "Mutuwhenua: The Moon Sleeps," in Landfall, Vol. 32, No. 4, December, 1978, pp. 372-75.*

PETER ALCOCK

"Stainless and shining, and as pure as the night of Mutuwhenua when the moon goes underground and sleeps." So Patricia Grace describes the cousin Toki, "whose soul is dark glowing black," the heroine of her second book [*Mutuwhenua*] and first novel, successor to her stories, *Waiariki.* It seems the brief and simple tale, told with very considerable integrity, economy, precision—fine and unrelenting, parsimony and poetry of phrase, relaxed yet unremitting control of structure—of a young Maori girl, only daughter, growing up in a Maori rural neighbourhood, say, somewhere on the west coast north of Wellington. Increasingly she becomes aware both of her own world and of distinction between it and that of the pakeha, yet she marries a pakeha teacher, Graeme, and, with him in the city, comes to an almost destructive realization that it is not to the pakeha world—if she is herself—she belongs, nor ever can.

"Mutuwhenua" is that phase when the moon is not seen—but it is there, even buried in darkness like "her" ancient mere, discovered, then bulldozed deeply over in a gully (out of pakeha reach) in chapter two. "The stone was my inheritance. It would always be so, but [my father] wanted me to have another inheritance as well." So the stubborn father accepts, welcomes, her pakeha marriage. Yet at the end of the book, after her psychological crisis in the city, then her father's death at the time of her son's birth, she rejoins Graeme in the city, leaving their child with her family. The final sentence of the book reads: "I went, remembering that day of Rakaunui, the time when you can see the shape of the tree that Rona clutched as the moon drew her to the skies." Rakaunui, full moon, is when the rakau, Rona's ngaio tree, can be seen plainly in the moon. Rona, going to the spring, cursed the obscured moon when she tripped. Patricia Grace's Ripeka (also Ngaio-"her" tree at home—and, temporarily, pakehafied Linda) remembers Dad's repeated words, ". . . you'll do right when the right time comes," and when that crisis comes upon her in the pakeha city, responds and recognizes the ineluctable stone within—unlike Rona's denial—asks and accepts the gathered wisdom of her kin, and is neither drawn out of this world nor alienated . . . from her soul's dark yet luminous inheritance.

The division of Ripeka's world begins with the shock of menstruation, a two-fold division both into pakeha/Maori and into things seen/unseen. This later theme develops subtly, first the mere, then careless impiety—and reactions and consequences—gathering seafood at Rakaunui, then awareness of Grandpa Toki's ghostly presence at this death (in a narrative context of Mutuwhenua), and then her major urban crisis, pregnant, far from her people, bare section, unfamiliar house, increasingly strange nights—"The dreams had in them a tall woman with moko on her chin a woman I didn't know, who beckoned from the corner of a room"—and unendurable days that drive her out to walk the streets till Graeme's afternoon return—" . . . I felt strongly and certainly the iced touch, the chill pricking across my shoulders and head and down my back—and I blocked the welling scream with my hand." From home they write, "It must be a burying place for this to happen"; she has no option but, with Graeme, to leave, and in the nick of time, upon her mother and Toki's arrival—for she has been too shy ever to reveal such Maori matters to her husband.

A fishbone in the pakeha throat—this climax? I can, myself, not easily accept it; the obstacle being not, certainly, in the impeccable writing, but in the implicit "rightness" of such experience and response. I would like to say, "sensibly," her past rises up against her in so unnatural, "alienated" urban life; more detailed "psychological" façades of "explanation" could be constructed. As already said, or possibly now apparent, the sustained integrity, economy, single-mindedness seems quite to rule out any such facile rationalization. This book very carefully says what it means. Is this what it means to *accept* "bi-cultural" literature, society? Other world-views, as other people, must no longer be converted, not even assimilated, but—accepted? "I began occasionally telling people that one should believe whatever had been believed in all countries and periods, and only reject any part of it after much evidence, instead of starting all over afresh and only believing what one could prove." Thus that giant among modern poets in English, W. B. Yeats, whose whole life and writing incidentally, were devoted exhaustively and with labyrinthine, occult complexity to what, perhaps, can only be called the Cycles of the Moon:

> Though grave-diggers' toil is long,
> Sharp their spades, their muscles strong,
> They but thrust their buried men
> Back in the human mind again.

In the above concern with content and controversy what may have become now not as apparent is the variety, versatility, and verve of this short book. Though the book's base is rural the "city scapes" are entirely adequate; in country or town Patricia Grace is mistress of her scene: ". . . a quiescent sea, burning silver from the flagellation of a full sun," "Wooden footfalls of the hundreds of wooden people and their unheard crying." The continuing comedies and errors of domestic trivia are exactly right. When she persuades her Nanny Ripeka to accept and attend her wedding, their spontaneous recitation of genealogies is a convincing and moving scene. The story moves swiftly, but can linger at need; the largely—by no means entirely—elliptic, oblique intrusion of the preternatural is tactful and delicately timed. (pp. 390-93)

> *Peter Alcock, "New Zealand," in World Literature Written in English, Vol. 18, No. 2, November, 1979, pp. 390-93.*

DAVID NORTON

I had expected to find this small collection better than I did. Patricia Grace's first collection of stories *Waiariki* showed . . . 'promise of good things', and her first novel *Mutuwhenua* even exceeded expectations and was well worth recommending to friends and sending to relatives overseas. Sadly, though, this present collection [*The Dream Sleepers and Other Stories*] seems to have gone back to being merely promising—promising that, given a sustained sense of structure and purpose, Patricia Grace could produce writing of real quality.

The collection is divided into two parts, the first of which has the best stories in it. These are stories in which a strong sense of character or of an emotional experience comes through, and they have a real vitality to them. **"Beans"**, the shortest, shows these strengths. The narrator tells of how he bikes into town every Saturday morning in the winter term to play rugby, and then bikes back again. It is a poem of youthful zest: 'Where the ball goes I go. I tackle, handle, kick, run, everything. I do everything I can think of and I feel good.' . . . This simple vitality and enjoyment is summed up by the old lady next door saying to Mum, 'He's full of beans that boy of yours. Full of beans.' It's an appropriate conclusion. The poem of mood is refreshingly satisfying and complete.

Strength of feeling, vitality of character and awareness of language such as **"Beans"** shows are present in all the better stories. **"Letters from Whetu"** consists of four letters, written by a boy who has stayed on in the sixth form, to his friends from 'the old gang'; it conveys the character's vitality well through the vigour of his language and perceptions. One feels convinced of his quality as a person. A brief passage such as when he describes his English teacher can only give an idea of this:

> She's trying to make us enjoy K. M. Kay Em is what she calls Katherine Mansfield, as though she and K. M. were best mates. Well I suppose Fisher could be just about old enough to have been a mate of K. M.'s . . .
>
> Do you know what? When she waves and flaps the book about she doesn't stop 'reading', so I suppose that means she knows her K. M. off by heart, bless her HART (Halt All Racist Tours), punctuation and all. I don't think her glasses will quite fall off— Beat Boredom, wait and hope for Fisher's glasses to fall off and cut her feet to ribbons.

K. M. may not come through to the narrator, but one sees his energy of mind. His vivid description of his classes, his critical awareness of them and his obvious joy in his adventures with his friends give real point to his doubts and fears about what he is doing.

In this story in particular, Patricia Grace has created a convincing fictional voice, but in two of the stories the voice, again convincing and interesting, appears to be her own: **"Between Earth and Sky"** . . . describes a woman's feelings through childbirth, and **"Mirrors"** simply follows a woman as she gets up before her family one morning to have half an hour to herself, and how her mood changes from joy to ill-temper. There is coherence and completeness in these stories.

The second group of stories, five in all, all concern the same characters yet lack focus of coherence. Half of the first one concerns the return of Uncle Kepa from the sea and the children's expectation that he will bring them a monkey. It is

hinted that Uncle Kepa has a son in Australia. The last part of the last one has this son appear, and one is reminded of the monkey. But this and the use of the same barely characterised children are not enough to give a sense of purpose.

Half a dozen of the stories (the last five and the title story [**"The Dream Sleepers"**]) show this lack of coherent purpose. By this I do not mean that they should have a moral point to them, that they should be earnestly message-laden, but (to be dangerously prescriptive for a moment) that the reader should have, as he reaches the last word of a story, a sense of the whole story he has read. A progressive sense of discovery is needed. Every detail should be felt to have earned its place so that the reader senses shape and meaning, if not in life, then at least in art. **"The Dream Sleepers"** is typical of the stories that lack these qualities. It starts in a fanciful, imitation-Mansfield way ('The houses sit on their handkerchiefs, and early in the morning begin to sneeze') and for nearly two pages follows the sneezings; but the bulk of the story concerns the sneezed-out children during a typical day at school. There is nothing to remind one of the opening, nor even anything in common with its manner of writing; the result is confusion.

Less important, but still a worry, is the minimal punctuation. Particularly in some of the earlier stories there is so little that reading is almost as difficult as making out a troublesome handwriting. Of course punctuation is the writer's servant, but it is also the writer's courtesy to the reader and the reader's guide to the words. This is a book likely to be used in schools, but such punctuation will not help to give young readers a sense of the clarity and meaningfulness of language.

And yet there is clarity and meaning in Patricia Grace's best writing. Let the following paragraph stand as a sample of what is best in this book (it is from **"Mirrors"**, as it becomes clear to the narrator that her try for a peaceful half hour has failed):

> And all I wanted was a half hour I tell you, not great rain bullets fired at me as I look for a spade, not skin lumping from the cold and a mess to clean. Only a warm few moments and breathing in and out, drinking tea. Time to look at the folds in the curtains and to watch the grey reels of darkness rotating in the room's corners and growing paler. A time to be you see.

(pp. 330-32)

David Norton, in a review of "The Dream Sleepers and Other Stories," in Landfall, *Vol. 35, No. 3, September, 1981, pp. 330-32.*

JOHN B. BESTON

The Dream Sleepers, Patricia Grace's second book of short stories, is essentially a non-narrative collection. Grace has always shown a fondness for idylls and vignettes . . . but her fondness has grown, given added impulse perhaps by the narrative and technical difficulties she encountered in writing the novel *Mutuwhenua.* She likes especially to portray the great cyclical events in the course of a human lifetime (birth, sexual maturing, marriage, and death), rituals (like courtship or parades), routines (like cooking or gardening), and recreations.

The sequence of the last five stories of *The Dream Sleepers*— **"Kepa," "The Pictures," "Drifting," "Whitebait,"** and **"Kip"**—represents the kind of thing that Grace writes most naturally, with least constraint. These are non-narrative stories about Maori children within a family context: various relatives are part of their daily life, and even their playmates seem to be an extension of their own family. The same figures recur throughout the five stories, giving them the character of a loose long short story. Uncle Kepa, the chief adult, especially interests Grace because as a Maori adult she has a deeper understanding of him than others would: while the children see his adventurousness and the *pakeha* sees his shiftlessness and irresponsibility, Grace sees the courage and acceptance in his adaptation to a life that has never offered him any direction. His repeated absences from New Zealand have not made him isolated; but Grace's characters are never isolated, for there are always other Maori ready to extend their *aroha*.

Grace's controlling purpose is to present universal situations, in which the Maori are the personages. In that way, she aims to give their lifestyle a human immediacy. It is the gentlest way of emphasizing their common humanity in a discriminatory society that likes to think it does not discriminate.

Although Grace is only part Maori, her sympathies and values are wholly Maori. What is especially Maori in her make-up is her strong sense of attachment to the land where one's ancestors have long resided (reflected in the old man in **"Journey"**); a belief in the anger of the disturbed dead (expressed in **"Journey"** and above all in *Mutuwhenua*); a faith in *aroha* and the warmth of personal relationships (conveyed in the story that closes this collection, **"Kip"**); and her anthropomorphism, in which the physical world is an extension of one's self and the changing seasons seem like changes in one's own mood or one's bodily state. Her awareness of *pakeha* attitudes to Maori, too, is that of a Maori—she sees clearly Reuben's contempt for Maori girls and his belief that they are all hungering for sex (**"Kip"**), and she portrays tellingly the obliterating effects of the *pakeha* attempt to integrate Maori into their way of life (**"Letters from Whetu"**). (pp. 667-68)

Grace is at her best when dealing with an exclusively Maori cast in a completely Maori context. In such a context, there are no tensions and there is no fear of offending, so that her vitality has free expression. The story most filled with life in *The Dream Sleepers* is **"It Used to Be Green Once"**; it was written with confidence and a good sense of humour. Normally Grace is a timid writer—as a Maori woman in male-dominated and *pakeha*-controlled New Zealand she could hardly have been otherwise—and is only truly relaxed when she can avoid sensitive areas. The assumption of a male persona in **"Beans"** allows her to assume a greater confidence than usual, too. One can almost hear Grace in this story saying, "If I had been a man, I would not have to be so wary."

In spite of her reluctance to treat racial themes, it was inevitable that Grace should do so; one wonders that she deals with such themes as rarely as she does until one remembers, again, that she is a Maori woman. With all her timidity bred into her by virtue of her sex and her race, one feels the passion underneath the control in her stories with racial themes, and it is these stories that stay longest with us; she may feel more at ease painting in the pastel tones, but it is her reds that most strike us. There are only two stories in this collection that deal with racial themes, **"Letters from Whetu"** and **"Journey."** The first consists of a series of letters written in class by a bored Maori highschool student, about to drop out or flunk out on the verge of becoming an honorable statistic by graduating from highschool. Ahead lies the *pakeha* prize, a

safe but dull office job, while outside lie friends and freedom and some kind of integrity. One sees in Whetu's resolute day-dreaming a resentment against the price of "success": for the lessening of *pakeha* antagonisms one must renounce one's Maori identity and accept subordination. The second story, **"Journey,"** tells of an old man who travels to the city to try to convey to some *pakeha* officials how important it is to his family to keep the land they live on, instead of being forced to sell it to the government for redevelopment. His mission is unsuccessful and his one gesture of frustrated rage merely impotent. The fertile land will in time be used as a parking lot, and *pakeha* houses will be built on the rocky land adjoining it. The story is technically very accomplished, told indirectly through anticipation and retrospect (before and after the meeting with the *pakeha* officials), a method that serves to soften the greatest tension in the racial confrontation. Like so many women writers, Grace avoids dealing directly with scenes of great friction.

If the fact of being a Maori woman in New Zealand has limited Grace's range and power, it has led her on the positive side to refine her technique. Carefulness and subtlety are characteristic of her work, like that of so many important women writers. Women have rarely dared to undertake grand themes, other than the sanctioned themes of love and the family, and Grace is no exception to the pattern. But their work is often immensely satisfying in areas like those just mentioned, carefulness and subtlety. Grace's style, for instance, is always carefully wrought and sometimes quite lyrical, and her technique is firmly under control. Like many other women writers, she makes her points by indirection and does not underline them too heavily. The appeal to the reader's intelligence and sensitivity is one we are bound to respond to with appreciation. (pp. 669-70)

John B. Beston, in a review of "The Dream Sleepers and Other Stories," in World Literature Written in English, *Vol. 21, No. 3, Autumn, 1982, pp. 667-70.*

BILL PEARSON

Memory plays an important part in [Patricia Grace's *Waiariki*], not only because it enables one to connect a lost past with a confusing present, but because it is a significant part of Maori folk tradition. Mrs. Grace follows the convention started by the *Te Ao Hou* writers by which the distinctions between a short story and meditative reminiscence were often blurred. It is notable how the predominant mode of her stories is first-person narration, usually from the point of view of a central character. . . . There are memories of childhood, one of a holiday by the sea; stories told by the very old; reminiscences by young or middle-aged adults recalling experiences of childhood in the old rural culture, mixed with a sense that they cannot communicate the meaning of those experiences to their children; the thoughts of an old man about to leave the country for the city 'to make a way for those who follow because I love', the thoughts of an old widower, waiting for death and reunion with his wife; the thoughts of a city-dwelling Maori woman, feeling the strain and the satisfaction of having coped with a fortnight's visit from seven relations. . . . There are only three third-person narratives, two of them comic and one angry.

Patricia Grace grew up in the city . . . aware of an imperfect understanding of her language and culture, and when she came to write made a conscious effect to use English to express Maori thoughts. She created a prose style based on the structure of Maori speech and evoking the rhythms of the speech of old people she had heard tell stories in her childhood. She told David McGill that she 'liked to sit and listen to their stories, their genealogies, talk of weather and tides, and food gathering'. Her style is suggestive of (not an accurate reproduction of) the speech patterns for rural Maori English more often than of Maori; but it is convincing and quite satisfying in the beauty of its leisurely rhythms:

> From the north he came, Toki, in his young day.
> Ah yes. A boaster this one, Toki the fisherman.
>
> ("Toki")

> Sad I wait, and see them come slow back from the river. The torches move slow.
>
> To the tent to rest after they had gone to the river, and while asleep the dream came. A dream of death. He came to me in the dream, not sadly but smiling, with hand on heart and said, 'I go but do not weep. No weeping, it is my time.'
>
> ("At the River")
> (pp. 176-77)

Norman Simms has remarked that in these stories there is a sense of timelessness, that it would be hard to say of **"Toki"** 'whether this story of a boastful fisherman from the north . . . happened today, yesterday, or a hundred years ago.' A sense of continuity with ancestors and land and seasons and tides quietly pervades Patricia Grace's best work. In the memories of the young and middle-aged adults the style is more conventional, but a sense of warmth and community is present. In one of them, a father recalls beaches he had gone to as a boy for sea-food, takes his children there, and though he finds much of what he looked for, he is unable to tell the children that to fill their kits with shellfish they should first urinate on them. They would misunderstand. . . . The father not only regrets that the custom has passed:

> And there was regret in me too for the passing of innocence, for that which made me unable to say to my children, 'Put your kits on the sand little ones. Mimi on your kits and then wash them in the sea. Then we will find plenty. There will be plenty of good kai moana in the sea and your kits will always be full!
>
> (*Waiariki*)

"Valley", which was at one time considered as the title piece for the collection is a cyclical account of a year at a country school, beginning in summer and ending with the start of the summer holidays. There is an awareness of the weather, light, the seasons, always the sound and movement of children, of the town as a community, of growth and death, and these are contained in a mood of contented acceptance. In the school it is as if we are getting from a Maori teacher's point of view those scenes from the infant room in Sylvia Ashton-Warner's *Spinster,* but without Miss Vorontosov's cranky theorising. On the gala day it is like revisiting A. P. Gaskell's "School Picnic", but from the point of view not of the racist Miss Brown but of one of the party preparing the hangi.

"Valley" is in four seasonal sections, each with its memorable event and appropriate incidents. Of the sixteen children enrolled in the infant room, some names begin to take shape.

One is Hiriwa, 'a small boy with a thin face and the fingers that press into the clay are long, and careful about what they do.' The children search the nasturtiums by the incinerator for butterfly eggs. The appropriate event of this section is the hatching of the eggs in the classroom, the caterpillars and the first of the butterflies. But Hiriwa has modelled a plasticine cricket, and suddenly smashes it.

The event of the Autumn section is Gala Day and the comedy of the cheerful preparation for the hangi, with Turei's uncontrollable dog upsetting the buckets of prepared vegetables, and a continual mutual teasing that only Noel Hilliard has approached. . . . Hiriwa's mother is there, 'pale and serious-looking and very young' with a white scar from her temple to her chin. Over at the chopping area is Hiriwa's father: 'Unsmiling. Heavy in build and mood. Blunt fingered hands gripping the slim handled axe.'

In the Winter section the dominant event is the death of one of the teachers from a heart attack, Auntie Mrs Kaa. There is sadness and she is buried, but the section closes on 'the sound of children's voices, laughter, a light guitar strumming.'

The last section is Spring. The children plant a garden. Hiriwa makes a gingerbread man of clay and smashes it.

> He writes in his diary. 'The gingerbread man is lost and I am lost too.' One side of his face is heavy with bruising.
>
> On the day of the pet show and auction his mother says to me, 'We are going away, Hiriwa and I. We need to go, there is nothing left for us to do. By tomorrow we will be gone.'
>
> (*Waiariki*)

It is only at the pet show and auction, which involves the town, that we become fully aware that we have been seeing things from a Maori point of view, when the pakeha auctioneer Joe Blow—no doubt, in the terms of the pakeha small town, a popular community figure—is shown up with all his glib sales patter, his glib fibs, his facile mateyness, calling every man by his first name, adopting a communal role but only for the occasion and on the surface. (pp. 178-79)

But the year ends on the note of expectancy of the last day of school when the children scramble into the bus. There are tuis in the pohutukawas, and the sequence ends with the children waving from the windows of the school bus and four of them staring from the back window. (pp. 179-80)

Patricia Grace told an interviewer she did not 'set out deliberately to be a Maori writer', and in some of her early stories, each one an inside view from a single character, usually a child, it would be hard to say whether the child was Maori or pakeha. In one of them, **"Beans"**, the boy biking past a pig farm takes a big sniff of 'a horrible great stink . . . a joyous big stink of pigs.' Then he goes home and eats lemons 'because I don't want to miss a thing in all my life'. It is so with Patricia Grace's writing. All experience is valid, and though it happens to a woman of Maori ancestry, much of it may be in common with the experience of other suburban women. So with **"Mirrors"** where a mother forgoes making love to get up and have a cup of tea before the family wake, goes out in burst slippers for the milk, gets caught in the rain, steps on some dog-shit on the path, puts her slippers in the incinerator and washes her feet. By this time the family is awake. An unimpressive series of events, but told in a mixture of stream-of-consciousness dialogue, (not 'interior monologue' but talking to herself as if to someone else) and observation of the early-morning scene, the waves on the shore, and on the rocks of Mana Island. There is a richness in the variety of experience to which she is alert. (p. 181)

In **"Pictures"** there is a detached, lovingly comic account of pictures night in a small Maori community, probably a few years ago. **"Journey"**, told in the third person, is about an old man clashing with incomprehensible pakeha bureaucracy when he goes into Wellington to try to arrange for the subdivision of his land for his nieces and nephews, kicked out of the office because he kicked the official's desk in frustration. On the journey into the city he has seen the hills being sliced. . . . It occurs to him that bones will be disturbed by the excavations and when he gets home he asks to be cremated.

In **"Valley"** there is a calm impression of life proceeding in its unpredictably expectable patterns. Patricia Grace showed that she had profited from her familiarity with such conscious stylists as Virginia Woolf, Patrick White, Katherine Mansfield, Janet Frame and Frank Sargeson. In her most recent stories she has shown a command of a wide variety of styles, passing subtly and deftly from one to another within a story. There is compassion and a maturity of judgement. Every experience of her characters strikes one as valid and interesting: she engages one at all levels. I do not doubt that she has a great deal more to say and that she will develop into a writer of considerable stature. (p. 182)

> *Bill Pearson, "Witi Ihimaera and Patricia Grace," in* Critical Essays on the New Zealand Short Story, *edited by Cherry Hankin, Heinemann, 1982, pp. 166-84.*

JOHN B. BESTON

New Zealand has produced the most distinguished of the ethnic literatures in English that have burgeoned in the South Pacific during the last fifteen years or so. The Maori represent a sizeable body (9%) in the total population of New Zealand and are the best educated of the native peoples of the South Pacific. In the course of their education, which in some cases continues beyond high school, they are introduced to English literature, whose conventions they follow in their own writings, for the literatures of the South Pacific islanders were oral and communal rather than individual in composition. (p. 41)

Although the Maori have not enjoyed the material benefits of New Zealand society on equal terms with the Pakeha (the Whites), they have not been excluded from the mainstream of that society to the extent that the native peoples have been in Australia or in Papua New Guinea. Consequently, the Maori have more confidence and pride in themselves than other Pacific peoples surrounded by an overwhelming White society, and the Maori writers are much more concerned with establishing what constitutes the essence of their identity as a people.

Grace's aim as a Maori author is to present the Maori people as comprehensively as possible, mainly to the Pakeha society around her, but also to her fellow-Maori and, ultimately, to the English world at large. Her main audience is of course the Pakeha: by virtue of numbers, education, and affluence, the Pakeha constitute the principal buyers of fiction in New Zealand. Works by Maori writers, beyond their inherent literary quality, would appeal to various impulses in Pakeha readers: the desire for novelty, interest in a people they commonly regard as inferior, a well-intended (if somewhat superficial) egalitarianism, and an element of self-gratulation that their culture has enriched the scope of Maori life. . . . Grace is aware that the quality of her work alone will not hold the continued interest of her predominantly Pakeha audience: she must make the Maori attractive to that audience and not alienate it. She must make it clear too that the Maori represent no threat to the privileges that the Pakeha have secured for themselves and, above all, must not accuse the Pakeha. In her Maori audience, Grace seeks to evoke the pleasure of recognizing themselves and to foster pride in their Maori identity. For Pakeha and Maori alike, she tries to establish what constitutes the essence of Maoridom.

In depicting her Maori characters, Grace is concerned most of all with establishing their common humanity. The activities she characteristically shows them engaged in are cyclic ones associated with the phases of life, familiar to all human beings: pregnancy and birth, schooldays, adolescence, courtship and marriage, aging, dying and death. In order to emphasize the universality of these cycles, she likes to link them to the progression of the seasons, like the spring births in **"Between Earth and Sky"** and **"Mirrors." "Valley,"** Grace's most typical story and perhaps also her best, tells of such cyclic events as the raising of a baby, schooldays, and one's first encounter with human death. It is divided into four sections headed "Summer," "Autumn," "Winter," and "Spring"; it is in the "Winter" section, appropriate to the cyclic nature of the story, that the teacher in the small school dies, while the "Spring" section celebrates renewal as gardens are planted again and preparations begin for the Spring Fair. Grace is also fond of portraying human routines to emphasize the similarities of Pakeha and Maori lives, as in the title story in *The Dream Sleepers* and in the story that follows it, **"Between Earth and Sky,"** where she depicts the routines of early morning. Her scenes of common recreational activities, too, would kindle in Pakeha and Maori alike an immediate response, the warm pleasure that comes from recognition. (pp. 41-3)

If it is her fondness for presenting the Maori in scenes of everyday human activities that establishes their common humanity, it is Grace's depiction of them as warm and expansive in their relations with one another that makes them attractive to her readers. Here her own preference for the Maori as a people shows through: when her Maori are together, their warmth and expansiveness contrasts sharply with the Pakeha's tight restraint and withheldness. Even in company, her Pakeha characters seem always alone, while her Maori characters are most alive in the company of others, unreservedly enjoying visits from relatives and friends.

Grace is careful to allay Pakeha fears by stressing that the Maori do not threaten the privileges the Pakeha have arrogated unto themselves. Her Maori characters never aspire very high: having learned early in life to make do with second best, they want only a modest slice of the pie. Only one minor character among her Maori cast is seen in a profession she shares with the Pakeha, the nurse Rawhiti in **"Between Earth and Sky"**; but while nursing is indeed a profession, it is a service profession in which one receives rather than gives directions. When Linda marries a Pakeha schoolteacher in *Mutu-*

whenua, her aspirations do not rise with her social position: they remain the common desires of a young married woman, to have nice clothes and to make her house attractive. But the house she lives in is rented, and she does not yearn for a house of her own. Continually in Grace's characters, and ultimately in Grace herself, one can perceive an aspect of deference to the Pakeha.

Grace is careful also not to alienate her Pakeha audience by showing her Maori as insisting on their rights. Her Maori are unaggressive, a gentle, noncompetitive people. They will fight for their rights only when it is a question of preventing the alienation of their land, for their land represents their very being. . . . The Maori's relation to the land is an intensely personal one: they *are* the land. The young man in **"And So I Go,"** about to leave his ancestral lands to find work in the city, makes no distinction between his love for his family and his love for the land. In his farewell to the land, he addresses the earth as his mother: "[I] Stretch out my arms on wide Earth Mother and lay my face on hers. Then call out my love." (pp. 43–4)

Grace never directly accuses the Pakeha of a basic contempt for the Maori; the closest she comes to it is in the story **"Journey,"** where her Pakeha characters behave with an obtuseness and indifference to Maori sensibilities and values that one has to acknowledge is widespread in Whites' dealings with people of other races who lack power. Throughout her stories (but much less in her novel) Grace illustrates clearly the Pakeha tendency to classify the Maori as a way of dismissing their importance. (p. 44)

[Stories] that deal with Pakeha condescension, **"Parade"** and **"Letters from Whetu,"** avoid direct accusation of the Pakeha simply by presenting graphically the state of affairs in New Zealand. Both stories describe a situation in which a character makes a sacrifice of personal dignity in order to assert his or her dignity as a Maori. . . . In **"Letters from Whetu,"** the student Whetu is about to opt out from becoming an "honorable statistic" within the high school system—that is, a Maori who graduates from high school, presumably going on to a low level but secure office job. Whetu's graduation would stand less to his credit than it would flatter the Pakeha image of themselves as elevating the lives of a people they consider to be in the main shiftless, lacking in persistence and ambition, and so would reinforce rather than dispel racism. Whetu sees fakeries within the school—the posturings of the English teacher and the mutterings of the Math teacher—that to him are a miniature of the Pakeha system. He comes to reject that system with a cynicism beyond his years, but is unable to replace it with anything worthwhile. In depicting a life blighted as it is about to begin its separate existence, **"Letters from Whetu"** is one of the saddest of Grace's stories. (p. 45)

Aroha, or love for one another as members of an extended family, is the most basic of Maori values. Because of *aroha,* Grace's Maori characters are never isolated, whatever the nature of the problem that besets them. Whetu, for instance, who seems so alienated in the classroom (**"Letters from Whetu"**), has a number of good Maori friends outside it; in fact, he counters the tedium of his schoolday by writing letters to them. His friends represent his freer Maori side, a life lived with others in contact with the sea and the open land. And Linda in *Mutuwhenua* owes her happiness, even her life itself, to her Maori family at a time when she feels she cannot communicate with her Pakeha husband. Throughout Grace's writing, but especially in *Mutuwhenua,* there is a persistent

contrast, pointed even though implicit, between the spontaneous *aroha* of her Maori characters and the emotional inhibitedness of her Pakeha characters. In *Mutuwhenua,* where her heroine and hero are Maori and Pakeha respectively, Grace is able to oppose the two sets of parents and grandparents and imply a value judgment upon the two cultures. Linda's parents are a vital couple with an ongoing relationship between them, but Graeme's parents are a drab couple of British origin such as one meets in the pages of Barbara Pym: sentient beings surprised early in their acquaintance by an access of enthusiasm and led by it into the long acquaintance of marriage. Even more marked is the difference between the grandmothers of Linda and Graeme: Linda's Nanny Ripeka is a lively and warm old woman who has remained an important member of the family, while Graeme's nameless grandmother is a truculent, cold woman who stands fiercely alone, tolerated rather than cherished. Grace does not actually say that the Pakeha are cold, but her attitude is clear from her portraits. (p. 47)

Grace endorses certain old Maori beliefs that do not clash with Christianity. In *Mutuwhenua* she presents the anger of the disturbed dead as an essential cause of the near tragedy. Although she does not explicitly state the Maori belief that it always rains when a Maori dies . . . she is clearly sympathetic to it, for rain falls at both the death and funeral of Tahi in **"Valley"**: "It is right that it should rain today, that earth and sky should meet and touch, mingle. That the soil pouring into the opened ground should be newly blessed by the sky . . .". There is a strong anthropomorphic strain in Maori thinking, a habit of seeing the physical world as an extension of oneself: the changing seasons seem like physical cycles in one's body, or like changes in mood. When in **"Between Earth and Sky"** the woman speaks to her slippers, sometimes as if they are an extension of herself, sometimes as if they are a blood relative, she seems to be indulging in this kind of anthropomorphic thinking.

Part of being a Maori, too, is the personal experience of Pakeha prejudice and discrimination, from which derives the ability to recognize quickly stereotyped Pakeha attitudes. In **"Kip,"** for instance, Mereana sees the contempt that Reuben has for Maori girls as she watches him dance with Lizzie; she has obviously seen it before. The ability to see from a Maori viewpoint is only possible if one is a Maori; the most sympathetic Pakeha is necessarily myopic. (p. 48)

Grace rarely treats situations of racial tension, and when she does, she contrives to reduce the tension. The one clash that occurs in her fiction, between the old Maori man and the Pakeha officials in **"Journey,"** has its roughness diminished by being narrated in retrospect: we see the clash as the old man relives it in his tired mind during his journey home. The fact that few Pakeha appear alongside the Maori in Grace's short stories is itself evidence of her wish to avoid dealing with interracial tensions. Nearly all her stories are told from the viewpoint of a Maori, in the first person; she is fond of the Maori and identifies with them. The Pakeha in her short stories are secondary figures with stereotyped attitudes and values. They are not portrayed favourably, although Grace is restrained in her criticism, showing them as obtuse or condescending rather than illwilled. Only the officials in **"Journey"** or Reuben in **"Kip"** are actually contemptuous towards the Maori.

Grace's desire to avoid offending her audience may be laudable, but it limits her artistic achievement. Nowhere is the force or even the relevance of her work so weakened by her earnest avoidance of giving offense as in *Mutuwhenua.* The novel deals with a Maori-Pakeha marriage, yet Grace avoids dealing with the very subject one would expect her to consider in undertaking such a theme: cultural gaps between the races that are possibly unbridgeable. Fears of problems that may develop in an interracial marriage are not given countenance in the novel, although such fears have a very real basis in everyday life; the problems that do arise are completely externalized, removed from Linda and Graeme personally, both before and after the marriage. Before the marriage, fears of difficulties arising from the marriage are transferred from Linda to her Nanny Ripeka, the family member most opposed to the marriage on the grounds that it would lessen Linda's Maori identity (as a grandparent, Nanny Ripeka stands for the preservation of traditional Maori values). Until her conversations with Nanny Ripeka, Linda has not had to contend with fears of her own devising. After the marriage, fears do breed within Linda of unbridgeable gaps between her world and that of her husband, and problems do arise from her Maori roots, but from an unexpected area—racial memories arising from her unconscious. The house where she and Graeme go to live is built over an old Maori burial ground, and she is beset by a series of dreams that call her to death. Not feeling sure of Graeme's understanding, she does not tell him about her dreams until it is almost too late. When appealed to, he responds with quick sympathy, and the threat to their marriage proves no threat—they simply move elsewhere. Thus Linda's fears are made by Grace to be built on incorrect assumptions: the problems in the marriage come from areas outside personal backgrounds. Grace plainly does not wish to deal with personal misunderstandings within an interracial marriage: she seems to hurry the couple into the ill omened house so that marital difficulties can arise from Linda's racial unconscious alone. Grace's guiding purpose in this novel is to avoid hurting anyone, especially the Pakeha; but that makes her wind and set the alarm when Linda and Graeme marry only to prevent it from going off. The result is that the book is anticlimactic.

Grace's desire to bring Pakeha and Maori close together, to avoid stirring up old prejudices or resentments, puts constraints also upon her characterization of the hero and heroine in *Mutuwhenua.* Graeme is idealized and, in the process, stripped of individualizing characteristics. He is made extraordinarily affectionate for a Pakeha man, using expressions like "my love" and assuring Linda that nothing else matters so long as she loves him; Pakeha men are more remarkable for their inhibition than their articulation of the softer emotions. Linda is not idealized but rather "universalized," made into almost any Pakeha woman; only occasionally is she distinctly Maori. Grace's attempt to establish her common humanity tends to drain her, not only of her Maori identity, but of any strong individuality. Only within her family does Linda have a personality of her own; in her life outside her family, she is timid and pallid. Her aspirations in marriage are those of the conventional Pakeha housewife, to keep house and buy things. What Grace has done in her characterization of her two main figures, in essence, is to endow Graeme with Maori qualities and Linda with Pakeha qualities. Graeme's warmth will win Maori approval and flatter the Pakeha, and Linda's pursuit of the Pakeha dream will allay Pakeha nervousness about Maori women. In trying to bring the two cultures closer, Grace has lessened the vitality of the main figures, and with them the novel.

By renouncing unique qualities of Maori life as subject matter, by avoiding scenes of tension or aspects of discrimination (a word that never occurs in her fiction), Grace considerably narrows the range of what she can write about. Her reluctance to give offense deprives her of a forceful stance, without which a strong narrative stance is difficult to maintain. She is not an outstanding teller of stories: her strength lies in presenting scenes where *aroha* rather than suspense or conflict prevails. Her stories remain within the dimensions she allots to them: her characters, for all their vitality, stay within their story, and her stories cover so short a period of time that narrative development is normally not an issue. Grace excels at vignettes: she is the master of the Maori pastoral. Even in her novel *Mutuwhenua,* the most memorable scene is the inset idyll, the gathering of the *kai moana* (sea food). Time dissolves and the adults become children again; all their usual preoccupations, which make up the substance of the narrative, evaporate. In simple pastoral scenes like this, Grace probably does more to promote understanding of the Maori than through her conscious efforts elsewhere to bring the two cultures together.

Although Grace's stories are for the most part non-narrative, they do not seem static, for there is in them a sense of ongoing life and continuing relationships. Appropriately, *Waiariki* is dedicated *mo aku tamariki* (for my children), for her children bear her blood to the generations that follow. The moral earnestness that runs through her writing is lightened by her humanity and enjoyment of life and the natural world around her, and by the lyricism of her style, as in her description of the various seasons in **"Valley."** Far from being alienated from her society, she is an acceptant person, and her stories overwhelmingly end in acceptance of the prevailing state of affairs. The young boy of **"Beans"** seems to reflect the rush of her own energy before she checks it and submits it to rigorous artistic discipline. Always these two aspects of Grace are present: on the one hand her exuberant enjoyment of life, on the other her moral seriousness, turned to advantage in her careful, exacting craftsmanship. (pp. 49-52)

John B. Beston, *"The Fiction of Patricia Grace,"* in Ariel: A Review of International English Literature, *Vol. 15, No. 2, April, 1984, pp. 41-53.*

PUBLISHERS WEEKLY

[In *Potiki*], Roimata Kararaina, her husband and their four children live peacefully in a tribal community along the unspoiled coast of New Zealand. But developers have big plans for the area—tourist facilities, roads and modernization—and they offer Roimata's Maori people huge sums of money for its lands. When the community refuses to sell, fearing the destruction of its environment and sacred traditions, the developers employ sinister means to change its mind, and the Maori find themselves united as never before as they battle for survival. Grace's characters are beautifully sketched, and their struggles evoke sympathy. The New Zealand author tells a vivid and mesmerizing story as she blends tribal myth with political realities and offers shrewd insights into human nature. The unique book is also full of exotic symbolism and language, but one wishes that Grace had provided a glossary of the numerous Maori words.

A review of "Potiki," in Publishers Weekly, *Vol. 230, No. 9, August 29, 1986, p. 390.*

MICHAEL OWEN JONES

"I became . . . a teller of stories, a listener to stories, a writer and a reader of stories, an enactor, a collector and a maker of stories," says Roimata at one point in [*Potiki*], the second novel by New Zealand writer Patricia Grace. Like the author, Roimata is a native Maori and a schoolteacher.

Some of Roimata's stories concerned childhood experiences, such as attending the white man's school where

> we were given holy pictures and toffees to help us do God's will. . . . It was his will that we pray, that we have clean handkerchiefs, wear aprons, bring pennies for souls, eat our crusts, hold our partner's hand.

Roimata's stories also included tribal myths and legends, "known stories from before life and death and remembering, from before the time of the woman lonely in the moon."

The novel begins with a myth about the carving of a pole for the community's meeting house. From the Prologue to the final chapter, called "Potiki," Grace's narrative flows beautifully in the rhythms of oral poetry—marked at times by stylized dialogue and description that seem more real and compelling for that.

Most chapters bear the names of various family members, each of whom tells stories or remarks on stories. In the fifth chapter, called "Roimata," the woman describes some of her family's traditions, including one son's "school stories," a daughter's "book stories," her husband's "work stories" and Granny Tamihana's stories, "which were weavings of sorrow and joy, of land and tides, sickness, death, hunger and work." There were also the stories from newspapers, library books and television.

"And this train of stories defined our lives, curving out from points on the spiral in ever-widening circles from which neither beginnings nor endings could be defined," says Roimata.

There were ancient narratives too. "It was a new discovery to find that these stories were, after all, about our own lives, were not distant," says Roimata, "that there was no past or future, that all time is a now-time centred in the being."

The "centred being" reaches out toward the outer circles called "past" and "future." "So the 'now' is a giving and a receiving between the inner and outer reaches, but the enormous difficulty is to achieve refinement in reciprocity, because the wheel, the spiral, is balanced so exquisitely."

Herein lie some of the themes of Grace's narrative, such as the pervasiveness and significance of traditions in our lives and the need in the present to cherish the past and respect the future. The literary form itself brings to life the past and celebrates the Maori heritage, exploring contemporary issues of native/white relations through the style of myth and structure of storytelling.

Potiki focuses on the conflict between the development interests of some whites and the rights of natives to their ancestral land. The situation involving Roimata and fellow villagers is similar to that of another community earlier. The songs, language and customs of the Te Ope had been "rubbished or ignored," their homes taken from them. Relocated to the city, they "did not have anything that belonged to them any more except they had each other, scattered as they were, and they had their stories." Their traditions helped maintain the identity and integrity of the Te Ope, necessary in their struggle to regain their homes.

The representative of white development interests, Dolman (called "Dollarman" by the community) entices, cajoles and threatens Roimata's own family and other villagers to sell their land for a quick profit to be made from turning their coast, meeting house and ancestral cemetery into a water playground and amusement park. It is "a much-needed amenity," he repeats.

"You're looking back, looking back, all the time," says Dollarman when community members resist. "Wrong. We're looking to the future," they respond, remembering the Te Ope. "If we sold out to you, what would we be in future?"

The villagers would not relinquish their land, "no matter how often the gold man came with his anger and his different way of thinking in his head," says Roimata's adopted child Toko-waru-i-te-Marama. "A misshapen and cauled baby boy," who is destined not to survive youth (but to live in myth and legend), this child prophet can foresee the future. Toko is afraid "because of a special knowing. I did not call out in sleep as my brother did, and I did not call out in anger as my sister did, but I had a special knowing that gave me fear."

The pressure to sell their land will—does—disrupt community members' lives. Ultimately, strife brings destruction and death. But it also creates new beginnings, which are connected to the past.

With great sensitivity Grace portrays the vicissitudes faced by her people, weaving together Maori legends and beliefs with some of the white man's own myths. Her style captures the rhythms of the finest oral poetry. Her imagery is memorable and her observations are penetrating.

This novel—composed of stories in which "story" is a central metaphor—transcends place and time. "(O)ur child, our precious one, our potiki," Grace seems to be saying, is the stories we tell whether we be Maori or anyone else. Traditions communicate our perceptions and perpetuate our values, helping us cope in now-time and survive in future. (pp. 1, 6)

Michael Owen Jones, in a review of "Potiki," in Los Angeles Times Book Review, *December 14, 1986, pp. 1, 6.*

PUBLISHERS WEEKLY

[In Patricia Grace's *Electric City and Other Stories,*] innocence clashes with a harsh and violent reality. Peopled primarily by children who appear in several of the stories, the spare tales focus on the daily and often mundane events in their lives, and the cruelty that lies dormant behind seemingly guileless faces. **"Going for the Bread"** transforms a routine household chore into a nightmare, as middle-class children wielding broken glass terrorize a peasant girl. **"Flies,"** the most disturbing story, details a favorite game: capturing flies, fastening strings around their necks (often at the expense of the flies' heads) and staging a mock battle in which most of the flies are mangled and killed. After the children tie the surviving flies together in one long chain, they let go and "off went the flies, crazily, pulling this way and that." The narrator observes: "It made you laugh your head off. It made you die." Actuality rears its ugly head as well in the few pieces set in the adult world: **"The Geranium"** depicts Marney who savors reading in the local paper about others' lives, steadfastly ignoring her husband's abuse. Throughout, Grace's dry, matter-of-fact tone effectively highlights the darker side of human nature.

A review of "Electric City and Other Stories," in Publishers Weekly, *Vol. 233, No. 12, March 25, 1988, p. 60.*

BOOK WORLD—THE WASHINGTON POST

A New Zealander of full Maori descent, Patricia Grace is a writer of considerable gifts: her stories (and one novel) have the slight, pastoral delicacy of Katherine Mansfield's, but at the same time Grace is tougher and more versatile. Her stories [in *Electric City and Other Stories*], for all their innocence, have a hard edge to them. Take **"Butterflies,"** a one-page epiphany of class and race differences which never so much as mentions class or race. A little girl lives with her grandparents so she can go to school, the first in her family. "Listen to the teacher. Do what she say," they admonish her. When the teacher corrects the child for having written a story about killing butterflies, the little girl is devastated. But the grandfather explains quietly, ". . . your teacher, she buy all her cabbages from the supermarket and that's why."

A review of "Electric City and Other Stories," in Book World—The Washington Post, *June 12, 1988, p. 16.*

ELEANOR J. BADER

Patricia Grace is a masterful writer, a Maori New Zealander whose words are to be savored and slowly digested. Lyrical and deceptively simple, her writing conveys soaring emotions wrapped in working-class, indigenous sensibilities. From the bantering of children on a fishing expedition to the aging process, from wife beating to the pros and cons of assimilation, Grace's work touches universal themes, yet her subject matter has a rare freshness to it, thanks to her observant eye and uncanny knack for describing the minute realities of day-to-day life. Her stories are compelling, raw. . . .

Being Maori in a predominantly Pakeha (white, European) world is a theme that winds through much of Grace's work, a river of mixed emotions that provides an undercurrent of uneasiness in the people she has created. Is assimilation always bad? Are all white people the enemy, to be feared and avoided? Are the old ways the only ways, or even the best ways? Questions largely without answers, making us think, making us pause in our hustle and bustle.

An old man in **"Journey"** (from *The Dream Sleepers*) is seen trying to reconcile urban development with respect for the land.

> Couldn't talk to a hill or a tree, these people . . . Couldn't go round, only through. Couldn't give life, only death. But people had to have houses and ways of getting from one place to another. A man had to eat. People had to have houses, had to eat, had to get from here to there—anyone knew that.

But Grace's acuity is visible in areas other than race and class as well, from her humorous look at childhood terrors to the many manifestations of sexism. One particularly sparse story, **"The Geranium"** (in *Electric City and Other Stories*), wastes no words in describing the agony of a battered wife and mother, whose only joy, sustenance even, comes from slowly reading every item in the weekly newspaper.

Linda, the main character in *Mutuwhenua,* raises troubling questions about how women learn sex roles. Although she chooses to marry a white New Zealander, breaking tradition and exhibiting a tenacity that is startling, she also falls into traps not of her own making. Thus, she relies on her spouse "to help and protect" her. Infuriating as it is to find such phrases in print, the reader is given a context for this assertion. What else could she—a poor Maori, daughter of a fisherman—expect? Real life and fantasy have conspired to provide her with few options. Women at home are respected and even revered, but their spheres of activity are well defined. Literature, a world that Linda relishes, also offers few role models. "We didn't become famous or have interesting or extraordinary lives of our own," she says of the books she has read,

> or even uninteresting and ordinary lives. We either got ourselves into what is known as 'trouble,' or we lay about giving some bloke hot sex. And that was all. Except sometimes we did ridiculous things in Pakeha kitchens, like ringing the fire-alarm instead of the dinner-gong because we didn't know the difference.

Children are present in many of Grace's short stories, giving the writing a spunkiness that lightens and embellishes the realities she presents. Perhaps their voices are what make her writing so precious and remarkably beautiful. Whatever it is, they—and the novel as well—are balm for the spirit and fuel for antiracist and antisexist activism.

Eleanor J. Bader, "Ridiculous Things in Paheka Kitchens," in Belles Lettres: A Review of Books by Women, *Vol. 3, No. 6, July-August, 1988, p. 7.*

Vicki Hearne

1946-

American poet, essayist, and novelist.

Hearne's writings reflect her experiences as a professional trainer of dogs and horses. Her works deal realistically with the relationship between humans and domesticated animals while alluding to the significance of nonhuman creatures as literary and mythological symbols. Hearne adopts a scholarly approach in her poetry and prose, making numerous references to literary figures and demonstrating the influence of such philosophers as Ludwig Wittgenstein and Stanley Cavell.

Hearne's first collection of verse, *Nervous Horses* (1980), consists of meditations upon horses and other animals. Her next volume, *In the Absence of Horses* (1983), delves into philosophical issues relating to humans, animals, and nature. Christopher Benfey observed: "To read [Hearne's] poetry with care is to probe some of the deepest questions in contemporary American poetry." *Adam's Task: Calling Animals by Name* (1986) contains essays on the training of animals as well as their coexistence with people. Michiko Kakutani described this work as "an informed defense of animals' capacity for understanding and commitment, and a philosophical meditation on the nature of learning, responsibility and language." Hearne's novel *The White German Shepherd* (1988) deals with similar issues amid the story of a love affair that develops between two trainers hired to prepare a dog to play the lead role in a film version of Jack London's novel *The Call of the Wild.*

DANA GIOIA

No one will accuse Vicki Hearne of publishing a conventional book of poems. The dustjacket informs one that she is "a professional horse and dog trainer in Riverside, California," and the title of her first book, **Nervous Horses,** proves absolutely literal. Of the forty-eight poems contained in the volume, twenty-eight of them are about horses. Not symbolic horses, real ones. Many of the remaining poems are about animals. . . . Such hippomania will certainly frighten away most readers, but **Nervous Horses** deserves a close look. There is a sense of real excitement in reading Hearne's best poems—the excitement of seeing the familiar world from an entirely fresh perspective. Like Ted Hughes's best poems in *Moortown,* Hearne's work stands in sharp contrast to "poetic" descriptions of the rural landscape. They are country poems by someone who really lives off the land.

In **"Riding a Jumper,"** which for me is the best poem in the book, Hearne manages to write a tough, unsentimental description of a landscape. Early one cold morning at the end of summer she rides along the fence bordering a familiar field keeping her eye on a herd of pastured mares. But she is more interested in the fence than the mares:

> Was this a place
> To reach after awkward travels? For us
> A fence shouldn't mark so fine a line
> Along the legal ground, one recorded length
> Of someone else's orchard. The fence should mark
> A fast hard leap that we could choose to make
> Or not, onto the brittle drought-dry ground.

Now no one, not even a woman on horseback, can go through the country talking about fences without bringing Robert Frost to mind. But here I think Hearne survives the comparison. She convinces the reader she is talking about a real fence, not a moral one, and even if she starts to philosophize, she ends up dismissing her fantasies for reality:

> Almost any line enclosing one
> Universe or separating two
> Or more will do for visions. This one serves
> To bring the horse and me limping back
> To measure it again, to judge a leap,
> To leap, or wait, or turn to find the mares
> Knee-deep in grass, irrevocably calm.

This is honest, admirable poetry. Anthologists of women's poetry should take special note. Here is an independent-minded woman who writes unpredictable, personal poems. Whatever the limits of Hearne's talent, it is honest and original. Curiously, the elegiac tone, which dominates so many first books of contemporary poetry, is entirely absent in Hearne's work. Even the poems about death are hard and unsentimental. Hearne is introspective without being sad, and it is refreshing to know that there is at least one cowgirl out there who doesn't get the blues. (pp. 623-24)

Dana Gioia, in a review of "Nervous Horses," in The Hudson Review, *Vol. XXXIII, No. 4, Winter, 1980-81, pp. 623-24.*

JOHN HOLLANDER

Hearne's **Nervous Horses** are both sinewy and agitated, as they are both actual and figurative—the horses of modernity. Her poems, largely in supple and controlled syllabic verse, are meditative but taut. In **"Genuine and Poignant"**, she shows she has learned Wallace Stevens's first lessons in poetic *dressage:* "Just that once, not to grieve, and the hill / To stand suddenly bare and pure / Confidently shaking its dust / Through the warm window." But she moves in other poems to the more animated subject of her horses and her dogs. Aware of the philosophical problem of other minds, of how (and even what) we know of others' thoughts and feelings, she treats the otherness of animals as intimate and terrifying. The consciousness of those animals, a beautifully hypothetical entity which keeps flickering in and out of interest, the more we know and are with them, is among the things this book so beautifully explores. The poems form a kind of romance in which our theories about how we ought sensibly to talk, and what the skilled experience of training animals leads one to say, are engaged in a dialectical sparring-match.

But she writes neither mock training-manuals, nor the journal notes of a self-conscious rider. Her poems often puzzle and are puzzled themselves; she is particularly concerned to avoid the way in which so much contemporary verse sets up and relates crude concepts of subject and object, experience and image, in an unacknowledged and unexplored realm of thought. The book's final, splendid **"The Metaphysical Horse"** is a poem about coming to terms with one's own metaphors—in this case, conceptions which are like mirror-images but which, having been lived with, allow her to end as follows:

> Circling elegantly we
> Glimpse the always receding
> True proposal in the glass
> And join the horses, who dance,
> Tremors of exactitude
> Flaring, still fresh on their limbs.

Hearne's practical experience of horses is at one with her interest in their mythologies. Plato's fable of horse and rider, Renaissance training manuals, the folklore of handlers, fall like shadows over her actual animals. She herself has what she calls in the title of one poem "The fastidiousness of the Musician"; exercises, lessons, set problems and puzzles are her typical occasions. The longest poem here, the penultimate **"St George and the Dragon"** has a quasi-narrative line, but records the quest not *of* the mounted knight, but rather *for* him, in the fragmentations of a picture-puzzle. The problem of piecing together an imaginative construction that will hold harks back to James Merrill's jigsaw puzzle of memory in "Lost in Translation". Hearne's poem modulates this into an amusingly domesticated metaphor in which friends and teachers help the poet cope with the epistemological puzzles,

trials and errors which occupy the whole of this distinguished first book.

John Hollander, "Tremors of Exactitude," in The Times Literary Supplement, *No. 4061, January 30, 1981, p. 115.*

JASCHA KESSLER

The title of a first book of poems by a young woman named Vicki Hearne is **Nervous Horses**. . . . It is an oddly-catchy title, and I puzzled about it until I realized that it is one of those verbal constructions that is asymmetrical: that is, it has no contrary—for to say "Calm Horses" would seem absurd or redundant, horses being our greatest, or noblest domesticated animal associated with beauty and power, force and conquest and nobility, it being hard even today, when one can follow a smelly little machine with almost a full horsepower engine around a lawn merely to trim the grass, to feel anything less than thrilled in the presence of such animals. When Jonathan Swift made his most savage satire on the wickedness and barbaric savagery of the human animal, inventing a lustful, naked, hairy, clawed and fanged species of upright ape and calling it the Yahoo, he made those creatures the slaves of a race of benevolent, strong and peaceful four-footed animals, the Houyhnhnms, splendid horses from muzzle to tail, for there was no other animal one can think of that is so emblematic of gentle, unlimited courage, strength and docility too, one that even when mastered and trained to complete obedience, with the human rider commanding it at will, is also graceful and glorious and shows its pride and self-respect in its every movement.

Nervous Horses, however, suggests that something is amiss: there is in the title a suggestion of alarm and anxiety. Now there is no poem by that title in this impressive first book, though there are horses riding, running, standing, falling, dying, appearing and disappearing in reality, fable, dream and myth, flying and frozen in art, horses materializing in the great majority of its fifty-eight well-crafted poems. Vicki Hearne must have become obsessed with horses, as so many adolescent girls do, very early on, and the evidence of her passion for the animals, and her knowledge of them, is clear everywhere. She does not write poems merely about the everyday relations a young woman has with horses, working around them, training and caring for them, which would be interesting enough if well-done and pretty; neither is she a sentimentalist, the sort of poet who would illustrate paintings of horses you find in the dens of people who are horse-proud: she is not of that class of owners and users. Rather, she is from the ordinary ranks of ordinary people, with the great exception that she has the gift of words, in the old sense, the gift of poetry, the kind of gift we think of when we think of the passion for contemplation of the world and the transformation of ideas and words into sentiments that are concerned with, as Plato put it, the Good, the True, and the Beautiful. That triad of essences of excellence is not really much regarded as the goal of poetry by most writers today: to many it would seem either naive or passé or irrelevant to the tasks of the poet, to our lives. But, to Vicki Hearne I think they are crucial: one has the feeling that she is a very serious and intense person indeed, serious and intense about horses, of course; but through horses to poetry itself. One recalls the title essay of Wallace Stevens' collection of essays about the art of poetry, "The Noble Rider and the Sound of Words." I would guess that, from horses in girlhood, Vicki Hearne

came to poetry, if she wasn't always writing something, as a way of giving reality to such a phrase as Stevens', although she is more concerned with the noble horse than the rider, and as for the sound of words, well, I have remarked that she is a skilled and serious writer. . . .

[Most] of Hearne's work is cast in a disarmingly simple speech, a speech that is full of stubborn verve, stubbornly true to her vision of the ideal world that poetry is for her. Her speech may be simple, but it is also formal and elevated too, in tone and in diction. I think she is someone who has earned the name of poet with her first book, and I hope that we will hear from her again. Meanwhile, . . . I hope [*Nervous Horses*] will find the place among the ranks of the poets that it deserves.

Jascha Kessler, in a radio broadcast on KUSC-FM—Los Angeles, CA, May 27, 1981.

SANDRA M. GILBERT

[As] the title of her *Nervous Horses* reveals, Hearne's thing is Horses. Indeed, the book's jacket tells us that she "is a professional horse and dog trainer" who is "writing a book on the nature of working animals." All very well, but also, at times, slightly questionable, since Hearne's horses often emerge in her poems more as literary artifacts, gotten by Stevens upon Swift out of Plato, than like real, twitching, jittery, itchy-skinned animals. For one thing, they seem to make this philosophical trainer think a lot about religion, and not very much about tackle, feed, stables, and other practical matters. . . . Alas, it seems clear that even though she's a real live horse-trainer Vicki Hearne is not always a poet of real live horses: her horses are, like Houyhnhnms or Christ figures, wise and alien—"*Divine,* as their throats pulse in the dark"—and they move goldenly through an "epiphanal landscape."

Still, in their mythologized grandeur, Hearne's sacred animals do from time to time generate a visionary glow that appears authentic, even, in **"A Note on Balance at the Trot,"** almost Blakeian. I quote this last poem in its entirety:

> Just so would horse trot,
> Approaching Bethlehem,
> Drums of Revelation
> Sounding in her hooves.

When she isn't writing about supposedly real but disappointingly mystical horses, moreover, Hearne's metaphysical imagination, well tempered by a command of the colloquial, opens up in lively meditations. I was particularly taken by **"St. George and the Dragon: Piecing It All Together,"** a dramatic monologue about doing a jigsaw puzzle picture of a dragon, a saint, and—yes, you guessed it—a horse. (pp. 39-40)

Sandra M. Gilbert, "On Burning Ground?" in Poetry, *Vol. CXXXIX, No. 1, October, 1981, pp. 35-51.*

CHRISTOPHER BENFEY

If you listen carefully to the poetry of Vicki Hearne you will discover something strange: she (or it) *is thinking.* Here is something new in American poetry, or something old that is periodically forgotten. Hearne's astonishing first book of poems, *Nervous Horses,* reminded readers that poetry could

think—about people, landscape, horses, language—and address the world with a philosophical reach and precision that we had almost given up asking from our poets. Now Hearne has added a second volume, *In the Absence of Horses,* which is darker and more brooding than the first, but no less exacting. (p. 9)

In her continuing meditation on elegance and acknowledgment, Vicki Hearne emerges as a philosophical poet, and in a richer sense than Santayana allowed that term. To read her poetry with care is to probe some of the deepest questions in contemporary American poetry. I think there is a growing impatience, among readers of poetry in this country, with the attenuated philosophical reach of so much recent writing. We have had enough "concrete imagery" and avoidance of ideas, and both poets and critics are to blame for the current state of poetry. Our poets have subscribed too readily to a naive and simplified New Critical model for poetry, and have been reluctant to inherit the more vigorous thinking of Dickinson, Stevens, and Frost. I am not saying that we need more ideas in poetry, as though it could be the task of poets to read a few books of philosophy, adopt a few "ideas," and versify them. That is a false picture of philosophy, and of poetry. We don't need more ideas, we need more *thinking;* and for thinking to occur we must shake off the old comfortable distinctions about "themes" and "imagery" and "ideas."

To challenge such distinctions is the task of criticism, but the possibility that poets can think is still something of a scandal to many American critics. . . . We are slow to accord our poets the seriousness we expect from "professional" thinkers, i.e., philosophers. So an overestimation of philosophy is one of the marks of both the New Critics and the more recent "advanced" criticism. If, as Harold Bloom has noted, "It is a truism of criticism from Aristotle through Sidney to Northrop Frye that poetry takes place between the concept and the example," we need to realize that the same is true of philosophy. *Thinking* takes place between the concept and the example. It may take the prodding of philosophers—such as Heidegger—to make us turn again to our poets for their thinking.

What then would a truly philosophical poetry look like? There are elements of it in Robert Hass's work and in Jorie Graham's. But the most cheering contribution I've seen is Vicki Hearne's poetry. Hearne has given thought to the sixth of Wallace Stevens's "Significant Landscapes," a little Kantian parable about rationalists who wear square hats, think in square rooms, and "confine themselves / To right-angled triangles." "If they tried rhomboids," Stevens speculates, "As for example, the ellipse of the half-moon— / Rationalists would wear sombreros." This surmise prompts Hearne's yearning apostrophe to her muse:

> Thought! Transparent, pellucid,
> Jaunty as a three-cornered
>
> Sombrero beneath our feet.
> Airy as love . . .
>
> **("The Charge of History")**
> (p. 11)

Christopher Benfey, "The Midas Touch," in The Threepenny Review, *Vol. VI, No. 1, Spring, 1985, pp. 9-11.*

WILLIAM LOGAN

Too much poetry has been wormed from obsession for it to be solely the product of a healthy imagination. The biographies of modernism are exercises in the crabbed insufficiencies of private lives, from Eliot's trusses and green makeup ("the colour of forced lily-of-the-valley") to Lowell's conviction while in a mental hospital that he was John Milton revising "Lycidas." The *Cantos,* the *Dream Songs,* the "sonnets" of Lowell's *Notebook:* these are one poem damned after another, their narrative impulse and even the thread of continuity thwarted by the compulsion to repeat and return, to become what they just became. These are the sequences of metastasis, replications in the disease of form that have as much to do with stasis as change, that are cancerous and brilliant.

Much of our poetry's neurosis has been formal, experience reduced or revised to fit the arbitrary structures the imagination demands. Such structures are not limited to sonnet or sestina, blank verse or dactylic hexameter. Even Pound's sprawling *Cantos* insist on a narrow range of formal gesture, the verse not free but foreseeable; compared to the liberating accretions of *The Divine Comedy,* their fussiness is constricting. Pound's obsessions were subject to their subjects as well, and few who have read the *Cantos* care to acquaint themselves further, or ever again, with the radical economics of Major Douglas. Formal obsessions are relatively transparent; only in the inscrutable recurrences of idea does the pathology of the imagination grow interesting. Obsessions afflict not only the major poets, but others as well; and few poets have traveled more deeply into the compulsions of subject than Vicki Hearne, who has been mastered, and perhaps even manufactured, by the image of the horse.

Hearne's first book, *Nervous Horses* (1980), was a fabulous *jeu d'esprit* whose poems repeatedly explored the history or habitation of the horse. From **"Riding a Nervous Horse"** to **"Rebreaking Outlaw Horses in the Desert,"** from **"The Metaphysical Horse"** to **"Daedalus Broods on the Equestrian Olympic Trials,"** such honorable allegiance to the strictures of equine ontology argued an imagination not only sufficient to its infatuation, but wholly defined by it. Whenever Hearne's poems deviated from her enthusiasms, her verse denied its passions. (pp. 463-64)

The title of her second book, *In the Absence of Horses,* is a shrewd commentary on the content of the first by someone who knows the value of obsession, if not caution. It is also a gesture calculated to mislead, since her horses are never more present than when they are supposedly absent. Like the ghost images on a television screen, through much of the book they broadcast from a station too remote to be more than echo, interference; but when the title poem is reached halfway through the book, scarcely a horse having trammeled its pages, the absence turns out to be an argument for presence:

> In the absence of horses
> The Beloved will suffice
> And will change on the brutal
> Turns of the tongue, becoming
> The Betrayer, betrayed, and
> Hollow figure of fullness
> For seventeen years until
> At last lovers, abandoned
> Again to their gazing are
> Figures of knowledge, figures
> Of action for which any
> Steady emblem is enough. . . .

("In the Absence of Horses")

Without the absorption provided by horses, then, lover turns betrayer (and it is a mark of the betrayal of the tongue that the eye wants to change *gazing* to *grazing*). Once their indispensability has been justified, the horses are released with an exhilaration almost giddy. They gallop through the remainder of the book as a reminder that art will always recover the agents of its pleasure, and that the strategy of a book's order may be as artful as its title.

Hearne's second book is a more abstract exercise than her first. . . . Though insinuated by the abstractions to which Hearne turns, the poems [in *Nervous Horses*] were line by line anchored in the ocean floor of image. In the new book image has given way to idea, and her style is less nervy than nervous. She begins with the skittish presentation of hypotheticals as if they were actuals:

> So: we don't nestle weightless
> In each other's hearts! The soul,
> Then, is a raptor—eagle
> Or falcon, and if the soul
> Is a raptor some other
> Soul must be prey. Is that it?

("The Language of Love")

That is the standard procedure of metaphor, which exists less often as a clarification than as a clearing away of other possibility: the soul is x rather than a-w or y-z. To be convincing, assertions must make their case by the accrual of particulars, or attend to the structures of thought, as in Stevens, in a way that may be attractive without being familiar or familiar without being attractive. Here the assertions are marshaled with a complacence that presupposes the reader's assent. The poem continues:

> Betraying is letting loose.
> The tame caged fox is betrayed
> To the hounds. Or: I betray
> My heart to you. Give it up,
> That is, into your keeping.
> Your treachery and rapture.
>
> But we must live, too, and somehow
> Understand that to love, how
> To love is how to believe.
> In a sacred tongue to say
> "Believe" is to say "about,
> At, or near to." And then, "love."
>
> Our tongue, I mean.

When an author is compelled to say "I mean," she acknowledges that the consensual relations between author and reader have broken down, that the rhetorical beckonings ("So," "hearts!," "The soul, / Then," "and if," "Is that it?," "That is") are not beacons. Such statements as these lines are composed of (and in them "is" makes almost as many appearances as the comma) are not evidence of an argument, only of sensibility.

Hearne's conjectures are so bereft of conviction that they cannot lead to an overwhelming answer, much less an overwhelming question. They lack the emotional pressure that might allow a reader to comprehend their necessity, if not their sufficiency; Hearne often seems to sleepwalk through her poems, out on the thin ice of pure language:

To pass over in silence
Is to acknowledge logic,
The necessity of form,

The stunning curve of language,
The curious way it seems
To turn out that "love" means "need"

Even in a lush garden.

                    ("Passing over Your Virtues")

There is no lush garden here, much less a stunning curve of language. For a poet with passions as profound and curious as Hearne's, the danger of such language and such logic, as dry as toast, is that they seem to require some rhetorical flourish to bring them to closure. After stanzas of self-denial, which in their rigorous thwarting approach something like self-contempt, poem after poem obliges the poet's nature by rising toward the vacuous sublime: "we must / Move closer, close enough to feel the inspiring heat, / Build walls of doubt against the flames," "This is why I fuss / Over the harmony I live with / Out hope of, why the song must go on," "we are / Ourselves after all, damaged, / Brutal, and speaking, brutal / And pure." Such endings would make an end to almost any poem.

Hearne is no more vacuous than she is sublime. In *Nervous Horses* the severity of idea and the grandeur of feeling existed in fruitful tension. Once an animal trainer, Hearne now teaches philosophy at Yale and is an essayist of distinction. That some mental divorce threatens the former co-existence of realms is evident, however, in the number of fatuous sentiments she breathes in utter sincerity: "Invoke what bright energies / You find here, breathe my name and / I'll breathe yours, into valleys," "Your eyes, ruined by calamaties [sic], / Jerk in the corners of bare chasms."

This is sentimental poetry of a curious sort, founded in the sentiment of ideas, not feeling. For all her talk of love and the sexual ("loins" is a favorite word), rarely has sexual passion seemed so chlorotic:

Sexual knowledge is still the trope

Of completion. Your heartbeats are still
The trope of the quest. My heartbeats are
Still anxious, knowing, under alien lights
That tranform [sic] posture into a plea,
The idea that we can make sense
In our skins.

                    ("The Shore")

Abstractions cannot engage when spun around the great verb "to be." Auden would make *trope* do an Astaire dance step. The great abstract poets blood their abstractions, and would make the endless talk of love and horses actual, not academic (that hardly means the numerous moments in Hearne's work when horses are dancing): "I will show you a horse, place / You around the horse so you / Circle with Horse at center / Instead of birth, death, love, / Or the best that has been said." Very well to say so, but the horsey system of abstraction is self-enclosed, self-supporting, and finally self-devouring.

Like many poets who have pondered the blank page too long, Hearne has found in poetry a convenient trope for itself, and for everything else. Most poets are occasionally tempted to use as tropes the tropes of their craft—to find simile and metaphor and even poem the adequate words of an inadequate

world. The ingenious critic may find every poem an *ars poetica,* but the ingenious poet doesn't need to make it so. Poems about poetry cripple before they are crutches, and the poet who too often succumbs to their attractions may find herself with few of her own. The tendency is early evident in Hearne's book, when nature suffers the metamorphosis into literature: "Now subtle oak trees, brilliant squirrels, / Rhythmical rains, the central poem." Soon the poems are everywhere, and hence nowhere: "and a giant poem / Struggles, just there, in the ocean," "The rider prevents / The approach of poetry," "in the poem's / Flesh a grain of sand," "Poems written "This poem of the only instinct. the poem now." Beyond the poem lies talk of texts, syllables, tropes, language, words, symbols, sentences, and syntax, the whole toolbox of self-conscious art.

Hearne's particular interest is speech. Though her poems about speaking often seem to reduce philosophical argument (two of the poems are dedicated to Stanley Cavell) to something neither philosophical nor poetical, she does in those poems reclaim some of the controlled passion that made her first book so delightfully eccentric. . . . The achievements of the poems in her new collection have been hazarded despite, not because of, their great limitation of poetic means. That limitation feels less like mastery than diminution. In a poet for whom saying is the crucial trope, it is odd how much is left unsaid, and odder how much is said over and over again, as if the repetition not of form but of information defined the act of poetry. These poems are speech acts in a double sense, and their duplicity is such that they can say without meaning far more often than they can mean without saying. (pp. 464-69)

William Logan, "The Habits of Their Habitats," in Parnassus: Poetry in Review, *Vol. 12, No. 2 and Vol. 13, No. 1, 1985, pp. 463-96.*

MICHIKO KAKUTANI

As a kid, a lot of us grew up reading such dog and horse stories as *Lad, a Dog, Black Beauty* and *The Black Stallion,* and from the movies and television, we were familiar, too, with the stories of Lassie and Rin Tin Tin. They were stories in which a brave dog or horse helped rescue someone in trouble, or stories in which a troubled child and an endangered animal saved and redeemed one another. From Vicki Hearne, those stories are not simply sentimental tales concocted for children, but fictions that reveal the possibilities of communication between domestic animals and man, and in this provocative new book [*Adam's Task: Calling Animals by Name*], she expounds further on the intricate moral relationship that can develop between dogs, cats, horses and human beings.

A poet and an assistant professor of English at Yale University, Vicki Hearne is also a professional animal trainer, and *Adam's Task* reflects her fluency in these two disparate worlds. Drawing upon Ms. Hearne's own experience, as well as a wide variety of texts—including works by Wittgenstein, Freud, Nietzsche and technical animal trainer's manuals—the book emerges, at once, as an informed defense of animals' capacity for understanding and commitment, and a philosophical meditation on the nature of learning, responsibility and language.

As Ms. Hearne sees it, a well-trained dog may possess a far more limited vocabulary than human beings, but his potential *respect* for language is far greater—in fact, is absolute in the sense that a command from his handler will elicit a response that is instantly "full, meaningful and serious." Proper obedience training, she argues, develops a dog's intellect and social skills, and in doing so also confers on him dignity and nobility of character. Further, by facilitating understanding between dog and man, it nurtures mutual autonomy, trust, reliance and a love that is based on shared commitments and collaboration.

In using decidedly anthropomorphic terms to talk about dogs and horses, Ms. Hearne points out she is using language that implies animals are capable of moral understanding. This is the same language employed by animal trainers and the authors of children's books, and it stands in sharp contrast to the coldly objective language of behaviorists and people who insist on referring to an animal as "it" instead of "she" or "he."

When Ms. Hearne herself relates a dog or horse story, the animals become full-fledged characters, as brightly delineated as people created by Dickens or Twain. There is Clever Hans, a famous horse who could answer questions with alphabet blocks by reading minute changes in his owner's facial expressions, a gallant police dog named Rinnie, who unlike his human handlers saw through a con man's elaborate deceptions, and Halla, a high-strung horse who won a Grand Prix jump even though a pulled muscle left her rider virtually incapacitated.

As for animals Ms. Hearne has trained herself, they are no less remarkable as personalities. Take, for instance, Belle, a beautiful and most serious pit bull, who refuses to put up with any sort of laziness on the part of her owner. One day, Ms. Hearne writes:

> it turned out that three days had gone by and I hadn't worked Belle on retrieving. I was lazing about, reading in bed, on the left side of the bed. Belle brought me her dumbbell and stared at me loudly. (Bull Terriers can stare loudly without making a sound.) I said "Oh, not now, Belle. In a few minutes." She impatiently dumped the dumbbell on top of the book I was trying to read, put her paws up on the edge of the bed and bit my hand, very precisely. She took the trouble to bite my right hand even though my left hung within easy reach. She bit, that is, the hand with which I throw the dumbbell when we are working. A very gentle bite, I should say, but also just—precise and justified. . . .

As a writer, Ms. Hearne occasionally diminishes the considerable force of her arguments by overstating an issue or stretching a metaphor beyond its bounds—at one point, she compares the risks horsemen are willing to take to those taken by soldiers in war. She also lapses, from time to time, into the convoluted syntax and pretentious posturing associated with the most tiresome sort of academics. One sentence, for instance, reads,

> But some horses (and this, alas, is part of the talent in them) are capable of responding to the knowledge art creates of what it feels like when there is complete congruence between the soul and the moment (that congruence Wittgenstein indicated when, at the end of the *Tractatus Logico-Philosophicus,* he says, "He who lives in the present lives in eternity") with a general anxiety that work should continue.

Such passages—which occur intermittently throughout the book—make reading *Adam's Task* a somewhat arduous process, and reflect, as well, a certain lack of clarity in thinking. All in all, though, Ms. Hearne's passion for her subject, along with her eclectic intelligence and technical expertise, succeeds in making even the most skeptical reader re-evaluate his relationship with animals and his preconceptions about communication. And in that alone, *Adam's Task* stands as a most intriguing and original book.

> *Michiko Kakutani, "Not So Dumb Animals," in*
> The New York Times, *August 16, 1986, p. 11.*

YI-FU TUAN

Why do automobiles bear animal names such as "Falcon," "Mustang" and "Jaguar"? Most of us know practically nothing about these animals, whereas we all know something about cars and most of us actually drive them. What new information can possibly be added by using such labels? Yet we feel much is added, as though we had been brought up chasing mustangs or hunting jaguars. Human relations with animals are mysterious, profound and passionate. Vicki Hearne's book, written with a philosophical purpose in mind, illuminates one relation—that of a skilled trainer to dogs and horses—but also adds to the mystery and the passion.

The philosophical purpose of *Adam's Task: Calling Animals by Name* is twofold: to define the nature of communication between human beings and the animals they train and domesticate, and to explain the right of humans to do so. In writing this book, Ms. Hearne . . . clearly wishes to refute two antipodal positions: that of psychologists who interpret animals in accordance with a mechanical, behavioristic model and that of what a fellow trainer and writer calls "humaniacs," that is, sentimental people who are fond of saying, "Gooood doggie!" and cringe at the words "discipline" and "punishment." Her own position reminds me of educators of the old school, trained in the classics. She believes profoundly in the intelligence of the animals she trains, in their vocation to fulfill themselves as beings of courage, responsibility and wisdom; at the same time, she believes in showing the whip if not actually using it. (p. 10)

Ms. Hearne reveals the intelligence, the will and the courage and, perhaps most significantly, the desire for challenge—even at the expense of comfort—in the dog and the horse. Her account of how she trains these animals is both illuminating and educational. She shows how mutual the process of learning complex tasks such as retrieving and hurdle jumping must be, and she tries to instill in us a greater respect for our fellow creatures, which means, among other things, resisting the "humaniac" temptation to extend a condescending, patting hand.

But I also have problems with her argument and rhetoric; with her anthropomorphism, for example. She is fully aware of the likelihood of this accusation and defends herself with confidence, armed with the thoughts on language of the Harvard philosopher Stanley Cavell ("the daily burden of discourse") and Ludwig Wittgenstein ("To imagine a language is to imagine a form of life"). But it seems to me that she goes out of her way to test her reader's credulity. The pit bull, Belle, is capable of sizing people up "not as bite prospects, but as problems in moral philosophy and metaphysics." After many excesses of this kind I, a person who seldom can size up another metaphysically, begin to feel so inferior that I find myself retaliating by refusing to grant even the management of a "happy grin" (as distinct from a happy smile?) to a puppy.

The second problem is one that constantly nags the author herself, namely, the images of authoritarianism, not to say of Nazism, that come up whenever the words discipline, control and training—but even more such words as collar, bridle, halter and whip—are used. Of course, Ms. Hearne is against cruelty: for instance, she doesn't use a bullwhip, but "a long light whip, called a longe whip, which is used for emphasis but not to touch the horse when the horse is being exercised on a longe line." On the other hand, certain practices slip by without comment, practices that bother me—for instance, the number tattooed inside the upper lip of the thoroughbred horse Drummer Girl. All harshness is forgiven if it is for the ultimate good of the animal herself. Drummer Girl "had enlarged herself, her soul was filled out" as a result of the training. But the tattooed number continues to nag. I can't for the life of me see it as somehow good for her soul, and that in turn throws doubt, not on Ms. Hearne's own high purpose and altruism, but on those of trainers and owners in general. (p. 11)

Yi-Fu Tuan, "Your Dog Is Sizing You Up," in The New York Times Book Review, *September 7, 1986, pp. 10-11.*

HARRIET RITVO

Poet and animal trainer Vicki Hearne has written a surprising book. In *Adam's Task: Calling Animals by Name* she uses ideas derived from her study of literary criticism and philosophy to interpret her hands-on experience in the ring and the field. . . .

At once sweepingly systematic and uncompromisingly anecdotal, Hearne's approach brings her into immediate conflict with the most widespread scientific method of investigating animal behavior. She wastes no opportunity to criticize what goes on in the laboratories of comparative psychologists, claiming in general that experimental conditions are so artificial as to suppress the animal behavior most worth knowing about. Further, the preconceptions of researchers—especially their disinclination to explain animal behavior in terms of intelligence and motive—may keep them from recognizing interesting questions when they do arise. (p. 70)

Her lack of sympathy for comparative psychology, however, does not league Hearne with the ordinary run of anthropomorphic anecdotalists. Indulgent pet owners earn her condescension at best, and her contempt for people who pride themselves on their humanitarianism can be scathing. . . . [She] characterizes self-centered people who combine superficial sanctimoniousness and underlying disrespect for animals as "humaniacs."

The term is borrowed from William and Dick Koehler, father and son trainers whose forceful methods have both provoked widespread controversy and attracted many disciples, Hearne included. Like them, she adheres to the animal version of "Spare the rod and spoil the child"—and "rod" is only a slight exaggeration, as several of the training stories make clear. It is the emphasis on physical correction (which is not the same as punishment, a distinction Hearne insists on) and the corollary absence of trivial rewards like baby talk or Liv-A-Snaps that inspire tenderhearted observers to com-

pare this technique to the tactics of oppressive regimes. Hearne confronts this accusation with another metaphor; what she offers the animals placed in her charge is not Nazism but education. She argues that discipline and obedience make animals not just better servants, but intrinsically better, just as we become better people as well as better citizens if we have been well and firmly trained as children.

Hearne's analogy is persuasive as far as it goes, but it restricts her analysis to a much smaller sphere than her subtitle suggests. She is not talking about animals in general, but about domestic animals—and only about those domestic animals that respond to training. Thus, although her dog and horse stories are compelling and illuminating, her chimpanzee and cat stories are not. And since she moralizes the training process, she implies that species that resist it are somehow inferior to those that can be transfigured by it. This view recalls an earlier scientific consensus about animal behavior, one untroubled by doubts about the position of human beings in the natural world. Enlightenment naturalists and their 19th-century successors devoted a lot of thought to identifying the top animal. They strenuously resisted installing the chimpanzee or the orangutan in that position, despite their obvious intelligence, preferring instead to elevate the horse and the dog, beasts that happily acknowledged human ascendancy. The recalcitrant cat inevitably occupied a low rank on such scales.

This evocation of the zoological past is probably unintentional; in general, Hearne rarely appeals to history. When she wishes to buttress her argument and broaden its significance, she calls on a battery of philosophers, from Nietzsche to Wittgenstein to Stanley Cavell, or she refers to such classics as *Othello* and *The Faerie Queene*. In addition, she draws heavily on the vocabulary of literary analysis to describe her interactions with her trainees and their responses to training. Although it offers an impressive index of her academic sophistication, most of this literary and philosophical baggage ultimately distracts the reader from the genuinely surprising and provocative material in *Adam's Task*—the description and analysis of the training process itself. As Hearne's stories make clear, animal training is not just an arcane technical pursuit, but an activity with far-reaching moral implications. She may be the only person who can talk valuably about both aspects at once, and a little pretentiousness is a small price to pay for such insight and fluency. (pp. 70-1, 74)

Harriet Ritvo, "The Moral Instruction of Animals," in Psychology Today, *Vol. 21, No. 2, February, 1987, pp. 70-1, 74.*

LOUIS MENAND

The jacket of Vicki Hearne's *Adam's Task: Calling Animals by Name* features blurbs by a variety of luminaries. One of these is the distinguished philosopher of mind A. J. Ayer, who offers this tribute: "I much enjoyed Vicki Hearne's book, and I learned a great deal from it about the possibilities of communicating with domestic animals." Since Ayer is not famous because of his way with dogs and cats, the newcomer to Hearne's book may feel justified in wondering what the fuss is all about. Reading the book may not be immediately helpful. . . . One confronts a book that seems to be a treatise on the proper training of dogs and horses but that reads like a study in moral philosophy, embellished with references to Aristotle, *The Faerie Queene*, Wittgenstein, and Stanley Cavell. The solution to this contradiction is that *Adam's Task* is a study in moral philosophy that works as philosophy only because its author is genuinely obsessed with the practical problems of training dogs and horses.

Still, it is easy to be put off. The writing is an engine that could not be more beautifully tuned. But like all good stylists, especially those whose prose seems perfectly transparent, Hearne has a domineering authorial personality. The reader chafes at the throat-clearing self-references ("I understand myself to be writing about Washoe's [a chimp's] *training*"), at the name-dropping ("I take *happiness* to have at least the range of significance Aristotle saw in it"), at the blanket pronouncements ("I do believe that things like education by and large serve to defraud humans of their own interests and sometimes thereby of their souls"), at the use of Ripley's Believe-It-Or-Not anecdotes about tracking dogs and jumping horses to make philosophical points.

This affective response to Hearne's text is not beside the point; in an important sense it *is* the point. For *Adam's Task* is one of the most perfect realizations of the conversational style of ordinary language philosophy: we resist the blandishments of its style at every stage because we are meant to resist them. If we find the writing pretentious, or extravagant, or obnoxious, or too smooth to be true, it is because its author wants to break us of the habit of reading passively and to force us to become active participants in a conversation.

The book's style enacts its program. Hearne's polemical point about animal training is that both the behaviorists and those she calls the "humaniacs"—people who are "kind" to dogs and horses—do not understand animals because they do not understand the way language works. "The investigation of animal consciousness, like the investigation of human consciousness, is centrally an investigation of language," she explains, "and this ought to remind us of what an investigation of language is." Skinnerians and sentimentalists confuse "talking to" with "talking at." They leave no room in their worldview for the notion that the animal they are addressing is simultaneously addressing them. They fail to realize that to talk—even to give commands or to murmur sweet nothings—is to engage in conversation.

But is this a book about people talking to dogs or is it "really" a book about people talking to people? To assume that the stories Hearne tells about animal training are merely allegorical is to miss the genuineness of her commitment to her subject. At the same time, though, the emphasis on the nitty-gritty of animal training is exactly what makes the metaphysics credible. Ordinary language philosophy and its offspring have always grounded themselves in the empirical: when the later Wittgenstein writes about language, he wants to know what happens at the level of everyday talk; when Stanley Cavell (Hearne's immediate model) writes about film, he keeps returning to the experience of actually sitting in a movie theater watching a movie. Hearne's meditations on the language of dog and horse training are meditations on the language of everyday life because she regards dogs and horses as part of the social, human world. There is, for her, no metaphysical difference between communicating with a horse by sitting on its back and tapping it with your heels and communicating with a colleague by standing in front of him or her and holding forth verbally. What is brilliant about the book is that it presents a compelling view of conversation by discussing relationships in which one of the partners cannot "talk" at all.

As impressive as the book is, there are sides to its argument that even the canniest literary style cannot make wholly appealing. This is a book about the nature of obedience; its subtext accuses the modern world of having abandoned, in its recoil from the horrors of fascist authoritarianism, the virtuous uses of authority. Thus the dignity of trained dogs and the nobility of trained horses are made to stand as mementos of what we lost when we shirked our responsibility to lead, to instruct, to command—and to be led and instructed by others.

Hearne's argument depends on the premise that the essence of dogness is, *mutatis mutandis,* the essence of humanness—that the experience of successful training, which she compares to the experience of creating a successful work of art, touches on the reality of what it means to be human. The trouble is that her notion of the human virtues is not universalist at all, but quite culturally specific. A sense of duty, selflessness, noblesse oblige—she wants all her dogs to be like Sir Philip Sidney. Those attributes of character were no doubt fine in the Renaissance, and retrospect makes them seem finer still. But this is not the Renaissance, and different cultural dispensations require different virtues.

Still, *Adam's Task* is a message to language prescriptivists. It reminds them that language is not a series of words, or a checklist of correct and incorrect usages, not the contents of the dictionary. Nor is it something that can be learned by rote: teaching someone not to say "hopefully" when he or she means "I hope" is not teaching someone how to use the language. If our future as a society somehow depends on the way we talk, it will help us to talk about talk with the tolerance and patience and even the inconclusiveness that is the spirit of a good conversation. (pp. 32-3)

Louis Menand, "Talk Talk: You Say Tomato, I Say Tomato," in The New Republic, *Vol. 196, No. 7, February 16, 1987, pp. 28-33.*

STEPHEN R. L. CLARK

Vicki Hearne teaches English literature at Yale, and is a professional horse and dog trainer. *Adam's Task* is her attempt to explain to her academic colleagues the language and form of life familiar to her as a trainer. In American academic circles—far more so than in Britain—it is the greatest of sins to be "anthropomorphic": "animals" should be viewed as controllable mechanisms, not as beings with whom we might have "moral" relationships. If an experimenter inadvertently describes his subject as "angry", "jealous" or "apprehensive", scare quotes must be emphasized, and such "loose", or "ordinary language" description eventually replaced by "scientific" jargon. If we cannot "prove" that animals are more than mechanisms, we are somehow required, without any proof, to assume that they are not. Professional trainers, on the other hand, simply cannot get by without the working assumption that the animals they deal with have individual points of view, characters and plans. Hearne makes clear how badly the charge of "anthropomorphism" misfires. Her dogs and cats and horses behave and feel like dogs and cats and horses, and she succeeds in training them away from (self-)destructive habits precisely because she can grasp their difference, their pride in being what they can, with her help, become. The real moral of the tale of Clever Hans, the horse who seemed to be able to solve simple arithmetical puzzles until it was realized that he was being cued, unconsciously, by his interrogator, is not "How stupid horses are if they can't tell that $7 + 5 = 12$!" but rather "How very interesting that horses can understand human beings so well!"

Much of Hearne's book is directed at a rather different target, people she calls "humaniacs", who disapprove of rigorous training methods or repressive commands. Imagining that what their animals need is sentimental affection, pity or a wild permissiveness, they allow destructive behaviour, sloppy or indolent technique, until the day when they at last require Hearne, or some other front-liner, to re-educate their murderous pet. Good working dogs and horses have a beauty and nobility of life and character that is insulted, outraged by the sort of contemptuous pity which thinks it cruel to impose discipline upon a youngster's moods, cruel to demand of horse or dog the very best they can deliver. Such human failure produces monsters, animals as confused as the schizoid products of a pathogenic household. And just as autistic or schizophrenic humans can, perhaps, be humanized by having to work with animals to create an accomplished performance, so can the animals themselves be restored to sanity. Sane dogs or horses inhabit much the same moral universe as we do, accept responsibility for what they do and seek to embody a natural perfection. Pity for the champion racehorse who has been "made" to run her best is as inappropriate as terror of the properly educated guard-dog, as if the latter were a "killing machine" or psychopath.

Hearne's stories, whether they are about her animals, or about the weird attitudes of those colleagues who express their "kindness to animals" by wishing her dogs dead, are always illuminating. Illuminating not only about animals—though it is impossible not to admire the fiercely unsentimental approach she makes to them—but about our own moral life, a life which needs to be structured by some vision of perfection, the full use of God-given ability, rather than by fear of pain or lust for passive pleasure. The high courage and capacity we see embodied in great dogs or horses are admirable for their own sake, and worth our pain and labour. Something like the same admiring love must be directed at wild animals, but they can never be—as dogs, cats and horses are—full members of our community, sharing the same stories.

This book is, inevitably, a product of its own culture. No one but an American could have written it; no one but a professor of English literature with a taste for the more aphoristic style of philosophy. The mostly anonymous philosophers who cross her pages seem to be there only to say silly things, as though none of us had ever argued for (or even against) the things Hearne admires. Wittgenstein and Stanley Cavell are her heroes: so much so that anyone who queries either is given much the same treatment of silent contempt as Hearne herself receives from mechanomorphic dogmatists. The style, in fact, is High American. British readers are unlikely—outside laboratories—ever to have encountered people who deny that dogs or cats or horses have their individual characters and preferences and plans; nor are there many people in Britain who think it cruel to train working dogs or horses to abide by the necessary rules of a humane society; nor does it ring bells with me to hear that modern children's literature has abjured heroism, imagination and humanizing identification with non-human creatures. On the contrary, every second book seems to be about disciplined and heroic beasts, and the move from self-absorption to heroic beauty. Our problems in Britain are not quite the same, but it is a great help

to see how subtly mechanomorphic and humaniac rhetoric distorts our view. (pp. 175-76)

Stephen R. L. Clark, "Beasts like Us," in The Times Literary Supplement, *No. 4377, February 20, 1987, pp. 175-76.*

CHRISTOPHER LEHMANN-HAUPT

The White German Shepherd is a novel about a dog, but it doesn't remotely resemble *Lassie Come Home* or *Lad a Dog,* or the more recent *Nop's Trials.* Its author, Vicki Hearne, is a former animal trainer turned writer whose widely praised previous book, *Adam's Task: Calling Animals by Name,* was a philosophical meditation on the relations between humans and animals. What she has done in her first novel is to apply the theories of her earlier book to fiction. It's an intriguing idea, but not an entirely successful one.

The story that Ms. Hearne tells is simple to the point of predictability. Diane Brannigan and Sam Carraclough, a couple of animal trainers, are approached by Hollywood for a dog to star in a remake of Jack London's *Call of the Wild.* The trouble is, what Hollywood wants for the part is a white German Shepherd, which, according to Diane, the story's narrator, will be about as easy to find as "snow in the Sahara Desert" because whites "were normally culled from the litter, so there were no real dogs, and if there had been, there was no tradition for them to plant their feet in."

Despite this handicap, they find a good-looking white named Jouster so close to home that they almost miss him, and when Diane starts training him for the film, he responds so well she begins to think they may have found some sort of a superdog. But when Jouster is asked in an emergency to track a kidnapper, his behavior throws every judgment of him into doubt. Has Diane lost her judgment as a trainer? Is Jouster nothing but a "trash" dog? Can he be trusted to behave on a movie set? Everything hangs in the balance, even the respective love lives of Diane and Sam.

But if the plot of *The White German Shepherd* seems simple and obvious, it contains considerable depths beneath its surface. Here Ms. Hearne explores the possibility that dogs not only "possess something very like conscience," as Charles Darwin observed in *The Descent of Man,* but that they can use that conscience to sniff out good and evil. The dramatic question posed by *The White German Shepherd* is whether Jouster's conscience is good or bad.

And then there are the esthetic issues raised by the novel. The feasibility of making a Hollywood animal film may seem a trivial matter on which to hang a story, but Ms. Hearne works hard to lend it meaning. . . .

Indeed, Ms. Hearne may work too hard. To judge from her prose, she feels so strongly about meaning that instead of allowing it to emerge from her story, she insists on cramming it into every line of her prose. Within the first quarter of the book, Captain Ahab and *Moby-Dick* get mentioned, and not two dozen pages later, a character informs Diane, "White is the color of death." References to Milton's *Aereopagitica,* Emerson's "Self-Reliance," Thoreau's "Civil Disobedience" and Yeats's "rag and bone shop of the heart" come not far behind.

Worse, Ms. Hearne so badly wants her characters to be among the instinctive who understand the animal world, that she forces language on them that sometimes collapses under the weight of its inarticulateness. "Sam and I say things," says Diane, "especially me, because things need to get said even though you can't say much, which doesn't always matter, except when you really have something to say, when there needs to be more room in the world for something."

To a degree, Ms. Hearne's prose technique is a matter of taste, and many readers may admire the way her diction trips you up and forces you to attend to its unusual rhythms.

Christopher Lehmann-Haupt, "Canine Consciousness and the Call of Hollywood," in The New York Times, *April 25, 1988, p. C22.*

CAROLYN SEE

I just wish Ernest Hemingway were still around in the Cosmos, bellied up to Harry's Bar and American Grill, so that he could have a nice talk with Vicki Hearne, author of **The White German Shepherd.** She'd set him straight, and quick.

"You know," Ernest might say to Vicki, "you don't look half bad for a girl. Let's go out to another bistro, or better yet, let's take in a bullfight. Because as a character of mine once remarked in *The Sun Also Rises,* 'Nobody lives their lives all the way up, except maybe bullfighters.'" At least he said something like that.

But Vicki would toss her head contemptuously: "I think you're mistaken, old man! Nobody lives their lives all the way up except dog trainers! Don't you know anything at all about the world? Only in the working of dogs do you see 'miracles as homely as milk.' I tried to explain it, and 'sometimes I think that maybe I was trying to talk about God, except when I heard other people talk about God. There's a way the light gets more real than anything, I see it mostly in the movements of certain dogs, all dogs but certain dogs especially, but you see it in paintings too, or I used to, when I wanted to paint. The light gets real, and for the sake of that light, training dogs is a matter of 27 hours a day and expensive.'"

Ernest might blink. "You sound like my kind of woman! You ought to write some of that stuff down. I could help you, maybe. I used to be a great American writer. People remember me for the close attention I gave to mundane detail. The sunlight on the scales of a newly caught fish, for instance, as it flops in the bottom of a shabby dinghy."

"Fish? Boats? Get real. Let's talk about cleaning dog runs, after you finish working the dogs: one person hosing down the runs, another following closely after, working the squeegee, so that in the lowliest job you contribute to a certain kind of perfection."

But by now the old master might be getting a little cranky. "Listen, lady! You're talking to a great American novelist! A white man! A member of the elite! So don't get smart with me! Remember what I did to the character of Robert Cohn in *The Sun Also Rises?* Remember what I did to Margot in 'The Short Happy Life of Francis Macomber'? I made Cohn look dumb not exactly because he was Jewish, but I made those two facts overlap, OK? And I made Margot less sensitive than a lion, because she was just a woman, so don't get smart with me or I might try a racial or sexist slur or two!"

"Anything you can do, I can do better," Vicki taunts her bar companion. "Because I am a dog trainer! So I am a member of the *real elite!* I take the position that first comes the dog, like when I say, 'The dog is the ultimate authority.' Right after that comes the dog trainer. In my book, the bad people call people on *my* side 'Nazis.' But *my* side calls those bleeding-heart liberals 'humaniacs.' And I say that 'Dogs were better at being dogs, in Vietnam, than men were at being men. . . .' Do you get my drift? So Ernest, I think we're even, except that I come out ahead."

"Strong stuff, daughter! Is this a *novel* you wrote that we're talking about here? What's it about?"

"Two dog trainers train dogs for a living. They look for a white German shepherd, find it and train it for a movie. Then the lady dog trainer gets dumped by her stupid boyfriend and marries her partner. But that's not what it's really about. It's about '. . . the quest or the imperfections of a possible order, a clearing, herding cattle, meals, sleep, loyalty to a few persons, because that was the only loyalty possible.'"

"Well, OK, but I bet it doesn't have any blood and gore. My work has lots of blood and gore, like when that Indian woman dies in childbirth and her blood drips down the wall in that Nick Adams story, or all that pus and stench when my hero gets infected in 'The Snows of Kilimanjaro.'"

"Get out of town! You're talking to a *dog trainer!* How about *this* for blood and gore? 'This bite started as puncture wounds and became two rips down my arm as well, tearing what felt like assorted tendons but actually only one, in my hand, and there was the fat poking out of the punctures like a new, mutant worm.' And guess what? My heroine goes on, with a bite like that, and trains her dog, and gets married, and gets in tune with the universe!"

Vicki Hearne turns her back on the King of American Lit. She has taken him on; she has fought him fair; and she has won on all counts. . . . And she has managed it all in the world of dog training. So Vicki smiles.

And Hem can only whimper, "Well, even though I've been dead for some time, my prose style was so distinctive that here in Los Angeles they've got something called the Bad Hemingway Contest. Because you can recognize my prose from a mile away and it's pretty lofty stuff."

But Vicki knows she has the old man on the ropes, and quotes tauntingly from her own novel about dog training: "'. . . That situation is already artificial enough to obscure the knowledge of how deeply you can and will fail a great-hearted dog, and if it is your own dog and great-hearted . . . then the demons would jitter-jitter-jitter death. . . .'"

But here Hemingway stands up and moves to the door of the bar. "Vicki, I . . . gotta get out of here. I'm going to hunt later this afternoon, ski, fish, something like that."

So Vicki's left alone, in the golden afternoon light of Harry's bar. She orders up another *fine* from the bartender. "Bud, did *you* know that nobody lives his or her life all the way up except dog trainers?"

"Well, miss," the bartender answers respectfully, "wouldn't it be pretty to think so?"

Carolyn See, "Vicki Hearne Meets Ernest Hemingway," in Los Angeles Times Book Review, *May 8, 1988, p. 8.*

LEIGH HAFREY

It would be pleasant to report that in [*The White German Shepherd*] Vicki Hearne has resurrected the dog story. She invokes a popular tradition, represented best for Americans by Jack London's *Call of the Wild* (1903), Albert Payson Terhune's *Lad: A Dog* (1919) and Jim Kjelgaard's *Big Red* (1945). As her narrator, Diane Brannigan, would have it, "there has to be something in the world that matters, and that's what a dog story is about."

But *The White German Shepherd* unfolds at a fatal remove from those originals, and Diane knows it. She and her taciturn partner, Sam, have been commissioned by an old-time Hollywood trainer to find and prepare a white German shepherd for a remake of *The Call of the Wild*. Unfortunately, the old-time trainer is now a lush; white German shepherds, as everyone in the world of this book knows, are "trash, every single one of them. No substance, no heart, no presence"; and though Diane and Sam finally find the dog they need, a canine redeemer named Jouster, for Diane their story belongs to the past, "the good old days . . . when citizenship, good or bad, wasn't on the run."

She is fighting a moral battle, and her author, hoping against hope, fights it with her. A former professional animal trainer, Vicki Hearne commented in her last book, the critically acclaimed *Adam's Task: Calling Animals by Name* (1986), that dog stories "have changed as radically as the stories about Pit Bulls . . . horror stories." So what's a good dog to do?

At the very least, a good dog should stay away from the likes of Diane Brannigan. She's a phony, and as Vicki Hearne herself would say, you can't lie to a dog. The story Diane is really telling is not Jouster's story, but the story of how Diane more or less deliberately levers her current lover—the disillusioned 60's New Journalist Luke Zeller—out of her bed and brings Sam in. She has been on constructively Platonic terms with her partner for some time when Luke arrives to disturb the peace at Neverland Kennel. True, Sam is grieving for a dog he brought back unharmed from the war in Vietnam, only to have Zeus die at home; but his all-seeing affinity for dogs keeps him from giving up on life, and eventually makes a meeting of the minds—and bodies—possible. As Diane comments: "We're all true visionaries in this business."

Maybe so. Certainly there is no end to the miracles dogs perform in *The White German Shepherd*, and the best passages are those illustrating dogs' interactions with each other and with human beings. . . .

Whether or not this is the final word on dog behavior, the animals are imagined in satisfying consonance with what Ms. Hearne, early in *Adam's Task*, calls the "literary tradition"

that informed her work as a trainer—a tradition both fictional and nonfictional, in commentaries on canine behavior going back to Xenophon. Yet Jouster's finest hour, when it comes, is a perfunctorily engineered subplot to the long narrative of Diane's vacillation between the seductive fantasies of the intellect (Luke) and the gritty reality of daily life (Sam), neither option delineated with anything like the sympathy or gift for telling detail that the dog episodes elicit.

There is nothing intrinsically wrong with focusing on the human situation: dog stories have always been about the people in dogs' lives, too, or at the very least about human nature. The contact between the human and the nonhuman throws a morally and emotionally nuanced light on our ways of being, certainly for the worse, but often for the best; and it leaves us wondering, if only in a happily undiscerning afterglow, how we and the world around us may still be cause for surprise.

That wonder, in part assured by a willingness to address the one audience that has wonder in plenty—the young—is what is missing from *The White German Shepherd*. For all Diane Brannigan's talk of seeing the truth in dogs, an adult resistance to the possibility of truth, a different or new truth, is the source of the drama that draws us through this narrative. In *Adam's Task*, which provides a theoretical underpinning to her new book, Ms. Hearne argues for an anthropomorphic reading of animal behavior rather than the mechanistic view she believes the "behaviorist" advocates—a view that, in her fictional protagonist's less discriminating analysis, is the reason why "intellectuals . . . can't work dogs." Yet the author specifically excludes from her discussion all but domestic and, more precisely, "working" animals—that is, animals worked by man—a decision that gives the lie to the title of her book. Perhaps we don't have the story that would account for the behavior of the other, wild animals. But we might find it even in dogs and the fiction they generate, if we were willing to read imaginatively—in Diane's terms, intellectually—in the tradition.

Along those lines, Ms. Hearne has Luke finally come up with a novel and the script for a movie—*Not Jack London*—that may do what good dog stories once did: give lessons in the continued possibility of citizenship. But we never see the movie, and *The White German Shepherd* we have remains a messy tale born of resistance to its own potential.

Leigh Hafrey, "You Can't Lie to a Dog," in The New York Times Book Review, *June 26, 1988, p. 24.*

John Clellon Holmes

1926-1988

American novelist, essayist, poet, and short story writer.

Holmes is best known as a chronicler of the Beat Generation, a group of American writers of the 1950s who rejected moral and artistic conventions and expressed disillusionment with the conservatism and materialism of the Cold War era. His novel *Go* is acknowledged as the first fictional account of the Greenwich Village bohemian scene that revolved around such figures of the Beat Movement as Jack Kerouac, Allen Ginsberg, and Neal Cassady. In his novels, which are marked by vivid characterizations and a meticulous, poetic prose style, Holmes depicted artists, hipsters, and outcasts whose dissatisfaction with traditional institutions of family, church, and state results in extreme lifestyles and unconventional social views. Holmes's essays on the Beat Generation are respected for their objectivity and lucidity in explaining the ethos of the movement. Discussing Holmes's nonfiction, Scott Preston noted: "In his adaptation of spontaneous beat prose techniques, weaving immediate, almost random nativistic imagery into sudden profound insights, Holmes now appears to have been a most intuitive pioneer of the so-called New Journalism as more popularly exemplified by Tom Wolfe or Hunter Thompson."

Holmes's first novel, *Go* (1952; published in Great Britain as *The Beat Boys*), portrays the New York underground scene of the late1940s. A *roman à clef* based on actual events and featuring several members of what would later be termed the Beat Generation, *Go* depicts young bohemians searching for identity and commitment in a time of stifling conformity. Holmes's persona in this book is Paul Hobbes, a writer composing his first novel who is torn between living a conventional married life and joining his hipster friends in their wild nocturnal exploits. While sympathizing with the Beats, Hobbes nevertheless remains wary of their self-destructive behavior. In his second novel, *The Horn* (1958), Holmes details the tragic decline of Edgar Pool, a black jazz saxophonist whose characterization is partially based on the lives of renowned instrumentalists Lester Young and Charlie Parker. Set in the 1930s and 1940s, *The Horn* examines rivalries among musicians and how financial need forces American artists to debase their work ethic in order to survive. Kenneth Rexroth commented: "As a social document *The Horn* is a shocking exposé of working conditions of the Negro in the entertainment business." *Get Home Free* (1964) concerns the failing love affair between Dan Verger and May Delano, two characters from *Go*. When the couple decide to part, they leave New York City for their respective home towns in hopes of learning about their pasts and better understanding themselves. While separated, Dan and May each meet a person who instills in them a will to survive. Upon returning to New York, they are again drawn together by their mutual zest for life and enjoy spiritual rejuvenation through sexual love.

After *Get Home Free,* Holmes published several nonfiction and poetry collections through small presses. *Nothing More to Declare* (1967) is an acclaimed volume of essays that contains Holmes's seminal pieces "This Is the Beat Generation"

and "The Philosophy of the Beat Generation." In the latter essay, originally published in *Esquire* in 1958, Holmes described "beat" as "a state of mind from which all unessentials have been stripped, leaving it receptive to everything around it, but impatient with trivial obstructions. To be beat is to be at the bottom of your personality, looking up; to be existential in the Kierkegaard, rather than the Jean-Paul Sartre, sense." *Nothing More to Declare* also includes profiles of Kerouac and Ginsberg, both of whom influenced Holmes, as well as pieces examining the assassination of President John F. Kennedy, the sexual revolution of the 1960s, and the effect of films on the youth of the 1930s. *Visitor: Jack Kerouac in Old Saybrook* (1981) and *Gone in October: Last Reflections on Jack Kerouac* (1985) comprise reminiscences and analyses of the work of the celebrated Beat author. Holmes's other publications include *Displaced Person: The Travel Essays of John Clellon Holmes* (1987) and the verse collections *The Bowling Green Poems* (1977) and *Death Drag: Selected Poems, 1948-1979* (1979).

(See also *Contemporary Authors,* Vols. 9-12, rev. ed., Vol. 125 [obituary]; *Contemporary Authors New Revision Series,* Vol. 4; and *Dictionary of Literary Biography,* Vol. 16.)

FREDERIC MORTON

[Lots of events happen] in *Go,* mostly adult variations on juvenile delinquency. There are scads of characters too, with and without quotations marks. After combing their stubble and straightening their T-shirts we shall present them, feeling a little like an over-worked police-sergeant at night court. There is drained, prematurely wrinkled Ancke, for instance, who allows himself to be arrested every three months so that jail may cure his drug-habit down to proportions he can afford: there is . . . Agatson, drinking Scotch by the quart and disliking most breakable objects until they lie broken on the floor. There is Hart Kennedy: he "doesn't care about anything"—except the next jag, the next joint. And Stofsky, a species of exuberant introvert, who likes both mystic poetry and homosexuality, has visions every second midnight, and believes in God, though usually under the assumption that God is mad. And Verger, the tubercular theology student who communes with bartenders. And Ed Schindel who steals groceries to save money for "weed." And Christine who has lovers by mail. And last but not least Paul and Kathryn Hobbes.

Paul and Kathryn are a little apart from their company. They love each other—an unorthodox circumstance considering the milieu—and that love saves them from much of the thrill-smothered sterility of their friends. Their marriage runs into difficulties but these only tighten the bond. It is through the Hobbeses—particularly through a heartbreakingly proud scene in which Paul pretends to be "big" about Kathryn's infidelity—that Mr. Holmes gives us a hint of the insights of which he is capable. It is again Paul and Kathryn who maintain what precarious continuity there is in the plot structure of *Go.*

But the howl and stomp of those cold water flat parties obliterates even that. The saxophones scream out of the portable while couples twitch against damp walls and a cry goes up that the reefers won't last. Before long somebody is sure to lick up spilled liquor from the dirty floor. And then, when all possibilities of debauch have been exhausted in one place, the "go" starts in earnest. . . .

Mr. Holmes' style is almost appropriately slack and erratic. Occasionally it bulges out into a cramped lyricism—only to retreat fatigued into a bare transcription of happenings. "A beat generation," philosophizes Paul Hobbes toward the end. We hope he is not right. But the adjective seems useful. This is a beat novel.

Frederic Morton, "Three A. M. Revels," in New York Herald Tribune Book Review, *October 12, 1952, p. 33.*

GENE BARO

[*The Horn*] is a novel centered in the world of jazz that is written with vivid intelligence and persuasive depth of feeling; it is a work of stature and maturity.

This story treats of the last days of Edgar Pool, Negro saxophonist, known as "The Horn," who became a legend in his lifetime, the musician whose style set the direction for modern jazz. It is the story of an idealist and individualist disillusioned, of a man used up by the life he has had to lead in order to express the sense of the truth within him. In his last fatal binge, "The Horn" is obsessed with the desire "to go home"; in his search for a few dollars Pool crosses again the paths of the woman he has loved and of some of the men whose music or way of life has owed so much to his own. In their retrospect and his, the life of Edgar Pool is unfolded. It is a life that springs from the page vibrantly and harrowingly real.

And the characters involved in Edgar Pool's story are given each his full dimension of reality. . . . Each of these lives varies the theme of creative aspiration and loneliness.

Indeed, it is really the idealistic and transcendental strain in American life that is the subject of this book. It portrays the romantic personality with its inarticulate yearning for some expressive essence, for the power of some word or deed or phrase of music to transform the eternal variability of experience into an absolute coherence, to merge opposites, to be fulfilled and absorbed timelessly; this is the story of what it means to follow after a vision of reality rather than after the common notions of what is real.

John Clellon Holmes writes with considerable distinction. Perhaps the structure of his novel shows a bit too strongly. Here and there, he has been betrayed by complexity into carelessness. But, mostly, he seems entirely to control his material. I know of no descriptions of the physical impact of jazz music, or of the stance and gestures of the musicians, to equal his. This book is studded with wise observations and moving scenes. Mr. Holmes speaks most often through an omniscient voice; he has managed nevertheless to give his work a unity of tone that combines the rhapsodic with the epigrammatic, like jazz itself.

Gene Baro, "A Novel Centered in the World of Jazz," in New York Herald Tribune Book Review, *July 20, 1958, p. 3.*

KENNETH REXROTH

The Horn is about Negroes and jazz, subjects about which the Beatnik, by definition, knows very much less than nothing. So *The Horn* is hung up on its own dilemma, but not badly hung up. Holmes shares the jazz mystique, the fascination with jazz as a way of life common to all—American and foreign—bohemia today. If (as Norman Mailer has characterized him) the hipster is an imitation Negro, the characters in *The Horn* are the kind of Negroes the hipster tries to imitate. Holmes is a conscientious craftsman, with considerable understanding of humans and their motives, and his fictional honesty redeems him. He says, "Finally Negro people are forever out of reach of white people, no matter how the whites strive or how they yearn." This is certainly the worst sort of Negrophile mystique. In jazz they call it "Crow-Jimism." The only answer to it of course is, "Well, what are you doing writing this novel?"

Nevertheless, his people are, for many pages at a time, simply people, with rather special conditions of tragedy, but finally with purely human tragedies, like you and me. The mystique distorts; this is not the life of Negro jazzmen, but it is remarkably close. As a matter of fact, *The Horn,* like *Go,* is a *roman à clef,* and the distortion of Negro life and of the jazz world is proportionate to Holmes's inventions and departures from the facts in the lives of his originals.

His people are close enough to real life for one powerful conclusion to come through and slap you in the face. What a horrible life! Now the hipster, the Beatnik, imitates the horror.

He likes it. The characters in *On the Road* don't have to live that way. The Negroes in *The Horn* do, and they don't like it a bit. As a social document *The Horn* is a shocking exposé of working conditions of the Negro in the entertainment business.

The writing is pretty dithyrambic. Algren and Kerouac are not the best models for Holmes, with his more pedestrian talents. In spite of this, the mystique slowly drains out. What finally emerges is a novel of tragedy and disgust—*The Jungle* of the life of a jazzman in the days of bop. . . .

On one point the mystique does not catch Holmes out. Carried away by the fervent bop propaganda, he does attribute far too much to the music as music. All the storm and stress of the bop revolution was about nothing more than the introduction of a few chords which were commonplaces to Beethoven, the use of the saxophone as a woodwind, which is what it is, rather than as a novelty instrument, and a slightly more flexible treatment of the standard jazz beat—8/8 or 12/8 instead of always 4/4. Even today the new "1958 Harlem Hard Bop" sounds like nothing so much as very simple, extra loud Berlioz. Like almost all jazz buffs, Holmes shows no signs of knowing what goes on musically in jazz—he digs it—it sends him. It doesn't really send the musicians, they just tell the customers that. They *know* what they are doing. The real touchstone of musical appreciation in modern jazz is the young bassist—called Billy James in the book, but obviously a real person well known to all modern jazz fans—whom Holmes puts down with a series of sneers. . . .

It so happens that in real life this man got his first date as a high-school boy with Kid Ory, who is jungly enough for anybody, was brought out in New York by Oscar Pettiford, who is pretty funky still, was known all through the bop era as "The Bird of the Bass" though still just a kid, and today is the foremost single pioneer of the kind of modernist jazz that Holmes mistakenly thinks bop was. He is anything but a snob and if he did walk to the mike once in Minton's and say, "Ladies and gentlemen, this is not jazz; these are very sick men," nothing shows how right he was more than the retelling of the episode in this very book. . . .

Fortunately, things are no longer quite so bad as they were in the days of this novel, the Thirties and Forties. A period of minor musical revolution in the till then extremely hidebound world of jazz happened to coincide with humanity's worst world war and with the concomitant social and cultural breakthrough of the American Negro. The story of Lester Young's persecution in Army stockades is far more awful than any of the episodes from his career reworked in this book. Los Angeles or Harlem, Buddy Collette or Don Byrd, the young Negro musician coming up today will never comprehend just how awful it was, what a cruel price, the price of life itself, older jazzmen paid to put him where he is. *The Horn* is a pretty accurate picture of that life—that life and that death. They can read about it there. I don't think they are going to have to live it. If some of them do, it will be because they want to—like the Beatniks who think it's kicks.

Kenneth Rexroth, "When the Joints Were Jumping," in The Saturday Review, *New York, Vol. XLI, No. 31, August 2, 1958, p. 11.*

RAY BENTLEY

In a prefatory note [in *The Horn*] Holmes warns:

The incidents in this book are not intended to reflect the factual history of jazz music during the Nineteen Thirties and Forties; nor are the characters intended to depict the actual men and women who made that history. The book, like the music it celebrates, is a collective improvisation on an American theme; and if there are truths here, they are poetic truths.

In this message the two major faults of the book are suggested; the one seemingly unavoidable as Holmes probably recognized; the other, a fault of his style. First, the book does strongly reflect the history of jazz and many of its people are individual or composite studies of living jazz personalities (the "Horn" himself seems three parts Coleman Hawkins and one part Lester Young). Secondly, Holmes is primarily a poet with a passion for the jazz tradition. His style and enthusiasm get in the way of the story of Edgar Pool's degradation, which is the heart of the book. The narrative is rosied o'er with a pale cast of "poetic truth" that the hip and the beat will accept as gospel, but the knowledgeable jazz fan and jazz musician will recognize as froth.

Ray Bentley, "Between Swing and Bop," in The New York Times Book Review, *August 10, 1958, p. 19.*

HASKEL FRANKEL

Near the end of *Get Home Free,* the hero, wanting to help a woman defeated by life, can only advise her, "Forget it, get drunk, take off your clothes, anything, anything—because it's all more impossible than you know." In this one sentence is embodied the mind and heart of John Clellon Holmes's third novel . . . , a neatly wrapped package of futility that is both depressing and impressive.

What is depressing lies within the story itself—a bleak look at life and love in the United States today. The plot is built like one of those gray, grainy European films that moves in a tarnished circle, taking the characters—in this case, Dan Verger and May Delano—from misery far afield, then back to where they began.

At the beginning, Dan and May are sharing a New York City loft and a crumbling affair. . . . The affair collapses and each of its lost participants tries to go home again—he to Connecticut, she to Louisiana—only to learn what Thomas Wolfe discovered long ago.

Dan and May eventually return to New York and begin again, more bleakly mature than before. . . .

What is impressive is the author's ability to create so much life in so barren an atmosphere. In the Connecticut section, he introduces Old Man Molineaux, the local tosspot, a giant character fully alive and totally engaging. He is both heroic and pathetic as he wheedles drinks, and at the same time roars his defiance against the town that is too small for him—but which he is never strong enough to leave.

Better still is the Louisiana section, which evokes a long night beginning among the ruins of white society and ending in a blur of jazz, dope and alcohol in the ruins of an old mansion. Mr. Holmes has a wonderful ability to make the mansion and every bit of filth in each of its rooms stand out in full dimension. Later, he takes the clutter and the people and slowly sets them adrift in bootleg alcohol, then floats them in and out of focus as drugs pump in on top of the booze. The scene is so well envisioned that it becomes a part of personal memory, something experienced rather than read.

If it were not for this gift of creating character and incident which continuously hurls fireworks into the gloom, *Get Home Free* might prove too depressing for consumption. After all, it's an unthinking person indeed who has not gotten past the age of 25 without discovering that life is difficult, that all our years, no matter how fierce the struggle, must end in death. Happily, whether the author likes it or not, the excitement of his creative ability overrides his grim trip from futility to resignation.

> Haskel Frankel, *"How Time Arms Us Against Itself,"* in The New York Times Book Review, *May 3, 1964, p. 36.*

WILLIAM BARRETT

In *Get Home Free,* John Clellon Holmes returns to the bohemian subject matter that he handled so well in his first novel, *Go,* more than ten years ago. That earlier work caught the mood of its period very well, and was a better and more mature presentation of the beat generation than the highly touted novels of Jack Kerouac. The hero and heroine of the present novel—Dan Verger and May Delano—belong to that same generation, and though they are still "beat," they have also become older, sadder, wiser, and a little more human.

Dan and May, who live in Greenwich Village, are having an affair. The relationship is sick and hysterical, and they break it off and return for visits to their separate homes, Dan to rural Connecticut and May to Louisiana. Most of the book, and by far the better part, is concerned with their adventures back home and the discoveries they make about themselves and their pasts when they return to their roots. When they meet again in New York, it looks as if they might take up where they left off, though this time the relationship will be very different, for they have both learned from their experiences to have a little compassion for each other.

Mr. Holmes is an honest and searching writer, who tries to look very closely at his material; his fault is that he does not distinguish well enough between where this material is significant and where it is not. Though he has matured, he still takes bohemian life and its sexual preoccupations a little too seriously. . . . Mr. Holmes is far more interesting when he is dealing with the town drunk, Old Man Molineaux, whom Dan encounters back home in his Connecticut village, and who overshadows all the other characters in the book. Dan and May are real in their own way, and if you have ever lived in New York, you have surely met them; but in comparison with the old reprobate Molineaux they are merely shriveled and neurotic children. (p. 136)

> William Barrett, *"Talent in Search of a Subject,"* in The Atlantic Monthly, *Vol. 213, No. 6, June, 1964, pp. 136-37.*

THOMAS LASK

Nothing More to Declare is John Clellon Holmes's spiritual customs declaration, made at age 40, at the border of a country to which he will never return. "I have outlived myself," he says, "as I was in the years recorded here, and I am done—

even with the celebrations of their end." Celebration is not precisely the term to best describe the feverish, restless, unanchored searching, the unfocused yearning that beset Mr. Holmes and the people he knew in the decade or so after World War II. It was a generation that called itself "Beat" and his pages tell how these people got to be that way, what they thought and felt, what they valued, what they sought. It was a generation that came between the socially conscious theoreticians of the nineteen-thirties and the New Left activists of the nineteen-sixties. . . .

Mr. Holmes, a novelist, was part of the scene. He knew the people who made it, was its sometime historian. More than facts or biographical sketches, his book is admirable in catching the atmosphere of those days and of the metaphysics that guided their behavior.

Fearing "spiritual death," the Beats made the journey into the interior, into themselves, using whatever was at hand: drugs, alcohol, poverty, mystic trances, long journeys—anything that would help them reach that inner element that was their true self and could sustain them. The story isn't new, of course, Mr. Holmes having told part of it himself. But no one has better caught the tone and mood of those years. I don't see how anyone who makes the nineteen-fifties his subject will be able to ignore it.

Four of the portraits, those of Jack Kerouac, Allen Ginsberg, G. Legman and Jay Landesman, would certainly seem to be basic material. These four were more than friends to Mr. Holmes. They were the most vital, stimulating and liberating people he knew. Sessions with them were not always easy, but they made up in sustenance what they lacked in harmony. . . .

Nothing More to Declare is also a personal chronicle of a man who started in the late nineteen-forties with great hopes and found the New York scene more and more disillusioning, with its parties, its publicity-ridden activities, its aimlessness. He found too that the conventional solutions in politics, morality and religion were unsuitable, and like the others in his group, was forced to turn inward for the answers to the questions that plagued him.

It is good to be able to report that there is enough in the book to argue about. He claims, I think, too much for the Beats. He says, for example, that the movement was apolitical and asocial; yet he asks us to believe that the young people of today's left stems from them. He pooh-poohs the social worker's view of society, but when he comes to look for clues to Lee Harvey Oswald's behavior, he drags out the old uprooted-home, selfish-parents argument. His emphasis on Existentialism is too often equated with action, as if any activity is superior to thought. And he can sometimes substitute one stereotype for another.

But his book does possess one quality that is both rare and admirable: A querying, questioning honesty that is free of rancor and petty accusation. He evidently wants to enter that new world absolutely free of encumbrances.

> Thomas Lask, *"Closing the Account,"* in The New York Times, *March 9, 1967, p. 37.*

RICHARD R. LINGEMAN

John Clellon Holmes, a proper Beat-generation "spokesman"

by dint of two articles on the phenomenon, as well as his novel *Go,* in which the phrase first appeared, has collected a variety of essays into a book which he titles *Nothing More to Declare* in rueful celebration of his 40th year. The book is a very kind, thoughtful and judicious consideration of his contemporaries in that hectic, grim frenzy of the late forties and fifties; it also scans an authentic American literary movement, whose influence—at least among the *outré* young—is still being felt in far-off, far-out places like Haight-Ashbury in San Francisco. (p. 42)

Holmes's perceptive essays on the Beat phenomenon, whatever one may think of the literary product of its espousers, provide a useful insight, from the vantage point of one foxhole, of the times we have recently lived through.

In the first of two Beat-generation pieces included in this book, Holmes wrote [in **"This Is the Beat Generation"**] (1952) that "the valueless abyss of modern life is unbearable" and that the current generation was seeking values—even false values—in desperate recoil from this vacuum. It was of course a postwar generation, too young for the most part to have participated in World War II, its emotions, rather, caught up at a distance by the world cataclysm. Then came the postwar let-down, the seediness of an America plagued by shortages, and then, in 1950, at war again and McCarthy beginning to be heard in the land.

Among the sensitive young men of the day, the search for some kind of faith began, and Holmes wrote, in *Go,* of a spiritual crisis in which his protagonist "was paralyzed by the vision of unending lovelessness." This vision was similar to Allen Ginsberg's Moloch in "Howl." The Beats were in a dark cave of the spirit and when they sounded their Whitmanesque barbaric yawps they were answered by a dull "boum" and a horrifying sense of meaninglessness. So they drank hard, raced back and forth across the country and talked extravagantly of "holymen" and "angel-headed hipsters." The devil was American life, and they diced with him for high stakes—their identities.

Holmes begins his book with four portraits of contemporaries who expressed differing concerns of those times—Ginsberg, Jack Kerouac, Jay Landesman, who edited a magazine called *Neurotica,* and the strangest of all, Gershon Legman, the underground Kinsey, who seems to be a character in a Wallace Markfield novel. Essays on the movies of the thirties, the sexual revolution and Lee Harvey Oswald follow, and the book ends with a long, beautifully sustained autobiographical threnody, in which Holmes charts his own course through his times.

Here he is at his best, interweaving the public world with his own private hells and small triumphs—the wartime marriage drawn out excruciatingly through the postwar years until finally it is ended; the early success (his first novel was sold to a paperback house for quite a few thousand dollars but never published); the fifties of Ike and Dulles and the button-down mind of Bob Newhart and very, very dry martinis; the second-book block—finally overcome; the new wife; another novel, squeezed out slowly around fallow periods; and finally the long hard look at oneself upon reaching the age of 40. It is a process of "molting," says Holmes, and now the people of his youth are scattered and he withdraws from the generational battles.

I am reminded of a story by Lafcadio Hearn. On Hearn's first day in Japan he is taken on a tour of a Buddhist temple. The priest leads him from one room through sliding doors to another, and to still another. At last they reach the altar in the innermost room, and there Hearn sees the end of his quest—a mirror; himself. And there Holmes's life, through the hue and cry of his times, has led him—to himself. Now he is "done declaring, exhorting, generationing. There are no Gentiles anymore, and there is no further need for Apostles who will speak to them." He hopes now only for the "solitary, incommunicable joy of work that is done for itself." He has laid aside the rusty sword of Beatism and turned toward . . . what? We are not sure. "What more is there to declare?" (pp. 42-3)

Richard R. Lingeman, "Charting the Course," in The New York Times Book Review, *April 9, 1967, pp. 42-3.*

DANIEL AARON

Now in his fortieth year and poised on "a frontier between the countries of experience," Holmes [in *Nothing More to Declare*] opens up his luggage of memories for inspection, concealing nothing, he says, from the Customs Official. His "Declaration" is an apologia for himself and his generation, at once a definition, explanation, and description presented with great charm and insight. Brilliant bravura passages, vivid portraits, artful accounts of dramatic encounters disclose the novelist behind the autobiographical historian; but his book, although occasionally "literary," never fakes or prevaricates. It is an absolutely honest testament in addition to being a kind of mosaic of a generation.

Nothing More to Declare opens with impressionistic sketches of four men whose composite views, visions, frustrations, and achievements define the mental boundaries of Holmes's expanding consciousness. Gershon Legman, "St. Jerome of the Bronx," carries on a lonely war against sadism and violence—the substitutes for sex in our culture—and converts Holmes to his "bravely avowed belief in the passional side of the human being." Jay Landesman, impresario of "happenings" and precursor of Pop, exposes the pomposities of high culture in the Fifties and illuminates the social blackness with black humor. Holmes learns from him "that sexuality is somehow the last sanctuary of the Real" and that one must adjust "not to the society but to the springs of life itself." Allen Ginsberg provides another "route to revelation." He is the rejected man who seeks the rejected, a creature of "ecstasies and premonitions" whose "Howl" is "the biography of a part of our era . . . the first statement of a point of view that was uniquely ours." And most important of all is Jack Kerouac, "a combination of Jack Armstrong and Thomas Wolfe," the "tramp transcendentalist" who helps the author to discover himself and his vocation. Kerouac reproduces "the dislocations and attritions of his generation's experience 'in great America'."

In an exhilarating essay on movie-going during the late Thirties and Forties, Holmes tells how films created a common fantasy for this age-group. Besides providing an escape from Depression dullness, they helped to dictate the responses to feminine beauty, literature, and even politics. Films took precedence over books. Holmes discovered Hemingway through Gary Cooper; Paul Muni sent him to Zola. In Bogart he and his friends beheld the incarnation of the "Existential Knight," and the bizarre comedy of the Marx Brothers, Laurel and Hardy, and W. C. Fields ("the secret Dutch Uncle of my generation") not only helped them to shape their surrealist vision of a corrupt and stuffy world but also to work out a desperate strategy for outwitting it.

An extended discussion of the Beat Generation that follows clears up a good deal of speculation and misinformation. The blurring of "Beat" and "Beatnik" has obscured the origins and significance of the "Beat Movement," and Holmes sets the record straight. His Beat Generation, he says, was a "literary group," not a social movement. It did not seek to clash with the Squares, only to avoid them, and its bent was quasi-religious—to go questing for revelations in the expanding consciousness of the Self. The Beats (his Beats) are largely responsible, he claims somewhat hyperbolically, for changing the social tone from one of prudence, irony, and impersonality "to the daring commitment and diversity of the creative artist." In so doing they made possible the dissent of the Sixties, although Holmes finds the New Left in many ways regressive, inclined to shock rather than to liberate, and blind to the discoveries of its Beat predecessors.

Throughout this far-ranging commentary, whether he is writing on President Kennedy as a touchstone of his generation, or brooding over the symbolism of Oswald's crime (the excluded man trying to make contact with society by assassinating his polar opposite), or reflecting upon the sexual revolution (the exploration of the last frontier), or recording his private struggles as a man and writer . . . , Holmes is invariably pertinent and unfailingly alive.

Perhaps he overstates the cultural importance of his Beat heroes and the profundity of their psychic and social disclosures, but exaggeration is usually undercut by wit and candor. Having emerged from "a disordered and wasteful past," he has come to appreciate the fatal truth of the cliché and is prepared "to persevere without rage." (pp. 211-12)

> Daniel Aaron, "The Beat Generation at 40," in Commonweal, Vol. LXXXVI, No. 7, May 5, 1967, pp. 211-12.

THE TIMES LITERARY SUPPLEMENT

Since the Beat Generation writers are no longer the subject of complacent scorn, Mr. Holmes's present memoirs [*Nothing More to Declare*] will have a wider reading public than the fans and the knockers. It contains a first-hand report on Jack Kerouac and Allen Ginsberg in the 1940s, and reprints Holmes's well-known pioneering essays, **"The Philosophy of the Beat Generation"** and **"This is the Beat Generation"**. These are placed in a framework of recent cultural history, refracted through autobiographical experience.

Nothing More to Declare is a personal report, and the weakest parts are where it concerns only the personal. The author is not a major figure and he knows it, but he has enjoyed the literary scene of the past twenty years, in spite of his sad reflections on his own "sad husks" of "fame, ambition, ego". He hands on his experience of other writers without jealousy, but he is not as good a writer on the literary scene as, for instance, Seymour Krim in his *Views of a Near-Sighted Canoneer*. His style is magazinish but the information does come through. . . .

Mr. Holmes's style has a generational imprint, but he strives too hard to suggest his representativeness: "My psyche, like that of the nation just then, suffered a series of numbing bruises to the self-esteem." It is the familiar, and slightly boring, "making it" urge, and it fades with the pundit. But Mr. Holmes at least, in 1968, understands that he has been "in a kind of thrall". His own novels, *The Horn* and *The Beat Boys,* are more documentary than fantasy, and his talent as reporter is not in doubt here either, except when he indulges in F. L. Allen "only yesterday" accumulations. References to Fitzgerald expose the gap in insights between Mr. Holmes's memoirs and the "crack-up" essays, and it is he who insists on the comparison.

What is done well is the record of Grub Street America in the 1940s and 1950s, written up with a certain appropriate scab-picking detail. His boredom with the 1940s is almost classically written up; echoes of *Howl* penetrate his prose, but the smell of authenticity arises from the namelittered smoke-filled rooms. His experience enables him, in **"The Silence of Oswald"**, to perceive that the president's assumed assassin was typically urban American, not eccentrically creative enough to be Beat and therefore emerging at the frontier of nonconformity and murder within the postwar social structure. . . .

Mr. Holmes does not have Norman Mailer's flair for the existential interiors of public life but he can decently suggest the darkness inside dullness. The main value of his book remains his first 125 pages. . . . If he is inadequate on Charlie Parker and uncritical in his definitions of being "high", he is excellent on the meanings of "beat" which radiate into American society. His chapters on prewar films stop short at nostalgia and fail to show their effect on literature, social attitudes towards war, and the changing images of the hero as Joel Macrea, Humphrey Bogart and W. C. Fields—the non-cooperative models for the 1950s. But being at one time reasonably close to Ginsberg and Kerouac, he does grasp their careers in his florid way. Kerouac's exuberance and melancholy, his dour New England, quixotically sympathetic character, his traditional hankering for the West and the Orient, his essential discursive inclusiveness—and Ginsberg's "manic verbal energy", erudition, "omnivorous hungers", "lust for an absolute metric order", obsession with hallucinations of consciousness: these come across clearly, enthusiastically and uniquely.

The sections on Gershon Legman and Jay Landesman are equally interesting, not the least because these are relatively less well known, although Legman's *The Horn Book, Love and Death* and *Rationale of the Dirty Joke* are essential reading. Legman apparently dismissed *Neurotica*, which Landesman so valuably edited, as "mostly garbage", because he was obsessed, long before the fashion with pop literature—perhaps, as Mr. Holmes suggests, the first to be seriously concerned with it. The chapter on Legman pins down something of this scholar of sex and language for the first time, but there is very little account of what he has actually written. As usual, Mr. Holmes concentrates on authentic reportage of his contacts with "representative men" and their climate. Whether or not his Generation premises are accurate or not, and in spite of his often souped-up style, he has produced a document for literary history.

> *"Keeping Pace with the Beats," in* The Times Literary Supplement, *No. 3511, June 12, 1969, p. 640.*

JAMES ATLAS

Before the beats had become the Beats—that occurred later on in the 1950s, after the publication of *On the Road*—Holmes charted in *Go* their manic exploration of the unconscious, their feverish quest for experience, their glorification of crime. (p. 24)

What distinguishes *Go* from Kerouac's own hectic testimony is its sobriety. Not that Paul Hobbes, Holmes's persona, is any less dissipated than his friends, any less susceptible to the blandishments of squandered evenings at nightclubs or drunken parties. But he is skeptical, conservative, unpersuaded by the ephemeral delight his friends derive from their indulgences. A solemn, industrious writer intent on salvaging his marriage, Hobbes is a reluctant participant in what Holmes elsewhere has called "futility rites"; he is a mere tourist in the underworld nightlife of Times Square dives, a realm "inhabited by people 'hungup' with drugs and other habits, searching out new degrees of craziness." Hobbes ventures into this world "suspiciously, even fearfully, but unable to quell his immediate fascination."

How different from the characters in *On the Road,* "mad to live, mad to talk, mad to be saved, desirous of everything at the same time. . . ." Yet Hobbes's very detachment is responsible for his insights. "The sense of freedom in his life, the idea of being able to control it, direct it, even waste it, of being able to entertain fancies that were detrimental or exercise a volition that was dangerous" comes to seem "a shameless illusion." Like Holmes himself, a New England Yankee from a venerable family, Hobbes is unnerved by a world where "his values are a nuisance and his anxieties an affront." He is more interested in self-preservation than in the *dérèglement de tous les sens* prescribed by Rimbaud and taken up with such ardor by the Beats. And if this reserve gives "a tinge of square moralism" to the novel, as one breathless chronicler of the period has observed, it also gives it a certain verisimilitude.

Go is the dispassionate record of one generation's self-destructive rituals. Disorderly parties in squalid apartments, "hordes of chattering people" leaping into cabs and racing up and down Manhattan, the incessant quest for "weed" or "tea"—as marijuana was then called: what Holmes has captured is that state of mind evoked by Norman Mailer in a glossary he once compiled of "The Hip and the Square," a list that included "wild," "Negro," "midnight," "orgy," and "a catlike walk from the hip." But what is so surprising about Holmes's portrait, apart from its archaisms, is its familiarity:

> Now the rooms were thronged with people [he writes of a party at Stofsky's], many of them unsure just what they were doing there, but intrigued by all the talk, the smoke and laughter, and the ceaseless movement by which people at a party disguise their self-consciousness. The brighter crop of philosophy and literature students from Columbia squatted on the floor, vying for repute in that elaborate game of intellectual snobbery which passes for conversation among the young and intense. They grouped themselves (at a safe distance so as not to appear too interested) around the one or two authentic literary figures that Stofsky had managed to ensnare: a poet of cautious output, a novelist whose work had been appraised as being 'not without talent,' and a soft-faced critic who spoke in terms of 'criteria and intention,' and whose articles were fashionably unreadable. Through the rooms, like

pale butterflies, flitted a number of young women, girl friends of the students, exchanging the gossip of the sets they traveled in with offhand arrogance, all the time snatching looks over their shoulders so as not to miss anything and quickly moving on.

This could be a scene from Edmund Wilson's *Memoirs of Hecate County,* the portrait of an earlier generation's rituals of decadence, or Delmore Schwartz describing a party spoiled by "the distortions of self-consciousness" in his story "New York's Eve." There is the same inauthenticity, the same thin accomplishments made much of, the same haze of alcoholic gossip. And, like these other writers' observant personae, Hobbes is made to seem the only sentient character. Toward the end of one chaotic party, he drifts off to a corner by himself,

> dizzy from the drinking and the marijuana, and snagged in the senseless return of an old inferiority, cherishing a fond sadness as though he had perceived in all the chaos a deep vein of desperation which everyone else refused to notice. 'Out of what rage and loneliness do we come together?' he thought drunkenly, certain some obscure wisdom lurked in the question.

What provoked this grim agitation, "this bleak eagerness for everything to happen at once"? In Holmes's later view, it was the prospect of nuclear war in that doom-haunted decade, combined with the restiveness that every postwar generation suffers and a rebellion against "conformist" values in favor of the "existential" (how dated those words have become!). Any mad adventure, he recalled in *Nothing More to Declare,* was justified by a conviction that "something had gotten dreadfully, dangerously out of hand in our world." If a rational civilization could produce world war, the death camps, weapons of universal destruction, why not cultivate the irrational? Ginsberg—and Holmes's Stofsky—found support for this idea in Blake, but he could have found it in Keats: "Oh for a life of sensation rather than thought!"

The consequences of such a life are painfully evident in Hobbes's marriage, which finally succumbs to the sexual liberation of the day (another instance of a phenomenon claimed by every generation as its own). When Hobbes's sensitive, unhappy young wife goes off with Pasternak, it is with great reluctance, compelled more by some inarticulate compulsion to be of her time than by any real desire. Hobbes, in turn, must affect to be free of jealousy—another impulse that, like fidelity, is considered archaic—and proceed with a joyless seduction of his own. To be unfaithful is a duty; freedom from the social contract involves just as many obligations as obedience to it.

The other notable character in *Go* is the city itself, the backdrop against which all these lurid scenes are set. In their feverish voyages to the end of the night, Hobbes and his friends speed up the West Side Highway, while "the river-girdled length of the island slipped by them and the George Washington Bridge up ahead hung across the dark throat of the river like some sparkling, distant necklace." (pp. 24, 26)

Hobbes's desperation has a more specific cause than his friends'; his frustrated struggle to write is what really drives him out into the streets. Holmes, writing *Go* is his early 20s, had a lively sense of young writers' anguish. His portrait of the vulnerable, manic Stofsky, producing "an endless flow of half humorous, half mystical ideas, mortared with bits of poetry and insights derived from religious paintings," conforms to what we know of Ginsberg's very uneven spiritual life during the early 1950s, when he was a perplexed, awkward boy uncertain of his talent; and he has managed to capture Kerouac when he was a bellicose young novelist whose destiny had yet to be decided, before he became a legend.

Three years after the publication of *Go,* Holmes abandoned New York for Old Saybrook, Connecticut, where he lives for half of each year (the other half he is professor of English at the University of Arkansas); Kerouac wandered out west; and the world depicted in the novel gave way to the legend of the Beats. But there is more of its essence in *Go* than in many subsequent records, for that novel was written before private experience became public myth. (pp. 26-7)

James Atlas, "A Novel of the Beat Generation," in
The New Republic, *Vol. 183, No. 19, November 8, 1980, pp. 24, 26-7.*

FREDERICK R. KARL

Everyone recognizes that *Go* is a significant document in the development of the so-called Beat movement. What appears less apparent is that the book looks backward as much as forward, backward to the type of fiction we associate with Nelson Algren, and only a little removed from naturalistic fiction. Holmes's Beats are versions of Steinbeck's dropouts, urbanized Okies. And we find a similar phenomenon in a lateral movement, in [George Mandel's] *Flee the Angry Strangers,* where the counterculture lives in Greenwich Village. Characteristic of all is the pursuit of leisure time, which may be filled in with drugs, booze, sex, talk, search for a transcendental being, self-destruction, frenetic movement, rearrangement of personal connections, reshuffling of lovers or mistresses, reliance on cars and spatial fantasies. Leisure is perceived as a form of liberation.

Go is representative in that Holmes was one of the first to prophesy the "counterfeit decade" in print. Searching for leisure is perhaps the most powerful way to indict a society hellbent on acquisition and property. One of the paradoxes of the Beat phenomenon, however, is that while materialism is eschewed, each individual has a favorite kind of property. For some, it is drugs, whose acquisition depends on money; or books, some of which can be stolen from the university bookstore; or a private pad, which requires payment of rent, however minimal; or a car, which may be stolen. In *Go,* even Stofsky (Allen Ginsberg), Holmes's most ascetic figure, requires refueling by way of books and his own place: possessions, albeit reduced.

Holmes's Paul Hobbes, like Kerouac's Sal Paradise, like Kerouac himself, is a somewhat unwilling Beat, caught between desire for freedom and the need to have stable relationships, a pleasant apartment, a dependable home life. Hobbes's name, that of the author of *Leviathan,* indicates a man who cannot depend on dreams, who is rooted in actuality. He must will himself into freedom, since his attitudes tend toward order. He has been married for six years to Kathryn, an Italian, who wants a stable life, but who dabbles in the counterculture because of Paul. One of the catalysts here is Gene Pasternak (Kerouac); an even stronger catalyst is Hart Kennedy, a toned-down version of Neal Cassady, Kerouac's Dean Moriarty, the legendary centaur, half man, half car. *Go* and *On the Road* serve as palimpsests of each other. What one stresses, the other places in the distance, with characters moving in and out of each other's books. Holmes's recreation of Kerouac, Ginsberg, Cannastra, and others, however, is closer to fact. Many episodes are direct representations of what occurred: Cannastra's death, Ginsberg's brush with the law, Kerouac's experiences with his first novel.

But the chief contribution of *Go* is Holmes's attempt to define a movement that was still inchoate, really only a small number of urbanized countercultural individuals.

> They made none of the moral or political judgments that he [Hobbes] thought essential; they did not seem compelled to fit everything into the pigeon holes of a system. . . . They never read the papers, they did not follow with diligent and self conscious attention the happenings in the political and cultural arena; they seemed to have an almost calculated contempt for logical argument. They operated on feelings, sudden reactions, expanding these far out of perspective to see in them profundities which Hobbes was certain they could not define if put to it.

Their habitats were "a world of dingy backstairs 'pads,' Times Square cafeterias, bebop joints, night-long wanderings, meetings on street corners, hitchhiking, a myriad of 'hip' bars all over the city, and the streets themselves." Their activity is characterized by yo-yoing, "rushing around to 'make contact,'" suddenly disappearing into jail or on the road, only to turn up again to search one another out. Their medium of entertainment, except for booze, drugs, and sex, was jazz, a black mode. We see how this movement would feed into Mailer's essay on the White Negro.

The question for Hobbes is how much of this he can absorb, for he is a man torn by many different sensibilities. Besides his desire for stability and escape, there is still another side, which he expresses in letters to Liza, a sickly, hysterical young woman he has met at Columbia. For Hobbes, the correspondence is a form of mental masturbation; he sees himself as Dostoyevsky's underground man ("how brittle and will-less I have become," he begins), while she, namesake of the prostitute in the second part of the Russian's novella, is "a fascinating and sickly plant that thrived on the stifling atmosphere of argument over coffee."

The letters to Liza, many of them not sent or answered, provide Hobbes with what Kathryn cannot give him. In his letters, he speaks of suicidal impulses, of antilife. "Life is a perpetual defeat for us. . . . We have no eagerness, no ecstasy, only the likeness of this sense of defeat." This transformation of European existentialism into American angst and defeat is, of course, part of the Beat adaptation of ideas; but it serves as well as the other side of 1950s productivity, expansion, economic optimism. With all its weltschmerz, it is an effort to penetrate counterfeit feelings and derivative thought.

Doomed lovers, whether straight, homosexual, or bi, characterize Beat associations. The young women who attach themselves to the figure of Agatson (modeled on Cannastra) identify with his doom, his destructiveness, his nihilism, which does not have even the force of strong denial. It represents simply a blind force of nothing, which is less than nothingness. In predominantly male-authored Beat fiction, there is little in the way of male-female give-and-take. Women become pawns, preyed upon rather than satisfied, and they attach themselves out of some blind belief in the man. For novels that insist on choice, women curiously give up all choice and let men treat them like dirt. Often, the women do have a voice—Kathryn here, Diane in Mandel's novel—but this does not prevent them from being subservient to male domination.

More cerebral than Kerouac, Holmes was more likely to reveal Beat paradoxes, chiefly that ideas outstrip literary performance. The Beats attempted to confront the counterfeit decade head-on, and to offer a counterculture which would be anathema to every aspect of that troubled period. . . . Even more, for the imitative happiness the decade offered, the Beats sought out pain; their attempts at joy compulsive, doomed to failure. They moved toward Dostoyevsky's sense of exalted suffering, while others, out there, settled for cheap happiness, counterfeit feelings.

Holmes perceived that the ideas would need far greater literary powers than the Beats could provide. While the latter indeed moved to extremes of behavior, toward compulsive Dostoyevskian themes, the novels themselves could hardly structure such themes into literary achievement. Recognizing the inadequacy of any single work, Kerouac from 1951 to 1956-57 tried to compensate with volume. But a problem common to all Beat novels is lack of moral differentiation. Since a recurring point is that each person has a distinct and worthy voice, then all experience becomes equally viable, or acceptable. Stofsky, for example, has no criminal intentions and is terribly frightened, but he does not try to prevent the use of his apartment to store stolen goods. If the author justifies all personal judgments equally, no moral, ethical, or even legal tensions are possible.

Corollary problems develop as well, particularly in Holmes's handling of Agatson. Bill Cannastra, who served loosely as the model for Agatson, had interesting qualities which countered his sense of doom. Among other achievements, he had a law degree from Harvard and worked responsibly for Random House, on an encyclopedia. Agatson has only Cannastra's destructive energy, his compulsive drinking habits, his need to destroy all relationships and humiliate women. The problem here is inherent in nearly all Beat literature: associations and relationships based on characters who wobble between fact and fiction.

The commitment to ideas in Holmes and Kerouac suffers. Hobbes strains for some dimension to give his life meaning. Holmes creates the brief fling between Pasternak and Kathryn, what he calls in the Introduction the "only completely invented incident in the book." The affair creates inevitable tension and gives Holmes the chance to plumb guilt, redemption, forgiveness. But this three-way relationship is so lacking in dimensionality that Hobbes treats Pasternak as if he had stolen his marbles, not his wife. Among good friends, some sharing of the little woman will not upset male bonding. The very lack of possessiveness feeds into flattened dramatic content; and the author's efforts to create tension are invalidated by his very premises. If everyone shares, then nothing is of value. (pp. 198-200)

Frederick R. Karl, "The Counterfeit Decade," in his American Fictions, 1940/1980: A Comprehensive History and Critical Evaluation, *Harper & Row, Publishers, 1983, pp. 176-253.*

ARTHUR WINFIELD KNIGHT

Gone in October consists of four essays, each previously published, and a poem, and they all deal with John Clellon

Holmes' relationship with Jack Kerouac. While the pieces examine Kerouac's psyche, they also examine what it means to be a writer in our time and the social forces that turn sensitive men to drink; but Holmes' book provides no easy answers, and he reveres life too much to turn away from it.

In the title essay ["**Gone in October**"] Holmes says Kerouac told him, " 'How glum life is without the booze' . . . raising his glass mockingly, able to say it right out . . . knowing I would understand just what it was made men like us feel glum—our disappointed expectations, and the novelist's necessity to accept into his work the irreconcilables that his own personal hopes struggle to deny." Partially because Holmes is "a boozer of sorts" he can understand what Jack meant, but their ties are more subtle than that.

Kerouac and Holmes almost felt like they were brothers because they shared the same birthday and they were both born in Massachusetts; also, both were "dogged by a dark sense of foreignness." But while Holmes was able to move to the country and adapt to the life there, Kerouac "never made it, and remained psychologically displaced and physically uprooted until it killed him."

Holmes speculates that he and Kerouac were "subtly different than Ginsberg or Burroughs or Corso" because John and Jack "wore a sense of the past like a birthmark" and guilt gave them "a fatal premonitory sense." Their New England heritage, which helped to shape them, is sensitively explored in **"Rocks in Our Beds,"** an essay that gives Holmes' claim that they were "Transcendentalists with hangovers" a lot of substance. Much of the essay borders on being mystical and Holmes, like Hamlet, might ask if "there is providence in the fall of a sparrow." But all of the essays in *Gone in October* are infused with metaphysical speculation.

The essays are also infused with an "autumnal" quality—it is a word Holmes uses often—and from the first page, in the poem **"Going West Alone,"** there is the sense that both men are old before their time; the "oldness" in Kerouac "burdens" Holmes because it seems to be "an omen of our common end." In **"The Great Rememberer,"** which was written four years before Kerouac died at the age of 47, Holmes says that, "in a special corner" of his mind Kerouac "always appears as an old vagabond going West alone," and Holmes felt "with a shiver, that Kerouac would not live much beyond forty." . . .

[The] four essays in *Gone in October,* along with Holmes' sensitive memoir, *Visitor: Jack Kerouac in Old Saybrook,* give us the "feel" of a man in a way none of the biographers have been able to. Holmes captures Jack's exuberance, his despair, and his lonesomeness as he tried to discover (and define) America, reconciling the contradictions in the land; but, most of all, Holmes shows us there can be something redemptive in a man's sorrow, in the tragedy of his life, and we come away from the book knowing more about what Holmes calls our "common humanity" and about the way the human heart works.

Arthur Winfield Knight, "Psychic Ground," in The Small Press Review, *Vol. 17, No. 8, August, 1985, p. 1.*

ROBERT J. CAMPBELL AND DAVID ROGERS

Gone In October: Last Reflections on Jack Kerouac affords

a particularly timely gathering of four previously published essays, all of which poignantly enhance our understanding of Kerouac, his work, and its place in the American literary tradition. . . .

Holmes shared for twenty-one years what he calls a "feverish" friendship with Kerouac that began with a party "on the second night of the July 4th weekend, 1948," when Kerouac was writing *The Town and the City*. This friendship deepened and matured during Kerouac's years of greatest achievement and public notoriety, and survived his long slide into hopeless alcoholism and premature death in 1969. The underlying strength of all of these pieces is that, although he treats his contemporary with the warmth and sensitivity that we might expect from such a friendship, Holmes neither lapses into unmerited aggrandizement nor permits his affection and admiration to circumvent his honest, clear-eyed assessment of Kerouac's flaws. Aided by his personal relationship and his first-hand acquaintance with Kerouac's manuscripts and work journals, Holmes critiques the media-myths and popular misconceptions that have obscured and trivialized Kerouac, who remains "as unique, primal and obscure as Niagara Falls, which has been looked at so long it can no longer be seen," and that have diverted attention from what should be our essential concern: the complex originality of Kerouac's style and vision.

In an effort to correct such myopia, Holmes explores the paradoxical, ultimately irreconcilable compulsions that dominated Kerouac's personality and fictional voice. Deeply traditional and conservative by nature and obsessed with a longing to find a home and settle down, Kerouac nonetheless was driven contradictorily by a kind of geographical and psychological uprootedness. In the opening essay, **"Rocks in Our Beds,"** Holmes argues that this divided nature was, at least in part, an inheritance of Kerouac's New England birth. Born, like Kerouac, in Massachusetts, Holmes contends that New England engendered in both of them, as it always has in its writers, the "curse" of a paradoxical sensibility or "double view." Writers such as Emerson, Hawthorne, Thoreau, Melville (the American writer to whom Holmes perceptively finds Kerouac closest in temperament), Dickinson, Frost, Olson, Creeley, and Wieners all inherited an outlook that "sees the human being as the fragile circuit between heaven and earth, life as a limbo state, and literature as a record of a passage-through—the continual dissolution of forms into other forms, the clearing of a field." Such a sensibility, writes Holmes, can never be satisfied with only the hard "fact," for in New England, "speculation is no further away than the woodpile, spiritual bliss comes to the swinger of birches."

Unlike many critics who have dismissed Kerouac, Creeley, and even Holmes himself as mere adolescent hipsters out for kicks ("Jazz, dope, and psychic anarchy"), Holmes aligns the group with the central American literary tradition, characterizing them as "transcendentalists with hangovers," "religious men without a creed" who were struggling to reconcile "the phantom vision" inherent in their New England psyche with the "factual reality" of the "New Yorks, Mexico Cities, Friscos, and Londons of the morally ambivalent world beyond." "We had moral rocks in our beds," Holmes writes, and he finds the group's literary endeavors motivated by a need "to write away the psychological bruises of nights spent in those rocky beds."

"The Great Rememberer," the collection's second essay and the only one written prior to Kerouac's death, was the first essay of its time to direct attention away from the controversial cultural figure and media cult hero that Kerouac had become and to focus it instead on the writing itself. Holmes repudiates Kerouac's know-nothing Bohemian image, noting, among other observations, that "a carefree do-nothing sensation-hunter" could not possibly have had the discipline necessary to write eighteen books: "a larger body of work than any of his contemporaries" and a canon embodying "a dense, personal world that is as richly detailed as any such American literary world since Faulkner's." As in the opening essay, Holmes emphasizes the moral and speculative restlessness underlying Kerouac and his attempts to connect the circuit between hard "facts" and the "phantom vision." He depicts Kerouac not as an undisciplined wordslinger who wrote (or typed) whatever came into his head in whatever order it arrived, but as a craftsman of words who labored prodigiously for years to find his own voice and to evolve a style capable of accommodating the "facts" and the "vision." Kerouac was, in fact, his own most demanding critic, as Holmes acknowledges. . . . Holmes also notes that Kerouac rejected the accepted formal and structural conventions (what Kerouac called "phoney architectures") then governing the novel in an effort to make consciousness itself the subject and protagonist of his prose. In so doing, Kerouac positioned himself squarely in the American literary tradition that Emerson and Whitman had prescribed. The first critic astute enough to perceive this innovation in Kerouac's prose, Holmes recognizes that Kerouac's work is "not so much concerned with events as it is with consciousness, in which the *ultimate* events are images." He quotes Kerouac's remark to the effect that he was trying to capture "the way the consciousness *really* digs everything that happens."

The lengthy title piece ["**Gone in October**"], derived mostly from his own personal journals, is Holmes's attempt to arrive at some personal reckoning and larger understanding of Kerouac's life and work in the context of Kerouac's death and funeral (the very task Kerouac had set for himself in his novels, as well). Alternately bitter, satirical, loving, world-weary, and meditative in tone, *Gone in October* weaves among and around Kerouac's family, relatives, and friends, and the media hounds and counterculture youth all brought together by the occasion of Kerouac's death and set against the backdrop of Lowell, Massachusetts, the decaying blue-collar milltown of Kerouac's birth.

[*Gone in October*] reconfirms a belief that many people have long held—that John Clellon Holmes is one of our most astute social commentators and adroit men of letters. The honest and gentle devotion that he gives to his understanding of himself, his generation, and Jack Kerouac demonstrates the wisdom and consciousness that American literature and criticism can infuse into a world to which the "only sane collective response" may well be, as he writes, "despair." Yet Holmes refuses to give in to any final despair or to opt for an equally easy and more fashionable cynicism. On the contrary, these recollections are characterized by an unillusioned optimism and sympathetic intelligence that make Holmes's continued reemergence a pleasure for us all.

Robert J. Campbell and David Rogers, "Rocks in Our Beds," in The American Book Review, *Vol. 9, No. 1, January-February, 1987, p. 15.*

SCOTT PRESTON

Holmes's greatest accomplishment came in his creative non-fiction. In his adaptation of spontaneous beat prose techniques, weaving immediate, almost random nativistic imagery into sudden profound insights, Holmes now appears to have been a most intuitive pioneer of the so-called New Journalism as more popularly exemplified by Tom Wolfe or Hunter Thompson.

It's interesting to hold the poems [in *Dire Coasts*] up against the essays in that light. Aside from the poems of personal, semi-confessional-mode insight, the majority of Holmes's poetry . . . consists of thumbnail sketches of various figures, mostly literary, mostly underground or at least alternative-cultured: Genet, Henry Miller, Malcolm Lowry, Billie Holiday, and, somewhat predictably, Rimbaud.

Holmes was considerably less successful than, for instance, Delmore Schwartz in incorporating other writers and artists into his work as compatriotly inspired touchstones. It is in the centerpiece poem of *Dire Coasts,* however, that Holmes finally and heroically merged his fraternal obsessions with pulsing language to create one of the saddest—and most compelling—literary self-assessments in the Beat canon or any other.

"Ode to Duplicitous Men," written, according to the note preceding it, after reading Ehrenburg's *People, Years, Life,* creates a most claustrophobic sense of survival-of-the-practical, of talented men squandering their abilities in the pure game of staying alive. But by the time the end is reached . . . it becomes devastatingly apparent that the real, secret master of duplicity was none other than Holmes himself, a decent, talented writer who by a quirk of time and place found himself associated with a literary movement his admitted "analytic Yankee cerebralness" was never wholly a part of.

Dire Coasts finally achieves a sense of inevitable, historical tragedy. Holmes's poetic line never managed to match the almost unconscious high-intensity wordstreams of Ginsberg or Gregory Corso, try as he might. This last book contains the work that came closest, up against the final edge of things in this life. In doing so, the inner themes of the best half dozen pieces take on an undeniably transcendent, sorrowful glow.

Consider the poems here against the suggestion of Holmes's "duplicity." **"The Old Saybrook House,"** an elegy for the home Holmes put years of handiwork into, only to be reduced to commuting to it for the summer after school in Arkansas was out, heightens itself against the subtext of his career—this was, after all, the house Holmes bought with the paperback advance from *Go,* an edition that never appeared, of a book whose early success was never approached again in his life as a writer.

> A home is where you have the chance
> of dying where you chose to live.

Or again, in the poem **"Skinning a Deer,"** for Gary Snyder, the recognition of the inextricable interrelatedness of being—surely a central preoccupation in the writing of all the great Beat figures—comes only in the presence of death, of a stripped animal carcass hanging in a hunter's garage.

It's difficult to say if this book will stand as Holmes's last great statement, although it's certain to be close. (pp. 12, 14)

Scott Preston, "Analytic Yankee Cerebralness," in The American Book Review, *Vol. 11, No. 1, March-April, 1989, pp. 12, 14.*

Israel Horovitz

1939-

American dramatist, scriptwriter, director, novelist, and poet.

A popular and prolific off-Broadway dramatist, Horovitz typically combines absurd humor with social commentary to expose moral ills in contemporary life. In his plays, Horovitz often utilizes physical and psychic violence to illustrate his view of society as a brutal game of survival. Influenced by Samuel Beckett and Eugène Ionesco, Horovitz employs extended metaphors, deft comic timing, realistic dialogue, and imaginative theatrical conceits to explore urban alienation, the impossibility of true communication, and the destructive forces of modern pressures. Ross Wetzsteon observed: "Over and over, [Horovitz's] plays brilliantly unite metaphor and meaning—content conveyed through stage imagery rather than through plot or dialogue—and in that sense he's one of the *purest* playwrights now writing."

Horovitz's first play, *The Comeback* (1958), was produced in Boston while he was a freshman at Harvard University; several early works were subsequently produced in New Jersey. In 1963 he earned the equivalent of a master of arts degree at London's Royal Academy of Dramatic Art, and two years later he became the first American playwright-in-residence at the Royal Shakespeare Company. Horovitz rose to prominence with several one-act plays in 1967 and 1968. His first successful production, *Line* (1967), is an allegory of the American ethos of success at any cost. This play depicts five undistinguished characters who use force and deceit to gain first position in a queue leading nowhere. Horovitz implies that the will to be first is inherent in the American psyche and that morality is secondary to success. In his next drama, *The Indian Wants the Bronx* (1968), which won an Obie for best American play, Horovitz utilizes humor and terror to explore the nature of random violence through a confrontation on a New York street between two young thugs and an Indian who speaks little English. Horovitz links the arbitrariness of the attack with the delinquents' inability to understand either their own emotions or those of others. *It's Called the Sugar Plum* (1968), a companion piece to *The Indian Wants the Bronx,* satirizes the anesthetized emotions of contemporary young people by focusing on a romance that develops after a college student accidentally kills a female classmate's fiancé. Both characters care more about the fame they hope to attain from the incident than they do about the death of a human being.

Several of Horovitz's subsequent plays further explore themes of social interaction and commitment. *Rats* (1968), for example, one of eleven short plays contained in the collection *Collision Course,* metaphorically explores the hopelessness of slum life in Harlem by depicting the devouring of a black infant by two rats. *Chiaroscuro* (1968; later produced as *Morning* in *Morning, Noon, and Night* by Horovitz, Terrence McNally, and Leonard Melfi) examines the conflicts and ironies that arise when a black family becomes white after taking pills that were dropped to earth by God. In *The Honest-to-God Schnozzola* (1969), Horovitz explores American moral depravity by portraying two businessmen intent on

hedonistic experiences while vacationing in Germany. *Leader* (1969) is an expressionistic parable about an American autocracy engineered by the media through mass hypnosis. The theme of noncommunication reappears in *The Primary English Class* (1976), a farce revolving around the incompetent efforts of a neurotic woman to teach English to five foreign students, all of whom speak different languages.

In his later work, Horovitz generally abandons realistic social plays in favor of introspective studies of character and mental confusion. This change is most evident in *The Wakefield Plays* (1979), seven interconnected dramas set in Horovitz's hometown of Wakefield, Massachusetts. Considered by some critics as Horovitz's masterpiece, *The Wakefield Plays* include *The Alfred Trilogy* and *The Quannapowitt Quartet.* In *The Alfred Trilogy,* Horovitz indicts a culture that places more value on material wealth than on ethics. The three Alfred plays—*Alfred the Great* (1972), *Our Father's Failing* (1973), and *Alfred Dies* (1977)—document the return of a famous millionaire with a faulty memory to his "cursed" hometown and his obsessive search for truth about crimes committed against his family. During his investigation, however, Alfred discovers that he and his family are guilty of adultery, incest, and homicide. In a fraudulent trial, Alfred's wife Emily blames him for her four stillbirths because he knew that she was his sister and purposely committed incest with her. Alfred, Emily, and their mother eventually take their own lives. The four one-act plays of *The Quannapowitt Quartet* (1976)—*Hopscotch, The 75th, Stage Directions,* and *Spared*—share thematic affinities with *The Alfred Trilogy. Hopscotch* focuses on the attempts of two former high school lovers who are also cousins to reconstruct their lives while playing a game of hopscotch. In *The 75th,* two nonagenarians humorously but unsuccessfully try to recall common experiences as the only surviving members at their seventy-fifth-year high school class reunion. *Stage Directions* portrays the responses of three children at their parents' funeral through recitation of stage directions by the characters. *Spared* consists primarily of a monologue by a resurrected and elderly Alfred in which he details his unfulfilling life by weaving past and present, memory and illusion.

In his plays of the 1980s, Horovitz has continued to explore many of his characteristic themes. *The Good Parts* (1982) is a comedy involving two long-time friends who leave their families and travel to Greece in order to reconcile mid-life crises. One character attempts this by reenacting his high school role of Electra at the Acropolis but realizes that he had been miscast and should have played Orestes. In *A Rosen by Any Other Name* (1986), set in Canada in 1943, Horovitz draws on childhood experiences to depict a Jewish boy preparing for his bar mitzvah amid air-raid drills, rumors of nazi evils, and threats of invasion. *North Shore Fish* (1987) is a realistic study of mistreated workers at a dilapidated frozen fish processing plant in Massachusetts.

In addition to dramas, Horovitz has written numerous television plays and screenplays, including *The Strawberry Statement* (1970), for which he won the Cannes Film Festival Prix du Jury, and *Author! Author!* (1982). Horovitz has also published the novels *Cappella* (1973), which he later adapted for the stage, and *Nobody Loves Me* (1975), as well as *Spider Poems and Other Writings* (1973).

(See also *Contemporary Authors,* Vols. 33-36, rev. ed. and *Dictionary of Literary Biography,* Vol. 7.)

DAN SULLIVAN

It's Called the Sugar Plum is a comedy with overtones of pity. *The Indian Wants the Bronx* starts like a comedy, but ends in terror. The variety in tone over the evening suggests that Mr. Horovitz has capacities for several kinds of plays.

He has been a playwright-in-residence with the Royal Shakespeare Company, our program tells us, and the first play can be taken as an ironic contemporary parody of the scene in *Richard III* where the hunchback king successfully woos Anne over the coffin of her husband.

But the world has grown considerably less heroic since Shakespeare's day. So here, a slightly eccentric Harvard student manages to seduce a not-too-bright coed after accidentally running over her skate-boarding fiancé.

It is a funny premise, just "sick" enough to be piquant, and Mr. Horovitz develops it skillfully. Both characters, true children of the age of publicity, are quite interested in the respective size of their pictures in newspaper accounts of the acci-

dent; indeed, the climax of the play involves a hat that the boy makes out of a newspaper. . . .

What keeps the play from complete success is the familiarity of the types. The boy is Holden Caulfield at Harvard; the girl, with her inane chatter about "commitment" and how terribly "basic" his part-time job is (delivering meat), is Elaine May at Radcliffe. . . .

It is the very pointlessness of their brutality that makes [*The Indian Wants the Bronx*]—with its awful final image of the Indian jabbering into a dead phone—so disturbing. We are convinced that this is exactly what would happen at this particular bus stop on this particular night; we see, again, that violence in the big city is as much a child of ennui as of anger.

But a reservation occurs. Didn't we know all this before? Has Mr. Horovitz really done more here than to drag a street fight into the theater? Would we care to see two teen-age punks torturing a cat on stage? Is it any more edifying to watch them torture an Indian?

I tend to think that the answer to the last question is "No." Yet the theatrical power of *The Indian Wants the Bronx,* the abstract beauty, if you will, of the violence, cannot be denied. That is another reason the play is disturbing.

> Dan Sullivan, "Two One-Acters," in The New York Times, *January 18, 1968, p. 47.*

MARTIN GOTTFRIED

Israel Horovitz is a playwright of unmistakable talent and the possessor of two of the most necessary qualities for stage writing—word sense and dramatic flair. These qualities have been present in the works of his that I have seen before and they are present in [*The Indian Wants the Bronx* and *It's Called the Sugar Plum*]. . . . But they are not the only qualities necessary to the stage and Mr. Horovitz still lacks the ability to create characters and situations. His people remain only types and their situations, once created, do not develop. As a result, his plays are at once too short and too long.

The Indian Wants The Bronx begins with a very strong stage situation. Waiting for a bus on a chilly, lonely, uptown Manhattan corner are two rough youngsters and a formal, turban'd Indian. The boys mess around for awhile and then, restless for action, they begin to tease the Indian. Soon their teasing turns ugly, growing from torment to sadism to murder. At each level, the intensity of the stage action increases, the Indian's innocence and torture heightened by his inability to speak English. The conclusion is frightening and pointed, as good a climax as any play might want.

But it is en route to that conclusion that Mr. Horovitz' weaknesses hurt his play. We are given two very familiar boys— the kind of boys that I have seen every day of my life in New York but never on a stage. Their good humor is superficial, their stupidity patent, their cruelty likely. They are the sort of boys much easier to sympathize with in theory than in observation and I think it both intelligent and original for Horovitz to have put them on a stage. But once having put them there, what has he done with them? Murph is the leader of the two, instinctively capitalizing on his friend Joey's inclination to sudden, unthinking, neurotic violence. He is humorous in the crude, one-tracked, obscene style familiar enough to anybody who can read scribblings on subway walls. . . . His dialogue is perfectly grasped by Horovitz, but if there is any explanation of his behavior none is in the play, and while I expect that Horovitz thinks there is no more to Murph than this (something with which I agree) how can we possibly be interested in him for very long? As for Joey, he is even less developed and in any case, why establish him as psychotically violent and then have Murph actually do the dirty work?

These questions suggest a playwright more involved with situation than with explanation and though explanations are not as important as situations, the stage demands something when the play is realistic. The contrast of a dignified, helpless Indian and two vulgar kids is striking but in the end it is only being used.

It's Called The Sugar Plum, which opened the evening, has the same faults. A Harvard boy has killed a fellow student in a car accident and now he is confronted by the victim's girl friend. She condemns him for murder only to reveal herself as being more concerned with her own role than with any kind of real tragedy. The boy is just as self-centered and the play proceeds to build type-humor (arty girl, almost-intellectual boy) upon this egocentricity, leaving the true tragedy of the dead boy quietly and effectively unspoken. But for all the humor and all the point, again nobody is developed and again there is repetition and padding.

> *Martin Gottfried, in a review of "The Indian Wants the Bronx," in* Women's Wear Daily, *January 18, 1968.*

EDITH OLIVER

[*The Indian Wants the Bronx*] is the over-all title of a pair of grisly one-act comedies by Israel Horovitz. . . . It is also the title of the second play, about an Indian named Gupta, in a white turban and Eastern dress, who speaks and understands no English. On his first day in New York, he has become separated from his son, Prem, whose name he carries on a card, and he is waiting alone, late at night, at a deserted bus stop. Behind him is an empty public phone booth. In the course of the action, he is picked on and teased and injured and tormented, in Pinteresque fashion, by a couple of young delinquents who happen by. The Indian is in an even worse situation than the old man in *The Caretaker,* since he doesn't understand a word of the verbal spate he is subjected to. The play combines jokey speech with savage action, and it evokes considerable uneasy, nervous laughter. Mr. Horovitz is a natural dramatist with a keen ear for regional talk—in this case, for cheap New York talk. (One of the boys goes into the phone booth to get the number of the Indian's son from Information: "How many Indians *in* the Bronx? *Two* Indians named Gupta? Is the both of them named Prem?") There are a few instances in which the lines seem too sharp or too bright for the speakers, but a more serious lapse is the introduction of casebook details about the background of the boys—details that, by their explicitness, break the nightmare spell and would far better be left to the imagination of the audience. (pp. 86-7)

It's Called the Sugar Plum, which opens the evening, is a satire about a pair of deadhearted children, aged about twenty-two. The setting is the room of a student in Cambridge, Massachusetts, who on the previous evening has run over and killed a young man riding a skate board. At the opening, we

see him pasting some newspaper clippings into a scrapbook, humming as he works, and the first we hear of the accident is in a report over his transistor radio, to which he listens with pleased attention. There is a knock at the door, and the fiancée of the dead man enters, in tears of accusation. She is a drama major and an art minor (or vice versa); his major is lit. Soon the air is thick with "total commitment," "symbolic," "empathy," and other passwords of the New Breed in the throes of enlightenment. Before they end up in each other's arms and his bed, they quarrel over the amount of space granted to each of them in the reports of the accident in the press. His outrage during the quarrel is the only emotion, other than embarrassment, that he shows from start to finish. Crocodile sobs are no problem for her. . . . *Sugar Plum* is, I think, the more original of the two plays—funny while it is going on but ultimately no less chilling than *The Indian.* Both plays are frightening, and the aimlessness of the utterly believable characters—their aimless cruelty and their aimless, solemn fatuity—is the most frightening thing about them. (p. 87)

> *Edith Oliver, "The Second Coming of 'Twelfth Night'," in* The New Yorker, *Vol. XLIII, No. 49, January 27, 1968, pp. 86-7.*

WALTER KERR

[*The Indian Wants the Bronx*] devotes itself almost exclusively to the idle, playful, improvised malice that begins with two buddies mauling each other casually and ends with their concerted physical attack, savage and utterly purposeless, on a stranger who is merely waiting for a bus. Mr. Horovitz's quiet nightmare depends upon a rage that rises randomly, indifferently, out of the often grinning twists and turns that minds make when they are going nowhere in particular. There is no logical pattern to follow; we must slip inside illogic to hear hate's heartbeat. . . . Each line of dialogue is a pebble skipped skillfully across the water's surface, its particular curve attended to; that a last well-aimed stone might kill is perfectly reasonable.

> *Walter Kerr, in a review of "The Indian Wants the Bronx," in* The New York Times, *June 30, 1968, p. 11.*

CLIVE BARNES

[In *Morning*], Mr. Horovitz, who persuasively believes that God is black, postulates also a God who let loose six little pills on the world, each pill potent enough to turn a black man white. Updike of Harlem, together with his wife, son and daughter, take the pill, and wake up to find themselves white. They are not unhappy about this, for while believing that black is beautiful, they have also noticed that white is better-paid.

Into this newly white-washed family comes Tillich. Tillich has a gun in his hand and revenge in his heart. He is a white sub-sub-intellectual (chiefly sub) whose unmarried daughter (just as well she is unmarried as she is only 14) has been impregnated—my word, not Mr. Horovitz's, for he is altogether much earthier on these matters—by Updike's now instant-whited son.

The outcome of this encounter is not altogether satisfactory, for Mr. Horovitz cannot quite resolve the bitter humor of blacks suddenly becoming whites, with all the wryly unjust opportunities such a transformation offers, and the more serious theme hinted at of black being beautiful in terms of black rather than in terms of pretend white. Yet it is a great attempt, and the writing is disturbingly funny, not least while using four-letter words to fantasticated comic effect.

Clive Barnes, in a review of "Morning, Noon and Night," in The New York Times, *November 29, 1968.*

BRENDAN GILL

[*Morning*] is based on a gimmick that [Mr. Horovitz] has not even troubled to make a neat one. A black family in Harlem have come into possession of some pills that God has carelessly let slip and that have the power to turn them white. (It is characteristic of Mr. Horovitz's kind of self-indulgence that he tries to get a laugh out of the stale jape that God is Himself black.) The family swallow the pills and begin a new life, safe for the first time inside their whiteness. We are expected to find it hilarious that, continuing to speak the cretinous scatological jargon of their immediate past, they succeed in totally befuddling a white man who, gun in hand, has come to avenge the rape of his fourteen-year-old daughter by the son of the family. Whitey breaks down and confesses that he was once black and was lucky enough to take a certain pill; for reasons that are not of the clearest, he thereupon strips and the family start daubing his naked flesh with black paint. In seeking to squeeze the last drop of supposed good theatre out of his not very clever gimmick, the author has chosen to turn his whitened blacks into stereotypes that would suit the fancy of the most brazen Southern racist. It may be that Mr. Horovitz sees this peculiar choice as the cream of the jest; if so, it is sour cream indeed. (pp. 139-40)

Brendan Gill, "Triumph and Disaster," in The New Yorker, *Vol. XLIV, No. 42, December 7, 1968, pp. 139-40.*

CLIVE BARNES

The double bill, *The Honest-to-God Schnozzola* and *Leader,* offers two jaundiced views of the present American condition. *Schnozzola* is concerned with the American character, while *Leader* suggests where that character might lead us.

Schnozzola is set in a dark and seedy Hamburg bar. Two visiting American businessmen—a young wise guy and a middle-aged innocent—arrive to paint the town bleary. . . .

Mr. Horovitz can simulate a hollow jollity and contrive to make it rather jolly. . . . The two men, the younger trying to play a cruel practical joke on his companion, are well-observed cartoon figures, probably taken as much from legend as from life yet nonetheless convincing for all that.

At first you imagine—at least I imagined, for I should'nt put stray thoughts in your head—that Horovitz is going along the old Brecht-Weill-Grosz route, and wonder vaguely where he is leading. The technique is neat enough. The characters grabbing microphones, as if in a nightclub act; the little midget asking questions of the audience (such as "Do you love your wife?"), and the younger man, Jimmy, occasionally lapsing into an unconvincing (yet therefore dramatically con-

vincing—if you will pardon the twist) imitation of Jimmy Durante, all this has style.

But what is happening? Then suddenly, like the blade of a well-oiled guillotine, the play clicks sickeningly into place. It would be wrong to say what occurs (itself a serious limitation of Mr. Horovitz's form) but afterward, when the play is dissolving itself in the embracing acids of the mind, there does appear to have been some kind of dramatic purpose and fulfillment, even a contrasted vision of reality and image.

The second play is an expressionist parable, I suppose, of the dictatorship—beyond the mere Presidency—that might arise with the wholesale seduction of American minds and consciences by mass media. . . .

Here again there is a certain theatricality, a certain show-biz pizzazz, but the idea is painfully ordinary and really sophomoric in that it does not lend itself to any dramatic extension outside of its initial statement. And the statement itself is obvious to the point of propaganda.

Clive Barnes, in a review of "The Honest-to-God Schnozzola" and "Leader," in The New York Times, *April 22, 1969, p. 40.*

EDITH OLIVER

The Honest-to-God Schnozzola, the first of two one-acters by Israel Horovitz . . . , and the one that gave the evening its title, was more properly *Honest-to-God Cabaret,* but with a change in point of view; this time, the contempt has shifted from depraved Germans to even more depraved Americans. The play . . . told of the events that befall two American television men, Jimmy and Johnny, a couple of good-time Charlies at loose in a bar-*cum*-brothel in Germany. Johnny, we learn, has raped and almost killed the wife of a German friend of theirs, and Jimmy pays him back at the brothel with as dirty a trick as can be imagined. They are a detestable pair, all right, and they are clichés—rancid Babbitts abroad. As a matter of fact, all the characters are awful, and everybody involved deserves everybody else. . . . For all my reservations, I found the play consistently interesting. If any man has earned the right to go his own way, it is Mr. Horovitz, but I do wish he would change his course. As he has already proved in *It's Called the Sugar Plum* . . . , he can delineate a character with a flick of a line or a piece of business, he can write dialogue that is dramatic and rings true, and he can explore an atmosphere or state of mind. I wish he would leave studies of corruption, evil, Fascism, mindlessness, and other abstract nouns to the lesser talents among us. . . . (pp. 108-09)

Leader, which closed the evening, was one of those Expressionist jobs, with everyone doing everything in unison, that unfailingly give me the pip. It was about a dictator—an automaton with only one line, "It isn't important," which he repeated at intervals—and his followers, who wanted to be rewarded for putting him in office and finally ganged up on him. (p. 109)

Edith Oliver, "Soft-Edge Pirandello," in The New Yorker, *Vol. XLV, No. 11, May 3, 1969, pp. 107-09.*

MARTIN GOTTFRIED

Line is a just slightly rough work, and if it were polished only the slightest bit more it would probably be an unqualified success. It runs an hour, is nearly always interesting, is frequently funny, always intelligent, and if its point were not so explicitly explored might be intellectually meaningful. The play is set on "a line," referring to both a line of people and the line behind which they are standing. We are never told what the line literally is for, nor does it make a difference. It could be for anything—people do wait on them. Metaphorically, it represents the accumulation of people hoping to outdo each other at whatever it is they want.

Mr. Horovitz created five distinct people to be waiting on his symbolic line, and just being able to create them proves his talent. What is theater if not a playwright's being able to conceive real, special, individual people? Not many playwrights can do it. Horovitz's people include a first-on-liner—the man who waits overnight and inevitably loses position anyhow. This man, a big, dumb beer drinker is immediately tricked out of first place by a young, psychotic composer who turns out to be the play's and the situation's moving force. Another person joining the line has a simpler, more mundane set of tactics. He believes in sticking with second place and being under the belly of the champion, where he can eventually kick him and get on top himself. The final two people on line are a married couple, the woman coarsely sexual and her husband a born loser. He is long since accustomed to being in last place, and her life is the story of a woman using sex to get ahead only to find that she is being used herself. The men just turn over and toss her out, and, in fact, all the men on line do.

The play, then, follows the metaphorical position-changing, almost everybody having a chance to be in front and then being tricked out of it, while the young man is spending what he hopes is the last day of his life, hoping to achieve first place as a composer by outstripping Mozart (who is in first musical place) in dying at an earlier age—that is, at younger than thirty-five.

It is a quite well-written play, although, as I said, not without flaws that make it slow going from time to time. (pp. 322-23)

> *Martin Gottfried, "Off-Off Broadway," in his* Opening Nights: Theater Criticism of the Sixties, *G. P. Putnam's Sons, 1969, pp. 313-28.*

CLIVE BARNES

Mr. Horovitz's purpose [in *Line*] is clear enough. He wants to tell us that the rat race is absurd, that our competitiveness only feeds our own need for competition, that we are our own judges of those plastic battles with which we litter our lives. He also wants us to know that Mozart died young, that youth does not endure, that sex is frequently a tangible object that can be passed around, that violence requires a victim and that suckers, by definition, can never be given an even break.

Mr. Horovitz believes in the theater of magic, and he is right. Here he takes a bare stage and fills it with five people and an allegory. He would have done better with, say, four people and a myth. There is too much logic here. The meaning beneath the words, the internal story, is far too obvious, so that we feel, eventually, a little cheated.

There are no real images here, only parallels. The line itself, with its crazy changes of fortune encompassed by accident and mayhem, is a very obvious and nonpoetic parallel for life

itself. The sexual availability of the girl finds symbolic expression in her dancing with each of the men. All the time Mr. Horovitz is explaining the ordinary in terms that overachieve the significance of the explanation. The insights are not worth the paraphernalia presenting them.

But Mr. Horovitz does have a rich and gorgeous theatrical sense. He can write true and dazzling dialogue, even when the dialogue has little to be true and dazzling about. Also he can create people—real breathing, living people.

We are told nothing about the man first on line. He is there, and shows himself to us with a word here and a word there. And yet at the end of this very short play we know him. We know his strange sense of fair play, his thwarted, regretted and abjured ambitions, even his middle-American culture. Mr. Horovitz tells us nothing of him in a particularly direct way, he just hints and nudges.

Mr. Horovitz also has that sense of heightened realistic speech that every good playwright must possess—the ear for the uncommon platitude, the gift for encapsulating a life-style in a foolish phrase, and that special creative wit that allows a character to say something witty that will not be witty in the internal context of the person but only, for the audience, in the external context of the play. Mr. Horovitz is a very technical playwright and he has a very fine technique. But here he is searching for something more immediate and arresting to write about.

> *Clive Barnes, in a review of "Line," in* The New York Times, *February 16, 1971, p. 26.*

EDITH OLIVER

"*Acrobats* and *Line*" is a first effort to produce works in the genre of post-Beckett New Comedy, a new form rooted in ancient tragedy tradition that redefines conventional comic rules." So runs a program note for this pair of one-acters by Israel Horovitz. . . . It is important, first of all, to reassure lovers of humor (and admirers of Mr. Horovitz) that the plays also have many attributes of *pre*-Beckett comedy— original ideas and situations, funny lines and . . . funny business to go with them, and odd, believable characters. Those who saw *The Indian Wants the Bronx* and that small masterpiece *It's Called the Sugar Plum* need hardly be reminded of Mr. Horovitz's extraordinary ability to create a group of people and to conjure up, by the words they speak and by the rhythm of those words, the atmosphere of the special segment of society that they represent, or of his ability to turn cruelty, heartlessness, and even suffering into the components of his comedy, as they are of Beckett's. *Line,* by far the more substantial of the plays, is a set of variations on the theme of people scrambling for position in a line that apparently goes nowhere (post-Beckett). It is these particular lunatic variations, plus, of course, these particular people, that give the play its backbone, tone, and color. They are small-time losers, and so much a part of this city that it took me quite a long while to realize that they were not waiting for seats in the bleachers of Yankee Stadium or Shea. At the beginning, only one man is standing on the stage—a large, dumb, burly soul with a denim duffelbag beside him. . . . He has been waiting all night, but once the action starts he loses his place in line and never gets it back. He is joined by three other men and a woman, one at a time. They are a rather crazy fellow and deadpan needler with a handy repertoire of Gems from Mozart, which he sings to the words on the credit cards in his wallet; a quiet, determined, tough man who gives the false impression of being more spectator than contestant for a spot at the head of the line; a wanton, whorish, pretty woman, as callous as anyone around, who goes off with each of the men in turn for strategic line-jumping purposes as well as sexual ones; and her straight, defeated, much older husband, in a business suit and a white shirt and a tie. The action, needless to say, is capricious, sometimes violent, and full of small jokes, and during its course we learn quite a lot about everyone concerned. The husband is almost impotent, and the wife, dis- and unsatisfied, has turned savage with frustration. His fumbling efforts to maintain a kind of offhand composure while in the throes of triple cuckoldry are sad and comical. (pp. 82-4)

Acrobats is a brief curtain-raiser—a variation, come to think of it, on Noël Coward's *Red Peppers.* An acrobatic team— husband and wife—are performing their act, and all their rage and their hatred of each other boil to the surface during its dangerous twists and turns and then completely evaporate once the act is over and the tension has dissipated. (p. 84)

> Edith Oliver, "Queue," in The New Yorker, Vol. XLVII, No. 2, February 27, 1971, pp. 82-5.

THE ANTIOCH REVIEW

[*Cappella*] is a moving examination of the writer's awkward self-distancing from "real life," articulated through separate, mutually uncomprehending monologues. Byron, the writer, is hospitalized after a violent stabbing incident. Sharing his room is the aged Jew Cappella, whose life of unending frustration pours forth in a voluptuous litany of suffering. Carefully recording it all—the agonies, the torturous gropings for understanding, their bleak determination to "continue"—is Byron's blind "copyist," a weirdly wraithlike creature; a device, for reducing rich human chaos to order.

Byron senses men's doubleness. . . . Cappella can only *feel,* their common burden of suffering. The copyist *organizes* their disunity. . . . But the copyist is blind. . . .

Cappella uses multiple dramatic monologues to render a "double" drama. It seems to dramatize a move away from the writer's technical dependence on his own psyche as the one reliable, judicial viewpoint. This has some interest as a dramatist's way of solving crucial fictional problems—and more, perhaps, as a reflection of the growing confidence of some of our best new writers to penetrate experience in all its variety, by methods that are continually reaching out beyond conventional practice.

> A review of "Cappella," in The Antioch Review, Vol. XXXII, No. 4, 1973, p. 697.

D. KEITH MANO

I think something fine has been achieved in *Cappella.* I think. The novel has absurdist affiliations: these irritate. Two men— an old Jew, a middle-aged writer—pass 30 years in a hospital: taxing their Blue Cross coverage somewhat. They have unhealed wounds, an absurdist favorite. The writer, Byron, is operated on 20 times plus, line of scar after line of scar, until his stomach skin resembles the Rosetta Stone. There is the standard paraphernalia: pains, exaggerations, nightmares,

super-meaningful glances, a clash of symbols. . . . A good deal is frankly impenetrable and annoying. God and gastronomy have the same liturgical significance. This comes with the absurdist franchise after all. Yet, quite reluctantly at first, I forgave. *Cappella* is also an entertainment.

This is the first novel of Israel Horovitz, a double-OBIE playwright. As might be expected, Horovitz has a glib knack for soliloquy. His words decant without sediment; they purl. And it is here that the enjoyment of *Cappella* is located. . . .

Three quarters of the book is an extended story telling. And the stories engross, they make thick laughter; their tone and accent, their circular movement is suave, accurate. By some ethnic prerogative the old Jew, Cappella, is the most articulate. His stories mature. They begin with a catalogue of proctological concerns. . . . But his range swells out, becomes less bodily parochial: trust grows between teller and listener. He passes on to snow—which, in the *Oxford English Encyclopedia of Symbolic Meaning* (Vol. IX, page 184c) invariably stands for death. Then Cappella and *Cappella* move even beyond that: toward grace, I suspect.

Wounds close. The painful but comfortable, orderly operations cease. A penchant for suffering and narcotics is outgrown. Lies told in the early pages are corrected. Cappella is no longer A. Cappella, unaccompanied; he becomes part of Byron. At first they live saprophytically on each other, trading character qualities, then there is symbiosis. Finally separate health. They leave the hospital for God knows where in an absurdist terrain. It is intriguing. (p. 2)

> D. Keith Mano, "The Novel as Oyster, Soliloquy, Folk-Legend, Anti-Climax," in The New York Times Book Review, February 25, 1973, pp. 2-3.

MEL GUSSOW

[*Dr. Hero*] is a life cycle comedy that is almost ruined by generality and coyness. The hero, who is named Hero, is born onstage. His mother dies in childbirth, and in the next scene he is in an orphanage where the actors imitate infants, mouthing baby-talk ("Do I have to get gwaphic?") while scooting around on Big Wheels.

Next there are scenes of childhood, education (with a Ph. D., he becomes Dr. Hero), marriage (to a lady named Heroine of course) and army. When Hero said, "There are no surprises here, just a few distractions along the way," I believed him, and wished for more distractions.

But the second act was a surprise. Dr. Hero enters the advertising business (a world that years ago included Horovitz before he became a successful playwright). At a conference Dr. Hero (by now a smug Sammy Glick) mobilizes his brainless agency to market a detergent which, when sprayed, produces mud. Machinelike, the actors mime the words as they speak them, until this skit becomes an insane little satire—one that could (and perhaps should) be extracted to stand on its own.

The rest of the play is not on that inspired plane, but the second act is still an enormous improvement over the first, bolstered by a competition for the title of "The World's Greatest Man," in which Dr. Hero beats the rest of the company in an aggressive game of riddles. Later, his strength ebbing, but his ego still soaring, Hero manages to overcome a bicepbound challenger, before he retires to a home for wheezing "charismatics."

Mel Gussow, in a review of "Dr. Hero," in The New York Times, *March 22, 1973, p. 55.*

WALTER KERR

[In *Dr. Hero*, Mr. Horovitz is summarizing a life,] though he has a distinctively oblique way of coming at it and a parodistic tone that ties its glimpses of everything from toilet-training to abandoned friends to ultimate defeat together.

His Hero is lonely, too, especially at cocktail parties: "Man invented the party so that he could experience *pure* loneliness," he suggests. The music of the past swirls about his birth and the first slapping he gets from a foster father: circus waltzes and "Dardanella" linger in the air. He has a friend, though an odd one, from who he parts. The friend . . . stiffly cocks his head to one side and begs for companionship even if he has, somehow, set fire to a house and killed his sister, whom he now sees smiling at him from the sky.

Hero's girl, like so many girls in remember-when plays, is a raunchy type, though she does seem less interested in him than in drugs. . . . Hero spends time on the battlefield: director Edward Berkeley has devised some highly evocative patterns for the sequence, spattering bodies about the stage floor in jittery geometric sprawls. And Hero, who meant to become not a film director but "the greatest man in the world," is of course reduced to the resignation that age imposes on all of us.

But Mr. Horovitz has taken his familiar material . . . and tossed them at us like so many eccentrically weighted basketballs. . . . When Hero is born, the doctors and nurses in attendance at once leap into a rousing cheer for Blue Cross. When he goes to college, he is subjected to a rat-a-tat inquisition by a manic faculty that wants to know why he possibly cared to enter this particular, obviously unworthy, school. When he joins an advertising agency, a minstrel show formation of hucksters tosses bad ideas about with the glee of endmen slapping knees over the glory of their own jokes.

In short, the evening is a game, insouciant mockery throughout. ("Think of your life condensed to its best 120 minutes," someone recommends, intimating perfectly clearly that there have been no best minutes anywhere.) Its contours are bold, its horrors are swiftly defined and swiftly dispensed with, its fantasy-quotient is consistent, its lens—the one we are allowed to look through—is sharply focused. If it fails, as I think it does, it is because Hero's ambition is much too generalized, nothing we can visualize with him, and because "the contest" in which he is defeated is similarly without an immediate, graspable base. Mr. Horovitz has got his outlines clean, his tonalities all in order; it's the ultimate innards of the piece that are spongy.

But his surface, at least, is controlled, pulled together; and that keeps us from drifting off on our own down memory's rag-tag lane.

Walter Kerr, in a review of "Dr. Hero," in The New York Times, *April 22, 1973, p. 11.*

CLIVE BARNES

[Horovitz's] latest project, and it is by far his most ambitious to date is a trilogy of plays he calls *The Wakefield Cycle.* Wakefield, Mass., was where Mr. Horovitz was born, and this cycle is intended as a tribute to his past, perhaps even as a tribute to the nation's past. . . .

In *Alfred the Great,* the hero, reasonably enough, is Alfred. He is a young man from Wakefield who has made it big. Mr. Horovitz never explains how—perhaps he is a movie star, a millionaire, a tennis champion or a politician. Sufficient for Mr. Horovitz that Alfred is a celebrity. But is it quite sufficient for us?

He is visiting Margaret and her husband, Will. It seems that Margaret and Alfred once had a boy-and-girl romance together, but perhaps, or so it subsequently seems not. Nothing is quite what it seems. Margaret has romanticized Alfred. And then there is Alfred's father, who may be dead, or may merely be in the local mental institution. Then there is Alfred's wife, Emily. An unhappy woman. For apart from all of Alfred's other troubles, it appears that he is impotent. This great man is impotent—the final trump in the all-American heroic myth. There is also perhaps a hint here that Alfred also suggests that brief American empire, an empire so powerful that it dared not employ its potency.

In most of his earlier writing, Mr. Horovitz tended toward the theater of the absurd and Eugene Ionesco, and one of his particular strengths was his uncanny knack of capturing the rhythms and banalities of human speech. He has moved to the ambiguous drama of Harold Pinter and Edward Albee, particularly perhaps Pinter. There is the same unspoken menace, the unlikelihood triggered by dramatic possibility and the same surging sense that life is somehow governed by the quiet sexuality of fathomless desire. . . .

The play, as now, does not work. But it has an intellectual substructure that is viable. The dramatic tone is not consistent—realism and fantasy are not always the easiest of bedfellows—but the dramatic idea is rewarding.

Clive Barnes, in a review of "Alfred the Great," in The New York Times, *August 14, 1974, p. 28.*

JOHN SIMON

In *Morning,* a Negro family wakes up one day turned white by a miracle of God. A white bigot with a gun is seeking Junior, the family's teenage son, for allegedly deflowering his daughter. The white man ends up painted black and becoming the victim of the new whites. The idea is simple and symmetrical, and though one condones its premise—*plus ça change* . . . —it is hardly news. But Horovitz has style. For one thing, he uses obscenity in a creative way, turning it into incantation, into an obsessive, funny, nightmarish obbligato. For another, his wit can brush you lightly even as it cuts deep. Someone says in passing, "for although black, God is a light sleeper . . ." In the most off-handed way a huge assertion is introduced; the wildness is heightened by the notion of God anthropomorphically in Morpheus' arms; and final absurdity is achieved by the seemingly meaningful collocation of "black" and "light," which traps us into a non sequitur. Ultimately this suggests that the whole black and white dichotomy may be likewise nonsensical. A playwright who can cram so much so comfortably into so little is to be watched with attention and delight.

What also makes *Morning* (originally called *Chiaroscuro*) remarkable is what it does with language. The white Negroes begin by sounding like minstrel-show characters but end speaking in toney Park Avenue accents. At first they use obscenities as casually as conjunctions; by and by, their language is purified and elevated. But, ironically, as their speech becomes more refined, their behavior becomes more outrageous—more outrageously white—and the comic disparity of form and content in human beings constitutes the play's strongest comment. (p. 187)

> *John Simon, "Spring, 1969," in his* Uneasy Stages: A Chronicle of the New York Theater, 1963-1973, *Random House, 1975, pp. 181-99.*

MARTIN GOTTFRIED

[*The Primary English Class*] seems the work of a primary playwright student. Too trivial for the 90 minute sketch it is, the play is dumb and irritating, a combination definitely to be missed.

Horovitz has always been plagued by gimmickry and preciousness and this new work is virtually a satire of his problems. It is set in a night school classroom where a half dozen immigrants of diverse nationalities have come to learn English from a teacher who has never taught the language.

So, one student speaks in Italian, another in French, another in German, another in Chinese, another in Japanese. Their dialogue is translated by a couple of unbearably cheerful, unseen actors. The students have trouble communicating with each other, which is presumably amusing.

The teacher, when she arrives, is a young woman whose bigotry and style, in speech and attitude, are meant to be satiric of contemporary college graduates. The contrast between her rudeness and her students' true education is intended to be ironic.

The play is a nuisance in almost all respects, the teacher because she is supposed to be. Horovitz may deserve some credit for that but not much, since her part is written with neither consistency, character nor organic humor. If he did in fact write the other parts in the actual languages, the translations suggest no character writing. It is merely foreign dialogue for the sake of poor and repetitious jokes.

There was doubtless a point being made. Amateurish plays usually make them. I fear all that Horovitz was trying to say was that aliens aren't ignorant merely because we don't understand their languages. Could he have meant something that obvious or is there even worse to fear? The fear isn't worth fearing.

> *Martin Gottfried, "A Tower of Babel," in* New York Post, *February 17, 1976.*

CLIVE BARNES

Communication is presumably what life is all about. It is undeniably what Israel Horovitz's play **The Primary English Class** is all about . . . . At one juncture Mr. Horovitz makes the shrewd point that "in this city we have a perfect balance between maniacs and nonmaniacs," and the play sets out to prove that contention.

It all takes place simply at a primary English class, where a flustered, confused, inexperienced but finally, if only in desperation, aggressive English teacher is trying to decline verbs in front of a veritable United Nations of pupils.

Much of it is extremely funny, if only because with a quite extraordinary flash of comic insight Mr. Horovitz has gone all the hilarious way and had his characters actually speak their presumably native languages. . . . In addition, Mr. Horovitz provides spoken subtitles, as it were, so the audience is afforded a simultaneous translation as the play proceeds.

It is possibly true that Mr. Horovitz is better at setting a situation than plotting a play. For all its humor, even with its suggestion of an allegory about noncommunication, **The Primary English Class** is more of a dramatic sketch than a drama. It is fairly brief, and although Mr. Horovitz maintains the wit and indeed the complete conceit, remarkably well—largely by introducing more and more absurd characters, a method that does have a kind of climactic effect—the play is still somewhat thin in its texture. I was reminded of another sketchlike play by Mr. Horovitz called **Line,** which was nothing but the behavioral patterns of characters standing in line.

Yet the humor in **The Primary English Class** is somehow even more basic than that in the earlier play. It finds its roots in the very human feeling that if you speak your own language very loudly and very slowly a foreigner will in some miraculous way understand. As a result we have this slow-talking Tower of Babel of a play, where everyone is intent in making him or herself understood to everyone else. It really is a gem of an idea.

> *Clive Barnes, "'The Primary English Class' Is Staged," in* The New York Times, *February 17, 1976, p. 38.*

EDITH OLIVER

Israel Horovitz's **The Primary English Class** is the first play of his in years that does not seem to me to be a composite—a pinch of Beckett here, a dollop of Pinter there. It is a one-act farce. . . . The setting is a classroom. One by one, five adult students enter—an Italian, a Frenchman, a German, an old Chinese woman, a young Japanese woman—and, last of all, the teacher, a young American woman. It is the first day of class; no student speaks English or a word of any other student's language, and the teacher speaks only English. All the jokes are misunderstanding jokes (most of which I found irresistible), and all the crises are misunderstanding crises. Every conceivable comic change is rung on bewilderment and—mostly in the case of the teacher—panic. Controlled chaos is what we aim at in farce, and controlled chaos is what Mr. Horovitz, his director, Edward Berkeley, and his proficient company have achieved. Mostly, Mr. H., who knows what he is up to with a script, is funny; occasionally he is just silly. My only complaint is that I ran out of laughter before he ran out of play.

> *Edith Oliver, in a review of "The Primary English Class," in* The New Yorker, *Vol. LII, No. 2, March 1, 1976, p. 79.*

PLAYS AND PLAYERS

Israel Horovitz's plays provide the best illustration of the difference between imitating the masters and building upon their work. Again and again, one sees the shadows of either Beckett or Ionesco falling across the stage—the lean but reverberating image of desolation, or the increasingly farcical insanity of logic. It's almost brazen, for instance, the way *Primary English Class* invokes Ionesco's *The Lesson*—the teacher-pupil relationship as a mixture of failed communication and sexual hysteria. Yet for all its glaring indebtedness, paradoxically it remains a tour de force of stunning originality.

Imagine a play in which none of the seven characters even speaks the same language. I can't think of a challenge less promising, or more intriguing. English, French, German, Italian, Chinese, Japanese, Polish—out of this Babel, as the teacher fails hopelessly to communicate more than a handful of the most innocuous phrases, Horovitz has created a stage image of both laughter and loneliness, building from the comedy of frustrated misunderstanding to the pathos of unbearable isolation. It's hilarious, the way we know so little of each other we have the most exasperating difficulty just learning each other's names. But it's desolating too, in Horovitz's brilliant image, the way we're so locked inside ourselves no one can even understand the words with which we moan our loneliness.

A review of "The Primary English Class," in Plays and Players, *Vol. 23, No. 10, July, 1976, p. 40.*

MEL GUSSOW

Just as David Storey drew from his football experiences for *The Changing Room,* Mr. Horovitz's revealing new play, **Sunday Runners in the Rain,** . . . is a report from the inside. (p. 313)

In common with Mr. Storey, Mr. Horovitz studies a closely allied group of people engaged in a shared athletic activity. Neither play deals with champions; the characters are serious amateurs or semiprofessionals, who are totally dedicated to a sport as a way of life. Metaphor rises naturally from the material.

Sunday Runners takes place in Gloucester, Mass., a road-run away from the marathon capital of America. The members of the Cape Ann Track Club dream about victory in the big race while tuning their bodies in their own club races, awarding one another prizes for their efforts. As the play begins, it is raining and a group of friends are gathered in a doughnut shop to prepare to beat one another's time. Simultaneously, Gus Swaddle, the president of the club, is being challenged for his office by an upstart, the formerly fat, eternally politicking Porker Martino. The presidential campaign and the club race are parallel bars of competition.

We never find out much about health habits or occupations, but we learn volumes about the role that running plays in the characters' individual lives. For Jonathan Hogan, running is a religion. He runs to win, even if it means subjecting his body to stress and pain. Many others in the club, including a hearty local minister, are Sunday runners; it is a pastime rather than a blood sport. For Maureen Anderman, it is a chance to be equal—or better. She faces her own dilemma: she is faster than her beau. Her role becomes a microcosm of the woman's movement. Most of Mr. Horovitz's runners are male racing chauvinists—the president conveniently forgets to order a women's trophy.

The ancient relic of a coach, one of the most colorful and idio-syncratic characters in the doughnut shop, is a man of pieties ("God's great foot is in every good runner's kick") and prejudices—and a retired cheat to boot. He is an absent-minded octogenarian who is totally obsessed with his sport.

Marital and extramarital squabbles—or "squibbles," as the word-twisting club president accidentally calls them—fill the stage, along with banter, comparative tales of bodily injury and memories of bygone days. Except for one speedy but bumbling teenager . . . , the characters are over 30. They have known each for a lifetime, or at least since grammar school—when the racing began, symbolically as well as athletically.

The play is frequently comic, but it has an underthread of seriousness. So many of the lives that unfold on stage are empty—except for their common avocation. Readying for action, putting on their racing shoes—when they can find two that match—flexing their leg muscles and prepping themselves for a workout, they are ordinary people who have hopes of being extraordinary, if only for one Sunday run in the rain.

Mel Gussow, "Living for a Sport," in The New York Times, *May 5, 1980, p. C17.*

KEITH GAREBIAN

Left to their own linguistic devices, the motley group of adult-students [in **The Primary English Class**], who become overpowered as much by their female teacher's neuroses as by their own helplessness in English, sound and behave like refugees from the Tower of Babel. Understanding becomes here an acutely comic problem in translation, and the play is structured like a foreign movie with English subtitles, offering great fun in the translator's deadpan voice that counterpoints the frenzied farce of garbled intentions.

In a violent one-act play, **The Indian Wants The Bronx,** where two punks terrorized an East Indian, Horovitz showed how language expresses psychoses. Now, though the surface is flashily comic and the rhythm zanily contrived, the deeper nuances are no less serious than those in **The Indian.** A Polish janitor, a nearsighted German, a rakish Italian, an anxious Frenchman, two female Orientals (one young and pretty; the other old and rickety), and an American female teacher establish Horovitz's view that "language is *not* the clarifier, neither a friend to thought, nor a twin to meaning." . . .

Horovitz's comedy exploits pinpoint timing and gross incongruity. The comedic arc is achieved through the same word-signals that ricochet from character to character, all of whom, nevertheless, manage to misunderstand them. To compound their confusion, their American teacher, Debbie Wastba, is a neurotic who is more than slightly xenophobic. Though she is a conglomeration of dress styles . . . she is paranoic about foreigners. Her pedagogical inexperience is matched by her racial intolerance, and though she makes irrelevant mundane chatter, she is a seething mass of sexual repression and cultural imperialism. . . . She wages war in order to teach, but her militant, racial sarcasm is totally lost on the uncomprehending class. In the end, they think she's crazy and leave her to her fear of failure. Language—her very own method of subjugation and assimilation—becomes her Waterloo. But her failure isn't simply hers alone, but that of the very society that insists on melting down cultural differences. . . .

Horovitz's play, then, becomes more than a whipped-up farce. It is a microcosm of confusion and prejudice, where the incomprehensible parley of strangers is gibberish or suspected insult to baffled ears. And the myth of Babel that underlies the comic situations, shows how absurd a punishment language can be. If these students and their teacher ever set about building another lunatic tower to the stars, they would savage one another with the splinters of their speech, although the American teacher would probably manage to regard the debris as a sign of a healthy work ethic, man's substitute for Eden. (p. 39)

Keith Garebian, "Benediction and Babel," in The Canadian Forum, *Vol. LX, No. 699, May, 1980, pp. 38-9.*

JOHN SIMON

The Good Parts is all *parts:* Scenes that function as set pieces in which two fortyish Hebrew-American (the term is Mr. Horovitz's) husbands have escaped to kick up their heels; and, in Act II, scenes in which they are pursued by their wives. It is all parts, though, with not even absurdist paralogic to hold them together; as for *the good,* the other half of the title, I can see very little of it here. The reference seems to be to the good part of Euripides' Electra, which Brian Levine, the more sophisticated and gallivanting of the husbands, once played in high school.

Brian now wants to re-enact it on top of the Acropolis, much to the indifference and, later, disgust of Eugene Jacoby, the more gallivanted against of the husbands, who only just now finds out that his best buddy, Brian, besides stealing his seven-year-old grade-school sweetheart as well as his current secretary, has been carrying on with his wife, Mildred, for eighteen years. Although Eugene's family has a history rather more purple than the House of Atreus, Eugene himself has no stomach either for Orestes' story or for reading his lines in support of Brian's Electra. As for Brian, who climactically discovers that Orestes is really the better part, he suffers a retroactive trauma over why his beloved drama teacher would have cast him as Electra in the first place.

The various—actually not so various—incidents concern mostly the husbands' and wives' brushes with assorted Greeks, who mistrust Americans even bearing gifts of dollars. The most dramatic encounter is that between Brian and Eugene, playacting atop the Acropolis, and an antihistrionic Greek guard, whose coming between Brian and his Electra complex results in his apparent demise and any number of unhilarious consequences for Brian, his wife, Brenda, Eugene, and his wife, Mildred. . . .

Now, I am not saying that the play is wholly without rewards. There is a talking-in-sleep scene that Tony Roberts (Brian) does very funnily; also a monologue about creeping—or, rather, galloping—memory loss. . . . Again, when, as fugitives from the Greek law, Brian and Eugene revert to a childhood language that consists of affixing the syllable *arb-* before every vowel, things become, though rather facilely, quarbite farbunnarby. And Horovitz does come up with the odd punchy one-liner, e.g., "Of course you're British—just look at your shoes."

But there is no claspable theme here, such as even a Jewish-Absurdist play needs to hold it together. It is not really about mid-life crisis or friendship or jealousy or marital relations or America versus Europe—or anything that the most desperate audience good-will can latch on to. Moreover, [Brian] is not *that* funny—and [Eugene] rather less so—to carry the heavy load of lacunae between the author's flashes of resourcefulness. . . . But the entire enterprise has something desperate about it—like sweat under the collar with delusions of grandeur of being a ring around a bathtub. (p. 70)

John Simon, "Half-Truths," in New York *Magazine, Vol. 15, No. 3, January 18, 1982, pp. 70-1.*

BARRY B. WITHAM

The Alfred Trilogy, a mammoth and as yet unproduced trio of plays by Israel Horovitz, is also about a man's search for the truth. It deals with an American town that has been "cursed" and the subsequent attempts to discover and punish the wrongdoer. In the first play, **Alfred the Great,** the successful American businessman returns to his boyhood town (Wakefield, Mass.) to seek out his brother's murderer and discovers that his quest is more complex than he suspected. For Alfred Webber is led into a maze of forgotten crimes and incestuous relationships in which he ultimately finds himself standing at the center. In the second play, **Our Father's Failing,** Alfred discovers the truth about his mother's death and his father's attempt to conceal the truth. And in the final play, **Alfred Dies,** his wife, Emily, conducts an illegal trial in which she negotiates a suicide pact and buries Alfred alive on the 4th of July.

While it is possible to deal with each of these plays separately, it is important to realize that the themes of crime and responsibility inform the design of them all as well as the four one-acts which Horovitz wrote to accompany them. In drawing conclusions about **Alfred Dies,** one has to rely on clues that the other plays provide. Is the curse ever vanquished, for instance? One is tempted to think so. In *The 75th* we learn that the old people are dying from causes other than murder, and in *Hopscotch* there are references to all the young families in that town, again implying that children are being born and the curse is over. But there are equally disquieting signs. *Hopscotch,* for instance, is not just about two former high school lovers. It is about two cousins (one of whom is Alfred's daughter) who have repeated the sins of their parents. Elsa's life style and sexual insatiability are a carbon copy of her mother (Margaret) as well as Sophie and Roxie, and Will's desertion and subsequent return recall Alfred's own behavior. More foreboding, however, is the symbolic design of *Hopscotch* in which everyone seems drawn inevitably back to "square one." In the same vein *Spared* suggests that the curse of the Webber-Lynch line may go on forever, because the old man of the piece—thematically related to Alfred—only brings death to others but never is released from life himself.

Alfred Dies is enormously complex and only a theatrical production can begin to reveal its artistry; some of the broad outlines are clear, however, particularly as they relate to Horovitz's use of the American character. It seems obvious that Alfred is guilty of matricide and incest, but his crime alone is not responsible for the curse. Indeed the incest, which is symbolic of the town's guilt, appeared long before Alfred's mad act at the age of ten. He is a scapegoat and convenient victim but he is not the cause.

How then do we fix the responsibility for the Wakefield

curse? It is a question that Emily is able to answer with absolute conviction and clarity: "It's rare, in this life, that it becomes really and truly possible to blame anyone for anything . . . In the matter of twenty years of my life, Alfred, I blame you. I hold you responsible." Emily recognizes that whatever the origin and however imperfect the justice, something must be done to end the personal suffering which hangs over the town. In a chilling final scene which recalls ancient tragedy she metes out her revenge under the village green while the fireworks explode and the marching bands celebrate America's birthday.

The archtypal associations, particularly those that link *Alfred Dies* with Greek tragedy are numerous and sometimes strained, but it is clear that Horovitz wishes to recall images of *The Oresteia*. The curse of incest, for example, which runs throughout the Webber-Lynch history is taken directly from the precipitating event in the House of Atreus tragedy, when Thyestes sleeps with his brother's wife. *Alfred the Great* is a homecoming play much like *Agamemnon,* and *Alfred Dies* is a trial in the tradition of *The Eumenides*. In fact, *Alfred Dies* is set underground suggesting a number of correspondences with the spirits of the Aeschelyan tragedy. Moreover, there are parallels to the Orestes legend throughout Horovitz's work. Alfred has killed his mother and is pursued for the crime of matricide and he has a scene with his sister which evolves out of a physical recognition of hair.

But *Alfred Dies* is not about Greece, it is about America and American values and where they have led us by Independence Day in the mid-1970s. Alfred is repeatedly referred to as the "boy wonder," the American success story. At 18 he sold a piece of swampland and embarked on a career which brought him all the outward symbols of the American dream. His name is in the newspapers, his face on television, and his material and physical needs satisfied by boats, cars, houses, and cash.

But the dream is a nightmare and the success is rotten. Alfred is haunted by half-remembered truths and old lies. He can't close his eyes. He is impotent. He is driven by a force which he can't understand to an accounting for the sterility which is his legacy. And what he discovers is that his life has been a lie. His wife is more than his wife: she is also his half sister. His father is not dead, but institutionalized for a crime he didn't commit—and the murderer whom Alfred sought is himself. *Alfred Dies* is a reckoning, an attempt to fix the responsibility for his crime and for the failure of the American promise.

His success is built—literally and symbolically—on a swamp. And his guilt is both the personal guilt of his own actions (abandoning Margaret, killing his mother) and the collective guilt of his country (defiling and trading the Indian's land, obliterating their race much as the Greeks did to Troy.) Thus Emily holds him responsible for the death of their children and he becomes the town scapegoat for the collective sins of the past.

Horovitz does not deal with values in quite the same way as either [Michael] Weller or [Lanford] Wilson. He is not so concerned with lifestyle as he is with the legacy and roots of being "American." The American success story is put on trial on the 4th of July in a cellar room stinking with feces and fetid air beneath a village bandstand where we can hear the incoherent strain of familiar songs and fireworks.

Alfred Dies is dominated by images of rot and decay. The air is overwhelmingly "foul" or "rancid" and there are frequent references to "vultures," "dumps" and "toilets." The Webber-Lynch bloodlines are polluted from their own inbreeding and can produce only stillbirths or barren wombs. In a like manner, the American dream is polluted from its own myth making and breeds not success but treachery and despair.

Alfred's trial is a mockery of due process but he is found guilty of his own crimes as well as the crimes of his people— murder, greed, lust and avarice. The Americans plundered their land rather than settling it. They destroyed the natives rather than embracing them, and they are all cursed because they share the collective guilt of the past by prolonging the myths. Images of incest, nymphomania, and impotency rush through *Alfred Dies* along with the recurring references to "stillbirths," "miscarriages," and "mutants."

Horovitz's America is a green park with a white gazebo built over a swamp. The facade is intact but only as a thin veneer covering the rottenness which festers underneath. We cannot go back to replenish the garden as we can with Wilson because the land is poisoned. And we cannot revel in the romance of a picture book past because the images are not the comfortable myths we would like to remember. It is not comforting, of course, in an age of nuclear waste dumps and chemical decay that his vision of an America which is Love Canal may be the most accurate of them all. (pp. 224-32)

> *Barry B. Witham, "Images of America: Wilson, Weller and Horovitz," in* Theatre Journal, *Vol. 34, No. 2, May, 1982, pp. 223-32.*

EDITH OLIVER

[*A Rosen by Any Other Name*] tells the story of a Jewish family in Sault Ste. Marie, Ontario. The time is 1943, a few weeks before the bar mitzvah of Stanley Rosen. His father, Barney, is a tailor, and his mother, Pearl, helps in the shop, but her main occupation at present is planning the reception that will follow the service, a reception whose pièce de résistance is to be a statue of Stanley made of chopped liver. Stanley's mortification is intense, his protests unavailing. The action is made up of little scenes—in and out of the house, or in the tailor shop, or with the rabbi, learning the ritual. Barney is afraid that the fate of the Jews of Europe will descend on him in Canada; to this timorous man everyone is a Jew-hater. When a rock is thrown through the window of his shop, he decides, to the disgust of his wife and the anger of his son, to change his name. "Royal" is the final choice. ("Royal Rosen?" asks the rabbi.) But Stanley, with the help of the rabbi and the encouragement of his cousin Manny, a veteran of the Navy who is staying with the family while recovering from shell shock, thinks of a way to outwit his father and retain his own name. Everybody lives happily ever after.

The story is serviceable enough, but it is the details that count—the vignettes that the author blends with some skill. A lot of the jokes pay off, and the characters are pleasant company. Horovitz is an experienced dramatist, with a sense of scale; he has deliberately kept the play small. That said, I must add that it is often too cute and too sugary for my taste.

> *Edith Oliver, in a review of "A Rosen by Any Other Name," in* The New Yorker, *Vol. LXII, No. 5, March 24, 1986, p. 111.*

CLIVE BARNES

Israel Horovitz is a playwright of many faces. It is his social-realism face that is looking at us foursquare in his play about the fading Massachusetts frozen-fish processing industry, **North Shore Fish**. . . .

It was probably Maxim Gorky, by leaping free from Chekhov's influence in his doss-house play *The Lower Depths,* who first suggested that a virtually unadorned, but not unedited, slice of life could offer its own social commentary.

The rest has been, in part, theater history, and in **North Shore Fish** Horovitz is returning to this almost documentary approach of showing men and women in the workplace.

Here they are workers, chiefly women, at an endangered fish-packing plant in Gloucester, Mass.

The work is dull and routine, dehumanizing, and the foreman is a cheap small-time Lothario who expects to enjoy sexual favors from any women in his employ who takes his fancy. And it is a wide ranging fancy.

But the job keeps bread on the table, there is a certain camaraderie among the workers, most of them having known each other since childhood, and the hours are regular, the labor involved comparatively undemanding.

There is now a hidden pressure: the plant is not particularly profitable, it would be more valuable to the owner to sell it as real estate.

The foreman is fighting like a cornered rat to keep it going—despite the disinterested ownership, and a government inspector pushing down on him with unyielding bureaucratic health regulations.

In some respects the play seems more English than American; it has something in common with Arnold Wesker's *The Kitchen,* and David Storey's *The Contractor* or *The Changing Room.*

But whereas the social-realist English playwrights were using reality as a metaphor for truth—with a little incidental symbolism thrown in on the side—Horovitz never moves away from the smaller issues.

What may be the play's wider purpose never seems quite apparent. The aged Arlyne—a link to earlier times in the Gloucester community—says at one point: "We are fish people doing what we are supposed to do."

Yet at the end . . . we know little more about fish or fish people than we knew at the beginning.

The play has many echoes of reality . . . but many fewer resonances of truth.

Perhaps the trouble is that in the theater facts very rarely speak for themselves. The playwright has to act as interpreter, and if you elect to document a process, a life-style if you like, rather than an incident of character, the process needs a more articulate sub-text than is here provided.

Watching people pack frozen fish, even with a little melodrama thrown in, is scarcely of itself a play.

Clive Barnes, "Fishing for Truth," in New York Post, *January 12, 1987.*

Kazuo Ishiguro
1954-

Japanese-born English novelist, short story writer, and scriptwriter.

In his novels *A Pale View of Hills* (1982) and *An Artist of the Floating World* (1986), Ishiguro examines modern Japanese society from a Westernized perspective. He depicts individuals who are deeply affected by the victory of the United States over Japan in World War II and by the subsequent impact of American culture upon his native country's traditional way of life. Writing in an understated, minimalistic style, Ishiguro often employs shifts in time to compare events from the past to those of the present. *A Pale View of Hills,* which Paul Bailey praised as "a first novel of uncommon delicacy," centers upon Etsuko, a former Japanese housewife and survivor of the nuclear bombing at Nagasaki who moved to England following World War II. The suicide of her daughter prompts Etsuko to recall the liberating and disruptive changes that accompanied the American occupation of postwar Japan. Francis King called *A Pale View of Hills* "a memorable and moving work, its elements of past and present, of Japan and England held together by a shimmering, all but invisible net of images linked to each other by filaments at once tenuous and immensely strong."

Set in a provincial Japanese town between 1948 and 1950, *An Artist of the Floating World* concerns Masuji Ono, an aging painter who attempts to convince his Americanized neighbors that his activities as a propagandist for Japan's imperialist regime during World War II were inspired by a naive sense of patriotism. While centering on Ono's attempts to arrange a respectable marriage for his daughter, Ishiguro juxtaposes his protagonist's attempts to adjust to Japan's modern social and political order with his recollections of youthful experiences at the "Floating World," the local entertainment district of bars and geishas. Geoff Dyer commented: "Ishiguro arranges Ono's uncertain reminiscences with the same elliptical skill displayed in *A Pale View of Hills,* coaxing nuances out of hinted ambiguities. His writing is clean, unharried and airy; full of inflections and innuendo, it touches the reader as lightly as a gentle breeze."

(See also *CLC,* Vol. 27 and *Contemporary Authors,* Vol. 120.)

PATRICK PARRINDER

The year 1945, like 1830 and 1914, now seems a natural watershed—above all in countries which experienced national defeat, social unheaval and military occupation. *An Artist of the Floating World,* a beautiful and haunting novel by the author of *A Pale View of Hills,* consists of the rambling reminiscences of a retired painter set down at various dates in the Japan of the late Forties. Americanisation is in full swing, national pride has been humbled, and the horror of the bombed cities and the loss of life is beginning to be counted. The young soldiers who came back from the war are turning into loyal corporation men, eager to forget the Imperial past and to dedicate the remainder of their lives to resurgent capitalism. Ishiguro's narrator, Masuji Ono, has lost his wife and

son but lives on with two daughters, one of whom is married. Were it not for his anxieties over his second daughter's marriage negotiations, Ono could be left to subside into the indolence of old age. As it is, 'certain precautionary steps' must be taken against the investigations to be pursued, as a matter of course, by his prospective son-in-law. The past has its guilty secrets which Ono must slowly and reluctantly bring back to consciousness.

Ono was trained as a decadent artist, an illustrator of the night-time 'floating world' of geishas and courtesans, but at the time of the 'China crisis' in the Thirties, he broke away from that style to create a more morally uplifting and patriotic form of art. In his painting *Complacency,* the image of three well-dressed men drinking in a bar was offset by three ragged youths brandishing sticks and wearing the 'manly scowls' of samurai warriors—the two images moulded together by the outline of the Japanese islands. In his declining years, however, Ono has relapsed into the decadence of the barfly and the maudlin old-timer: and now it is his turn to confront the anger of the young with a Polonius-like complacency.

Some of Ishiguro's most delightful scenes portray the mutual incomprehensions of the old and the young. Ono is frustrated in his attempts to initiate his eight-year-old grandson into the male mysteries of sake-drinking and the samurai warriors, for example: the youngster is more exercised by cowboys, monster movies and Popeye the Sailorman. (At least it makes him eat up his spinach.) But there is more serious business afoot. At the height of his career Ono had won an 'auction of prestige', in which the most suitable buyer was chosen for an imposing town house. . . . Now, as he tries to marry off his daughter, Ono's prestige as a former Fascist painter is a rapidly dwindling asset. For who needs a father-in-law who was once official adviser to the Committee on Unpatriotic Activities, and who turned over his favourite pupil to the secret police?

There is in Japan an honourable way out of such dilemmas, as Ono is only too well aware. A famous composer of patriotic songs has committed suicide. The director of a company involved in 'certain undertakings' during the war is reported to have gassed himself after an ineffectual attempt—betrayed by minor scratches around his stomach—to perform harakiri. Every day brings more news of such deaths 'in apology' to the nation's war widows and bereaved families. What will Ono do? Ishiguro gives a delicate and wholly convincing account of the evasions, the self-justifications and the pride of a man willing to bend with the breeze, but accustomed to a position of dignity. Through Ono's mental detours, and the little hypocrisies of those around him—his daughters' deferential and half-mocking manner towards him is exquisitely caught—Ishiguro gives us a vignette of a moment of cultural history which is as complete, in its own way, as *Washington Square* or *Castle Rackrent*.

The core of Ono's shame is that he betrayed his pupil; but recollecting the incidents of his own apprenticeship, he constructs a view of the artistic profession in which, thanks to the 'anxiety of influence', mutual betrayal is almost a natural termination to the relationship between a master and his most gifted follower. Eventually, at the *miai* or formal meeting between his daughter and future son-in-law and their respective families, Ono rouses himself to speak the words of apology and self-humiliation that he feels are expected of a man of his former political sympathies. It is an act of moral exertion sufficient, at least, to preserve the honour of a conscientious mediocrity who whiles away what is left of his time by drinking in the city's 'pleasure-district' or taking walks to the aptly-named Bridge of Hesitation. History may not be able to forgive the defeated, but at least Ono himself can finally bestow his blessing on the brave new Japan of democratic values, Hollywood movies and Nippon Electronics. Far from embodying the samurai tradition which he had extolled in his paintings, the hero of this gentle, moving tragicomedy reminds us of nothing so much as a Japanese Vicar of Bray. (p. 16)

> *Patrick Parrinder, "Manly Scowls," in* London Review of Books, *Vol. 8, No. 2, February 6, 1986, pp. 16-17.*

GEOFF DYER

[In *An Artist of the Floating World*], Masuji Ono, a retired painter, looks with bemused approval at a country in the process of regenerating itself as a capitalist power, succumbing to crass Americanisation and eager to atone for atrocious memories of the recent past. The complex business of arranging his daughter's marriage, however, leads Ono meandering back to his past, to his days as a young man serving his ap-

prenticeship as an 'artist of the floating world'—the twilight district of geishas and bars. The deepening crises and Japan's expansionist ambitions of the Thirties lead Ono to reject this 'decadent' art in favour of a propagandist art addressing itself directly to the problems of the day; Ono himself meanwhile explicitly identifies himself with the extreme right, serving on the Committee on Unpatriotic Activities and reporting a pupil to the secret police.

Ishiguro arranges Ono's uncertain reminiscences with the same elliptical skill displayed in *A Pale View of Hills,* coaxing nuances out of hinted ambiguities. His writing is clean, unharried and airy; full of inflections and innuendo, it touches the reader as lightly as a gentle breeze. While Ono abandons the 'fragile lantern beauty' of the floating world for a strident, political art of thick black outlines and bold calligraphy Ishiguro impresses by how much history he can contain within—and between—his frail lines. (p. 25)

> *Geoff Dyer, "On Their Mettle," in* New Statesman, *Vol. 111, No. 2871, April 4, 1986, pp. 25-6.*

KATHRYN MORTON

It is not unusual to find new novels by good writers, novels with precise wording, witty phrases, solid characterizations, scenes that engage. Good writers abound—good novelists are very rare. Kazuo Ishiguro is that rarity. His second novel, *An Artist of the Floating World,* is the kind that stretches the reader's awareness, teaching him to read more perceptively.

As the retired gentleman Masuji Ono chats with the reader, the words are simple, but where is the reality? Postwar Japan is a world of shifting values, of behavior complicated by polite formalities, of undeserved pride or unnecessary humility, of memories that swell to smug importance or disappear to suit convenience. The "floating world" of the title is the Japanese term for night life in the pleasure districts. But its meaning grows.

An aspiring artist, young Ono began as a hack artist, then became the star pupil in a school of bohemian artists who enjoyed and celebrated bars and sake, hostesses and lantern light. Led by a member of the Okada-Shingen (New Life) Society, Ono's eyes were opened to social needs, and so he broke with the school and became an influential artist and propagandist for Japanese imperialism and the war effort. . . .

Ono meets with the reader four times between October 1948 and June 1950, addressing him as he would an acquaintance who may not remember that most pleasing pavilion that once stood in the Takami Gardens, or the Nishizuru district in its squalor, or the Migi-Hidari, newly established as a night spot for the young imperialists, with its décor of marching boots and its name meaning "right-left." During these encounters the reader moves from accepting Ono's decorous version of the past to wondering what kind of a man Ono really was. . . .

Often with Japanese novels the Western reader may suspect he is missing the point and feel that important references may be getting by him. That is not a problem here. Mr. Ishiguro, though born in 1954 in Nagasaki, has lived in England since 1960. He writes in English and does not require that the reader know the Orient to understand his book. His unnamed city is generic, full of Japanese place names that give it the sound of authenticity. Its people are so embedded in the particulars of their own history and so bound up with their own culture that their conversations alone betray what we need to know of their background. True to a traditional Oriental delicacy and circumspection, the characters are forever emitting small laughs, saying, "indeed," while essentially disagreeing. As the author never fails to reveal their true intentions, they seem no more "inscrutable" than any of us. The tensions stay tight. And this is what makes Mr. Ishiguro not only a good writer but also a wonderful novelist.

Kathryn Morton, "After the War Was Lost," in The
New York Times Book Review, June 8, 1986, p. 19.

PAUL STUEWE

The artist-protagonist of Ishiguro's second novel [*An Artist of the Floating World*] is highly skilled at interpreting the signs and symbols that make up his society's frames of reference; his explanations of what the most seemingly innocuous words and gestures actually mean constitute a kind of basic course in the country's social context. Ishiguro, an expatriate who writes in English, uses a sparse, understated vocabulary that at first seems simplistic but gradually rivets our attention to the crucial nuances of his characters' actions. *An Artist of the Floating World* confirms the positive impression made by his first book, *A Pale View of Hills.* It is now clear that Ishiguro's somewhat distanced vantage-point is an ideal spot from which to sympathetically understand and trenchantly communicate his perceptions of Japan's fundamental national characteristics.

Paul Stuewe, "Genuine Japanese . . . Slush-Pile
Saviour . . . for God and Greed," in Quill and
Quire, Vol. 52, No. 12, December, 1986, p. 31.

NIGEL HUNT

[In *An Artist of the Floating World,* Ishiguro] has found an approach to his themes which does not keep us on the outside trying to peer in to the foreign nature of his setting. Instead he brings us along by allowing us inside the mind of his main character, Masujo Ono, an aging painter. . . . Beautifully written, Ishiguro's book presents his themes clearly but without sacrificing any of the integrity of his story. The features of his system reach us in a way which enables us to feel something of the place between the pages.

Thematically, *An Artist of the Floating World* concerns itself with the influence and responsibility of the artist to society as well as the way in which the present changes our perceptions of the past. The story begins with Ono describing the house in which he lives and the way that he acquired it. Previously owned by a wealthy family, the house was sold to him because of his prestige rather than simply his ability to afford the highest amount. Ono approves of this principle: "How so much more honourable is such a contest, in which one's moral conduct and achievement are brought as witnesses rather than the size of one's purse."

In tandem with nostalgia for the former glory of the local pleasure district which has since declined, and memories of his apprenticeship as an artist, Ono is forced to examine his own past actions in order to secure his younger daughter Noriko's chances of marriage. The previous year, marriage negotiations with a suitor's family had fallen through. The reason given to Ono was that the suitor's family felt them-

selves unworthy to marry into Ono's family, an explanation that Ono is able to accept without question. Ono's older daughter, Setsuko, however, suggests that "it is perhaps wise if Father would take certain precautionary steps. To ensure misunderstandings do not arise," implying that it is his past which may be misunderstood.

In the course of the novel, we discover that Ono had produced paintings for propaganda purposes which endorsed the rising militarism in Japan at that time and eventually led to the country's demise in World War II. He even participated as an official adviser to the Committee of Unpatriotic Activities where he had occasion to denounce a former student of his who subsequently suffered harsh punishments, far beyond the reprimands which Ono had anticipated. Ono is forced to recall this incident after he tries unsuccessfully to visit the former pupil in his efforts to ensure that the customary investigations into the family's past will not hinder Noriko's chances of marriage with her new suitor. Ono is, in fact, considered by some of the younger generation to have been a traitor and to have helped lead Japan astray into needless suffering. For the purposes of his future, contained in the marriage hopes of Noriko, Ono professes: "Indeed, I would be the first to admit that those same sentiments are perhaps worthy of condemnation. I am not one of those who are afraid to admit the shortcomings of past achievements." Yet he also concurs with an old friend and former colleague who says, "But there's no need to blame ourselves unduly. . . . We at least acted on what we believed and did our utmost. It's just that in the end we turned out to be ordinary men." His admission also turns out, perhaps, to have been unnecessary. After admitting his past mistakes in front of his potential son-in-law's family, Ono is admonished for thinking himself more influential than was the case: "But father is wrong to even begin thinking in such terms about himself. Father was, after all, a painter." Opinion, it seems, is never fixed. We are left to wonder with Ono to what degree his fears were real or existed only in his mind.

Ono's young grandson, while displaying more openly the changing importance of respect for the older generation manifest in his unruly manners, also shows the post-war generation's hunger for things American in his imitations of Popeye and the Lone Ranger. In a charming scene when Ono suggests to his grandson that it's "more interesting, more interesting by far, to pretend to be someone like Lord Yoshitsune," his idea is met with something less than enthusiasm: "It occurred to me he was about to burst into tears or else run out of the room."

What Ishiguro has captured so deftly is the fact of change and rebellion between the generations. Ono remembers his own growth as an artist, the time when he realized that he must betray his teacher by painting in a radically different style from the one he was taught. Ono's *sensei* made his career from painting pictures of the pleasure district and its inhabitants. He is forced to confront his teacher and Ono tells him: "It is my belief that in such troubled times as these, artists must learn to value something more tangible than those pleasurable things that disappear with the morning light. It is not necessary that artists always occupy a decadent and enclosed world. My conscience, Sensei, tells me I cannot remain forever an artist of the floating world." Ono's daughters contradict his subtle ways, teasing him about his age or his habit of moping around the house. Often the rules of conduct insist that criticisms must be made metaphorically rather than so directly. Noriko, anxious because of her father's actions, reproaches him while he is gardening. "Father tends to meddle too much. I think he is going to ruin that bush too." With such subtlety, Ishiguro captures the formal requirements of his characters' use of language and the heartfelt sentiments beneath. When Ono as a young man betrays his *sensei* by his paintings and he is summoned to bring his work to show the master, Ono tells him: "I regret, Sensei, that I will not be able to find the remaining paintings." The need for the rebellion, for betrayal, for growing up, for revaluating the past is always present no matter how it may be couched in the words which suit the speaker's age and circumstances.

We also see with Ono, because it is his mind through which the story is revealed, that memory is always subject to reinterpretation. Ono brackets off incidents and their relevance which he does not wish to consider at the moment. The knowledge and perception gained from events which transpire, and from past actions which are recalled, are woven by the author with such skill and insight that we cannot help but feel that the "floating world"—the world which breathes and expires with the change of light—is our world. (pp. 37-8)

Nigel Hunt, "Two Close Looks at Faraway," in Brick: A Journal of Reviews, *No. 31, Fall, 1987, pp. 36-8.*

Ivan Klíma
1931-

Czechoslovakian short story writer, dramatist, novelist, essayist, and author of children's books.

In his fiction and drama, Klíma documents everyday life in a totalitarian society. He is praised for his use of satire and black humor to examine the effects of political and economic repression upon ordinary individuals. Although Klíma enjoyed a degree of autonomy over his writings during Czechoslovakia's period of liberalization in the mid-1960s, his works were banned by the Communist government following the Soviet Union's invasion of his homeland in 1968. Since that time, Klíma's works have appeared in the East only in underground editions; several of his books are available in the West in English translation, and some of his plays have been produced by experimental theater groups and university drama departments in the United States.

Klíma's earliest fiction is collected in the short story volumes *Bezvadný den* (1960) and *Milenci na jednu noc* (1964). His first novel, *Hodina ticha* (1963), concerns the futile attempts at organization by a group of Czech farmers upon discovering the government's plan to seize their land for collectivization. Klíma's first book to be translated into English, *Lod jménem Nadeje* (1969; *A Ship Named Hope*), consists of two novellas that develop allegorical condemnations of communism and Soviet dictator Joseph Stalin. In the title piece, the passengers of a cruise ship find themselves at the mercy of a malevolent crew member when the vessel strays off-course. The second novella, *The Jury,* depicts twelve jurors of a murder trial who are forced to render a verdict despite their discovery that the defendant has already been sentenced and executed. A reviewer for the *Times Literary Supplement* commented that *The Jury* "provides a unique insight into the moral and psychological problems faced by people caught in the judicial trap set up by a totalitarian system from which there is no escape."

Má veselá jitra (1979; *My Merry Mornings: Stories from Prague*), Klíma's first book to appear in English translation following his censure, consists of tales revolving around characters who attempt to manipulate Czech bureaucracy. In "A Christmas Conspiracy" for example, Klíma relates the misadventures of an ostracized literary scholar who decides to sell carp on the black market but lacks the shrewdness necessary to make his venture profitable. The stories in *Moje první lásky* (1985; *My First Loves*) relate the experiences of an unnamed youth during and immediately following World War II. "Miriam," which is set in German-occupied Prague, depicts the narrator's attraction to a girl who works in a soup kitchen. The girl abruptly ends their friendship after the deportation of local Jews to Nazi death camps. Jack Sullivan observed: "*My First Loves* is a deeply personal book, more given over to restless fantasies about sex, death, and coming of age than to political commentary. . . . [These] stories carry the burning authority and desperate eloquence of a survivor."

Klíma is also regarded as an accomplished dramatist. His first play, *Zámek* (1964; *The Castle*), a reworking of Franz

Kafka's novel *Das Schloss,* is generally interpreted as a satire directed at state-supported artists. *Mistr* (1967; *The Master*), is a mystery involving a carpenter who delivers a coffin to a family despite their insistence that they did not order it. Klíma's dramas produced in off-Broadway theaters include the black comedies *Café Myriam* (1968; *The Sweetshoppe Myriam*), which depicts a restaurant owner who poisons elderly people in order to sell their apartments on the underground market, and *Ženich pro Marcelu* (1969; *A Bridegroom for Marcela*), which concerns a clerk who receives official notice of his upcoming marriage to a woman whom he hardly knows.

(See also *Contemporary Authors,* Vols. 25-28, rev. ed. and *Contemporary Authors New Revision Series,* Vol. 17.)

THE TIMES LITERARY SUPPLEMENT

Ivan Klíma's two short novels [*The Jury* and *A Ship Named Hope*] are in many respects the very opposite of Josef Škvorecký's [*The Cowards*]. They do not refer directly to any events that actually occurred, were published in Czechoslovakia only last year and, as for literary tradition and influences, Mr. Klíma remains on home ground. Like some other contemporary Czech writers, Jaroslav Putík for instance, he has evidently found much of his inspiration in Franz Kafka.

The first novel, **The Jury,** is about a group of ordinary citizens called upon to pass a verdict on an alleged murderer. During the trial it becomes obvious, however, that a verdict of "Guilty" has been taken for granted and the accused in fact already executed. The jurors react in different ways to the pressure to which they are exposed. In the end, only one of them dares to maintain his view that the defendant is, or rather was, innocent, but finds out that even this is part of the game and that his dissent merely helps to keep up the semblance of the jury's independence.

While Mr. Škvorecký is mainly a story-teller, Ivan Klíma's aim is to convey an idea. **The Jury** is an allegory based on the Stalinist trials, which provides a unique insight into the moral and psychological problems faced by people caught in the judicial trap set up by a totalitarian system from which there is no escape. The theme of nightmarish helplessness recurs in the second novel, **A Ship Named Hope,** another highly complex allegory about people being taken to their death in the name of hope. Mr. Klíma's writing is admirable. . . . It seems though, that the second novel is slightly overburdened by symbolic details, which get more and more involved, until a baroque structure is built up that tends to obscure rather than clarify the original statement. On the other hand, this may well reflect the nature of contemporary totalitarianism, which is more sophisticated than that once described by Arthur Koestler.

"Prehistoric Historian," in The Times Literary Supplement, *No. 3581, October 16, 1970, p. 1184.*

PETER VANSITTART

[Klima's] two allegorical novellas [**The Jury** and **A Ship Named Hope**] are a balance between B. S. Johnson's plea that, with other media commandeering the Novel's traditional territory, the serious novelist must increasingly 'go on writing about whatever can be found inside himself'—and the individual's relations not only to himself but outside himself, but to family, friends, community, State. Both stories focus on the hesitations of an average man belatedly forced to take a decision, hesitations that swiftly become gruesome. Statements and solutions are seldom plain, nor, in what are not party tracts, should they be. One recalls Rebecca West's remark that, whether we like it or not, we must admit that there is very little in Shakespeare that can be used as propaganda for adult suffrage. In **The Jury,** a shy, obscure historian, juryman in a murder trial, realizes that the whole process is rigged, nothing but chilly non-sequiturs leading to pre-arranged condemnation; essentially a reproduction of a medieval witchcraft trial, with lawyers as privileged priesthood, the public a purposeless mass unless galvanized by a dynamic individual gesture. Meanwhile, the prisoner is 'shot while trying to escape', but the historian's unexpected protest leads to the discovery that he has actually been guillotined. Nevertheless, the trial must continue, indeed, it is only now beginning, and the juror continues his education in the reality of guilt, evidence and punishment: the difference between legal and moral guilt, the savage motivations, conscious and unconscious, behind Law itself. 'Nothing,' he reflects, 'can break a man's spirit like the realization that some higher power is de-

termined to carry through its intentions without regard to any norms or standards, not even to those which it has itself set up.'

This is also pertinent to the more complex **A Ship Named Hope.** Passengers board a ship for a brief trip between two local ports, but find themselves in open sea heading for the far north, at the mercy of a totalitarian Chief Officer for an unseen, perhaps imaginary Captain. One passenger, Jacob, is mistaken for a priest and, elected spokesman for the passengers, continues the masquerade though ignorant of almost all religious beliefs. Throughout his petty life he has followed convention, yet has felt himself capable of profounder thought, action, love. Here is his chance, the crisis quickens him to extremes of selfishness, vanity, responsibility, understanding, and to truths for the most part shocking. Filled with biblical undertones and analogies, this is a variation on the Messiah theme, with Jacob as a guilty, ambitious, fault-ridden potential saviour, anxious to succour but usually paralysed by too much thought, too many alternatives and conflicting motives. Messiahs can break the iron circle of power in which officers ruthlessly, mechanically, obey orders however mistaken, absurd, or made monstrous by perverted idealism. He fails, partly because, deep down, he wishes to fail, as perhaps messiahs generally do. Retribution is due, for lifelong indifference to life and people, by him, by most of his fellow-passengers. And many people have obscure cravings to love their executioners, a pronounced and drastic strand in political history. The condemned ship carries a cargo of urgent contemporary dilemmas rising from the abstruse nature of individual choice, the pressure on politics and behaviour from shadowy, archaic religiosities, the fading of organized Belief in a nebulous age, the tragedy when, with all its secret motives and desires, the unconscious is heaved into appalling light. Whatever one's reservations about dramatic, skilfully-told stories, these are not analogous to horse-riding. (pp. 94-5)

Peter Vansittart, "Horse-Riding," in London Magazine, *n.s. Vol. 10, No. 11, February, 1971, pp. 93-5.*

MARKETA GOETZ-STANKIEWICZ

Despite its openly sailing under Kafka's flag—this is reflected not only in the title but also in the hero's name, Kan—[Ivan Klíma's play, **The Castle,** and its] relation to Kafka's novel is curiously inverted. (p. 118)

The plot of **The Castle** concerns Josef Kan's arrival at the Castle in order to work together with the renowned scientists, artists, and 'deserving' politicians who inhabit it. The play begins with a shock effect. The stage instructions are as follows:

> In the darkness a long choking scream is heard. The scream is heard again; the terrible scream of a man who is being choked and frees himself for an instant from the choking grip. It dies away, stifled. A moment of silence. Quick steps of a person; the partition is moved to the side. The light illuminates a hand that is extended toward the string of the chandelier. The chandelier is lit. Centre scene is a bed with dead Ilja, at the bed stands Cyril, putting something into his pocket. Bernard as always at the window, which he opens. Emil is sitting motionless on a chair that faces the cupboard with a mirror. In the room there are several more chairs and an old fashioned writing desk. At the side wall a large decorated partition. When the light goes on Filipa

comes running in, her hair loose obviously as if she were just going to comb it.

As the characters on stage begin to discuss this event, the hero, Josef Kan, arrives, apologizing for the clearly inconvenient time of his visit. During the following scenes we find out more about the inhabitants of the castle. Their alleged work, to which Kan refers initially with deep reverence, consists of doing precisely nothing. . . . They squabble and obviously suspect each other of the young scientist Ilja's death, but it gradually becomes clear that they murdered him in unison. It also appears that Kan has taken the victim's place in every sense of the word. The very night of his arrival he is forced to sleep in the bed where his predecessor has just died.

As Kan begins to realize that the circumstances surrounding the death are highly suspect, justice seems to be on the way. An official arrives who has been delegated to find out the truth about the murder. He stages interrogations and finally reconstructs the circumstances of the deed by asking each of the group to play the role he played during the murder. Kan tries to add his own observations but is silenced. The final irony comes as a shock: the face of justice was a mask. The official, satisfied with what he has found, delivers an ambiguous speech and withdraws with polite wishes for successful further work, leaving the scene free for the inevitable final scene: the murder is re-enacted with Kan as the victim. The play ends with the lamp being turned off by the same hand that had lit it in the first scene and another terrible scream rises from the darkened stage as the curtain falls. (pp. 118-19)

To use Kafka as a spring-board was a good idea because the famous borrowed name of the play helped it to be staged in Germany and sparked immediate attention among Western commentators who never fail to mention it in even the briefest assessments of Czech theatre. But the real merit of the play lies elsewhere, in its being the first work openly to integrate the work of Kafka into Czech literature. (p. 121)

Kafka's great novel is about a young man who is trying to get into the Castle to do some work there but who never succeeds and who becomes old in the process of trying to find his way into the complex alien hierarchy. Klíma's play is about a young man who arrives at the Castle in order to work there but is murdered by its inhabitants. Kafka's hero is prevented from what he considers to be his duty—carrying out his calling—by having to cope with endless difficulties so that all his emotions and mental energies are used up in constantly intensified efforts directed toward a constantly diminishing goal. Kafka's hero cannot get *into* the Castle; Klíma's hero cannot get *out* of it. The struggle to find out about the reality of the Castle has turned, for Klíma's hero, into an awareness of that reality. The unknown enemy has become known. This, of course, is no longer Kafka. But then, Klíma did not want to become Kafka's follower and we must free him from this image for which he himself was responsible. (p. 122)

Klíma returned to Kafka once again in 1974 when he collaborated with Pavel Kohout on a dramatic version of *Amerika*. Was his spiritual affinity with Kafka so strong that he felt he had to steep himself in the work which had received less dramatic attention than the other two? Was he encouraged by Kohout, whose clown character August . . . shares certain psychological aspects with Karl Rossmann, the victimized yet strangely indomitable hero of *Amerika*? These are questions that may be answered by future commentators. The fact is that in a unique bout of cooperation, the two writers shaped

a play from Kafka's novel in which they kept meticulously to Kafka's original text. This was possible by means of a narrator who bridges the various scenes and provides a commentary on the events. (pp. 122-23)

The two adapters' loyalty to the original is so consistent that it raised sceptical comments among German critics after the première at the Krefeld Theatre in March 1978. One of them, for example, felt that the Czech authors had radically reduced the complex novel to the 'external shape of the various events.' This judgment was partly justified because of the unfortunate nature of the production which ignored the carefully worked out psychological dynamics of the play as well as the finer philosophical points which the adapters had taken care not to obstruct.

[*Amerika*'s] production . . . came closer to the secret chiaroscuro pattern of the novel which reveals how the land of unlimited dreams gradually becomes a land of unsuspected horrors. An initially mercurial and chaplinesque but later more and more tormented Karl Rossmann tries to cope with a surrounding which was undergoing an increasingly grotesque and uncanny metamorphosis (a ship, a hotel, a brothel, and the big theatre in Oklahoma were suggested with minimal but powerful props on the revolving stage set).

A close analysis of the Czech dramatization and a comparison with the original work should yield most interesting results, but in this context we must limit ourselves to one aspect only—the treatment of law and guilt. Karl Rossmann, during his employment as an elevator operator in the Hotel Occidental in New York, abandons for a short while the elevator of which he was in charge. He is found to have neglected his duty and thus broken the regulations governing the hotel staff. To be sure, he had begged one of his colleagues, whose work he had taken on that night, to oblige him in return and take charge of the elevator for a little while (while he, Karl, quickly took care of a drunken friend who would have caused disturbances of all sorts in the elegant hotel). The neglect of his duty, therefore, weighed against the possible embarrassment to the hotel management if the drunk had been noticed by the guests, was indeed much the lesser of two evils (after all, nothing at all went wrong with the elevator during Karl's brief absence).

However, the powers that be in the hotel took a different view. During a cross-examination, conducted by the Head Waiter and the Chief Desk Clerk, Karl's guilt towards the letter of the law as well as towards persons of authority in the hotel hierarchy is amply proved. He is cross-examined, humiliated, and fired. (pp. 123-24)

His 'guiltlessness'—not having consciously done anything wrong—therefore turns to 'guilt' in the absolute eyes of the law—not having observed the law precisely, and having depended on a private promise rather than on a legal agreement. The personal aspect had taken the upper hand in his actions; complex human loyalties had led him to ignore the letter of the law. But such considerations have no room in Kafka's universe. The human being is deformed into performing mechanized functions according to abstract and absolute instructions. On Kafka's heroes these gradual and painful deformation experiments are performed, and with meticulous care Kafka observes the various stages of deformation. (p. 124)

On the face of it, Klíma's *The Master* (1967) looks like a conventional detective story. A carpenter delivers a coffin to a family home, and claims that it has been ordered. None of the inhabitants of the house knows anything about it. Yet later it appears that the delivery of the coffin was not based on a mistake, for one member of the family is found to have died in his room upstairs. Moreover it appears that he died under suspicious circumstances, after having drunk poisoned milk. This is, of course, a perfect situation for a detective story: the four inhabitants of the house are all under suspicion; even the master-carpenter who brought the coffin is a possible suspect. He becomes a sort of confessor for every single member of the household, and discovers each of them to be a potential murderer. Again, in the tradition of the detective story, the circle of suspects decreases, and the members of the household die, one after another, until only the dead man's daughter is left. The revelation of the truth seems imminent.

Unlike a detective story, however, this play has no revelation. Obviously none of the suspects committed the murder, and the fact that the master-carpenter might conceivably be the guilty one seems not only unsatisfactory but also irrelevant. This feeling of the irrelevance of the whole 'case' has been wedging its way into the mind of the reader since he first has the inkling that he is being led up the garden path by a false detective story. However, the playwright's deception of the reader as to the actual nature of his play is counteracted by the fact that he provides clues that would reveal this deception: he does this by suggesting that the conventional detective secret—who is the murderer?—conceals within itself a further, much more complex secret.

It is the secret of the hidden forms of guilt every man—unless he be a saint—incurs by not fighting constantly for what he believes to be true and good. In the play the paralysis of moral indifference is represented as a kind of death. Klíma has embodied it in the strangely aloof figure of the master-carpenter who stalks death with his ever-ready coffin but who also dispenses a consolation that results in euphoric numbness and submerges the will to act.

The master-carpenter constantly refers to an ideal place which he describes as a desert where the stars are near and anguish is burned away in the clean sand. All the inhabitants of the house fall prey to the reassuring beauty of this vision; only the young woman Františka withstands it. No longer able to distinguish between guilt and innocence (all her relatives have fallen dead and the murderer remains unknown), she still refuses to be lulled into irresponsible oblivion of the here and now. When the master-carpenter wants to take her to his 'desert,' she says she would rather go to the police station. 'You know how to speak beautifully,' she tells him, 'but what are these words in a world where words have been completely separated from deeds? Your desert? What is that desert of yours? . . . Do you believe in it? And what if you long ago stopped believing in anything except those words which flow from your lips of their own accord, still beautiful and still alluring? . . . You care for nothing but your vision. You would be capable for its sake . . . to use everything . . . even our pain . . . And the fear you awakened in us.' (Softly) 'It is so close: consolation and death-hope and despair . . .'

The implication of such a passage is obvious to anyone aware of the Communist vision of an ideal future in the name of which deeds of violence are justified. But Klíma has written more than a topical play. Descending to a deeper and more universal level of meaning we find that self-justification by means of a selfless aim is a widespread disease—and as soon as we have said so, we are bound to question the use in this context of the word 'disease,' wanting, perhaps, to substitute it with a non-committal term like 'phenomenon,' and having thereby provided a perfect illustration of the general confusion about the meaning of 'guilt.'

The Master was never performed in Czechoslovakia. Apparently no director could be found who could understand it. When it appeared in print the heady intellectual excitement of the times was not favourable to a speculative study of this sort. People were not in the mood for detective stories that ended in metaphysical question marks. Although the problem of an individual's guilt was highly topical material, there was a need for more clarity. Even if the nature of justice was revealed as remaining beyond human grasp, there was some need to define the villain more clearly than by means of a passive death-wish in man. Although Czechoslovaks of the sixties were ready for Beckett and Pinter, they seem to have been able to accept a local work of metaphysical complexity only if it was a work of poetry. It was Josef Topol who provided this type of writing for the stage. Klíma never pretended to be a poet. (pp. 126-28)

The second and last of Klíma's plays to be performed in Czechoslovakia was **The Jury,** a remarkable tour de force that takes up the question of a man's guilt with a combination of philosophical ambiguity, grotesque legalism, and dramatic momentum. . . . The absurd twist of Klíma's play—as the audience and the jury find out about half-way through the play—is that the accused man is dead already and the jury's verdict will be merely a theoretical judgment of a case that has in effect been closed. (p. 128)

The man on whom the group is to pronounce judgment has been accused of murdering a young woman but the event remains so vague and is referred to in such contradictory ways that the audience is unable to form its own judgment. Gradually, however, they realize that the accused is of minor importance; it is the jury who is on trial here—a group of ordinary people faced with the choice between making a decision to the best of their conscience and putting a stamp of approval on a case that has already been decided. Clearly, the authorities want the verdict to be 'guilty.' They make sure that the jury realizes this. Not long after the beginning of the play the question in the minds of the audience is no longer 'is the accused guilty or not guilty?' but rather 'will the jury perform its task as puppets of an authority that has made up its mind?'

The verdict has become merely a matter of principle, no longer related to the actual fate of the defendant. The playwright subtly suggests the characteristics of the members of the jury and reveals how their minds give in under steadily mounting pressure. Even after learning that the accused is already dead—beheaded, as the Engineer finds out, and not shot while escaping, as the authorities claim—the jury is not allowed to close deliberations; they have been locked into the building and soldiers are marching up and down outside, urging them on to pass a 'just' verdict. And so they begin to realize what the audience has known for some time, that they must pass a verdict not on the alleged murderer but on themselves.

Gradually they become aware of a predominant feeling that is directly connected with the moral decision they are facing. It is the fear of contradicting the authorities. The army captain, accustomed to act rather than to think, is the first to pronounce the verdict 'guilty.' Gradually he is joined by the Barber and the Milkmaid and finally even the Engineer who, realizing that the whole thing is a show prepared for public consumption, no longer cares.

Only the Archivist, conscientiously repeating the contradictory aspects of the accusation, remains unswayed and makes his ethical gesture by pronouncing the accused 'not guilty.' However, even this act of moral courage becomes part of the system it is trying to oppose. In the words of the Judge the Archivist's verdict 'contributed to the certainty of the complete independence of the tribunal; in other words, it helped to provide the image of justice before the public eye. Alone on the stage during the last few minutes of the play, the Archivist bitterly assesses the role he has played in furthering manipulation and injustice.

The Czech reviewer who compares the gradual change of the jury's attitude to that of the citizens in Ionesco's *Rhinoceros* seems to have overlooked the basically different motivation. Klíma's jury changes on the premises that 'it's all the same anyway,' whereas Ionesco's people change because 'one has to keep an open mind . . . and we must move with the times.' The former decision is based on the awareness that heroism is not only dangerous but also useless; the latter is prompted by thoughtless gregariousness and the refusal to be different. On the whole Klíma's people *know* that their decision has nothing to do with what they think is right; Ionesco's people think their decision is based on what is right. The characters in the Czech play watch themselves changing into rhinos, never losing sight of the human image they are abandoning; the characters in the French play invert the values: the rhinos become people and the people become monsters.

It is surprising that *The Jury* was staged in Prague as late as April 1969 when, naturally, it caused agitated applause and obvious excitement among the audience. The reason that it was censored only at a later date may be found in the fact that the play could be and indeed was interpreted as a comment on the false claims of democracies that pretend to let the people have their share in decisions. That the play can be taken as a comment on the problem of justice in entirely different social systems shows that Klíma's play plumbs greater depths than the manipulations of justice in a country that is being 'normalized' back into a system. (pp. 129-30)

Four highly theatrical one-act comedies followed *The Jury,* and at first sight one would hardly recognize the author of *The Castle* and *The Jury.* The author's vivid stage sense seems to have come with his decision to provide amusement because 'what sense is there in torturing minds that are already filled with anxieties. Despite this rather gloomy incentive Klíma has written very funny plays, though the laughter they evoke is none too comforting. But then—as we have been shown from Aristophanes to Molière and Shaw—laughter somehow rarely is. (p. 131)

Klara and Two Men had its first production in German at the Atelier-Theater in Vienna in 1971. It is an amusing yet deeply serious one-act play about how and whether to enjoy life. 'I like to be happy,' says the naïve heroine of the play who is surprised that there seem to be people who do not seem to share this preference. Her world is one where pleasures are considered the only legitimate goal in life and the harassments which stem from problems perennial or topical are simply pushed aside gently with the reminder 'don't think about that now.' We are reminded of the lesson the tensely conscientious English writer learned from Zorba the Greek who believed that a man should dance as often and as long

as possible. However, Klíma does not grant his Klara the full victory of the passionate Greek. The play, written rapidly during a short spring holiday, starts out looking like a bedroom farce and ends with an existential outcry into silent darkness. The scene is Klara's room, cluttered up with potted plants, radios and transistors because, although she likes many things, one thing she does not like is silence.

When the curtains open, Klara enters with a bunch of flowers and a man. The first line explains the situation: 'Man: (looking around . . .) So this is where you live.' The audience has been alerted for what is likely to follow: a first attempt at love-making interrupted by all kinds of difficulties. This is indeed what does happen, but the difficulties are different from what we expect. It turns out that in the next room Klara's former lover is dying of cancer and his faint voice carries through the wall, begging for forms of help that seem as absurd to Klara's visitor as they do to the audience: the voice asks for wire and dogs. Klara, who has been providing both for the last weeks, calmly explains to her puzzled visitor that there is nothing strange about these requests. . . . The faint but insistent voice on the other side of the wall keeps interrupting the Man's increasingly half-hearted attempts to make love to Klara (who obviously is perfectly prepared to do so). . . . (pp. 132-33)

Soon the fall of a body is heard. Under Klara's orders he has to help her bring the dead man into her room and put him on the couch where he remains until the end of the play, by which time the Man predictably leaves without having done what he intended.

So much for a realistic obstacle regarding the Man's endeavours—a death (though not his own) thwarted the embrace. But there is another dimension to the play which opens up a quite different reality. Throughout the action all sorts of inexplicable things keep happening. Several times the phone rings and voices ask for the Man although he protests 'no one knows that I am here. Half an hour ago not even *I myself* knew that I'd be here.' Another tenant rings the bell at midnight with suspicious requests. All these incidents visibly unnerve the Man, whereas to Klara they seem perfectly normal occurrences. Everything is natural for Klara. At one point, when the Man has gone into the room next door, she actually picks up the phone and talks to God, to her 'friendly, fat God who wears sandals,' to whom she has always prayed whenever she has broken off with a lover. But now her God does not answer, she cannot even see him as she is used to; her desperate assertion 'But I want to—I want to be happy!' and her plea 'This one time, a last time, one more last time . . . Don't leave me!' remain unanswered and the only sound that is heard as the light goes out is water running from the tap she has turned on in her desperate attempts to break the unbearable silence.

And so the bedroom farce has turned out to be a play about human fear: the whole spectrum of fear beginning with the concrete fear of being caught in an illicit love affair, moving on to a more general anxiety generated by mistrust of other people (the Man is uneasy about the woman tenant at the door), and ending with a constant sense of some kind of persecution (he examines the phone, worries about who might have seen him come). (pp. 133-34)

Café Myriam, written in 1968, is an entertaining black comedy which ostensibly deals with the shortage of places to live. It is perhaps ironic that this most localized of Klíma's plays was performed in the United States [in 1971 under the title *The Sweetshoppe Myriam*] where shortage of apartments is certainly not one of the main problems [American] society faces. The author, although he refuted the idea that the play was meant as social criticism—'I had a lot of fun trying out that black humour for the first time'—tells us that it was inspired by the desperate shortage of apartments in Czechoslovakia. In a situation where young couples have to wait for six or seven years for an apartment, live in the meantime in cramped conditions with in-laws, and have to pay a horrendous deposit in order to be put on the waiting list, an apartment gradually becomes the focus of dreams and desires. The disastrous psychological consequences for the characters of otherwise harmless and kind people provide the background for *Café Myriam.*

The café sells a 'speciality of the house': delicious cakes in the shape of a mushroom, covered with marzipan and soaked in brandy. . . . The chief pastrycook of 'Myriam'—a burly muscleman who looks more like a butcher—bakes two kinds of sweet mushrooms: both are equally delicious but one kind is poisonous, causing certain death to the consumer.

A young couple appears in the café, lured by an advertisement that 'Myriam' can provide apartments within a few days for a relatively low price. As the couple try to find out how this splendid proposition works, they are gradually enlightened as to its real nature. Apartment-seekers find an elderly person who has an apartment, establish friendly relations, take him or her for a treat to the pastry shop, attend the funeral a day or two later, and are promptly presented with the papers for the apartment by the efficient manager of Café Myriam.

Not only have the police and the representatives of justice availed themselves of this successful housing service, but a government minister is actually the founder of the establishment. In impassioned speeches he explains to the young couple that it is all being done 'for you, my children, so that you have a roof over your heads. So that you can procreate in peace.' The young man is appalled: 'Can you live where murderers live unpunished? Where the authorities protect the murderers?' Admirable ethics, to be sure. But, like the honest Archivist in *The Jury,* Klíma's young man is denied a role of honour. He is carried off on the shoulders of the butcher-cook, cheered by the others as keeping alive the image of purity and idealism so badly needed in this guilt-ridden world to which we all belong. Stunned with what is happening to him, he is integrated into the poisonous production as a holy picture of innocence that punctually revives the theory of guilt-lessness while everyone around shares in guilt.

The black comedy here has given another sardonic twist to the theme of *The Jury.* Although we are likely to laugh throughout this vivacious and fast-moving play, the question that forces itself on our minds is no less serious than the one posed by *The Jury.* A system that is able to arrange things in such a way that the most elementary needs of man are presented as privileges has the power to control people to a frightening degree. Moreover, there is an equally frightening power in the pull of togetherness; if everyone does it, it surely can't be all that wrong? Collective guilt, although we have done much talking about it in the last few decades, does not weigh as heavily as individual guilt. In fact, it strangely loses the face of guilt for those who do not want to see it. There is, it turns out, only a short step from the absurd Café Myriam to the great social questions that rock our age.

A Bridegroom for Marcela concentrates openly on the themes of arbitrary guilt, free will, and violence. Again the fable that illustrates these questions is amusing, at least at the start: the quiet clerk Kliment is asked to present himself at a higher office because, he is told, he apparently wants to marry a young woman, Marcela Lukášová, who lives in the same apartment block. This is a complete surprise to Kliment whose connection with the girl is limited to having once helped her with the groceries. Far from having amorous designs on Marcela, he says he has his own girl whom he intends to marry. When he is finally ushered into the office after having had to wait for eight hours in the unheated waiting-room, he is tired, hungry, and cold, but he is certainly not guilty of what he is accused of—namely, having seduced Marcela Lukášová who is now expecting his child.

In the course of the play three officials work on Kliment with methods varying from moralizing rhetoric about conscience and love, to blows and a loaded pistol. At one point they actually bring in the 'bride' who shows obvious signs of a similar official interrogation and considers Kliment no less a stranger than he considers her one. The play ends with Kliment, reduced to a babbling, croaking bundle of wretchedness, collapsing of a heart attack.

The author, who had written the play in feverish haste while on a visit to London during the fateful month of August 1968, felt disappointed on later hearing about the Viennese audience's reaction to the play. Protesting against what they regarded as cynicism and violence, they completely misunderstand its intention. The beatings on stage which had offended their sensibilities were actually quite unimportant. This was proved in the later radio-play version where the author eliminated any reference to physical violence which he considers only a minor aspect of spiritual violence, for 'what could human brutality achieve without the murderous deafness, deadly dissembling and lies which are the forces that activate brutality?'

It would, of course, be easy to interpret the play—particularly if we consider when it was written—as an allegory on the political events of August 1968. But while these events may have provided the momentary impulse, the play is conceived on a deeper level and deals with questions related to the great fables of mental violence of our age, like Ionesco's *The Lesson,* Dürrenmatt's *The Visit,* or Max Frisch's *Andorra.* The core of the play is actually a critique of language used as an instrument of power. Klíma had long been aware of a general and potentially dangerous development, 'the increasing distance of words from their original meaning.' We can all think of instances in this cliché-ridden world of ours when the confusion between concepts such as 'conviction' and 'prejudice,' 'conformist' and 'individualist,' 'right' and 'privilege' is such that we throw up our hands at a loss for any word to define the situation. (pp. 134-37)

The usual laws of language and logic have lost their value in the office where Kliment has to account for his life. When he assures the officials that he does not love the woman they want him to marry, he gets a lecture on emotions 'that beautify human relationships and are a prerequisite for a happy future of all citizens;' when he tells them that he loves his own girl, he is reminded that the office is not interested in old memories but rather 'in what you are doing today;' when he tries logic and argues that, after all, he cannot love the girl they have for him because he does not even know her, he is told that he is 'emotionally confused;' when, in the end, exhausted and delirious, he crouches on the floor and calls for 'one human being . . . At least one human being . . .' the officials interpret triumphantly: 'He is calling for her.' They mean Marcela, of course.

It is here rather than in *The Castle* that Klíma brings Kafka 'up to date.' The conversations in Kafka's work often give the impression that the other characters speak on a different level from the hero and attach a different meaning to words. This secret change of meaning—a source of irritation and anguish to Kafka's character—Kafka sees as something mysterious and incomprehensible because the reader shares the hero's frame of mind with all its suspicions, hopes, and perception of limitations.

Klíma formulates this change in a concrete way: words are used in full awareness of their changed meaning. Take the phrase 'service to our youth' repeated by the clientele of *Café Myriam* in several variations. The word 'service' here actually means 'murder.' Or consider the way the officials who try to find a bridegroom for Marcela use terms designating humanity: 'We too are human,' says one official when it is getting late and he wants to go home. 'Are you even human?' another asks of Kliment. The words are used in full awareness of their changed meaning. We are reminded of Ionesco's Professor who uses language literally as a tool to commit murder. 'After all we are civilized,' writes Klíma, 'and know how to humiliate, violate, torture and kill without a single blow, without any noticeable use of force.'

The Double Room, written in 1970, is a farce about a young couple, Roman and Juliet, who have rented a hotel room for a horrendous price in order to be alone together—a luxury which they have never enjoyed during their previous love-making on sofas and floors with relatives sleeping, or not sleeping in the next room. As in *Klara and Two Men* the initial situation—'finally alone together'—quickly changes. But instead of the phone calls and a dying man next door, *The Double Room* is invaded by a motley group of people who intend to settle down for the night. The stage becomes a scene of increasing confusion, as characters pour into the room, invade the bathroom, pull out fold-away beds, beat a big drum (some of them belong to a travelling band), bicker and make passes at Juliet, as her lover looks on helplessly.

Communication between the couple and the intruders is impossible. In this respect the play reminds us of *A Bridegroom for Marcela.* However, unlike the wretched 'bridegroom,' the young couple here learn how to use the weapons that are being used by the intruders. By accepting aggressiveness, egotism, lies, and total disrespect for others as the basic rules of conduct between people, they manage to get rid of the whole crowd. Finally they are again alone in their room but their attitude has changed. The night of love can no longer take place. Sitting next to each other on the bed, their faces buried in their hands, they know that they will never be the same again. The author, surprised that one of his friends thought the work his first 'optimistic' play, tells us that, on the contrary, he feels this to be 'the strongest expression of his scepticism,' because it shows people who overcome their problems by accepting and perpetuating the workings of inhuman surroundings. (pp. 137-38)

Thunder and Lightning (1972) is a hilarious one-act farce about life in one of the many regimented recreational establishments at which totalitarian regimes excel. A number of citizens arrive for what is to be a relaxing holiday at a moun-

tain resort and soon find themselves in situations diametrically opposed to what one imagines by the free and easy holiday spirit. They are forced to take part in classes learning how to make beds according to a certain method; failure to cooperate results in not being given any breakfast, or lunch, for that matter. They are handed out keys with confusing instructions as to which doors they unlock, and soon they find out that the rooms have neither furniture nor water-tight ceilings.

As the audience laugh their way through an hour of fast-moving slapstick they get to know the individual characters: the couple who kowtow to any regime; the he-man who volunteers for jobs to impress the ladies rather than for idealistic reasons; the sceptic who resents being pushed around but who backs down when he is reprimanded 'officially' through a loudspeaker; the paranoid with the persecution complex who enjoys other people's fights; the adolescent who translates manuals on sexual behaviour to any female who will lend an ear; the military vacation-group leader who mouths completely arbitrary and absurd rules and regulations with a gospel teacher's intensity and a robot's mechanistic phraseology.

From the first moment the audience know that the vacationers are bound for disaster. As the speed of the action increases, a thunderstorm begins to roar outside and the group leader assigns the vacationers to a variety of incredible jobs, such as holding up the lightning rod on the roof or the grounding cable near the oil-storage and handing out rubber-soled boots and notebooks for meteorological notations for greater efficiency. When, after a terrible clap of thunder and a flash of lightning, one of the characters comes staggering onto the stage with singed clothes to call for help because lightning has struck, the leader of the group cannot be found. He has departed with the most attractive of the lady-vacationers to provide her with refuge and holiday pleasure in his sheltered villa in the valley, which has not only a swimming pool but also a canopy-bed and a lightning-rod.

The message is clear: the rules are arbitrary and exist for their own sake; truth, as the cynical saying goes, has been buried so deep that no one can find it; people who have come to escape routine and seek freedom and play find another form of regimentation; people's sense of guilt is used as a lever for any action; crass rule of power masquerades as objectivity; the slogan 'equal opportunity' provides a smoke screen for arbitrariness, favouritism, and force alike. (pp. 139-40)

Games was written in 1973 and translated into German from the typescript (the playwright made some changes to the Czech original while the translation was taking place). Here Klíma takes up the theme of guilt and innocence in yet a new way. As was apparent in the four black comedies, the initial atmosphere of the play seems miles away from Kafka's world. However, while the characters play the 'games' announced in the title, a dark, threatening reality begins to emerge from the cheerful surface like a terrifying monster from the bubbling waves of a peaceful lake. . . .

Games shows Klíma's dramatic genius at its best. The action consists of a group of people meeting at a friend's house for an evening of games. The friendly hostess, Irena, had thought it would be nice to invite a few people and 'just play games rather than talk about politics and such awful things.'—'You know,' she explains to the guest who arrives first, 'simply forget that we are grown-ups and that the whole ugly world pushes itself on us.' Gradually the other guests arrive and several games are played—though with resistance for various reasons by the people taking part.

There are six games: three in the first act and three in the second. The scenes are named after the particular games: Meddling, Charades, Taking Hostages, Court Procedures, Spiritual Affinities, and Execution. The games become increasingly sinister and dangerous. (p. 141)

[The] characters are a cross-section of modern society. There is the perfect hostess and excellent cook, Irena, the naive inventor of the disastrous games idea, a sentimental, motherly woman who would not harm a fly but who, if something terrible is happening close by, bends over her salad bowl, slicing and measuring, paying meticulous attention to the delicate balance of the ingredients. Obviously she is too busy to notice anything else. Besides, although she knows that 'fate is evil,' she is also convinced that 'we people are not.'

Her husband Filip, a former judge, is haunted by the accusing ghosts of his past verdicts. He cannot stand games in which people are blind-folded and the thought of loaded guns makes him shiver. When, during the charades, he is made to represent the Statue of Liberty (incidentally a dramatically brilliant and hilarious scene), no one is able to recognize his representation of freedom. In a later game, he prefers to act the Court Attendant who simply ushers people in and out and watches the proceedings as an outsider who is not responsible for anything. (p. 142)

Among the guests is the fat and prosperous Deml, who can afford a beautiful young actress for a mistress. It is Deml whose past, as the games reveal more and more clearly, is the truly criminal one. He has murdered a young woman whose body he disposed of in a garbage truck. But this crime seems melodramatic, crass, and unreal amidst the complex games of right and wrong. As the surface of the game cracks and Deml's murderous past comes to light, his crime seems like a decoy, realistic yet unreal, somehow out of step with the vast dimensions of the rest of the play.

Eva, his mistress, is the most enthusiastic game-playing guest. Apart from sexual games, which she plays to perfection, she likes any game at all. She eagerly acts any part, from charade guesser, to hijacked passenger, to prosecuting attorney, to henchman's assistant. She does it all with panache, finds everything fascinating, and does not mind much which of the other eligible males she will seduce the next evening—the muscleman or the bookworm.

The former, Jacob, is an avid sportsman who flies around the world wherever his team is sent, who communicates in the clipped sentences of the sports 'pro,' who acts the witness for the prosecution with the same slow-witted pedantry with which he does muscle-building exercises 'according to the Kaiserschad-Kowalski method.'

His opposite, Peter, a thoughtful scientist, cool and collected behind the book he insists on reading most of the evening, is the ironic observer of the cruel ways and games of man. His occasional aphorisms reveal him as the author's spiritual kin: he remarks that 'not only he who carries out violence serves its purpose but also he who submits to it;' or else he refers to 'judgments which will be made only years later. Or centuries later, or never.' It is Peter who plays the Judge during the trial of the real crime, who knows whenever anyone plays the part best suited to him, who, after having asked in vain whether anyone wants to hear the verdict before they hang

an innocent man, draws the conclusion which makes up the last words of the play: 'They don't hear me. How very busy they are.'

Then there is Bauer, a nondescript bully of fifty, who becomes sociable only when he talks about guns or tells stories from his own—if we are to believe him—colourful past. . . . It appears that Bauer 'made always good,' as he would put it himself in his crude lingo. Fascinated by the loaded gun which he has detected on the wall, he begins to handle it playfully and soon wields it with much pleasure and know-how, whether acting the part of a Revolutionary or a member of the State Militia. The last game, Execution, is Bauer's own idea, and he organizes and casts it with great efficiency. At the end it is Bauer who gives the command for the hanging which is interrupted, not by anyone shouting 'Stop it!' as the guests had hopefully imagined, but by the falling curtain. The audience will never know the end of the game.

Last but not least there is Kamil Sova, a gentle homespun philosopher who is the first guest to arrive. He is intrigued by Madame Irena's salads from the culinary as much as from the philosophical point of view (because he realizes that the relationship of certain ingredients and how they affect each other could be transferred to an abstract argument of values with most revealing results). Sova—incidentally the only character who has both a first and a last name—is rather a poor actor but he has a lot of imagination. Too much, in fact. He has imagined what it is like to be a prisoner, what a man feels before he is executed, how one would talk to a man before he goes to his death; he used to dream of being a revolutionary but somehow he has lost the belief that the world can be changed. The ingredients are such that the salad—or the world—is bound to turn out to be of a certain kind.

But it is Sova who recognizes the symbol of freedom even in its most awkwardly represented form: Filip impersonating the Statue of Liberty. Sova's roles, we realize, probably run parallel to the roles he played in his real life. They progress from an idealistic hijacker (who has written books like *On Truth, Justice, and its Enemies*) to witness for the defence of a real criminal, to innocent victim at the Execution. However, as his hands are tied, he lifts them into the air and calls out his own credo of freedom: 'These are not the worst fetters. Power and false beliefs put us into much tighter chains.' To be chained and rendered helpless is for Sova 'an extraordinary experience . . . only now do I become aware of its [the world's] real dimension . . . all of a sudden, by means of this (lifts his tied hands) I feel unified with all those who perhaps have not even a notion that their hands are tied too.' As he climbs the improvised scaffold, appealing to his friends not to abandon an innocent man to the henchman's hands, Peter, the commentator, raises his eyes from his book: 'He acts brilliantly! Finally he has found the part that's right for him.'

If in *The Double Room* Kafka was turned inside out, in *Games* he is conjured up. As Kafka's seemingly innocuous corridors, offices, pubs, or studies become threatening places where dark forms of guilt are relentlessly revealed, so the cosy living room where a hostess welcomes her guests for an evening of fun gradually turns into a solemn court of justice—a grim place of execution. Kafka's haunting metamorphosis of an average young man into a giant beetle is at work in Klíma's play: a sex bomb becomes the henchman's helper; a kindhearted matron, who would unlock the chains of any prisoner if she got the chance, becomes an indifferent witness of brutality; a judge becomes a robot; an academic becomes a policeman. Kafka's salesman had changed into the beetle in his sleep before the story started. In Klíma's case the metamorphosis takes place before our very eyes; when we realize what has happened, it is too late. The deformation has taken place. The one man who has not joined the general behaviour is isolated and stares in horror at his fellow men.

Klíma's Kamil Sova expresses three emotions when he mounts the scaffold at the end of the play and the end of the 'Game': horror of his fellow men, conviction that he is innocent, and regret about the loss of human dignity. 'It is all so undignified!' are his last words. It was Kafka who spent his life drawing for us a meticulously graphic picture of modern man's loss of dignity, of his deformation into performing mechanized functions, of his loss of human consciousness. Jan Grossman, calling Kafka 'the first poet of automization of the modern world,' put it in these words: 'Dostoevsky's characters are people subdued by deformation who strive against it. In Kafka's case the main character is deformation itself which still keeps its human likeness and strives against humanity.'

In 1974 Klíma and Kohout decided to dramatize Kafka's novel *Amerika,* six years after the Prague Spring and after all creative voices except those who completely adhered to the Communist party line had been silenced. Theirs was a poignant attempt once more to illuminate—literally, put into the limelight—Kafka's prophetic and, in the most basic sense of the word, *political* vision of the horrendous danger of man's automatization. The danger can manifest itself in the organized murder of people or in—a spiritual kind of murder—the organized destruction of human individuality and dignity. From *The Castle* to *The Jury,* from *Amerika* to *Games,* this realization is the deep bond between Kafka and Klíma's work. (pp. 142-45)

Marketa Goetz-Stankiewicz, "Ivan Klíma," in her The Silenced Theatre: Czech Playwrights without a Stage, *University of Toronto Press, 1979, pp. 116-45.*

RICHARD DEVESON

One of the subtler ways in which totalitarianism oppresses writers is to force them to write about oppression. The banned author writing stories told by an 'I' who is an author who has been banned for writing stories that criticise the authorities for banning authors—it is harsh to have to say it, but one's ready political and human sympathies are liable to be frightened off by the sight of such literary self-cannibalisation, however understandable it may be. Being banned not only doesn't mean you must be a good writer; it can also be bad for your writing—as it's meant to be.

Ivan Klíma's *My Merry Mornings* isn't, I think, entirely free of the Czech government's clutches in this sense. Some of its stories remain anecdotal, shaped only by the fact that they seem actually to have happened to the 'I' who is very like Klíma. Others, however, escape into art. Klíma was an established writer before 1969 but, since then, his work has appeared only in typed 'padlock editions'. His *alter ego* here has to do occasional stints as a hospital porter and selling Christmas carp on the streets; he encounters wise-guy black marketeers and cheerful skivers who tend to worst him; he is obliged to waste hours in run-down car-repair workshops and on building sites surrounded by mud and nettles, scanned by

the huge skeletons of unfinished high-rise blocks. Sex, as so often in Czech writing, is plentiful, farcical and an anarchic defiance of the puritanical tyranny of the state.

The best stories are ones in which Klíma manages suddenly to illuminate an abstract or moralised pattern from within an apparent mishmash of incidents. He succeeds in convincing one, for example, that an image of a writer and a randy reform-school girl and an absent-minded ex-philosopher, all floating in a rowing boat in a flooded South Bohemian field—the professor's briefcase is full of banned Charter 77 documents and the combination to the lock is the year when Carneades of Cyrene began lecturing in Rome, only the professor's forgotten the date—is a true symbol of the condition of contemporary Czechoslovakia. Not everyone will care for this Czech shrug of ironic self-mockery, but it is arguably, under the circumstances, a profound assertion of freedom. (pp. 31-2)

Richard Deveson, "Nor Iron Bars," in New Statesman, *Vol. 109, No. 2824, May 3, 1985, pp. 31-2.*

MISHA GLENNY

My Merry Mornings is Ivan Klíma's first collection of stories to appear in English since 1970; it has only appeared in *samizdat* in Prague. It comprises seven autobiographical tales, one for each morning of the week. The mundane narrative style contrasts with the stories' contents, which are alternately grimly funny, shocking or absurd. The ghosts of Kafka and Hašek often visit the pages of this book: a Habsburgian *malaise* still lingers in Czechoslovakia, nurtured by an inefficient bureaucracy and a weird combination of national pride and self-deprecation.

At the start of each story, Klíma fleetingly indicates that this morning, like every other, is not going to be ordinary: a six-year-old boy drops ten feet on to his terrace; he agrees to rise at five o'clock to sell carp. With the exception of casual sex, which he seems to stumble on daily in some form or other, there is no routine or repetition in Klíma's world. In **"Sunday Morning: A foolish tale"**, which is set just after the drawing up of Charter 77, he is accused by the press of being a signatory, which he was not. As a consequence he soon becomes embroiled against his will in the politics of the Charter. . . .

Unfortunately several of his strange encounters are not very interesting. The techniques used by carp salesmen at Christmas to cheat the customers are described with reverence and at some length but Klíma is not successful in assimilating their pitch and the results are predictably Chaplinesque. The reader is more likely to be impatient than amused by the author's puerile discovery of his incompetence; combined with the banal prose, the effect is deadening.

Like so much recent Czech literature, *My Merry Mornings* is obsessively autobiographical, and in Klíma's case, this is a weakness. When he concentrates on the problems and dilemmas faced by others, his writing carries a stronger, moral conviction. **"Friday Morning: The orderly's tale"** is a triumphant example. He writes a moving story for a nurse at the hospital where he works. In it he quietly admonishes her for lacking compassion in her work with terminally ill elderly patients. In response she confides to him something that exposes his naive complacency. The secret (which it would be unfair to reveal) contrasts the brutal cynicism of the hospital administration with the nurse's essential innocence. . . .

The prose is marred by the occasional arcane phrase, but there have been few better translations of Czech slang.

Misha Glenny, "Carping and Confiding," in The Times Literary Supplement, *No. 4292, July 5, 1985, p. 756.*

GABRIELE ANNAN

[In *My Merry Mornings: Stories from Prague*], Mr. Klíma tells you what it's like being a dissident, a second-class citizen—not that there are many first-class citizens in Czechoslovakia anyway. He tells you what it's like getting up in the morning, traveling home at night, working, eating, shopping, weekending, having sex. There is a lot of sex, and no wonder; it's the only activity unaffected by the regime, except when the authorities separate lovers by sending one to prison or driving the other abroad. Meanwhile, buttons pop, trousers fly through the air, and every junkyard, forest clearing and cupboard shelters a not even particularly furtive couple. Men and women share a merry randiness that may be a Czechoslovak specialty. Anyway, it's familiar from Milan Kundera's work and films like *Closely Watched Trains.*

Most of the stories are funny, at least on the surface, but that is because scrounging, fixing, corruption and the black market are prime subjects for comedy. In a totalitarian society, no one is honest or expects anyone else to be. Peter, for instance, in **"A Christmas Conspiracy Tale,"** is a banned lecturer, literary critic and philologist who finds it impossible to make ends meet as a night watchman and stoker. So he decides to sell carp for Christmas outside a supermarket. The carp have to be stolen first, of course, so he needs money to bribe a fish warden as well as the supermarket manager. The narrator goes in with him. The manager, quickly won over with a bottle of brandy, kindly instructs the amateurs in cheating on the scales. The tank leaks overnight, and next morning many of the fish are dead. The manager is undismayed—cut into chunks, the victims can be sold at a higher price per kilo. But even so, the two friends take a loss, because too many carp are pilfered from them—you need talent and experience to be a successful crook. Still, the narrator gets down among the fish heads with one of the supermarket girls.

This is the most rumbustious of Mr. Klíma's tales. Most have a strong, sad undertow emanating from the narrator's frustration at not being allowed to write or even live freely—his passport is confiscated, his telephone tapped, his chronically ailing car followed when it hasn't broken down because of a shortage of spare parts. He is driven to read the *Canine News* in the vain hope that at least the dog breeders' journal won't be full of lies. He is equally disgusted by the materialism all about him; he can't, for instance, bear the sight of people lining up for things. And, naturally, religion attracts him—another forbidden area. In **"A Thief's Tale,"** a miracle of healing occurs—possibly. The man concerned is a Catholic who resists his fellow citizens' tendency to muddle through, if necessary by dishonest means. "I wouldn't like to adopt *their* way of life," he says—but helps to pilfer timber just the same.

In his preface to a collection of Milan Kundera's short stories, Philip Roth wrote that dissidents do not want their work judged on compassionate grounds. Well, then: [Mr. Klíma's] stories are readable and entertaining, though unsophisticated both psychologically and technically. There are sentimental passages. The criticism of the regime is too explicit for the short-story form, where the meaning should emerge without overt commentary. But the bonuses are the feel of everyday life in Eastern Europe and the acquaintance of an extremely likable literary personality, decent, humorous and engagingly down-to-earth.

Gabriele Annan, "All That's Left Is Sex," in The New York Times Book Review, *July 28, 1985, p. 8.*

INA NAVAZELSKIS

There is a sadness that permeates [*My Merry Mornings*], something not at first apparent because of Klíma's light, ironic style. It is the sadness of someone who realizes that despite being rejected by and alienated from his own society, he is nevertheless irrevocably bound to it. Loneliness—that of the narrator and of the people he describes—is a by-product of the dulling, dehumanizing atmosphere in which they all live. Yet the narrator had the option to leave [Czechoslovakia]—as did Klíma himself. Many of his contemporaries, such as Milan Kundera and Josef Skvorecky, took that option.

In one story, he explains why he did not leave. The narrator is speaking to a former lover, who left several years before, and who, on a visit back, cannot understand why the narrator has chosen to remain.

> The freedom that exists out there, which I have played no part in creating, could hardly give me satisfaction or happiness, just as I couldn't hope to feel the sorrows of those people. . . . It so happens that life often presents you only with a choice between two kinds of suffering, two forms of nothingness, two varieties of despair. All you can do is choose which you think will be the less unbearable. . . .

Unable to earn a living by writing, the narrator supports himself and his family with odd jobs—stints that bring him into contact with those who, more often than not, live by a different code of ethics. His world is populated by operators, wheeler-dealers, people who know the score and the ropes, cynics who are bemused and more than a little bewildered by the likes of the narrator and his contemporaries.

The state, the secret police, the censorship apparatus, do not figure prominently in these vignettes. They are a fact of life, acknowledged but not dwelt upon. Klíma focuses attention elsewhere. He writes of his own would-be audience, and their often seeming indifference to his own destiny and to those like himself. The narrator meets these people daily. They are the fish-peddlers who teach him how to cheat customers when selling carp. They are the hospital orderlies who steal everything from bedsheets to radiators to toilet doors. They are old acquaintances who acquire building permits for cooperative apartments and bribes from hopeful occupants. . . .

While all seven stories are well written, not all are equal in quality. Some are interesting for the description of contemporary Czech daily life; others for how deftly Klíma describes human reactions and adjustment to "the system." But the strongest stories are those in which Klíma allows his narrator to become involved with the people he encounters. These are the moments when the reader can feel as well as intellectually understand why he has chosen to remain in Czechoslovakia.

His affection for and his commitment to his fellow country-men come through.

In one story-within-a-story, the narrator writes a tale of the last few days of an old woman's life, as experienced by her husband. The setting is the hospital, where the orderlies steal whatever they can, and the tale is written for a lonely nurse assigned to the dying woman's ward. In this piece, Klima drops his usual ironic tone and writes with a clean, spare emotion that makes this story the most moving and powerful in the book. It is the story that makes Josef Skvorecky's comments about *My Merry Mornings* ring true: "One of the lovely and significant works of fiction that fade from the memory very, very slowly."

Ina Navazelskis, "Ivan Klima: Alienated Yet Bound to His Homeland," in The Christian Science Monitor, *August 2, 1985, p. B4.*

PETER KUSSI

Ivan Klíma is among the important Czech authors who chose to remain in his homeland and to persist as a writer in spite of political obstacles (the bulk of his work has never been officially published in Czechoslovakia and exists in the Czech original only in *samizdat* form and in editions printed by émigré publishers abroad). Klíma is prolific, skilled in a variety of genres including the novel, the drama, and children's literature. He is probably best known for his short stories; they all have strong autobiographical elements, evoking the atmosphere of his youth while reflecting the realities of wartime and postwar Czechoslovakia.

The most characteristic feature of the stories in *Moje první lásky* [published in Great Britain and the United States as *My First Loves*,] is Klíma's light, deft touch, the attitude of a bemused observer mocking his own attempts to cope as well as the absurdities of a harsh world. Even when the setting is a concentration camp, as in **"Myriam,"** the touching first story of the collection, the narrator maintains a tone of detachment and ironic humor. . . . **"Myriam"** is the story of an unfulfilled adolescent love affair. The point of view of a sensitive adolescent growing up amid frightening yet fascinating realities is maintained in the other three pieces as well, but the settings vary widely: **"Má vlast"** (**"My Homeland"**) is rooted in Czech village life, whereas **"Provazolezci"** (**"The Tightrope Walkers"**) tells of a young man's early encounter with the fate of artists. Klíma's casual, reminiscing style works well in suggesting mood and atmosphere but is less suited to philosophical reflection. When overt philosophizing comes to the fore, as in the story **"Hra na praydu"** (**"A Game of Truth"**), the writing seems contrived and unconvincing. (pp. 137-38)

Peter Kussi, in a review of "My Merry Mornings: Stories from Prague by Ivan Klíma," in World Literature Today, *Vol. 60, No. 1, Winter, 1986, pp. 137-38.*

RICHARD DEVESON

My Merry Mornings, Ivan Klima's collection of stories that came out in this country last year, had a rather oppressed—and depressed—air. Not surprisingly, especially as his writings are all banned there, Klíma found it hard not to be infected by the daily pettinesses of life in contemporary Prague.

In this new book he has a subject guaranteed to be more inspiriting: early love. And, masterfully resisting the obvious poisons of sentimentality and self-pity, *My First Loves* emerges as a triumph: attractive, humane, comic, elegiac and moving.

The book consists of four semi-separate stories, each told in the first person, each describing a stage in the narrator's discovery of love. In the first story, **"Miriam"**, he is a young teenager in a wartime prison (unnamed, but clearly Theresienstadt) who realises that a girl doling out milk is smiling at him, is giving him an extra ration, is hoping that he will speak. The transports are leaving for Poland; but he can't bring himself to say a word.

"My Country" is about a family summer holiday in a hot South Bohemia just after the war: the country is poised between coalition and dictatorship, the inn is peopled with characters who seduce the shy boy away from his improving 'great' literature, the doctor's wife is restless . . . 'I was stunned by the realisation that . . . she could yearn for me and make love to another and weep for another, yet that life was like that.' In **"The Truth Game"** the 'I' meets a woman who is a compulsive liar. But does he have cause to complain? While she is there, she is there; once she is gone, he has lost some naive illusions—illusions about truth and seriousness, including his idealistic Stalinism. Never trust outward appearances, his father writes to him: don't repeat my own mistake. The letter comes from a prison camp.

In **"The Tightrope Walkers"**, finally, the narrator arrives teetering on the edge of loving someone who seems to be teetering on the edge of loving him. Is he going to dare to walk the tightrope of life? Is he going to walk it alone? The story ends with the questions unanswered.

Political themes echo through the book, like the trumpet hymn from *Má Vlast* in the second story which echoes over a lost Bohemia, 'this small, painful, blessed piece of earth'. But *My First Loves* isn't really about politics. It isn't really about love, either; or only inasmuch as love itself is also about aspiration and energy and discovery, about the pull of life as against the view from the tightrope.

Richard Deveson, "Acrobat's Apprentice," in New Statesman, *Vol. 113, No. 2910, January 2, 1987, p. 24.*

ROGER SCRUTON

Klíma's literary preoccupations tend to be as minute and personal as Škvorecký's are public and vast. It is indeed hard to see how he could have retained his literary persona had he moved away from a narrow field of experience. The moments described in his stories are flat, sad, eerie, usually centred on some erotic sentiment through which the loneliness of the characters and the utter otherness of their world is made apparent. Klíma offers us the everyday life of Communism—bleak, stagnant, meaningless, with every gesture cut off from its fulfilment and hanging uncompleted in the air. No one can be trusted; no love or liking can find its cheerful outward expression. In unforgettable images, Klíma describes the backrooms, bars and rubbish dumps, the abandoned places where informer meets victim in a momentary embrace and where no one seems answerable to anyone.

The stories in [*My First Loves*] are set in the decade of the

Communist coup and the show trials. They are concerned with a young, shy, self-centred hero, as he searches for the needed sexual opportunity. All four of his first loves prove to be vacillating, treacherous, nymph-like. There is a wealth of subsidiary characters—bandsmen and schoolmasters, doctors, firemen and trapeze artists, characters from the old Central European world of settled roles and proudly sported uniforms. But the poison of Communism has been breathed on all of them and as it steadily conquers them, the hero meanders through the débris, kicking it over in the hope of solace, and finding here and there a sudden, but illusory, moment of passion.

Even in the seediest of the episodes there is a kind of candour, an innocent openness to experience, which is the mark of a true narrator. Until recently Klíma has concentrated his talent on the writing of stories and novellas—forms suited to his delicate sense of irony. Now, however, after many years' work, he has produced a full-length, ambitious novel—*Soudce z Milosti (A Judge on Trial)*—which tells the story of a good judge, existing miraculously in the nightmare world of "socialist legality", in which he seeks a personal redemption. This, one of the saddest novels to have been written in contemporary Czechoslovakia, contains incomparable descriptions, not only of the extent of the moral corruption sanctioned and encouraged by Communism, but also of the quiet voice of true religion which Klíma and his contemporaries are increasingly disposed to hear.

Roger Scruton, "Vanished Consolations," in The Times Literary Supplement, *No. 4373, January 23, 1987, p. 83.*

LESLEY CHAMBERLAIN

David Krempa, [the protagonist of *A Summer Affair*], is a dull married scientist whose life is confined to his research until he meets Iva, who brings him perfect pain. Shamelessly and unreasonably, not enjoying the hurt, he abandons his family and his work for a humiliating and temperamental sexual arrangement. For most of this simply written novel neither the reader nor David nor Iva knows whether their affair involves love, only that it causes David to lose faith in his work on human longevity. The crazy girl with a scar on her wrist who abuses him makes him wonder what he lived for until he involved himself in her beautiful, lustful, childlike doubt. Theirs is a life-like tale, which after many pages of gently gripping narrative reaches a daunting conclusion. . . .

[David] thinks in stereotypes. His girl is sexy, young, boundlessly attractive to other men, while his wife is tired and fat and his children more irritating than vulnerable. Yet it is not thinking that makes him act. It is as if the moral life were a matter of two orbits coinciding. Now that he circles a different sun, his wife's suffering is merely tangential. He drove slowly on the old planet, now he is reckless; he used to save, but now he has become extravagant. The new life is diffuse and unpredictable, whereas the defects of the old are precise and nameable. At this point David tries to pick up the intellectual thread linking his will to his work and finds that *that* dream of infinity was pitifully small.

David's spiritual removal allows for some superbly laconic destructive characterization, as when he muses on his wife: "There was nothing exceptional in her appearance and no militancy in her mental make-up. The world of the arts had,

happily, never touched her at all." His monitoring of his own feelings is kinder, but exact about his muddle. "I've never driven anywhere without knowing where I was going. But now I'm driving just for the drive." Though Ivan Klíma does not quite condone, these are facts, not matters inviting judgment. Love is a condition, not a controllable sin, and Klíma writes about it with disconcerting Flaubertian wisdom.

Lesley Chamberlain, "Cabaret-Time," in The Times Literary Supplement, *No. 4404, August 28, 1987, p. 932.*

JACK SULLIVAN

An ecstatic vertigo is the main feeling that suffuses *My First Loves,* a new collection of stories by the Czechoslovak writer Ivan Klíma about sexual awakening and political upheaval. Again and again, the nameless young narrator of these interconnected stories . . . experiences a dizzying but momentary empathy with an object of desire, often from a great distance or depth. In a particularly radiant moment, he gazes up at, then becomes one with, a beautiful girl "dangling in the void" from a rope ladder on a hot-air balloon, swinging over a "deep emptiness" that afterward becomes his own; in another, he swoons in terror as he watches a miraculous tightrope artist, longing to tell her afterward how he "shared in her vertigo." Only at the end, as he gropes toward an uncertain adulthood, does he begin to lose this continual tingle of another's anxiety.

Unlike mysterious moments of empathy in modern fiction by James Joyce or Virginia Woolf, these imaginative flights are from real holocausts rather than spiritual or interior ones. In the opening story, the narrator crouches in a claustrophobic Prague ghetto, hoping he won't be the next to be hauled away by the SS; by the middle of the book, he is struggling to understand why his father has been incarcerated, not by Nazis, but by the very Communist regime he has so eloquently and idealistically championed.

In **"The Truth Game,"** as the narrator's own idealism begins to crumble, he becomes involved with Vlasta, a mysterious woman who continually changes her name and otherwise lies to him for no apparent reason. This paralleling of romantic initiation and political trauma, Mr. Klíma's main structural device, sometimes occurs through collagelike juxtapositions. In the slyly ironic, sumptuously composed **"My Country,"** a novella in the form of an opera, the main story of an encounter with a married woman named Paula is interrupted again and again by arialike song lyrics and political speeches; Mr. Klíma also inserts some violently erotic passages from Balzac, Stendhal and other "great masters" the hero's teacher has assigned to elevate his mind and inspire him as a budding writer. These quotations simply erupt on the page, without comment or transition, giving voice to the narrator's sexual longing and political confusion.

Sometimes the romantic layer in a story is a displacement of a larger, infinitely more tragic one. In **"Miriam,"** the most moving piece in the book, a young girl working in a ghetto soup kitchen (another angelic stranger) begins illegally offering the narrator extra milk, along with what seems to be a smile of love. When she suddenly withdraws both, he is thrown into a trauma far worse than the anxiety occasioned by the parallel story of his aunt Sylvia, who offers stolen food to the family to celebrate her wedding, only to be deported to a concentration camp with her lover on what was to have been their honeymoon.

Like all of Ivan Klíma's work (including *A Ship Named Hope* and *My Merry Mornings*) this haunting and disorienting collection has not been published in his native Czechoslovakia. This seems a peculiarly defensive kind of repression, even for a totalitarian state, for *My First Loves* is a deeply personal book, more given over to restless fantasies about sex, death, and coming of age than to political commentary. . . .

Mr. Klíma is most compelling when he is willing to trust the power and odd lucidity of his hero's adolescent musing. He is least so when he occasionally (as in the opening and closing of the final story) explains the work's symbolism and significance. No explanations are necessary, for these stories carry the burning authority and desperate eloquence of a survivor.

Jack Sullivan, "Prague, with Balloons and Angels," in The New York Times Book Review, *February 21, 1988, p. 31.*

Rhoda Lerman

1936-

American novelist.

In her fiction, Lerman utilizes satire and fantasy to examine sexual relationships, urban anxieties, and religion. Often classified as a feminist writer, Lerman frequently combines elements of realism, myth, and theology to comment upon the role of women in history and contemporary society. Although occasionally faulted for her complex and unorthodox style, Lerman is consistently praised for her perceptive and imaginative wit. Erica Abeel observed: "Reality is canted through Rhoda Lerman's slyly irreverent sensibility, one of the most idiosyncratic in contemporary prose. Her comic range is enormous. . . . [She] is funny because she hears us so right."

In *Call Me Ishtar* (1973), her first novel, Lerman draws upon the Bible, Classical and Middle Eastern mythology, and European fairy tales to comment upon patriarchal elements of Judaism and Christianity. This work details the incarnation of Ishtar, the Babylonian goddess of war and fertility, into the body of a contemporary Jewish housewife through which she hopes to subvert the influences of Moses and Jesus Christ and to reclaim her spiritual dominance. *The Girl That He Marries* (1976) revolves around a sophisticated Gentile woman who sacrifices her integrity and individuality to win a superficial Jewish man through manipulative ploys. While some critics regarded Lerman's style as occasionally awkward, most lauded her acute satire of sexual game playing and urban Jewish life, comparing her comedic talent to that of Philip Roth. Harriet Rosenstein asserted: "Her eye for the give-away detail, her ear for the mad half-phrase, her ability to sustain the cadences of a comic scene, all have that peculiar mix of energy, lucidity, and hysteria at which Roth excels."

In *Eleanor* (1979), the fictional voice of former First Lady Eleanor Roosevelt narrates her struggle to overcome personal insecurities during her husband's affair with Lucy Mercer and later when he is diagnosed as having polio. Frances Taliaferro commented: "This splendid novel transcends its careful scholarship; Lerman's poetic, impressionistic version of Eleanor has a 'reality' truer and more haunting than the most scrupulous notes of the biographer. *Eleanor* is distinguished historical fiction." *The Book of the Night* (1984), a fantasy novel, concerns a young woman who enters a tenth century monastery disguised as a man. Upon falling in love with the abbot, the woman metamorphoses into a white calf to avoid expulsion from the order. *God's Ear* (1989) garnered praise for its humorous portrait of an insurance salesman who is called upon by the ghost of his rabbi father to establish a synagogue in the Colorado desert.

(See also *Contemporary Authors*, Vols. 49-52.)

HARRIET ROSENSTEIN

Call Me Ishtar is an anti-Mosaic mosaic, a patchwork satire of patriarchy, sublimation and suburbia. The book has two stars: Ishtar, once the Sumerian deity of love and war (in later incarnations Mother Goddess, Queen of Heaven, Angel of Death, Whore of Babylon), and Rhoda Lerman, American first-novelist of formidable gifts. Sometimes, like good sisters, they cooperate; sometimes, like prima donnas, they compete. The result is an imaginative *embarras de richesses,* an unresolved esthetic rivalry between narratives and narrators.

Lerman resurrects Ishtar and establishes her in upstate New York — supernatural housewife and sexual subversive. Interlarding that crazy tale are rewrites, many brilliantly done, of both Testaments, Classical and Middle Eastern mythology and European fairytales. And, to make the mosaic more Byzantine yet, there are comic mini-lectures on matriarchal lore — on the vulvular significance of cookies and *sukkahs,* for example. Everything — language, objects, history — becomes the object of playful revision; pure play exhausts; the novel cannot contain its own inventiveness.

Although an enterprise like this would have been unthinkable five or six years ago, it cannot be called feminist fiction. First and least importantly because Earth Mothers, however powerful, are hardly what the age demands. And because dominance, however humorously, is still the issue: putting Mama on top merely reverses the missionary position. And because

175

the attitudes toward sexuality here are contradictory in the extreme — at moments, surpassingly humane; at others, macho-adolescent. It is often like listening to Philip Roth impersonate the Wife of Bath, self-consciously reciting what he still believes to be dirty words. Bloodless bawdiness. The self-titillating talk of spare parts. Or a disconcerting archness: the effort, as Ishtar puts it, to be both "cunning and lingual."

Another parallel to Roth is inevitable and here Lerman equals him in his own good game—the Jewish absurd. Her eye for the give-away detail, her ear for the mad half-phrase, her ability to sustain the cadences of a comic scene, all have that peculiar mix of energy, lucidity and hysteria at which Roth excels. At a bar mitzvah:

> Except for the Cleveland aunt and the strangling rabbi, no one in the entire congregation misses a shiver of David's glen plaid jacket and his golden Farah slacks as he looks into the eyes of heaven. . . . By itself, truthfully, the electric organ in the organ loft explodes and its pipes, as they burst, plotzing in pleasure, howl maniacally and go sailing, little golden spaceships, through the memorial windows, stained.

Yet Lerman's comedy can be as sweet as her bar mitzvah scene is broad. . . . The book abounds in creations to relish: Cinderella fleeing the Foot Fetishist; a Joycean novocaine trip while Ishtar is under the drill of "the Tooth Pharaoh, this latent Jewish dentist." Ritual seduction — "I would get you in the bathtub!" — in water rendered Aegean by three drops of Durkee's Food Color. . . . *Call Me Ishtar* is great fun and often wonderfully funny. It should probably be read slowly, as an anthology, and savored, as a promise. Though it attempts too much and never settles formal or tonal questions, it announces a writer of genuine talent. Rhoda Lerman is a find. Go out and find her.

Harriet Rosenstein, "Supernatural Housewife, Sexual Subversive," in The New York Times Book Review, *November 25, 1973, p. 46.*

THOMAS R. EDWARDS

[In *Call Me Ishtar*], the small and seemingly hopeless details of Middle American housewifery get infused with wild strains of myth, as the archetypal mother—call her Ishtar or Astarte or Aphrodite or Arianrhod or whatever else Robert Graves or Norman O. Brown may suggest—descends into the fallen world of rational male order somewhere around Syracuse, New York, in the incarnate form of a sexy, Jewish [homemaker]. . . . (p. 470)

Call Me Ishtar reflects a sense of what could fairly be called oppression, a sense Lerman obviously shares with many other women. But I think that women face a special difficulty in expressing this sense, one that black writers, for example, may not face. Lerman's book reminds me interestingly of Ishmael Reed's *Mumbo Jumbo,* which also relates the culture of an oppressed group to a body of lore drawn from mythography and comparative religion and in which the myths invoked unexpectedly make more sense than the satiric occasion requires. But if women are an oppressed group, they are not an oppressed *minority* group; in practical terms, at least, they have less to gain and more to lose than blacks do, and a sense of qualified oppression can create imaginative uneasiness. Where Reed uses his mythic materials with a fine, incisive arrogance, Lerman seems a little nervous, unsure about

what's "serious" and what isn't where Reed doesn't bother to discriminate, over-anxious to make something, preferably something dignifying, of the housewife's lot.

Virginia Woolf once remarked that "when a woman speaks to women she should have something very unpleasant up her sleeve." Rhoda Lerman finally doesn't. . . . (p. 472)

Thomas R. Edwards, "Women Beware Women," in Partisan Review, *Vol. XLI, No. 3, 1974, pp. 469-76.*

ERICA ABEEL

As I read Rhoda Lerman's outrageous and hilarious account of the New York mating game, *The Girl That He Marries,* I kept wondering about the different responses of male and female readers. Women, I thought, would experience delicious little shocks of recognition, an oh yes, how *right* sense. The novel has received advance accolades from Gloria Steinem, Lucy Freeman, and Susan Brownmiller, and been compared with *Fear of Flying.* But men would instinctively bristle at Lerman's Portrait of the Hero as Asshole. Though men could accept a horrific female . . . they might deny that Lerman's Richard Slentz could exist outside a zoo, and dismiss as well her nightmare vision of premarital transactions. Unfortunately for all of us, though, her vision is woefully accurate, give or take a bit of comic distortion; and men, if they have the courage, ought to read this novel and meet their mate.

Stephanie Boxwell, pushing 30, would rather not grow old and die alone. She wants to get married. A Ph.D. in art history, Stephanie is on loan to the Cloisters where she's assembling an important show of Cornish crosses, but she could care less about Cornish crosses—which is, of course, the real trouble. She wants "something meaningful" in her life, i.e., a husband, and isn't unduly picky: "I didn't want a hero," says Stephanie, "I wanted a man who wasn't crazy."

Enter Richard Eligible, who may just be "the right one," since he hums "The Girl That I Marry" in her ear, is grooming to be governor, and tells her that *she* may be "the right one." But Richard, as Stephanie is quick to realize, is less an individual than a species, a Balzacian type she often refers to as "the Richards," only he wants to conquer the South Bronx instead of Paris. He lunches at the Four Seasons where he orders "the usual," avoids Jewish ties, had an ear job, speaks a *patois* of Broadway lyrics, pop therapies, and 1950s lines, murmurs endearments in Spanish without the tilde, lives with a nurse called Innocent Marie, [and] won't sleep with Stephanie. . . . He is also a master manipulator, running his "fiancee" over to Stephanie's office to deliver the keys to their apartment, and unloading lines like "when we begin to expect something of each other the excitement is over," "you're just too wonderful a girl to be small-minded and jealous," and "with you I'm not afraid to feel."

Yet, unfathomable perversity of woman, Stephanie wants her Richard. . . . She seems to have a split vision of Richard: in moments of lucidity she sees him as the devil-man with a heart on his tail as depicted on one of her crosses, for this figure suggests that "the man's heart is directly related to his asshole." The rest of the time, though, she wants the dream of Richard, marriage at any cost, and not to die alone.

But mainly she wants Richard because she gets hooked on "the game." At some point the goal of bagging Richard becomes an irresistible intellectual challenge, obscuring the truth of who he is, and Stephanie gets hot for The Win. With the female folk wisdom, the accumulated guile and ruse of forced passivity, Stephanie psychs out Richard's "program" and plots her strategy, aided by Sissy, her Sapphic secretary (Stephanie sees the alternatives as lesbianism or Scarsdale), and Miriam the psychiatric social worker, who warns her: "Remember, once you get him you're stuck with him."

According to Lerman's antiromantic vision, a woman "gets" a man by practicing Skinnerian mind manipulation: If she can figure out his pattern of gratification, she can control his behavior. If he wants nice, he gets nice. If he wants bitch, he gets bitch. Only the truth is out of the question, because "men don't marry women who tell them the truth." Innocents that they are, men, Lerman's saying, may think they're directing the action—and they are, up there in the Legislature. But in the sexual arena Stephanie Everywoman is running her man through the tracks, go-backs, tilts, and free games of an intricate pinball machine.

But at what price women entrap their men, Lerman cautions in this moral fable. Though Innocent Marie loses Richard because she is sincere, loving, and kind—wrong "program"—at least she keeps herself. Stephanie wins by becoming a nagging bitch, the duplicate of Richard's mother that his program requires. . . .

Though the book is peppered with sentences such as "What is it with men?" and "no wonder men have to go after power externally. They have so little internally"—it's far from a simplistic man-hating diatribe handing women all the points. While a shade too accurate for men to accept—without wincing—as reality, Richard is too subtly drawn to dismiss as propagandistic caricature. Lerman seems to feel that women have a monopoly on humor and the capacity to *feel* (we specialize in Affect, it seems), but she doesn't let her narrator off the hook. Women don't have a monopoly on decency or maturity. When Stephanie screams at Richard that he, "the Richards," have made her, "the Stephanies," into nagging bitches, it sounds suspiciously like that old shtick: blaming another. Better to die alone, Stephanie.

In a sense, Lerman's is a voice in the feminist backlash because her novel implicitly attacks the way women treat each other. Stephanie and Miriam are old-style female allies: The basis of their friendship is fortification against men whom they regard as a species of mule that has to be bonked over the head to catch its attention. Even worse, women who are not specifically allied against the enemy kill off their own kind. . . . What she really wants, in the end, is not to "get" Richard, but to fuck over Innocent Marie.

When Stephanie closes in for the kill, after acing out her rival, she's responding, she realizes, to some vile "primitive instincts." "My smile when I greeted Richard," she says, "was a thoroughly atavistic baring of teeth." In a final nightmare sequence, Stephanie, in her lovelessness, recognizes that her competition is a better woman. . . .

Despite its bleak view of our mating habits, this novel is antically funny. Reality is canted through Rhoda Lerman's slyly irreverent sensibility, one of the most idiosyncratic in contemporary prose. Her comic range is enormous. In a tour de force, Richard, who has lots of lines (both senses) never speaks an *authentic* phrase. Lerman is funny because she hears us so right. Stephanie's lyrical meditation on the mystery of the Cloisters' Unicorn flips over into a raunchy

Woody Allenesque anachronism. Lerman has a trick, too, of repeating pop slogans and cliches, like "in the name of love" and "going off the wall," and worrying them about the page until they lie there, dead husks of language. Her prose lurches forward, stops, and tracks back in a loony sequence of ellipses and nonsequiturs and flagrantly ungrammatical sentences composed of stumps of phrases, oddly jointed with "buts," "excepts," and "yets," the better to translate Stephanie's multiple contradictions.

Like her characters, Lerman's language plays games. Spinning us on a swift whirligig through the sexual nastiness of our culture, she sets us down laughing.

Erica Abeel, "Laughing, Sort of, All the Way," in The Village Voice, Vol. XXI, No. 29, July 19, 1976, p. 35.

ALIX NELSON

Read it and weep. With unrelenting manic ferocity, this savage, sexist, hilarious romance à la Kafka [*The Girl That He Marries*] demonstrates the truth of H. L. Mencken's assertion that "to be in love is merely to be in a state of perceptual anesthesia—to mistake an ordinary young man for a Greek god." Pursuers of ordinary men (is there some other kind?) can hardly afford to miss this cautionary tale.

Never has an ordinary man been rendered with such glee. For those of us who've been waiting around for Alexander Portnoy to get his, author Rhoda Lerman here "hulls him from the belly button like an overripe strawberry" to prove that writing well is the best revenge.

Outstripping Philip Roth in his own milieu, she lays to rest, in all their Bloomingdaled, Brooks Brothered paraphernalia, those narcissistic scions of Jewish families. . . . (p. 10)

"Maybe they've just run out of emotion, the way the world runs out of fossil fuels," the female protagonist of *The Girl That He Marries* observes—an indictment the author herself applies impartially to the entire gender.

In determined pursuit of this elusive quarry (known hereafter as Richard Slentz) . . . is one Stephanie Boxwell, an attractive gentile from the Midwest who has a Ph.D.in art history and a collection of Sumerian fragments. She is, obviously, in Richard's scheme to become The Governor, "the right one, an intellectual decision, a vote-getter." He is, obviously, in Stephanie's scheme to join the Pound Ridge married four-wheel drivers, a man with whom "to walk arm-in-arm into the Executive Mansion . . . permanent, rock-solid, lasting."

Also pompous, banal, pure cliché. Nonetheless, Stephanie joins the battle armed with such a brilliant arsenal of psychologically debilitating tactics that even the most Machiavellian princesses among us are forced to wince with recognition and shame.

Richard, it must be noted for the squeamish, is a Grand Master of The Game. Since he essentially dictates the rules (now you see me, now you don't), he is free to change them every time Stephanie moves in close.

Rallying around this pas de deux is a corps de ballet of armchair generals, ruthless relatives and fearless advice-givers who contribute scene after scene of splendidly stylish satire. . . . (pp. 10-11)

What Richard correctly perceives is that Stephanie will eat him alive. What Stephanie fails to grasp is that a boring elusive man, once caught, is—simply boring, and that what wives get is "loyalty, life insurance, birthday cards, a new outfit each season, the paycheck every week and wait forever for an emotional commitment." That's in reserve for the Innocent Maries at the piano singing "I'm Just a Girl Who Can't Say No."

"I'd prefer the Big O," says Stephanie, in a last wistful moment of truth before launching the ultimate attack that earns her an engagement ring, plus a crack at a week in Bermuda.

Will Stephanie settle for five fun-filled days? Will she hit Richard on the head with his Yamaha racket before she drowns in The Times Travel Section? It looks like Steph is down for the Big Count, but it's possible to imagine that she foresees her own end in time to make the big bolt.

Rhoda Lerman's first novel, *Call Me Ishtar,* has become an underground classic among the few who have read it. For those interested in the total Lerman oeuvre, I can only repeat the injunction given by a reviewer when that book was published [see excerpt above]: Rhoda Lerman is a find. Go out and find her! (p.11)

Alix Nelson, in a review of "The Girl That He Marries," in The New York Times Book Review, *August 8, 1976, pp. 10-11.*

DORIS GRUMBACH

Rhoda Lerman's "novel" *Eleanor* is what has recently been dubbed a "faction"—a portmanteau word for a work of fiction based on fact. The title of the novel indicates its subject: Eleanor is Eleanor Roosevelt. The time for Lerman's fictional exploration of her as a character is 13 years after her marriage to 36-year-old Franklin. She is 33, has five children, the youngest 2 years old. The time is 1918.

Eleanor tells her own story, describing herself in the painfully self-conscious terms the youngish woman we know from Joseph Lash's biography might have used: "I was too thin, too tall, and too tense. I had shingles, nightmares, constipation, a world of daydreams to ease the pain of my days, twice as many teeth and three times as much energy as anyone I knew except my Uncle Ted and very little courage."

World War I is almost over. Eleanor works in a canteen for soldiers and sailors in Union Station in Washington and in New York, dancing with the doughboys, serving them drinks and doughnuts, while her husband is abroad serving as Assistant Secretary of the Navy. He writes to her: "I have seen the war. I have found four Heppelwhite chairs with our crest." And she thinks: "I have feet of lead and hammer toes and shingles."

What Rhoda Lerman has achieved in this re-creation of the crucial and personally troubled years in the life of a great American woman—a lonely and sensitive wife of a charming, unfaithful husband—is an imaginative success. On occasion, it is true, Lerman creates for Eleanor some overheated prose. Of Louis Howe, Roosevelt's close friend and adviser, she allows Eleanor to think: "He is a medieval horror. . . . He sucks on our dreams, on Franklin's dreams, and stokes up the madness in us both. He has a face full of holes, and fills his holes with our beauty." (p. R12)

After the war, on the outskirts of Paris and seeing the devastation, she tells "a silent woman silently" that "Yes, I lost my home and lived in a cellar of my despair with weeds in my garden, choking on my fruits, chewing on my wings."

If these introversions seem excessive at times for the woman whose prose we came to know through her newspaper column, "My Day," and if, as is inevitable, sometimes we bridle at the liberties Lerman takes with Eleanor's interior life, they do not appreciably disturb the whole accomplishment: In spite of them, Lerman brings what has always been a stick figure in history to glowing, aching life.

The novel ends with Roosevelt's severe illness and Eleanor's profound compassion for him. She is pictured here as "a woman filled with her own lead." And Lerman imagines Eleanor saying early in the book that "the performed may turn and become the performer." We know from history, the natural agent that ends this hypothetical but fascinating book, that this is just what happened to Eleanor. (pp. R12-R13)

Doris Grumbach, "Four Compelling Novels about the Lives of the Young," in The Chronicle of Higher Education, *Vol. XVIII, No. 8, April 16, 1979, pp. R12-R13.*

WEST COAST REVIEW OF BOOKS

Legends about Eleanor Roosevelt are legion. And the facts about the extraordinary person are surely more startling and fascinating than a lot of fiction. [With *Eleanor*] Lerman has written a novel, not a biography, about Eleanor Roosevelt, and we have found it difficult to understand or condone why she has chosen to do so. Whatever Joseph Lash wrote in the biographies of Eleanor and Franklin Roosevelt, whatever other biographers and interviewers have written, we have gained a veritable mine of insight and information about the person who was the great Eleanor. We already were well aware of her relationship with her mother-in-law, her insecurities about her person, her weaknesses and strengths, her torments and bents. Lerman, in her novel, offers little to justify the book. The prose is stilted and formal, and the entire account is written in first person. Her sentences are convoluted and endless. . . . Her dialogue has that unreal ring: "Darling!" Franklin smiles at me so. "You are splendidly, absolutely Delphic. I've thought of aeroplanes only as warships that fly. But, Babs, what of that terrific moral suppository you've offered me all these years . . . that Science will ruin Spirit! What of that?" Can you believe it? We didn't . . . and fidgeted continuously throughout the reading of this unnecessary novel.

D. H. R., in a review of "Eleanor," in West Coast Review of Books, *Vol. 5, No. 3, May, 1979, p. 23.*

FRANCES TALIAFERRO

Rhoda Lerman's *Eleanor* looks at Eleanor Roosevelt in the critical years 1918-21. In 1918 Franklin Roosevelt was Assistant Secretary of the Navy, long married to Eleanor and in love with Lucy Mercer; the three years of this book take him through postwar politics and end at Campobello, where he was stricken with polio. The political events of the period are only incidental to the fine portrait of the Roosevelt marriage and of Eleanor herself. Here, in her thirties, she is not the grand old lady we remember from her latter years. Emotionally ungainly, she seems to have been pressed unwillingly into the Roosevelt pattern of aristocracy. She calls herself "the question, the family emergency." She is a figure of heroic melancholy, of lead not yet alchemized, of immortal longings unreconciled to the proper world of orderly linen closets and dinners for eighteen. This splendid novel transcends its careful scholarship; Lerman's poetic, impressionistic version of Eleanor has a "reality" truer and more haunting than the most scrupulous notes of the biographer. *Eleanor* is distinguished historical fiction.

History in its first sense is narrative, and a historical novel without *story* runs the risk of being becalmed. But our present quirky sensibility demands more than a corking tale about high and far-off times. The artistic success of *Eleanor* . . . suggests that the best historical novels are those in which an emphathetic imagination takes great leaps into unpredictable forms. They are to be valued not as history but as art. (p. 98)

> *Frances Taliaferro, "History Enhanced," in* Harper's, *Vol. 258, No. 1549, June, 1979, pp. 94, 98.*

SUSAN MERNIT

"It was a dangerous time for me, a time between the daydream and the real, a time when the walls between them bent and I couldn't tell if I were holding them up or pushing them down. I cried often." Thus speaks Eleanor Roosevelt, narrator and protagonist of *Eleanor, A Novel,* Lerman's inventive story of the Roosevelts' early years 1918-1921, during which Eleanor painfully evaluated her life while Franklin pursued love and political ambitions. Through exclusive use of first person narration and lightning-quick episodes similar to cinematic vignettes, Lerman adds to the canon of Roosevelt literature by providing Mrs. Roosevelt with a voice which biography cannot. On a journey of self-discovery, this Eleanor deals with an unfaithful husband, a domineering mother-in-law, the domination of her life by the demands and expectations of others, sexual fear and longing, all of which interest us because of their prevalence as twentieth-century problems and popular motifs in fiction, and because it is stimulating to imagine they concerned her.

Eleanor's inner life focuses on two issues: the nature of her being and her relationship with the dull but ambitious Franklin. . . . Our last glimpse of her is of a disillusioned nursemaid keeping alive the man she will make President of the United States.

The elements in Eleanor's struggle for selfhood are so familiar they must be drawn from "women's fiction" and the genre novel of self-discovery, rather than from the historical fact on which the book is based. One wonders why Lerman shaped her portrait from such tired clay. Eleanor's struggles are admirable because Lerman does such a good job of inventing them, not because they have particular freshness or daring, or because they involve the reader. The *tour de force* is not in the material, but in the strength of Rhoda Lerman's imagining, her careful integration of research and reportage into a fictional document. Lerman's emotional realism suggests what Mrs. Roosevelt might have been like if these problems were of concern to her. Since we have no way to know that, we can only applaud Lerman's total immersion in her character.

Fiction illuminates character; biography shapes history into some coherent path. Fiction looks in; biography looks back.

As our ideas about fiction break down, biography seems as arbitrary as fiction, and no more capable of narrating the history of a time. . . . [But] *Eleanor* is distinct in using imagination and fictional techniques for the purpose of illuminating an inner life, not history.

In this determination to illuminate character lies the novel's strengths and weaknesses. Lerman's fictive act is impressive, but the novel is flawed. Filtered through Eleanor's consciousness, character development and plot are minimal. Lucy Mercer is sweet, Henry Adams is clever, Mama is ramrod proper, Franklin is a bombastic child. Events happen at a distance, and there is little of the conflict/drama/resolution we anticipate in a quest story of this type. However, Eleanor gives herself a narcissist's willful attention throughout. Her predicament is well drawn, but one wishes for a more commanding story, with more interaction between the characters. Readers who share Lerman's fascination with Roosevelt's character will be fascinated as they turn the pages, while the less historically inclined will find *Eleanor* well written but slow.

> *Susan Mernit, in a review of "Eleanor, a Novel," in* The American Book Review, *Vol. 2, No. 3, February, 1980, p. 8.*

DIANE K. BAUERLE

[In *The Book of the Night*], Lerman takes us to 10th century Celtic Iona, an island where "the veil between Heaven and earth is thin" and Druid/Christian monks sing time on its course and preserve the balance between the fruitful daylight Gods and the God of Darkness, Seth. To this place Celeste, disguised as a boy, is brought by her father. He teaches her a provocative set of approaches and truths: litanies of bizarrely connected words, catechisms of questions with no answers, and the startling idea that in "the moment of chaos . . . change becomes not evolution but exaltation." During a crisis, Celeste does achieve this moment when she can transform herself and she becomes a little white cow. When the miracle is discovered by the monks, she becomes the center of the struggle between the Irish and Roman churches; Celeste's main concern, however, is not the date of Easter, but self-perfection and a return to human form.

Although Lerman weaves an eccentric and sometimes fascinating tapestry, too many ends are left hanging. The odd relationship between time on the island [900 A.D.] and that of the world outside remains hazy and not fully worked out. Lerman's knowledge of various mythologies, philosophies and sciences, as well as the connections between them all is very impressive, but it overwhelms her story which becomes mainly a vehicle for her pyrotechnic displays of language and learning. At times her poetry and comments on the nature of God combine in epiphanies; elsewhere symbols and events are merely obscure. While in the end I found the whole to be intriguing, I still was missing many answers. This could be intentional. . . . However, most readers will find the effort this book requires hardly worthwhile. Those who are heavily into the poetics of modern fiction, unique combinations of mythologies, their symbols and philosophies of human self-fulfillment may find *The Book of the Night* interesting.

> *Diane K. Bauerle, "An Eccentric, Sometimes Fascinating and Obscure Tapestry," in* Fantasy Review, *Vol. 8, No. 1, January, 1984, p. 17.*

VALERIE MINER

This collage of *Yentl, The Empire Strikes Back, Dr. Dolittle* and *The Gnostic Gospels* [*The Book of the Night*] is long on obscure metaphor and short on narrative power. The earnest author takes readers back to the 10th century and the Celtic island of Iona where good wars with evil, passion vies with intellect, and pagan forces sap Christian conscience. The arcane, almost precious language is counterpointed with fantastical flash forwards to the present. The result is a sometimes glittering but often confusing mishmash of ideas and images. The narrative structure consists of journal entries alternating between the voice of the monk Generous and that of the main character, who undergoes various metamorphoses. The protagonist begins as a lonely young girl, Celeste. Celeste masquerades as a young man, Cu Roi, so that she can apprentice in a monastery. Eventually Cu Roi falls in love with the abbot. She turns herself into a cow to avoid being banned from the monastery. Thus, much of the book is narrated by a small white cow. . . .Rhoda Lerman creates in *The Book of the Night* a fantastic narrative voyage that is as unpredictable as an acid trip in which one's imagination is the primary determinant of reality; it is replete with luscious detail and intriguing wordplay—"Now this Enlightened One descends to Naught, Nicht, Noch, Not." The shimmering symbols and sparks of originality, however, can't compensate for the lack of a credible, engaging story. Ultimately, readers finish the book—or don't—confirmed in the understanding that, as with all acid trips, you had to be there to understand it.

Valerie Miner, in a review of "The Book of the Night," in The New York Times Book Review, *October 28, 1984, p. 27.*

KIRKUS REVIEWS

After a couple of ambitious but disappointing outings, . . . Lerman triumphs with [*God's Ear*], the story of a Jewish insurance salesman, conned by his dead father's ghost into ministering to the spiritual needs of a congregation of losers and crazies.

Hasidic Rabbi Fetner "lived in a universe in which absolutely everything is God's intention, where there's no coincidence, where an angel stands behind every blade of grass, singing 'Grow, darling, grow.' " His son, Yussel, can't be bothered with all that and lives a comfortable life with his wife and children, selling insurance instead of following the family tradition: he has no intention of sacrificing his life as his father did. . . . But then Rabbi Fetner dies and is punished in the hereafter for unkindness to his wife. As his ghost explains—though he may be lying—he won't be allowed into Heaven until Yussel accepts his rabbinical destiny. In spite of himself, Yussel establishes a religious community in the Colorado desert where—after magically inventive happenings, misadventures with the locals (and with his father's pathetic followers), and much suffering brought on by desire for a beautiful, provocative neighbor—he finds he must defy tradition and look at women in a new light, a discovery which leads him to open his heart and attach himself to God.

Lerman effortlessly works an immense amount of Jewish learning and Hasidic lore into a novel that's moving, wise, and very, very funny.

A review of "God's Ear," in Kirkus Reviews, *Vol. LVII, No. 4, February 15, 1989, p. 238.*

PUBLISHERS WEEKLY

Like a Chagall painting translated to print, this passionate, hilarious, God-infused novel [*God's Ear*] centers on Yussell Fetner, Hasidic rabbi turned rich insurance salesman. His clients think he has the gift of prophecy, inherited from his rabbi father, whose own prophetic gifts descend directly from King David. Summoned from Far Rockaway to Kansas by his dying father, Yussel finds himself on a journey into the desert to locate an assemblage of three palm trees and a tent, where, the Rabbi announces, God has decreed that Yussel must found his congregation. Yussel explodes: he doesn't *want* a congregation, especially not in Kansas; he wants to be in Rockaway selling insurance. But he hasn't time to argue because his father dies almost at once (though he returns from time to time to guide Yussel in his ascent toward oneness with the Almighty). The incongruities of Talmudic worship in Kansas are further leavened by ribald Yiddishisms, and solemnized by informed reference to Jewish law. The very opposite of a minimalist, Lerman . . . proves herself mistress not only of side-splitting one-liners but also of pregnant perceptions about faith and virtue.

A review of "God's Ear," in Publishers Weekly, *Vol. 235, No. 9, March 3, 1989, p. 86.*

Arnost Lustig

1926-

Czechoslovakian novelist, short story writer, and scriptwriter.

A prolific author of Holocaust literature, Lustig illuminates the courage displayed by victims of Nazi atrocities by tempering the horror of the World War II Jewish experience with hopeful insight into human nature. A Czechoslovakian Jew who spent his adolescence in several concentration camps, Lustig often explores the irrevocable loss of innocence suffered by children who endured this terrifying ordeal. Although his writing is highly personal, Lustig avoids self-pity, and critics praise his spare, unsentimental prose, which offsets the brutality of his subject matter. Alex Raksin observed: "Lustig's stories chronicle survival, not only suffering, during the Holocaust. They are sagas of adventure and endurance as well as parables with a timeless, humanistic message: Ultimately, any attempt to eclipse the individual will fail."

As a child, Lustig lived outside Prague in Terezín, a Nazi-occupied ghetto that served as a model for more violent concentration camps. His family was imprisoned and transferred to Auschwitz and Buchenwald, where most of them were killed. Lustig himself escaped a deportation train bound for Dachau and returned to Prague, where he became active in anti-Communist revolutionary activities. He left Czechoslovakia in 1968 after Soviet troops invaded his homeland, and he emigrated to the United States in 1970.

Noc a nodeje (1958; *Night and Hope*), Lustig's first fiction work to be translated into English, is a collection of short stories set in Terezín that describe the strength and compassion of the community's inhabitants. Critics were impressed with Lustig's controlled tone and his accounts of children who begin to comprehend the realities of the ghetto and the possibility of death. *Demanty noci* (1958; *Diamonds of the Night*) pays homage to the enduring humanity of inmates of the camps, as in "Lemon," the story of a boy who trades his dead father's trousers and gold fillings for a lemon to feed his dying sister. *Dita Saxova* (1962; *Dita Sax*) explores the repercussions of adolescent internment in concentration camps. Set in Prague in 1947, this novel illustrates the plight of teenagers left orphaned by the war. As survivors of the Holocaust, they are too tenacious to be treated as children yet too young to cope with adulthood. Representative of their dilemma is Dita Sax, a Jewish girl whose inability to dismiss the past or endure the present causes her to shun human contact.

In *Modlitba pro Katerinu Horovitzovou* (1964; *A Prayer for Katerina Horovitzova*), which was nominated for the National Book Award in 1974, Lustig attacks the materialism and ignorance of American Jews during World War II. This book centers on twenty American Jews who are trapped while vacationing in Italy during the 1943 German invasion and are deported to a prison camp. There they are joined by Katerina, a young Pole whose family has just been murdered. The wealthy Americans bribe the German officers to set them free but are swindled of their funds and remain oblivious to the realities of Auschwitz even as they enter the camp's gas showers. Only Katerina, aware of the chamber's real pur-

pose, tries to save herself. Critics regard *Darkness Casts No Shadow* (1977) as Lustig's most autobiographical work. Like Lustig, the protagonists of this novel escape from a train that is leading them to their deaths. As the famished youths flee toward Prague, their pasts are recalled through flashbacks involving concentration camps. The humanity of the characters is ultimately tested when they realize that they must murder an elderly woman for her food. *The Unloved: From the Diary of Perla S.* (1985) depicts a highly ethical seventeen-year-old girl living in Terezín whose resilient spirit is reflected in her diary entries after she becomes a prostitute as a means of survival. As Nazi control of the ghetto increases, Perla's entries become more perceptive and complex. Several critics maintain that the strength of Lustig's narrative stems from the detachment of his characters as they contemplate their chances for survival. Peter Lewis commented: "[Perla's ability to] remain sane and retain her humanity in the face of institutionalized insanity and inhumanity, gives the novel a positive force. There is an important sense in which 'the unloved' Perla achieves a human victory, even a victory of love, over the forces of evil and darkness surrounding her."

In the recent *Indecent Dreams* (1988), a collection of three novellas, Lustig deviates from Jewish experience to address problems faced by the citizens of Nazi-occupied Prague. The collapse of Hitler's regime is observed from the perspectives of a German prostitute who is forced to hide a Nazi colonel, an orphaned Aryan schoolgirl who falls in love with the soldier who arrested her activist parents, and a young theater cashier working below the headquarters of a ruthless Nazi military court. In addition to his novels and short stories, Lustig has written scripts for both Czechoslovakian and American television and is also an acclaimed filmmaker.

(See also *Contemporary Authors,* Vols. 69-72.)

THE TIMES LITERARY SUPPLEMENT

The seven stories in [Arnost Lustig's] *Night and Hope* are about the life of Jewish people in Czechoslovakia during the Nazi persecution. The author was in the Terezin ghetto as a boy and his fiction has the authority of personal involvement in the world he revives in these tales with the objectivity that time and maturity have given him. This is not merely the work of a reporter, nor memoirs arbitrarily shaped to read as short stories. Each tale has a genuine unity of its own and is a small work of art in its own right, though all are dominated by the pitifully epic theme of the whole Jewish experience.

The oddly quotidian character of life under the darkest oppression and the most abject apprehension is particularly well conveyed. Mr. Lustig's tales never sacrifice this vital commonplaceness to the exigencies of plotting. No one reading them could ever feel that they were *only* stories. The man on the run with false identity papers, the old woman keeping shop in the ghetto, the boys and girls growing up in their own self-conscious society, the unlucky lovers, the corrupt Jewish official, the sick old people who still look forward, all have their due place in a larger context than any of their individual visions can comprehend.

Compassion is a word perhaps too often used with too little meaning nowadays but it is certainly one of the qualities of this writing. These are handsome tales, well translated, focusing a colossal and horrible phase of this century's history, and they fulfil the artist's mission of communicating to others what he has in him of the truth about mankind. They make a strangely reassuring book.

> *"Light into Darkness," in* The Times Literary Supplement, *No. 3146, June 15, 1962, p. 441.*

MARK SAXTON

[Arnost Lustig, the author of seven controlled, perceptive stories contained in *Night and Hope*], spent part of his boyhood in the Terezin concentration camp near Prague, and that ghetto town is the setting of his narratives. Varying greatly in length and immediacy of point, they have the frightening quality of making the ghetto a living organism separate from the world it came from, bringing the reader inside by an unspoken kind of inclusion. Germans are rarely mentioned except in **"Rose Street,"** in which a German non-com unwillingly befriends an elderly Jewess, and in **"Blue Flames,"** in which a Jewish Elder of the Council connives with the Commandant on lists of inmates for the transports who are to go "not for return"—that is for extermination. The long opening story, **"The Return,"** tells of a middle-aged

man who cannot bear to be either outside the ghetto or in it and tries both. Perhaps the most vivid are the two stories about children, **"The Children"** and **"Moral Education,"** showing how the young organize themselves along the lines of authority and prowess, how the whole perspective of their future is foreshortened by the limits of the ghetto and the fear of the next list of transports east. Fittingly the volume concludes with a gently told story called **"Hope,"** the ordeal of an elderly couple waiting for final liberation by the Russians.

> *Mark Saxton, in a review of "Night and Hope," in* Books, New York, *August 26, 1962, p. 7.*

IRVING WARDLE

Arnost Lustig, a Czech survivor of Auschwitz, is known in this country as the author of a collection of wartime ghetto stories. In *Dita Sax* he is concerned with the immediate aftermath of war as it affects a group of parentless adolescents who have grown up during the barbarities of the Occupation. A good many of them crowd through the book, each with his own obsessive memories and vague plans for the future, but only one gets detailed attention; presumably Lustig regards her predicament as representative.

Dita lives in a girls' hostel and puts in half-hearted attendance at an art school; most of the time she stays in her room playing records, gently fending off all serious relationships. The only authority she acknowledges is that of a classic Czech novel by Victor Dyk called *The Rat Catcher,* in which the Pied Piper figures as an aphoristic Mr K. Dita governs her life by his doctrine of non-attachment, which finally leads her to death in the Swiss mountains.

The form of the book is well defined and an apt reflection of the girl's inability to escape from the past and make contact with her present surroundings. The writing is scrupulously honest and unemotional, and minor figures are sketched in with the same transitory vividness with which they flicker across the consciousness of the heroine. At the same time, it is easier to respect the book than to enjoy it. Emotionally it seems less held in control than burned out; and, legend or no legend, the ending is uncomfortably Germanic.

> *Irving Wardle, "On Inactive Service," in* The Observer, *February, 1966, p. 27.*

THE TIMES LITERARY SUPPLEMENT

At first sight *Dita Sax,* set in Prague in 1947, has a straightforward moral: Czechs—even young Jews orphaned by the gas-chambers—should not desert their country. According to Erich Munk, an idealistic schoolmaster writing just after the 1948 Communist *coup d'état,* "Now there will be no more rich and no more poor, only justice . . . red is the colour of hope". His letter fails to reach Dita, who has emigrated: she has already fallen to her death from a Swiss glacier.

But the novel judges Dita less simply than Munk. The Prague hostel she lives in is a transit camp for the future, where books become "a private emigration office". The mingled fear and hope of these adolescents reaching nervously into womanhood without a childhood is immensely moving. One by one they decide whether to stay in Prague or to emigrate. Their sparse possessions—Dita's paper shoes, her two records, the empty shell of a Phillips radio—are not introduced for pathos but are simply facts in the quality of their lives and experience. Dita's willing seduction by D. E. Huppert, a student on the make, and her final love-making with a pair of twins, are presented with equal neutrality. Dita stands by herself in all her contradictions. Like the novel itself, she has the split face of a Cubist portrait. If she thinks herself a whore, she can also realize, "Oh, well, I'm still more of a nun than the other thing!" If she claims, "I don't think I could live anywhere but in Prague", she nevertheless leaves. Like Munk her concern is "To live! To live!"—yet she dies.

Dita's frequent quotations from Victor Dyk's novel about the Pied Piper enforces this doubleness. Should we feel pity or gladness for the children of Hamelin? The Piper might be the Nazis who brought the group together, or the West which beguiles them from Prague, or Dita's dream of a clean white house amid green lakes ("Nature's so pleasant and clean. . . . Not like people!"). In Switzerland Dita finds her dream, and also the glacier which is both the instrument of her death and the embodiment of her vision of purity. Lustig moves surely from the opening's incisive realism to the realistic symbolism of Dita's death. On the glacier she almost realizes the truth she has sought, a truth entirely of her generation. Munk writes, "The sickness of mistrust and loneliness is strongest in the handful of you who came back from the war too young to be left to your own devices, and yet too old to suffer anyone to look after you": but what Munk terms "sickness" is, in fact, tragedy. In Dita's words: "I'm afraid to sleep with anyone, for fear of startling him if I start to scream in the night."

> *"Blank Czechs,"* in The Times Literary Supplement, *No. 3336, February 3, 1966, p. 77.*

H. T. ANDERSON

[In *A Prayer for Katerina Horovitzova*], Arnost Lustig tells yet another story of the Holocaust of Jews in 1943. It is a novel of death whose plot unfolds in a bizarre kind of hope.

Considering the subject, it almost seems awkward to refer to it as a "suspense novel" but it is—and of a most unusual kind. In the summer of 1943 twenty extremely wealthy Jews are trapped by the Germans invading Italy. They are all European born, but they all also have American passports. The entire group is sent to a death camp in Poland where a young Polish girl who is about to be sent to the gas chamber with the rest of her family is allowed to join them. Within yards of stench and the smoke from the crematory ovens, negotiations begin for an exchange and for their lives. They are offered freedom for the return of high-ranking German officers held in American prison camps.

A Prayer for Katerina Horovitzova is a gripping novel—short, simple, but powerful. It is indeed a suspense tale. It is also a tale of horror, deceit, and the dilemma of a young, innocent girl.

I think it was Elie Wiesel who was asked once if there was need for still another book about the extermination of millions of Jews. He answered "yes" simply because many people found it impossible to conceive. Read this one and believe.

> *H. T. Anderson, in a review of "A Prayer for Katerina Horovitzova," in* Best Sellers, *Vol. 33, No. 14, October 15, 1973, p. 328.*

ABRAHAM ROTHBERG

[*A Prayer for Katerina Horovitzova*] concerns a group of twenty very rich American Jewish businessmen who were captured by the Nazis when the Wehrmacht overran Italy in the summer of 1943. The Nazis, in the person of a Gestapo officer, Friedrich Brenske, wish to exchange them for several high-ranking German officers who are American prisoners, and they also wish to milk these rich Jews of whatever financial assets they have. As a consequence, the Americans are given "special treatment," including permission to save a young and beautiful Polish dancer, Katerina Horovitzova, whom the leader of the American businessmen, Herman Cohen, sees at the Auschwitz railway siding and hears saying, "I don't want to die."

It turns out that Brenske is toying with them, that the German "authorities" have no intention of exchanging them or of permitting them to live. All of them, including Katerina, end in the gas chambers and the crematoria at Auschwitz, where Katerina's parents and six sisters have preceded them.

The novel is a curiosity in the holocaust literature because its cast of characters is largely American; and this fact and the way in which Lustig portrays those American Jews is doubtless what not only made the book palatable to the Czech government when the novel was first published in Prague in 1964, but even permitted that government in 1967 to award the book the Klement Gottwald Prize. Not only does Lustig show a corroding hatred for the Germans, but he also betrays a contemptuous distaste for these American Jews who think "money buys everything," that their wealth and passports will save them. The Americans are delineated as materialistic, cowardly, complacent, selfish, interested only in saving their own skins, and willing to blind themselves to what is happening at Auschwitz. When they are finally herded into the gas chamber, they go "like sheep to the slaughter"; only Katerina, seizing one of the guard's pistols, manages some resistance: "She simply understood and killed." The Americans, like the Germans, are cardboard figures, stereotypes; we neither understand them nor particularly care what happens to them. Only two of the minor characters come to life: a Jewish tailor called upon to make Herman Cohen a suit, and a mad Rabbi who is in charge of the room where the hair cut off the victims' heads is kept and dried.

The prose style is flat and understated, interrupted by occasional spurts of rhetoric and long passages of repetitive Nazi self-justification propaganda of the *Deutschland muss leben* variety. Though Lustig is aware that "a new system of human relationships operated in the camp; a different scale of sensibilities and obligations had been established, different from the ones in the Five Books of Moses or in the writings of socialist scholars or even in sociology textbooks," nowhere does he confront the nature of the evil he is dealing with, nowhere does he bring imaginative skill or creative insight to bear on the people and the situation he is now portraying. If the *Prayer for Katerina Horovitzova* is, indeed, the *Kaddish,* the Jewish prayer of mourning for the dead, for the "six million," as Lustig clearly intended it to be, it is a most conventional and ceremonial prayer. It fails to move us; it fails to become, as any threnody must, a litany for the living. (pp. 88-9)

> *Abraham Rothberg, "Chant for the Dead," in* Southwest Review, *Vol. 59, No. 1, Winter, 1974, p. 87-9.*

CURT LEVIANT

Arnost Lustig, the noted Czech novelist and prize-winning filmmaker who now lives in the United States, has devoted his entire creative career to his vision of the Nazi holocaust and the Jewish tragedy. His acclaimed novel, *A Prayer for Katerina Horovitzova*, was published in 1973; now another novel and a story collection have been published simultaneously.

Darkness Casts No Shadow tells of two adolescents who escape from a German death train while it is being strafed by an American plane. The two boys, Manny and Danny, make their way into a forest and hope to walk to their hometown, Prague. In a clearing, the starving boys see a woman giving food to her farmer husband. The turning point in the story comes when the youths decide that to save themselves one of them must kill the woman in her house. There, and later in the woods, the drama . . . is concluded.

Since films are as important to Lustig as fiction, it is not fortuitous that cinematic touches predominate in his prose. Take, for instance, the opening pages of the novel. I can imagine the footage of the scene where the exhausted boys clamber slowly up the hill and dodge the guard's rifle shots. No dialogue would be needed; perhaps an occasional, breathless, "Hurry!" The camera would focus on the boys' agony as they—and we—try to reach the top and tumble down out of gunshot range.

This scene is paradigmatic of Lustig's approach to holocaust reality. Honed descriptions, taut dialogue. One might justifiably expect an endless outcry; yet, like the holocaust itself, the fiction about it has created its own laws. As if in antithesis to the suffering, Lustig's writing is superbly understated. One is almost tempted to say that his objective narrative sans emotion is reminiscent of Hemingway; surely Lustig has learned from him the art of paring down. But Lustig is more consciously a national writer. If Hemingway described lost souls, Lustig limns a lost people.

The author's accent on the friendship between Manny and Danny (the choice of names is unfortunate; the reader occasionally confuses the two) is an artful substitute for doses of emotion. In an era when the Nazis tried to pervert "love they fellow man" to "every man against his neighbor," Lustig shows that love is alive. Survivors' accounts of deeds of kindness in a collapsing world are legion—and even if it is a small victory (something the Jews are used to), it is nevertheless a large accomplishment in the cavernous time/space borders of evil. But Lustig is not nostalgia-ridden; his books are not filled with saints. For example, although the boys are close friends, when one gives the other a piece of turnip, the price is a pair of shoes. And when one shoe works up a nail, the suspicion is that the shoes were given up so readily *because* of the nail.

Nevertheless, all these are childish thoughts—and we must remember it is children who are being led to extermination, and it is children who are making their way—alone—across the terrible terrain of Germany. Despite these normal suspicions, each lad feels that he is his brother's keeper. Not only are they survivors, Lustig seems to assert, but they are an island of surviving decency. Shoes and turnips are one thing; life is another.

As a counterpoint to their forward movement in the woods—lacking food, the youths are nourished by hope, future, Prague—come scenes of various concentration camps and factories, memories of a father slain, their life in the kingdom of night. In the forest—their "real" world, their first freedom—the lads promise to extirpate the past. Nevertheless, it leaps back at them. Lustig, unlike his fellow Praguer Kafka, is not a symbolist; yet he repeats clusters of images that reinforce the unforgettable past. In the italicized holocaust passages, the rain of ashes returns again and again; in the forest, as the boys stumble along, they are constantly aware of the ominous cawing of the ravens overhead. One of the boys remembers stoking coal in the crematorium and leaning against the wall for warmth. He knows what makes the bricks warm. Still, the farther they go from the flames, the hotter the fires become.

In *Darkness Casts No Shadow,* the two protagonists have been stained: Auschwitz is behind them, a tattoo that cannot be erased. In the seven stories of *Night and Hope,* everyone—children and adults—is still in the kingdom of twilight. They are aware of cruelty and death in Terezin (or Theresienstadt), that "model" Czech camp that the Germans used for propaganda purposes. (In his brilliant film, *Transport from Paradise,* Lustig actually uses German footage that shows a band welcoming new residents to Terezin; an old woman is courteously helped from the train . . . happy smiling faces . . . awaiting paradise.) The Jews know about the transports, but they do not clearly know what will befall them. That is why life in Terezin is nearly normal. Children play hookey from work assignments; they have secret hideouts; Danny—still in his state of pre-Auschwitz innocence—appears in adventures with his friends; a youngster can muse about "the finest day of his life." A young couple falls in love, briefly, before a transport separates them.

The opening tale, **"The Return,"** serves as a bridge between the outside world and the sealed camp. The hero, Hynek Tausig (what a sad name!), is a 40-year-old bachelor who had been hidden by an elderly gentile couple after avoiding a transport to Terezin. A frightened, decent man, he is trapped by time and history; unable to bear his cramped hiding place, he walks out into the streets of Prague, hoping to join a transport and reunite with his people.

This beautiful evocation of a haunted man in doomed, grey Prague is a stylistic anomaly: as an introspective interior monologue it is an exception to Lustig's usual crisp diction. Yet **"The Return"** is as cinematic as the other stories, because the inanimate objects, on which Lustig zooms in with his lens, become as palpable as speech and action. As Tausig emerges into the street for the first time, without his Jewish star, afraid he will be recognized, his painfully slow progress through the street is measured by the blue and white paving stones. (pp. E1, E6)

"Rose Street"—almost novelistic in intensity—shows both sides of the fence: the German commandant and his family and staff, and an old woman in the ghetto who runs a junk shop. Here Lustig succeeds in the difficult task of individualizing the Germans. He depicts their pettiness, their infighting; he even succeeds in creating a conscience-stricken German guard who, remorseful at hitting the elderly shopkeeper, later returns and gives her a can of sardines. *Night and Hope* contains a miniature world of variegated Jewry—including despised members of the *Judenrat.* In this disjointed world, people at times have nonconversations; their thoughts reverberate in wordless dialogue, frightened, waiting, hopeful. This is the hope in the night; hence the title of the collection.

Arnost Lustig's books are powerful and moving because he celebrates *mentshlichkeit* at a time when the Germans delighted in sandpapering a person's humanity before taking his life. One man gives a sick women a drink of water. Another gives an old lady a boiled potato; a gentile tram driver, knowing that Hynek Tausig is a homeless Jew, gives him a jam sandwich—all, under the circumstances, are gifts of gargantuan proportions. In modern French literature we have the gratuitous act; in Lustig, the meaningful act. "I met so many very beautiful people during those years and most of them died," Lustig has said. "The only way to bring them back to life is to write about them. This is my responsibility . . ." Indeed, he has ressurrected them. Under the sentence of death, his people freeze time, preserve decency. They luminesce like light crystals in the dark. (p. E6)

> Curt Leviant, "Moving Pictures of the Holocaust," in Book World—The Washington Post, *June 12, 1977, pp. E1, E6.*

KIRKUS REVIEWS

[*Diamonds of the Night* is another] in a series of story collections based on the Holocaust: concentration camps, burning villages, and—in the last two tales—the wake of the defeated German army. Lustig's most successful characters are children—starving, orphaned, fragile as ancient skulls, drenched in horrors. A boy tries to trade his dead father's trousers, and then gold from the corpse's teeth, for half a lemon to save his dying sister; another survives a day of atrocity to dream at last of "a land of warmth and sun"; and a young killer who has blown up German tanks with a fire bomb arranges for the merciful suicide of his grandfather before he is himself reduced to ashes. After "liberation," camp survivors witness a new kind of "justice": a child who has experienced unspeakable atrocities at first exults in the killing of Germans—a river filled with bodies, rags, blood, and oil—but then decides to examine the meaning of the "right" and then the "duty" of killing. In his stark narrative and spare dialogue—as skeletal as the starved bodies of the speakers—Lustig sustains the reality of people scoured by obscene torture and loss, discovering islands of sanity in nightmare. . . .

> A review of "Diamonds of the Night," in Kirkus Reviews, *Vol. XLV, No. 19, October 1, 1977, p. 1063.*

MICHAEL HEIM

While sharing a basic point of departure, writers who deal with the World War II concentration camp experience display an amazing degree of variety. Arnost Lustig's picture of camp life is wholly his own. The reason his characters make so strong an impression is that they are adolescents first and Czech Jews in concentration camps only incidentally. In other words, Lustig gives the reader a new perspective on the ordeal of adolescence because of the conditions under which it must take place. At the same time—and again, incidentally—he draws him into the world of the Holocaust. By amalgamating universal problems of maturation with the day-to-day horrors of the concentration camp, he shines new light on the former and makes the latter more real, more accessible to those who did not live through it.

In the novel *Darkness Casts No Shadow* two boys escape from a train on its way to Dachau. Wandering through the woods in search of Prague, they slip from the present—the forest is in its own way as hostile as the camp—into the idolized past of their childhood and the idealized future of manhood. In the seven stories that make up *Night and Hope* the setting is Terezín, the "model" camp north of Prague that in reality served as a way station to the gas chambers. The shorter genre enables Lustig to expand on several aspects of growing up (love, sex, friendship, loyalty) and explore growing old (marriage, dignity, self-esteem) as well.

> Michael Heim, in a review of "Darkness Casts No Shadow" and "Night and Hope," in World Literature Today, *Vol. 52, No. 1, Winter, 1978, p. 139.*

RALPH A. SPERRY

Literature of the Holocaust, the genre which draws its material specifically from the events of the persecution of the Jews by the German Nazi regime, must pass two crucial stumbling blocks if it is to succeed as writing: its inevitable narrowness of theme, and the temptation to present that theme in an unrelentingly narrow way. Since holocaustic writers are almost always people who suffered at the hands of the Nazis, they must, if they are to do well, be far greater writers than ordinarily, because, in order to reach those of us who could not otherwise possibly grasp what happened to the Jews in the 1930s and '40s, they must wrench their perspective on their own lives terribly, or else produce parochial works comprehensible only to others like themselves. In [*Diamonds of the Night*, a] collection of nine holocaustic stories, however, Lustig only occasionally transcends the limits of his material; he is a good writer by ordinary standards, but unfortunately not quite good enough to accomplish everything he, and we, would like.

The holocaustic theme is that of the acceptance of utter, banal annihilation as a way of life. However much the characters seek reasons for the mindless cruelty imposed upon them, they take the cruelty as fact, to live with, to exist despite, to continue in the face of for as long as possible—even to manipulate for their individual goals, albeit that those goals are necessarily shortsighted and often virtually ephemeral. Thus, the denouement being an inevitable given—that is, certain death without the least comprehensible rationale—such writing must rely on characterization for its vehicle and on the wryness embodied in pure horror for its impact. Otherwise, sad to say, holocaustic fiction becomes boring, its tragedy numbing rather than insightfully repellent, its theme itself banal. And in *Diamonds of the Night,* with only a couple of exceptions, this is pretty much what happens, for Lustig writes too sparely. He is too concerned with events to give his characters the depth necessary to highlight those events. He is too somber to allow us that chilling humor to be found in, for example, [Tadeusz] Borowski's *This Way for the Gas, Ladies and Gentlemen,* a humor which, in its essential sadness, touches us as no recitation of the depravity behind that humor alone ever could.

There are, to be sure, fine moments here, such as in **"The White Rabbit,"** a story of a boy who tries to show a hospitalized encephalitic girl a rabbit in order to cheer her, only to find that she's disappeared, simply gone without clear explanation. There is true poignancy in **"The Lemon,"** as a young man realizes he must remove his dead father's gold cap in order to secure food for his dying and, in any event, doomed sister. And there is a rather unusual departure in **"Early in** the Morning," a narration of the liberation of Prague as seen by a survivor of the concentration camps. But on the whole these stories prove to be too much of the same thing—futility without end, quiet despair without respite, or, as one character puts it, *"hope* without *believing."* Unhappily, there are few things more tedious than sheer inhumanity presented unrelentingly.

To approach this book, if you are not a survivor of the Holocaust, you must at least be already familiar with other, consistently better examples of this genre. Then, ***Diamonds of the Night*** becomes, as it were, a supporting document by which to put the whole of this literature in perspective. But if you do not know anything of this disaster, either first-hand or vicariously, Lustig will too rarely make you care to know, and that is, perhaps, even a greater disaster.

> *Ralph A. Sperry, in a review of "Diamonds of the Night," in* Best Sellers, *Vol. 37, No. 11, February, 1978, p. 341.*

ERNST PAWEL

What matters, in novels about the holocaust, is not the line between fact and fiction but the abyss that divides the genuine from the fake. The banality of evil is still with us, spurred on by sales figures and ratings; the wave of meretricious trash that brought us a televised Auschwitz in living color has not yet crested. Its cheap sentiments and media-sized ideas falsify, desecrate and pervert both the reality of what happened and our memory of it. Those with the courage to examine their wounds in pursuit of the truth face a struggle. The unspeakable resists language. Yet in the end their voices are the only ones that matter. We may choose to ignore them, but ignorance will not restore our innocence. . . .

[**Diamonds of the Night**] matters. Its author's credentials as a witness are dismally impeccable. Born in Prague in 1926, Arnost Lustig was interned at Terezín, shipped to Auschwitz, and eventually ended up in Buchenwald. His father was killed; he and his mother returned to Prague after the war. . . .

Mr. Lustig is not only an eyewitness but also a skillful, gifted writer, even though his manifest professionalism has not, in the past, always worked to his advantage. ***A Prayer for Katerina Horovitzova,*** for instance, seems flawed by cinematic touches and forced melodrama despite some deeply moving passages. But with age, exile and distance, he appears to have outgrown mere brilliance and learned to deal with the past in his own way.

The result is a projected multi-volume series entitled ***Children of the Holocaust,*** of which ***Diamonds of the Night*** is the third volume to be published in this country. Each book is self-contained, but they have a common focus: The heroes and victims are children.

Chronologically, that is; those who clung to childhood, who weren't able to grow up overnight, didn't last long in the shadow of the chimneys. Their world was a death camp run by mass murderers who killed around the clock and made soap out of the corpses. How children learned to live with this reality—and the alternative was a secret to no one—is the theme of these stories, as it was of Mr. Lustig's earlier work.

Other survivors—Elie Wiesel, André Schwarz-Bart, Michel del Castillo—have dealt with childhood in the camps. But

Mr. Lustig attempts to show not only how these youngsters died or survived, but how some of them managed to live, even to retain their humanity.

Not all the stories in the present volume are as effective as his novels; some, moreover, suffer from lumpy prose congealed in infelicitous translation. But four of the 10 rank with the best work he has done: the nightmare vision of a boys' barracks in the camp, caught in the midst of an Allied air raid; an encounter between two youngsters, one a callow Hitler youth, the other a seasoned veteran of death, that turns into a test of ultimate self-knowledge; the story of two survivors, scarecrows with shaven heads, who seek to rekindle their numbed sense of life by watching Germans being killed; and, most moving of all, an evocation of the tenderness between a doomed old man and his grandson, rendered without a trace of spurious pathos:

> Hope can be a damned messy business. . . . Hopelessness is much better. Hopelessness puts a stone in your hand, at least, if not a dagger or a bomb. When someone has nothing left to hope for, then at least he is sure of it.

Such is the message of hope in our time.

> *Ernst Pawel, "In the Camps," in* The New York Times Book Review, *March 18, 1979, p. 21.*

LAWRENCE L. LANGER

Arnost Lustig writes about the Holocaust experience with a modest authority that is virtually unique among his peers. . . . The most recent of Lustig's works to be translated, ***The Unloved: From the Diary of Perla S.,*** can only add to the stature of an author still not well-enough known for his contributions to Holocaust literature.

Lustig's genius lies in his ability to understate themes and situations which cry out for melodramatic treatment. Perla S. is a 17-year-old Jewish girl turned prostitute as a means of survival, who is quartered in an attic of one of the buildings in the Theresienstadt concentration camp. Grim details of existence there infiltrate her diary entries as casually as the items she receives in exchange for her sexual favors, although some apparently visit her simply for a few moments of human intimacy.

One of these, old man O., is a painter, whom Perla describes with a few deft verbal strokes that nearly pass by the careless or innocent reader: "He's got mutilated fingers; they were scorched off at the Little Fortress because he had painted what he had seen, what his interrogation officer called Greuel Geschichten, horror stories." Were it not for details like these, we might not at first know where we are, since Little Fortress (the notorious *kleine Festung* at Theresienstadt) and interrogation officer awaken few echoes of atrocity for the uninformed. Horror stories are on the periphery of this fiction, in the future, toward the east, the fate of those who have gone, not the history of those who remain.

How does the reader learn about this? Together with Perla, who gradually pieces together her doom and that of her fellow Jews. She discovers, as we do, that deportation signifies more than resettlement. But the truth encroaches slowly, as it must have for the victims too. One might expect such revelations to be devastating; but in fact, as one of Perla's friends admits, they quickly seem to belong "to the normal course of things, just as much as the fact that the earth turns or that the sun rises and sets again." Part of the emotional intensity of the narrative derives from the clinical detachment with which the potential victims themselves discuss the prospects of survival. . . .

Slowly but insistently, the details in Perla's entries transform before our eyes memories of normal pleasures into auguries of abnormal death. The Holocaust redefines everything. Recording a dialogue with her closest friend, Perla admits that she no longer perceives light and dark as she once did. "Nowadays," she confesses, "I'm beset by dread when night sets in . . . I no longer regard darkness as more than just light, as I did back home." Perla thinks often of "back home," but since all her family members have already been deported to the east, the memories associated with it constitute roughly amputated fragments of a vanished past.

As the teen-age diarist expands her entries, she rapidly matures, turns reflective, and meditates challengingly on the implications of her experience. She decides to gather the last words everyone spoke just before leaving on a transport for the east, only to discover how trivial and unmemorable they were. She imagines proceedings against God, who for everything He has permitted, is condemned to become a man. She sets the fate of the Jews into a cosmic context: "Isn't the memory of people in fact something akin to the light of the stars that long ago became extinct?" Early in her diary Perla had written that life in Theresienstadt was not a choice between good and bad, but worse and worst, still preserving a minimal moral terminology. Much later, in a dream, she acknowledges that the only option now remains surviving or not surviving, with no assurance that actions based on these alternatives will be permanently successful.

One of Perla's clients is a Luftwaffe officer, who unconcernedly describes to her in vivid detail what awaits her at Auschwitz. Her response to the officer, once more effectively understated, is the dramatic climax of the novel. After that, Perla must confront her fate. She feels the temporary shame of children surviving their parents, but more profoundly, the shame that comes from "the impossibility of sparing someone from things he ought to be spared from." She envies the rat, who shares her garret with her, because rats don't worry about tomorrow. But in her last entry, she internalizes the people "who have gone away, are going, and are still to go." This is her final human gesture, though it leads to emptiness, terror, and an unredeemable grief.

Lustig's novel in the form of a diary provides an uncompromising vision of the small consolations and large fears that constitute daily existence in Theresienstadt. Through the sensibilities of its young Jewish protagonist, it gives us access to the inner lives of the victims as no history could possibly do.

Lawrence L. Langer, "Paying the Price of Survival," in Book World—The Washington Post, *January 12, 1986, p. 10.*

URSULA HEGI

Despite its setting—a Nazi concentration camp—Arnost Lustig's latest novel [*The Unloved: From the Diary of Perla S.*] is strangely affirmative in its vision of innocence and courage. Mr. Lustig traces five months in the life of Perla S., an adolescent prostitute in the Theresienstadt camp. In her diary, Perla keeps track of how often she has sold her body by the items the men bring her: bread, men's galoshes, a chocolate bar, an umbrella, a vial of blue ink. Surrounded by the horrors of the camp, Perla escapes into fantasies, dreams and stories told by old Mr. O., a prisoner whose travels have taken him to a subterranean city near the Sahara. She forms close friendships with Ludmila and Harychek, two other adolescents. At times they forget about death as they talk about love, parents, early memories and clothes. With Ludmila she can speak of her infatuation with a German Luftwaffe officer, and with Harychek she can play his ghostly version of Monopoly which he has expanded with squares that reflect life in a concentration camp: "Get ready for transport." To be transported east means death, a fate Mr. L., one of Perla's clients, has protected her from by switching her card in the Central Registry. The perspective of a 17-year-old is convincing whenever Mr. Lustig writes about Perla's experiences and feelings, but occasionally, when Perla philosophizes about the nature of life and death, her voice loses that authenticity and sounds considerably older. Mr. Lustig, the survivor of three concentration camps, has written a stunning and unsentimental novel, celebrating moments of normality amid corruption and death.

Ursula Hegi, in a review of "The Unloved: From the Diary of Perla S.," in The New York Times Book Review, *January 19, 1986, p. 20.*

PETER LEWIS

[Arnost Lustig's] latest novel *The Unloved* carries the subtitle "From the Diary of Perla S." and takes the form of a diary kept between August and December 1943 by a seventeen-year-old girl in Theresienstadt. Much Holocaust literature has understandably been cast in quasi-documentary form to bring home the objective reality, but Lustig concentrates more on the subjectivity of the victims, especially young people and children. Perla's diary, which differs markedly from Anne Frank's but inevitably brings it to mind, records her feelings, memories, fantasies, dreams and aspirations rather than the physical actualities of life in a concentration camp, although she keeps a list of the bizarre assortment of things she obtains by prostitution. After a couple of years in Theresienstadt, Perla has come to accept the camp as her home. She manages to maintain as normal a life as possible while constantly being aware of the transports regularly taking her friends and associates to the East and to death, the fate which awaits her at the end despite her success in cheating the system and surviving for so long. Although implied and understated, the horror of the situation is no less intense than in graphic descriptions of it, yet Perla's ability to rise above the situation, to remain sane and retain her humanity in the face of institutionalized insanity and inhumanity, gives the novel a positive force. There is an important sense in which 'the unloved' Perla achieves a human victory, even a victory of love, over the forces of evil and darkness surrounding her. (p. 73)

Peter Lewis, "Centrality and Marginality," in Stand Magazine, *Autumn, 1986, pp. 71-5.*

PETER Z. SCHUBERT

[Arnost Lustig] seems to be fascinated with the notion of a weak woman who uses violence to defy the powerful oppressor of her people. The Czech émigré author employed the theme in his best-known novel . . . *A Prayer for Katerina*

Horovitzova, and he returns to it in the present book. His interest in defiance is again manifested by his choice of setting for *The Unloved.* The symbolic value of the Terezín (Theresienstadt) ghetto has often gone unnoticed. The small North Bohemian town was the scene of a brave and desperate attempt to resist the Nazis' aim of breaking the Jews spiritually and destroying them bodily. It was here that a struggle took place to create within the ghetto an independent and autonomous framework for the unhampered development of Jewish life by ignoring, time and again, the decrees of the Germans. The revolt of the spirit was impeded by the incessant change in the population of Terezín, which became a transition point on the way to the extermination camps. More than 50,000 inhabitants lived in Terezín at the peak of its history in 1943, before the town was declared a "model ghetto" and had its population reduced by almost 80 percent.

The situation is reflected in the fictionalized diary of the adolescent prostitute Perla S., who keeps record of all her transactions and payments, conversations, dreams, and memories. The candid, matter-of-fact account of Perla's last five months in Terezín evokes the atmosphere of the ghetto. The journal does, however, more than just subtly describe the horror and the absurdity of life in an isolated world. It shows how, under these cruel circumstances, Perla's youthful attempts to fathom the mysteries of sex, consciousness, and death are intensified beyond the usual brooding of a seventeen-year-old. The heroine's complex psychological makeup, which combines the profession of a prostitute with high ethical values, would attract attention even of the reader not informed that *The Unloved* belongs . . . to a series of narratives dealing with moral values exposed to unusual pressures.

The compound thematic nature and the attempt to evoke an atmosphere in a relatively static story put great demands on the composition and style. Lustig manages his task very well.

Peter Z. Schubert, in a review of "The Unloved: From the Diary of Perla S.," in World Literature Today, *Vol. 60, No. 4, Autumn, 1986, p. 655.*

KIRKUS REVIEWS

[Lustig] has consistently focused on the fragile terror of youthful femininity counterposed against the Holocaust. Most often the young girls of his fiction are Jewish, all facing destruction; but in this volume [*Indecent Dreams*], consisting of three novellas, the women are not Jews but, rather, [in *Blue Day*], a German prostitute who is in Prague as the Nazi war machine collapses; [in *The Girl with the Scar*], a schoolgirl whose politicized parents have been sent away to the camps but who herself, as pure-Aryan stock, is put into an orphans' school for later disposition (perhaps as a field prostitute for the S.S.); and [in *Indecent Dreams*], a young woman who works as a cashier in a Prague movie theater that doubles (upstairs) as a Nazi court where German deserters are killed summarily with injections directly into the heart. In each story, Lustig captures the almost swoony perversity produced when hormonal confusion finds itself in fascinated thrall of cruelty. In each, too, he makes these women creatures of utter fear—only waiting until greater male strength (*evil* male strength, at that) turns next to them.

The novella form doesn't perfectly suit Lustig—the pieces often seem here repetitious, there attenuated; but together they have a rinsing action whereby feelings become clear-

sightedness and then, on occasion, acts of tragic bravery. (pp. 563-64)

A review of "Indecent Dreams," in Kirkus Reviews, *Vol. LVI, No. 8, April 15, 1988, pp. 563-64.*

RICHARD LOURIE

In the three tales that comprise his recent book, *Indecent Dreams,* Lustig demonstrates . . . considerable daring and talent. He sets himself the same problem in each tale—describing the last days of World War II from a woman's point of view. The tales are self-contained and each stands on its own, but they can also be taken together as a single composition, variations on a theme. The tales are also strongly united by their structure and atmosphere. In each a mood is built, gathering like a storm, and only in the final moments is that energy discharged in the lightning of violence.

The first tale, *Blue Day,* centers on Inge Linge, a German prostitute in Nazi-occupied Prague. As the author slyly and subjunctively notes in his opening lines: " . . . if you'd seen her early last spring, training on the sports fields reserved for the *Wehrmacht* and officers' wives, you'd have said she was . . . a woman whom life had not yet overwhelmed." Inge Linge is, of course, about to be overwhelmed by life.

She begins to be haunted by the Jewish woman whose disappearance afforded Inge the apartment she now lives in. She fights it off with contempt: "Why were all the Jews she had ever known, like Ida Geron, bent over as though they were looking for something in the dirt and dust beneath their own and other people's feet?" Like most prostitutes, Inge is morally retarded; she lives for pleasure and has only the vaguest sense that her actions have consequences.

Germany has surrendered but the killing continues. Inge is visited by a fleeing Nazi judge who barricades himself with her in her apartment. When she confides her misgivings about what she has heard about death camps, he replies: "When those who survived our baths and showers grow up, they will be astonished at how mild we were—as mild as lambs." The tension between Inge and the judge is perfectly built and the violence, when it comes, is also a measure of the force required to transfigure a Nazi whore into a human being.

After her parents were executed, Jenny Thelen, the heroine of *The Girl With The Scar,* was sent to study at the Prague Institute for Girls of Pure Race from Non-German Territories. The only thing more murderous than the name of the school is Jenny's teacher, Elzie Mayerfeld, in whose "smile was Germany itself." Before becoming a teacher Mayerfeld had served in the female guard at the Sobibor death camp near Lublin. By her words, aura and example she educates her adolescent students in sexuality and hatred.

All blossom in Jenny as spring comes to Prague. They mix in with longings she cannot understand: "The second bell rang, piercing the girl with the scar like needles—needles threaded with heat and sunlight, with words and their most secret meanings, with silence." But Jenny has borne a scar since the men dragging off her parents had slammed the door on her, splitting open her forehead. And her soul. In a device that simply must be accepted, the man who awakens desire in her is one of the men who arrested her parents. By giving us the arresting officer's point of view in all its workaday banality, Lustig succeeds brilliantly in rendering this too-symbolic situation real. . . .

Although Jenny Thelen is also a virgin to violence, the act with which the story ends proves simpler and more inevitable than she had imagined possible.

The young movie theater cashier in *Indecent Dreams* is another virgin tormented by impulses and fantasies that mix with those of the movies she sees. They too lead her to violent death, but hers is not one of repentance or retribution as in the first two stories. Somehow, Lustig lost his perfect focus in the final tale. Previously, he had not only kept the lyrical and the cruel in balance but had made them augment each in other in an ironic symbiosis. The cashier is never as real as the German prostitute or the adolescent school girl and her fate, itself somewhat gratuitous, is less moving for that reason.

> *Richard Lourie, "Three Women at War's End," in* Book World—The Washington Post, *June 19, 1988, p. 10.*

JOHANNA KAPLAN

The Czech-Jewish writer Arnost Lustig, a survivor of three concentration camps, emerged from that infernal *Gymnasium* to wrest from it the stark—but paradoxically enlivening—vision that makes his fiction remarkable. Wholly unsentimental, and clean of self-pity, Mr. Lustig returns in his novels and stories to the harrowing landscape of his youth, discovering within its brutal boundaries the grim but still achingly recognizable panoply of a last, vast, various neighborhood of man. In this murderous realm, he has carved out his turf, much as Isaac Babel staked his early claim with Odessa's Moldavanka, or Saul Bellow with Jewish Chicago. Like these writers', Mr. Lustig's prose is smart, spare, tough-minded and then, abruptly, piercingly lyrical in its evocation of the natural world or of a city-scape; unlike theirs, alas, in Mr. Lustig's old neighborhood the canvas, by necessity, is too often monochrome.

Until now, Mr. Lustig, the too-little-known author of over half a dozen works of fiction . . . has concerned himself with the Holocaust's primary Jewish victims. But he is also a city boy, from Prague, and in *Indecent Dreams,* a collection of three novellas, he turns his hard gaze to the war's secondary victims, the ordinary citizens of Prague, and, in a stunning imaginative foray, to their about-to-be-defeated Nazi masters.

Thus, a leisurely, confiding, almost turn-of-the-century *mitteleuropisch* voice coaxes us into the chilling universe of *Indecent Dreams*—but oh, how quickly, how subtly the accent changes. . . . In each of these novellas, we are plummeted into the chaos, cruelty and moral squalor that engulf daily life in war-torn, Nazi-occupied Prague, and into the dim, struggling minds of characters who can only imperfectly grasp the enormity of their situations. Yet even these, the author suggests, revealing with each denouement the rigor of his vision—even these people, already severely bruised and, moreover, limited by age or by mental endowment, may one day defy their apparent life scripts with an outburst of conscience. (pp. 1, 24)

In these three novellas, the protagonists erupt into deadly, decisive "heroic" acts that are utterly uncharacteristic, deeply shadowed and barely understood. All three seemingly rise to an occasion that, only a moment before, each would have failed to perceive or wished to deny. Does extreme circumstance induce self-transcendence, then? Is the heroism of an ordinary person invariably accidental?

In *Blue Day,* set in Prague on the eve of the German surrender, a provincial German prostitute, frightened by the rumors of defeat, sits alone in her hard-won, confiscated apartment, desperate for a soldier-customer to appear and dispel her forebodings. . . . At last, a visitor arrives; but the haughty, elegantly appointed colonel at her doorstep will have nothing to do with her. He is a Nazi military judge, abruptly trapped in about-to-be-liberated Prague; his single, disdainful demand is that she provide him hiding.

A brilliantly evoked atmosphere of sinister, perfumed apprehension overhangs the novella, especially as the hours wear on and the rebuffed young prostitute's confused, claustral anxiety mounts to panic. Dimly perceiving in the colonel's many cruelties a thin, familiar, evil thread of the collective Nazi design, Inge, by now in a frenzy of humiliated terror, conceives a hideous unity with the tubercular old Ida Geron, her apartment's deported Jewish owner, "that ugly living ghost with its hooked nose." In this unhinged but heightened state, Inge Linge embarks on the cunning, retributive gesture that betrays her high-ranking fugitive and seals her own doom.

In the barricaded gloom of two end-of-the-road Nazis, Mr. Lustig has set up a shockingly unsympathetic *mise en scène,* yet *Blue Day,* with its dense, crepuscular mood, sparse, chilling dialogue and murmurous, accusing shadows achieves a hard, creepy, morbid power.

A far more conventional tale of heroic vengeance, **The Girl With the Scar,** is the least bleak of the three novellas, and the least complex. In this sensuously rendered account of a moony Czech schoolgirl's befogged, festering accession to avenging angel . . . , Mr. Lustig has created a darkly stirring story and a ghastly, illuminating portrait of the dwindled universe of oppression.

Prague, in the explosive imminence of liberation, again provides the dynamic for the sprawling, pageantlike, ambitious title novella **Indecent Dreams;** the city itself—a frightening trajectory of raging, disjointed, war-ruptured lives—is this selection's most forceful imaginative presence. A scattering of intentionally "small" nameless characters shifts urgently across the anguished, perilous landscape all through this chaotic "day of the animal, not the day of victory." And though a terrifying big-city sensation of desperate, shuttered simultaneity is powerfully conveyed here, a perplexing equality of character and incident continues, as all quickly disappear into the narrative maw and the novella is deprived of resonance.

Certainly, a broad-lens, distancing effect is central to Mr. Lustig's design in the novella **Indecent Dreams,** yet here, his technical virtuosity and thematic devotion to characters envisioned as "small" sadly unite to frustrate the reader's root fictional craving. Still, this is a literary landscape littered with by-the-way riches, so that if the confused young cashier-protagonist fails to wholly convince, there are characters—the resistance fighter called "the lanky fellow," and his murdered sweetheart—whose vividness transcends the authorial scheme, and episodes, like the trial of the German deserters, of icy, harrowing power.

A world so entirely bound by suffering can be painful to enter; but Mr. Lustig, searching out a code of honor in this most defiled, inhuman sphere, has come upon a maximalist human canvas. His view is oddly invigorating and his work invites a maximal audience: it will quarrel, it will recognize, it will marvel and yes, of course, sometimes it will have to look away. (p. 24)

> *Johanna Kaplan, "Savage Boulevards, Easy Streets," in* The New York Times Book Review, *June 19, 1988, pp. 1, 24.*

Alistair MacLeod

1936-

Canadian short story writer, poet, and editor.

MacLeod is regarded by critics in both Canada and the United States as an important contemporary short story writer. Raised on Cape Breton Island, Nova Scotia, MacLeod is usually placed in the tradition of such Maritime authors as Alden Nowland and Ernest Buckler, who often depicted the harsh landscape and ethnic milieu of eastern Canada. In a review of MacLeod's second book, *As Birds Bring Forth the Sun and Other Stories,* Russell Brown asserted: "[These] are pieces that speak eloquently to MacLeod's Maritime heritage without defensiveness or condescension, and, with their understated passions and their lovely blend of folk narrative and modern sensibility, they define the continuing possibilities of traditional fiction."

MacLeod established his literary reputation with his first collection of short fiction, *The Lost Salt Gift of Blood* (1976). Several stories from this volume garnered MacLeod international recognition after being published in such prestigious anthologies as *Best American Short Stories* and *Best Canadian Short Stories.* In *The Lost Salt Gift of Blood* and his subsequent collection, *As Birds Bring Forth the Sun and Other Stories* (1986), MacLeod emphasizes the power of the past to affect the present, often depicting the educated descendants of Scottish-Canadian miners and fishermen who either abandon their impoverished homes in Nova Scotia for the modern mainland or, having become alienated by their new urban surroundings, return to their forsaken families and Gaelic traditions. While occasionally faulting his stories as overwritten, reviewers have commended MacLeod's authentic, unsentimental portrait of the cultural decline of Nova Scotia, which he links in a larger sense to his perception of a loss of traditional Canadian values. Critics have also commended MacLeod's lyrical use of the historical past, a narrative technique by which past events are described in the present tense to convey the immediacy of cultural and personal memory.

(See also *Contemporary Authors,* Vol. 123 and *Dictionary of Literary Biography,* Vol. 60.)

JON KERTZER

As its title hints, ***The Lost Salt Gift of Blood*** explores inheritance: the ambiguous challenges, honours, and betrayals involved in family relationships. Its seven short stories are united by their Cape Breton setting, and by their concern with the tensions between and within members of the Island's sturdy Scottish families. Alistair MacLeod presents a theme with variations. Husband, wife, child, parent and grandparent confront each other in varying configurations and, as opponents or allies, work their way to mutual understanding or hostility, acceptance or rejection, self-confidence or self-doubt. But because these are tales of divided loyalties and conflicting impulses, the victories and defeats are often equivocal.

The domestic conflicts are set against turbulent landscape and seascape and the dangers each offers to Cape Breton miners and fishermen. In a wider view, they are amplified by a more complex conflict between island and mainland. Island life is traditional, clannish, violent, deep-rooted, sustaining yet confining. Mainland life is modern, lonely, comfortable, sophisticated yet shallow and unsatisfying. Characters are torn between the two and . . . the troublesome passage from island to mainland mentality is usually prompted by education. Semi-literate parents encourage their children to study and better themselves, only to find that they have learned to be dissatisfied with their rustic lives and their restricting family heritage. Several stories deal with these rites of passage, and focus on the critical moment of leave-taking or homecoming. A brooding narrator records his feeling of confinement and his attempt to escape from his family and the Island; or he describes his feeling of exile and his attempt to return. But the one who escapes will regret what he has forfeited; the one who returns will feel at home in neither world. The domestic conflicts, therefore, are bound up implicitly with a wider Canadian drama: the modernization and erosion of traditional, rural communities. This is a losing battle which stands behind the family antagonisms and contributes to the sense of loss in most tales. . . .

The great merit of these stories is their power and authenticity of detail. MacLeod presents a setting which he seems to know well. When describing the cramped horrors of coal mining, the repairing of a lobster trap, the superstitions of an old Scottish grandmother, or a fisherman's wardrobe, he writes with precision and authority. He provides a background rich and palpable enough to bring life to the characters and to give urgency to their problems. The weakness of the book is a tendency to excess.

One tale ceases to dramatize and lapses into moralizing; another indulges in a poolroom melodrama; another allows its tone to become remorselessly elegiac. But at his best, MacLeod weds his characters to their locale so that each is enriched by the other. . . .

> Jon Kertzer, "Equivocal Victories," in The Canadian Forum, Vol. LVI, No. 662, June-July, 1976, p. 51.

LAURENCE RICOU

[Alistair MacLeod is] content with illuminating the commonplace. Each of the stories [in *The Lost Salt Gift of Blood*] moves toward that moment of determining, or appreciating, otherness, of discovering that another's perception of exactly the same experience can be completely different, and yet just as valid. MacLeod builds to his quiet revelations mainly through the subtle power and pain of family ties, most established in the fishing and mining communities of Cape Breton. . . . Several of MacLeod's stories are told in the historical present: "We are in the kitchen of our house and my mother is speaking as she energetically pokes at the wood and coal within her stove." But this formula, which should mark an intimate and confiding narrative, can feel, ironically, austere, as if the narrator were speaking into a tape recorder, setting his experiences down for history, as artifacts, rather than telling a story. The immediacy of "we are" is disrupted and diminished by the obvious retrospective, with the result that the narrative seems coy rather than revealing.

It is this danger, no doubt, which makes the historical present so rare among modern storytellers. MacLeod's repeated use of it indicates that he values its aura of the old-fashioned, its suggestion of stories being swapped around a hot stove. And even the stories which don't use the technique share a tone of thoughtful nostalgia. An incident in "**The Boat**," for example, demonstrates the contradictory responses evoked by the reconstructing memory. The narrator, who teaches in a midwestern university, recalls his Cape Breton boyhood, and particularly his father's harsh life and cruel death on the sea. One of the most vivid memories is of his father drunk, singing for hours through his repertoire of sea shanties, war songs, and Gaelic drinking songs for a group of tourists. As the narrator recalls his own response: "I was ashamed yet proud, young yet old and saved yet forever lost, and there was nothing I could do to control my legs which trembled nor my eyes which wept for what they could not tell." The narrator is delighted, yet hurt by his own insensitivity, to discover that his father is a frustrated artist, linked through song with generations of primitive suffering. On the other hand he is embarrassed at the prodigality of the emotions, and the fawning of the tourists. So it is, in a sense, with reading MacLeod: the

stories, especially "**The Return**" and "**The Road to Rankin's Point**," are often emotionally subtle, but the self-conscious remembering can turn revelation into contrivance. The quoted passage, for example, quivers on the edge of excess, and drifts into increasingly vague sentiment. The self-assertive narrator . . . is always adjusting to try to put things straight: "I say this again as if it all happened at once and as if all of my sisters were of identical ages and like so many lemmings going into another sea and, again, it was of course not that way at all." But his hesitations and repetitions do more to deflect interest from the guts of a father/son relationship than to arouse concern for the narrator's struggle with his story. (117-18)

> Laurence Ricou, "Story and Teller," in Canadian Literature, No. 76, Spring, 1978, pp. 116-18.

RICHARD LEMM

When Alistair MacLeod speaks to creative writing students, he stresses the connection between a short story and an evening snack. If the writer has successfully crafted an engaging short story, he says, the reader will not be tempted to put down the story and go fix a cheese sandwich. MacLeod's own fiction lives elegantly on every page with the crafting of a perfectionist. Cordon bleu cuisine could not tempt the reader away. . . .

[Following the publication of MacLeod's first book, *The Lost Salt Gift of Blood,* readers], critics and fellow-writers recognized a superb talent, powerful sensibility and disciplined skill. Yet the book went out of print, and a loyal following searched libraries and used bookstores until it was reissued in paperback last year. Meanwhile, those familiar with his prose were comparing him favorably with Canada's finest short fiction writers. . . . At a time when so many Canadian writers were being lionized, MacLeod seemed to be one of those quiet workers cutting fictional gems outside the CanLit spotlights.

Born in Saskatchewan, MacLeod grew up in the coal-mining country of Alberta and in farming communities of Cape Breton. His parents were farmers, and his father worked for a time as a miner. MacLeod was a school teacher, miner and logger, before undertaking a university teaching career. . . .

MacLeod's family background, particularly in Cape Breton, and his work in a variety of jobs, underlie the deep experience of his fiction. . . .

Yet the appeal of MacLeod's stories is not at all confined to local Maritime colour or a narrow regionalist savvy. Like the fiction of Alice Munro, or the novels of Margaret Laurence, MacLeod's stories grow from their roots in a particular place and people to a universality of human experience and insight.

MacLeod's writing strikes home with immediacy, intensity and poetic beauty. Most of the stories are told by first-person narrators, and MacLeod is so skillful with his use of time that the narrators' memories of the past become living moments. He writes from the centre of an individual's consciousness where past, present and future are interwoven into a single fabric of awareness. "**The Return**" begins: "It is an evening during the summer that I am ten years old and I am on a train with my parents as it rushes toward the end of eastern Nova Scotia." MacLeod reveals how the physical and emotional landscapes of the past permeate our present existence.

Relationships between children and parents, within the contexts of economic and emotional survival, are a central aspect of MacLeod's fiction. Initiation into adulthood, separation from family, return to the place of origin from an adult life faraway, become occasions and themes for the narrators' reflections. Sometimes, instead of parents, there is a grandmother clinging to her isolated home on a sea-cliff's edge or a meat-packer who plays a sharp game of pool: these adults profoundly affect the main characters' perceptions of life and death. Like the tides in the Cape Breton fishing village where **"The Boat"** is set, the currents of experience and outlook and feeling flow back and forth between children and parents, and eddy in the narrators' minds.

A writer who works with all five senses in high gear, MacLeod brings his characters, landscapes and events to life with vivid and exacting detail. The most ordinary things are infused, again, with the real significance they once had for us. . . . In MacLeod's stories, the sensory, tangible world triggers recollection and the need for insight.

The poetic quality of his prose is evident in his rhythms, evocative imagery and musical resonance. The poetry comes through not only in descriptive passages, but in reflective moments:

> Oh I would like to see my way more clearly. I, who have never understood the mystery of fog. I would perhaps like to capture it in a jar like the beautiful childhood butterflies that always die in spite of the airholes punched with nails in the covers of their captivity . . .

MacLeod's poetic prose tells us something of what it is like to be a coal miner or a fisherman's son who abandons his family for an academic career. Even more, it shows us what it is like to be ourselves: to pass through the stages of life and always wrestle with our inheritance. . . .

[Why], given MacLeod's tremendous talent, isn't he more visible in Canadian letters? *The Lost Salt Gift of Blood* did not exactly receive high-profile promotion when it was first published. Moreover, MacLeod is not an ambitious promoter of his own work. Yet this low-profile is deceptive. . . .

A superb and dedicated teacher, he selflessly gives a great deal of time to students and fellow-writers. He is a man of high integrity, industry, and admirable modesty. As well, he may have the best sense of humour this side of W. O. Mitchell, one of his close friends and academic colleagues. MacLeod is, in fact, rapidly gaining the recognition he so richly deserves, on the basis of his writing and his numerous other contributions to literature. . . .

A good short story, [MacLeod] says, is like a V-8 engine finely-tuned and cruising flawlessly down the highway. As a craftsman, he knows precisely what goes on under the hood of a short story. And when the story starts, when the reader climbs inside and drives off, MacLeod's intricate invention takes us on a journey into the regions of pathos and beauty. His writing truly is a gift, like salt, and like blood.

> *Richard Lemm, "Alistair MacLeod: The Invention of Inheritance," in* Atlantic Provinces Book Review, *Vol. 9, No. 4, December, 1982, p. 9.*

COLIN NICHOLSON

[*The essay excerpted below incorporates criticism by Colin Nicholson with MacLeod's comments taken from an interview conducted during his visit to Edinburgh University's Centre of Canadian Studies from 1984 to 1985. MacLeod's remarks appear in indented form.*]

Alistair MacLeod's characters and contexts are miners and their families, fishermen or farmers and their communities. His are, in the proper sense of the word, elemental fictions. The driving wind that blows through the pages of **"In The Fall"** both strains and secures a family under economic and emotional duress. Coalmines in **"The Vastness of the Dark"** play a comparable role for the eighteen-year-old narrator, imprisoning him but also lending him a strength of which he is at the time of telling only dimly aware: a history of mining disasters in the region of his upbringing both confining him yet paradoxically giving him definition. "This grimy Cape Breton coal-mining town whose prisoner I have been for all of my life," is not something easily shaken off. But the remembered words of his grandfather lend an urgency to the boy's desire to set himself free from a history which fascinates and repels him simultaneously: "once you start it takes a hold of you, once you drink underground water, you will always come back to drink some more. The water gets into your blood. It is in all of our blood. We have been working in the mines here since 1873." As these twin and rival themes of entrapment and escape, enclosure and release mutate through the volume, the language registers a history of hardship and of endurance. In the words of the itinerant miner desperately searching for work, whose comment ends **"The Vastness of the Dark,"** "it seems to bust your balls and it's bound to break your heart." (pp. 90-1)

Born in Saskatchewan, Alistair MacLeod grew up in the coal-mining area of Alberta, moving when he was ten years old to the farming communities of Cape Breton. (p. 91)

Gaelic songs, Scottish history, Highland allusions and Scots-Canadian place names like Truro, Glenholme, New Glasgow—all of these are woven into the fabric of his writing. A question which the dying schoolteacher who narrates **"The Road to Rankin's Point"** asks himself springs naturally to mind: "what is the significance of ancestral islands long left and never seen?"

The answer is direct:

> My parents were both from a place in Canada called Inverness County—named that for the obvious reason. When people from Scotland went over there, they went to a large extent in family groups from individual islands, like Eigg, and intermarried, and carried with them the whole body of whatever it is that people carry with them—folklore, emotional weight. Because it was all open to them, they settled pretty much where they wanted to. Cape Breton Island and Nova Scotia remained rural for a long time, and fairly isolated. And because there was no-one else to integrate with, they stayed very much to themselves almost for six generations. . . . When you think that this is good you say that people were stable for several generations: when you think of it in negative terms, you could say that they were static. Although my wife has adequate Gaelic, we are really the first generation where the breakdown of that culture is beginning to occur.

It is a breakdown which will return to haunt the writing in a number of ways.

But it is all the more notable, in the light of that clear enunciation of historical awareness, that as a collection, *The Lost Salt Gift of Blood,* is characterized by a narrative predilection almost exclusively dedicated to the present tense.

> In that mode you can be tremendously intense. I just like that. I think that individuals are very interested in telling their own stories, and to adapt this persona is very effective in just riveting the listener.
>
> (pp. 91-2)

Closely focused upon the experiential now of the narrator and the reader, these stories also achieve a similar kind of immediacy and intensity for the recollection of emotions from the past in a troubled, untranquil present. Moreover, by presenting this recall in a style of lyric elaboration, MacLeod's narratives conjure both the bright surfaces of life and their implicit emotional undertow, bringing them into what William Carlos Williams once called "that eternal moment in which we alone live." It is in the sculpting of the emotional infrastructure of any given situation that MacLeod's talent shines, so that his lyricism "celebrates the poetic self despite every denial." And his narrators are, all of them, poetic selves. While the verbal unspooling of first-person narration counteracts a relative paucity of dialogue, the cross-weaving of time past with time present signifies the ubiquitous presence of history in his writing, as narrating memory speaks. Thus, an account of a middle class family going back to working class origins in a mining community, simply called **"The Return,"** opens with "It is an evening during the summer that I am ten years old and I am on a train with my parents as it rushes towards the end of Eastern Nova Scotia." After exploring that moment in an earlier and a later direction, a reentry is subsequently effected—"And now it is later"—after which the present moves forward in the narrating memory: "It is morning now and I awake to the argument of the English sparrows outside my window and the fingers of the sun upon the floor." (Argument defines the relationship, on this visit, between the child-narrator's mother and father, and between them and his grandparents: and identity and relationships are very much prefigured in imagery associated with the human hand.)

On the two occasions in the volume where the more traditional past tense is used as the vehicle for fictionalized recall, in **"The Golden Gift of Grey,"** and **"The Boat,"** other techniques are used to persuade the reader of the enriching if troubling immediacy for the narrator of what is being narrated. Indeed, from its opening utterance, **"The Boat"** may be accurately described as a technical meditation upon remembered events and imaginings as the past folds in on the present: "There are times even now, when I awake at four o'clock in the morning with the terrible fear that I have overslept," thereafter unobtrusive iterations mark the affective passing of time, as the process of memory inscribes its intricate divagations. "And I know then that that day will go by as have all the days of the past ten years, for the call and the voices and the shapes and the boat were not really there in the early morning's darkness and I have all kinds of comforting reality to prove it." Meanwhile, rhythms of acute discomfort are registered. Or, to slightly different effect, "I say this now as if I knew it all then," and later, "I say this again as if it happened all at once and as if all of my sisters were of identical ages . . .

and again, it was of course not that way at all." The narrative consciousness in these stories repeatedly demonstrates its ability to enter their constructed worlds at will, at any point, and from that chosen present range backwards or forwards in time.

In the process, **"The Boat"** reflects post-modernistically upon its own procedures, so that when we read an instance of apparently more straightforward recall we encounter, rather, an image which encodes the fictive strategy both of this story and of the collection as a whole:

> The floor of the boat was permeated with the same odour and in its constancy I was not aware of any change. In the harbour we made our little circle and returned.

The image is a paradigm of a mode of writing where circling and returning constancy and change and sameness and difference are central to its concerns. For what strikes the reader all the more tellingly for being implicit, is the narrator's prior, and the reader's subsequent awareness of a change so profound that it jeopardizes any sense of constancy either might otherwise enjoy. It is an image which reinforces our own subliminal involvement in the circlings and returns of the past into the present and the present upon the past, and which illuminates MacLeod's narrative technique everywhere else as much as it advances narrative event in this story. And in common with stylistic procedures widely adopted in [*The Lost Salt Gift of Blood*], the shaping agency of personal, familial, and community history is felt along the pulse of practically every sentence in **"The Boat,"** as an emergent consciousness is adumbrated: "I first became conscious . . ."; "My earliest recollection of my mother . . ."; "I learned first. . . ." It is, then, appropriately typical of MacLeod's method that the past lights up memory's retina with the shock of first cognition. . . . The past is recalled with a sensuous immediacy as if present, while the story's final image subsequently enshrouds this earlier remembering.

"The Boat" begins in the present tense, and maintains this mode for a page and a half before reverting to the conventional mode of recall. For the reader, this too structures a contextual immediacy of recurrent nightmarish intrusions of the past into the present which technically glides as easily into that past. It is, then, a semantically functional technique, offering the reader a kind of analogous exposure to the process whereby, for the narrating self, the past actively shapes his present. The reading present slips into a narrative past just as the narrator's past exfoliates, always already shaping the self he now is. In this way a textual web of two-way entrapment is created. The narrator gives this voice. "I say this now with a sense of wonder at my own stupidity in thinking I was somehow free." In **"The Boat,"** as throughout the volume, both time and experience appear to be duplicitous, possessing the quality of being double in action, and, then, of double-dealing, almost deceiving the characters, being understood by them in two ways at different times; time passing openly and secretively at the same time.

> I was interested [in **"The Boat"**] in the idea of choice, of the price we all have to pay for the choices that we make; in the idea that sometimes people choose to do things that they don't want to do at all, somewhat like the father in that story. This is a man who is caught up in a kind of hereditary pattern, where people fish, and the only son inherits the father's boat—that kind of life. But what

I was getting at with the father was that here was a person who maybe didn't want to do that at all, but who is just caught up in this inherited life. Throughout this story, nobody ever thinks of him as ever having a side to him that yearns for something else. They just see him as doing what everyone else does. Which he does. I was interested, towards the end of the story, in the son who is an ambiguous kind of person—can do things well at school as well as handle the boat. It never enters the boy's mind, until his father becomes sick, or something like that, that maybe he has to choose between this or that. And then he realizes that his father has made this choice before. So when I was writing the story, I realized that there were several things I had to do: I've got to make the father old, because if he was a thirty-eight, or even a forty-eight year old man with a son who doesn't want to fish with him, then I've got a very different kind of situation on my hands. But what you've got here is a man who is fifty-six when he fathers this child, and his wife is maybe around forty-two. Six daughters before—none of whom marry local people and the mother is left alone—and this is the only son. The mother is thinking of future security and the father is thinking of other things. So that by the time the son has to make these decisions, what he's got for a father is someone who is around seventy-three. Very different indeed from a father who is thirty or forty. You've got a grandfather for a father.

Within this family configuration, only the briefest of gestures towards a specifically colonial history—"the houses and their people . . . were the result of Ireland's discontent and Scotland's Highland Clearances, and America's War of Independence. Impulsive emotional Catholic Celts who could not bear to live with England and shrewd determined Protestant Puritans who, in the years after 1776, could not bear to live without"—helps to contextualize deeper significations for both a loveless marriage and a mother's attitudes to the relative merits of literature and work. So it seems inevitable that one of the ways this literature works is to make, of a father singing "the laments and the wild and haunting Gaelic war songs of those spattered Highland ancestors he had never seen," a historical epiphany by modulating past tense into fluid continuous present: "and when his voice ceased, the savage melancholy of three hundred years seemed to hang over the peaceful harbour . . . and the men leaning in the doorways of their shanties . . . and the women looking to the sea from their open windows with their children in their arms." Conversely, the light but firm embedding of the narrative in an interfusing past and present enables extensions from concrete immediacy out towards timelessness. . . . (pp. 92-5)

Finally, **"The Boat"** returns us to the now with which it opened, playing a fugue in memory of the dead father whose presence is everywhere felt. The syntax moves from "is" to "was" to "had been," to repetition: "but neither is it easy to know that your father was found . . . at the base of the rock-strewn cliffs where he had been hurled and slammed so many many times," and then from "was" to an image whose haunting and continuous immediacy first triggered the narrative act of memorial homage. "There was not much left of my father, physically, as he lay there with the brass chains on his wrist and the seaweed in his hair." It is the word "physically" which provides the clue. The father who exists no more, exists all the time in the boy's mind.

All the time. I think what I was trying to deal with there was, as the father makes the choice, and so may always be haunted by that choice, you know, haunted by "the road not taken," so the son has made the opposite choice, and the haunting passes to him. Still his mother and all these people who stay there wonder when he's coming back. And of course he's never coming back physically in a permanent sense.

Narrative strategy floats the possibility that the father has committed suicide in order to free the son.

Nobody knows, not even the son. All that the son knows is that when this fishing season is over then it's really over. But as it turns out, it's as if they get through the last season and there isn't any more father; like it's on the last day and the weather is now too bad to continue. The boy looks around, and there's more finished than he thought! Remember that when the boy had said that he would stay and fish with him as long as his father was alive, the father had said I hope you remember what you say. So, when the father's no longer there, one way of looking at it is that the son has been freed. When you're dealing with the possibility of suicide, hindsight becomes very different. Cryptic remarks assume strange significance, and nobody really knows what they mean. So, after the old man is washed overboard, and the son looks back on all this, he is left to puzzle out what the old man really meant. But what does happen is that the son goes away, and does not pursue that career as a fisherman; then the mother just thinks of it as disloyalty. And with that final image comes the recognition that you're never free of anything.

As the boy remembers it, his dead father was once described by a party of visiting tourists as "Our Ernest Hemingway," and it may not be entirely accidental that Alistair MacLeod's writing opposes itself to one central attribute of the American's style. In common with many of the protagonists in Hemingway's short stories, in "The Snow of Kilimanjaro," a fear of contemplation, or indeed of any recuperation by thought, combines with a celebration of sensuous immediacy to construct a fictive terrain of recrimination and failure. The immediacy of the senses displaces conceptual thought, and the narrative of the dying writer Harry is characterized throughout by a devotion to the "now" of lived experience, even as his life has been characterized by a squandering of that experience. Harry himself recognizes the betrayal implied in selling "vitality in one form or another" in his writing. As he acknowledges elsewhere, "you kept from thinking and it was all marvellous." Only in his moment of dying is Harry able to substitute a sense of duration for the effects of intensity, with the word "then" displacing the word "now" in his terminal experience of consciousness. In marked difference, by playing upon the ambiguity of the different adverbial forms of "then" in **"The Boat,"** MacLeod registers the emphasis of immediacy in its lexical dance with "now," but makes of it a process and a style which renders *both* words durable. The Canadian's "now" is a deepened, meditative, historical experience.

In contrast with Hemingway's preferred American usage, the "now" in which MacLeod's first-person narrators tell their stories is one of ruminative awareness, one that is densely historical, resonant with the history of a local community. And exploring an immediate present both backwards and forwards in time is, as we have seen, a narrative technique he favours. So to think of him as a kind of fictional historian of the "now," begins to seem natural. (pp. 95-7)

[There exists] in MacLeod's writing an abiding note of loss and of regret, with the Scottish allusions seeming to operate like a kind of choric threnody. So there is, co-existing with his lyrical celebration of living, a pervasive sense of sadness, as if the style itself were keening.

> Well, I'm not sure, but there may be among those people a kind of sadness that they brought with them, the sadness of which we still hear. I don't know how long we can be saddled with Culloden, or with The Clearances, but while some obviously couldn't care less, perhaps meditative, thoughtful people brought that kind of sadness with them.

It is a remark which brings into focus a feeling generated by reading MacLeod's work, that one of the things he is doing is memorializing an immigrant culture from the Highlands and Islands at a time when its historical purchase in Nova Scotia begins to slip: both memorializing and, since he is writing in English, enacting that moment of slippage. (p. 98)

MacLeod's earlier remark about belonging to the first generation in which the old Gaelic culture is beginning to break down suggests that there are further ways in which he is involved in a kind of historical elegizing, playing a pibroch in his own behalf, perhaps, as well as for the purposes and places of his characters. In its invocation of a phase of irreversible transition, his writing is reminiscent of some of Thomas Hardy's concerns, and the tone of regret which suffuses these stories, amounting almost to a characteristic sense of foreboding, might best be intimated through a story not included in *The Lost Salt Gift of Blood.* **"The Closing Down of Summer"** deals with a gang of miners who roam around the world following work and who are at the peak of their powers, but is narrated by the gang-leader whose intimations of his own forthcoming death suffuses the texture of the writing. As he reveals how itinerant mining ruined his own marriage much as it damaged that of his parents, time passing becomes time future in particularly ironic ways—"perhaps we are but becoming our previous generation"—and he wonders whether, in a rapidly transforming world of work, "we have perhaps gone back to the Gaelic songs because they are so constant and unchanging and speak to us as the privately familiar."

> One of the things I was interested in when writing that story, was the problem of the intelligent, reflective, inarticulate person, someone who thinks a lot. He has been away from his family for so long that he hardly knows them; and his closest friends are those he works with. I think of these men as athletes—but without fans. They're laying their bodies on the line, but with no-one to see them! And as they become more handicapped—deafened or whatever—they revert to the Gaelic which they can also use in the lip-reading conditions underground. In my own life, as my grand-parents became older, my grandfather became deaf; and they became almost Gaelic speakers again. He could "hear" Gaelic better than he could English. This was in them anyway, and I think they just had some kind of pre-lapsarian return. So I think that this happens to these men in the shaft, when they're in Africa or wherever, they just speak Gaelic to each other.
>
> I was also interested, with the Gaelic singing, in the idea of whether art ever makes converts, or whether it just speaks to the converted all the time. That

miner, looking at the Zulus dancing and wondering about what it might mean. He realizes that no matter how long he watches them, he will understand very little. And these undercurrents lead to the reflection that when he sings his Gaelic songs, and looks out at the audience, he does not know them, and they understand very little of what he is singing. They see him as he sees the Zulus. So the miners stop singing professionally. Then, with that Medieval lyric he had read during his short time as a university student, it stayed with him, and his daughter reads it as a student. He has changed so much, and his daughter has changed so much, but this little statement about man becoming clay—which he misquotes, changing it to suit himself, though he doesn't know that—continues. He had no way of knowing that it would stay with him. Now he wonders whether he, too, will soon be clad in clay.

Throughout **"The Closing Down of Summer,"** the narrator's brooding intimations of mortality seem to owe as much to the alienating effect of a single year at university as they do to art's longevity. Certainly one of the constancies running through many of these tales, playing like a patina over their surfaces but also mining their structures with a calculated uncertainty, is a web of literary allusions which functions in paradoxical ways, at some point involving, whether consciously or not, the author's own literary intervention. For the narrator of the title story, **"The Lost Salt Gift of Blood,"** self-conscious comparison to a literary figure ("like a foolish Lockwood I approach the window although I hear no voice. There is no Catherine who cries to be let in"), or reference to Yeats's *Cuchulain* or to Arnold's *Sohrab and Rustum* serve not to buttress his confidence but to mark his separation. All of these references are concerned with trying to get the lost person back, and thus they enforce a sense of his isolation. Perhaps, outsider that he is, this is why the word "within" holds such fascination for him. It does, anyway, soon become clear that in the world of these stories, education, and particularly a literary education is very much a two-edged sword, serving to alienate characters from their origins even as it releases them from the more gruelling demands of necessary labour. From Dickens to Hemingway, from Hopkins to Dostoievsky, "book-learning" is both envied and feared, cherished and despised as simultaneously a salvation and a curse.

It is a problematic which gathers to a focus in the closing story in the volume, **"The Road to Rankin's Point,"** where a schoolteacher returns to his grandmother's farm to die at the age of twenty-six, the same age at which his grandfather had died (though, as with **"The Boat,"** whether suicidally or not is left uncertain). Whatever wisdom he has acquired seems to be of little use to him now, and the biblical three score years and ten which separates him from his grandmother—the term of a natural life—only reminds him of what he can never enjoy. Paradoxically, then, in Alistair MacLeod's loving inscription the people and places of *The Lost Salt Gift of Blood* find a refuge and a permanence which life and history seem destined to deny them, while the dying schoolteacher muses in a way which provides a fitting epigraph for the collection as a whole and for the reader's encounter with it. "The hopes and fears of my past and present intertwine. Sometimes when seeing the end of our present our past looms ever larger because it is all we have or think we know. I feel myself falling into the past now, hoping to have more and more past as I have less and less future." (pp. 99-100)

Colin Nicholson, "Signatures of Time: Alistair Mac-
Leod & His Short Stories," in Canadian Literature,
No. 107, Winter, 1985, pp. 90-101.

THOMAS P. SULLIVAN

One of the drearier things about hoary old bromides is how
often they contain a grain of truth.

Take the notion of finding out all you need to know about life
"right in your own backyard". How many generations of
dreamers and drifters have been stopped in their tracks by sa-
gacious killjoys preaching the stay-at-home gospel? . . .
[Yet, MacLeod's collection *As Birds Bring Forth the Sun and
Other Stories* reveals] more of the truth in that advice than
romantics might hope for. . . .

Although MacLeod sticks [close] to home, he's no homey old
story-teller spinning yarns about the quaint folks down on the
jetty. He's a tough, precise stylist capable of superb, dazzling
prose. He may find his truths in the material at hand, but he
polishes them until they're fit for export to anywhere people
read.

That polish may account for the scarcity of his output. His
lone previous collection, *The Lost Salt Gift of Blood*, contained seven stories, written in as many years. Now, 10 years
later, his *As Birds Bring Forth the Sun and Other Stories*
contains six new short stories.

The opening piece, **"The Closing Down of Summer"**, is barely
a story at all, but a finely wrought meditation on death by the
leader of a mining crew whose members are about to leave
their Cape Breton homes for yet another far-flung mining
camp, this time in South Africa.

Death is never far away in these stories. In the title piece, a
family is haunted by the legend of a grey dog that brings
death to generation after generation. In **"Winter Dog"**, a vicious collie saves its young master's life in an eerie race across
shifting pack ice, only to be destroyed later as a menace. The
boy, now grown, recalls the story while he watches his own
children playing with a neighbour's dog and waits for news
of a dying relative. This is memory as private myth (another
of MacLeod's recurring themes). The effect is hypnotic; the
imagery is burned into the brain and lingers.

Not all death portrayed in the collection is physical. In **"Tuning of Perfection"**, an old man watches the death of traditional Scottish culture, even as the forces that celebrate it twist
it to their own ends. In **"To Every Thing There Is a Season"**,
a boy confronts the truth about Santa Claus and childhood
dies. The subject is so potentially mawkish, it's exhilarating
how MacLeod brings it off with neither soap nor saccharin.

MacLeod—ex-miner, ex-logger, ex-farmboy, professor of English and creative writing—blends a country man's clear-
eyed and unselfconscious awareness with a sometimes stunning ability to write, to succeed in virtually everything he
tries.

In fact, it's almost a fault. No writer who deals seriously with
boys and dogs and Santa Claus, with the singing of Gaelic
story songs, is playing it safe, exactly, but neither is he straining to reach beyond his formidable grasp.

Thomas P. Sullivan, "Atlantic Writers Find Divergent Worlds in Their Own Backyard," in Quill and
Quire, Vol. 52, No. 5, May, 1986, p. 25.

JANICE KULYK KEEFER

Alistair MacLeod's Cape Breton is by now a firmly defined
fictive world on this country's literary map, but it is not merely another picturesque region about which you like to read
but in which you wouldn't want to bother living. MacLeod's
fiction is empowered by his vision of life itself as our one common and obligatory journey, whether we live in Saskatoon,
Toronto or Inverness. And while the ethos, the landscapes
and forms of labour his fiction describes are distinctively
Cape Breton, the experiences his characters undergo are, as
the indispensable formula has it, universal. While many other
contemporary writers create fictions which distract or 'de-
centre' us from the stark and mysterious givens of our personal, social and historical lives, MacLeod forces our attention
to life's incontrovertible processes and ends, as in [the story
"As Birds Bring Forth the Sun"]—a fable upon the 'tangled
twisted strands' of love and death, life and fate.

Yet if MacLeod's fiction [in the volume *As Birds Bring Forth
the Sun*] is 'universal' in its scope and focus, it achieves this
distinction by its passionate commitment to a region which
is not so much geographical as imaginative and racial—
everything that is conjured up by the term Gaelic. . . . Mac-
Leod establishes a storyteller's compact between narrator
and reader—one wants to say 'listener', given the compelling
cadences of his prose. And MacLeod, too, has created fictive
worlds whose interstices are haunted by the fantastic and the
supernatural. In the story **"Winter Dog"**, for example, a
man's remembering of a traumatic incident of his childhood—his helpless complicity in the killing of the dog who'd
once saved his life—is turned from conventional flashback
into a kind of 'second seeing' as the dog which triggers off the
recollection becomes not just symbolically, but supernatural-
ly, the dog who had bled to death so many years before. The
collection's title story begins as a fairy tale: 'Once there was
a family with a Highland name who lived beside the sea', and
ends in the realm of Greyhound bus stations and Toronto
hospitals, but the great grey dog who brings about the death
of the man who lovingly raises her inhabits both worlds, a fusion of symbol and flesh, physical force and mystery. (Fittingly, the story has both the simplicity of a fable and the sophistication of fiction: the knowledge of mortality associated with
the dog is positively Jamesian in its necessary indirection:
'You cannot *not* know what you do know.') Finally, **"Vision"**
brings about an intricate interconnection between the brawl-
ing lives of present-day fishermen and their children, and
those of the direct ancestors who, in their dark possession of
second sight, of catastrophic loves and hates, seem more rooted in St. Columba's Ireland than in Cape Breton. There is,
at the finish of this otherwise masterful story, perhaps a little
too much tying-up and tidying of already tightly-woven ends,
but the reader eagerly accepts the array of violent coincidence, visionary experience, symbolic and physical blindness,
so inspired—no other word will do—is MacLeod's recreation
of a story which goes into the listener the way a knife goes
into the skin, leaving a 'scar forever on the outside' and a
'memory . . . forever deep within.'

These 'visionary' stories seem to have sprung from the same
source as did **"The Road to Rankin's Point"**, the final story
of MacLeod's *The Lost Salt Gift of Blood.* Yet other stories
in *Birds* recall and at the same time transcend the heart of
this earlier collection. Where it was given over to exploring
the emotional reality of betrayal, loyalty and loss, with characters always guiltily leaving or as guiltily returning to family

and homeland, *As Birds Bring Forth the Sun* represents a mature and complex acceptance of the problematic and ultimately tragic nature of experience. In this context the story **"The Tuning of Perfection"** is representative. Its hero, the solitary, seventy-eight-year-old Archibald, brings into difficult and costly balance his loyalty to the integrity of the past, personified in the beloved wife he lived with so briefly, and his recognition of the permanence of loss and change for the worse, as signalled by the crude and yet poignant ignorance of his own grandchildren towards the Gaelic songs which to them are incomprehensible and expedient rather than sacred. Moreover, the collection's opening story, **"The Closing Down of Summer"**, is a kind of requiem for the heroism and beauty which is the essence of the miner's life. Whereas MacLeod's first collection featured anguished protagonists who had rejected their fathers' way of life in the mines, **"The Closing Down of Summer"** is narrated by a miner who eloquently, intelligently and almost serenely defends the choice he has made with his life—to quit not the mines, but the university. . . . (pp. 113-15)

Finally, this collection features two stories which allow their heros to 'know what they cannot not know' in other than tragic or resolutely elegiac ways. The first, **"To Every Thing There is a Season"**, is comparatively lightweight, but **"Second Spring"**—the story of a boy's loss not so much of innocence as of arrogance, as he realizes that the forces of nature are not his to curb or plot—is a beautifully comic piece, one which varies the prevalent tone—*lacrimae rerum*—of this collection.

One last observation—it is revealing that the female features most powerfully in MacLeod's fiction in the form not of women but rather of animals. I say this not to raise a feminist howl, but rather to point to MacLeod's connection with that tradition in Maritime fiction . . . whereby women are not only silent but also actively hostile to any literary use of language. In *As Birds Bring Forth the Sun* the cow Morag of **"Second Spring"**, the *cù mòr glas a'bhàis* of the title story, are much more present and convincing characters than are the dead wife of **"Tuning"** and the wife who, 'permanently into a world of avocado appliances and household cleanliness' is 'unavailable for communication' in **"The Closing Down of Summer"**. It is only in the last story, **"Vision"** that a true heroine appears—blind, filthy, sharing a disintegrating house with animals and referred to only as 'the woman'. Yet MacLeod's evocation of what she once was—passionate, willful, magnificently strong—suggests that he can, if he so chooses, make not only his miners but also his women 'articulate in the accomplishment of what [they] do.' (pp. 115-16)

Janice Kulyk Keefer, in a review of "As Birds Bring Forth the Sun and Other Stories," in The Antigonish Review, *Nos. 66-67, Summer-Autumn, 1986, pp. 113-16.*

JACK HODGINS

Several years before Alistair MacLeod published his first book [*The Lost Salt Gift of Blood*], I came upon one of his stories in a *Best American Short Stories* anthology and became an admirer even before I'd got to the end of its first paragraph:

> There are times even now, when I awake at four o'clock in the morning with the terrible fear that I have overslept; when I imagine that my father is waiting for me in the room below the darkened stairs or that the shorebound men are tossing pebbles against my window while blowing their hands and stomping their feet impatiently on the frozen steadfast earth. There are times when I am half out of bed and fumbling for socks and mumbling for words before I realize that I am foolishly alone, that no one waits at the base of the stairs and no boat rides restlessly in the waters by the pier.

It now seems clear that this single paragraph, which opened **"The Boat"** (later included in his first collection, *The Lost Salt Gift of Blood*), was a strong signal of what would continue to stand at the centre of MacLeod's fiction: the past's insistence on intruding upon the present; the inescapable pull of life on the seacoast; the haunting figure of the admired father. It was also a demonstration of the sort of intelligent and sensitive care this writer would be willing to put into his choice of words, his creation of rhythm, his shaping of sentences, and his subtle engineering of the reader's response.

Ten years of this sort of care have gone into MacLeod's second book of stories. . . . *As Birds Bring Forth the Sun* includes seven fine stories, all set in Atlantic Canada, or in the places Atlantic Canadians came from, or in places they have gone to. In every one of these stories the past forces itself in some form upon the present: a childhood memory of a heroic dog betrayed, a returned brother, a radio station's renewed interest in the old Gaelic songs, a recalled family legend of a big grey dog that has attended deaths of fathers back through several generations, a recurring talent for the "second sight" in a blinded eye. Sometimes the present is illuminated by the visiting past; always it is haunted.

What MacLeod may be best at is the short narrative passage in which an individual labours, in spite of surprising obstacles, in pursuit of an important if unusual goal. In this book there are at least three of these passages I expect to remember for a long time. In each case, I discovered myself sitting forward, grinning, ready to whoop aloud with admiration.

In **"The Closing Down of Summer"** the narrator is struggling to dig his brother's grave in the crowded family plot while his father's disintegrating coffin must be held back from falling in from the adjoining site. In **"Winter Dog"** the boy-narrator has gone out with his dog on the heaps of ice that have crowded in close to shore, and has pried loose the frozen corpse of a seal that seemed "more real than reality." Bringing the seal home on his sleigh, he discovers a gap has widened between the ice and the land.

In **"Second Spring"** a farm boy who wants to breed and raise his own calf for a local club is finally given permission to take the chosen cow to visit the perfect bull five miles away over a narrow dirt road. At the top of the hill the boy and the cow are spotted by a most undesirable bull. . . . This bull knows nothing of the club's high standards and will not be distracted from his need and his intention. The unasked-for and frightening romantic encounter is recounted in some of the best narrative writing I've read in a long time.

The title story [**"As Birds Bring Forth the Sun"**] is perhaps the most inventive in the collection, in terms of technique. I expect it will be, for me, the most memorable as well. It appears to announce its particular slant in the language of its beginning:

> Once there was a family with a highland name who

lived beside the sea. And the man had a dog of which he was very fond.

Though beginning like a fairy tale, this becomes the legend of the narrator's great-great-great grandfather, who lovingly raises a pup left at his gate. When the dog grows too large for male dogs to mount, he—being a man used to breeding animals—goes so far as to find a large enough male and to assist the pair in the process of mating. Some years after the dog and her pups have run off, he comes upon them on an island and calls to the dog. Misunderstanding their mother's reasons for running to this human, the wild pups leap upon him and kill him in full view of his horrified sons.

The story shifts at this point, in a quite wonderful manner, to become a contemporary account of the narrator's own vigil, with his brothers, at the bedside of his dying father. The entire family down to the present generation has inherited the fears and superstitions that attend the legend of the big grey dog of death. (pp. 12-13)

While very much aware of the hardness of life for the people he writes about, MacLeod's wise heart perceives their secret longings, admires their patient strengths, and records with great authority the small triumphs in their struggle for dignity, pride, and love. The last story in the collection, **"Vision,"** which is the longest and certainly the most complex, makes the greatest demands upon the author's heart as upon his writing skills. Another writer might have needed the space and freedom of a novel in order to tell this multi-generational tale of blinded eyes and vision, of sex and love, of friends and neighbours and enemies. In the final paragraph, which is also the final paragraph of the book, MacLeod acknowledges the difficulty of the task he has set himself:

> And when the wet ropes of the lobster traps came out of the sea, we would pick out a single strand and then try to identify it some few feet farther on. It was difficult to do because of the twisting and turning of the different strands within the rope. Difficult to be ever certain in our judgements or to fully see or understand. Difficult then to see and understand the twisted strands within the rope. And forever difficult to see and understand the tangled twisted strands of love.

This is the task he has set himself in all the preceding pages, a task he has performed—for all its difficulty—with originality, strength, care, wisdom, and remarkable talent. I'm an admirer still. (p. 13)

Jack Hodgins, "Home Is the Haunter," in Books in Canada, *Vol. 15, No. 6, August-September, 1986, pp. 12-13.*

FRASER SUTHERLAND

"Once there was a family with a Highland name who lived beside the sea." So begins **"As Birds Bring Forth the Sun,"** the title story in Alistair MacLeod's latest collection [*As Birds Bring Forth the Sun and Other Stories*] and a clue that this book is closer to myth or folktale than it is to modern realistic narrative. MacLeod's Cape Bretoners belong to some Celtic heroic age in which men are proud, wilful, and unhobbled by hubris. (I say men because the protagonists of the six stories are male.) Unlike Hugh MacLennan, with whom he has some affinities, MacLeod does not superimpose Greek myth on the local scene but mines the original stuff.

Mining is the operative word, since the opening story, **"The Closing Down of Summer,"** concerns what is "perhaps the best crew of shaft and development miners in the world." Spellbound by a heat wave on the west coast of Cape Breton, the crew awaits a signal to fly to South Africa for yet another job. The crew leader, like some ancient chieftain, speaks for his tiny itinerant community and this insistent "we" lends considerable power to a story that is structured by means of metaphor, not action. (p. 35)

These stories contain much sentiment but little sentimentality. An unforced Celtic melancholy informs not just the action but the rhythm of the prose itself, sometimes reinforced by quotations from the Gaelic. Little spoken today, Gaelic is rudimentary for expressing how or why to do things but superb for conveying intuitions and feelings. The intense purity of the latter is what MacLeod values most in his people. Archibald, the old singer in **"The Tuning of Perfection"**, mourns not just his long-dead wife but the loss of all she represented: a perfected wholeness of being. Only in a young knife-scarred troublemaker does he improbably find this "closeness," "fierceness," "recklessness," and "tremendous energy." . . . The real thing cannot be faked because, embodied in singers like Archibald, it is a mode of being, not the synthetic acquisitions of academic folklorists and tourism promoters.

In all these stories, the past is coexistent with the present. The *cù mòr glas,* the big grey dog in the title story, haunts successive generations of a family. In **"Winter Dog,"** the animal who frolics with the narrator's children reincarnates the mutt who saved his life when he was a boy. In **"To Every Thing There is a Season"** another speaker says, "I am not sure how much I speak with the voice of that time, and how much in the voice of what I have since become." MacLeod's characters do not live in the past. The past lives in them.

Since the stories lean toward timeless myth rather than contemporary social realism, they occasionally call for suspension of disbelief. Would a rough-living miner like the one in **"The Closing Down of Summer"** be quite so lucidly eloquent? Would a two-and-a-half-year-old construct sentences like "Who are you going to dress up as at Christmas? . . . I think I'll be a snowman" (**"To Every Thing There is a Season"**)? Why does the father in **"Winter Dog"** with the faraway gravely ill relative think that he may have to drive—not fly—his family 1500 miles to see him?

Such questions do not persist because the stories are elementary, in the original sense of the word, and therein lies their power. The elements are often polarized—**"Second Spring,"** which contains a welcome vein of comedy, presents a boy's attempts to impose order on the unruly natural world—but nowhere are they more masterfully balanced than in **"The Closing Down of Summer."** In that story the dichotomies of wet/dry, earth/air, freedom/confinement have the force of fate and the story itself has the inevitability of the best fiction. MacLeod creates a small and in some respects narrow world but, like the tunnels his miners dig, it is capable of infinite expansion. (pp. 35-6)

Fraser Sutherland, "Modern Myths," in The Canadian Forum, *Vol. LXVI, No. 761, August-September, 1986, pp. 35-6.*

DAVID HELWIG

Ten years passed between the publication of MacLeod's first

collection of stories, *The Lost Salt Gift of Blood,* and the recent appearance of the seven stories included in *As Birds Bring Forth the Sun.* It takes time for MacLeod to discover and inscribe his potent short narratives. MacLeod's stories present themselves in a direct, somewhat plain fashion. He does not practice urbanity or any of the more obvious narrative ironies. His stories are concerned with characters who have their roots in Cape Breton, and the directness of the story telling reflects the directness of the men told about. Men: not men and women. There are women in the stories, sometimes to powerful effect, but they are studied as they affect male lives. Yet the stories are powerfully rooted in traditional family life, and its warmth is almost the only comfort in the face of the death and disaster that haunt these men. It isn't easy to give sufficient emphasis to the hardness of these stories, their weight, brutality almost, without stinting the qualities of complexity, poetry, and delicacy that they show as well. Take the opening story, **"The Closing Down of Summer."** In it, a miner—one of an expert crew sent all over the world—tells about himself and his life. Nothing fancy, no structural tricks here, just a man trying to get across the nature of his life, increasingly shut away from his wife and children, his body scarred and damaged by his work, his mind more than a little obsessed by death. His narrative of the digging of his brother's grave, in an autumn rainstorm when the clay begins to collapse, and the coffin of his father, who was blown up in a mine accident five years before, begins to fall on him, has about it the startling hard poetry that is characteristic of the book. Death, sexual love, and the power of the past: these are the themes that run through all the stories and unify the book. The power of love is not scanted, not for a minute, but the context of human love is the brutal animal breeding that occurs throughout.

As Birds Bring Forth the Sun has a powerful poetic unity. It expresses a moment in history when the Gaelic songs of the past and the mythic world they embody is for the last time imaginatively available. The fathers are dying, and these deaths invoke dangerous, important spirit presences from the past. In a world where fatuous television and impersonal conglomerates are carelessly in power, Alistair MacLeod has sought out the links to the Cape Breton and Highland past and listened for the intimations they can still offer. (pp. 1022-23)

David Helwig, in a review of "As Birds Bring Forth the Sun and Other Stories," in Queen's Quarterly, *Vol. 94, No. 4, Winter, 1987, pp. 1022-24.*

RUSSELL BROWN

[Many] readers have already discovered the pleasure offered by [MacLeod's] writing. Although *As Birds Bring Forth the Sun* is only his second volume of stories, he is not a new writer: his first book, *The Lost Salt Gift of Blood,* was published over ten years ago, and that single volume brought him considerable recognition. MacLeod is one of the best literary craftsmen in Canada, capable of conveying intense emotions in a prose that never strains for effect. Partly because they are not very susceptible to short quotation, there isn't space here to demonstrate how good his new stories are. Each is an elegy—sometimes for the lost moments of childhood and the lost companions of adulthood, sometimes for a vanishing way of life, a disappearing language, a culture in peril—yet none is sentimental or manipulative. Neither metafictional nor minimalist, these are pieces that speak eloquently to Mac-

Leod's Maritime heritage without defensiveness or condescension, and, with their understated passions and their lovely blend of folk narrative and modern sensibility, they define the continuing possibilities of traditional fiction.

Russell Brown, "A Gathering of Seven," in The American Book Review, *Vol. 10, No. 2, May-June, 1988, pp. 10, 21.*

LOUISE ERDRICH

Ranging in style from studious and plain to fiercely lyrical, these short stories [in *The Lost Salt Gift of Blood*] by the Canadian writer Alistair MacLeod impart a sense of the daily drama of life in and around Cape Breton Island, Nova Scotia. Occasionally they sentimentalize, more often celebrate with a tough eye, the lives of men and women close to the earth and sea. **"The Boat," "Second Spring," "Island"** and **"The Lost Salt Gift of Blood"** recall the romantic intensity and regional descriptiveness of Ivan Turgenev, and seem almost of a former century in their elemental concerns. . . .

The elegiac title story [**"The Lost Salt Gift of Blood"**] (perhaps an intentional tribute to Turgenev's "Bezhin Meadow") begins with a lengthy, poetic description of sun, water and "blunt gray rocks that loom yearningly out toward Europe," and then the narrator is caught up in the interaction between young fishermen whose accents are "broad and Irish." This is also a story, as are all of the stories in the collection, about an immigrant society in which the older generations speak Gaelic and the young eventually realize that though they speak English, the old language is internalized, that the sound and meaning of it rise to haunt them in the same way that the ancient mythologies and superstitions, spun through generations, exert an ineluctable hold. . . .

Although the work sags when the voice is not sufficiently compelling to bear the weight of long, precise observations, and lapses when the writer works with clichéd situations such as that of a boy saved by his dog, most of the stories are rich, considered and quietly moving. **"In the Fall"** manages to rise above the inherent sentimentality of its theme, the ignominious end of a faithful horse, through passionate attention to detail. Scott, the gray horse who once hauled coal in the mines, follows his master, trustingly, into the back of the cart that will take him to his death. . . .

After the death of the horse the son observes his mother and father in their vulnerability, shame and tenderness. "My parents are there, blown together behind me. They are not moving, either, only trying to hold their place. They have turned sideways to the wind and are facing and leaning into each other with their shoulders touching, like the end-timbers of a gabled roof."

The most extraordinary of these stories, **"Vision,"** gathers all of Mr. MacLeod's concerns—the passing of a way of life, family allegiance, fate, rough destiny and the interdependence of human and animal. Everything is at work here. The texture of the language is both colloquial and literary, the symbolism drawn straight from the surroundings. The driving narrative pulls the reader from one paragraph to the next almost before the meaning is absorbed. **"Vision"** is a tale of precognition, fatalism and sexual passion, in which every incident and image collects and bears a secret meaning. The narrator, whose grandfather was possessed of *Da Shealladh,* in Scots Gaelic "two sights or the second sight," pieces snatches of memory and hearsay into a tale that is mysteriously coherent and whole, for all the wide variance of sources. The language, throughout, is . . . beautiful and evocative. . . .

Louise Erdrich, "Songs of the Earth and the Sea," in The New York Times Book Review, *September 11, 1988, p. 15.*

François (Charles) Mauriac

1885-1970

(Also wrote under pseudonym of Forez) French novelist, nonfiction writer, essayist, critic, autobiographer, biographer, dramatist, poet, short story writer, journalist, critic, and scriptwriter.

Mauriac is considered one of the notable Roman Catholic authors of the twentieth century. Most of his works offer vivid depictions of his native region of Bordeaux and feature individuals tormented by the absence of virtue in their lives. The tribulations of Mauriac's protagonists reflect his concern with sin, redemption, and other issues relating to Christianity and morality. James M. Mellard stated: "For Mauriac's characters, mankind's sins may rest on their shoulders, but each man, not mankind, must work out his own redemption; the communal Church seems less crucial than the individual soul." A recipient of many honors and literary prizes during his lifetime, Mauriac was elected to the Académie Française in 1933 and was awarded the Nobel Prize in Literature in 1952.

Mauriac's writings reflect his conservative, Jansenist interpretation of Catholicism, the precepts of which stress personal sanctity, austerity, and predestination. He portrays his characters as essentially evil human beings who are redeemable only after they renounce all pleasures outside the worship of God. While Mauriac's novels emphasize the necessity of chastity in a Christian life, they often feature sensuous depictions of illicit sexual activities. André Gide claimed that Mauriac injected religion into his fiction in order to make its erotic content palatable to Church authorities. In a letter addressed to Mauriac, Gide commented: "This reassuring compromise, which allows you to love God without losing sight of Mammon, causes you anguish of conscience and at the same time gives a great appeal to your face and great savour to your writings; and it ought to delight those who, while abhorring sin, would hate not to be able to give a lot of thought to it." Mauriac was aware of and distressed by the possibility that his novels might offend Catholic readers, yet he resolved, in his words, to "[reach] the secret source of the greatest sins."

Mauriac's early publications are semiautobiographical studies of youthful characters on the verge of adulthood. The protagonist of his first novel, *L'enfant chargé de chaînes* (1913; *Young Man in Chains*), experiments with political activism and sexual promiscuity before choosing religious devotion as the basis of his life. *La robe prétexte* (1914; *The Stuff of Youth*) depicts a young man in the process of becoming a writer. The maturation of the young artist is also the focus of his next two books, *La chair et le sang* (1920; *Flesh and Blood*) and *Préséances* (1921; *Questions of Precedence*). Although regarded as relatively minor works, both novels reflect the thematic preoccupations of Mauriac's later writings, notably his concern with Christian ethics.

Mauriac's fifth novel, *Le baiser au lépreux* (1922; *The Kiss to the Leper,* also published as *A Kiss for the Leper*), is regarded by many commentators as his first serious exploration of religious issues. This book concerns the physical and emotional

rejection of an unattractive man by his beautiful spouse. After her husband's death, which is indirectly caused by her coldness, the wife belatedly realizes her love for him. Throughout the 1920s, Mauriac wrote novels depicting characters who suffer, or generate suffering, because of their sinful actions. *Le fleuve de feu* (1923; *The River of Fire*) concerns a woman who tries to protect her former schoolmate, an unwed mother, from the attentions of a lascivious neighbor. *Génitrix* (1923; *Genitrix*) is the story of a weak middle-aged man who allows his possessive mother to destroy his relationship with his young wife. In *Thérèse Desqueyroux* (1927; *Therese*), Mauriac introduces his best-known character, a woman who unsuccessfully tries to poison her husband. After the crime is discovered, Thérèse becomes an outcast, tormented by guilt yet stubbornly refusing to ask God's forgiveness. Mauriac followed the adventures of the unrepentant Thérèse in several other works, including *La fin de la nuit* (1935; *The End of the Night*). Illicit passion is the subject of *Destins* (1928; *Destinies*), a novel about a handsome young Parisian vacationing in Bordeaux who becomes an object of desire for two lonely women.

During the early 1930s, Mauriac entered a new phase in his development as a novelist. While his earlier works portray humanity as incorrigibly evil, many of his later novels, beginning with *Ce qui était perdu* (1930; *That Which Was Lost*), depict individuals who successfully overcome their sinful tendencies. These books focus less on the destructive effects of sexuality than his previous works, concentrating instead on broader intellectual and social issues. *Le noeud de vipères* (1932; *Vipers' Tangle,* also published as *The Knot of Vipers*), considered one of Mauriac's finest accomplishments, concerns an elderly man who becomes embittered by the lack of affection shown him by his coldhearted relatives. After finally receiving the love he craves, the man experiences a joyful religious conversion. *Le mystère Frontenac* (1933; *The Frontenac Mystery,* also published as *The Frontenacs*) centers on a young man who renounces his ambition to become a scholar in order to take over his family's winery after his father's death. *Les anges noirs* (1936; *The Dark Angels*) examines the process by which an unregenerate criminal converts to a Christian lifestyle. Mauriac's more humanistic approach to religion is especially evident in *La Pharisienne* (1941; *A Woman of the Pharisees*), which satirically depicts the disastrous effects of a middle-aged woman's overly zealous Catholicism on the lives of her young relatives. In *L'agneau* (1954; *The Lamb*), a young seminary student sacrifices his life in order to save the soul of a corrupt older man.

The last novel completed by Mauriac before his death, *Un adolescent d'autrefois* (1969; *Maltaverne*), returns to the autobiographical mode of his earlier fiction. Set at the turn of the century, this work concerns a young writer who refuses to enter into an arranged marriage with the daughter of a wealthy neighbor. After the girl is murdered, however, he is plagued by remorse. An unfinished sequel to this novel, posthumously published as *Maltaverne* (1972), features the same protagonist, now an elderly writer, engaged in a homosexual liaison with a young admirer.

Mauriac is also regarded as an accomplished dramatist. His play *Asmodée,* which was translated in 1938 and produced in 1945 as *Asmodée; or, The Intruder,* involves a seminarian who interferes with a romantic intrigue between an attractive widow and her daughter's fiancé. *Les mals aimés* (1945) details a woman's struggle to suppress her love for her sister's husband while dutifully accepting her role as nursemaid to her unloving invalid father. *Passage du malin* (1948) portrays a female school director who attempts to help another woman overcome her passion for an undeserving man but falls in love with him herself. *Le feu sur la terre; ou, Le pays sans chemin* (1951) involves a woman whose incestuous attraction toward her brother provokes her to destroy his marriage.

Mauriac offered his views on religious and ethical issues in several essay collections. In *Dieu et Mammon* (1929; *God and Mammon*), for example, he details his attempts to reconcile his fictional depictions of sinful behavior with his duty to uphold Christian values in art. *Souffrances et bonheur du chrétien* (1931; *Anguish and Joy of the Christian Life*) chronicles Mauriac's conversion from a narrow Jansenism to a philosophy more accepting of human frailty. Mauriac also published other nonfiction works on a variety of subjects, including *Le cahier noir* (1943; *The Black Notebook*), an anti-Nazi document published under the pseudonym of Forez during the German occupation of France, and *Lettres ouvertes* (1952; *Letters on Art and Literature*). In addition, Mauriac published several volumes of poetry, including *Les mains jointes* (1909), *L'adieu à l'adolescence* (1911), *Orages* (1925), and *Le sang d'Atys* (1940).

(See also *CLC,* Vols. 4, 9; *Contemporary Authors,* Vols. 25-28; *Contemporary Authors Permanent Series,* Vol. 2; and *Dictionary of Literary Biography,* Vol. 65.)

WILLIAM A. DRAKE

Among the younger novelists of France, there is none whose work affords at once greater promise and less encouragement for the hope that that promise will be achieved, than that of François Mauriac. Coming, in this curious generation which learns to write before it learns to read, somewhat late to literature, Mauriac won recognition and ardent admirers with his first novel [*L'Enfant Chargé de Chaînes*]. Fine writing is almost as scarce in France as it is in America, and when a mellow, well-balanced style is accompanied by a genuine gift of story-telling, excellent psychology, and familiar types and situations, it becomes well-nigh irresistible. So it proved with Mauriac. He wrote well; his themes were vital; he had found his orientation in the soil of his native province, and he was unimpeachably serious and circumspect before his art. Any of these attributes, in a young novelist, would constitute promise. All of them together, when found as Mauriac combines them, are enough to seduce the enthusiasm of the most cautious. So François Mauriac was hailed, upon his first conspicuous appearance, as a writer destined to great accomplishments. He may still be so destined. But, although novel after novel has come from his pen beneath the impetus of that first enthusiastic acclaim, he has not, it would seem, approached appreciably closer to a fulfillment of those generous expectations.

The rise of François Mauriac justified extravagant hopes. One felt that in him, throughout the ordinary period of youthful endeavors, a splendid talent had been laying fallow, close to the heart of France and the well-springs of human passion, to emerge at last, mature, rounded, and full-voiced, like that of Thomas Hardy. The two volumes of poems which Mauriac published about 1911-1912 seemed but a youthful overflow of that still mysterious faculty. Even that strangely powerful, strangely revolting study of adolescent concupiscence, **L'Enfant Chargé de Chaînes,** which he published in 1913, seemed to be, so to speak, merely a testing of his wings, an approach to a style, a method, and an orientation. This story of a young Frenchman, tortured from childhood by the devils of the flesh, who, after seeking satisfaction vainly in several liaisons, enters a Jesuit cloister to purge himself of his torments, and thereafter marries his cousin in order to keep himself in that happily innocuous state, is perfectly absurd. *La Chair et le Sang* is thrice so, because it describes three protagonists suffering from the same preposterous disquietudes. But in these early efforts, Mauriac accomplished three important things. He showed himself to be the master of a literary style worthy of the great French realists. He definitely localized his art in the southwest of France: in La Lande, the place of his parental origins, and in Bordeaux, the city of his birth. Finally, he identified himself with the little group of writers who, shortly before the war, had arisen to describe what André Beaunier terms "the quest of a dogma," the inverse evolution of the spiritually starved modern from skepticism to faith—Ernest Psichari, Emile Baumann, Robert Vallery-Radot, and André Lafon—and in so doing, clearly indicated that the via dolorosa by which he would lead his troubled characters back to the ancient faith was that of the passion of love.

The Catholic ascetic ideal is indeed the motivating factor of all Mauriac's work, despite the circumstance that only his first novels are directly concerned with strictly religious subjects. His unique conception of love as something terrible, disturbing, and destructive, lends an undercurrent of somber presage and irresistible significance to his themes. Thus, although *Préséances* is outwardly an excruciating satire of the snobbishness of the rich wine merchants of Bordeaux, as seen by the two superior members of their community who wish to escape its leveling influence in behalf of their own spiritual goals, the book reflects a horror of sordid ideals so passionate that it distorts an otherwise charming masterpiece of irony. *Le Baiser au Lépreux,* the finest novel of Mauriac's first creative period and the book which, upon its appearance in 1922, definitely established its author's reputation, is a serious evangelistic document, directed against the system of intellectual rejection represented in the philosophy of Nietzsche.

Le Baiser au Lépreux is a masterpiece of its kind, a gloomy and terrible novel, but one filled with strength and beauty. But Mauriac is not destined to regular excellence. *Le Fleuve de Feu* fails in substance and, as it stands, is little more than the outline of a not-too-promising romance. (pp. 268-70)

Génétrix is considerably more than the best novel of an extremely interesting contemporary writer. It is the best short novel produced in France since the war; one of the best short novels, indeed, in the French language. A stark and terrible story, charged with the rancor of those who come too close, it describes implacable and unlovely characters, thwarted and warped by a wretched, plundering sort of love which, grimping to their very souls, torments and desolates them and fills them with cruel hate. Characters and emotions like these are hideous and, happily, infrequent, but they exist none the less; and beneath the magic of Mauriac's art, and beneath, we must add, the somber fanaticism of his point of view, they are invested with a disquieting life and imminence.

Only François Mauriac could have written such a story as *Génétrix,* but even Mauriac, it would appear, cannot write another quite like it. The novels which he has published at regular intervals since 1923 represent a conspicuous falling-off of the richly promising art which, in *Génétrix,* proved that it was capable of perfection. There is, in each of these books, a creative flaw, possibly originating in the author's attitude to life, which fatally limits their accomplishment. But *Le Désert de l'Amour* represents, for all that, a very high accomplishment within itself. Here Mauriac is back again in the milieu which he knows and hates best—the smug, unimaginably snobbish, bigoted wine merchant bourgeoisie of Bordeaux. Unlike *Le Fleuve de Feu,* which fails chiefly because an arbitrary and fundamentally unsubstantial plot is made to carry the whole weight of the characters' conversions, *Le Désert de l'Amour* is an admirably reticent and luminous study of a group of characters who, brought together in various juxtapositions, develop their own story. Mauriac's Maria Cross is one of the most unusual heroines in French literature. She is a quaint little pedant, much given to reading and to quoting what she has read, still young, and, although not beautiful, possessed of an indefinable charm that lingers forever in the memory of the men who have loved her. But she bears, in every feature of her being, a sloth and decay which deprive her of volition, of dignity, even of the capacity of loving or suffering or being happy, and which smirch with a sort of un-

conscious indecency her slightest thoughts and actions. Widowed at twenty, she has become the mistress of Larouselle, the richest wine merchant of Bordeaux, who, to the horror of the community, has openly installed her in his country house. In the next villa lives old Doctor Courrèges, who had attended Maria Cross's seven-year-old son in his last illness. Love had never before entered his life, and though, being wise and middle-aged, he does not now give it utterance, it casts a luster upon his placid, scholarly universe. It is not the beautiful devotion of the old doctor, but rather the brilliant youth of his seventeen-year-old son, Raymond, that receives the responses of Maria Cross. But even that distorted passion passes with the merest of gestures; and when Larouselle's wife at length dies of her cancer, Maria Cross becomes the wife of her protector—"J'ai fait un mariage morganatique," he remarks—and the slave of her saintly stepson. An unclean and disquieting story, of which old Doctor Courrèges is the solitary wholesome element. Yet, with the precision of its style, the incisive veracity of its analyses of character, the actuality of its setting, and the author's extraordinary skill and persuasiveness in story-telling, it is a work of pure literary genius.

It seems to be the portion of François Mauriac to produce fine novels and indifferent ones in precise rotation. *Thérèse Desqueyroux* is almost as flimsy as *Le Fleuve de Feu.* It is merely the commonplace history of a commonplace woman who, mismated with a commonplace burgher of Lande, suffers the commonplace trials of her kind and at length, in order to gain her wished-for freedom, which she would not in any case know how to utilize, resorts to the most commonplace of expedients—she poisons him. Here again we are brought sharply against what we have termed the flaw in Mauriac's creative talent, the fatal obsession and limitation of his point of view. Another woman, in Thérèse's situation, would have left her husband, hanged herself, resigned herself to the consolation of minor adulteries, or comforted herself with the reflection that, imbecile though he was, she had at least found a husband. Not so Thérèse; she must needs commit murder, thereby affirming Mauriac's conviction that the mating of the flesh is a conjuration of the devil. We shall not dispute his point. We merely point out that, for the purposes of fiction, as Mauriac has exemplified it in *Le Fleuve de Feu, La Désert de l'Amour* and *Thérèse Desqueyroux,* any so arbitrary attitude as this, when adopted toward the most fertile subject of realistic fiction, deprives a novel of emotional variety and imaginative resiliency, painfully limits its scope, and ultimately perverts its reality.

Since we have no data to explain the personal genesis of François Mauriac's strange obsession, it is the more difficult to justify its persistence in an artist of his undoubted magnitude and intelligence. But this horror of earthly love lays upon his spirit and his genius as a pervading blight. His Catholicism only partly accounts for it, for Catholic writers have never attempted to set up Nitrean asceticism as an exigent ideal. Mauriac's asceticism possesses a certain medieval flavor, and indeed, in French literature, one must needs go back to the passages on the misfortunes of Abélard in the *Roman de la Rose* to find a similarly passionate description of the manner in which carnal love misdirects and enervates the aspirations of a man. Yet Mauriac is certainly not, like the medieval ascetics, a misogynist. His whole principle is an unconsolable aversion to love—to maternal love in *Génétrix,* to physical love in *La Chair et le Sang* and *Le Fleuve de Feu,* to conjugal love in *Le Désert de l'Amour* and *Thérèse Desqueyroux.* In human matings, he sees only the incessant yearning for a union more perfect than can ever be consummated on earth; brutal selfishness, senseless cruelty, defeat, exhaustion, distortion, and the desperation of accumulated trifles. There is something minutely but inescapably unclean about it all. Perfection and integrity he believes to be qualities which every person must nurture within himself, without squandering his moral forces upon another whom he can never really know.

Yet François Mauriac is not lacking in tenderness. He knows and loves these men and women, these suffering convicts of life, whose torments he describes with so much sober understanding. But his is the tenderness of the Holy Inquisition, which tortured and burned the heretical in order to save their souls. He is, in a word, inclined to a sort of physico-religious fanaticism, which at present appears seriously to hamper his development as an artist. The pure flame of an obsession can justify itself by producing a single masterpiece; after that, it is likely to grow tiresome. Mauriac has written *Le Baiser au Lépreux, Génétrix* and *La Désert de l'Amour,* which, even if he were to produce nothing more, are sufficient to give him remembrance. But he is not yet fifty, and one *Baiser au Lépreux,* one *Génétrix,* one *Désert de l'Amour,* are all that one writer can produce without debasing the creation. François Mauriac must enlarge his scope. But he cannot enlarge his creative scope until he has widened his spiritual horizons. His future achievement as a novelist intimately depends upon his willingness and his ability to accomplish this miracle. (pp. 274-78)

William A. Drake, "François Mauriac," in his Contemporary European Writers, *The John Day Company, 1928, pp. 268-78.*

MILTON H. STANSBURY

Mauriac's election to the French Academy rekindled interest in this distinguished writer. His sensitive, almost tragic features were photographed for every French newspaper and illustrated review. It is a sad face which suggests some inner torment. Harassed by the lifelong struggle between his religious and literary integrity, this good Catholic and brilliant novelist appears never to have enjoyed an easy moment. Not since Racine—whose problems were in some respects identical—has a writer professed such qualms of conscience. But fortunately for us, Mauriac has not yet followed the example of his illustrious predecessor and ceased to write. The world—the Roman Catholic world, at least—is still eagerly awaiting his final stand. In the meanwhile, Mauriac suffers—and we have good novels.

To the layman, the polemics waged in Mauriac's name resemble a tempest in a teapot. Neither Mauriac himself, nor the people he portrays, seem so very reprehensible. Indeed, these characters are almost virtuous when compared with the creations of many of his contemporaries. It may appear incredible that a twentieth-century novelist should concern himself so seriously with winning the good graces of the Church. By this, I do not mean that the modern man has ceased to scrutinize his soul; in truth, most of our writers do little else. They are all seeking salvation in some form or other, and many, like Mauriac, preach a return to God. But there are few who identify themselves so closely with religious dogma. Mauriac has done everything in the world to win the approbation of the Church—everything, that is, except comply servilely with her demands. (pp. 33-4)

His literary beginnings were made under Roman Catholic auspices, and from the first he complains of the Church's disapproval. It demanded that he be a proselytizer. As an artist he claimed the privilege of detachment. How reconcile the artistic instinct with the writing of books intended primarily to edify? Convinced that the clergy were exhibiting a form of stupidity peculiar to the Catholic mind, he continued to write in his own fashion.

However, this decision brought him little peace, for he suspected that his critics were not altogether wrong in detecting a decadent element in his works. He sought every opportunity to vindicate himself; in numerous pamphlets he defined—and he hoped, justified—his relation and responsibility towards his public and his Church. He would not admit that Catholicism itself was unsound, but he pronounced it impracticable because of the shortsighted interpretation of the priests. Was he not discharging some part of his religious responsibility, he asks, by attracting the world's attention to existing discrepancies in Catholic teachings?

As a Christian writer, he was obliged to choose between his own convictions and the creation of characters whose views he did not share. In either case, if these views were found to be unorthodox, the Catholics would condemn him. Mauriac contends that the Catholic novelist is no more privileged than any other to falsify the life he sees around him, and he asks why those who profess to believe in the original fall and corruption of humanity are unwilling to look either squarely in the face? "Impossible to reproduce the modern world," he writes, "without portraying the violation of some holy law," and he laments the necessity of altering his creation through fear of wounding the susceptibilities of impressionable readers. What, for instance, is his own responsibility towards the young man who, as a result of reading *Génitrix,* sent him his photograph with the inscription: "To the man who almost made me kill my grandmother!"

It is interesting to recall that Gide—though the last to worry about responsibilities—expresses much the same idea when he says: "How many secret Werthers were ignorant of themselves, were only awaiting the reading of Goethe's novel, to commit suicide! How many hidden heroes needed only the example of a book, some spark escaped from this fictitious life, before following the lead!"

Mauriac is well aware of the truth of Gide's statements that "exalted feelings are the stuff of which bad literature is made"; that "there is no work of art to which the Demon is not a cosignatory"; and that "there are no artists amongst the saints, no saints amongst the artists." He knew also that souls in a state of pristine purity do not exist; that they are to be found only in fiction, and bad fiction at that. In order to obey the strict letter of religious law, the Christian would have to abandon all idea of writing novels, and Mauriac wonders if the genuine novelist could ever make so great a sacrifice. He believes that the real artist is no more master of his creative imagination than he is of his own destiny. "The moment a character conforms docilely to what is expected of him, the author may rest assured that no life remains in his inanimate puppet." (*Le Romancier et ses personnages.*)

To follow the development of Mauriac's art is to follow the various stages of his moral growth, for his life and his art are inextricably interwoven. The novels which reflect his spiritual evolution gain in depth and strength as Mauriac climbs arduously the rungs of his own moral ladder. He was to find no lasting protection or solace in his faith until he accomplished his own conversion. Nor was he persuaded at a single stroke and for all time; it was a long, ever renewed fight, demanding the greatest fortitude and perseverance.

Defining the art of writing novels as "a transposition of the real and not a reproduction of the real," he believes that a novelist must pass his characters through the sieve of his personal experience and then conceive them as living individuals who work out their own destinies. "There comes that moment in every novelist's life," he writes, "when, after having struggled for years to create what he believes to be new types, he ends by discovering that it has only been the same character reappearing in one novel after another. Indeed, the books which a novelist has already composed are only the earlier drafts of a work which he has been striving to realize without success. His problem is not to multiply his types, but with infinite patience to renew the same character in the hope that some day he will produce that masterpiece which he has been pursuing from the beginning, but which, perhaps, he will never be able to write." This character, of course, is Mauriac himself. He has transported his own inner conflict into each new book, and it is this recurrent theme which gives, in spite of the variety of its wrappings, a fundamental unity to his work. "When my critics demand that I try something new, I say to myself that the essential thing is to go to new depths in my original subject. If people complain that the hero of *Le Noeud de vipères* resembles too greatly that of *Génitrix,* this criticism does not disturb me, because in this later work I am assured of having penetrated deeper into the knowledge of this man, of having brought to light a more hidden layer of his being." In these potential Mauriacs the author seeks some solution, or at least some compromise for his own difficulties. His books are so many conquests over his own timidities and uncertainties; in short, so many scenes in his own moral drama. Hence, he says: "For a long time, I believed that an author's work delivered him from all that lay dormant in him, such as desires, angers, spites; that his erring characters were the scapegoats for all his own potential sins; that, on the other hand, the superman, the demigod, accomplished the heroic acts of which he was incapable; thus, he transferred to them his own good or evil impulses."

Mauriac's novels fall into three rather sharply defined divisions. The first group comprises *L'Enfant chargé de chaînes, La Robe prétexte,* written just before the War, and *La Chair et le sang,* which appeared soon after it. His first novels, portraying very youthful souls, reveal the author's hesitations as a Catholic in face of religious doubts, worldly ambitions, and his craving for a frankly voluptuous life. In conformity with Catholic teaching, he was expected to represent all earthly love as antagonistic to the love of God. As a young man, Mauriac strove to reconcile the two, but found the experiment disastrous. "It is difficult," writes Lucien Dubech in commenting on Mauriac's early work, "to love or take very seriously these young Catholics, who, scarcely issuing from the church, lose all their illusions at Montmartre, where they go to dissipate between vespers and morning prayer. Returning home with pasty mouths at early dawn, they shed a tear over the fate of the workmen and maidservants they see hastening to their daily labor."

After his next novel, *Préséances,* which marks a period of transition, Mauriac emerges from the troubled, adolescent groping characteristic of his early work, and with *Le Baiser au lépreux* (1922) begins a series of infinitely more mature

and skilful novels: *Le Fleuve de feu; Génitrix; Le désert de l'amour; Coups de couteaux; Thérèse Desqueyroux;* and *Destins* (1928). In this second period of his career, Mauriac may be called a Catholic and a novelist, but not a Catholic novelist. If, as Charles du Bos points out in *François Mauriac et le problème du romancier catholique,* Mauriac the novelist gains much from Mauriac the Catholic, the contrary is not true. The Catholic in Mauriac reaps nothing from this association, unless it be the hatred which was to burst forth one day in *Destins.*

Mauriac limited his field of observation almost exclusively to Bordeaux and its countryside. No one was better equipped to scourge the numerous defects found in certain old provincial Catholic families. Who but an eye-witness could evoke so faithfully this world of petty vanities and dissension, of demoralizing avarice, jealousy, spite, hatred, pride, and snobbery? His *dramatis personae* may be divided into those central figures whose psychology is the special object of his study, and the minor characters who serve as buffers or motivators. Among these lesser figures are representatives from all classes of Bordeaux society. Treated with bitter scorn because of their bestiality and lack of true spirituality, they create a somber and depressing atmosphere through which his main figures struggle and meet defeat. His satire is directed most keenly at members of the Catholic faith whose religion consists of a strict adherence to prescribed forms. In *Le Noeud de vipères,* Janine, the granddaughter of the old man who is writing the story, has been abandoned by her husband; to the question "Do you have faith?" she replies: "Of course, I am religious, I fulfill my duties. Why ask me that? Are you making fun of me?" And the old man comments in his journal: "That is exactly what all my life I have hated most, just that: for what is it but a coarse caricature, this mediocre employment of the Christian life?" Mauriac is equally pitiless towards the crass and self-complacent bourgeois, whose desires are limited by a well-rounded paunch, a comfortable income, a family to fall back upon in case of need, and the opportunity to indulge in his favorite occupations. He likewise attacks the tyrannical bourgeois family with its narrow-minded bigotry, its attempt to control the private life of its individual members, its censorship of all independence. (pp. 36-40)

Mauriac believes that innate in man is some taint which may assume various outward forms. The revelation and development of this taint—apt, in his earlier books, to be carnal desire—its corroding and, in the end, fatal effect on a character, form the theme of Mauriac's work. . . . Throughout his work, Mauriac assumes that passion and love are unclean and bestial. He speaks of "the ineffaceable defilement of the wedded union." When a young man, in *Le Noeud de vipères,* seeks to rejoin his wife, the furious old father-in-law inscribes in his diary: "Like a cat entering through a window, he has stealthily penetrated into my house, attracted by the odor." For to Mauriac, passion is not transfigured by the married state.

Whatever blemish man possesses Mauriac believes has been present since early childhood. In opposition to this inherent stain are portrayed the constant swirl of emotions, of habits, prejudices, and desires. Man has no unity in himself, nor can he acquire any in this unceasing turmoil. The logical result is that he must remain as enigmatic to himself as to others. As an epigram for the title-page of *Le Noeud de vipères,* Mauriac quotes from Saint Theresa of Avila: "God, take into consideration that we do not understand ourselves, that we do not know what we want, and that we are always wandering farther away from that which we desire."

Moving in a sphere of complete isolation, Mauriac's characters find that every attempt to seek aid or consolation only emphasizes their utter solitude. He has vouchsafed them no understanding friend, no sympathetic parent to relieve the burden, no wife or husband to share confidences or troubles. The doctor Courrèges, in *Le Désert de l'amour,* hoping for solace from his wife, asks her for the first time in years to walk in the garden with him, but she only speaks of her quarrels with the servants, and reproaches him for forgetting to turn out his light.

There is no refuge from this conflict and isolation except in final defeat and resignation, no oblivion except in a living death or death itself. Noémi, entombed in the family life, "recognized that her fidelity to her dead husband (whom she had never loved), would be her humble glory and that it was her duty not to seek to avoid this obligation." Irène, dying as a suicide, thinks of the empty lives she is leaving behind; she has a presentiment that in continuing to live "there perhaps exists another form of renunciation, another night, another death than this she had sought and desired." *(Ce qui était perdu.)* These men and women, who from lack of faith live in an atmosphere devoid of light, have been analyzed by Marcel Arland as "people who believe themselves to be alone because they are not loved or do not love themselves; let love come and they feel equally alone. Thwarted beings who seek each other with arms deprived of hands, with eyes that cannot see; if they do succeed in reaching one another, it is only to wound each other and themselves."

Mauriac's specialty is to render the sinner more attractive than the so-called righteous man. The more unworthy the character, the more it endears itself to him. "I am like a severe schoolmaster," he writes, "who has all the trouble in the world not to have a secret preference for the inferior nature, rather than the soul so good that it is no longer capable of reacting. Alas! we novelists have this misfortune that inspiration takes its source in the least noble, the least purified of our being, in all that which subsists in us in spite of our better selves. People used to say to me 'Paint virtuous characters.' I replied, 'But I always miss the mark with virtuous ones.' They then would say, 'At least, try to raise the moral level.' But the more I strove to do so, the more obstinately my characters refused to lend themselves to any sort of grandeur." (pp. 41-3)

It soon becomes apparent that Mauriac spends a great deal of his time and talent evoking the pleasures he expects his readers to condemn. If he is resentful of Mammon's sway, he is also fascinated by it. Not that Mauriac's characters are permitted a lusty sinful time to be atoned for later by suffering and repentance. On the contrary, these people undergo such tortured consciences and moral discomfort that even in the act of sinning, their stolen ephemeral moment is robbed of all pleasure. Mauriac's treachery was to idealize and beautify carnal desire only to condemn it as a snare and delusion. Or as Edmond Jaloux has phrased it: "Mauriac makes us think of a young Levite who accompanies his martyr to some evil place, but not always to protect him." Can it be that Mauriac is a Christian in just so far as a feeling of guilt adds piquancy to his scenes of love? "That anguished conscience," writes Gide, "which lends such charm to your features, and gives so much savor to your writings, must gratify immensely those among your readers who, though abhorring sin, would be an-noyed if they were no longer obliged to concern themselves with it. And you know, my dear Mauriac, that in such a case the doom of literature would be sounded, and you are not sufficiently a Christian to give up writing. Your great art is to make accomplices of your readers. Your novels are less calculated to convert sinners than to recall to Christians the existence on earth of something more than Heaven."

Mauriac excels in painting sensual pictures, and this is the one talent his faith enjoins him not to exercise. If to be acclaimed a Christian author is the goal of his desire, it is easy to understand his qualms and misgivings. He may well ask himself what his work has accomplished for the cause of Christianity. At most, he has shown the insufficiency of lives deprived of God. The invariable failure of any two of his characters to attain a mutual and permanent harmony may be one method of decrying a lack of faith. The reader, being supplied solely with negative examples, can only surmise the happy results of righteous living. A few positive illustrations would undoubtedly have pleased his Catholic brethren better. Love and emotion are not lacking in his books, but these are invariably aroused by earthly idols. In most cases their faith reveals itself as little more than a cloak to hide the real nature of their desires, and these, when analyzed, bear a disconcerting resemblance to ordinary physical love. After reading Mauriac it is equally impossible either to blame him for representing evil as victorious or praise him for causing good to triumph. The objections of his Catholic friends can be readily understood. They find his analysis of passion too keen and sympathetic, his depiction of the world too alluring. On the one hand, reproaches from the Church for undermining morals; on the other, sarcasms from the Gides, whom Mauriac is equally loath to displease. No wonder his exasperated critics cried: "Where do you stand?"

Whether Mauriac has merely capitulated before the unremitting onslaught of the Church, or whether his religious convictions have really strengthened, he has finally adopted a more deferential attitude towards Catholicism. In his most tormented moments he never lost his faith, and now, even though a sinner, he has decided to remain a Catholic. So, in a third phase, coincident as it is supposed to be with his conversion, Mauriac says he is striving to purify his art by first purifying his life. (pp. 44-5)

Milton H. Stansbury, "François Mauriac," in his French Novelists of Today, *University of Pennsylvania Press, 1935, pp. 33-51.*

JEAN-PAUL SARTRE

[*The essay from which this excerpt is taken was originally published in* La nouvelle revue Française *in February, 1939.*]

It occurred to me, as I was about to begin *La Fin de la Nuit,* that Christian writers, by the very nature of their belief, have the kind of mentality best suited to the writing of novels. The religious man is free. The supreme forbearance of the Catholic may irritate us, because it is an acquired thing. If he is a novelist, it is a great advantage. The fictional and the Christian man, who are both centres of indeterminacy, do have characters, but only in order to escape from them. They are free, above and beyond their natures, and if they succumb to their natures, here again, they do so freely. They may get caught up in psychological machinery, but they themselves are never mechanical.

Even the Christian conception of sin corresponds to one of the principles of the writing of fiction. The Christian sins, and the hero of the novel must err. If the existence of the error—which cannot be effaced and which must be redeemed—does not reveal to the reader the irreversibility of time, the substantial duration of the work of art lacks the urgency that gives it its necessity and cruelty. Thus, Dostoevsky was a Christian novelist. Not a novelist and a Christian, as Pasteur was a Christian *and* a scientist, but a novelist in the service of Christ.

M. Mauriac is also a Christian novelist, and his book, **La Fin de la Nuit,** tries to penetrate to the inmost depths of a woman's freedom. He tells us in his preface that he is trying to depict "the power accorded to creatures who have all the odds against them, the power to say *no* to the law that beats them down." Here we touch the heart of the art of fiction and the heart of faith. Nevertheless, I must admit that the book has disappointed me. Not for a moment was I taken in, never did I forget *my* time; I went on existing, I felt myself living. Occasionally I yawned. Now and then I said to myself, "Well done." I thought more often of M. Mauriac than of Thérèse Desqueyroux—of M. Mauriac, subtle, sensitive and narrow, with his immodest discretion, his intermittent good will, his nervous pathos, his bitter and fumbling poetry, his pinched style, his sudden vulgarity. Why was I unable to forget him or myself? And what had become of this Christian predisposition for the novel? We must go back to the question of freedom. What are the processes by which M. Mauriac reveals to us the freedom he has conferred upon his heroine?

Thérèse Desqueyroux struggles against her destiny. Well and good. There are thus two elements in her make-up. One part of her is entirely an element of Nature; we can say this of her as we would of a stone or log. But another whole side of her defies description or definition. because it is simply an absence. If freedom accepts Nature, the reign of fatality begins. If it rejects and resists it, Thérèse Desqueyroux is free, free to say no, or free, at least, not to say yes. ("All that is asked of them is that they not resign themselves to darkness.") This is Cartesian freedom, infinite, formless, nameless and without destiny, "forever starting anew," whose only power is that of sanction, but which is sovereign because it can refuse sanction. There it is—at least as we see it in the preface. Do we find it in the novel?

The first thing to be said is that this suspensive will seems more tragic than novelistic. Thérèse's oscillations between the impulses of her nature and the action of her will are reminiscent of Rotrou's stanzas. The real conflict in a novel is rather between freedom and itself. In Dostoevsky, freedom is poisoned at its very source. It gets tangled up in the very time it wants to untangle. Dmitri Karamazov's pride and irascibility are as free as Aliosha's profound peace. The nature that stifles him and against which he struggles is not God-made but self-made; it is what he has sworn to be and what remains fixed because of the irreversibility of time. Alain says, in this connection, that a character is an oath. While reading M. Mauriac—and this may be to his credit—we dream of another Thérèse who might have been abler and greater. But it is the venerable antiquity and orthodoxy of this conflict between freedom and nature which finally commend it to us. It is the struggle of reason against the passions; the rebellion of the Christian soul, linked by the imagination to the body, against the body's appetites. Let us accept this

theme provisionally, even though it may not seem true; it is enough that it be beautiful.

But is this "fatality" against which Thérèse must struggle merely the determinism of her inclinations? M. Mauriac calls it destiny. Let us not confuse destiny and character. Character is still ourselves; it is the combination of mild forces which insinuate themselves into our intentions and imperceptibly deflect our efforts, always in the same direction.

When Thérèse gets furious with Mondoux, who has humiliated her, M. Mauriac writes, "This time it was really she speaking, the Thérèse who was ready to tear things apart." Here it is really a question of Thérèse's character. But a little later, as she is leaving, after managing to make a wounding reply, I read, "This sure-handed blow helped her to gauge her power, to become aware of her mission." What mission? Then I remember the following words from the preface: "the power given her to poison and corrupt." And there we have the destiny which envelops and prevails over the character and which represents, within Nature itself and in M. Mauriac's work, basely psychological as it sometimes is, the power of the Supernatural.

It is a fixed law, independent of Thérèse's will, that governs her acts as soon as they escape from her, and that leads them all, even the best-intentioned of them, to unhappy consequences. It reminds one of the fairy's punishment: "Every time you open your mouth, frogs will jump out." If you do not believe, this spell will have no meaning for you. But the believer understands it very well. What is it, after all, but the expression of that other spell, Original Sin? I therefore grant that M. Mauriac is in earnest when he speaks of destiny as a Christian. But when he speaks as a novelist, I can no longer follow him. Thérèse Desqueyroux's destiny is composed, on the one hand, of a flaw in her character and, on the other, of a curse that hangs over her acts. But these two factors are incompatible. One of them is visible from the inside, to the heroine herself; the other would require an infinite number of observations made from the outside by an observer intent on following Thérèse's acts to their ultimate consequences.

M. Mauriac is so keenly aware of this that, when he wishes to show Thérèse as a predestined character, he resorts to an artifice; he shows her to us as she appears *to others.* "It was not surprising that people turned to look back as she passed; an evil-smelling animal betrays itself at once." Here, then, is the great hybrid presence we are made to see throughout the novel: Thérèse—though not limited to her pure freedom—Thérèse as she escapes from herself, to lose herself in a world of baleful fog. But how, then, can Thérèse know she has a destiny, if not because she already consents to it? And how does M. Mauriac know it? The idea of destiny is poetic and contemplative. But the novel is an action, and the novelist does not have the right to abandon the battlefield and settle himself comfortably on a hill as a spectator musing on The Fortunes of War.

But we must not think that M. Mauriac has accidentally surrendered for once to poetic temptation. This way of first identifying himself with his character and then abandoning her suddenly to consider her from the outside, like a judge, is characteristic of his art. He has, from the first, given us to understand that he was going to adopt Thérèse's point of view to tell the story, but, as a matter of fact, we immediately feel the translucent density of another consciousness between our eyes and Thérèse's room, her servant and the noises that rise from the street. But when, a few pages further on, we think we are still inside her, we have already left her; we are outside, with M. Mauriac, and we are looking at her.

The reason is that M. Mauriac makes use, for purposes of illusion, of the ambiguity of the "third person." In a novel, the pronoun "she" can designate *another,* that is, an opaque object, someone whose exterior is all we ever see—as when I write, for example, "I saw *that she* was trembling." But it also happens that this pronoun leads us into an intimacy which ought logically to express itself in the third person. "She was astounded to hear the echo of her own words." There is really no way of my knowing this unless I am in a position to say that I have heard the echo of my own words. In actual fact, novelists use this quite conventional mode of expression out of a kind of discretion, so as not to demand of the reader an unreserved complicity, so as to screen the dizzying intimacy of the *I.* The heroine's mind represents the opera-glass through which the reader can look into the fictional world, and the word "she" gives the illusion of the perspective of the opera-glass. It reminds us that this revealing consciousness is also a fictional creation; it represents a viewpoint on the privileged point of view and fulfills for the reader the fond desire of the lover to be both himself and someone else.

The same word has thus two opposing functions: "she-subject" and "she-object." M. Mauriac takes advantage of this indefiniteness in order to shift us imperceptibly from one aspect of Thérèse to another. "Thérèse was ashamed of her feelings." Very well. This Thérèse is a subject, that is, a *me,* kept at a certain distance from myself, and I experience this shame *inside Thérèse* because Thérèse herself knows that she feels it. But, in that case, since I read into her with her eyes, all I can ever know of her is what she knows—everything she knows, but nothing more.

In order to understand who Thérèse really *is,* I would have to break this complicity and close the book. All that would remain with me would be a memory of this consciousness, a consciousness still clear, but now hermetically closed, like all things of the past, and I would try to interpret it as though it were a fragment of my own earlier life. Now, at this point, while I am still in this absolute proximity with his characters, their dupe when they dupe themselves, their accomplice when they lie to themselves, M. Mauriac, suddenly and unbeknown to them, sends streaks of lightning through them, illuminating for me alone the essence of their beings, of which they are unaware and on which their characters have been struck as on a medal. "Never had the slightest relationship been established in Thérèse's mind between her unknown adventure and a criminal affair . . . *at least, in her conscious* mind," etc. . . . I find myself in a strange situation; I *am* Thérèse, and, at a certain aesthetic distance, she is myself. Her thoughts are my thoughts; as hers take shape, so do mine.

And yet I have insights into her which she does not have. Or else, seated in the centre of her consciousness, I help her lie to herself, and, at the same time, I judge and condemn her, I put myself inside her, as *another person.* "She could not help but be aware of her lie; she settled down into it, made her peace with it." This sentence gives a fair idea of the constant duplicity M. Mauriac requires of me. Thérèse lies to herself, reveals her lies and, nevertheless, tries to hide them from herself. This behavior is something I have no way of knowing except through Thérèse herself. But the very way in which this

attitude is revealed to me involves a pitiless judgment from without. (pp. 8-13)

And now here is the real reason for his failure. He once wrote that the novelist is to his own creatures what God is to His. And that explains all the oddities of his technique. He takes God's standpoint on his characters. God sees the inside and outside, the depths of body and soul, the whole universe at once. In like manner, M. Mauriac is omniscient about everything relating to his little world. What he says about his characters is Gospel. He explains them, categorizes them and condemns them without appeal. If anyone were to ask him how he knows that Thérèse is a cautious and desperate woman he would probably reply, with great surprise, "Didn't I create her?"

No, he didn't! The time has come to say that the novelist is not God. We would do well to recall the caution with which Conrad suggests to us that Lord Jim may be "romantic." He takes great care not to state this himself; he puts the word into the mouth of one of his characters, a fallible being, who utters it hesitantly. The word "romantic," clear as it is, thereby acquires depth and pathos and a certain indefinable mystery. Not so with M. Mauriac. "A cautious and desperate woman" is no hypothesis; it is an illumination which comes to us from above. The author, impatient to have us grasp the character of his heroine, suddenly gives us the key. But what I maintain is precisely the fact that he has no right to make these absolute judgments. A novel is an action related from various points of view. And M. Mauriac is well aware of this, having written, in *La Fin de la Nuit,* that " . . . the most conflicting judgments about a single person can be correct; it is a question of lighting, and no one light reveals more than another." But each of these interpretations must be in motion, drawn along, so to speak, by the very action it interprets. (p. 15)

La Fin de la Nuit is not a novel. How can anyone call this angular, glacial book, with its analyses, theatrical passages and poetic meditations, a "novel"? How can anyone confuse these bursts of speed and violent jamming of the brakes, these abrupt starts and breakdowns, with the majestic flow of fictional time? How can anyone be taken in by this motionless narrative, which betrays its intellectual framework from the very start, in which the mute faces of the heroes are inscribed like angles in a circle? If it is true that a novel is a *thing,* like a painting or architectural structure, if it is true that a novel is made with time and free minds, as a picture is painted with oil and pigments, then *La Fin de la Nuit* is not a novel. It is, at most, a collection of signs and intentions. M. Mauriac is not a novelist.

Why? Why hasn't this serious and earnest writer achieved his purpose? Because, I think, of the sin of pride. Like most of our writers, he has tried to ignore the fact that the theory of relativity applies in full to the universe of fiction, that there is no more place for a privileged observer in a real novel than in the world of Einstein, and that it is no more possible to conduct an experiment in a fictional system in order to determine whether the system is in motion or at rest than it is in a physical system. M. Mauriac has put himself first. He has chosen divine omniscience and omnipotence. But novels are written *by* men and *for* men. In the eyes of God, Who cuts through appearances and goes beyond them, there is no novel, no art, for art thrives on appearances. God is not an artist. Neither is M. Mauriac. (pp. 24-5)

Jean-Paul Sartre, "François Mauriac and Free-

dom," in his Literary and Philosophical Essays, *translated by Annette Michelson, 1955. Reprint by Collier Books, 1962, pp. 7-25.*

NEIL C. ARVIN

One cannot understand Mauriac fully without taking account at the outset of two fundamental parts of his make-up, both of which are dynamic and beyond the reach of reason and which are at the same time, in his eyes at least, mutually hostile: he is an ardent, intransigent Christian and, at the same time, a man in whom the urge to literary creation is overpowering. "I must write," he notes in his *Journal,* "and my books must be a running commentary on my soul; in my books I must recognize my most secret self." He was born in Catholicism, but to explain why he was such fertile soil for Catholic culture would, as he himself says, involve many things extraneous to his immediate self—his family for instance—but above all God's will toward him. He never for a moment thought of abandoning Christianity, for he always knew he could never escape the Christian grip. At the same time, confronted with the problem of sin, he realized that all he could do—in order, as he put it, to express and make more palpable that which he could not conquer—was to throw himself heart and soul into writing. (p. 364)

Although in his early years his Catholicism seems to have been tinged with more than a trace of Jansenism and although he has always believed fully in the doctrine of grace, his conception of grace later lost the character of despairing acceptance of a rigid determinism. It is true that as a writer he seems to have the conviction, of Jansenist origin, that the only real Christians are those who have given everything to God and that God demands absolute and unshared submission. Nor has original sin ever lost any of its terrible reality for him. Yet he is at the same time overwhelmed by the realization of the infinite love of God for His creatures and is sure that human love, even passion, is in essence only a manifestation of man's love for his creator. For Mauriac, God's command that we should love no one except for Him and in Him does not destroy human love, it only makes it sublime. "Even passionate love for another creature," he writes, "needs only to change its direction to lose itself at once in love of God." At the same time, however, he is haunted by the certainty that all human love that does not have in it the seeds of divine love leads, sooner or later, to frustration and sterility. "We love only that which we can never possess," he says, "and possession of the object loved only destroys it; the objects of our love are mere shadows, phantoms which keep us from seeing the true light, which is the love of God."

Perhaps the best way to characterize Mauriac's religion would be to say that for him the power of religion on someone who believes in it is this, that everything is concentrated in religion, even things that seem to be at the opposite pole. He would say that although a Catholic may, of course, escape from Grace, falling into sin is not escaping from Christianity and would agree with Charles Péguy that the sinner is an integral part of Christianity, that he is indeed at the very heart of Christianity, and that, as Péguy puts it, the saint and the sinner form two complementary and uninterchangeable—yet within each other interchangeable—parts of Christianity. Mauriac thus not only conceives the unhappy characters in his novels as fitting into the world of Christian doctrine and Christian values, for him they are sick souls in whom human love, or love of power, or intellectual pride or thirst for re-

venge, is not accompanied and purified by divine love and yet for whom, in his eyes, salvation is still possible.

But we must remember that Mauriac is not only a Christian but an artist, a writer in whom the creative impulse is as irresistible as his religion. His conception of the role of the Catholic novelist he has stated in these words: "To serve," adding: "I do not want to die before I have written the drama of the world and its creatures as I have seen it in my own life. I must write nothing that is not immediately useful." But to know how best to serve, how to know always what is immediately useful and how to avoid what is harmful and yet at the same time to compromise not one iota of his integrity as an artist has not been for Mauriac an easy task.

This conception of the writer's grave responsibility will determine every feature of his work—subject-matter, style, and method. "The writer is a messenger," he says in his essay on the novel, and elsewhere he approves Baudelaire's contention that a writer is a light-house. With dilettantism of any sort Mauriac has little patience. Being, as he is, almost obsessed with a Christian concern with original sin, Grace, and salvation, it is imperative for him that his art should serve not only his own progress toward good, but that of his readers. He would say, as does Psichari, that "one must write in fear and trembling under the eyes of the Trinity", and that those who believe in the immortality of each individual soul therefore believe in the extreme importance of their writing as affecting each mortal destiny. Mauriac thus has no patience with the literary dogma so widely proclaimed during the last hundred years of the absolute independence of the artist, the claim that a work of art has no object beyond itself and that anything written to be of any use is disqualified from the realm of art. With André Gide's assertion that the moral issue for the artist is not that he should present an idea that is useful, but that he should present an idea well, Mauriac takes uncompromising issue and shares MacLeish's distrust of the writer who ignores the world of the relation of ideas, of intellectual association, and of moral preference.

Yet the claims of the artist upon him are as inescapable as those of religion. Speaking, in his essay on "God and Mammon" of the creative instinct, Mauriac avers that no human power could possibly reduce a man to silence during his period of fertility. "We do not know," he goes on to say, "whether Grace has ever been able to triumph over writing-sickness; we are still awaiting the miracle of a writer reduced to silence by God." That he is as much an artist as a messenger has . . . made his problem a difficult one, yet in his entire work there is not the slightest evidence of any compromising with his Christian conscience nor, except perhaps in his earliest novels, any indication that he has ever sacrificed the exigencies of art to religious scruples.

It is clear then that for Mauriac, as for Montaigne and the Classicists, the real goal of the writer is the knowledge of man. Simply to observe, however, is not enough for him. He goes beyond the Naturalists and claims that the novelist is much more than an observer, that he is really a creator of fictitious life, not content with watching man from some lofty vantage point but bringing living people into the world. Man, then, being the novelist's proper subject and the study of man his purpose, human passions should be the only object of the novelist's inquiry. But man is evil. And here begin the difficulties of a writer who is a scrupulous artist but who is at the same time a religious man. Can one examine and portray evil without thereby running the risk of demoralizing the reader?

Should he say, with Maritain, that the essential point is not to know whether a novelist may or may not portray a given aspect of evil, but to know at what altitude he is when he makes his portrayal and whether his art and his soul are pure enough and strong enough to make it without conniving at it? To write the work of a Proust, as it should be written, Maritain tells us, would require the inner light of a St. Augustine. Here surely is the dichotomy between the disinterestedness of the artist and the utility-sense of the apostles of which Mauriac speaks.

Faced with this issue he has never thought of evading it. André Gide's taunt that he has reached a reassuring compromise which allows him to love God without losing sight of Mammon he says is groundless, because the impossibility of serving two masters does not necessarily mean forsaking one for the other to the extent of losing sight of the forsaken One and losing awareness of His presence and power. Writers like Gide, Mauriac asserts, who claim that a book which scandalizes is nearly always a book which sets people free, are wrong from the Christian point of view since they take into account neither the fall of man nor the fact that man is born defiled. Should a novelist then falsify life in order not to unsettle his readers? This dilemma between profane art and Christianity is sometimes of course, as in the case of Tolstoy, solved by the abdication of the artist, by giving up the attempt to reconcile the conflicting claims of art and of faith by turning one's back on literature. To Mauriac, even with Racine's example before him, this renunciation seems unnecessary. For even though a writer can draw only upon what is in him and although what is in him is largely evil, the creation of sinners and of characters ruled by passion can serve a moral purpose if the writer not only portrays sinners, but shows them living and struggling in the deserts of love, or of pride or of sloth, unconcerned with their spiritual life and turning into worldly channels the love which through faith and Grace could be directed toward God. If, as a Catholic writer, Mauriac creates not virtuous characters but sinners, he does so because it is in these sinners that he can best show the merit of Grace. Although he does not share Gide's contention that good literature cannot be made out of fine sentiments and that the worse the characters the better the book, he nevertheless maintains that it is not easy to make good literature with good sentiments only. Moreover, in the world of reality one does not find beautiful souls in the pure state; these are to be found only in novels, so Mauriac assures us, and most often in poor novels.

But, he asks, must one then stop writing, even if one feels that literary creation is as natural to one as breathing? Perhaps someone, somewhere, he says, knows a way in which a conscientious novelist can escape from these three choices: either changing the object of his observation, or falsifying life, or running the risk of spreading scandal and misery. If the novelist but busy himself with his personal purification will nothing harmful then emerge from his mind? But the practice of superhuman virtue is no easier for a novelist than for other men. Then should a deeply religious man not refrain from writing novels? And so although as we have already seen, Mauriac says that one can serve both God and Mammon, when Mammon requires one to write novels, he seems nevertheless to have found for this problem no solution satisfactory both to his religious and his esthetic probity. (pp. 365-69)

Neil C. Arvin, "François Mauriac," in The Sewanee Review, *Vol. L, No. 3, July-September, 1942, pp. 362-73.*

PAUL DOMBEY

[In a short essay,] **"The novelist and his characters,"** which is distinguished no less by the modesty of its tone than by its complete insight into the subject, M. François Mauriac places himself, by implication, among those creative writers whose concern for the living soul raises them above the contingencies of journalism and of party. "The distinction," he says, "is not between bourgeois [*mondains*] and proletarian writers, but between good and bad writers." And further on he fills out this distinction by a more explicit statement of the true novelist's aim: "I believe it is our justification . . . that we create an ideal world thanks to which living men may see more clearly into their own hearts and so may show each other more understanding and more pity."

It is refreshing to come upon a contemporary, imaginative writer whose moral values do not wear a provisional air. Pity and understanding are certainly the most striking qualities of Mauriac's novels; but both are edged with the sternness that comes of an absolute religious conviction, bred in the bone and fostered by strong attachment to a traditional way of life in a remote and self-contained corner of France. With its tracts of sand dune and pine forest, its vines, its lost and crumbling manors, its proud peasantry, its torrid summers and dank winters, the Gironde is a gift to a novelist, for it contains those extremes of habit and circumstance which he need not describe but of which he must be constantly aware. Though backed by the Mediterranean, the face of this uncompromising land is turned towards the Atlantic and its mists. So Mauriac derives the simplicity and vigour of his style from the classical south, but from the north and west his passion for the human soul. If he does not really count among the "regional" novelists, this is because the fervently Catholic cast of his mind gives to his picture of life a universal quality which is lacking in the deliberate and emphatic provincialism of writers like Giono and Frank O'Connor. Mauriac writes always of the Gironde, not in order to celebrate it, but because a lifetime's knowledge of the place and its inhabitants offers him all the material he needs for the exploitation of his theme.

Unlike most contemporary novelists, Mauriac is primarily interested in the problem of Good and Evil; and here it must be remembered that while to the atheist or agnostic evil is simply the anti-social urge within an ill-balanced personality, to the Christian it is an hierarchy of its own, beside the human system. Yet it is also essentially parasitic—a wandering force which, in order to maintain itself, fastens upon the unwary, the violent, or the desperate soul so that this becomes literally possessed, separate, terrible. "Every time we do good, God works in us and with us; on the other hand, our bad actions belong wholly to us. Where evil is concerned, we are in some sense gods." And in *Les Anges Noirs,* which is Mauriac's most unflinching examination of the hierarchy of evil, the action of the story is constantly being snatched away from the characters themselves, so that everything is made deceptively easy for them, as in some kinds of dream. . . . This strong conception of the nature of evil renders it terrifying to the imagination in a manner, and with a power, which are not available to those writers . . . who entertain a negative idea of this reasonless force. Mauriac—like Graham Greene and (in a different way) Kafka—is a great adept in the art of gathering two or three together so that Evil is conjured to make a fourth in the game. A suddenly intensified *usualness* in the appearance of everything—a quietness replete with signs: the fire burning just too brightly; the pictures on the wall edged with intent; outside the burnished window the landscape dissociating itself. There is no escape, and the scene is set for a proud exaltation of the self which organises a cold and careful demolition of the subtle structures of love. The agents of evil in these novels are superficially various: they range from weaklings like the gigolo, Bob Lagave, of *Destins,* and the furtive rake, Hervé de Blénauge, of *Ce Qui Etait Perdu,* to professional artificers of ill like Gabriel Gradère *(Les Anges Noirs)* and Hortense Voyod *(La Pharisienne).* These are extreme cases, and it is perhaps natural that Mauriac's most famous character, the murderess Thérèse Desquéyroux, should also be that which has aroused the liveliest interest and sympathy among his readers.

Mauriac's most recent creation *[A Woman of the Pharisees]*—and, I think, his finest, just because so rich in complexities of motive still observable in the "average" person— is a woman whose character suffers all but total ruin through the irreconcilable claims of the religious and the secular forces within her. In other words, Brigitte Pian is a Pharisee whose life is devoted to the forging of an "armour of perfection" around her soul, the corruption of which is hidden from her by egotism and a self-righteous love of power. In this wonderful portrait, which has the grandeur and pathos of a Rembrandt, Mauriac observes his subject with perfect detachment and with a dry humour which exposes Mme Pian's pretensions as essentially comic. . . .

Mauriac has shown us the male, and even more sinister, equivalent of Mme Pian in the spoiled priest of his play, *The Intruder,* and has commented upon the type in an interesting essay on Molière's Alceste, which contains the following acute remark: "He feels no horror for what is horrible— beginning with himself: all his attacks are turned outwards; he compares himself with others only to his own advantage." In the Christian sense, then, Brigitte Pian's self-satisfaction is comic; but meanwhile the harm it does to others is frightful, and nowhere does the power of this novelist's imagination operate to such admirable effect as in the success with which he engages our sympathy for the miserable woman, when, at long last, the results of her acts begin inevitably to recoil upon herself.

The subject is a large one; it requires both time and space for its deployment; and the author's management of both is that of a great master of fiction. When the story opens, three of the principal characters—Mme Pian's step-children, Louis and Michèle, and Louis's school friend Jean de Mirbel—are children; but so cunningly is the story told that years have passed and they are grown up before we realise it. The tragedy of the saintly Abbé Calou, the deterioration of Jean de Mirbel, are contributory stages in the same sequence; but the factor of space is equally important, and the irregular intersection of diverse destinies (a constant feature in all Mauriac's novels) is here contrived with an effortless ease and a completely firm grasp on realities of the situation which make the laboured counterpoint of Aldous Huxley and others look very clumsy indeed. For although the progress of the Pharisee is the centre of the book, the individual stories which contribute to it are made to seem no less interesting, because the author's hold on his character is both firm and tender.

It is an absorbing spectacle, not only because we feel so lively an interest in these people, but because—to put it very mildly—M. Mauriac knows how to tell a story. In fact, I can think of no other living novelist whose sheer narrative power is at all comparable with his. Impossible to stop reading any of his novels, especially this one. His method is traditional and presents no difficulties or obliquities such as we find in writers like Bernanos or Elizabeth Bowen (to take two very dissimilar examples). Reserving all complexity for the analysis of character and the interplay of shadowy moral forces, Mauriac's prose has the close, economical texture, the hard definition and the smooth serenity of Racine's verse. And because he never flinches before the worst, he is an entirely unsentimental writer. In the hands of a cynic or existentialist a novel like *Les Anges Noirs* would become a revolting piece of Grand Guignol; Rose Révolou, the only character to survive the general cancelling out in *Les Chemins de la Mer,* would be a first cousin of the Constant Nymph; and Jean de Mirbel would be indistinguishable from one of Mr. Koestler's emaciated heroes. Mauriac, on the other hand, regards his creations, not as figures in a daydream nor yet as social or economic pawns, but as individual objects of love. Since he loves them, he can afford to display their vileness, as well as to conceal, if necessary, their nobility, for "not all mysteries are shameful," as he says in the second volume of his *Journal.* In the same way, he knows that his Pharisee will never wholly outgrow her evil propensities, even when events have shown her to herself as she really is. So he allows us to witness the change in her, reasonably confident that we shall not be deceived. This judgment is so beautifully balanced, so just and sober, that the effect of pathos is overwhelming. . . .

With the possible exception of *Les Anges Noirs,* in which, I feel, it is very difficult to accept the author's belief in Gradère's salvation, all Mauriac's novels achieve a perfect catharsis, so that the sense of disaster, though predominant, does not leave behind it an impression of gloom or futility. This is perhaps due in the main to the charm and sincerity of his pictures of young people. Those of us who saw *The Intruder* acted in London before the war will scarcely have forgotten the beautiful simplicity with which the boy and girl were drawn; and it is the same with the three young victims of Brigitte Pian. Our pity for and understanding of their agonies evoke all the helplessness and ineptitude of our own youth, and leave besides a conviction of the ultimate value of their ordeal.

Paul Dombey, in a review of "A Woman of the Pharisees," in New Statesman & Nation, *Vol. XXXI, No. 796, May 25, 1946, p. 379.*

WALLACE FOWLIE

Mauriac's province, which was Montaigne's also, plays a much more significant part in his novels than that of a mere setting. The somber and somewhat sad city of Bordeaux and the countryside around Bordeaux, composed of pine forests, vineyards, stretches of sand and large isolated houses, have helped to form the sensitivity of the novelist. He is no regionalist writer in a narrow sense, but the physical and spiritual qualities of his province exist in close alliance with the characters of the novels. The province is part of the poetry and part of the drama in each of the books, to the same degree, so difficult to measure, as in the novels of William Faulkner about the deep South. Mauriac does not sing directly or blatantly about his province, as Barrès did about his. He is always concentrated on the landscape of the soul, but this first landscape reflects the romantic wildness and solitude of Les Landes. (p. 39)

Mauriac's meditations on the moral and religious problems of man have been closely associated with his meditations on the role of the writer, and more especially on the function and the responsibility of the novelist. The work of the writer is for Mauriac the justification of his life. He would consider that his novels contain the essential truth about his life and his mind. His pages of fiction represent a closer approximation to truth than any purely factual rehearsal of his life. In every page of his novels, the novelist is at the bar defending himself and his ideas and pleading for the justification of his existence.

The novelist draws upon the memories of a lifetime. Rather than being dispersed or effaced, each memory is recorded permanently within him: each face he saw, each word he heard, every anecdote that was told to him, every accident he witnessed. The rooms, the houses and the gardens, which serve as the background for Mauriac's novels, are inevitably monotonous because they were all observed by him in Bordeaux and in the family estates outside of Bordeaux. Friends and neighbors of Mauriac have been startled in recognizing in his novels their own rose garden or their own living room. But they were even more astonished at reading the somber dramas which unfolded in the familiar setting. The secret of the novelist was the discovery of the hidden monsters in the seemingly inoffensive characters who lived in the houses and walked about the gardens. Against the background of decorous conventionality in a Bordeaux household and the logically patterned gardens, Mauriac has projected characters of illogicality, of passion and complexity. These are his creatures and his creations. He is concerned with the deepest motivations within them, with their suppressed desires and the unspoken dream fantasies.

If therefore the content of Mauriac's novels is somber and passionate, the actual form of his writing, like the symmetrically ordered gardens of his settings, is lucid and classically direct. The chastity of his style permits him to say anything he wishes about his characters. The disorder of crime and chaotic mental states in the novels of Mauriac is offset by the sense of order which controls his writing. The total absence of melodrama in his style permits the violent drama of the characters to take on its full objectivity. The simplicity and understatement of the sentences help to increase the torment of the creatures, which in many cases is unarticulated.

Mauriac believes that behind each novel there exists to some degree a part of the novelist's own life, a personal drama either directly experienced or imagined. Thus the writing of the books becomes a deliverance of personal suffering or passion, of suppressed anger or desire. And the characters in the books almost resemble scapegoats, mystically loaded with the sins which had been committed or imagined by the novelist. The literal defect in the life of a novelist, when it is transplanted, may easily grow to monstrous proportions. The novelist's art is a transposition and not a reproduction of the real.

François Mauriac occupies a very special place among the Catholic writers of contemporary France. His work, completely innocent of didacticism or proselytism, is devoted to the study of sin, evil, weakness, suffering. Sanctity is not one of his themes. He has confessed that he always fails in the depiction of virtuous characters. Pietistically minded Christians as well as non-Christians have found it difficult to accept this trait in Mauriac. Gide at one time chided Mauriac for the preponderant place he gives to evil in his novels, for the compromise, as he defined it, which permits Mauriac to love God

without losing sight of Mammon. Gide continued his argument by saying that if he were more fully a Christian, he would not be able to follow Mauriac quite so easily.

The major attack on Mauriac's conception of the novel (whereby Mauriac believes the novelist comparable to God, having full knowledge of his creatures, although never denying them freedom of will) came from Jean-Paul Sartre, in an article written before M. Sartre enjoyed the fame he does today [see excerpt above]. The existentialist argues that the Christian writer, because of his belief in man's freedom, is admirably suited to write novels. Dostoevski would be a leading example. But Mauriac, according to Sartre, sees the whole of his universe at all times. His dialogue, like that of a play, is always efficacious and moves rapidly ahead. Whereas the characters of Dostoevski, Faulkner, and Hemingway do not know what they are to say next. They are freer than the creatures of Mauriac. And M. Sartre concluded that God is not an artist and neither is François Mauriac! This criticism of Sartre greatly limits the art of the novel. Mauriac is a descendant, not from other novelists, not from the realists Balzac, Flaubert, and Zola, but from Pascal, Racine, and Baudelaire, whose sense of tragedy demanded a certain aloofness of attitude and an abstraction or purgation in style. (pp. 41-4)

One of the constantly reiterated themes in the writings of Charles Péguy is the important position which the sinner occupies in Christendom. . . . The novels of Mauriac illustrate this significant and dramatic role of the sinner. It was particularly after the publication of *Les Anges Noirs,* in 1936, that the criticism of Mauriac's themes grew almost into a storm of protest. Wasn't it a sign of morbidity and unhealthiness, his detractors questioned, that the world of evil depicted by this novelist was so uniformly black and despairing? Doesn't this perpetual preoccupation with sin and perverseness indicate a connivance or a compliance with them? His work has often been called a scandal and Mauriac has been asked repeatedly to defend and justify himself.

His answer is always the same. He is interested in the problem of evil, and finds nothing exceptional or outrageous in his characters. The newspapers alone furnish sufficient proof that in every city every day crimes are committed which are not more strange or more monstrous than those in his novels. The novelist simply isolates one of those cases and analyzes its genesis and its development. A novel is a steady floodlight focused on one of the lurid stories of passion which the journalists dispatch with flagrant irony and disinterestedness. Mauriac has called his novels a matter of "lighting."

The characters of Mauriac represent that kind of human nature, formed and conditioned by a long background of orthodox Christianity. Even if in many of the characters there is only a nominal or hypothetical adherence to the Catholic faith, the deepest part of their natures reacts to the forces in them and around them as if Christianity, acknowledged or unacknowledged, governed the beginning and the end of human existence. In such natures as these, the struggle between good and evil is clearer and more dramatic than it would be in others. It is true that the Calvinist as well as the Catholic may experience a kind of terror when he has committed sin or when he is alone with his passions, but it would seem that the Catholic, more than other Christians, feels a more metaphysical or historical terror in the presence of sin and in the memory of sin. Every sin committed by others affects him in some way and augments his personal drama. There is a profound solitude in many of Mauriac's characters, but the solitude is controlled by an ancient knowledge of sin. They are immobilized, not so much by their own personal experience of sin, as by some ancient sense of responsibility for the sins of mankind. The Catholic is more attached than other men to the imperfections and the failures of the world. Each day, even if he performs his religious obligations in the most perfunctory manner, even if he does not perform them at all, he ties himself up with the sins of the dead, he fills his solitude with the terror which comes from the sense of solitude created by the alienating force of sin. The barrenness of the Mauriac scene is in constant complicity with the barrenness of his creatures' hearts, but it would be difficult to discover in any literary tradition a more cosmic sense of evil.

The general climate of Mauriac's novels may appear unhealthy to many readers because it is dominated by the more somber aspects of passion. The sexual problem, never blatantly stated, is at the center of each of the books. The drama takes its origin in the most secret of all meeting places within a human being: there where religious aspiration, or at least religious conditioning, collides with sexual desire. In most of Mauriac's characters, this sexual desire is repressed and continues half hidden, half forgotten until it breaks out in some tense abnormality. The problem is always there, waiting in the dark, so to speak, but its presence is felt in all the actions and decisions of the characters, as well as in their periods of loneliness and in their attitudes of waiting. Although Mauriac seldom gives any direct expression to the sexual problem, he is concerned with the degree to which it adumbrates and even controls all other problems. Concupiscence ties up the soul with the body, and becomes in itself an indistinguishable commingling of spiritual aspiration and passionate urgency. Mauriac finds in the sexual origin of each life, not an absolute determinism, but a bent and an inclination which constantly threaten the possible sanctity of human life. Each one is tested to a degree proportionate with his nature, because of this dark origin of the flesh. This is the world of evil, for Mauriac, whose site is the heart. The other world in his novels, of Bordeaux and Les Landes, serves only to delineate more sharply and more poignantly the ancient world of the heart. (pp. 44-7)

Mauriac's dark hero (cf. Jean Péloueyre in *Le Baiser au Lépreux,* Fernand Cazenave in *Génitrix,* Raymond Courrèges in *Le Désert de l'Amour*) illustrates an entire aspect of Pascalian psychology, which still remains, especially in France, the chief source of psychological inquiry in the Christian tradition. According to this aspect of "Pascalism," the human heart is the microcosm of the universe. Each individual heart is the reflector of the universe, the container of immensity. Mauriac studies in his hero's heart its tragic precision and uniqueness. Dostoevski's writing is very close to this conception of the heart, but Mauriac's art is more concentrated, more precipitous, and therefore more Pascalian.

Mauriac as a novelist combines in a subtle and well-nigh indistinguishable way the roles of Freudian analyst, in his study of the secret of disorder, and of theologian, in his study of the origin of sin. Throughout the Mauriac novel, the deepest part of man is imperiled. It is the dramatic representation in characters of Pascal's wager passage, and one can't tell which state will win out: grace or damnation. The typical novels, such as *Génitrix* and *Le Désert de l'Amour,* are inconclusive, because the novel, as Mauriac conceives of it, is the story of the peril (or the disorder) in which the dark hero finds himself, and the novel stops at the moment when the peril may come to an end.

Jansenist by temperament, both Pascal and Mauriac carry on in their writings a constant dialogue between appearance and reality. Pascal, abstractly as moralist and philosopher, and Mauriac, concretely as psychologist and novelist, depict the mysterious dignity of sin and the blindness of men who do not love what they think they love. If Mauriac appears Jansenistic by inspiration, he is not so doctrinally because of the freedom of his characters. In them he sees the constant unpredictable interplay of nature and grace. The leading trait of Mauriac's dark hero is perhaps his nostalgia for a lost purity. His hero's soul, no matter how perverted it has grown, is always considered by Mauriac in its quality of eternality. He is concerned, as Pascal was, with the existential character of the soul, with the wretchedness of the soul without God. Once Mauriac defined himself as being the metaphysician working with the concrete. His excessive use of the word "drama" is a clue. In Mauriac's mind everything becomes a drama: love, passion, family, poverty, nature, evil, religion, grace.

Pascal and Mauriac appear as two lawyers pleading before God for the case of man. The somberness of Mauriac's world recalls that of Proust, but there is nothing of the pleader in Proust. Mauriac believes that each man bears within him much more than himself. An out-and-out sinner is a myth. A man represents an accumulation of inherited tendencies. He is all his ancestors at once, as well as himself. The divisioning and bestowal of grace come from an unknowable system of economics where unpredictable correspondences occur. At the end of [*Génitrix* and *Le Désert de l'amour*], the dark hero stands, not alone, but in an intricate relationship with his ancestors. He represents them as well as himself before God. But his will is not entirely bent to God, because in that case the devil as well as the novelist would lose his rights over the man's soul. (pp. 56-7)

Wallace Fowlie, "Mauriac's Dark Hero," in The Sewanee Review, *Vol. LVI, No. 1, January, 1948, pp. 39-57.*

WALLACE FOWLIE

During the 1920's, when he was publishing his early novels at regular intervals, Mauriac spoke of the theater in various articles and referred to the seventeenth century (when Pascal was writing his spiritual letters to Mlle de Roannez) as the only period in French history when the theater could reach a high degree of perfection. "Every Frenchman," he stated, "is a casuist." . . . Casuistry is today pursued in journalism and politics rather than in the domain of theology.

Mauriac claims he is a dramatist who happened to write novels. His characters are presented at a moment of crisis in their lives and remain throughout the story in a state of crisis. This characteristic of his novels explains the swiftness and intensity of the action. (pp. 151-52)

The power of *Asmodée* seems to come from the fact that the play can have an almost edifying effect on convinced Christians, but that its supernatural intentions may pass unnoticed by non-Christians. There is no need for a theological disposition or knowledge in order to follow the play. An atheist might find some confirmation for his views in the unhealthy Catholicism the play reveals, and a communist would find in it confirmation for desire to terminate the reign of the bourgeoisie.

The central character, Blaise Couture, a contemporary Tartuffe, a former seminarian, has become the spiritual director of a provincial family in which he is employed as a tutor. He exercises an unusual power over women, and in particular over the lady of the house, Mme de Barthas, widowed for eight years and still young. A young Englishman, Harry Fanning, spreads dissension in the family so rigorously governed by Couture. The daughter of the family, Emmanuèle, aged seventeen, falls in love with Harry. Couture encourages this marriage in order to remain alone with Marcelle de Barthas. This is complicated by the fact that for a while mother and daughter are rivals for the affection of Harry, and also because of a possible religious vocation in the daughter.

The title of the play is drawn from the eighteenth-century novel *Le Diable boiteux* by Lesage. In the book, the devil Asmodius flies over Madrid and removes roofs in order to observe domestic scenes. Harry Fanning, on his arrival at the home of Mme Barthas speaks of this. He wanted to see French homes and possibly some of the dramas in these homes. . . . Marcelle de Barthas assures him that he is entering a peaceful house where he will come upon no dramas of passion. The truth, of course, is just the opposite, and Harry becomes the instrument of the crisis. Blaise Couture, a powerful and sinister personality, holds together all the strands of the varied relationships in the drama. He is not literally a Tartuffe, because he is not a religious hypocrite. He quite directly incarnates a force of evil. Marcelle, like many heroines of Mauriac, represents a sense of solitude and a marked weariness of life. She is easily the prey of such a strong character as Couture. He recalls Molière's hypocrite only insafar as he has retained the manner, the speech, and the subtleties of thought of a seminarian. The unfolding of Marcelle's personality dominates the lesser dramas in the play: the rivalry between Emmanuèle and her mother for the love of Harry, and the struggle between divine love and human love in the heart of Emmanuèle.

Mauriac's second play, *Les Mal Aimés,* of 1945, is more Racinean in form than *Asmodée,* more close-knit, more unrelieved in its depiction of an intense human conflict. The action of the play concerns four characters: M. de Virelade, a slightly transposed figure of Couture, who mounts guard over his elder daughter, Elizabeth, whose life is totally devoted to her father. She is in love with Alain, the man who married her younger sister Marianne, and she even contemplates flight with this man. At the end of the play, Alain returns to his unloved wife, and Elizabeth to her unloved father. The concept around which the work is built is expressed by Elizabeth when she says that we are bound to those we do not love. (pp. 152-53)

Many reasons account for the failure of Mauriac's third play, *Passage du malin,* first produced in the fall of 1947. All the critics spoke of the inadequacy of the cast, but more seriously of weaknesses of theatrical devices, of comic scenes, and deficiencies in composition. The theme of the play is the temptation of a character, in this case the directress of a school, to dominate another character, a young girl, and free her from the physical love she has for a young man who is an opportunist and thoroughly unreliable. Momentarily she succumbs to the seductiveness of the man, but at the end of the play she returns to her duties.

Le Feu sur la terre, of 1951, was inspired, according to Mauriac, by the spectacle of a forest fire in the Landes which he had witnessed in the summer of 1949. But the literal forest fire is far less important than the symbolic fire of passion which is the subject of this fourth play. The setting of the Landes, the family house, the possessive love of a sister for her brother are themes that recall the Mauriac novels. When the brother returns home from his studies in Paris, with a wife of his own choice, the sister's plans (she had chosen an inconspicuous girl for her brother) are thwarted. The main action is her effort to break the marriage. Her love was perhaps too glibly called "abnormal" by the early critics of the play. It is a demanding powerful sentiment, but to call it "unnatural" would be to contradict one of Mauriac's most tenacious beliefs: that there is no distinction between normal and abnormal. All men are driven by the same inclinations and desires. Only external circumstances alter the patterns of love and defeat in love.

Of these four plays, the first two seem the most assured of some continuing success. Dramatic technique is not so suitable as the technique of a novel to Mauriac's great skill in depicting and utilizing an atmosphere. The religious theme is almost absent from his plays. It has often been argued that the believer, as believer, is not a suitable character for the theater. There are few exceptions to this rule in the contemporary theater. The leading exceptions would be, not Mauriac's plays, but Claudel's *L'Annonce faite à Marie* and Bernanos's *Dialogues des Carmélites.* Despite Mauriac's disavowal of the theme of abnormality in his plays, most readers and spectators will look upon each of these plays as centering upon an abnormal or at least unusual relationship, such as that between Marcelle and Harry in *Asmodée,* between Elizabeth and her father in *Les Mal Aimés,* and between the brother and sister in *Le Feu sur la terre.* And yet Mauriac has insisted that in this latter there is no incest because it is a nonreciprocal relationship.

Anouilh, in a famous quip, described life as a long family dinner. Mauriac's quip, if he were to answer Anouilh, might well be: life is family relationships, the setting where each member of the family watches over and even spies on all the other members. The playwright himself is a member of this family if we remember his oft-repeated statement that his characters, in the novels and plays, are born from the most obscure and the most troubled part of himself, that they are formed out of that part of his own substance which continues in spite of all his efforts to eradicate it.

Mauriac's Catholic sensibility is in the sometimes visible and sometimes invisible background of his plays. Even when they do not refer to Him, God exists for his characters as a reproach or a source of exaltation. It has been said, with some degree of justice, that Mauriac's heroes are less free and more directed and controlled than are the heroes of other contemporary French writers. This seems to come from the fact that in Mauriac's universe sin is a presence, and evil is someone. The playwright-novelist fully realizes his intermediate position of not pleasing the world and of displeasing the saints. (pp. 153-55)

Wallace Fowlie, "Religious Theater," in his Dionysus in Paris: A Guide to Contemporary French Theatre, *Meridian Books, 1960, pp. 127-55.*

DENIS DONOGHUE

Maltaverne, "that arid anguished land with its bleeding pine trees," is more than a setting for François Mauriac's latest novel, *Un adolescent d'autrefois* : It is the objective equivalent of a young man's feeling. "I cannot give up this land, these trees, this stream, the sky between the tops of the pine trees, those beloved giants, that scent of resin and marshland which—am I crazy?—is the very odor of my despair." The young man is Alain Gajac, who tells the story of his life from the age of fourteen to twenty-two. Near the end, Maltaverne appears to him as "a bleak arid heathland," and he knows that it has been transfigured by his own gaze. His relation to the place is a kind of black magic, until he releases himself from its claims. At the end, the young man leaves the pine trees and commits himself to the solitude of Paris. . . .

Mauriac has announced that this is to be his last novel. It is appropriate, therefore, that it resumes so many of his grand themes and motifs—the nature of evil, the relation of outer and inner landscape, the sense of place, God's hand in the world. Alain speaks of

> the secret point where the truth of life as we experience it joins revealed truth—the revealed truth that has to be extracted from the matrix that has hardened round the word of God through the Church's two thousand years of history.

This is Mauriac's special area of feeling, the place of Incarnation, where personal truth and revealed truth converge, like choice and chance. Sartre asks, in *Being and Nothingness,* whether it is possible for freedom to take itself as the source of all value; or whether freedom must necessarily be defined in relation to a transcendent value which haunts it. Mauriac chooses the second answer. His Alain is determined to assume responsibility for his own life, but this decision is animated by his sense of an even greater responsibility to God. At the age of twenty-two he crosses a shadow line in his life, when the question of happiness ceases to be important, and everything aspires to the condition of faith. "But I, my God, whatever I may do, am responsible to you." This is the ghostly responsibility which surrounds the entire novel: In the early chapters it merely appears as a lurid gleam, theatrical, melodramatic; at the end it makes a glow, a bright halo of meaning and value.

Perhaps the novel is somewhat brisk, too brief to be fully convincing as a pilgrim's progress. Some of its significance is reflected from Mauriac's earlier novels on similar themes, where the figures and patterns were first defined, as in *The Desert of Love* and *The Knot of Vipers.* The book has an air of summary, like a phrase from Pascal lodged in a young man's mind; but it is beautiful and noble.

> Denis Donoghue, "A Master's Farewell," in Book World—The Washington Post, *June 14, 1970, p. 13.*

WALTER CLEMONS

Un adolescent d'autrefois [Maltaverne] appeared last year in France when François Mauriac was 84, after a period of 15 years in which he published no novels and was thought to have written his last. The fact of the book's existence is a marvel. The book itself is not. It is deftly and elegantly written, but it is remote in impact and deficient in energy. It is difficult to feel the novel's crucial event as more than a blackboard diagram of the Problem of Evil.

Those who don't already know what a powerful novelist Mauriac was at his best, more than 40 years ago, should start not with *Maltaverne* but with the five novels included in the generous *Mauriac Reader.* Of these, I am not an admirer of *The Knot of Vipers* (1932), which I dutifully read 20 years ago on the assurance of a Catholic friend that it was Mauriac's masterpiece and was deterred from further exploration for some years thereafter. Reread now, its "monstrous" narrator's gloating accounts of his villainies and of his mysterious turn toward God ring as hollow as before.

However, two of the others, *Genetrix* (1923) and *The Desert of Love* (1925), are brilliant. The first is a tightly detailed, implacable study of a domineering mother defeated by her son's obsessive devotion to the memory of his wife whom he neglected when she was alive and whose death the mother helped bring about. It is a short novel of horrifying, savage energy.

The Desert of Love is even better. In a famous, and very funny, attack on Mauriac as a novelist, Jean-Paul Sartre rapped him for having limited the freedom of his characters by the godlike high-handedness with which he judged them and meted out their fates. ("God is not an artist. Neither is M. Mauriac") [see excerpt above]. In *The Desert of Love* Mauriac commits all the violations of Point of View that Creative Writing classes and Jean-Paul Sartre warned us against. He slips in and out of the minds of a father and son and the commonplace woman they both love; and we are asked to believe that their unconsummated infatuation determines the lives of both men during 15 years they pass without seeing her. While reading, we don't question it; the exact observations sting, the air is so charged that we can believe the distraught Dr. Courreges stumbling away from Maria Cross's villa in such a state that "he imagined he saw fire burning in the branches and realized it was the rising moon." The novel's final scene, the desolating, trivial good-bys of father and son in a Paris railway station, is one of the most heartbreaking in fiction.

Sartre—and *Maltaverne*—to the contrary, Mauriac is an artist, when he is at his best, of astonishing power.

> Walter Clemons, "Mauriac Then and Now," in The New York Times, *July 15, 1970, p. 37.*

GERMAINE BRÉE

I find it difficult today when rereading the novels of François Mauriac not to entertain some misgivings about their ultimate viability. It may be that a critic like me who approaches them without sharing Mauriac's Catholic beliefs is at a disadvantage. It may be too that it is difficult today to respond wholeheartedly to some of Mauriac's themes and stylistic idiosyncrasies. Mauriac's fictional world developed in the 'twenties—the 'thirties did not greatly add to its basic characteristics—at a time when, under the impact of Freud, some French writers were revising traditional conceptions concerning the processes of individual experience and the nature of human motivations; while, under the impact of World War I and the Russian Revolution, others were re-examining the foundations on which their culture rested. By temperament and perhaps because of his provincial upbringing, Mauriac seems to have remained insulated from the more extreme ideological currents, attitudes, and literary experiments of those years. But instinctively, almost surreptitiously, at the very outset of his career as novelist, he broke away from the then decried novel of analysis with its smooth cause-and-effect mechanisms and its preoccupation with the surface of everyday reality. The particular realm he exploited—the essentially elusive modalities of sexual attraction and obscure individual revolts—the vivid but not logically explicable narrative line of his stories and their intensively personal atmosphere all appealed to readers avid for new literary experiences. His techniques as novelist were freer. Steeped in an atmosphere of sustained emotion, his short narratives relied for their dynamism on a visionary kind of lyricism reminiscent of Chateaubriand and the Romantics. Barrès was his literary patron. What endeared Mauriac to some critics was this "beautiful harmonious language," the "spiritual music" of his style, the familiar cadences of the Romantics. Today these cadences have lost their seduction, an obstacle rather than an advantage.

It is not easy for most of us to share Mauriac's intense but vague anguish concerning the omnipresent but seldom concretely evoked "sins of the flesh." Half a century of research into the workings of human emotions have accustomed us to more searching inquiry into our own. Sensuality is no longer solitary or hidden, a hideous form of disease; and we can no longer indiscriminately attribute the human perturbations it causes to the fascinating voice of Satan avid for the possession of our souls. Nor is it easy, in our strife-torn society, to accept unquestioningly as a criterion of moral lucidity Mauriac's contemptuous rejection, at least for fictional purposes, of the simple joys of private affections and everyday living. It is not, however, these peculiar components of Mauriac's fictional universe that limit his efficacity as novelist but rather a certain conflict and confusion apparent in the patterning of his style and which deeply affect the basic coherence of his fictions.

Mauriac is the author of many kinds of books: twenty novels or so, a few plays, essays on the novel and narrative techniques, memoirs, a *Journal,* and poems. Whole sentences and paragraphs could be shifted from one category to the other without causing the slightest disturbance in atmosphere. Their relevance then, when they appear in the novels, is not to the specific concrete situations and individual experiences narrated. They refer us to the private world of the author, a realm of discourse common to characters and novelist alike whereby the ones are absorbed into the inner life of the other. (pp. 141-42)

Mauriac's own uneasy relation with his stories was brilliantly attacked by Sartre, though on rather specious grounds. And indeed, . . . Mauriac's fictional world is not self-contained. This characteristic seems to point to a deep fissure in Mauriac's own personality. Yet undoubtedly his world has a certain power of imaginative persuasion and undeniable intensity and coherence. This is perhaps because Mauriac's direct intervention in his narrative, as manifest in his stylistic mannerisms, engages his emotions, not his intelligence, or, in fact, any system of belief. As he has very often made quite explicit, what he pursued as novelist was the concrete dramatization of inner fantasies based on the intense emotions that welled up inside him. Mauriac has never been reticent about his work and has made it quite clear over the years that as writer he took only slight interest in the commonplace reality about him. Until the Spanish Civil War—that is, until he was in his

fifties—he lived, he said, withdrawn in a private universe of dream. Houses, land, people observed all served to give shape to the dramas and "monsters" of his imagining. It is because the narrative and the commentary originate in the same violent emotivity that, in the best of Mauriac's stories, they can coexist in an uneasy equilibrium, contributing thereby to the dramatic impact of the work. Where the equilibrium is not maintained, fiction turns into a particularly insidious form of self-dramatization. Mauriac is not really, as he would have it, engaged in a "drama of salvation" as much as in a specious kind of equivocation, unwilling to take the responsibility for his own imaginings.

From this point of view he was well served by one of the current literary ideas of the day concerning the relation between the novelist and the characters he creates. The character, so it was argued, once he or she emerged, took on in Pirandellesque fashion an autonomous life which the novelist could record but was powerless to mold. So Mauriac, in relatively good faith, could claim a kind of innocence with regard to Thérèse Desqueyroux in the famous apostrophe placed by Mauriac as foreword to the novel,

> Thérèse, there are many who will say that you do not exist. But I know you exist, I who for many years have watched you, waylaid you, stopped you as you went by, unmasked you.

Metaphor and reality neatly overlap. But the confusion can hardly excuse Mauriac's incredibly pharisaic "envoi,"

> I should have liked your suffering, Thérèse, to have delivered you up to God. . . . But many of those who nonetheless believe in the fall and redemption of tormented souls would have denounced the sacrilege. . . . At least on the pavement where I abandon you, I hope you are not alone.

This is doubly equivocal coming from the man who claimed at one time that it was his self-appointed task "to make perceptible, tangible, and odorous the Catholic universe of evil." And the equivocation is only compounded when we consider that Mauriac also stated his intent in slightly different terms "to make perceptible, tangible, and odorous a world full of criminal delights." The equivalence established is curious.

In point of fact, Mauriac's universe draws its visionary power from what seems to be an imagination mired in a latent semi-unconscious sexuality rather than from the "Catholic universe of evil." The dramas enacted in the stories, the characters that emerge in them, live in a kind of interzone between two realities connected through the particular rhetoric of Mauriac's language: intense sexual desires felt by characters enclosed in the "prison" of flesh, verbal frustration, and impotence; and a vague sense of impending spiritual doom suggested from without by the writer. "The river of fire," "the fetid swamps," "the prison bars" link the two worlds of lust and damnation, not logically but by the force of insistent evocation. To these two realms Mauriac relates the conduct of his characters, and not to any objective system of reference, Catholic or otherwise. What we see enacted are not moral conflicts, nor even, as Mauriac sometimes suggests, the ravages of destructive passions, but a submerged ritual of possession, destruction, and punishment. In *Le Baiser au lépreux,* Jean Péloueyre expiates his single night of possession of his wife's alluring body; Thérèse all her life must pay for that moment of intense delectation when she held power over Bernard's life; in *Genitrix,* Félicité Cazenave, the strongest, most unforgettable of Mauriac's characters, and her son are in turn "possessed" and destroyed by each other.

At the source of Mauriac's creations there is a turbulent power, a fear and a revolt manifest in the nature of his stories. Their simple narrative line, as Mauriac progressed, acquired somewhat more complexity through the use of the flashback or the fictional journal. But it remained uncluttered, involving only a very few characters. Timeless, anachronistic stories, in spite of a few vague attempts at establishing temporal perspectives, they are played out against the static hierarchical background of a society clearly outlined and projected in the typical Mauriac "décor," the isolated estate surrounded by its vineyards or pine forests. The vivid pictorial scenes depicted can be, on occasion, unforgettable in intensity: a gigantic Félicité dancing with fury on one of the platforms she had had erected in every room so that she could watch her son, refusing to accept his marriage; Thérèse, sequestered in her room, imprisoned behind the endless rows upon rows of pine trees, endlessly stubbing out her cigarettes. A few outside characters trapped and passively going to their doom—unchanged, unchanging, inexplicable; a world of "dead paths," of moral irresponsibility in which every character, submissive or not, unique or mediocre, is eventually preyed upon or preys. These are the well-known characteristics of his best novels. Schopenhauer, not Christ, is at the heart of Mauriac's world with an added dash of Nietzschean contempt for the "sick animal," man, and his addiction to mediocre happiness. A book, Mauriac once said, is a violent act, a kind of rape. The force of his own work comes perhaps from the intensity of an inner struggle, Schopenhaueresque in kind.

Guilt-ridden, Mauriac seems to have sensed that his attempt to extinguish in himself the turbulent "lust," which he denounced as "the will to evil," was to extinguish his own power to create. He seems to have associated that power with the Satan of his childhood anguish, a Satan feared because of the invisible fascination of his appeal and whom he felt he must resist, and yet could not resist, trapped thereby in his own closed hell.

The weakness of his work seems to me to stem from an inner cleavage, from an unwillingness to accept his fictional world, in all its ambivalence, as coming from himself, and from his paradoxical fear of being contaminated by the proliferation of his own myths. Hence, his refuge in the fiction that the "evil" embodied in his stories, like the evil in the world, did not come from himself as creator, but from the world itself. Hence, too, Mauriac's tendency to draw the reader away from the narrative toward the commentary and to replace the unresolved tensions in his writing by a rhetorically imposed unity. He is undoubtedly sincere when he claims, as he has claimed ever more emphatically with the years, that he aims at direct or indirect edification and that his fictional universe has a metaphysical dimension. The claim is not convincing. It is apparent that, Sartre notwithstanding, Mauriac was primarily an artist, albeit a reluctant and hesitant one, who did not fully accept the artist's responsibility for an involvement in his creation. (pp. 145-49)

> Germaine Brée, "The Novels of François Mauriac,"
> in The Vision Obscured: Perceptions of Some
> Twentieth-Century Catholic Novelists, edited by
> Melvin J. Friedman, Fordham University Press,
> 1970, pp. 141-50.

WILLIAM R. MUELLER

We are indebted to some of François Mauriac's more disapproving critics for many of his revealing, and sometimes defensive, remarks about his fiction and his faith. Representative of such criticism is the comment of Georges Bernanos, quoted in Mauriac's *Mémoires Intérieurs* and comparing his fiction "to a cellar, the walls of which are sweating with moral anguish." The eloquent simile is understandable: the Mauriac reader, quickly surfeited with accounts of man's sin, wretchedness, and obsessive propensity toward bringing suffering upon others (even upon himself), must look far for examples of happy and loving human relationships. But Mauriac is charged with more than a blindness to the generally purported joys and redemptive qualities of the religious life: he is accused of a perverted fascination with the subtle, demonic delights of sin, a perversion thought more likely to tempt than to inspire his readers. Such criticism has been made by various Christians, but no criticism has been more personally directed, or more smartingly received, than that of André Gide, who argued a great gulf between Mauriac the accomplished writer and Mauriac the professing Christian. In a letter to Mauriac, Gide writes:

> . . . what you are searching for is the *permission* . . . to be a Catholic without having to burn your books; and it is this that makes you write them in such a way that you will not have to disown them on account of your Catholicism. This reassuring compromise, which allows you to love God without losing sight of Mammon, causes you anguish of conscience and at the same time gives a great appeal to your face and great savour to your writings; and it ought to delight those who, while abhorring sin, would hate not to be able to give a lot of thought to it. You know, moreover, what the effect would be on literature and especially on your own; and you are not sufficiently Christian to cease to be a writer. Your particular art is to make accomplices of your readers. The object of your novels is not so much to bring sinners to Christianity as to remind Christians that there is something on earth besides heaven.
>
> Once I wrote—to the great indignation of certain people—"It is fine sentiments that go to make bad literature." Your literature is excellent, my dear Mauriac. Doubtless if I were more of a Christian I should be less your disciple.

In his book of essays entitled *God and Mammon,* in which Gide's letter is quoted, Mauriac seeks to counter the imputation that, under the guise of a Christian position, he derives from his excursions into the more salacious aspects of human behavior a certain forbidden joy, one generously shared with his readers. Whether or not Mauriac's self-defense is in practice substantiated by his novels, it is theoretically impeccable. The novel, he affirms, is above all a study of human nature and must portray man as he is, not as the writer wishes he were. More than this, the novelist's art (certainly that of the Christian writer) "is concentrated on reaching the secret source of the greatest sins." To write of sin and probe its sources is hardly to commend it. In *God and Mammon* and other writings, Mauriac argues the indefensibility of a literature which promotes a spurious optimism and confuses itself with moral homily. His major goal is an accurate reflection of the fallen creatures of this world, showing both the condition of the man at least temporarily beyond the touch of

God's grace and the transfiguration following upon the renewed flowing of that grace.

To read Mauriac's fiction is to find grounds both for his detractors' arguments and for his self-defense. Though his novels observe no depravity unobserved by the Bible, their composite picture of depravity is less leavened by evidences of tenderness. His analyses of man's fallen nature, of the sources and workings of sin, are brilliant, though most readers are inclined to sense an imbalance, an excessive grimness, in his view of humanity. Mauriac, of course, sees his view as grim but hardly distorted: in life itself he finds the quality of purity in few individual hearts and of impurity in the large body of mankind. In *The Son of Man,* for example, he acknowledges the presence of saints, while at the same time insisting that the world at large has remained obdurate to them: "The course of history," he writes, "has not been influenced by the saints. They have acted upon hearts and souls; but history has remained criminal." From a Frenchman who endured two world wars on his own soil such judgment is not surprising. We find among the essays comprising *Cain, Where Is Your Brother?* reflections on Buchenwald, Auschwitz, Ravensbrueck, and Dachau. The Allied advance into Germany late in World War II was to Mauriac a descent into hell and brought into sharp focus the concentration camps' incredible atrocities: "We . . . [saw] with our own eyes, heard with our own ears, the witnesses of the most extensive outrage which the dignity of man has ever suffered since there have been men on earth who killed each other."

Through his attempt to portray mankind as he sees it, Mauriac, I believe, seeks to protect his readers from the self-deception of wishful thinking without casting them into despair. He wishes both to dissuade men from what he believes is their mistaken view that Satan no longer exists, and to persuade them that Satan's net is not so thickly woven as to prevent escape for those persons given the faith to accept the faith. In *The Son of Man* he writes that Christians of the twentieth century, like those of the first, are called upon "to persevere in the faith in a world without faith, to remain pure in a society delivered to all manner of covetousness." And in this respect his tribute in *Letters on Art and Literature* to Georges Bernanos (of whose work he *might* have said what Bernanos said of his own—that it resembles "a cellar, the walls of which are sweating with moral anguish") is relevant:

> If you were to ask me what I admire most about him, I would say that it is his faith, the fact that he never doubted God's mercy, although he was face to face with evil; that his work bears witness to the love of the Creator for His creatures; that in this murderous world in which he lived (and in which we continue to live), where this divine love is insulted, rejected, held in contempt by many, and completely ignored by many more, he held fast; that he did not lose heart when for him holiness remained crucified on the very brink of despair.

Mauriac's words about Bernanos are equally applicable to himself. Face to face with the evils of a century lacerated by the most devastating conflicts in history and with the sins and crimes of his fictional characters, Mauriac yet believes that there remains a remnant of men who bear witness to their cre-

ation in God's image and to the continuing presence of his grace. The binding force between God and man is manifested above all in the Incarnation, the God-man, Jesus Christ, the living promise that life has a purpose and man a destiny beyond the human frailties which Mauriac so persistently underscores in his fiction. (pp. 215-19)

In his Nobel Prize acceptance speech, **"An Author and His Work,"** delivered in Stockholm in 1952, Mauriac acknowledges his reputation as a writer who presents a museum of horrors and specializes in monsters—a familiar and frequent charge made against his novels. It is important to note the kind of monsters his characters are. They are *not* accomplished villains, not Iagos or Edmunds or protagonists of the kind found in the plays of Christopher Marlowe or John Webster. There is about them a morbidity, an unwholesomeness, rather than a greatness; they are objects of loathing or despisement rather than hate or grudging admiration. At worst their reduction to sickly caricature evokes a reader's impatience and distaste. I think, for example, of those relatively early companion pieces, *A Kiss for the Leper* and *Genetrix,* in which the characters of Jean Peloueyre or of Félicité and Fernand Cazenave are of caricatural proportions to strain our credulity. And *The Lamb,* a much later novel, does indeed resemble a chamber of horrors where we meet again with Jean, Michèle, and Brigitte, older than they were in *Woman of the Pharisees.* Both *The Desert of Love* and *The Knot of Vipers* come off considerably better, especially the former. From a Christian writer one would expect, of course, full recognition and portrayal of man's ingenuity in sinfulness, but in much of Mauriac we find attention not only to depravity of spirit but to sheer sordidness and physical repulsiveness. Mauriac's eye is fascinated, not unlike Graham Greene's, by outward loathsomeness of the human body, with the result that Jean Péloueyre, the Cazenaves, even the Puybarauds are repulsive to the reader's physical senses. *Woman of the Pharisees* is relatively free of this quality, though in the Puybarauds and in the brief sketch of the schoolmaster, Monsieur Rausch, near the novel's beginning, we find traces of it.

However Mauriac might define the chamber of horrors of which he is accused, he asks in his Nobel speech that we look beyond its blackness to "the light that penetrates it and burns there secretly." He asserts that in one essential respect his characters are almost unique in contemporary fiction: "They are aware that they have a soul." Even though some of them, responsive to the hypothesis of God's death, "do not believe in the living God," they are nonetheless "all aware of that part of their being which knows evil and which is capable of not committing it. They know what evil is. They all feel somehow that they are responsible for their actions, and that their actions in turn affect the destiny of others." (pp. 230-31)

William R. Mueller, "François Mauriac: The Mysteries of Evil and Grace," in his Celebration of Life: Studies in Modern Fiction, *Sheed & Ward, 1972, pp. 215-31.*

Ron(ald) Milner
1938-

American dramatist, lyricist, director, essayist, poet, short story writer, and editor.

Milner is acknowledged as one of the leading black dramatists of the late 1960s and 1970s. Along with such playwrights and directors as Ed Bullins, Lonnie Elder III, and Woodie King, Jr., Milner sought to redefine the goals of contemporary black American theater by affirming the importance of traditional familial values and self-determination. He stated: "We're at the end of a catharsis. . . . We're no longer dealing with 'I am somebody' but more of who that 'somebody' really is." Many of Milner's dramas revolve around ethical individuals struggling to maintain optimism despite the crime, drugs, and limited opportunities that plague their communities and modern society in general. Because his protagonists are often propelled into situations that challenge their basic values, Milner is often labeled as a moralist. While some reviewers consider his work melodramatic and contrived, Milner has garnered praise for the stark realism of his settings and his authentic recreation of urban dialogue and idioms.

Most of Milner's dramas are set in the inner city of his native Detroit. His first play, *Who's Got His Own* (1966), concerns Tim Bronson, a youth who reaches emotional maturity after the death of his father, a bitter and abusive man who rarely demonstrated love toward his family. Examining his feelings toward his father, Tim discovers that the elder Bronson's destructive behavior evolved from a childhood tragedy during which he witnessed the rape of his mother and his father's murder by a white mob. Milner's next drama, *The Warning—A Theme for Linda* (1969), is a one-act play that was performed as a portion of *A Black Quartet,* which also included short works by Ben Caldwell, Ed Bullins, and Imamu Amiri Baraka. Milner's piece centers on a young woman's determination to remain with her boyfriend despite her family's interference.

Milner's best-known drama, *What the Wine Sellers Buy* (1973), is often regarded as a contemporary morality play. This work revolves around Steve, an innocent ghetto youth who falls under the influence of Rico, a pimp. Although Steve's family desperately needs money, Rico's suggestion that he procure his girlfriend Mae conflicts with his principles and beliefs. At the play's conclusion, Steve rejects Rico's advances and vows to make a permanent commitment to Mae. While noting stylistic flaws and predictable scenes in the play, reviewers lauded Milner's strong characterizations and authentic dialogue. Edwin Wilson commented: "[*What the Wine Sellers Buy* pulls] no punches and it is out of a raw, ruthless environment that the moral emerges."

Milner's works of the 1980s focus upon maladies of the black middle class. *Don't Get God Started* (1987), which features gospel music composed by Marvin Winans, contains several sketches written by Milner depicting affluent men and women tormented by such problems as drug addiction and marital infidelity who turn to God for spiritual guidance. The comedy *Checkmates* (1988) examines how shifting social val-

ues have shaped the experiences and altered the expectations of two married couples representing successive generations. By comparing modern marriages with those of the past, Milner suggests that contemporary couples are too engrossed with careers and material values to achieve lasting commitments. While some critics faulted *Checkmates* for plot and structural contrivances, others concurred with Clive Barnes's assessment that "[Milner's] seriousness, his brisk and adroit humor . . . and his pertinence are unquestionable."

Milner has also produced musicals for which he wrote both the lyrics and text. These works include *Season's Reasons* (1977), which depicts a man imprisoned for political subversion who discovers that his compatriots have compromised their revolutionary idealism for material comfort; *Crack Steppin'* (1981), which concerns several inner-city youths who establish their own construction business under the guidance of a kind-hearted retiree; and *Jazz-Set* (1982), which resembles an impromptu jazz session during which several musicians gather to discuss the vicissitudes of their lives.

(See also *Contemporary Authors,* Vols. 73-76; *Contemporary Authors New Revision Series,* Vol. 24; and *Dictionary of Literary Biography,* Vol. 38.)

WALTER KERR

At the American Place Theater last evening I strained to hear [*Who's Got His Own*] in two different ways.

The first problem is merely vocal. For Ronald Milner's *Who's Got His Own,* the director Lloyd Richards has brought together three restless, volatile, fever-pitch players who can scarcely contain the furies they feel. . . .

The play *should* be done in the round because it is composed almost entirely of passionate fists and faces, but the round becomes a menace when the pitch is low and the pace close to breathless. One [character] turns his head away and more than words are lost. The shape of the sequence disintegrates and we are forced to patch meanings together as best we can, by long-distance and with a faulty connection.

The strain goes beyond that, though. Mr. Milner has certain admirable intentions, at least, as a playwright. He would like to use the stage as though it were really a bear pit, with a point at the center where all angers must cross. He would like to make his play out of words, a hundred thousand harsh words and no window dressing. And he would like us to see his victims gored to death in full view, harried and helpless and beyond hope. The Negro family of the play no longer have anything to conceal; they have reached the point where only truth-telling and blood-letting will do.

Mr. Milner does make us listen, or try hard to. The formalization that brings a bitter brother, a trembling sister, and a bereaved mother into separate spotlights to rasp out their private agonies creates a confinement with some tension to it. We are curious to know precisely why the boy, immediately after his father's funeral, wants all pious mourning dispensed with as so much fraud, why he cannot bear the memory of seeing the old man, in work clothes, hunched over a cigarette on the street looking as though he had just stolen something in broad daylight.

We are curious to understand why the shaken sister's white lover has looked at her, one morning, with a disgust he cannot explain. We certainly want to know, at the beginning of the play's final act, why the son of the family—desperate with everyone's grief—has gone to a white friend for consolation and, on impulse, beaten him senseless against a wall.

In part, we come to grasp these things. The love-hate relationship between the whites and blacks has left each of the frustrated blacks with a residual impulse, "like he had to kill one of *them* before he could have any peace." Yet there is no peace in the killing. The killing is meant to atone for yesterday. But, a resigned mother sighs at evening's end, no one can wait in ambush for yesterday. It's not coming this way again.

With effort, we make our own connection with Mr. Milner's circling, unsettling thought. . . . But the connection remains remote even when we have heard what is being said, the heat on the stage is a dry heat. The [characters] cry real tears now and again; but we are merely alert, strictly attentive, still detached from the felt heart of the matter.

Why? Possibly Mr. Milner works at too high a pitch too much of the time; soon the room becomes airless. Possibly he has made the mistake of taking us only backward, never forward, in time. . . . [*Who's Got His Own*] takes place in "the continuing past," the program tells us; and it does seem always to be retreating.

More than that, Mr. Milner is not yet a poet. He has a poet's habits of style and a dramatic poet's eagerness to crack heads together to see what new sound may be forced from them. But the language itself is still prose, prose in an incredible hurry, prose in such a hurry that it escapes us before we are quite touched. Language need never be tame; but it must take the time to steal closer to us.

Walter Kerr, in a review of "Who's Got His Own,"
in The New York Times *October 13, 1966, p. 52.*

LARRY NEAL

[*The essay from which this excerpt is taken was originally published in* The Drama Review, *Summer, 1968.*]

Ron Milner's *Who's Got His Own* is of particular importance. It strips bare the clashing attitudes of a contemporary Afro-American family. Milner's concern is with legitimate manhood and morality. The family in *Who's Got His Own* is in search of its conscience, or more precisely its own definition of life. On the day of his father's death, Tim and his family are forced to examine the inner fabric of their lives: the lies, self-deceits, and sense of powerlessness in a white world. The basic conflict, however, is internal. It is rooted in the historical search for black manhood. Tim's mother is representative of a generation of Christian Black women who have implicitly understood the brooding violence lurking in their men. And with this understanding, they have interposed themselves between their men and the object of that violence—the white man. Thus unable to direct his violence against the oppressor, the Black man becomes more frustrated and the sense of powerlessness deepens. Lacking the strength to be a man in the white world, he turns against his family. So the oppressed, as Fanon explains, constantly dreams violence against his oppressor, while killing his brother on fast weekends.

Tim's sister represents the Negro woman's attempt to acquire what Eldridge Cleaver calls "ultrafemininity." That is, the attributes of her white upper-class counterpart. Involved here is a rejection of the body-oriented life of the working class Black man, symbolized by the mother's traditional religion. The sister has an affair with a white upper-class liberal, ending in abortion. There are hints of lesbianism, i.e. a further rejection of the body. The sister's life is a pivotal factor in the play. Much of the stripping away of falsehood initiated by Tim is directed at her life, which they have carefully kept hidden from the mother.

Tim is the product of the new Afro-American sensibility, informed by the psychological revolution now operative within Black America. He is a combination ghetto soul brother and militant intellectual, very hip and slightly flawed himself. He would change the world, but without comprehending the particular history that produced his "tyrannical" father. And he cannot be the man his father was—not until he truly understands his father. He must understand why his father allowed himself to be insulted daily by the "honky" types on the job; why he took a demeaning job in the "shit-house"; and why he spent on his family the violence that he should have directed against the white man. In short, Tim must confront the history of his family. And that is exactly what happens.

Each character tells his story, exposing his falsehood to the other until a balance is reached.

Who's Got His Own is not the work of an alienated mind. Milner's main thrust is directed toward unifying the family around basic moral principles, toward bridging the "generation gap." (pp. 199-200)

Larry Neal, "The Black Arts Movement," in The Black American Writer: Poetry and Drama, *Vol. II, edited by C. W. E. Bigsby, 1969. Reprint by Penguin Books Inc., 1971, pp. 187-202.*

EDITH OLIVER

The best new play to come along in months is Ron Milner's *What the Wine Sellers Buy*. . . . The action takes place in the black ghetto of Detroit—in various rooms and alleys, in a corner bar and a dry-cleaning establishment, and on the street outside. The hero is a seventeen-year-old high-school senior, subject to the usual tugs and pressures of adolescence, and especially stifled by his rotten environment, who is almost conned into becoming the errand boy for a hustler in whores and dope and stolen clothes, and almost conned into becoming the pimp for his own loving girl. Virtue triumphs, I'm pleased to report, and, as distinct from many enterprises of this kind, the only corpse at the end is that of the villain. The struggle for the boy's soul between the hustler, on the one hand, and the boy's widowed mother, a friend of hers, and the girl, on the other, is Faustian in its intensity. . . .

The plot has a classic simplicity, but theatrically the play is extremely complex, rich in small, seemingly inconsequential scenes that bring a whole neighborhood to life, and rich, too, in characters and emotions and humor and truthfulness. . . . The running time is almost three hours, and it might be trimmed some, I suppose, if the trimming could be done without weakening its urgency and vitality. (p. 56)

Edith Oliver, "Suffer, Little Children," in The New Yorker, *Vol. XLIX, No. 14, May 26, 1973, pp. 54, 56.*

EDWIN WILSON

More and more, black theater appears to be a movement which has found its own voice and is here to stay. The latest evidence is *What the Wine-Sellers Buy*. . . . Written by Ron Milner, it reiterates themes and forms which have become the hallmarks of black theater and which confirm its authenticity.

What the Wine-Sellers Buy is first and foremost a morality play. Steve, a young high school student whose father died when he was a small child, is being corrupted by Rico, a pimp. Rico is a modern Mephistopheles who argues that the only way a black man can get ahead is to have money and the only way to get money is through illegal means—dope, prostitution, etc. . . . Opposed to Rico in the struggle for Steve's soul is Steve's mother and her friend, Jim Aaron. The latter is a contractor and like Steve's mother, a churchgoer.

As in all good morality plays there is a physical confrontation between the opposing forces, in this case between Rico and Jim, and in the showdown Jim proves to be more than Rico's equal. Steve's mother enters the struggle as well, explaining to Steve that his father, though a hustler, held some things

in his life pure, which is not the case with Rico. In the end, after a tempestuous internal battle, Steve rejects Rico's way. The title of [*What the Wine-Sellers Buy*] comes from the Rubaiyat of Omar Khayyam: "I wonder often what the vintners buy one half so precious as the stuff they sell." Rico wanted Steve to sell his soul and turn his girlfriend—a basically decent person—into a prostitute. The moral of the play is that if you sell your total person, no matter what you receive, it is not "half so precious" as what you sold.

But Steve does not accept the acquiescent course of his mother and Jim either. He determines to be his own man, neither subservient to whites nor a prey to corrupting forces in his own group. This moving toward a new direction, rejecting white models on the one hand and black extremism on the other, is characteristic of the note struck again and again in today's black theater. So, too, is the positive, moral tone. The latter is all the more remarkable because of the violent, profane picture painted of the urban ghetto; the plays pull no punches and it is out of a raw, ruthless environment that the moral emerges.

The concern with a young man coming of age is another feature of black theater. As in last season's *The River Niger*, to which [*What the Wine-Sellers Buy*] bears a strong affinity, the emphasis is not on past grievances and injustices, but on the future—on the problems and perils young people face growing up in broken homes and a hostile environment, and their determination to overcome these forces. Hand in hand with this attitude goes an enormous vitality in the work itself both in the writing and the playing. . . .

What the Wine-Sellers Buy is a sprawling play, and like others of its type, overwritten at times but the play gives further evidence that black playwrights today, like its hero, Steve, are determined to find their own way, in this case, a way to speak out in the theater.

Edwin Wilson, "A Black Morality Tale," in The Wall Street Journal, *February 21, 1974.*

WALTER KERR

If you have ever gone to any of the summertime festivals of street plays—exceedingly simple moralities in which Virtue and Vice contend for the souls of ghetto youngsters . . . you will recognize Ron Milner's *What the Wine-Sellers Buy* right off. Its bones are the bones of all such exhortations to "stay clean," its neighborhood pieties the same neighborhood pieties, its warnings the very same warnings. At the end of the evening a lad who has *almost* been seduced by a Mephisto-like figure into pimping his thoroughly nice girl reaches out to the girl, clutches her tight, and firmly announces "We ain't goin' his way, it costs too much." The homily has simply been moved indoors . . . , opulently mounted, opened up by its author to cram just as much lifelike detail—and perhaps as much dramatic truth—into its elementary design as possible.

How much? At what point does a slogan stop being a slogan and begin to dissolve into the ambiguity and abrupt candor and restless complexity we're willing to call art? There are three or four suddenly hushed moments in Mr. Milner's play when we can very nearly hear the metamorphosis taking place, the evening gliding upward into felt personal truths that are not necessarily suitable for placards.

[Mae], the girl trapped between her love for a boy and the

boy's mistaken notion of what will best secure their futures, is taking a severe dressing-down from her mother. The piece, like all such pieces, is full of scoldings: there must be spokesmen for the Right. But, halfway through the older woman's entirely conventional tirade, the girl cuts her off with a cry. The cry is not what we expect. The girl is begging her mother to hit her, hit her hard. Not to wake her up, to drum some sense into her. She scarcely needs that. She simply wants her mother to touch her, to put a hand to her, never mind how fiercely or what for. "When you stopped whipping, you just took your hands away," [Mae] says. . . . Something over and above the rhetoric has crept in, and its presence has an authority that no amount of righteous finger-wagging will ever equal.

[Mae] is given another such opportunity to escape the strict programing of Our Lesson for Today (Mr. Milner seems to write best for this reluctant, defiant changeling). Under too much pressure from the boy, who is now daydreaming that prostitution will earn them enough money to buy a service truck and turn legitimate, she tries flight. Phoning her father in another city, she asks if she can come to him.

The scene itself is resolutely sentimental, unabashedly stock. The girl fondles a teddy bear as she listens to the refusal we know is certain, a faltering "Oh?" trickling out of her as she absorbs a father's lame excuses. But the conversation goes on a bit longer, grows lighter, and she has pretty well swallowed her disappointment by the time talk turns to Christmas. What would she like for a present this year? The answer pops out of her, eyes glinting maliciously. "A truck," she says.

Of course she knows that the request is absurd. She has suddenly seen herself as absurd, her situation as absurd; she is laughing at her own pain, and the flash of bold humor cuts through everything that is saccharine about the sequence like an honest-to-God breadknife.

As Mr. Milner goes on with his work, he will do well to let impulse interrupt him oftener, let people speak for themselves instead of steadily saluting the evening's cause. He has a certain gift for decoration, even when it is being applied to the all-too-obvious. His Mephisto, for instance, emerges as a spider-legged, flair-skirted, sombrero-crowned cock of the roost who cannot discuss the prospects of chicken farming without turning his throat into a barnyard pianoforte. . . .

[The panderer Rico] is often mesmerizing to watch as he sidles through what seem to be no more than cracks in the hall doorway, dressed in everything from zebra-stripes to tapes tried red-and-golds that would look well on the backs of playing cards. If he resembles anything at all it is a Fifth Musketeer, recently cashiered from the King's service for good cause.

Mephisto, however, is still Mephisto, and what he has in mind for his prey is Hell. As soon as one of the Virtues—in this case a bourgeois contractor—begins an impassioned speech that may persuade our young hero to think twice, we know that the devil in the back room will slink instantly from his lair, ready to tug the other way. While the boy propositions his girl, [Rico] stands above them in a pale blue spotlight, dictating the boy's ploys, sometimes reciting them with him. . . .

A debating-society regularity haunts the play: a high school coach speaks sharply on the subject of sex; the boy traps the girl immediately afterward. The first act lights fade away on the boy's first taste of marijuana. The second act lights fade away on the *girl's* first taste. Motivations stand in the corner, waiting, until they are needed: if the boy requires new prompting along a wrong path, his mother becomes ill and there is no money for medicine. This done, we lose the mother for up to an hour afterward.

And the slogans keep on raining. "If you don't respect us, we got to respect ourselves," the girl declaims, as likely as not to automatic applause. "If I sell you, then what am I gonna buy, huh?" the boy finally asks, repenting his plans. It's very much an "I'm gonna tell you somethin'" play, with the speaker promptly making good his word.

Graham Greene once remarked that it was no more than a single step from the medieval morality play—with, perhaps, a central figure named Ambition—to *Macbeth*. But it is the step that makes all the difference, so great a difference that by the time we get to *Macbeth* it is no longer possible to say precisely where the most urgent ambition lies. **What the Wine-Sellers Buy** hasn't yet made the step. Though it comes teasingly close a few times . . . , the formula locks it in as tightly as though Mephisto's claws *were* inescapable. In the service of virtue, a theatrical vice wins. The characters haven't freedom enough to act for themselves.

Walter Kerr, in a review of "What the Wine-Sellers Buy," in The New York Times, *Section II, February 24, 1974, p. 1.*

LANCE MORROW

Steve Carlton is a bright and loving son to his widowed mother. He wears a Northeastern High School jacket, dribbles a basketball round the house and spoons with his sweet girl friend Mae, the cheerleader. But Steve falls in with a bad companion from next door, and before long his mother hardly knows him.

[**What the Wine-Sellers Buy**] is essentially a sentimental domestic morality play of wayward youth, a play that is a dramatic refugee from the 1950s. Except that here the characters are black and the setting is the Detroit ghetto. The bad influence arrives in the form of Rico, a wonderfully reptilian pimp who means to apprentice Steve to his trade by having the lad peddle Mae in the streets. Will Steve choose the life of vice? Will he break his old mother's heart, not to mention Mae's?

The answer is not much more interesting than the question. It is, of course, both dislocating and diverting to have such small-time Chayefsky framed in a raw ghetto context. Much of the wild street talk is funny, and the acting often superb. . . . Steve is a skillfully subtle combination of pride and confusion. . . . [The] dazzlingly evil pimp [Rico] sweeps round the stage, almost a production unto himself, costumed like a Liberace with soul.

At last, a sort of Middle American virtue triumphs in the victory of mother, church and romantic love. In the final scene, when Steve rejects the life of sin and sweeps up Mae . . . in his arms, her feet leave the floor and you almost expect her, slowly and sensuously, to kick off high-heeled shoes in Hollywood abandon to the last cuddle.

Lance Morrow, "Ghetto Chayefsky," in Time, *New York, Vol. 103, No. 8, February 25, 1974, p. 69.*

CLAYTON RILEY

Unfortunately, the text of Ron Milner's *What the Wine-Sellers Buy* succeeds primarily in battling itself to a draw by first defining its dramatic equation superlatively, then destroying that value with a trite, implausible ending.

The setting is today's Detroit, a Black neighborhood where a vicious and predatory hood named Rico pimps everything in sight.

Rico's logic is unassailable: America is a hustler's paradise. He contends that working yourself to death for the profit of a faceless oppressor class is the only real prostitution.

Young Steve Carlton's mother is forced to rent Rico a room and soon her impressionable son is taking lessons in The Life from him. Steve wants a taste of it—the spectacular outfits Rico wears, his expensive shoes and massive car, the abundant women around him. Steve cons his girl, pretty and innocent Mae, into becoming a prostitute for him, but breaks down during their first hustle. Reforming, he vows to support his dying mother with the sort of factory job Rico disdains as urban share-cropping. . . .

Though the play is structurally unsound, in several areas, especially with Rico, brother Milner has embroidered his text with some excellent writing. In a crucial scene, when Mae first rejects the proposal Steve makes to set himself up in business with her body, . . . [Mae asserts] powerful grace and strength. . . . But shortly thereafter, for no dramatically viable reason, she returns to the stage and cancels the urgency of her earlier work by begging for a chance to do Steve's misguided bidding.

As one of the characters asks: "What the wine-sellers (hustlers) buy, is it half so precious, half so sweet as what they sell?" Presumably they sell human beings, those they love, for fast cars, cash and clothes. Ron Milner will, we hope, provide us with a stronger answer to that question in his next play.

> *Clayton Riley, "The Black Man in Search of His Own Soul," in* The New York Times, *Section II, March 3, 1974, p. 3.*

XAVIER NICHOLAS

The praise that has been poured so lavishly on Ron Milner's play, *What the Wine-Sellers Buy,* reflects the ideological confusion in which the Black movement now finds itself. Why on earth is there all this excitement over this one play? There should be discussion of the play in order to clarify the confused thinking that revolves around it.

The mission of art is to raise the level of political consciousness of the broad masses of the people to struggle against their oppression. Our artists, therefore, must project a vision of what the broad masses of the people must struggle *for.* What vision should Black artists project for an oppressed people in urgent need of some sense of direction and purpose in life? Is the question simply "to be or not to be a pimp"— which is the decision that Steve, a Black youth, has to make in the play? If we all agree that the answer is not to be a pimp—at which Steve finally arrives—the question arises: then what? The failure of *What the Wine-Sellers Buy* is that it never comes close to dealing with this vital question.

The play, in short, does not rise to a vision of human grandeur—it does not unfold the creative capacities of man to move mountains. Only once are we given a glimpse of what this play could possibly have been—and that's when Mae, the modest young girlfriend of Steve, refuses to "play the game" when he tries to turn her out on the streets as a prostitute. During the course of the play, Steve falls for the smooth talk of his Uncle Rico who is a pimp and has "been one for a long time and been wanting to be one longer." But Mae knows "what the deal is." "Rico got you," Mae tells Steve, "but he ain't got me." The scene fades out with Mae screaming frantically, "Do you hear me?"

From this early point on, the play progressively degenerates. . . . Not only Mae but all of the women characters in Milner's play—including Steve's long-suffering, church-going mother—value themselves only in relation to a man. They have no concept of themselves as human beings separate and apart from a man. But what value should women place upon themselves? That question is never asked. Then along comes Deacon Aaron, the nondescript escort of Steve's mother, talking about women being a "supplement" to a man . . . With no concept of self-worth except through the eyes of a man, the women characters in this play will literally do *anything* for a man in the name of "love." Mae, we must remember, never decides *not* to be a prostitute. Steve decides for her by deciding *not* to be a pimp. But let us ask: Why can't Mae decide for herself? After all, it is her body that will be sold on the auction block. Milner's portraits of women have nothing of substance in them to even suggest the qualities of dignity which are the endowment of all human beings. And this in the midst of a period of momentous changes in the way women are beginning to view themselves!

What the Wine-Sellers Buy is a history of particular conditions of a particular time. Art, however, is truer than history precisely because it is larger than life. History records what-was and what-is. Art projects what-should-be and what-can-be. Which is why the play is so narrow, so one-dimensional in its scope, in its world-view. There is no vast canvas upon which the conflict between characters is painted. How else are we to account for the play having no connection whatsoever with the tremendous struggles of Black people over the last 20 years to gain human and social liberation? From watching this play, one would think that the ultimate question facing the Black movement today is "to be or not to be a pimp." Is this what we have come to? There is absolutely no grasp of the Black movement in this play because all movements are based on human beings struggling to grasp the infinite. And to envision a new society of more *human* human beings is to project revolution. And to project revolution is to evoke the powers of the imagination. This play simply has no imagination.

More than anything, *What the Wine-Sellers Buy* reflects the limitations of a narrow Black cultural nationalism that does not make the great leap forward to revolution which is "a leap," as Mao says, "in the social development of man." It expresses essentially a narrow *bourgeois* point of view. In this sense, *What the Wine-Sellers Buy* is a very middle-class play. For the dreams, the aspirations of Steve and Rico are really the same—only the means are different. (pp. 95-6)

What the Wine-Sellers Buy does not end with a bang but a whimper—the whimperings of a drunken youth deprived of any concept of his identity with the advancement of man/womankind. Because Milner's mind is imprisoned in the present, he cannot project a vision of the future. Consequently, *What the Wine-Sellers Buy* has nothing to say to the young or to the old. (p. 97)

Xavier Nicholas, in a review of "What the Wine-Sellers Buy," in Black World, *Vol. XXV, No. 6, April, 1976, pp. 95-7.*

MEL GUSSOW

The stage is filled with the gleeful sounds of **"These Streets,"** a musical tribute to carefree days and nights in the urban outdoors. Then, suddenly, the ingenuousness is contradicted by seven strident black sisters swinging into a cynical response, **"Ain't No Love in These Streets,"** a testimony to all subjugated, abused black women. Though written by two men—the playwright and lyricist Ron Milner and the composer Charles Mason—the song has the urgency of a poem by Ntozake Shange.

If all, or even most, of *Season's Reasons* . . . maintained this high level, it would be a show to extol. . . . However, in its present condition, *Season's Reasons* is ill-formed and indecisive, not so much a musical as songs interrupted—and often undercut—by spoken words.

Mr. Milner, the talented author of *What the Wine Sellers Buy* . . . , has constructed an interesting platform for social commentary. A young black man named R. B. (read Righteous Brother) had been jailed for inciting riots in the 1960's. Escaping from prison, he—and his decade—confront the 70's. Commitment has been replaced by compromise, activism by self-indulgence.

In the first act, Mr. Milner aims satiric shafts at these lifestyle changes—a street rebel turned preacher, a formerly repressed woman campaigning for Congress, an angry black poet who now makes a living writing scripts for "The Jeffersons" and "Good Times."

This half, particularly the songs, is pungent; but already there are clues to the show's disability—for example, the thunderstruck public reaction to R. B. "He must be"—long pause—"one of the men of the 60's!" It is as if R. B. were carrying the plague.

In the second act the author recants, issuing footnotes and corrections. R. B. wanders gloomily across the stage as his former friends try to convince him that the 70's are not all bad, that they are really working for progress through existing institutions (schools, churches, government). As delivered, the message is unconvincing and the lyrics are contrived.

Mel Gussow, in a review of "Season's Reason's," in The New York Times, *July 19, 1977, p. 31.*

JAY CARR

[From the sidewalks of Detroit] comes *Crack Steppin'*, and if the economy were as upbeat as this show, we'd all be in clover. At this stage, the show seems to personify its title. It's a bit too sketchy to work as a play, yet doesn't quite have enough singing and dancing to work as a musical. The pacing and direction need beefing up, too. But its young cast is terrific.

Once you'd see shows about kids who'd get together to do a show. *Crack Steppin'* is more up to date. It's about black kids who get together to get jobs. One of the production numbers sends the chorus on like gangbusters, singing, "A job, a job, a real live job!" . . . Obviously, it's filled these kids with a kind of can-do pride and self-esteem.

From beginning to end this effort is absolutely without self-pity, and brimful of self-reliant pragmatism. When these kids sing, "We're gonna make it because we've found a way," you not only believe it, but want to cheer. In the show, they become their own bosses after they meet a kind old-timer who helps them form and run their own construction and contracting company.

Earning money solves their problems and straightens out their lives. A teen-age couple with a baby finally moves out of their respective mothers' houses. A drifting orphaned teenager finds a home base and focus. A street hustler survives a dope drop and matures. A would-be composer gets his hard-driving father to listen to him and take his musical ambitions seriously. Another black teen-ager gets her parents to ease up on their frantic suburban social climbing.

Certainly Ron Milner has succeeded in putting characters and a message on the stage with a heartful of compassion. . . .

Keeping heart, soul, dreams and self-respect alive in hard times is what *Crack Steppin'* is about.

Jay Carr, "'Crack Steppin' Makes You Want to Cheer," in The Detroit News, *November 21, 1981, p. 3C.*

FRANK RICH

Ron Milner's *Jazz Set* looks like a play that has been rethought so many times that the author finally forgot what he was thinking about in the first place. It's full of half-baked ideas, blurry characters and fractured narrative lines that lead nowhere. . . .

Mr. Milner, best known for *What the Wine Sellers Buy,* has tried to construct this work like a jazz composition. The characters are identified only by the instruments they play in a sextet; the free-form writing contains repeated rhetorical phrases, rhythmic group chants and incoherent poetry that one assumes to be scat-dialogue. While there's nothing wrong with this stylistic ground plan, Mr. Milner executes it sloppily, using it as a license to commit all manner of self-indulgent theatrical sins.

The content that lies beneath the obfuscatory words is soap opera. As we gradually learn through some embarrassingly bathetic flashbacks, the musicians have been variously victimized by drug addiction, jail sentences, homosexual rape, familial betrayals and wartime horrors. After three acts, these interchangeable people finally realize that "the music is what's important"—and that it can lead them all to "harmony and peace," not to mention future club bookings.

The play gets better as it goes along only because each act—or "set"—is briefer than the one before. . . .

Jazz Set ain't got that swing and don't mean a thing.

Frank Rich, "In Free-Form," in The New York Times, *July 21, 1982, p. C17.*

CLIVE BARNES

There is a kinship between the theater and three quite diverse human activities—a court trial, a political meeting and a religious service. And the more intense, more overtly dramatic any of these theatrical kin become, the more they take on the trappings of a performance.

The actual ritual of any religious observance is extraordinarily close to a theatrical experience, and not only did the medieval world, with its miracle and mystery plays, see the link between religion and religious drama, but the connection has never been lost on the more modern gospel revivalists.

Most gospel revival shows on Broadway—perhaps the best was *Your Arms Too Short to Box With God*—have been, in effect, staged cantatas.

In a purely dramatic sense the new gospel musical, *Don't Get God Started* . . . , is more ambitious, although not necessarily better. . . .

What makes *Don't Get God Started* a different kind of gospel show is the contribution of black playwright Ron Milner, best known for his play, *What the Wine Sellers Buy.*

Amidst the gospel imprecations and admonitions to mend our ways and find God, Milner has inserted five dramatic vignettes, all intended to show the decadence of the world in general and the rising black middle class—who it seems are not all like that nice, wise old Mr. Cosby—in particular.

The sins of the younger generation—much to the disdain and disgust of their elders—are demonstrated by three troubled couples and two sex perverts.

In one couple, the wife, a snobbish doctor's daughter, deserts her honest, hardworking, blue collar husband, and becomes a cold-slabbed victim of adultery, booze and pills.

In another the husband, before his redemption by the Church, sacrifices his life, family and honor to demon cocaine, while with a third, a good-natured but badly duped hairdresser puts her boyfriend through law school only to have him leave her for a rich white girl.

Other God-steppers are a comic sex addict, Silk, who cannot get enough of his habit, and a parishioner, Sister Needlove, who confuses Christian love with earthly love and gets the hots for the hot gospel.

All these vignettes are as naive and simplistic as the comic episodes in a medieval miracle play—but, as staged by Milner himself—they make their point. . . .

The preview audience I saw [*Don't Get God Started*] with was very free with its cries of assent and obviously heartfelt "Amens!," and individual feeling about the show will unquestionably depend upon one's feeling toward gospel teaching and singing.

Because if you yourself don't get started, from a pure entertainment point of view (if such a viewpoint is not irreverent or even sinful), whether God gets started or not is fundamentally irrelevant.

> *Clive Barnes, "Gospel Fills 'Don't Get God Started',"* in New York Post, *October 30, 1987.*

JOHN BEAUFORT

[*Don't Get God Started,* an] ebullient gospel musical, is forthrightly dedicated to promoting spiritual values by making a joyful noise unto the Lord.

Author-director Ron Milner and composer-lyricist Marvin Winans have gone a step beyond the format of such concert-style shows as *Your Arms Too Short to Box With God.* Their upbeat, ment intersperses vignettes of black urban life with rich outpourings of gospel music.

Mr. Milner has described *Don't Get God Started* as "a semiopera combining drama, comedy, social commentary, and spiritual enlightenment. . . . We're trying to get back to the sense of God first, family second, country third, and the self organized around the other three entities. We all need to change our commitment from 'I' to 'we'—or there won't be any 'I' or 'we.' "

Mr. Milner's intertwined episodes involve the familiar evils of drugs, promiscuous sex, marital infidelity, and selfish exploitation of others. Each segment—dramatic or broadly comic—is followed by a musical interpretation. . . . Central to the inspirational theme are . . . a pair of Bible-quoting elders who provide spiritual aid, comfort, and rescue to both backsliders and their victims. Although *Don't Get God Started* makes no bones about the wages of sin, it is even more assuring about the powers of self-redemption. And while the musical morality play aims its message at a black urban middle class, the applications are universal. (p. 25)

> *John Beaufort, "Gospel Musicals Resound with Joy and Praise,"* in The Christian Science Monitor, *November 5, 1987. pp. 25-6*

THOMAS M. DISCH

If the simplistic political schema of [Mbongeni Ngema's] *Sarafina!* is redeemed by the show's soul, then why can't soul accomplish the same redemptive purpose for *Don't Get God Started* . . . ? Superficially the two shows are up against a similar difficulty—how to bring alive a didactic script of elemental simplicity with high voltage music. Milner's book takes the form of a temperance tract, contrasting the sorry fates of those who surrender to the temptations of sex and drugs with the glory of sinners who are born again in Jesus. Milner's dramatic vignettes are at once broad and genteel, burlesque that has been sanitized for family consumption. As in *Sarafina!* it is left to the music to solve the problems defined by the drama, to move from the black-and-white verities of the writer's prose into the sublimities of the composer's songs. And it is precisely at this task that *Sarafina!* so excels and that *Don't Get God Started* funks and fails. . . . [The] music has all the spontaneity and charm of a high school pep rally. Only the stars get solos, only they get glitzy costume changes. . . . As the evening advances, the two singers come to seem the musical equivalents of Jim and Tammy Bakker, grinning bullies who consider themselves God's gift to an audience of rubes and yokels. . . . Their oppressiveness is never more apparent than in the larger choral numbers, when the backup chorus has to march in place double-time, smiling glassily and clapping like hyperactive metronomes. The show reaches its pinnacle of coerciveness at the final curtain when the song lyrics actually insist that we stand up to give the performers an ovation. (pp. 694-95)

[*Don't Get God Started*] preaches "Christian" values, but it practices the star system at its most hierarchic. (p. 695)

Thomas M. Disch, in a review of "Don't Get God Started," in The Nation, *New York, Vol. 245, No. 19, December 5, 1987, pp. 694-95.*

HOWARD KISSEL

Let's be blunt. If *Checkmates,* a play about two black couples, one elderly and nostalgic, the other young and aggressive, were about whites, it probably wouldn't have been done.

Yes, there should be black plays on Broadway, but let's not accept the mediocre just to make A Statement.

This play never goes anywhere. The young couple either argue or dance off to the bedroom. He takes umbrage at her career independence, at her gay friends. (There is something unsettling about the virulence with which one minority attacks another.) She, in turn, is unsympathetic to his job problems. Even when something real happens—she gets an abortion without telling him she's pregnant—it seems too pat.

When the older couple are not dashing to the bedroom, they reminisce about World War II, a key turning point for American blacks.

The playwright, Ron Milner, is more interested in scoring points than telling stories. At times he's successful, as when the young husband throws a stack of women's magazines to the floor, derisively reading the titles of articles all focusing on The Self. Some of the older man's reminiscences are vivid and his wife's ironic remarks are sharp.

But Milner is a bit too reverential of the old folks, too contemptuous of the young. Nothing seems thought through, and often scenes fade out feebly, a suitable prelude to a commercial but not theatrically effective. . . .

Checkmates reflects an almost cynical economic awareness of a new black audience eager to come to Broadway. It has been shrewdly cast, handsomely mounted and well-directed. If only this effort had been expended on a real play.

Howard Kissel, " 'Checkmates' Really Fails to Check Out," in Daily News, *New York, August 5, 1988.*

CLIVE BARNES

Ron Milner's social comedy *Checkmates* . . . has a great deal going for it, but don't judge too quickly, for you may judge it too harshly.

For one thing the first act of this play, about two generations testifying on love and life, is markedly inferior to the second act—Milner takes a long time to clear both his throat and his mind.

Also it would be possible to look at this determinedly simplistic story of two black couples—one in its early 60s, the other in its late 20s—and categorize the play as just another of those Bill Cosby-like discoveries of the black middle-class, and how whitish it is, that seem to appeal equally to the aspirations of black achievers and the sensibilities of white liberals.

Yes, and I do admit that there were times—especially at the beginning—when it seemed that the play's main interest was indeed just its blackness.

But slowly and surely, Milner won me round to the realization and acceptance of what is clearly his own view, that *Checkmates* is about neither blacks nor whites but it is about Americans and America today and the change in contemporary mores between now and, say, 40 years ago.

Milner naturally colors the details of the play black—and one of his main themes is the emerging role of the black in American society—but the central conflict of the play, that between the us-generation and the me-generation, is very clearly colorblind.

Frank Cooper and his wife Mattie, after 45 years of marriage, four children and six grandchildren, finding themselves lost in a large house in a moderately prosperous Detroit suburb, have rented out the top floor to a young yuppie couple, Sylvester Williams, a liquor salesman, and his wife, Laura McClellan-Williams, a fashion executive.

The Coopers have survived World War II, racism and, even, marriage. The Williamses—glossy, pampered, smart and chic—seemed ill-prepared to survive anything more taxing than a common cold, and even that might be in doubt.

Their concerns—like the Coopers, and like most people basically—are sex and money, but whereas the Coopers handle both with tender, loving care, the Williamses, totally self-absorbed, make a competitive game out of both.

As you might imagine it all works out in the end, but perhaps not quite as you did imagine it. . . . Milner holds back a few gambits right to the end, and although his perceptions are not particularly profound, they are well put, and dramatically angled.

Checkmates is a far glossier work, but it does not completely fulfill the raw talent suggested by Milner's earlier play, *What the Winesellers Buy.* Still, his seriousness, his brisk and adroit humor—it is often very funny—and his pertinence are unquestionable.

Clive Barnes, "Well Worth Checking Out," in New York Post, *August 5, 1988.*

FRANK RICH

While it's easy to name a recent Broadway play or two as awful as *Checkmates,* it may be necessary to get out the scrapbooks to recall one quite so amateurish and boring. *Checkmates* is a comedy in which the characters say such lines as "A man's home is his castle" and "It's a whole new ball game"—and aren't joking. It's a play in which [a character] can finish a speech with the question "What the hell am I talking about?" and be absolutely certain that no one on stage or off would dare vouchsafe an answer. . . .

As written by Ron Milner, *Checkmates* often seems to aspire to emulate reruns of "All in the Family" and "Three's Company." In a two-family home in Detroit, we meet a square older couple, the Coopers, and their swinging young upstairs tenants, the Williamses. The crotchety but lovable Coopers were shaped by the Depression, World War II and assembly-line drudgery. The upwardly mobile Williamses have his-and-her careers, a personal computer and an affinity for the advanced social ideas propagated by magazines like *Cosmo-politan* and *Self.*

That both couples are black neither adds to nor subtracts from Mr. Milner's inexhaustible supply of clichés. The generation-gap conflicts, starting with the many raised eyebrows over the younger couple's noisy sexual antics, may well predate the settlement of Detroit by citizens of any race. Though Mr. Milner is the author of an authentic play about the urban ghetto, the 1973 *What the Wine-Sellers Buy,* most of the Afro-American sociological background in *Checkmates* comes in the form of canned speeches that have been inserted into the domestic tiffs like boilerplate.

The play's tedium, however, derives not so much from its bland content as from its lack of dramatic propulsion. The younger couple's scenes are so frequently interrupted by a ringing phone that one begins to wonder if *Checkmates* might not be a call-in show. The older couple's sequences also fail to move the play forward—indeed, they shift it into reverse. The Coopers, who have been married 45 years, not only recite family history as if they had just met each other, but they also re-enact that history in flashbacks drenched in purple lighting that precisely matches the tone of the prose.

Such is Mr. Milner's theatrical aptitude that the two couples don't even intersect on stage until Act II. By then—over two hours after our arrival—*Checkmates* is ready to yield its single incident of truly hilarious looniness, in which one warring wife suddenly confronts her husband with a gun. To inject a loaded weapon into a play as fluffy as this one is an act of artistic overkill akin to bringing down the curtain of *The Nerd* with the detonation of an atomic bomb.

> Frank Rich, "Milner's 'Checkmates,' Story of 2 Households," *in* The New York Times, *August 5, 1988, p. C3.*

EDWIN WILSON

There used to be a type of show on Broadway known as an "audience show," a play that the critics tore apart and the audiences loved. The classic example was *Abie's Irish Rose,* which was roundly panned and ran for 5½ years in the 1920s. Like so many other kinds of popular theater—mysteries, romantic comedies, musicals with songs you can hum—the audience show has all but disappeared.

Recently, though, a play with the earmarks of an old-fashioned audience show opened on Broadway. It won't have a run like *Abie's Irish Rose,* but it does get audiences stirred up.

Checkmates . . . is about two black couples, one married 45 years and the other relative newlyweds. The older couple, Frank and Mattie Cooper, represent the generation that believed in family, church and hard work. Frank fought overseas in World War II and later made a success of his own small construction company. He and his wife, Mattie, have four children who also are doing well.

The Coopers live in the lower half of their two-family house and rent the upstairs to Sylvester and Laura. He's a silver-tongued salesman and she's a department store buyer about to begin her own business in fashion. The play's faults are fairly obvious. First of all the setup—with two generations, one upstairs and the other downstairs—is overly schematic, and this is accentuated by [the] set in which the high-tech

apartment of Sylvester and Laura (black, white and gray with computers and cordless phones) makes an overly pat contrast with the simple kitchen of the Coopers.

Then there are the scenes in which playwright Ron Milner wants to fill us in on the Coopers' past life. In these, an eerie light strikes an empty space on stage right and [Frank and Mattie] enact moments from their courtship and early marriage, and his Army career. There is one particularly awkward monologue in which [Mattie] recalls a passing affair she had while her husband was away in the service. This episode, as well as the other flashbacks, is not only contrived but unnecessary.

There also is Mr. Milner's dependence on the hoary device of the telephone. Sylvester is trying to land a big account at the same time that he fears he may be eased out of his job. This entire part of the play is carried out in lengthy, one-way phone conversations.

Critics may dwell on these problems all they want, but the night I saw the play the audience could not have cared less. The fact is that Mr. Milner . . . [has] hit on some basic, if obvious truths: ones with which the audience strongly identifies.

Laura is the new woman, into psychology, power and paranoia. She is determined to have her own career and not be a mere housewife or chattel to her husband. Sylvester, meantime, has his own problems.

But the real difficulty is that they are both on divergent paths. He lands a big account on the same day that she gets her promotion, so neither can enjoy the spotlight alone. And then she begins traveling, and he begins staying out late, and the spiral of estrangement is underway. In the end the only thing that seems to hold these two together is sexual attraction. But their relationship is what makes this an audience show. . . .

In plays of this kind the playwright often walks a thin line between a television sitcom and real drama. But this sort of flirting with popular art is not unusual in theater. A good deal of Greek or Shakespearean high tragedy has a large component of out-and-out melodrama. Mr. Milner is on to something and his audiences know it.

> Edwin Wilson, "Theater: An Old-Fashioned Crowd Pleaser," *in* The Wall Street Journal, *August 12, 1988.*

MICHAEL FEINGOLD

Three and a half decades ago, in my childhood, black American life was represented on television by "Amos 'n' Andy." Though this was racially offensive and humiliating, it was not esthetically outlandish, given a medium in which the white American housewife was represented by Lucille Ball, the white American workingman by Jackie Gleason, and the American educator by Eve Arden as our Miss Brooks. Socially speaking, our representations do progress: who would deny that Bill Cosby is an improvement on "Amos 'n' Andy"—the televised version of which was itself an improvement on the radio show, in which the black characters were played by white performers.

One medium's social improvement, however, might be another's artistic poison. *Checkmates* . . . is to contemporary black TV series pretty much what Neil Simon and his clones are to white sitcoms—an extension of reductive network-television over-simplifications into the theater. It may be a little freer in spirit and a little less well organized in structure than its white counterparts, but it caters to the same sensibility and triggers the same effects, including Pavlovian bursts of laughter whenever sex is mentioned.

The subject is marriage, the characters are an older couple who own a two-story Detroit house and their yuppie tenants, and the rather muddled plot has to do with the older marriage staying put while the younger one shatters on the rocks of neo-affluence and women's independence. Given this recipe, the script cooks itself up as easily as a TV dinner, and with about as much flavor. . . . The younger wife, whose magazine-tutored feminism the author seems to blame for the breakup, is carefully given a pathetic past, both to explain her aspirations and to ease the burden of blame: she wants to be independent because she grew up watching her stepfather beat her momma.

Though Milner has carefully covered his tracks in this area, his juxtaposition of the wife's restless unhappiness with the old folks' cozy ability to ride past disagreements inescapably makes the play an exercise in middle-class, middle-aged nostalgia—an emotion that is common enough on Broadway but a little surprising to find in a black writer, given the struggles of the last hundred years. It is, I suppose, another sign of progress: there are now black American artists and audiences, as well as white, with a comfortable banality to defend. In a society without a defined culture, bad taste becomes a democratic ideal, and the second-rate art form a goal toward which upwardly mobile ethnic minorities can strive. In a hundred years, when the North American continent is one vast shopping mall and we have all stopped noticing color differences, black and white actors will be mingled in dinner-theater revivals of Neil Simon and Ron Milner, without provoking any particular comment—or contributing in any way at all to the art of the theater.

Michael Feingold, "Black Marketing," in The Village Voice, *Vol. XXXIII, No. 33, August 16, 1988, p. 85.*

Czesław Miłosz

1911-

(Has also written under pseudonym of J. Syruc) Polish poet, essayist, novelist, critic, nonfiction writer, translator, and editor.

The recipient of the 1980 Nobel Prize in Literature, Miłosz is generally considered Poland's greatest contemporary poet, although he has lived in exile from his native land since 1951 and his work was banned by Polish authorities for over thirty years. Deeply informed by his youthful experiences in rural Lithuania, his knowledge of literature, and the horrors he witnessed while Poland was violently subjugated by both German and Russian occupying forces during World War II, Miłosz's works address harsh realities of existence yet frequently celebrate nature, ordinary life, and the values of culture. While affirming a moralistic outlook that encompasses humanistic, Christian, and Manichean values, acknowledging multiplicity of meanings, and musing upon the uncertainties of life, Miłosz's writings blend social concerns, history, metaphysical speculations, and continual pursuit of self-definition. Jonathan Galassi noted: "[Miłosz's] entire effort is directed toward a confrontation with experience—and not with personal experience alone, but with history in all its paradoxical horror and wonder. . . . His own work provides dramatic evidence that in spite of the monumental inhumanities of our century, it is still possible for an artist to picture the world as a place where good and evil are significant ideas, and indeed active forces."

Miłosz was born in Lithuania, a small Baltic nation that has been alternately controlled by Poland or Russia since medieval times. The heavily wooded, pristine landscape of this area and the influences of folktales and Catholicism that helped shape Miłosz's sensibility are frequently alluded to in his work. During his years at the University of Vilnius, Miłosz won respect for his poetry and became associated with a literary group called the "Catastrophists," who prophesied the subversion of cultural values and a cataclysmic global war. Miłosz lived in Nazi-occupied Warsaw during World War II, working as a writer, editor, and translator for Polish Resistance forces. After the war, he served as cultural attaché in Paris for the postwar Communist regime in Poland. Disgusted by the hypocrisy and authoritarianism of his government, Miłosz defected to the West in 1951 rather than return to Warsaw. Miłosz lived in Paris until 1960, when he accepted a teaching position at the University of California, Berkeley and established permanent residence in the San Francisco area.

While Miłosz has established a strong reputation in the West through English-language translations of his verse, critics frequently emphasize his important contributions to the development of contemporary Polish poetry. These commentators cite his application of modernist as well as classical verse forms and his lyricism, which blends formal and informal language, aphorisms, and tones appropriate to his subject matter. Critics attribute the clarity of his verse to his command of synechdoche and irony. Miłosz's first three volumes, *Poemat o czasie zastyglym* (1933), *Trzy zimy* (1936), and *Wiersze* (1940), the latter published by an underground press

under the pseudonym J. Syruc, include pastoral lyrics, meditations on the poetical process, and commentary on social problems. In many early poems, Miłosz evokes grim urban images imbued with a sense of impending catastrophe. Most critics agree that Miłosz's talents matured with *Ocalenie* (1945), a volume that contains several of his most famous poems. Among these pieces are "The World," a series of short lyrics in which a speaker offers vivid impressions from his past. Helen Vendler described "The World" as "the most opalescent of Miłosz's sequences; it exists as pure light against a background of abysmal darkness, preserving that doubleness of perspective—extreme joy recalled in extreme despair—which is Miłosz's unique discovery in the art of poetry." This volume also includes "Voices of Poor People," a sequence in which Miłosz adopts the perspectives of various common citizens to comment on representative social concerns; "In Warsaw," in which a poet's attempts to be celebratory are contrasted with violence and hardships; and "Dedication," a meditation on the role of art in which Miłosz asks, "What is poetry which does not save / Nations or people?"

In his next two volumes, *Swiatlo dzienne* (1953) and *Trakat poetycki* (1957), Miłosz characteristically blends lyrical, classical, and modernist forms to create poems that are alternately discursive, visionary, and somber. In the latter collection, which is structured as a treatise on poetry, Miłosz expresses dissatisfaction with traditionalism that stifles originality and avant-garde forms that compromise the dignity of art. *Krol Popiel i inne wiersze* (1962), *Gucia zaczarowany* (1965), and *Miasto bez imienia* (1969) contain many poems that Miłosz composed after relocating to California. In addition to metaphysical speculations, Miłosz explores contemporary culture, comments upon California lifestyles and landscapes, and, in several poems, adopts a voice and method similar to that of Walt Whitman to celebrate nature and personal freedom and to examine social pressures.

Gdzie wschodzi slonce i kedy (1974) contains some of Miłosz's best-known poems, in particular "From the Rising Sun," which is structured as a journey from Lithuania to San Francisco and blends prose and poetry, historical detail, and personal reminiscence. Terrence Des Pres stated: " 'From the Rising Sun,' which is [Miłosz's] most ambitious and perhaps his greatest poem, is likewise the outstanding example of his kind of poetry. . . . [While] it takes as its subject the development of Miłosz's own unique and unlikely career, it is also a wonderful poem about its own becoming. . . . [It] stands as his successful integration of self and larger world, of destiny both private and collective." Many of the poems in this book were published in English translation in *Bells in Winter* (1978). *Hymn o perle* (1981; *The Separate Notebooks*) collects poems from throughout Miłosz's career as well as lyrical ruminations and observations on such topics as language, self, the physical world, and the imagination. *Nieobjeta ziemia* (1986; *Unattainable Earth*) comprises notes, letters, poetic and prose passages, and quotations from works by other writers to form a comparison between the real and intangible elements of existence and to explore the possibilities and limitations of language, religion, and metaphysical concepts. English translations of pieces from the various phases of Miłosz's career appear in *Selected Poems* (1973; revised 1981) and *Czesław Miłosz: The Collected Poems, 1931-1987* (1988).

Miłosz's experiences, his interest in history and politics, and his aesthetic theories are delineated in several nonfiction works. *Zniewdony umysel* (1953; *The Captive Mind*), which elaborates his reasons for defecting from Poland, studies the effects of totalitarianism on four creative individuals who are forced to alter or compromise their convictions in order to survive. Miłosz's autobiographical work, *Rodzinna Europa* (1959; *Native Realm: A Search for Self-Definition*), won praise for its lyrical recreation of the landscape and culture of his youth, his horrific descriptions of war-torn Warsaw, and his investigation of the influence of environment, education, religion, and history on his intellectual development. The essays in *Widzenia nad Zakota San Francisco* (1969; *Visions from San Francisco Bay*) offer sardonic reflections on European culture and American society. In *Ziemia Ulro* (1977; *The Land of Ulro*), Miłosz evokes a symbolic land that appears in several of William Blake's mythological poems. Ulro, according to Miłosz, denotes "that realm of spiritual pain such as is borne and must be borne by the crippled man." In this work, Miłosz laments the modern emphasis on science and rationality that has divorced human beings from spiritual and cultural pursuits. *The Witness of Poetry* (1983), which collects Miłosz's presentations as a visiting lecturer at Harvard University, includes comparisons between contemporary East European and American verse. Miłosz contends that historical events have forced Eastern European writers to focus on social, political, and cultural issues, and concludes that the freedoms and relative absence of censorship

have freed many American poets to explore personal interests.

Miłosz has also written two novels. *La prise du pouvoir* (1953; translated from the Polish manuscript *Zdobycie wladzy*), which was published in the United States as *The Seizure of Power* and in Great Britain as *The Usurper,* explores the fortunes of intellectuals and artists within a communist state. Blending journalistic and poetic prose, this work examines the relationship between art and ideology and offers vivid descriptions of the Russian occupation of Warsaw following World War II. In *Dolina Issa* (1955; *The Issa Valley*), Miłosz evokes the resplendent river valley where he was raised to explore a young man's evolving attitude toward nature. The mythical structure of this work pits such dualities as innocence and evil, regeneration and death, idyllic visions and grim realities. Miłosz is also well-known in his homeland for his translations of Biblical passages and works by T. S. Eliot, Whitman, and Shakespeare. Two of Miłosz's books originally published in 1969 and revised in 1983, *The History of Polish Literature* and *Postwar Polish Poetry,* are considered standard introductions to Polish literature.

(See *CLC,* Vols. 5, 11, 22, 31; *Contemporary Authors,* Vols. 81-84; and *Contemporary Authors New Revision Series,* Vol. 23.)

HELENE J. F. DE AGUILAR

Like most poetry lovers I have, over the years, read scrupulously in Czeslaw Milosz's work and have acquired in the process a guilty conscience. Milosz has been acclaimed so fervently and consistently by so many notable critics—most recently by Helen Vendler, [see *CLC,* Vol. 31], whose *New Yorker* commentary is quoted on **The Separate Notebooks'** jacket cover—that I have become uncomfortable. (pp. 127-28)

Joseph Brodsky has "no hesitation whatsoever in stating that Czeslaw Milosz is one of the greatest poets of our time, perhaps the greatest." He too is quoted to this effect on the jacket cover of **The Separate Notebooks** and, whatever the original context of the remark, it is certainly a silencing, as well as puzzling, notion: *the* greatest?? I do not think Milosz is a Great Artist and I would be very much surprised indeed were he to prove an enduring one. (p. 128)

Cultural estrangement is often advanced to account for a foreign writer's lack of impact, and it constitutes a pyrrhic, if impregnable, line of defense since it leads to the conclusion that works in translation ought not to be published in the first place. A more convincing exoneration of lyrical lapses is the futility of translating Polish rhyme. Milosz himself stresses the centrality of rhyme in the classical poetry of his mother tongue; and although I know no Polish, a glance at the original texts printed in **The Separate Notebooks** convinces me that these poems do rhyme, emphatically. We are clearly missing a lot. As non-Polish speakers—a cultural impediment of unimpeachable validity—we are limited to the English version of Milosz which evokes, at least in this reader, a blend of fitful appreciation and malaise.

To begin with, Milosz is puzzlingly comfortable in America, perhaps *too* comfortable. "I did not choose California. It was given to me," he tells us in *The Separate Notebooks.* Apparently the soul's inextricable entanglement in a more-or-less ancient civilization poses no difficulties for Milosz, whatever its ill consequences for the rest of us, because he writes prolifically and assertively about America. Throughout his work, however, the poet's sense of representative or significant American resonance is odd and somehow always a trifle "off." One essay from the 1982 *Visions from San Francisco Bay* bears as an epigraph the pathetically shopworn whimsy, "God is dead. Nietzsche. Nietzsche is dead. God." What in the name of all the gods at once—the essay is entitled **"On the Turmoil of Many Religions"**—induces Milosz to quote tedious clichés and embarrassingly unwitty tidbits of Berkeley juvenilia as though some Great Truth lurked therein? Chronic throughout his writing runs this taste for the trite and the boring. Irreparable harm may be inflicted upon Milosz's poetry through the sacrifice of rhyme, but such damage is not a factor in *Views,* nor, for that matter, in *The Captive Mind* or *The Seizure of Power.* Why then is the prose so weak, the perceptions so flattened? "The nineteenth century was a century of the spirit." **("On That Century")** "Religion has its inexpressible sides, but its symbols must constantly be revived in the imagination and take on the juices of life." **("On the Turmoil of Many Religions")** "Full human equality will come to pass, but that may well be the equality of the subjugated. People will be guaranteed bliss, but on condition that they do not interfere with the processes of government." **("The Dance of Death and Human Inequality")** (pp. 130-31)

Precisely what Milosz does see from San Francisco Bay rarely emerges into any clear focus and almost never into an interesting one. For a long time I feared I was missing the point of the prose, but there are limits to my modesty. Would I miss, on page after page of book after book, *so* many points were they there to be noted? "The United States is a land of virtue," says the Polish poet, "Through virtue it arose and achieved its technical might." De Tocqueville's observations were somewhat similar, but they were accompanied by a redeeming cynical wryness altogether lacking in Milosz. I trust I love my country, but the Nobel Laureate's solemnity baffles and discomforts me. Surely he means something more specific than "virtue," but what can the something be? Over and over again *Visions from San Francisco Bay* refuses identification. Milosz is least convincing, because least original, in sociological or political postures. It is for this reason, perhaps, that *The Seizure of Power,* a novel dear to its author's heart and reissued some years ago to considerable critical acclaim, is so unimpressive in so predictable a manner. (p. 131)

Lest these weaknesses be dismissed as entirely genre-linked occupational hazards, let me state that it is not only in political novels that Milosz's mode of expression is so disappointing. Discerning some wonderful idea within a drab or glossy wrapping is an active challenge to readers of *The Separate Notebooks,* a collection of poems, fragments of poems, prose-poems and near-poems of great, if sometimes plodding intensity. Frequently singled out by Milosz fans for its beauty and emotional power is **"The World,"** a very long (eleven pages) and much subdivided poem which resurrects the poet's childhood with a wealth of sensual detail. **"The World"** is a work of re-creation, summoning up the way life felt in a time now so far behind us that it appears mythical. Its subtitle, "A Naive Poem," is repeatedly confirmed in the simplicity of each stanza.

> The word *Faith* means when someone sees
> a dewdrop or a floating leaf, and knows
> That they are, because they have to be. . . .

Such self-contained, unassailable realizations of joy do seem appropriate to childhood; not, however, to poetry. To the adult imagination a faith urged upon us in terms—literally—of dewdrops and leaves is less than sustaining. Hope cannot be sought in a garden, like a flower or a star, because we must *recover* childhood before we can respond like children to such stimuli.

"Through poetry . . . I wanted to save my childhood" says Milosz in his personal history, *Native Realm.* But the restoration of innocence involves the subtle manipulation of nostalgia and Milosz's language is decidedly not subtle. There is a good deal of the blunt instrument in the English diction of **"The World"**; and though the West may have been won in this style, childhood cannot be. . . . Perhaps we as readers have simply lost the capacity to take the abrupt believer's plunge into the naiveté the poet treasures, but in that case, while the loss is surely ours, the problem is certainly his. "Without much exaggeration it can be said that poetry, for the majority of poets, is a continuation of their school notebooks or is, both literally and figuratively, written on their margins." Here, no doubt, are the origins of *The Separate Notebooks* and all their difficulties. Milosz trusts too much in the automatic power of the margins.

By way of contrast, **"Father in the Library"** respects the distance between the long-lost child's vision and the grown man's recollection thereof:

> A high forehead, and tousled hair
> The sun at the window pouring light
> Father wears a crest of downy fire
> As he opens, slowly, the great book.
>
> His gown covered with devices
> Like a wizard's, he murmurs spells:
> Only one whom God has taught magic
> Could know the marvels his book reveals.

The patience and balance of this segment are characteristic of Milosz at his near-best. Memory stands perfectly still, effortlessly accurate. The surface stillness of the image renders it changeless; the changelessness makes the scene appear eternal, and the deceptive but irresistible eternity redeems the remembered afternoon from mere life, immortalizing both incident and sunset. Visual impressions are important to Milosz; therefore his tendency to rush or overload his lines can prove seriously disruptive. . . . The first quatrain of **"Father in the Library"** is hushed, full of repose. Sufficient time is allowed for its atmosphere to collect and for a scene half a century behind us to regain real presence. The stanza's deliberate, suspended serenity is emphasized by the adverb "slowly" which modifies the only movement in the scene. Note too the integration of images: everything aspires to the condition of *magus:* halo, gown, book, murmurings. Since it is the nature of magic to remain magical, we do not find explained "the marvels his book reveals." Their mystery abides even unto this day, and this *open* closure proves effective, almost disturbing, in exactly the proper way. There is a lightness of touch, or *grace* in these closing lines, compatible with the yearning Milosz wishes to evoke but which he often stamps out, like campfire embers, through the excessive certainty and solidity of his images.

Elsewhere in **"The World"** the textures of the poet's nostalgic evocations are unattractive, either lumpy or strained. We look at too much too hastily; everything is pretty, little exceptional, nothing unique. . . . As philosopher-poet, however, bent on extracting messages and meanings from sentiment and sense perception, Milosz can wax positively embarrassing. . . . [In **"Love,"** the] soft, somehow moldy romanticism is largely the result of Milosz's desire to recapture childhood naiveté *without having to stalk it,* by poetic fiat, as it were. The mood he seeks to wake by *will* must be evoked instead by extreme verbal sophistication which he rejects. That Milosz is perfectly capable of supplying such sophistication is unquestionable, and why he would rather not do so is likewise understandable. The outcome of the refusal, however, is unfortunate.

It is true that certain inspirational poems by Milosz make the heart beat faster, but in these cases once again the author tends to rest upon laurels not in the strict sense his. . . . **"Incantation"** begins with echoes of *Wisdom of Solomon* ("Wisdom is more beautiful than the sun," etc.), proceeds to a paraphrase of Paul to the *Romans,* and concludes with two lines of enormous power, powerful because they are a typical *Psalms* closure. Heavy-handed and inducing winces are, in comparison, the few wholly original contributions of the poet: "It establishes the universal ideas in language, / And guides our hand so we write Truth and Justice / With capital letters, lie and oppression with small."

All this, including even the laborious and slightly sanctimonious symbolism of the capital letters, is true enough. And of course some degree of reliance upon echoes and overtones and allusions is inevitable—maybe laudable—in a poem of exhortation, especially when the poet speaks openly for a broad and ancient culture. What then is wrong with **"Incantation"**? To my mind the poem fails because it exerts no influence over its echoes, its overtones, and its allusions. As a twentieth-century gloss on and affirmation of some splendid staples of western philosophy, **"Incantation,"** like much of Milosz's best work, can hardly be faulted. But it *adds* nothing to the original texts (*Wisdom, Romans, Psalms*) from which it derives, and the emotional component of the poem is in fact supplied largely by the remembered resonance of these earlier formulations.

A similar taste for paraphrase characterizes the work of Ernesto Cardenal, the Nicaraguan "poet priest" who bears many resemblances to Milosz. Like his Polish contemporary, Cardenal is a self-conscious Catholic of extensive education and vast erudition. He too is a poet of historical anguish, a chronicler of his generation and an active citizen. (He now occupies a Nicaraguan government post.) **"Incantation"** is strikingly comparable to Cardenal's *Psalms,* with the equally striking difference that Cardenal really does radicalize his biblical source. (pp. 132-37)

The Cardenal/Milosz connection interests me because the world, in the case of both celebrities, is too much with us. The reputation of Eastern European and Central American artists tends to precede them politically. They are in vogue for suspicious reasons. (The Eastern Europeans have an advantage over their Latin counterparts in that Europe is popularly regarded as exporting talent in rather the same fashion that the Banana Republics export bananas.) Stylishness is no impediment to genius, but it does have deleterious effects on critical assessment and analysis. The fanfares resound so loudly that one can scarcely read in peace, and the consequences of such hurried, induced, even harassed enthusiasm include hyperbo-

le and random exaltation—a disservice to artists made unduly conspicuous by life's numerous non-artistic factors. (p. 138)

Six poems chosen from his own work by the Nobel laureate himself compose the Milosz section of the anthology [*Postwar Polish Poetry* he edited]. Like a well-designed Rorschach test each one provokes a distinctive response. They are all trustworthy compositions, but not his best. **"My generation was lost,"** a fourteen-line poem which serves as an introduction to *The Witness of Poetry* is far superior: is, in fact, exquisite. Milosz is interesting when he bites; the success of his wit and acerbity is notorious while his desire for poignancy, not his mastery of it, catches our notice. Poignancy cannot easily accommodate his intellectual preoccupations, for Milosz is a teacher and a guide. He likes to show the reader what surrounds him and then insist that he reconsider its meaning. A short tone and an air of incontrovertible conviction are more useful to this end than a gentle melancholia. Hence Milosz' poetry often exhibits strong irony or avant-garde sharp edges. Paradoxically the poems which truly reveal him as a master and not as one more "important Polish poet" are altogether lacking in causticity. They are few and far between but they are worth the wait. (p. 145)

Moods of unabated misery frequently overtake Milosz. When this happens he is deprived of the loving sense of possible preservation which is essential to his aesthetic. As he loses heart his language loses finesse. Urgency and remorse replace it, but poorly. (p. 148)

The initial apostrophe [in **"Dedication"**] is powerful but it is immediately undermined by the self-consciousness and indifferent imagery of the rest of the stanza. The language falls victim to the kind of verbal slipped-disc to which Milosz is susceptible. "I speak to you with silence like a cloud or a tree." Does he really *mean* "a cloud or a tree" or are these merely the first nouns that came to mind? Inexplicable translation weakens the poem further. What sort of a verb is "mixed up"? What are its implications? What, exactly, is the "inspiration of hatred"? Off-balance, Milosz has a habit of lecturing in the middle of a poem; his professorial and lyrical modes then operate at cross-purposes, especially where, as in this case, he appears to be reproving the deceased.

The central conundrum of **"Dedication,"** namely, "What is poetry which does not save / Nations or people?" impresses me as strange, since most readers would undoubtedly be more interested in knowing what poetry it is that does perform these tasks. Or is this question not asked in earnest? In that case it is a bothersome rhetorical flourish, another reprise of an old complaint, and curiously unworthy of a major artist. It is typical, too, of the dejected Milosz to repeat the tired old rebuke of "Readings for sophomore girls" (he hasn't the heart to invent his own slurs) a scant three lines after so quintessentially "sophomoric" a display of ingenue idealism. The final four lines return the poet's attention to the dead he addressed in the beginning and restore us to them, that is to say, however briefly, to the realm of true poetic imagination.

Odd as it may seem, Milosz's lyrical work is not very imaginative. I am not bemoaning a shortage of mythical beasts. I mean that the poetry settles down on ideas we already entertain rather than on flying to others we know not of. This is odd in a poet deeply affected by late nineteenth-century French writers and so intimately connected with the twentieth-century avant garde. In the 1944 poem **"A Song on the**

End of the World," also included in *Postwar Polish Poetry,* we find that "The voice of a violin lasts in the air / And leads into a starry night." Later on "the bumblebee visits a rose" and "rosy infants are born." Granted, the staleness of these images is partially deliberate, but the dullness of the poem as a whole is surely not. . . . Compare **"A Song on the End of the World"** with Jules Supervielle's conception of the same event [in his poem, "Prophecy"]. . . . Because there is no surprise in Milosz's apocalypse it does not stun; indeed, it scarcely seems to touch us. Supervielle's vision is euphoric in comparison, yet its terrible loneliness is breath-taking in its sudden totality.

Nothing in Milosz approaches the raptness of such a vision, the utter conviction and soaring regret of the French poet's world's end. Rapture, needless to say, is not incumbent upon a poet, still less upon a survivor of, *inter alia,* the Second World War. Exiles are condemned to love the world which destroyed them and this eats away, perhaps, at their capacity for fantastical awe. Milosz can only revere the goldfinch *he* has heard, the swallow he saw while being driven away forever from his childhood in that well-remembered cart. He loves what he has lost, not what God may find.

In any event, Milosz is not readily prompted to soar. There is much activity in his poems, but it is almost always earthbound, or at best a hovering movement. . . . In **"A Poor Christian Looks at the Ghetto,"** one of the strongest pieces in *Postwar Polish Poetry,* moles bore through the earth, "Bees build around the honeycomb of lungs, / Ants build around white bone," and the decomposition of the dead is as relentless as the death-bound survivor's guilt:

> My broken body will deliver me to his sight
> And he will count me among the helpers of death:
> The uncircumcised.

Even where resurrection is the theme (for Milosz would favor an afterlife), transfiguration is not on the agenda. (pp. 149-51)

A poetry of ideas, mostly general, conveyed in great part by an ego which while present is not intensively characterized, and expressed in a vocabulary shy of exhilaration but always agitated, presents many difficulties. Milosz's long poems, in which the reader might hope to get to know the poet better, are convulsive and jerky. *The Separate Notebooks* are studded with spectacular lines all splendidly detached from each other so that whole pages read like lists of opening gambits for a book of still-unwritten poems to come. . . . [He] remembers so much, so passionately, that there is no space in the present for so rich, if tormented, a past. Excellent opening lines slip past him like invaluable experiences never to be recovered for want of storage space, and in such profusion that concentration is hard to maintain. Milosz has, as a poet, too much to attend to.

The cultish excesses of his critics, moreover, have fixed Milosz's poetry in an uncompromisingly exposed position. Lauded for its lucidity, for its profound insight into Polish reality in our century, it proves insufficiently revelatory; after all, Milosz himself presents twenty-four other poets whose statements on Polish reality might reasonably share such critical acclaim. Extolled as a triumph of private sensitivity, the poetry proves inconsistent. Its intensity is unstable. When good, Milosz is very, very good; when bland, he is very bland. Many Milosz poems seem underseasoned. They resemble complicated dishes expertly prepared and ready for serving, except that some vital condiments were left out. One can

guess what is missing but one cannot actually taste it. Worrisome, and significant, is the fact that Milosz's prose is often barely distinguishable from his poetry; he communicates almost as much about himself when engaged in describing his colleagues-in-art as he does through his own creative work. Milosz's genius requires enormous calm—the kind of calm from which **"My generation was lost"** emerged; but other facets of his character preclude his enjoying such stillness for any extended period of time. More specifically, Milosz's roving, analytic, academic intellect is an obstacle to his poetic realization. (pp. 152-53)

That he is a generous, moral, and fiercely alive individual seems obvious. That he is "the greatest poet of the twentieth century," as billed, less so. In fact, as Milosz might be inclined to agree, he is not Prince Hamlet nor was meant to be. Like Fortinbras he is sometimes ruthlessly unfanciful, a pose as convincing, although for reasons entirely opposite, as his Childhood Revisited posture which it in fact contradicts. In **"Advice,"** another poem included in his anthology of Polish poets, Milosz seems to admonish the little boy who clung to that vanishing prewar landscape as if to a paradise lost. This advice is terrible in its shrewdness—it is demonic advice, but perhaps the best available. Milosz is surprisingly effective as devil's advocate, a role with which readers and critics somehow do not associate him, and it is with the final lines of **"Advice"** that I shall take leave of a poet who if he does not shine fixedly like a planet most certainly twinkles brilliantly as a star.

> We created a second Nature in the image of the first
> So as not to believe that we live in Paradise.
> It is possible that when Adam woke in the garden
> The beasts licked the air and yawned, friendly,
> While their fangs and their tails, lashing their
>   backs,
> Were figurative and the red-backed shrike,
> Later, much later, named Lanius Collurio,
> Did not impale caterpillars on spikes of the black-
>   thorn.
> However, other than that moment, what we know
>   of Nature
> Does not speak in its favour. Ours is no worse.
> So I beg you, no more of those lamentations.
>
>   (p. 154)

Helene J. F. de Aguilar, " 'A Prince Out of Thy Star': The Place of Czeslaw Milosz," in Parnassus: Poetry in Review, *Vol. 11, No. 2, 1984, pp. 127-54.*

STANISLAW BARANCZAK

At least in one respect Czeslaw Milosz's work resembles that of Blake, Mickiewicz, Dostoevsky, Gombrowicz, and other favorite subjects of his essays: it is a work that thrives on contradictions. Some of the more penetrating Polish critics have been aware of this for a long time: hence the constant "yes, but . . ." that goes together with almost all critical formulas. Catastrophism?—yes, but an "eschatological catastrophism." Moralism?—yes, but full of deceitful irony. Classicism?—yes, but sprouting, paradoxically, from romantic roots. Poetry of culture?—yes, but who understands the world of nature better than Milosz? One could easily find an analogy in Milosz's spiritual father, William Blake, whose *Songs of Innocence* reveal their full meaning only when read together with their counterpart, *Songs of Experience.* The same is true of Milosz, who could be understood in quite contradictory ways if a reader tried to isolate his ostensibly sententious statements from the whole system of his dialoguing opinions and arguments.

This also applies to that particular component of Milosz's work that we can call his concept of poetic language. There are several basic contradictions here, even if we limit our observation to the poet's explicit opinions formulated in some of his essays, in his long poem **"Traktat poetycki,"** and in other works. The most striking of those contradictions is probably the fact that Milosz, at the same time, *is* and *is not* interested in the problems of poetic language. We can find in his work quite a few statements resulting from his "conscious and stubborn anti-aestheticism", his refusal to acknowledge any seriousness of purely literary dilemmas, of that "make-believe land" poetry is or sometimes is. His aversion to pure poetry involves also an aversion to all the problems that arise from overestimating the role of language: here Milosz attacks both certain trends in the humanities ("I read with aversion and hostility various structuralists who preach that it is not we who use language, but language that uses us,") and certain currents in literature (those avant-garde movements that were interested in linguistic self-thematicism, "rather in the poetic work in itself than in the wide world,"). Against a "narrowed" poetry, against the avant-garde "atrophy of heart and liver"—in favor of all attempts at "punching holes through the wall which a modern poet erects with his own hands around his laboratory fortress". Such, apparently, would be the basic distribution of Milosz's sympathies and antipathies.

But only apparently. In fact, it would be hard to find another contemporary Polish poet whose work is so deeply permeated by literary self-analysis—including also a consideration of poetic language problems, a reflection on the development of a "new diction" ("I want not a new poetry, but a new diction"—one of the central statements in **"Traktat poetycki,"**). Once again we could quote from Milosz's work numerous sententious opinions concerning those problems, and who knows if, statistically, there wouldn't be more of them in Milosz than in such an apparently "self-thematic" poet as Julian Przyboś.

We meet a contradiction in the very beginning, then; and there will be more further on—especially if we do not confine ourselves to Milosz's "formulated poetics," but try to consider his "immanent poetics," his practical use of poetic language as well; in other words, if we try to define why and in what way Milosz's "diction" is really "new" against the background of twentieth-century Polish poetry.

Like many other poets, Milosz is tormented by a basic shortcoming of language: its being out of proportion to reality. "Everything would be fine if language did not deceive us by finding different names for the same thing in different times and places" (***Bells in Winter***); everything would be fine, let us add, if on the other hand language were not so insufficient in relation to the abundance of the real world. Due to the nature of language, we are "banished from the paradise of the world's lucidity," for

> A word should be contained in every single thing
> But it is not. So what then of my vocation?

This dilemma of words being out of proportion to things is, of course, as old as poetry itself. What makes Milosz's method of solving the problem more specific is the basic assumption of his *Weltanschauung:* the preeminence of reality. All

things of this world "participate in the universal, existing separately", but their importance lies exactly in their particular existence, from which we are separated by the threefold veil of our imperfect senses, memory, and language. The imperfection of language presents a special problem here, because it consists not only in the above-mentioned lack of proportion between the system of words and the system of the world's elements; it also consists in the fact that language by its nature is not able to denominate a particular being, since it always more or less tends to a generalization (a follower of the school of General Semantics would say that a denomination, even the most concrete and precise, always lifts a thing to this or that rung of the "abstraction ladder"). What in a sensual experience—or even in a reminiscence—appears as a clear, concrete, substantial, individual thing is, by receiving a name, automatically subsumed into a superior class: it becomes not a thing, but the representation of an idea of a thing. Hence a persistent feeling of disappointment. . . . (pp. 319-21)

The extensive fragment of the long poem **"With Trumpets and Zithers"** discusses this semantic difficulty in a direct way:

> I wanted to describe this, not that, basket of vegetables with a redheaded doll of a leek laid across it.
> And a stocking on the arm of a chair, a dress crumpled as it was, this way, no other.
> I wanted to describe her, no one else, asleep on her belly, made secure by the warmth of his leg.
> Also a cat in the unique tower as purring he composes his memorable book. . . .
> In vain I tried because what remains is the ever-recurring basket.
> And not she whose skin perhaps I, of all men, loved, but a grammatical form.
> No one cares that precisely this cat wrote *The Adventures of Telemachus.*
> And the street will always be only one of many streets without name.

"In vain I tried" is the central sentence of that passage; its meaning depends on which of its two parts is stressed by a reader. If "in vain" is stressed, the whole sentence becomes a sign of frustration and disappointment in language. But "I tried" is equally important: the poet knows very well that language has its defects, but in spite of that he repeatedly *tries* to give the things their exact names. Milosz's private question of universals ("Who would have guessed that, centuries later, / I would invent the question of universals?") consists also in an active struggle against the abstractness of language: he tries to find words as precise, concrete, and unique as possible, to descend as low as possible down the semantic "abstraction ladder." (pp. 321-22)

Naturally, Milosz never gives up his lexical quest; as a rule, he always tries to find the most concrete among all possible synonyms, even at the cost of transgressing the limits of the ethnic language. . . . However, his most characteristic stylistic inclinations appear not so much within the field of lexical options as within the field of figures of speech. Compared to most lyrical poets, Milosz stands out as someone who almost completely rejects figures near to the metaphorical pole (especially metaphors as such and symbols) and who instead strongly favors metonymical figures (especially synecdoche and within it especially *pars pro toto*). Milosz is a poet of synecdoche: I think Polish critics have never sufficiently emphasized this, even though it is a peculiarity both conspicuous and increasing in the course of time.

It is interesting, though, that synecdoche does not dominate in Milosz's poetry from the beginning. In his prewar work there are still a good many metaphors typical of the avant-garde disease of "metaphoritis" (as critic Karol Irzykowski liked to call it). During the war years this tendency underwent a significant change: since that time Milosz uses language mostly in a synecdochic way, only incidentally introducing some enclaves of "small" metaphors. In the first stanza of his **"Równina,"** for instance:

> For years, for years, the same, inconceivable,
> With herds of women on its potato fields,
> With its plot where unreaped clover glitters,
> With its long spark of gnats around the horses'
>   mouths.

There is, of course, a felicitous metaphor based on a visual similarity (a gnat ["komar"] equated with a "long spark" ["dluga skra"]), but it functions mostly as an intensification of the image's concreteness. However, the image itself contains a whole chain of synecdoches. The plain ("równina"), mentioned in the title, is seen as a series of *partes pro toto:* first the general panorama of potato fields ("kartofliska"), next a concentration on a single clover plot ("pólko koniczyny"), then at last a close-up on some horses' mouths ("końskie pyski") with gnats flying around them.

I have used the technical film expressions "panorama" and "close-up" not without purpose: as early as 1946, in his famous review of Milosz's book *Ocalenie,* Kazimierz Wyka noticed that in this poetry "film is a principle of meanings." As a matter of fact, Wyka meant rather the general technique of merging images or of montage "cuts." One could add to that observation that the sequences divided by the cuts adjoin each other in a synecdochic way. For example, in the above-quoted fragment of **"Równina,"** we have a typical sequence of film shots, from a panorama to a close-up. Each next shot makes the general *totum* of "równina" more particular and detailed by showing its more and more concrete *partes.* A sequence of shots can be, of course, more complicated. (pp. 322-23)

The analogies with film techniques go even further: sometimes we may notice, for example, that the images can not only be divided by montage cuts, but can also merge as if by use of a zoom lens that provides a fluid passage from one shot to another. This fluid mixing of perspectives can be additionally motivated by the specific poetics of a dream (used especially in a longer poem **"Album of Dreams,"** but also in many other poems from Milosz's latest period).

Milosz himself quite recently gave an autobiographical key to his synecdochic technique of film montage, when in his Stockholm address he mentioned Nils Holgersson, his favorite childhood hero. Holgersson, a boy from Selma Lagerlöf's novel *A Wonderful Voyage,* is "the one who flies above the earth and looks at it *from above,* but at the same time sees it in every detail," which can be "a metaphor of the poet's vocation." Milosz also adds that after many years he discovered an identical motif in one of the Latin odes by Maciej Kazimierz Sarbiewski. We should emphasize here that in Milosz's poetry this fusion of extremely incompatible perspectives— the point of view of a bird and that of an ant—is not a manifestation of the poet's omnipotence; on the contrary, it is a manifestation of the poet's submissiveness in the face of reality, which demands to be regarded from as many points of view as possible. Hence Milosz's synecdochic style and his gradual elimination of metaphors and symbols: in the long

poem **"Bobo's Metamorphosis"** (the hero of which, a boy "changed into a fly," is one more incarnation of Nils Holgersson) these sentences, referring to a certain painter, can be ascribed to the poet as well:

> How much he envied those who draw a tree with
>   one line!
> But a metaphor seemed to him something indecent.
>
> He would leave symbols to the proud busy with
>   their cause.
> By looking he wanted to draw the name from the
>   very thing.

It is not the "ideal object," "the object which does not exist," that is important, but "the accidentals of life", every object that "is what it is". Milosz is not only a poet of synecdoche, a poet of life seen as an assemblage of concrete "accidentals": he is, in addition, a consistent (if we do not count the earliest phase of his work) antisymbolist. (p. 324)

This antisymbolism does not mean, though, that in Milosz's opinion one has an easy and direct access to the object in itself. On the contrary, Milosz clearly sees numerous obstacles dividing us from the object: natural limitations of our senses and intellect, semantic pitfalls inseparable from the nature of language, and the unreliability of human memory, which in the course of time destroys primary experiences by adding to them subsequent ones. . . .

If Milosz's ontology accepts being, his epistemology is skeptical: we are not able to reach the essence of what "is what it is"; at least we are not able to communicate it verbally to other people. Because of the mediation of language, every attempt at giving things their names causes a constant and irremovable tension between generality and concreteness: the "question of universals" is unsolvable. One can, perhaps, blend the general idea and the particular existence only in a flash of a mystical illumination; however, the latter can be achieved only beyond language. What is left? Only the accumulation of details, of the "accidentals of life" that are imperfect representations of a whole. Only the analytical crumbling of reality into numerous *partes pro toto,* each of which seems to be another attempt at saving the world from the tyranny of universals and, at the same time, from the tyranny of transitoriness and death. . . . (p. 325)

But there is another method left. To be fair to reality, one can not only just multiply its synecdochic fragments, *partes pro toto,* "accidentals of life"; one can also multiply various testimonies to the same reality. Testimonies belonging to various points of view, various value systems, various voices:

> It's incredible that there were so many unrecorded
>   voices
> Between a toothpaste and a rusted blade,
> Just over my table in Wilno, Warsaw, Brie, Mont-
>   geron, California.

Both methods bear a resemblance to a court hearing, during which an objective truth has to be established both by reporting as many details as possible and by summoning as many eyewitnesses as possible. The latter is a method well known in narrative prose (at least since Dostoevsky, if we do not count previous forms of specific narrative polyphony, such as epistolary novels or novels with a Chinese-box narration). Polyphony has its traditions in poetry as well (and they are known to Milosz: see his comments on the role of dramatic monologue in Mickiewicz [**Kontynenty**] or in European poetry from Browning to Cavafy [*Prywatne obowiazki*], but a poem based on a dialogue structure or using *dramatis personae* is always to some extent balancing between literary genres; thus "pure poetry" (at least in the Polish literary tradition) always preferred lyrical homophony and tended to reject the polyphonic structure.

Milosz, however, has never felt close to the ideals of "pure poetry"; on the contrary, he has always considered the genre barriers inessential when compared with the duty of rendering justice to the visible universe. Since, on the other hand, Milosz—as [Jan Blański] put it—"cannot imagine poetry otherwise than in a historical and most of all anthropological dimension," that duty must also consist in a frequent use of "not his own" words, "someone else's" voice, "another person's" point of view. [Milosz's] essay of 1946 entitled **"A Half-Private Letter on Poetry"** (an answer to the above-mentioned review [of *Ocalnie*] by Wyka) contains already, in an embryonic form, his later theory of polyphony, and of irony, which is one of its effects. The application of polyphonic technique has also been described by some critics who, following Milosz's own remarks on the subject, point out that his later poetry (from the war poems **"Voices of Poor People"** on) more and more often uses the method of quoting "someone else's word." Here we can mention the phenomenon known in Polish descriptive poetics as "liryka maski" (for example, the whole long poem **"The World,"** where a child is a lyrical speaker and a subtle interplay of identification and alienation between the speaker and the author is arranged) or "liryka roli" (apart from **"Voices of Poor People"** also such poems as **"Child of Europe," "Greek Portrait,"** or **"On the Other Side,"** where the distance between the speaker and the author is much more essential than the possible identification). We should also add several examples of poems based on a dialogue structure, either openly (**"Rozmowa na Wielkanoc 1620 r."**) or implicitly (when the whole poem is a kind of reply to a question of a hidden partner, for example, **"Readings"**). These are, however, rather traditional solutions, engaging mostly the level of the lyrical speaker. The same problem seems to be more interesting on a lower level, not that of "someone else's voice" but that of "someone else's word." In other words, more interesting are situations when the polyphonic technique manifests itself on the level of poetic language, sometimes (but not necessarily always) finding its counterpart on the level of the lyrical speaker. (pp. 325-26)

Milosz's "someone else's word" is, most of all, "another poet's word"; his texts are [according to Edward Balcerzan] "many-storied constructions of allusions." Not only indirect literary allusions, but also direct quotations; also "latent" quotations and allusions; also more general "quotations of a genre," "quotations of a style," "quotations of a structure"; also—sporadically—self-allusions and self quotations. There are many possibilities, then, and their differentiation results additionally from the fact that Milosz very often hints at literary sources that are by no means well-known to an average reader. In such situations the border between direct quotation or allusion and stylization becomes intentionally unclear. Intentionally, because Milosz aims very often not at a precisely indicated literary source, but rather at a general suggestion of "someone else's word," of a message from the dark past, recognizable at once by its different stylistic features even if we cannot identify the author of the message.

In this respect it is also very significant that Milosz's "someone else's word" does not have to have a literary provenance:

apart from being "another poet's word" it can also be "another epoch's word" or "another country's word." Literary allusions or even quotations are not substantially different from other linguistic signals of antiquity or outlandishness. A cursory glance at Milosz's vocabulary makes a reader aware of his extremely unconstrained use of words from various times and geographical regions. At the same time, in each particular case the reader is compelled to notice the purposefulness of the poet's choice of a word. (p. 327)

This polyphony of "voices," traditions, styles reaches its peak (thus far) in the last of Milosz's long poems, **"The Rising of the Sun."** Alongside purely lyrical fragments we can find here, *inter alia,* the author's prose commentary, elements of dialogue, quotations from an authentic old-time story for children, extracts from encyclopaedias, bibliographies and ancient documents, fragments in Latin, Byelorussian and Lithuanian, a poem by prewar poet Tadeusz Bujnicki, quotations from William Blake (in Milosz's own translation), a pastiche of Old-Polish poetry, etc., etc. The principle of multiplying the various testimonies about reality reaches its apogee here, all the more so as the poem presents not a mosaic of separate voices, but rather their stylistic interaction and osmosis.

The evolution of Milosz's poetic language consists in another process as well: the poet more and more seriously tries to get rid of the "flaw of harmony" (**"Skaza harmonii"**), which in his opinion constituted the major fault of the prewar Skamander poets but which in his own poetry has a deeper, existential significance as well. Ideas like "harmony," "happiness," "tranquility" are always suspect here (in a prewar poem **"Siena,"** Milosz invokes: "Save us, O star—save us from happiness and calm"). Analogically "the training of the hand" of a writer means that finally "it is sent to the school of blots and scrawls/Till it forgets what is graceful". From the reader's point of view, moreover, one can say that the most outstanding among Milosz's poems are those in which—apart from other merits—he succeeds in creating an unstable balance between harmony and disharmony, regularity and irregularity, discipline and freedom, "high" and "low" style, poetry and prose. Poetic irony—achieved by means we have mentioned above—offers a method of confronting and, at the same time, reconciling these opposites with each other.

Milosz's struggle against the "flaw of harmony" starts from the very bottom: from the sound level; its nature can be grasped most surely in the field of versification. In his first volumes there is no equilibrium yet between the harmony of the verse and the flexibility of syntax: the former too often prevails and unnecessarily deforms the sentence. . . . (p. 328)

His struggle against the "bawds of euphony" (to use the phrase of Wallace Stevens), his "dislike for poetry that is too slick", documented in his essays by many accurate observations and analyses of other poets, in his own practice assumes a series of particular forms.

The proportion of regularity vs. irregularity, harmony vs. flexibility varies from such regular forms as hexameter and traditional syllabotonic schemes (very often broken by accentual or syllabic disturbances), through various types of irregular verse (fluctuating around traditional syllabic forms) to a biblical verset (employed especially often in Milosz's last volumes, though it has its beginnings in poems from the forties and fifties). The critic Jerzy Kwiatkowski was right when he indicated that what he called "Milosz's magic" consists, among other things, in a specific interplay between more or less traditional versification and modern, individual, colloquial, and flexible syntax and vocabulary. He failed to emphasize, though, that in Milosz's later poems the biblical verset offers much broader possibilities: here the "breath of ordinary syntax" is by no means tamed by the poetic rhythm, but in a complicated way coexists with it and even generates it.

The evolution of Milosz's versification and syntax represents only one side of a more general development in his poetic language. The ultimate goal of that development is an artistic utterance located somewhere between "poetry" and "prose". . . . In one of his later poems (**"Ars poetica?"**) Milosz speaks about this in an almost programmatic way, though, let us not forget, not without a dash of irony:

> I have always aspired to a more spacious form that
> would be free from the claims of poetry or prose
> and would let us understand each other without ex-
> posing the author or reader to sublime agonies.

Milosz's poems really are "free from the claims of poetry or prose" ("[ani] zanadto poezja ani zanadto proza"), but not only for the simple reason that they avoid metaphorical condensation of meanings and prefer metonymical presentation of the "accidentals of life." Another important reason is Milosz's ever-present inclination to counterpoint pathos with irony, sublimity with coarseness, high style with low. The latter opposition seems to be a particularly interesting phenomenon from the linguistic point of view. It could be argued that the least successful poems in Milosz's output are those in which the author fails to tone down his high style with a low one. A typical example is the poem **"Do polityka"** (from the volume *Swiatlo dzienne*), where pathos does not have its sufficient counterbalance in irony or concreteness of the image: the whole poem is somewhat empty, rhetorical, not very interesting as poetry. However, the internal principles of development in Milosz's poetry can be distinctly seen in the fact that many poems of this kind were excluded from later selections—and thus doomed to oblivion—by the poet himself. On the other hand, the best of his poems are based on an opposition between pathos and irony, the high and low styles. Elements of the low style appear particularly often since the series of war-period poems **"Voices of Poor People,"** in which the new technique of dramatic monologue ("someone else's voice") facilitated the introduction, as if in quotation marks, of "someone else's word" with its low stylistic features. In **"Song of a Citizen,"** for instance, the tragic and timeless pathos:

> On city squares lifted up by the glaring dawn,
> beneath marble remnants of blasted-down gates,

is broken by a prosaic and trivial anticlimax:

> I deal in vodka and gold.

It is a contrast of realities, but also a contrast of styles: for all we may say, in Milosz's prewar poems words like "wódka" and "handlować" ("vodka" and "to deal" in a mercantile sense) did not have the right to permanent residence. In the course of time Milosz more and more strongly opposes another dogma of the postsymbolist tradition (including, from his particular point of view, also the Cracow Vanguard, poets like Peiper and Przyboś). This dogma consists in separating poetic from "nonpoetic" language, from all those

words, expressions, and styles that are prohibited or at least "not recommended" for a poet. Milosz—"Having more respect for what is real / Than for what's petrified in name and sound"—protests such limitations in an active way: by broadening the sphere of poetic language with new territories, forbidden in the past because of their "prosiness."

However, such poetic language "which would withstand a confrontation with reality" is imperiled not only by literary conventions that restrain its drifting toward undiscovered and unnamed territories. There is also a peril from the other side: from the side of the nonpoetic language of everyday life, especially contemporary life. It presents itself to the poet as a tremendous pressure of shapeless and senseless information that brings to light "devilish possibilities of language" and makes one "resist constantly the omnipresent machine producing turmoil". Besides, there are also the instigations of History, which urges: "Fashion your weapon from ambiguous words. / Consign clear words to lexical limbo". Only taking all that into account can we fully understand the message of such concise but weighty poems as **"A Task"**. . . . (pp. 329-31)

Here we have another of Milosz's attempts to overcome some basic contradictions: this time he tries to find a way between the Scylla of poetic convention (a language that is organized but limited) and the Charybdis of colloquial spontaneity (a language that is unlimited but also unorganized). He sympathizes neither with Scylla (as some contemporary Polish neoclassicists do) nor with Charybdis (the best representative of which in Polish poetry is Miron Bialoszewski). He chooses the third way: the language of "pure and generous words," "strict and clear sentences", following the unattainable example of the Bible with its "true dignity of speech". At this moment we do not have to emphasize that the "dignity" of language is not synonymous with pathos and the high style, while "purity" has also a different meaning than in the esoteric "pure poetry" of the symbolists. Milosz is concerned with the language that is open to every way of speaking, every recess of vocabulary, every possible style—as long as they save the "true dignity of speech" that lies in its basic task: "ponazywać rzeczy" ("to give the things their names").

In the poem **"Wezwanie,"** from which this simple formula is taken (written in 1954 and printed only twenty years later), Milosz speaks about "a great hope" of a poet who in spite of everything tries "to give the things their names." This is a tragic hope, because it defies everything: it defies the natural pitfalls of language, it defies the limitations of an individual perception, memory, and ability to speak, it defies the pressures of literary conventions, and it defies the turmoil of everyday life. Against all of these only one thing can stand: a firm belief in the preeminence of reality that ends in a logical conclusion that, since we have a language—even an imperfect one—to speak about that reality, we should make the best of what we have got. We are—says Milosz—endowed with language, just as we are endowed with existence. In both cases we must draw the same conclusion. (pp. 331-32)

Stanislaw Baranczak, "Milosz's Poetic Language: A Reconnaissance," in Language and Style, *Vol. XVIII, No. 4, Fall, 1985, pp. 319-33.*

STANISLAW BARANCZAK

At first sight, [*Unattainable Earth*] seems to be a poet's scrapbook rather than a book of poems. It reminds one of the *silva rerum*, a "forest of things," the 17th-century term for a fascicle containing loosely arranged notes, occasional poems, copies of letters and memorable quotations. In the same way, ***Unattainable Earth*** consists only in part of Mr. Milosz's own poems. The rest of the volume is filled with his prose notes or aphorisms, letters from his friends and what he calls "inscripts"—fragments from sources as diverse as "Corpus Hermeticum," Casanova's memoirs, Zen philosophy, the Russian émigré philosopher Lev Shestov, the poet Oscar Milosz and the French philosopher Simone Weil. There are even several poems by Walt Whitman and D. H. Lawrence, translated by the author into Polish in the book's original edition and here restored to their English versions and included as "an homage to tutelary spirits."

A veritable mosaic, then; yet its diversity is carefully arranged. Unlike Mr. Milosz's three previous collections in English [***Selected Poems*** (1973; revised, 1981), ***Bells in Winter*** (1978), and ***The Separate Notebooks*** (1984)], each of which offered a mix of his older and more recent poems, ***Unattainable Earth*** is a faithful replica of his latest Polish book, published in 1984. A few minor omissions and additions are all that distinguish the translation (a splendid job done by Mr. Milosz himself with the help of one of his steady collaborators, the poet Robert Hass) from the original. This fact alone indicates that Mr. Milosz's forest of things is not as wild as it seems to be; that, as the author's preface puts it, "under the surface of somewhat odd multiformity, the reader will recognize a deeper unity."

What provides this unity is, first and foremost, Mr. Milosz's basic philosophical problem, compressed in the two words that form the book's title. In its Polish version, the meaning of the title is, more precisely, "earth too huge to be grasped." This notion is, indeed, the key to Mr. Milosz's poetic philosophy. On the one hand, his is a poetry obsessed with the very fact of the world's being. "What use are you? In your writings there is nothing except immense amazement," he addresses himself in one of his prose notes. Despite the ironic tone, there is much truth in this. Mr. Milosz's constant, perpetually renewed "amazement" with the richness of "The Garden of Earthly Delights" (as he calls the world in a poem that borrows its title from Hieronymus Bosch's triptych) can often reach the heights of an ecstatic hymn of praise and thankfulness: "You watch what is, though it fades away, / And are grateful every moment for your being."

On the other hand, Mr. Milosz's certainty that the earth is something real and tangible is coupled with his incessant awareness that the earth is "unattainable," "too huge to be grasped." We humans have our share in it, but we are separated from its essence by the dim screens of our imperfect senses, our fallible memory, our limited language. . . .

Here we encounter the metaphysical and religious poet, one who is able to note down, apparently with an approving nod, this statement from the philosopher René Le Senne: "For me the principal proof of the existence of God is the joy I experience any time I think that God is." But Mr. Milosz is also able to record this thought: "A decent man cannot believe that a good God wanted such a world." That is because the world—both the world of nature and the world of human history—is tainted by the constant presence of evil. In other words, the earth is unattainable to our imperfect senses, intellect or language; it is unattainable because the coexistence of

a good God and unwarranted suffering is something beyond our comprehension.

For Mr. Milosz, one answer to the problem of evil is the very act of being aware that "good is an ally of being and the mirror of evil is nothing," and that what we call the devil is actually "The Great Spirit of Nonbeing." As a consequence, "searching for the Real," futile and unsatisfactory as that usually is, is the only defense of good accessible to the poet. He affirms being through naming it, and his affirmation has an ethical dimension.

But the poet's search for the Real, if it is to bring any result at all, cannot be done within the limits of one mind, one place, one language, one epoch. It must involve his repeated attempts "to transcend my place and time," to "multiply" himself and "inhabit" objects and people, so that finally the voice of the poet speaks on behalf of all the things of this world, all forms of being, past and present, dead and alive. This is why the ultimate point of Mr. Milosz's unique development as a poet has been, paradoxically, pursuing the ideal of dissolving his individual voice in an all-encompassing polyphony—in the immense dialogue of different voices that resounds in the pages of ***Unattainable Earth.***

Stanislaw Baranczak, "Garden of Amazing Delights," in The New York Times Book Review, *July 6, 1986, p. 10.*

J. P. WHITE

Like other writers from Eastern Europe (or Latin America), Milosz has had little to imagine. His problem has been just the opposite: making reality believable. His poems remember the upheavals that have been erased by ideology, and they touch again the individuals who fell victim to the abstractions of history.

Milosz's new book, ***Unattainable Earth,*** includes poems, prose, quotations, letter fragments, and translations—all of which attest to his unshakable questioning approach. This is Milosz's most personal book to date—intimate, quiet, and pensive, with an undercurrent of praise for what may happen next. Some of the shorter poems like **"My-Ness," "Thankfulness,"** and **"Theodicy"** are too precious in their affirmation, but nearly all of the longer poems strike a more paradoxical note of cool detachment and quickened discovery.

Although most of the pieces here turn on a personal memory, Milosz always keeps one eye on civilization, on what happened or failed to happen in the nightmarish stretch of history that left his native Poland "the backyard of empires, / Nursing its humiliation with provincial daydreams." What's remarkable about the tension he creates between private and public history is how it slips into his poems like a casual intermezzo in a conversation between old friends: "Cold borscht is served and I am abstracted / With disturbing questions from the end of my century / Mainly regarding the truth, where does it come from, where is it?" Milosz is in his seventies and can look down the vistas and cul-de-sacs of his time on earth and give a chill to a impromptu question like this. We listen because it carries the weight of lived experience. The question remains unanswered in the poem **"Rustling Taffetas,"** and throughout this book the unfinished pursuit of truth is the only state of mind, embattled though it is, that offers some degree of solace and hope. Memory can awaken the names and faces that clung to our personal history, but the meaning of that history remains beyond our grasp. The world, then, as Milosz conceives it, is always "unattainable," and therefore always worthy of love as it lives for one more day in perilous balance between good and evil.

Freighted by his search for the unknowable, Milosz is also aware that his passions and appetites, born in youth, are ready to be rekindled at any moment. In **"Father Ch., Many Years Later,"** Milosz recalls the vicar of his childhood parish and considers his own lack of fidelity to the vicar's principles, which included an abstinence from earthly pleasure. What's memorable about the poem is how Milosz allows the drama of personal trial to suggest a larger predicament in the world. The poet laments that he would not have been among the disciples of Jesus as the Roman Empire collapsed. . . . This dual focus—beginning with an imagined personal failing and ending with a collective spiritual doubt—represents Milosz at his most original and insightful. *Unattainable Earth* honors the human struggle to create form and meaning in a world that teeters on the brink of annihilation. It is an old-fashioned excavation examining what we are capable of, where we are going, what has happened up to this moment. (pp. 168-69)

J. P. White, in a review of "Unattainable Earth," in Poetry, Vol. CXLIX, No. 3, December, 1986, pp. 168-69.

CHRISTOPHER CLAUSEN

[Milosz's] poems since 1960 balance past and present, native and alien life and language. They are the work of a man who has led two lives in radically different times and places and is trying to unite them in thought and art. The result is a major and unique contribution to American literature, one that has gone virtually unnoticed by commentators who have been content to think of Milosz simply as an exile whose career since 1960 has been no more than a prolongation of his earlier life on native soil.

Milosz's first reaction to exile, he explains in **"To Raja Rao"** (significantly, the only poem in his *Selected Poems* that was written originally in English), was very much what one might expect:

> For years I could not accept
> the place I was in.
> I felt I should be somewhere else.
>
> . . . .
>
> Somewhere else there was a city of real presence,
> of real trees and voices and friendship and love.

Exchanging Poland for France and then America was no help; like Solzhenitsyn, although less apocalyptically, he found East and West animated by opposite vices.

> Ill at ease in the tyranny, ill at ease in the republic,
> in the one I longed for freedom, in the other for the
> end of corruption.
>
> (pp. 142-43)

There is a subsequent stage in exile, however, at least if the one exiled is fortunate and brave enough. The poem continues:

> I learned at last to say: this is my home,
> here, before the glowing coal of ocean sunsets,
> on the shore which faces the shores of your Asia,

in a great republic, moderately corrupt.

This stage marks not an end but a new beginning. It does not, needless to say, fully resolve the problems that have been left behind, the guilt and disorientation of the witness to history, the émigré, the survivor in lotus-land. Guilt of this kind is a major theme in the poetry that Milosz has written over the last forty years. He speaks again and again of scenes of horror half-recalled in dreams, of friends and strangers killed by the Gestapo, of various forms of desertion. In many of his poems, the landscape itself is deformed by history into nightmare. (p. 143)

The brief section of *Selected Poems* that contains works written before the war is entitled, with a wistful irony, "How Once He Was." That section is followed by "What Did He Learn," which comprises poems written during and after the German occupation. The last section, including nearly half the poems in the book, is "Shore." As in the poem quoted above, the shore is that of California. It is in "Shore" that the ghosts of Europe are—not exactly exorcised, but made to cast a different shadow in a landscape whose paucity of rooted things bears some relation to the clarity and intensity of its sunlight. The lowering clouds of history may encourage richer vegetation; they also sometimes obscure things that are close at hand.

The English-bound reader whose interest in Milosz is as an American poet of European background, rather than a European poet accidentally resident in America, will be delighted to discover rumors of Walt Whitman in a poem entitled **"Hymn,"** written as early as 1934. . . . Milosz's admiration for Whitman and the visionary tradition has been an abiding influence, one which naturally reappears in the poems written after he came to this country. In **"Album of Dreams,"** Whitman's name is even mentioned ("With a broad white beard and dressed in velvet, / Walt Whitman was leading dances in a country manor / owned by Swedenborg, Emanuel."). More significantly, **"Throughout Our Lands,"** a long work in which present California and past Lithuania are contrasted in a series of concrete meditations, begins with an invocation of a valued predecessor. . . . (pp. 144-45)

It would be going too far to say that Milosz finds Whitman an altogether kindred spirit. No skeptical twentieth-century intellectual could possibly make such an affirmation, whatever his background. The following passage from [**"Throughout Our Lands"**] is both like and unlike Whitman's dream sequences:

> Between the moment and the moment I lived
>   through much in my sleep
> so distinctly that I felt time dissolve
> and knew that what was past still is, not was.
> And I hope this will be counted somehow in my defense:
> my regret and great longing once to express
> one life, not for my glory, for a different splendor.

The distinction in the last line would have been alien to Whitman, even after his own harrowing encounters with history. Nevertheless, in the tormented dreams, the merging of past and present, the aspiration (however thwarted) towards universal celebration, the similarities run deep.

A California poet whom Milosz has long admired in a more qualified way is Robinson Jeffers. Like Whitman and Milosz, Jeffers yearned for what critical prose can identify only as a mystical sense of the wholeness and saving beauty of reality, a lasting vision of the world's oneness in which all the accidents and terrors of actual life cease to be important. Milosz is drawn towards such a vision even while he remains skeptical of it; Jeffers found its fulfillment, rather precariously, in nature at its most inhuman. For both poets, history is a personal burden. But while Jeffers' solution was to apotheosize predatory hawks, cruel splendor, a rocky coast with few human inhabitants, Milosz finds nature in the raw just as repellant as the mindless atrocities of conquerors. The psychic problem of history has many possible solutions, with varying degrees of satisfactoriness. **"To Robinson Jeffers"** is Milosz's answer to one of the most seductive. The opening is suitably brusque:

> If you have not read the Slavic poets
> so much the better. There's nothing there
> for a Scotch-Irish wanderer to seek.

The "Slavic poets," as Milosz conceives them here, inhabited a peaceful, anthropocentric landscape where "the sun / was a farmer's ruddy face" and nature a place where humans found themselves (naturally) at home. Jeffers' landscapes, on the contrary, are filled with violence and solitude, the heritage of a northern warrior race that listened too long to the ocean. (pp. 145-46)

Nevertheless, human values—however fragile—remain at the center of the poet's vision. The inhumanity of Jeffers' God is no more admirable than the inhumanity of historical processes. Perhaps direct experience of the latter is an inoculation against falling in love with the former. . . . Far from being Eden, the wilderness is simply a void. Civilization with its morality may be a frail creation, but there is no substitute for it. How could there be, for a poet whose mind is filled with such images of nightmare as the following (from **"Album of Dreams"**)?

> They ordered us to pack our things, as the house
>   was to be burned.
> There was time to write a letter, but that letter was
>   with me.
> We laid down our bundles and sat against the wall.
> They looked when we placed a violin on the bun-
>   dles.
> My little sons did not cry. Gravity and curiosity.
> One of the soldiers brought a can of gasoline. Oth-
>   ers were tearing down curtains.

The category of experience here is altogether outside Jeffers' awareness, despite his professions of complacency towards the destruction of civilization.

And yet the comparatively historyless California landscape does make a healing difference. Vanished Lithuania and burning Warsaw look different in its light. . . . There is a serenity about California that is profoundly appealing. The softer features of the landscape offer a vision of an order that is not human, but at the same time is by no means inimical to the values of civilization. Even basalt cliffs, even birds of prey, may have their place in easing the burdens of history. Here, one feels, is a good place for civilization to flower. If it has not altogether done so, Milosz seems at times to be thinking, neither has tyranny. (The works of humanity are always ambiguous; Berkeley and Hollywood are equally products of California.) There is the sweetness of air (though, alas, neither in Berkeley nor in Hollywood), the clarity of light, the mystery of fog, the grandeur of mountains in the distance— an inviting place even to the unwilling exile; a combination, perhaps, of a Van Gogh painting and a Japanese print, those pictorial legacies of great troubled civilizations. If it is not the fulfillment of history, it is more than lotus-land. . . . To be sure, painful memories come back immediately—of childhood, of war, of the remote historical past of Europe. But the context is different from what it was. It is too much to say that images of the Golden State overpower the sad past. But they certainly change it into something richer and more universal. Looked at this way, the tragedy of Eastern Europe ceases (for the reader) to be remote and becomes part of the American landscape of imagination, even as (for the writer) something of the opposite process occurs. For each party, a new relationship is established between two disparate and important experiences, one alien, the other relatively familiar, in which each element is enriched by the other.

California is not as devoid of history as all that, of course; it only seems so because of the fluidity of life there and because few of its inhabitants have lived there for more than a generation or two. One of the ways in which Milosz the poet assimilated himself to his new home was by meditating on its history. It would have been very surprising if such a writer had rested content with landscape. In fact he has had more to say about California's past than most native poets. In **"Throughout Our Lands"** . . . he casts his mind back to the first Europeans who lived in the Far West: among them Junipero Serra, the Franciscan friar who founded the California missions in the eighteenth century. Perhaps Milosz sees (at least playfully) a certain parallel between his own situation and that of the missionary who wandered earnestly west from Spain and north from Mexico. . . . The focus soon shifts, however, from the exile to his flock, and Junipero comes to seem a rather naive bearer of European civilization to barbarians who are probably better off without it. His message of salvation falls at first on deaf ears ("poor people, they had lost the gift of concentration"). In fact, it is to the soon-displaced Indians that Milosz feels a deeper sense of gratitude. The Indians lacked writing and had primitive tastes.

> Nonetheless it was they who in my place took pos-
>   session
> of rocks on which only mute dragons
> were basking from the beginning, crawling out of
>   the sea.
> They sewed a cloak from the plumage of flickers,
>   hummingbirds, and tanagers,
> and a brown arm, throwing back the mantle, would
>   point to: this.

An earlier explorer than Junipero Serra, Cabeza de Vaca, met an even less enviable fate among the pre-European inhabitants of the West. Not a missionary whose journey was deliberate, he was only an exile who landed from "a boat thrown up on the sand by surf, / crawling naked on all fours, under the eye of immobile Indians." Alternately worshipped as a long-expected god and punished when his miracles miscarried, he endured a life not altogether dissimilar to that of the European intellectual exile in the twentieth century. Whether such a parallel was in Milosz's mind it is impossible to say, but the episode comes at the end of the poem in which he goes furthest to set up reverberations between the settler of the past (Indian, missionary, castaway) and himself; between memories of Europe and images of the American West; between simple realities like a pear and the difficulty of naming it when one has had to live in too many languages. Perhaps the best writing about places is often done by exiles. It is nonetheless surprising, but true, that some of the best poems ever written about California and the West were composed in Polish.

In **"Ars Poetica?"** (from *Bells in Winter*), Milosz writes:

> The purpose of poetry is to remind us
> how difficult it is to remain just one person,
> for our house is open, there are no keys in the
>   doors,
> and invisible guests come in and out at will.

For obvious reasons, that difficulty is one of which Milosz has been unusually aware. In *Native Realm* (1958; English translation, 1968), he wrote, "My own case is enough to verify how much of an effort it takes to absorb contradictory traditions, norms, and an overabundance of impressions, and to put them into some kind of order." The continuing effort to do so, in the second stage of his exile and at an age when most poets have long ceased to assimilate new experience into their art, is what gives Milosz a special claim on American readers. Its success is what most amply justifies, at least to the reader who has no Polish, his Nobel Prize.

> The first movement is singing,
> A free voice, filling mountains and valleys.
> The first movement is joy,
> But it is taken away.

So Milosz declared in **"The Poor Poet,"** in the burning Warsaw of 1944. His "first movement," of course, was life as a young writer before 1939, sometimes prophesying bad days to come but living nonetheless in a sort of prehistorical present. The "second movement" was the war, defeat, what has come to be known as the Holocaust (which, he reminds us in his Nobel address, was not restricted to Jews), and then the greater betrayal that followed the coming of peace. For the first half-decade of Soviet rule, Milosz chose not to become an exile, just as he had chosen to witness and resist the German occupation. But of the taking away of joy there was no end, and in 1951 his "second movement" ended in emigration.

It is with the American poems of his "third movement" that I have been mainly concerned, not only because they are the ones most accessible to American readers, but also because in them some of the harshness of history is mitigated, if not quite overcome. In them Milosz finds himself—sometimes—in a present that is no longer haunted, that has room for other things besides memory, even for joy. His passage through the horrors of history to a degree of posthistorical serenity testifies powerfully to the resources of both imagination and poetic art—resources which have been greatly in demand during his lifetime. (pp. 147-52)

One of the spiritual dangers of exile is that the one exiled may believe his own experiences, his own history, to be the only kind that lead to wisdom. This belief may manifest itself in an arrogant condescension towards those people among whom his exile is spent, a condition as unfavorable to art as the fanaticism of a Pearse. To judge by his poems of exile that have appeared in English, Milosz's art has avoided this fate by remaining open to the possibility of making a new home for itself, without of course forgetting the old one. Three concerns have preoccupied—one might almost say obsessed—Milosz's writings since the war: the value of European civilization, the persistence of history, and the artist's duty to tell the truth, both for his own sake and for the sake of his society. Dwelling on these preoccupations in the benign but alien setting where they seem at first to be drastically out of place; al-

lowing the literal and symbolic extremes of past and present, old Europe and new California, to interpenetrate and illuminate each other; at his frequent best, doing all this with great power and inventiveness—it was these accomplishments that signalled his transformation from a promising young poet of early-twentieth-century Eastern Europe into a major poet of worldwide significance in the late twentieth century. (pp. 152-53)

> *Christopher Clausen, "Czeslaw Milosz: The Exile as Californian," in his* The Moral Imagination: Essays on Literature and Ethics, *University of Iowa Press, 1986, pp. 139-53.*

ALEKSANDER FIUT

By strongly and frequently emphasizing the anthropocentric tendency of his creative work, Czesław Miłosz challenges those modern philosophical trends which claim the decline of the concept of human nature. At the same time he challenges that literature which considers this state of affairs to be irreversible. . . . He believes that destruction of the metaphysical foundation of human existence does not simply degrade man by depriving him of any meaning or value. An equally negative result is the collapse of that vision of the universe which had assumed significant hierarchical divisions both of space and moral values. Science, which had evolved from the great schism between reason and faith, destroyed the traditional divisions and then relativized such basic categories as the ethical, esthetic, and cognitive. Since that time, thought and imagination have tried ineffectually to overcome the chaos which has been produced.

Given this state of affairs, where can man find the support he needs? Religious images and symbols appear in this quotation not by chance, since Miłosz believes that

> Catholicism is the most anthropocentric of religions, and in some sense, through its own excess of divine humanity, it resists the exact sciences which annihilate the individual, and thus, paradoxically, is less susceptible than other religions to the disintegrative influence of science and technology. (*Visions from San Francisco Bay*)

Therefore, Miłosz calls on literature to defend Christian vision and to restore—at least in the word—a spatial hierarchy which will provide the sovereign individual with a place at its center. How can that be achieved in an age which has proclaimed the death of God, the death of man, and the death of art? How can one avoid being accused of naiveté and anachronism without degrading contemporary science at the same time? Finally, how can one reconcile this kind of anthropocentrism with the experience of unleashed nihilism? These questions and dilemmas are recurring themes throughout Miłosz's poetry.

At the same time it must be emphasized that Miłosz does not simply illustrate theological or philosophical problems but embodies them in the conventions of poetic language. He not only "philosophizes" poetry, but "poeticizes" philosophy. . . . [His] ultimate goal is to re-create language that is both poetic and philosophical. In the context of this concept of poetry, I will demonstrate that Miłosz's search for a definition of the essence of human nature is closely related to the ambiguity and elusiveness of the speaker's identity.

Definitions of human nature, according to Miłosz, have always depended on the particular perspective from which an individual is observed. Experience teaches that man is simultaneously—but not exclusively—a historical, social animal and metaphysical being. Therefore, none of these dimensions should be given priority, and man should not be reduced to any one. The scope of this assertion would seem sufficient to distinguish Miłosz from other contemporary Polish poets. They usually concentrate on just one sphere of man's existence. For example, for Herbert it is predominantly the historical dimension; for Szymborska—that of nature; for Białoszewski—human interactions. According to Miłosz, however, man should try to define himself, always keeping in mind that he interacts with nature, history, the sacred, and his fellow man as well.

These efforts at self-definition must be individual, momentary, and unique: individual, since only what is refracted through the experience of one man, immersed in his own existence, is considered to be true by the poet; momentary, for such an act is unique and defined by the time and space in which it occurs; unique, because only one distinct aspect of the above-mentioned interactions can be elucidated at one time. Miłosz's hero discovers himself through his contact with a bird, a beaver, or another man; through his presence in the ruins of a town and in ardent prayer to a silent God.

Does the hero really appear in the poem as a different entity? What unifies these flashes of self-knowledge? What suppresses the threat of relativism and protects *humanitas* against its diffusion into these diverse relations? Miłosz's answer sounds provocative in the context of the fashionable theories of today, for he persuades us—in spite of numerous doubts and reservations on both our parts—to believe in the existence of an undiminished element in human nature. Furthermore, this belief should remain the keystone of man's self-definition, and obviously it cannot be maintained in its former shape since its base has been undermined by the theory of evolution, psychoanalysis, and historical determinism. (pp. 65-7)

Attempts to grasp what is stable and unchangeable in human nature are marked in Miłosz's poetry by uncertainty and indecision. Dramatically suspended between the elusiveness of the object and the constantly changing criteria, these efforts search for this justification as much in the individual's needs as in the history of the culture which testifies to these efforts. In other words, Miłosz's writing can be read as a record of the devastating test to which the Christian concept of a person . . . has been submitted. This concept has been tested most acutely by those modern scientific conceptions, philosophical systems, and socio-political doctrines whose nihilistic implications can be seen both in the concept of man and his imagination.

These beliefs are naturally not present in all of Miłosz's poetry; all four dimensions of human existence cannot be traced in every poem, and the poet puts different emphasis on this importance in successive periods of his writing. However, with a striking insistence, he returns again and again to the questions of what institutes human nature, what marks its limits, and how it manifests itself. In addition, he multiplies the signs of the dissociation, sprinkles on paradoxes, and piles up contradictions. . . . (p. 67)

Miłosz seems to be asking, what can be said about that which forms human nature? In spite of scientific progress it remains an unsolvable puzzle. Any given definition of man which juxtaposes definitions can easily be challenged. Such notions as *homo faber, homo ludens, homo ritualis,* and so on grasp no more than a part of the phenomenon and tend toward generalization. Traditional theological and philosophical systems also diminish in importance. What can be done besides listening intently to the voice of intuition, juxtaposing it to knowledge and experience, and always doubting the certainty of resulting conclusions? As in Miłosz's poem **"Świadomość"** (*Nieobjęta ziemia;* **"Consciousness,"** *Unattainable Earth,* "człowieczość" (humanness), veiled in negation and trapped in paradox, can only be sensed, but not expressed; separated from its potentiality, humanness congeals immediately in yet another frozen formula. "Our humanness becomes more marked" when we are in contact with nonhuman reality, specifically expressed in this poem when the speaker reflects on the essence of a dog's nature. Miłosz even coins the word *psiość*—"dogishness." At this point a direct sensation is reinforced by philosophical knowledge, in this case the knowledge of universals. The claim that "humanness *becomes* more marked" seems to indicate that cognition can be described as a continuous and infinite process, simultaneously open to the past and to the future. This process combines the insistent question, "Who am I?" which everyone asks himself privately, with a variety of ready-made answers furnished by the history of mankind.

Miłosz is as interested in the very phenomenon of aspiring to self-knowledge as he is in the forms in which this aspiration expresses itself in the cultural tradition of a given time and place. His poetic imagination animates the multiplicity, diversity, and richness of forms, at the same time strongly emphasizing their mutable quality. He achieves this by distancing himself from these forms and juxtaposing them. Perhaps the true subject of Miłosz's poems is not the finished *concept* of human nature, but the *process* of attaining this concept. Each time this process occurs it is different and unique. Miłosz reminds us that human nature does not inhabit the heaven of abstractions, but rather evolves in history, suffused with new meaning in its different periods. The innumerable formulas and images with which man, through the centuries, has tried to illuminate his own uniqueness in the cosmos may sometimes seem ridiculous and naive. However, something elementary is present, something which is beyond the language of ideas and which cannot easily be questioned. I have in mind the dualism of human nature. Referred to differently throughout history, it can be reduced, as Miłosz states, to the basic opposition between what is "the divine in man" and what is "the natural in him," or more explicitly expressed:

> Consciousness, intelligence, light, grace, the love of the good—such subtle distinctions are not my concern; for me it is enough that we have some faculty that makes us alien, intruders in the world, solitary creatures unable to communicate with crabs, birds, animals. (*Visions*)

Embodied in the signs and symbols of culture, "the divine in man" changes and at the same time endures throughout history owing to collective memory. This "divine" is opposed to "the natural in man," to that which obeys mathematical necessity and the laws of instinct and which is excluded from the sphere of sense and value. (pp. 68-9)

Miłosz's reflections are impossible to contain in the framework of a single philosophical school or impossible to explain through a single philosopher's system. The poet asks questions rather than giving answers, sharpens contradictions rather than resolving them. Instead of tracing the philosophical sources of Miłosz's poetry, we should more closely observe the tension between the scope of the basic questions implicit in his poems, and the variety of answers which these texts give. In addition to the concept of meditation on existence, the problem of humanhood is also important. There are, logically speaking, two sides of the same issue: as the world cannot be imagined without human presence in it, human nature is equally unable to exist without acknowledging the world's reality.

The assumption of the importance of only that which has passed through the filter of individual experience has another consequence that deserves mention. Namely, the silent question in Miłosz's poetry, "Who is man?" corresponds to the spoken questions of his heroes and *personae:* "Who am I, unique and placed in a particular historical age, a certain space?" In short: questions concerning individual identity or, rather, doubts about identity. In these poems one often finds such statements as: "Ten sam i nie ten sam" ("The same and not quite the same") ["Śroczość" ("Magpiety" in *Selected Poems*)]; "nie pamiętam kim jestem i kim byłem" ("I do not remember who I was and who I am") ["Natrabach i na cytrze" ("With Trumpets and Zithers" in *Selected Poems*)]; "młody człowiek, ja dawny, niepojęcie ze mną tożsamy" ("a young man, my ancient self, incomprehensibly identical with me") ["Osobny zeszyt," the title poem of *The Separate Notebooks*].

To be oneself is then a serious issue and not at all self-evident. The ego of Miłosz's character is still threatened by the passage of time, the pressure of his subconscious, the burden of heritage, social milieu, and caprices of memory. He searches for his own identity by delving into the depths of his personality or by projecting his cognitive uneasiness on the environment.

It is interesting that Miłosz expresses all thse problems simultaneously through the complicated network of the relationship of three entities: the implied author, the speaker, and the lyric hero. He questions the traditional divisions of lyrical poetry, which silently assumed their relative stability and interior coherence. He questions the identity of this person who speaks as well as the distinctness of his act of enunciation: "the direct monologue" in Miłosz's poetry constantly leans toward "the indirect monologue" and "the dramatic monologue." This is achieved through various kinds of stylization, by transforming some of the poet's personal experiences into parables, and by traveling freely through the time and space of someone similar to him. (pp. 69-70)

Miłosz obviously prefers above all that kind of poetic narration which is usually situated between "the direct monologue" and "the dramatic monologue." It would be wrong to term it simply "the indirect monologue," since the identities of the *persona* and the implied author are problematical; their relationship is not clearly defined and in part depends upon the decision of the reader. An example of this is found in "Dużo śpię" ("A Magic Mountain"), where the question of who is speaking at any given moment is quite difficult to answer. . . . (p. 71)

In creating a mood of intimate confession, the first line evokes the traditional model of lyrical poetry. In order to reinforce the realistic features of his vision, the author exploits his own Californian setting: the Bay Area, San Francisco, Sacramento Valley, and the dry landscape of Nevada. Even the references to the books read by the speaker recall Miłosz's own

reading. Certainly, their choice and interconnection bring the poem additional, symbolic meanings. But even in his own books, such as *Native Realm* and *Visions from San Francisco Bay,* Miłosz often refers to St. Thomas Aquinas. Moreover, as he stated in an interview, Gabriel Vahanian's *The Death of God* is a work with which he is quite familiar.

Starting with the plaintive cry: "Please, Doctor, I feel a pain," the speaker separates himself gradually from the author. The only remaining aspects of their former resemblance are the confession of pain of existence and an allusion to Vilnius (St. George Street was one of the main streets of this city). The identity of this man, who addresses himself to the "Medicine Man" is not certain. It might be the same person, but it could also be the Mexican peasant who "believes in spells and incantations" and is sure that "women have only one, Catholic, soul," but men have two. Simultaneously, it could be a disappointed intellectual who has read many books but no longer believes them.

It is not difficult to recognize some of the motifs that frequently occur in Miłosz's poetry. He returns often in his imagination and memory to the banks of the river of his childhood. Those "crosses with chiseled suns and moons" appear in "To Robinson Jeffers" (*Visions*). Miłosz solemnly declares his own belief in "spells and incantations" in "Bypassing rue Descartes" (*The Separate Notebooks*). In short, he creates here a person who differs from himself, but at the same time he gives him some of the features of his own personality. Or, in other words, the poet has taken the shape of someone else without giving up his own sovereignty. The strong suggestion of the unity of speaker and author made at the beginning of the poem is in serious doubt at the end.

This change is evidenced by the fact that the *persona*'s personality is based upon contradictory features. The evolution of the monologue itself has a similar importance. One can see a change from direct monologue to indirect monologue; from the speech in the first person, through "Du Lyrik" (speech in the second person) the monologue evolves into "the interior dialogue." The latter is marked by spoken answers to unspoken questions and commands such as: "Put on," "Send," "Tell me."

Thus "A Magic Mountain" can be viewed as a model of the evolution of Miłosz's poetry as a whole. This evolution fluctuates between two major poles: an identification of the speaker with the author, and their total separation. To be more precise, this evolution proceeds from a rather unclear distinction between the author, the speaker, and the hero, through a growing independence of the speaker until the moment when the latter's identity and the degree of his identification with the author become a structural feature of the text. This is characteristic of the majority of Miłosz's poems written in California. (pp. 73-4)

Miłosz creates a new type of lyrical poetry, while retaining the traditional topos of the poet as seer. But—and this is his original invention—this seer not only resembles the author in many respects, but is also uncertain about his identity. We can sense different and unidentified voices within his speech, voices which often cannot be distinguished from his own. The result of this multiplicity is the speaker's interior diffusion. The identity of the *persona* is no longer obvious, but has become a conflict which the reader himself must resolve. In short, this kind of monologue not only provides an exceptional opportunity to see the world from various viewpoints but it has also become a way to restore the poet's ego. This restoration, however, can be as hypothetical and momentary as the very definition of humanhood is hypothetical and momentary. (pp. 74-5)

Aleksander Fiut, "Czesław Miłosz's Search for 'Humanness'," in Slavic and East-European Journal, n.s. Vol. 31, No. 1, Spring, 1987, pp. 65-75.

A. ALVAREZ

Milan Kundera published in [*The New York Review of Books* (April 26, 1984)] an essay called "The Tragedy of Central Europe." The tragedy in question was not so much war and occupation, the massacres, destruction, and humiliation at the hands of ignorant invaders; it was, instead, the loss of what Central Europe once embodied: European culture. Central Europe, for Kundera, was not just a collection of small and vulnerable nations with difficult languages and tragic histories; it was the intellectual and artistic center for the whole of Western civilization and the last stronghold of the intelligentsia, a place where essays counted for more than journalism, and books had more influence than television.

Long before Kundera wrote his article Czeslaw Milosz had described a typical day in the life of Central European man. On August 1, 1944, the day the Warsaw uprising unexpectedly began, Milosz and his wife were caught in heavy gunfire while on their way to a friend's apartment to discuss—what else?—poetry in translation. Face down for hours in a potato field, with machine-gun bullets zipping over his head, Milosz refused to let go of the book he was carrying. After all, it was not his to throw away—it belonged to the library of Warsaw University—and anyway, he needed it—assuming the bullets didn't get him. The book was *The Collected Poems of T. S. Eliot* in the Faber & Faber edition. All in all, it was a very Polish situation: bullets and modernism, the polyglot in the potato field, ashes and diamonds.

Milosz has all the other characteristics of Central European man. He was born in Lithuania, a country that has vanished utterly into the Soviet maw, the bulk of its people transported by Stalin to somewhere beyond the Urals. Like his great Lithuanian predecessor Adam Mickiewicz, Milosz writes in Polish and is fluent in several languages. He has also suffered a typically Central European fate—exile. Half his long life has been spent teaching in Berkeley. In other words, he is a man whose only true home is in books, in language; he carries his country around in his head.

The one language Milosz might be expected to speak is German. He claims, however, to understand only two phrases, *Hände hoch!* and *Alle männer vrraus!,* mementos of the five years he spent in Warsaw during the Nazi occupation. His fellow Polish poets, Zbigniew Herbert and Tadeusz Rozewicz, also got their education during the war; whence the starkness of their poetry—Rozewicz's minimalism, Herbert's austere, ironic morality. But they were both teenagers when the Germans marched in and the terrible years of Hans Frank's Government-General were their high school. Milosz, however, was born in 1911 and had published two books of poetry before 1939, so his style was formed in less savage times and what was lost—"a world gone up in smoke" he called it in a poem ["**A Book in the Ruins**"] written in 1941—concerned him as much as what was being done. . . .

The experience of total war taught him the supreme value not of art but of life itself, of being, of brute survival in a wholly destructive element. . . .

Before the war Milosz's sense of impending doom had earned him the title of "catastrophist." In the face of a catastrophe greater than he could ever have imagined his own early prose appeared to him paltry and self-indulgent. So did his youthful literary ambitions. He peddled a pamphlet of his verse—printed by an underground press and sewn together by his wife-to-be—in the same spirit and for the same motive as he peddled black-market cigarettes and blood sausage: because he was penniless. Poetry had become, in every sense, a means of survival, a matter of life and death.

The poems he wrote during the war and published in 1945 as ***Rescue*** [***Ocalenie***] are a kind of atonement for his earlier frivolity and a reparation made to those who did not survive. (p. 21)

The war released Milosz into an adult world where rhetoric, dogma, and ambition seemed so much childishness. This adult world, however, did not exclude childhood. At the heart of ***Rescue,*** among poems about ruined Warsaw and the destruction of the ghetto, about grief, deprivation, and random death, is a beautiful sequence called, ironically perhaps, "**The World.**" The poems are short, calm, so simple as to seem almost translucent, and their subject is the lost world of Milosz's childhood in the deep Lithuanian countryside (the same world that he later wrote about—less convincingly, I think—in his autobiographical novel, ***The Issa Valley***). In their restrained and tender way, they bring "news / From a world that is bright, beautiful, warm, and free," and they make Milosz's subsequent exile seem inevitable. They confirmed him as a poet whose continuing theme, however stern and "naked" the reality he dealt with, was always that of loss.

In Central Europe the war did not end when what Richard Eberhart called "the fury of aerial bombardment" was over. The Stalinist repression that followed merely translated the problem of survival into different terms: moral instead of physical, personal truth in the face of state-imposed hypocrisy. The kind of poetry imagined by Milosz and those like him—poetry that occupies the moral high ground yet is proof against ridicule and impervious to pretension—became more urgently necessary and correspondingly less easy to publish. "A new, humorless generation is now arising, / It takes in deadly earnest all we received with laughter," Milosz wrote in 1946, when he was a Polish diplomat in New York. Five years later, having decided that historical inevitability and the good of the cause were no longer excuses he was willing to tolerate, he went into exile, first in France, where ***The Captive Mind*** was vilified by Sartre's captive left, then in California. It was not an easy decision. "I was afraid to become an exile," he wrote, "afraid to condemn myself to the sterility and the vacuum that are proper to every emigration." For the poet, whose work partly depends on nuances and allusions that only his countrymen can pick up, the vacuum of exile is inevitably more absolute than for the prose writer:

> Novels and essays serve but will not last.
> One clear stanza can take more weight
> Than a whole wagon of elaborate prose.

But not in translation. Although Milosz supervises the English versions of his work and has been well served by his collaborators, his poems have a richness and sinuous flow that make you believe that a good deal has been lost in translation.

The vacuum of exile exists in many forms, the two foremost being the loss of audience and the loss of subject matter. Eventually, Milosz's poems did filter back into Poland, but not officially until long after he had defected, so for years his effective audience was reduced to bickering and malicious café clubs of fellow exiles. But for a poet whose subject matter was loss, who already considered himself to be in exile, like Adam, from some lost Eden of Lithuanian childhood, physical exile merely strengthened him in his themes and preoccupations. As a result, "the sterility of exile" has never been Milosz's problem. *Czeslaw Milosz: The Collected Poems, 1931-1987* runs to more than five hundred pages and his serious, wondering, adult tone of voice never lapses into affection or self-consciousness.

Perhaps this is because Milosz has always been a poet of place, a marvelous describer of everything from details—"the tiny propellers of a hummingbird"—to atmosphere. It is ironic that he should have written so vividly *in Polish* about California:

> With their chins high, girls come back from the ten-
>   nis courts.
> The spray rainbows over the sloping lawns.
> With short jerks a robin runs up, stands motionless.
> The eucalyptus tree trunks glow in the light.
> The oaks perfect the shadow of May leaves.
> Only this is worthy of praise. Only this: the day.

His long years in the perennial Californian spring, however, have not softened his vision of the world or of his business in it. "Ill at ease in the tyranny, ill at ease in the republic," he says of himself, and from that unease is born his steady concentration on the essentials of the poet's task when everything superfluous has been removed: "gradually, what could not be taken away / is taken. People, countrysides. / And the heart does not die when one thinks it should." All that is left is language. "You were my native land; I lacked any other," he writes in a poem on **"My Faithful Mother Tongue."** And the poem ends, "what is needed in misfortune is a little order and beauty." This need for the beauty and order of poetry as an alternative to the disorder of homelessness has been Milosz's constant theme. At the end of *Unattainable Earth*, published in 1986 and his last book before the *Collected Poems,* there is a poignant poem on the **"Poet at Seventy."** It is followed by a kind of prose footnote that encapsulates his whole life's effort:

> To find my home in one sentence, concise, as if
> hammered in metal. Not to enchant anybody. Not
> to earn a lasting name in posterity. An unnamed
> need for order, for rhythm, for form, which three
> words are opposed to chaos and nothingness.

Milosz's pursuit of order and beauty has been curiously disinterested. Someone once said that 90 percent of the *Oxford Book of English Verse* is about God or death or women. Not so in Milosz's poetry. He is a Catholic and the Church figures in his verse, but less for God's sake than because its rituals recall his early upbringing. As for women: in his whole *Collected Poems* I found only a single love poem—an exceptionally beautiful one called **"After Paradise."** That leaves death, and the truth is that the people who appear in his poems are mostly ghosts from the past. Milosz is a poet of memory, a witness; his real heroes are the dead to whom his poems make reparation. Perhaps exile makes it hard to forget the past and part of its burden for the poet is the need to bring the imagination to bear on people and places that no longer exist. But,

as he explains in a marvelous late poem called **"Preparation,"** living emotions keep getting in the way:

> Still one more year of preparation.
> Tomorrow at the latest I'll start working on a great
>   book
> In which my century will appear as it really was.
> The sun will rise over the righteous and the wicked.
> Springs and autumns will unerringly return,
> In a wet thicket a thrush will build his nest lined
>   with clay
> And foxes will learn their foxy natures. . . .
> No, it won't happen tomorrow. In five or ten years.
> I still think too much about the mothers
> And ask what is man born of woman.
> He curls himself up and protects his head
> While he is kicked by heavy boots; on fire and run-
>   ning,
> He burns with bright flame; a bulldozer sweeps him
>   into a clay pit.
> Her child. Embracing a teddy bear. Conceived in
>   ecstasy.

I haven't learned yet to speak as I should, calmly.

Like other major witnesses of this century—Primo Levi, Zbigniew Herbert—Milosz is a moralist: his work does not pronounce or make judgments; it simply takes as its criterion human decency—disinterested, modest, and not willingly misled:

> poems should be written rarely and reluctantly,
> under unbearable duress and only with the hope
> that good spirits, not evil ones, choose us for their
>   instrument.

(pp. 21-2)

A. Alvarez, "Witness," in The New York Review of Books, *Vol. XXXV, No. 9, June 2, 1988, pp. 21-2.*

C. H. SISSON

[Milosz] has broken into the large public afforded by the English language through a series of translations in which he has himself collaborated. This phenomenon, without parallel in the earlier centuries of Western literature, raises questions about the diffusion and assimilation of literary cultures, and raises them so acutely because Mr. Milosz was formed so deep within the troubled world of Poland in the first half of the century. Educated at the University of Wilno (now Vilnius), he lived through the German occupation and from 1945 to 1950 served in the Polish diplomatic service in Washington and Paris. That is a far cry from the world of the American academic poets with whom he has more recently been associated.

It is to this association that we owe the existence of an English-language Milosz. . . . Mr. Milosz must have learned a lot about his own work in the process, as no doubt his English-speaking translators learned a lot about it, from their very different perspectives. As a translator of some experience, I confess that I have never understood how a poet could attempt to translate a text he has not directly wrestled with in the original, but the situation here is admittedly a special one, in view of the involvement of the author of the original text—an author with, of course, a great familiarity with both the languages involved.

As one himself entirely ignorant of Polish, I can approach

this volume only by taking it at its face value as a contribution to the literature of the English language. From this point of view, I share what seems to be Mr. Milosz's own reservation about the earliest poem here [**"Artificer"**], included "at the insistence" of Robert Hass, "who found in it a 'wild, anarchistic energy.' " I would say that in its present form it is only wild and anarchistic. The second poem [**"The Song"**], dated from the same place, Wilno, three years later (in 1934), is different altogether. It is a piece for several voices that seems to gather within itself a particular location, certainly a vision of a place unspeakably significant to the poet. It is at once troubled and suffused by a great calm: "I am the wind going and not returning."

In a number of these poems of the 1930's we have the "faithful son of the black earth," and things seen on the earth. . . . (p. 6)

The war found the poet already irrevocably oriented, and indeed no poet has ever been known to recover completely from his first findings. **"Campo dei Fiori,"** written in Warsaw in April 1943 and published in an underground anthology that was dedicated, a note in this volume says, "to the Jewish tragedy by poets living 'on the Aryan side,' " is clearly a work of great maturity, and perhaps a crucial one in Mr. Milosz's development. The Campo is the square on which "they burned Giordano Bruno" and "Before the flames had died / the taverns were full again."

The lines place contemporary events, as well as those of 1600, in the context of history, and they are a link with the **"Child of Europe"** who writes bitterly in New York in 1946:

> We, who taste of exotic dishes,
> And enjoy fully the delights of love,
> Are better than those who were buried.

"You swore never to be / a ritual mourner," the poet had told himself a year before, in Warsaw:

> never to touch
> The deep wounds of your nation
> So you would not make them holy.

And never thus to feed the rancors that follow one another through the centuries; but there is never any doubt about the hold these ancient griefs have on him. . . .

"Who serves best does not always understand": the subtlety, modesty and (so far as may be) realism of Mr. Milosz's mind are summed up in this line from a wartime poem. It is because he has persisted in his "unnamed need for order, for rhythm, for form," as all that can be opposed to "chaos and nothingness" that he has left, over so many years now, so valuable a deposit as a poet. It must be admitted that not all the later work fulfills the promise of the earlier. It is interesting, but as the discursive element grows, the tension of the verse as well as the solidity of perception becomes less convincing; it may be because the technique is not equal to the complexity of the material. It could possibly be argued that, as the earlier poems are inspired by Mr. Milosz's native milieu, the poems from the volume titled *From the Rising of the Sun* represent the new cosmopolitan world of California; but, though the new milieu has obviously left its mark, the old loyalties as well as the old skepticisms remain.

With all the matter of this volume, the reader who knows the work only in English must be left with a profound regret that he has no access to the original words and rhythms of the poems. One wonders how Mr. Milosz himself, in the quiet of his own mind, reflects on the deprivation he has suffered in what must always count as an exile. No doubt he is glad to have found such competent and devoted collaborators to help him make his work available to an English-speaking public. But he is, after all, not a writer like Conrad who, through the unlikely medium of the British merchant fleet, found himself so in love with the English language that he chose to write in it rather than in his native Polish. He has continued—and what poet's sense of rhythm could allow him to do otherwise?—in the language of his first days, and a translation, even controlled by the poet himself, is not the original poem. In the extraordinary collaboration that produced this volume, the process is necessarily a willful one, far removed from that unity of word and perception that must have given rise, no doubt more or less involuntarily, to the original text.

Does the volume as we have it belong to the literature of Poland or Lithuania, or of California? To the latter, no doubt, as to its language and techniques. But as to its profound content? To the former, rather, and not merely in the localized poems, but because the poet's mind was made by the history, including the religion, of his native country. It can perhaps be argued that California has drawn its cultures from all the corners of the earth, and that it is to a new synthetic world that Mr. Milosz now intimately belongs. Whether such a synthetic world can really exist, and how boring the new monoculture would be, are large questions, but these novelties can hardly be exemplified in a Polish poet who arrived in Berkeley at the age of 50 and became a professor of Slavic languages and literatures. It is the rootedness of the content, and the relative superficiality of the language and techniques, that make this book so tantalizing. (p. 7)

> *C. H. Sisson, "Old Loyalties, New Language," in* The New York Times Book Review, *June 19, 1988, pp. 6-7.*

IRVING HOWE

In an essay Czeslaw Milosz wrote in 1963, he remarked upon the ability of certain lyrical poets like Boris Pasternak and Julian Tuwim

> to elude the dilemma which for my generation was insoluble but oppressive: for us a lyrical stream, a poetic idiom liberated from the chores of discourse, was not enough, the poet should also be a *thinking* creature; yet in our efforts to build a poem as an "act of mind" we encountered an obstacle: speculative thought is vile, cunning, it eats up the internal resource of a poet from inside.

When the youthful Milosz was writing in Poland during the Second World War, he did not seem to experience this "dilemma" strongly. He wrote out of a persuasion that the work of poets like himself must "contain history." There was no choice; and as far as one can tell from these poems, he did not yet believe that "a lyrical stream" necessarily meant "liberation" from "the chores of discourse." With one major exception, these early poems are sharply phrased lyrics, pungent and bitter in evoking the helplessness that Milosz and others felt during the Nazi occupation of Warsaw. These are the kind of poems that the last century has made familiar, but to which we can still respond directly.

Today, however, in the "conversations" with Milosz that two

admirers have put together (*Conversations with Czeslaw Milosz* by Ewa Czarnecka and Aleksander Fiut), Milosz expresses impatience with these "civic-minded" poems of his youth, just as he has recently bridled against A. Alvarez's description of him in the *New York Review of Books,* as a "witness" to 20th-century Europe. "I rebel against any attempt to reduce me to those poems," says Milosz; and one feels a certain sympathy, for which writer has not "rebelled" (though seldom with any success) against being "typecast"?

Yet the later Milosz, the writer of "speculative thought" drawn to theology and metaphysics, is finally helpless before the presence of his own career. Such lyrics as **"Campo dei Fiori"** (1943) and **"In Warsaw"** (1945) have by now gained an autonomous life. **"Campo dei Fiori"** returns to a carousel at the edge of the Warsaw ghetto where "the bright melody drowned / the salvos from the ghetto wall," and **"In Warsaw"** asks, "Was I born to become / a ritual mourner?" These poems survive in memory, and I don't see how anyone can deny that, as Alvarez wrote, they are the work of a "witness." Which is not to say *only* a "witness."

The major achievement of the early Milosz—a masterpiece, I think—is a rather strange, quasi-pastoral poem called **"The World,"** written, as he notes, "in the style of school primers, in neatly rhymed stanzas," and superbly translated by the author himself. **"The World"** consists of 20 short lyrics imagining—in Warsaw, 1943—"the way the world should be." It offers a vision of utopia, a utopia of ordinariness, almost Biedermeier in its stimulated naïveté, where children go to school ("Crayons rattle among crumbs of a roll"), read picture books (in which a moth "flits over a chariot that speeds through the dust"), Father sits in the library explaining geography to the children, and birds bring news from "a world that is bright, beautiful, warm and free." This Song of Innocence depends crucially on its dateline, "Warsaw 1943:" text and dateline teetering in unstressed poignant irony.

My little anthology of favorite Milosz poems, about two dozen lyrics, might be called Songs of Experience. In part, they are written by the Milosz against whom Milosz now chafes, by the poet "actively involved in history," but in part they are also the work of a poet who detests history and struggles to break away from it. I see this Milosz as a writer who can no more escape his century, however, than flee his skin; who is embroiled in a recurrent, sometimes irritable struggle of the self "not to appear other than I am"; and who keeps returning to a recognition of his own vulnerability.

This Milosz—let's say "my" Milosz— is a lyricist *and* "a meditative poet," if not quite yet a metaphysical one. He is a meditative poet in his lyrics, and these prove to be adequate for carrying his meditation. This Milosz is a poet of deep uneasiness, bruised by the roles into which circumstances thrust him, harried by shame over real or imagined lapses of conduct, struggling with a vanity he cannot quite contain, seeking to achieve the stability of faith while honest enough to admit his distance from it. He writes as a man of divisions ("I am not my own friend / Time cuts me in two"), and with a poet of divisions, even alien divisions, one can feel kinship.

Here are a few instances, spanning six decades, of the Milosz I want to bring to the foreground. His work has been nicely translated into a high-middle English, neither rhetorical nor colloquial, by poets like Robert Haas, Robert Pinsky, and Milosz himself. Reading through the collected poems, I have felt an excessive evenness or sameness of tone in these transla-

tions—mostly plateau, few peaks or valleys—but that must have been how Milosz wanted them, since by now his English is quite as good as that of native speakers.

"Child of Europe" (1946), an instruction to the heartless:

> Love no country: countries soon disappear.
> Love no city: cities are soon rubble . . .
> Do not love people: people soon perish.
> Or they are wronged and call for help.

"In Milan" (1955), a defense against the charge (it now seems ironic) of being "too politicized". . . .

"Veni Creator" (1961), one of the poems in which Milosz reaches toward a faith that seems to come only in spasms:

> Come, Holy Spirit,
> bending or not bending the grasses,
> appearing or not above our heads in a tongue of
>   flame . . .
> I am only a man: I need visible signs.
> I tire easily, building the stairway of abstraction.

"Gift" (1971), a lyric in which the poet, distancing himself from the demons of history, affirms pleasure in simple being. (p. 26)

The Milosz of these poems [and **"On Prayer"** and **"Six Lectures in Verse"**], not the man who wrote them but the figure that appears in them, is a poet in whom "thought fights with thought" (the phrase is W. S. Landor's), memories gnaw at the mind, the homelands of Eastern Europe abut the new lands of California. The self turns to accusation against itself, and at times an oddly Calvinist sensibility breaks into the work of this poet born Catholic. Perhaps strongest of all is the testimony, from Vilna and Warsaw to Paris and Berkeley, of what it has meant to live in this century, entangled (alas) "in history." The moral consciousness encompassing these poems is utterly scrupulous, earning the deepest respect. When Milosz writes about faith he means exactly that, and not any sort of fashionable aestheticizing of either experience or belief.

At least in English translation, Milosz does not emerge as one of those blessedly "natural" poets—like, say, Frost, Amichai, Drummond de Andrade—who can strike an image or sketch a scene that is absolutely right. He does not overpower one through force of imagination or virtuosity of language. He writes thoughtfully, in sustained reflection, in a gentlemanly Polish way.

But there is another Milosz, by some accounts, including his own, the major one. Donald Davie, in a fine little book *(Czeslaw Milosz and the Insufficiency of Lyric),* writes that in mid-career Milosz came to feel "the insufficiency of the lyric mode for registering, except glancingly, the complexity of 20th-century experience." Abandoning what Davie calls "the fixed standpoint of the lyrically meditative 'I,' " Milosz in his later years began to use longer and more complex forms, struggling up "the stairway of abstraction." Milosz himself speaks of wanting "a more spacious form / That would be free from the claims of poetry or prose." What that form might be, is hard to say. (p. 27)

[In] my perhaps constricted reading of Milosz's long poems, I find much unevenness, striking passages next to arid stanzas. And if Milosz's idea really was to surmount "the insufficiency of the lyric," he may not have succeeded, since most of his longer poems break down into lyrical fragments.

But is it really true that the lyric is "insufficient" to speculative thought? It may be insufficient to system-making, or to an extremely rarefied order of abstraction, but to speculative thought? My impression is that Milosz's mind is at its strongest in his lyrics, and that his natural gift, as distinct from the pressing of his will, remains for the lyric, which is an endlessly flexible and tensile mode able to accommodate as much meditative substance as a poet needs or provides. True, by its very nature the lyric lacks extension or duration; but in the work of the great lyric poets there is a compensating interplay of thought among lyrics. And I think Milosz's own work bears this out.

Still, it is only fair to add that my problems with Milosz's longer poems may be due to my deficiencies as a reader, as well as to my distance from his intellectual concerns. Christian theology, gnosticism, Polish history, the writings of Lev Shestov and Simone Weil, all discussed in Milosz's conversations with Czarnecka and Fiut, have been major preoccupations of his later years; if not in the foreground of his long poems, they evidently are somewhere behind them. For a reader like myself, lamentably cool to metaphysics (though not, I hope, indifferent to meditation), these long poems, and the concerns winding through them, result in dryness of voice—or as Milosz himself has said, they "eat up the internal resources of a poet from inside."

And yet Milosz the lyricist breaks through now and again in these long poems. **"City Without a Name"** (1968) is a meditation on the workings of memory, with the poet moving from American locales to Warsaw scenes, and in one splendid section turning to a natural setting that "matches" the colors of the self:

> Yet what is too dazzling and too high is not for me,
> So when the clouds turn rosy, I think of light that
> is level
> In the lands of birch and pine coated with crispy
> lichen,
> Late in autumn, under the hoarfrost when the last
> milk caps
> Rot under the firs and the hounds' barking echoes,
> And jackdaws wheel over the tower of a Basilian
> church.

More engaging still is another long sequence, **"With Trumpets and Zithers"** (1965), a gathering of 11 dithyrambic poems in long, loping Whitmanesque lines ("I address you, my consciousness"). . . . (pp. 27-8)

Here the philosophical or "speculative" motif finds a subdued place in a flow of rhapsodic particulars, and what is, is enough: "a dress crumpled as it was, this way, no other." (p. 28)

> *Irving Howe, "A Velvet Bridge," in* The New Republic, *Vol. 199, No. 14, October 3, 1988, pp. 26-8.*

HELEN VENDLER

Emerson, at the end of his famous "Ode: Inscribed to W. H. Channing," pronounced an epitaph on Poland:

> The Cossack eats Poland,
> Like stolen fruit;
> Her last noble is ruined,
> Her last poet mute.

But Polish literature, Czeslaw Milosz once wrote, "is energy incessantly renewed against all probabilities," and the publication of Milosz's *Collected Poems, 1931-1987* ratifies Emerson's instant revision of his initial despair:

> Straight, into double band
> The victors divide;
> Half for freedom strike and stand;—
> The astonished Muse finds thousands at her side.

The publication and the reception of Milosz's work in Poland assure the astonished Muse of her thousands there as well as abroad. Those of us able to read Milosz only in English know that we can have no idea of what his Polish commentators testify to—his intimate and extensive reworking of current and archaic language in his poetry, and also in his translations of various books of the Bible (the Psalter, Ruth, Ecclesiastes, the Gospel of Mark) into modern Polish.

Greatness in poetry is always marked by unusual felicity and condensation in the handling of language, and, seduced by words, we may take poetry in our own language on its tactile and musical terms without inquiring whether there is a second, inner greatness by which we are being, almost unconsciously, touched. When we read a translation, we are forced to ask what we are admiring, if not language. Reflection on a greatness in poetry which survives the absence of the original words tends to leap instantly to ethical or philosophical praise, and there are reasons to offer that praise to Milosz. But an American reader may perhaps be allowed to linger over the irreproachable construction of these poems. They anchor themselves in the memory in a way so unusual that it cannot be simply the effect of discreet and gifted translations (carried out for the most part by poets, notably Robert Hass, some with Milosz himself as collaborator). Even in English, the poems have a structural contour so strong that it strikes with the force of an originally conceived shape. This contour, in the typical Milosz poem, encloses a still-life of a few poignantly sketched objects, a passage of personal reminiscence (often bitterly self-lacerating or mordantly comic), a rhapsodic hymn to being, some historical or social glimpses, and an epistemological or metaphysical moral. It is in the conjunction of these unlikely bedfellows that the Milosz lyric distinguishes itself. It is as though Milosz were at once Chardin, Rembrandt, Matisse, Géricault, and Cézanne, or—to turn to poetic analogues—as though he were from moment to moment Clare, Whitman, Lawrence, Auden, and Marvell.

As the poet Donald Davie has remarked, the crystalline lyric is a form that Milosz mastered early. He has never abandoned it, but it is also a form that he has consistently pressed beyond, writing sequences of poems, "mixed" sequences of prose and poetry, and poems containing a multitude of voices. . . . Faced with the past's crowd of events, chorus of voices, and throng of perceptions, Milosz undertakes, as his first aesthetic act, an almost inhuman reduction of moments of life to a single gesture or a framed object, which must at the same time be imbued with the weight of almost inexpressible feeling. This, he says, is a religious duty:

> The landscape lacked nothing except glorification.
> Except royal messengers who would bring their
> gifts:
> A noun with an attribute and an inflected verb.

Milosz was raised as a Roman Catholic, and that upbringing is everywhere in his symbols, his thought, and his self-image as a theologian manqué. But he is also given to sensual rapture and to an aesthetics of the erotic. Prey to the headiness of the physical moment, the artist, in Milosz's definition, always retains the appetites and stubborn intensities of the child. . . . The avid child persists in the sensuous obsessiveness of the poet, who must enumerate one by one the ecstasies of touch and vision; and the child's watchful, onlooking stance becomes the poet's dislocating psychological perspective:

> Like Peter Breughel the father he fell suddenly
> While attempting to look back between his spread-
>   apart legs.

It would not be far wrong to say that Milosz's poems have their forcible structural impact because in them the world is seen upside down from a distance, or through a variety of comic and tragic "distorting" lenses (telescope, microscope, field glasses). Another name for these perspectives and lenses is scenic form. A second kind of form is conferred on a poem by the type of sentence in which a perception or a thought is cast. Each sentence has its own philosophical and formal "weight"—from its vocabulary first of all, but also from its length and complexity, its rhythm, and its emphasized grammatical features. (pp. 122, 125)

Milosz may have constructed the obdurate solidity of his lyrics as a bulwark against the chaos and exile of his life. . . . On the other hand, the exceptional stability of his lyric form may be simply a reflection in him of the talent behind his father's profession, engineering.

Emotionally, by its compressed passion, a Milosz poem obtrudes a fiery screen—almost the heat of the Cherubim—between us and its struts and girders. It seems a violation to look into the underpinnings of such poetry. However, if we are to explain how Milosz makes his poems "real," we can say that the structural supports for any given poem must (in the Miloszian scheme) comprise sensual, aesthetic, metaphysical, and ethical elements. For Milosz, these categories, when we first received them in infancy, existed in primal interrelation, and are therefore, taken inseparably, exactly what we mean by the "real." Lacking one of them, a poem would seem hollow, as would life. . . . (p. 125)

This politically defiant and hardwon poetics is voiced in **"One More Day,"** which bears as its sensual ornaments the voices of birds, iridescent morning light, a peach-colored sky meeting dark-blue mountains, and a columnar, green-crowned tree—the ephemera of "one more day" in Berkeley (where Milosz is professor emeritus of Slavic literature). The conduct of the poem, as we see it pass from the mother's arms to the idea of beauty, thence to the morning light and the argument for the inseparable connection of beauty with knowledge and being, is characteristic of Milosz as he strides between the phenomenal and the Platonic, defending the middle air of the aesthetic as the continuum between the senses and the mind.

The "unattainable earth" of Milosz's passionate senses is finally incommensurate with language, yet, as he says in an epitaph for himself and his poetic generation in Europe, "great was that chase with the hounds for the unattainable meaning of the world." For an American reader, the European contexts of the collected poems come to life in the personally reticent but intellectually electric volumes of essays that Milosz has published between 1953 and the present: *The Captive Mind* (1953), *Native Realm* (1968), *The Emperor of the Earth* (1977), *Visions from San Francisco Bay* (1982), *The Witness of Poetry* (1983), and *The Land of Ulro* (1984).

These have now been supplemented by the more informal *Conversations with Czeslaw Milosz,* by Ewa Czarnecka and Aleksander Fiut, translated by Richard Lourie. The conversations take up, in order, the life, the books, and more general ideas—philosophical, religious, and aesthetic. Milosz's contorted theology is here, emphasizing the pain, catastrophe, and injustice of the world, yet professing a faith—oddly compounded from Marx's belief in the power of man to change history and a Christian assertion of ultimate justice—that human intuitions of value, preserved by virtuous human action, by art, and by just institutions, establish in history an absolute by which all human endeavor is judged. Always, in these conversations, the metaphysical is saved by the memory of the physical:

> What do we have to build a world of our own
> from—the flutter and twitter of language, lipstick,
> gauze, and muslin, which are to protect us from the
> galactic silence.

This may be the first time that lipstick and the galactic silence have coexisted in a reasonable sentence; and it is just this vertiginous turn from close-focus tenderness to Mt. Palomar chill that makes Milosz's ambitious poetic structures so memorable. In the transcribed conversations, Milosz is deprived of his lyric honeycombs, but his epigrammatic wit, his scorn of cant, his historical reference are all present. The conversations naturalize us to the Miloszian atmosphere—its myths, its recollections, its European moment.

In fact, Milosz's world is half myth, half recollection. Mythical counters from his Catholic inheritance—God, the World, the Flesh, and the Devil—play powerful roles in the poetry as he re-creates his youth in Lithuania and Poland. The "untranslatable" parts of his poetic work (some of which have now been translated) linger over the Lithuanian and Polish historical past in an effort of resuscitation, inventory, and commemoration which must be inestimably precious to Polish readers, the more so because the poems (as a Polish critic like Stanislaw Baranczak can tell us) are labors of linguistic memory as well. In a previously untranslated segment (**"Lauda"**) of the sequence **"From the Rising of the Sun,"** Milosz writes:

> Who except me has pondered the life of Jasiulis
> And his wife, and their son Gregory, and their four
>   daughters,
> And Matulis, Pranialis, Ambrozej, and their sisters
>   Polonija,
> Rajna, Dosjuda, and Bujkis? . . .
> Who sifts in his hand their ashes, changed now into
>   words?

Milosz feels a survivor's duty to the dead, since the prewar environment of which he is one of the last inhabitants has almost vanished. He has said that when he went to Salem, Massachusetts, he recognized in the architecture and implements of the seventeenth-century houses precisely the environment of his childhood ("In Salem, by a spinning wheel / I felt I, too, lived yesterday"); he is himself a living bridge from the almost medieval rural life of Europe before the First World War to the postmodern life of California.

Like Milton before him, Milosz has wanted to understand the whole culture of his era, and to see what can be truly said of our life in the vocabulary available to this century. His poetry faces up not only to moral evil but to the irremediable physical evil of the universe. Milosz admits the present powerlessness of literal images of an eternal afterlife (whether Heaven or Hell). He substitutes for those lost images the eternal "now" of memory and art. And yet the elegiac vein in Milosz is powerfully corrected by a sardonic and contemptuous laughter. . . . In a famous passage from a poem of 1961 (**"Throughout Our Lands"**) Milosz presents with comic grotesquerie his own perspective on the world:

> If I had to tell what the world is for me
> I would take a hamster or a hedgehog or a mole
> and place him in a theater seat one evening
> and, bringing my ear close to his humid snout,
> would listen to what he says about the spotlights,
> sounds of the music, and movements of the dance.

Even here, we can see the elements of the Miloszian poetic construct: the moral meaning ("what the world is for me"), the lens that distorts and thereby renews perspective (the rodent eye), the distance from the spectacle (the theater seat), the foregrounding of expressive language ("what he says"), the items and rhythms of the *theatrum mundi* (spotlights, music, dance), and, chiefly, the oddity of the poet's viewpoint. No other poet has wanted to bring ear to snout for epistemological information.

Milosz often treats his own life with the same economical contempt he bestows on others. . . . And yet, when occasion demands, he can combine scorn for his own ambition with veneration for the powers of art. He may begin [as in **"Preparation"**] in hubris:

> Tomorrow at the latest I'll start working on a great
>   book
> In which my century will appear as it really was.

But this ambition, ironically represented, falters before a welter of anguished emotions not yet disciplined to form. . . . [The] poet's preparation embraces an enormous historical ambition ("my century . . . as it really was"); a lifelong linguistic preparation (symbolized glancingly by the Biblical allusion to "man born of woman"); a sensual initiation that can speak knowledgeably of the utmost reaches of bodily sensation ("conceived in ecstasy"); a storehouse of personal memory ("embracing a teddy bear"); self-analysis ("I still think too much"); and an instinctual revulsion from evil—torture, napalm, indifferent mass burial. All the preparations are to be brought into the finality of art-speech—that "calm" of aesthetic poise achieved when every linguistic weight and counterweight is in place. Here one feels that poise in the balance of "tomorrow . . . No, it won't happen tomorrow;" in the shocking slippage from the universal "man" born of woman to the particular body being kicked, set afire, bulldozed; in the cinematic reverse from corpse to ovum ("bulldozed" to "conceived"); and in the supplanting of the speech-pitch of horror by the moral effort of making art (to "speak calmly").

Anyone curious about the larger aesthetic effects in Milosz can see how often pity and indignation struggle in him with the effort to balance all, bring all to mind. The unspeakable invention of war—which will surely appear one day as inconceivable as public drawing and quartering—must be rendered, not propagandized against; and Milosz's incomparable

gift for the astonishing detail (the bright flame of the body, the baby with the teddy bear) is his best weapon against cliché. His brief vignettes of the European past have some of the theatrical chiaroscuro of painting, as his spotlight picks out a hat adorned with one red plume, a silk bathing suit, a "horseflesh-colored city in ruins." The very first poem in the **Collected Poems**—**"Artificer,"** written when Milosz was twenty—defines the artist's work as the detaching of such elements from the continuum of temporal experience and their recombination into the new constellation of a poem. . . . The effect here is rather strained: chop a building open, see society (art, children, violence), feel emotion, extract the honey of import. Nonetheless, the poem betrays the young Milosz's restless voyeurism of the whole—his wish to be a poet of society rather than of nature alone—and it suggests as well his distinctive combination of thought and sensual expectancy: pensive, he looks at honey.

Milosz's **Collected Poems** is an enthralling and commanding book. What it must mean to a Polish reader I can only imagine. Its great poems, already known to many, stand in imposing array: **"The World," "Incantation," "From the Rising of the Sun," "The Separate Notebooks," "The Garden of Earthly Delights."** The poetry becomes, as Milosz ages, less choral and incantatory, more historical and precise. The sobriety of Milosz's style (based not on metaphor but on the telling detail) seems to have increased as his narratives of penitence, pride, and ecstasy have become sparer. I can imagine that each period of his writing life will have its advocates. What is certain is that many of his poems have already passed into the canon of poetry in English—that is to say, they are admired and imitated by poets. **"The World"** is one of these; another is a chant called **"Incantation"** —Milosz's hymn to human thought and human art. . . . [The opening and close of this poem] exhibit Milosz's enchanting capacity for mixing religion and fairy tale, the prophetic and the humorously tender, the personal and the liturgical. . . . (pp. 125-30)

One does not go to Milosz for relaxed domesticity, social brilliance, indolent luxury, or fantastic arabesques; no poet's work can be as large as the imagination. But he is one who knows the "mountain ridges in the heavenly forest / Where, beyond every essence, a new essence waits." These pages unfold a new essence with each new title. The **Collected Poems** makes me want to read a good book on Milosz by a Polish-speaking poet—one who will describe to me not those structural and focussing powers visible even in translation but the gracious, denunciatory, nostalgic, and sublime powers of Milosz's inventive Polish. At this moment, even though he has received the Nobel Prize for his poetry, Milosz is known chiefly as a political exile, a polemicist, a memoirist, and an analyst of the Marxist state. In time, the poems will eclipse the rest. (p. 130)

Helen Vendler, "Sentences Hammered in Metal," in The New Yorker, *Vol. LXVI, No. 36, October 24, 1988, pp. 122, 125-30.*

Georges Perec

1936-1982

French novelist, dramatist, poet, scriptwriter, translator, and nonfiction writer.

An author of experimental literature, Perec was among the most innovative members of the Ouvroir de Littérature Potentielle (Oulipo), or Workshop of Potential Literature, a Parisian literary society founded in 1960 by novelist Raymond Queneau and mathematician François LeLionnais with the goal of combining mathematical and literary concepts. This group is devoted to inventing precise, often constrictive prose forms and procedures based upon structures that supersede aesthetic concerns. By using anagrams, acrostics, and algorithms, among other devices, Perec sought to create literary puzzles in which plot, characters, and situations relate directly to the craft of creating fiction. Italo Calvino, an Italian novelist who shared similar interests with Oulipo, praised Perec as "one of the most singular literary personalities in the world, a writer who resembled absolutely no one else."

The son of Polish Jews who had emigrated to France in the 1920s, Perec became an orphan during World War II when his father was killed in the German invasion of France in 1940 and his mother was deported to the Nazi concentration camp of Auschwitz in 1943. Raised by relatives, Perec studied sociology in college and began publishing reviews in literary journals at the age of twenty. His earliest fiction, written prior to his membership in Oulipo, reflects his desire to explore a wide variety of literary forms. Perec's first novel, *Les choses: Une histoire des années soixante* (1965; *Les Choses: A Story of the Sixties*), which Robert D. Cottrell described as a "kind of sociological survey," uses a minimalistic documentary style to depict a young middle-class couple who become obsessed with material and luxury items despite their limited income. Black humor and intrusive narration characterize Perec's next novel, *Quel petit vélo à guidon chromé au fond de la cour?* (1966), in which a group of young Parisian intellectuals attempt to keep a friend from serving in Algeria's war for independence. *Un homme qui dort* (1967), written entirely in the second person singular tense, describes the surreal experiences of a young social misfit who analyzes various models of behavior before rejecting the entire world.

Perec became a member of the Workshop of Potential Literature in 1967. While admitting the adoption of technical restrictions to be entirely gratuitous, members of Oulipo insisted that formal constraints could provide fresh literary perspectives on overused conventions and should be embraced for their potential as art. Although related to Dadaism and Surrealism, Oulipo relies more upon closely defined structures than chance association. An example of Oulipian procedure is the "n plus seven" method invented by French poet Jean Lescure, in which the nouns of a preexisting text are replaced with the seventh nouns that follow their entries in a dictionary. According to the "n plus seven" method, Shakespeare's famous soliloquy from *Hamlet* begins: "Whether 'tis nobler in the mineral kingdom to suffer the slipcovers and arsenates of outrageous Forty Hours. . . ." In his first Oulipian novel, *La disparition* (1969), Perec revives the ancient form of the lipogram, avoiding the vowel "e," the most com-

mon letter in the French language. Perec's repression of the character "e" produces life-and-death conflicts in the novel's central narrative; for example, a bartender explodes while trying to enunciate the French word for eggs, "oeufs," which retains the sound of the pronunciation of the letter "e." In *La disparition,* a search for a missing bachelor leads to a château where various accidents, intrigues, and crimes that occur are revealed to stem from a mysterious curse. Harry Mathews commented: "What began as an apparently sterile and arbitrary device has turned into a dramatic enactment of our inescapable, paradoxical, hopeless struggle with language." In his subsequent novel, *Les revenentes* (1972), Perec excludes all vowels except "e" from his text.

Perec's novel *W; ou, Le souvenir d'enfance* (1975; *W; or, The Memory of Childhood*), according to Paul J. Schwartz, "has inspired remarkably diverse interpretations, as a condemnation of the capitalist system, as an oedipal search for identity, and as an affirmation of Jewish identity and an allegory of [Palestine Liberation Organization] fanaticism." Drawing on the styles of such diverse literary figures as Marcel Proust, William Faulkner, and Franz Kafka, Perec juxtaposes personal reminiscence with recreated childhood fantasy. The autobiographical portions of *W,* written in roman typeface, revolve around Perec's dislocated memories of his childhood.

The novel's fantastical chapters, presented in italic typeface, center on a French army deserter who escapes to Germany during World War II by using the papers and name of a missing child who resembles Perec. Requested to search for the child, the deserter becomes fascinated with an island in the Tierra del Fuego called W, where sadistic contests involving physical hardships serve as an allegory of Nazism. In the poetry collection *La clôture et autres poèmes* (1976), Perec uses a variety of literary, textual, alphabetical, and mathematical constraints to produce, among other experiments, long palindromes and bilingual poems that may be read in either French or English.

In Perec's most popular and acclaimed work, *La vie mode d'emploi* (1978; *Life: A User's Manual*), the scaffolding of a Paris apartment building serves as the literal structure for the narrative. Focusing on a dying painter who has created a large fresco of the building with its outer facade removed, Perec minutely describes the objects and personal history of the inhabitants of each room. In detailing one room per section in a total of ninety-nine chapters, Perec also sketches the path of a chess piece that eventually covers all spaces on the chessboard. A similar Oulipian enterprise is attempted by Percival Bartlebooth, a millionaire whose boredom with wealth leads him to study painting for twenty years, to spend another twenty years painting pictures of seasides and ports, and to have the pictures cut into jigsaw puzzles by a resident of his apartment building. After spending his remaining years attempting to reassemble the jigsaws, Bartlebooth returns each completed puzzle to the location that it depicts; once there, the painting's image is dissolved. Paul Auster declared: "Like many of the other stories in *Life,* Bartlebooth's weird saga can be read as a parable (of sorts) about the efforts of the human mind to impose an arbitrary order on the world."

THE TIMES LITERARY SUPPLEMENT

That the solipsistic attitude to life of *le nouveau roman* may after all be specious and on the way out is suggested by this year's major literary awards in France, of which only one . . . is representative of this dead-end genre. . . .

[Perec's] first novel, **Les Choses,** subtitled *une histoire des années 60,* was the choice for the Prix Renaudot. . . . The author, M. Perec, is a twenty-nine-year-old medical research worker educated in sociology, who makes capital use of his background to describe a young student couple in their mid-twenties, Jerome and Sylvie, turned market researchers of a sort, in their relation to the world of things: furniture, clothing, the whole gamut of manufactured luxury objects. But before they reach thirty, driven by that old bogey of bourgeois prosperity, conformity, still riches-minded, they go to Tunisia where Sylvie takes a teaching post. They soon miss the social and physical amenities they enjoyed in Paris, however, and return to what is for them "semi-poverty" as the heads of an advertising agency in Bordeaux. In detailing their total preoccupation with affluence and the acquisition of inanimate possessions ("They loved wealth more than life"), the novelist is indicting the Gaullist Consumer Society from which non-material interests and aspirations of a higher (?), more spiritual order are vanishing. This sad, thoroughly modern *éducation sentimentale* is the most significant example of "the

(collective) non-fiction novel" that has been published in France. The spare, documentary style finds apt expression in the description of the ideal apartment carefully culled from [the magazines] *Elle* and *Jardin des Modes,* at the beginning of the book.

"Father-Frustrations," in The Times Literary Supplement, *No. 3339, February 24, 1966, p. 147.*

THE NEW YORKER

The couple sketched in this wistful, brilliant, and accurate short novel [*Les Choses: A Story of the Sixties*] . . . happen to be French, but they are true for any country in the affluent West. Jérôme and Sylvie are romantically in love with possessions, and they weave dreams of wealth and happiness around stylish knickknacks that they either own or covet. Their youth passes amid fantasies of acquisition and ends with practical surrender to dull security. M. Perec leaves it to the reader to decide whether the couple's destruction is due to that peculiar idealism "taste," or to greed, or to social snobbery, or to a wicked society. The work succeeds as much because of the author's restraint as because of his original, profound, and humane concept.

A review of "Les Choses: A Story of the Sixties," in The New Yorker, *Vol. XLIV, No. 14, May 25, 1968, p. 158.*

PETER LENNON

I have never felt it to be a particular virtue, in describing a world in which objects have come to have an obsessive and tyrannical power (thanks to advertising), for the writer to reduce his scope to a monotonous litany of spiritless gestures or a catalogue of items. If urbanized man can be seen as the depressed victim of our consumer society, there is no reason why the novel should be. Or if so, it's nothing to celebrate.

If you can no longer walk a city street without being ambushed by insistent suggestions to BUY, . . . then it is more a subject for the complex hysterics of [Nathanael West's novel] *Day of the Locust* than a low-powered, cautious essay like **Les Choses.** . . .

Les Choses won the fashionable Prix Renaudot, which guaranteed it an extensive readership largely among those who only read the annual "literary prizes." People like its heroes, a young Parisian couple, Jerome and Sylvie, market-research workers obsessed with the doubtful joys of possessing, not necessarily beautiful objects, but *objets à la page,* as indicated by such publications as *Elle* and *L'Express.* . . . Their agitation and discontent is all the more intense since they do not have the income to satisfy these artificially stimulated needs. They are the victims, but—Perec makes it clear—not really the dupes, of the consumer society. Like most addicts, they know they are wasting their lives.

It is a genuine theme of the sixties. But Perec's insight into the problem is not rewarding enough. Deprived of dialogue which could give direct signals of the state of mind of his characters, the author makes the fatal mistake of repeatedly telling you what you are supposed to think about them. More than once, you have the feeling he does not understand them sufficiently. In this world, of what the French would describe as "Americanized Parisians," there is a complex fabric of confusion and anguish which this novel barely touches.

> Peter Lennon, "English Shoes," in The New York Times Book Review, *June 16, 1968, p. 32.*

ROBERT D. COTTRELL

The Things designated in the title [of *Les Choses: une histoire des années soixante*] are strung along on the most tenuous of story lines: we learn that a young middle-class Parisian couple works for an advertising agency and take marketing polls. The novel itself is a kind of sociological survey of their colorless daily lives and an enumeration of the fashionable and snobbish Things they wish to possess. . . . Neither rich enough to buy their Things, nor alive enough to create their own happiness, they are bored. Their brief attempt to escape by going to Tunisia proves a failure, because they take their boredom with them. . . . And Perec's dry and lifeless style, almost a caricature of Robbe-Grillet's style, does not make this "vie sans rien" any more interesting to the reader than it is to the limp couple.

As in most sociological studies, there are elements of truth in *Les Choses:* no doubt, the dream of Perec's couple embodies the myth of things in a consumer-oriented society; and surely most of us recognize the truth contained in that old adage, "Men do not live by tape recorders and Brooks Brothers shirts alone." But these nuggets of truth are so self-evident that, unless vitalized by a genuinely creative imagination, they seem feckless and, worse still, dull.

> Robert D. Cottrell, in a review of "Les Choses: une histoire des années soixante," in The Modern Language Journal, *Vol. LIV, No. 7, November, 1970, p. 531.*

E. SELLIN

There are obviously limits to the whimsicality with which words may be used and yet taken seriously, but there is a certain serious charm in those texts which test the credible limits of whimsicality. Such a text is Perec's *La clôture et autres poèmes.*

To understand what Perec . . . intends in this collection, it is necessary to consult what he calls the "Bibliographie" at the end of the work. It tells the history and definition of the various short segments of the collection. Many of the texts are what Perec terms "heterogrammatical" and are characterized by a fragmented syntax. The ambiguous juxtapositions, the mysterious insights afforded by the typographical *ulcérations* (to borrow one of Perec's titles) and the bilingual puns afford us a wonderful showcase of linguistic flutter-bys.

One short sequence of poems, entitled **"Trompe l'oeil,"** though less dense than such texts as **"La clôture"** or **"Palindrome,"** is literally and figuratively central to this collection. It is a suite of six brief poems composed entirely in capital letters (presumably to obviate the necessity of compromising accents in French) and which may be read as French and/or English. (pp. 434-35)

Ultimately, if these texts have some truth, it lies in the phoneme and the word-symbol and not in the sentence or paragraph. But then, who is to determine what unit of poetry is

that with the highest priority? I know what Perec's words mean even if I do not understand his book. (p. 435)

> E. Sellin, in a review of "La clôture et autres poèmes," in World Literature Today, *Vol. 55, No. 3, Summer, 1981, pp. 434-35.*

HARRY MATHEWS

The reissuing last year of Georges Perec's fourth novel *La Disparition* rescued a very intriguing work from the shades of unavailability. The book tells a funny, mysterious, bafflingly complex tale, in the course of which all the main characters disappear one by one. First to go is the Parisian bachelor Anton Voyl, whose obsession with an enigmatic motif in a rug he owns propels him into hallucination, insomnia, a life of fantasies, even a desperate resort to surgery, at the end of which he vanishes without a trace. Several friends and two detectives begin examining the circumstances of his disappearance. All eventually gather in Agincourt, in a chateau belonging to a certain Augustus B. Clifford, and there uncover a concatenation of accidents, plots, and crimes stemming from a terrible curse, of which they themselves have been designated as future victims. (p. 4)

The final sentence of *La Disparition* reads: "Dying marks this book's conclusion." The novel begins:

> Four cardinals, a rabbi, a Masonic admiral, a trio of insignificant politicos in thrall to an Anglo-Saxon multinational inform inhabitants by radio and by mural displays that all risk dying for want of food.

These two sentences share a peculiarity, one which remains constant through the book's three hundred pages: they lack the letter of the alphabet that occurs most frequently in French as in English, the vowel e. Perec's novel is an example of lipogram, a procedure, dating back to classical times, by which a writer voluntarily excludes one or more letters from his resources. Whatever the point of using such a procedure in the past, it seems natural to ask why, in our day, a novelist would want to forego all the words in the language containing an e. (pp. 4-5)

A first clue to Perec's intentions is his membership in the Ouvroir de Litterature Potentielle, or Oulipo. Founded in 1961 by Raymond Queneau and Francois LeLionnais, both of whom wanted to combine mathematics and experimental writing, this Paris-based group is dedicated to the creation and recreation of constrictive literary structures—that is, of forms and procedures so imperious that no writer using them can avoid (at least initially) subordinating his personal predilections to their requirements. The difference between constrictive and ordinary forms (such as rhyme and meter) is essentially one of degree. Composing a good sonnet may be as difficult as ever, but not because of the sonnet form itself. On the other hand, writing a series of ten sonnets all of whose first lines are interchangeable (this gives a possible total of 10 x 10 sonnets,) whose second lines are no less interchangeable (multiply by another 10,) and where such interchangeability is maintained throughout the fourteen lines of the ten original poems, thus creating the cosmic potential of 1014 sonnets in all, is a task in which the formal act itself acquires an inescapable primacy. It was the realization of this very task— Queneau's *100,000 Billion Poems*—that precipitated the founding of the Oulipo. . . .

An easily overlooked fact is that the Oulipo is not a literary school. It produces no literary works; it does not claim that constrictive structures are the writer's salvation. It proposes such structures only for the sake of their *potentiality*. The name of the group means "workshop of potential literature." . . . In isolating new or neglected structures in experimental conditions, the Oulipo's aim is to provide methods that writers can use according to their needs. To the Oulipo, the value of a structure is its ability to produce results, not the quality of those results, which will be demonstrated elsewhere, if at all. The most the Oulipo ever does is supply one or a few examples of each structure, to show that it works. These examples are intentionally "frivolous": they are meant to avoid prejudicing the structure's future yield; no one should be able to mistake them for models. . . .

[Queneau] observed that the Oulipo's work constituted an *anti-hasard,* an anti-chance. In mathematics, chance does not exist; and Queneau the mathematician felt that whenever a writer resorted to chance—either directly or by relying on such notions as automatism, spontaneity, or inspiration—he risked trapping himself in systems of "low-level regularity." (By analogy, Queneau said that when you try and think up an irregular series of numbers out of your head, it invariably turns out to follow a rather ordinary pattern.) For the Oulipo, even an apparently mechanical structure will, when it is deliberately chosen, offer an escape from the "low-level" systems that impose themselves on us without our knowing it. . . .

While the Oulipo itself creates no true works of literature, it would be surprising if those of its members who are practicing writers did not sometimes test the group's discoveries in their own undertakings. It was, after all, the existence of Queneau's *100,000 Billion Poems* that inspired the Oulipo at its beginnings. The most notable of such works are probably Jacques Roubaud's ϵ in poetry, and in prose (aside from *La Disparition* itself) Italo Calvino's *The Castle of Crossed Destinies* and Perec's monumental *La Vie Mode d'Emploi.* . . . *La Disparition,* in which Perec creates a book-length work of fiction out of a particularly unpromising and arduous constrictive procedure, is a fascinating example of the poetic functioning of Oulipian ideas.

Jacques Roubaud says that constrictive form has three effects: it defines the way a text is to be written; it supplies the mechanism that enables the text to proliferate; ultimately, it gives that text its meaning. His statement reads like a summary of Perec's approach to *La Disparition.* His problem was: having reduced my vocabulary this viciously, what do I do now? There is no value inherent in the product of a constrictive form, except one: being unable to say what you normally would, you must say what you normally wouldn't. Without e, what has become unspeakable and what remains to be said? Perec's genius was to make this question the subject of his fiction; to make it his fiction. Instead of trying to inhibit the inhibiting constriction, he expanded it into absolute law. In Oulipian terms, he transformed a syntactic construction into a semantic one.

The first disappearance in the novel is one imagined by Anton Voyl. A captain in mufti goes into a bar and orders a porto flip. The barman refuses to make one. The captain insists. After desperate protestations, the barman dies, because he has no. . . . To make a porto flip, you need eggs: the word the barman cannot speak is *oeufs,* which to a French ear sounds the same as the letter e. An e is not only a forbidden letter but a forbidden egg; not only an egg but a bird (born from an egg.) E is the number 3 (because of the three bars in E) and the number 5 (e is the fifth letter of the alphabet; there is no chapter 5.) E is, of course, *The Purloined Letter.* E is absence, in many ways, not only all manner of holes and voids but *le blanc,* meaning blank, also meaning white: and e through this whiteness becomes not only Moby Dick but (via the Latin *albus*) Albion and Albania. (If white e is Moby Dick, three-pronged E is a harpoon.) Finally, because in this book e decides matters of life and death, e becomes king (a "white dead king"), the Pied Piper, the vengeful father—the terrible Bearded Man who in his ultimate incarnation is none other than the author.

Perec has drawn from his constrictive procedure not only the material but the dynamic of his story. It isn't (for example) merely that Augustus B. Clifford's son Douglas *Haig* (the last name in its French pronunciation sounding like egg), meets his doom when, playing the Commendatore in *Don Giovanni,* he is costumed in white plaster to become his own egg-like self . . .: all the characters in the book are in flight from a similar doom; every event concerning them involves the agency of an Enigma that will destroy them *whether it is resolved or not.* One protagonist describes this enigma with her dying breath as *la maldiction*—malediction minus its e becoming "ill-speech." An onlooker comments: evil is incarnate in the act of speech; the more we say, the more we become victims of what we can't say; salvation can only mean enunciating one word that would dissolve our problem along with our existence, and that word is taboo. There is no way out. In the last chapter, a character confronted with a text that is a double lipogram (without a or e) says: "Not only no a's but no—" and immediately, on the verge of this impossible truth-telling, swells like a balloon and explodes. He leaves behind him only a minute pile of gray ash.

Those ashes are the book we have been reading: a gray of black vanishing into white; and they are The Book. By the end of *La Disparition,* e has become whatever is unspoken or cannot be spoken—the unconscious, the reality outside the written work that determines it and that it can neither escape nor master. E has become what animates the writing of fiction; it is the fiction of fiction. What began as an apparently sterile and arbitrary device has turned into a dramatic enactment of our inescapable, paradoxical, hopeless struggle with language. The bearded Perec knows that, even as Author, he cannot escape his own law, which decrees that once his children are dead, the father must die.

In a postscript to his story, Perec says that he began writing *La Disparition* on a bet, that after becoming entertained and then fascinated by his project, he decided to try and make a useful contribution to the creating of fiction. Starting from the current notion that the *significant* has absolute primacy, he would attempt to expand the writer's knowledge of the nature of his materials. The seriousness and brilliance with which he realized this ambition produced a book that is not only funny, stimulating, and, in its prodigious digressions on the duplicity of language, extraordinarily moving, but one which must remain untranslated: not because of the technical obstacle (not all that hard a one,) but because an indissoluble unity determines every facet of the book (even, on occasion, its punctuation.) The novel could only be recreated in a foreign language by inventing new characters, new events, new texture; by writing a brand-new book. In this, too, *La Disparition* can serve as provocation and exemplar. (p. 5)

Harry Mathews, in a review of "La Disparition," in The American Book Review, *Vol. 3, No. 6, September-October, 1981, pp. 4-5.*

MICHAEL BISHOP

Georges Perec is a rather prolific and versatile writer. The pieces presented in [*La Clôture et autres poèmes*] are texts published in the main in review (*Change, Les Nouvelles littéraires*) or in special limited editions often accompanied by photographs or other work by contemporary artists.

To enter the world of *La Clôture* is to enter a space of at once limited, somewhat closed, and yet potential and distinctly feasible appeal. The space is cerebral, essentially unemotional, and unaesthetic. It is that zone enamoured of crossword puzzle and scrabble enthusiasts, though at times more literary in its aspirations, a zone eminently literal, textual, indeed alphabetical, centered upon the *gramma* and tending frankly, boldly, even merrily towards the "lipogrammatic" or what Perec also terms the "heterogrammatic," towards an *écriture* always somehow *autre,* not quite what it appears to be. . . . [In] his **"Histoire de lipogramme,"** which appeared a few years ago in Oulipo's *La Littérature potentielle* (1973), Perec, while endeavoring to shift appreciation of lipogrammatic texts from the severely critical or dismissive to the basically positive and the crucially aware, nevertheless is drawn to stress the notion of minimality. . . . (p. 441)

The texts we are invited to read—palindromes of great virtuosity, stretching to five thousand letters; illusionist *franglais* poems, which may be read either as English or French texts; and, for the most part, heterogrammatic-lipogrammatic poems offering varyingly consistent adherence to an array of consonantal-vocalic models—conform to a poetics of minimality and yet crucial worth, a poetics of play and yet discipline. They cannot be judged according to the criteria we may apply to writers such as Reverdy, Perse, Proust, or Sarraute, for they lack the aesthetic and affective charge that gives the work of these writers their particular depth and urgency. And yet it is not altogether inappropriate to speak of Perec's *La Clôture* in the context of the work of a Beckett or a Ponge, even a Mallarmé at moments.

For despite the profound differences between them all, Perec maintains a residual contact with them—and indeed others such as the surrealists, only to think of the modern period—precisely for his insistence upon factors such as the intellectuality of man's linguistic activity, its intricate, ludic, yet not quite ludicrous character, language as pastime, as ephemeral, re-creative and recreational *parole, objeu* rather than quasi-transcendent medium of attaining to the real, and so on. If, then, Perec betrays no anguish, no evident deeply ontological sensitivity—and the *distance* from Beckett, Ponge, and Mallarmé becomes immediately apparent again—this, ultimately, does not mean that these poems are at a total remove from such considerations—how could they be?—but rather that they articulate themselves at the intersection of minimal sense and significance, asceticism and simple fun, nothingness and smiling, stubborn ingeniousness. (pp. 441-42)

Michael Bishop, in a review of "La Clôture et autres poèmes," in The French Review, *Vol. LV, No. 3, February, 1982, pp. 441-42.*

WARREN F. MOTTE, JR.

More than any other aspect of Perec's work, the metaliterary element remains constant, and strongly so, from text to text. His writings demonstrate a lucid awareness of their literary character and call attention with insistence to themselves as works of literature.

Indeed, Perec alludes frequently to his own texts in both temporal directions (to anterior texts and works in progress); he refers to himself as author and to the literary goals to which he aspires. He also cites and alludes to other texts as well, referring to writers from Sophocles to Spillane. Apart from their obvious role in the metaliterary commentary, these allusions serve another, less evident purpose: they function as cues intended to direct the receptive process. They encourage the reader to receive Perec's texts in a certain manner, to situate his works hierarchically according to the tenor of the allusions to other texts and writers whose situations in the literary hierarchy are more stable. (p. 114)

From the outset, Perec's textual worlds are dominated by literature; even on the intradiegetic level, literary concerns remain manifest. In his first major text, **Les Choses,** the principal characters, Jérôme and Sylvie, are presented as *readers.* Allusions to their books and other readings recur frequently in the text, participating in the pattern of metaliterary commentary. In Perec's second novel, *Quel petit vélo à guidon chromé au fond de la cour?*, the pattern continues, with references to Henri Pollack's "chers bouquins." References to books abound again in both **Un Homme qui dort** and **La Disparition.** In the latter text, the characters' literary interests are carried even further: Anton Voyl is writing a novel, and Aloysius Swann kills Savorgnan with a Smith-Corona, having rejected, one supposes, the more traditional (if in some respects no more deadly) Smith and Wesson.

In all four of these novels, then, the principal characters and the milieu in which they circulate are presented as cultured and, more specifically, literate. Alongside these general references to literature exist abundant citations from and allusions to individual writers, philosophers, historians and critics. (p. 115)

[The] domain upon which Perec draws for citation and allusion is very broad indeed. [His] references and borrowings range from the minimal, the seemingly offhand, to the maximal. Examples of the former sort, as might well be expected, are far more prevalent than those of the latter. . . . [In one minimal allusion in **Les Revenentes**], the narrator recalls memories from his youth [and alludes] . . . to another project of rememoration, [Marcel Proust's] *A la recherche du temps perdu.* (p. 118)

An example of maximal intertextual borrowing is offered by **Die Maschine,** a radio play commissioned by Saar Radio in 1968 and translated into German by Eugen Helmlé. The text is an experiment in "technological esthetics": it attempts to simulate a computer analysis of Goethe's "Wanderers Nachtlied." For the computer, Perec postulates a group of six data banks containing, respectively, the poem in question, information about Goethe, a German vocabulary, alphabets arranged according to a phonological key permitting words to be formed, a syntactical key (a grammar) and a selection of poems from world literature. The logical unit of the computer, the control, issues the commands to the data banks. There are four voices in the radio play (three speakers and the voice of the control) which communicate the output of the computer. The analysis of the "Wanderers Nachtlied" which constitutes the text of *Die Maschine* proceeds according to categories (or registers) which the computer applies to the poem successively: an analysis of the language material of the poem in the broad sense, an analysis of the individual word material, a modification of the semantic element, an examination of the relations between the poem and its author and, finally, a comparison of the poem to other poems in order to extract that which Perec calls "the essence of the poetry."

Perec's stated intention is to describe both the workings of a machine and the "inner mechanism of poetry," suggesting, through the confrontation of machine and poem, both the poetic nature of the machine and the mechanistic nature of the poem. It is this, perhaps, which is the prime concern of "technological esthetics": a recuperation of the science-art schism. (pp. 118-19)

Thus, Perec's allusive technique ranges from the minimal to the maximal, from the "throwaway lines" . . . [in] *Les Revenentes* and *Quel petit vélo* to the use of the "Wanderers Nachtlied" as the *texte de base* in *Die Maschine*. The intertextual element in the rest of Perec's work situates itself between these two poles.

I have noted [elsewhere] the Sartrian echoes which color *Un Homme qui dort*. . . . But the intertextual reference in *Un Homme qui dort* is by no means limited to Sartre. Perec uses allusion as a closure device, when the hero rejects successively the models of behavior proposed by the 20th-century novel. . . . (pp. 119-20)

The allusions function on two levels. Intradiegetically, the hero rebels against the literary models, as he rebels against his previous comportment, his "sleep." On the extradiegetic level, they may be read as resolutions taken by Perec as author, as he situates himself with regard to the literary *chefs-d'oeuvre* which dominate his cultural heritage. . . .

Literature which presents itself as "serious" or elitist (rather than popular) is historically patrophagous: successive generations implicitly or explicitly reject that which precedes them. "Tout le reste est littérature" [or, "The rest is just literature"], proclaims Verlaine in the final line of "Art poétique"; Perec's tactic at the end of *Un Homme qui dort* is similar. And he is crafty enough to see that such a ploy may function in two opposing manners: while he apparently rejects the literary traditions which precede him, his allusions encourage the reader to consider *Un Homme qui dort* in light of those traditions, to accord Perec's novel a favorable place in the literary hierarchy. (p. 120)

Perec continues to use allusion to direct the receptive process in *La Poche Parmentier,* but here the allusive technique is parodic, as is the tone of the play as a whole. Just as *Un Homme qui dort* reviews a certain novelistic tradition, *La Poche Parmentier* reviews a tradition of the theater, and this through parody. The initial stage directions are calculated to confuse the distinctions between illusion and reality. The curtain is to be raised fifteen minutes before the "start" of the play, the actors being already in their places. . . . After the bell which calls the audience to their seats and the traditional three knocks announcing the "beginning" of the play, the dialogue begins. . . . [A character alludes] to Ionesco, specifically to the *chef-d'oeuvre* of the theater of the absurd, *La Cantatrice chauve.* After this tip of the hat, much of the play passes under the sign of Ionesco, with allusions not only to *La Cantatrice chauve,* but also to *Jacques ou la soumission* and *La*

Leçon. If Ionesco constitutes the prime target of parody in *La Poche Parmentier,* there exist, nonetheless, allusions to other playwrights and their works. The deaf and dumb servant recalls Camus's *Le Malentendu;* Perec also alludes to Sartre, Genet and Labiche. Finally, as in *Un Homme qui dort,* Perec uses intertextual reference as a closure device: *La Poche Parmentier* ends as the characters perform a pastiche of *Hamlet.* This final play within a play is the culmination of the pattern of metaliterary commentary which Perec develops in *La Poche Parmentier.* Apart from its status as a venerable theatrical device, the play within a play renders manifest that which is suggested throughout *La Poche Parmentier*—the systematic confusion of illusion and reality. . . . In spite of Perec's claim to the contrary, *La Poche Parmentier* is a play about the theater, more specifically about 20th-century theater and one of its most privileged themes, the infinite regression of the *jeu.*

Both *Un Homme qui dort* and *La Poche Parmentier,* then, situate themselves explicitly with regard to that which precedes them. If Perec criticizes the 20th-century novel and theater, he does so lovingly and generally with humor. Despite his apparent rejection of tradition, it is clear that he profits from recent literature; the high degree of metaliterary commentary in his work testifies to this. In fact, through this metaliterary element, Perec's works implicitly inscribe themselves in that literary tradition. (pp. 120-22)

Granted the importance which Perec accords to the intertextual allusion, it is less than astonishing to find that in *La Vie mode d'emploi* the allusive element is augmented, since, in this long novel, Perec unites and amplifies all the diverse themes, techniques and literary directions which he had explored up to that point. . . .

But in *La Vie mode d'emploi* the difference in Perec's use of intertextual allusion is not merely quantitative, but qualitative as well: it moves from the thematic to the structural level, forming thus one more element in the general system of formal constraint upon which the text is built. (p. 122)

Intertextual allusion is only one aspect of the broader metaliterary phenomenon. Perec exploits another aspect thereof in all his writings, indulging in a high degree of metacommentary. The latter may be divided for analytical purposes into two principal subsets, the first including those passages wherein the field of reference is limited to the individual text itself, the second including passages which focus on literature in general and on Perec's own literary goals.

The intrusive narrator of *Quel petit vélo* . . . provides a rich stream of metacommentary in his discourse with the narratee. *Quel petit vélo* is full of the narratorial asides and apostrophes which are so characteristic of the intrusive narrator. Many of these passages comment upon that which immediately precedes them in the text and are intended to direct the reader's reception thereof. (p. 123)

Most of the passages, however, are baldly coercive; they are, for all that, appealing, since the narrator takes no pains to conceal his tyranny. . . .

[In] *L'Augmentation,* a play first performed in 1970, intertextual allusion and obvious autocommentary are, for once, absent. This is not to say, however, that all metaliterary concerns are equally banished. Indeed, *L'Augmentation* is an investigation of the essential nature of the story, of the process by which stories are told. The basic conceit is that of a worker asking for a raise: in doing so, he follows his company's organigram. The play traces his fortunes (more properly, his misfortunes) in the quest. (p. 124)

La Disparition, the experimental text *par excellence,* is full of autocommentary. Perec, for instance, explicitly inserts *La Disparition* in "la tradition du plus strict roman" [or, "the tradition of the strict novel"], playing, of course, both naïvely and ironically. In certain passages . . . , Perec mixes autocommentary and allusion. . . . Perec's metaliterary discourse in *La Disparition* is self-serving, but one would be hard-pressed to find one which was not: in Perec's case, his pretensions are largely unmasked and rendered manifest in the text and indeed, especially in *La Disparition,* constitute one of the principal areas of concern.

In an analogous manner Perec draws attention to the problem of closure, just as he does in *Un Homme qui dort, La Poche Parmentier* and *Quel petit vélo:* he invites the reader to trace the various esthetic choices which he makes as author. . . . The intent of this commentary is to furnish an illusion of openness; it appears to invite the reader's participation. In fact, it invites the reader to read more closely and, ultimately, to consider the text in a favorable light. (p. 125)

[Within *La Vie mode d'emploi*], there is a great deal of commentary dealing directly or indirectly with the structure of the text, intended, thus, to direct its reading. The theme of the puzzle and the many passages which discuss the theory of the puzzle point, as I have demonstrated, not only to Bartlebooth's obsession (the principal thematic on the intradiegetic level), but also to the work as a whole, since the text imitates the form of the jigsaw puzzle in its structure. If writing is, in any case, a process of encoding, and reading one of decoding, these processes are rendered far more apparent in *La Vie mode d'emploi* through both theme and structure. This is why Perec's attempts to direct the reading, already apparent in his earlier works, becomes so insistent in *La Vie mode d'emploi.* . . . (p. 126)

In addition to intertextual reference and autocommentary within individual texts, Perec's work is filled with a broader sort of metaliterary discourse dealing with literature in general and with his own project in particular. Perec has spoken of the readings which were critical in his formation as a writer. Indeed, the importance of his readings may be deduced from the richness of the intertextual allusion in his work: like any other writer who relies heavily on allusion, he considers himself first a reader. In *W ou le souvenir d'enfance,* Perec says that his first memory is of deciphering a letter in a Yiddish newspaper. Later he speaks of the readings which colored his childhood: *romans-feuilletons,* adventure novels, Westerns. Afterwards, he moved to detective novels and science fiction. . . . It is clear that these readings left their mark on Perec's work; like many writers of his generation, he admired the efficacy of the detective novel as a narrative form. But he suggested that these early readings of popular literature, so formative for him, affected him to such an extent that he became intimidated by more "serious" literature and by the idea of writing. . . . (pp. 126-27)

Granted this, it is interesting to note that most of the allusions in Perec's work are drawn from elitist literature. The tenor of some of these is ironic. . . . But in most cases Perec uses them straightforwardly. Moreover, as I have suggested, Perec consistently attempts to inscribe his own work in the tradition of elitist, rather than popular literature. Perhaps he

accepted the *défi* posed by elitist literature and apprenticed himself to it. In any case, as he states in *W ou le souvenir d'enfance,* his adult readings are far more "serious" than those of his youth and adolescence. . . . *W ou le souvenir d'enfance* may, in fact, be read as a Künstlerroman, tracing the hero through the loss of his parents to his eventual literary apprenticeship and vocation. Literature (both the reading and the writing thereof) is that which finally eases Perec's sense of exile: this is evident within *W ou le souvenir d'enfance* and is also clear from an examination of Perec's work as a whole.

If literature in general comes to serve this parental role, there is one writer in particular who has exerted an enormous influence on Perec, assuming the status of a godfather: Raymond Queneau. Perec's admiration for Queneau is unqualified; he unhesitatingly characterized himself as one of his "acolytes." . . . Many of Perec's Oulipian exercises are, thus, inspired by Queneau: his two **"Morales élémentaires"** are exercises on a form elaborated by Queneau, while his syllabic palindrome, **"Dos, caddy d'aisselles,"** first appeared in the Bibliothèque Oulipienne's fourth publication, entitled *A Raymond Queneau.* In *La Disparition,* Perec includes two lipograms written by Queneau. . . . And, whereas other authors are mentioned by name in *La Disparition* only if their names contain no E, Perec refers to Queneau twice, as "Raymond Quinault" and "Ramun Quayno." Perec's prime model for his work in experimental literature is the *Exercices de style,* which may be viewed, moreover, as the seminal Oulipian text. But, even in Perec's texts which are not so heavily influenced by the Oulipo, he nonetheless pays homage to Queneau. (pp. 127-28)

If Queneau's relation to Perec, then, is that of a *maître à penser,* surrogate father, literary godfather, the most fundamental influence may perhaps be seen in the fact that Perec, like Queneau, steadfastly refuses to divorce theory from practice. At every step in his career Perec posed theoretical questions; every text responds in some fashion to a theoretical problem or set of problems, generally enunciated or implied in the text itself. . . . The "Post-scriptum" of *La Disparition* is a good example. There Perec defends his apparently gratuitous conceit, the lipogrammatic form, on theoretical grounds: "L'ambition du 'Scriptor,' son propos, disons son souci, son souci constant, fut d'abord d'aboutir à un produit aussi original qu'instructif, à un produit qui aurait, qui pourrait avoir un pouvoir stimulant sur la construction, la narration, l'affabulation, l'action, disons, d'un mot, sur la façon du roman d'aujourd'hui."

That which constitutes the *enjeu* of the novel is clearly the novelistic form itself: the principal discourse of the text is metaliterary in nature. Perec was never reluctant to speak of his own literary theory and the practical directions which he felt should be pursued. In 1967 he wrote an article on the influence of the mass media on literature and suggested that literature recuperate techniques elaborated by the mass media: "l'implication, donc, la simultanéité et la discontinuité forment, me semble-t-il, les trois axes de la sensibilité contemporaine telle que les mass-media l'ont forgée. Leur adaptation à l'écriture nous permet peut-être d'esquisser une structure ouverte de l'oeuvre littéraire, y compris du roman."

In his own work Perec chose various means of putting this theory into practice. Through the devices of which I have spoken—intrusive narrators, metaliterary *rappels* in the text, heavy dosages of allusion—he attempts to achieve "l'implication du lecteur dans l'oeuvre." For simultaneity Perec encourages multi-level readings: this is precisely the reason why he amplifies the metaliterary element of his works with such insistence: each text may be read as a story *and* as the story of the story, each text is a chronicle of its own writing. . . . Paradoxically, for all his seemingly ferocious modernism, Perec proposes a return to former models of narrative offered by the 18th century: [Pierre Ambroise François Choderlos de Laclos's] *Les Liaisons dangereuses,* [Denis Diderot's] *Jacques le fataliste* and especially [Laurence Sterne's] *Tristram Shandy.* These are the essential models for Perec's novelistic enterprise. . . . (pp. 129-30)

But Perec's theory of the novel is only a part of his larger poetic theory. In consequence, his work as a whole is remarkably heterogeneous; it is as if Perec had set out to practice every literary form available. (p. 130)

Perec, more than most other writers, even those of our time, led his literary life in a goldfish bowl, and voluntarily so: his insistent metaliterary discourse invites the reader to participate, if vicariously, in Perec's own project. If any text comments implicitly upon the tradition from which it springs, Perec's works do so explicitly, overtly, establishing webs of correspondence with the literature of his own time and that which precedes. . . . Rhetorically Perec returns thus to his puzzle, like Borges to his labyrinth. Images of art and artifice, they serve as figures of both the microcosm and the macrocosm, both the individual text and the body of tradition from which it arises and by which it is nourished. (pp. 130-31)

> *Warren F. Motte, Jr., in his* The Poetics of Experiment: A Study of the Work of Georges Perec, *French Forum, Publishers, 1984, 163 p.*

PAUL J. SCHWARTZ

In *W ou le souvenir d'enfance* (1975), Georges Perec has woven together two narratives, an attempted autobiography and a re-created childhood fantasy, into a rich literary tapestry which has fascinated readers and earned the appreciation of critics as a major literary work. . . . Superficially, the weaving is rather a coarse grafting with obvious seams, for Perec has merely alternated chapters of the two narratives. The odd-numbered chapters tell the story, created when Perec was 13, of the fictional Gaspard Winckler, his missing namesake, and his fascination with an island in the Tierra del Fuego called W, where sport is king; the even-numbered chapters represent Perec's attempt to piece together memories and reminders of his childhood. The final chapter quotes at length David Rousset's *L'Univers concentrationnaire* to bind together the autobiography and the fantasy. For the athletic hierarchy on W evolves throughout the novel into a . . . [machine] comparable to the Nazi occupation of France which scarred Perec's childhood and separated him from his mother.

There is a further weaving which takes place, however, a more subtle creation of intertextual relationships which unite the two narratives, creating a complex "whole" which is greater than the sum of its parts, and which has inspired remarkably diverse interpretations, as a condemnation of the capitalist system, as an oedipal search for identity, and as an affirmation of Jewish identity and an allegory of PLO fanaticism.

Perec's project is self-consciously literary; critics have cited many likely sources: Proust, Faulkner, Dickens, Beckett, Kafka, Verne, Leiris, Queneau, Flaubert, Roussel, and Melville. The project is also immensely personal. At age 38, . . . Perec stops to meditate upon his past and the light it may throw upon his future. Two epigraphs from Queneau beginning the first and second halves of the book reflect this intention. At a crossroad in his life, Perec seizes upon the doubleness of the route going before and after, and constructs a book based on doubling effects with X as a major symbol. As he explains in the course of the narrative, Perec was fascinated in his childhood by the values of X as a letter, a word, and a symbol. He built upon it a complex network of associations, a "géometrie fantasmique" which groups X as a symbol of words crossed out, removal, multiplication and unknowns, with permutations of the geometric components of X, two V's, which can be manipulated to form the symbols of Nazism, the Gestapo, and Judaism, as well, of course, as W.

Robert Misrahi has analyzed the structural relationships of the different parts of the book, specifically their doubling and mirroring effects. He divides the book into four parts: W_1, W_2, P_1, and P_2. The W sections tell the story of Winckler and the island W. The P sections are Perec's memoirs. Parts 1 and 2 of the novel are divided by titles (Première partie, Deuxième partie), by an ellipsis in parentheses on page 85 and by the Queneau quotes.

Gaspard Winckler's search for his namesake, the sickly child lost at sea or perhaps abandoned by his mother, introduces a detective motif which is common to W_1 and P_1. The parallels between the investigation of the disappearance of Gaspard Winckler and Perec's search through old photographs and documents for evidence of the orphaned boy he once was and doesn't remember are obvious and disturbing. . . . Both narrators use similar language to describe their searches; in both narratives the city of Venice is the site of a sudden memory, the word "bretzel" assumes an unexpected importance, and the narrator stresses his passive role as observer. (pp. 71-2)

On the back cover of the book, Perec calls attention to the apparent discontinuity of his work, focusing not on the alternation between W and P, but rather on the break between the two halves of *W* . . . [There is an] ellipsis on the otherwise blank page 85, which interrupts the proposed search for Gaspard Winckler and precedes the description of W. This break in the text, this blank page, is central to Perec's conception of his book. . . . (p. 72)

[Page 85] presents on one hand a perfectly neutral ground, a suspension, in Perec's geometric terms the crossing points of the two axes ($x = 0$; $y = 0$). On the other hand, it is ground zero, "l'explosion de l'univers." . . . It has the same value as the page inserted by Victor Hugo between the second and third poems of the Fourth Book of *Les Contemplations,* bearing the date "4 Septembre 1843" and a series of "points de suspension" to mark, for the bereaved poet, the before and after of the death of his beloved daughter, his silence, and the eventual conception of the book of poems.

Perec relates the notion of *suspension* directly to his departure from Paris for Villard at the beginning of the occupation. His vague memory of the scene includes three details: his mother had given him a Charlie Chaplin comic book on whose cover Chaplin is floating from a parachute attached to his suspenders. Perec's arm was in a sling, or (because his aunt denies the presence of a sling) he was wearing a bandage for a hernia, a "suspensoir," Perec analyzes these uncertain details. . . . Sixteen years later, as he is about to make his first parachute jump, he suddenly relives the departure. . . . His childhood was irrevocably severed at the Gare de Lyon when he was thrown into the emptiness of the train, exiled and orphaned in one traumatic moment, which his childish imagination buries under images of suspension.

Despite his perception of the pathos of the repressed memory, Perec refuses to dwell upon it. Instead he observes and analyzes the birth of his artistic imagination through his unconscious attempts to adjust to the loss of his mother. With remarkable lucidity, he continues to explore the notions of "cassure" and "rupture" as they reappear in his life as a series of dislocations: of his memories, and of his early attempts to write and draw. He catalogs a rich network of obsessive imagery relating notions of suspension, dislocation, and fracture which become part of his creative imagination, from which will spring a fascination with puzzles, with missing elements and with the notion of *coupure.*

An additional personal anecdote and Perec's interpretation of it further relate these associated images to the childhood separation. He remembers in the spring of 1942 . . . a sledding accident, a broken shoulder blade, and his right hand tied behind his back in a sling, which earned for him much consoling pity. Later information convinces Perec that the accident actually happened to another boy, and that the broken shoulder, a "reparable" fracture is really a metaphor for a more traumatic and irreparable break in his life. The real wound, only whispered and not fully understood by the child is the absence, the silence which steals his mother from him.

The absence itself explodes within Perec's imagination; the mature Perec's recognition of the source and role of his broken and suspended imagery has . . . founded the text. To present the splintered images of a shattered childhood, Perec employs a form which mirrors its content and which calls forth associated images which have accompanied him since the childhood experiences which the book evokes. The book is for Perec an essential effort to accept his past and to affirm his future by assuming the responsibility of memorializing his lost parents and his subsequently lost childhood. (pp. 72-3)

Paul J. Schwartz, "The Unifying Structures of Georges Perec's Suspended Memoirs," in The International Fiction Review, *Vol. 12, No. 2, Summer, 1985, pp. 71-3.*

ALAN ASTRO

If we think of allegory as a narrative where figural meaning eclipses literal meaning, then it is clear that the works of Georges Perec demand allegorical readings. The title of his best-selling work, **Les Choses,** suggests that it be understood less as the life of Jérôme and Sylvie than as an allegory of consumerist society: hence its subtitle, *Une Histoire des années soixante.* Similarly, one could hardly read **La Vie mode d'emploi** as the stories of various tenants in a Parisian apartment house without being constantly aware that each chapter is determined by its place in a puzzle. The very title **La Vie mode d'emploi** makes explicit the allegorical import: as in medieval allegory, the literal story matters less than its didactic significance, the lesson it teaches us about how to live. Unlike medieval allegory, of course, Perec's texts do not convey a

specific moral meaning; they simply remind us to read life in some sense other than the most immediate one. (p. 867)

Perec's novel **La Disparition** functions as allegory. It would be misplaced to read this work literally as the tale of the disappearance of Anton Voyl, for every word in the text, even more so than in **La Vie mode d'emploi,** is dictated by an underlying structural principle: the scrupulous avoidance of the letter *e. La Disparition* is the story of a missing character in both senses of the word: a missing person and a missing letter. Moreover, since *e* is the most frequent letter in Perec's own name, its absence from **La Disparition** may stand for the disappearance of Perec's parents during the war . . . as well as the disappearance of Hebrew letters from Perec's life (his parents were Yiddish-speaking Polish Jews).

We learn these facts about Perec in his allegorical and autobiographical work, **W ou le souvenir d'enfance.** As the title suggests, the text is double. Its alternating chapters—the odd ones in italic, the even ones not—tell two different tales. The chapters in regular typeface are composed of fragmented memories from Perec's childhood in occupied France. The chapters in italics recount the imaginary, even fantastic, tale of a French army deserter who escapes to Germany; the historical epoch is recent but unrecognizable, and the style is classically novelistic, complete with names and dates designated by their first letters or digits followed by dots. . . . The deserter has been given the identity papers of Gaspard Winckler, a child who is believed to have disappeared in a shipwreck in the Tierra del Fuego; and he has been requested to join in the search for the child. At this point, the text in italics turns abruptly into the meticulous description of an island in the Tierra del Fuego named W, site of a sports camp which pits athletes against each other in inhuman competition. It soon becomes clear that *w,* in French a foreign letter used mainly in words of Germanic origin, represents the *w* in Auschwitz; the barbaric sports camp on the island W symbolizes the extermination camp at Auschwitz. On W, losers in the athletic competitions are deprived of food, tortured and even put to death; the women's quarters are surrounded by an electrified fence; and unfit children born there are killed. The athletes, designated officially by numbers instead of their names, are cheered on in German. Throughout the text, nouns like "Athlètes," "Sport," "Victoire," "Vainqueur" and "Stade" are capitalized, as they would be in German—or in an allegory.

Thus there is an apparently stable structure whereby the text in italics ending up in the sports camp is the allegorical version of the story in regular typeface which ends up in the death camps. We can decode the text in italics as follows: the deserter is Georges Perec, the sole member of his immediate family to have survived the war; and the deserter's search for the child whose name he bears is Perec's own search for his childhood in **W ou le souvenir d'enfance.** The first time we encounter the deserter, he is on the Giudecca, the Venetian island whose name attests most probably to its early Jewish settlers; likewise, Perec's familial history begins in the Jewish *shtetlekh* of Poland. The deserter's use of false papers recalls how Jews hid their identities during the war. . . . The depiction of Auschwitz as a barbaric sports camp is equally symbolic. Perec ends the book with a quotation from David Rousset's *L'Univers concentrationnaire,* which describes the sadistic athletic competitions which Nazi torturers made their victims engage in; there was also the *rafle du Vel' d'Hiv',* when thousands of Parisian Jews were herded into a bicycle-racing stadium before being sent to their deaths. Even the abrupt switch in the fantastic narrative from the story of the deserter to the description of the sports camp can be read as figuring the disruptions in Perec's life as a child who, after leaving his family in Paris, was sent to various places in the unoccupied zone.

Despite the rigorous parallelism between the autobiographical and fictional texts, between the literal and allegorical planes, a cross-over occurs: the autobiographical text functions allegorically and the fantastic text becomes real. (pp. 867-69)

[The autobiographical section of *W ou le souvenir d'enfance*] approaches allegory in its emblematic and typical quality, in its "arbitrary and schematic image[s]" (my trans.), and in the eschatological import inherent in its reference to the death camps: allegories ultimately tell the story of humanity's salvation or perdition. Contrarily, the properly allegorical *récit*—the fantastic tale of the barbaric athletic camp—becomes real. The quotation from David Rousset reminds us that Auschwitz *was,* among other things, a barbaric sports camp; and Perec remarks that it was prophetic that he set *W* in the Tierra del Fuego because the Pinochet government has turned some of the islands there into deportation camps.

Moreover, the allegorical narrative approaches the real because the referent of the allegory—its underlying reality, Auschwitz—seems fundamentally unreal. . . . Because Auschwitz is unconceivable, and its horror unspeakable, descriptions of it cannot approach its reality and function as allegories for what Auschwitz must have been like. Perec's version of Auschwitz as a barbaric sports camp moves towards real description of Auschwitz by assuming the necessarily allegorical component of such description. (pp. 870-71)

The crossing-over between allegory and real and vice versa in *W ou le souvenir d'enfance* can be related as well to Perec's slight dyslexia. Left-handed at birth, he was forced to write with his right hand, a fact which he believes may explain his confusion of right and left, of concave and convex, of grave and acute accents, of less-than and greater-than signs, of the difference between hyperbola and parabola, numerator and denominator, dividend and divisor, metaphor and metonymy. The chiasmus between allegory and real is also figured in the crosses and *x*'s in the text. Perec's father's grave in a military cemetery is marked by a cross, despite his having been a Jew; Perec himself was baptized supposedly to protect him from the Nazis and recounts that he went through a devout period; and he remembers seeing in his childhood a man sawing wood on a sawhorse formed by two parallel crosses. Such a sawhorse is called in French an "x." . . . Perec reads his memory of the sawhorse according to Lacan's theory that the unconscious is structured like a language and inhabited by the agency of the letter. If *W ou le souvenir d'enfance* generally undermines the distinction between the autobiographical narrative and its allegorical reëlaboration, the passage on the letter *x* crosses the boundary between a literary text and its psychoanalytic interpretation.

Perec goes on to remark that the letter *x* is formed by two *v*'s—one right-side up and one upside-down—aligned vertically; and we then realize that a *w* is formed by two *v*'s aligned horizontally: the title *W* is a rearranged *x*. Next, Perec notes that by prolonging the branches of an *x* by equal but perpendicular segments one can form a swastika, and that when the two cross-sections of the swastika are separated and lined up

in parallel manner, they form the sign of the Waffen SS. (pp. 871-72)

Perec lived his childhood under emblems based on *x*'s, the cruelest letter. . . . Perec's writing career can be understood as the wish to restore those whose every trace was to have been wiped out. . . . (p. 872)

Elie Wiesel has stated that, for him, writing is "an invisible tombstone, erected to the memory of the dead unburied"; likewise, the insistence of the letter in Perec's work can be traced to the lack of epitaphs. Like most victims of the death camps, Perec's mother has no grave. Even when, towards the end of the 1950's, Perec received the official certification of his mother's death, it was marked by an absence. He was informed that because she had not had French citizenship, she could not be awarded the honorific title "Mort pour la France." (pp. 872-73)

So great is Perec's expectation of the absence of his name that upon reading his father's tombstone, he is taken aback by seeing his own surname, which none of his surviving relatives shares. Perec's name is almost literally *le nom du père:* it is pronounced *Pé*rec or *Per*rec despite the lack of an extra *r* or the acute accent. The elided diacritical mark recalls how Perec's most illustrious forebear signed his name. We learn in *W* that Perec is the great-great-nephew of the Polish-Yiddish writer Y. L. Peretz (*c* in Polish is pronounced *ts*). Now while Yiddish uses the Hebrew alphabet, it places its vowels on the lines, whereas Hebrew either puts the vowels under the consonants in the form of diacritical markings or leaves them out altogether. Though Y. L. Peretz wrote in Yiddish, he signed his name in Hebrew: *pe, resh, tsadik* (*p, r, ts*). Like the characters in *La Disparition,* Peretz wrote his name without the vowel *e;* the title itself contains Perec/Peretz's signature in the Hebrew form *PRTs: disPaRiTion,* where the *tion* contains a *t* graphically and an *s* phonetically. (p. 873)

Thus, in *La Disparition* and *W ou le souvenir d'enfance,* the literal plane—in the most literal sense, as letter—assumes significance, as the embodiment of an otherwise absent past. This reflects Jewish tradition, where the letter of the sacred text is itself sacred. Despite the emphasis in this article on the war and the deportations, this tradition is not only assumed tragically. Perec's oeuvre is full of playful uses of letters: anagrams, palindromes, and, significantly, crossword puzzles. If in Yiddish the name Perec harks back to the classic writer Y. L. Peretz, the associations are lighter in Hungarian, where the word *peretz* means "pretzel." (pp. 873-74)

Perec's playfulness signals the completion of his mourning. . . . His acceptance of an irrevocably lost origin is reflected in his recourse to allegory. As Paul de Man writes in "The Rhetoric of Temporality": "Whereas the symbol postulates the possibility of an identity or identification, allegory designates primarily a distance in relation to its own origin. . . ."

However, the cross-over between allegory and real in *W* suggests that the distance from the origin collapses: based in historical fact, the representation of Auschwitz as a barbaric sports camp approaches a symbolic mode. Thus Perec portrays how we cannot achieve a stable distance from Auschwitz, ever present; *W ou le souvenir d'enfance* recounts the impingement of that untenable reality on the desire to elaborate it into allegory.

One question remains with respect to allegory in *W ou le souvenir d'enfance.* Perec had originally published the allegorical tale of the barbaric sports village alone; only in book form does he supply the referent of the allegory as well, the personal history by whose means we can interpret the allegory. Even if, as we have seen, the allegorical and real planes come to intersect, the two-tiered structure gives us cause for wonder, since allegories generally provide only a figural narrative. Usually, it is up to the reader to decipher the underlying meaning, but in *W* Perec furnishes the exegesis of his own text.

This procedure is in keeping with Perec's tendency elsewhere to comment upon his writings. In *W ou le souvenir d'enfance,* the exegetical principle is psychoanalytic: as in a Freudian case history, Perec provides us both with the manifest content of the fantasy and its latent meaning. Moreover, the fantasy is a repressed one: Perec tells us in the first pages that he originally imagined the island of W at the age of thirteen, only to forget the fantasy until it resurfaced during a trip to Venice. But as Freud pointed out in "Creative Writers and Day-Dreaming," there is a difference between a fantasy and a literary creation. Hence Perec makes it clear that his text does not simply reproduce his fantasy; rather, it is an elaboration of his fantasy, much as his fantasy is an elaboration of his life. . . . Hence *W ou le souvenir d'enfance* is not simply an account of Perec's psychoanalysis; it is rather an allegory of psychoanalysis, a literary reworking of his fantasy and its interpretation. (pp. 874-75)

> Alan Astro, "Allegory in Georges Perec's 'W ou le souvenir d'enfance'," in MLN, Vol. 102, No. 4, September, 1987, pp. 867-76.

ALBERT MOBILIO

Harry Mathews, Jacques Roubaud, and the late Georges Perec are all members of a Paris-based group of experimental writers dedicated to the high art of game. Founded in 1960 by mathematician François Le Lionnais and novelist Raymond Queneau, Oulipo (*Ouvroir de Littérature Potentielle,* or Workshop of Potential Literature) produces literary puzzles whose spirit and shape derive from mathematical formulae and linguistic high jinks. Inspired by Lewis Carroll, Stein, Joyce, and Raymond Roussel, Oulipians craft puzzle-palace poems and novels for which solutions are not nearly as crucial as the process of solving. Some typical bits of Oulipo business include palindromes like Perec's "Straw? No, too stupid a fad. I put soot on warts," [or] snowball sentences adding one letter to each successive word. . . . These games are not as flat as they sound. The N-7 algorithm takes a familiar passage and replaces each noun with the seventh noun that follows in the dictionary. Try it. Any domesticated phrase— Our fathom who art in hebetude hallowed by thy nannyberry—yields laughs and a glimpse of sound and sense at work. . . .

Georges Perec's comic novel *La Disparition (The Disappearance)* undoes the dictionary by employing the lipogram—a linguistic ruse, dating back to ancient Egypt, which requires the elimination of one or more letters from use. Perec chose the letter e, the most common in French, setting the difficulty dial on high for this 300-page book. The result proved so readable few noticed anything odd. In effect, Perec invented a new language while suggesting the possibility of alternative vocabularies obtained from perforated alphabets.

Now Perec's grandest game, *Life: A User's Manual,* has been translated (no mean task) . . . a decade after being hailed a masterpiece in France. Without a doubt, it's quintessential Oulipo. Through the governing metaphor of a jigsaw puzzle, Perec invites readers to reenact the novel's composition. In his brief preamble on the "ultimate truth" of games, he says,

> puzzling is not a solitary game: every move the puzzler makes, the puzzle-maker has made before . . . every blunder and every insight, each hope and each discouragement have all been designed, calculated and decided by the other.

The novel is truly a "user's manual," a guide for assembling itself.

A Paris apartment building, 11 Rue Simon-Crubellier, provides the literal structure for reconstruction. Having lived in No. 11 most of his life, dying painter Serge Valène conjures up a painting, a vast fresco depicting the entire building as if the façade were peeled away to expose the front rooms, halls, stairs, and inhabitants. . . . Like an exacting geographer, he surveys roomfuls of Second Empire flotsam, pausing to invest particular objects—a bracelet, a vase, especially paintings—with a story. Gradually the fictive canvas acquires an archaeological aspect, as the histories accumulate, layer by layer, to include fantastical tales of Sumatran tribal life, dictionaries of lost words, decades-old art swindles, and Arabian myth. The digressions veer off unpredictably: In the empty bedroom of Geneviève Foulerot hangs a painting of another room. . . . It becomes increasingly difficult to find the story's center, as difficult as finding the center piece in a jigsaw-puzzle box.

The dizzying self-reflexiveness—a painter imagines a room containing another painting containing another room, another painter—captures Perec's regressive riddle: does the puzzle make the puzzle-maker's moves? Percival Bartlebooth, the English millionaire dandy whose presence hovers throughout the book, personifies the dilemma; he's puzzle-maker as puzzle. Consider his strange life. For 10 years he studies painting with Valène (they're neighbors in the building). For the next 20 he travels around the world, painting seasides and ports in identical formats, allowing two weeks per painting. Canvases are dispatched to Paris where puzzle-maker Winckler (another tenant) turns them into jigsaw puzzles of 750 pieces. With 500 paintings completed, Bartlebooth returns to spend his last 20 years reassembling the jigsaws in the order they were painted, at the same two-week intervals. Solved puzzles are "retexturized," the painting sent to its place of origin. There it's dissolved and the clean sheet returned to Bartlebooth.

The lifelong exercise rests on guiding principles that read like an Oulipo manifesto: the plan is "logical: all recourse to chance would be ruled out," and "the plan would be useless, since gratuitousness was the sole guarantor of its rigour." Leaving no trace of a pointless game is Bartlebooth's joy and intent, just as the novel's complicitous game with the reader seeks to dissolve Perec's position as author. Driven by mathematical formulae (the Graeco-Roman square of 10 determines the number of rooms and objects described; progress through the 100 chapters, one per room, follows the path of a chess knight covering the entire board without hitting any square twice), *Life* is a perpetual-motion machine, its maker lost inside the gears.

The tension between the elegance of its scheme and the

ragged complications of other lives, their infinitely digressive histories, charges *Life* with a sense of boundlessness. A meta-novel made to house not just a hundred other stories, it embodies the very feeling of connectedness, the suspicion you have watching faces hurtle by on the downtown express that somehow these lives are bound to yours. Perec has engineered a methodical sprawl, a toy, a dream; he's cut pieces for the puzzle we're solving every day.

Among *Life*'s many novels lurks a *roman policier,* the how and why of Bartlebooth's mysterious death. Obviously, sleuthing is a natural for Oulipians. Perec in *La Disparition* [draws] . . . on the genre's mythic dimension—the riddle as quest—but [neglects] its hardboiled colorations. (p. 11)

Albert Mobilio, "Perpetual Notion Machines," in VLS, No. 60, November, 1987, pp. 11-12.

PAUL AUSTER

Georges Perec died in 1982 at the age of 46, leaving behind a dozen books and a brilliant reputation. In the words of Italo Calvino, he was "one of the most singular literary personalities in the world, a writer who resembled absolutely no one else." It has taken a while for us to catch on, but now that his major work—*Life: A User's Manual* (1978)—has at last been translated into English it will be impossible for us to think of contemporary French writing in the same way again. . . .

To read Georges Perec one must be ready to abandon oneself to a spirit of play. His books are studded with intellectual traps, allusions and secret systems, and if they are not necessarily profound (in the sense that Tolstoy and Mann are profound), they are prodigiously entertaining (in the sense that Lewis Carroll and Laurence Sterne are entertaining). In Chapter Two of *Life,* for example, Perec refers to "the score of a famous American melody, 'Gertrude of Wyoming,' by Arthur Stanley Jefferson." By pure chance, I happened to know that Arthur Stanley Jefferson was the real name of the comedian Stan Laurel, but just because I caught this allusion does not mean there weren't a thousand others that escaped me.

For the mathematically inclined, there are magic squares and chess moves to be discovered in this novel, but the fact that I was unable to find them did not diminish my enjoyment of the book. Those who have read a great deal will no doubt recognize passages that quote directly or indirectly from other writers—Kafka, Agatha Christie, Melville, Freud, Rabelais, Nabokov, Jules Verne and a host of others—but failure to recognize them should not be considered a handicap. Like Jorge Luis Borges, Georges Perec had a mind that was a storehouse of curious bits of knowledge and awesome erudition, and half the time the reader can't be sure if he is being conned or enlightened. In the long run, it probably doesn't matter. What draws one into this book is not Perec's cleverness, but the deftness and clarity of his style. . . .

Life: A User's Manual is constructed in the manner of a vast jigsaw puzzle. In it, Perec takes a single apartment building in Paris and uses 99 short chapters (along with a preamble and an epilogue) to give a meticulous description of each and every room as well as the life stories of all the inhabitants, both past and present. Ostensibly, we are watching the creation of a painting by Serge Valène, an old artist who has lived in the building for 55 years. . . .

What emerges is a series of self-contained but interconnecting stories. They are all briskly told, and they run the gamut from the bizarre to the realistic. There are tales of murder and revenge, tales of intellectual obsessions, humorous tales of social satire and (almost unexpectedly) a number of stories of great psychological penetration. For the most part, Perec's microcosm is peopled with a motley assortment of odd-balls, impassioned collectors, antiquarians, miniaturists and half-baked scholars.

If anyone can be called the central character in this shifting, kaleidoscopic work, it would have to be Percival Bartlebooth, an eccentric English millionaire whose insane and useless 50-year project serves as an emblem for the book as a whole. Realizing as a young man that his wealth has doomed him to a life of boredom, Bartlebooth undertakes to study the art of watercolor with Serge Valène for a period of 10 years. Although he has no aptitude whatsoever for painting, he eventually reaches a satisfactory level of competence. Then, in the company of a servant, he sets out on a 20-year voyage around the world with the sole intention of painting watercolors of 500 different harbors and seaports.

As soon as one of these pictures is finished, he sends it to a man in Paris by the name of Gaspard Winckler, who also lives in the building. Winckler is an expert puzzle-maker whom Bartlebooth has hired to turn the watercolors into 750-piece jigsaw puzzles. One by one, the puzzles are made and stored in wooden boxes. When Bartlebooth returns from his travels and settles back into his apartment, he will methodically go about putting the puzzles together in chronological order. By means of an elaborate chemical process, the borders of the puzzle pieces have been glued together in such a way that the seams are no longer visible, thus restoring the watercolor to its original integrity. The painting, good as new, can then be removed from its wooden backing and sent to the place where it was originally executed. There it will be dipped into a detergent solution that eliminates all traces of the painting, yielding a clean and unmarked sheet of paper. In other words, Bartlebooth will be left with nothing, the same thing he started with.

The project, however, does not go according to plan. Winckler has made the puzzles too difficult, and Bartlebooth does not live long enough to finish all 500 of them. . . .

Like many of the other stories in *Life,* Bartlebooth's weird saga can be read as a parable (of sorts) about the efforts of the human mind to impose an arbitrary order on the world. Again and again, Perec's characters are swindled, hoaxed and thwarted in their schemes, and if there is a darker side to his book, it is perhaps to be found in this emphasis on the inevitability of failure. Even a self-annihilating project such as Bartlebooth's cannot be completed, and when we learn in the epilogue that Valène's enormous painting (which for all intents and purposes is the book we have just been reading) has come no further than a preliminary sketch, we realize that Perec does not exempt himself from the follies of his characters. It is this sense of self-mockery that turns a potentially daunting novel into a hospitable work, a book that for all its high jinks and japery finally wins us over with the warmth of its human understanding. . . .

Georges Perec's reputation in France was well deserved. He is not a writer who will appeal to everyone, but those who have a taste for the unusual, for books that create worlds unto themselves, will be dazzled by this crazy-quilt monument to the imagination.

Paul Auster, "The Bartlebooth Follies," in The New York Times Book Review, November 15, 1987, p. 7.

PATRICK PARRINDER

Like Hoyle and Stephen Potter, Georges Perec was a devotee of indoor games. . . . He saw reading as a pastime and literature as a strenuously recreational art. The writer, he thought, was at his best when, like an obsessed games-player, he was struggling to comply with some rigid system of formal constraints. Perec was often dismissed as a mildly amusing exponent of *la folie littéraire,* but he was far more than this.

Perec was the least pretentious of writers. He wanted to write exciting narratives, books which could be 'devoured face downwards on one's bed'. (*Life: A User's Manual* is a rather bulky volume for this purpose, though it qualifies in other respects.) Nevertheless he was a dedicated avant-gardist whose best works were inspired by his membership of the experimental group OuLiPo (*Ouvroir de Littérature Potentielle*). It was to OuLiPo that he owed his interest in palindromes, anagrams, crosswords, acrostics and mathematical algorithms as sources of literary structures. . . .

[Perec employed Oulipian constraints] in a variety of literary forms. For example, there is a brief play, *Les Horreurs de la Guerre,* in which the dialogue consists entirely in the enunciation of the letters of the alphabet from *A* to *Z*. (It opens with the words *Abbesse! Aidez!*) Not surprisingly, much of his work is regarded as untranslatable. *Life: A User's Manual* is an exception. . . .

The theme of puzzles, especially jigsaw puzzles, is the main hint we are given that this is a novel as carefully patterned as Joyce's *Ulysses*. The 'subject' is a Parisian apartment block: *Life: A User's Manual* is, more or less, a room-by-room inventory of its contents, its inhabitants and their life-histories. If the 99 chapters (plus Preamble and Epilogue) are somehow reminiscent of *The Thousand and One Nights,* it is worth noting that Perec's choice of setting contains powerful allusions to the realist tradition in French fiction. Behind *Life: A User's Manual* there is the taxonomic 'human comedy' of Balzac, the sociological and clinical precision of Zola and the synaesthesia and imaginative claustrophobia of Proust. Perec shares the encyclopedic aims of his predecessors, taking us through endless rooms cluttered with meticulously-described pictures, books and *objets d'art*. It is like wandering through some vast museum of narrative painting, piling story upon story, storey upon storey. The inhabitants themselves are almost all, in a broad sense, artists (painters, writers, craftsmen, actresses, film-directors) or their servants and hangers-on (such as art-thieves and antique dealers). At the top of the building is an artist, Valène, engaged on a picture of the building, and an empty flat where Gaspard Winckler, cutter of jigsaws, formerly plied his jigsaw in a cork-lined room.

But however much it owes to the realist tradition, this is an Oulipian novel based on mathematical structures. Its compositional principles were outlined in an article that Perec published four years before it was completed. The sequence of 99 chapters, it turns out, follows an unbroken series of knight's moves across a checkerboard of ten squares by ten, corresponding to the vertical elevation of the apartment building. Within each chapter, a mathematical algorithm produces a list of 42 elements which have the effect of shaping the text at every level. The book concludes with a rough elevation diagram, a chronological table, a checklist of incidental stories, and an enormous (and, I would say, superfluous) index. Such a rigidly Cartesian procedure is also appropriate, so Perec assures us, to the design and solution of jigsaw puzzles.

In the ideal hand-cut wooden jigsaw the skill of the solver is exactly matched against the cunning, trickery and subterfuge employed by the puzzle-maker. The reconstruction of a jigsaw piece by piece resembles the work of a detective patiently solving a crime: the moment the solver relaxes his attention or gives way to enthusiasm he is likely to be taken in by false resemblances of colour and shape. . . .

The dream of a perfect system, attainable but for a single slight error, is an ancient theme of fiction and even of religion. *Life: A User's Manual* aspires to the condition of a perfect system, being a novel with (in the words used of one of the tidier rooms in the apartment building) 'a place for everything and everything in its place'. In an essay included in his posthumous collection *Penser/Classer* (1985), however, Perec treats the idea of a perfect system with some disrespect. Here he speaks of 'taxonomic vertigo', and argues that utopias are dissatisfying to the human spirit because they leave no room for chaos. Chaos is subtly present in *Life: A User's Manual,* which plunges the reader into a taxonomic vertigo with the effect of subverting the very systems that the novelist is at such pains to observe. Far from escaping, life pours in through the cracks of Perec's plan, so that the methodical inventory of an apartment block and its inhabitants comes to resemble nothing so much as a cluttered and cobwebby Old Curiosity Shop. If you want to read about, say, animated watches, early maps of the New World, the golden age of French cycling, or a hundred other unrelated things, then this is undoubtedly the book. One could become as obsessed with it, however, as Bartlebooth was with his jigsaws. The cascade of curiosities threatens never to stop.

Perhaps life, as this user's manual outlines it, is meant to be summed up in the story of Polonius the hamster. Polonius is the 43rd descendant of a pair of tame hamsters which had been trained to play dominoes. Like all his predecessors, he has been introduced to the game by his parents. An epidemic attacks the hamster community, and Polonius is the only survivor. He cannot play dominoes on his own, but neither is he capable of ridding himself of his obsession with the game. To preserve his sanity he has to be sent back to his original trainer for a weekly domino lesson. Another slave to obsession and victim of information overload is Cinoc, a 'word-killer' employed by [the publisher] Larousse to eliminate obsolete words from its dictionaries. The better Cinoc is at his job, the more it contrives to haunt him. He ends by spending all his leisure hours compiling a lexicon of forgotten words. (Perec being Perec, we are given a generous sample.) The narrator speculates inconclusively on the way in which Cinoc's (Jewish) name ought to be pronounced; oddly enough, of the twenty phonetic variants that he lists, not one corresponds to the English (or Welsh?) 'Kinnock'.

Gaspard Winckler, the puzzle-maker, was once a devotee of Jules Verne. The epigraph to Perec's novel—'Look with all your eyes, look'—is also taken from Verne. The act of looking, in its turn, leads to speculation, puzzling and surmise; it teases the brain. For example, a reader of *Life: A User's*

Manual may notice a certain similarity in the names Verne, Cinoc and Perec, and may even link them by means of a word-chain, a type of puzzle expounded in Chapter 85. Can Perec's outspoken interest in Verne be attributed to their shared double *e* (neither name could appear in the text of *La Disparition,* for example) and to their mutual passion for classifications and lists—or is there some deeper symbolic affinity? In one of his essays Perec refers wistfully to the library on the *Nautilus,* a uniformly-bound collection of 12,000 volumes which remained fixed in time and frozen in their places on the shelves at the moment when Captain Nemo began his voyage. Perec's apartment block is as utopian as Verne's submarine. Though it has a sufficiently mundane address (11 Rue Simon-Crubellier, Paris XVII) and though the narrative present can be precisely located in time (it is just before 8 p.m. on 23 June 1975), the last thing that *Life: A User's Manual* sets out to do is to portray or comment on Parisian life in the Seventies. The rich life of Perec's building is as cut off from the world around it and as subservient to its creator as the *Nautilus* was to the calculations of Captain Nemo.

> Patrick Parrinder, "Tall Storeys," in London Review of Books, *Vol. 9, No. 22, December 10, 1987, p. 26.*

LANIE GOODMAN

Founded in 1960, the Oulipo (*Ouvroir de Littérature Potentielle,* Workshop of Potential Literature) was conceived as a collaboration of interests between two old friends, French novelist Raymond Queneau and chess wizard Francois Le Lionnais. In light of the whopping 300-year success of the alexandrine, arbitrarily organized around the number 12, their idea was simply to take up where the rhetoricians of the 16th century had left off. (p. 1)

If one accepts that every literary work is essentially the mirror of another, then all writing is, by definition, a game of "plagiarism by anticipation," to employ an Oulipian term. Consequently, any existing literary passage can be "prepared," gutted like a chicken, emptied of its nouns, verbs or adjectives and "stuffed" with new vocabulary from another known work. . . .

One might object that these self-imposed strict rules of writing appear to be entirely gratuitous, and the Oulipians would tend to agree. Declaring that it is neither an esthetic movement, a pedagogical institution, nor a literary school, the Oulipo also shrugs off being categorized as a group of "serious" scientists, although certain members are indeed affiliated with universities. How would they describe themselves? Like "rats who must construct a labyrinth from which they then propose to escape" or, as one member of the group summed it up: "Every writer is in a cage; the difference is we just choose our own cages."

But why should any author voluntarily put himself through the conundrums of such a task? Paradoxically, the demands of a constrictive form only serve to liberate the imagination, since one is obliged to write in a way that one would never do otherwise, thereby eliminating sticky problems of ego or divine inspiration. . . . Writing for the Oulipian becomes a process of discovery, an ever-expanding puzzle, a solution to a problem that is all in the storytelling.

In Georges Perec's *Life, A User's Manual,* the most obvious game plan of the novel is based on a Parisian building without a facade, such that every room and stairway is simultaneously visible. Although everything takes place within the architectural framework, . . . *Life, A User's Manual* not only tells of its past and present tenants but develops into a massive catalogue of stories within stories and inexhaustible lists of objects and activities. . . .

Yet, regardless of the variety of staggering constraints, . . . what is so utterly compelling about this Oulipian tour de force is that it is also a mosaic of endearingly eccentric characters and life's little dramas.

Take, for instance, Percival Bartlebooth, an English millionaire, indifferent to power, women or his own fortune, who confronts the incoherence of the modern world by engaging himself in a lifetime project that is founded on a completely arbitrary premise. Bartlebooth studies art for 10 years with his neighbor Serge Valène so that during the next 20 years he may travel to 500 seaports all over the world to paint one picture every two weeks. Each new port scene is promptly expedited to a gifted artisan, Gaspard Winckler (also a tenant of the same building), who glues the watercolor onto a block of wood and then cuts it into a 750-piece jigsaw puzzle.

Upon his return, Bartlebooth plans to spend the next 20 years holed up in his apartment, reassembling the 500 puzzles. . . . When Bartlebooth mysteriously dies holding the last piece of the 439th puzzle, the joke may be on him, but perhaps on the reader as well, which is all part of the fun. For those who enjoy the occasional little narrative trick, Perec's sly craftsmanship invites us to grope for clues, discover hidden games, realign discrepancies and ultimately carve our own zig-zagging itinerary in the novel. (p. 14)

> Lanie Goodman, "Fiction at Play: Welcome to the Fun House," in Book World—The Washington Post, *December 20, 1987, pp. 1, 14.*

SVEN BIRKERTS

The underlying assumption [behind *OuLiPo*] is simple: that customary procedures within genres tend to ossify and become automatic; that a well-conceived formal limitation can force the creator to break new ground. Perec, who came to *OuLiPo* in 1967, found that this playful new mode allowed him to overcome a long-standing writer's block. From that time until his death from cancer in 1982 (he was 46), he was a model group member. . . . [He] reserved his greatest artistry for *La Vie mode d'emploi* (now translated as *Life: A User's Manual*), which is sure to stand as one of the great literary anomalies of our time—an experimental work that is a pleasure to read.

Life: A User's Manual is the elegant product of several rather unusual constraining conceptions. To begin with, we are invited to regard the whole work as the verbal transcription of an enormous visionary painting undertaken by an aging artist named Serge Valène. Valène has lived in the same Parisian apartment block for the past 55 years. He has conceived a Saul Steinbergesque—or, if you will, Simultaneist—work that would capture, from a single vantage point, the lives and surroundings of all of the building's residents at a given time, the evening of June 23, 1975. (p. 38)

Perec has, further, arranged his novel so that there are 99 chapters, plus an epilogue. One hundred narrative units, then, that have been set up as a Greco-Latin square of ten, that is, ten by ten. The *OuLiPo*-ean constraint is that we should cover every square by following the forking move of the chess knight. The reader need not know any of this—the hobbles are there mainly to guide the author's hand.

The reader's progress from room to room, into the depths of this old building, is at every step a temporal as well as a spatial movement. We are made privy to every last visual detail of what is there before us:

> Madame Marcia is in her bedroom. She is a woman of sixty or so, tough, broad, and bony. Half-undressed, wearing a white lace-edged slip, a girdle, and stockings, and with her hair in curlers, she is sitting in a modern-made moulded wooden armchair upholstered in black leather. In her right hand she is holding a large barrel-shaped glass jar full of pickled gherkins and is trying to get hold of one between the index and medius fingers of her left hand.

Perec delights in precise description of this sort, here and everywhere. He goes on and on, sometimes covering pages, bringing scrupulosity to the edge of comedy. And often enough, as in the image of Madame Marcia struggling to get hold of the gherkin, he steps right over.

But then there is the other—the temporal, or narrative—aspect. A quick flip to the back of the book reveals that Perec has included not only a comprehensive index of proper names (unheard of in a novel!), but a no less comprehensive chronology of principal dates in his characters' lives and, most unconventionally of all, an "Alphabetical Checklist of Some of the Stories Narrated in this Manual." . . . The list is as inventive and entertaining as any of the inventories in Rabelais, and the matching tales—one per chapter, more or less—make up a modern day *Arabian Nights.*

Picking from this list quite at random, let's follow up The Tale of the Overweight Girl and her mast. The checklist sends us to Chapter 40, which is entitled "Beaumont, 4"—meaning that this is the fourth account thus far about a member of the Beaumont family. As the chapter opens, we find ourselves looking in on an eclectically appointed bathroom. The description picks out the main features, then comes to focus on "a green satin dressing gown with a cat silhouette and the symbol designating spades at cards embroidered on its back." The gown, we learn, has a colorful—though possibly apocryphal—history, having once belonged to a black boxer named Cat Spade, who was the reputed lover of the grandmother of Anna Breidel (Beaumont). It is Anna who we now see lying on the floor beside the bathtub. "She is wearing a white buckram nightdress pulled halfway up her back; on her stretchmarked buttocks there lies an electrical thermal massage vibrator, about fifteen inches in diameter, covered in a red plastic material."

Anna, it seems, has a weight problem. She works on herself daily with the vibrator cushion, at the same time studying a brochure entitled *Complete Table of Energy Values of Customary Foods.* There follows an itemized list of the caloric contents of the various foods that Anna consumed the previous day. We have scarcely digested this information, however, before we learn that Anna also does a good deal of between-meal snacking (representative items listed) that she does not log in.

Then the narration shifts. "In 1967," writes Perec, "at the age of nine, Anna discovered her vocation to be an engineer."

The girl had read in a newspaper that a Panamanian tanker, the *Silver Glen of Alva,* had capsized off Tierra del Fuego, and that her crew had perished. Some claimed that the loss of life could have been averted if there had been receiving aerials with the power to pick up the ship's maydays. Anna thereupon became obsessed with the desire to build the world's largest radio beacon. For the next five years she spent every minute of her spare time drawing, calculating, and so on. . . . But then, quite anticlimactically, the growth of satellite telecommunications as well as her own need to study for college exams "finally got the better of her project." End of tale.

Well, nobody said that all of the stories were going to be show-stoppers. There is, rather, a dazzling variety. Scandal, violence, and mystery alternate regularly with drolly commonplace tellings. The procedure, though, is well illustrated by the Anna example. So many of the chapters begin with precise and neutral visual detailings, which then open out into histories of an object or person. These too are recounted in cool, neutral tones. What's more, few of the tales connect; the majority are taken up and then abandoned forever. By intention, the kaleidoscopic narrative does not add up to a sum greater than the assembled parts. On the page, as in life, individuals are granted their simultaneous, yet essentially separate, orbits.

What results is a most intricately imbricated hybrid, a work neither wholly visual nor wholly narrative. And this is the place to remark yet another of Perec's subtle structural feats: that the final forking knight's move lands the reader in Valène's studio, positioning him before what turns out to be a near-empty canvas. . . . But we are more enlightened than confused by this sudden turn. For when we realize that Valène has not actually been filling in the visual specifics, but merely surveying them in the mind's eye, then we understand the easy narrative transitions from precise descriptions of three-dimensional objects and surfaces to the fourth dimension of a story-telling. The novel, we grasp, has been unfolding as a reverie inside the mind of a dying artist. Everything that Valène has seen, heard, remembered, imagined, and read fuses together as he surveys the apartment boxes that he has sketched on his canvas. (pp. 39-40)

Perec is playing a double game. He is having his richly confected cake and eating it too. On the one hand, he has achieved a kind of apotheosis of formal inventiveness, both beguiling and, in a curious way, profound. For while there is nothing intrinsically deep or meaningful about the subtly concealed limitations that he has put on his practice (they are as arbitrary as they are rigid), they make us feel that the work, like the engine of a DC-10 or the world banking system, will forever exceed our complete comprehension. We accept that, and we submit to it as to a fate. The profundity, then, derives not from a surplus of meaning, but from what appears to us as a transcendent structural intricacy.

But there is, again, the other hand. While indulging his *OuLiPo*-ean pyrotechnics, Perec can also see their limitations. And by concluding with the ultimate failure of Bartlebooth's stratagem, he administers a sly elbow-poke at his own enterprise. The move is at once serious and comical. Though it looks like a well-timed absurdist pratfall, and evokes a smile or a shake of the head, it is also Perec's way of articulating the paradox at the heart of *OuLiPo* and, by extension, of all hyperaesthetic undertakings: that structures, however clever and inclusive, and however productive of new arrangements and new angles of regard, always break down before the entropic chaos of real life. Like the jewelled bird in Yeats's "Sailing to Byzantium," they serve to keep us drowsing emperors awake, and they attend and refresh whatever insomnias may afflict us. But even at the height of their crafted complexity, they cannot fend off or cancel the relentless momentum of time. We are asked to consider both the beauty of the artifact and the sublimated need that underlay its making. Every formal pleasure wears some nimbus of sadness. With that last recognition, Perec completes his own puzzle; he turns a construction of dazzling design into true art. (p. 40)

Sven Birkerts, "House of Games," in The New Republic, Vol. 198, No. 6, February 8, 1988, pp. 38-40.

JAMES SALLIS

One of the few *unsurprising* things about [*Life: A User's Manual*], truly an extraordinary and often astonishing work, is its dedication to the memory of Raymond Queneau, a writer who deserves to be far better known outside France. Surrealist, pataphysician, Freudian and mathematician, general editor of *L'Encyclopedie de la Pleiade* and editorial director at Gallimard (for many years virtually *the* French publisher) Queneau was a polymath who for almost five decades turned out a prodigious amount of work seminal in ways not yet fully acknowledged even in France.

Among Queneau's books are a long poem embracing the entire history of the solar system, a remarkable autobiographical novel in verse, and several novels which in their structure and concerns foreshadow what became known as *le nouveau roman*. *Exercises in Style* recounts a brief narrative in ninety-nine widely diverse styles, including some written within quite arbitrary parameters (in words of only two to five letters, for instance). Of *Le Chiendent's* profoundly arithmatical structure, Queneau once remarked, "I always compelled myself to follow certain rules which had no justification other than their satisfying my taste for figures or some purely personal whims."

Queneau was also a founder of, and Perec a member of, OuLiPo, a peculiar society it's hard to imagine existing anywhere besides France, one given to the inclusion of anagrams, acrostics, and other such language games in "serious" literary work. Perec, for instance, wrote an entire novel in which the letter *e* does not appear. He was also a crossword enthusiast, contributing to *Le Point*, until his death in 1982, a weekly puzzle of exceptional difficulty.

Just so, Perec's novel is riddled with word games, with lengthy (and camouflaged) quotes from other writers, recipes, chess diagrams, facsimile labels, and typed lists, with secret correspondences and recondite jokes.

Both Queneau and Perec are very funny writers. Nor does either forget that primarily, whatever claims we make for it, art is play.

The second great shadow here, alongside Queneau's, is that of Julio Cortázar, whose own game-playing novel *Hopscotch* virtually defined the type. Much of *Life's* humor is reminiscent of Cortázar; its basic scheme could easily have been his own conception. Even the novel's opening lines put one in mind of Cortázar's rhetoric, in which all time seems somehow suspended, or simultaneous:

Yes, it could begin this way, right here, just like that, in a rather slow and ponderous way, in this neutral place that belongs to all and to none, where people pass by almost without seeing each other, where the life of the building regularly and distantly resounds.

It is with "the life of the building," first and finally, that Perec's novel concern itself, somewhat in the manner of a naturalist detailing the strata and discrete activities of an anthill or apiary.

The building in question is 11 Rue Simon-Crubellier, in the 17th *arrondissement* of Paris, and at the book's center (where it is always 8:00 PM, June 23, 1975) resides one Percival Bartlebooth.

Wealthy, doomed to a life of boredom by that wealth and his own mediocrity, Bartlebooth early adopts *life as artifice* for creed. For ten years he studies watercolor, and for the next twenty he travels throughout the world, painting a different seascape each fortnight. These paintings, 500 of them all told, are sent back to Paris where they are turned into complicated jigsaw puzzles by another inhabitant of the building, Gaspard Winckler, and packed away in individual boxes. For the next twenty years, Bartlebooth reassembles, again each fortnight, one of the jigsaws. He dies sitting over the final puzzle in his room at 11 Rue Simon-Crubellier, holding in his hand a W-shaped piece. The remaining blank in the puzzle is X-shaped.

On that bare and unsubstantial frame, moving freely among the coinhabitants of Bartlebooth's building, their histories and memories and the things which surround them (these things in turn pursuing their own impenetrable life), Perec constructs a world of miraculous depth and appeal. Much like novels by Gaddis and Pynchon, *Life's* reach is encyclopedic, grasping towards all human experience, all knowledge, all history.

But above all else, *Life* is a compendium of wonderful stories. Even the partial index of "tales" which concludes the book is revelatory: The German Chemist's Tale, The Tale of the Argentinian Airman, The Tale of the Clown from Warsaw, The Tale of the Jazzman who was never satisfied, The Tale of the Lady who made up nieces, The Tale of the Man who bought the Vase of the Passion, The Tale of the NCO who died in Algeria, The Tale of the Thespian Cook . . .

Published in France in 1979, winner of the Medicis Prize and named novel of the decade by *Le Monde*, *Life: A User's Manual* in Europe has gained an acclaim and currency similar to that given *Hopscotch* in past years. One hopes that American readers also will discover, acknowledge, and embrace this wonderful novel whose windows, mirrors, and multitudinous drawers open onto the many structures—historical, social, neurotic, illusory, artistic—through which we all redeem our lives, or die trying.

James Sallis, "Art & Artifice," in The Bloomsbury Review, Vol. 8, No. 2, March-April, 1988, p. 16.

HARRY MATHEWS

Nearly ten years after its publication in Paris, Georges Perec's monumental *La Vie mode d'emploi* has at last been published in this country as *Life A User's Manual*. . . . Where for the French the novel came as the culmination of a distinguished twenty-year career, for most Americans it coincides with their discovery of its author. They could hardly pick a better place to start; although I must, at the outset, declare my opinions in this matter altogether partial. Two chapters of this translation of *Life* are my doing; Perec and I were close friends—I am biased in favor of his work simply because it is his. I hope that the familiarity underlying this bias will make it possible for me to provide useful information for Perec's English-speaking readers.

Georges Perec was born in 1936 of Polish Jews who emigrated to Paris in the Twenties. By the age of six he had lost both his parents. His father died during the fall of France in June 1940. Arrested in 1942, his mother was deported to an unidentified death camp. Perec spent the occupation years with relatives who had taken refuge in the Vercors, a mountain region south of Grenoble. . . .

Autobiography, or at least concern with autobiography, underlies much of Perec's writing, even in those works in which it is least obvious. . . . While *La Disparition* and *Life A User's Manual* are not overtly autobiographical, I think they can be read, among other ways, as products of Perec's preoccupation with autobiography or, perhaps more accurately, of his obsession with the autobiography he felt he could never write.

Two passages in which Perec writes about himself may help to explain what I mean. The first, from [*W ou le souvenir d'enfance*] describes how his lost and ever-present parents inform his writing:

> I do not know if I have nothing to say; I know that I say nothing. I do not know if what I might have to say remains unsaid because it is unspeakable (the unspeakable is not ensconced in writing, it is what instigated it long before). I know that what I say is blank and neutral, a sign for all time of an annihilation for all time. . . .
>
> That is what I say, that is what I write, and nothing else is to be found in the words I inscribe. . . . It would do me no good to track down my slips . . . or to daydream for two hours about the length of my father's greatcoat. . . . I shall never find anything . . . besides the last reflection of a speech absent from the written word, the outrage of their silence and my silence. I do not write in order to say that I will say nothing, I do not write in order to say that I have nothing to say. I write. I write because we lived together, because I was one among them, a shadow among their shadows, a body next to their bodies. I write because they left in me their indelible mark, whose trace is writing. In writing their memory is dead. Writing is the remembrance of their death and the affirmation of my life.

Perec once said that he had been deprived not only of his mother and father but of their deaths. They had been taken away from him behind his back.

Perec considered his Jewishness as another condition of deprivation. In the commentary he wrote to the film *Chronicles of Ellis Island,* he contrasts his attitude with that of the director, Robert Bober, to whom being Jewish "means continuing to reaffirm one's place in a tradition, a language, and a community":

> What I find present [on Ellis Island] can in no way be called references or roots or remnants, rather their opposite: something shapeless, on the outer edge of what is sayable, something that might be called closure, or cleavage, or severance, something which in my mind is linked in a most intimate and confused way with the very fact of being a Jew. . . .
>
> [Being a Jew] isn't a sign of belonging. . . . It seems closer to a kind of silence, emptiness, to being a question, a questioning, a dubiousness, an uneasiness, an uneasy certainty, and looming beyond that, another certainty . . .: that of having been labeled a Jew, Jew therefore victim, and so beholden for being alive to exile and luck. . . .
>
> (p. 34)

The pretexts of writing, for Perec, are "silence," emptiness, and death: "I know that I do not say anything" means not "I have nothing to say" but rather "nothingness cannot be said." But if silence and emptiness seem a reasonable response to the historical deprivation to which Perec found himself condemned, how then explain the abundance of his output? Why did he become a writer in the first place?

A partial answer to the last question can be found in another passage in *W,* in which he describes his experience as an adolescent reader. Speaking of Dumas's *Vingt ans après,* he tells of reading it over and over again to make sure all its familiar details are still in place: "I not only felt that I had always known them but that they had almost provided me with my own story: [they were the] source of unfathomable memory, of perpetual renewal, of certainty." As an adult, he finds in rereading the books he loves the joy of "complicity and, beyond even that, of kinship restored at last."

Many of us who are not orphans have had the experience of literature as "family," even if we can only guess at its intensity in Perec's case. However, the experience suggests also one origin of Perec's desire to write: since the sense of loss and of being lost is inexpressible, what can you say in its place? How can you say anything at all?

Instead of struggling to find an answer to these questions, Perec sidestepped them, by becoming what used to be called a formalist, ignoring history, looking for things to do inside language, inside writing. Instead of trying to find words to describe the world, he tried to invent interesting ways to use words in their own right. He set himself "precious" tasks. In *Les Choses,* for instance, he methodically explored Flaubert's method of using syntax for stylistic purposes (Perec's opening chapter is written entirely in the conditional tense, the final one in the future tense), using the advertising pages of glossy magazines as his subject matter. The book was read as a realistic commentary on the perils of the consumer society. There is no denying the vividness and authenticity of *Les Choses;* but it must also be said that the subject of the book became "real" as it was invented in the arbitrary tasks the author set himself, without which he might not have written the book at all.

Perec's approach to writing was conveniently codified when, in the mid-Sixties, he became, as later did Italo Calvino and the present writer, a member of the Oulipo—the Ouvroir de littérature potentielle, or Workshop of Potential Literature, a group of literary and mathematical persons founded in 1960 by Raymond Queneau and François LeLionnais. (pp. 34-5)

Perec distinguished himself at many levels of Oulipian experiment, which has ranged from the trivial (spoonerisms) to high art (Calvino's reader-writer chapters in *If on a Winter's Night a Traveler*). Such difficult abstract procedures appealed to him as a writer of fiction because, I suggest, they take formalism to its extreme limit in providing ways of composing that are empty, autonomous, and self-propagating. Empty in that they presuppose no particular content, thus finessing the question of what to say, of how to deal with history; autonomous in that they require no justification beyond obedience to their rules; self-propagating in that, through a simple application of those rules, works are almost automatically generated. Oulipian procedures offer a clear escape from the paralysis of writer's block, or, in Perec's case, a deep sense of historical displacement. More positively, the procedures can become tasks as inspiring as the creation of any hero or heroine. . . .

How Perec filled his "severities" is typically illustrated by *La Disparition,* his most purely Oulipian novel. The book is written without any word containing the letter *e,* a procedure even harder in French than in English, so hard that whenever I try it I have to glue an upturned thumbtack on the *e* key of my typewriter to keep the forbidden vowel at bay. Perec took this absurdly confining idea and made of it a way of creating incident, situation, and plot. (p. 35)

The central story tells of the disappearance one by one of all its main characters, victims of a nameless, terrible power that threatens at any moment to destroy everything in sight—a power that ultimately takes the shape of a bearded king that devours his offspring (resembling not only Saturn but the author himself) and that is at one point defined as an "enigma that will destroy us whether it is solved or not." In the world of *La Disparition,* threatened by the absent but ever-menacing *e,* people can neither speak nor remain silent: it might be said that in this plot that combines elements of a detective story, a tale of adventure, and a Marx Brothers movie, Perec has also replicated his historical situation—the sense of historical loss—without even mentioning it.

No such simple procedure characterizes *Life A User's Manual. La Disparition* wears its torn-out heart on its sleeve; Perec's later and longer work depends on multiple artifices, some of them mathematically complex, all of them virtually invisible. The importance of abstract procedures nevertheless remains the same: they enable the author to choose and organize his material, and in this case to produce an almost Balzacian "world" teeming with characters and events. But I think the time has come to forget about Oulipian structures, and Perec would probably agree: he repeatedly compared the devices used in writing *Life* to the scaffolding of a building, something to be discarded once the work was completed. *Life* is not a puzzle, or else it is one that the author has already solved, leaving every piece in place. It presents with almost nonchalant transparency a prodigious variety of objects and of both ordinary and exotic characters.

The narrative conceit of *Life A User's Manual* . . . is to imagine a nine-story, turn-of-the-century Parisian apartment building from which the façade has been removed. Each chapter of the novel corresponds to one of the streetside rooms thus revealed and describes the objects it contains, the present occupants of the room or of the apartment to which it belongs, sometimes the former occupants. The conceit might seem likely to produce no more than a catalog of lives and things; and *Life* often seems to present such a catalog, replete with accounts of kitchen equipment, bric-a-brac, and undistinguished works of art, all detailed in meticulous and

neutral terms. But this is only pretense, an elaborate display of hyperrealism veiling the reality of what we slowly and almost unwittingly learn as we wend our distractible way from room to room.

Among the thirty-odd characters whose stories are told at length, three are soon recognized as central: Bartlebooth, Winckler, and Valène. . . . Percival Bartlebooth is an Englishman endowed with . . . virtually unlimited wealth. . . . To fill up the vain time ahead of him, he conceives in his youth of a preposterously demanding and altogether gratuitous scheme that will require several decades to carry out. . . . [He will] travel around the world to paint views of five hundred widely scattered seaports, at the rate of two a month. The watercolors will then be transformed into jigsaw puzzles that Bartlebooth, once his travels are over, will reassemble, after which each will be dispatched to the place where it was painted, there to be destroyed. Gaspard Winckler, a craftsman of genius, is hired by Bartlebooth to turn the watercolors into puzzles. Serge Valène is a painter who teaches Bartlebooth the skills he needs.

At the start of the book, Bartlebooth's scheme is nearing its conclusion. The watercolors have all been made into puzzles, and Bartlebooth has almost completed the 439th of them. Winckler has died after a life of disillusion and heartache; Valène and Bartlebooth by now are old men. Valène is engaged in a project of his own, which resembles that of Perec's novel. He is painting the building in which he, Bartlebooth, and Winckler have lived, with the façade removed so that each room behind it lies open to view. An intensely compassionate man, Valène is obsessed by a sense of the transience of things and of human life. (pp. 35-6)

As a background to these three lives we are told a multitude of stories about the other inhabitants of the building. One can hardly say that these lives remind us of the three principal ones, except in one respect. Like Bartlebooth with his insane scheme, Winckler with the revenge he has plotted against his employer through his five hundred puzzles, and Valène with his gigantic painting project, most of the secondary characters are dominated by some obsession. Henri Fresnel sacrifices his family and his career in his determination to become an actor. His wife devotes her life to waiting for him so that she can throw him out when he comes back. The ethnographer Appenzzell wastes away, haunted by the memory of an elusive primitive tribe. Bartlebooth's uncle James Sherwood squanders a fortune because of his mania for collecting *unica* (one-of-a-kind objects). Sven Ericsson spends many years and most of his money in order to murder the accidental agent of his child's death. (p. 36)

The accumulation of such stories, together with that of the three main characters, produces an effect of inevitability, of fatality, almost of futility: less that these obsessive human lives allow no room for choice than that knowledge and self-knowledge not only do not modify fatality but confirm it. It is as if no possibility existed outside a single narrative possibility, as if human life was confined by a syntax as unyielding as language itself, as if life were the outcome of some arbitrary, abstract, formal constraint.

The relations of Bartlebooth, Winckler, and Valène underscore this sense of fatality. It is tempting to describe the three men in Marxist terms (Perec after all was a socialist): Bartlebooth the capitalist, the master; Winckler the exploited laborer condemned to work at the production of goods he will never use; Valène the sympathetic but expendable parasite, full of petit-bourgeois sensibility. While such an account would be absurdly reductive, it does suggest something of Perec's view of fatality and choice, with respect to a particular form of production, that of the artist, especially the writer.

If we look at our triumvirate as a composite portrait of the artist, we can identify Bartlebooth as the passionless inventor of abstract and gratuitous formal procedures; Winckler as the rebellious agent who nevertheless submits to such procedures; Valène as the compassionate witness who freely invents his own forms. Each of the three depends on the others: Valène and Winckler are both employed by Bartlebooth, who of course cannot carry out his scheme without them. Naturally Valène's position strikes us as the most enviable: if you have to adopt demanding forms, you are surely better off choosing your own. But the events of *Life* do not confirm our bias. Valène barely manages to begin his great painting. Bartlebooth will never solve the remaining puzzles. Only Winckler, bitter and resentful, succeeds, by creating (in a Proustian cork-lined room) his own unforeseen and hermetic strategy of revenge while executing the years-long task that has been imposed on him. So choice—at least the kind of choice that produces results—lies not in the unconstrained will but in the circumstances of fatality itself, as though choice and fatality were anything but opposites.

Life does not have a conclusion. It only comes to an end, with the disappearance of its two surviving protagonists. The final pages proceed toward a last image of the dying Bartlebooth bent over a puzzle of which every segment is in place but one. We realize that everything that has taken place so far is shown to be only a prelude to this moment, an elaborate and delusive preparation. The abundance of stories, the multiplicity of lives, have brought us to a conclusion empty of life and possibility; all we have read now collapses in a hopeless finality. The effect is of "something," in Perec's words, "that might be called closure, or cleavage, or severance." We are left, as the author elsewhere remarked, with nothing "except this object you have shut, a few images, blank shadows or dark ghosts that have flitted through your head and mine."

One of the transient inhabitants of Perec's apartment building, Emilio Grifalconi, "a cabinet maker from Verona," gives Valène an unusual object in appreciation of a family portrait the artist has painted for him. The object resembles "a large cluster of coral," and it has been produced by the solidification of a liquid mixture Grifalconi once injected into the tangle of minute tunnels that termites had bored inside the base of an antique wooden table. Even reinforced, the base proves too fragile to support the table top and has to be replaced; but Grifalconi salvages

> the fabulous arborescence within, this exact record of the worms' life inside the wooden mass: a static, mineral accumulation of all the movements that had constituted their blind existence, their undeviating single-mindedness, their obstinate itineraries; the faithful materialisation of all they had eaten and digested as they forced from their dense surroundings the invisible elements needed for their survival. . . .
>
> (pp. 36-7)

Since the object is referred to at one point as a *réseau de vers,* which can mean a network not only of worms but of verses, we can claim it for literature; most usefully, for this very

book. The novel is certainly a "record of life" in all its "obstinate itineraries," at least as it has manifested itself in a particular place during a longish time. The book's pretext of methodically reviewing the inhabitants of a variously populated apartment house guarantees as much. But as I have suggested, this pretext does not necessarily correspond to what actually happens. Perec's deliberate cataloging enables him to reinforce his personal narrative with an apparently authoritative objectivity. . . . Perec has used his systems to discover exactly what he needs to say as a novelist. . . . [Visions] recur throughout the novel, and they are what to me make Grifalconi's salvaged arborescence such an appropriate emblem of the book: life, and lives, leave nothing behind them but a faint or ossified residue. Once gone, they "mean" no more than these traces. And writing, like Grifalconi's sculpture, sometimes is such a trace.

I wrote that *Life A User's Manual* might be read as part of Perec's preoccupation with the autobiography he could never write since, in his case, the "historical" pretext of writing was a dumbfounding sense of emptiness and death. So the novel ends in the fatal, futile "closure" of its protagonists' careers; but it achieves this by following one exceptionally bright strand across a varied universe of high and low life:

> One day, well before his fatal hibernation had gripped him, [Grégoire Simpson] had told Morrelet how as a little boy he had played drum major with the *Matagassiers* on mid-Lent Sunday. His mother, a dressmaker, made the traditional costume herself: the red-and-white-squared trousers, the loose blue blouse, the white cotton bonnet with a tassel; and his father had bought him, in a fine circular box decorated with arabesques, the cardboard mask which looked like a cat's head. As proud as Punch and as grave as a judge, he ran through the streets of the old town along with the procession, from Place du Château to Porte des Allinges, and from Porte de Rives to Rue Saint-Sébastien, before going up into the high town, to the Belvederes, to stuff himself with juniper-roast ham and to slake his thirst with great gulps of Ripaille, that white wine as light as glacier water, as dry as gunflint.

It hardly matters if this episode comes from observation, memory, or another book. Its value, that of a small item from a large repertory, can perhaps be best discerned through one of Perec's definitions of his aims as a writer: "to pluck meticulous fragments from the deepening void, to leave somewhere or other a furrow, a trace." Just as in the novel James Sherwood collects *unica,* Perec gathered many such fragments and assembled them into a replica of his most treasured *unicum* of all. Death may come first and last; in between we find life. . . . (p. 37)

Harry Mathews, "That Ephemeral Thing," in The New York Review of Books, *Vol. XXXV, No. 10, June 16, 1988, pp. 34-7.*

JOHN LEE

[*In the essay excerpted below, translator and critic John Lee discusses the problems he encountered while translating Perec's novel,* La disparition.]

Georges Perec's *La Disparition* is an outstanding example of modern French fiction—not least for its humour, within a complex network of elements where the relationship between the world and the book is only indirectly established. . . .

[A] constraint applied in *La Disparition* is the "lipogram", or "letter-dropping": in this case the commonest letter in French, e, is proscribed. . . . What is so peculiar to Perec's use of the lipogram, however, is the fact that the formal constraint governs the story rather than the other way round. The unspoken disappearance of the letter takes human form in a series of mysterious deaths and disappearances, and the search for an explanation becomes the novel's plot. As this penultimate scene shows, and—almost—explains, any character about to pronounce the unpronounceable, having discovered his narrative strait-jacket, gets killed off in mid-sentence.

Along with rhymes, puns, grammatical slips, and all kinds of intertextual linkages, quotations, translations and cross-fertilizations, the book contains smatterings of Latin, Italian and German, as well as plenty of English. In this sense, it positively invites its own translation. But can this be done merely by translating the sense, without regard to the lipogram? Clearly not, since the sense and the lipogram are one and the same thing. The medium is the message, or rather, "the medium is the message" is the message. As it is, the lipogrammatic solution is difficult enough, not so much in itself, but because of the *heightened* importance of the sense, but because so much of the linguistic content is, inevitably, specifically French. This entails an unavoidable stylistic constraint (apparently not to everyone's taste: on these grounds, Collins Harvill, who own the rights, have refused my completed version of *La Disparition,* deciding, finally, to release the rights rather than to publish themselves). In my view, any non-lipogrammatic rendering would be a far more radical transformation of the text—a completely different novel, in fact.

It takes ingenuity, for example, to explain the absence of eggs in terms of the absence of e's, in other words to render the pun "pas d'oeufs/pas d'e". Using e's, this is easy enough: in the terms of the fiction, however, one might say it is "difficult inough"—ie not really *eesy* at all, for *un oeuf* is more than *enough* (the unorthodox spelling copying "infant" for "enfant" in the accompanying extract). None the less, it can be done. . . .

The novel is full of wordplay which must be rendered in translation because it is an integral part of the whole—that is, carries meaning. One or two examples: if a spoonerism on the name Carcopino gives *Cocopinar* ("coco", a derogatory diminutive for a communist, combining with "pinard", or low-grade table wine, to form an ambiguous "red plonk"), something like *Karlovino* must be found. But "coco" also means "egg" in baby talk—hence "e", which explains the banning, on another page, of the Communist Party, where "coco" may be rendered "commy nignog" (close to "egg-nog"). There is alcohol on nearly every page, mainly because of the peculiar combination of letters in the word *whisky*. . . . The word has an additional property in English: its dual spelling, Scotch whisky/Irish whiskey. All it takes to draw attention to the missing "e" is to write . . . "Irish whisky".

The book raises an interesting theoretical question about the status of author and translator. On the one hand, Perec's technique is largely one of rewriting (I have recently discovered the presence of vast quantities of literary borrowings previously only suspected). On the other hand, he makes great demands on his translator's own inventiveness. This apparent contradiction undermines the popular notion of the author as an original genius, and the translator his faithful servant—barely a writer at all, even. What we have in Perec, then, is a fictional justification of two ideas crucial to modern theory since Lautréamont: writing as a shared, democratic process; and translation as writing, in the fullest sense of the word.

John Lee, in a commentary on his translation of "La Disparition," in The Times Literary Supplement, *No. 4457, September 2-8, 1988, p. 958.*

NIGEL WILLIAMS

[One] of the cheering things about *W or The Memory of Childhood,* by Georges Perec, is that it is as different from the author's masterpiece *Life: A User's Manual,* as it is possible to imagine. That is not to say that it reads as if written by someone else—the obsession with game-playing, the penchant for humorous names and the bemused fascination with material objects that characterise Perec's great novel are to be found in these pages. But if *Life: A User's Manual* was a shatteringly complete look at a moment in the history of a building, and at the histories of those living in it, *W* is a deliberate attempt at raggedness, a cultivated turning away from the aesthetic, since what it describes cannot, or perhaps must not, be spoken about too gracefully.

When he was six, in 1942, Perec's mother, Cyrla Szulewicz, a Warsaw-born Jew who had come to Paris just after the end of the First War, took him to the Gare de Lyon and put him on a Red Cross convoy bound for Grenoble in the Free Zone. A year later she died, at Drancy, on her way to Auschwitz. Perec's father had died of abdominal wounds received from machine-gun fire on the very day of the Armistice, 16 June 1940, and the heart of *W* is an attempt to set down, as accurately as possible, the memories of the orphaned, Jewish child that the adult writer seems hardly to recognise. Accuracy is very important, since Perec is not, in this section of the book, attempting the kind of subjective sketch in which early impressions are set down with the sole intention of making the reader see them. He wishes, in a very non-literary way, to disentangle false memory from true, and to this end transcribes a passage from his first attempt to recall those years, written 15 years before *W,* and annotates it, informing us that his first account gets his father's death date wrong by a day, elevates his father's family's status and spells his mother's maiden name wrong. Older Perec seems suspicious of younger Perec, as if the mature writer had become infected with Platonic moral doubt about the enterprise of fiction, asking himself, even in the act of writing itself, why it is he has chosen to include or omit this or that detail. What he is most frightened of is style, artifice, false cunning, and false emotion.

Perec offers up his childhood through childhood's purest eye, and his conscientious rendering of the immediate makes this section of the book both haunting and compelling. But *W* is not simply a memoir of childhood. Intercut with memories, of being given the wrong toy by a Canadian soldier at the Liberation or of seeing a group of German soldiers visit the children's home where he spent the war, Perec tells the story of the search for a ten-year-old boy, lost from a ship somewhere off the Azores. An agency, entitled the Bureau Veritas, needs to find him, and yet the boy, who bears the name of Gaspard Winckler (familiar to all readers of *Life: A User's Manual*) is as irretrievable as the childhood of his creator. The only evidence of his survival is an account of the mysterious island of W, where a society has evolved in which success is based on athletic prowess. This Olympian sounding ideal is, in fact, a repressive bureaucracy designed to humiliate and degrade its citizens very much in the way Perec's own mother suffered.

The slow exposition of this society's customs—rather as if one had begun to describe any Fascist or totalitarian state in terms of its paper constitution, and only gradually got around to the torture chambers and death cells that were in fact the heart of the system—is chilling and totally effective. . . . Is W an island created by the lost boy, Gaspard Winckler? Should we read anything into the fact that the name Pfister crops up in the scrupulously truthful memoir and in the extravagantly designed myth of the island of W (which, by the way, seems to have been a very early fictional effort by the young Perec)? What, exactly, are we reading here? Isn't it too wilfully fragmented for a reader to assimilate, neither fiction nor autobiography, but an awkward mixture of the two? Well, if it is, it is intended so to be, and . . . [W] convinced this reader that this is the way it should be, since the heart of the text is an attempt to describe the life of a child whose fate was determined by events so horrific as to stun the fiction writer into silence before the facts.

Once again this writer is asking us to look with all our eyes. His concentration and honesty in that exercise must rank this book alongside the really crucial texts in the literature of the Holocaust, the testimony of the survivors. (pp. 34-5)

Nigel Williams, "The Past Is Another Island," in The Listener, Vol. 121, No. 3085, October 20, 1988, pp. 34-5.

PIERS BURTON-PAGE

In the post-Olympic depression [described in *W or the Memory of Childhood*] there is no respite in ultima Thule. W is a lost mythical island, whose sole raison d'etre is an endless series of sporting (and unsporting) contests; not just Olympiads, but Atlantiads and Spartakiads too. These cyclical encounters govern the entire sociological fabric of W. The terrifying totalitarian regime thus imposed on the island is climactically exposed by Perec as an uncannily apt metaphor for the *univers concentrationnaire* of both past and present—and which made Perec himself an orphan. He died in 1982, tragically early, leaving a body of work that is essentially a voyage of self-discovery.

So *W* develops startlingly from its Jules Verne-like opening, complete with shipwreck. Chapters of fantasy and autobiography alternate, illuminate each other in strange ways, and slowly blend in an extraordinary literary fusion, half fiction, half fact. Such originality should not surprise us, coming from the author of that magisterial novel *Life: A User's Manual*. . . . *W,* though, is altogether different, an earlier work that nevertheless embraces many of the novel's themes—memory, childhood, identity, success and failure, guilt and expiation—and uses many of the same literary devices—puzzles, cryptic clues, cabbalistic signs. The W of the title stands not only for the island, but also for the lost identities of the protagonist, Gaspard Winckler. . . . Inverted and superimposed, W can also be both swastika, and star of David.

The memory of a star pinned on is one fragment among many that make up the searing autobiographical collage that forms the other half of *W.* Gradually the focus clears on Perec's

nightmare of war, injustice, separation and loss, recalled with dry-eyed objectivity. *W* is a spell-binding book, a major addition (despite its slimness) to the Perec canon in English. Now we desperately need his third masterpiece, *La Disparition*. . . . We need it because Perec is unique: as *W* shows, in the hollow cleft between fiction and the self, he finds an authentic note of tragedy. (pp. 36-7)

Piers Burton-Page, "World of Sport," in New Statesman & Society, Vol. 1, No. 21, October 28, 1988, pp. 36-7.

MICHIKO KAKUTANI

In France, a country that prizes formalism and cerebral innovation in its arts, Georges Perec (1936-1982) emerged as one of the most daring and admired of contemporary writers. . . .

[*W, or the Memory of Childhood*] defies conventional narrative rules. Told in alternating chapters, the novel actually consists of two separate stories; the first deals with Mr. Perec's own childhood in Nazi-occupied France; the second with a mythical island nation called W that is somewhere off Tierra del Fuego. The story of W, it seems, is an embellishment of a tale written by the author when he was 12 or 13. A kind of allegory about the Nazi atrocities of World War II, it serves to illuminate the autobiographical portion of the book by parable and indirection.

In the chapters devoted to his own life, Mr. Perec attempts to piece together a picture of his childhood. The past does not return to him in a liberating rush of Proustian reminiscence; rather, it has to be extracted painfully from fragmentary memories, photographic clues and other people's recollections. Sometimes, Mr. Perec observes, he does not even know when he is telling us the truth and when he is giving us imaginative re-creations of what really happened.

We learn that the author's father enlisted the day war broke out and that he "was taken prisoner after being wounded in the abdomen by machine-gun fire or a shell splinter" in 1940 and died. We learn that his mother sent him off with the Red Cross to be evacuated from Paris and that she was subsequently picked up during a German raid, then interned at a camp in Drancy, where she died in 1943.

The young Mr. Perec, meanwhile, was adopted by relatives and enrolled in a Catholic school. Although the presence of soldiers and refugees made him aware of the war, many of his memories of this period deal with fairly conventional matters: competing with classmates for special privileges, collecting bilberries in the summer and skiing in the winter. He says he has "no visual memory" of the Liberation or "of the waves of enthusiasm that accompanied and followed it and in which it is more than likely that I took part."

Juxtaposed with Mr. Perec's own story is the story of W, an island society supposedly dedicated to the Olympian ideal, "a land where Sport is king, a nation of athletes where Sport and life unite in a single magnificent effort." Competitions in track and field events take place regularly between the island's four villages, and a strict Darwinism appears to rule.

Winners are given sumptuous feasts and privileges, while losers are mocked, starved, sometimes even killed. Further, this barbarism permeates the entire social structure. Four out of five female children are killed; the remaining girls grow up to be raped by the winners of certain competitions. All manner of foul play is allowed during these events (including tripping, shouldering, elbowing, kneeing, even the ripping out of eyeballs) and the island's administration reinforces such unsportsmanlike behavior by perpetuating what is known as "organized injustice."

"It is necessary that even the best be uncertain of winning; it is necessary that even the feeblest be uncertain of losing," Mr. Perec writes. "Both must take an equal risk and must entertain the same insane hope of winning, the same unspeakable fervor of losing." As a result, arbitrary handicaps are imposed on contestants; umpiring is frequently biased and disruptive elements (unevenly placed hurdles, etc.) are regularly introduced into the competitions.

W's institutional unfairness, of course, comes to stand for the randomness and moral chaos of the real world, and it also underscores the terror experienced by Mr. Perec's family and the other victims of World War II. In addition, specific parallels between W and the Nazi regime are implied. We're told that the colonizers of W are "almost exclusively Aryan," that they subordinate all questions of morality to the brutal esthetic of the state and that all residents of the island participate in the officially sanctioned atrocities, if not overtly, then by silent acquiescence.

None of these parallels are ever explicitly discussed by Mr. Perec. In fact, there's an almost willful reluctance on his part to connect the story of W with the story of his own youth—a self-conscious narrative strategy that in calling attention to itself distracts the reader from the larger moral questions raised by the entire novel. At the same time, however, Mr. Perec's gift for grounding his literary pyrotechnics in precisely observed details lends an immediacy to both stories: in the case of the story of W, the urgency is an illusion created by a skillful storyteller; in the case of the memoir, the urgency comes from knowing that the facts related are real.

More important, *W, or the Memory of Childhood* manages to transcend the rarified realm of contemporary esthetics by taking on one of the central questions of our age: How could the Holocaust have happened, not on a mythical island, but in 20th-century Europe?

> *Michiko Kakutani, "An Allegory and a Memoir of Nazi Rule Entwined," in* The New York Times, *November 26, 1988, p. L14.*

KEITH WALDROP

Every book by Perec is an experiment, each one a *different* experiment, but they share the security of style, a sense of bedrock that seems anything but restless. It is reported that he wanted to write every kind of book, but no kind twice. Had he not died at 46 (in 1982), he might have come close. . . .

[*W or the Memory of Childhood*] has two strands, both in transparent prose. One is autobiographical, told from a scant store of childhood memories and from conjectural interpretations of a few photographs, words jotted on the backs of photographs, and such obscure traces. This is a story of recall, beginning "I have no childhood memories," but going on to recover some.

The second strand, interwoven with the first in alternate chapters, is the account of an imaginary island called W, where a society has been founded on "the Olympic ideal,"

that is to say on a glorification of sports and the ethic of winning. The description, quite objective, as if by an anthropologist or by Jules Verne, seems itself at first a harmless sort of game—following the logic of a bizarre premise. But it darkens rapidly as the game is played and the parallel with the Nazi regime comes clear.

The two strands, opposed as they are, are interwoven. On the simplest level, the island is an attempt of the adult Perec to work out a project of his own childhood. At the same time, it is a reminder that Perec's parents were victims of the Nazis. No novel of the Holocaust could be more oblique than this or, in another way, more direct. Starting with the author's "absence of history," that history becomes terribly concrete, genuinely terrifying. . . .

I find *W or The Memory of Childhood,* in French or English, a wonderful book.

> *Keith Waldrop, "The French Novel: Writing as Wordplay," in* Book World—The Washington Post, *January 8, 1989, p. 11.*

LINDA SIMON

[Perec] was brought to the attention of American readers in 1987 with the translation of *Life: A User's Manual*. . . . Fragmented, surrealistic and irreverent, the novel established Perec's reputation as an innovator in post-modern literature, an outrageous, energetic voice.

He is not outrageous in *W: Or The Memory of Childhood,* a darker, more fragile work. . . . Perec, characteristically, does not present us with a straightforward narrative. *W* interweaves two texts: one is an assemblage of Perec's memories of his childhood in Nazi-occupied France, the other a fable he wrote when he was 13 and later reconstructed in an effort to retrieve even one story from the near extermination of his past.

The latter is a grotesque fantasy of life on an island called W, off Tierra del Fuego. Like most dystopias, it is a totalitarian state, a place where women are used for sexual recreation, children are separated from adults and men are set one against the other in ruthless athletic competitions. . . . The story of W, read outside of its historical context, would be a predictable tale. But as we witness the violence that is unleashed in Perec's imaginary world, we are repeatedly interrupted by the autobiographical fragments, and this juxtaposition makes both the fiction and the reality all the more terrifying.

Perec tries to penetrate "History with a capital H . . . the war, the camps," to find his own history, that of a child born to Polish Jews in France in 1936, soon to lose both family and heritage. . . .

The certainty with which Perec narrates the tale of W contrasts with his tenuous groping for the past. He struggles to make sense of contradictions. He ventures an anecdote, then qualifies it with pages of annotations. He does not trust himself; he does not believe the stories he is told. He does not trust literature. "Whether I added true or false details of greater precision, whether I wrapped them in irony or emotion, rewrote them curtly or passionately, whether I gave free rein to my fantasies or elaborated more fictions," he writes, still he cannot say what is essentially unsayable; still he cannot resurrect what was annihilated.

If the shattering of reality seems a literary device in *Life,* here it becomes an accurate representation of history. Only incoherence, Georges Perec tells us, can serve to reflect a past that is not merely elusive but incomprehensible.

> *Linda Simon, "The Unspeakable Life of a Child,"
> in* The New York Times Book Review, *January 8,
> 1989, p. 16.*

Emily Prager

1952-

American short story writer, novelist, and journalist.

Prager is known for comic parables in which she employs exuberant prose and biting witticisms to satirize sexual politics, race relations, and ecological issues. Her first book, *A Visit from the Footbinder and Other Stories* (1982), was praised for its provocative and humorous parodies of such masculine institutions as the combat unit and the "bull session," gatherings at which men boast of their sexual conquests. Prager also comments on the subjugation of women and the social customs that encourage sexist behavior. In the title story, for example, she details the mutilating footbinding ceremony of a six-year-old daughter of medieval Chinese aristocrats. Phyllis Raphael remarked: "These stories made me aware of how much I had missed feminist troublemaking and how necessary it still is to identify that part of myself in the art of an intelligent, tough and eminently witty writer."

Prager's first novel, *Clea and Zeus Divorce* (1987), is a futuristic work about two internationally famous performance artists whose productions revolve around the major events of their ten-year marriage. The narrative centers on "Clea and Zeus Divorce," their final performance, which is being telecast live throughout the United States from Times Square. The tension as well as the comic possibilities in the novel are heightened after Clea's psychic predicts that a nuclear bomb will explode at John F. Kennedy Airport before the third act of the program. Prager intersperses depictions of this performance with flashbacks of the characters' first meeting, their previous productions, and events leading up to the dissolution of their marriage. Some critics have interpreted Clea and Zeus's relationship with their entourage, which includes a Chinese Maoist poet and an African medicine woman, as emblematic of Western civilization's alternately exploitative and charitable association with Third World countries. Although several reviewers considered Prager's characters one-dimensional and unsympathetic, many commended her authentic rendering of backstage anxiety and interaction. Cynthia Cotts asserted: "[*Clea and Zeus Divorce*] is a work of seamless prestidigitation, a multi-tiered narrative concealing a thousand surprises. Though it careens between melodrama and contrivance, this camp tragedy is delivered with cutting style."

ANN HULBERT

Tolstoy may have been right when he wrote that all unhappy families are unhappy in their own way, but the consensus among authors seems to be that unhappy women, at least, are strikingly similar. "In sorrow thou shalt bring forth children," God told Eve and all her descendants, according to one ancient book. According to newer books, written mostly by women, the fair sex shares more than labor pains and a legacy of social and political oppression. There are many peculiarly female psychological woes as well, and they seem to

be multiplying: authors tell of mother troubles and Cinderella complexes, "pressure points" and "passages," that lie in store for girls as soon as they turn into women at the witching hour of puberty. Every week the "Hers" column in *The New York Times* has even more up-to-date news on a wide variety of unhappinesses women might share with their sisters. In fiction too, the shape of a distinctively feminine, and arduous, *Bildungsroman* has been discerned by literary critics (mostly women) looking back at lady novelists of the past. Meanwhile, women writers of the present are at work updating female ordeals and adventures. This fall three collections of short stories by women present a bevy of unhappy heroines who share an often burdensome self-consciousness about their common woes.

Virginia Woolf, a pioneer on feminist literary terrain, identified two essential difficulties women faced both in writing and in living. The first was obedience to a phantom she called The Angel in the House and described this way:

> She was intensely sympathetic. She was immensely charming. She was utterly unselfish. She excelled in the difficult arts of family life. She sacrificed herself daily. If there was a chicken, she took the leg; if there was a draught, she sat in it.

Woolf turned upon this selfless sprite and caught her by her delicate, yielding throat. However, women's other problem—telling the truth about their passions, about their "own experiences as a body"—was more intractable. . . . But many of these stories, published half a century after Woolf's essay, suggest that women now—both the writers and their characters—have far more trouble with Woolf's first problem than with the second. Bodies and passions now lie bare in books, carefully scrutinized in countless contortions. It is how to behave as a self in the house, in the world—not as a body in bed—that poses greater difficulty for women in these stories: if not as an Angel, then as what? (pp. 40-1)

Emily Prager's [*A Visit from the Footbinder and Other Stories*], her publishing debut, is wry and irreverent, rare qualities in feminist fiction. Like almost all of her female characters, Prager is adventurous. She begins [this volume] with the tale of the footbinding of a little girl named Pleasure Mouse in thirteenth-century China and resists conventional accounts of women and their contemporary complaints in the stories that follow. Instead of finding pathos in women's acquiescence to cultural and personal constraints, she discovers comedy and irony, often dark, in their efforts to liberate themselves. In the medieval Chinese court, women's only hope for a good marriage and luxurious life was to have bound feet, "no longer than newborn kittens," forced into tiny shoes at a tender age, a gruesome rite supervised by the ladies of the court. Prager's story of the subjugation of six-year-old "perky Pleasure Mouse's" scampering feet is at once poignant and pointed, thanks to an active imagination and inventive prose—far more effective than the heavy-handed parable it all too easily could have been. Prager is distinctly less deft in **"The Lincoln-Pruitt Anti-Rape Device: Memoirs of the Women's Combat Army in Vietnam,"** where she attempts the broadest social and sexual satire of the collection.

In the least outlandish of the five stories, **"Agoraphobia,"** Prager comes back home to Manhattan and conventional realism and writes what could almost be a Margaret Atwood tale of female neurosis, except for the liberal lacing of irony.

> Marian had read about herself in *The New York Times*. An article in the 'Hers' column had convinced her that she was an 'agoraphobe,' a term she preferred to 'shut-in' for the visions it conjured up of a white-pillared marketplace in ancient Greece.

Along with her neurosis, however, Marian has a down-to-earth phantom named Dolores (she files her nails and cracks her gum—not at all an Angel) who has been impatiently scolding and prodding Marian ever since she was four. This time imaginary Dolores bullies Marian into venturing out to a cocktail party—where her courage is rewarded by bumping into Russell Baker, whose column Marian has the good sense and humor to follow even more avidly than "Hers." (p. 42)

Ann Hulbert, "Femininity and Its Discontents," in The New Republic, *Vol. 187, Nos. 12 & 13, September 20 & 27, 1982, pp. 40-2.*

CHRISTOPHER LEHMANN-HAUPT

In the longest, wildest, most blackly humorous piece in [*A Visit from the Footbinder and Other Stories*, an] audacious collection of five stories, a platoon of female soldiers goes into the Vietnam jungle armed with Lincoln-Pruitt Anti-Rape Devices—L.P.A.R.D.'s, or leopards—lethal mechanisms de-

signed by one Maj. Victoria Lincoln-Pruitt, the highest ranking female officer in the United States Army.

As Major Lincoln-Pruitt tells the Joint Chiefs of Staff while promoting what she calls Operation Foxy Fire: "The L.P.A.R.D. has given rape a new meaning. And for this reason, is the long-sought-for answer to the problems of female combat. With the L.P.A.R.D. for the first time women will be able to kill easily and fully, and with complete security that no one will be taking obscene Polaroids of them after the battle. Guns are clearly for men, but the Leopard is for a woman." To this, "The Joint Chiefs winced, but they recognized her logic as invincible."

Does this sound a bit like adolescent fantasy—an exaggerated female counterpart of boyhood dreams of glory? Of course it does, because that's exactly what Emily Prager is up to in some of these stories. **"The Lincoln-Pruitt Anti-Rape Device: Memoirs of the Women's Combat Army in Vietnam"** is a blatant and very funny parody of masculine war fiction, even down to precombat flashbacks in which the "girls," one by one, recall how they came to be members of Foxy Fire.

Similarly, **"The Alumnae Bulletin,"** in which three Brearley School graduates convene for their annual reports on recent sexual activities, is, among other things, a takeoff of those bull sessions in which the guys get together to boast of their conquests. . . .

The danger of this sort of humor is that the idea can sometimes seem funnier than its execution. And indeed Miss Prager . . . is occasionally guilty of overcerebration. Every so often this reader had to stop and reflect for a while before he could see the wit of what Miss Prager was up to.

Fortunately, there's a lot more going on in these stories than jokes and sexual warfare. This is evident in the following wonderfully ambiguous descriptive line from a scene in the antirape story in which warfare works its malign influence on pastoral beauty: "The sun, in its decline, shot its rays like deadbolts through the open water, and portions of the bank were bathed in the most golden and secret of lights."

It is further evident in the book's two shorter stories. **"Agoraphobia,"** about a young woman struggling to get herself to a party with the help of an imaginary friend who "had refused to vanish at adolescence"; and **"Wrinkled Linen,"** in which another young woman uses her strength to articulate her fragility. In both these pieces, Miss Prager is more concerned with the social constraints on women than she is with fantasies of getting even.

Her considerable depths are even evident in the antirape story, where nothing turns out as one expects it to, and the ending is a twist of a twist of a twist. But most of all they are apparent in the title story, **"A Visit From the Footbinder,"** where Miss Prager combines her talents most frighteningly. The feminist in her seethes at the horror and injustice of the not-so-ancient Chinese practice of mutilating the feet of aristocratic women. The psychologist in her understands how the weight of tradition can crush individual protest. The comedian in her renders an aptly subtle parody of that tinkly literary cliché that results when Western muscles try to conjure up the delicate Orient. Together, they make a powerful statement about the crippling power of tradition. . . .

What we have here then in Emily Prager's collection is the collaboration of an ideologue, a comedian and a literary artist. When they cooperate, the book is splendid and original. When they fight, it declines into cleverness. It will be most intriguing to follow the future adventures of these multiple talents.

> *Christopher Lehmann-Haupt, in a review of "A Visit from the Footbinder," in* The New York Times, *October 4, 1982, p. C17.*

JAMES WOLCOTT

Emily Prager isn't a jolly satirist, retracting her claws so that we'll know she's just funnin'. Suavely heartless in the manner of the early Evelyn Waugh, Prager is a feminist fantasist of bright, cruel gifts, and the stories in her first collection, *A Visit from the Footbinder,* are speckled with eerie moments, like beads of blood squeezed through an eye-dropper. Set in thirteenth-century China, the title story is about the lunatic tyranny of ritual. Pleasure Mouse, a frisking child of six, visits her sister Tiger Mouse, who boasts of having the teeniest of tiny feet, little nubbins as small as kittens. Pleasure Mouse grows fearful and restive as the footbinding ceremony draws near, as well she might, for white stabs of pain will forever end her frisking. Perhaps it's unfair to call Prager heartless—the spectacle of mothers crippling their daughters in the call of Duty and Tradition has a chilling poignance, because the suffering is so baroque, so *needless.* Far more slapstick is **"The Alumnae Bulletin,"** about a group of graduates from The Brearley School (former students of Frances Taliaferro?) who also partake of exotic ritual. This story boasts a cameo appearance by Jerzy Kosinski, . . . [and] it was weirdly clairvoyant of Prager to have one of her characters grab Kosinski and demand to know if he "really" wrote *The Painted Bird.*

The book's major showpiece is **"The Lincoln-Pruitt Anti-Rape Device,"** a bizarre tale of a women's combat unit in Vietnam that leaves a trail of disturbing brilliancies. Under Operation Foxy Fire, a group of women are disguised as Buddhist monks (shaved heads, saffron robes) and equipped with hidden weapons that are manifestations of men's worst castration fears. "Once a bevy of luscious breasts and thighs, in a trice the platoon of women had become: a cache of human punji sticks." Funny, frightening, and ruthlessly worked out, this story ends in carnage—"*Guernica* in pink"—and a feminist fillip that reveals what sisterhood under fire truly means. The book's only miss is the story about a squabbling couple entitled **"Wrinkled Linen,"** which settles for comfy brittle neurotic chatter in the style of Woody Allen's urban fussers.

A Visit from the Footbinder is a macabre treat, and it's puzzling that after an initial buzz of anticipation, the book strayed off into the thickets of critical neglect. Perhaps critics and readers were put off by the book's freaky-deaky aplomb; they may prefer more domestic writers, who kindly drop lumps of marshmallow into the reader's cocoa. But if Emily Prager doesn't go sugary and accommodating, she may someday write a book as sardonically chill as *Vile Bodies.* Not that this book is a slouch. *A Visit from the Footbinder* was, I think, the best book of fiction in 1982.

> *James Wolcott, in a review of "A Visit from the Footbinder," in* Harper's, *Vol. 266, No. 1593, February, 1983, p. 75.*

HARRIETT GILBERT

[Some writers] have condensed the horrors of history into pill-like symbols. American writer Emily Prager has concentrated on two of these in her first collection of stories, *A Visit from the Footbinder.* Even before it was over, the war in Vietnam had begun to represent all Western imperialist aggression—or, to a number of feminists, all *male* imperialist aggression; while the ritualistic crippling and deforming of upper-class Chinese girls has long ago shifted from being an example to being a metaphor for women's oppression. Prager approaches these icons via comedy. There is nothing intrinsically outrageous in this—it may, indeed, be the only sane route—but there is something worrying, nonetheless, in her tale of an all-woman combat troop luring 'gooks' into 'raping' them, in order to kill them with the devilishly cunning Lincoln-Pruitt Anti-Rape Device.

The trouble is, Prager keeps pulling back from the edge. By refusing to state unequivocally that *all* men deserve violent death, she turns her choice of the Vietcong, as victims, into a tacit acceptance of the racism expressed by the rest of the war. Stylistically, too, by retreating from total bad taste, by stepping back into harbours of 'reasonable' feminism, she forces us to react to her story seriously. Seriously, it is ill-conceived and naive.

[**"A Visit from the Footbinder"**] is not quite that, but falls between so many stools—social satire, realism, fable—that the genuine horror of the footbinding ceremony loses itself in the confusion. It is the shorter, more personal stories that finally redeem this collection—the reunion of school friends to test the truth of the penis-envy theory; the woman stuck in a taxi with agoraphobia; the couple trying to have a row in New York's Russian Tea Room. With a confidence and wit not evident before, these describe, with vicious precision, the emotional mutilation of women forced, by men, to 'be women'. (pp. 27-8)

> *Harriett Gilbert, "Stomaching It," in* New Statesman, *Vol. 105, No. 2711, March 4, 1983, pp. 27-8.*

SAVKAR ALTINEL

Although described on its dust-jacket as "dispatches from the front line" where "provoked women and provocative men meet", [*A Visit from the Footbinder and Other Stories*] is more like the jottings of a mercenary determined to keep out of the fighting and prosper by serving both sides. . . . Emily Prager writes with a keen awareness that there is more than one market to exploit, and the results of her efforts to be all things to all persons are rich with ambiguity.

In [**"A Visit from the Footbinder"**], set in China in the thirteenth century, foot-binding serves as an emblem of female bondage. This is familiar territory, and the message seems reassuringly simple and straightforward. What is less reassuring, however, is the way in which the story unnecessarily dwells on the details of the process, gradually building up to a climax in which a girl bound to a chair with leather thongs has her toes painfully bent into place by a leering Buddhist nun with a shaven head and a round body like a "carved ivory ball". Despite the jokiness of the tone, there is no disguising the intention of the writing to titillate.

The same also goes for the novella-length **"The Lincoln-Pruitt Anti-Rape Device"** in which a group of American women fitted with a castrating gadget are sent into the jungles of South-east Asia in search of unsuspecting Vietcong men. Once again the point is clear: no matter how intelligent, sophisticated and self-assured she may be, a woman will not be completely free as long as she has to live with the fear of sexual assault. Unfortunately, this cannot be underlined without the women baring their breasts, massaging each other with oils, painting dazzle spots on their bodies, and performing other acts supposedly designed to lure the enemy. Even worse is the description of the Major in charge of the operation. . . .

The story is ultimately as assiduous in pandering to male fantasies as it is in supporting the cause of liberation.

The three remaining stories are slight. Although one shows Jerzy Kosinski confronted by three women wearing eight-inch dildoes who, like everyone else, want to know if he really wrote *The Painted Bird,* and another offers a glimpse of Russell Baker in an elevator, they are remarkable chiefly because of their ability to wed the clichés of feminist propaganda to those of soft porn, dressing their heroines in tight skirts and "very high heels" and having them tied to beds and flagellated. Interestingly, at one point we meet an emancipated woman called Edda who writes pornography for a living, but feels compelled to pay a middle-aged English charlady named Mrs. Bainbridge to pretend to be the author of her books. Clearly, incongruity bothers Ms Prager much less, and she is happy to play both roles herself.

Savkar Altinel, "Bound to Please," in The Times Literary Supplement, No. 4171, March 11, 1983, p. 248.

PHYLLIS RAPHAEL

Not for a long time have I read such intensely feminist fiction as the collection of five angry, funny stories in Emily Prager's *A Visit from the Footbinder*. . . .

Masochism . . . penis envy . . . paralysis . . . dependence . . . castration as revenge . . . and male impenetrability and insensitivity . . . this is prototypical genre fiction in the tradition of Sue Kauffman and the early Lois Gould; wild comedy underpinned by healthy, ferocious rage. Ms. Prager, a former contributing editor to *The National Lampoon,* is funny and her lunatic turns of wit drive the writing forward. She's had a good time with her mischief . . . that's clear. In **"The Alumnae Bulletin"** Jerzy Kosinski's favorite food is Mrs. Paul's frozen fish sticks. While a couple quarrels in The Russian Tea Room "Sylvia Sydney leaves the restaurant and Sylvia Miles enters and is given the same table." . . .

The flaw in these stories is that there are few nuances of character. Perhaps it's the comedy, the original springboard for the writing of these stories, that's blinded Ms. Prager to the people in them. Often it's difficult to tell the women apart and in **"The Alumnae Bulletin"** I had to read parts over and over again to differentiate between the three women. And inventive as the use of Jerzy Kosinski may be, using the real man relieves Ms. Prager once more of the obligation to create a character. Kosinski is simply there. His predilection for odd hours and sadistic sex is revealed but outside of asking a few questions . . . he does nothing to advance the action of the story. It might have been better for Ms. Prager's fiction if Kosinski had to reveal himself on the page. The same is true in **"The Lincoln-Pruitt Anti Rape Device."** The women exist as

so many good ideas, but they never complete themselves in the tale.

However, this is a forgiveable sin in view of what Ms. Prager *has* done. At a time when potential Medeas are enrolled in MBA programs and women's fiction is colored by such gentle voices as Lynne Sharon Schwartz and Laurie Colwin, it's easy to forget about footbinders. Ms. Prager jogged my memory and I'm grateful. These stories made me aware of how much I had missed feminist troublemaking and how necessary it still is to identify that part of myself in the art of an intelligent, tough and eminently witty writer. [*A Visit from the Footbinder*] is always good and often shattering. It should be read.

Phyllis Raphael, "Feminist Troublemaking," in The American Book Review, Vol. 7, No. 3, March-April, 1985, p. 24.

CYNTHIA COTTS

[*Clea and Zeus Divorce*] is no slice of life, no slow dance to the tunes of adolescence and motherhood. The protagonists are already hardened, exotic, staring dead on at mortality. And this Emily Prager is way out of the mold. She spins a tale in the tradition of Tom Robbins or Thomas Pynchon, deploying a repertoire of black humor, arch sexual insight, wild metaphor, and Jungian synchronicity. Her Clea recalls Oedipa Maas in *The Crying of Lot Forty-Nine,* the only sane woman in a world on the brink of collapse.

Clea and Zeus are renowned for the illusionist psychodramas they perform on stage and in live TV specials. As celebrities, they wield the power of gods, a power that results from his dancing, her acrobatics, and their preternatural sex appeal. In confessional fiction, the protagonist's hormonal draw is often more labored than convincing; here a few strokes establish Clea and Zeus as emblems of desirability.

Prager's world is deracinated by war, and the lyricism of childhood has given way to mass culture and the technological imperative. Raised in Rhodesia, Zeus saw his mother murdered during an insurgency, while Clea studied acrobatics as an American military brat in China. Their assistants, a Red Chinese poet and a Xhosa witch doctor, still resort to magic in times of crisis; Zeus's Cambridge pals include Ruth, who lives with the apes, and De Quincy, who wears only Victorian clothes and deals only Victorian drugs. In their idiosyncrasies, each of these characters has crafted a defense against depersonalization.

The events that coincide to bring on Clea's breakdown and divorce are as follows: Zeus fucks a groupie, Clea's mother dies of leprosy contracted from armadillos, and Clea's psychic predicts the start date of World War III. . . .

The jam involves the scheduling of their final performance (live, on prime-time TV) the night the bomb is to hit JFK. . . . The resolution to this central issue, though chilling, doesn't offer much retroactive insight into character.

Prager's narration is soundly engineered. "Clea and Zeus Divorce" is the title of the show they're performing, and in it they act out a microcosm of the story that unfolds in the book. Parallel time schemes stretch from the first page to the last: the real time that passes on the night of the fated performance and the cyclical time that draws on several characters' memories of the past.

These thumbnail histories are funny and pungent, perfect little crystals indicating the residue of a burning imagination. But unlike the vernacular histories that turn up in novels by Prager's realist contemporaries, character is not the focus [in *Clea and Zeus Divorce*]. In the stylized Zeus and Clea, Prager doesn't offer the full disclosure that renders a character inhabitable and indelible. What she does offer is a work of seamless prestidigitation, a multi-tiered narrative concealing a thousand surprises. Though it careens between melodrama and contrivance, this camp tragedy is delivered with cutting style.

> *Cynthia Cotts, in a review of "Clea and Zeus Divorce," in* VLS, *No. 59, October, 1987, p. 3.*

ROBERT PLUNKET

When Emily Prager's first book, a collection of very odd short stories entitled *A Visit From the Footbinder* was published . . . people took notice. Here was a voice not just quirky and original but dangerous—critics were upset with her troubling insights into women, pornography and masochism. Her technique also drew fire, for her stories were the literary equivalent of comedy skits . . . , and in her world of hip young women in stiletto heels using sex or being used by it, some people saw brilliance while others saw only ambiguity. Ms. Prager's first novel, *Clea & Zeus Divorce,* will heighten the debate. The concept is audacious; the singular prose style intact and flourishing, as sharp as a brand-new Lady Schick. But talk about ambiguous!

Clea and Zeus are dancers, but like no dancers you've ever seen. . . . Their extravagant shows combine music, dance, television and just about every other art form with special effects so elaborate they have to be rehearsed in the antigravity chamber at NASA. . . . Their fans adore them; they are the ultimate fantasy couple. "They seemed the same, lithe and magnetic . . . their fate predetermined long ago in a shadow play on the wall of a cave."

But tonight things are different. Clea is undergoing a crisis that threatens to change everything. She feels that Zeus doesn't love her anymore, that she doesn't love him, that sexual love has made her weak, that "her talent was robbing her of her life." Since art and life are one as far as Zeus and Clea are concerned, they will act out their breakup on a prime-time TV special being broadcast live from a theater in Times Square. The timing couldn't be worse, though. Clea's mother is dying of leprosy in Hawaii (she contracted it from her job, skinning and stuffing armadillos for a man out in Oklahoma who painted them gold and sold them as gewgaws); Jerry, Clea's astrologer, is calling in from Vegas with the news that an atomic bomb will be detonated at Kennedy Airport at 10 P.M., just before the third act begins.

Clea takes the bomb threat seriously, and soon the reader does too. Jerry has always been right in the past, and Clea, who has her own war room with access to the Norad computers, confirms the prediction in a fortune-telling ceremony performed by her faithful retainer, Miss Florie. Nuclear war will be traumatic but it may have its good points; if she survives "there's just got to be a return to innocence." It is Clea's effort to get everyone—including the audience and a performing cat named Pilar ("an animal actress with a résumé that spelled trouble: one cat food commercial after another, a ca-

reer of downers and starvation")—to wear special radiation suits that propels the action of the novel forward.

Obviously, Ms. Prager is a writer who requires interpretation. In *A Visit From the Footbinder* this was great fun. She teased the reader along, layering irony, comedy and horror in the title story, about how women acquiesce in their own oppression and, paradoxically, acquire power from it. If there are any high school English teachers out there I suggest they use it as subject matter for those "What does the author mean?" type essays. It's right up there with Shirley Jackson's classic story "The Lottery."

In *Clea and Zeus* the teasing is still there, but the interpretation turns into an unwelcome chore. Somewhere there's an organizing principle in all this, but where? Is it a heavily ironic fable about a woman driven to madness, or a wicked parody of Joan Didion's writing at its most overwrought? How seriously are we supposed to take all this nuclear war business? Is it all just a big joke? We're never quite sure, so all we have for consolation is the aura of glamorous despair that pervades every page.

This problem of not knowing how to take things extends to the characters. Zeus's life is mostly external. He is described by admiring fans as a cross between Lord Byron, Robert Donat, Frédéric Chopin and Mel Gibson. He is a white Rhodesian, a laudanum addict because he killed his mother (accidently, sort of.) . . .

We learn more about Clea; this is definitely her book. I'm not sure what Ms. Prager thinks of her, but to me she comes across as your worst nightmare of a stereotypical Sarah Lawrence girl—so cool, so talented, so hip in her little deer-hoof boots, so very obsessed with herself. "Beneath her dolly exterior lurked a raging little animal that bit and clawed and threw itself around rooms, causing destruction." But we never really learn why. She and Zeus remain enigmas. "Equally charismatic and sparkling, equally talented, equally larger than life, equally—what was it?—lost, no, hidden, no, bereft."

Even though *Clea & Zeus Divorce* eventually sinks under the weight of too many ill-matched metaphors (colonialism, art, Western gods vs. Eastern gods, stardom, Vietnam, the Bomb and so on), Ms. Prager emerges with her reputation as a stylist and innovator intact. No writer around is quite so visual; her prose is a series of images out of Calvin Klein ads and MTV (she's constantly describing the lighting), made all the more remarkable by the beauty and significance she finds in such commercial trash. She loves a good show-biz joke. She positively revels in clothes and makeup. And even though the book does not succeed, there is a very skillful artist at work here, trying to articulate the unexplained and maybe unexplainable terror of modern life.

> *Robert Plunket, "The End of a Marriage, Live from Times Square," in* The New York Times Book Review, *November 22, 1987, p. 9.*

SAVKAR ALTINEL

In the Ted Harris Theatre near Times Square, a television special is being filmed before a live audience. The stars are Clea and Zeus, who for a decade and a half have enchanted thousands all over the world as much with their obvious devotion to each other as with their singing, dancing, juggling, and comedy routines. Sadly, this is to be their last appearance, for not only has Clea announced that she is divorcing Zeus, but she has also been informed by her personal psychic that at exactly 10pm, while the show is still in progress, a hundred-and-fifty-kiloton nuclear device will explode over New York, setting off a war which will end all civilization.

How have things come to this pass? The answer is provided in part by the sketches performed on the stage and in part by the reminiscences of the two principal characters as time and again they wait for a cue in the wings. It was evidently in Addis Ababa that Zeus, a white Rhodesian, sanction-busting on behalf of Ian Smith's State Tobacco Monopoly, first ran into Clea, then a virtually unknown young acrobat graduated only a few years ago from a special academy in Taiwan. It was love at first sight. . . . They gave their first joint performance at the Cairo Hilton, causing the *Egyptian Gazette* to remark: "She is the flute to his snake . . . unless she is the mongoose." Then it was on to Athens, ecstatic posters screaming: "*Clea kai Zeus! Eseis agapoume!*", and a tearful reunion with Doran and his Seven Golden Lieutenants, childhood friends of Zeus's from Africa. Later came married bliss, the Hammersmith Odeon and Carnegie Hall.

Now, however, the couple have drifted apart and begun to pursue their separate interests. Meanwhile, the minutes are ticking away, bringing 10pm closer. . . .

Is there an allegory lurking here somewhere, with the "almost British" Zeus and the American Clea standing for the English-speaking world, burdened by imperialist guilt and headed for nuclear annihilation? Or do they perhaps represent the entire human race?—which, after all, went on from origins in Africa and China to a high point of civilization in Egypt, and then achieved even greater glory in Greece before proceeding steadily westwards to its apotheosis, or, depending on one's point of view, doom, in the New World. Certainly, the blurb speaks of a "chilling perspective on global affairs"; but ultimately the only global affair that is really in sight is Clea and Zeus's globe-trotting romance. Although Emily Prager is an anthropologist by training, what interest her are not social relationships but sexual ones—love as a "colonial tragedy" involving subjection to an alien power and the end of love as a form of dissolution no less devastating than nuclear fission. In so far as civilization and its discontents get a look in, they, too, are apprehended in essentially sexual terms.

[*Clea and Zeus Divorce*] is a striking first novel, better in every respect than *A Visit from the Footbinder,* the self-consciously outrageous collection of short stories with which Ms Prager made her début [in 1982]. She handles the complex narrative with great dexterity, writes with intelligence and wit, and displays an impressive store of esoteric knowledge on subjects ranging from Enid Blyton books to the precise ringing tone of an African telephone. She can be deemed already to have reached the Cairo Hilton stage in her artistic career: with any luck, Athens should not be far away.

Savkar Altinel, "The Wrong End of Love," in The Times Literary Supplement, No. 4425, January 22-28, 1988, p. 81.

HELEN BIRCH

It takes a while to get orientated in Emily Prager's [*Clea and Zeus Divorce*]. The opening pages seem to be lost between the glittery high-tech nostalgia of Fellini's *Fred and Ginger* and a tipsy carnivalesque reminiscent of Angela Carter. (p. 28)

At the beginning of the novel, Clea wants to divorce Zeus and bow out to their public in a final, explosive break-up beamed to the nation on primetime TV. The daughter of an American army general, she has become obsessed with the imminence of nuclear war and is feverishly preparing for survival. It's this tension which pushes the narrative on: will the world end before their marriage does?

As the stage is set for the most tragic performance of a lifetime, Zeus, the fallen god from Rhodesia who "fought for freedom on the wrong side", sits in colonial splendour and stones his guilt with laudanum, while Clea taps into her War Room computer and calls up her psychic on the nuclear hotline. It seems an Absurd, self-referential game of life parodying art, or the other way round. But, as the narrative flicks back and forth from '70s New York to Clea and Zeus' first meeting in Addis Ababa, to Greece, Rhodesia and China, the camera closes in on their spectacular aerial *pas de deux*, reminding us that this is performance of a unique kind: sex as act; war as theatre. Tiny, doll-like Clea is crazed with a kind of fast-forward longing; she's a despotic fantasist who believes that issuing radiation suits and building bunkers can save the world. "There must be a return to innocence," she says to her estranged husband. But even her zeal cannot rescue Zeus from the terminal guilt he carries, remembering the raid on his Rhodesian tobacco farm and the moment, unknown to Clea, when he shot his own mother who danced and sang and paraded in blackface and nappy wig.

The drama of divorce bristling on-screen tears open a web of betrayals. Clea and Zeus' is a "union based on electrochemicals and a spiritual coincidence", founded on little more than the love of the same childhood story and Clea's dream of a shared loss. "Love is always a colonial tragedy," she tells Zeus' sister Ruth, a zoologist who lives among apes. This is love story turned global: romance touching down to the crack of guns on the veld; the sexual sparring of sitcom tuned to grim power struggles as the world threatens to self-destruct.

These links become explicit when Clea's tough Texan mom is told that she has caught leprosy from the armadillos she hunts, stuffs and sells to museums. Leprosy, the wasting disease, the rotting of the body; bodies flayed and slowly eroded by radiation. "It's the end honey," she tells Clea. "The end of the world as we know it." Through Prager's black imagination the American dream of innocence is relocated as survivalist aftermath, found sleeping peacefully in the bunker where Clea hopes flowers might grow. As the climax edges closer, anger subsumes performance: it's "fight turned theater", the splitting of two dream worlds dissolved into newsreel.

The tone of [*Clea and Zeus Divorce*] is sardonic; here as in her earlier short stories, *A Visit From the Footbinder,* ideas are carefully layered, her images glancing off and contradicting them. The photograph of Zeus' great-grandfather, the pioneer, is "brown and hazy like an old thought"; Clea and her performing cat in their radiation suits look to Zeus "like a nuclear madonna and child". In a recent TV interview, Prager said that the book was about "the marriage of American militarism and Southern African racism", but to read it as political allegory would be crude. Like Clea and Zeus dancing on wires, Prager's novel defies gravity, spinning passion and cynicism and wit into the air and catching them all as neatly as Clea the juggler. (pp. 28-9)

Helen Birch, "Dance of Death on a High Wire," in New Statesman, *Vol. 115, No. 2966, January 29, 1988, pp. 28-9.*

JOHN NAUGHTON

[*Clea and Zeus Divorce*] is a tale of two fruitcakes. Clea is a tiny, captivating juggler, dancer, acrobat and computer freak who has allegedly hacked her way into the NORAD computer system. She also believes that the End—in the form of a nuclear war—is Nigh. She hails from Texas. Her papa is a four-star general (which may be why Clea is also a martial arts expert), her mama is a leper who contracted the disease from her hobby of stuffing armadillos. Zeus, a former Rhodesian tobacco salesman and sanctions-buster, is Clea's pardner. He is a dancer and sex-symbol who has stuffed everything in his time, bar armadillos. Quaintly, he is also a laudanum abuser. Once, during a guerrilla raid on the family farm, he blew his ma's head off after she winged him with a pistol. This information he has kept from Clea, but the guilty secret continues to haunt him, as well it might. For some reason, he is guarded night and day by a squad of gorgeous heavies with machine-guns. They are called the Seven Golden Lieutenants.

As a showbiz couple, our pair are a stupendous success. . . . But now, the old black magic has ceased to work. Clea is obsessed by the impending holocaust; Zeus is stoned most of the time and aloof in manner on account of his matricidal past. So they decided to divorce. But, since this is showbiz, they plan to go out with a bang, with a show entitled (surprise, surprise) "Clea and Zeus Divorce." It goes out live on primetime American television, and is scheduled to end just as the first nuke hits JFK airport—or so Clea thinks.

Now if you're thinking that it must be hard to take these cookies seriously, then let me tell you something: it is. In fact, I got to page 140 before agreeing to suspend disbelief. This is the point where Clea's mama gets leprosy in the heart of the Lone Star State. Ha, ha, very droll, said I, pull the other one while you're at it. But then I came across an interview with Ms Prager in which she said reports of leprosy among Texan armadillo stuffers had appeared in the *Wall Street Journal*. At which point, I surrendered.

Clea and Zeus Divorce is structured around the final performance of the eponymous duo. The progress of the show is interwoven with fragments of flashback from their earlier lives, and is quite sophisticated in its way. Ms Prager's style is fruitly evocative, sometimes to the point where it both invites and defies parody. Consider the case of Rita and Peg, two supporting dancers whose figures describe the kind of parabolic arcs which can cause cardiac arrest in elderly males. At one point in the show they 'leaned against one another, naked shoulder to naked shoulder. Their nipples were stiff and the light bounced off them like beach balls off a seal's nose.'

There is a good deal more where that came from. Zeus's room, for example, 'pulsated moodily in the purpling light'. Some of the dialogue isn't much better. Lamenting her husband's aloofness, Clea wails: 'There was a vacuum I couldn't hope to fill . . . a grief in him I couldn't even hope to assuage. Over time, he formed a laager around his meteoric crater.' On stage, she complains about him to the audience: 'When he's

guilty he cowers behind the voluminous skirts of the existential.' And all the poor chap has done is smoke his pipe and mutter 'That's life, baby,' whenever he's hassled.

What all this suggests is that *Clea and Zeus Divorce* is the fictional equivalent of a Richard Rogers building—fascinating to look at but not much fun to inhabit. It is bursting with fancy ideas and has a most ingenious and complex structure, much of it exposed to the elements. The central idea, which is to build everything round an account of the final show, works well enough to keep one reading to the end. The atmosphere of raw energy and near-panic which characterises live performances is brilliantly evoked. But, overall, one is left with a feeling of someone trying rather too hard to pump life into a singularly implausible pair of hoofers. (pp. 24-5)

John Naughton, "The Gods Must Be Crazy," in The Listener, *Vol. 119, No. 3048, February 4, 1988, pp. 24-5.*

MICHAEL GORRA

Emily Prager's [*Clea and Zeus Divorce*] like [Jay McInerney's] *Bright Lights, Big City,* is one of those coolly-packaged Vintage Contemporaries Originals, the literary novel as an up-market brand name, the Ben and Jerry's of the book trade. But this flavor isn't as successful. *Clea and Zeus Divorce* might be described as a music video in the form of a novel. The title characters have made a career out of enacting scenes from their life in a series of television specials. So there's no Clea or Zeus, properly speaking, but only "Clea" or "Zeus," only the role and not an actualized self, as Clea realizes in thinking that "Her performing emotion was useless in a human context." Nor can she summon the emotions appropriate for that context, because they've taken "poetic license with their life, theatricalizing it, decorating the tedious parts . . . they couldn't quite distinguish what happened from what they had designed." They perform a self as an alternative to having one. Now they've decided to announce their divorce by doing another show, which opens with them on-stage, sharing out their possessions, recalling scenes from their lives together. And the novel itself cuts between an account of the show and one of their earlier life—how they met, their childhoods, and above all Clea's conviction that Kennedy Airport is going to get nuked about two-thirds of the way through the performance.

But the ideas Prager plays with about theatricality and the self are more interesting abstracted from the novel than in the work itself. "When Clea returned from the awards taping, it was eight P.M., prime—as the TV people were wont to call it—time, like prime rib, juicy lean time not fatty, gristly time, not, as they called the period one A.M., the graveyard shift." The pun seems labored and the metaphor clumsily mixed, without the high Wildean frivolity and verbal inventiveness such mannered material needs. And I'm bothered by other things too. Zeus is an exiled white Rhodesian whose entourage includes some machine-gun-toting childhood friends called "The Seven Golden Lieutenants"; the Aryanism is camp, but only just. Though I suppose that's meant to be balanced by a sort of third world chic—there's an African medicine woman and a Chinese sage in the entourage as well. Like all those spots on MTV that flash a half-second image of a mushroom cloud or a riot across the screen, *Clea and Zeus*

Divorce invokes a number of weighty issues, but is finally far less meaningful than it appears to be. (p. 404)

> *Michael Gorra, "American Selves," in* The Hudson Review, *Vol. XLI, No. 2, Summer, 1988, pp. 401-08.*

Raja Rao

1909-

Indian novelist, short story writer, editor, critic, and essayist.

A leading English-language Indian author, Rao is best known for novels in which he examines metaphysical themes by involving characters with diverse ideas, outlooks, and backgrounds. As these individuals establish relationships, they are prompted to compare and reexamine their personal, political, spiritual, and cultural values, and through them Rao frequently contrasts Indian philosophy and spiritualism with Western society's emphasis on dualism and rationalism. While often entangled in irreconcilable conflicts with those they love, Rao's protagonists gain insights into the nature of identity, existence, illusion, and reality. Edwin Thumboo stated: "Rao's greatest achievement, which I suspect only he can pass, is the degree to which his works . . . contain the insights, emblems, mantras, metaphors, and other carriers of meaning and instruction that enable the individual to achieve, through his own meditations, a better understanding of self through Knowledge and Truth." In 1988, Rao became the tenth author awarded the Neustadt International Prize for Literature, a biennial honor bestowed upon a living writer who has made significant contributions in poetry, fiction, or drama.

To authentically recreate the local color of Indian life and speech patterns, Rao often experiments with English language, syntax, and fictional forms. This interest is particularly evident in his first novel, *Kanthapura* (1938), where he combines an anecdotal, stream-of-consciousness style with slight use of punctuation to capture the dialect and upbeat lifestyle of an Indian village. In this work, which is narrated by a grandmother, a young man returns to his native village after having left to study at a university and promotes the ideals and values of Mohandas Gandhi. The man is mocked by several residents and violently apprehended by authorities for his nonviolent defiance of traditional social norms. While relating these incidents in colloquial language replete with colorful aphorisms, the grandmother embellishes her tale with numerous references to local customs, daily activities, superstitions, rituals, and legends. Santha Rama Rau stated: "[*Kanthapura*] is written in an elegant style verging on poetry; it has all the content of an ancient Indian classic, combined with a sharp satirical wit and clear understanding of the present."

In his next novel, *The Serpent and the Rope* (1960), Rao examines themes relating to illusion and reality. In this work, a young Brahmin named Rama gains greater understanding of identity and truth from experiences with his extended family in India, his encounters and studies in France, and his visits to England. Rama attempts to assimilate into a Western lifestyle after marrying a French woman, but a visit to India reawakens ties to his heritage. While vividly detailing daily life in France and India, this deeply symbolic metaphysical novel contrasts Western rationality and Hindu mysticism, explores ideals pertaining to Catholicism, Marxism, Freudianism, and fascism, and develops numerous parallels between myths, legends, and histories of different cultures.

Rao's third novel, *The Cat and Shakespeare: A Tale of India* (1965), is a comic fable narrated by an Indian bureaucrat who is implicated in adultery, murder, and thievery. This novel features such symbolic events as droughts and illnesses, sudden appearances by a cat during portentous misunderstandings, and the actions and pronouncements of a mystical man who frequently transcends a metaphorical wall between appearance and reality. *The Chessmaster and His Moves* (1988), first of a projected trilogy of novels, is narrated by a man named Sivarama, who pursues absolute truths through mathematics and relationships with women. Employing Hindu myths to shape and order the narrative, Rao introduces characters from various cultures who are defined by their ideas and opinions on such matters as politics, history, love, art, and religion. Through their encounters, these individuals reassess their ideals, discover self-perpetuated myths, and come to a greater understanding of their individual identities.

Most of Rao's fictional pieces collected in *The Cow and the Barricades and Other Stories* (1947) and *The Policeman and the Rose* (1978) are vignettes of village life in India that focus upon traditions, social unrest, and various other representative concerns. "The Policeman and the Rose" is a symbolic story that illuminates differences between India and the West. In *Comrade Kirillov* (1976), Rao examines the influence of history on the individual and develops an extended comparison between Vedantism and Marxism. The title character of this novella is the namesake of an individual in Fedor Dostoevsky's novel *The Possessed*. Both protagonists represent their author's suspicions about individuals who promote political reform by drawing upon ideas and models from outside their native lands. Rao's character, for example, champions change through means that are antithetical to the principles of Gandhi.

(See also *CLC*, Vol. 25 and *Contemporary Authors*, Vols. 73-76.)

RAJA RAO

[The Foreword reprinted below was originally written in 1937 and published in 1938 in the first edition of Kanthapura.*]*

There is no village in India, however mean, that has not a rich *sthala-purana*, or legendary history, of its own. Some god or godlike hero has passed by the village—Rama might have rested under this pipal-tree, Sita might have dried her clothes, after her bath, on this yellow stone, or the Mahatma himself, on one of his many pilgrimages through the country, might have slept in this hut, the low one, by the village gate. In this way the past mingles with the present, and the gods mingle with men to make the repertory of your grandmother always bright. One such story from the contemporary annals of a village I have tried to tell [in *Kanthapura*].

The telling has not been easy. One has to convey in a language that is not one's own the spirit that is one's own. One has to convey the various shades and omissions of a certain thought-movement that looks maltreated in an alien language. I use the word "alien," yet English is not really an alien language to us. It is the language of our intellectual make-up—like Sanskrit or Persian was before—but not of our emotional make-up. We are all instinctively bilingual, many of us writing in our own language and in English. We cannot write like the English. We should not. We cannot write only as Indians. We have grown to look at the large world as part of us. Our method of expression therefore has to be a dialect which will some day prove to be as distinctive and colorful as the Irish or the American. Time alone will justify it.

After language the next problem is that of style. The tempo of Indian life must be infused into our English expression, even as the tempo of American or Irish life has gone into the making of theirs. We, in India, think quickly, we talk quickly, and when we move we move quickly. There must be something in the sun of India that makes us rush and tumble and run on. And our paths are paths interminable. The *Mahabharata* has 214,778 verses and the *Ramayana* 48,000. The *Puranas* are endless and innumerable. We have neither punctuation nor the treacherous "ats" and "ons" to bother us—we tell one interminable tale. Episode follows episode, and when our thoughts stop our breath stops, and we move on to another thought. This was and still is the ordinary style of our storytelling. I have tried to follow it myself in this story.

It may have been told of an evening, when as the dusk falls, and through the sudden quiet, lights leap up in house after house, and stretching her bedding on the veranda, a grand-

mother might have told you, newcomer, the sad tale of her village. (pp. vii-viii)

Raja Rao, in a forward to his Kanthapura, *1938. Reprint by New Directions, 1963, pp. vii-viii.*

TIME (NEW YORK)

No philosophical thicket seems denser to the Western eye than Hinduism, and no country more confusing than India. In this long, densely packed novel [*The Serpent and the Rope*] of the intellectual and emotional odyssey of a high-caste Brahman, Indian author Raja Rao offers an intimate look at Indian family life seen from the inside, and a sometimes illuminating, sometimes bewildering tour of the strange-blooming intricacies of Hindu thought as his hero grapples with the mundane practicalities of the West. With a novelist's illusionist skill, Rao makes it all as fascinating as a basketful of talking cobras.

Author Rao's credentials are impressive. André Malraux sought him out as a cicerone for a tour of India; Lawrence Durrell has pronounced *The Serpent* a work "by which an age can measure itself"; and E. M. Forster, whose *Passage to India* remains the classic of Anglo-Indian intellectual commerce, has praised Rao's *Kanthapura* (not yet published in the U.S.) as perhaps the best novel in English to come out of India.

Rao's hero Rama is an orphan, but life for a rich Indian orphan is very crowded. He inherits, besides Little Mother (his stepmother), numerous stepsisters, cousins, aunts, ancestors, household gods, pets, servants, and a system of ceremonial obligations that would burden a Byzantine bishop. . . .

When eventually Rama takes off for Europe to become a "holy vagabond," he has difficulty explaining himself to Europeans, let alone the Europeans to himself. But Rama does his best to embrace and smother with love the barbarous tribes of Paris, and records an impulse to lead a cow up to the altar at Notre Dame. Before long he is studying for his doctorate in southern France (author Rao attended the University of Montpellier) and married to Madeleine, a blue-stocking blonde who smells wonderfully—of thyme mostly. Soon they have a son, symbolically called Krishna, who symbolically dies.

The honeymoon of East and West is over, and Rama's intellectual career runs into a terrible occident. Logic seems to be the trouble (Hindus have a system of their own, a very non-Aristotelian affair). To the Western reader, Rama—whether in conflict with a Catholic, a Communist or a Freudian—appears, in the female manner, to counter an argument with a story about something else. Rama's efforts to Orientalize Europe's recent social and intellectual history are puzzling. He may be "devoted to Truth and all that," but what are Westerners to make of his theory of Naziism and Communism, which has Hitler representing the male principle and Stalin the female? What would Freud himself make of Rama's explanation of psychoanalysis in terms of the Indian rope trick? Or Madeleine's gallant effort to see origins of the myth of the Holy Grail in the begging bowl of an Indian holy man?

The female majority of novel readers may enjoy being told that "to worship woman is to redeem the world." The Western male, however, may feel as mixed up as the lady who called Rama a "lecherous eunuch," and wonder about the Eastern profundities that sprinkle the book like sacred coconut in the curry.

"Truth and All That," in Time, *New York, Vol. LXXXI, No. 8, February 22, 1963, p. 96.*

NANCY WILSON ROSS

The noted Indian writer, Raja Rao, frequently referred to in the literary press of England and France as his country's "greatest novelist," is presented to the American public for the first time in *The Serpent and the Rope.* Whether or not one can agree fully with the critical superlative it is not possible to read this remarkable novel, dealing with East-West confrontations on the most subtle subjective plane, without reaching the conclusion that Raja Rao is a writer of singular originality, perception and power.

The heart of the plot (though it can hardly be said to have a plot in the conventional use of the term) concerns the marriage of Rama, a cultivated South Indian Brahmin, and Madeleine, a young French intellectual from the Charente, who have met one another while attending the same French university at the end of the Second World War. The story, told by Rama in the first person, carries a strong suggestion of autobiography. Around the central theme of the intimate relationship between two exceptional people of totally unlike orientation and social background, Mr. Rao has woven an intricate and leisurely web that moves from India to France to England to India again, in and out, back and forth, with India the everrecurrent and dominant theme. And, as he tells the story of Rama and Madeleine, their families, friends and loves, in Mysore, Aixen-Provence and London, Raja Rao also contrives in an unhurried style—only occasionally a little prolix for Western taste—to present an intense and illuminating personal awareness of the contrasting "souls" of his homeland, of France, and, to a lesser extent, of England.

Rama, coming to Europe from the ancient traditional Brahmin world of South India, is a man who, in his own words, wants "to absorb more than to know." He plans to return to India to assume a professorship there and is in France working on a thesis that concerns the Albigensian heresy. His studies and research bring him into a circle of friends who talk constantly of various kinds of faith: Communism, Catholicism, Buddhism, Vedanta. . . . [With] detachment, and with only the faintest surprise and irony, Rama . . . looks on while his wife, by now a *Professeuse* at the local college, begins to find "the true and sacred" only in whatever is not her childhood faith, Catholicism. This change of direction she attributes to a subtle Brahmanical influence that her husband has exerted though never in any conscious or wishful way. In time Madeleine becomes so absorbed in various yoga practices and elaborate Eastern disciplines and ritual (in none of which Rama participates) that she even undertakes a strict forty-one day fast—superbly and specifically described in all its aspects—as her way of helping to cure her husband of his chronic, long-standing illness, tuberculosis.

A great deal happens to the characters in Mr. Rao's book, but it all takes place without any dramatic high-lighting. The physically unfulfilled "timeless" love of Rama for Savithri, the English-educated daughter of a North Indian raja: his final separation from Madeleine—to name only two of his personal crises—transpire in a dreamlike fashion, curiously outside the "self," as the West understands it. . . .

An enormous amount of legendary, historical and literary lore, French as well as Indian, is to be found in the pages of this widely acclaimed novel. There are extraordinary descriptions of incidents and landscapes, both in India and in Europe, and many East-West comparisons that catch sharply at the reader's attention, particularly if he knows the parts of the world familiar to Mr. Rao. . . .

The most arresting of Rama's numerous (though unpressed) comparisons is one he makes between the famous Indian mystic teacher, Sri Aurobinde, and the Russian dictator, Stalin. Seemingly poles apart, Rama finds them alike in their "materialism;" in their emphasis on the attainment of the state of "Superman;" a condition which must always be, in his opinion, "the enemy of man."

Perhaps the best clue to a fuller understanding of this book's unfamiliar stylistic qualities lies in a comment once made by the author on Indian novels in general. This form of literature, says Mr. Rao, "can only be epic in form and metaphysical in nature. It can only have story within story to show all stories are parables." The ideal Indian novel would, therefore, consist not only of stories within stories but of many odd bits of philosophic musing, myths, anecdotes, poetry, humor, theory, and descriptive set-pieces, with the human events transpiring in a sustained mood of "self-surrender."

When one closes the pages of *The Serpent and the Rope* the image that comes to mind is that of a mighty river like the Ganges, along whose shores and in whose waters, life and death meet and commingle in one eternal rhythmic continuity.

Nancy Wilson Ross, "Subtle Marriage of East and West," in Books, *New York, April 7, 1963, p. 14.*

GERALD SYKES

We are familiar with the yogi who comes to our shores, reacquaints us, with the ancient thought of India, and goes home. . . . In this beautiful, semi-autobiographical novel [*The Serpent and the Rope*] Raja Rao presents a new and different kind of Hindu sage, a Brahmin who is equally attracted to East and West, commutes frequently between the two, and dramatizes in his own person their irreconcilable conflict. This new Vedantist talks well, but he is still more interesting for his private pathos. He is a man of our time, a victim who longs to be a hero.

Rama is his name. He is born into the priestly caste, but takes no monastic vows. . . . He goes young to France, to prepare for a professorial career in India, and marries an uncommonly *sympathique* young Frenchwoman, also a scholar, whose family loves him almost as much as she does.

To reveal what happens to his marriage would be grossly unfair to his story, which depends for its subtle suspense upon an exact and slow appreciation of each nuance. I wonder if any writer of our time has done such sensitive justice to the minutiae which are the substance of any marriage. Rama has been schooled since birth in the mystical doctrine that all one's failures are failures in love, and he applies this axiom tenderly and rigorously to his wife and his friends—though perhaps not as rigorously to himself. . . .

A thoroughgoing Vendantist might perhaps see Rama as a "householder" in an unhappy stage of his progress toward complete asceticism. A Western psychologist might perhaps attribute his inordinate love of metaphysical dispute—he argues constantly in Aix, Paris, London, Cambridge—to a desire to cling to early instruction, rather than risk full exposure to other modes of thought. Such criticism would miss the point. Rama is tragically divided against himself, and his division makes possible a new and very pertinent kind of Indian writing.

Who has given us a more intimate sense of Indian home life than Raja Rao? For that matter, what foreigner has done Provence better? *The Serpent and the Rope* was originally written in French, then "translated" by its author into English. One can understand the enthusiasm of E. M. Forster for his art, and of André Malraux for his insight.

Gerald Sykes, "An Indian Man of Our Time," in The New York Times Book Review, *April 14, 1963, p. 53.*

SANTHA RAMA RAU

Raja Rao is perhaps the most brilliant—and certainly the most interesting—writer of modern India. The reason is, of course, that he is more than a writer. An advanced student of philosophy, a novelist, an essayist and a man trying to find both himself and the meaning of life—this may sound very grand, but he expresses it with no pretension—he wrote [*Kanthapura*], first published in England, in 1938. . . .

Kanthapura was written when he was 21—and it is a novel that illustrates most beautifully his combination of the "insider" explaining and the "outsider" looking in. Kanthapura is a village in South India, one of the many caught by the influence of Mahatma Gandhi, by the nonviolence movement for independence from the British—which, in turn, was resisted by the vested interests of Indian landlords and hirelings of the colonialists as much as by the foreigners. It is this situation that brings out Raja Rao's special talents, the knowledge of the deep Hindu mystique of *ahimsa*, (the principle of not taking life and consequently of nonviolence) and the ability to put in dramatic fictional form the way a village and its people are affected by such ideas. . . .

His story is told by a wise old woman—one who knows her village in every aspect and all the people in it. She recounts the return of a liberal young man who has, in the city, picked up "new ideas" about a better life for all—and, on his expression of them in the village, blows up a storm. *Ahimsa* is too dangerous a doctrine to follow. Nonviolence brings on violence. (One can see it happening these days in the American South.) Yet morality and philosophy must prevail. The only way to fight is not to fight. Even when the young man's ideas seem doomed, even when the instant, repressive measures of landlords and police seem too strong to overcome, the author makes us see the pattern of the future.

There is more to Raja Rao's book than a morality tale. It is written in an elegant style verging on poetry; it has all the content of an ancient Indian classic, combined with a sharp, satirical wit and a clear understanding of the present. The author's extensive notes (printed as an appendix) will prove invaluable to the general reader unfamiliar with Indian myths, religions, social customs and the background of the independence movement.

Santha Rama Rau, "Through the Village Gate Came Some Disturbing Ideas," in The New York Times Book Review, *January 5, 1964, p. 6.*

GEOFFREY GODSELL

[*Kanthapura*] is a story fascinatingly told, building up like Rossini's famous aria on calumny to a crashing climax that well-nigh shatters the little village and its traditional organization of society.

Prospective readers of Raja Rao's novel should not be deflected by the fact that, although now appearing in the United States for the first time, it was first published in Britain a quarter of a century ago, a decade before the withdrawal of the British raj from the Indian subcontinent. All these years later, it does not seem dated: Mr. Rao's skill as a writer (part-philosopher, part-poet, part-chronicler) and the enduring importance of the Gandhian movement in the history of our times combine to prevent that.

For American readers, the novel has added actuality. Woven into it is an illuminating exposition of ahimsa (not-hurting), one of the two chief components of the Gandhian teaching of non-violence, so much of which has been adopted by the Rev. Dr. Martin Luther King Jr. and his followers in the struggle for civil rights for Negroes. And indeed there are many moments in *Kanthapura* that seem to have a parallel in the events of the recent past in the United States.

"The great enemy is in us," says Moorthy, " . . . hatred is in us. If only we could not hate, if only we would show fearless, calm affection toward our fellow men, we would be stronger, and not only would the enemy yield, but he would be converted." . . .

Can one not hear Martin Luther King saying virtually the same things?

After demonstrating his full commitment to Gandhian teaching by consorting with the Pariahs of Kanthapura, Moorthy fasts for three days further to purify and strengthen his dedication—as he sees it through Hindu eyes. And while fasting, he is insulted by one of the village termagants, Waterfall Venkamma, who is outraged by his defiance of the traditional order. She takes from her clothes-basket a wet roll of sari, holds it over his head and squeezes it. Then "she laughs . . . and laughs again, and then she jabbers and shouts and goes away, still chattering to herself." Moorthy remains silent and motionless—like those Negroes, seen in a television newsreel last summer, "sitting-in" at a lunch counter in a Southern state, silent and motionless while their foes poured ketchup and sugar and mustard over their heads.

These are but moments in a story teeming with life, full of Asian color, and shot through with references to Hindu mysticism and the Hindu pantheon. . . .

Kanthapura is saved from leaving the reader now with a sense of tragedy because of the knowledge that Gandhiism—despite the disappointments of the 1930's and the early 1940's—did indeed prove the motive force that took India to the triumph of independence in 1947. Yet the near-destruction of Kanthapura in the process long before independence was assured, leaves one wondering whether nonviolence if not coupled with practical political direction of the highest order can of itself obtain desired political ends.

With unconscious dramatic irony, Mr. Rao's Moorthy writes in a letter in the concluding moments of the story: "... Things must change. Jawaharlal will change it." Without Jawaharlal Nehru's political skill, would Gandhi's ahimsa have triumphed of its own in 1947?

> *Geoffrey Godsell, "Does a Gandhi Need His Nehru?" in* The Christian Science Monitor, *January 16, 1964, p. 7.*

MARTIN TUCKER

[*Kanthapura,* written before *The Serpent and the Rope*], is a much more simply narrated story. It has only one setting, the symbolic town of Kanthapura, and it speaks in folk rhythms of the transformation which Gandhi's philosophy achieved in a tradition-ridden society.

Whereas *The Serpent and the Rope* was philosophical and abstract, *Kanthapura* is poetic and concrete. In many ways it seems the work of a young man, or at least of a man who has remained young. It has few pretension to intellectual complexity, and all its meaning is conveyed in spare, ballad-like rhythms. The novel is really a lyric on the expansion of man's spirit, and it carries with it the purity and intensity of youthful ardor. Its music is haunting: Rao has achieved one of those rare simple tales that is perfect in mood and declaration.

Kanthapura is really any town in India before the advent of Gandhi released a flood of longings. To this town returns Moorthy, the educated Brahmin, "honest as an elephant," who "had been to the city and knew things" which people in the sleepy town had forgotten or buried. Moorthy visits the Pariahs, or untouchables, and attempts to teach them to read and write. He invites the Pariahs to the religious festivals which he and his aunt organize. His acts are at first pacific, not meant to disturb, but they are soon opposed by those in the town who have a vested interest in a caste society. Eventually the opposition achieves its purpose—to make Moorthy an outcast.

The struggle, however, has only begun. Moorthy, after a fever and exaltation, realizes his destiny. He throws away his European clothes, eats at the doorways of houses like a Pariah, and continues to incite his townspeople to nonviolent action. The awareness of their growing strength leads the Pariahs, and many Brahmins, to protest against the government. . . .

The struggle initiated by a belief in nonviolence leads to bloodshed. At the end of the novel Moorthy has been beaten and jailed many times. Yet though the struggle seems to have ended in defeat, a triumph has been assured.

The narrator of the novel is the old aunt of Moorthy, a woman who has never been interested in politics, but who, through love of her nephew, is caught in the spirit of the new movement. Rao's use of this point-of-view technique is a brilliant stroke, for it allows for a simple rendering of the tale, one in which the human element is at all times in view. It also seems faintly reminiscent of E. M. Forster, who knows Rao and admires his work. Rao's old aunt is much like Forster's old woman—the steady matriarchs who hold society together while it is going through its convulsions. She is present in the final scene, a symbol of the stability of the human tradition. (pp. 242-43)

> *Martin Tucker, "Perfect in Mood," in The Com-*
monweal, *Vol. LXXX, No. 8, May 15, 1964, pp. 242-43.*

S. NAGARAJAN

In spite of the serious interest in the United States of America in contemporary Indian literature, the work of Raja Rao, the Indo-English novelist whom the London *Times Literary Supplement* hailed some time ago as "India's greatest novelist," does not seem to be quite well-known. It is true that he has not published much: besides [*The Serpent and the Rope*] he has written another—on the Indian struggle for independence—*Kanthapura* and a volume of short stories, *The Cow of the Barricades.* But this small output is distinguished not only by an authentic Indian quality but by genuine literary merit. *The Serpent and the Rope* has the additional interest of translating into intimate human terms the current dialogue between the Orient and the Occident and the debate within India itself of the Indian experience of time and history. It is a long novel—Raja Rao himself prefers to call it a history—rather loosely knit and partly autobiographical, and it has been announced as the conclusion of Raja Rao's quest over many years for the spiritual roots of his motherland. He himself has been living for a long time in France, and this expatriation may have something to do with the rather aggressively metaphysical definition of India that he has adopted in the novel.

It is the history of the marriage of an Indian student with a French girl. Rama is an Indian *par excellence*. Raja Rao's India is not the peninsula marked on the map, but an idea, a metaphysic, "philousia," as another student of East-West contrasts calls it, distinguishing it from "philosophy." [In *The Destiny of the Mind,* Wilhelm Haas noted: "Philousia is the love of Is-ness or essence, while philosophy is the love of wisdom"]. India is contiguous with time and space, but is anywhere and everywhere. "Can you understand," Rama asks his wife, "that all things merge, all thoughts and perceptions, in knowledge? It is in knowledge that you know a thing, not in seeing or hearing. That is India. *Jnanam* is India." In short, India is the metaphysics of Samkara's Shuddadwaita, pure non-dualism. The world is not real except in the way that illusions are while they last. Raja Rao's hero contends that only two attitudes are possible toward life. Either you believe that the world exists, and so you; or you believe that you exist, and so the world. "There is no compromise possible." (pp. 512-13)

Madeleine, the French wife, is very different from all this. She "smelt the things of the earth, as though sound, form, touch, taste, smell, were such realities that you could not go beyond them—even if you tried." She believes in the actual reality of the world and of the human person. In the marriage of Rama and Madeleine, two contrary world-views, two contrary epistemologies, come together, and the novel is a study of that encounter.

News comes to Rama in France that his father is dying, and he returns to India. He performs the obsequies, and escorts his Little Mother (a deliberately literal translation of the Kannada word for step-mother) on a pilgrimage to the holy places of North India. The novel opens with splendidly evocative descriptions of Benares and Haridwar, which give us the feel of a country where the past is an ever-brooding presence. At Allahabad he is introduced to Savithri, the Western-educated daughter of a minor raja. Her family has affianced her to Pratap, but she does not greatly fancy him. What could be the secret of this indifference to a very desirable match? Rama, who lives in Europe and has even a French wife, is requested to probe her real mind. He meets her duly, and though nothing much happens at the moment, the meeting has an important part later in the development of both. Rama returns to France soon after to resume his studies.

In a sense, however, his Indian sojourn begins precisely on his return from it. On the day he comes back, he dresses his French wife in the *saree* which he has brought for her, and they sit down to supper. "My hand just would not lift," writes Rama, who is himself the narrator. "Mado, something has happened." "Yes," she agrees. "Something has. . . . To whom?" "To everything," he answers. What has happened is clear enough in the novel, though not very explicit. Rama has had a traditional upbringing as prescribed in the Hindu books for a Brahman boy—though I wonder whether Raja Rao does not slip up when he claims that his hero read the Upanishads at the age of four before he was invested with the holy thread—and his visit to the holy places of North India and his new status as head of the family after the death of his father renew his awareness of whatever it is that goes to create a Hindu home. This awareness wells up in him when he sees his French wife, dressed in a *saree*, sitting down to that eminently homely event, the evening supper. His wife senses the great change in him, and in pain and longing asks him: "Have I failed your gods?" "No," he says, "you have failed me." The novel sets out to suggest the nature of this inevitable "failure."

On a later occasion Rama explains to his wife that all women are perfect, for they have the feminine principle in them, the *yin, prakrati;* and all men are perfect when they turn "inward and know that the ultimate is man's destiny." In terms of the definition of India taken up in the novel, man is *purusa,* the Lord of Creation, and woman is *prakrati,* the inherent power of *purusa* whereby the *purusa* creates. Woman's function is to give herself as *prakrati* to man as *purusa* so that man may know that in his true self he is *purusa* himself. Madeleine, however, with her belief in "person" tries to take her husband. The pain that she feels is not of love, explains Rama, for it springs from her refusal to transcend the subject-object relationship of lover and beloved into "the hypostasis of a cosmic order." (Of this pain of separation there is a graphic description in the diary of Rama himself.) The cosmic order which unites the lovers is the subject of the great Upanishadic pronouncement which is quoted more than once in the novel: "Not for the sake of the husband is the husband loved, but for the sake of the self in him. Not for the sake of the wife is the wife loved, but for the sake of the self in her." (pp. 513-15)

On her way to Cambridge, where she is reading for the English Tripos, Savithri visits Rama and Madeleine in France, and when Rama himself goes to England soon after, a deep friendship develops between him and Savithri. Once she visits him in his room in London, and mythicizing him as Krishna, the divine lover, and herself as Radha, the beloved of Krishna, offers him a ritual worship. Every traditional Hindu bride still sees herself as Radha married to Krishna, as Sati wedded to Siva, for only so is the marriage felt to be real. . . . The *purusa* knows himself only in knowing his power of *prakrati.* Therefore all denial of womanhood is wrong, whether in the Gandhian-ascetic way or the Western way "in which virginity was lost by too much knowledge and womanhood had lost

its rights by forsaking that involved slipping secrecy, that mendicant shyness with which woman hides her truth." In the ideal Indian marriage, husband and wife try to adjust themselves not primarily and directly to each other—that, of course, takes place, though incidentally—but to a *dharma* which is intended to lead them to the *jnanam,* the sole reality of the self (*atman*) and its identity with knowledge and existence. In a modern Western marriage—and let us remind ourselves that East and West are not geographical localities in Raja Rao's thought and the Western is not necessarily the Christian—husband and wife recognize themselves as independent entities and try to adjust themselves to the precise curve of each other's personality. If a maddening sense of personal frustration is the risk in a marriage oriented toward the Indian ideal, unfaithfulness is the risk in a Western one. Both risks are realized in the other examples of marriage illustrated in the novel. Madeleine's failure from Rama's point of view consists simply in her dualism, the assertion that *purusa* and *prakrati* are separate.

She gradually drifts away from him into an ascetic form of Buddhism and comes to feel that marriage is irrelevant to this body composed of the elements. Buddhism attracts her because Buddhism also believes in the separate existence of the object. (pp. 515-16)

The novel is interesting for a stylistic experiment. Raja Rao has tried to endow his hero with a style that will enable the reader to obtain a clear impression of "personality," which in the Indian sense evoked in the novel is something, as Madeleine says, "as evanescent and tangible as mountain-air, the fragrance of the honey-pine of the heights, the smell of incense while the mist arises." He has also tried to convey the feel of a world-view very different from that which has shaped the idiom of the English language. . . . Raja Rao's aim is to create a style which will reflect the rhythms and sensibilities of the Indian psyche, and since it is in Sanskrit that the Indian mind has found its most consummate linguistic expression, he has tried to adapt his English style to the movement of a Sanskrit sentence. He says that Sanskrit is rooted in primary sound, and when it is read aloud, it creates, as it were, an aura of emptiness around one and one feels the breath of oneself, sees the sight of oneself. Here is an example of the style that is the consequence of these aims:

> I could see in myself a vastness, as it were, a change of psychic dimension, an awareness of a more ancient me. There was no joy in this knowledge, no, no exaltation. There was just a rediscovery, as though having lost a brother in famine or on pilgrimage I had wandered hundreds of miles, had asked policeman and mistress of household for him, had asked barbers, tradesmen and sadhus for him; as though walking back through time I had asked men with a more antique form of tuft on their heads, with voices more grave, with lips more lecherous; as though from Muslims as they consolidated their ramparts, sentry-chambers, palaces, "Brother, have you seen my brother?" I had asked; from Kings, and going beyond the Ganges or the Cauvery, from saints and sages I had asked, backwards in history to the times of the Upanishads, even unto Yagnavalkya and Maitreyi; and as though at each epoch, with each person, I had left a knowledge of myself; and in this affirmation had been the awareness of the Presence that I am, that I am my brother. Thus it was as I walked about in my Kensington room. . . .

This long sentence is controlled by the central concept of the novel: "I am" is the sole truth. The first-person pronoun is repeated with every change of epoch to proclaim that the "I" remains the same throughout time. It is Presence itself, Existence itself. The brother whom Rama feels he has lost is none other than the "I" in "I am." The sentence begins with contemporary time, and goes back through medieval and primeval past to end in simple Presence, the unchanging Now which we call eternity. But perhaps the most striking feature of the sentence is the structure of the sound. The rhythm has been lengthened, as it were, by clustering together the heavily accented syllables and separating these clusters with less accented ones. This lengthened rhythm helps in a curious way to draw the reader close to the spokesman of the sentence. (pp. 516-17)

> *S. Nagarajan, "An Indian Novel," in* The Sewanee Review, *Vol. LXXII, No. 3, Summer, 1964, pp. 512-17.*

NANCY WILSON ROSS

[*The Cat and Shakespeare: A Tale of India*] is tantalizing, poetic, symbolic—and brief. It may well come as a surprise to those Western readers who associate Rao with such major works as . . . *The Serpent and the Rope* or his early powerful and brilliant *Kanthapura*. . . .

Although the *mise en scène* of the [*The Cat and Shakespeare*], as in *Kanthapura,* is a South Indian community, the two novels are quite unlike. . . . [The earlier work] flowed with the torrential vigor of a brilliant folk epic, sweeping the reader into an almost physical experience of participation in the rise of the Indian masses under Gandhi. In *The Cat and Shakespeare* the style is leisurely, oblique and ruminative.

It is not that of the times of which Rao is now writing are any less eventful, for the action of the new novel takes place during World War II and even those residents of the Trivandrum community who can not, or do not, read the daily papers are aware of Hitler's assault on Europe, Japanese suicide squads, the defeat of the British in Burma, the denunciation of Jews in France and other equally disturbing occurrences. . . .

There are . . . mysterious plagues of boils, and various new, and frequently fatal diseases which, like the current drought, are attributed by some residents to the indirect effects of universal conflict. Ration cards play an important part in the development of the tale, along with marital infidelity, children born out of wedlock, a false murder charge, sudden deaths, vilification, falsehood, loss and some eventual personal triumphs.

Listed in this manner the events in the book may sound violent. Actually its tone is curiously serene, for somehow, as Mr. Rao quietly unwinds his unconventional narrative, all events of whatever nature—whether taking place in the world outside or within the confines of this specific locale—appear in the end to equate with one another. Myth and fact meet and commingle in that delusive "reality" which, to many Indian minds, is only a timeless "illusion."

Govindan Nair, the philosopher hero of this brief tale, is presented to the reader through the first-person chronicle of his neighbor and friend, Ramakrishna Pai. Wisdom, for Govindan, is exemplified in the way a kitten, being carried by the scruff of its neck, submits to the mother cat's rough tongue and sure grasp. Says Govindan to his friend, "Without Mother the world is not." . . .

Within the symbolic frame set by the author it naturally follows that a real, though rather magical cat, helps to rescue Govindan from a charge of murder, just as he, in turn, enables the neighbor he has proselytized to realize some improbable private wishes.

The cat and kitten part of the hero's view of life was, for me, far easier to follow than the role played by Shakespeare in Govindan's personal philosophy, and this in spite of a long speech "in the manner of Hamlet" which, taking off from the familiar "to be or not to be," plays evocatively back and forth on the themes of the I and Is-ness and dream versus fact.

Occasionally, too, in spite of Rao's extraordinary facility—and felicity—in the use of the English tongue, there are lapses into a kind of overblown phraseology that he himself describes to one of his characters: "a mixture of *The Vicar of Wakefield* and Shakespeare." But to be sometimes puzzled, or to have one's ear jarred a bit, are hardly valid reasons for putting down (or failing to take up in the first place) any of the remarkable works of Raja Rao.

Rao's writing has the power to pierce below the surface of visible India into hidden layers of his country's ancient, complex and long-enduring culture. On page after page of the new book fleeting references tease the reader's mind: the local maharajah making a ritual journey to dip his sword in the sea; the beautiful god in a nearby temple lying asleep on the coils of the cosmic serpent; the old grandmother who could stop a flood by reciting a sacred *mantram* in classical Tamil.

In Rao's novels one experiences an acute awareness of India's innumerable subtle paradoxes and poetic contradictions. One cannot come in contact with this exceptional creative mind without understanding a little more clearly the nature of the confrontation between the technological, scientific We and a land and people nourished by a still-living mythology and personally viable metaphysics.

> *Nancy Wilson Ross, "Where Myth and Fact Meet," in* The New York Times Book Review, *January 17, 1965, p. 5.*

ELIOT FREMONT-SMITH

The Fable is an ancient teaching from which, if it is to work, must first of all be precise in meaning. There have been effective modern fables—George Orwell's *Animal Farm* comes to mind—but on the whole it does not seem a form especially well suited to the modern (Western) literary temperament.

Perhaps we know too much, or think we do, so that the discovery of what is "true" and "right" no longer easily surprises or explains (except for children). Accustomed to ambiguity, we are suspicious of the proverb. Thus a serious modern fable is handicapped from the start by our resistance to the very simplicity of the moral point or principle of behavior which it is the fable's purpose to illustrate and to reveal. At the same time, if the point or principle is obscure or missing, we are left dissatisfied or laughing.

These remarks are occasioned by the publication of two slim books [Raja Rao's *The Cat and Shakespeare* and Ronald L. Fair's *Many Thousands Gone*] that attempt the fable form. Neither is successful. In [*The Cat and Shakespeare*], simplicity becomes so artfully reductive as to be incoherent; the reader is left picking away at paradoxes among the ruins of a narrative. . . .

[*The Cat and Shakespeare*] concerns the philosophic development of Ramakrishna Pai, the narrator, under the metaphysical tutelage of his friend and neighbor, Govindan Nair.

Nair's method of teaching is to "twist a thing into its essence and spread it out." In the words of Pai: "To him all the world is just what he does. He does and so the world comes into being. He himself calls it: "The kitten is being carried by the cat. We would all be kittens carried by the cat.' " . . .

The cat is also Mother (or the central feminine power in Hindu theology) as, in another sense, is Pai's pregnant mistress, Shantha: "Shantha is not just a woman, she is woman."

The setting is a small South Indian community in 1941-42. The war is present in bureaucracy. Pai and Nair are government clerks. "Everybody must do something," Nair says, "the clerk must correct his files, the fleas must bite."

But these are only the outer trappings of life—as the book's plot, which includes infidelity, a case of boils and a murder trial, is merely the wrapping for its epistemology—and every reality has its synthesizing opposite. Sometimes it makes the whole: "Life is a riddle that can be solved with a riddle. You can remove a thorn with another thorn, you solve one problem through another problem. Thus the world is connected."

At other times, opposites cancel each other out. The point is further made that if one, or the world, is a kitten in the mouth of the mother cat, it does not see the mother cat: so existence may be nothingness.

Well, the Westerner may well become impatient with such conundrums—even in a story which has, as this one does, an overlay of humor. Precisely what the point of it is, is hard to say, and the many passages that read like "Who's on First?" are not encouraging. A provincial judgment perhaps, but even Eastern paradox can have diminishing returns. Here they seem inscrutable.

> Eliot Fremont-Smith, "Proverb Hunting in Paradox Land," in The New York Times, *January 20, 1965, p. 37.*

ROBERT MAURER

"I have a system of no logic, and that is the story," says the narrator of this delightful "metaphysical comedy" [*The Cat and Shakespeare*], by Raja Rao, an Indian who writes in English. The narrator's good friend, Govindan Nair, follows no logic either. Between the two they share a madcap poem in prose that makes a reviewer sorry he hasn't more space to quote and to commend.

Nair will recall Kazantzakis' Zorba and Cary's Gulley Jimson, beings whose super-human vitality is both joyous in its overthrow of reason and humorous in its abnormality. He bounds up stairs two at a time to increase the fun and save energy. He leaps over walls, even non-existent ones. Speaking metaphorically in a weird mixture of *The Views of Wakefield* and Shakespeare, he describes himself as a kitten carried by a mother cat to whom he surrenders his will. When you learn the way of the kitten, Nair tells his friend, you free your mind, deliver yourself from desire. Passive though his way

seems, it miraculously supplies the two men their multiple desires—for a house with three stories (two, actually, the third being the terrace, open to openness), a mistress, a cure for boils, the grace of Shiva, success at the government offices where they work as clerks, and even acquittal in court when Nair is charged with thievery.

Just how much of this Eastern outlook can be understood by us is hard to say, for the simplest of comic actions (a trip to a doctor's office suddenly metamorphosed into a brothel) are convoluted beyond Occidental recognition. While some of the numerous epigrams strike a familiar chord in our ears ("Milk is never an immediate friend like coffee") others sound as discordant as two meows ("To gulp is sin, to purge is bounty"). And always there are poetic passages that are tantalizingly obscure but luminous. . . .

> Robert Maurer, "Landing Right Side Up," in Book Week—The Sunday Herald Tribune, *January 31, 1965, p. 16.*

DANIEL CURLEY

[*The Cat and Shakespeare*] is narrated by Ramakrishna Pai, a minor official at the Revenue Board. His work has taken him away from his native place, and his wife has chosen to remain behind with the children, a choice that Mr. Pai finds rather to his liking, for he has discovered that his wife is really unsympathetic: She insists that two and two always make four. She will admit that in dreams the answer is often seven, but she says, "I am not living in a dream." Ramakrishna Pai rather thinks he is living in a dream, and he is so fortunate as to find a really womanly woman who is very bad at arithmetic. In the course of the book, this woman bears his son, and they seem to live happily ever after, although the technicalities and legalities of the situation must continue to perplex the Western mind haunted by dreams of the most precise kind of arithmetic.

More important, however, than this idyl is the character of Govindan Nair, neighbor and best friend to Ramakrishna Pai. Govindan Nair is a mystic and perhaps a confidence man. He works at the Ration Office and is perhaps corrupt—at least he has more money than is easily accounted for and is actually tried for some vague irregularity. His great contribution to the book is his theory of the cat. Life is the cat. We must know how to be the kitten, to submit. "Learn the way of the kitten. Then you're saved. Allow the mother cat, sir, to carry you."

This is a fine theory—related in a distant way to Conrad's "to the destructive element submit"—but its application to the book is very hard to see. After all, when the book opens, Ramakrishna Pai had abandoned his wife, and his mistress is four months pregnant. It looks very much as if Mr. Pai were already dangling happily under the cat's chin and as if no opposition remained to be overcome.

The main problem confronting the reader is to make up his mind whether or not his usual standards apply to an Indian novel, whether there is a special Indianness that requires a special standard. Narayan's novels do not raise this question, nor do any Indian films released in this country. They are strange to be sure but no stranger, say, than Dostoevsky. Ultimately, of course, the usual standards must be applied, and by those standards this is a bad novel. There is always a chance that something new and unrecognized is going on, but the reader dangling from the mouth of the mother novel can only say, Why, the Emperor is buck naked.

Specifically, a depressing cloud of philosophy envelops the book. It is full of sentences that should be read only in a cave in the Himalayas or in a coffee shop in the Village. An exchange between Mr. Pai and his five-year-old daughter: "Father, what is life?" "Daughter, it is where no flame can burn." Again: "One can be and not be but be." There are moments of charm, but the price is too high. (pp. 27-8)

Daniel Curley, "Pretension without Content," in The New Leader, *Vol. XLVIII, No. 13, June 21, 1965, pp. 27-8.*

M. K. NAIK

The epigraph on the title page of [*The Cow of the Barricades and Other Stories*] is perhaps the key to the heart of these stories. The quotation is from Kabir, the fifteenth-century Indian saint-poet: "When I tell them the truth, they are angry, / And I cannot lie." In these sharply etched vignettes of Indian village life, Rajo Rao does not lie; and this accounts for the appeal and the power of the book.

The India of these stories is mostly rural South India (except in **"In Khandesh"** where the setting shifts slightly farther up to Maharashtra; in **"Companions,"** where the author goes up north and in **"A Client,"** where, for once, we are taken to a city). [Except for **"Companions,"** the stories] are set in the Thirties—a most eventful period in modern Indian history, for it marked the beginning of Gandhi's non-violent struggle against the British. Yet these stories are by no means of merely topical interest. For, though the impact of the modern Indian resurgence brought about by the contact with the West is very much in evidence in them, they also reveal how the traditional mores of Indian life are still a vital force working for the good as well as to the detriment of the community. Furthermore, though the locale of these stories is India, the "heartbreak at the heart of things" which the best of them capture is ultimately true to the kindred points of home and the universal human condition.

The unrest of the Thirties is mirrored in three stories—the title story **"The Cow of the Barricades," "Narsiga,"** and **"In Khandesh."** The holy cow named after the goddess Gauri, in [**"The Cow of the Barricades"**], is an expressive symbol of the Indian synthesis, of India's power of "carrying on the old tradition and yet ever adapting it to changing times." The sacred cow, dedicated to a god or a temple and therefore inviolable, is part of the ancient Indian tradition; yet Gauri, who dies of a bullet fired by a British Officer during the freedom riots and thus probably saves the lives of many in the village, is a martyr in the cause of the modern Indian freedom struggle. **"Narsiga"** shows how the national consciousness roused by Gandhi percolates into the mind of a small illiterate orphan, though, in that process, ancient myth and legend get inseparably mixed with Gandhi's life and character, as Narsiga the orphan imagines the great man "going in the air, with his wife Sita . . . in a flower-chariot drawn by sixteen steeds." In **"In Khandesh,"** the Viceroy's special train is to pass by the village and the Village Headman's orders are that the villagers should stand by the railway line to show their loyalty to the British emperor, but that they should stand with their backs to the train—for "You know how some devilish, prostitute-born scoundrels tried to put a bomb beneath the train of the Representative of the Most High across the Seas."

The traditional mores of Indian life are vividly depicted in most of the stories. Raja Rao knows his Indian village through and through; and, true to the motto borrowed from Kabir, he is determined to tell the truth. A perfectly intimate picture of Indian village life thirty years ago emerges from these stories: You can reach a village only after a ten-mile cycle ride on a bare, dusty road. The village crier beating his drum, "tom-tom, tira-tira," is a walking gazette making important announcements. Time is not reckoned by calendar and clock here, but by significant landmarks either in the life of the community or in one's own. (pp. 392-93)

Religion—not in the restricted sense of a theory of God and a creed, but in the wider sense of *Dharma,* a whole way of life—is a potent force here. Belief in *Karma,* rebirth, and transmigration of souls is strong. . . . The division of society into rigid castes is still sacrosanct here. Hence, "A Brahmin is not meant to work." He is the "chosen one," for the sacred books are his; he is the twice-born. The lowly-born are his servants. Early marriages are the rule. Akkayya the child bride loses her husband, but is perfectly unconcerned since she fails to understand the significance of the event; she enjoys the festival doll-show. "They only asked her not to put on the vermilion mark and she did not mind that in the least." Wife-beating is normal, and a widow's life is a long chronicle of austerity, self-denial, drudgery, and misery.

Ignorance and credulity foster a lush crop of superstitions here. A plague epidemic becomes a terrible goddess from whose clutches there is no escape. The idea of the hospital horrifies plague-stricken Rati for, "All that they did there, nobody knew. They cut you, pierced your flesh and did a million unholy things. Death was better." If the morning fire in the kitchen refuses to burn with a "hard, gem-like flame," it is an evil omen to Beti; so is the sight of a cat, first thing in the morning, to Ramu. But a lizard falling upon your right shoulder is sure to bring good luck, thinks Motilal. Little wonder then that the world of the villager should be full of magic, witchcraft, and ghosts. (p. 393)

Winds of change are already astir in this world of age-old tradition, in which the inevitable clash between the old and the new has set in. If the village elders, Dattopant and Govindopant, who are all excitement at the Maharaja's passing by their village, imagining how they would bow to him and how he might perhaps send them "bags and bags of gold," represent a deeply entrenched feudalism, the dangerous clique of Bolopant, Vithobopant, and Pandopant with their city chatter and subversive talk show the new democratic and nationalistic urge at work. Again, while young Ramu chafes at the rigid social code, his married sister, who loves the lowly-born Javni as if the latter were her mother, will not eat with her, for that is irreligious, and "affection does not ask you to be irreligious."

It is a motley crowd that lives in this world. There is the Bania, the village grocer, who comes down from Gujarat, "poor as a cur," who soon runs up a prosperous business as a moneylender; the professional matchmaker, skilled in the art of catching prospective eligible bachelors; the snake charmer; the *sadhu* in his Ashram; the saintly, pontifical Brahmin who has a vision of God; the simple peasant boy; and the city-educated young man, questioning traditional values. They are all vividly realized. But the most memorable characters in the book are the women, especially the widows—Javni and Akkayya. A modern Hindi poet, Maithilisaran Gupta, has summed up woman's destiny as "Even such, O woman, alas! is your lot; There is milk in your breasts, and there are tears in your eyes." This description, almost meaningless (for more than one reason) in the modern European (and to some extent in the modern Indian) context, is seen to be only too apt in the case of the women in these stories. Whether it is Javni, the ill-fated widow whose sister-in-law would not let her touch the latter's child, for she is "a witch and an evil spirit"; or Akkayya the child-widow who spends her long life in bringing up other people's children, but is in death as in life only an irritating nuisance to her relatives; or Beti, whose husband does not spare the rod in correcting what to him appears to be a spoilt spouse; or pretty Rati, daughter of rich parents, turned into a slave of her mother-in-law and a "casual wife of a husband with a mistress"—they all suffer and continue to exist, though hardly to live.

Raja Rao is no dreamy-eyed romantic however, and not all his women are angels or Griseldas. Narsiga's shrewish aunt; and Sata, the good Ramakrishnayya's widowed daughter, "greedy, malicious and clever as a jackal"—"they" even said she had poisoned her husband because he was too old for her—these provide admirable foils to Javni and her ilk.

The people in her village describe Javni as "good like a cow," in the typical Indian way; and, curiously enough, the Cow in the title story is as living a character as Javni herself. By no means an officially "god-dedicated" cow, Gauri has that within her which makes her more saintly than the trappings of orthodox sanctions. Strange indeed are her ways. . . . (pp. 393-94)

It must be remembered that the picture of village life in these stories is now more than thirty years old. Much water has flowed in the Ganges during this most eventful period, and the face of rural India—a face upon which time left little impression for centuries—has been, since Independence, rapidly changing, and changing, on the whole, for the better. Economic and social betterment is being vigorously attempted, though the actual progress is none too rapid; efforts are afoot to break the strangle hold of ignorance and superstition upon the rustic mind; the Brahmin is no longer the "chosen one"; the woman's lot and the widow's are definitely improving, if a trifle too gradually. Yet there is much in this picture that is more or less true, even today.

"For me literature is *sadhana*—not a profession but a vocation. That's why I've published so few works," declared Raja Rao to an interviewer [in *The Illustrated Weekly of India,* January 5, 1964]. His literary technique, therefore, can hardly be considered in isolation from his vision. It is indeed a part of the vision, and shapes and is shaped by it. For instance, in narrating the ancient legend of Kanakapala, "protector of gold," the author ends the introduction with a benediction in the traditional Hindu style: "May those who read this be beloved of Naga, King of Serpents, Destroyer of Ills." Raja Rao's style, too, captures the very feel and flavor of the life it describes, itself transformed in the process into truly "Indian" English. . . . His similes smell of the Indian soil: "She was as red as the inside of a pumpkin"; Kanakapala's "Old, old skin . . . shriveled like the castoff skin of a plantain"; Akkayya's face "all wrinkled like a dry mango"; "Death had entered the house like a cobra," Hosakere Nunjundayya's "dust-covered feet seemed bluish green like cow-dung"; "My

father's face turned grey as a coconut," "A heart pure as the morning lotus"; brides "beautiful as new-opened guavas."

Like Mulk Raj Anand, Raja Rao also literally translates Indian vernacular idioms and phrases, oaths and imprecations into English, thus securing a strong local color: "Always the same *Ramayana*" (it is always the same old story); "Else it would have been your marriage day" (else you would have had it); "When one has a guest like you, even a miser will turn the Generous Cow" (i.e., the fabled Kamadhenu, the legendary divine cow which gratified all desires). The village habit of prefixing an appropriate adjective to a proper name is well exemplified in names like Eight-verandahed-house Chowdayya, Cardamomfield Venkatesha, and Plantation Subayya. The appellation of "the Red man" for the white man is equally typical. Rustic speech is also larded with picturesque terms of abuse such as "wife of a donkey," "son of a prostitute," "dog-born," and the like.

But local color is not the only forte of Raja Rao's style. He is a master of descriptive prose, and his picture of the summer landscape in **"In Khandesh"** is as evocative as the descriptions of the seasons in *Kanthapura:*

> In Khandesh the earth floats. Heaving and quivering, rising and shriveling, the earth floats in a flood of heat. Men don't walk in Khandesh. They swirl round and round upon their feet—and move forward. Birds don't fly in Khandesh. They are carried on the billows of heat. . . . In Khandesh the earth is black. Black and grey as the buffalo, and twisted like an endless line of loamy pythons, wriggling and stretching beneath the awful beat of the sun. . . .

As a short story writer, Raja is no more of an experimenter than Tagore, Anand, or Narayan. In fact, the modern Indo-Anglian short story writer has always erred on the side of traditionalism in the matter of form. At one or two places, Raja Rao indeed carries the process a little too far, ending two of his best stories in a rather hackneyed manner. . . . (pp. 394-95)

How does Raja Rao, the short story writer, compare with Tagore, Anand, and Narayan? He clearly lacks their range and variety. In his wide sweep, Tagore ranges over themes as diverse as the decadent Bengali aristocracy, as in *The Babus of Nayanjore;* the mind of an invalid, as in *Mashi;* and child and adolescent psychology as in *The Postmaster* and *The Home-Coming.* His tone and temper, too, can swing from the pathos of *Cabuliwallah* to the somber tragedy of *The Trust Property;* from the sharp satire of *The Parrot's Training* to the light-hearted humor of *My Fair Neighbour.* Mulk Raj Anand is equally at home with rural or urban life. . . . And, with his socialistic sympathies, he is a committed writer. Narayan with his delicate touch brings out both the humor and the pathos in the lives of ordinary men and women—both rustic and city-bred—a beggar, a domestic servant, a college-student, a farmer, a clerk, and others. But none of these writers has felt the pulse of village India with a surer touch, nor seen the traditional, the transitional, and the universal in it more clearly than Raja Rao has done in his one book. This is perhaps the reason why he has the most distinctive style of all the Indo-Anglians.

It is to be regretted that Raja Rao has written so few short stories. The comparatively freer form of the novel has been a fatal Cleopatra to him in *The Serpent and the Rope,* that occasionally exasperating exercise in style and in metaphysical ingenuity. "The caste mark was not on his face but on his soul," says Raja Rao about his Brahmin hero Ramu, in **"A Client."** The caste mark on Raja Rao's own soul has made his intellect run away with story and character in *The Serpent and the Rope,* though in the earlier novel, *Kanthapura,* the damage was limited because of the much smaller framework. The sonnet's "narrow plot of ground" proved a most salutary discipline for Wordsworth. Indo-Anglian writing is certainly the poorer because Raja Rao did not submit himself oftener to the relatively more exacting discipline of the short story. (pp. 395-96)

> M. K. Naik, " 'The Cow of the Barricades and Other Stories': Raja Rao as a Short Story Writer," in Books Abroad, *Vol. 40, No. 4, Autumn, 1966, pp. 392-96.*

ROBERT J. RAY

One of the most satisfying of vicarious literary experiences is the close scrutiny of an author's development from rudimentary beginnings to artistic fulfillment. Such development is manifested in form and structure, in characters, in theme and plot, in symbolism, and especially in style. With a novelist like Raja Rao, whose native language is not English, style becomes particularly important because [as he stated in his foreword to *Kanthapura* (1938) excerpted above,] he is attempting to embody within written English the rhythms of Indian life and the traditional qualities of Sanskrit. . . . In *Kanthapura,* what Raja Rao produced from such a theory is a stylistic texture dominated by *and, then, but, when,* and *now.* One sequence follows another without emphasis or control, and the result is a book that reads much like the following passage, which describes a typical scene in the South Indian village of Kanthapura:

> and they clapped hands again, and they wiped the tears out of their eyes, and more and more women flowed out of the Pariah street and the Potters' street and the Weavers' street, and they beat their mouths the louder, and the children ran behind the fences and slipped into the gutters and threw stones at the police, and a soldier got a stone in his face and the police rushed this side and that and caught this girl and that. . . .

The description loses force at *this side and that;* it becomes completely diffuse at *this girl and that.* The effect, of course, is breadth: violence touched all sides (places, areas, etc.) at all times, and all violence was equal, and the police and the soldiers were all equally violent and the people were all equally victimized, but especially some of the girls. For a novel of almost two hundred pages, the effect is not speed, as Raja Rao hoped in his Introduction, but monotony, and even the most socially concerned reader has trouble digging into the story.

Like most Indo-Anglian novels, *Kanthapura* is a didactic work of social criticism, and its message to the world of India in the troubled Thirties is reinforced and clarified by some fifty-odd pages of notes. These notes provide necessary historical and cultural background on the Gandhi movement, which motivated the villagers of Kanthapura to action against the British-controlled government. Unfortunately, the clarity of meaning is contained not in the novel itself, but in these notes, where the didactic voice of the novelist is stronger and more convincing than the sonorous tones of the

female narrator. These notes, when added to the monotonous style and the plural point of view ("and we rush down the aloe lane,") make *Kanthapura* an artistic failure.

More than twenty years separate *Kanthapura* and *The Serpent and the Rope* (1960), Raja Rao's second novel. During this time the novelist went through a psychological and spiritual transformation, and the subsequent change in his artistic craft is the most profound in the history of Indo-Anglian literature, perhaps even in the history of contemporary literature. He has replaced the obvious theme of social criticism with a probing examination of the human psyche. The limited setting of the tiny village of Kanthapura he has expanded into a gigantic geographical triangle that covers England, France, and India. He has embodied new power in conventional symbols (like city, bridge, mirror, mountain), and the fifty-odd pages of notes have shrunk to a glossary of two pages. But the most significant difference in the two novels, and the key to the change in the novelist himself, is style; through his new first-person narrator (a South Indian Brahmin historian named Ramaswamy), Raja Rao moves far beyond monotonous co-ordination to paradoxical language patterns that are stunning, subtle, profound, and beautiful. The explanation for this change is simple enough, and occurs as part of the texture of the novel, not in an introduction. . . . Instead of simply reflecting Indian life (the stylistic credo of 1938), style is completely a part of the author. And this is the change that made *The Serpent and the Rope* Raja Rao's best novel and one of the deepest and most serious literary efforts of the twentieth century.

As we discover the stylistic elements of *The Serpent and the Rope,* we must remember that they belong deep in the texture of the novel, and when we isolate and describe them we are not describing *the* novel, but only a part that reveals significant tone, atmosphere, or essence. For the novel's style is a complex network of subtle repetitions, crossing pronoun references, rhythmical parallels, and delicate (and impossibly paradoxical) equations. All of the style is a part of Raja Rao himself, and as the novel is one long human perception, so the style mirrors the nature of that perception. . . . (pp. 411-12)

If the stylistic essence of any book is revealed more by one pattern or part of speech than another, then the essence of *The Serpent and the Rope* is revealed by reflexive pronouns. . . . [The] reflexives control the metaphoric center of Ramaswamy's philosophy, and turn even his most carefully contrived objective symbols into extensions of the self. This symbolic extension is evident in the development of Ramaswamy's concept of Love ("Love, my love, is the self"), and of Woman ("Woman shows that the world is oneself seen as the other"); but it is especially apparent in his Brahmanic view of Benares, Paris, and London. Benares, where Ramaswamy flies from Europe to cremate his father, is "indeed nowhere but inside oneself." And when he returns to Europe, he finds the same to be true of Paris: "Paris somehow is not a city: it is an area in oneself." And when he looks again, he sees Paris as "a sort of Benares turned outward," the whole image mirroring the spatiality of the reflection . of perception. . . . The essence of the symbolic city emanates from the true perception of self, this perception is the constant major quest of the narrator, and the moment of perception is both illusory and eternal:

> Seeing oneself is what we always seek; the world,
> as the great Sage Sankara said, is like a city seen in
> a mirror.

The circle that binds the narrator to style is constantly turning inward, and it is this same motion that characterizes our perception of *The Serpent and the Rope.* Discovering the "reality" of the novel is like Raja Rao's mythical man "trying to walk into a road that he sees in a hall of mirrors." We can see the details, and we can isolate them on the page and in the mind, but the total pattern of the whole is obscured in the paradox of their presentation.

Raja Rao's third novel, *The Cat and Shakespeare* (1965), is an extension of *The Serpent and the Rope:* the narrator is an unnamed South Indian; the controlling symbols (*wall, house, cat*) are simple and strong; the main subjects are women, philosophy, and the paradox of the perception of perception; and the key to the novel is again the reflexive pronoun. *The Cat and Shakespeare* takes its name from a symbolic cat and a parody of Hamlet's soliloquy. The cat is symbolic of motherhood in all its protective qualities, even when it is eliminated from the Shakespeare parody. The parody itself is delivered by Govindan Nair, neighbor of the narrator and the central character in the novel:

> A kitten sans cat, kitten being the diminutive for
> cat. *Vide* Prescott of the great grammatical fame.

A kitten sans cat, that is the question. This speech by Govindan Nair occurs in the Ration Office where he works, and it occurs just before Boothalinga Iyer, the head of the Ration Office, dies. From Raja Rao's oblique prose, we can only assume that the cat *and* Shakespeare were the cause of death:

> "I'll tell you a story," said Govindan Nair, and lifted the cat and placed her upon his shoulder.

> "Once upon a time," he began, and before he could go on, the cat jumped onto Boothalinga Iyer's head. Boothalinga Iyer opened his eyes wide and said, "Shiva, Shiva," and he was dead.

This scene in the Ration Office is typical of the key scenes in the novel: linked together only by the voice of the narrator, Govindan Nair, and tricks of illustory perception, they form points of intensity at different levels in the network of action that is almost a non-plot. A short time later, for example, Govindan Nair is arrested, "not on a charge of attempted homicide [for the death of Boothalinga Iyer?] . . . but on a charge of bribery," and the trial that follows forms another point of intensity in the narrator's reverie. But the most striking point of intensity is Govindan Nair's visit to a doctor's office, which turns out to be a brothel, Govindan Nair the symbolic doctor, and the dancing prostitute a patient in disguise: "The patient may undress while the doctor is getting ready."

With the illusory non-plot of *The Cat and Shakespeare* held together only by these mystifying points of extreme intensity, the texture of the novel becomes even more important: symbols and elements of style turn in on themselves, mirroring each other as they disclose paradoxical data about Govindan Nair, the narrator, and our illusory perceptions of perception. Govindan Nair, for example, transports himself from place to place across a wall that becomes gradually a symbol. The wall exists at the edge of the narrator's garden, and Govindan Nair jumps across it so that he can philosophize with the narrator. He jumps back across it to go into the world and into the several intense scenes of the non-plot. But

when the narrator himself crosses the wall near the end of the novel, we see the return of the mirrored self, a symbol from *The Serpent and the Rope:*

> That was the first time I went across the wall. I found a garden all rosy and gentle. . . . The air was so like a mirror you just walked toward yourself. How is it I never knew my neighboring wall went up and down the road, and up again toward the hospital.

The wall extends to the narrator's experience of Woman, as he learns from his beloved not-wife, Shantha, who says: "I can see you have never been across the wall. For there you could touch me and see yourself touch me." The wall is also the symbolic resting place and transit point for the kittens:

> What is death to a kitten that walks on the wall? Have you ever seen a kitten fall? You could fall, I could fall. But the kittens walk on the wall.

The singular kitten on the wall is probably representative of the dimensions of the self, which Raja Rao carries with the familiar reflexive from *The Serpent and the Rope:*

> There's only one depth and one extensivity and that's (in) oneself. It's like a kitten on a garden wall. It's like kittens walking on the garden wall.

In a sense the reflexive pronoun is the key symbol of *The Cat and Shakespeare,* linking the objects of the universe to mankind, the obvious center. A watch, for instance, is "a thing that turns on itself and shows the moon"; the moon is "the thing that turns on itself and (elliptically) goes around the sun." The reflexive pronoun is the beginning and end of all things, forming a convenient circle for all didactic problems raised by the narrator's conversations with Govindan Nair and with himself. . . . Intuitive recognition of such a device reveals the depth of Raja Rao's understanding of English, which is, I repeat for emphasis, not his native tongue. Our problems with such a device, if we have them, reveal our lack of understanding of our native tongue, and produce other problems with philosophy and worldview. We are perhaps more at home with abstractions, e.g., "perfection of perfection," but Raja Rao's deepest talent is in the concrete. . . ." (pp. 413-14)

Robert J. Ray, "The Novels of Raja Rao," in Books Abroad, *Vol. 40, No. 4, Autumn, 1966, pp. 411-14.*

HARISH RAIZADA

Raja Rao has a very high sense of the dignity of his vocation as a writer. He looks to his work in the spirit of dedication. For him literature is *sadhana*—not a profession but a vocation. It is why all his writing after *The Cow of the Barricades and Other Stories* has been mainly the consequence of a metaphysical life, what he means by *sadhana.* (p. 158)

According to Raja Rao, a man must be a man first and a writer afterwards. By man he means the metaphysical entity. One can, however, realize one's metaphysical entity only by following the Indian way and seeking the guidance of a "Guru". Though Raja Rao is a man of great literary cultures being equally at home in the knowledge of classical Sanskrit and modern European literature, he is basically an Indian. His whole approach to life and literature has been outlined against the broad perspective of the Indian philosophy and tradition.

Raja Rao believes in the Advaitic truth of "Shivoham, Shivoham; I am Shiva, I am Shiva," as Sankara says. According to him, Shiva is the opposite of *shava.* Shiva is not a god. He is the absolute Truth and can be realized when a Guru, who is himself a realized being, gives one the *upadesam.* Otherwise Shiva is an empty word. Though born in a Vedantic family, Raja Rao could not realize the full significance of *Vedanta* till he met his Guru, Shri Atmananda, to whom he dedicates **The Serpent and the Rope.**

Life is duality and the perfection one dreams about can never be achieved on the material or mental plane. If the perfection is to be attained, duality is to be resolved not into oneness but into nonduality. Life then becomes nothing but meaning.

Raja Rao felt the sincerity and spirit of dedication even when he wrote his first novel, **Kanthapura.** He was, however, then a "confused and a lost person" and had not realized his metaphysical entity. It is why he gave up writing entirely for a long time. (pp. 158-59)

Kanthapura, though not a mature and spiritually satisfying work from his point of view, is one of the most remarkable Indian novels in English because of its distinctive treatment of thought content, form and expression. It reveals Raja Rao's social and political preoccupations which he shared with the writers of the 'thirties. He wrote it during his stay in the High Provence in France. The distance from the real scene of action helps him to portray the violence and waste and the courage and glory witnessed by India during the terrible years of its struggle for liberation, with the artistic detachment and objectivity rare in the novels of the period.

In this novel Raja Rao relates the story of a South Indian village Kanthapura—from which it derives its title—as it rallies to Mahatma Gandhi's call of non-cooperation. It gives a graphic and moving description of the National Movement in the 'twenties when thousands of villages all over India responded in much the same way. They shook off their lethargy and joined the Congress Movement and Gandhi's militant programme of *Satyagraha* and *Civil Disobedience.* They took to hand-spinning on the spinning wheel, shed their prejudice of caste and creed, and relented in their attitude towards the untouchables, often admitting them into their social circle. Kanthapura is India in microcosm: what happened there is what happened everywhere in India during the early stages of its struggle for freedom.

Raja Rao's preoccupation with Indian religious traditions which finds its fuller expression in his later novels, is revealed in this novel as well. What he describes here are, however, the popular beliefs of the illiterate and unsophisticated villagers with their faith in superstitions, local rituals and the benign influence of gods and goddesses. The story-teller, an old village grandmother, blends the tale of the political resurgence in her village with these religious beliefs in the stream of her reminiscent narration. The undercurrent of the religious traditions running throughout the novel not only adds to the impact of the national movement on the readers but also unfolds the sensibility of Indian villagers for whom religion counts more than anything else and who are very prone to viewing the important events in their lives from the religious point of view and mythicising them. That is why every village in India has its own local legends connected with its ideal men and women or its association with the mythical heroes of the country. . . . **Kanthapura** is the tale of Moorthy, a dedicated and selfless soul, who is regarded by the villagers as the "learned master", the local Mahatma—"he is our Gandhi"; "the saint of our village". It is at the call of Moorthy that the whole village plunges itself in the non-violent national struggle of Mahatma Gandhi.

Higher than Moorthy, the local *avatar,* is, however, the greater deity Mahatma Gandhi, the real *avatar* of *Kalayuga,* born to free the Mother Bharatha from the tyranny of the imperialist demon. (pp. 159-60)

Mahatma Gandhi was often portrayed as an *avatar* and compared with Rama and Krishna in the patriotic poems, folk ballads, and *bhajans* and *kirtans* of the 'thirties all over India. Raja Rao also uses these analogies to describe the temper of the age and illustrate the devotion of Indians for the Mahatma. The *Harikatha*-man in one of his recitals compares Mahatma Gandhi with Krishna who killed the serpent Kali. (pp. 160-61)

Not only is this mingling of myth and fact appropriate to the point of view of the narrator who is an old illiterate grandmother but it also helps to reveal the ethos of the villagers and the atmosphere of the village of which the narrator is herself a part. Raja Rao makes this picture of village life rich in the religious faith of the unsophisticated villagers appear more effective by describing their rituals and festivals such as Sankara-*jayanthi,* Rama festival. . . .

No other Indian novel reveals so realistically as **Kanthapura** the various facets of the village life with its socio-economic divisions, superstitions, religious and caste-prejudices, blind faith in gods and goddesses, poverty, petty jealousies, dusty lanes, shady gardens, snake-infested forests, dirty pools, hills, rivers and changing seasons. (p. 161)

Raja Rao is endowed in the highest degree with the one essential gift of the novelist, the power to create living characters. All the characters portrayed in the novel, though static and simple, are alive and realistic and have an individuality of their own. They are living men and women, not mere symbols. Like the Russian masters, Raja Rao is able to put his finger on the pulse of the deepest factors in man's life and character. Though the village Kanthapura itself is the real hero of the novel, the people who live in it are made alive and distinguished from one another by the few masterly strokes of his pen. (p. 162)

For catching the thrilling atmosphere and fleeting pictures of the village life, Raja Rao has forged his own bold narrative technique such as old grandmothers follow for telling legendary tales to children at night. The whole story is put in the mouth of an old woman of the village who is supposed to tell a modern story about her village. As the old woman moves to and fro in time, the story turns to be the stream of her memory. Thus while using the old technique of the ancient myths and legends, Raja Rao makes use of the innovations in style of Conrad, James Joyce and Virginia Woolf to suit the narrator's rambling and reminiscing speech. For conveying the tempo of the nightmarish and fast moving episodes, he has evolved a racy rhythmic style with long and interminable sentences connected with numerous "ands" and containing few punctuation marks. (pp. 162-63)

It is likely that besides native influences which moulded his style, Raja Rao benefited from the examples of the French writers Gide and Malraux also who write with emotions and intensity. He admits himself "Gide influenced my literary form and Malraux my literary expression." The most decisive influence on his style was, however, of the Kannada authors and their works. In his article, **"Books Which Have Influenced Me"** [published in *The Illustrated Weekly of India,* February 10, 1963], he confesses:

> In Kannada, the *Vechnakaras* and then *Kanakadasa* and *Purandaradasa* affected me so profoundly that they seem to have changed my style of writing.

Raja Rao has evolved not only his own technique and style but also his own peculiar English—Indian English—to suit his material. He is aware of the difficulty an Indian writer faces in describing the Indian life and conversation through a language which is not Indian. (p. 163)

[Raja Rao] takes enough linguistic liberty of expression in his effort to develop "Indian English" and express his thoughts accurately. In Raja Rao's language therefore we find richness of local colour, set forms of Kannada expression, metaphrased idiom and an imagery that is nearer to the Indian way of thinking. The sentences such as, "I know you are not a man to spit on our confidence in you" or "We shall be there before you have swallowed your spittle thrice", may appear peculiar, but ideas embodied in them cannot be better and more effectively expressed in context with the village life in the Kannada speaking region. There is freshness, vitality and novelty about Raja Rao's imagery and figures for they are derived from "coconut", "elephant", "banana", etc. which are peculiar to life in the state of Mysore.

The Serpent and the Rope is the most mature of Raja Rao's works. It took ten years in shaping itself and was published thirteen years after his earlier work, *The Cow of the Barricades,* a collection of short stories. No other Indian novel in English has aroused so much of commotion in the Indian literary world and evoked so much of critical attention. It won for Raja Rao Sahitya Akadami Award in 1966 and Padma Bhusan by the President of India in 1969.

In *Kanthapura* Raja Rao experimented in the language and form of the novel and gave them distinctly Indian character, in *The Serpent and the Rope* he has extended the scope of the novel by giving it a new subject matter, the quest for metaphysical wisdom or the meditations on the nature of existence from the Indian point of view. The popular beliefs of unsophisticated and illiterate villagers in gods and goddesses based on the traditions of the peasant India which figured in the first novel are here replaced by the authentic Vedantic vision based on the traditions of the philosophic India of the *Vedas, Upanishads, Brahma Sutras,* the *Gita,* Yagnyavalkya, Sankara, Madhava and their descendents who left hearth and riverside fields and wandered to distant mountains and hermitages to see God "face to face".

In *Kanthapura* the story was told from the witness-narrator point of view by an old illiterate village grandmother, a minor character in the novel, who like a chorus in a Greek tragedy reflected on the circumstances which she witnessed. *The Serpent and the Rope,* because of its philosophical subject matter, requires a sophisticated and intellectual narrator. As the theme is the knowledge of the self and the action takes place in the thought process and psyche of the hero, the narrative perspective is focussed on him. The story of *The Serpent and the Rope* is therefore unfolded from the protagonist-narrator point of view. As the hero-narrator is interested not so much in the events of his life as events, but in terms of the meaning hidden in them, not so much in the physical action as in the philosophical meditations, the novel turns out to be his spiri-

tual autobiography. In order to communicate his meditations and the thoughts of the innermost recesses of his mind, the hero-narrator uses the devices of introspective diary entries containing his feelings and reflections on the nature of his relations with others, self-revealing letters received from friends and relatives, jottings of recapitulated poetry quotations from the *Vedas, Upanishads,* Hindu lore and French poetry. In his narrative perspective he moves to and fro in space and time "to apprehend the point of intersection of the timeless with time", he mixes memory and reverie by switching back and forth from the present to the past and by making present and past aspects of one reality and he scatters with a seeming recklessness aphorisms, witticisms, cynicisms, and profound metaphysical comments.

The hero, Ramaswami, is a young man of great literary cultures. (pp. 164-65)

Being a product of many cultures Rama's mind is a seething whirlpool of cultural currents and cross currents. Unlike the simple story-teller in *Kanthapura,* who knew only Indian myths and legends, Rama is familiar with myths and legends of different civilizations and he can discern parallels between them and forge a link between the past and the present by comprehending the essential oneness of history. . . .

At some places the legend of one civilization is blended into that of another while at other places the mythical incident is related to the historical one. The love of Iseult for Tristan is analogous to that of Rada for Krishna or of Savitri for Satyavan. Holy Grail has its origin in Buddhism and Chalice is the mendicant alms-bowl upturned. (p. 166)

Raja Rao has used the myths and legends to highlight the situation of characters or the relationship between them and to substantiate or concretize the abstract thoughts of the hero, Ramaswamy. While Madeleine describes her yearning for Rama who had gone to India by using the analogy of Penelope and Ulysses ("Like Penelope I sat on the sea-shore, weaving my web. When will you come, O Ulysses?", Ramaswamy likens her to a devotee who "would want her Shiva or Krishna to be big and grand, that she might make a grand *abhishkea* with milk and honey and holy Ganges water". Though Savithri sometimes calls Rama her Shiva and sometimes Satyavan and Tristan, the relationship between them is described by the recurrent mythical allusion of Radha-Krishna legend. The mythical allusions which are used by the author to elucidate and support Rama's reflections, are integral parts of the theme of the novel. They enforce Rama's metaphysical meditations which constitute the real subject-matter of the novel. The intellectual protagonist-narrator does not only employ the new machinery for unfolding his story but also uses the style different from that of the village grandmother in *Kanthapura,* to express adequately his metaphysical meditations. The concrete imagery (taken from the South Indian regional life) which was prominent in the previous novel is here replaced by general reflections and abstract speculations.

The style is marked by high seriousness befitting the Vedantic theme treated by the author. The quotations from Sanskrit, Kannada, Hindi and French verses are sprinkled here and there. The syntax and accent of the English language are changed to lend it the beat and rhythms and the incantatory effect of the Sanskrit language. Aphorisms, paradoxes, clever inversions, and rhetorical expressions are very common in the novel as in the Vedic scriptures. (p. 167)

What gives *The Serpent and the Rope* its distinctive character is, however, its thought content which is the revelation and assertion of the life-giving Vedantic vision. The hero, Rama, is "born a Brahmin—that is devoted to Truth and all that". Explaining Vedantism he points out that Vedantism is complete in itself and no one can improve on it. (p. 168)

Vedantism represents the idea of the Absolute which makes the relative meaningful, but man must not learn to confuse the relative with the Absolute, the moment for Eternity, the particular for the Universal, the shadow for the Substance, the serpent for the rope. Talking to Madeleine before the break up with her, Rama taking the analogy of the serpent and the rope used by Sankara, gives a brilliant exposition of the difference between the illusion and reality from which the novel derives its title.

It is why Rama who has known Vedantism intellectually but not yet realized it spiritually cries at the end of the novel:

> "No, not a God, but a Guru is what I need. 'Oh Lord, My Guru, My Lord'. . . . 'Lord, Lord, my Guru, come to me, tell me; give me Thy touch, vouchsafe 'the vision of Truth. Lord, my Lord'."

In a sense it is this India, the land of Vedantic wisdom, which may be called the hero of the book. However, in this apotheosis of India, there is no deliberate disparagement of any other religion, culture or country. It is wrong to exaggerate the confrontation of the East and the West in the novel. Rama has an assimilative mind and absorbs the best of every culture. He has a great respect for the West and often identifies himself with its towns, rivers and mountains. The separation of Madeleine and Ramaswamy should not be considered as symbolic of the East-West antithesis. The main cause of Madeleine's alienation is not the cultural difference between India and Europe. It is true that Rama "is born a Brahmin" and Madeleine has Catholicism in her blood, but this difference was there when they married and lived happily. It alone is therefore not a sufficient reason to separate them. Madeleine is not wrong when she contends Rama's assertion that it is "India" which has separated them for she points out, "But I am a Buddhist". We know that she even reads Sri Aurobindo and finds a great deal to approve of in his philosophy. Earlier she has said in all earnestness, "Everything good for me has only come from India".

In fact the separation is due to several reasons and one of the most important of these is the incompatibility of their temperaments. Rama is meditative and serious. Abstract ideas matter more for him than the tangible objects of life. Madeleine on the other hand is not metaphysical but practical and decisive in her ways. Religion for Rama is realization, for Madeleine it is a matter of faith, that is why she believes even in superstitions and miracles. For him what counts is wisdom, for her goodness and compassion are more important. It is why Madeleine is drawn towards Buddhism and asceticism. Perhaps the disparity in their age (Madeleine is five years his senior in age) also adds to the incompatibility of their temperaments. Madeleine's attraction for Georges and Rama's for Savithri might have also caused some cleavage in their relations. A still more plausible reason for their separation is, however, the death of their second child. The sad incident may not have affected Rama much but the grief-stricken Madeleine's superstitious mind is likely to attribute its cause to their inauspicious marriage. Madeleine is drawn more and more towards asceticism after this calamity and it ultimately

leads to her alienation from Rama. Their separation therefore does not represent the East-West conflict.

Rama describes the narrative of *The Serpent and the Rope* as "the sad and uneven chronicle" of his life. This has led some critics to consider *The Serpent and the Rope* as "essentially a spiritual autobiography" and to ignore its fictional character. It is an autobiography in the sense "all books are autobiographies". While being interviewed by Annie Brierre, Raja Rao pointed out, "Everything one writes is autobiographical. But it is a metaphysical novel." Owing to its distinctive character *The Serpent and the Rope* should not be judged by the canons of the traditional Western novel. (pp. 169-70)

In *The Serpent and the Rope,* the real action takes place not on the tangible plane but in the mind and psyche of the hero. We have therefore to seek for the movement and crests and troughs of the action in the thought process and metaphysical reflections of the hero. Action is not born here out of the motives of characters or their conflicts with each other as in dramatic novels. . . . In *The Serpent and the Rope,* the destinies of different characters run parallel to each other's. Little Mother, Saroja, Madeleine, Savithri, Catherine and Lakshmi, each carries on her own pilgrimage of life separately without ever crossing another's path. What the author is interested in is not their contact with each other but with Rama. Even Rama's life they touch at a tangent without intersecting it and creating a crisis. Each of these encounters and experiences gives a new meaning to Rama's sensibility but it does not change the tide of his physical life. Raja Rao is interested not so much in the destiny of his characters as in the destiny of man as seen through the mind of initiated Ramaswamy.

The Serpent and the Rope has all the known characteristics of the novel form—story, plot, social criticism, characterization and dialogues. Their treatment, however, differs from the traditional pattern owing to the newness of the subject matter dealt in the novel. It has a story, though in the greatest fiction story does not figure as an important aspect and is subordinated to the rendering of life.

Though *The Serpent and the Rope* is epical in form, it has an architectural symmetry which is connected with its thematic development. It can be divided into six movements or intermeshing blocks dealing with Rama's encounter with different women characters in the novel—"Little Mother" block, "Madeleine" block, "Catherine" block, "Savithri" block, "Saroja" block, and "the metamorphosed—Madeleine's" block. All these blocks are interrelated for other women characters also figure in each of these blocks, though one of them occupies the most prominent place. Each block takes a new meaning in Rama's life and adds to his metaphysical awareness. The climax reaches in "Savithri" block which is almost in the middle of the novel. Here Rama realizes his "self" as is evidenced by his remark, "One cannot possess the World, one can become it: I could not possess Savithri—I became I". It is therefore wrong to think that structurally the novel is discursive and it lacks unity of form.

Though primarily concerned with metaphysical reflections of the protagonist, the author is not completely oblivious of the tangible reality. It is obvious from his ironical comments on the weak spots of social and political life in India. . . . The author ridicules the decayed and false modernity of the small Indian Rajas with their vulgar tastes, Babu English and sycophancy for English officers. There is a biting satire on the subjugation of women in India in Saroja's angry outburst against the arranged marriages. Equally harsh is Savithri's criticism of the type of India that was emerging after independence.

Raja Rao's skill in portraying living characters is amply displayed in *Kanthapura. The Serpent and the Rope* reveals a further advance in his technique of characterization. He is no more concerned with delineating characters in their private aspects. He now portrays them in relation to the broader and more impersonal objects that occupy mankind—their relations to public affairs, philosophy, art and religion. In *Kanthapura* he had shown a discerning eye for the surface personality of his characters. He could visualise their outward idiosyncrasies vividly and unerringly, their manner, their charm, their tricks of speech. In *The Serpent and the Rope,* he realizes the psychological organism that underlies speech and manner. With his lucid knife-edged mind he penetrates beneath the external impressions to discern the peculiar combination of qualities that go to make up their conduct and individuality. There is also a greater variety of characters in *The Serpent and the Rope* than in *Kanthapura.* Characters are here drawn from different races and nationalities and they are all real and alive. If Little Mother represents the Indian women of the older generation, Saroja does those of the younger generation with her resentment and revolt against the arranged marriage. Savithri, a daughter of the prince of a rich state, is one of the emancipated girls. The author has breathed life by a few strokes of his pen, even into minor character like Savithri's Cambridge friends, Lakshmi, Sharifa, Swanston, a Marxist, Stephen, a logical positivist and his girl friend, the beautiful Julietta. Equally convincing are Henri, the taxi driver, Madame Petensir, the patronne of Hotel du Roi Jean, Madame Chimaye who hates the man doing business in birds opposite her restaurant more than she hates Americans, Sukumari, the younger sister of Rama, who marries a Communist and makes his politics an act of her faith and Uncle Seetharamu who helps Rama during Saroja's marriage.

Raja Rao has an uncanny knack of framing natural dialogues. He changes their tone and style to suit his characters and situations. They are formal, intellectual and witty in Rama's philosophical discussions with Georges, Lezo, Madeleine and Savithri, while chatty and colloquial in his conversation with his family relations in his home town in India. (pp. 170-72)

Between *Kanthapura* and *The Serpent and the Rope* there lies a gap of almost a quarter of a century. During this period Raja Rao has lived a fuller and freer life of mystical experience and contemplation and attained spiritual fulfilment. In *The Serpent and the Rope* and his other later writings he has, therefore, attempted to communicate his metaphysical reflections and reveal the basic spiritual tradition of India lying hidden under the changing surface reality of the contemporary life. Even in *Kanthapura,* though engaged in dramatising the social and political turmoil of the ('thirties), Raja Rao was not oblivious of this spiritual tradition of India. He, however, treated it from the point of view of the peasant sensibility. Besides, his interest was at that time divided between the social and political issues of the country on one side and its spiritual ethos on the other. From *The Serpent and the Rope* onwards he is more and more concerned with the revelation of the deeper sensibilities of Indian life. The external actualities of the contemporary life, though not completely ignored, provide only a superficial background for the enactment of the more profound drama of the spirit. In *The Serpent and the Rope,* there are references to Hindu-Muslim riots at the time of partition of India, the merger of princely states in the newly-born Indian Republic, the role of Pandit Nehru and Congress Ministers who waver in their choice of building the new India after the pattern of China or England, the Korean War, and the coronation of the Queen of England. Similarly while in *The Cat and Shakespeare* there figures the India of the Second World War and the Rationing Office as the background of the action, the changing political world situation during the Second World War and the fluid state of Indian political life after independence do in *Comrade Kirillov.* The political and social issues are, however, no more the chief concern of Raja Rao. His approach to life and literature is now outlined against the broad perspective of philosophy and spiritual tradition.

In *The Serpent and the Rope* he deals with the metaphysical quest for Absolute Truth where man can distinguish the rope from the serpent. In *The Cat and Shakespeare,* the author goes a step ahead and describes the state of spiritual serenity which descends in the life of a man who leads the life of detachment and resignation. Govindan Nair, the protagonist of the novel, though a man of modest education and living (being a mere clerk in the Ration Office), is a humanist and possesses Shakespeare like all-embracing catholicity. He detaches himself from *Maya* symbolized by the corruption rampant in the Rationing office and follows the metaphysic of life as suggested by the symbol of cat in the *prapatti marge* in *Yoga:* "Learn the way of the kitten" i.e. surrender to destiny.

In *Comrade Kirillov,* too, published in 1976 though originally written in the early 'fifties, Raja Rao emphasises the superiority of Vedantism, which recognizes the basic reality, over Marxism which is concerned with the ephemeral and the changing. . . . (pp. 172-74)

According to Raja Rao "the Indian novel can only be epic in form and metaphysical in nature. It can only be story within story to show all stories are parables' ". Raja Rao has followed this technique in his novels from *The Serpent and the Rope* onwards and thus given them a distinctive Indian character. (p. 174)

Harish Raizada, "Literature as 'Sadhana': The Progress of Raja Rao from 'Kanthapura' to 'The Serpent and the Rope'," Indo-English Literature: A Collection of Critical Essays, *edited by K. K. Sharma, Vimal Prakashan, 1977, pp. 157-75.*

EDIRIWIRA SARACHCHANDRA

Raja Rao's *Kanthapura* has been described as "the most satisfying of Indian novels" and it deserves this praise for many reasons. Although written in English, it satisfies the Indian ego in as much as it does not follow any of the usual techniques of western fiction. It reads like something written in an indigenous Indian language, and yet is a modern novel by any standards. There are characters that stand out; there is the setting of the village of Kanthapura, the ambience of which is skilfully evoked; and there is the development of the plot to its catastrophic conclusion. It inspires us with feelings of patriotism and the grandness and vigour of the Gandhian movement, its loftiness, its heroism, and its uniqueness—its uniqueness because, being a political movement, it was still not only that, but much more. It had its roots deep in the great culture of India and that is why it both fired a fervour in the heart of almost every Indian, and also baffled all attempts of the British to understand it or to cope with it. When a political movement takes on a cultural form it is almost invincible. And nothing ever written about the Indian independence movement brings out this aspect of it better than *Kanthapura*. Nothing ever written is as evocative of the mood or explains better how an unarmed people were able to fight successfully against the might of the British Empire. (p. 107)

Kanthapura can be styled a prose poem, a *gadya kavya* as it would be called in the language of Sanskrit literary criticism. Every novel is a prose poem in the broad sense of the term, but in *Kanthapura* the author makes a conscious attempt to make his diction evocative, and one marvels at the control Raja Rao has over a language that is not his mother-tongue, the independence and courage with which he moulds it into his native thought-forms. A significant achievement of the novel is its linguistic virtuosity. The description of Moorthy's experience in meditation is an example of what the author is able to achieve by a creative handling of the English language.

> And the beating of the clothes sank into his ears, and the sunshine sank into his mind, and his limbs sank down into the earth, and there was a dark burning light in the heart of the sanctum, and many men with beards and besmeared with holy ashes stood beside the idol, silent, their lips gently moving, and he, too, entered the temple like a sparrow, and he sat on a handle of the candelabra, and as he looked fearfully at the holy, floods suddenly swept in from all the doorways of the temple, beating, whirling, floods, dark and bright, and he quietly sank into them and floating away like child Krishna on the pipal leaf.

The coming of the rains is described in language that is remarkably redolent of the Indian scene:

> The rains have come, the fine, first-footing rains that skip over the bronze mountains, tiptoe the crags, and leaping into the valleys, go splashing and wind-swung, a winnowed pour, and the coconuts and the betel-nuts and the cardamom plants choke with it and hiss back. And there, there it comes over the Bebbur Hill and the Kanthur Hill and begins to paw upon the tiles, and the cattle come running home, their ears stretched back, and the drover lurches behind some bel-tree or pipal-tree, and people leave their querns and rush to the courtyard, and turning towards the Kenchamma Temple, send forth a prayer, saying, "There, there, the rains have come, Kenchamma; may our houses be white as silver", and the lightning flashes and the thunder stirs the tiles, and children rush to the gutter-slabs to sail paper-boats down to Kashi . . .

Although Raja Rao himself says, along with several of his critics, that he follows the old Indian tradition of story-telling, his technique is not as simple as this description might suggest. It is only superficially that the technique appears to be that of the medieval story-teller. There is a great deal of conscious art in it, careful organisation of plot so as to create suspense and drama, and a good deal of subtle characterisation that he achieves by means of the dialogue. And Raja Rao solves the problem of dialogue more successfully than, perhaps, any other Indian writing in English. Narayan's dialogue uses a neutral, literary idiom without any phonetic or syntactical idiosyncrasies peculiar to the speaker, so that it has a sameness throughout and does not help characterisa-

tion. We have to assume, in most instances, that the characters talk in an indigenous tongue and that we are given only a standard rendering of their speech into English. Raja Rao does not use dialogue to the extent that a writer who is following a conventional fictional technique does. But whenever he does, he translates the native idiom so skilfully that we get the feel of the original language the characters would be using. It is not surprising that native speakers of Kannada like A. K. Ramanujan and Anantha Murthi have said that they hear the cadences of their mother-tongue in the English of *Kanthapura.* The native flavour is enhanced by the use of imagery drawn from the raw speech of the people, as in "Everybody saw that Narsamma was growing thin as a bamboo and shrivelled like a banana bark", or "Stitch up your mouth, do you hear?" or "In Kashi, for every hymn and hiccup you get a rupee".

In his next novel, *The Serpent and The Rope,* however, we see Raja Rao the mystic, the Brahmin proud of his birth, who traces his ancestry to the sages Yajnavalkya, Madhya and Sankara, and the nationalist, over-shadowing Raja Rao the artist. At the time it first appeared (1960), it was hailed both in Europe and India as a great work and something that portrays the East-West relationship better than any novel written up to that time. Eminent literary men like Denis de Rougement and Lawrence Durrell have showered unstinted praise on it. Perhaps there was reason for this enthusiasm at that time. Some features that give distinction to *Kanthapura* are discernible in *The Serpent and the Rope* as well. We see in it the same poetic language and the same creative use of English that we saw in the earlier novel. But one wonders what purpose all that virtuosity serves in this novel. There are superb evocations of Benares and some parts of Europe as well. And there are effusive extravaganzas on the delights of love and on Woman, and exquisite paeans to the holy river Ganges. But these are only purple patches in a story that is interminably dull, pointless, and rambling. One looks in vain for the human story behind the jungle of digressions.

The main flaw in *The Serpent and the Rope* seems to be that it is written in the first person, so that the reader does not get the opportunity of disengaging the narrator from the author and of seeing how the author views his hero. For, before the reader gets through half the novel, the narrator appears to him to be an insufferable bore, a self-opinionated and muddle-headed egoist who wants to pontificate on everything that comes to mind, talking in paradoxes that create an impression of great profundity but really makes no sense. One even wonders whether the author has to be understood as being ironical when he makes his hero say the absurd things he says—the things that seem to confound his wife Madeleine and drive her to take refuge more and more in Buddhist meditation and ascetic practices. (pp. 108-110)

Since personal relations are not dealt with in any depth, the characters flit about the pages of the book like shadows or silhouettes. Since they do not get involved with one another emotionally, the novel lacks any dramatic quality. Even most of the dialogue that ensues between Ramaswamy and Savithri, who, the reader is led to believe, have entered into some kind of emotional relationship with each other, is on a level of a philosophical conundrum. (p. 110)

It is strange that even in one of Ramaswamy's last meetings with his French wife, Madeleine, they discourse on what purports to be philosophy, when we would expect to get a glimpse of the emotional communion between them. And although we do not read a novel to learn philosophy, it must be pointed out that some of the philosophy expounded by Ramaswamy could convey to Western readers, in particular, a wrong impression of Indian habits of thinking. In fact, classical Vedanta (Ramaswamy ostensibly is attempting to expound the Advaita Vedanta of Sankara) is far from the obfuscated version of it that Ramaswamy gives us. (p. 111)

Sankara is no mystic of the type that Ramaswamy is. He does not use language for the purpose of confusing things. It is only when we try to speak of the ultimate reality, the noumenon behind the phenomena, that language fails us, or we have to speak in riddles or conundrums. Sankara uses the serpent and the rope image as well as the silver and mother-of-pearl image to illustrate the illusory nature of the phenomenal world, the seeming diversity in the world as presented to the sense-organs, behind which is unity, the reality. The rope is seen to be a serpent because of the activity that Sankara calls *adhyasa,* or superimposition, that is, the superimposition of the attributes of one thing on another. When superimposition does not function any more, the rope is seen to be a rope. As a substrate of the illusion, the rope exists. Sankara does not attempt to do away with the serpent and the rope both. Nor does he dismiss the "I" as non-existing, or as Nothingness. Even when there is false knowledge, there must be a knowing person. And the cause of *adhyasa* is *avidya,* or ignorance, which in its cosmic aspect is called *maya.* The distinction between subject and object, the knowing person and the thing known, exists as long as *avidya* persists. When it is realised, by right knowledge, that the individual self or *jivatman* is nothing but the Transcendental self or *paramatman,* which is another word for *Brahman,* the perception of diversity disappears and you see the world as One. In that condition of Release, the subject-object relationship ceases to exist, and the subject becomes the object. This is what is meant by the statement, *brahmavid brahmaiva bhavati* (the knower of Brahman becomes Brahman itself).

All the confusion created by Ramaswamy, therefore, when he talks of seeing the serpent as the same as becoming it, is not only unnecessary but quite misleading. What he means by saying that "the world is either real or unreal . . . and all that is in-between is poetry or sainthood" is the kind of talk that gives westerners the impression that Indian philosophy is all moonshine. (p. 112)

[Neither] Sankara nor any of the commentators on the *Upanishads* postulated that the world was subjective illusion. It was the Buddhist Vijnanavadins, called "idealists" somewhat misleadingly, like Vasubandhu and Dinnaga, who maintained that external objects do not exist and that they are projections of the mind—that, in other words, only consciousness (*vijnana*) exists. Sankara postulates three orders of reality; the order of the completely illusory, such as dreams, hallucinations and such (*paribhasika satya*), the order of practical reality, that is, the phenomenal world in which we move about and interact with our fellow-beings (*vyavaharika satya*) and the order of ultimate reality, which, alone, has true existence (*paramarthika satya*). The serpent and the rope imagery could apply to the relationship between any two of these orders of reality. When illusions disappear we see things as they are; that is, we see that the rope is a rope and not a serpent. But, in an ultimate sense, the phenomenal world has no independent existence. When *avidya* is removed, we see the true nature of things, the identity of Atman and Brahman, the unity in diversity.

This solves the problem of morality which might otherwise crop up in a philosophy like that of the Vedanta. The phenomenal world is relatively real, good and evil exist, and human relationships carry with them moral responsibility. When a person attains the higher realisation, he would be a *jivanmukta,* one who, while yet in this life, has attained release from *samsara.* Such a person is above morality, that is, it is not that he can do evil and escape its consequences, but that it is impossible for him to do evil. And we wonder whether in the character of Ramaswamy, the author was trying to portray such a *jivanmukta.* If this was in Raja Rao's mind, we must say that he does not accomplish this end convincingly. What sort of a character would a *jivanmukta* possess? We cannot say. No one has attempted to portray such a character in fiction. And if Raja Rao is attempting it, it is he who must give us a convincing picture of it. It would be doing the concept an injustice to identify Ramaswamy of the novel with a *jivanmukta,* a man above morality, above even the level of discursive thinking. And the questions arises, could a *jivanmukta* ever be portrayed as a character in fiction? If Raja Rao was really attempting it, was he not attempting the impossible?

There is no doubt that Ramaswamy is a saint of sorts. Most of the time he is shown as strutting around engaged in intellectual discussions with the people he meets, and words of wisdom fall from his lips. But he is engaged in mundane activities as well. Evidently he has no financial problems, for he is able to move to and fro between France and India and England as he pleases, which is a luxury that very few Indian students would have been able to enjoy in Europe. He is married, and, on his own confession, loves his wife deeply. But at other times he is not sure that he loves her. When his first son dies, he takes a handful of Ganges water and pours it back into the river, professing an inability to love; and when news of his second son's death reaches him, he laughs and says, "I was neither in pain, nor was I relieved; I felt above both, like a child looking at a kite in the sky". Is this the saint who has freed himself from all attachment, who looks at things from the perspective of ultimate truth, and knows that there is no life, no death, there is no one who lives or loves or dies?

What of Ramaswamy's relationship with Savithri, then? He deliberately talks about it in vague terms, throwing a mystic aura round it and even quoting the Upanishads, to suggest, perhaps, that between them there was love of a spiritual sort, on a higher plane than physical desire, like the yearning of the Atman for Brahman. However, what can the mundane reader make of statements like the following:

> When Savithri fell into this state I feel into myself, and forgot all but the feeling that existence is I. I am, therefore the world is. I am, therefore Savithri is. How I would have loved to have taken Savithri into my arms, how natural, how true it would have been! But we were not one silence, we were two solitudes. What stood between Savithri and me was not Pratap, but Savithri herself. . . .

But Savithri is more down to earth. She writes to him and puts the situation directly to him:

> "If you stood by me there is a grave question I would ask you: If I asked you, would you really marry me, will you? Father may object and say you are just a professor. But mother, whose values are more right, would say, 'Oh, a Brahmin!' She would

think your presence amidst us august, holy. But I am too poor, too wretched a creature. . . . Tell me, Rama, tell me truly and as before God, 'Come', and I'll come".

But Ramaswamy has no reply to give her. He applies Upanishadic philosophy to this mundane question as well, and ends up chanting Sankara but far from the point. . . .

Poor consolation for Savithri to be told that Ramaswamy would marry her "when the becoming was stopped" or when "there is no one to marry another"!

In a scene which gives a hint of there being a closer intimacy between Ramaswamy and Savithri than an etherealised, spiritualised communion of the self with the Self, Savithri makes what appears to be (if we are to read behind the riddles) a poignant appeal to Ramaswamy to take her (as his wife?) and even suggests that she is prepared to leave her husband for his sake. To the ordinary reader Ramaswamy appears to be taking her along the devious paths of myth and mysticism to avoid giving her an answer. . . . (pp. 112-115)

It is obvious, by ordinary moral standards, that Ramaswamy has deserted both Savithri and Madeleine. Madeleine seems to take Yogic practices more seriously than her husband, through whom she first learned about them. The way she inflicts suffering on herself, undertakes long fasts, taking Buddhism so literally that she begins caring for wounded caterpillars and nurses plants and butterflies, and even believes she has attained supernormal powers, is the one place that moves the reader in the novel. One finds she has at last found a way to escape from the boredom of her husband's interminable philosophisings and his incurable egoism: by practising seriously what he was only preaching all the time.

If Raja Rao intended to depict the character of a *jivanmukta* in his novel, the question to ask is, is this how a *jivanmukta* is expected to be? A *jivanmukta* is described as being "*in* the world but not *of* it." Sin may touch him but he is not defiled by it. Does this mean that he could sin and yet not have to face the consequences of sinning? Could he sleep with his friend's wife, as Ramaswamy does with Sham Sundar's wife, and yet not be guilty of immorality? Does his avoidance of responsibility in his relationship with Savithri mean that he is above morality? And can his strange behaviour on hearing the news of the death of his sons be interpreted as detachment?

The failure of *The Serpent and the Rope* as a novel is, of course, due to the inchoate character of its hero Ramaswamy on whom the events and the relationships hinge. Perhaps Raja Rao, always pursuing the ideal of a truly Indian novel, was attempting to create a character that we see cannot be depicted in fiction. If the author had not succumbed to the temptation of making his hero look like an oracle who would pronounce the last word on every conceivable subject under the sun, and given us a picture of a more sincere devotee of the Upanishadic philosophy who tried to live it in his practical life but failed, the novel would have deserved less to be dubbed "a compendium of interminable commentary and philosophising . . . a book of discursive inquiry rather than narration." (p. 115)

Ediriwira Sarachchandra, "Illusion and Reality: Raja Rao as Novelist," in Only Connect: Literary Perspectives East and West, *edited by Guy Amirthanayagam and S. C. Harrex, Centre for Research in the New Literatures in English & East-West Center, 1981, pp. 107-17.*

V. Y. KANTAK

It is in *Kanthapura,* Raja Rao's first essay in full-scale fiction, that a whole new dialect seems to emerge fully formed and, in his hands, fully responsive to the intricate tasks of the narrative structure. He has gone on, it is true, to fashion subtler modes for his purpose—a highly involved blend of autobiography and metaphysical probing in *The Serpent and the Rope,* and a unique combination of the symbolic, the fabular and the comic in *The Cat and Shakespeare.* It is arguable that in these more ambitious enterprises where more is at stake, lies his greater achievement. That at least is the presumption. On the other hand, *Kanthapura* within its humbler intention lays claim to the profound simplicity of a classic, something that the more self-conscious artistry of the later work seems to miss. One reason is, *Kanthapura* is essentially a triumph of the new dialect; its artistically deployed 'Indian' English no longer strikes one as an innovative device but is wholly absorbed in the larger 'folk-epic' purpose, is so congruous with it.

And it glints as though fresh from the mould. The novel opens with a swift initial sketching of the *locale*—a village up the Western Ghats from where slow-moving bullock-carts bring cardamom, rice, coffee and sugarcane to the coastal towns for export, by narrow, dusty, rut-covered roads that

> wind through the forests of teak and of jack, of sandal and of sal, and hanging over bellowing gorges and leaping over elephant-haunted valleys, they turn now to the left and now to the right and bring you through the Alambe and Champa and Mena and Kola passes into the great granaries of trade.

With that, we are already introduced to some of the salient features of *Kanthapura* prose, especially its cumulative particularizing quality, and transported besides to that village community—there to be greeted by Water-fall Venkamma roaring 'day and night against Rangamma'. From then on we are on the same wave-length with Kanthapura characters throughout, as far as the English is concerned. Marks of individuation are caught above all by the ear in the pace and the rhythm of speech, in the tendency to repetition, in the quality of diction and phrasing, in the peculiar intonation and speech mannerisms. . . .

Raja Rao seems to work primarily by the aural imagination, seeking to give the English the native (rural) Kannada speech tunes. These are readily recognizable, for instance, in the functional 'address' of "No, no, Bhattare," as much as in the non-functional 'address' of expressions like "Yes, sister", or for that matter, in the general habit of using 'sister', 'brother', 'father' and so on, simply as fraternizing tags that lubricate conversation and confirm intimacy. But the new intonation pattern runs through whole paragraphs, showing up poignantly in sentences like:

> But, *Rama-Rama,* really, if we have to hang the sacred thread over the shoulders of every pariah . . . it's impossible, impossible

where the *Rama-Rama* is not an 'address' but rather the invoking of God's name to emphasize the depths to which we have fallen.

Reiteration, one of the readily identifiable features, takes many forms. There is the communal habit of repeating things for intensification as in the ubiquitous of course, of course, for solicitation and appeal as in "Do not drink, do not drink, in the name of the Mahatma", or under the pressure of anticipation and suspense as in "Now, we are safe, we are safe" and "Sister, who is dying? Sister, who is dying?" and so on. Often this undulation acquires a crooning quality induced by emotional stress or gathers an incantatory force in devotional singing. . . . Or it may be the sheer hunger of the Andhra poor that lends incantatory force to their hopes of a wage. Trudging all the way from the Godavari to the Skeffington Estate, they chant the formula that holds the promise: 'a four-anna bit for a man and a two-anna bit for a woman,' like a *mantra* of the Kaliyuga.

Another element in the sound structure of *Kanthapura* English, and a curious one, is a kind of reiteration laced with *alternation*. . . . [When] Moorthy is arrested he is led away 'with a policeman on this side and a policeman on that side'. To say, 'a policeman on either side' would have hurt the rhythm and the reporter's imagination perception no less. And this lilt sometimes continuing through extended descriptions contributes to the building up of a sense of looming crisis. . . . Perhaps, ultimately, it is the sheer *pace* so alien to English and so evocative of colloquial Kannada that accounts for the power of this style of narrative, it being but the tempo of Indian life that has been, as Raja Rao claimed, infused into our English expression. In respect of the English medium, therefore, what appears at first to be done in despite and a blemish is actually an example of the adaptive power of a living tongue. It's a result of our inescapable bilingualism that Raja Rao talked of and refused to deplore, considering it rather our strength:

> We are all instictively bilingual . . . We cannot write like the English. We should not. We can write only as Indians.

And this concern to make the English echo the Indian speech tones is of special relevance to the present novel in that it lends authority to the figure of the narrator and her 'point of view' as it comes through in the fiction.

However, a preoccupation with the sound aspects of language and too great a reliance on the 'aural' rather than the 'visual' imagination may have its risks. It may happen that in the flow of description, mere similarity of sound may bring words together in total or partial disregard for semantic content or consistency of visual image, thus giving rise to an awkwardness that jars the sense. For instance, we are told that the day Ramakrishnayya died rains set in and that "It *poured* and it *plundered* all the fields and the woods." Apart from the innovation involved in extending the idiomatic use of 'It poured' (reflexive) to 'It plundered' (transitive), one suspects, 'plundered' is coupled with 'poured' for no more valid reason than alliterative effect. Though, of course, we recognize that, in a sense, too much rain has the effect of plundering the village. A more frustrating example of sound-sense disharmony may be this: In the final attack on the village, we read, " . . . there was a charge and the soldiers came *grunting* and *grovelling* at us, bayonets thrust forward . . ." Here again, 'grovelling' may link up with 'grunting' by virtue of the initial sound agreement, but its visual image clashing with it sharply presents an attitude contrary to that of the ruthless soldier and may be seen to belong rather to his victim. (pp. 35-8)

Such minor infelicities apart, the essential soundness of Raja Rao's insight is borne out by the result and beyond cavil: to be truly expressive of Indian life the English has, above all, to sound like Indian speech. And how magnificently does *Kanthapura* English absorb the villagers' strong sense of rhythm, iteration and tunefulness that is so marked a characteristic of their native dialect! One instinctively likens it to a 'mutation', *Kanthapura* being probably the finest specimen of its kind in Indo-English fiction to-date. What is important, at the same time, is to see that the semantic component of that transformation is equally effective and convincing. For instance, one of the features distinctively rendered into English is the villagers' passion for inventive *sobriquets* and evocative labelling of persons. (And often, not only persons but things—fields, houses . . . may be similarly individualized.) It obviously conduces to the community sense of belonging to know everyone by his defining, individuating, mark whether high or low in the social hierarchy—whether it be the one-eyed pariah, Linga, fig-tree-house Ramu, Waterfall Venkamma, husking Rangi, corner-house Moorthy, Jack-tree Tippa or front-house Suranna, and so on. And often, the innocent sobriquet may easily be extended to a searching character assessment, as it is, for instance when we are told of the Gandhi fanatic Shankar who 'makes everyone fast for every cough and sneeze of the Mahatma', or of Postman Subbaya 'who had no fire in his stomach and was red with red and blue with blue'. Allied with this is the condensed power of phrasing we sense in the stigmatizing of the youthful interest in the movement as 'this Gandhi vagabondage' or describing the movement itself as 'Don't touch the government campaign' and the Government forfeiture of the villagers' lands in terms like, "There's not a *ragwide* field left."

Rustic speech so meticulously characterized and integral even in its English *avatar,* one expects, would carry a strong charge of folk-wisdom conveyed through aphoristic expressions. Indeed, the language of an ancient peasantry such as the South Indian with its rich *Subhashita* tradition couldn't do otherwise. Needless to say, the form this takes wouldn't always be that 'display' string of rare maxims such as village Poloniuses might trot out on proper occasions at short notice, but rather the common harvest of everyday experience that has gone into the warp and woof of the villagers' language—a thoroughly unselfconscious acquisition. Often the novelty may consist in a slight shift—mainly verbal—in an otherwise well-worn proverbial usage in English. Thus, for instance, the *Kanthapura* expression 'a crow and sparrow story' supplants the familiar but jaded 'cock and bull story', just as in the expression "Every *squirrel* has his day," the gentle little arborial rodent is allowed to supplant the over-worked 'dog'. The more significant of these expressions that have a varied aphoristic force relate to the *ethos* and value system of the villager; the words have a freshness and variety purely of native brew. (pp. 39-40)

And there are those exquisite language mutations which bring the cultural matrix into sharp focus giving it body in wholesome English. Such a gem from the common resource you come across when a young girl's attaining of the age of puberty is referred to in the statment: "She will come home in a few weeks' time."—a delicate euphemism for an event which imposes the onerous task of finding a bridegroom for the girl and not only on her parents but also on the whole village. The expression itself existed before and is of the soil. The wonder is how perfectly harmonized it is when adapted to *our* English dialect, with no loss of its original suggestive force and no harm to the new language structure. That's, in a way, the process continuously at work in **Kanthapura** English.

A language that has gained such inwardness with Kanthapura's life as to become the authentic vehicle of its vitality would do two things at once—firmly establish the cultural context and equally firmly individualize the narrator's voice. (And it is appropriate to the 'epical' purpose of the fiction that the narrator should be one among the village women, obviously a Brahmin widow as can be inferred, and mother of Seenu, one of the village Gandhi, Moorthy's disciples.) The two lines of significance run smoothly together throughout. The usage, the language texture, is in fact replete with clues to the double purpose; so that the very strangeness of the idiom and the 'queer ring' of the English declare the inviolableness of the speaker and the speaker's world. Almost every page offers distinguished examples:

> Well, well, one must close one's eyes and ears or else the food will not go down one's throat these days.
> O Sage, is it greater for you to ask or for me to say 'yea'?
> There is such a silence (at the meeting) a moving ant could be heard.

And when someone calls him 'our Protector' the jovial Patel must quip, "Protector, yes, Protector of the village fowl!" (pp. 40-1)

Nor is it only in the singularity of usage and tone—a kind of lucid oddness—that the cultural background and the narrator's rural identity are registered. They are reflected just as well in the imagery, the choice of simile, and the metaphorical force of the language on occasion. Thus, we are told, Range Gowda, after the struggle, becomes, 'as lean as the arecanut tree', Narasamma when her son Moorthy's revolt shatters her world, grows 'as thin as a bamboo' and shrivels 'like banana bark', Waterfall Venkamma 'plants herself like a banana trunk' in front of Rangamma who was 'as tame as a cow' and stands watching Narasamma's misery 'helpless as a calf'. In the same way, Nanjamma can rise to the occasion and describe her vision of the Mahatma:

> No sister, I do not imagine the Mahatma as a man or a god, but like the Sahyadri Mountains, blue, high, wide, and the rock of the evening that catches the light of the setting sun.

And not only poetry that thus shyly peeps through the simpleness of mind. There is much compressed poetry below the unpretentious surface that yet sounds in no way discordant with the narrator's voice. As it happens, for instance, when the women are locked up in the Shiva temple at the height of the battle. " . . . the light went down and the sanctum's hooded darkness thrust itself over us." And when they are let out: "We slowly rose upon our clayey legs, and when the morning light threw itself upon us we felt as though a corpse had smiled upon the burning pyre."

That strikes a fine balance, the authorial prerogative working within the narrator's imaginative range and capabilities. The imagery and the language bear the clear markings of their provenance and yet blend harmoniously with the author's over-all artistic designing. While the *Indianness* of the dialect seems to be confirmed and even intensified if anything in that process. Such features of the English are not confined to the give and take of rustic encounters but are operative equally well when large seasonal harmonies of the countryside, for instance, call for lyrical description. That's how the grand onset of the Monsoon, always one of nature's spectacular displays in the South-west, is being described in the novel. . . . Thus, the dialect meets the demands that the fiction makes upon it with no loss to its distinctive character, adapting itself freely to the lyrical, 'dramatic' and narrative requirements of the moment. The effect is that, from the first page to the last, we have an assurance of the language's uniform competence and a sense of its organic unity. One's impression is that of a seamless garment, a word-body that is whole, a self-contained medium adequate for any mode of articulation.

But not quite. There are at least two or three places in the novel where it may be found wanting, where it comes short of making good the claim of being a self-sufficient dialect affined to the Indian village *ethos*. Even less can it claim to being the voice of the illiterate narrator. The occasions that prove so searching and revealing are worth pondering. One such is Moorthy's espousal of the Gandhi evangel. As a college student, while attending a Gandhi meeting he comes under the Mahatma's spell. But his response to that transforming experience—a vision of the Mahatma mighty and God-beaming—finds expression in language that seems to have suddenly dropped its dialect form, its naivete, and has donned refinement. As Moorthy stood by him, 'the very skin of the Mahatma seemed to send out a mellowed force of love' and there seemed to be between the Mahatma and his audience, 'the silent communion of the ancient books'. . . . The transformation in the idealistic young man is not in question and raises no cavil. But what has happened to the narrator that she should suddenly start talking about 'silent communions' and revelations of the 'sheathless' beings of souls, playing false to that magnificently alive *lingo*, her birth-right, and all without so much as an alibi for the defection?

More disconcerting still is her reportage of the newly initiated Moorthy's purificatory fast that he undertakes after the Master's fashion:

> . . . and closing his eyes tighter, he slips back into the foldless sheath of the Soul, and sends out rays of love . . . and he feels such exaltation, creeping into his limbs and head that his heart begins to beat out a song, and the song of Kabir comes to his mind: 'The road to the City of Love . . . '

And when he meditates:

> Thoughts seemed to ebb away to the darkened shores and leave the illumined consciousness to rise up into the back of the brain, he had explained to Seenu. Light seemed to rise from the far horizon . . . and rise to the sun-centre of his heart. There was a vital softness about it he had hardly ever felt.

Yes, but one asks, what of the language? Even the pretense of the narrator's voice has disappeared. It's clearly Raja Rao's own voice. And where is that 'colourful Indian speech' he had praised and, in a manner sworn by? Once again, it is not the validity or credibility of Moorthy's experience that is in question. What is at stake is the truth of articulation within the fiction's ambit. And admittedly here there is more involved than merely the failure to authenticate the device of the narrator's *persona*. Reports of the action-filled scenes are all done in dialect and vividly render what's afoot—the arrest of Moorthy, the Toddy Grove affair, the Picketting, the no-tax campaign and the bestial attack on the village, the sacking and the firing. Why should there be a flight from the dialect when it comes to Moorthy's idealistic response to the Mahatma's call or the landscape of his inner experience during the fast? Why, if not because, somehow, these are no fit occasions for it, supposedly? And yet that should have been true of the villagers' experience as well; for they, too, have a shrewd sense of what is happening even of the principles and issues involved, though, of course, in their own manner of apprehending them.

In fact, one of the finest successes of the book—and a crucial event in that it turns the tide in favour of the Gandhian movement—is the scene where Moorthy wins over the Patel, Range Gowda, to the Gandhian cause and the strict 'ahimsa' code of conduct it enjoins. What is at issue may be no less than lofty belief and the Gandhi *charisma,* but we can see that the Patel is being his own natural self in the way he reacts, that he speaks his own dialect and that the narrator reports him faithfully: "At this rate," he grumbles "I shouldn't howl at my wife and let my son-in-law go fooling with concubine Siddi's daughter . . ." But the Mahatma was a holy man, his word was the word of God, and he, Range Gowda, "was not with the jackals but with the deer." We sense at once that he has, in his rough-grained manner grasped the essence of the situation, but his mode of expression is still the same virile home-grown brand which the English preserves.

This is still a far cry from the *Kanthapura* dialect that might prove adequate for experience like Moorthy's inward strivings and illuminations. The short-comings, it would appear, are mainly linguistic. It's as though *Kanthapura* English equivalents for those indefinable wisps of thought, feeling and articulatory gesture are yet in the process of formation—with language itself functioning as *gesture.* Sometimes, the miracle does occur, however infrequently, and subtle inner experience gets described in English that has thoroughly imbibed the native speech tones. That's how we find the effect of the women's yogic breath-control exercises is conveyed: "The women began to feel stronger and stronger, the eyes stuck brighter in the sockets, and the mind deeper in the spirit." . . . The manner of speech and language here does no violence to the image of the narrator—we can imagine, this is how she might sound at some felicitous moment—nor does it rupture the verbal unity that the English of the novel presents.

Why should the language of Moorthy's inner world remain the big exception? Does it wholly explain the deviation simply to say, those are Moorthy's experiences, that it would be natural for his cultivated sensibility to find utterance in sophisticated phraseology? But there is, after all, the narrator's voice not to be so unceremoniously silenced. And then we are aware of the author's special closeness to the transformation he describes as taking place in his hero. It is clearly a central part of the artistic 'intention' and is meant to be taken seriously. (pp. 42-6)

The position is obviously, far from simple. Firstly, to find the English equivalents for those lit-up spots, luminous introspections, in the narrator's manner of speech would not be easy. She would either see them differently—in which event, it is true, there would be no occasion for an 'expression block' but then what is described could hardly be the same—or else, she would not see them at all. Secondly, the problem seems somehow basically concerned with the difference between *action* and *contemplation* and the articulation appropriate to them, in the fictional context. As soon as a character reflects on the acts of the mind itself we sense a certain inadequacy

in the *Kanthapura* English dialect. Raja Rao said, English 'is the language of our intellectual make-up, not of our emotional make-up'. Presumably self-communings and reflections on the act of the mind carry an emotional charge, and the language of the 'Moorthy' passages in question is not adequately the language of our emotional make-up. When a mode of expression that is native to the Indian peasant is found for these experiences in English, it will not only differ from the language of those passages but will be closer to the Indian articulation in general. For it is clear, this is a problem common to the elite and the illiterate alike. Finally, our dissatisfaction might amount to this: The 'Moorthy' passages are really addressed to the task of making the meaning of the experience clear rather than embodying the experience itself. To do that, we shall have first to find its emotional correlative in language.

Despite this lacuna—which is rather the sign of a continuing process of maturation of the new dialect—Raja Rao's *Kanthapura* is a confident affirmation of the integrity of English as the Indian fiction writer's medium. To evolve a whole new way of articulation in English and to maintain it consistently through an extensive action-filled drama speaks of the advanced level of language naturalization I had earlier spoken of. It's like setting a test for our claim to use English for expressing Indian sensibility, like asking ourselves how convincingly we make good that claim. The theme as it is developed provides but poor occasion for philosophic speculation or for reflecting on the acts of the mind. Here's hardly promising material for that purpose. How could this lowly group of Indians, largely illiterate, come alive and find a voice in English, the language of our intellectual make-up? But they do; and the adopted tongue subjugates itself to their uses and their accents to create a fictional monument to their common deed. The account of their *agon* is even touched with a certain nobility. Something of the brightness that lights on the high peaks of history rests upon their story, making it a little saga of a rural Indian community facing its moment of destiny. The way the challenge is met and the style of the reportage are marvellously adapted to each other. The genuineness of the fiction compels credibility, confers distinction.

So Raja Rao's *penchant* for a tensely reflective kind of prose or for indirections of the symbolic power of words, evident in his other novels, shows up here to disadvantage as though trenching on an unblemished harmony. What builds up that harmony is primarily the rustic women's naivete, their unconscious propulsion into action, their interminable, ebullient talk,—all concretely and objectively realized. That group, the narrator among them, are the real protagonists. And naturally it is the direct impress of their accent, of their impulsive gesture, that the English language is made to carry; which means in effect, the bustle and vivacity with which Kanthapura's men and women carry on their private and public affairs. And the Indian nuance of the English gains intensity as the action climaxes in the tumult, the noisy confusion, and the feral violence of the establishment; so that one is aware of a many-sided triumph as the book closes with the redoubtable Range Gowda's valedictory gesture addressed to the vanished Kanthapura whose legendary history or *Sthalapurana* has just been composed and sung:

> I drank three handfuls of Himavathy water, and I said, "Protect us, Mother!" to Kenchamma and I said, "Protect us, Father!" to the Siva of the promontory, and I spat three times to the west and three times to the south, and I threw a palmful of dust

at the sunken wretch, and I turned away. But to tell
you the truth, Mother, my heart it beat like a drum.

Actions like the ritual spitting and the throwing of a palmful
of dust—a kind of libation in reverse to the manes of the departed village—are, of course, all of a piece with the rest from
the beginning, and, in the cultural context, profoundly authentic. No less so (and that's the greater wonder) is the new
usage that announces itself in such things as the unaccustomed placement and force of 'mother' and 'wretch' (which
may be applied to the nuisance of rain—"Oh, this *wretch* of
a rain!"—as well as to a devastated and defunct village, as
here), and the new intonation pattern blended with the lively
undulating rhythm of Range Gowda's utterance, making a
music that we hear throughout the narrative. To those who
can respond to it, the effect is at once magical and fresh. For
they recognize the native habit of articulation wholesomely
imaged in the extended English.

It is as though the English-speaking world is served notice of
a new English dialect's coming of age. (pp. 47-49)

> *V. Y. Kantak, "Raja Rao's 'Kanthapura'," in* The
> Literary Criterion, *No. 13, Summer, 1985, pp. 35-
> 49.*

RAJA RAO

[*Reprinted below is Raja Rao's acceptance speech upon receiving The Tenth Neustadt International Prize for Literature.
The ceremony took place on June 4, 1988.*]

I am a man of silence. And words emerge from that silence
with light, of light, and light is sacred. One wonders that
there is the word at all—*Sabda*—and one asks oneself, where
did it come from? How does it arise? I have asked this question for many, many years. I've asked it of linguists, I've
asked it of poets, I've asked it of scholars. The word seems
to come first as an impulsion from the nowhere, and then as
a prehension, and it becomes less and less esoteric—till it begins to be concrete. And the concrete becoming ever more
earthy, and the earthy communicated, as the common word,
alas, seems to possess least of that original light.

The writer or the poet is he who seeks back the common word
to its origin of silence, in order that the manifested word become light. There was a great poet of the West, the Austrian
poet Rainer Maria Rilke. He said objects come to you to be
named. One of the ideas that has involved me deeply these
many years is: where does the word dissolve and become
meaning? Meaning itself, of course, is beyond the sound of
the word, which comes to me only as an image in the brain,
but *that* which sees the image in the brain (says our great sage
of the sixth century, Sri Shankara) nobody has ever seen.
Thus the word coming of light is seen eventually by light.
That is, every word-image is seen by light, and that is its
meaning. Therefore the effort of the writer, if he is sincere,
is to forget himself in the process and go back to the light
from which words come. Go back where? That is, those who
read or those who hear must reach back to their own light.
And that light I think is prayer.

My ancestors and, yes, the ancestors of some of you or of
most of you who speak the English tongue, came from the
same part of the world thousands of years ago. Was it from
the Caucasus or the North Pole? One is not certain yet. They
spoke a language close to my own language and close to your

language. There is in America a remarkable dictionary called
the *American Heritage Dictionary.* It offers almost a hundred
pages (at the very end) of the Indo-European roots of many
of our words. Most of you are of European origin. At least
your thinking has been conditioned by European thought.
There is thus a common way of thinking, an Indo-European
way of thinking, between us, so that we are not so far from
each other as we often think we are. And beyond the Indo-
European way of thinking in Asia, Africa, Polynesia, is *that*
same human light by which all words become meaning. Finally, there is only one meaning, not for every word, but for
all words *where* the word, any word, from any language, dissolves into knowledge. It is only there at the dissolution of
the sound of the word or of the image of the word that you
say you understand. And *here* there is neither you nor I. That
is what I have been trying to achieve. That I become no one,
that no one shine but It.

Many good things have been said by distinguished speakers—
about me—this evening. But I want to say to you in utter
honesty: I would like to be completely nameless, and just be
that reality which is beyond all of us who hear me—that reality which evokes in me you, and I in each one listening to me
this evening, that there be no one there but light. And it is
of that reality the sages have spoken. The sage is one, someone beyond the saint. He is no one. He is the real seer. In fact,
we are all sages, but we don't recognize it. That is what the
Indian tradition says. In the act of seeing—that is, of the seer,
the seen, and the seeing—in seeing alone is there pure light.
Where this comes from, nobody can name. I once asked Dr.
Oppenheimer, the scientist, who told me his hands were
soiled by the atom bomb: Have you ever seen an object? And
he answered: Never. If a scientist like Dr. Oppenheimer says
he has never seen an object—yet I am hearing him say what
he has in all honesty declared—it is that level of knowledge
I would like to reach from where I truly write. It is to that
root of writing I pay homage. The Neustadt Prize is thus not
given to me, but to That which is far beyond me, yet in me—
because I alone know I am incapable of writing what people
say I have written.

> *Raja Rao, "Laureate's Words of Acceptance," in*
> World Literature Today, *Vol. 62, No. 4, Autumn,
> 1988, p. 534.*

EDWIN THUMBOO

[*The encomium excerpted below was originally delivered by
Edwin Thumboo on June 4, 1988 at the ceremony honoring
Raja Rao, receipient of the Tenth Neustadt International Prize
for Literature.*]

Religions characterized by a duality rest on the belief that
God—or the Absolute, if you prefer—is external to man. He
creates, is compassionate, lays down. He judges, punishes,
forgives. Out of such sets of beliefs arises an ethos, a way of
life governed by the sacred and the secular, a distinction that
deeply influences morality and action; you render unto God
and you render unto Caesar. Thus the potential of conflict,
in which the overriding anxiety is whether soul or spirit, immortal and God-given, redeemed from sin, whether original
or incurred, is protected from evil and therefore damnation.
A state of grace for life, a state of grace for death, for without
grace there is everlasting darkness instead of eternal joy in the
presence of God.

In contrast, the Vedantic tradition is nondual. As embodied

in the Vedas, commented upon, expanded, and given greater precision by Sankara (788-820 A.D.) and other sages-gurus-teachers, including Rao's own guide Sri Atmananda, it is the basis of all his thinking and, consequently, of all his writings. To refer to his *thinking* and to his *writing* is to posit a dichotomy, a duality almost, which is not there, for the two activities are intrinsically bound, singular and seamless, as they are in Vedanta, which, Rao asserts in *The Serpent and the Rope,* "must become real again before India can be truly free." Its creative, linguistic, stylistic, ideational, psychological, analytical, social, philosophical, metaphysical nature, power, and reach derive from the totality of resources that are Indian, tested and refined over some four thousand years. It is underpinned by two key features: the conviction of nonduality, and the capacity to note the concrete in order to move beyond it to abstractions. Axles upon which the circles of Rao's epistemology turn, both are intimately linked to lie compacted at the core of his efforts "to move from the human to abhuman" through a dialectic defined and propelled by the continuities of the Indian tradition. There are fundamental consequences as well. First, the primary and secondary notions of the numinous in nonduality, such as the pantheon of Hindu deities, would appear exotic and/or confusing to those committed to a thoroughgoing monotheism—God above man—whose strictly parceled morality is likely to misjudge the true, abstract relationship between, for example, Krishna and his Gopis. Such monotheism posits a duality, separating the numinous from the human. On the other hand, in Vedantic nonduality man contains divinity; religions of duality shut him out. This leads to Rao's distinction between what he calls the horizontal and the vertical.

> There are, it seems to me, only two possible perspectives on human understanding: the horizontal and (or) the vertical. They could also be named the anthropomorphic and the abhuman. The vertical movement is the sheer upward thrust toward the unnameable, the unutterable, the very source of wholeness. The horizontal is the human condition expressing itself as concern for man as one's neighbour—biological and social, the predicament of one who knows how to say, I and you.
>
> The vertical rises slowly, desperately, to move from the I to the non-I, as the Buddhists would say—the move towards the impersonal, the universal (though there is no universe there, so to say) reaching out to ultimate *being*—when there is just being there are no two entities, no I and you. The I then is not even all, for there is no other to say I to. It is the nobility of *sunyata,* of zero, of light.
>
> **("On Understanding")**

Societies and psyches are identified accordingly: India is vertical, China horizontal in *The Chessmaster and His Moves,* in which Siva is vertical and Jean-Pierre horizontal, whereas Suzanne attempts the vertical but fails because she cannot go beyond horizontal gestures and excursions. Neither is birth into a vertical setting an automatic advantage—Raja Ashok is still a Turk, his self, his "I" unreleased because he is captive to the sensualities of the concrete, in contrast to Ratilal, who has left these behind. The distinction is crucial, as it helps, for instance, to clarify and reassert the centrality of the feminine principle in Rao's thinking/works. Woman is essential to man's progress up the vertical, for only with and by woman can man and woman find the Absolute. The relationship is deeply intrinsic, not poised, complementary, or bal-

anced as in yin and yang, which represent a horizontal relationship, one not integrated. It is Savithri who makes Rama holy in *The Serpent and the Rope,* Jayalakshmi Siva in *The Chessmaster and His Moves,* and they through them. (pp. 530-31)

I eschew any brief summary of Rao's individual works. Those who have read *The Serpent and the Rope, The Cat and Shakespeare,* and *The Chessmaster and His Moves* know how rapidly they defeat such attempts. The expansion and deepening of his fiction centers on the search by the self for a self capable of fulfillment in a world shaped by a tradition that is alive, inexhaustible, subtle, and on the move, a broad and complex continuum whose matrix consists of metaphysics, religion, and ritual as embodied in texts ranging from the Vedas to the emblematic tales from the *Ramayana* that carry, as appropriate to the capacity of reader or listener, religious, social, and political linguistic instruction and reaffirmation. Key texts and narratives are shared, pan-Indian, and connect with those that are regional—such as the collection of *vacanas* in Kannada—down to ones associated with the rhythms of life presided over by a village deity, a village history. The continuum is marked at one end by the most abstract, taxing metaphysics, at the other by humbler religious practices. It has the mutually reinforcing power of written and oral traditions—the retelling of episodes from the *Ramayana* or the stories of the gods by traveling narrators of *harikathas*—that instruct and nourish priest and villager.

Characters in search of self on various levels offer the major fictional foci and energies. More often than not they must contend with change arising from the pressure of events or the challenge of understanding the ethos of another culture. The young orphan Narsa in **"Narsiga"** (from *The Cow of the Barricades and Other Stories*), who herds sheep and goats and is abused by some but protected by the master of the ashram and whose growing awareness of the image of the Mahatma is described with deep insight and precise delicacy, belongs to the large Rao cast of characters that includes Rama *(The Serpent and the Rope)* and Comrade Kirillov, who both rise to the challenges but at an infinitely more sophisticated level and in a much broader, more universal, international context. The fictional ground between is established by characters such as Little Mother, Catherine, Savithri, Madeleine, Georges *(The Serpent and the Rope);* Moorthy, Rangamma, and Ratna *(Kanthapura);* Ramakrishna, Pai, and Govindan Nair *(The Cat and Shakespeare);* and Siva, Suzanne, and Jayalakshmi *(The Chessmaster and His Moves).*

Rao's themes include the metaphysical apprehension of God, the nature of death, immortality, illusion and reality, duality and nonduality, good and evil, existence and destiny, Karma and Dharma; the quest for self-knowledge, the place of the guru, the influence of religion and social concepts and patterns and prejudices on individual and group behavior, corrupt priests; the ideal and meaning of love and marriage, the impact of tradition on the individual and collective life and the meaning of India's real and symbolic content, and the historical or contemporary meeting of East and West in religious, political, and psychological terms tested against the vertical/horizontal distinction. The list is by no means exhaustive. Neither does it suggest the way themes conflate, complement, or construct oppositions depicted through the increasing psychological authority of the characters from the early short stories, through *Kanthapura, The Serpent and the Rope,* and *The Cat and Shakespeare,* to the firm, monumental authority of *The Chessmaster and His Moves.* This listing belies Rao's achievement of bringing into the life of each character and his or her relationships the extraordinarily complex worlds they each occupy—Indian, French, Greek, Hebraic, African, Chinese—and which overlap and contain, in a single moment, the mundane and the metaphysical.

That is a major achievement, as is Rao's remarkably successful reorientation of a language and his assembling of a narrative mode to articulate life fully within the continuum of tradition and change in which life is played out against the larger movements of personality, situation, and environment. (pp. 531-32)

The uniqueness of Raja Rao's style is its apt flexibility, demonstrated in how it incarnates the thoughts and emotions of characters ranging from relatively "simple" peasants to the Brahmin prone to disquisitions. His prose is resonant, bare, or poetic as required. His language accords with the Indian spirit, its speech, gestures, proverbs, and metaphysical thrust. Still, this rootedness in the Indian scene and the Indian tradition does not circumscribe his language. In fact, the sharp management of syntax, of sentence structure, the revealing use of its symbolic and metaphorical resources, gives both clarity and power.

Rao's basic narrative structure, particularly in *Kanthapura,* a majority of the short stories, and *The Cat and Shakespeare,* derives from Puranas, *sathala-puranas,* and *harikathas,* which between them bring together, inter alia, religious and metaphysical discourse, folklore, local legend and quasi-history, straight description, dramatic insets and well-managed digressions. In *Kanthapura* the first-person narrator (a favorite Rao device) is a villager. The style is fluid and simple, with the flow of narrative relieved by digression. The structure which carries the narrative voice is determined to a considerable extent by the status of the narrator himself or herself. Though this may seem obvious, it is considerably less so in that merging of a new language to an old environment. Consequently, in *The Serpent and the Rope,* narrated by Rama the young Brahmin, we find a combination of Indian and "Western" modes. It blends the scope of the notebook and the quest, both of which offer room for autobiographical excursions. The Indian elements derive from the Puranas, which mix religion, philosophy, history, and literature. Given its theme of the discovery of self and illumination through the apparently tangential instruction of a "guru," *The Cat and Shakespeare* reverts to the style of the *sathala-puranas.* The comedy and whimsy are deceptive because the message is fundamental, put across with subtlety and an indirection that is clarified by the concluding paragraphs.

Rao's greatest achievement, which I suspect only he can surpass, is the degree to which his works, especially *The Chessmaster,* contain the insights, emblems, mantras, metaphors, and other carriers of meaning and instruction that enable the individual to achieve, through his own meditations, a better understanding of self through Knowledge and Truth. They lead us, in Rao terms, from the human to the abhuman, to the Absolute or, if you will, from god to God to GOD, thus moving from the horizontal to the vertical. (pp. 532-33)

Edwin Thumboo, "Encomium for Raja Rao," in World Literature Today, *Vol. 62, No. 4, Autumn, 1988, pp. 530-33.*

EDWIN THUMBOO

Raja Rao's considerable achievement derives substantially from the uniquely Indian spirit and thrust of his work. The underpinning vision, steadied from its inception by that search for self-understanding, is embodied in a variety of characters, some with contrasting antecedents, who each chose their own path and ultimate goal. These pilgrimages are tested against that sense of an Absolute inspired and shaped by an immemorial inheritance stretching from the Vedas down to Rao's teacher, Sri Atmananda Guru, from whom the epigraphs to *The Serpent and the Rope* (1960), *The Policeman and the Rose* (1978), and *The Chessmaster and His Moves* (1988) are taken. As Sivarama Sastri, the protagonist-narrator of *The Chessmaster,* says:

> My home, my real home, was the forest, the forest where the Vedic debates took place, and Aranyakas, the forest wisdoms, from which came the Upanishads themselves. And from the Upanishads to Sankara is one straight leap, and from Sankara to Ramana Maharshi, another leap, and I was within the recognizable space and time boundaries of my own existence.

This cumulative tradition's relentless, ancient power constructs a richly suggestive epistemology that looks diagnostically at the past and at contemporary life in terms of themes, contexts, and, increasingly, international points of view, which are unraveled, developed, and connected on a number of levels. The constituents of the epistemology help separate Indians from non-Indians and is crucial in identifying and posing the choice between "two different categories of thinking. Either you accept logic and go beyond man, or be fulfilled by faith, and so, to God, man's archetypal image. Tagore or Sankara is the question, and there is no half-way house to it".

Rao's latest novel, again set in India, France, and England, is obviously more intricately encompassing than *The Serpent and the Rope.* The cast of characters, who are cross-cultural, draw sustenance and identity from these countries as well as from Israel, Greece, Senegal, and the Maghreb and from the major religions. *The Chessmaster* offers perhaps the broadest, deepest internationalism we have in fiction and, in a sense, enables fiction to catch up with life. Still, Rao's works are profoundly Indian. Very demanding, they are generally more praised than read, posing a major challenge to reader and critic alike regarding how to approach, assess, and place them. Their intrinsic interest apart, they raise basic questions about the new literatures in English. . . .

It is ironic that although linguists are prepared to accept varieties of English springing from nativization—"We indians never forgot our native tongue, while speaking english," says Sivarama—literary critics, scholars, and comparatists remain less inclined to see the literatures in these varieties as possessing their own rubric, their distinctive quartet of spirit and pulse, form and function. Rao himself touched succinctly on the main issues as early as 1938 in his foreword to *Kanthapura* [see excerpt above]. He had occasion to remark later that "unless word becomes *mantra* no writer is a writer, and no reader a reader." That is the condition his language aspires to, at least in certain moments. Inevitably, this view of the word allied to the demands of the rubric, the quartet, requires some reconstitution of English that, indubitably, makes the results unique in a special way. It is not a matter of judgment and value but of ascertaining and giving credence to the nature, origin, and thrust of the writer's vision and creative procedures which shape his view of life, of writing, and, beyond them, to his growing Indo-Anglian tradition. The more the work is that of a native son—Rao's is among the preeminent instances—the more it locks into the distinctive parts of his inherited traditions, thus making it less accessible to those from the culture, the society of another variety of English with *its* distinctive literary ethos. (p. 567)

The Chessmaster and His Moves is a massively demanding work that addresses perhaps the most central issues in life, depicted from many points of view and on different levels. The relationships of characters are marked by a continual contact that converts into the discussion and adjustment in ideas touching God and the Absolute: "Each one of us, the french sensibility or the indian, the arab or the chinese, has his own way of coming to the same centre, like the poet or the physicist". The sentence preceding this refers to "illuminations," Poincaré's as "mathematical experience," Pascal's "in the mystical," with Sivarama linking them as "the contribution of indian sensibility to contemporary science." Encyclopedic in scope and content, Rao's close treatment of the thought and action of individuals moves from the most public to the most intimate moments and interests. The present account can only hope to note briefly certain aspects of the novel in order to show its scope, methods, and spiritual reach, which attains its greatest height in the conversation-cum-dialogue between Sivarama and Michel in "The Brahmin and the Rabbi," the third and final book of *The Chessmaster.*

Rao's are unusual novels. To begin with, his characters are seen partially, leaving much implied through descriptions. This is true even of the first-person narrators: we do not see Ramaswamy in *The Serpent and the Rope* wrestle with Albigensian history or Sivarama with his mathematics per se. Sivarama describes and comments, building the reader's knowledge of and insights into various characters. It usually starts with a profile in detail at or near the point where we meet the character. Our sense of each enlarges and refines. For example, of Jean-Pierre Vauxgrand, "half-Greek and half-Senegalais," we are told: "He was most inventive in his myths, the fact became a myth the moment it occurred, and Jean-Pierre added so many facts to it, drawn to his myth from anywhere that it all made for an apt story. The beauty of it is, Jean-Pierre believed in it, and would swear on his mother". Also,

> He liked secretive things, he wanted something that he did not know, some sort of nothingness that was real, concrete, healthy, trustworthy, and maybe heroic. He had read Pericles of course, and he dreamt of a hero-god he could die for, an Alexander who would build a united humanity, of all races and tribes, drinking the libations of the gods. To be Greek is to live in two worlds at the same time, the Asian and the European—the French, after all, the natural heirs of the Greeks. Jean-Pierre's ambition was to become a doctor, and help humanity, and write, if possible, like Balzac. His family had so many connections, and connections with higher connection, that any combination would work—a language, as it were, that used numbers as the sure means of communication, whether one or a million, would mean one or a million—remember the French franc had lost all value, how did this matter for the proper rudiment of expression, tout-de-même? But it did. He however sought in words what his family had found in numbers—he wanted

a clear definition of any object. The object here meaning any three dimensional, rather four dimensional, entity, or any feeling or thought.

There is much more at work in these descriptions—which are typical—than meets the eye. Taking the second quotation alone, we see how the first sentence suggests an uncertainty in an active, thinking person. As we read on, we get a feel of the heroic unrealized in a sedentary life, having been told in earlier pages of Jean-Pierre's bravery as a teen-ager. The reference to Balzac arches back to his "myth-making" propensity: Balzac's books were measured with "a foot rule," and he was paid "according to the number of lines his text made". Like Sivarama, he is searching, but toward something "real, concrete, healthy etc.," away from zero. Moreover, numbers for his family do not lead to the Absolute, but rather to power and influence. He wanted words to have the same effect. We begin to understand Jean-Pierre and Sivarama and why they are mutually attracted, share certain views, yet differ passionately on others, such as the significance of de Gaulle. Above all, we are given help that illuminates such later comments, revelations, and pungent self-descriptions as "this complexity of blood and temperament, this greco-negritude . . . and his aristocommunisme".

We find a pattern, basic but unconfining. When Sivarama tells us of Jean-Pierre or Mireille or Suzanne, it seems a natural part of his thought or conversation. Each initial sketch is carefully modulated to reveal as much as possible of the character's views on life, politics, history, art, and religion and of his impulses and interests, his search for meaning in life. The main description of Jean-Pierre is succeeded almost immediately by one of his wife Mireille, which continues, interspersed with Sivarama's conversation (apropos Gandhi, de Gaulle, and others) with Madame X(enakapoppulos), her mother, to which she and Suzanne contribute. Company and conversation adjourn to the Kiang-Su for dinner, where they are joined by Jean-Pierre. The setting extends the conversation and Sivarama's thoughts. . . . (pp. 568-69)

This brief summary suggests only the frame in which the curve and association of individual thought, the cut and thrust in dialogue, are developed and contextualized by Sivarama's account. Incremental disclosures and comments continue to build after a first large deposit of information, which holds our attention and makes up for the fact that we do not, for instance, see parts of their lives. They lunch together, love, converse, and set off to work. We know their professions—or their intellectual interests, in the case of Mireille—but in all the novel's 708 pages we are not given any comprehensive description of them at work. There is, for example, no account of Suzanne's acting in any play, which seems odd, given her intimacy with Sivarama the narrator.

Rao's primary interest lies elsewhere. Emotional and intellectual life matter most when converted to metaphysical inclinations, of which Madeleine's deepening interest in Buddhism (in *The Serpent and the Rope*), declared and intimated, is an example of a fundamental theme forcefully treated in *The Chessmaster and His Moves* with greater confidence, clarity, spaciousness, subtlety, and resonance in the "immortal longings" of Suzanne, Uma, Jayalakshmi, Mireille, Michel, and, above all, Sivarama himself. The characters argue; they are defined by their ideas and opinions, their basic philosophical stance. Moreover, love is not love unless it metaphysics finds, which is why the dialogue is at times intensely philosophical. Consequently, when readers compare their work, Narayan's is seen to have a richer, more variegated "life" than Rao's, which partly explains the former's greater popularity in America and England. Paradoxically, however, critics tend to judge Rao as the more significant writer, whose abiding achievement includes the major contribution so far to the development of the Indian novel in English. Implicit in his work is the conviction that the novel should be ahead of its time and place, that it should both reflect experience and influence it.

The Chessmaster and His Moves goes beyond *The Serpent and the Rope,* which is its forerunner in some ways. Rao's narrative methods are more sophisticated, and his themes and preoccupations are developed with greater complexity on different levels, which are presumably still in process, as two further installments of the trilogy await publication. At the core is still his knowledge/conviction that "unless one goes beyond the real, the mental, the essential, that is, beyond cause and effect, and this one, he, he will have, as you well know, neither birth nor death." For the individual it is the discovery of his or her "isness," though the routes for man and woman differ, as we shall see. When in *The Serpent and the Rope* Ramaswamy asks Savithri, "What is Truth?," she answers, "Isness is the Truth." Early in *The Chessmaster* Sivarama, thinking of men and women, of being, of death and rebirth, asserts, "What *is* can never die". Being central to that search for final answers by the main characters, the point, the Vedantic answer, is reiterated at various moments in the novel. This inner conviction is the basis of axioms, apophthegms, and equations that help reveal the nature and significance of different cultures and how they cope with ultimate questions such as birth and death and the nature of God, of the Absolute.

The two key formulations are the notions of the *human/abhuman* and the *horizontal/vertical.* Sivarama asserts, "There are only two races of men: those that look the horizontal way, the way of infinity. And those that look vertically, the creatures of dissolution, the zero way". Broadly, the pairs are extensions of each other and therefore interchangeable as referring to common aggregates or qualities: *human* equals *horizontal,* and *abhuman* equals *vertical.* We build upon their contrasts and differences, whose value and usefulness are easily demonstrated. (p. 569)

As we have seen, the characters are as much described as analyzed by Sivarama the first-person narrator. Rao has to rely on the sum of his sensibility, his locus and encounters, to create his fiction, his mantras, his insights. What we know of a character—or the unfolding of the theme—can only come, after all, from one or more of four sources in the text: the narrator, the character's conversations with him as he recalls, conversations that refer to other characters, and by way of letters, diaries, and telegrams. Like Ramaswamy in *The Serpent and the Rope,* Sivarama is on a quest, a pilgrimage, seeking equations of illumination. That quest moves on at least two levels, which take on very subtle and varied forms in terms of his relationship with the other characters, chiefly women, including his sister, and his mathematical explorations.

Sivarama is himself in search of the absolute. A mathematician, he sees the primacy of numbers providing a crucial statement: "From pure nothingness do all objects emerge, from zero all numbers". The contrary is true: all objects return to nothingness, all numbers to zero. Here are the two phases in a cyclic process. You can move in either direction—

clockwise or counterclockwise—but the process is the same: creation/dissolution/creation/dissolution (*srsti/pralaya/ srsti/pralaya*). Within this large cycle, the individual has his cycles according to his karma. The individual search for the Absolute, being to nonbeing, is part of that binary contrast between human and abhuman, between horizontal and vertical. Sivarama's interest in the irreducible—i.e., the primary—marks the whole thrust of his mind and his perceptions. (p. 569-70)

That is part of man's constant search for a sense of reality. It complements and is simultaneous with the understanding of the self—"uncovering aspects of your own self"—reflected in the question which Sivarama asks at almost regular intervals as he ponders the insights that move him further toward an answer: "To what country did I belong? And to whom, lord, to whom?" Sivarama the narrator is not altogether the Sivarama who speaks and describes himself and others. He has the maturity derived from his experience, which is *The Chessmaster and His Moves,* for the narrative implies his growth.

> Man has to grow to see splendour constantly. The splendour of today is the left-back acquisition of tomorrow. (This was in fact my case, I had begun to see, with Suzanne.) Unless you grow you cannot give. And growth needs search. And search fearlessness. And all search is inward—the outer leads one to repetition, to monotony.

His is the major structuring consciousness: "growth," "search," and "fearlessness" mark his first-person accounts, especially when he reflects upon his thought-experience, when he analyzes himself and others, chiefly Suzanne, Jayalakshmi, Mireille, and Jean-Pierre and the common ground that he and Michel find. The female relationships are crucial to his self-awareness, maturing sensibility, and search for Truth: "The woman is the miracle. She subsumes you with her presence, and makes you know yourself. She gives not only bone and blood to your abstractions, but the sense of the real". Man and woman need each other in different ways, but that which brings the miracle of completion is ultimately the most important: "Woman and man rose out of the concept of extension and dissolution, hence inversely it is the woman which receives being, there where she lies, and man prolongs himself for birth of becoming, where he is truly and wholely become".

The three women—the fourth is Uma, his sister—influence Sivarama's life as much as he theirs. He meets Jayalakshmi first, in Calcutta, then Suzanne in Paris, then Mireille as his circle of friends widens. His relationship with them differs in what he gives and receives, in the gathering of insight and understanding of them and of himself and the increasing sophistication of his frame of reference and analysis of life and contacts—the history, politics, religion, the personal interests, attitudes, and expectations that move people. That with Jayalakshmi is abstract, spiritual, moving toward the marriage of being; the second, sexual but with growing metaphysical force; and the third, although sexual, turns into a litany, an epiphany. Uma's suffering makes him more concerned and sensitive.

To Jayalakshmi, Sivarama says, "I was only a Brahmin, my brain ready for cerebral adventures, my heart uneducated. You, beloved, you gave it its truth, gave back, almost its physiological reality". They share what is for each the most complex and comprehensive coming together on the level of abstraction, the vertical, the abhuman, where "the two seeks not the one but oneness". Both must journey. She knows the way but "would go one step forward and half a step backward, pulled by the beauty of the nondual, and fearful of the abhumanity of it". So subtle is Rao's mode of narration that we may overlook the fact that the first two hundred pages of **The Chessmaster** are dominated by her. Sivarama's self-inspection and discussions on a variety of subjects are chiefly with and for her. Their extended dialogue, which includes recollections of earlier ones, covers a great deal of ground and returns constantly to the two aspects of that fundamental woman-man nexus in the search for the Absolute. Jayalakshmi's understanding is in advance of his. His visits to her in the hospital, where she lies stricken by a brain tumor, draws them very close, to the point of oneness.

> Finally she opened her eyes and, smiling almost like a child, said: 'Tell me, promise me, if I die, you will incarnate as the Siva in the temple, the temple they are going to build. Our marriage then will be consummated.'
>
> 'What marriage?' I asked, surprised. She had never talked of that to me ever.
>
> 'The only marriage. There is but one marriage for any woman.'
>
> 'And so?'
>
> 'Let this concubine body go elsewhere, to where it is in such regal demand. Promise our marriage is complete.'
>
> 'Come to Paris, Jayalakshmi. Paris, you know, is like my own hearth and home somewhere. Come to Paris, and we will consummate it there—'

Sivarama misunderstands her: *oneness* is marriage, is—at the risk of appearing contradictory—metaphysical consummation. He mistakes its *abstraction* for a physical promise, more conveniently realized in Paris. He obviously and disappointingly fails to perceive why she rejects the body, the physical. He has yet to understand the difference between "abstraction" and "dissolution." That will come with the catechism of ideas and experience to which Jayalakshmi contributes. At the moment, however, he is uncomprehending. Hence her reaction, carried in her tone and sapped by her despairing question.

> 'Where?' she asked almost in astonishment.
>
> 'In De Gaulle's Gaul—in Paris—in holy Paris, in royal Paris. Will you come?'
>
> 'Of course, I will.'
>
> 'You know, I have to leave tomorrow, my sister is arriving the day after.'
>
> 'The gods have decided everything,' she added, pressing my hands firmly, yet in deep sorrow.
>
> 'And anyway, you will have all your family here.'
>
> 'Yes, I know. And they will be talking of business, and Nehru, or even of the next tiger shoot!'
>
> 'Or of the temple.'
>
> 'Who are you?' she asked brusquely, once again, as though I would reveal myself because of the suddenness of her questioning.

We see why Jayalakshmi is deeply sorry. Only on the following day, when she hints, inserts correlatives, and lays her head on his lap after saying "Fortunately, the hindus believe in reincarnation. . . . Because what is not now can be then. . . . Lord, why don't you make it now? Why not then be now? Lord make it so", does Sivarama begin to realize her true meaning. Jayalakshmi is married, however, and therefore has to find an alternative, which she does. For Sivarama the physical was part of the route to the Absolute. We recall those moments of intensity shared with Suzanne and Mireille. . . . (pp. 570-71)

Of [Mireille] we are told, "She seemed . . . to play the mystery woman, half-sphinx, half-goddess . . . her femininity could change flesh into steel, the male into a hero, a god". She had her lovers but chose, significantly, "her moment and her men". Mireille's personality, interests, and openness, her obvious intelligence and physical attractiveness strike Sivarama and the others. Sivarama is aware that she searches among men yet is moved to observe, "There is, don't you see, a certain virginity in Mireille, a marvellous purity". For her, "Every man was first and foremost a man, a male, whom you awakened to be awakened in return to your own final feminine depths". The word *play* is significant, as it is the apt description of how Mireille and Sivarama relate after they come together for the first and last sharing.

> 'Sorry,' she said, 'I played a trick on you.'
>
> 'In India we say the world is lila, play. So you played.'
>
> 'Did I?'
>
> 'Yes—and in playing, I forgot myself. So I became I,' I said, 'not me, but maybe the principle, the inner-arising Siva, the self-manifesting birth of form.'

This is a prelude to her litany. She and Sivarama converse about the traits and expectations of man and woman, particularly their attitudes toward love. She likes "greek precision, and cartesian logic," needs "clarity in everything", and believes, "The body, Siv, is just not a body. It's not prose. It is poetry. We treat the body as if it were made just of straight lines. It has curves, its own wisdom." When they renew their lovemaking, she finds her completion. . . .

All three women contribute powerfully and comprehensively to Sivarama's growth. It would be interesting to trace that growth in terms of his emotional and intellectual life, his metaphysics, and his perception and understanding of others. That growth deepens in one vital direction through his friendship with Michel, taking it into areas beyond—yet remaining complementary to—the personal, the sensual, the mathematical, toward the true universality of the Absolute.

Michel and Sivarama are the "1" and the "0" of a binary system. They are the archetypes of the horizontal and the vertical, the human and the abhuman, the dual and the nondual. Sivarama is aware of this when he says, "Michel's mind was scientific, that is deductive. . . . My mind was essentially metaphysical, hence my aptitude for mathematical solutions to all problems". As a Jew—and given his and his family's tragic experience—Michel carries the sum of man's enmity to man, as reflected primarily in the whole history of Western civilization, including the diaspora and the struggle to return to and hold the land of the twelve tribes. There are also those images in literature, such as Shylock, whose hardness and intransigence seem harsh if we disregard the provocation. Michel's account is specific, archetypal; it is part of contemporary memory and experience. (p. 571)

Michel, who is said to have "a rich hassidic background", is not introduced in the usual way. Apart from a few scattered references, what we know is provided by Sivarama and interspersed with his conversation with Michel about the Jews, the Indians, the word as image, the image of God, duality and nonduality, and his feelings about the marriage of Suzanne and Michel. The linear sense of time is displaced as we see them first meet. The dialogue revolves around certain major themes invoked by Rao's terms—dual, nondual, horizontal way, vertical, dissolution, zero, Truth, God—and introduces what is perhaps the most important them in *The Chessmaster and His Moves.*

> 'Michel, the real dialogue in the world is not between the East and the West, but between, but between you and me, between the brahmin and the rabbi.' Michel closed his eyes, as if in reminiscence of something (or maybe he thought of Moses and the Sinai), and slowly opening them again, he remarked, 'You are probably right.'

It is the resolution of the issues raised in the intensive and narrowing discussion between Sivarama and Michel that makes *The Chessmaster* truly universal, rising above the individual and offering a way to the Absolute, the *It.*

The decisive meeting between Sivarama and Michel is preceded by the letter to Malraux, Sivarama's discussion with Suzanne (during which she predicts her death at thirty-nine, his at fifty-six, and that he will have a son), his meeting with Hungarian scientists, with Mireille—"Hebrew is the sacred language of the jews, like Sanskrit is of the hindus. . . . We in Europe are dualists"—and with Jayalakshmi and Uma. Conversation, dialogue, and his own thoughts prepare for that encounter between Brahmin and rabbi. Michel starts to talk about himself and the Jews, especially of their history, destiny, relations with God: "We were made for books—for the Book and the Torah"; "Remember, as I was saying, God forgot us"; "You do not know hell. I do"; "We were the priests of the western world". There is the story of Isae, which leads into a dialogue wherein Michel urges the primacy of God, Sivarama that of Truth. The latter says, "The quarrel of man is between zero and infinity, between Truth—and God". Their positions begin to overlap with Sivarama's answer to Michel's question, "Who is the other God then?"

> 'The No-God, the highest God. He is not even a He but an It.'

> 'Maybe that's the only true God,' he said, and fell into his usual silence, scratching his face. Even after all these years, his whip-cut wound in the face, he said, ached. It wanted the nazi knout back, or so it seemed, he joked. Man loves even his slavery, he had once explained. 'And now, allons enfants de la patrie,' he said, rising. 'Let us make the pilgrimage to the No-God.'

The pilgrimage first requires settling on suitable terms for an equation satisfactory to Michel and Sivarama, rabbi and Brahmin, from God to No-God, from Him to It achieved "through Him that is It." This moves Michel: " 'So, my brother,' he said, lifting his head suddenly, his eyes shining up with love. 'My brother,' and, coming to me, kissed me on both cheeks, hugging me with a deep, long, forlorn sigh". For

Sivarama, "In that knowledge, in that wisdom, Michel and I were brothers".

Still, as with Mireille's completion of self-understanding, brotherhood must be capped. Sivarama, who wishes to go home as the ladies are waiting, is about to catch a taxi when Michel rushes back to him and suggests they take a walk. He does not say no, as he feels Michel "wanted to say something yet more important". There is a similar building up of a sacerdotal mood similar to the one preceding Mireille's experience. Michel's poem, his prayer, his litany, scribbled in the hope that God, "that august fellow would come down." His mood at this point is compounded of tenderness and love and an anger rooted in his tragedy and the accumulation of bitter persecution suffered by his race. Paradoxically, he "would like to take a machinegun and shoot all of them," yet "He was sorry for mankind". He thinks of his father, his mother, and of his brother Sasha and his uncle Dinka, both taken from the ghetto, creating a terrible image for the young Michel. Such intensities are only augmented by moments of relatively light banter. When "a thaumaturgical spell appeared to have pulled Michel desperately in", it is Sivarama who starts chanting from the *Purusa-sukta,* attracting a few boys. . . . One discovers later that the poem, the litany, "poured out of an artificial intelligence machine. Not from the computer, but from me". We recall Rao's declaration about "the word" and "mantra" and also Sivarama's statement (quoted earlier): "Indeed there must be primary sounds, like particles in our nuclear universe, which act and react according to as yet unknown laws". In any case, the drama, the ritual, is meaning-making. Sivarama's chant had started the mood into which Michel erupts. He sings and claps his hands, looking at an imaginary throne, eyes uplifted in awe, the children—two are named, Pierre and Nicos (French and Greek? Potentially of the vertical and the horizontal?)—repeating what Michel says in solemnity with clasped hands. Sivarama dances round the imaginary throne and they follow, the rhythm of the chant turning more rapid until he stops,

> . . . as though he'd lost his breath, and lifting his hands up, gently bowed to the Being, only he saw, and none others ever saw, and in that evening light, I promise you, I saw, maybe, the most ancient face—a face of supernal beauty, I should have said—of the whole Western world, he the zadik, the miracle maker, who loved all of man.

He runs "with an intense, withdrawn power," picks up the rose, chants, and puts it down. At his command the children kneel and Pierre (who leads them) distributes its petals as a sacrament. The effect is so holistic that Sivarama feels life is renewed and restored: "Everyone, as anybody can see, is saved." In answering his question as to whom he paid homage, a smiling Michel says, "Certainly to Him. Maybe to It". The Brahmin and the rabbi have gone beyond dialogue toward a sharing, as the latter is now able to contemplate the vertical, the nondual. The dialogue between Brahmin and rabbi offers the final mantra to which the other mantras, arising from other relationships and meditations, contribute. It is an end; it is a beginning. (p. 572-73)

Edwin Thumboo, "Raja Rao: 'The Chessmaster and His Moves'," in World Literature Today, *Vol. 62, No. 4, Autumn, 1988, pp. 567-73.*

S. C. HARREX

[There] is a progression during the three decades in which [his] short stories were written which, experimentally, became a model that provided the groundwork for Rao's metaphysical novel [*The Serpent and the Rope*]. This progression is modal, evolving from the mode of "history" into the mode of "romance." I use these terms in accordance with the theory of "modal approach" elaborated by Robert Scholes [in "Towards a Poetics of Fiction: An Approach through Genre"] and Ulrich Wicks [in "The Nature of Picaresque Narrative: A Modal Approach"]. (p. 592)

Perhaps the best of Rao's early short stories—for instance, **"Akkayya," "The Little Gram Shop,"** and **"Javni"**—are in the mode of history, being studies of character and family life in the context of social hierarchy. Arousing compassion and presenting a clearly documented sense of place and psychology, these stories are essentially humanist and realist. Satisfying as these achievements were, however, one may speculate that the history mode did not adequately satisfy the needs of what C. D. Narasimhaiah in his afterword to *The Policeman and the Rose* refers to as Rao's "religious impulse and . . . metaphysical imagination". Rao was to discover that such needs could be best expressed and explored in a poetic mode—to be more specific, in Indian equivalents of romance. An examination of an early story, **"The Cow of the Barricades,"** and a typically later one, **"The Policeman and the Rose,"** demonstrates how the abiding model of progression and pilgrimage in Rao's work is from history to romance, culminating to date in romance as metaphysical identity and illumination in *The Serpent and the Rope* and romance (incorporating surrealism, symbolism, fantasy, allegory, and absurdist comedy) as spiritual quest and discovery in *The Cat and Shakespeare.* In *The Serpent and the Rope* Vedanta and Ramaswamy's use of the European discipline of history to undermine the concept of objective history provide the philosophical foundation of the novel's romance mode. His dismissal of materialism—"Materialism . . . can only lead to the acknowledgement of the object as real," "Nobody has yet known an object-in the whole history of humanity"—is the corollary argument in support of his romance, specifically his belief that India "has no history, for Truth cannot have history". Another characteristic of the romance mode of Rao's metaphysical novel is the postmodernist metafictional tendency in *The Serpent and the Rope.* This is seen, philosophically supported by the subject-centered interpretation of Brahminism, in the narrator's endorsement of the self-reflexive principle as ultimate and absolute: namely, that "all books are autobiographies" in which the textual intricacies and elements are synonyms of the physical and psychological characteristics of the author's personality.

In **"The Cow of the Barricades"** the tragedy of history is redeemed by romance in the shape of Indian idealism, holiness, and godliness. The history in question is the struggle for independence as exemplified by a confrontation between the people and the army under British rule, at a time (presumably in the thirties) when colonialism became intensely oppressive under the pressure of the Quit India movement. This history, which in the story is transmuted into romance and sentiment, highlights the moral test which Gandhi's program of civil disobedience and nonviolence imposed on those fighting for independence. The natural tendency to respond to violence with violence is averted in the story by the heroic sacrifice of the cow Gauri, who walks the barricade dividing army and people and who exudes such compassion and holiness that both sides lay down their arms, except for the army's "Chief, the red-man." He shoots her dead, and so she falls "a vehicle of God among lowly men." Gauri's martyrdom heralds the spiritual triumph of Mother India, as well as celebrating Gandhi's saintly philosophy of compassion and nonviolence. The story ends (as it has been narrated throughout) in what resembles a biblical style: "Therefore it is said, 'The Mahatma may be all wrong about politics, but he is right about the fulness of love in all creatures—the speechful and the mute' ".

A familiar typology within genres of fiction is structured around protagonists or heroes who are animal instead of human, and India has produced many examples ranging from the religious-methodological (Hanuman, Ganesha, et cetera) to modern literary works like Kipling's *Jungle Book* and R. K. Narayan's novel *A Tiger for Malgudi* (1983). What **"The Cow of the Barricades"** introduces, however, is a specialized version of this typology in which the protagonist is also—symbolically—a culture heroine. Gauri is in the Hindu sense God—or, more strictly, God in the form of an avatar— "a vehicle of God" and codivine therefore with other such vehicles like the Nandi bull. In terms of typology, then, Rao has devised a model of the short story which exhibits nationalistic aspirations embodied in the fictional heroine who is God (or the principle of God's love and compassion) as well as holy Mother India. Her response to India's suffering is a quintessential image of piety and spiritual love: "She looked very sad, and somebody had even seen a tear, clear as a drop of the Ganges, run down her cheeks, for she was of compassion infinite and true". As a result of her epic deed she keeps alive iconographically the power of worship and faith which in turn sustains the ideal life that permeates and transcends the ephemeral world of maya and death. (pp. 592-93)

Rao presents the evil world of history redeemed, in the communal context of Gandhian sentiments, by a metaphysical reality or principle which—in terms of fictional mode—we can call romance. Akin to the allegory of *The Faerie Queen,* such romance—in Wicks's words—"satisfies our craving for divine harmony, integration, beauty, order, goodness, and ultimate fulfilment." This is Indian romance, however, and the referents and the style are culturally codified accordingly: "Mango Street," "kumkum," "Lakshmi," "the red-men's Government," "Copper Seenayya's house," "Suryanarayana Street," "Venkatalakshamma Well," "Mahatma Gandhi ki jai." India is a world or society in which religious veneration, personal desire, and social ambitions are interrelated, as we see from the description of people who approached Gauri as a kind of deity while she was alive: "And students came to touch her head and touch her tail, saying, 'Let me pass the examinations this year!' And young girls came to ask for husbands and widows to ask for purity, and the childless to ask for children". Such faith or hope is characteristic of a traditional, mythological society in which the collective or communal psyche conceives the goals and ends of life religiously in terms of what we can call a romance world view. This cultural fact, together with the folkloric form of storytelling in an Indian-English dialect which aims to simulate inflections and rhythms of Indian oral narrative, gives credence to the symbolic or romance typology which Rao has created in **"The Cow of the Barricades."**

"The Policeman and the Rose" contains a different version of this fictional typology, of the protagonist as God manifest in terrestrial form. In this autobiographical story the narrator is foregrounded, cultural symbols are perplexed by personal symbols, and the protagonist is (S)self in a complicated, obscure metaphysical sense. I would argue, nevertheless, that **"The Policeman and the Rose"** is in the typological romance mode of the God hero in a quest or pilgrimage story, because the symbolic and surreal narrative traces the hero's aspiration and destiny toward the realization of God in self.

As in most of Rao's work since **The Serpent and the Rope,** **"The Policeman and the Rose"** brings together cultural metaphors from the European tradition and the Indian tradition and matches these with his own private symbols, which somehow merge with the cultural symbols. Illustrations are the two roses in the story: the red "Rose of Compassion" which the narrator brings to India from Avignon, and the white rose of Travancore. At one level the red rose is the medieval symbol of romance: its chivalric aspects are passion and compassion. But what is the white rose? An ascetic Indian corollary of a European ideal of love, or beauty, or truth? The personal and private appropriation of traditional symbols, then, is one of the reasons why a reliable reading of the story is difficult, if not impossible, to arrive at.

The problem is at its zenith, however, in the case of the policeman symbol, which would suggest that its creator, like God, is a law unto himself. As Narasimhaiah puts it [in his afterword]: "The reader is totally at the mercy of the author—author, because the policeman remains a private symbol. . . . What does he stand for in the story? For soul? Guru? God? the transcendental principle? Or is it Evil? Ignorance or Illusion?". Narasimhaiah's conclusion is that "the policeman is most likely to be the law of Karma and, paradoxically, when it 'arrests' you, you become 'free', for it must work itself out". This is, of course, a plausible interpretation in that karma is law (divine and human law) and a policeman is a civil image signifying embodiment of law, an agent whose responsibility it is to uphold and enforce law. It is also a profound theme in Indian literature. The opening paragraphs of **"The Policeman and the Rose"** contain the following statements:

> I was arrested when I was born. . . . All men are arrested the moment they are born. So are the women. . . . Every living *man* has a policeman, and his name is your name, his address your address, his dreams your dreams. . . . In the last life too he was a policeman—he always was a policeman. . . . God once got angry with him and killed him, but he became many. Today God does not know what to do—so I have to remind God all about it. . . . I want to be free. . . . Your policeman is naked but he's all blind. He knows all there is to know, but he does not know the knower. When he knows the knower there is no knower. Knowledge is knowledge.

> The story of the policeman is my own biography.

By juxtaposing these quotations we not only appreciate how Indian philosophy in Indian fiction rearranges the traditional character-fate relationship in European literature; we also observe a philosophical paradox. This is a dialectical opposition of dharma and karma, moksha and maya, Truth and ignorance, Reality and illusion. It has been argued that symbolism expresses paradox, and that Vedantic nondualism resolves paradox; Raja Rao's writing depends on both propositions, as the above example indicates. The dual meaning of

the term *arrest* is telling. We are told that the law arrests the individual from birth, and the narrator, in consequence, postulates liberation from arrest as the ultimate climax of the human story, of history. Rao's symbolic proposition expressed logically submits that to arrest that which arrests is the path to freedom.

Rao's story traces this progression. Considered philosophically, the dual narrator—the "I" and his doppelgänger policeman—is a cultural specimen of an Indian kind: both his aspects are products of Godhead and are in quest of Godhead. Perhaps their duality is intended to reflect the Truth or Reality/Maya or Illusion duality. The "I" is a confidant-advisor of God: "Today God does not know what to do—so I have to remind God all about it". The policeman is one become many. The policeman's account of his past includes his vegetable incarnation in the time of Rama; as grass and weed he knew Rama and Ravana and saw Sita bathing. In the twentieth-century present he is the "I's" policeman, and this relationship of double identities of the double self is explained by the policeman thus: "When I was born, he said: 'My child, I know your antecedents, or rather I know why you are hot and cold. . . . Grow and become free, and my happiness is in my dissolution. You seek your death of me, the death of deaths. Death happens to me. Never to you' ". This statement implies that the "I" is the eternal self (the soul or spiritual principle) and the policeman is the self as ego, the reincarnated corporeal being destined for dissolution just as the other self is destined for moksha, for nirvana. The policeman's narrative emphasizes his bodily, carnal, sinning identity: "I excrete and try to fornicate," "I have genitals," "The policeman alone is sin," et cetera. He also achieves fame as a holy man in France, being revered by the virgins of Avignon: "God is my business, I cried—Hindu gods . . . all the virgins came to my confessions"; "I was the Policeman of God. . . . I became a legitimate divinity. . . . I was God." He acquires the "fabular and fantastic" red rose and goes on "pilgrimage" to India "to become a pukka God." This is the false egoism of Godliness, however, because the policeman does not know Truth. He learns the compassion of the red rose but still does not know Truth until the end of the pilgrimage when he is in retirement. This would seem to be in contrast with the spiritual capability of the self's other identity. Earlier this persona declares: "How I saw God is a story that nobody shall know. That is the only thing the policeman did not note correctly in his diary. . . . That was written in the stars. . . . The policeman had suddenly grown two inches shorter". With the wisdom of hindsight, the narrator introduces the pilgrimage as follows: "The rose is red . . . in Avignon or Paris, and white in Travancore. The rose of Travancore is the story of a pilgrimage. I went with my red rose of aught and naught. . . . Truth is Travancore".

In Rao's Vedantist philosophy knowledge of Truth is the purpose of existence, the Reality principle. The story concludes by identifying Truth not with the rose but with the Lotus. . . . His red rose has disappeared, thus suggesting its illusory status; its traditional spiritual value as sensual love (passion) and compassion is of maya (or illusion), because the red rose celebrates desire and feeling for another and is therefore synonymous with being imprisoned, arrested, in ego-bondage. In such a state the higher Truth cannot be known because the red rose is mistakenly seen as Truth. Thus the Romance of the Rose is ephemeral, not infinite. The protagonist does see the white rosebush, however. "And I knew," he says. The white rose presumably is closer to Truth because it is ascetically desensualized. Perhaps punning on Shakespeare's "That which we call a rose / By any other name would smell as sweet" (*Romeo and Juliet*, 2.2.43-44), Rao concludes the story with three basic statements: 1) "The rose knew its perfume was of the rose. . . . So it smelt of the Lotus. . . . I became . . . free"; 2) "In the kingdom of Travancore there are no prisons. . . . That is the beautiful Truth, said the white rose to me"; 3) "And the trouble, brother, all the trouble is that we mistake the Lotus for the Rose". I interpret the first statement as defining the necessary connection between self-knowledge, knowledge of Truth, and spiritual liberation; the second statement as reinforcing this by implying that Truth involves the distinction between the bondage of attachment (the red rose) and the freedom of Truth in the land of the Lotus, with the white rose serving as a kind of mystic intermediary; and the final statement, which is somewhat reminiscent of *The Serpent and the Rope,* as defining Truth as avoidance of the error of ascribing Truth to other than itself, to the rose instead of the Lotus. Illusion is imprisonment; Truth is freedom.

Whereas the fictional form or type of **"The Cow of the Barricades"** is the traditional folktale, the form of **"The Policeman and the Rose"** is symbolist, metaphysical, and modernist. The modernism is evident in Rao's surreal and Kafkaesque use of the romance quest narrative, which begins with the imprisonment of the hero, who is also his own policeman-jailer; the action requires of this dual identity that he find himself by defeating himself—and by learning the difference between the compassion of the rose and the serenity of the lotus. The victory of ideal Truth over impermanent beauty reveals, in modal terms, the supremacy of metaphysical romance. It is this supremacy, first summoned in his short stories, which later becomes the guiding light of Raja Rao's novels. (pp. 592-95)

S. C. Harrex, "Typology and Modes: Raja Rao's Experiments in Short Story," in World Literature Today, *Vol. 62, No. 4, Autumn, 1988, pp. 591-95.*

PERRY D. WESTBROOK

In an introduction apparently intended for the first English edition of **Comrade Kirillov** (1976), Raja Rao described how he wrote the short novel twenty-five years earlier, in 1949, in the village of Brosses, France, a few miles from Vézelay, in whose cathedral Saint Bernard preached the Second Crusade in 1147 A.D. The author writes of the "summer silence of the hills, and the silvery Yonne, meandering so full of grace in the expansive valley below," as seen from the room where he wrote of the 1930s and 1940s, when India was struggling for independence and the world was aflame with war. Even in pastoral Brosses citizens had died before firing squads, first Pétain's and later those of the Résistance. Rao muses: "Thus the drama of man, wheresoever one goes, trying to find his Jerusalem. And Comrade Kirillov is just one of these men, caught in this mighty theme of history." . . .

As a title for his book and as a sobriquet for its protagonist, Rao chose the name of one of the most appalling characters in Fyodor Dostoevsky's novel about Russian nihilism, *The Possessed* (also known as *The Devils*). In Rao's novel Comrade Kirillov is a South Indian Brahmin whose real name is Padmanabha Iyer. When he was very young, Theosophy "had carried him westward on its proselytising flood . . . to the California coastline where perforce all new religions are

born". He soon abandoned Theosophy, however, and in its place dedicated himself to political reform, especially the cause of Indian independence, inspired perhaps by Annie Besant, a leading Theosophist who herself had championed Indian freedom. Still, for Comrade Kirillov, Theosophy was now irrelevant; hope for humanity, especially for India, now lay solely in social, political, and economic revolution. Thus he studied German, French, and Russian so that he could read Marx, Fourier, St. Simon, and Lenin. Having left America, he settled in London, where he earned a meager living as a translator of German texts. Soon, in conversations "on the benches of Bloomsbury parks . . . [he] found the veracity of Karl Marx"; and emulating Marx, he immersed himself in the British Museum researching an anticapitalist and anticolonialist treatise. Later he married a Czech and became more and more active in the Communist Party as a faithful and unquestioning member. He readily espoused the party line regarding the Moscow trials in the 1930s, applauded the Hitler-Stalin pact of 1939, and, after the Nazi invasion of Russia, had no problem in accepting Stalin's decree that agitation for India's liberation be suspended until an Allied victory had been won. In his research Kirillov relied on statistics in reaching his conclusions; in his political thinking he relied on the Politburo.

How, then, does Comrade Kirillov come by his Dostoevskian nickname? In *The Possessed,* one remembers, Kirillov had been a member of a revolutionary group of so-called nihilists, whose purpose included the total destruction of the existing social, political, and religious order and the replacement of it with some vaguely conceived form of socialism. Atheism was, of course, axiomatic in the thought of the movement; and Dostoevsky's Kirillov, assuming that there is no God, concludes that he himself is God or has Godlike powers, reasoning as follows: "If God exists, all is His will and from His will I cannot escape. If not, it's all my will and I am bound to show self-will." He proposes to express his self-will "on the most vital point" of life and death by killing himself, yet he consents to make himself useful to the cause by assuming, in a suicide note, responsibility for any specific crime his comrades choose to commit. To Dostoevsky, then, Kirillov represents the extreme to which atheism can lead: the assertion of self by killing oneself.

Raja Rao's Kirillov is far different. (p. 617)

Neither an "intellectual" suicide nor a sadhu's yellow robe, it is clear, awaits Rao's protagonist, though he has the potential for either one. Kirillov is devoted to communism to the extent that he has submitted to the party line, but so far this subservience has not completely dehumanized him. Also, he shuns the asceticism of a fanatic, either political or religious. He is married, apparently happily, and he takes joy in his son, to whom, significantly, he has given the Hindu name Kamal Dev instead of "Stephanovich, or Electricity". Neither is he self-centered like Dostoevsky's Kirillov, whose energies have been redirected from "the cause" to proving his total independence and freedom of will by killing himself. The difference between the two Kirillovs is enormous; one rejects life and the other affirms it, each on both a personal and a political level.

Still, Rao's choice of a nickname for his Indian communist expatriate is entirely defensible, as readers acquainted with Dostoevsky's novels will see. To Dostoevsky the gravest intellectual or spiritual sin that a Russian could commit was to reject his or her Russian cultural heritage and substitute for it values and practices and, worst of all, innovative social and philosophical theories drawn from Western Europe. (pp. 617-18)

Rao's views regarding India in relation to the West parallel those of Dostoevsky regarding Russia and the West, though Rao is somewhat less rigid and expresses himself less strongly, softening his strictures with irony. To him, it would be fair to say, India is a "god-bearing" country or culture—a state of mind or of spirit as much as a political entity. Frustrated in achieving its freedom, the subcontinent with its many languages and cultures could rely only on its ancient Hindu religion for the unity necessary for true nationhood. Philosophically and theologically important in Hinduism is Vedanta, and Rao is an avowed Vedantin, thus averse to the materialism of Marxism and many other Western philosophies. Vedanta is to Rao what Eastern Christian Orthodoxy was to Dostoevsky.

In the movement toward Indian independence as presented in *Comrade Kirillov,* Mahatma Gandhi is the embodiment of the country's spiritual traditions and aspirations. It is through him, therefore, that the narrator R. believes that national liberation will be won. Kirillov the communist, however, though he resents criticism of Gandhi by non-Indians, considers the Mahatma a "Sadhu reactionary who still believed in caste and creed and such categories, and whose birth in this world had set history many centuries backwards"; he brands Gandhi's program of "non-violence . . . a biological lie." He is "the one enemy of [the] new dispensation" promised by Marx. Kirillov adds: "More insidious than Hitler is this intellectual venom [Gandhi's teachings] that is spreading over vast and ignorant humanity. Beware!". That such views are utterly antithetical to Rao's own estimate of Gandhi is apparent to anyone who has read *Kanthapura* and *The Serpent and the Rope.*

As an epigraph for *Comrade Kirillov* Rao has chosen an excerpt from a conversation between Shatov and Stavrogin, two characters in *The Possessed.*

> STAVROGIN: Tell me, have you caught your hare? To cook your hare you must catch it, to believe in God you must first have a god. Do you believe in God?
>
> SHATOV: I,—I *will* believe in God.

Shatov, having rejected the nihilism which he had once helped to promote by means of a clandestine printing press, struggles to believe in the Russian Orthodox God and the divine mission of the Russian people. His change of heart is evidenced in the scene—referred to in *Comrade Kirillov*—in which he takes into his house his long-absent estranged wife, pregnant by another man, and rushes out in the middle of the night for a midwife to deliver the baby. That R. imagines Comrade Kirillov acting in the same way indicates a potential, whether its source lay in Marxian logic or in the power of love, that goes far toward humanizing Kirillov; and later in the novel manifestations of Kirillov's love of his son have much the same effect. Thus Rao is attributing to Kirillov some of the qualities of Dostoevsky's Shatov. Here, then, is a reason for the novel's epigraph.

There is, however, another, paradoxical reason for the epigraph. Shatov's struggle is to rid himself of his former nihilistic state of mind and substitute for it a belief in the Russian God. Comrade Kirillov, on the other hand, strives to convince himself of the infallibility of Russian Marxism-Leninism, at the cost of suppressing his intellectual and spiritual heritage as a Brahmin. He succeeds, for a time at least, but his success is not easy; for as a sincere and thoroughgoing Marxist, he has been expected to accept and approve Stalin's pact with Marxism's deadliest enemy, Adolf Hitler. Further, he has been required to renounce until after the war his dearest project of independence for India. His allegiance to communism has indeed been put to the test, and many a time he may have cried, "I—I *will* believe in Marx—and Stalin!" In different words he says as much to R.: "Logic my religion, Communism my motherland".

This brings us to the thematic center of the novel, which has to do not so much with the tensions between Eastern and Western thought as with the tensions between logic, on the one hand, and feeling, intuition, and spirituality on the other. . . . R. can marvel at his friend's Marxist logic, his singleness of purpose, his spirituality that underlies his materialism, yet he knows that a wide and deep gap saparates his own Vedantism and Kirillov's communism. What the two friends have in common is their Indianness, which, despite any superimposed Western modes of thought, must dedicate itself to the life of the spirit. Indeed, Kirillov, during a sojourn in India, has visited a famous ashram. He has enjoyed getting back in touch with his roots and assures R. that he can excel him four to one in reciting Sanskrit verses, but he remains condescending about Gandhi and about Nehru, whom he characterizes as "a well-meaning, Utopian liberal, sitting crosswise on the hedge between socialism and liberalism". Kirillov is still a communist but now seems to have shifted his sights from Moscow to Peking, confident of the triumph of Chinese communism.

In the meantime Kirillov's wife has died after giving birth to a second child, who also dies. Though fascinated by Indian culture, Irene had always dreaded the prospect of going to her husband's homeland. After her death, her son Kamal Dev, whose name bears witness to his father's essential Indianness, is sent to live with his grandparents in Trichinopoly in South India. The death of Kirillov's European wife and the transplanting of his son into his ancestral soil seem to symbolize the waning of Western influence not only on Kirillov—he has already begun to be known as Padmanabha Kirillov—but on India as a whole.

As the novel ends, R., happening to be in Trichinopoly, takes Kamal on a "pilgrimage" to Cape Kanyakumari (Cape Cormorin), the southern tip of India and one of Hinduism's most sacred places. . . . (pp. 618-19)

There at the Cape R. told Kamal a story of Shiva and Parvati, and one evening he dressed the boy "in sacred silk, gave him his silver waist-band, and sandal on his face, [and] showed him to Mother Kanyakumari. Between the lamps and the bright Goddess, we heard the leaping adoration of the ninth moon ocean". India has thus received back her own, the son of a Western woman and a Brahmin of ancient lineage who, in the world of politics and economics was a Marxist but in the spiritual world was willy-nilly as much a Vedantin as R. himself.

In a footnote to the novel Rao definitely identifies R. as himself and then proceeds, in the text, to describe him as others see him. Kirillov, writing to his wife from India, states that he does not wish to meet R., who is also in India at the time, because R. would "madden him with aesthetics and Sanscrit" and make him feel "ten years younger and an undergraduate." Furthermore, he believes R.'s "leanings are still Trotskyite, and worse, the rank reactionary going back to the *Vedas* and all that". Irene finds R. sincere yet verbose, too much the Brahmin, too dependent on abstractions. He is, she thinks, an Alyosha, but a Dimitri added—a Karamazov, all right"—that is, a mystic and a sensualist but one wary of Western ways and thoughts, as are the two Karamazovs.

Structurally, **Comrade Kirillov** is essentially a long short story or novella. Its very brevity restricts its focus to only three characters; and, with a notable exception on the final pages, where the action shifts to South India, the setting is in London, mainly during World War II. A break in the unity of the narration occurs with the abrupt insertion of Irene's diary, apparently with the purpose of providing Western and feminine reactions to the Indian characters (all of them men) and their thoughts and doings. Though this purpose may be accomplished, a discordancy in the narrative flow results.

The story is told in unpretentious prose with frequently recurring overtones of irony that reflect R.'s amused puzzlement regarding Kirillov. In effect, the style is that of a highly literate journalist—"a newspaper Tagore," as Kirillov says—which indeed R. actually is. Only when R. and Kamal visit Kanyakumari does the writing become lyrical, as is appropriate to this section's purpose of affirming the greatness of India. (p. 619)

Perry D. Westbrook, "Raja Rao's 'Comrade Kirillov': Marxism and Vedanta," in World Literature Today, *Vol. 62, No. 4, Autumn, 1988, pp. 617-20.*

J(erome) D(avid) Salinger
1919-

American novelist and short story writer.

The following entry presents criticism on Salinger's novel *The Catcher in the Rye* (1951). For overviews of Salinger's career, see *CLC*, Vols. 1, 3, 8, 12.

Best known for his controversial novel *The Catcher in the Rye*, Salinger is recognized by many critics and readers as one of the most popular and influential authors of American fiction to emerge after World War II. Salinger's reputation derives from his thoughtful, sympathetic insights into the insecurities of both adolescence and adulthood, his mastery of symbolism, and his idiomatic style, which helped to rejuvenate the colloquial idiom in American literature. While his young, endearing protagonists have made him a perennial favorite among high school and college audiences, establishing him as a spokesperson for the goals and values of a generation of youths during the 1950s, *The Catcher in the Rye* has been recurrently banned by public libraries, schools, and bookstores due to its presumed profanity, sexual subject matter, and rejection of some traditional American values. Robert Coles reflected general critical opinion when he lauded Salinger as "an original and gifted writer, a marvelous entertainer, a man free of the slogans and clichés the rest of us fall prey to."

Salinger was expelled from several private preparatory schools before graduating from Valley Forge Military Academy in 1936. While attending a Columbia University writing course, Salinger had his first piece of short fiction published in *Story,* an influential periodical established by his instructor, Whit Burnett. Salinger's short fiction soon began appearing in *Collier's, The Saturday Evening Post, Esquire,* and, most notably, *The New Yorker.* Along with such authors as John O'Hara and John Cheever, Salinger helped to develop the sharp, ironic style that characterizes what critics term the "New Yorker" school of fiction. His many contributions to the magazine include "For Esmé—With Love and Squalor," a highly popular and acclaimed story in which a soldier's ingenuous friendship with a young English girl saves him from a nervous breakdown. "I'm Crazy" and "Slight Rebellion off Madison," both of which were published in periodicals during the 1940s, were revised for inclusion in *The Catcher in the Rye.* These stories introduce Holden Caulfield, the novel's adolescent narrator.

Self-critical, curious, and compassionate, Holden is a moral idealist whose attitude is governed by a dogmatic hatred of hypocrisy. *The Catcher in the Rye* opens in a sanitarium, where Holden is recuperating from physical illness and a mental breakdown. Holden begins by describing his expulsion from Pencey Prep, a select preparatory school, prior to Christmas vacation. Before leaving his dormitory, Holden seeks friendship with Stradlater, his athletic, womanizing roommate. Upon discovering that Stradlater has a date with Jane Gallagher, a girl with whom Holden once enjoyed a chaste relationship, Holden becomes angry and jealous. This incident reveals two aspects of Holden's moralism: he fears his roommate's sexual prowess and he values children for

their sincerity and innocence, seeking to protect them from the immorality that he believes permeates adult society. Both Jane and Holden's younger brother, Allie, who died at eleven years of age, function for Holden as symbols of goodness. Caught between adolescence and adulthood, Holden seeks the stability that his childhood relationship with Jane allowed him, yet experiences a personal crisis while attempting to embrace a mature adult role. Despite being jealous of Stradlater, Holden agrees to complete an essay assignment for his roommate in which he affectionately describes Allie's baseball mitt. However, Stradlater returns and rejects the composition. Fearing that Stradlater has had sex with Jane, Holden picks a fight with him and is humiliated. Following a futile attempt to become friends with Ackley, a social outcast, Holden runs away to New York City. Several critics have commented that the characters at Pencey Prep represent facets of Holden's personality. His sexual confusion, for example, is often interpreted as being embodied in the extremes of Ackley, whose repression leaves him socially and sexually undeveloped, and Stradlater, whose sexual prowess arouses Holden's arrogance. The two people he most respects, Allie and Jane, never appear in the novel and symbolize the absence of compassion and decency in Holden's world.

As the narrator of *The Catcher in the Rye,* Holden offers comments on the flaws and merits of American society, through which readers may evaluate Holden's own morals and values, particularly his need for human clemency. To delay confronting his parents about his expulsion, Holden decides to loiter in New York City. While on a train to Manhattan, he meets the mother of an unpopular student he knew at Pencey and purposely embellishes her son's reputation to spare her feelings. Once in the city, Holden struggles between wanting to return to scenes of his youth and venturing into a mature adult lifestyle. Arriving at a jazz club where a friend of his older brother plays piano, Holden becomes disillusioned with the gifted musician's contrived performance and is reminded of his brother, whose career as a Hollywood screenwriter Holden regards as a waste of creative talent. In one pivotal scene, Holden decides to lose his virginity to a prostitute but sympathizes with her plight and is unwilling to consummate the act. While many critics have noted that Holden is hypocritical because he frequently complains about the "phonies" that surround him yet lies to the mother of his schoolmate, others cite his reaction to the prostitute as indicative of his compassionate nature.

Wandering through Central Park toward the Natural History Museum, a favorite place of his childhood, Holden reflects on the comfort and stability he has always found there. He decides to remain outside, however, a choice critics have interpreted as a step toward his impending adulthood. Holden's subsequent date with a young woman at a local theater leads to ambivalent feelings when he is besieged by the artificiality of the evening's social proceedings. Afraid that he too will become a "phony," Holden despises his own conventionality yet causes his date to reject him following his immature and unrealistic proposal to elope in rural New England. Arranging to meet an older schoolmate, Carl Luce, at a hotel bar, Holden becomes intoxicated and asks Luce personal questions about his sex life. Commentators have noted that much of the humor in *The Catcher in the Rye* stems from Holden's misconceptions of adulthood. Although Luce is more experienced than Holden, the older man is not as mature as Holden believes him to be. After this attempt at communication has failed, Holden flees to his younger sister, Phoebe, the only person he completely trusts.

Many critics concur with S. N. Behrman's comment that Phoebe Caulfield is "one of the most exquisitely created and engaging children in any novel." A clever, precocious ten-year-old, Phoebe functions as Allie's living counterpart and Holden's salvation. After discussing her brother's problems, Phoebe asks if Holden likes anything about his life. Revealing his obsession with the past and inability to cope with the present, Holden can think only of Allie and a former classmate who committed suicide rather than apologize to a bully. In this section, from which the novel's title derives, Holden tells his sister of his wish to be a "catcher in the rye"—one who stands on the edge of a cliff near a rye field where thousands of children play. Holden explains: "What I have to do, I have to catch everybody if they start to go over the cliff. . . . That's all I'd do all day." Holden's intentions are honorable yet quixotic, and Phoebe expresses disgust at her brother's unrealistic goals. John Romano remarked of this passage: "This seems to me one of those arresting moments when a writer bravely elects to put in question the very point of view on which, by and large, he has staked his art. Such questioning of its own visionary standpoint is not the least of the reasons why, in the end, *The Catcher in the Rye* is so noble and honest a piece of work."

After informing Phoebe that he intends to escape his responsibilities and travel west, Holden visits Mr. Antolini, one of the few teachers he admires. Although Salinger leaves the incident ambiguous, the man's advice is tainted by gestures that Holden construes as homosexual advances. Arriving at Phoebe's school to leave her a note, Holden notices obscenities scrawled on the building's wall. Horrified that schoolchildren might glimpse them, he erases the vulgarities but later encounters the same graffiti in the Natural History Museum. Despondent at this perversion of his idealized past, Holden finally accepts that the world will change despite his attempts to preserve it. When Phoebe announces her intention to go west with Holden, his forbiddance reveals his impending maturity. In the novel's climactic scene, Holden watches as Phoebe rides the Central Park carousel in the rain and his illusion of protecting children's innocence is symbolically shattered. Critics regard this episode as Holden's transition into adulthood, for although his future is uncertain, his severed ties with the dead past have enabled him to accept maturity. James Bryan observed: "The richness of spirit in this novel, especially of the vision, the compassion, and the humor of the narrator reveal a psyche far healthier than that of the boy who endured the events of the narrative. Through the telling of his story, Holden has given shape to, and thus achieved control of, his troubled past."

The Catcher in the Rye is written in a colloquial prose style enhanced by teenage slang of the 1950s. Many critics concur that Holden's candid outlook reflects aspects of adolescence still relevant to contemporary youth. *The Catcher in the Rye* is often compared to traditional picaresque literature, particularly Mark Twain's novel *The Adventures of Huckleberry Finn*. Both works feature naive, adolescent runaways as narrators, both comment on the prevailing problems of their times, and both have been recurrently banned or restricted. Early critics often faulted the narrative style of *The Catcher in the Rye* as erratic or unreliable, claiming that Holden possesses many of the middle-class values that he rejects. Later commentators, however, have praised Salinger's wry humor, technical virtuosity, and skilled mockery of vocal speech, contending that the novel's structure ideally personifies Holden's unstable state of mind. Alastair Best remarked: "There is a hard, almost classical structure underneath Holden's rambling narrative. The style, too, appears effortless; yet one wonders how much labour went into those artfully rough-hewn sentences."

Salinger's subsequent works have also contributed to his fame and popularity. Sensitive to criticism and protective of his privacy, Salinger retreated to a secluded home near Cornish, New Hampshire in the 1950s but continued to publish short fiction until 1965. Following *The Catcher in the Rye,* Salinger again provoked controversy and commentary with *Nine Stories* (1953; published in Great Britain as *For Esmé—With Love and Squalor and Other Stories*), a collection of previously published fiction about the Glass family, a group of precocious characters whose quests for personal serenity in a superficial world prefigure those of characters in Salinger's ensuing works. One of the most popular stories in this collection, "A Perfect Day for Bananafish," recounts the puzzling suicide of Seymour, the eldest Glass sibling. Although occasionally faulted for commercialism, *Nine Stories* was generally praised for its incisive, revealing dialogue. "Franny" and "Zooey," which were originally published in *The New Yorker* as separate stories, achieved wide acclaim after being collected and republished as *Franny and Zooey* (1961). "Franny" delineates Franny Glass's emotional and spiritual breakdown while attending college; "Zooey" depicts the attempts of her brother Zooey to alleviate her problems. Several reviewers faulted Salinger's anecdotes about the Glasses in *Raise High the Roofbeam, Carpenters and Seymour: An Introduction* (1963) as convoluted, asserting that sentimentality had overwhelmed the author's artistic control. Salinger's last published story under his own name, "Hapworth 16, 1924," appeared in *The New Yorker* in 1965. This piece is written from a summer camp in the form of a letter home by seven-year-old Seymour Glass. According to several reviewers, "Hapworth 16, 1924" ties together the Glass family saga by suggesting reasons for Seymour's later suicide. Although Salinger has published no works since 1965, critics continue to acknowledge the value of his fiction, his influence on the style of other writers, and above all, his place of honor among young readers.

(See also *Contemporary Authors,* Vols. 5-8, rev. ed.; *Dictionary of Literary Biography,* Vol. 2; *Concise Dictionary of American Literary Biography: The New Consciousness, 1941-1968;* and *Short Story Criticism,* Vol. 2.)

PAUL ENGLE

[*The Catcher in the Rye*] is a novel about a 16 year old boy which is emotional without being sentimental, dramatic without being melodramatic, and honest without being simply obscene. The language has the authentic sound of a boy's voice without ever being childish or seeming to be written down to that age level. Nor is it merely one more account of adolescence, complete with the usual meditations on youth. The effort has been to make the text, told by the boy himself, as accurate and yet as imaginative as possible. In this, it largely succeeds.

The narrative begins in a boy's prep school in Pennsylvania where the narrator, Holden Caulfield, is seeing one of his teachers for the last time, after having been informed that he is being expelled for failing almost all of his courses.

After various incidents with other students, with none of whom is he able to make any close or congenial relationship, he suddenly packs his bags and takes a night train to New York. . . .

The balance of the novel deals with his adventures in New York while hiding out from his family and friends.

Various efforts to establish communication with other people fail, and he sneaks home to talk to his younger sister while his parents are out. He decides to run away and Phoebe, the sister, decides to go with him. It is her decision which ties him down and keeps him home, so he does, in the end, find a human warmth.

The book ends with Holden in a mental institution for which the earlier events have hardly prepared the reader. But the story is an engaging and believable one for the most part, full of right observations and sharp insight, and a wonderful sort of grasp of how a boy can create his own world of fantasy and live forms.

*Paul Engle, "Honest Tale of Distraught Adoles-*cent," in Chicago Sunday Tribune Magazine of Books, *July 15, 1951, p. 3.*

VIRGILIA PETERSON

[*The Catcher in the Rye*] by J. D. Salinger, whose short stories in *The New Yorker* and other magazines have caused considerable comment, should provoke a tempest of reactions. Those who have read Mr. Salinger's stories will remember his special concern for youth and, for its despairs, a kind of crazy tenderness. In *The Catcher in the Rye,* these feelings of the author reach their apex. Couched in the first person singular, the book is the story of a few climactic days in the life of a sixteen-year-old prep-school boy as he himself recounts it a few months later. In it lies the implication that our youth today has no moorings, no criterion beyond instinct, no railing to grasp along the steep ascent to maturity. This is the importance of *The Catcher in the Rye,* and it is upon the integrity of his portrait of a so-called privileged American youth that Mr. Salinger's novel stands or falls.

Holden Caulfield begins his account of himself on a December day, the week before Christmas vacation, when he decided to leave Pencey Prep ahead of the other boys, since he had failed in four subjects and was not to return for the winter term. Holden had had "trouble" in two previous schools, chiefly because he hated them. Pencey, no worse than the others in Holden's view, was merely another "phony." . . . After writing a theme for his roommate, paying a good-by call on an ailing teacher, and selling his typewriter for extra cash, he assembled his clothes and equipment and set off for the station, late in the evening, on foot. Determined not to appear before his parents till the day they expected him, by which time the school would have informed them that he was fired, Holden spends two incredible days and nights in the city, lost, uprooted, lifted by hope, dashed by despair, trying to be a man and enjoy a man's pleasures but succeeding only in more deeply humiliating himself except in the intervals when he revisits the places of his childhood or tiptoes clandestinely into his own home late at night to talk with "little old Phoebe," his ten-year-old sister—the only being he completely trusts.

Like most of his literary predecessors—that host of sad twigs being arbitrarily bent to make twisted trees—Holden Caulfield is on the side of the angels. Contaminated he is, of course, by vulgarity, lust, lies, temptations, recklessness, and cynicism. But these are merely the devils that try him externally; inside, his spirit is intact. Unlike so many of his literary predecessors, however, he does not oversimplify his troubles. He is not tilting against the whole adult world (there are some decent adults); nor does he altogether loathe his worst contemporaries (he hates to leave them). He sees the mixtures, the inextricably mingled good and bad, as it is, but the very knowledge of reality is what almost breaks his heart. For Holden Caulfield, despite all the realism with which he is supposedly depicted, is nevertheless a skinless perfectionist.

Had Ring Lardner and Ernest Hemingway never existed, Mr. Salinger might have had to invent the manner of his tale, if not the matter. *The Catcher in the Rye* repeats and repeats, like an incantation, the pseudo-natural cadences of a flat, colloquial prose which at best, banked down and understated, has a truly moving impact and at worst is casually obscene. . . .

Mr. Salinger speaks, no doubt, for himself as well as for his hero, when he has Holden say to little Phoebe:

> I keep picturing all these little kids playing some game in this big field of rye and all. Thousands of little kids, and nobody's around—nobody big I mean—except me. And I'm standing on the edge of some crazy cliff. What I have to do, I have to catch everybody if they start to go over the cliff—I mean if they're running and they don't look where they're going I have to come out from somewhere and catch them . . . I'd just be the catcher in the rye and all . . .

But before it is possible to nominate Mr. Salinger as the top-flight catcher in the rye for the year or the day, it would be interesting and highly enlightening to know what Holden Caulfield's contemporaries, male and female, think of him. Their opinion would constitute the real test of Mr. Salinger's validity. The question of authenticity is one to which no parent can really guess the reply.

> *Virgilia Peterson, "Three Days in the Bewildering World of an Adolescent," in* New York Herald Tribune Book Review, *July 15, 1951, p. 3.*

JAMES STERN

This girl Helga, she kills me. She reads just about everything I bring into the house, and a lot of crumby stuff besides. She's crazy about kids. I mean stories about kids. But Hel, she says there's hardly a writer alive can write about children. . . . [But she] came hollering to me one day, her hair falling over her face and all, and said I had to read some damn story in *The New Yorker*. Who's the author? I said. Salinger, she told me, J. D. Salinger. Who's he? I asked. How should I know, she said, just you read it.

"For Esmé—with Love and Squalor" was this story's crumby title. . . . Hel, I said when I was through, just you wait till this guy writes a novel. Novel, my elbow, she said. This Salinger, he won't write no crumby novel. He's a short story guy.—Girls, they kill me. They really do.

But I was right, if you want to know the truth. You should've seen old Hel hit the ceiling when I told her this Salinger [had written a novel, *The Catcher in the Rye*]. . . . For crying out loud, she said, what's it about? About this Holden Caulfield, I told her, about the time he ran away to New York from this Pencey Prep School in Agerstown, Pa. Why'd he run away, asked old Hel. Because it was a terrible school, I told her, no matter how you looked at it. . . .

Then Hel asked what this Holden's father was like, so I told her if she wanted to know the truth Holden didn't want to go into all that David Copperfield-kind of business. . . . You see, this Holden, I said, he just can't find anybody decent in the lousy world and he's in some sort of crumby Californian home full of psychiatrists.

That damn near killed Hel. Psychiatrists, she howled. That's right, I said, this one psychiatrist guy keeps asking Holden if he's going to apply himself when he goes back to school. (He's already been kicked out of about six.) And Holden, he says how the hell does *he* know. "I *think* I am," he says, "but how do I know. I swear it's a stupid question."

That's the way it sounds to me, Hel said, and away she went with this crazy book, *The Catcher in the Rye*. What did I tell

ya, she said next day. This Salinger, he's a short story guy. And he knows how to write about kids. This book though, it's too long. Gets kind of monotonous. And he should've cut out a lot about these jerks and all at that crumby school. They depress me. They really do. Salinger, he's best with real children. I mean young ones like old Phoebe, his kid sister. She's a personality. Holden and little old Phoebe, Hel said, they kill me. This last part about her and Holden and this Mr. Antolini, the only guy Holden ever thought he could trust, who ever took any interest in him, and who turned out queer—that's terrific. I swear it is.

You needn't swear, Hel, I said. Know what? This Holden, he's just like you. He finds the whole world's full of people who say one thing and mean another and he doesn't like it; and he hates movies and phony slobs and snobs and crumby books and war. Boy, how he hates war. Just like you, Hel, I said. But old Hel, she was already reading this crazy *Catcher* book all over again. That's always a good sign with Hel.

> *James Stern, "Aw, the World's a Crumby Place," in* The New York Times Book Review, *July 15, 1951, p. 5.*

ANNE L. GOODMAN

[In] the climactic scene of [Salinger's] first novel, *The Catcher in the Rye,* the sixteen-year-old hero who has been wandering around New York alone for three days, ever since his expulsion from boarding school, in a state somewhere between reality and unreality, abandons his dream of running away to the West and goes home (and subsequently to a sanitarium) when his ten-year-old sister, whom he has met secretly, is clearly broken-hearted at the thought of his leaving. . . .

The final scene in *The Catcher in the Rye* is as good as anything that Salinger has written, which means very good indeed. So are a number of other episodes. But the book as a whole is disappointing, and not merely because it is a reworking of a theme that one begins to suspect must obsess the author. Holden Caulfield, the main character who tells his own story, is an extraordinary portrait, but there is too much of him. He describes himself early on and, with the sureness of a wire recording, he remains strictly in character throughout. . . .

In the course of 277 pages the reader wearies of this kind of explicitness, repetition and adolescence, exactly as one would weary of Holden himself. And this reader at least suffered from an irritated feeling that Holden was not quite so sensitive and perceptive as he, and his creator, thought he was. In any case he is so completely self-centered that the other characters who wander through the book—with the notable exception of his sister Phoebe—have nothing like his authenticity. *The Catcher in the Rye* is a brilliant tour-de-force, but in a writer of Salinger's undeniable talent one expects something more. (p. 21)

> *Anne L. Goodman, "Mad about Children," in* The New Republic, *Vol. 125, No. 3, July 16, 1951, pp. 20-1.*

HARVEY BREIT

The two summer novels I have just read, J. D. Salinger's *The Catcher in the Rye* and Kenneth Fearing's *Loneliest Girl in the World,* are nearly good enough of their kind for the reader to be immensely grateful—and to let it go at that. What is more interesting, and necessary, is to attempt to find out why Salinger's novel is a near miss and Fearing's a loud one.

Somewhere about halfway in Salinger's novel, the bright, terrible, and possibly normal sixteen-year-old protagonist follows a little boy who is singing quietly to himself "If a body catch a body coming through the rye." Later when the youthful hero's younger sister challenges him, demanding to know if there is anything in the world that he likes or wants to be, he can only think he wants to be "the catcher in the rye." It is significant because the novel, for all its surface guilelessness, is a critique of the contemporary, grown-up world.

It isn't important whether Salinger had it in mind or not, but reading *The Catcher in the Rye* made me think of *The Adventures of Huckleberry Finn.* Holden Caulfield struck me as an urban, a transplanted Huck Finn. He has a colloquialism as marked as Huck's. . . . Like Huck, Holden is neither comical nor misanthropic. He is an observer. Unlike Huck, he makes judgments by the dozen, but these are not to be taken seriously; they are conceits. There is a drollery, too, that is common to both, and a quality of seeing that creates farce.

What is crucial is where Huck and Holden part company. T. S. Eliot once pointed out that we see the world through Huck's eyes. Well, we do not see it through Holden's. We see Holden as a smiling adult sees a boy, and we smile at his spectral, incredible world. I think that is the decisive failure: whatever is serious and implicit in the novel is overwhelmed by the more powerful comic element. What remains is a brilliant *tour de force,* one that has sufficient power and cleverness to make the reader chuckle and—rare indeed—even laugh aloud.

> *Harvey Breit, in a review of "The Catcher in the Rye," in* The Atlantic Bookshelf, *a section of* The Atlantic Monthly, *Vol. CLXXXVIII, No. 2, August, 1951, p. 82.*

S. N. BEHRMAN

Holden Caulfield, the sixteen-year-old protagonist of J. D. Salinger's first novel, *The Catcher in the Rye,* . . . refers to himself as an illiterate, but he *is* a reader. One of the tests to which he puts the books he reads is whether he feels like calling the author up. He is excited about a book by Isak Dinesen and feels like calling her up. He would like to call up Ring Lardner, but an older brother has told him Lardner is dead. He thinks *Of Human Bondage* is pretty good, but he has no impulse to put in a call to Maugham. He would like to call up Thomas Hardy, because he has a nice feeling about Eustacia Vye. (Nobody, evidently, has told him the sad news about Hardy.) Mr. Salinger himself passes his unorthodox literary test with flying colors; this reader would certainly like to call *him* up.

Mr. Salinger's brilliant, funny, meaningful novel is written in the first person. Holden Caulfield is made to tell his own story, in his own strange idiom. Holden is not a normal boy. He is hypersensitive and hyper-imaginative (perhaps these are synonymous). He is double-minded. He is inexorably self-critical; at various times, he refers to himself as yellow, as a terrible liar, a madman, a moron. He is driven crazy by "phoniness," a heading under which he loosely lumps not only insincerity but snobbery, injustice, callousness to the tears in

things, and a lot more. He is a prodigious worrier. . . . He is moved to pity unconscionably often. He has few defenses. For example, he is driven frantic by a scrawled obscenity some vandal has chalked on the wall of his ten-year-old sister Phoebe's school. Grown men sometimes find the emblazoned obscenities of life too much for them, and leave this world indecorously, so the fact that a sixteen-year-old boy is overwhelmed should not be surprising. (p. 71)

The book covers Holden's last day at Pencey, a fashionable prep school, from which he has flunked out, and the following two days, which he spends in hiding in New York City. Stradlater, Holden's roommate, is handsome, gross, and a successful amorist. On Holden's last night at school, a Saturday night, he is in a frenzy of jealousy because Stradlater has dated up Jane Gallagher, with whom Holden is in love. The hero and heroine of this novel, Holden's dead brother Allie and Jane Gallagher, never appear in it, but as they are always in Holden's consciousness, together with his sister Phoebe—these three constitute his emotional frame of reference—the reader knows them better, finally, than the characters Holden encounters, who are, except for Phoebe, marginal. It is characteristic of Holden that although he is crazy about Jane, always thinking of her, always wanting to call her up, he never does call her up. He is always about to but doesn't, because he's never "in the mood." ("You really have to be in the mood for that stuff.") Perhaps he means that circumstances and his feelings are always too chaotic at the particular moment—that he wants to appear before Jane when everything is in order and he is in control of himself. Or perhaps he wishes to keep his memory of Jane inviolate and consecrated, like his memory of Allie; perhaps he is afraid of finding her innocence tarnished—not in a sexual sense, because eventually he is sure that Stradlater didn't "get to first base with her," but simply of finding her no longer what she was, possibly finding that she has become, in short, a phony. He keeps calling up a girl named Sally Hayes, whose manifest phoniness gives him "a royal pain," but he writes that off as the overhead of sex. He can never risk it with Jane.

While Stradlater is shaving before going to meet Jane, he asks Holden to write a classroom composition for him. "Anything descriptive," Stradlater says. "A room. Or a house. . . . Just as long as it's as descriptive as hell. . . . Just don't do it *too* good, is all. . . . I mean don't stick all the commas and stuff in the right place." The implication that all there is to writing a composition is a sense of direction about commas also gives Holden "a royal pain." "I mean," he explains, "if you're good at writing compositions and somebody starts talking about commas. Stradlater was always doing that. He wanted you to think that the only reason *he* was lousy at writing compositions was because he stuck all the commas in the wrong place. . . . God, how I hate that stuff!"

While Stradlater is out with Jane, Holden, knowing his roommate's technique on the back seats of cars, takes terrific punishment from his imagination. Nevertheless, he sits down to write a composition for the absent Don Juan:

> The thing was, I couldn't think of a room or a house or anything to describe the way Stradlater said he had to have. I'm not too crazy about describing rooms and houses anyway. So what I did, I wrote about my brother Allie's baseball mitt. It was a very descriptive subject. It really was. My brother Allie had this left-handed fielder's mitt. He was left-handed. The thing that was descriptive about it, though, was that he had poems written all

over the fingers and the pocket and everywhere. In green ink. He wrote them on it so that he'd have something to read when he was in the field and nobody was up at bat. He's dead now. He got leukemia and died when we were up in Maine, on July 18, 1946. You'd have liked him. He was two years younger than I was, but he was about fifty times as intelligent. He was terrifically intelligent. His teachers were always writing letters to my mother, telling her what a pleasure it was having a boy like Allie in their class. . . . They really meant it. But it wasn't just that he was the most intelligent member in the family. He was also the nicest, in lots of ways. He never got mad at anybody. . . .

(pp. 71-2)

Holden copies Allie's poems from his baseball mitt. He tells you casually, "I happened to have it with me, in my suitcase." Very much later, we discover that the only person to whom Holden has ever shown this mitt is Jane. ("She was interested in that kind of stuff.") Allie is always there. Sitting in his hotel room in New York, Holden feels he is sunk, and he starts talking to Allie. He remembers that he and another boy were going on a bicycle jaunt with their BB guns, and Allie asked to come along, and Holden wouldn't let him:

> So once in a while, now, when I get very depressed, I keep saying to him, "Okay. Go home and get your bike and meet me in front of Bobby's house. Hurry up." It wasn't that I didn't use to take him with me when I went somewhere. I did. But that one day, I didn't. He didn't get sore about it—he never got sore about anything—but I keep thinking about it anyway, when I get very depressed.

Holden is always regretting that you didn't know Allie. "You'd have liked him," he keeps saying: the human impulse to make a silent voice audible to others, a lost essence palpable.

By the time Stradlater returns from his date with Jane, Holden is sure that he has slept with her, and Stradlater helps him to think so, without being actually caddish. Stradlater asks for the composition; he is furious when he reads it, because it is about a baseball glove rather than a room or a house. Holden tears the composition up. He has a fight with Stradlater and gets a bloody nose. Shortly after that, he decides he can't stay another minute in Pencey and will go to New York, though his parents don't expect him until Wednesday.

Holden goes to say goodbye to Mr. Spencer, his nice old history teacher. It worries the boy that while his teacher is saying edifying valedictory things to him, he becomes acutely concerned about the winter quarters of the ducks in the Central Park lagoon. . . . This worry about the ducks stays with Holden all through his adventures in New York. On his second night, he has an irresistible impulse to go to Central Park and see what the ducks are doing. In his avidity to find them, he pokes in the grass around the lagoon, to see if they are sleeping there, and nearly falls in the water. No ducks. Beginning to shiver, he is sure he is going to die of pneumonia, and he decides to sneak into his parents' apartment to see Phoebe once more before he dies.

This Phoebe is one of the most exquisitely created and engaging children in any novel. She is herself a prolific novelist, who is not deterred from starting a new book merely because she hasn't finished the last one. They are all about an attractive girl detective named Hazle Weatherfield. Hazle's father is "a tall attractive gentleman about 20 years of age." When Holden tiptoes into Phoebe's room, she is asleep. As befits an author, Phoebe has numberless notebooks. Before Holden wakes Phoebe, he has a look at her notebooks and her schoolbooks. Phoebe's middle name is Josephine, but Holden finds "Phoebe Weatherfield Caulfield 4B-1" written on the flyleaf of her "Arithmetic Is Fun!" Phoebe keeps changing her middle name, according to caprice. In a little list of variations, Holden finds "Phoebe Weatherfield Caulfield, Esq." "Kids' notebooks kill me," Holden says. He devours Phoebe's.

Holden wakes Phoebe. The moment she opens her eyes, she wants to know whether Holden has received her letter announcing that she is going to appear in a school play, *A Christmas Pageant for Americans.* "It stinks but I'm Benedict Arnold," she tells him excitedly. "I have practically the biggest part." Then, after her theatrical excitement simmers down, she remembers that Holden wasn't expected home until Wednesday, and she learns that he has been kicked out of school. She hits him with her fist. "Daddy'll *kill* you!" she cries. Holden lights a cigarette and tries to explain, but can't get much further than saying that the school was full of phonies and they depressed him. "You don't like *any*thing that's happening," she says. This accusation, in which Holden recognizes that there is a fundamental truth, also depresses him. He tries desperately to justify himself. He enumerates things and people he does like—his brother Allie, for instance. Phoebe replies sagely that it is easy to like people who are in Heaven. Holden, miserable, cannot marshal all his likes. There was, he remembers, a frail boy who was so bullied by some thug schoolmates that he jumped out of a window to escape them. A teacher, Mr. Antolini, picked the boy up and put his own coat around him—"He didn't even give a damn if his coat got all bloody"—and for this teacher Holden has always had a special feeling. Near Phoebe, Holden begins to feel better. (pp. 72-4)

Everybody, says Holden, accuses him of acting twelve years old. It's partly true, he admits, but not all true, because "sometimes I act a lot older than I am—I really do—but people never notice it." These perpetual insistences of Holden's—"I really am," "I really do," "It really does"—after he has explicitly said something, reveal his age, even when he is thinking much older, as when he says, "People always think something's *all* true." Although Holden thinks lots of things are funny, he hasn't much sense of humor; he has the deadpan literalness and the all-or-nothing combativeness of the passionate adolescent. Salinger's use of reiteration and redundancy in Holden's self-communion conveys this. After a passage describing his schoolmate Robert Ackley as pimply, dirty, disgusting, and nasty, and as having a terrible personality, he tells you, "I wasn't too crazy about him, to tell you the truth." . . . He is so aware of the danger of slipping into phoniness himself that he has to repeat over and over "I really mean it," "It really does." When he is not communing with himself but is in actual situations, these reiterations disappear; the dialogue and the descriptions are economical and lean.

The literalness and innocence of Holden's point of view in the face of the tremendously complicated and often depraved facts of life make for the humor of this novel: serious haggles with belligerent taxi-drivers; abortive conversational attempts with a laconic prostitute in a hurry; an "intellectual" discussion with a pompous and phony intellectual only a few years older than himself; an expedition with Sally Hayes, which is one of the funniest expeditions, surely, in the history of juvenilia. Holden's contacts with the outside world are generally extremely funny. It is his self-communings that are tragic and touching—a dark whirlpool churning fiercely below the unflagging hilarity of his surface activities. Holden's difficulties affect his nervous system but never his vision. It is the vision of an innocent. To the lifeline of this vision he clings invincibly, as he does to a phonograph record he buys for Phoebe (till it breaks) and a red hunting cap that is dear to him and that he finally gives to Phoebe, and to Allie's baseball glove. He has a hunger for stability. He loves the Museum of Natural History because the figures in the glass cases don't change; no matter how often you go, the Eskimo is still there catching fish, the deer drinking out of the water hole, the squaw weaving the same blanket. You change the circumstances of your visit—you have an overcoat on one time when you didn't before, or you may have "passed by one of those puddles in the street with gasoline rainbows in them," but the squaw and the deer and the Eskimo are stable. . . . Holden knows things won't remain the same; they are dissolving, and he cannot reconcile himself to it. He hasn't the knowledge to trace the process of dissolution or the mental clarity to define it; all he knows is that he is gasping in the avalanche of disintegration around him. And yet there is an exhilaration, an immense relief in the final scene of this novel, at the Central Park carrousel with Phoebe. ("I felt so damn happy all of a sudden, the way old Phoebe kept going around and around.") Holden will be all right. One day, he will probably find himself in the mood to call up Jane. He will even become more tolerant of phonies—it is part of the mechanics of living—as he has already had to endure the agony of saying "Glad to've met you" to people he isn't glad to have met. He may even, someday, write a novel. I would like to read it. I loved *this* one. I mean it—I really did. (pp. 75-6)

> S. N. Behrman, "The Vision of the Innocent," in The New Yorker, Vol. XXVII, No. 26, August 11, 1951, pp. 71-6.

JOHN W. ALDRIDGE

Mr. Salinger's **The Catcher in the Rye,** like *The Adventures of Huckleberry Finn,* is a study in the spiritual picaresque, the journey that for the young is all one way, from holy innocence to such knowledge as the world offers, from the reality which illusion demands and thinks it sees to the illusion which reality insists, at the point of madness, we settle for. But the great difference between the two novels is the measure not merely of the change in time and history of a cultural situation, but of the changed moral circumstances in which innocence typically finds itself in crisis and lends itself to drama. The innocence of *Huckleberry Finn* is a compound of frontier ignorance, juvenile delinquency, and penny-dreadful heroism. It begs for the challenge of thugs, thieves, swindlers, and feuds, and that is what it gets and delights in, takes such delight in, in fact, that even when the dangers become real and the escapes increasingly narrow, we know it is all in fun. . . . Still, in the suspension of our disbelief, in the planned illusion of the novel itself, the innocence and the world of violence appear to be seriously and effectively opposed. The innocence is the raft to which Huck and Jim, in flight from the dangers of the shore, make their narrow escapes. It is the river itself, time, faith, continuity, moving endlessly and dependably beside and between the temporary and futile altercations of men. (pp. 129-30)

The innocence of Mr. Salinger's Holden Caulfield, on the other hand, is a compound of urban intelligence, juvenile contempt, and *New Yorker* sentimentalism, and the only challenge it begs for, the only challenge it has left to beg for, is the challenge of the genuine, the truly human, in a world which has lost both the means of adventure and the means of love. But it is in the nature of Holden's dilemma, his spiritual confinement in this world, that he lacks a concrete basis, can find no concrete embodiment, for the ideal against which he judges, and finds wanting, the life around him. He has objects for his contempt but no objects other than his sister for his love—no raft, no river, no Jim, and no Tom. He is forced, consequently, simply to register his contempt, his developing disillusionment; and it is inevitable that he should seem after a time to be registering it in a vacuum, for just as he can find no concrete equivalent in life for the ideal which he wishes life to embody, so the persons on whom he registers his contempt seem inadequate to it and unjustly accused by it. The boorish prep school roommate, the hypocritical teacher, the stupid women in the Lavender Room, the resentful prostitute, the conventional girl friend, the bewildered cab driver, the affected young man at the theater, the old friend who reveals that his interest in Holden is homosexual—these people are all truly objectionable and deserve the places Holden assigns them in his secret hierarchy of class with its categories of phonies, bores, deceivers, and perverts. But they are nonetheless human, albeit dehumanized, and constitute a fair average of what the culture affords. They are part of the truth which Holden does not see and, as it turns out, is never able to see—that this is what one part of humanity *is;* the lies, the phoniness, the hypocrisy are the compromises which innocence is forced by the world to make. This is the reality on which Holden's illusion is finally broken, but no recognition follows, and no conversion. He remains at the end what he was at the beginning—cynical, defiant, and blind. And as for ourselves, there is identification but no insight, a sense of pathos but not of tragedy. It may be that Mr. Salinger made the most of his subject, but his subject was not adequate to his intention, just as Holden's world is not adequate to his contempt, and that is probably because it does not possess sufficient humanity to make the search for humanity dramatically feasible. (pp. 130-31)

> John W. Aldridge, "The Society of Three Novels," in his In Search of Heresy: American Literature in an Age of Conformity, McGraw-Hill Book Company, Inc., 1956, pp. 126-48.

DAVID STEVENSON

It is a curiosity of our age of criticism that J. D. Salinger, one of the most gifted of the young writers to emerge in America since World War II, is rarely acknowledged by the official guardians of our literary virtue in the quarterlies. He was extravagantly praised by the nation's book reviewers for his best-selling novel of 1951, **The Catcher in the Rye.** . . . His work has become standard reading in Freshman English. One hears his name occasionally above the noise of a cocktail party when a new story appears, in the last few years usually in *The New Yorker.* But he has remained outside the interest of our seriously dedicated critics.

Perhaps the most obvious reason for this neglect is the fact that, as a writer, he exists almost wholly beyond the fixed orbit of their attention. He has never been an artist in residence at a summer session. He has published no critical treatise in a literary quarterly on the mythic symbolism in Faulkner, no "thoughts" on the conversion of Edith Sitwell or on Wimsatt's theory of the intentional fallacy. He is not a proper man of letters who occasionally publishes a short story or a novel; he is that rare thing among contemporary writers who take their craft seriously, a complete professional.

Because of this diffidence to things dedicatedly literary, Salinger is usually identified by book reviewers, and properly, as a *New Yorker* writer, implying thereby both city wit and surface brilliance in his use of prose and stylized irony of situation in his use of plot. Such an identification suggests that his published work is meant to satisfy the reading tastes of a fairly heterogeneous audience, composed more of the highly literate men and women of the upper middle-class than of the "avant garde" or of the peer group of the quarterlies. (p. 215)

Salinger's most ambitious presentation of aspects of contemporary alienation, and his most successful capture of an American audience, is in his novel *The Catcher in the Rye.* It is the brief chronicle of Holden Caulfield, a sixteen-year-old boy who escapes to New York after flunking out of his third prep school. The novel is written as the boy's comment, half-humorous, half-agonizing, concerning his attempt to recapture his identity and his hopes for belonging by playing a man-about-town for a lost, partially tragic, certainly frenetic weekend. *The Catcher in the Rye* is a full-length novel, and yet gives much the effect of his shorter pieces. Its dimensional depth is extrinsic to the narrative, and is measured by the reader's response to the dialogue, and the background of city America. It is supplied by one's recognition that Holden Caulfield, sensitive, perceptive, is too aware of the discrepancies between the surface intentions and the submerged motives of himself and of his acquaintances to feel at ease in any world. Through him, Salinger has evoked the reader's consciousness of indefinable rejections and rebellions that are part of the malaise of our times.

As we have come to expect from Salinger's other work, the main devices of characterization in *The Catcher in the Rye* are an apparently effortless verisimilitude of dialogue and an unerring sense of the appropriate in details of gesture, or bodily movement. There is a further fictional device, used elsewhere in his short stories, but of paramount importance in his novel in creating a hold on the reader. It is his use of almost Chaplin-like incidents and dialogue, half-amusing, half-desperate, to keep his story always hovering in ambivalence between comedy and tragedy. Whenever a character approaches hopelessness in a Salinger sketch, he is getting there by the route of the comic. It is usually both the character's way of holding on for a moment longer . . . and, at its sharpest, a way of dramatic irony, a way of heightening the intensity of a character's predicament (as when Holden attempts to be bored with sex to get rid of a prostitute). But no single scene from his novel completely demonstrates this peculiar strain of comedy in Salinger: it pervades, seeps into, almost every incident.

When one is reading Salinger, one accepts his carefully placed "New Yorkerish" style and tone, and surrenders one's mind almost completely. It is only when you put the story aside and turn to other contemporary writers and to other fictional methods and techniques that you begin to wonder whether the immediacy and vividness of Salinger might be limited in power. Nowhere in Salinger do we find ourselves plunged into the emotional coiling and recoiling provoked by passages from Styron's novel, *Lie Down in Darkness.* Nowhere in Salinger is a character moved against the murky intensity-in-depth of a Nelson Algren Chicago scene, in *The Man with the Golden Arm.* Nowhere is a character revealed by the great clots of heterogeneous detail yoked together in single crowded sentences, as by Saul Bellow in *The Adventures of Augie March.*

But despite the temptations of comparison there remains one's conviction that Salinger is deeply and seriously committed in his fiction. Further, a little research into the Salinger canon reveals that two of his major creations, Holden Caulfield and Seymour Glass, the young husband of **"A Perfect Day for Banana Fish,"** have deep roots in Salinger's own imagination. His novel, in its way, is as much a final version of "work in progress" as are the novels of his more literary contemporaries. . . . (pp. 216-17)

This extrinsic information helps verify one's feeling that there is actually more weight to his explorations of human alienation than his bright dialogue and his frugal use of background and event might suggest. Moreover, Salinger's nonliterary status leaves him, as a serious writer, almost unique as a wholly free agent, unhampered by the commitments of his more dedicated contemporaries to one or another school of critics. One might guess that this is Salinger's most precious asset. Rather than wishing quarterly significance or "greatness" on him, we can be content to take him for what he is: a beautifully deft, professional performer who gives us a chance to catch quick, half-amused, half-frightened glimpses of ourselves and our contemporaries, as he confronts us with his brilliant mirror images. (p. 217)

David Stevenson, "J. D. Salinger: The Mirror of Crisis," in The Nation, *New York, Vol. 184, No. 10, March 9, 1957, pp. 215-17.*

CHARLES H. KEGEL

[*The essay excerpted below was originally published in* Western Humanities Review, *Spring, 1957.*]

Admirers of J. D. Salinger's *The Catcher in the Rye* ought to have welcomed the exciting analysis of that novel in the Spring, 1956 issue of *Western Humanities Review.* One may not agree in every particular with Heiserman and Miller's "J. D. Salinger: Some Crazy Cliff" [see *CLC,* Volume 12], yet the article serves as a very convincing notice to students of recent American fiction that *The Catcher in the Rye* deserves careful, critical attention. Notwithstanding the rather insensitive and highhanded action of puritanical censorship groups like the Detroit Police Department, which removed the work from Detroit book stalls as "pornographic trash," many once-through-quickly readers have sensed in Salinger's novel a dignity which transcends the apprehension of prudish minds. Heiserman and Miller have gone still further and have shown that that dignity governs both the theme and the structure of the novel. By doing so, they have sent us back for a fresh and more serious look.

The Catcher in the Rye can certainly be read, as Heiserman and Miller suggest, as a double-barreled quest: first, for "acceptance, stability, a life embosomed upon what is known and can be trusted," second, for "a Truth which is unwarped by stability." Without contradicting this interpretation, however, the novel can also be read as Holden Caulfield's quest for communicability with his fellow man, and the hero's first person after-the-fact narration indicates, of course, that he has been successful in his quest.

Like Stephen Dedalus of [James Joyce's] *A Portrait of the Artist as a Young Man,* Caulfield is in search of the Word. His problem is one of communication: as a teen-ager, he simply cannot get through to the adult world which surrounds him; as a *sensitive* teen-ager, he cannot even get through to others of his own age. (pp. 53-4)

Caulfield places most of his attention . . . on the sympathetic rapport which must exist between communicators. He asks but one thing of those he talks with, sincerity; he asks only that they *mean* what they say. If they tell him, as does Maurice, the elevator operator, that the price of goods is "Five bucks a throw," Caulfield expects to pay only five dollars. If they ask, as did Mrs. Antolini, about the health of his mother, Caulfield expects sincere concern about his mother's health; he expects that the questioner *actually* wants an answer to her question and will not interrupt him half way through it. Throughout the novel, he is troubled with people who are not listening to what he says, who are talking only to be polite, not because they want to communicate ideas. Like Hamlet, a "sad, screwed-up type guy" like himself, Caulfield is bothered by words and word formulas which only "seem," which are "phony." The honesty and sincerity which he cannot find in others, he attempts to maintain in himself. His repeated assertions that something he has said is *"really"* so demonstrate his attempt to keep faith with the Word. He is particularly distressed by the occasional realization that he too must be phony to exist in the adult world. With regard to the insincere "Glad to've met you" formula, he laments that "if you want to stay alive, you have to say that stuff, though."

As I have indicated, the main reason for Caulfield's communicative difficulty lies in his absolute hatred of phoniness. And he finds that phoniness, that hypocrisy, not only in the world of his personal contacts, but in the world of art as well. He detests phony books, phony music, phony movies and plays. He sees Hamlet as a "sad, screwed-up type guy" and wants him played that way instead of "like a goddam general." Likewise he is bothered by the way people "clap for the wrong things" and hence corrupt the promising artist. Very poignantly he understands the plight of Ernie, the piano player, or of brother D. B., once a sincere writer, but now "out in Hollywood . . . being a prostitute." (pp. 54-5)

Holden Caulfield's inability to communicate satisfactorily with others represents itself symbolically in the uncompleted telephone calls and undelivered messages which permeate the novel. Seeing a phone booth is almost more than he can stand, for he almost constantly feels like "giving somebody a buzz." On fifteen separate occasions he gets the urge to communicate by phone, yet only four calls are completed, and those with unfortunate results. Usually the urge dies without his having even attempted to place the call; he seems fearful of what the results will be and rationalizes, "I wasn't in the mood." Likewise, none of the several verbal messages he asks others to deliver for him gets through to the intended receiver; he simply cannot succeed in making contact.

Growing logically out of this prolonged incommunicability is Caulfield's intention to become a deaf-mute. So repulsed is he by the phoniness around him that he despairs of communicating with anybody, and in a passage fraught with import, he contemplates a retreat within himself.

> I figured I could get a job at a filling station somewhere, putting gas and oil in people's cars. I didn't care what kind of a job it was, though. Just so people didn't know me and I didn't know anybody. I thought what I'd do was, I'd pretend I was one of those deaf-mutes. That way I wouldn't have to have any goddam stupid useless conversations with anybody. If anybody wanted to tell me something, they'd have to write it on a piece of paper and shove it over to me. They'd get bored as hell doing that after a while, and then I'd be through with having conversations for the rest of my life. Everybody'd think I was just a poor deaf-mute bastard and they'd leave me alone. . . . I'd cook all my own food, and later on, if I wanted to get married or something, I'd meet this beautiful girl that was also a deaf-mute and we'd get married. She'd come and live in my cabin with me, and if she wanted to say anything to me, she'd have to write it on a goddam piece of paper, like everybody else.

Significantly, the fact that a message does get through to Phoebe—the only successful communication in the entire novel—leads toward the abandonment of the deaf-mute retreat. The Rousseauistic-Wordsworthian theme of childhood innocence and sincerity which Salinger had played upon so effectively in **"For Esmé—with Love and Squalor"** works its magic again. It is Phoebe who furnishes the clue to the solution of his problem, and when he refuses to ride the carrousel with her and thus gives up his idealistic attempts "to grab for the gold ring," he has initiated his transition from adolescence to adulthood. He does not, of course, capitulate to the phoniness of life, but he attains an attitude of tolerance, understanding, and love which will make it endurable. There can be no doubt but that when he returns to New York—for he, unlike Dedalus, will return home—he will be in the mood to give "old Jane a buzz." (pp. 55-6)

Charles H. Kegel, "Incommunicability in Salinger's 'The Catcher in the Rye'," in Studies in J. D. Salinger: Reviews, Essays, and Critiques of 'The Catcher in the Rye' and Other Fiction, *edited by Marvin Laser and Norman Fruman, The Odyssey Press, 1963, pp. 53-6.*

MAXWELL GEISMAR

He worked on **The Catcher in the Rye** for about ten years, J. D. Salinger told us, and when it appeared in 1951, it evoked both critical and popular acclaim. . . .

Salinger's short stories in the *New Yorker* had already created a stir. In undergraduate circles, and particularly in the women's colleges, this fresh voice, which plainly showed its debt to Ring Lardner, but had its own idiom and message, began to sound prophetic. (p. 195)

But just what is the time spirit that he expresses? The **Catcher**'s hero has been expelled from Pencey Prep as the climax of a long adolescent protest. The history teacher who tries to get at the causes of Holden Caulfield's discontent emerges as a moralistic pedagogue, who picks his nose. ("He was really getting the old thumb right in there.") During his farewell lecture, Holden is restless, bored—"I moved my ass a little bit on the bed"—and then suddenly uneasy. "I felt sorry as hell for him all of a sudden. But I just couldn't hang around there any longer." This refrain echoes through the narrative; and the rebellious young hero ends up by being "sorry" for all the jerks, morons, and queers who seem to populate the fashionable and rich preparatory school world.

He is also scornful of all the established conventions as "very big deal." (Another standard refrain in the story.) He seems to be the only truly creative personage in this world, and, though he has failed all his courses except English, he has his own high, almost absolute, standards of literature, at least. (pp. 195-96)

[The novel's action is] centered around the athlete Stradlater, who is "a very sexy bastard," and who has borrowed Holden Caulfield's jacket and his girl. Stradlater is "unscrupulous" with girls; he has a very *sincere* voice which he uses to snow them with, while he gives them the time, usually in the back seat of the car. Thinking about all this, Holden gets nervous ("I damn near puked"). In his room, he puts on his pajamas, and the old hunting hat which is his talisman of true rebellion and creativity, and starts out to write the English theme (which Stradlater will use as his own) about his dead brother Allie's baseball mitt. Yet when the athlete returns from his date, full of complacency about Holden's girl and of contempt for Holden's essay, this weakling-hero provokes him into a fight. (p. 196)

Later, nursing a bloody nose as the price of his defiant tongue, he wanders in to old Ackley's room for companionship. . . . But he can find no comfort or solace in the room which stinks of dirty socks. Ackley is even more stupid than Stradlater. "Stradlater was a goddam genius next to Ackley." A familiar mood of loneliness and despair descends upon him. . . . He counts his dough ("I was pretty loaded. My grandmother'd just sent me a wad about a week before.") and says good-by. . . . (pp. 196-97)

The Catcher in the Rye is eminently readable and quotable in its tragicomic narrative of preadolescent revolt. Compact, taut, and colorful, the first half of the novel presents in brief compass all the petty horrors, the banalities, the final mediocrity of the typical American prep school. Very fine—and not sustained or fulfilled, as fiction. For the later sections of the narrative are simply an episodic account of Holden Caulfield's "lost week end" in New York City which manages to sustain our interest but hardly deepens our understanding.

There are very ambiguous elements, moreover, in the portrait of this sad little screwed-up hero. His urban background is curiously shadowy, like the parents who never quite appear in the story, like the one pure adolescent love affair which is now "ruined" in his memory. The locale of the New York sections is obviously that of a comfortable middle-class urban Jewish society where, however, all the leading figures have become beautifully Anglicized. Holden and Phoebe Caulfield: what perfect American social register names which are presented to us in both a social and a psychological void! Just as the hero's interest in the ancient Egyptians extends only to the fact that they created mummies, so Salinger's own view of his hero's environment omits any reference to its real nature and dynamics.

Though the book is dedicated to Salinger's mother, the fictional mother in the narrative appears only as a voice through the wall. The touching note of affection between the brother and sister is partly a substitute for the missing child-parent relationships (which might indeed clarify the nature of the neurotic hero), and perhaps even a sentimental evasion of the true emotions in a sibling love. The only real creation (or half-creation) in this world is Holden Caulfield himself. And that "compassion," so much praised in the story, and always expressed in the key phrase, "You had to feel sorry"—for him, for her, for them—also implies the same sense of superiority. If this hero really represents the nonconformist rebellion of the Fifties, he is a rebel without a past, apparently, and without a cause.

The Catcher in the Rye protests, to be sure, against both the academic and social conformity of its period. But what does it argue *for?* When Holden mopes about the New York museum which is almost the true home of his discredited childhood, he remembers the Indian war-canoes "about as long as three goddam Cadillacs in a row." He refuses any longer to participate in the wealthy private boys' schools. . . . Fair enough; while he also rejects the notion of a conventional future in which he would work in an office, make a lot of dough, ride in cabs, play bridge, or go to the movies. But in his own private vision of a better life, this little catcher in the rye sees only those "thousands of little children" all playing near the dangerous cliff, "and nobody's around—nobody big, I mean—except me" to rescue them from their morbid fate.

This is surely the differential revolt of the lonesome rich child, the conspicuous display of leisure-class emotions, the wounded affections, never quite faced, of the upper-class orphan. This is the *New Yorker* school of ambiguous finality at its best. But Holden Caulfield's real trouble, as he is told by the equally precocious Phoebe is that he doesn't like *any*thing that is happening. "You don't like any schools. You don't like a million things. You *don't.*" This is also the peak of well-to-do and neurotic anarchism—the one world of cultivated negation in which all those thousands of innocent, pure little children are surely as doomed as their would-be and somewhat paranoid savior. "I have a feeling that you're riding for some kind of a terrible, terrible fall," says the last and best teacher in Holden's tormented academic career. But even this prophetic insight is vitiated by the fact that Mr. Antolini, too, is one of those flits and perverty guys from whom the adolescent hero escapes in shame and fear.

He is still, and forever, the innocent child in the evil and hostile universe, the child who can never grow up. And no wonder that he hears, in the final pages of the narrative, only a chorus of obscene sexual epithets which seem to surround the little moment of lyric happiness with his childlike sister. The real achievement of *The Catcher in the Rye* is that it manages so gracefully to evade just those central questions which it raises, and to preserve both its verbal brilliance and the charm of its emotions within the scope of its own dubious literary form. It is still Salinger's best work, if a highly artificial one, and the caesuras, the absences, the ambiguities at the base of this writer's work became more obvious in his subsequent books. (pp. 197-99)

Maxwell Geismar, "J. D. Salinger: The Wise Child and the 'New Yorker' School of Fiction," in his American Moderns: From Rebellion to Conformity, *Hill and Wang, 1958, pp. 195-209.*

DONALD P. COSTELLO

[*The essay excerpted below was originally published in* American Speech, *October, 1959.*]

A study of the language of J. D. Salinger's *The Catcher in the*

Rye can be justified not only on the basis of literary interest, but also on the basis of linguistic significance. Today we study *The Adventures of Huckleberry Finn* (with which many critics have compared *The Catcher in the Rye*) not only as a great work of literary art, but as a valuable study in 1884 dialect. In coming decades, *The Catcher in the Rye* will be studied, I feel, not only as a literary work, but also as an example of teenage vernacular in the 1950's. As such, the book will be a significant historical linguistic record of a type of speech rarely made available in permanent form. Its linguistic importance will increase as the American speech it records becomes less current.

Most critics who looked at *The Catcher in the Rye* at the time of its publication thought that its language was a true and authentic rendering of teenage colloquial speech. . . . [Only] the writers for the *Catholic World* and the *Christian Science Monitor* denied the authenticity of the book's language, but both of these are religious journals which refused to believe that the 'obscenity' was realistic. (pp. 92-3)

In addition to commenting on its authenticity, critics have often remarked—uneasily—the 'daring,' 'obscene,' 'blasphemous' features of Holden's language. Another commonly noted feature of the book's language has been its comic effect. And yet there has never been an extensive investigation of the language itself. That is what this paper proposes to do.

Even though Holden's language is authentic teenage speech, recording it was certainly not the major intention of Salinger. He was faced with the artistic task of creating an individual character, not with the linguistic task of reproducing the exact speech of teenagers in general. Yet Holden had to speak a recognizable teenage language, and at the same time had to be identifiable as an individual. This difficult task Salinger achieved by giving Holden an extremely trite and typical teenage speech, overlaid with strong personal idiosyncrasies. There are two major speech habits which are Holden's own, which are endlessly repeated throughout the book, and which are, nevertheless, typical enough of teenage speech so that Holden can be both typical and individual in his use of them. It is certainly common for teenagers to end thoughts with a loosely dangling 'and all,' just as it is common for them to add an insistent 'I really did,' 'It really was.' But Holden uses these phrases to such an overpowering degree that they become a clear part of the flavor of the book; they become, more, a part of Holden himself, and actually help to characterize him.

Holden's 'and all' and its twins, 'or something,' 'or anything,' serve no real, consistent linguistic function. They simply give a sense of looseness of expression and looseness of thought. (pp. 93-4)

Holden's informal, schoolboy vernacular is particularly typical in its 'vulgarity' and 'obscenity.' No one familiar with prep-school speech could seriously contend that Salinger overplayed his hand in this respect. On the contrary, Holden's restraints help to characterize him as a sensitive youth who avoids the most strongly forbidden terms, and who never uses vulgarity in a self-conscious or phony way to help him be 'one of the boys.' *Fuck,* for example, is never used as a part of Holden's speech. The word appears in the novel four times, but only when Holden disapprovingly discusses its wide appearance on walls. The Divine name is used habitually by Holden only in the comparatively weak *for God's sake, God,* and *goddam.* The stronger and usually more offensive

for Chrissake or *Jesus* or *Jesus Christ* are used habitually by Ackley and Stradlater; but Holden uses them only when he feels the need for a strong expression. He almost never uses *for Chrissake* in an unemotional situation. *Goddam* is Holden's favorite adjective. This word is used with no relationship to its original meaning, or to Holden's attitude toward the word to which it is attached. It simply expresses an emotional feeling toward the object: either favorable, as in 'goddam hunting cap'; or unfavorable, as in 'ya goddam moron'; or indifferent, as in 'coming in the goddam windows.' (p. 96)

Other crude words are also often used in Holden's vocabulary. *Ass* keeps a fairly restricted meaning as a part of the human anatomy, but it is used in a variety of ways. It can refer simply to that specific part of the body ('I moved my ass a little'), or be a part of a trite expression ('freezing my ass off'; in a half-assed way'), or be an expletive ('Game, my ass.'). *Hell* is perhaps the most versatile word in Holden's entire vocabulary. . . . So far is Holden's use of *hell* from its original meaning that he can use the sentence 'We had a helluva time' to mean that he and Phoebe had a decidedly pleasant time downtown shopping for shoes. The most common function of *hell* is as the second part of a simile, in which a thing can be either 'hot as hell' or, strangely, 'cold as hell'; 'sad as hell' or 'playful as hell'; 'old as hell' or 'pretty as hell.' Like all of these words, *hell* has no close relationship to its original meaning.

Both *bastard* and *sonuvabitch* have also drastically changed in meaning. They no longer, of course, in Holden's vocabulary, have any connection with the accidents of birth. Unless used in a trite simile, *bastard* is a strong word, reserved for things and people Holden particularly dislikes, especially 'phonies.' *Sonuvabitch* has an even stronger meaning to Holden; he uses it only in the deepest anger. When, for example, Holden is furious with Stradlater over his treatment of Jane Gallagher, Holden repeats again and again that he 'kept calling him a moron sonuvabitch.'

The use of crude language in *The Catcher in the Rye* increases, as we should expect, when Holden is reporting schoolboy dialogue. When he is directly addressing the reader, Holden's use of such language drops off almost entirely. There is also an increase in this language when any of the characters are excited or angry. Thus, when Holden is apprehensive over Stradlater's treatment of Jane, his *goddams* increase suddenly to seven on a single page. (p. 97)

Holden's slang use of *crazy* is both trite and imprecise. 'That drives me crazy' means that he violently dislikes something; yet 'to be crazy about' something means just the opposite. In the same way, to be 'killed' by something can mean that he was emotionally affected either favorably ('That story just about killed me.') or unfavorably ('Then she turned her back on me again. It nearly killed me.'). This use of *killed* is one of Holden's favorite slang expressions. Heiserman and Miller are, incidentally, certainly incorrect when they conclude: 'Holden always lets us know when he has insight into the absurdity of the endlessly absurd situations which make up the life of a sixteen-year-old by exclaiming, "It killed me." Holden often uses this expression with no connection to the absurd; he even uses it for his beloved Phoebe. The expression simply indicates a high degree of emotion—any kind. It is hazardous to conclude that any of Holden's slang has a precise and consistent meaning or function. These same critics fall into the same error when they conclude that Holden's use of the adjective *old* serves as 'a term of endearment.' Holden appends this word to almost every character, real or fictional, mentioned in the novel, from the hated 'old Maurice' to 'old Peter Lorre,' to 'old Phoebe,' and even 'old Jesus.' . . . All we can conclude from Holden's slang is that it is typical teenage slang: versatile yet narrow, expressive yet unimaginative, imprecise, often crude, and always trite.

Holden has many favorite slang expressions which he overuses. In one place, he admits:

> 'Boy!' I said. I also say 'Boy!' quite a lot. Partly because I have a lousy vocabulary and partly because I act quite young for my age sometimes.

But if Holden's slang shows the typically 'lousy vocabulary' of even the educated American teenager, this failing becomes even more obvious when we narrow our view to Holden's choice of adjectives and adverbs. The choice is indeed narrow, with a constant repetition of a few favorite words: *lousy, pretty, crumby, terrific, quite, old, stupid*—all used, as is the habit of teenage vernacular, with little regard to specific meaning. Thus, most of the nouns which are called 'stupid' could not in any logical framework be called 'ignorant,' and, as we have seen, *old* before a proper noun has nothing to do with age.

Another respect in which Holden was correct in accusing himself of having a 'lousy vocabulary' is discovered in the ease with which he falls into trite figures of speech. We have already seen that Holden's most common simile is the worn and meaningless 'as hell', but his often-repeated 'like a madman' and 'like a bastard' are just about as unrelated to a literal meaning and are easily as unimaginative. Even Holden's nonhabitual figures of speech are usually trite: 'sharp as a tack'; 'hot as a firecracker'; 'laughed like a hyena'; 'I know old Jane like a book'; 'drove off like a bat out of hell'; 'I began to feel like a horse's ass'; 'blind as a bat'; 'I know Central Park like the back of my hand.'

Repetitious and trite as Holden's vocabulary may be, it can, nevertheless, become highly effective. For example, when Holden piles one trite adjective upon another, a strong power of invective is often the result:

> He was a goddam stupid moron.
> Get your dirty stinking moron knees off my chest.
> You're a dirty stupid sonuvabitch of a moron.

And his limited vocabulary can also be used for good comic effect. Holden's constant repetition of identical expressions in countless widely different situations is often hilariously funny.

But all of the humor in Holden's vocabulary does not come from its unimaginative quality. Quite the contrary, some of his figures of speech are entirely original; and these are inspired, dramatically effective, and terribly funny. As always, Salinger's Holden is basically typical, with a strong overlay of the individual:

> He started handling my exam paper like it was a turd or something.
>
> He put my goddam paper down then and looked at me like he'd just beaten the hell out of me in ping-pong or something.
>
> That guy Morrow was about as sensitive as a goddam toilet seat.

> Old Marty was like dragging the Statue of Liberty around the floor.

Another aspect in which Holden's language is typical is that it shows the general American characteristic of adaptability—apparently strengthened by his teenage lack of restraint. It is very easy for Holden to turn nouns into adjectives, with the simple addition of a *-y:* 'perverty,' 'Christmasy,' 'vomity-looking,' 'whory-looking,' 'hoodlumy-looking,' 'show-offy,' 'flitty-looking,' 'dumpy-looking,' 'pimpy,' 'snobby,' 'fisty.' Like all of English, Holden's language shows a versatile combining ability: 'They gave Sally this little blue butt-twitcher of a dress to wear' and 'That magazine was some little cheerer upper.' Perhaps the most interesting aspect of the adaptability of Holden's language is his ability to use nouns as adverbs: 'She sings it very Dixieland and whorehouse, and it doesn't sound at all mushy.'

As we have seen, Holden shares, in general, the trite repetitive vocabulary which is the typical lot of his age group. But as there are exceptions in his figures of speech, so are there exceptions in his vocabulary itself, in his word stock. An intelligent, well-read ('I'm quite illiterate, but I read a lot'), and educated boy, Holden possesses, and can use when he wants to, many words which are many a cut above Basic English, including 'ostracized,' 'exhibitionist,' 'unscrupulous,' 'conversationalist,' 'psychic,' 'bourgeois.' Often Holden seems to choose his words consciously, in an effort to communicate to his adult reader clearly and properly, as in such terms as 'lose my virginity,' 'relieve himself,' 'an alcoholic'; for upon occasion, he also uses the more vulgar terms 'to give someone the time,' 'to take a leak,' 'booze hound.' Much of the humor arises, in fact, from Holden's habit of writing on more than one level at the same time. Thus, we have such phrases as 'They give guys the ax quite frequently at Pencey' and 'It has a very good academic rating, Pencey.'' Both sentences show a colloquial idiom with an overlay of consciously selected words.

Such a conscious choice of words seems to indicate that Salinger, in his attempt to create a realistic character in Holden, wanted to make him aware of his speech, as, indeed, a real teenager would be when communicating to the outside world. . . . Sometimes Holden stops specifically to interpret slang terms, as when he wants to communicate the fact that Allie liked Phoebe: 'She killed Allie, too. I mean he liked her, too.' (pp. 98-101)

In grammar, too, as in vocabulary, Holden possesses a certain self-consciousness. . . . Holden is, in fact, not only aware of the existence of 'grammatical errors,' but knows the social taboos that accompany them. He is disturbed by a schoolmate who is ashamed of his parents' grammar, and he reports that his former teacher, Mr. Antolini, warned him about picking up 'just enough education to hate people who say, "It's a secret between he and I".'

Holden is a typical enough teenager to violate the grammar rules, even though he knows of their social importance. His most common rule violation is the misuse of *lie* and *lay,* but he also is careless about relative pronouns ('about a traffic cop that falls in love'), the double negative ('I hardly didn't even know I was doing it'), the perfect tenses ('I'd woke him up'), extra words ('like as if all you ever did at Pencey was play polo all the time'), pronoun number ('it's pretty disgusting to watch somebody picking their nose'), and pronoun position ('I and this friend of mine, Mal Brossard'). More remarkable, however, than the instances of grammar rule violations is Holden's relative 'correctness.' Holden is always intelligible, and is even 'correct' in many usually difficult constructions. Grammatically speaking, Holden's language seems to point up the fact that English was the only subject in which he was not failing. (p. 102)

Now that we have examined several aspects of Holden's vocabulary and grammar, it would be well to look at a few examples of how he puts these elements together into sentences. The structure of Holden's sentences indicates that Salinger thinks of the book more in terms of spoken speech than written speech. Holden's faulty structure is quite common and typical in vocal expression; I doubt if a student who is 'good in English' would ever create such sentence structure in writing. . . .

There are other indications that Holden's speech is vocal. In many places Salinger mildly imitates spoken speech. Sentences such as 'You could tell old Spencer'd got a big bang out of buying it' and 'I'd've killed him' are repeated throughout the book. Yet it is impossible to imagine Holden taking pen in hand and actually writing 'Spencer'd' or 'I'd've.' Sometimes, too, emphasized words, or even parts of words, are italicized, as in 'Now *shut up,* Holden. God damm it— I'm *warn*ing ya.' This is often done with good effect, imitating quite perfectly the rhythms of speech. . . . (p. 103)

The language of **The Catcher in the Rye** is, as we have seen, an authentic artistic rendering of a type of informal, colloquial, teenage American spoken speech. It is strongly typical and trite, yet often somewhat individual; it is crude and slangy and imprecise, imitative yet occasionally imaginative, and affected toward standardization by the strong efforts of schools. But authentic and interesting as this language may be, it must be remembered that it exists, in **The Catcher in the Rye,** as only one part of an artistic achievement. The language was not written for itself, but as a part of a greater whole. Like the great Twain work with which it is often compared, a study of **The Catcher in the Rye** repays both the linguist and the literary critic; for as [Charles Kaplan] has said, 'In them, 1884 and 1951 speak to us in the idiom and accent of two youthful travelers who have earned their passports to literary immortality.' (pp. 103-04)

> *Donald P. Costello, "The Language of 'The Catcher in the Rye'," in* Studies in J. D. Salinger: Reviews, Essays, and Critiques of 'The Catcher in the Rye' and Other Fiction, *edited by Marvin Laser and Norman Fruman, The Odyssey Press, 1963, pp. 92-104.*

GEORGE STEINER

[*The essay excerpted below was originally published in the* Nation, *November 14, 1959.*]

Writing in *The Nation* in March 1957 [see excerpt above], Mr. David L. Stevenson expressed surprise at the fact that Salinger is "rarely acknowledged by the official guardians of our literary virtue." He can now rest assured. The heavy guns are in action along the entire critical front. Salinger's unique role in contemporary letters has been accorded full recognition. . . .

Obviously, critics are interested to find out why this should be so. Salinger has caught with uncanny precision the speech and thought-rhythms of the young. "The talk of his charac-

ters is, so to speak, righter than right" [according to Granville Hicks (see *CLC,* Volume 12)]. He can make a kind of poetry of "the simplest occasion," giving the shapes of art to the swift, raw, undigested materials of urban and college life (Mizener). The crisis of a Salinger fable makes the reader aware of how we are "members all of the lonely crowd" (Stevenson). (p. 113)

One might have thought that that was more than enough to account for the success of a good minor writer with an audience which is, by any traditional tokens, largely illiterate. But no. Where the Higher Criticism is at work more portentous issues are invoked. . . . Professors Heiserman and Miller tell us that *The Catcher in the Rye* belongs to an ancient narrative tradition, "perhaps the most profound in western fiction" [see *CLC,* Volume 12]. . . . In the course of exegesis, Salinger's young lout is also compared with Alyosha Karamazov, Aeneas, Ulysses, Gatsby, Ishmael, Hans Castorp and Dostoevsky's Idiot, and always rather to his own advantage.

With Salinger firmly enthroned in the critical pantheon, the gates were open to the happy hunt for literary influences and analogues. (p. 114)

In short: Salinger's tales are "comic masterpieces" (Charles Kaplan, *College English* . . . , 1956), and they may safely be compared with the classic in literature. The scholarly apparatus which such stature implies is also forthcoming. Professors Gwynn and Blotner provide a "Check-List of J. D. Salinger's Fiction" and a list of "Critical Studies of Salinger's Fiction." They devote a learned monograph to their man and come up with a pronouncement which caps the entire Salinger Industry:

> The problem he [Salinger] has set himself in this last period is no less than the utilization of transcendental mysticism in satiric fiction, something (as far as we know) never attempted before by an American writer, and by only a few in Western literature.

Roll of drums; exeunt Cervantes, Chekhov and other lesser souls.

In themselves, all these pomposities and exaggerations are of no great importance. But they do point to some of the things that are seriously wrong with contemporary American criticism.

First of all, they get Salinger's work badly out of focus and could do him a great deal of harm if he were so misguided as to read them (most probably he does not). Mr. Jerome David Salinger is neither Molière nor Chekhov. He is not yet Mark Twain (and by a long shot). Why should he be? He is a gifted and entertaining writer with one excellent short novel and a number of memorable stories to his credit. He has a marvelous ear for the semiliterate meanderings of the adolescent mind. He has caught and made articulate the nervous, quizzical, rough-edged spirit of the moment. He very obviously touches on major or traditional motifs: the failure of the bridges that are meant to link young and old, the mending power of a general, non-sexual love between human beings (something between friendship and compassion). **"For Esmé—with Love and Squalor"** is a wonderfully moving story, perhaps the best study to come out of the war of the way in which the greater facts of hatred play havoc in the private soul. **"The Laughing Man"** and **"Down at the Dinghy"** are fine sketches of the bruised, complicated world of children. But neither holds a candle to Joyce's *Araby* or to the studies of childhood in Dostoevsky. (pp. 115-16)

Salinger's virtues account for part of his vast appeal. But only for part. The rest is less exalted. The young like to read about the young. Salinger writes *briefly* (no need to lug home a big book or something, Lord help us, not available in paperback). He demands of his readers nothing in the way of literacy or political interest (in my time, college bull-sessions raged over *Doctor Faustus;* but that meant having heard of Hitler or Nietzsche or being dimly aware of a past writer called Goethe). Salinger flatters the very ignorance and moral shallowness of his young readers. He suggests to them that formal ignorance, political apathy and a vague *tristesse* are positive virtues. They open the heart to mystic intimations of love. This is where his cunning and somewhat shoddy use of Zen comes in. Zen is in fashion. People who lack even the rudiments of knowledge needed to read Dante or the nerve required by Schopenhauer, snatch up the latest paperback on Zen. "Salinger's constant allusions to the Bhagavad Gita, Sri Ramakrishna, Chuang-tsu, and the rest are only efforts to find alternate ways of expressing what his stories are about," says Mizener [see *CLC*, Volume 12]. I wonder. They are more likely a shrewd insight into the kind of half-culture which the present college generation revels in. (pp. 116-17)

These are the main facts. Why is literary criticism so determined to get them out of proportion?

First, there is a matter of language. Having added to the legacy of Germanic scholarship the jargon of the New Criticism, many American academic critics are no longer able to write with plainness or understatement. They have a vested interest in the complex and the sublime. . . . A new, probably rather minor achievement comes along, and at once critical language soars to sublimity. The result is a serious devaluation of critical coin. If one writes about Salinger as do Gwynn and Blotner, just how is one to write about Cervantes or Turgenev? The entire sense of discrimination between values which should be implicit in a critic's language goes lost. (p. 117)

American literary criticism has become a vast machine in constant need of new raw material. There are too many critical journals, too many seminars, too many summer schools and fellowships for critics. . . . With Eliot, Pound, Leavis, Edmund Wilson, Trilling, Blackmur, Tate and Yvor Winters in the field, just how much use is there in writing yet another essay on Dante or Shakespeare or Yeats? The quarry of greatness having been exhaustively mined, younger critics turn their big guns on to the smaller targets.

All this has serious consequences. There is, at the moment, a gross devaluation of standards. . . . If criticism does not serve to distinguish what is great from what is competent, it is not carrying out its proper task. . . . Of course, Salinger is a most skillful and original writer. Of course, he is worth discussing and praising. But not in terms appropriate to the master poets of the world, not with all the pomp and circumstance of final estimation. By all means, let us have Esmé, Daumier-Smith and all the Glasses. But let us not regard them as the house of Atreus reborn. (pp. 117-18)

> *George Steiner, "The Salinger Industry," in* Studies in J. D. Salinger: Reviews, Essays, and Critiques of 'The Catcher in the Rye' and Other Fiction, *edited by Marvin Laser and Norman Fruman, The Odyssey Press, 1963, pp. 113-18.*

EDWARD P. J. CORBETT

[The 1955 dismissal of a professor from a West Coast college for requiring his freshman students to read *The Catcher in the Rye*] may have been the earliest instance of a teacher getting into serious trouble over J. D. Salinger's book. Since that time, reports of irate protests from school boards, principals, librarians and parents have multiplied. . . . Curiously enough, the same kind of censure was once visited upon the book to which *The Catcher in the Rye* has most often been compared—Mark Twain's *Huckleberry Finn*.

Adult attempts to keep *The Catcher in the Rye* out of the hands of young people will undoubtedly increase, for it is the one novel that young people of the postwar generation have been reading and discussing avidly. I had firsthand evidence of students' reactions when *The Catcher in the Rye* was one of the three novels (the other two were Huxley's *Brave New World* and Conrad's *Under Western Eyes*) eligible for review two years ago in the Jesuit English Contest, an annual event among ten Midwestern Jesuit colleges and universities. At least 90 per cent of our students elected to write on Salinger's book. In fact, I have never witnessed on our campus as much eager discussion about a book as there was about *The Catcher in the Rye*. . . .

To the many people who have come to love the book and its hero, Holden Caulfield, all this controversy is puzzling and disturbing. They regard even the suggestion that the book needs defending as sacrilegious—almost as though they were being asked to vindicate the Constitution. Although their feelings of outrage are understandable, I feel that in view of the vast and continuing popularity of the book the objections should be confronted and appraised. My arguments in defense of *The Catcher in the Rye* are the common ones, quite familiar to those acquainted with other controversies about "forbidden" books.

The language of the book is crude, profane, obscene. This is the objection most frequently cited when the book has been banned. From one point of view, this objection is the easiest to answer; from another point of view, it is the hardest to answer.

Considered in isolation, the language *is* crude and profane. It would be difficult to argue, however, that such language is unfamiliar to our young people or that it is rougher than the language they are accustomed to hear in the streets among their acquaintances. But there is no question about it, a vulgar expression seen in print is much more shocking than one that is spoken. Lewd scribblings on sidewalks or on the walls of rest-rooms catch our attention and unsettle our sensibilities; and they become most shocking when they are seen in the sanctity of the printed page. (p. 441)

Granting the shock potential of such language, especially to youngsters, must we also grant it a corrupting influence? To deny that words can shape our attitudes and influence our actions would be to deny the rhetorical power of language. But to maintain that four-letter words of themselves are obscene and can corrupt is another matter. Interestingly enough, most reports about the banning of this novel have told that some principal or librarian or parent hastily paged through the book and spotted several four-letter words. That was evidence enough; the book must go. It is natural, although not always prudent, for adults to want to protect the young from shock. And this concern may be sufficient justification for adults wanting to keep the book out of the hands of grade-school children or the more immature high school students. But one of the unfortunate results of banning the book for this reason is that the very action of banning creates the impression that the book is nasty and highly corrosive of morals.

As has happened in many censorship actions in the past, parts are judged in isolation from the whole. The soundest defense that can be advanced for the language of this novel is a defense based on the art of the novel. Such a defense could be stated like this: Given the point of view from which the novel is told, and given the kind of character that figures as the hero, no other language was possible. The integrity of the novel demanded such language.

But even when readers have been willing to concede that the bold language is a necessary part of the novel, they have expressed doubts about the authenticity of Holden's language. Teen-age girls, I find, are especially skeptical about the authenticity of the language. "Prep-school boys just don't talk like that," they say. It is a tribute, perhaps, to the gentlemanliness of adolescent boys that when they are in the company of girls they temper their language. But, whatever the girls may think, prep-school boys do on occasion talk as Holden talks. As a matter of fact, Holden's patois is remarkably restrained in comparison with the blue-streak vernacular of his real-life counterparts. Holden's profanity becomes most pronounced in moments of emotional tension; at other times his language is notably tempered—slangy, ungrammatical, rambling, yes, but almost boyishly pure. Donald P. Costello, who made a study of the language of *The Catcher in the Rye* for the journal *American Speech* [see excerpt above], concluded that Salinger had given "an accurate rendering of the informal speech of an intelligent, educated, Northeastern American adolescent." (pp. 441-42)

Holden's swearing is so habitual, so unintentional, so ritualistic that it takes on a quality of innocence. Holden is characterized by a desperate bravado; he is constantly seeking to appear older than he really is. Despite that trait, however, Holden's profanity does not stem from the same motivation that prompts other adolescents to swear—the urge to seem "one of the boys." His profanity is so much ingrained by habit into the fabric of his speech that he is wholly unaware of how rough his language is. Twice his little sister Phoebe reminds him to stop swearing so much. Holden doesn't even pause to apologize for his language; he doesn't even advert to the fact that his sister has reprimanded him. And it is not because he has become callous, for this is the same boy who flew into a rage when he saw the obscenity scribbled on a wall where it might be seen by little children.

Some of the episodes in the book are scandalous. The episode commonly cited as being unfit for adolescents to read is the one about the prostitute in the hotel room. A case could be made out for the view that young people should not be exposed to such descriptions. It would be much the same case that one makes out in support of the view that children of a certain age should not be allowed to play with matches. But a convincing case cannot be, and never has been, made out for the view that vice should never be portrayed in a novel.

One shouldn't have to remind readers of what Cardinal Newman once said, that we cannot have a sinless literature about a sinful people. That reminder, however, has to be made whenever a censorship controversy comes up. The proper distinction in this matter is that no novel is immoral merely because vice is represented in it. Immorality creeps in as a result of the author's attitude toward the vice he is portraying and his manner of rendering the scene.

Let us consider the scene in question according to this norm in order to test the validity of the charge that it is scandalous. First of all, neither the novelist nor his character regards the assignation with the prostitute as proper or even as morally indifferent. The word *sin* is not part of Holden's vocabulary, but throughout the episode Holden is acutely aware that the situation in which he finds himself is producing an uncomfortable tension, a tormenting conflict, within him. And that vague awareness of disturbance, of something being "wrong," even if the character doesn't assign the label "sin" to it, is enough to preserve the moral tone of the scene in question.

Some readers seem to forget, too, that Holden didn't seek this encounter with the prostitute. He was trapped into it; he was a victim, again, of his own bravado. "It was against my principles and all," he says, "but I was feeling so depressed I didn't even *think*." Nor does he go through with the act. Embarrassment, nervousness, inexperience—all play a part in his rejection of the girl. But what influences his decision most, without his being aware of it, is his pity for the girl. That emotion is triggered by the sight of her green dress. It is that pity which introduces a moral note into Holden's choice. . . . All of the scenes about sexual matters are tastefully, even beautifully, treated. Is it any wonder that devotees of the novel are shocked by the suggestion that some of the scenes are scandalous?

Holden, constantly protesting against phoniness, is a phony himself. With this objection we move close to a charge against the novel that is damaging because it is based on sounder premises than the other two objections. No doubt about it, Salinger likes this boy, and he wants his readers to like the boy, too. If it could be shown that Salinger, despite his intentions, failed to create a sympathetic character, all the current fuss about the novel would be rendered superfluous, because the novel would eventually fall of its own dead weight.

Holden uses the word *phony* or some derivative of it at least 44 times. *Phoniness* is the generic term that Holden uses to cover all manifestations of cant, hypocrisy and speciosity. He is genuinely disturbed by such manifestations, so much so that, to use his own forthright term, he wants to "puke." The reason why he finds the nuns, his sister Phoebe and children in general so refreshing is that they are free of this phoniness.

But, as a number of people charge, Holden is himself a phony. He is an inveterate liar; he frequently masquerades as someone he is not; he fulminates against foibles of which he himself is guilty; he frequently vents his spleen about his friends, despite the fact that he seems to be advocating the need for charity. Maxwell Geismar [see excerpt above] puts this objection most pointedly when he says: "*The Catcher in the Rye* protests, to be sure, against both the academic and social conformity of its period. But what does it argue *for?*" Because of this inconsistency between what Holden wants other people to be and what he is himself, many readers find the boy a far from sympathetic character and declare that he is no model for our young people to emulate.

These readers have accurately described what Holden *does,* but they miss the point about what he *is.* Holden is the classic portrait of "the crazy, mixed-up kid," but with this significant difference: there is about him a solid substratum of goodness, genuineness and sensitivity. It is just this conflict between the surface and the substratum that makes the reading of the novel such a fascinating, pathetic and intensely moral experience. Because Holden is more intelligent and more sensitive than his confreres, he has arrived prematurely at the agonizing transition between adolescence and adulthood. He is precocious but badly seasoned. An affectionate boy, yearning for love and moorings, he has been cut off during most of his teen-age years from the haven of his family. Whatever religious training he has been exposed to has failed to touch him or served to confuse him. Accordingly, he is a young man adrift in an adult world that buffets and bewilders him.

The most salient mark of Holden's immaturity is his inability to discriminate. His values are sound enough, but he views everything out of proportion. Most of the manners and mores that Holden observes and scorns are not as monstrous as Holden makes them out to be. His very style of speech, with its extraordinary propensity for hyperbole, is evidence of this lack of a sense of proportion. Because he will not discriminate, he is moving dangerously close to that most tragic of all states, negation. His sister Phoebe tells him: "You don't like *any*thing that's happening." Holden's reaction to this charge gives the first glimmer of hope that he may seek the self-knowledge which can save him.

Holden must get to know himself. As Mr. Antolini, his former teacher, tells him: "You're going to have to find out where you want to go." But Holden needs most of all to develop a sense of humor. One of the most startling paradoxes about this book is that although it is immensely funny, there is not an ounce of humor in Holden himself. With the development of a sense of humor will come the maturity that can straighten him out. He will begin to see himself as others see him.

The lovely little scene near the end of the book in which Phoebe is going around and around on the carrousel can be regarded as an objective correlative of Holden's condition at the end of his ordeal by disillusionment. Up to this point, Holden has pursued his odyssey in a more or less straight line; but in the end, in his confusion and heartsickness, he is swirling around in a dizzying maelstrom. In the final chapter, however, it would appear that Holden has had his salutary epiphany. "I sort of *miss* everybody I told about," he says. Here is the beginning of wisdom. The reader is left with the feeling that Holden, because his values are fundamentally sound, will turn out all right.

I suspect that adults who object to Holden on the grounds of his apparent phoniness are betraying their own uneasiness. Holden is not like the adolescents in the magazine ads—the smiling, crew-cut, loafer-shod teen-agers wrapped up in the cocoon of suburban togetherness. He makes the adults of my generation uncomfortable because he exposes so much of what is meretricious in our way of life. (pp. 442-43)

[Some] concession must be made, I suppose, to the vigilantes who want to keep *The Catcher in the Rye* out of the hands of the very young. Future controversy will probably center on just what age an adolescent must be before he is ready for this book. That may prove to be a futile dispute. But I would hope that any decisions about the book would be influenced by the consideration, not that this is an immoral, corrupting book—for it is certainly not—but that it is a subtle, sophisticated novel that requires an experienced, mature reader.

Above all, let the self-appointed censors *read* the novel before they raise the barriers. (p. 443)

> Edward P. J. Corbett, "Raise High the Barriers, Censors," in America, Vol. CIV, No. 14, January 7, 1961, pp. 441-43.

IHAB HASSAN

[*Portions of the essay excerpted below were originally published in* Western Review, *Summer, 1957.*]

The Catcher in the Rye inevitably stands out as Salinger's only novel to date. As a "neo-picaresque," the book shows itself to be concerned far less with the education or initiation of an adolescent than with a dramatic exposure of the manner in which ideals are denied access to our lives and of the modes which mendacity assumes in our urban culture. The moving, even stabbing, qualities of the novel derive, to some extent, from Salinger's refusal to adopt a satirical stance. The work, instead, confirms the saving grace of vulnerability; its protest, debunking, and indictments presuppose a willing responsiveness on the part of its hero.

On the surface, Holden Caulfield is Salinger's typical quixotic hero in search, once again, of the simple truth. Actually, Holden is in flight from mendacity rather than in search of truth, and his sensitivity to the failures of the world is compounded with his self-disgust. In comparison with his dear, dead brother, Allie, a kind of redheaded saint who united intelligence and compassion as no other member of the family could, setting for all a standard of performance which they try to recapture, Holden seems intolerant, perhaps even harsh. The controlling mood of the novel—and it is so consistent as to be a principle of unity—is one of acute depression always on the point of breaking loose. But despair and depression are kept, throughout, in check by Holden's remarkable lack of self-interest, a quality of self-heedlessness which is nearly saintly, and by his capacity to invoke his adolescent imagination, to "horse around," when he is most likely to go to pot. These contrary pressures keep the actions of the novel in tension and keep the theme of sentimental disenchantment on the stretch; and they are sustained by a style of versatile humor.

The action begins at a prep school from which Holden has flunked out, and continues in various parts of Manhattan; it covers some three days of the Christmas season. The big city, decked out in holiday splendor and gaudiness, is nevertheless unprepared for Holden's naked vision, and it seldom yields any occasions of peace, charity, or even genuine merriment. From the moment Holden leaves Pencey behind, leaves its Stradlaters and Ackleys, its oafs, creeps, and hypocrites, and dons his red hunting cap—why not, it's a mad world, isn't it?—we know that we are on to an adventure of pure self-expression, if not self-discovery.

In New York, it is once again the same story of creeps and hypocrites revealed in larger perspective. We hardly need to recapitulate the crowded incidents of the novel to see that Holden is motivated by a compelling desire to commune and communicate, a desire constantly thwarted by the phoniness, indifference, and vulgarity that surround him. He resents the conditions which force upon him the burden of rejection. In protest against these conditions, he has devised a curious game of play-acting, of harmless and gratuitous lying, which is his way of coming to terms with a blistered sensibility, and of affirming his values of truth and imagination. But above all, he is continually performing the quixotic gesture. Thus he socks Stradlater, who is twice his weight, because he suspects the latter of having seduced Jean Gallagher, without any consideration of the fact that she is the kind of girl to keep all her kings, at checkers, in the back row. He gives money away to nuns. He can read a child's notebook all day and night. He furiously rubs out obscenities from the walls of schools. (pp. 272-73)

A closer look at *The Catcher in the Rye* might allow us to separate its real from imaginary failings. Mr. Aldridge, for instance, taking his cue perhaps from Phoebe's comment to her brother, "You don't like *anything* that's happening," has recently observed—Maxwell Geismar makes exactly the same point [see excerpts above]—that Holden "has objects for his contempt but no objects other than his sister for his love." It is true that Holden has *more* objects for his contempt than his love—this is the expense of his idealism and the price of his rebellion. But it is impossible to overlook his various degrees of affection for Allie, his dead brother, for James Castle, the boy who was killed because he wouldn't retract a statement he thought true, for the kettle drummer at Radio City, the nuns at the lunch counter, the kid humming the title song, or even the ducks in the park, without missing something of Holden's principal commitments. And his answer to Phoebe, "People never think anything is anything *really*. I'm getting goddam sick of it," may do for those who find these commitments rather slim. Nor can we disallow the feeling of pity which often modifies Holden's scorn, his pity for Ackley and the girls in the Lavender Room, or his confession to Antolini that he can hate people only part of the time, and that he quickly misses those whom he may have once hated. Holden, of course, is not in the least cynical; nor is he blind except to part of the truth which he can otherwise entertain so steadily. Still, there are those who feel that the novel accords no recognition to its hero, and that it fails to enlist our sense of tragedy. The lack of recognition, the avoidance of conversion and initiation, is almost as inherent in the structure of the novel as it is consonant with the bias of the American novel of adolescence. The action of the book is recollected by Holden who is out West recuperating from his illness, and Holden only chooses to tell us "about this madman stuff that happened to me around last Christmas"—nothing more. He refuses to relate incidents to his past or to his character, and he refuses to draw any conclusions from his experience: "If you want to know the truth, I don't *know* what I think about it. . . . About all I know is, I sort of *miss* everybody I told about. Even old Stradlater and Ackley, for instance. . . . Don't ever tell anybody anything. If you do, you start missing everybody." This is an embarrassed testament of love, full of unresolved ambiguities, the only lyrical and undramatic recognition the novel can afford. The partial blindness of Holden, which has been correctly attributed to Holden's juvenile impatience with the reality of compromise, is made more serious by Salinger's failure to modify Holden's point of view by any other. . . . There is also some danger that we may be too easily disarmed by the confessional candor of Salinger's novel. When Holden says time and time again, "I swear to God I'm crazy," the danger is equally great in taking Holden at his word as in totally discounting his claim. Holden does succeed in making us perceive that the world is crazy, but his vision is also a function of his own adolescent instability, and the vision, we must admit, is more narrow and biased than that of Huck Finn, Parson Adams, or Don Quixote. It is this narrowness that limits the comic effects of the work. Funny

it is without any doubt, and in a fashion that has been long absent from American fiction. But we must recall that true comedy is informed by the spirit of compromise, not intransigence. Huck Finn and Augie March are both, in this sense, closer to the assumptions of comedy than Holden Caulfield. This once understood, we can see how *The Catcher in the Rye* is *both* a funny and terrifying work—traditional distinctions of modes have broken down in our time—a work full of pathos in the original sense of the word. But suffering is a subjective thing, and the novel's sly insistence on suffering makes it a more subjective work than the two novels which relate the adventures of Huck Finn and Augie March. Adventure is precisely what Holden does not endure; his sallies into the world are feigned; his sacrificial burden, carried with whimsey and sardonic defiance, determines his fate. The fate is that of the American rebel-victim. (pp. 274-76)

Ihab Hassan, "J. D. Salinger," in his Radical Innocence: Studies in the Contemporary American Novel, *Princeton University Press, 1961, pp. 259-89.*

HUBERT I. COHEN

While recuperating in the sanitarium Holden Caulfield has probably told the institution's psychiatrist about "the madman stuff that happened to me around last Christmas," and we know for certain that he has told his brother D. B. about it. The psychiatrist seems not to have provided any insight, and Holden appears to have received no satisfaction from D. B., who was either unwilling or unable to interpret Holden's story for him. . . . (p. 355)

Having exhausted the possibility of getting help from people he knows—Sally, Carl Luce, Phoebe, Mr. Antolini (whose advice, whatever its merits, Holden is certainly too tired to understand and almost too tired to listen to), the psychiatrist, and D. B.—to whom can he turn? Like the Ancient Mariner, he turns to tell the "so many people," the people who do and "don't live in New York." He turns to us; to anyone who will listen. And what he expects from us is best stated in his own pathetic comment on Phoebe's response to his attempted explanation: "I'm not too sure old Phoebe knew what the hell I was talking about. I mean she's only a little child and all. But she was listening, at least. If somebody at least listens, it's not too bad." Desperate to be understood and to understand, Holden hopes that some one of us who hears his story will explain it to him, or, if that is too much to expect, will listen patiently while he tells it over and over—until he himself comes to understand the events and feelings he is relating. (pp. 355-56)

[Holden is] wont to evade discussion of certain of his feelings and actions. . . . He may find the truth too painful and himself not strong enough to face it. His evasive tactics embrace a number of common techniques: blatantly to suppress the facts (e.g., his having been kicked out of school); to change the subject; to give a misleading excuse (e.g., his reasons for not sleeping with the prostitute); or, perhaps, to plead ignorance, claiming that he does not "know" why he felt and acted the way he did. . . . Finally, as when he fails to call Jane, the one person who, besides Allie and Phoebe, fills his thoughts and daydreams, he will tell us that he does not "feel in the mood."

These are all effective means of evasion; a still better means of evading a subject is to talk about it vaguely. It is this vagueness, this blurring his feeling (or the facts), and not simple rationalization, suppression, or silence that Holden resorts to most frequently and most successfully. Although his language is often vital and arresting, he uses certain formulary words and phrases that blur the feeling or experience he is describing: "crazy," "madman," "funny," "stuff," "old," "always," "stupid," "know," "corny," "phony," "lousy," "goddam," "bastard." . . . The very repetition of these words and phrases, furthermore, establishes a ritualized language which augments the imprecision.

That Holden is being purposely imprecise may strike us initially as strange. We have seen that even though he says he has a "lousy vocabulary," he has and relishes the knack of using that vocabulary (and his metaphorical talent) to pin down the essential quality of a person or situation. Why, then, does he, both as the storyteller and as the troubled boy seeking understanding, use words that obscure the experiences he wants us to listen to and possibly interpret to him?

The answer to this question is rooted in Holden's attitude toward experience itself: in his consciousness of and anxiety over the fleeting quality of experience and in his distrust of the very stability which he urgently needs.

In the last section, Holden tells us that the psychoanalyst asked him what he thought about going back to school and applying himself. Holden's comment is: "It's such a stupid question, in my opinion. I mean how do you know what you're going to do till you *do* it? The answer is, you don't. I *think* I am, but how do I know? I swear it's a stupid question." This sense that life is in a state of flux is fundamental to Holden's thought and feeling. Each experience is different and must be responded to uniquely. Hence "phoniness," which involves playing a role or acting in a prescribed or habitual manner, is a cardinal folly. In not spontaneously expressing what one feels at the moment, one distorts the very nature of sentient life. This explains how Holden, while looking out of his hotel window, can admit that "it might be quite a lot of fun, in a crumby way, . . . if you were both sort of drunk and all, to get a girl and squirt water or something all over each other's face." It is all right, in other words, depending on the mood and the moment—but, says Holden, "the thing is, though, I don't *like* the idea."

Since Holden seems to accept completely the fluid nature of experience (it is the basis for many of his value judgments), he should have become at least partly reconciled to disorder. The truth is, however, that the fleetingness of experience is beginning to oppress him. There is too much flux. He keeps finding himself borne off balance, being unable to cope with his experiences because either he or the external circumstances have changed so radically. After Holden has told Sally he loves her, for example, he laments: "I *meant* it when I said it. I'm crazy. I swear to God I am," and we hear the same cry after Sally has refused to escape with him. Unable to understand why he asked her in the first place, he explodes: "The terrible part, though, is that I *meant* it when I asked her. That's the terrible part. I swear to God I'm a madman." (pp. 357-59)

Because of this unsettling sense of the flux of things, there has developed within Holden a compensatory desire for permanence. We encounter it first in his attempt to distill from his memories an impression of Pencey: "What I was really hanging around for, I was trying to feel some kind of a good-by. I mean I've left schools and places I didn't even know I was

leaving them. I hate that. I don't care if it's a sad good-by or a bad good-by, but when I leave a place I like to *know* I'm leaving it. If you don't, you feel even worse." And in his discussion of what the museum means to him his desire for stability is crystallized. . . .

> The best thing . . . in that museum was that everything always stayed right where it was. Nobody'd move. You could go there a hundred thousand times, and that Eskimo would still be just finished catching those two fish . . . and that squaw with the naked bosom would still be weaving that same blanket. Nobody'd be different. The only thing that would be different would be *you*. Not that you'd be so much older or anything. It wouldn't be that, exactly. You'd just be different, that's all. . . . I mean you'd be *different* in some way—I can't explain what I mean. And even if I could, I'm not sure I'd feel like it.

Although Holden insists he is unable (or unwilling) to explain, his examples of what he means make it clear that becoming "different" involves the loss of a frame of reference. What is devoutly to be wished, he says, is that "certain things they should stay the way they are. You ought to be able to stick them in one of those big glass cases and just leave them alone. I know that's impossible, but it's too bad anyway. Anyway, I kept thinking about all that while I walked."

Again and again we observe him thinking he has permanently realized a degree of stability and each time we witness his frustration as that is lost. In this scene, as Holden moves toward the museum thinking of the simultaneous desirability and "impossibility" of things' remaining the same, he is not depressed over the "impossibility" because it seems less absolute than usual. An experience of a few moments before has reassured him that not only people, but experiences could remain, in some degree, the same. On his way to the museum he had stopped to tighten a little girl's skate: "Boy, I hadn't had a skate key in my hand for years. It didn't feel funny, though. You could put a skate key in my hand fifty years from now, in pitch dark, and I'd still know what it is." The sense of stability that the skate key engenders is reinforced by the girl's being a "very nice, polite little kid." Holden seems to say that this kind of honesty, innocence, and genuine humanity is something one can almost *always* count on in children. "God, I love it when a kid's nice and polite when you tighten their skate for them or something. Most kids are. They really are." But the sense of stability and well-being derived from his thoughts of the museum and his contact with the skate key and the little girl are upset when, before he enters the museum, he stops to watch two boys on a seesaw: "One of them was sort of fat, and I put my hand on the skinny kid's end, to sort of even up the weight, but you could tell they didn't want me around, so I let them alone." Rejected by the boys, Holden re-enters the world of inconstancy and flux, lapses into his previous depression and again conceives of permanence as unattainable. "Then a funny thing happened. When I got to the museum, all of a sudden I wouldn't have gone inside for a million bucks. It just didn't appeal to me—and here I'd walked through the whole goddam park and looked forward to it and all." The reason for his sudden turnabout is left inexplicit, but perhaps it was that going into the museum at this time would heighten his sense of flux. Once inside he would find that he had changed too much or that the glass cases and their static exhibits made the instability of the outside world unbearable.

Holden's security and stability are further upset after his encounters with Sally, Phoebe, and (most shatteringly) with Mr. Antolini. Deciding to carry out his escape fantasy, he wants to say good-by to Phoebe before he leaves, but when he tries to get a message to her in his old school, he confronts the problem of stability and flux once again. He is worried that he will not "remember what it was like inside." "But I did," he says, momentarily reassured. "It was exactly the same as it was when I went there." He goes through a detailed description of the things that have stayed the same, and his feeling of security grows until he discovers that the obscene outer world, in the form of a word, has violated even this sanctuary: "I saw something that drove me crazy." His mind filled with pictures of himself protecting the children and killing the offender, he rubs out the obscene expression only to find it cut into the wood in another spot: "It's hopeless, anyway. If you had a million years to do it in, you couldn't rub out even *half* the 'Fuck you' signs in the world. It's impossible."

Waiting to meet Phoebe, Holden seeks refuge in another sanctuary, the museum. Before she comes, he meets and is charmed by two little boys who want to see the mummies. "Boy," says Holden, "I used to know exactly where they were, but I hadn't been in that museum in years." Nevertheless, he finds the mummies and gives the boys a lecture which is nearly a facsimile of his answer to the "optional essay question" he had written for Mr. Spencer after having studied the ancient Egyptians for nearly a month. Holden *"chose"* what concerned him—the ways to keep things from changing:

> The Egyptians are extremely interesting to us today for various reasons. Modern science would still like to know what the secret ingredients were that the Egyptians used when they wrapped up dead people so that their faces would not rot for innumerable centuries. This interesting riddle is still quite a challenge to modern science in the twentieth century.

The scene and the problem of flux and stability come to a climax when Holden finds the same haunting obscenity in the depths of his museum sanctuary—the Egyptian tombs. . . . With his disillusionment at its crest, his physical condition, which parallels his mental state, deteriorates, and he passes out in the museum's lavatory.

The intensity of Holden's need for stability is underscored in his final meeting with Phoebe. He is horrified by the fact that Phoebe has packed a bag and is ready to run away with him. Because he feels that Phoebe's not appearing in the school play will destroy what little order is left in his world, he turns on her. . . . (pp. 359-62)

Yet, a few minutes later, they arrive in the park and while watching Phoebe on the carrousel Holden briefly achieves a sense of stability once more. Present is an element of experience that has remained the same—"It [the carrousel] played that same song about fifty years ago when *I* was a little kid. That's one nice thing about carrousels, they always play the same songs." In addition, there are Phoebe's kiss and forgiveness, Holden's own decision to return home, and the unique movement of the carrousel—the flux (movement up and down and around) held to a fixed, circular pattern. This resolution seems to symbolize the kind of stability Holden has been longing for—flux and stability at one, movement within an orderly design.

> Boy, it began to rain like a bastard. . . . All the parents and mothers and everybody went over and stood right under the roof of the carrousel. . . . I got pretty soaking wet. . . . I didn't care, though. I felt so damn happy all of a sudden, the way old Phoebe kept going around and around. I was damn near bawling, I felt so damn happy, if you want to know the truth. I don't know why. It was just that she looked so damn *nice,* the way she kept going around and around, in her blue coat and all. God, I wish you could've been there.

The stability reached in this scene is momentary. There is no indication that Holden has lastingly resolved his conflicts. The flux and Holden's anxiety in the face of it both persist. As he finishes his story, we learn that he is in an institution, sick in body and mind alike.

We shall proceed to connect this ambivalent attitude of Holden's—this desire for change but anxiety in its presence, and the concomitant need for but distrust of stability—to the problem . . . [of] the disparity between Holden's language and his therapeutic need in telling his story. It is first necessary, however, that Holden's reason for telling his story to *us* be clear. His apparent irritation with us (in the very first line, in fact, he sounds as if we had begged him to tell us his story—"If you really want to hear about it") should not put us off or make us ignore his legitimate complaints against the advice he has been receiving (it has been either "phony," irrelevant, or badly timed). His annoyance with "a lot of people, especially this one psychoanalyst guy" who asked him if he thought he was going to do all right in the future is understandable in the light of his belief that no one can ever know what he is going to do until he does it. Since he does not know what has brought him to this institution in the first place, moreover, he is hardly in a position to predict. As for being irritated when D. B. asks him what he thinks about the events of those three days before Christmas, Holden insists that he has had no insight and, therefore, cannot give his older brother a neat analysis. Nevertheless, Holden's language and tone continue to create the impression that he wishes people would stop pestering him. But if he wants merely to be let alone, why, after so short a time (he says it was "last Saturday" that he told D. B. the story he has just finished telling us) *is* he telling us? The only answer seems to be that he *has* to tell, and that, as he said, "if somebody at least listens, it's not too bad." We are his last resort. By going over and over the events that have led to his breakdown, hopefully he will elicit the reasons for it; either he will come spontaneously to understand or someone will be able to explain them to him.

Yet in telling and retelling his story to a mass audience, Holden runs into a difficulty that is not therapeutic, but artistic. Although a close friend, a brother, or a psychoanalyst can listen to a story, sift the facts, note evasions, and ask questions to fill in conscious and unconscious omissions, a mass audience has to take what is given. It therefore demands that the storyteller present everything important as clearly and precisely as possible. This demand would seem to be in harmony with Holden's own therapeutic aims. He should want all important information out in the open so that his hearers can understand him and so that he himself can come to self-knowledge. Returning to the question posed earlier—why, then, is there so much blurring of feeling and fact, so much imprecision and evasion throughout the book?

The explanation is rooted not in that part of Holden which yearns for stability in the midst of flux—that is behind his telling the story in the first place—but in the Holden who believes that no two experiences *can* be the same. It is rooted in his rational opinion that to render events as fixed and rigid is to falsify them and in his emotional fear that such fixity kills and embalms. That is why he fears telling his experiences to himself or to us. To recapitulate them he must formulate them to some degree and thereby destroy their fluidity, their life-likeness. You cannot "put down" flux and have it remain true. It is like pinning a live butterfly to a display board. Suddenly, one no longer has a butterfly, but a dead thing that is *like* a butterfly. Holden regretfully admits that this is exactly what happens when he tells his story: "I'm sorry I told so many people about it. About all I know is, I sort of *miss* everybody I told about. Even old Stradlater and Ackley, for instance. I think I even miss that goddam Maurice. It's funny. Don't ever tell anybody anything. If you do, you start missing everybody." At least one reason why Holden is vague and imprecise, then, is to protect himself and his experiences. If one does not "fix" the experience "exactly" (Holden tries to make his listeners *think* they are getting things "exactly") one does not completely destroy its truth, its living quality. Thus, Holden's record of his experience is not written, as Mr. Antolini suggested it should be. The written word is too definite, too final. It "fixes" things forever. (pp. 362-64)

For Holden, telling about "the madman stuff" is merely a means of coming to grips with his experiences, but *The Catcher in the Rye* seems to have a somewhat larger significance for Salinger. By making Holden Caulfield a storyteller and involving him with unity and digression, flux and stasis, vague and precise language, the written versus the spoken word, problems that the literary artist has to face, Salinger seems to be suggesting something about art and artists, literary art in particular. He seems to suggest that the process which Holden is going through for the sake of his own sanity is analogous to the process the artist goes through, and that Holden's decision to persist no matter how painful the task resembles the choice of the artist. Holden shadows forth the trials the artist undergoes as he begins to look carefully and critically at his family, his friends, his society's conventions and facades, and his own illusions. In one of its aspects, *The Catcher in the Rye* is a portrait of an artist as a young man. (p. 366)

Hubert I. Cohen, " 'A Woeful Agony Which Forced Me to Begin My Tale': 'The Catcher in the Rye'," in Modern Fiction Studies, Vol. 12, No. 2, Autumn, 1966, pp. 355-66.

KENNETH HAMILTON

"I'm Crazy" presents the gist of the story of young Holden Caulfield which ten years later became *The Catcher in the Rye.* The first story tells how Holden, who fails at school and has a searching exchange of ideas with his young sister Phoebe, goes on to take up his first job convinced that he is not going to be "one of those successful guys." Although changed in details and filled out with many significant episodes resulting in a highly complex texture of narration, the novel is basically in line with the short story. At the same time, it also reflects the style of Salinger's writing coming to the fore from 1948 on. Thus the *Catcher* is as good a starting-point as any for looking at the works of his maturity. At this time the success-failure paradox is still a dominant theme, but the place of youthful innocence in explicating the theme is coming to the fore. Another way of speaking of this change in emphasis would be to say that Salinger is turning to write specifically

about love. But "love" in this context means, first and last, the power latent in innocent youth to meet the ravages of experience and win its peculiar kind of victories, victories in which the tensions between the outside and the inside of things are partly resolved, yet still remain. Existence in time and space represents, even in the presence of love, at once a threat and an opportunity, an illusion and the means of breaking through to reality.

The revulsion of the sixteen-year-old Holden against phoniness in each and every form is the most obvious facet in his character. The word "phony" has become associated so closely with Holden that it now carries the overtones of his use of it. And Holden applies the word to the false values of the materialistic adult world, with its unrestrained egotism and consequent double standards, subterfuges, venality, and violence. This world is all around him in his preparatory school, but so far he has been able to avoid surrendering completely to it. That he has compromised already we know from his style of speech, which is largely indistinguishable (on the outside view) from the profane, repetitive, debased coinage of his school fellows. He is as aware as we are, however, of what he calls his "yellow" side that gives in to conformity's pressures. Now at last he sees that childhood's evasions will no longer serve. His expulsion from school, being the third in a row, will precipitate an immediate crisis in relation to his parents. So, unprepared to act for himself, he runs away to lie low in New York City until he makes up his mind about the future. His flight from the small world of school into the big one of New York scares him badly when he faces, alone, the massed strength of the powers that stand against him. His only wish is to escape, and he persuades himself that he can actually run away permanently from society and live entirely without communicating with others. But his three-day descent into mental hell is ended with a resurrection through contact with the innocent strength and intuitive wisdom of his ten-year-old sister Phoebe, who has not yet been contaminated by the adult world.

There is an antithesis to "phony," and it is, as Warren French has pointed out, the word "nice" [see *CLC*, Volume 1]. Why these polar opposites have been so often overlooked is not really very puzzling. After all, the "phony" world is ever around us while the "nice" world appears only in quick glimpses on the occasion where the interior world shines through, like a light looming up out of heavy fog. When Holden has to decide whether he can avoid being pressed into the mould favored by his successful father, what are his resources? Against him stand both parents, the school that defers in all things to the successful, his elder brother D. B. who is prostituting his writing gifts in Hollywood, and the whole weight of the American way of life. His strength—and here lies the pathos of the story—is a failing one; for the integrity of his childhood vision has been broken, and he can find no new source of courage. What finally reduces Holden to almost complete despair is the discovery that the allies he is counting upon are all dead and unable to support him as once they did. There is his younger brother Allie, the child-poet whose baseball mitt was covered with poems, and who taught him that Emily Dickinson, not Rupert Brooke, was a true war poet (i.e., genuine conflict is inward, and poetry *is* as relevant to the war-game of life as it seems irrelevant to baseball). Allie is dead, although Holden calls out for his help on the streets of New York. The writers he admires are mostly dead, too, and certainly not available for intimate conversations over the telephone, as he thinks would happen in an ideal world. Physical death or distance would matter much less, all the same, were his own inner vision living. But at the moment it is not. It is attached to the dead past of a childhood innocence that cannot be revived. "Certain things should stay the way they are," is his futile command to the universe to come over to his side. But the ducks on the pond in Central Park, remembered with such affection, have gone long ago. And, in the very place erected to conserve the past unchanged, The Museum of Natural History, and in the very room where Egyptian embalmers' art of defying time is exhibited, he finds the obscene word reminding him of his loss of the innocent past through the invasion of the defiled present. You cannot make the world "nice," he concludes, since never in a thousand years could you wipe all the dirty words off the walls where children might see them. Nevertheless, he continues to dream of being a "Catcher in the Rye," who watches children at play beside "some crazy cliff" and is ready to catch them before they fall.

It is Phoebe the playing child who keeps *him* from falling to entire destruction. She reminds him that Allie is dead, and that the line of the song he overheard is not about *catching* but about *meeting*. Because she has innocence to trust him without fear of consequences, Holden is compelled to reconsider his irresponsible dreams of escaping in order to live a personal family life completely cut off from the human family. Finally, watching her happily riding on the carrousel in the park, he discovers that the "nice" world is still accessible and powerful. Phoebe before had accused him of not loving anything living. Now he discovers love. "It was just that she looked so damn *nice,* the way she kept going around and around, in her blue coat and all. God, I wish you could've been there."

Salinger's artistry in the *Catcher* is taut, complex, and balanced. Consider, for example, the associations exploited in the picture of Phoebe on the carrousel. Against the empty, brittle pleasures of the jostling millions of city-dwellers, Salinger balances the delight of two persons in personal intimacy free from the frenzies of sex. The relationships of brother and sister, lover and beloved, parent and child are fused. Swearing being a low form of prayer, Holden is not simply wishing his readers could have shared his experience, for he is actually appealing to the God before whose face the little ones on earth are always spiritually present. The picture of a girl in a blue coat on a carrousel echoes the subject of one of Rilke's poems, linking the event with the world of poetry. That is not all. Since blue is the traditional color of the Madonna's cloak, the image of the child who belongs both to the Kingdom of Heaven and to the Kingdom of Poetry coalesces with the image of the Pure Virgin, the Handmaid of the Lord and Mother of God. Of course Phoebe (i.e., Diana, the chaste goddess) looked "damn nice"—an oblique way of saying in our modern non-religious idiom, "*blessed.*" And all the time, in the midst of the wasteland of New York, the rain that brings to life the barren earth (it is the Christmas season) is falling. The carrousel's circular movement represents eternity, living time that cannot die. But Holden also realizes that, when children like his sister want to grasp "the gold ring" and are in danger of falling off the carrousel, you must not interfere. . . . The "nice" world is present for those who have eyes to see it. (pp. 22-5)

The balance as well as the complexity of Salinger's art is evident in the *Catcher.* The portrayal of Holden is realistic enough to satisfy those who see in him just an impetuous, ro-

mantic, undisciplined adolescent projecting onto society his own disturbed condition. The final scene leaves the issue, on the face of it, unresolved. Holden is in a psychiatric ward, evidently in California since his brother D. B. visits him from Hollywood. (Though Salinger now identifies Hollywood with *phony* dreams, the cinema is by no means universally condemned; and Phoebe adores all the proper non-Hollywood movies.) But he has not decided to submit to being "adjusted." He has discovered, however, that love is possible and that it must be extended to the phony. He *misses* every one, and specifically those who have recently wronged him. Therefore he has learned from Phoebe that the song he heard was not about catching but about meeting, when "coming through the rye." Life has its inescapably "wry" aspect; for example, the symbolically healing rain is also the physical cause of his being in the hospital. Yet the pilgrim soul must pass joyfully through the ambiguities of existence in order to meet others in love. Thus Holden's future is uncertain. Nevertheless he has grown in wisdom. His inner vision is no longer tied to a dead past. Underground the spirit spreads its greenery, and this knowledge supports the frightened adolescent who had previously watched with terror his foliage turn "yellow" as it became exposed to the frosts of the adult world that kill the creative imagination. (pp. 25-6)

Kenneth Hamilton, in his J. D. Salinger: A Critical Essay, *William B. Eerdmans, Publisher, 1967, 47 p.*

CLINTON W. TROWBRIDGE

To some, I fear, what I am about to argue will seem the most blatant form of mistruth, horrendous, even, in its lack of taste, a kind of literary sacrilege, in fact. Surely we have reached the end, they will say, when one can consider comparing the immortal Hamlet, Prince of Denmark, with the adolescent protagonist of Salinger's **The Catcher in the Rye.** And I can sympathize with their feelings of outrage. Salinger's "hero" has been compared to many literary figures, from Huck Finn to David Copperfield. So many different attitudes have been taken toward him. Let's stop talking about him and write about something else. Isn't the subject getting boring? Perhaps so, but Holden, at least for me, will not go away. He continues to pester the mind, and recently, while reading A. C. Bradley's analysis of Hamlet's character [in *Shakespearean Tragedy* (1905)], I couldn't resist the idea that much of what Bradley was saying about Hamlet applied to Holden as well. So, let the critics carp. I, at least, have felt illumined. And perhaps the comparison is not as absurd as it first appears. (p. 26)

After demolishing the theories of other critics, Bradley concludes that the essence of Hamlet's character is contained in a three-fold analysis of it. First, that rather than being melancholy by temperament, in the usual sense of "profoundly sad," he is a person of unusual nervous instability, one liable to extreme and profound alterations of mood, a potential manic-depressive type. Romantic, we might say. Second, this Hamlet is also a person of "exquisite moral sensibility," hypersensitive to goodness, a moral idealist who, when he cannot wholly love the world chooses wholly to despise it rather than live in it with its imperfections. He is also a person who tends to see only good as real but who, when evil is forced upon him as a reality, loses his awareness of good almost altogether. Third, there is Hamlet's particular type of intellectual genius: an unusual quickness of mind, a great agility in shifting mental attitudes, a remarkable ability to penetrate appearances once they are seen as such, a passion for generalizing about life, and a curiosity about life, ideas, and people that is so strong that one doubts the possibility of his ever satisfying it.

Bradley goes on to say that the tragedy of Hamlet is that these very characteristics, which formerly were the reasons for his superiority, . . . are now the very qualities that bring about his destruction. Bradley sees his inability to act as being the result of an intense moral disillusionment, one that produces a depression so great as to constitute utter world-weariness and a frustration as well as perversion of intellectual genius. The Hamlet of the play, then, as Bradley sees him, *is* melancholy in the sense that he is almost continually depressed and thus incapable of positive action, is moving toward death, spiritual as well as physical, and yet is a figure whose story is tragic because we are constantly made aware of the greatness that he once had. As Bradley says, the tragic feeling is the profound awareness of waste.

Before discussing the manner in which these remarks apply to Holden, let me hasten to say that Holden is redeemed from the tragic catastrophe. He is, at least minimally, brought back to life; in fact, . . . he might be said to have been saved from tragedy. That is one supreme and vital difference between them. Another, of course, is that I would hardly argue that Salinger's depiction of the Hamlet character is as profound or as deeply moving as Shakespeare's. But let us now look at the evidence. (pp. 26-7)

[Everyone] seems to agree, detractors and worshipers alike, that Holden is some crazy kid. To say that he is moody is to understate indeed. Surely his nervous instability, his tendency toward a manic-depressive form of Romanticism, needs no corroboration.

His "extreme moral sensibility" is also pretty obviously there. Virtually everything in his world is regarded as "phony"; nor does he exempt himself from "calumny." And there are other more exact parallels. His idealization of Allie, the only perfect person he has ever known, he says, is similar to Hamlet's attitude toward his father. As Hamlet's "almost blunted purpose" is sharpened by the reappearance of his father's ghost, so Holden's suicidal tendencies are held in check by the memory of Allie, who keeps Holden from destruction as he crosses the city streets. Holden's disillusionment with people is on the same vast scale as Hamlet's and encompasses an even greater variety of people: his brother, D. B., who has prostituted his talents by writing for Hollywood; his history teacher, Mr. Spencer, who laughs at the headmaster's jokes; his former English teacher, Mr. Antolini, who is seen, momentarily at least, as a pervert; most of all the "rogue and peasant slave" that is himself.

The process whereby each universalizes the significance of a particular disillusioning experience is also strikingly similar. Just as Hamlet's disillusionment with his mother's character extends itself to Ophelia and finally to women in general, so does Holden's conviction that to grow up is to grow phony force itself upon him.

Both characters are left virtually alone at the end, having either been betrayed by or alienated themselves from those who could have helped them. Holden's friends, Stradlater, Ackley, Carl Luce, Sally Hayes—the Rosencrantzes and Guildensterns of *The Catcher*—betray him and are rejected. . . . There are also, however, what might be called Horatio char-

acters in *The Catcher,* figures who are relied on mainly for their steadfastness but who also have a quality of innocence and what might be called rationality about them: the nuns, the drummer at Radio City Music Hall, Jane Gallagher, who keeps her kings in the back row. Phoebe is certainly the most important of these characters, though she finally goes beyond her prototype and prevents the "noble heart" from "cracking."

Most important, surely, in considering the similarity between Hamlet and Holden as disillusioned, moral idealists, is the sense so deeply embedded in each of them that death is preferable to life in a world in which evil seems to predominate. Yet neither is capable of suicide.

If differences in age and in depth of mind are remembered, the thought that Holden is of the same type of intellectual genius as Hamlet should not be too offensive a suggestion, and, once again, the similarities are striking. Holden's remarkable quickness of mind shows itself most clearly in the spur-of-the-moment fantasies he weaves for Mrs. Morrow, for the nuns, and for Sunny. His agility in shifting mental attitudes is perhaps best seen in connection with Mr. Antolini who falls from savior to seducer "overnight." Holden's ability to see beneath appearances is one of the reasons why *The Catcher* can be read purely on the level of social satire. Combined with his passion for generalizing about life, it is this ability in him that helps produce his disillusioned ruminations on the phoniness of the world. As with Hamlet, this capacity to see the real behind what appears becomes a cynical habit of mind and so, ironically, finally places each in a nightmare world whose abominations as effectively hide reality as did the former fantasies of the world of appearance. Holden is perceptive when he sees the difference between the appearance and reality of Stradlater, "the secret slob," when he sees through the false charity of Sally Hayes's mother, when he senses the egotism behind Ernie's false humility; and taken all together, his vision constitutes a valid indictment of the phoniness of man and society. But Holden's perceptiveness, like Hamlet's, leads him too far. He condemns too rapidly and too harshly. The fact that he suspects that he does so proves that he can be equally perceptive about himself, that he cannot stop from doing so, that his perceptiveness is degenerating into cynicism. He forgets the nuns, Mr. and Mrs. Spencer, Mrs. Morrow, Horwitz, the divinely mad taxi driver, the drummer at Radio City Music Hall, and he concludes that to grow up is to become hopelessly corrupt. Not to grow up, then, must be to remain good; and there is the consequent false idealization of childhood, the past, ultimately the changeless world of the dead. Just as Claudius is no satyr, and just as Hamlet's father was probably no Hyperion, so the adult world cannot be seriously imagined as wholly evil and the world of the child as entirely good. While there is obviously truth in both heroes' conclusions, it is certainly equally obvious that what begins as perceptiveness degenerates into unperceptive melancholia.

Yet, in spite of the utter dejection, the only momentarily alleviated world-weariness of both characters, both keep to the end what is essentially an insatiable curiosity about life, ideas, people; and at the end, Holden, having been saved from catastrophe by Phoebe, can start again with all the questions that he has been so unsuccessful in answering, having been given one answer that will enable him to ask them all over again in a different light. He has been told, and he has come to realize, that the world can be, in fact must be, loved in spite of its imperfections. (pp. 27-9)

[There] is a great importance in recognizing the basic similarity between the characters of Hamlet and Holden; and it lies chiefly in the following "truths." Such recognition helps clarify Salinger's attitude toward his "hero" by giving additional support to those of us who, for other reasons, already view Holden as symbolizing the plight of the idealist in the modern world. Most importantly, however, it suggests why Holden Caulfield won't go away, why we can't stop thinking about him, why after almost as many words have already been spilled over him as over Hamlet himself, he continues to fascinate us, why he continues to remain so potent an influence on the now aging younger generation that he first spoke to, and why he continues to brand himself anew on the young. In fact, in this age of atrophy, in this thought-tormented, thought-tormenting time in which we live, perhaps it is not going too far to say that, for many of us, at least, our Hamlet is Holden. (p. 29)

Clinton W. Trowbridge, "Hamlet and Holden," in English Journal, *Vol. 57, No. 1, January, 1968, pp. 26-9.*

CLINTON W. TROWBRIDGE

Once we recognize that J. D. Salinger's depiction of Holden Caulfield as symbolizing the plight of the idealist in the modern world provides the primary structural framework of *The Catcher in the Rye,* we can see every other aspect of this concise, symbolically compressed novel as reinforcing that design. Whether we look at the significance of the briefly drawn but highly individualized minor characters or at the use of concrete details, whether we consider the major or the minor emphases, we recognize each in turn as symbolic extensions of the protagonist. Thus *The Catcher in the Rye* stands on every count as one of the masterpieces of symbolist fiction.

By utilizing many of his secondary characters so purposively, as exaggerated or distorted forms of Holden himself, Salinger succeeds in rendering the character of his "hero" more objectively than he could otherwise. In fact, it is largely this technique that makes Holden the extraordinarily "round" character that he is. We see him not merely from the highly limited first person point of view, but also in a series of dramatic self-portraits.

Some of the characters, like Stradlater and Carl Luce, dramatize Holden's man-of-the-world image of himself. The paradoxical attitude that he adopts toward these—he both admires and despises them—are resolved when we realize that these are really attitudes that he has adopted toward images of himself. Others, like Antolini, Allie, Phoebe, and to some extent, Mr. Spencer, are Catcher figures, symbols, that is, of Holden in his imagined role of protector of innocence and goodness. James Castle represents the apparent inflexibility of Holden's idealism and thus dramatizes for us the fearful image that Antolini has of Holden—that of his dying nobly for some highly unworthy cause. Not only does Holden say he admires Castle's behavior, but he and Castle are symbolically identified through Holden's sweater. But the genuineness of Holden's admiration is tested and found to be wanting when he refuses to jump out of the window after the Maurice episode. That Holden's idealism is anything but inflexible is further shown by the fact that Maurice himself represents another and completely different ideal of behavior to Holden: that of the tough guy who gets what he wants when he wants it. By being an extension of the assertive personality that

Holden would like to have, Maurice dramatizes both the phoniness of that ideal and the fact that Holden actually despises it.

With some of the characters a recognition that they are symbolic extensions of Holden himself is absolutely necessary if we are fully to understand his attitude toward them. His treatment of Sunny, for instance, is not just the result of adolescent inexperience; he cannot treat her as a prostitute because she is too close to being a pathetic image of himself; she so depresses him because his pity for her amounts to self-pity, because she contributes to the gradually encroaching vision of himself as the homeless wanderer, alienated from man and society. So, too his admiration for the drummer at Radio City Music Hall can only be fully understood when we recognize that to Holden he represents a kind of saintliness. If the aim of life is to retain, or regain, youthful innocence and goodness, the drummer, with his total absorption in perfecting a relatively simple and uninteresting task, has achieved a kind of beatific state.

We fail to see the significance that Holden attaches to Jane Gallagher's keeping her kings on the back row unless we realize that both Holden and Jane are scared of the adult world into which they are plunging. . . . Stradlater's date with Jane so upsets Holden not just because he knows what a lady's man Stradlater is but because he would like to approach her romantically himself but no more dares to upset their childish relationship than she to move her kings from the back row. That Stradlater symbolizes Holden's romantic ideal of himself in this scene is underlined by the fact that Stradlater is actually wearing Holden's jacket. It is significant that only after Holden feels momentarily secure at the Antolinis does he actually decide to call Jane on the telephone. His failure to call her is a symbolic reminder to us of two things: that he cannot reestablish contact with what he believes to be goodness and innocence; and secondly, that he is experiencing a growing alienation from his world. That he never does call her and that there is no specific mention of her at the end also reminds us that, although he has been saved from figurative and perhaps literal death, he is still far from being "romantically" adjusted to the adult world.

Salinger's method of using other characters to dramatize various images that Holden has of himself does more than just increase the "roundness" of his character, however. It reinforces the structural pattern of the novel in that it allows Holden to sort out the true from the false images of himself through direct confrontation with them. He thinks he admires James Castle, for instance, but he cannot act like him. Actually, he comes to the final stages of his quest by discovering whom he can and cannot act like, and the person he most acts like at the end is Mr. Spencer.

At first glance, Mr. Spencer does not seem to embody any of Holden's ideals. He is old, sickly, and generally pathetic; he is phony enough to laugh at the headmaster's jokes; in the lecture he gives Holden, he is by turns blunt, sarcastic, and woebegone about Holden's future. In marked contrast to Antolini's sympathetic understanding of Holden's condition, all Mr. Spencer can offer is to underline the headmaster's observation that life is a game and must be played according to the rules. Perhaps his parting cry: "Good Luck!" sounds so terrible to Holden because taken literally it puts the outcome of Holden's quest wholly on the level of chance, whereas what Holden is so desperately seeking is a plan whereby he can control his life. But behind all this is Mr. Spencer's loving concern for Holden and the fact that Mr. and Mrs. Spencer both seem to get a bang out of life. Holden's whole treatment of Phoebe at the Museum is similar to Mr. Spencer's treatment of him (It is in fact much harsher); and, at the end, he is getting a bang out of the counterpart to Mr. Spencer's Navajo Indian blanket: Phoebe's blue coat.

That Mr. Spencer represents the nearest thing to a dramatization of Holden's final image of himself is suggested in several other ways by Salinger. They are both tall and stooped in posture. Like Mr. Spencer, Holden constantly uses the term "boy," nods his head, repeats himself, and is often sarcastic. While he criticises Mr. Spencer bitterly for his phony laughing at the headmaster's jokes, one of the most obvious things about Holden's behavior is that he is outwardly conventional. Though he hates saying "Glad to've met you" to someone he is not glad to have met, he is constantly doing so. (pp. 5-8)

Many of the characters in the novel can be understood as exaggerated portraits of Holden as he is. All of these characters are treated with a greater or lesser degree of pity, scorn, or annoyance by Holden, and, as we have seen to be the case with two of these—Sunny and, to some degree, Mr. Spencer—his attitudes are only fully understood when we see that Holden is really concerned with these traits in himself. Again Salinger's method is to take one of the traits or attitudes that Holden deplores in himself, exaggerate it, and dramatically portray it in the form of another character. The three "grools" from Washington who are going to get up early to go to Radio City Music Hall are pathetic examples of tourism and of the hold that phony values, as epitomized by Hollywood, have on Americans; but not only does Holden himself go to two movies and a play in the course of the action of the novel, he goes to Radio City Music Hall as well. What he says about the movie that he sees there expresses succinctly the dilemma he is in, the manner in which he is trapped in the very world he is so hostile to: "It [the picture] was so putrid I couldn't take my eyes off it." Holden does not look for his initials on the bathroom doors, as does the old alumnus of Pencey Prep, but the smells of the Natural History Museum and of his old public school make him just as nostalgic and sentimental, and what he does find engraved on the walls of both places symbolize not a romanticized version of lost youth—the initials—but a crass reminder of the defeat of innocence. (p. 8)

While many of the characters in *The Catcher in the Rye* take on an additional interest and importance once their symbolic connection to Holden is seen, Salinger's deepest and most suggestive symbols are found not in them but in some of the apparently minor details of the novel. Of these the most important is Holden's red hunting hat. The effectiveness of this symbol lies in its great suggestiveness. Not only does it operate on several different levels of meaning, but Salinger is so careful to make it unobtrusive as a symbol that to most readers it is simply a funny hat, just the sort of thing that a rebellious adolescent would wear. Even the circumstances of Holden's buying the hat, however, suggest that we must go beyond this understanding of it. Holden purchases it just *after* he notices that he has lost all the fencing foils. As manager of the fencing team he is immediately ostracized by the other boys, and thus, from the very beginning, the hat is comforter, a consolation prize for failure. He feels comfortable in it when he is reading alone in his room; but partly because he likes to wear it with its long peak toward the back of his head, he does not feel at ease wearing it in public. On its sur-

face level the hat is simply a detail by which Salinger dramatizes an important part of Holden's character.

Yet there is a deeper meaning. Holden is outwardly conventional in manner and particularly in dress; but, as we discover when he ruminates about his Gladstone bags from Mark Cross, he sees this conventionality as a sign of phoniness in himself. Through his conventional dress and manner he dimly sees himself as supporting the very world that he is so hostile to. Thus, wearing the cap also symbolizes his desire to break through the phony conventions of his world; not wearing the cap dramatizes his failure to destroy what is phony, either in himself or in his world, as well as reminds us of the power that the conventions have over him. (pp. 8-9)

The hunting hat, then is closely associated with the basic structural pattern of the novel: Holden's quest for truth. In fact, it is even more intimately connected to it than we have so far indicated. To Ackley the hat is simply a hunting hat, a deer shooting hat, as he calls it. Holden's response is: " 'Like hell it is,' I took it off and looked at it. I sort of closed one eye, like I was taking aim at it. 'This is a people shooting hat,' I said. 'I shoot people in this hat.' " At the core of Holden's personality lies the double vision, and therefore double nature, of the idealist. The essential paradox of his being is his love-hate for humanity. He sees with frightening clarity the difference between what is and what ought to be, and that vision is the basic motivation for whatever he does. (p. 9)

[One other important aspect of the hat is reflected in] the fact that Holden likes to wear it backwards. This detail leads us to the full richness of the symbol. With the peak to the back, he looks far more like what he really is, a catcher rather than a killer. Nor is the literal image of a baseball catcher inappropriate to consider here. One of Holden's most prized possessions is his brother Allie's fielder's mitt. In the fact that it is a left-handed mitt and that Allie had covered it with poems so that he could read them when no one was up at bat, the mitt is a rich symbol in its own right. Holden idealizes Allie as by far the brightest as well as the nicest member of his family. When Allie died Holden so damaged his hand by breaking out the garage windows that, as he tells us, it still hurts him when it rains and he can no longer make a proper fist. Part of what is suggested here is that Holden, equipped by his brother with a means of catching the good and the innocent, has, because of his love for his brother, made himself ineffective as a hater (the broken fist) and, like his brother, has dedicated himself to an impossible ideal. When the impossibility, and more importantly, the undesirability of the ideal is finally grasped (as it is by Holden while watching Phoebe on the merry-go-round), the idealist is saved from self-destruction and uselessness and led back to man and the world by means of love.

The fact that Holden likes to wear his cap with the peak reversed not only provides us with an ironic visual picture of the catcher ideal but also dramatizes for us the very direction of Holden's search. In many senses of the phrase, Holden is trying to go backwards. He is between childhood and adulthood, a condition that is symbolically represented in the fact that the hair on one side of his head is grey. More than anything else he wants to keep for himself and others what he imagines to be the untarnished goodness and innocence of the child. The reversed peak, then, suggests his idealization of and yearning for the childhood condition. (p. 10)

[When Phoebe wears Holden's hat outside the museum, she

reveals that] she has accepted his quest as her own. When she meets him she throws the hat at him in fury because she recognizes that his refusal to accept her as a companion is really an admission of phoniness, both in himself and in his plan. In reality, of course, she has saved him by symbolically showing her willingness to die with him. Instead of looking to the past, he is now going to try to deal with the future. This is the affirmation with which the novel ends, and Salinger has very unobtrusively underlined it by the use he makes of the hunting cap in this final scene. He has forced the hat upon her—given up the quest, that is; and her forgiveness of him for disappointing her is again symbolically portrayed in her giving him back his hat, his identity as an idealist. That he has changed the direction of his quest and that she is the person responsible for his doing so is told us by her putting on his hat for him and putting it on his head with the peak facing the front. It is clear that she does so place the hat on his head, but Salinger is clever enough not to force the symbol on us in so direct a manner. Rather he chooses that we discover it. While Holden watches Phoebe ride around on the carrousel, it begins to rain. He sits there in the rain and Salinger tells us: "I got pretty soaking wet, especially my neck and my pants. My hunting hat really gave me quite a lot of protection, in a way, but I got soaked anyway." The "especially my neck" is Salinger's master stroke in the use of symbolic technique, a technique that so often in modern fiction results in lifeless allegory. Holden has thus been re-born into at least a partial acceptance of life. His direction has been radically changed. It seems to be no mere happenstance, then, that Salinger should set this final scene in the Zoo, the place of life, after leading Holden from the Egyptian tombs, the place of death. Nor, particularly as we know that Salinger himself is deeply interested in Zen, does it seem improbable that Salinger means us to see the carousel as symbolic of the wheel of life, the constantly changing pattern of the Eternal One. (p. 11)

> *Clinton W. Trowbridge, "Salinger's Symbolic Use of Character and Detail in 'The Catcher in the Rye',"* in The Cimarron Review, *No. 4, June, 1968, pp. 5-11.*

G. S. AMUR

[*The Catcher in the Rye*] seems to have cast a permanent spell on the critics not only as a literary masterpiece—[Brian Way praised it as] "a classic novel of adolescence"—which is understandable, but as one of the most powerful myths of our time.

In spite of the large body of Salinger criticism, however, with the exception of a few critics like Brian Way, Carl F. Strauch [see *CLC,* Volume 12] and D. B. Costello [see excerpt above], very few have spoken with the actual literary object before their eyes. The appeal of *The Catcher in the Rye* as a psychological, social and philosophic myth seems to have been far more powerful than its artistic and literary appeal. . . . [The] basic question whether the novel has "a firm and complex controlling intention"—a question which Arthur Mizener poses and answers in the negative—has not been satisfactorily answered. The object of this paper is to attempt such an answer.

Primarily, *The Catcher in the Rye* is neither a story of social rebellion nor one of philosophical quest. Holden, the central character whose experiences provide the subject-matter of the novel, is neither a revolutionary, nor a saint or seeker of Truth. He is an American adolescent facing a psychological crisis and in desperate search of personal relationships powerful enough to pull him through. The search, which ends, after a series of frustrations, in Holden's surrender to his child-sister Phoebe, is the basis of the novel's thematic unity as well as the source of its tensions. The role of the catcher-in-the-rye—the preserver of innocence—which Holden is romantically ambitious to assume but which is limited to the erasing of obscene writing on the walls of a school—and the diametrically opposite role of the recluse which also attracts him temporarily but which he never assumes—are not central to his experience as it is presented in the novel, and it is highly doubtful whether they would fit him at all.

Holden's search for genuine and satisfying personal relationships—essentially a simple search—becomes a tragic search in the context of his complicated personality, his unusual family background, his passion for discrimination, and his adolescent immaturity.

"Holden," says Edgar Branch, "is essentially homeless, frozen out." But he is only partially right because, though Holden, the only "dumb one" in the family, as he describes himself, never seems to have aroused more than parental solicitude in his wealthy but "touchy" father and his "not too healthy," "psychic" mother; and, though the house is for him a place where "everything creaks and squeaks," he is a "wanderer" only in a limited sense. It is with Phoebe—for him the centre of the family after the death of Allie and the fall of D. B.—and with Phoebe alone that he finds tranquillity. He quietly returns home when the crisis is over, and is unable to sever himself from it. (pp. 11-12)

Holden's inability to sever himself from home may be a result of a lack of courage to which he often confesses, but it is more likely that it is caused by a paralysis of the will brought about by his allegiance to Phoebe, Allie and D. B., his utter dependence on personal relationships.

Holden as Ihab Hassan points out [see excerpt above], has a natural and powerful urge "to commune and communicate" with his fellowmen, and it is this urge that decides for him the quality of things and people. Phoebe is "nice" because "she was somebody you always felt like talking to on the phone." A book like Isak Dinesen's *Out of Africa* is a very good book because "you wish the author who wrote it was a terrific friend of yours." But this urge in Holden is continually thwarted by another urge—the urge to discriminate—which is equally powerful. . . . [His] discriminations range from the purely instinctive and idiosyncratic, such as his dislike for pimples, sickness and old age, to the deeply deliberate and purposeful, like his hatred of the movies, the Hemingway school of fiction, and the Ivy League colleges. For him, the differences—like the one between "phoney" and "nice" or that between the child and the adult—are real and fundamental. . . . What particularly maddens Holden is the horror of the ordinariness of life that he tells Sally Hayes:

> But it isn't just it's everything. I hate living in New York and all. Taxi cabs, and Madison Avenue buses, with the drivers and all always yelling at you to get out at the rear door, and being introduced to phoney guys that call the Lunts angels, and going up and down in elevators when you just want to go outside, and guys fitting your pants all the time at Brooks. . . .
>
> (pp. 12-13)

"You don't like *anything* that's happening," Phoebe tells her brother. This is the beginning of "a special kind of fall, a terrible kind" against which Antolini, Holden's English teacher at Elkton Hills, warns him. Holden's tragedy, however, is not that he hates everything—he does find several objects for his approval—or that he gives up the search for what he is looking for—because he doesn't. What is really tragic is his involvement in a kind of situation which Zooey Glass describes to his sister Franny, who is caught in a crisis similar to that of Holden [in *Franny and Zooey*]. " 'God damn it,' he said, 'there are nice things in the world—and I mean *nice* things. We're all such morons to get sidetracked. Always, always, always referring every god-damn thing that happens right back at our lousy little ego.' " Holden is a "lousy" egoist, trapped in the web of his own highly individualistic discriminations, and a good example of this is his attitude to institutionalised education. A whole system stands condemned because an immature and egotistical adolescent who has no use for academic knowledge, cannot get anything out of it. . . . [Holden] is not even consistent in his attitude, for, in spite of his declared hatred for schools and colleges, he is proud of the academic achievements of Allie and Phoebe and is deeply disturbed when Phoebe wants to give up school and follow him into exile.

Thus, Holden's discriminations, which result in a rejection of the ordinary as well as the exceptional in the human condition, are ultimately to be traced to his practice of referring all experience to his own ego, a practice which leads him away from the objective world into the world of his own fantasies, and seriously damages his relationships with people. Concrete examples of this phenomenon in the novel are the Sally Hayes and Antolini episodes.

Keats, one of Salinger's favourite poets and a man who knew, more than any one else, the agonies of adolescence, in his preface to *Endymion* has an interesting passage, which is of great help to us in our efforts to understand Holden:

> The imagination of a boy is healthy, and the mature imagination of a man is healthy; but there is a space of life between in which the soul is in ferment, the character undecided, the way of life uncertain, the ambition thick-sighted; thence proceed mawkishness and all the thousand bitters.

One of the most important sources of Holden's difficulties is immaturity. Antolini suggests this to him, when he quotes from Wilhelm Stekel; "The mark of the immature man is that he wants to die nobly for a cause, while the mark of the mature man is that he wants to live humbly for one." But Holden is too tired to listen. Holden has an acute intellect, and though he confesses now and then that he does not understand a few things, he apparently believes in his own maturity, as can be seen from his constant habit of generalising for the benefit of others. But many of Holden's attitudes to things and people are characterised by immaturity. Very often, the immaturity is the direct result of the illusion of maturity from which Holden suffers. Holden rejects knowledge because he believes that it can only buy Cadillacs, and pursues wisdom; but this search, instead of bringing him illumination, as it does in the case of Zooey, succeeds only in leading him to the verge of madness. Much has been made of Holden's revulsion from materialism, but we cannot be too sure that it springs from purely spiritual sources. We can, for instance, think of it as a predictable social reaction of an adolescent belonging to the privileged classes, who takes material security for

granted and indulges in a romantic form of social discontent. (pp. 13-15)

To identify the controlling theme of *The Catcher in the Rye* with the personal theme of Holden's search for human relationships in the context of a psychological crisis is not . . . to deny the validity of other approaches to the novel, which can be of help to us in understanding the complex nature of its thematic content and the variety of its appeal to readers and critics. "American fiction," [one anonymous reviewer has stated], "is nothing if not critical," and *The Catcher in the Rye* has been read as a story of contemporary alienation, or as a merciless exposure of falseness and perversity in American urban culture. . . . [Attempts] have also been made to visualise the novel in terms of the archetype of death and rebirth, or as a defence of innocence against the evils of experience, and to place it firmly in the Romantic tradition. There has also been the suggestion that *The Catcher in the Rye* is essentially an enactment of Holden's search for identity and belongs to the Proustian tradition in the novel. But these interpretations, powerful as they are as statements of the value of *The Catcher in the Rye* as myth, are highly vulnerable as explanations of its literary structure.

"For all its brilliance," writes Arthur Mizener, "*The Catcher in the Rye* does not quite come off as a whole." The reason for this failure, he believes, is the "claustrophobic" and "random" quality of the novel, the lack of a complex and firm controlling intention. For him, as for David Leitch, the value of the book is as a "lyric monologue," as an expression of "complex feelings." (pp. 15-16)

What exactly is the basic movement in *The Catcher in the Rye?* It has not been easy to decide. In Brian Way's analysis, it is a movement which originates in Holden's "rejection of the ethos of his society" and ends in his double collapse—a collapse into madness, and into childhood. For Strauch, it is something quite different and consists in Holden's unconscious preparation for the catcher role, for the "burdens of maturity." (p. 16)

The confusion that has arisen over this issue, a result of myth-making rather than genuine literary criticism, could have been avoided, since the movement of *The Catcher in the Rye* is a simple one. It is a movement which involves the beginning of a psychological crisis in Holden, the deepening of this crisis owing to a series of frustrations Holden has to suffer in his efforts to overcome it, and his final recovery. The highly organic nature of this movement gives unity to the novel's structure.

Holden's crisis is the result of an accumulated experience of isolation. Its immediate cause is his getting the axe at Pencey Prep., and the ostracising by the school fencing team—of which he was "the goddam manager" for his "responsibility" in the episode of the missing foils and equipment. But there are other and more important causes, his hatred for schools and things in general, the shocking disillusionment over D. B. his elder brother, and the death of Allie, his younger brother, to whom he was deeply attached.

Holden's visit to the Spencers, "to feel some kind of a good bye," is the first of several efforts he makes to fight the crisis. Holden likes old Spencer—the history teacher at Pencey—but the visit ends in failure and frustration because of Holden's passion for discriminations ranging from his physical revulsion at Spencer's "terrible posture," his "yelling," his "nodding routine," his habit of secretly picking his nose and missing the bed whenever he chucked something at it, to sharp differences with his views on the Life-game. Holden's next effort is with Stradlater, his room-mate, with whom he has an ambivalent relationship. He is critical of Stradlater and dislikes him for his "piercing whistle," his slobby personal habits, his conceitedness and his technique with girls, but he is also attracted to him in a way because Stradlater was "very generous in somethings," was a "very friendly guy," and had a sense of humour. Holden's conversation with Stradlater in the Can, where he follows him, and his fight with him later over Jane Gallagher illustrate Holden's attempts to stimulate himself into establishing some kind of relationship with him. This attempt which ends more grievously than before—in Holden's chastisement at the hands of Stradlater—brings out Holden's immaturity in matters of sex. Holden's sudden attack on Stradlater in the Can, when he jumps on him, holds him in a half-nelson is playful no doubt, but it is caused by a remark which Stradlater makes about Fitzgerald, [a girl Stradlater dated but quickly broke up with]—"She's too old for you"—that hurts Holden's sexual pride, though, in his immaturity, he is hardly aware of it. One of the powerful factors involved in his more serious fight with Stradlater is the sexual jealousy which Stradlater arouses in him by his highly ambiguous statements about the details of his dating with Jane. Holden's visit to Ackley after his fight with Stradlater, around eleven or eleven thirty, in spite of his intense dislike for him, is a desperate and pathetic effort on his part to fight the feeling of overwhelming isolation. But the effort leaves him more exhausted and bitter than ever before. Holden has to do something to save his sanity and decides abruptly to leave Pencey and go to New York "to take it easy till Wednesday," when he was expected to return home for Christmas. His midnight cry, "Sleep tight, ya morons" sounds deeply misanthropic, but it is more truly a cry of pain and frustration. Holden's train journey, which he enjoys, gives him a temporary release from his tensions, but his need to communicate is still strong and urgent. This explains his phoney talk with Ernest Morrow's mother in the course of which he paints a highly flattering picture of Ernest, in spite of the fact that he knew him to be "the biggest bastard that ever went to Pencey." Holden's lying is a defence mechanism which releases him from the pressures of the ego and of actuality, by providing an escape into the private world of fantasy. But Holden is fully aware of the instability of such escapes and does not indulge in them too long or too often. Another defence mechanism, a mechanism which he frequently uses and which is opposed to lying, is his indulgence in sarcastic humour. There is more to his indulgence in sarcastic humour. This is more to his liking, since it involves an active participation of the ego and comes to him naturally.

Holden continues his fight with loneliness and the threat of insanity in New York, and the first thing he does when he gets off at Penn station is to go to a phone-booth, but he ends up not calling anybody. He checks in at Edmund Hotel and fouls up a plan to get Faith Cavendish for a cocktail. Holden's attitude to sex has the same ambivalence as his attitude to movies, to night clubs and to many other things. He hates sex, but allows his mind to be obsessed by it. Unlike the grown up Stradlater or Carl Luce, he is not mature enough to establish normal and satisfactory sex relationships, though he likes girls and women. But in his desperate search of companionship, he gets involved in several abortive sex adventures. There is also, at the unconscious level, the urge to play the

adult (Holden often lies about his age), perhaps to imitate Stradlater.

Holden is fond of dancing and music, and his visit to the Lavender Room of the Hotel, where he meets the "three witches"—movie maniacs from an insurance office in Seattle and later, his visit to Ernie's night-club, where he finds good music, but spoilt by people clapping for the wrong ones, offer him a temporary relief from the growing threat of loneliness, in spite of the fact that the sight of the Waste Land leaves him more depressed than before. But, immediately after this, on his return to the Hotel, he gets himself involved in the "big mess" about Sunny, the prostitute. The Sunny episode brings out some of the important aspects of Holden's predicament— his desperate need to find a foothold in some kind of relationship and his inability to find it in sex. Holden's courageous but, under the circumstances, quixotic stand against Maurice results in the severest torture, physical as well as psychological, that Holden ever went through, and leaves him in a truly sad plight.

Holden's meeting with the nuns the next day, on Sunday, at the sandwich Bar and his highly successful attempt to communicate with them, especially the nun with the glasses, are of the highest importance in the structure of the novel. Holden's gift of money to the nuns—exactly the amount which Maurice had demanded and Holden had refused to give— represents his ability to discover the "nice things" in the Inverted Forest, Salinger's symbol for contemporary human situation, and to respond to them adequately transcending the limitations of his strong discriminations. Holden has a prejudice against all institutions and groups, including the religious, but, for once, these do not interfere in his relations with human beings.

The Sally Hayes episode, the next important development in the action of the novel, marks the beginning of an acute stage in Holden's neurosis. Holden rings up Sally, makes a date with her and, after a visit to the Broadway (where he buys a record for Phoebe), the Park and Museum (where he expects to find Phoebe), he goes to the Baltimore and waits for Sally. Sally arrives, and her "terrific" looks make an immediate sexual impact on Holden. They go to see the Lunts in a show. At the end of the first act, when they come out ("with the other jerks"), Sally meets the boy from Andover, "George something," and her enthusiasm for him upsets Holden and, though he is not aware of it, arouses in him the feeling of sexual jealousy. After the show, they go for ice-skating at Radio City, where they prove to be "the worst skaters on the whole goddam rink." The humiliation which has a terrible effect on Holden's nerves, explodes in his violent outburst against schools and people in general. Holden seeks refuge from this fury in his private world of fantasy and makes a "fantastic," (and as he realises later, phoney) proposal to Sally that they should run away and live in a cabin. Sally's refusal, which destroys this fantasy, produces his final insult to her, and the "loud stupid laugh." The Sally Hayes episode is yet another illustration of Holden's ambivalent attitude to sex and his immaturity in dealing with its problems.

Holden's next attempt is at intellectual companionship. He rings up Carl Luce who had been his student-advisor at Whooton, and asks him for a drink at the Wicker Bar of the swanky Seton Hotel, with the intention of having an intellectual conversation with him. He had tried something of this kind with Sally Hayes as well, though at the end he was sorry he had started it. But when he actually meets Luce, all that he does is to get brutally personal about Luce's sex-life and to tell him about his own sex problems. The meeting breaks up abruptly and Holden, once again "lonesome as hell," gets drunk and tries to make it up with Sally on the phone. And, later, in the Central Park, where he is haunted by the fear of getting pneumonia and dying, he decides to sneak home and see Phoebe. This decision, which launches him on the road to recovery, marks the end of yet another phase in his experiences.

Holden knew all the time that he would find in Phoebe the island of peace and understanding for which he had been groping on the dark sea of his suffering. What had kept him away from home was his conviction that his parents would not be able to understand his problems. He feels the change the moment he steps into Phoebe's (D. B.'s) room. He regains his mental health and relaxes. Even his tone changes and becomes sentimental. He freely discusses with Phoebe his problems—his failure at Pencey, the ostracising to which he was subjected there. When Phoebe accuses him of cynicism, he calmly points out the things he *has* liked—the nuns, James Castle who would rather kill himself than take back what he had said, Allie, and sitting with Phoebe. He confides to her his dreams and ideals and tells her how he would like "to catch everybody if they start to go over the cliff." The dance with Phoebe, the climax of this new experience of his, leaves him in the ecstasy of joy and at least, he finds the release— "Then all of a sudden, I started to cry. I couldn't help it." Holden's relationship with Phoebe is completely satisfying, because it is so entirely free from the two obsessions of his mind—sex and society.

"The more I thought about it . . . the more depressed and screwed up about it I got," says Holden about the Antolini episode, the most baffling experience he undergoes. Holden respects Antolini, formerly his English teacher at Elkton Hills, and remembers with pride the way he had carried James Castle's body all the way to the infirmary "without giving a damn if his coat got all bloody." His visit to the Antolinis starts on a quiet note in spite of the fact that the subject of discussion is himself and schools. Holden defends the students' right to digress in Oral Expression, rejects the suggestion that he is heading towards "a terrible fall," and listens politely to Antolini's sermon on the meaning of maturity and the need to apply oneself in school. But then later, after he has gone to bed, he suddenly wakes up from his sleep and finds Antolini "sitting on the floor right next to the couch, in the dark and all" and "petting," or "patting" him on his head. Holden is shocked and his suspicions are fully aroused. He also knew that Antolini was drunk and he quits the apartment, "shaking like a madman" and sweating, as he goes down in the elevator.

Later, sitting up on a bench in a waiting room at Grand Central, and remembering how kind Antolini had been to him and to the other boys earlier, he wonders whether he had been "wrong about thinking he was making a flitty pass at him," and the mood of depression, from which he had emerged in his meeting with Phoebe, returns to him in full force. "I think I was more depressed than I ever was in my whole life."

The nightmare of the fall which Antolini had spoken about the previous night, becomes almost a reality for Holden, as he walks up Fifth Avenue on Monday morning. He wants to talk to Allie—exactly as Franny wants to talk to the dead Seymour in her crisis [in "Franny"]—and prays to him in the

language of his private litany—"Allie, don't let me disappear. Allie, don't let me disappear. Allie, don't let me disappear. Please Allie." Holden's dream returns to him, and he suddenly decides to go west and lead a hermit's life. He changes his mind, however, when he meets Phoebe at the Museum and, finding her insistent on following him into his exile, realises his responsibility and accepts the inevitability of returning home. He and Phoebe walk down to the Zoo, and Phoebe has a ride on the carousel. As Holden sits on a bench, watching her go round and round, the rain comes down. He gets soaked, but doesn't care, and feels happy.

Holden's crisis is over, but he does not change very much. Most of his characteristic attitudes remain with him. Is he going back to school next September, and is he going to apply himself? Holden thinks these are stupid questions. The acceptance has come to him through his growing faith in the reality of personal relationships. The ending of *The Catcher in the Rye* is neither "a pat Happy Ending" [as Leslie Fiedler asserted] nor a scene of pathetic collapse. It is, simply, the conclusion of Holden's slow and difficult recovery from the crisis he faced and a quiet affirmation of his will to live.

"As symbol can serve structure," writes William York Tindall [in his *The Literary Symbol* (1955)], "so structure can serve as symbol." This is very true of *The Catcher in the Rye* which has been to many a highly effective symbol of American urban culture, representing various things—from a triumphant assertion of saintly innocence to a shocking spiritual bankruptcy. But what is of great interest to us in the context of a demonstration of the literary integrity of the novel, is the fact that though *The Catcher* is not a symbolic novel in the sense in which [Herman Melville's] *Moby-Dick* or [Ernest Hemingway's] *Old Man and the Sea* are symbolic novels, it involves a good deal of conscious symbolism, which has been skillfully worked into its theme and structure.

The symbols in the *The Catcher in the Rye* perform both the important functions which Tindall discusses in his book, viz., (i) the creation of an inner world and (ii) the mediation between the inner world and the external world. We have a series of concrete and symbolic images in the novel, without whose assistance the inner world of Holden would hardly be accessible. These range from the purely romantic and private symbols like the red hunting hat to traditional and archetypal water symbols like the rain and the lake. The red hunting hat is one of the most striking of Salinger's private symbols. "This is a people shooting hat; I shoot people in this hat," Holden explains to Ackley. But he never wears it in his aggressive public acts. The hat has ear laps and Holden often uses it as a protection against cold. In spite of its associations with deer hunting, the hat is a symbol of withdrawal into a psychic world where Holden seeks refuge from the stresses and shocks of social life. (pp. 16-21)

Allie's baseball mitt, with the poems written all over the fingers and the pocket and everywhere in green ink, is Holden's "secret goldfish," a treasure jealously guarded from others (The only person to whom it was shown was Jane Gallagher). Holden's attachment to his dead brother has been interpreted as the symbolic expression of a death wish and traced to a feeling of guilt, but Allie, who was the nicest and most intelligent member of the family, and in whom Holden finds one of the few objects which he could love in the phoney world around him, is a redeemer image and not a death symbol. Holden turns to him, as has been noted earlier, for life and not for death. "I know he's dead," he tells Phoebe, "Don't you think I know that? I can still like him though, can't I? Just because somebody's dead, you don't just stop liking them, for God's sake—especially if they were about a thousand times nicer than the people you know that're *alive* and all." (p. 22)

The half-frozen lake and the ducks of the Central Park lagoon, the rain that comes down as Holden watches the carousel, and the carousel itself belong to a different order of symbols. These are the literary symbols which have external as well as internal references. The ducks in the half-frozen lake hold a lot of interest for Holden because at the unconscious level, he feels the similarity that exists between his own situation in the half-frozen environment and theirs. He wants to know whether the ducks fly away, because flight is something which he himself has been contemplating. The rain is the rain of baptism which revives in him the will to live, and the carousel . . . symbolises for him the possibility of peace in the flux of life.

Thus Salinger's symbols are, like the theme and structure of the novel, the choice of a firm controlling intention and, illuminating as they do the inner world of Holden and relating it to the external world, they give us a fuller insight into the nature of his struggle, more than his words and actions do, and add depth and concreteness to the novel, which in its form is essentially an organisation of memories. (pp. 22-3)

G. S. Amur, "Theme, Structure & Symbol in 'The Catcher in the Rye'," in Indian Journal of American Studies, *Vol. I, No. 1, July, 1969, pp. 11-24.*

MALCOLM BRADBURY

At first sight, *The Catcher in the Rye* seems to be a fairly loose comic novel of adventures, some of them amusing and some not, which happen to a boy of sixteen when he slips away from his prep-school in Pennsylvania and goes off to New York on his own. Over a period of forty-eight hours, from the time he is expelled from the school to the time he rejoins his family, Holden Caulfield, who narrates his own story, is in a kind of limbo, a state of extreme freedom. He has escaped both from his responsibilities and from those who are responsible for him, and it would seem that, in the big city, almost anything could happen to him. A great deal does; once he is in the city, the novel's action moves rapidly through a great many settings and involves many different kinds of characters, people met casually from the crowd and then lost to sight again. In short, the novel is picaresque, proceeding not through old-established relationships in a stable community but by passing encounters in a constantly changing one. These adventures can be in significant sequence, which can be of a very loose kind, illustrating how very various and unexpected life is, or of a very tight kind. And I think that normally, as we reflect on a novel, we would start looking for lines of development that link the sequence together or explain *how* it develops, why these events should follow in this order. So we can ask all sorts of questions: about the world that is explored, and about the character. Does that world have any features that make it consistent? By the end of the novel, have we acquired a sense of the workings of one whole sector of society? Or is it perhaps consistent in a different way: do, for instance, most of the episodes seem in some way to illustrate how immoral or corrupt society, or this society, is? And what of the character's way of experiencing his movement through the novel? Does he or she develop, under-

go a psychological or emotional change, or learn something from his experiences? (pp. 58-9)

[Is *The Catcher in the Rye*] a picaresque novel of adventures, perhaps mainly calculated to produce a comic effect? Is it a novel about the squalor of the world and how it cannot really be lived in, a novel presenting Holden as a 'rebellious saint' trying to overcome squalor with love and protect the innocent against life? Or is it a novel about a boy who sees through the sham of his society, recognises it as commercial and exploitative: in short, a classic work of protest, as other critics have suggested? Or is it perhaps a novel less reacting against the given world than a novel of quest, involving a psychological development in which Holden seeks to see how his beliefs and attitudes square with those of an adult world that he is on the verge of entering? All these amount to very different suggestions about how the novel coheres: about the primary basis of its development and structure. And to come to a view of it, we will need to look closely at the whole book and try to come to some conclusions about what Salinger is seeking to develop as he writes. There is not space enough to do this in the kind of detail we should, in our own minds. And even if we have done it properly we could, of course, still disagree; indeed the book itself may thrive on such an ambiguity.

How, then, does the novel develop? Let us look first at the world in which the action is conducted, and how we are led through it. Clearly, we are led by a narrator who is not the novelist but is an agent implicated in the action: who is, in fact, at its very centre. The world is formed entirely around him and what happens to him. He leads us through the two main settings of the story: Pencey Prep, the exclusive boys' school in Pennsylvania where he is a boarder, and New York City, or rather those parts of it that are likely to be known to a college boy who is a resident. The social world of the book is a middle-class one, and Salinger/Holden creates it with a kind of lovingness, a realistic fascination with places and *mores,* tones of voice and styles of behaviour, that give the book a dense specificity. Holden is a very exact recorder of his situation and what is more, of his environment, which he fills out even as he reacts to it. He is always observing, watching, registering; the world is a crucial lesson in all its detail. And because he reacts to what he understands, we see more than the surface of this world; we see its inconsistencies, its oddities of behaviour, its primary obsessions. The obsessions are with wealth and getting on, with money and success, with ordering and systematising experience so that it fits those forms of success, with refusing to be interested in failure. So many of the events and settings illustrate all this, in precise ways; Holden moves from one scene to another in the narrative present, then illustrates from the narrative past, in order to build up the web, a web from which the human centre is often missing. The events through which he passes are vignettes of a fairly consistent culture, in which—at least by Holden's view—most people behave in the same kinds of way.

So the society has a general tendency, as we see it through Holden and through the novelist. But it is not a society created as a social realist would create it; Salinger isn't attempting to show us the dark underside of American society or the complex social tensions of urban life. He illustrates through manners and interludes, and as the novel builds up and we relate those vignettes, we recognise a squalid consistency in the entire order while not, I think, finding only a basically social *origin* for that consistency. In other words, it does involve a consistency in the particular society of America in the late 1940s in which Holden lives; but it also involves a consistency in the world of adult life as such. Adulthood is seen very much as a state of social acceptance—or at least is seen, as in Mr. Spencer and Mr. Antolini, as a way of thinking about life in terms of being mature and thinking about the future and having a realistic view of one's place in the world. But that is because adults tend to think like that, by a kind of adult necessity. And of course Holden is trying to be an adult, to be mature, in certain respects at least. He wants to appear sexually and socially sophisticated, and a lot of the comedy derives from his assumption of very sophisticated attitudes. But at the same time he stands somewhat outside this society. This is not because he protests in a general way about its basic relationships as such; it is not in that sense a novel of protest. It is rather because he stands at a time of life when he must neither accept nor reject it completely; where he is innocent enough to gaze in bewildered wonder at its inconsistencies; but where of course he is ironically implicated, because boys of sixteen must grow up into men.

This society is of course created by the author, who invents all its details, but it is created in relation to Holden and he is made capable of providing a judgment on it. The judgments need not be the author's; that, too, is something we must sense out. As far as Holden is concerned, it is not an invention but the given world he has to live in. So how is it evaluated? To a large extent, of course, it is evaluated through Holden's judgments, which at first often seem comically quirky but which gradually take on a consistency and depth. By choosing to evaluate it through Holden, Salinger of course is able to explore not only the society but Holden too. And in doing that he is able to make Holden's perspective, which at the beginning seems simply one of amusingly created responses, into a moral integrity. And that too is a principle of the novel's development; the events and episodes being calculated toward doing that as well as toward exploring the social world. That is to say, most of the events in the novel, however episodic they may seem at first, are calculated either to extend his knowledge of the world as it is or to reinforce or extend his particular values and preferences. This means that Holden's values don't just come out of the world as it is, the world we explore, but have certain more personal sources. Holden sees, as we have said, from an adolescent perspective; but it isn't the perspective of all adolescents, as the school scenes at Pencey show. Rather they come from Holden's way of grouping certain significant moments in his life and putting a special value on these. And these moments usually have to do either with nostalgia about childhood, or children, or about his own family: especially his sister Phoebe and his dead brother Allie. This gives him a localised moral world from which to see life. So the ethic Holden expresses is more or less present in him from the first. He normally expresses it in terms of strong immediate responses and preferences, stated through an evocative, value-laden, adolescent slang ('It made me puke'; 'She gave me a pain in the ass'). Holden is perfectly open to experience; he does, however, have strong convictions about it. And to see all these effects working—the creation of a broad world, the creation of values and attitudes toward it, and the creation of a smaller world of the family and children out of which these attitudes come—we need to start grouping certain of the scenes of the book and getting them into perspective.

There is not space to do this in detail, but a few broad hints here can be given; rather they are tentative suggestions. In the early part of the book, the events of the day at Pencey, on the Saturday of the football game, are given in loose sequence. Holden does this and that; people come in and out; from time to time Holden remembers something in the past and introduces it in the telling. The sequence builds up to Holden's 'impulse' to leave that night and rest up in New York for a few days. But there is in fact a certain degree of consistency about what we are told. For instance, we see the school in two different lights: the light of its function in the world, to minister to the needs of society, to attempt to mould boys for their social roles; the light of its more 'real' culture of dormitories, dating, bull-sessions in which the boys compare sexual experiences. Holden is in fact separated from both cultures, which in fact link up with one another. He is not separated completely, though. He clearly needs to withdraw from the school's world of damaged innocence, but at the same time he needs to involve his affections in it, and 'miss' it. His emotions take him backwards toward nostalgia but forward to new events.

When he gets to New York, the same pattern extends and also gets complicated. On the one hand it is a confusing, anonymous and vast city, a city for growing up in; a city of adulthood where things are not what they seem and the signs of turmoil are finally those dirty words about sex that are written on the walls and cannot be erased. But it is also the city of Holden's childhood, and of other children. Holden's movements and emotions again seem casual; but he does have certain set patterns to follow deriving from both of these versions of the city. He knows college-set New York, sophisticated and mildly experienced: you meet girls under the clock at the Biltmore, you go to the theatre and the skating rink at Radio City, you go to Eddie's in the Village and listen to jazz. You ask for liquor and if the waiter thinks you are under age you drink coke. But behind that map of Manhattan lies another—the schoolchild's New York, an unsophisticated world of the lake in Central Park, the Museum of Natural History, the zoo, the carousel. Holden explores both worlds at once and tries to bring them into relation. So the episodes of this section are very mixed but again have certain patterns to them. Some involve salutary shocks about the world ahead (the episode with the whore and the elevator man); others are both instructive and salutary (the conversation with Luce or Mr. Antolini, with its ambiguous conclusion in Antolini's apparent homosexual advance); and some seem to suggest a role for Holden in relation to childhood—he can be a catcher in the rye, the adult who is the protector of childish innocence. Over these episodes, Holden obviously develops and his attitudes change. He is hunting for his own adulthood, but doesn't want to lose his childhood. He sees his childhood dropping away from him (as in the scene . . . when, after recalling the joys of going to the museum, he decides not to go in). He realises the impossibility of rubbing out all the dirty words from the world. He also realises that many of the characters who might help him to an adult world finally disappoint him. He ends up in the middle of a complex of contradictions. He thinks he will leave town and 'go out west and all'. But he doesn't, because Phoebe persuades him not to; and he ends the sequence apparently as the catcher in the rye, watching from the sides as Phoebe turns and turns on the carousel of her childhood and feeling 'so damn happy all of a sudden'. (pp. 60-4)

The scene is, in a sense, more than Holden says it is, because it not only tells his happiness but draws together various themes and depends on various contrasts—with the commercial Christmas-time we have just been seeing, for example. It recreates the pattern of the 'catcher in the rye' story: Holden as the older, protective watcher observing the happiness of childhood and its lack of concern about where it is going. Holden wears his hunting cap, a protective device he has kept donning through the story, and which has been associated with childhood: Phoebe has just been wearing it, and it has almost become for us a mildly symbolic badge of innocence. It is the novelist who creates this sense of significance, finally; particularly in the interesting verbal ambiguity of the last line, which suggests that religious feeling is what, in an oblique and unstated way, Holden has been looking for. The absence of God, the absence of veneration for things, seems here to be redeemed; we recall other moments like this one, such as the scene where Holden refuses to throw snowballs at the car and the fire hydrant because they 'looked so nice and white'. If the image serves Holden as a secure moment of happiness, it serves the reader even more. But there are also ironies in it that are surely beyond Holden's seeing. It starts to rain, and the hunting cap gives him 'a lot of protection, in a way' but doesn't stop him getting soaked. Holden has already been feeling ill, and the next thing we learn— Holden deliberately doesn't give the reasons or the details—is that this is followed by illness. 'I practically got T. B.,' Holden has earlier told us, from his post-narrative position. Holden's real power to protect childhood, moreover, is already in question; and, as in the image of the catcher on the cliff, with Holden himself threatened with toppling over backwards too, the scene suggests that his position is neither lasting nor safe. He does not belong on the innocent roundabout of the young; he is out and exposed to the weather. His idealised image is real enough here, but also qualified—and really by the novelist, who would seem to be suggesting in the situation more than Holden actually understands or knows.

This brings us back to the question of the point of view of the book. The main action takes place some time before the time of writing; but between those two points in time something has happened to Holden, which is not stated directly by him. Holden has indeed gone 'out west and all', but not in the way he intended—he is in hospital on the west coast, apparently with something like T. B. but also under psychiatric treatment. . . . All this brings alive in the story those signs of oncoming illness we have had touched into the telling; Holden's feeling 'spooky' and his getting wet in the rain; the warnings of Mr. Antolini about 'This fall I think you're riding for'. This involves additional meanings—meanings beyond Holden's way of looking at these events at this time and place—and these have to be worked into the story by the novelist: the novelist who in some fuller sense *does* know what the story means. Salinger has created a world of very immediate experiences and actions; created a narrator who is very open to experience and does to a considerable extent interpret it for us; but there are certain touches of distance that separate novelist and his narrator Holden.

The question of whether Holden is a reliable narrator, a sane or honest one, is one possible area of separation, but perhaps not the most important. Holden's engaging admission that the story is 'crazy', 'madman stuff', doesn't so much throw doubt on his accuracy or viewpoint as encourage us to respect his independence. But it does provide a way in which he is seeing the story in a different way from us. The real touches of distance come from tone and technique. At one level, they come from the comedy, which makes Holden sympathetically farcical. But even that is understandable in terms of his

viewpoint. More important is the way Salinger creates a contradiction in Holden; between his essential openness to experience and his essential innocence. All that is important to Holden comes out of life, and so his attitudes can be presented as moments of immediate emotional response that flow out of the run of the living. But it is innocence that makes Holden open to experience; and it is also experience that is the obverse of innocence. One has to grow up, face 'reality', be mature. The childish eye cannot *remain* childish. So Holden's adventures bring him to the edge of the crucial cliff that brings the innocent out of childhood and which is—in this novel, surely—a version of the fall of man. 'I think that one of these days', he (Mr. Antolini) said, 'you're going to have to find out where you want to go. And then you've got to start going there'. Holden sees himself that simply by continuing through the line of experience one reaches a point where the vision is questioned. Hence perhaps his getting run down; hence perhaps the gap between novelist and narrator; hence the discovery that Holden is thinking of going back to school, and his experiences must start opening out again. (pp. 65-7)

The story, then, focuses on a crucial phase in Holden's life, the point at which one crosses the line from innocence to experience. The crossing involves a fall and a decline; it also involves a kind of moral schizophrenia. The innocent eye involves a love of the world, an appreciation of it, an attempt to reconcile the love and the squalor in it. But the squalor itself threatens to engulf the innocent eye. Holden comes to learn that 'you can't ever find a place that's nice and peaceful, because there isn't any'. The theme of the novel is indeed in some sense religious: how do we come to accept a world in some respects evil and corrupt, yet is our only world. The presence of the novelist in the themes and episodes raises these questions, and raises them beyond and outside Holden. He, in fact, must go on to grow up; but the innocence of vision he presents may help us to perceive the world in a different way. So we, in seeing not only Holden but the way the novelist has created Holden and his world, see the book as a much more enduring meaning than Holden does. We know, more than he does, what to think about it; we know it as a fictional work, a created whole. (p. 67)

To a considerable extent, *The Catcher in the Rye* is a book that follows life through with an empirical curiosity, and many of the things in it are surely designed to interest in that life for its own sake. At the same time, it is also concerned with making central and crucial a particular point in human experience—the point at which the child becomes adult and at which an innocent and hopeful love, a desire to protect life, becomes a profound human problem. Holden's special world does not stay intact, but it has been imagined and created up to the limit of its possibilities, and out of it a value and a meaning emerges. It is a value and meaning that comes from Salinger's control and management; and we will not really understand it unless we respond, whether consciously or unconsciously, to that control and management. It consists of a story that moves us through a social world and a moral world internal to that story, and it is up to us to look how the values by which we judge the story come out of what is given of that internal world. (pp. 67-8)

Malcolm Bradbury, "Reading a Novel," in his What Is a Novel? *Edward Arnold (Publishers) Ltd., 1969, pp. 57-69.*

ROBERT COLES

By now J. D. Salinger's Holden Caulfield would be approaching 40, and perhaps (with him one can't be certain) would have fathered one or two of those children he dreamed of catching, in case their frolic in the rye led them dangerously astray. By no means have readers wearied of Holden. As of April 1972 his youthful preoccupations had gone into their 33rd paperback printing. It is hard to estimate the influence of a widely read book, but surely few writers have affected certain young people of a generation as strongly as Salinger did in the 1950s and into the early 1960s. (p. 30)

Holden Caulfield is yet another quizzical adolescent, scornful of what he does see and quite sure there is even more to unearth and condemn. He is kin of Maisie in Henry James' *What Maisie Knew* and of Portia in Elizabeth Bowen's *Death of the Heart;* like them, he serves the author's purpose: to scrutinize the banalities and cruelties that the rest of us, grown-up and so sure of our right to preach to children, often make a point of ignoring or justifying. But Salinger is not only a shrewd and winning observer or critic; he is also a rather active proponent of certain values—and it turns out, a man of considerable vision. In the late 1940s, when Holden first began to appear men wore their hair short, the nation was hopeful that its industrial productivity, so accelerated by World War II, would continue to increase by leaps and bounds, psychoanalysis was becoming a virtual religion among the agnostic *haute bourgeoisie* of cities like New York, Chicago and San Francisco, and certainly the idea of being a soldier and fighting a war was not looked down upon—the worst tyrant in history having just been defeated through the efforts of millions of American, British and Russian troops. Nevertheless Holden differed strongly with those and other habits or assumptions of postwar America. If his differences were destined to be overlooked or unduly taken in stride by his admirers, then one has to ask whether *any* criticism could really unnerve Eisenhower's America.

Much of the criticism of *Catcher in the Rye* . . . centers on Holden Caulfield as the *enfant terrible,* or the mixed-up, if not seriously "disturbed" adolescent. True, he is praised for his social commentary, or condemned as a snotty kid who sees the obvious, all from the vantage point of obvious money and power. (His father is a corporation lawyer.) But the emphasis is always on the private schools he attended, one after the other, or the New York scene that keeps coming up: the Hotel Biltmore, Central Park, the museums, the theater, the skating rink, a movie, a cafeteria, a train terminal, a swanky apartment building or two. That is, Holden is given credit for getting the number of all the phonies he meets in those places, or is called a self-indulgent brat who has no real "depth," only a kind of smart-aleck, superficial shrewdness.

In fact, Holden long ago addressed himself to the most serious of concerns; and they are ones which still hold our attention. He can't imagine himself fighting in a war. He is aghast at the tawdriness of urban life; he yearns for a place that is quiet, that is "nice and peaceful"—not surrounded by defaced buildings and noisemaking machines and air that one can't enjoy breathing. His girlfriend wonders why people have to wear crewcuts. And he extends his criticism of a particular culture a lot further than that: the dreariness and rigidity of the "best" education; the smugness and narrowness that a certain kind of psychoanalytic ideologue can demonstrate, and for doing so, be worshiped as a virtual messiah; and not least, the subtle nature of that social and psychologi-cal "adjustment" most of us make to the various "powers and principalities" we recognize both dimly and quite clearly (depending upon which moment it is) as our ultimate masters—always to be taken into consideration and appeased, if not followed blindly. (p. 31)

I have no idea why Salinger has not in recent years graced us with more stories. It is no one's business, really. He has already given us enough, maybe too much: we so far have not shown ourselves able to absorb and use the wisdom he has offered us. . . . A while back one could read Salinger and feel him to be not only an original and gifted writer, a marvelous entertainer, a man free of the slogans and clichés the rest of us fall prey to, or welcome as salvation itself, but also a terribly lonely man. Perhaps he still feels lonely; but he is, I think, not so alone these days. The worst in American life he anticipated and portrayed to us a generation ago. The best side of us—Holden and the Glasses—still survives, and more can be heard reaching for expression in various ways and places, however serious the present-day assaults from various "authorities." I put down *Catcher in the Rye* and *Franny and Zooey* this year again grateful to their author. I wondered once more how to do justice to his sensibility: his wide and generous responsiveness to religious and philosophical ideas, his capacity to evoke the most poignant of human circumstances vividly and honestly, and with a rare kind of humor, both gentle and teasing. No doubt that sensibility continues to attract the many young men and women who read him; it can be said that they read him out of a special and occasionally desperate kind of thirst and hunger which he has all along appreciated and, "a certain Samaritan" that he is, tried both to comprehend and assuage. (p. 32)

Robert Coles, "Reconsideration: J. D. Salinger," in The New Republic, *Vol. 168, No. 17, April 28, 1973, pp. 30-2.*

JAMES BRYAN

Standing by the "crazy cannon" on Thomsen Hill one sunless afternoon, listening to the cheers from a football game below, "the two teams bashing each other all over the place," Holden Caulfield tries to "feel some kind of a good-by" to the prep school he has just flunked out of. . . . A careful look at this first scene in the novel provides clues for interpretation, by no means crucial in themselves, but illustrative of a pattern of scene construction and suggestive imagery which does yield meaning. Appropriate is this adolescent's sense of his "darkling plain" where, if an extravagant metaphor be allowed, "ignorant football teams clash by afternoon." In a pattern repeated throughout the novel, he thinks back to a time when he and two "nice guys" passed a football around, shared rather than fought over it, though even then the idyllic state seemed doomed. Holden is poised between two worlds, one he cannot return to and the other he fears to enter, while the image of a football conflict is probably an ironic commentary on Holden's adolescence, football's being a civilized ritualization of human aggression.

What is forcing Holden's crisis? Everything in the idyllic scene points to the encroachment of time—the season, the time of day, even such verbal echoes from his friends' names as "ticking," "bell," and "pall." Accrual of this sort of evidence will justify what may seem overinterpretation here, especially of the significance of a biology teacher's ending the boys' innocent pleasures—their idyll already sentenced by time, darkness. More than anything else Holden fears the biological imperatives of adulthood—sex, senescence, and death. . . . (p. 1065)

Much of the *Catcher* criticism has testified to Holden's acute moral and esthetic perceptions—his eye for beauty as well as "phoniness"—but the significance of his immaturity in intensifying these perceptions has not been sufficiently stressed nor explained. Precisely because this sixteen-year-old acts "like I'm about thirteen" and even "like I was only about twelve," he is hypersensitive to the exploitations and insensitivity of the postpubescent world and to the fragile innocence of children. A central rhythm of the narrative has Holden confronting adult callousness and retreating reflexively into thoughts and fantasies about children, childlike Jane Gallaghers, and especially his ten-year-old sister, Phoebe. These juxtapositions render both worlds more intensely and at the same time qualify Holden's judgments by showing that they are emotionally—or, as we shall see, neurotically—induced.

While a fair number of critics have referred to Holden's "neurosis," none has accepted Salinger's invitation—proffered in the form of several key references to psychoanalysis—to participate in a full-fledged psychoanalytical reading. . . . As a step toward psychological understanding, I shall consider certain manifestations of Holden's disturbances. An examination of the structure, scene construction, and suggestive imagery reveals a pattern of aggression and regression, largely sexual, which is suggested in the Pencey Prep section, acted out in the central part of the novel, and brought to a curious climax in the Phoebe chapters.

One implication of the novel's main motif, that which polarizes childlike and adult responses, concerns the dilemma of impossible alternatives. Here characters suggest human conditions that Holden either cannot or must not make his own. In the novel's first paragraph Holden tells us that his brother D. B. has "prostituted" his writing talents by going to Hollywood—a failure implicitly contrasted throughout with the purity of Allie, the brother who died before the temptations of adulthood. Holden's first encounter is with Spencer, the old teacher who fills his mind with thoughts of age and death, while his last is with Phoebe, his emblem of unattainable childhood beauty. Stradlater and Ackley are antithetically placed to represent what Holden fears he may become if he is either sexually appropriative or repressed. Because the novel is built around these impossible alternatives, because Holden's world provides no one he can truly emulate, the many critics who read *Catcher* as a sweeping indictment of society have virtually drowned out those who attack Holden's immaturity. One feels the justice of this, yet the novel's resolution, like all of Salinger's mature fiction, transcends sociological indictment in affirming individual responsibility. When Holden answers for his own life as he verges toward some rather dreadful appropriation of his own, he begins to come to terms at once with himself and society.

At the outset of traditional quest narratives, the hero often receives sage advice from a wise old man or crone. The best old Spencer can do is to wish Holden a depressing "good luck," just as another agent of education, a woman "around a hundred years old," will do in the penultimate chapter. (pp. 1065-66)

[Though the episode between Holden and Spencer establishes that] Holden has flunked the administrative requirements of education, we learn immediately that he draws sustenance

from art. He returns to his room to reread in Isak Dinesen's *Out of Africa* that chronicle of sensitivity surrounded by primitive id forces. At this point he is interrupted by eighteen-year-old Robert Ackley, a grotesque possibility of what Holden may become if his manhood is similarly thwarted. Unleavened sensitivity will not be enough as we see Holden vacillating through five chapters between Ackley and Ward Stradlater, the equally unacceptable model of male aggressiveness. Stradlater's vitality is dramatized in his "Year Book" handsomeness, "damn good build," and superior strength, while Ackley's impotence is reflected in acned, unsightly looks, general enervation, and repulsive habits. Stradlater is slovenly too—Holden calls him a "secret slob"—but he elicits some admiration where Ackley is only pathetic.

Stradlater's date for the evening is Jane Gallagher, a girl with whom Holden has had a summer romance. That relationship was characterized by Jane's habit of keeping her kings in the back row when they played checkers—later on, Holden says specifically that their lovemaking never went beyond the handholding stage. In Holden's request that Stradlater ask Jane if she still keeps her kings in the back row, [Carl F. Strauch] sees Holden signaling warnings about her "sexy" date [see *CLC*, Volume 12]. (p. 1066)

Stradlater's strength and sexuality cause Holden to discountenance his own. This night, for example, Stradlater uses Holden's "Vitalis" hair tonic and borrows his "hound's-tooth" jacket, leaving Holden "so nervous I nearly went crazy" as he thinks of this "sexy bastard" with Jane. Conversely, Holden this same night endures Ackley's droning narrative of his sexual exploits with a final comment, "He was a virgin if I ever saw one. I doubt if he ever even gave anybody a feel." Not until Holden faces the Ackley and Stradlater in himself will he be able to do the purgative writing that is of course the form of the novel itself. They are almost like doppelgangers; one will interrupt him when he reads to escape while the other rejects the composition he ghostwrites because it is escapist. Even when he attacks the cocksure Stradlater after the latter's date with Jane, Holden's brief blood initiation is, as we shall see, a needful battle against himself. Right after the fight, getting no consolation from that other polar figure, Ackley, Holden leaves Pencey Prep.

The five Stradlater and Ackley chapters make for closely woven, dramatized exposition of Holden's psychological quandary which prepares for the loose, episodic middle section of the novel where Holden goes questing after experience and wisdom. Rejecting the alternatives implicit in Stradlater and Ackley, Holden wants his life to be vital without appropriation, innocent without retrogression. In the Phoebe section where the novel tightens up again, we shall see that Holden nearly becomes *both* appropriative and retrogressive and that it is precisely Holden's awareness of this that points the way to maturity.

Immediately after arriving in New York and checking into a hotel room, Holden is treated to a fresh installment of the Ackley-Stradlater antithesis. Through one window across an airshaft he sees a transvestite dress himself and mince before a mirror, while in the window above a couple squirt water "out of their mouths at each other." Holden confesses at this point that "In my *mind,* I'm probably the biggest sex maniac you ever saw" and that he might enjoy such "crumby stuff" as squirting water in a girl's face. . . . Later in a bar he is flanked on his left by "this funny-looking guy" nervously reciting to his date "every single goddam play" of a football game he had seen, and on the other side by a suave young man giving a beautiful girl "a feel under the table," over her embarrassed objections, "at the same time telling her all about some guy in his dorm that had . . . nearly committed suicide." All around him Holden sees distorted reflections of his own spasmodic aggression and withdrawal. And in the last instance cited we get an early hint of one of the most dangerous manifestations of his neurosis: his association of sex with death.

When he retreats in a panic to Grand Central Station, for example, he begins to read a discarded magazine to "make me stop thinking" about Antolini's apparent homosexual advances. One article convinces him that his hormones are "lousy" and another that he would "be dead in a couple of months" from cancer. What seems burlesque here ("That magazine was some little cheerer upper") becomes urgent in Holden's response to an obscene legend he sees shortly after in Phoebe's school:

> Somebody'd written "Fuck you" on the wall. It drove me damn near crazy. I thought how Phoebe and all the other little kids would see it, and how they'd wonder what the hell it meant, and then finally some dirty kid would tell them—all cockeyed, naturally—what it meant. . . . I figured it was some perverty bum that'd sneaked in the school late at night to take a leak or something and then wrote it on the wall. I kept picturing myself catching him at it, and how I'd smash his head on the stone steps till he was good and goddam dead and bloody. But I knew, too, I wouldn't have the guts to do it. I knew that. That made me even more depressed. I hardly even had the guts to rub it off the wall with my *hand,* if you want to know the truth. I was afraid some teacher would catch me rubbing it off and would think *I'd* written it. But I rubbed it out anyway, finally.

As we shall see, Holden is more repelled by the "obscenity" of the sexual act itself than by the obscene word. And his fear of being identified with the sort of "pervert" who planted it in Phoebe's school is reiterated when, in one more withdrawal, he goes to the mummy tomb in the museum and again finds the legend. At this point he decides,

> You can't ever find a place that's nice and peaceful, because there isn't any. You may *think* there is, but once you get there, when you're not looking, somebody'll sneak up and write "Fuck you" right under your nose. Try it sometime. I think, even, if I ever die, and they stick me in a cemetery, and I have a tombstone and all, it'll say "Holden Caulfield" on it, and then what year I was born and what year I died, and right under that it'll say "Fuck you." I'm positive, in fact.

It is not enough to leave it that Holden's sickness has brought about this odd commingling of lovemaking and dying in his mind. Looking back at Holden's ostensibly random comments on various fascinations and aversions, one sees a subtle but coherent psychological pattern taking shape. Early in the novel we learn of his interest in Egyptian mummification and his particular fascination—mentioned again in the tomb scene—that the process ensured that "their faces wouldn't rot or anything." (pp. 1067-68)

If there are sexual inhibitions reflected in Holden's curious

concern with the "preservation of faces," they must also be implicit in his general and constant longing for a state of changelessness. He laments, for instance, that though his beloved museum never changed, he did. . . . (p. 1068)

The expository sections of the novel dramatize Holden's problems as essentially sexual and moral. Yet most critical readings of the novel's ending either ignore these things or imply their absence by declaring that the resolution is "blunted" or else "humanly satisfying" while "artistically weak." Those critics who attest to a harmonious resolution generally do so on philosophical grounds, the effect being a divorce of theme from Holden's human situation. To deny a fused sexual and moral resolution of some sort in the closing emotional crescendo of the Phoebe section would, it seems to me, impugn the integrity of the novel.

I am suggesting that the urgency of Holden's compulsions, his messianic desire to guard innocence against adult corruption, for example, comes of a frantic need to save his sister from himself. It may be Phoebe's face that Holden unconsciously fears may be desecrated; hence the desire to protect Phoebe's face that compels his fascination with mummification. And it may be Phoebe who provokes his longing for stasis because he fears that she may be changed—perhaps at his own hand. Holden's association of sex with death surely points to some sexual guilt—possibly the fear that he or Phoebe or both may "die" if repressed desires are acted out.

I do not mean to imply that Holden's desires, if they are what I suggest, drive him inexorably to Phoebe's bed. The psychoanalytical axiom may here apply that a sister is often the first replacement of the mother as love object, and that normal maturation guides the boy from sister to other women. At this point in his life, Holden's sexuality is swaying precariously between reversion and maturation—a condition structurally dramatized throughout and alluded to in this early description:

> I was sixteen then, and I'm seventeen now, and sometimes I act like I'm about thirteen. It's really ironical, because I'm six foot two and a half and I have gray hair. I really do. The one side of my head—the right side—is full of millions of gray hairs. I've had them ever since I was a kid. And yet I still act sometimes like I was only about twelve. . . .

The narrator's overall perspective is thus mapped out: his present age representing some measure of maturity, and thirteen and twelve the vacillation that normally comes at puberty and that is so much more painful when it occurs as late as sixteen. This vacillation is somehow resolved in a climax beginning in Phoebe's bedroom (or rather the bedroom of D. B., the corrupt brother, where she sleeps) and ending at the carrousel after Holden has refused to let her run away with him. However one interprets the ending, it comes as a surprise which is dramatically appropriate precisely because it shocks Holden. Hence, also, the aptness of providing only scattered hints of things to come through the quest section, hints which, in my presentation, will necessarily seem tentative.

One notes in passing, for example, Holden's sudden infatuation with Bernice, one of the prosaic Seattle girls, while they are dancing. "You really can dance," he tells her. "I have a kid sister that's only in the goddam fourth grade. You're about as good as she is, and she can dance better than any-body living or dead." (pp. 1068-69)

More can be made of an assertion Holden is constrained to repeat that Phoebe is "too affectionate." After retreating from making the date with Faith, he describes Phoebe at length. . . . Later, when Holden awakens Phoebe and "She put her arms around my neck and all," he blurts out:

> She's very affectionate. I mean she's quite affection-ate, for a child. Sometimes she's even *too* affection-ate. I sort of gave her a kiss.

One begins to recognize the brilliant stratagem of imprecise adolescent qualifiers such as "sort of," "I mean," "and all," and the nervous repetition of "affectionate" which dramatize Holden's confusion of restraint and desire. (p. 1069)

Then, there is the curious matter of "Little Shirley Beans," the record Holden buys for Phoebe:

> It was about a little kid that wouldn't go out of the house because two of her front teeth were out and she was ashamed to. . . . I knew it would knock old Phoebe out. . . . It was a very old, terrific re-cord that this colored girl singer, Estelle Fletcher, made about twenty years ago. She sings it very Dix-ieland and whorehouse, and it doesn't sound at all mushy. If a white girl was singing it, she'd make it sound *cute* as hell, but old Estelle Fletcher knew what the hell she was doing, and it was one of the best records I ever heard.

The significance of the record is underscored by Holden's anxiousness to give it to Phoebe and his inordinate dismay when he breaks it. . . . One wonders if the accident wasn't psychically determined. If the Shirley Beans affair were a sub-ject of dream analysis, the missing teeth, the shame, and the translation through "whorehouse" jazz by a singer who "knew what the hell she was doing" would conventionally suggest the loss of virginity. Hence, Holden's unconscious forces would dictate the destruction of this "record" as well as its purchase. (pp. 1069-70)

At one point Holden hears a child singing the song that be-comes the anthem of his savior fantasies: "If a body catch a body coming through the rye." Yet in the next paragraph he buys the "Little Shirley Beans" record—the pairing symboli-cally dramatizes his conflict of protecting and of violating. . . .

After a series of abortive adventures with women, Holden rather desperately seeks the counsel of a former classmate who was regarded as the dormitory's resident expert on sexu-al matters. Luce is too pompous to help, but his cutting as-sessments are probably accurate. He tells Holden that his "mind is immature" and recommends psychoanalysis, as he had done the last time they had talked. Holden's self-diagnosis at this point—that his "trouble" is an inability to get "sexy—I mean really sexy—with a girl I don't like a lot"—raises questions when one recalls his fraternal affection for Jane Gallagher and the relatively sexy episodes with the likes of Sally Hayes and "a terrible phony named Anne Lou-ise Sherman." A probable answer, as we shall see, lies in his confused feelings about Phoebe.

All chances for normal sexual expression or even sexual un-derstanding now depleted, Holden gets drunk and goes to Central Park to find "where the ducks go in winter." . . . It ought to be pointed out that Holden's breakdown occurs after

the events of the narrative. His desperation in the park is cer-tainly one extreme of his vacillation, the withdrawing ex-treme which is imaged by coldness and thoughts of death. Fi-nally, he decides to see Phoebe, "in case I died and all," more explicitly associating Phoebe with death.

Holden makes his way into the apartment furtively—ostensibly to keep his parents from learning that he had flunked out of school. Yet his guilt seems obsessive. "I really should've been a crook," he says after telling the elevator op-erator that he was visiting the "Dicksteins" who live next door, that he has to wait for them in their hallway because he has a "bad leg," causing him to limp "like a bastard." Though his mother "has ears like a goddam bloodhound," his parents are out and he enters Phoebe's room undetected. (p. 1070)

Suddenly Holden feels "swell" as he notices such things as Phoebe's discarded clothing arranged neatly on a chair. Throughout the Phoebe section, double entendres and sexu-ally suggestive images and gestures multiply, most flowing naturally from Holden's mind while others, once the coding is perceived, become mechanical pointers to the psychologi-cal plot.

When Holden awakens Phoebe and is embarrassed by her overaffection, she eagerly tells him about the play in which she is "Benedict Arnold." . . . When the Benedict Arnold image recurs at the end, we shall see that the role of "traitor" is precisely the one she must play if her brother is to weather his crisis. . . .

Through the next chapter Phoebe hears Holden out on his "categorical aversions," in Salinger's phrase, to all the "pho-niness" that has soured his world. The conversation begins in a curious manner:

> Then, just for the hell of it, I gave her a pinch on the behind. It was sticking way out in the breeze, the way she was laying on her side. She has hardly any behind. I didn't do it hard, but she tried to hit my hand anyway, but she missed.
>
> Then all of a sudden, she said, "Oh, why did you *do* it?" She meant why did I get the ax again. It made me sort of sad, the way she said it.

Holden spells out his dissatisfactions at length—and indeed he cites valid and depressing instances of human failings—until Phoebe challenges him several times, "You don't like *any*thing that's happening." "Name one thing," she de-mands. "One thing? One thing I like?" Holden replies. "Okay." At this point he finds he can't "concentrate too hot." . . . He can't concentrate, I suggest, because the truth is too close.

> About all I could think of were those two nuns that went around collecting dough in those beat-up old straw baskets. Especially the one with the glasses with those iron rims. And this boy I knew at Elkton Hills.

(p. 1071)

None of this will do for Phoebe and she repeats the challenge:

> "I like Allie," I said. "And I like doing what I'm doing right now. Sitting here with you, and talking, and thinking about stuff, and—"

When she objects that "Allie's dead," Holden tries to explain but gives up. . . . Her insistence drives him to the loveliest—and most sinister—fantasy in the novel:

> "You know that song 'If a body catch a body comin' through the rye'? I'd like—"
>
> "It's 'If a body *meet* a body coming through the rye!'" old Phoebe said.

Holden proceeds to conjure up the daydream of himself as catcher in the rye, the protector of childhood innocence. As Phoebe implies, however, the song is about romance, not romanticism. Because he has to, Holden has substituted a messianic motive for the true, erotic one.

In the next chapter Holden and Phoebe seem to be acting out a mock romance, much the way Seymour Glass does with the little girl in **"A Perfect Day for Bananafish."** The episode is at once movingly tender and ominous. (pp. 1071-72)

[Later, the parents return] and the scene that follows, Holden gathering up his shoes and hiding in the closet as the mother interrogates Phoebe about the (cigarette) "smoke" in the bedroom and asks "were you warm enough?" is reminiscent of nothing so much as that mainstay of French farce, the lover hiding in the closet or under the bed as the girl ironically "explains" to husband or parent. . . .

When the mother leaves, Holden emerges from his hiding place and borrows money from Phoebe. Phoebe insists that he take all of her money and Holden "all of a sudden" begins to cry. . . . Holden's breakdown, his visiting of his own suffering on the child, the chill air, and the innocence of their intimacy in this moving scene signal his growing, frightening awareness of the other sort of intimacy. From now until he sees Phoebe again, Holden is in full flight. Nonetheless, their parting is filled with suggestions of a sort one might expect after a casual, normal sexual encounter. (The emphases in the following passage are my own.)

> Then I *finished buttoning* my coat and all. I told her I'd *keep in touch with her*. She told me *I could sleep with her* if I wanted to, but I said no, that I'd better beat it. . . . Then I took my hunting hat out of my coat pocket and *gave it to her*. She likes those kind of crazy hats. She didn't want to take it, but *I made her*. I'll bet she *slept with it* on. She really likes those kinds of hats. Then I told her again I'd *give her a buzz* if I got a chance, and then I left.

It is almost as if Holden is acknowledging the real content of the sexual charade and escaping while he can. (p. 1072)

Holden leaves Phoebe to spend the night with Mr. Antolini, a former teacher who during the course of the evening offers sound if stilted assessments of Holden's future which become particularly relevant in the epilogue. Antolini has been drinking, however, and disrupts the peace he has provided (Holden feels sleepy for the first time) by awakening the boy with tentative homosexual advances. Certainly Holden is victimized ("I was shaking like a madman. . . . I think I was more depressed than I ever was in my life"), but the encounter may torment him most for its parallels to his own unconscious designs on a child. Now one begins to see the significance of Holden's unfounded suspicions about Jane Gallagher's stepfather and his murderous rage at the "perverty bum" who wrote the obscenity on Phoebe's school wall—inordinate reactions pointing to fears about himself.

At this point Holden's neurosis verges on madness. Each time he crosses a street, he imagines he will "disappear" and "never get to the other side of the street." I do not take this so much as a symbolic manifestation of "identity crisis" and of his fear that he "may never reach maturity"—although both are implicit—but rather as a literal, psychologically valid description of the boy's breakdown. He retreats into wild fantasies of running away forever, living in a cabin near, but not in, the woods ("I'd want it to be sunny as hell all the time"), and feigning deaf-muteness, all to escape the confusion about to engulf him. Phoebe betrays these plans—the first ironic level of the Benedict Arnold motif—by joining in his escape. When she appears, bag in hand and the hunting cap on her head, Holden reacts wildly:

> "I'm going with you. Can I? Okay?"
>
> "What?" I said. I almost fell over when she said that. I swear to God I did. I got sort of dizzy and I thought I was going to pass out or something again. . . .

[This near-hysterical response] can be understood, it seems to me, only in the context that Phoebe is the very thing he is fleeing. He somehow realizes that she *must* be his "Benedict Arnold."

Holden's fury at Phoebe having set the climax in motion, Salinger now employs a delicate spatial strategy. Phoebe returns the hat, turns her back on Holden, announces that she has no intention of running away with him, and runs "right the hell across the street, without even looking to see if any cars were coming." Positioning here signifies the end of their relation as possible lovers, but love remains. Holden does not go after her, knowing she'll follow him "on the *other* goddam side of the street. She wouldn't look over at me at all, but I could tell she was probably watching me out of the corner of her crazy eye to see where I was going and all. Anyway, we kept walking that way all the way to the zoo." (pp. 1072-73)

[Holden finally] promises not to run away and they rejoin as brother and sister in the presence of the carrousel—miraculously open in winter. Phoebe wants to ride and Holden finds a mature, new perspective:

> All the kids kept trying to grab for the gold ring, and so was old Phoebe, and I was sort of afraid she'd fall off the goddam horse, but I didn't say anything or do anything. The thing with kids is, if they want to grab for the gold ring, you have to let them do it, and not say anything. If they fall off, they fall off, but it's bad if you say anything to them.

The substitution of a gold ring for the traditional brass one may point to Phoebe's future as a woman. In any event, Holden has renounced his designs on Phoebe and thus abrogated his messianic role. . . . One need not search for literary sources to recognize that the carrousel finally represents everyone's sacred, inviolable human destiny. (pp. 1073-74)

In the epilogue we learn that Holden went West—"after I went home, and . . . got sick and all"—not for the traditional opportunity there but for psychotherapy. This would be a bleak ending were it not for the fact that Holden has authored this structured narrative, just as Antolini predicted he might:

> you'll find that you're not the first person who was ever confused and frightened and even sickened by human behavior. You're by no means alone on that score, you'll be excited and *stimulated* to know.

Many, many men have been just as troubled morally and spiritually as you are right now. Happily, some of them kept records of their troubles. You'll learn from them—if you want to. Just as someday, if you have something to offer, someone will learn something from you. It's a beautiful reciprocal arrangement. And it isn't education. It's history. It's poetry.

The richness of spirit in this novel, especially of the vision, the compassion, and the humor of the narrator reveal a psyche far healthier than that of the boy who endured the events of the narrative. Through the telling of his story, Holden has given shape to, and thus achieved control of, his troubled past. (p. 1074)

> James Bryan, "The Psychological Structure of 'The Catcher in the Rye'," in PMLA, Vol. 89, No. 5, October, 1974, pp. 1065-74.

DUANE EDWARDS

Salinger's admirers have responded in a variety of ways to *The Catcher in the Rye,* but most have something in common: they idealize Holden. In order to do so, they play down the seriousness of his ambivalence, exhibitionism, and voyeurism and assign the blame for his severe depression entirely to society, to the world of perverts and bums and phonies. Failing to respond to the first person narrator as ironic, they assume that Holden should be taken at his word; that he is right and the world wrong; that there is a sharp dichotomy between Holden and the world he loathes. . . . What these writers ignore is that Holden shares in the phoniness he loathes; that he lives by his unconscious needs and not the values he espouses; that he withdraws from rather than faces the challenge of personal relationships.

It's not difficult to understand why readers have ignored, or have failed to perceive, Holden's grave deficiencies as a person. After all, he is very appealing—on the surface. He genuinely appreciates brief and isolated instances of kindness and accurately pinpoints phoniness in both high and low places; he is witty and his love for Phoebe is touching. But he himself is a phony at times, and he has virtually no self-awareness. Furthermore, he has no intention of gaining awareness. . . . [He] cannot name one *living* person, or even one occupation, that he likes. Nevertheless, he believes he is a lover of people in general because he wants to be the catcher in the rye.

When Holden says that he wants to be the catcher in the rye, he reveals a great deal about himself—a great deal more than he knows. He reveals that he does not seriously want to learn about himself. He simply won't make the effort. After all, he hasn't bothered to read Burns's poem; he isn't even able to quote accurately the one line he heard a small boy recite; he doesn't know that Burns's narrator contemplates kissing the "body" he meets in the rye field. So when Holden changes the word "meet" to "catch" and talks not of love but of potential death (falling off a cliff), he reveals his willingness to distort the truth by ignoring—or even changing—the facts. He also reveals his use of displacement: he substitutes one response for another. He focuses on danger and potential death instead of love and a personal relationship. Ultimately, he reveals his unreliability as the narrator of his own life's story.

Fortunately, the fact that Holden distorts doesn't matter to anyone concerned with the *significance* of the events and dialogue recorded in *The Catcher in the Rye.* Like the psychoanalyst analyzing a dream, the reader can analyze what matters most: the distortions. What emerges from this analysis is an awareness that Salinger's narrator is ironic: he doesn't understand (or know) himself, but he unwittingly lets the reader know what he is like. In fact, he does so at the very beginning of the novel when he promises to give the reader none of "that David Copperfield crap" about his "lousy childhood." Normally, such a statement would be innocent and unrevealing, but Holden isn't "normal": he's a severely depressed adolescent telling the story of his youth while in a mental institution. He is, by his own admission, sick. So his refusal to talk about the incidents of his childhood signifies that he will remain ill, as does his chilling advice, "Don't ever tell anybody anything," at the end of the novel.

Elsewhere in the novel there is evidence that Holden will remain ill because he refuses to assume responsibility for his own actions. For example, when he is "the goddam manager of the fencing team," he leaves the "foils and equipment and stuff" on the subway. Although he admits that he left them there, he hastens to add: "It wasn't all my fault." Here and elsewhere he simply will not or can not let his mind rest without ambivalence or qualification on a conclusion.

Ambivalence is, in fact, characteristic of Holden and the surest evidence of his mental instability. If he loathes what he loves and does so intensely, he is by no means well. He is also not what he and many readers assume he is: an anti-establishment figure whose disgust is directed entirely at other people. (pp. 554-56)

What is Holden's problem? Whatever it is in specific form, it's reflected in his inability to relate sexually to females. Holden himself suggests this when he says, "My sex life stinks." But even when he speaks the truth he fools himself: he believes that he cannot "get really sexy" with girls he doesn't like a lot whereas, in reality, he cannot get sexy with a girl he does like. In fact, what he likes about Jane Gallagher is that a relationship with her will not go beyond the hand-holding stage. In his other attempts to establish connections with girls or women, he fails sexually and, in fact, deliberately avoids both affection and serious sexual advances. He kisses Sally Hayes—but in a cab where the relationship cannot go beyond "horsing around." He consents to have a prostitute sent to his hotel room but asks her to stop when she starts "getting funny. Crude and all," that is, when she proceeds from words to action. Aroused by watching the "perverts" in the hotel, he does call up Faith Cavendish, a woman he has never seen, but at an impossibly late hour and so ensures that she will refuse his request for a date. Clearly, Holden has a problem with females.

This problem is reflected in his response to Mercutio in *Romeo and Juliet.* Acting in character, Holden identifies with Mercutio, the character in the play he has most in common with. . . . Mercutio assigns the role of lover to Romeo just as Holden assigns the role of lover to Stradlater. Then, too, both young men ramble on when they talk. Mr. Antolini reminds us that this is true of Holden; Romeo calls Mercutio's long speech "nothing" and Mercutio himself admits that he talks of "dreams / Which are the children of an idle brain, / Begot of nothing but vain fantasy." Finally, both Mercutio and Holden like to "horse around." Holden does so repeatedly; Mercutio does so even when he's dying.

What these two characters have in common at the level of speech and overt behavior reveals how they are alike in subtler ways. For example, both talk about, but do not engage in, sexual love. Both are more enamoured of words than facts. Both are victims—from Holden's point of view. Mercutio is the victim of the Capulets and of Romeo's desire to live at peace in the world; Holden sees himself as the victim of snobs, perverts, and phonies. Since Holden identifies with victims in general and, in fact, projects his suffering onto them, he has sympathy for the ducks in Central Park, for Selma Thurmer, and for the lunatic in *Mark V.* It follows logically that he likes Mercutio.

It also follows logically that he did not like "Romeo too much after Mercutio gets stabbed." Clearly, Romeo is the antithesis of both Mercutio and Holden. He is passionate; he speaks without irony; he goes to bed with Juliet. He is by no means sexually shy although he, like Holden, is very young. In contrast, Holden is sexually shy; paradoxically, he also has an exhibitionistic attitude, that is, he has a *need* to attract attention to himself by attempting "to amuse, to stir, or to shock others." Acting on this need, he performs for Stradlater in the men's room; he pretends to have a bullet in his stomach; performing for Ackley, he pulls his hunting hat over his eyes and says in a hoarse voice, "I think I'm going blind"; he wears a red hunting cap in the streets of New York. He even calls himself an exhibitionist to attract attention to himself.

It's true that each of these examples of exhibitionism is, in itself, both harmless and normal, especially for a boy of Holden's age. (Holden himself would say that he was simply "horsing around.") But Holden has a need to show off, and he has more serious problems eventually. After all, he does end up in a mental institution. Consequently, his exhibitionistic attitude serves as a clue to his state of mind; it also helps to explain why Holden "got sick and all." Since he himself won't tell us, this clue is especially important.

Other important clues to Holden's problem are included in Chapter 25, the chapter following Holden's flight from Mr. Antolini and preceding the one-page concluding chapter which reveals that Holden is in a mental institution. Near the beginning of Chapter 25, Holden's mental breakdown (which is not recorded in the novel) is anticipated: Holden has a headache and feels "more depressed than [he] ever was in [his] whole life." He also has the desire to catch what he assumes is "some perverty bum that'd sneaked in the school late at night to take a leak or something and then wrote [an obscenity] on the wall." And, finally, he notices—and comments on—a little boy who "had his pants open." Since Holden likes children more than adults and dead people more than the living, he is in character when he enters the tombs of the mummies with the little boy and his brother. He is also in character when, left alone in the tomb, he finds peace among the dead—at least temporarily. But then the words "Fuck you" written in red crayon on the wall remind him that he has not escaped from people, not even from the "perverty bums." Furthermore, he realizes that there is no escape even in death: some day someone will write this same obscenity on his tomb, he assumes. So when he leaves the tomb he is not cured but is, in fact, very ill: he "sort of had diarrhea" and finally passes out.

Commenting on this scene, [Carl F. Strauch (see *CLC*, Volume 12)] stresses that Holden feels better after he faints and "is reborn into a world of secure feelings and emotions, with himself fulfilling the office of catcher in his mature view of Phoebe." Since Holden is reconciled with Phoebe and says that he felt "so damn happy all of a sudden," there is some basis for this statement. However, Holden is not "reborn." Instead, by his own admission, he "got sick" (that is, mentally ill) *after* the fainting incident and the expression of happiness and is *subsequently* in an institution. Furthermore, his identification with the lunatic in *Mark V* prepares us for this.

Although Carl F. Strauch sees in Holden's response to the lunatic an anticipation of the fact that Holden "will subsequently break his morbid psychological fetters," there is too much evidence to the contrary. It's true that Holden and the lunatic have something in common: both spend time in the tombs; both suffer; both are mentally ill. But they are also unlike one another in some important ways. To begin with, the lunatic participates in his own cure by running up to Jesus, adoring him, and calling out to him. In contrast, Holden withdraws from people, including Phoebe. . . . He watches her "going around and around" on the carrousel, but he remains at a distance and stands apart from "the parents and mothers and everybody" who seek shelter from the rain under the roof of the carrousel. It's true that he, like the lunatic, does go home, but the lunatic goes home cured while Holden goes home only to leave in order to enter an institution. Finally, whereas the lunatic tells everybody what has been done for him, Holden regrets having told anybody anything. So it's not surprising that when Holden says he likes the lunatic "ten times as much as the Disciples," he refers to him as "that poor bastard" who lived in the tombs and kept cutting himself with stones" and does not refer to the lunatic's cure or his re-entry into the world of people, including adults. Acting consistently, he responds to *Mark V* the way he responds to Burns's poem: he cites what pleases him and ignores what doesn't.

This subjectivity and tendency to distort explains a great deal about Holden. Specifically, it explains his interest in the "perverty bum" and the little boy whose pants are unbottoned. Both appeal to him because of his voyeuristic tendencies.

That Holden has voyeuristic tendencies should surprise no one. He himself admits that he finds it "sort of fascinating to watch" bizarre sexual activity through his hotel window. Besides, anyone "who in the unconscious is an exhibitionist is at the same time a voyeur" in psychoanalytic terms. So it is not surprising that Holden is interested in the "perverty bum" and the little boy. What is surprising is the degree of his response. In the first instance he responds with extreme hostility; he wants to catch the bum urinating and/or writing on the wall (Holden is a bit ambiguous here) and "smash his head on the stone steps till he was good and goddam dead and bloody." In the second instance he responds with extreme concern and embarrassment; he says the boy's behavior "killed" him and adds that he wanted to laugh when the boy buttoned his pants without going behind a post, but he didn't dare to; he was afraid he'd "feel like vomiting again." (pp. 556-60)

It shouldn't be surprising that Holden has severe sexual conflicts: his family situation is far from ideal. The father barely exists as far as Holden and Phoebe are concerned, and the mother is not emotionally involved in the lives of her children. This is revealed in the scene in which the Caulfields return from a party. First of all, they are indifferent to Phoebe. Although she is still a child, they have left her home alone. When they do return home late at night, only Mrs. Caulfield bothers to look in on her daughter. But she is by no means greatly concerned. She doesn't object seriously to what she assumes is smoke from a cigarette Phoebe has been smoking; she moves randomly and nervously (like Holden) from one subject to another, including Holden's return from school; she fails to react to Phoebe's statement that she couldn't sleep. In brief, she is a mother incapable of affection.

Meanwhile, the father has gone into another room without bothering to inquire about Phoebe. Since Phoebe has said that he will not attend her Christmas pageant, it's safe to assume that he is generally absent from his children's lives. He is the aloof father whose inaccessibility makes it impossible for his son to identify with him and thus to develop "normally."

But he does have a connection with Holden: he punishes him. Confirming this, Phoebe says repeatedly that Mr. Caulfield will "kill" Holden, and Holden himself acknowledges that "it would've been very unpleasant and all" if his father had found him at home. Since Mr. Caulfield remains a vague and powerful figure, his effect on his son is inevitably exaggerated and debilitating. He joins forces with his wife to stifle and stunt his son's sexual development.

Because Holden's home situation is so unfortunate, it's easy to sympathize with him. It's even tempting to see the conclusion as affirmative. Besides, Holden is very appealing when he criticizes bums and phonies and perverts—so appealing that it's easy to forget that he's a bum, a phony (at times) and a potential pervert. And when he expresses his love for Phoebe, his hostility and egotism seem relatively unimportant. So it's tempting to see Holden as a person who doesn't need a psychoanalyst because he has gone beyond affirmation and denial. But at the end of the novel Holden is depressed and subdued. He has lost interest in life: he doesn't want to think about the past; he isn't interested in his future. When he tells D. B. that he doesn't know what to think about "all this stuff I just finished telling you about," he reveals that he is still confused. And when he says that he misses everybody—even Stradlater and Ackley and Maurice—he reveals that he is still sentimental. Although his sentimentality has often been sentimentalized as love, it is not love at all. It is a symptom of his inability to express his feelings easily and naturally.

Nevertheless, Holden is likable. He also deserves sympathy because, as William Faulkner has said, he "tried to join the human race and failed." But Faulkner is not quite accurate when he says that there was no human race for him to enter. Phoebe loves him; D. B. expresses an interest in him by visiting him in the mental institution; Mr. Antolini offers him shelter and good advice. Ultimately, people are as good to Holden as he is to them. So Holden should not be idealized. It may be true that he is "more intelligent than some and more sensitive than most," but his response to his own experience results in deep depression and may have culminated in mania. Nor does Holden resist the establishment that makes it difficult for him to love and develop. His rebellion is all fantasy. He tells off no one—not even the prostitute or the phonies at Pencey. And his overt behavior is conventional except when he is acting out his exhibitionistic attitude. He doesn't become a recluse or a beatnik; instead, he returns home, enters an institution, and will *again* return to school in the fall.

He does have what Faulkner calls an "instinct" to love man, but this makes him a typical, rather than extraordinary, teenager. It's what causes him to want to join the human race.

What does make him extraordinary is his special ability to de-

tect phoniness everywhere (except in himself). Of course it's unfair to emphasize, to the exclusion of everything else, that Holden shares in the phoniness he loathes. After all, Holden conforms to phoniness because he wants so badly to join the human race. But in doing so he makes it difficult for others like himself to find a human race to join. (pp. 561-63)

Duane Edwards, "Holden Caulfield: 'Don't Ever Tell Anybody Anything'," in ELH, *Vol. 44, No. 3, Fall, 1977, pp. 554-65.*

GERALD ROSEN

Now that over a quarter century has passed since the publication of **The Catcher in the Rye,** it is possible to see the book in the light of the enormous body of writing that has been done on it. . . . It is also possible to see the book in the context of Salinger's other work, especially the writings about the Glass family, most of which were published after **Catcher.** These stories reveal themes not immediately apparent in a reading of **Catcher** and stem from a side of Salinger that has been of less importance to his critics than to Salinger himself. I refer to the importance of Eastern thought and religion to Salinger, and of Buddhism in particular, especially the form which we in the West refer to as Zen.

The Zen masters have a saying, "Sometimes we go east, sometimes we go west," and it appears that Salinger, after a brief attempt to "go west" in the American army during World War II, became disillusioned with his native culture and society and turned to a study of Eastern thought. This disillusionment can be seen in Holden's approving remark about his brother D. B.: "My brother D. B. was in the Army for four goddam years. He was in the war, too—he landed on D-Day and all—but I really think he hated the Army worse than the War. . . . He said the Army was practically as full of bastards as the Nazis were." Of course I don't mean to identify Salinger with D. B., but like D. B. Salinger himself participated in the Normandy invasion and his story, **"For Esme—with Love and Squalor,"** embodies the vision which Holden attributes to D. B.

In Buddhism one is asked to give up one's illusions. **Catcher** was given final shape in the post-war period, and it is basically a novel of disillusionment. The radical nature of Salinger's portrayal of disappointment with American society, so much like Twain's in *Huck Finn,* was probably as much of the reason that **Catcher** (like *Huck*) was banned from schools and colleges as were the few curse words around which the battle was publicly fought. (pp. 547-48)

Since Salinger seemed to achieve instant success with the appearance of **Catcher** in 1951, it is important to remember that he was already in his early thirties by this time, had been publishing stories in slick magazines like *Saturday Evening Post* for ten years, and had been working on **Catcher** through much of this decade during which time he was studying Buddhism. . . . (p. 548)

The Buddha, like most great ancient religious teachers, now exists at the point where the lines of history and legend cross. . . . A Raja of the Sakya clan (he is sometimes referred to as Sakyamuni—the sage of the Sakyas), the Buddha, according to tradition, was born in what is now Nepal in 563 B.C. His name was Siddhartha Gotama. Raised in a protective, affluent environment, the young prince was shielded from the suffering of the world and not taught to deal with it. The turning point in the story of the Buddha's life occurs when he is confronted with old age, sickness, and death. They so shake him he decides to leave the shelter of his surroundings and the distractions of his involvement in his everyday life in order to wander in the world in search of a guide who will teach him to come to terms with old age, sickness, and death. He doesn't find one, is forced to work out his salvation on his own, persists in his detachment and alienation, has a vision of the truth, and returns to the world out of compassion for his fellow living suffering beings.

I would suggest that, in rough outline, and without the Buddha's final conscious mature understanding, this is the form of the story of Holden Caulfield. When we first meet Holden in the affluent, protective environment of a prep school, we are prepared for his lonely journey by immediately being given a picture of his alienation from the non-seeing groups of people around him. (Alienation is the negative side of detachment or non-attachment which the Eastern religions see as a virtue.) Salinger presents us with our first glimpse of Holden on the day of the big football game. Holden's detachment from the game is emphasized by having him view the stadium from a distance where the excitement and involvement of the crowd over "the two teams bashing each other all over the place" appears ridiculous. Holden comments, "The game with Saxon Hall was supposed to be a very big deal around Pencey. It was the last game of the year and you were supposed to commit suicide or something if old Pencey didn't win."

The reference to suicide is not fortuitous for we soon come to see that it is precisely a continuing preoccupation with death that keeps Holden from participating in the games of those around him. It prevents him from concentrating on those activities like day-to-day school chores which we don't ordinarily think of as games but which, in the presence of death, tend to recede toward the unimportance we usually ascribe to games.

And, in fact, just as in the story of the Buddha, it is sickness, old age, and death, which we the readers, along with Holden, encounter when we begin our journey through the pages of *The Catcher in the Rye.* We meet sickness and old age in the form of Mr. Spencer, Holden's teacher. . . . (pp. 548-49)

Holden explains to Mr. Spencer that his problem relates to the idea of life as a game. "He (Dr. Thurmer—the headmaster) just kept talking about life being a game and all." To which "old" Spencer responds, "Life *is* a game, boy." Holden agrees with him outwardly, but he tells us, his confidants, "Game my ass. Some game." At this point Holden believes his objection to life as "a game" is that it's only fun for the winners. But he has deeper, unconscious objections to life, since ultimately in life there are no winners, only corpses. And immediately after introducing sickness and old age, Salinger presents us with the third member of the Buddha's problematic triad—death.

Holden, like the young Buddha, is obsessed by death, and by its corollaries, time and change. He has turned Spencer's exam question about ancient Egypt into a short essay which Spencer cannot see as springing out of this obsession: "Modern science would still like to know what the secret ingredients were that the Egyptians used when they wrapped up dead people so that their faces would not rot for innumerable centuries." And Holden flunks, because on this exam, as in his life, no one has ever taught him how to get beyond this primary question, in the shrill light of which all secondary questions are obscured. (p. 550)

Holden has no one to teach him how to cope with death. In a stable culture, one would ordinarily turn to the oldest people for this kind of wisdom. They've been around the longest and presumably would have had the most experience with these matters. But in a rapidly changing culture like ours, the old people and their knowledge appear obsolete to the young. To Holden, the older people he meets are generally all right, but they seem "out of it": "I have this grandmother that's quite lavish with her dough. She doesn't have all her marbles anymore—she's old as hell . . ." and in "old" Spencer's case, "he was a nice old guy that didn't know his ass from his elbow."

Seeking protection himself, Holden is forced to protect the adults he encounters. He forgives Spencer in advance for failing him, writing on his exam, "It is all right with me if you flunk me. . . ." Several critics have noted the contradiction between Holden's hatred of phoniness and his lying to Ernest Morrow's mother when he meets her on the train on his way to New York from Pencey. Yet he lies to her to protect her from having to face the fact that "Her son was doubtless the biggest bastard that ever went to Pencey. . . ." And it is interesting that when he lies to her about his name, he doesn't do it for the usual reason one lies—to aggrandize oneself—but rather he takes on the name of Rudolph Schmidt, the dorm janitor.

After he fails to get the guidance he needs from his teachers or from the other adults he meets, one would expect Holden to turn to his parents. But in the entire novel, his father never appears and his mother appears once and then only speaks to Phoebe as Holden hides in the closet. The absence of Holden's parents (along with the absence of real religious guidance in the form of a school chaplain or family minister) is so important it amounts to a presence. On the failure of religion, Holden tells us, "my parents are different religions, and all the children in our family are atheists. If you want to know the truth, I can't even stand ministers. . . . They sound so phony when they talk." And, about his family, in the first paragraph Holden explains, "my parents would have about two hemorrhages apiece if I told anything pretty personal about them." Here is the genesis of his hatred of phoniness. His parents live in two worlds: the real world and the world of appearances. The surface does not reveal the underlying reality and Holden has been taught not to talk about what lies beneath. Yet, at times, indirectly, he does. When Phoebe suggests he become a lawyer like their father, he says, "Lawyers are all right, I guess—but it doesn't appeal to me. . . . All you do is make a lot of dough and play golf and play bridge and buy cars and drink martinis and look like a hot-shot." This occurs right after Phoebe asks him to replace their father at her play (the father will be in California on business).

Holden's mother, though well-meaning, won't be of much help either. "She still isn't over my brother Allie yet," and, "She's nervous as hell. Half the time she's up all night smoking cigarettes." Like the other adults, parents can't be relied upon to see, much less give good advice. Holden says of insensitive Stradlater, the secret slob, "he was mostly the kind of a handsome guy that if your parents saw his picture in your Year Book, they'd right away say, 'Who's *this* boy?'"

Holden sorely misses being able to turn to his parents in his time of trouble. He doesn't say this, but he reveals it obliquely in his movie-fantasies of being shot by the mob. In the first, he pulls the peak of the hunting cap over his eyes and shouts about being blind. . . . "Mother darling, everything's getting so *dark* in here," and "Mother darling, give me your *hand*. Why won't you give me your *hand*?" This seems like clowning, but in fact it is a revelation of his terrible anguished isolation from his family. In a later fantasy, Holden reveals, "I didn't want anybody to know I was even wounded. I was *concealing* the fact that I was a wounded sonofabitch." Then he calls Sally and explains the source of his wound: "They got me. Rocky's mob got me." This is clarified three pages later, when he refers to his family at Allie's funeral as "a mob," thereby revealing the source of his wound and the traumatic occasion when he first really felt the pain of it. And he begins to speak of Allie as if he were alive but underground: "I certainly didn't enjoy seeing *him* in that crazy cemetery" [italics added].

So Holden can not get advice on how to leave the world of childhood from the adults around him. Nor can he find suitable models to emulate. (pp. 551-52)

Holden possesses the necessary but painful gift of the novelist—the intuitive ability to perceive that words are instruments used to create effects and have no necessary attachments to non-verbal reality. So he needs more than even good advice, he needs a living adult, a mature person within the culture who, by his or her living presence, will *demonstrate* a possibility that Holden might achieve if he gives up the non-defined personality of his childhood and accepts a role as a mature member of the society. Holden's brother D. B. who once offered this possibility has sold out to Hollywood which produces images such as the great lover with the violin and the courageous guy with romantic wounds. Since the viewer can't hope to live up to these images, they contribute to making him feel small and uncourageous and add to his wounds. As Holden notes, "The goddam movies. They can ruin you. I'm not kidding." And he isn't. And Mr. Antolini, who gives Holden what might seem to be good advice, cancels any effects his words might have had by his actions and his mode of life. (p. 553)

Holden fantasizes a Thoreau-like existence in the country, outside of the limits of institutional roles and of social norms and manners. He tells Sally, "we could drive up to Massachusetts and Vermont, and all around there, see. It's beautiful as hell up there . . . we could live somewhere with a brook and all . . . I could chop all our own wood in the wintertime. . . ."

Sally, who has been successfully acculturated, explains to Holden about his obligation to fulfill the traditional male role of husband and provider, and then she promises, "There'll be oodles of marvelous places to go." In responding to Sally, Holden gives us the novel of his future which haunts him and which is one more factor preventing him from accepting an adult role and "growing up" into the society:

> I said no, there wouldn't be marvelous places to go to after I went to college and all. Open your ears. It'd be entirely different. We'd have to go downstairs in elevators with suitcases and stuff. We'd have to phone up everybody and tell 'em goodbye and send 'em postcards from hotels and all. And I'd be working in some office, making a lot of dough, and riding to work in cabs and Madison Avenue buses, and reading newspapers, and playing bridge all the time, and going to the movies. . . .

It is important to note here that Holden's rejection of an adult role is not a case of sour grapes. He believes he *will* succeed and it is the successful life he fears. And this passage, in which he tells Sally to open her eyes and ears, "Open your ears. . . . You don't see what I mean at all," further highlights his desperate isolation. Like the adults, his contemporaries don't see what he sees or hear what he is saying either.

With such a dead-end vision of the trap of adulthood and marriage, it is no wonder that Holden fears initiation into that most adult and most involving and non-detached form of relationship—sex. In a society in which human relationships are infected by market-place values of competitiveness and surface appearance, and humans are measured in terms of social status and money income, Holden is seeking a deeper, more real relationship with someone—a more human relationship. Holden is against many things, but he isn't nihilistic. "Human" is one of his values, as he reveals comically in his preference for the horse over that sacred American object, the automobile: "A horse is at least *human* for God's sake."

Another positive value of Holden's is that it is wrong to hurt people. He reveals this when he says, in attempting to forgive bores, "They don't hurt anybody, most of them. . . ." So Holden is very careful not to use people as a means for his own ends, to try to be certain that he treats each person as a human being and not as a commercial object available for his use in the manner sanctioned by his culture. Yet he is a member of his culture to a degree, so it is not surprising that when he is offered the teenage dream of being indoctrinated into sex in a nonresponsible situation, in which all he has to pay is money, he jumps at the chance, and then, when he is confronted by the human reality of the situation, his tremendous empathy surfaces and he feels sorry for the girl. Of course, Maurice victimizes him here, because Holden allows himself to be victimized by virtually everyone who tries; the culture's emphasis on "winning" in encounters with other people is so threatening to him that he plays it safe by always losing—his scissors to Ackley, his coat to Stradlater, his sweater to James Castle, and so on.

Pure sex, like the myth of rural peace, is a romantic good place Holden is struggling to hold onto in the face of the urban-commercial society determined to pollute both. But Holden's mistrust of sex goes deeper than the merely social level. For Holden, sex is the ultimate involvement in the world; it is the final entry into time. Holden cannot accept change and time is the measure of change. Time is the medium in which change lives. Time is the silent partner of death. And sex is the passageway through which one is seduced into entering time. Salinger makes this connection clear when Sunny, the prostitute, first comes to Holden's room and asks him, three times, whether he has a watch. Of course, he doesn't. He is still a virgin. He has not yet left the timeless world of childhood. (pp. 553-55)

Thoughts of sex seem to lead Holden to thoughts of death. After the fight with Stradlater over Jane, Ackley asks Holden what the fight was about, and Holden tells us, "I didn't answer him. . . . I almost wished I was dead." In his New York hotel room, when he is thinking about sex and then considers calling Jane at college, an excuse for the late-night call pops into his mind: "I was going to say her aunt had just got killed in a car accident. . . ." And after Sunny, the prostitute, leaves his room he begins to talk out loud to his dead brother Allie.

In both Holden's mind and in his culture, besides the link between sex and death there is a connection between sex and aggression, and aggression is an extremely negative quality to Holden. As in his reaction to the culture's emphasis on winning, Holden is so anxious to avoid aggression that he makes himself defenseless. He fights Stradlater, but loses and tells us, "I'd only been in about two fights in my life, and I lost *both* of them. I'm not too tough. I'm a pacifist, if you want to know the truth."

One reason he loses the fight is that he can't make a fist, and it is interesting to note that he injured his fist, and thereby partially rendered himself incapable of aggression, by punching it through a window after Allie died. Aggression, at its extreme, will lead to someone's death and, as Holden comments about the death of Mercutio, "it drives me crazy if somebody gets killed . . . and it's somebody else's fault." Here we have a clue as to why Holden has crippled himself—he has been so shocked by Allie's death that he is afraid to act in the slightest manner that might implicate him in the injustice of it. At bottom, beneath Holden's quarrel with his culture, there is always his quarrel with God whom Holden can't forgive for killing his brother. (pp. 555-56)

The connection between sex and death in the culture surfaces in the famous scene near the end of the book where Holden attempts to erase the "Fuck You" signs in Phoebe's school. The culture uses the same word for its highest aggressive insult and for its term for sexual intercourse. In the culture's mind and in Holden's, sex is something men *commit* on women and it is clear that this view of sex, built into the culture's language and value system, has poisoned it for Holden.

So here we come full circle: Holden fears aggression because it may lead to death, sex is equated with aggression, and, once again, sex is thus connected with death and with its agent, the grim-reaper Time.

In opposition to this vicious circle, Holden dreams of an Edenic world, outside of time, beyond aggression: a world prior to the anxiety caused by the Fall. In his romantic imagination, this world is equated with the pre-pubescent world of childhood. No one in Holden's world understands natural forces (no adult ever *does* tell him what happens to the ducks in the winter) and puberty resembles death in the way it places man at the mercy of tremendous natural forces which come with one's body and are the price one pays for living in the changing material world. (p. 556)

Holden holds on to many things to keep from dealing with the reality of change. In the museum, there is glass which keeps things out of time and decay. Holden especially likes the museum for this reason. . . . "Certain things should stay the way they are. You ought to be able to stick them in one of those big glass cases and just leave them alone." It is at Allie's funeral that Holden is jolted out of this timeless world that he has seen preserved behind the glass, and, as if in revenge against this fraud, his response is to punch his fist through a window, breaking the glass which has deceived him. Later in the book, beneath the glass in the wall in the Museum of Art, he sees a "Fuck You" scrawled in red crayon and this verbalizes the traumatic insult the timeless world gave him when it broke with Allie's death.

The presence of these "Fuck You" signs in the book points to a crucial difference in attitude between Salinger and his young narrator. The closeness of Salinger and Holden in terms of certain values and aspects of vision is emphasized by Salinger's use of Holden as a first-person narrator. Any distance between them tends to be obscured by Salinger's obvious sympathy for Holden, and by the tone of his writing which succeeds in its scrupulous efforts to get Holden's speech down exactly, creating an intimate effect which is almost like having Holden in the room, telling the reader his own story.

Yet, to ignore the distance between Holden and his creator is to do a disservice to Salinger. In the instance of the "Fuck You" signs, Salinger is doing precisely the opposite of what Holden is attempting to do. Quixotically, Holden attempts to erase the "Fuck You" signs, thereby trying to keep children from learning about sex in this misguided (and even aggressive) context. He is trying to be the catcher who keeps children in their Eden before the Fall. Yet Salinger, by *including* these "Fuck You" signs, is actually scrawling them on the walls of his book, forcing the reader to acknowledge their presence and deal with them. At the time the book was published this caused a controversy and was one reason the book was deemed "dirty" by many readers and was taken from libraries and the reading lists of high school courses. Salinger here is not playing the catcher at all, but is asking the reader to grow up and accept the fallen world in which he finds himself.

Interestingly, the readers who attempted to ban the book from libraries and from the schools of their children were acting in exactly the immature manner which causes Holden so much pain and which Salinger is trying to diagnose and prescribe for in the novel. Yet here we see what must be a conflict in Salinger's own mind: after 1947, he has identified himself with the *New Yorker* magazine, publishing almost all his stories in its pages. **Catcher,** however, was not published in the *New Yorker,* and it is clear it couldn't have been published there because of these same "Fuck You" signs. (pp. 556-58)

Thus, by serving up a fare that includes "Fuck You" signs, Salinger is rebelling against his literary parents at the *New Yorker,* giving them a dish they can't chew and thereby, by implication, putting them in the position of poor immature Holdens, trying to serve as catchers for their readers. And, by the way, perpetuating the same standards of sex and language which are causing Holden so much of his pain. (p. 558)

"Life is suffering." This is the first "Noble Truth" of the Buddha, and it stands like a neon sign over the entrance to Buddhism, acting like a filter that only lets in those who are willing to accept this premise as the price of admission. By the time Holden goes to see his sister Phoebe, one can certainly say that *his* life is suffering in the true Buddhist sense. (Another translation of "suffering" would be "continued irritation" or "anxiety.") The other of the four Buddhist Noble Truths say there is a cause for suffering and a cure. The cause, most briefly termed "desire" or "selfish craving," is said to stem from the failure to accept change (and the failure to deal with sickness, old age, and death) and the concomitant attempt to avoid change by holding on to things, grasping at false possibilities for stability and illusions of permanence. The cure is to let go of desire and selfish craving for ways out of time, be they promised by public gods or private fantasies.

Holden is holding on to many things besides his virginity. He is holding on to his old character patterns which lead him to be unable to let go of saying yes to virtually everything anyone asks him for, and to losing in almost every encounter with other people (especially where money is concerned). He also holds on to objects, such as Allie's glove, and the broken pieces of Phoebe's record (symbolically so like a corpse—the matter is still there, but not the music). He holds on to old opinions as well, such as his (and Allie's) veneration of the kettle drummer at Radio City Music Hall. By avoiding a meeting or a telephone conversation with Jane Gallagher, he holds on to his old image of her which is clearly no longer applicable since she is dating Stradlater; apparently Holden has been defending this image and avoiding her present reality for quite a while since he doesn't even know which school she goes to.

The Buddha said the greatest source of suffering is the belief in a single, continuous, unchanging personality, and the attempt to hold on to it. By not letting go of his old character traits and images of the world, Holden is doing precisely this. Of course, Holden is most strongly holding on to (is most attached to) Allie. When Phoebe challenges Holden to name one thing he likes, he appears to be at a loss for an answer at first, getting stuck on thoughts about James Castle, the boy who committed suicide. Holden is identified with Castle by Castle's having killed himself while wearing Holden's sweater and by Castle's appearing just before Holden on the roll call at school. This carries the implication that Holden may be next in line for Castle's fate. (The fact that Mr. Antolini attempts to help Castle, but is too late, prefigures Holden's experience with Mr. Antolini.) From this image of the dead James Castle, when Phoebe again challenges him, Holden's mind moves back to the image of his dead brother, which he carries with him wherever he goes, and he responds, "I like Allie." (pp. 558-59)

Holden's meeting with Phoebe is the turning point of the book. For the first time he admits, "I just felt good for a change." And the reason he feels good is clear. He is with a person who sees. He tries to lie to her about his getting kicked out of school and she sees through his lie immediately. He tells her, "I'll probably be in Colorado on this ranch," and she responds, "Don't make me laugh. You can't ride a horse." She isn't easy, but she *sees*. And Holden quickly begins to pour out what is bothering him, as if she were a little doctor. When her mother returns with a headache, she prescribes a few aspirin. And she lies to protect Holden, taking the blame for his smoking. These upside-down situations, in which the younger person protects the older ones and gives them advice, are in line with the whole pattern of the book. And the failure of the older people to protect and guide the young not only results in botched initiations like Holden's, it also leads the younger people to try to be their own parents, forcing them to act older than they are by cursing, affecting a false cynicism, lying about their age, drinking, and wearing falsies.

The Zen masters say, "Cold eye, warm heart," and besides seeing, Phoebe is also compassionate. The *Dhammapada* says, "Let us live happily then, we who possess nothing," thereby defining Buddhists. Holden includes Phoebe within this definition when he says, "She says she likes to spread out. That kills me. What's old Phoebe got to spread out? Nothing."

But Phoebe does have a small amount of money, her Christmas money. Eight dollars and sixty-five cents. It isn't much, but it's all she has and she gives it to Holden. And this *act* of compassion breaks through the shell of Holden's fearful isolation: "Then, all of a sudden, I started to cry."

What we have here in miniature, in 1951, is the prescient portrait of an attempt to create a counterculture. The children, unable to connect with the prevailing culture, begin to separate from it and to attempt to care for each other. As the Buddha said, "Brothers and sisters, you have no mother and father to take care of you. If you will not take care of each other, who else, I ask, will do so." We also have the reason for the failure of the counterculture. Holden and Phoebe have charge accounts. The money they give away so freely still comes from their parents and their parents' culture.

Culture is a form of hypnosis and it dies hard. Holden makes one last try to connect. He leaves Phoebe and plays his ace-in-the-hole: Mr. Antolini. Mr. Antolini is full of advice, much of it good, but he is blind to the existential reality of Holden's condition. Once again, when Holden needs a guide, he gets words. They aren't enough. Phoebe remains the only person who has *seen* where he is and who has *acted* truly in his behalf.

So he returns to Phoebe and, in opposition to Antolini's treatment of himself, Holden *watches* the situation and doesn't chase her away, explaining, "I didn't put my hands on her shoulders again or anything because if I had she *really* would have beat it on me. Kids are funny. You have to watch what you're doing." And he accompanies her to the carrousel in Central Park where he gives up his desire to be a catcher and his craving for an Edenic world and accepts the world in which he finds himself at present. . . . (pp. 560-61)

In a scene which parallels the one in his parents' apartment when Phoebe gave him her money and his body responded by beginning to cry, here Phoebe gives him a kiss and nature itself seems to respond as it begins to rain. Holden, who has been obsessed with Allie's being out in the rain, stays out in the rain himself, accepts the rain, thereby identifying himself with Allie and Allie's fate, accepting his own death and vulnerability to natural forces. He turns away from what he has lost, letting go of his obsessive hold on the vision of the dead Allie, and turns toward the happiness which comes in seeing what he still has—a living Phoebe, with him, right there in the present. When Holden says, "God, I wish you could've been there," he isn't just talking to us. He is talking to God. (pp. 561-62)

Gerald Rosen, "A Retrospective Look at 'The Catcher in the Rye'," in American Quarterly, *Vol. XXIX, No. 5, Winter, 1977, pp. 547-62.*

LAWRENCE JAY DESSNER

Thieves steal, the brutal strike and when they are apprehended, confronted with their cache of booty or with their bruised victims, society is vindicated by their shamefacedness, however verbally denied. There are other violators of the public order, whose crimes are less obvious. They may even believe that what they are doing is preventing crime. When these are confronted by their accusers, there is no shame, no outpouring of defensive rhetoric. Yes I did it, they will say, but look what a wonderful thing it was to do. The accusers may be the ones to lower their eyes.

It is with such a culprit that we have now to deal. His act is the writing of a best-selling, widely and loudly acclaimed novel, one that more than twenty-five years later is still in print, still read, still publicly admired by many of those professors of higher learning who ought, at least by now, to know better. J. D. Salinger's *The Catcher in the Rye* has long since been accused of several million counts of impairing the morals of a minor. . . . [While] a few have found Salinger a pernicious influence, the many have gratefully applauded what he did to them. He gave them Holden Caulfield, an idealization of their worst selves, to cherish. While they were doing so, their best selves, their potential to be, in whatever way, better, was ignored, despised, unexercised, indefinitely postponed.

In the ten years after its publication in July of 1951 *The Catcher in the Rye* sold over one and one half million copies. It was adopted as a text in some 300 American colleges and universities, and in countless secondary schools. A great deal of what is called "research" was published on it. In dismay, George Steiner did what he could to stem the flood [see excerpt above]. He disparaged what he named "The Salinger Industry," called Holden Caulfield "the young lout," and bemoaned comparisons of him with "Alyosha Karamazov, Aeneas, Ulysses, Gatsby, Ishmael, Hans Castorp, and Dostoevsky's Idiot." (p. 91)

The Catcher in the Rye has been most often compared to Mark Twain's *Adventures of Huckleberry Finn,* compared, that is, in terms of form, characters, plot, humor and all this so assiduously that comparison of value, that comparison which would justify making all the others, is ignored, value tacitly assumed. The novels are "akin also in ethical-social import." "Each book," [Edgar Branch maintains in his essay "Mark Twain and J. D. Salinger: A Study in Literary Continuity"], "is a devastating criticism of American society and voices a morality of love and humanity." . . . I cannot forbear asking about that "morality of love and humanity." Is there some other kind? Is there a morality of love but not of humanity, or of humanity and not of love? Is this morality "voiced" by Salinger, by Holden? Have we been reading the same book? May one professor turn another one over on his knee and deliver corporal punishment? Is the view of American society which Salinger's novel devastatingly criticizes a fair and accurate view of that society? Is Pencey Prep more than an ill-tempered caricature of some lesser Andover? Is there, in all of *The Catcher in the Rye,* any reference to the historical or political or economic conditions of its moment? Well, I guess there must be, because [Ihab Hassan], one of the more eminent commentators on modern literature, after quoting Thoreau and breathlessly wondering "what is the sound of one hand clapping," assures us that "Salinger proves . . . to be seriously engaged by a current and a traditional aspect of reality in America" [see *CLC,* Volume 1]. Wow! Both a current *and* a traditional aspect of reality. (p. 92)

Since the earlier days of Salinger's prominence, criticism has followed the method of praise by association and implication. Some of the more imaginative professors have found it useful, in considering Salinger, to discuss Beckett and Camus, Saul Bellow, and Martin Buber. And no doubt many other giants have been hitched to Salinger's wagon. Nor should we be surprised to learn that *The Catcher in the Rye* [according to Clinton W. Trowbridge (see excerpt above)], "is a masterpiece of symbolist fiction." There are even signs that the period of evaluation, such as it was, is over, and scholars can turn to source studies. [James Bryan] prints his speculations on the possibility of Sherwood Anderson's influence on Salinger. Confirmation of Salinger's place in the pantheon comes from [Peter Freese], an energetic German scholar who reviews over one hundred critics and concludes that Salinger has made it into the canon of American literature. Here is a fine chance for us to brush up on our German—what a reward for learning the language for our degrees!

Literary judgments of value are usually made tacitly, as assumptions, not logically argued. Merely to write about Salinger, to mention him in the same breath as Mark Twain or, heaven help us Dostoevsky, is to make the claim for his place with the immortals. We must assume that these valuations are made in full sincerity. Many critics, like many readers, enjoyed *The Catcher in the Rye,* felt, in the reading, and in the remembering of the reading, the kind of satisfaction they had come to know as aesthetic pleasure. About their pleasure there is no room for dispute. One does not speculate, nowadays, in public, on one's colleagues' taste. But on the morning after, when mind awakes from its binge or its sleep, and pleasures are re-evaluated, criticism has its opportunity. The present critic leaps, no doubt bruising shins and egos, to seize it.

Beware of the novelists bearing gifts. The more delicious and enthralling the gifts, the more wary we must be. Best of the sweets Salinger has Holden giftwrap and deliver to us is the idea that to the degree that we like Holden Caulfield we were better than anyone who doesn't. The method of Salinger's flamboyant and insidious flattery goes like this: Line up all the people in the world who we, in our weakness, our failures of sympathy, our ignorance, our narrow-mindedness, have ever allowed ourselves to hate. Include in this line-up caricatures of people we know we should not have hated. (Once having hated them, we have a vested interest in seeing them worthy of hatred.) Include persons we hated because we knew they were better than we were. (There is nothing like jealousy to prompt and sustain hate.) Now introduce before that line-up a tortured, bleeding and sublimely "cute" victim of all the insults and injuries all of us have ever imagined ourselves to have suffered. Let this victim be on the edge of insanity, the result, of course, of what others have done to him. Let him ooze the sentimental notion that the doctrine of Original Sin, and all its modern parallels, have been revoked. This is crucial. Not only does it let our victim be perfect, it removes any excuse the evil-doers might otherwise offer on their behalf. Let our victim believe that what the world needs now is not love, not even Coca-Cola, but that fool's gold, Sincerity. He himself has it of course, and some of it rubs off on his admirers, but no one else has it at all. Now the scene is set and the action commences. Blood in his eyes and trickling from his battered little nose, our victim raises a machine-gun and shoots everyone lined up before him. And he cries, weeps, as he does so. You see, utterly guilty as his tormentors are, he forgives them, he likes them! What super-human magnanimity! What delicious revenge, too! Who could resist enjoying this spectacle? Few have. (pp. 92-4)

We have no reason to assume that Salinger's attitudes differ from those of Holden Caulfield. It is the author's obligation to unmistakably untangle himself from his hero, or at least to give the reader the means to discover their relationship. But Salinger does neither. It seems absurd that a grown man, and a literate man at that, should hold the jejune opinions of Holden Caulfield. But he does and he lacks the grace or courage to say so outright, in or out of the novel. There isn't a whisper of any other view of life emanating from either quarter. We must take Salinger's silence in the novel to give consent. He is evidently angry that with the exception of himself—and his Holden—sincerity is in very short supply. "Then, after the Rockettes, a guy came out in a tuxedo and roller skates on, and started skating under a bunch of little tables, and telling jokes while he did it. He was a very good skater and all, but I couldn't enjoy it much because I kept picturing him practicing to be a guy that roller-skates on the stage." Perfect sincerity requires and implies perfect spontaneity. And of course this utterly denies all the arts of life as well as the arts of Art. How does one know, Holden inquires, if the lawyer who has saved his client's life did so because "he really *wanted* to save guys' lives, or because . . . what [he] *really* wanted to do was to be a terrific lawyer, with everybody slapping [him] on the back and congratulating [him] in court when the goddam trial was over." This is the question Holden asks of everyone. Its force is rhetorical. Holden wants a guarantee of the purity of human motive. He has been given everything else he wanted, but this complete absolution, of himself and his world, he cannot have. He cries "phoney," and takes up his bat and ball and leaves the game. We are to play by his rules or His Holiness will not play with us.

There is little point in using Salinger's text to show that Holden himself behaves with less than perfect kindness, less than Saintly sincerity. And to take that line against this novel is to accept its premise. *The Catcher in the Rye* urges the young to destroy their own, their only world, and to take refuge in their own soft dream-world peopled by themselves and by shadows of their perfected selves. No adolescent has ever entirely avoided this temptation. All of us had what used to be called "growing pains," fell into what used to be called a "brown study." Among the very rich, in our very rich country, all pleasures, no matter how self-deluding and self-defeating, no matter how selfish, are seized upon, and sold, and admired. Holden is a child of wealth, and most children wish they were too. The richer one is, the longer one may prolong one's adolescence. That is what Holden Caulfield is doing, and what Salinger and his admirers, are praising. (p. 95)

Those of us of a "certain age," brought up in the same streets and schools as Holden Caulfield, may be especially susceptible to Salinger's siren song. The present writer, along with a goodly percentage of our country's literati, shared Holden Caulfield's environment. We wondered about the ducks in Central Park lakes. We enjoyed a good cry about the sadness of life, the disappointments, the rain falling on our tennis courts. We too, in Salinger's most un-mean streets, discovered puberty, the painful way. But we managed to grow up, more or less; to see that it was not true, ever, that everybody was out of step but ourselves, to see that the words "compromise," "compassion," "tact," even "hypocrisy," were not obscenities which desecrated God's creation, but marks of the fact that none of us was, himself, God.

Holden's youthful idealism, his bitterness toward the world he never made might have, had a Holden himself come before us, made for a successful novel. What could be funnier than the confessions of such a one as he? . . . But Salinger's Holden Caulfield is made of soggy cardboard. The death of his younger brother Allie hangs over his story forbidding anyone in it more than a momentary laugh. That death, utterly unrelated to the vapid social criticism which is Holden's prime activity, should have made Holden atypical, a special case whose opinions may be regarded only as pointers to his private distress. But Salinger ignores this; evidently he wants Holden's opinions on the general condition of society to be

highly regarded, and he wants no one involved, character, author, reader, critic, to see his story as a comedy. We must, out of courtesy, courtesy that has been uncourteously forced upon us, take it all with high seriousness. Salinger needs the dead Allie in his novel so that we may not laugh. Yet the story itself is the quintessential comedy, the story of maturity looking back, with a wince and a smile and a guffaw at its own immaturity.

No character of Holden Caulfield is the only certifiable "phoney" in the novel. No youth, no matter how emotionally shaken, goes so long, so seriously single-mindedly after his real and imagined enemies. When the real Holden Caulfields encounter the terrors, such as they are, of their gilded ghettoes, they stumble every now and then on those insights which will add up to their definition of being grown-up. Not Holden. His larger considerations are bogus. He meanders about as if he were free to find out about things for himself, free to stumble on the other sides of the "phoney" question, to learn why people behave the way they do. But Salinger has put blinders around the boy. He never learns anything; never considers anything antagonistic to his sustaining faith that everything and everybody is wrong. It is as if Holden grew up at the knee of Abbie Hoffman—but even that is more funny than true. No matter how doctrinaire the upbringing, bright boys have a way of seeing around the blinders their elders set in place. But then Holden is not a real boy at all; he is Salinger's dream-boy, the boy who will not grow up. He is immaturity's best defense, a non-stop assault on maturity.

But after all this we really should petition the court to reduce the charge brought against Mr. Salinger. Boys being what we know them to be, despite the example of Holden, the crime is not impairment of the morals of a minor, but only attempted impairment. No real harm will be done by this book, unless professors succeed in making it a classic. *The Catcher in the Rye* is no more than an insult to all boys, to us who have been boys, and to the girls and ex-girls too. It is an insult to childhood and to adulthood. It is an insult to our ideas of civilization, to our ideal land in which ladies and gentlemen try to grow up, try to find and save their dignity. (pp. 95-7)

Lawrence Jay Dessner, "The Salinger Story, Or, Have It Your Way," in Seasoned Authors for a New Season: The Search for Standards in Popular Writing, *edited by Louis Filler, Bowling Green University Popular Press, 1980, pp. 91-7.*

WILLIAM RIGGAN

Among the most important works of literature in the Western world, there are to my knowledge very few which match *Huckleberry Finn*'s exhaustive exploration of the possibilities of the naïve narrator. That is, few of these works use a child or adolescent or child-man or unconsciously good individual as a narrator to begin with, and fewer still use such a narrator as much more than a persona or a vehicle for satire, with only minimal characterization of the narrator himself. (pp. 157-58)

Perhaps the only work which really comes close to *Huckleberry Finn* in the sense adduced here is another American novel, J. D. Salinger's *The Catcher in the Rye* (1951). Like Huck, Holden Caulfield is an adolescent (seventeen years old at the time of narration) and runaway (from a prep school) who tells his story in the current vernacular from a point in time not far removed from the actual narrated events (the time of narration is less than a year following those events). At the time of narration Holden is a patient in a California sanatorium, where he has been sent for professional help in sorting out his emotional problems. Like Huck, he is in a lull, poised between the adventures recounted and the promise of a new world of experience to come (Huck's lighting out for the frontier; Holden's release from the clinic and return to the outside world). Holden has already told his story twice (once to the clinic psychiatrist and once to his brother D. B., a Hollywood writer) and is now transcribing it for an imagined reader in what amounts to an effort at communicating and at unburdening himself in a kind of talk-therapy fashion, just as he constantly seeks someone to talk with (through phone calls, bar chatter, visits) during that December weekend in New York City which forms the subject of his narrative. And as in Huck's case, the act of narration proves rather exhausting and not particularly satisfying for Holden, who finds himself at the narrative's conclusion no clearer about himself and his experiences than when he started, even a trifle regretful of the fact that he has gone to all the trouble.

Holden is, however, very different from Huck in a number of more basic respects, and his narrative points up some interesting differences in the use of the naïve narrator. First, he is slightly older and more educated than Huck, though not necessarily more intelligent or industrious—he does not really care for school and is flunking everything except English literature. He is therefore a more self-conscious artist of sorts in narrating his story, at least to the extent that he chooses not to recount his "whole goddam autobiography" and include his childhood experiences and "all that David Copperfield kind of crap," focusing instead on that "madman stuff" of one weekend some six months earlier. He is competent enough in writing to ghost term papers for others, as he does to no avail for his prep-school roommate Stradlater; he sees through the sham of the sentimental film at Radio City; he is conversant with the names of public figures and movie stars; he enjoys listening to good intellectual talk from persons such as his older friend Carl Luce and his former English teacher Mr. Antolini; he is familiar with writers from Shakespeare to Hardy to Isak Dinesen; and he has done at least some thinking on his own and possesses some appreciation of subjects such as ancient history—in fact, the historical museum is one of his favorite haunts.

Second, Holden is a city youth, not a frontier child like Huck, and hence has never enjoyed and does not display an intimate contact with nature. Within limits, however, he demonstrates a certain sensitivity toward the natural world—his love of Central Park, his concern for the ducks there in winter, his disapproving comment on the workmen who refer to a large, unwieldy Christmas tree as a "sonuvabitch"—and talks on occasion of an eventual idyllic retreat to a cabin in the New England woods where everything and everyone would be required to be "natural" at all times. And third and most important, he is far more subjective than was Huck, given to reflection on and personal reaction to virtually everything that he sees, hears, and experiences.

This third aspect in particular makes Holden radically different from Huck in regard to narrative style, a fourth point of distinction between the two. Where Huck was basically a chronicler of the events and characters in his story, rendering whole episodes such as the Shepherdson-Grangerford feud and the Evasion virtually devoid of narrative asides, Holden cannot report even the briefest incident or conversation without adding his own commentary or reaction. Huck gives us Emmaline's poetry and the King's "To be or not to be" soliloquy with only grace notes of approval at the ends of the respective passages; but Holden interlaces his accounts of the Radio City movie and the Lunts' stage performance with a running barrage of largely disapproving criticism. Huck reports his encounter with Mrs. Loftus in straight dialogue style with only enough narrative filler to let us know his uneasiness as the conversation proceeds; Holden's account of his train conversation with the mother of a fellow student is interrupted every several lines with opinionated remarks on luggage, the woman's readiness to believe anything good about her son, the son's utter loathsomeness, and the negative features of Pencey Prep. And where Huck can narrate with nearly complete self-effacement those events and conversations in which he is not directly involved (the Sherburn-Boggs episode, Tom's explanation of the elaborate escape plans to Jim), Holden punctuates description with personal reaction, speaking, for example, of the "perverts" whom he watches through his hotel window and of the "phony" conversations at neighboring tables in a bar. In brief, where Huck rarely sees or reports anything beyond the surface facts of his experience, Holden's narrative consists at least as much in his commentary on the events and people of his experiences as in the actual narration of those experiences; and where Huck's narrative unreliability was a product of his largely literal, conscious acceptance of reality as he had experienced it, the source of Holden's unreliability must be sought elsewhere.

The very language used by Holden is perhaps the first indicator of a certain unreliability in his narrative. Whereas Huck's vernacular was both indigenous to his native region and a consequence of his only minimal literacy, Holden's slangy speech is an acquired argot typical only of a certain age group in a particular era and indicative more of an assimilated attitude than of a natural heritage. This jargon is also imprecise in many respects, so that a number of its stock phrases become so clichéd and/or vague as to be rendered almost meaningless. . . . [As Donald P. Costello has noted (see excerpt above), Holden's language is] for the most part typical teenage slang, "versatile yet narrow, expressive yet unimaginative, imprecise, often crude, and always trite," and therefore indicative of a mind which is not yet sufficiently perceptive or discriminating to render a reliable account of its experiences.

Second, while Holden does realize that he possesses a "lousy vocabulary," he fails to see a number of other shortcomings in his own character. Some are verbal, such as his disdain of inarticulate people who try to sound intelligent by saying things like "that's between him and I," when he himself makes that selfsame grammatical error on numerous occasions. Others are a bit more serious and reveal a discrepancy between attitude and action on his part; he complains that Ackley always seems to stand right in a person's light, then does the same thing himself to Stradlater; he abhors the pedantic snobbery of people like old Professor Spencer and the pseudo-literati at the theatre, yet himself entertains pretensions of intellectuality when trying to converse with Luce and comments condescendingly on the low intellect of the girls from Seattle; he decries the phoniness of such role-playing types as Stradlater and one of his brother's old girl friends, yet tries to assume the air of an experienced man-about-town in the bars he visits; and he finds fault with the excessive attention paid to style and appearance by many in the city nightclub crowd and by show-business types, yet picks his roommates on the quality of their luggage. His perceptiveness regarding the nature of his own character is thus still quite undeveloped and again most untrustworthy.

Third, Holden is admittedly inexperienced in many of the areas in which his adolescent personality is undergoing some form of conflict. The most obvious of these, of course, is sex, in which he confesses his basic ignorance—that is, his virginity—and his lack of understanding. This bit of information, if not already apparent during Holden's desperate defense of Jane Gallagher's supposed virtue from the imagined onslaught of Stradlater's unscrupled charms, affords the older reader an added dimension of insight and enjoyment not only in the reading of the fight scene but also of later incidents such as the cavortings of the "perverts" at the Edmont Hotel, the encounter with the young prostitute Sunny, and the close of the scene in Antolini's apartment when the teacher puts a reassuring hand on the boy's leg. Because of Holden's inexperience in such matters, his declamatory judgments are at least open to question, particularly regarding the nature of Antolini's actions.

Similarly, Holden's charges of phoniness are applied in such profligate, undiscerning, and unmoderated fashion as to be rendered again at least somewhat suspect: old folks and academics, people who work in Hollywood, people who frequent certain nightclubs, people who go to Radio City, people who cater to an audience's whims, people who don't care about the ducks in Central Park—all are condemned without exception or qualification. The very absoluteness and generalized inclusiveness of the judgments render them not wholly acceptable. Their wanton use deflates their efficacy to such an extent that Holden often appears a total misanthrope, fully open to Phoebe's charge that he doesn't like "*anything* that's happening" and to Antolini's prognosis that he is "riding for some kind of terrible, terrible fall" and is fast approaching the point where he will hate everything and everybody.

That Holden is *not* misanthropic, however, despite the abundance of negative personality features elucidated by his narrative, is indicated in the youth's reactions to these two charges and borne out by that same narrative. Phoebe's demand that Holden name one thing he likes sets off an extended but confused memory sequence in Holden's mind, touching first on the two nuns in the city to whom Holden had given ten dollars when he himself was getting very low on cash, then recounting at length the suicide of a quiet fellow student named James Castle. Both incidents convey a strong compassionate streak in Holden and mark him as possessing charity and sensitivity to a degree far in excess of those around him. Significantly, however, he cannot articulate these two incidents to Phoebe and instead brings up his deceased younger brother Allie as one thing he likes, only to see his choice refuted by Phoebe's correct and unsparing remark that Allie is dead and so "that is nothing really."

Holden's choice of what he would like to be, again in response to the precocious Phoebe's questioning, is just as "unreal" and as romantic as his evocation of Allie: instead of finding satisfaction with any conceivably real activity, Holden longs only to play "the catcher in the rye," eternally saving children from falling over "some crazy cliff." Holden's vision is not only again "nothing really" in its ephemerality and otherworldliness; it is also, significantly, based on a misconception—namely, his oft-cited mistake (Phoebe notes it in the text) of thinking that Burns's poem runs "if a body catch a

body, comin' through the rye," when in fact the verb is "meet" and the context one of a lovers' meeting, not children's games. The vision is of course an inspired one, again indicative of a beautifully sensitive and compassionate strain in Holden's nature, but it is one which has yet to come to terms with the actual business of living. It is again a mark of Holden's immaturity, a kind of groping for some base which will conform to his adolescent idealism and counter the encroaching realizations born of maturity. It represents a retreat from the disappointing "phoniness" of the world he is in the process of discovering and back to the idyll of childhood and innocence where people like Allie were "about a thousand times nicer than the people you know that're *alive* and all."

To Antolini's prediction that Holden will eventually find himself hating all human types, Holden manages a slightly more articulate reply:

> You're wrong about that hating business. I mean about hating football players and all. You really are. I don't hate too many guys. What I may do, I may hate them for a *little* while, like this guy Stradlater I knew at Pencey, and this other boy, Robert Ackley. I hated *them* once in a while—I admit it—but it doesn't last too long, is what I mean. After a while, if I didn't see them, if they didn't come in the room, or if I didn't see them in the dining room for a couple of meals, I sort of missed them. I mean I sort of missed them.

The remark has much truth in it, for even when Holden had been most disgusted by Ackley's hygiene or outraged by Stradlater's *macho* insensitivity, he found himself often feeling sorry for the former and respecting some of the latter's better qualities such as his generosity. Similarly, his improvised falsehoods regarding his classmate Ernest Morrow to the boy's mother on the train to New York, his impassioned championing of Jane Gallagher's virtue against the stronger Stradlater, his harmless kidding of the three girls from Seattle, his "feeling sorry" for D. B.'s old girl friend despite his dislike of her phoniness, his spontaneous charity to the nuns, his compassion for the young prostitute Sunny, his regret about criticizing Sally Hayes's lack of imagination, his love for Phoebe, and his disgust at the obscenities scrawled on the toilet walls at the museum and at Phoebe's school all demonstrate a good heart essentially like Huck's in its basic self-heedlessness and naturally positive moral instinct.

At times Holden seems to empathize so fully with others as to shoulder their burdens and their guilt for them, as in the cases of Jane and Sunny; and this same Christlike tendency is at least somewhat evident, though in distorted form, in his vision of playing "the catcher in the rye." Holden's profanity and offhandedness of manner and speech would seem to indicate a combination of extreme belligerence and utter indifference toward others. Yet he actually fights only to defend Jane's honor, not in cases where he himself is victimized (as when the pimp Maurice pummels an extra five dollars out of him), and otherwise feels considerable emotional involvement with the problems of people encountered and recalled along his weekend odyssey. And despite the harsh jargon, the studied disinterest, and the grudging reluctance to tell of more than the one weekend, all three of which traits mark the beginning of his account, Holden is moved by the mere recollection of his experiences. . . . [The] portrait that results is one of a compassionate spirit undergoing the painful and disorienting process of physical and emotional maturation, of the development of self-consciousness with all the attendant confusions, agonies, and extremes of mood and perception.

Hence Holden's wild fluctuations of tone between swaggering belligerence—the profanity, the refusal to talk about certain topics and experiences, the roundhouse criticisms of phoniness—and genuine intimacy with his reader: "God I wish you were there," "you shoulda seen her," "it would've knocked you out," and so forth. Unless scores of readers and critics are guilty of misreading Holden's narrative, the youth is to be taken in a positive light. He is culpable only in his bitter disillusionment and in his overly harsh reaction to that disillusionment as he begins to pass from childish innocence and to realize some of the harsh facts about adult life. Not yet mature enough to be able to face this disillusionment with anything approaching full perspective, unable to run away from his dilemma for fear of dragging Phoebe down with him, and unable to contemplate suicide seriously, all he can do is lash out verbally at all the phoniness he both sees and believes to see and simultaneously seek to withdraw into the static world of childhood—to play "the catcher in the rye."

The sweeping criticisms Holden utters are, however, as seen, more than offset by his basic sincerity and his respect for simple decency and human dignity. And it is also a positive sign that, despite his wish to protect all children from a similar disillusionment—saving them from the "crazy cliff," erasing the profane graffiti—he decides not to try to protect Phoebe and the other children from falling in reaching for the gold ring on a carousel. . . . Besides having revealed his basic goodness through his narrative, Holden here shows signs of ultimately surviving his adolescent crisis and growing up. His story, like Huck's, harbors distinct and often damning criticism of the society through which he moves; but he himself emerges as a sort of moral yardstick against which that society is measured and found considerably wanting. If he is not as exact a yardstick as is Huck, the reason lies in the fact that he is slightly older and consequently closer to the adult world against which he reacts so strongly. [In his essay "Mark Twain and J. D. Salinger: A Study in Literary Continuity"], Edgar Branch summarizes the comparison well:

> Each book is a devastating criticism of American society and voices a morality of love and humanity. In many important matters . . . Huck and Holden—not to speak of others like Jim and Phoebe—affirm goodness, honesty and loyalty. Huck does so almost unconsciously, backhandedly, often against his conventional conscience, and Holden does so with agonizing self-consciousness and a bitter spirit. In each the perception of innocence is radical: from their mouths come pessimistic judgments damning the social forms that help make men less than fully human.

(pp. 159-69)

William Riggan, "The Naïf," in his Pícaros, Madmen, Naïfs, and Clowns: The Unreliable First-Person Narrator, *University of Oklahoma Press, 1981, pp. 144-70.*

ALASTAIR BEST

J. D. Salinger's 'picaresque, and often appallingly funny novel' [*The Catcher in the Rye*]—I quote blurbs which have long since been removed at the self-effacing author's behest—was first urged on me in a Strasbourg café in 1959. Nowadays

I am proof against books I 'ought to read'; but at the time I was fresh out of school and painfully conscious of the gaps in my education. It was a *coup de foudre*. Much of the book's attraction lay inevitably in a tremendous sense of fellow-feeling with its narrator. I was a year older than Holden Caulfield. His pangs and misgivings and confusions were also, to some extent, my own. But there was something more: Holden's charm, his tenderness. Re-reading the book now I am even more impressed by the sweetness of his character than I was all those years ago.

The Catcher in the Rye is a sort of odyssey. Using Holden's 'lousy vocabulary' with extraordinary skill, Salinger describes 'this madman stuff' that happens to his hero after his premature departure from Pencey Prep. He tells of adventures and conversations in bars, hotel-rooms, taxi-cabs. There are plenty of sirens en route; even a cyclops, supplied by the repulsive pimp, Maurice ('he snapped his finger very hard on my pyjamas; I won't tell you where he snapped it, but it hurt like hell')—but there is no real reconciliation at the end. Holden's Penelope figure, Jane Gallagher—the girl who always keeps her kings on the back row at draughts—remains tantalisingly out of reach. . . .

When *The Catcher in the Rye* was published in 1951 the *Times Literary Supplement* accorded it a couple of paragraphs of tepid approval, but entered the incredible reservation that the work was too subjective. 'One would like to hear more of what Holden's parents and teachers think of him,' wrote the anonymous critic. I have long relished this piece of book-reviewing fatuity. For in fact it is always clear what Holden's mentors think. The trouble is that they, like old Spencer, are always handing out stale maxims of the 'life is a game, boy' variety. Holden's reflections on these threadbare homilies are pungent and to the point. 'Game, my ass. Some game. If you get on the right side where all the hot-shots are, then it's a game all right—I'll admit that. But if one gets on the *other* side, where there aren't any hot-shots, then what's a game about it? Nothing. No game.' This passage reveals two sides of Holden's character. His hatred of phoniness and also his compassion, bordering at times on sentimentality. Holden exists on that other side. In wilder moments he regards himself as a bulwark between the lost world of innocence and the phoney world of adults. . . .

Holden is still clinging to the vestiges of innocence ('I've had quite a few opportunities to lose my virginity and all, but I've never got around to it yet') while at the same time trying to penetrate the sophisticated world of adults. Although to some extent bemused by the grown-up milieu of sex, fast cars and night club entertainers, he pierces through its affectations with the mercilessly clear eyes of a child. Salinger is everywhere present in his novel; but never more so than when spearing the 'phoneys' and pinning them to the page.

There is, for example, Stradlater—a debased Steerforth figure—with this 'very sincere, Abraham Lincoln voice'; or Ernie the piano-player, who turns round on his stool and gives this 'very phoney, *humble* bow. Like as if he was a helluva humble guy besides being a terrific piano player'; or, my own favourite, the mean-spirited recluse, Ackley. 'I once sat next to Ackley at this basketball game. We had a terrific guy on the team, Howie Coyle, that could sink them from the middle of the floor . . . Ackley kept saying, the whole goddam game, that Coyle had a perfect *build* for basketball. God, how I hate that stuff.'

I know nothing of the circumstances in which *The Catcher in the Rye* was written. The book has been described as sprawling, but it is, in fact, nothing of the kind. There is a hard, almost classical structure underneath Holden's rambling narrative. The style, too, appears effortless; yet one wonders how much labour went into those artfully rough-hewn sentences. If *The Catcher in the Rye* is a classic then it is also a literary freak. For Salinger has produced nothing to equal it since.

Holden's definition of a good book is also mine. He liked a book that 'when you're all done reading it, you wish the author was a terrific friend of yours and you could call him up on the phone.' Alas, Holden's creator cannot be smoked out. He is no Gore Vidal, old J. D. Salinger. You have to hand it to the crazy sonuvabitch. You really do.

Alastair Best, "A Book in My Life," in The Spectator, *Vol. 250, No. 8062, January 15, 1983, p. 25.*

William Saroyan

1908-1981

(Also wrote under pseudonyms of Archie Crashcup and Sirak Goryan) American dramatist, short story writer, novelist, autobiographer, scriptwriter, essayist, and songwriter.

The following entry presents criticism on Saroyan's drama *The Time of Your Life* (1939). For discussions of Saroyan's complete career, see *CLC*, Vols. 1, 8, 10, 29, 34.

In many of his works, Saroyan drew upon his Armenian-American childhood in California and celebrated the potential of the human spirit for reciprocity and love. Saroyan is probably best known for his play *The Time of Your Life,* for which he received both a Pulitzer Prize in drama and a New York Drama Critics Circle Award. This play reflects Saroyan's early exposure to vaudeville and popular folk theater as well as the influence of proletarian literature of the 1930s. Saroyan eschewed the anger, indignation, and pro-Marxist sentiments characteristic of many works of social protest during this era in favor of a nostalgic evocation of romantic idealism. The play's moral philosophy is expressed in Saroyan's program notes: "In the time of your life, live—so that in that good time there shall be no ugliness or death for yourself or for any life your life touches." Although Saroyan's egoism and disregard for conventional dramaturgy have prompted some commentators to fault *The Time of Your Life* as carelessly written or sentimental, most have commended his exuberance and originality, and several contemporary critics suggest that his indifference to plot and use of colloquial dialogue contribute to the play's rich improvisational texture and sense of urgency.

Immediately prior to *The Time of Your Life,* Saroyan established himself as a dramatist with *My Heart's in the Highlands* (1939). This play was originally produced by Harold Clurman, a critic and influential figure in the development of American drama who founded Broadway's Innovative Group Theater with Lee Strasberg and Cheryl Crawford to create a format for modernist expression. Although he later characterized *The Time of Your Life* as "a little classic of the American theatre," Clurman initially declined the opportunity to produce it, faulting the work for "a certain self-indulgence, a flagrant braggadocio of undiscipline, a thoughtless and almost cheap bathos. . . . It was as if after the directness and simplicity of *My Heart's in the Highlands* Saroyan was seeking to popularize not only his message but his reputation." Clurman soon reconsidered and offered to produce the drama, but by that time Saroyan had sold the work to the Broadway Theatre Guild. Although Saroyan had specified a drab, realistic setting, Robert Lewis, the director of the original production company in New Haven, Connecticut, interpreted the play as a fable and opted for a fantastical setting. With characteristic self-assurance, Saroyan soon assumed the directorship of the production, since, he contended, "a play is achieved or miscarried on the boards by its director." Shortly thereafter, on October 25, 1939, the play moved to New York, where it ran for 185 performances but failed to recoup its production costs until its Broadway revival the following year.

Set in a bar on the San Francisco waterfront, *The Time of Your Life* revolves around Joe, a wealthy philanthropist whose guilt over accumulating a vast fortune at the expense of others has led to ennui and an indulgence in charitable acts. Drinking champagne and observing the actions of those around him, Joe states that he wants "to find out if it's possible to live . . . a civilized life . . . , a life that can't hurt any other life." The play's other characters, most of whom are lonely romantics in pursuit of beauty and social interaction, are stock dramatic figures that reflect the influence of melodrama and vaudeville on Saroyan's work. These individuals include a muscular longshoreman who considers himself an intellectual, a policeman who hates his duties but appreciates people, and a frontiersman, nicknamed Kit Carson, who boasts of such implausible feats as herding cattle on a bicycle and falling in love with a thirty-nine-pound midget. The drama's central conflict revolves around Blick, a fascistic vice squad detective who periodically harasses the bar's patrons. Blick's mistreatment of Kitty, a young prostitute who seeks a permanent family, climaxes in a scene where Joe arranges for Kitty to be married to his assistant and Blick is assassinated by Kit Carson outside the bar.

Most commentators interpret the conclusion of *The Time of Your Life* as implying that all problems have their solution and that benevolent individuals must necessarily overcome evil. While several critics disapproved of Saroyan's indifference to plot and character conventions, the original production of *The Time of Your Life* received largely positive notices for its rich sense of pageantry, and the play prompted comparisons to the works of Sherwood Anderson for its unpretentious philosophy and mystical reverence for human existence. Many reviewers regarded the drama as essentially optimistic, observing that Kitty is given the chance to change her lifestyle, Kit Carson is not expected to suffer legal repercussions despite murdering the detective, and Joe overcomes his state of immobility. Some contemporary scholars, however, have suggested that *The Time of Your Life* is characterized by a profound sense of pessimism, citing the arbitrary and uncertain nature of Kitty's marriage to Joe's assistant as well as a refrain uttered throughout the play by a disillusioned Arab: "No foundation. All the way down the line." Despite these differing critical views, *The Time of Your Life* has been revived by professional theater organizations on several occasions and remains a standard work of American community theaters and high school and university drama departments, reflecting Brooks Atkinson's assertion that the work "is seething with originality and spirit."

(See also *Contemporary Authors,* Vols. 5-8, rev. ed., Vol. 103 [obituary]; *Dictionary of Literary Biography,* Vols. 7, 9; *Dictionary of Literary Biography Yearbook: 1981;* and *Something about the Author,* Vols. 23, 24.)

JOHN MASON BROWN

[*The essay excerpted below was originally published in the* New York Post, *October 26, 1939.*]

William Saroyan continues to serve the theatre well. He has much to bring to it—his vitality, his compassion, his originality, his courage, his genuine writing skill, his love of people and of words, and his magical ability to create a mood which in itself not only makes a comment but takes the place of plot.

My Heart's in the Highlands showed what Mr. Saroyan could do to extend the theatre's dimensions. In it he wrote a fantasy about mankind's eternal hunger for beauty which was more of a melody than a play. (p. 189)

What Mr. Saroyan did charmingly about beauty . . . in *My Heart's in the Highlands* he has done even more charmingly on the subject of the purpose of existence and the pursuit of happiness in *The Time of Your Life.* His new play is, one suspects, the kind of drama Philip Barry meant to write and came near to writing in last season's *Here Come the Clowns.* It, too, finds a playwright looking into the heart of life. Where Mr. Barry lost his way in the philosophical confusions of his brave allegory, Mr. Saroyan steers a surer, simpler course, if only by virtue of the ever-warming compassion of his writing.

To respond to *The Time of Your Life* one does not have to know precisely what it is about. What matters in Mr. Saroyan's playwriting more than what is being done is our willingness to have something done to us. If Mr. Saroyan has dispensed with plotting as plotting is commonly understood, it is because he wants mood in the theatre to serve as the equivalent of melody in music. (pp. 189-90)

To relish such a play as *The Time of Your Life* one has only to be willing to feel. It is a quickening play—gay, tragic, and filled with revelations even when it may seem meaningless. Its people—all characters wandering in and out of a saloon on San Francisco's waterfront—are not grease-paint creations. They have blood in their veins, fresh air in their lungs, and joy in their hearts. They leap to life as Mr. Saroyan, with a vigor matched only by the suddenly revealing sensitivity of his perceptions, states their small hopes, their secret pleasures, their mean worries, and minor tragedies. (pp. 190-91)

[For those] who insist upon knowing exactly what is happening at every moment during a play, who feel cheated if they are not told precisely what Jack is doing to Jill, or, in a more modern script, what Jill is doing to Jack, Mr. Saroyan offers the compensation of a story of some sort. It is not much of a story. So far as action is concerned it could be told in one act. But action, surface action, is the least of Mr. Saroyan's interests. His fable is no more than how a man, a strange, kindly, and inquiring fellow, a delectable, heartsick, Irish Mr. Fix-It, whose search, between gulps of unexplained champagne, is for happiness and an answer to the far-reaching enigmas of life, manages to marry a two-dollar prostitute off to his amiable henchman and thus save her from the pryings of an odious busybody on the Vice Squad.

To pretend that *The Time of Your Life* is only concerned with such a story is to miss its point. It is a formless play. It suffers somewhat by the unnecessary change of scene in the second act which for the moment removes it from its saloon setting. It has its undeniable moments of monotony. And it includes two characters as feebly written as are its two unfortunate rich people.

Yet, formless or not, Mr. Saroyan's script has enormous vigor. It has beauty, too. Its compassion is as irresistible as its humor is gay or as its insight is exceptional. Such scenes as the ones in which the policeman describes his hatred of his duties; or the prostitute is brought a mechanical toy, symbolical of what is wrong with the machinery of life— . . . these are outstanding moments in a rewarding evening. (pp. 191-92)

Unlike most of our dramatists, Mr. Saroyan does not content himself with surfaces. He gives us a bifocal exposure in time, inviting us to look behind the present into the past. He asks us to consider not the prostitute who is, so much as the girl who was. In other words, his challenge is to make us realize how, in the case of such a character . . . , the machinery in the toy of life has failed to operate. What is true of Mr. Saroyan's writing of his prostitute is no less true of the constant spiritual disclosures, the spurts of revelation, which add to the joys and fascination of such a sample of the originality he has brought into the theatre as *The Time of Your Life.* (p. 194)

> John Mason Brown, "America's Yield," in his Broadway in Review, W. W. Norton & Company, Inc., 1940, pp. 132-97.

BROOKS ATKINSON

[*The essay excerpted below was originally published in the* New York Times, *November 5, 1939.*]

When William Saroyan's *My Heart's in the Highlands* stirred the town's reviewers out of their vernal lassitude last

April the unbridled Armenian sent them telegrams of congratulation. "Congratulations!" he exclaimed over the wire into this office. "I'm sure my play is great." Although his second play, *The Time of Your Life,* has been on view for more than a week now, this office has been waiting pensively for another wire of rollicking reassurance from the author. So far in vain, but no matter. Whether or not these are immortal plays is something that need not worry us at the present moment. For the simple fact is that Mr. Saroyan, whirling through our climate like an explosive comet, has an extraordinary gift for writing about human beings, and *The Time of Your Life* is an original, breezy and deeply felt play.

It springs naturally out of his personal response to the artless human comedy that dances across the country. It is as spontaneous as an improvisation. If Mr. Saroyan's enthusiasm for life extends to the things he is contributing to it, no one is likely to raise serious objections. For the main thing is to recognize the abundant goodness of the work he is doing. It is the freshest thing in the theatre just now.

At some time or other nearly every normal person, especially if he is young, is intoxicated with life, full of affection for the creatures of the world and eager to make a song in praise of everything in sight. That is how lyric poetry gets written. Something of that lyric ecstasy goes into Mr. Saroyan's association with the characters in his sketches, stories and plays. They delight him as figures on the bizarre screen of the world, and he believes in the innocence of their hearts. In *My Heart's in the Highlands* last Spring he was in his most exultant mood. . . . In the current *The Time of Your Life* Mr. Saroyan's mood is more contemplative, but his enjoyment of the characters remains unalloyed and his play about them is wholly disarming.

This time they are rubbing elbows in a hospitable barroom along the San Francisco waterfront. Behind the bar stands the amiable proprietor, regarding his customers with the friendly amazement that must overcome most bonifaces as they stare at the people who take refuge in dingy saloons. Nothing very constructive is going on there now, for Mr. Saroyan's mind runs from the specific to the general. But most of these drinkers and ruminators represent various forms of the human ego in search of fulfillment. The chief one among them . . . is an enigmatic man of some means who has a profound sense of dissatisfaction with the ways of the material world. He regards himself as a student of life; the others defer to his judgment, probably because he has money. For they are all simple people, . . . and as the day and evening wear on they talk, joke, make a little music and savor of mortality.

If Mr. Saroyan's emotions were less turbulent and his intellect cooler, he might find a dramatic story to bind all these random characters into an organic play. Nothing of much constructive significance is accomplished in *The Time of Your Life.* It is loosely put together; it is casually contrived. There are dead spots in it. Theatregoers accustomed to the taut pace of the well-made play may be confused by the seeming aimlessness of the narrative. But there is also a place in the theatre for the drama that goes a little to one side of center and throws out fiery particles centrifugally. [Sean O'Casey's] *Within the Gates* was that sort of play. It combined music, poetry, dance and prose with rare virtuosity and made the great affirmation by an orchestration of theatre arts. Although Mr. Saroyan's gifts as an artist are less magnificent, for his reach is short and his prose style undistinguished, he,

too, uses the stage for incantation and makes an affirmation about life that he does not specifically declare.

He has a genius for people. He has an uncanny ear for turns of phrase and casual talk, and his thumbnail sketches are perfectly drawn. Listen to the braggadocio of the thinking longshoreman who declares that he is too muscular to be an intellectual all the time; or to the dull-witted cop who has misgivings about the mad world he is trying to keep in order—all that is grand talk. For animal exuberance there is nothing to beat the cattle ranger who bursts into the saloon, rushes up to a stranger and shouts: "I don't suppose you ever fell in love with a midget weighing thirty-nine pounds," and goes on from there. That is the sort of crazy quilt comedy that suits Mr. Saroyan down to the ground, and *The Time of Your Life* is full of laughter and giddiness and barroom drollery. As a free hand sketch of human beings it is a triumph of the author's good nature. (pp. 129-31)

The Time of Your Life would be a sturdier play if Mr. Saroyan were less romantically indifferent to the practical details of the central character. Since it wields so much influence on the drama as a whole, where did it get all that money, which is one of the most essential facts of life. But little things like that hardly interest Mr. Saroyan, who does his writing with a Roman candle. *The Time of Your Life* is seething with originality and spirit. (p. 132)

> Brooks Atkinson, " 'The Time of Your Life'," in his Broadway Scrapbook, *Theatre Arts, Inc.,* 1947, pp. 129-32.

GRENVILLE VERNON

William Saroyan's play [*The Time of Your Life*] according to old time canons may not be a play at all, but it is certainly the most interesting work the theatre has revealed thus far this season. In fact taken in conjunction with last season's *My Heart's in the Highlands* it gives us the hope that Mr. Saroyan may become one of the leading figures in the American theatre. It would be useless to attempt to tell the story of *The Time of Your Life;* it has no story. It is rather a few hours in a saloon on the San Francisco waterfront, in which people come and go without apparent will from the author, while all the time an alcoholic philosopher and philanthropist sits at a table drinking champagne. It is fantasy with a realistic background. There are sailors, women of the street, slummers in evening dress and drunken hangers on. This is the realism, and so far the characters are the stock figures of melodrama. But against these are other figures, a troubled cop and a philosophical longshoreman, a bar-tender who is the real thing, a teller of tall tales, a hoofer who thinks he is a comedian and back of it all, both as Greek chorus and god from the machine, the philanthropist.

Mr. Saroyan is a somewhat orphic writer. He often emits dark sayings whose exact meanings are difficult to understand. But one is never in doubt as to what the characters feel. Mr. Saroyan's people are warm and human; they know that this is not the best of all possible worlds, and therefore their hearts are filled with tenderness and pity, but they also know they are incapable of making crooked things straight except through kindness and understanding of each others' troubles. He is a poet of little people, and he sees the beauty in their souls and lives. He writes with his heart rather than his brain, and . . . his work itself has a humbleness of approach which is disarming. Indeed it is this, with his imaginative fancy, which makes him unique among American writers for the theatre. He may believe in himself, but he knows he hasn't the key to the mystery of life. He asks only that people treat one another in the simple Christian way. He has at present no sense of form, and this is his weakness and his strength. It is his weakness because it prevents a final compression of power; it is his strength because it permits him liberties which are fascinating and often delightful. To be a complete artist he must attain the first, but let us be thankful that at present we have the latter to enjoy.

The Time of Your Life, despite one or two lines lacking somewhat in taste, is a play to be seen.

> *Grenville Vernon, in a review of "The Time of Your Life," in* The Commonweal, *Vol. XXXI, November 10, 1939, p. 78.*

BROOKS ATKINSON

Although the delight that theatregoers are taking in Saroyan's *The Time of Your Life* testifies to the sanity and flexibility of public taste, some of the grammarians are not convinced. They complain, on the one hand, that it is not a play because it does not have a plot; and, on the other hand, that it is old hat because the characters are familiar in the theatre. I know *The Time of Your Life* is a play because I saw it in a theatre with actors playing the parts of imaginary characters—which is always a hint to the judicious.

As for the characters being old stuff, who isn't? Romeo and Juliet were old stuff long before Shakespeare got around to writing about them. The vital thing about a play is what the author contributes to the characters out of his own insight or enthusiasm. Art is creation; and the creative process consists not merely in imagining a new world, if such a thing is really possible, but in discovering something fresh and exhilarating in material that has been kicking around for years. What impresses Saroyan most about the characters in his waterfront saloon is their purity of heart under a raffish exterior. They are quite unlike the barroom characters in Philip Barry's *Here Come the Clowns* of last season because Saroyan has a wilder imagination. They echo Saroyan's gayety and enthusiasm. He transmutes them. That is art, and that is why in spite of certain superficial resemblances his characters resemble no other characters under the sun.

But the complaint that *The Time of Your Life* is not a play discloses a bewilderment about art in the theatre that is of older standing and goes back to first principles. Time out for a classroom discussion! Should a play be constructed on a plot like a building or should it be written with the spontaneous exultation of a poem? As a matter of fact, plays can be written in both ways. In rare instances both ways are the same way, as in the best of the Ibsen plays. But to come down to cases, the deliberately constructed play, like [Lillian Hellman's] *The Little Foxes,* can provide superlative excitement in the theatre by proposing a theme, working it out in terms of characters and events and arriving at a concrete conclusion. As in the case of the sonnet and the old French verse forms, the problems it presents are intricate, for the form can easily tyrannize over the characters and influence the course of the story. But when everything drops sweetly into place, like the rhymes in gracefully written formal poetry, the deliberately constructed play can be triumphantly exciting and

vivid in the theatre and result in giving thought a terrific impact. It will always be the favorite type of play with audiences. It asks the least from them.

To insist that all plays be written that way would be reducing the art of drama to the status of a jig-saw puzzle. Not everything can be expressed in set form. . . . Although a play of set craftsmanship, like *The Man Who Came to Dinner,* is remarkably intelligible in the theatre to large numbers of people, many themes would be strangled by taut play construction. They need space and air. . . .

[Saroyan has succeeded in writing *The Time of Your Life*] without tricking it up like a moral lesson. In a cheap dive in San Francisco he finds a rag-tag and bobtail of representative tipplers, all of whom are obsessed with one phase of life or another. The natural hospitality of a saloon loosens their tongues. They go on for hours, chewing on the fringes of philosophy. When the law comes in at the door to sniff for sin, cruelty comes in at the same time and things take on an ugly look for a few moments. But leave these people to themselves, Saroyan says, and they will behave like normal human beings and creatures of decent impulse. Although each one of them has some private grievance that impedes his personal happiness, each one has also a sense of good-fellowship and goodwill.

And since Saroyan has considerable capacity for enjoyment in his own right, *The Time of Your Life* becomes hilariously funny and includes some vastly humorous conversation. The intellectual longshoreman, the meditative cop, the fanatical vagrant with only one phrase in his head, the young swain on fire with love and the braggart cattle wrangler—these are some of the most flavorsome characters we have had in the theatre. Having no concrete theme to argue or issue to win, Saroyan lets them shuffle through a slow barroom folk-dance, and the result is a bright and joyous pattern in the comédie humaine. What comment Saroyan has to make on the way of the world is implicit in the characters, the talk and the setting.

Not that he is artist enough to create his ragtime poem perfectly. Although he has abandoned the play of plot and set craftsmanship because he cannot work inside that straitjacket, he has not created a play in free style that is vibrant all the way through. There is a false scene in a prostitute's hotel room, a false denial of love in one brief scene in the saloon and there are places when the whole play is at loose ends. The improvised mood was easier to sustain in the short *My Heart's in the Highlands* than in the full length *The Time of Your Life.* So far Saroyan lacks the hardness of mind that makes a solid basis for artistic virtuosity—viz., Sean O'Casey. In an article in the current *Theatre Arts* Saroyan says: "I mean to behave freshly and spontaneously and supernormally." Leave off the "supernormally" as so much word swagger and we still have enough to go on. "Spontaneity" is as rare as creation. It is the one thing grammarians cannot account for.

> *Brooks Atkinson, in a review of "The Time of Your Life," in* The New York Times, *Section IX, November 26, 1939, p. 1.*

STARK YOUNG

Almost everyone who likes *The Time of Your Life* will speak of its abundance and be sure that he is making an original remark. Original or not, the word is inevitable for this play, which has fullness rather than power, and has flexibility rather than force, but which carries all its varied content with gusto and a kind of open delight in itself.

In something like this sense Mr. Saroyan's play is poetic, far more so than some of the blank-verse efforts that help to give what is called poetic drama a black eye. He has created a plentiful life that pours up constantly; the mind behind the play is rich with curiosity, wide music, variety, an instinct for human color, a patter of human words, and a passion, almost gay, for half-tragic human experience. As Mr. Brooks Atkinson says in *The New York Times,* Mr. Saroyan uses "the stage for incantation and makes an affirmation about life that he does not specifically declare" [see excerpt above, November 5, 1939]. The main setting, that barroom along the waterfront in San Francisco, helps to frame and carry all this, a place whose doors all the world may stream through, and whose soul, which is alcohol, has the Dionysian function of releasing the souls, memories, moods, passions of those that come there.

The rambling technical defects of Mr. Saroyan's play make good illustrations of the inexorable—you could very well call them biological—exactions of the theatre. The theatre has its distances, physical, mental and emotional, as we have, beyond which nothing can be truly seen or felt. The needs, too, of the actors parallel those of our bodies: just as, for instance, you cannot walk out of a room without legs, so the actor cannot get out of a scene without something contrived for him to get out on.

[The] saloon of Nick's on Pacific Street is constantly stated in the play as a favored resort; we are to believe that there is no variety of human being or number of them that does not come here. But throughout the entire play, as Mr. Saroyan has written it, we are never presented for a moment with any frequented interval, any crowded scene, in the saloon, that might without effort convince us through our eyes of this essential point.

That practical instinct that is in artists will help Mr. Saroyan to study these matters and consider, with imagination, the laborious imagery and projection special to the stage. Meanwhile his play furnishes us with an illustration of the artist as distinguished from the craftsman—in any art. Which is to say that the basic, underlying, fecundating and generalizing principle of life is there in him, in his theatre writing; and that the transition to theatrical form is but partially achieved. But it is achieved sufficiently to carry a long way already. Moreover, it should be said—and this will mean very little except to professionals—that at this stage of the game it is a certain innocence in Mr. Saroyan, as to what is hackneyed theatre and what is not—this rushing in where the angel playwrights fear to tread—that sometimes lends the play its charming and lovable quality. On the other hand Mr. Saroyan might ask us who these angels are, and make us quite sick.

Stark Young, "New Abundance," in The New Republic, Vol. CI, No. 1304, November 29, 1939, p. 169.

CHARLES ANGOFF

The Time of Your Life, Mr. William Saroyan's new play, presents even more serious doubts than his first, *My Heart's in the Highlands.* A series of sketches of the goings-on in a San Francisco saloon, its thin story has to do with a wealthy patron, a chronic dipsomaniac, who hands out largesse to nearly all and sundry, and who finally rescues a prostitute by throwing her into the arms of a somewhat thick-witted protégé of his. All the characters spring out of ancient vaudeville programs—the phony cowboy who talks big and mooches drinks, the newsboy who thinks he can sing, the big-hearted cop, the society couple come to see life in the raw, the young man in love who calls up another girl by mistake and tries to date her up but lies out of it when she shows up with all her ugliness, the omniscient bartender, and so on.

These skits appear on the stage almost precisely as they appeared fifteen, twenty, and twenty-five years ago, with not a breath of freshness added. The prostitute-rich man episode forms one of the most embarrassingly callow pieces of drama to have reached Broadway in decades. Poor Mr. Saroyan seems to harbor the opinion that all prostitutes carry great dreams deep within them, and that a little kindness from a stranger immediately brings those dreams out.

The whole script oozes cheapness. . . . [Five] minutes after the curtain rises, [Joe's] character collapses in the tedious lines, and thereafter the entire evening mounts in boredom. Toward the end, when the . . . [prostitute] starts to climb over Mr. Saroyan's extraordinarily undistinguished writing, the play almost shrieks for a doctor to save it. (pp. 403-04)

Charles Angoff, in a review of "The Time of Your Life," in The North American Review, Vol. 248, No. 2, Winter, 1939-40, pp. 403-04.

ROSAMOND GILDER

William Saroyan is a dangerous fellow, a destroyer of accepted shibboleths. Listen to his Joe in *The Time of Your Life:* 'I don't do anything. I just live all the time.' What is this poet-playwright up to? What is he doing with America's puritan conscience, with its past and present gospel of work? (p. 11)

In content [*The Time of Your Life*] is much the same as is everything that Saroyan writes, a hymn to the human heart expressed in terms of a poet's imagination. It abounds in vitality and humor, but at the same time it is, as was its predecessor, suffused with nostalgic melancholy. A plaintive minor note runs through it, like the sound of the shepherd's flute in *Tristan*. Music haunts Saroyan's plays, not only in their form and in their poetic idiom, but also in actual fact. It weaves in and out of the very structure of the plot, supplementing and enlarging its meaning and enriching its fabric. In *My Heart's in the Highlands* the old man's golden horn is the core of the play, and in Nick's waterfront saloon no less than four instruments play their part. . . . [Even] though the score at first planned for *The Time of Your Life* was in the end eliminated in favor of greater realism, the whole play moves to music. . . . [For] all its pin-games and nickelodeons Mr. Saroyan's saloon is frankly a land of dreams.

Nick, its proprietor, is a warm-hearted Italian who dispenses drinks, handouts and philosophy while his chief client, the mysterious Joe, sits at one of the little round tables consuming champagne and contemplating life. Joe has plenty of money but his legs are bad. He cannot walk on his feet but his mind roams the world and climbs its high places. Such plot as the play possesses is concerned with a wispy love affair between a golden-haired, gentle prostitute and Joe's protégé, a young man whom he had befriended and who runs his odd errands for him. From time to time various waifs and strays charge into the saloon seeking physical food and spiritual release. . . . It is all inconsequential, ingratiating, witty and full of laughter.

Mr. Saroyan looking at the world about him seems to see objects more clearly than he sees character. His little-boy pockets are still full of shoes and ships and sealing wax. As Joe says about the toys he has sent Tom to fetch: 'I like to study them. I'm interested in things. I'm trying to understand them.' People too, he implies, are mechanical dolls who, if they could only be set free as the poet's imagination can set them free, would cease to jerk and stagger, fight and kill, and would live the kindly, generous, creative life which is theirs by nature. (pp. 11-12)

There are actually no 'minor roles' in *The Time of Your Life,* for all the characters, two-dimensional as they are, have such bright colors and stand out so boldly from the melodic background, that they demand attention. Even Nick's mother, who rushes in for a split second only, pours out a stream of greetings, news, endearments and admonitions, all in voluble and quite incomprehensible Italian, and rushes out again, is a vivid and somehow significant figure. . . . [The play's characters] are fresh and unforgettable creations of a poet's imagination. (p. 13)

Rosamond Gilder, "The Worlds They Make," in Theatre Arts, *Vol. XXIV, No. 1, January, 1940, pp. 11-13.*

JOHN GASSNER

[*The essay excerpted below was originally published in* One Act Play Magazine, *February, 1940.*]

No play demonstrates the potential vitality of our stage at the end of the 1930's more convincingly than William Saroyan's fugue, *The Time of Your Life.* In most countries his first effort, *My Heart's in the Highlands,* would have been hooted off the stage as the work of a charlatan. Here it was recognized by most critics as a thing of beauty, even if its charm was found to defy analysis. It was not the masterpiece some commentators thought it was; its thinking was decidedly muddled and its assault on the penumbral regions of the mind grew somewhat wearying. Nevertheless, few of us failed to respond to the advent of a fine talent. . . . Disaster seemed imminent at [the first showing of *The Time of Your Life*], and so discouraging seemed its prospects that it might have normally been discarded as hopeless. Instead, however, the author . . . refused to accept defeat, and . . . [the work is at present] one of the outstanding plays of the season.

Theoretically, the play should have been a disastrous failure, and purists must exclaim that it is not a play at all. So must writers, young and old, who have gone to the trouble of learning the rudiments of dramatic technique only to find that their efforts are unrewarded or are less rewarded than the seemingly scrambled lucubrations of a short-story writer who does not hesitate to proclaim himself a genius. What they fail to see is that there may be direction in indirection, and that the theatre which lives by nuances of acting has always been grateful for nuances in the drama except in the most embattled episodes of its history. Moreover, there is a lasting power in obliquity, in leaving implications to the audience, in asking it to participate in an experience instead of driving the spectator to an acceptance of a philosophy of action that he will very probably forget the moment he leaves the theatre unless

he is preconvinced. It is generally safer to steep him in the substance of the life of his times and to let him try to make sense and purpose out of it. For the record, it is necessary only to go back to Shakespeare, whose disapproval of both feudalism and Renaissance Machiavellism was so implicit that it could be more explicit than any preachment—and far more persuasive. (pp. 407-08)

The truth about *The Time of Your Life* is that its uniqueness resides in its form rather than in its content or meaning, and even the form departs from convention only by a greater degree of obliquity and by a more persistent employment of nuances than we have found customary. If the play is to be measured by the yardstick of social criticism, it is not likely to be as exasperatingly negligible as some young critics are inclined to believe. If it is to be measured by the yardstick of conventional dramaturgy, it is also not to be dismissed as a hopeless object of curves and angles. Only those who believe that social drama must be hortatory . . . will not know how to measure it. It may also be argued with some validity that we need not measure a work of art at all; it is necessary only to feel its magic. That too is criticism or a form of judgment, and the trouble with this absolutely valid approach is only that one cannot argue about it. (p. 408)

The prime condition of dramatic structure is not actually the principle that everything in a play must be tied up in a knot, . . . but that there should be no inconsistencies in the development of character and plot. A writer who keeps us in one groove and then suddenly jolts us out of it is far more culpable than a Saroyan. . . .

[One may] ponder the question whether this play is a fantasy; I do not think it is—one does not consider Brueghel's crowded canvases or Igor Stravinsky's *Sacre du Printemps* fantastic. The assumption that anything not completely integrated constitutes fantasy is an illusion of reason-inebriated members of the intelligentsia; to them we recommend the platitude that a good deal of private and social life is unintegrated and illogical. (p. 410)

John Gassner, "Saroyan's 'The Time of Your Life'," *in his* Dramatic Soundings: Evaluations and Retractions Culled from 30 Years of Dramatic Criticism, *edited by Glenn Loney, Crown Publishers, Inc., 1968, pp. 407-10.*

EDMUND WILSON

[*The essay excerpted below originally appeared in slightly different form in the* New Republic, *November 18, 1940.*]

The refrain becomes monotonous; but you have to begin by saying that Saroyan . . . derives from Hemingway. The novelists of the older generation—Hemingway himself, Dos Passos, Faulkner, Wilder—have richer and more complex origins, they belong to a bigger cultural world. But if the most you can say of John O'Hara is that he has evidently read Ring Lardner and F. Scott Fitzgerald as well as Hemingway, the most you can say of Saroyan is that he has also read Sherwood Anderson. . . . When you remember that Lardner and Anderson were among the original ingredients in Hemingway, you see how limited the whole school is.

But what distinguishes Saroyan from his fellow disciples is the fact that he is not what is called hard-boiled. What was surprising and refreshing about him when he first attracted notice, was that, although he was telling the familiar story about the wise-guy who went into the bar, and I said and the bartender said and I said, this story with Saroyan was never cruel, but represented an agreeable mixture of San Francisco bonhomie and Armenian Christianity. The fiction of the school of Hemingway had been full of bad drunks; Saroyan was a novelty: a good drunk. The spell exerted in the theater by his play, *The Time of Your Life,* consisted in its creating the illusion of friendliness and muzzy elation and gentle sentimentality which a certain amount of beer or rye will bring on in a favorite bar. Saroyan takes you to the bar, and he produces for you there a world which is the way the world would be if it conformed to the feelings instilled by drinks. In a word, he achieves the feat of making and keeping us boozy without the use of alcohol and purely by the stimulus of art. It seems natural that the cop and the labor leader should be having a drink together; that the prostitute should prove to be a wistful child, who eventually gets married by someone that loves her; that the tall tales of the bar raconteur should turn out to be perfectly true, that the bar millionaire should be able to make good his munificent philanthropical offers—that they should be really Jack the Giant-Killer and Santa Claus; and that the odious vice-crusader, who is trying to make everybody unhappy, should be bumped off as harmlessly as the comic villain in an old-fashioned children's "extravaganza."

These magical feats are accomplished by the enchantment of Saroyan's temperament, which induces us to take from him a good many things that we should not accept from other people. With Saroyan the whole trick is the temperament; he rarely contrives a machine. The good fairy who was present at his christening thus endowed him with one of the most precious gifts that a literary artist can have, and Saroyan never ceases to explain to us how especially fortunate he is:

> As I say, I do not know a great deal about what the words come to, but the presence says, Now don't get funny; just sit down and say something; it'll be all right. Say it wrong; it'll be all right anyway. Half the time I *do* say it wrong, but somehow or other, just as the presence says, it's right anyhow. I am always pleased about this. My God, it's wrong, but it's all right. It's really all right. How did it happen? Well that's how it is. It's the presence, doing everything for me. It's the presence, doing all the hard work while I, always inclined to take things easy, loaf around, not paying much attention to anything, much, just putting down on paper whatever comes my way.

Well, we don't mind Saroyan's saying this, because he is such an engaging fellow; and we don't mind his putting down on paper whatever happens to come his way. It is true that he has been endowed with a natural felicity of touch which prevents him from being offensive or tiresome in any of the more obvious ways; and at their best his soliloquies and stories recall the spontaneous songs of one of those instinctive composers who, with no technical knowledge of music, manage to finger out lovely melodies. Yet Saroyan is entirely in error in supposing that when he "says it wrong," everything is really all right. What is right in such a case is merely this instinctive sense of form which usually saves him—and even when he is clowning—from making a fool of himself. What *is* wrong, and what his charm cannot conceal, is the use to which he is putting his gifts. . . . [A columnist] is what William Saroyan seems sometimes in danger of becoming—the kind of columnist who depends entirely on a popular personality, the

kind who never reads, who does not know anything in particular about anything, who merely turns on the tap every day and lets it run a column. (pp. 26-9)

Rudyard Kipling said one very good thing about writing: "When you know what you can do, do something else." Saroyan *has* tackled in his plays something larger and more complicated than his stories; but these plays seem now to be yielding to a temptation to turn into columns, too. (p. 30)

In the meantime, Saroyan goes on with his act, which is that of the unappreciated genius who is not afraid to stand up for his merits. This only obscures the issue. Most good artists begin by getting bad reviews; and Saroyan, in this regard, has been rather remarkably fortunate. So let him set his mind at rest. Everybody who is capable of responding to such things appreciates what is fine in his work. The fact that a number of people who do not know good theatrical writing from bad or whose tastes lie in other directions have failed to recognize Saroyan is no excuse for the artist to neglect his craft. He will be judged not by his personality act or by his ability to get produced and published—which he has proved to the point of absurdity; but by work that functions and lasts.

With his triumph there has crept into Saroyan's work an unwelcome suggestion of smugness. One has always had the feeling with his writing that, for all its amiability and charm, it has had behind it the pressure of a hard and hostile environment, which it has required courage to meet, and that this courage has taken the form of a debonair kidding humor and a continual affirmation of the fundamental kindliness of people—a courage which, in moments when it is driven to its last resources and deepest sincerity, is in the habit of invoking a faith in the loyalties of straight and simple people—Armenians, Czechs, Greeks—surviving untouched by the hatreds of an abstract and complex world. In Saroyan the successful playwright, for whom that pressure has been partially relieved, there seems to be appearing an instinct to exploit this theme of loving-kindness and of the goodness and rightness of things. . . . [Let] not Mr. Saroyan deceive himself: no writer has a charmed life. (pp. 30-1)

Edmund Wilson, "The Boys in the Back Room," in his Classics and Commercials: A Literary Chronicle of the Forties, *Farrar, Straus and Company, 1950, pp. 19-56.*

GEORGE R. KERNODLE

William Saroyan, even more than Odets, feels that compassion is the greatest need of the world to-day. His characters, like those of Odets, are unable alone to triumph over evil. In *The Time of your Life,* Joe, a rich guardian angel, sits all day and all night in a dock-side honky-tonk to seek out goodness. He gives money, but also what is more important—faith, the courage to believe in dreams. When Kitty, the streetwalker, discovers that Joe will listen to her daydreams and that Tom really loves her, she has strength to leave the hated life. When the detective bullies her, she becomes what he thinks her.

The theatre waited for half a century to see the romantic optimism of Walt Whitman put on the stage. In both the play and the several essays published with it, Saroyan repudiates the whole pessimistic age of realism. While Aldous Huxley has written the swan-song of the debunking period, Saroyan sees in his beloved America the possibility of a passionate reaffirmation of life.

The Time of your Life seems to me the most suggestive image of the American psyche in 1940. The characters are surrounded by darkness and evil, but with compassion and faith they rediscover the possibility of goodness. The play reassures us that the optimism of Whitman is still possible in 1940—that the Oriental and European elements in America can unite with our own Kit Carsons to preserve both the warmth of human kindness and a picturesque racy flavor that will make your time a time of life. (pp. 422-23)

> George R. Kernodle, "Plays of War and Peace Time," in The Yale Review, Vol. XXX, No. 2, December, 1940, pp. 421-23.

PHILIP RAHV

When William Saroyan first began boosting his own "genius," it was taken for granted that this was but a passing phase in the career of a talented and spirited young writer. But Saroyan, persisting in his campaign, was knowingly or not acting on the principle that people are bound to believe you if you speak your piece loudly enough, and with sufficient frequency and self-confidence. Thus one noticed that a good many reviewers were beginning to support Saroyan's account of his own merits. And with the publication earlier this year of *The Human Comedy,* his first novel, it became altogether plain that most of them had finally been induced to abandon their previous reservations. (p. 371)

It is some months after seeing the reviews that I read [*The Human Comedy*]. It seemed to me a puerile performance. Puerile not merely because it is a bad novel, but because of the glaring contradiction between its actual content and truly grandiose pretensions. . . . In most cases the commercial writer makes no bones about what he is up to. Saroyan, on the other hand, has been so oversold to the public that he can now pass himself off as a seer, a moralist, and a philosopher in a work which is in fact part and parcel of the escape literature of our time.

There would be no point, of course, in taking Saroyan quite so seriously if it were not for the significance of his career as a symptom of the age we live in—as an object lesson in the atrophy of taste and decay of values to which the national literature has been exposed since the early 1930's. The fine level achieved by American writing in the past has virtually been forgotten. A new gentility now prevails, and those affected by it see nothing amiss in our creative life. (pp. 371-72)

In his plays Saroyan recovers his losses to some extent. This is particularly true of the shorter pieces. In some of the skits, . . . the lyrical strain in Saroyan and his talent for spoofing combine to form a kind of stylized vaudeville which has deep roots in urban folk life and in the popular traditions of the theatre. . . .

But in his plays, as in his stories, Saroyan imitates himself *ad infinitum.* Having hit it off once in *My Heart's in the Highlands,* he has used the same dramatic scheme ever since. In the longer play this scheme invariably gets out of hand, spoiling the excellent fun of the vaudeville passages. The vaudeville is very good in *The Time of Your Life,* for example, especially in the Kit Carson episodes; but the stuff about the angelic streetwalker and the millennial person called Joe is pure corn. And as usual Saroyan goes too far in advancing his claims. Not content to let us enjoy his pastoral sentiments for

what they are, he must needs try to persuade us that they contain deep ideas—a complete system of values, in fact. (p. 375)

> Philip Rahv, "William Saroyan: A Minority Report," in American Mercury, Vol. LVII, No. 237, September, 1943, pp. 371-77.

HAROLD CLURMAN

A few weeks after *My Heart's in the Highlands* opened, Saroyan wrote *The Time of Your Life,* the most popular of his plays, which made his mood of lyric anarchism and confused benevolence the characteristic tone of the early forties. Saroyan brought it to me on completion.

My rejection of this play was a serious error. It came about this way: During my reading of the script I was asked what I thought of it. "Every page of it has points of genius," I answered. It made me laugh; it touched me. Yet it annoyed me more than it amused me. There was about it a certain self-indulgence, a flagrant braggadocio of undiscipline, a thoughtless and almost cheap bathos that I could not abide. It was as if after the directness and simplicity of *My Heart's in the Highlands* Saroyan was seeking to popularize not only his message but his reputation—to say what he had to say and to call attention to his boldness and originality at the same time. This was much too severe a judgment, I am sure. The play, despite its blemishes, was an authentic expression of a true state of mind, both immature and generous, a state of mind not only personal to the San Francisco poet who is Saroyan but closely related to the wistfulness and humor of many Americans during this zero hour of history, when very few were quite sure what they thought except that they wished each other well, hated evil, sorrowed, wondered, and blinked. "No foundation; all the way down the line" (an actual phrase Saroyan had picked up in a bar) was at once the play's masterpiece of perception and the cause for my impatience with it.

When Saroyan discussed the play with me, I enjoined him to write with more precision and plot line. He answered quite truthfully that he wasn't able to do this. He was right about his method, and I was wrong about trying to correct it. In a few days I reversed my professional attitude toward the play and called Saroyan back in the hope that the Group might still be able to do it. It was too late; Eddie Dowling had just bought it. (pp. 251-52)

> Harold Clurman, "High Point," in his The Fervent Years: The Story of the Group Theatre and the Thirties, 1945. Reprint by Da Capo Press, 1983, pp. 233-52.

FREDERIC I. CARPENTER

Of all American authors who have achieved fame since 1930, William Saroyan is perhaps the most original, the most versatile, and closest to the mood of the common people. His stories, his plays, and his novels have not only achieved popularity with the reading public, but have appealed vividly to that public which does not usually read. Some professional book reviewers also have acclaimed him. But at the same time, other professional reviewers have expressed a hearty disapproval. And, strikingly, every serious literary critic who has discussed his writing in book or in essay form has enthusiastically damned William Saroyan. The abyss in America between popular opinion on the one hand, and critical judgment on the other, has never been illustrated more graphically.

Of course there are good reasons for the critics' disapproval. Even Saroyan's best work is faulty, and very little of his work is "best." The bulk of his writing, although vivid, is careless and formless. His many volumes of stories contain few masterpieces, and much third-rate material. His plays are amorphous; and many of his prefaces are bumptious. He has produced, I think, only two really first-rate things: *The Human Comedy,* and a one-page preface to *The Time of Your Life.* Judged by purely literary and artistic standards, the formal critics are often right in condemning him.

But Saroyan's obvious artistic faults do not explain the hostility of the formal critics. All of them have specifically attacked his "morality" or his "philosophy." Grouping him with "The Boys in the Back Room" [see revised excerpt below], Edmund Wilson deprecated his "barroom philosophy." Philip Rahv used his writing to illustrate the "atrophy of taste and decay of values" [see excerpt above] in modern literature. Edwin Berry Burgum—certainly no reactionary—described him as evidencing a "flight from maturity and responsibility." And Joseph Remenyi characterized Saroyan as "a sentimental romanticist." If these critics grudgingly admitted the vitality of his work, they had little good to say of its intellectual or moral qualities.

Yet it is just these intellectual and moral qualities which make Saroyan's work most interesting and most important. If he were merely a romantic and sensationalist, we might dismiss him as a second- or third-rater. But the fact that he arouses such enthusiasm combined with such hostility suggests that he has something important to say.

In his artistic and moral faults and virtues alike, Saroyan suggests comparison with Walt Whitman. Like Whitman, he is an American "natural." Like Whitman, he celebrates himself and his America, but above all the America of his dreams. Not only his personality and his method suggest the good gray poet, but most of all his philosophy and his moral values are those of Whitman, Emerson, and the American transcendental tradition.

But obviously Saroyan is no traditionalist. Rather he is a product of the California of the twentieth century. If he seems to repeat the pattern of transcendental individualism, it is because that pattern has again become natural to the time and place in which he lives. Certainly he is as closely akin to the other California writers of his time—to Steinbeck, Sinclair, and Jeffers—as he is to Emerson and Whitman. For contemporary California has produced a school of writing which may well be called "the new transcendentalism." Seen in relation to the transcendental past and to the California present, William Saroyan takes on new stature.

If the most striking thing about Saroyan's writing is its originality, the most striking thing about Saroyan himself is his egotism. He shows a whole-hearted contempt for other people's rules, for society's customs, and for traditional values. In his prefaces he appears almost insolent. But this same egotism makes his creative writing fresh, vivid, and exciting. In the realm of morals, or philosophy, it creates an emphasis on the "transcendental" values of individual freedom and integrity. Perhaps Saroyan's combination of egotism, originality, and integrity may best be described by the old phrase: "self-reliance."

Saroyan's self-reliance produces much the same impression that Emerson's and Whitman's did a century ago. Indeed his first and most famous story ["**The Daring Young Man on the Flying Trapeze**"] repeated the theme of Emerson's early poem, "Good-bye, proud world! I'm going home." The daring young writer of the 1930's ventured forth to an employment agency, learned that the work-a-day world considered "writing" a mechanical and somewhat anomalous occupation, and returned home to live on the flying trapeze of the imagination. But his story made dramatic the contrast between the worldly values, and the esthetic or spiritual values of "writing." And this conflict of values has motivated all his subsequent work. (pp. 88-90)

[Saroyan's] later writings have emphasized the value of "faith to the mass," or of belief in social democracy to all Americans. Not only have his values become more clearly defined, but they have become more social. The most successful realization of them occurs in *The Human Comedy.* The best statement of them appears in the prologue to *The Time of Your Life.* Since this prologue sums up his whole democratic philosophy, it may be read in full:

> In the time of your life, live—so that in that good time there shall be no ugliness or death for yourself or for any life your life touches. Seek goodness everywhere, and when it is found, bring it out of its hiding-place and let it be free and unashamed. Place in matter and in flesh the least of the values, for these are the things that hold death and must pass away. Discover in all things that which shines and is beyond corruption. Encourage virtue in whatever heart it may have been driven into secrecy and sorrow by the shame and terror of the world. Ignore the obvious, for it is unworthy of the clear eye and the kindly heart. Be the inferior of no man, nor of any man be the superior. Remember that every man is a variation of yourself. No man's guilt is not yours, nor is any man's innocence a thing apart. Despise evil and ungodliness, but not men of ungodliness or evil. These, understand. Have no shame in being kindly and gentle, but if the time comes in the time of your life to kill, kill and have no regret. In the time of your life, live—so that in that wondrous time you shall not add to the misery and sorrow of the world, but shall smile to the infinite delight and mystery of it.

Where Saroyan's earlier writing was often rebellious and negative, his later writing has become almost wholly positive: "In the time of your life, *live!*" Indeed he may have tended to "accentuate the positive" too much. But he has also tended increasingly to face the problem of evil, and has made clear—both in his prefaces and in his fiction—that he belongs to the *interbellum* generation, when "the time comes to kill." Living in this time he has sought to reaffirm the old American faith, and even in war to treat all men as brothers and equals. In this also he recalls the faith of Walt Whitman during the Civil War.

But this transcendental optimism which Saroyan reaffirms is more than a faith; it is also an American philosophy of equality. All men are equal; under the skin "every man is a variation of yourself." Like Whitman, Saroyan has sought to convert this idea into reality through the chemistry of the creative imagination, not only embracing all men with a vague, cosmic sympathy, but imagining individual characters who realize the ideal values stated in the prologue. (pp. 91-2)

William Saroyan has not yet realized the full potentialities of his talent. His work has often been shoddy and his idealism fuzzy. But he has shown a capacity for steady growth, both in art and in thought. He is firmly rooted in the rich soil of his California reality. And he has absorbed—no matter by what mysterious processes of photosynthesis—the ideal truths of the American tradition. Far from being a decadent sensationalist or immature romantic, he has progressively realized a consistent American philosophy and has steadily advanced toward individual maturity and toward social responsibility. (p. 96)

Frederic I. Carpenter, "The Time of William Saroyan's Life," in The Pacific Spectator, Vol. 1, No. 1, Winter, 1947, pp. 88-96.

JOHN GASSNER

[Portions of the essay excerpted below were originally published in One Act Play Magazine, *February, 1940.]*

When William Saroyan's celebrated fugue on the futilities and joys of living [*The Time of Your Life*] opened in the fall of 1939, the troubled anticipations of its producers were quickly dispelled. By rights the play should have failed, according to Broadway showmen, since it departed from the rules of playwriting. According to ordinary Broadway playwrights, too, failure awaited the seemingly scrambled improvisations with which a short-story writer violated both practical and academic precepts. The difficulties the . . . production encountered in Boston suggested a dire fate. Directors were changed midstream and the original setting, an abstract one, was scrapped in favor of a realistic one. And even after the play, instead of being abandoned in Harvard's backyard, reached Broadway, puzzled logicians wondered how illogic and inattention to dramatic action-plot could win plaudits from usually harsh critics. Saroyan, who had proclaimed himself the wild man of the theatre and—with touching candor—also a genius, was now admitted to respectable company (he had a Broadway "hit") while his claims to transcendent merit were wholeheartedly accepted by all but a small minority of the theatre's devotees. In time, the New York Drama Critics Circle and The Pulitzer Prize Committee, long at odds, . . . put their seal of approval on *The Time of Your Life,* voting it the "best play" of the first war-time season.

Actually, the mystery of Saroyan's success was no mystery at all. It was the result of an instinctively arrived at accommodation between two schools of theatre that had been at war with each other during the depression-harassed thirties—the school that made social awareness the primary test of playwriting and the school that would have preferred playwrights to sublimate the times into poetry, fantasy, and abstraction.

Saroyan, himself a depression period writer ever since he wrote about starvation in **"The Daring Young Man on the Flying Trapeze,"** obliged in the play in a variety of ways. He not only drew a picture of poverty and unemployment with characterizations of an actor and a Negro musician, but painted a backdrop of "social significance" by supplementing the foreground action with a waterfront strike which provided conversation for a class-conscious dockworker and a voluble policeman. . . . Saroyan ranged himself on the side of the common people, too, by sympathizing with a hapless

young harlot. . . . He consigned her persecutor, the Vice Squad detective Blick, to scorn and ultimate assassination by "Kit Carson," an ex-frontiersman with delusions of grandeur—a symbol, no doubt, of the gallant West and the good old American spirit of freedom. Saroyan also had uncomplimentary words for wealth based on economic exploitation, and gave Joe, his wealthy hero who plays the roles of observer, intercessor, and philosopher in the play, an acute case of social conscience. (pp. 297-98)

There was little doubt that this mélange was frequently refreshing and evocative on the busily occupied stage. And the very fact that Saroyan put virtually everybody except the villainous Vice Squad officer, himself a psychological mess, into the same boat helped to "sublimate" the social content of the play. Here, in other words, there was no evidence of the sharp cleavage between capital and labor favored by the doctrinaire political left. The moral to be drawn from Saroyan's picture, and the moral the author himself explicitly drew, was that life being as full of frustration as it is, we should make the most of our time—"in the time of your life" *live.* Not content, however, with this counsel, hardly novel and surely not so challenging as to suggest any passionate involvement in the conflicts posed by the depression and by the rise of Hitler, Saroyan proved the possibility of "living" by extracting as much courage and spirit from his honky-tonk habitués as anyone could wish. Both the common and the uncommon people of the play were, in one respect or another, marvelously vital, imaginative, or sensitive. . . . And for very good measure, Saroyan spun a world in which everything was possible: Thus, Kitty the magdalen is redeemed and married, with help from Joe, to Joe's handsome and simple-hearted protégé, and villainy is destroyed when "Kit Carson," using his antique frontier-weapon, stalks the Vice Squad insect and shoots him dead for insulting a lady—to wit, Kitty Duval. No consequences to "Kit Carson" are expected from this act of private reprisal, so much simpler in dramatic fancy than resistance to Hitler's battalions of evil outside the theatre. And since even Saroyan did not allege that the war of good and evil was at an end, he made Joe bequeath his own, unused, gun to "Kit Carson" for further exploits when and if called for. (pp. 298-99)

Curiously enough Saroyan's extravagance, which, coldly considered, is infantile, proved to be quite entrancing; and not merely because all of us indulge in wishful thinking or because, as the cliché goes (and cliché and Saroyan were bizarrely related), there is a child in the heart of each of us, but because Saroyan's bravura carried the day. His bravura had been tender and casual in his first play *My Heart's in the Highlands,* produced earlier in the same year, and it had made that long one-acter a unified fancy. *The Time of Your Life* was disunified and sprawling; it was less completely self-contained than its predecessor. But here, too, Saroyan did not withhold his hand from dispensing the bounty of an Americanized, plebeianized fairyland, and he poured a good deal of robust humor and even some tonic of irony into his largesse.

Saroyan, in short, was able to live in two worlds—those of social reality and fantasy—at the same time. The play, coming as it did at the beginning of World War II which ended a decade during which those worlds had stood miles apart in the consciousness of writers, was a fitting valedictory to the militant social theatre movement of the thirties soon to be memorialized in Harold Clurman's book about the Group Theatre under the title of *The Fervent Years.* (p. 299)

[The] Group Theatre, the most talented company to follow social consciousness as an article of faith in the thirties, . . . gave up the ghost in 1941. Henceforth, this prodigy and victim of history belonged to history—as a memory of the best ensemble acting Broadway had ever known and as an "influence" through its directors and actors—especially through Elia Kazan, Harold Clurman, and Lee Cobb, who became variously associated with the emergence of the new decade's foremost playwrights Tennessee Williams and Arthur Miller. As for Saroyan himself, the decline of his fortunes in the theatre actually became more rapid and marked than that of many less gifted and robust playwrights. Only two other full-length plays by him, *Love's Old Sweet Song* and *The Beautiful People,* and his one-act play *Hello, Out There,* all produced within the next two or three years, won any plaudits.

It would be wrong to attribute his misfortunes as a playwright to the very qualities that first drew attention to him. His breezy style and carefree inventiveness would have continued to sustain him on Broadway, which is anything but unappreciative of gusto and unconventional playwriting. Nor can it be maintained that he was always so unconventional that he taxed the tolerance of American playgoers. It is true that for a short time in a few plays, such as *Sweeney in the Trees* and especially *Jim Dandy,* he played the extreme *surréaliste* like a hod-carrier carrying a needle. But *Jim Dandy* was widely circulated during the war on the circuit of the National Theatre Conference, the Rockefeller-supported confederation of our most active university and community theatres. And, actually, the plays with which he won his reputation as the most promising new playwright at the close of the thirties were less extreme than press reviews had suggested.

Both *My Heart's in the Highlands* and *The Time of Your Life* made only moderate demands for a suspension of disbelief on our part. Their dialogue was colloquial and clear, and their characters were recognizably human, if eccentric. Their "philosophy," when they had one, was individualistic and genial in a manner traditional in the United States. Saroyan's brassy affirmativeness was that of an American street-Arab, his irreverence that of traditional American humorists. His fancies were moderate, consisting as they did largely of propositions favored in American "low-brow" and "middle-brow" circles—namely, that the common man is the salt of the earth, that somehow things usually turn out well for him, and that he has a high-hearted capacity for endurance. . . . [The] fact that Saroyan presented his faith with whimsy and compassion and that he added a spray of rue to his bouquet for "the beautiful people" endeared him to critics.

The structure of *My Heart's in the Highlands* and *The Time of Your Life,* as well as of several later plays, was actually as realistic as his dialogue; only their premises seemed somewhat extreme and askew. He made no literary allusions. He fiddled no harmonics on the strings of bohemian alienation or left-bank sophistication. By comparison with Apollinaire's *Les Mammelles de Tiresias,* Cocteau's *Orphée,* E. E. Cummings' *Him,* and any number of *surréaliste* and expressionist plays, his work was actually that of a conformist.

The Time of Your Life is a genre picture with a wealth of chiaroscuro, enlivened by the characters who reach out differently for their desires and dreams, and are roused out of various degrees of egocentricity by a conventional enough crisis when the Vice Squad detective tries to intimidate the saloon's inhabitants and jail the gentle harlot "Kitty Duval."

Packed into a "honky-tonk," a saloon that supplies entertainment as well as hard liquor, are a number of people. They are, superficially considered, hopelessly miscellaneous. But they have one thing in common—their burden of aspiration or of frustration or of both. The young marble-game addict, the melancholy comedian, the Negro who collapses of hunger and plays divinely when he is revived, the overzealous comedian, the naïvely persistent young man at the telephone, the prostitute who veils her past in dreams, the sensation-seeking wealthy woman married to a comically straitlaced husband, the policeman who detests his job, the frontiersman who blusters and lies himself into a glorious past—who are these and others but waifs of the world, impressing upon us the fact that we are all waifs of one kind or another!

The interplay of these characters, the mere fact, indeed, that they constitute a world, provides cohesion to the play on a level of simple intelligibility. And more cohesion is provided by the central character, Joe. Everything, every event or presence in the play, impinges upon him. He is many things in one, this man who acquired money and sickened of it, who is alone and inscrutably so.

Out of his loneliness and sensitivity he has developed a pity for all mankind and a sense of justice. And having money and time at his disposal, he has made himself a paraclete or comforter of his fellow creatures, giving understanding where it is needed and material help where it is imperative. One cannot attribute supernatural or social leadership to this figure. But as a very human person, he is the catalytic agent of a large portion of the play. He has a mystic prototype in the Paraclete of Evreinov's *The Chief Thing,* and a realistically characterized one in the interfering Luka of Gorky's *Night's Lodging* or *Lower Depths.* Saroyan's honky-tonk, itself, is an Americanized "Night's Lodging."

In its rambling way, *The Time of Your Life* even affords a theme. It is the need to make the most of life, which requires endurance, compassion, and opposition to the enemies of life represented by the vice-hunter and bully Blick. All mankind is pitiful, indeed, in Saroyan's stage world; even the sadistic Blick—who bullies the prostitute and maltreats the Negro who comes to her defense—is a pitiful specimen. And at the same time Saroyan suggests obliquely that there is a degree of evil that can be overcome only by the application of force. Joe wants to give his gun to "a good man who can use it," and he gives it at the end—to Kit Carson. Compassion and perception, and laughter and pity are fused in Saroyan's play. Nothing is basically vague here, although everything is fugitive. If the work does not come to a single point (and there is no reason why every play must, provided it is richly alive), all its separate points are vividly realized. Only a certain sweet tenderness dissolves them, particularly in a bedroom scene between a simple-minded boy and a broken-hearted young harlot.

We cannot, therefore, say that Saroyan won his early place in our theatre with a really radical departure from American playwriting. On the contrary, he epitomized both its virtues and defects in the plays which gave him a reputation on Broadway. Nor did he lose his place in our professional theatre because he offered a new dramatic form which was cravenly or obtusely rejected.

Saroyan's vogue in the theatre, which he has been unable to

recover to date, though not for want of trying, was a casualty of sheer wilfulness on his part. Like so many of us in America, he quite appealingly wanted to remain young forever, and therefore performed canters that did not become his subject matter. He was wont to start themes that required serious application on his part with a view to developing them, but he was too self-indulgent to do more than doodle around the edges. Self-indulgence, however, is the privilege of the young, and not of writers of whom maturity is expected after promise has been granted. Many American playwrights failed to mature, and we may well wonder what it was in our theatre that encouraged an arrested adolescence. Perhaps the indulgent education to be had in our schools gave the playwrights an insufficient sense of discipline. Perhaps the belief that success can be had with little effort made them too balky when hard thought was required. Saroyan certainly made too little effort to *think* things through and *work* things out. If the Group Theatre was a casualty of "history," Saroyan, like other writers, was a casualty of our culture. Indeed, he nearly made a cult out of the flouting of responsibility and discipline. Buoyancy and sentiment proved to be inadequate substitutes for meaning even in his often vital kind of playwriting. (pp. 299-302)

> *John Gassner, "Saroyan: 'The Time of Your Life',"* in his The Theatre in Our Times: A Survey of the Men, Materials and Movements in the Modern Theatre, *Crown Publishers, Inc., 1954, pp. 297-302.*

HAROLD CLURMAN

[*The essay excerpted below was originally published in the* Nation, *New York, February 5, 1955.*]

William Saroyan's **The Time of Your Life** is a little classic of the American theatre. I do not use the word "little" to indicate any lack of value or the word "classic" to signify any pretension of profundity. The simple fact is that in **The Time of Your Life** Saroyan has not only given us the essence of his talent, his personality, and his sense of life, but in doing so has expressed in delightfully theatrical terms a certain American dream and a certain American tradition. It is the dream of freedom in an almost child-like aspect, the tradition of a lovable vagrancy.

Americans believe in work, in accomplishment, in success. What we have built as a result of this credo is the most complicated and gigantic civilization the world has ever known. (p. 57)

The typical hero of such a civilization is the supercolossal achiever of the greatest amount of financial, social or physical displacement—some sort of personal atomic explosion. But such heroes—and we produce them constantly—soon become as stupefying as the works they create. We seek relief from them in anti-heroes—those with whom we can laugh, those toward whom we can feel kindness, those whom we envy not because of their greatness but, on the contrary, because of their littleness, their endearing inconspicuousness.

This sentiment produced such symbols as Chaplin's early pictures and motivates the hobo figure of our popular literature and stage. Saroyan's **The Time of Your Life** is a charmingly effusive, drunkenly dreamy, deft and darling piece of hoboism. We are nuts, but we are good, says the hobo poet; we know that life can be sweet because there is sweetness in all of us, but we allow ourselves to become bewildered—we have

lost our "foundation"—through the fraudulent mechanism of the world which has been elaborated around us. People who are full of hate may be brushed aside without malice, like bugs. For the rest we have only to accept the life process— inhale and exhale; there is romance, fun, genius and song on all sides.

Saroyan's play is wayward and airy. It is inspired by the bonhommie of the bar, the mildness, good nature, and cosmopolitan color of San Francisco itself. It moves in circles like a carrousel to beer-hall music spiced with strains of Orientalism and a gently drugged jazz. The dialogue is like a delicious babel of homespun jokes mingled with the strange clamor made by all the languages and races of a port town. There is the constant echo of laughter, and now and again the faint suspicion of a sob. The pervasive quality, as well as the "philosophy" of the play, is one of lyric anarchism.

If I speak with unabashed affection of **The Time of Your Life** it is not without a certain pang of regret. For I must make a public confession now—sixteen years after the event: I once turned down the opportunity to produce this gay and lovely play. It has always been difficult for me to explain or even fully to understand the reason. Perhaps there is in this play, besides the things that endear it to me, a certain cloying infantilism, exemplified by the scene in which the play's central vagabond and his companion vie with each other as to which can consume the greatest number of jellybeans, the "wiser" of the two exclaiming, "I've been wanting to do this all my life."

It is this trait in the play that spoils it for some people and probably spoiled it for me on that lamentable occasion sixteen years ago. But every work suffers from the defects of its qualities, and it is a serious critical weakness to detect the vice before one has a chance to appreciate the virtue of what is fundamentally a healthy, joyous dramatic spree in praise of folly. (pp. 58-9)

> *Harold Clurman, "The American Playwrights" in his* Lies Like Truth: Theatre Reviews and Essays, *The Macmillan Company, 1958, pp. 23-86.*

MARY McCARTHY

[*The essay excerpted below was originally published in slightly different form in* Partisan Review, *March-April, 1940.*]

William Saroyan has been in the writing business for eight years. He still retains his innocence. . . . To keep it, he has, of course, had to follow a strict regimen—no late hours, no worries, and only a limited responsibility. That is, he has had to fight off Ideas, Movements, Sex, and Commercialism. Some of the benefits have been remarkable. He has stayed out of the literary rackets—the Hollywood racket, the New York cocktail-party racket, and the Stalinist racket, which became practically indistinguishable from both the others. What is more important, the well of inspiration, located somewhere in his early adolescence, has never run dry. He is still able to look at the world with the eyes of a sensitive newsboy, and to see it eternally brand-new and touched with wonder. The price is that the boundaries of this world are the boundaries of the newsboy's field of vision.

Saroyan is genuine, Saroyan is not mechanical, Saroyan is the real thing; he tells you this over and over again in the prefaces to his two plays, [**My Heart's in the Highlands** and **The Time** *of Your Life*]. It is true. If you compare him with his contemporaries, Odets and Steinbeck, the purity of his work is blinding. Puerile and arrogant and sentimental as he may be, he is never cheap. Both Odets and Steinbeck are offering the public a counterfeit literature: Odets is giving an imitation of a lacerated Bronx boy named Odets who once wrote a play; Steinbeck is giving an imitation of a serious novelist. Saroyan as a public figure does an impersonation of Saroyan, but as a writer he plays straight. Moreover, both Odets and Steinbeck suffer from a kind of auto-intoxication; they are continually plagiarizing themselves; and their frequent ascents into "fine writing" are punctuated with pauses for applause that are nearly audible. Now Saroyan, as I say, has created a public character for himself, and the chief attribute of this character is exhibitionism, but he has incorporated this character boldly into his work and let him play his role there. Vanity has become objectified and externalized; it has no need to ooze surreptitiously into the prose. Saroyan's writing remains fresh and crisp and never has the look of having been pawed over by the author. Furthermore, though Saroyan's work is all of a piece, and the same themes and symbols recur, you will rarely find a constellation of symbols repeating itself, you will rarely get the same effect warmed up for a second serving.

It may be that Saroyan's world of ice-cream cones and toys, of bicycles and bugles, and somersaults and shotguns, of hunger and of banquets that appear out of the air, of headlines that tell of distant disasters, of goodhearted grocers and lovable frauds, of drunk fairy princes and pinball games that pay, is naturally more at home in the theatre than in fiction. Or it may be that, his scope being necessarily as narrow as it is, he has exhausted the permutations of the short story and requires the challenge of a new medium. At any rate, he has written [*My Heart's in the Highlands* and *The Time of Your Life;* the former] caused a furore and the other is a hit. (pp. 46-7)

[*The Time of Your Life*] is almost pure vaudeville, a play that is closer to *Hellzapoppin* than to anything else in the theatre.

The action of this play takes place in a San Francisco waterfront saloon in the year 1939. . . . [There] is a group of relatively simple people. . . . [These] characters seem to be trailing clouds of glory; they are beautiful and terrible just because they *are* people, Saroyan thinks. Each of them wants to do his own job, to do it tenderly, reverently, and joyfully, and to live at peace with his neighbors. Unfortunately, there are Frustrators at work, monstrous abstractions like Morality, and Labor and Capital, whose object is to flatten out these assertive individualists. The chief of these Frustrators is a Vice-Squad man named Blick, who stands for Morality, but Finance Capital is in the room in the shape of a gentleman slummer, and the voice of Labor can be heard outside in the waterfront strike. But if this universe has its devil in Blick, it has its God in Joe, . . . a charming, indolent alcoholic, whose mysterious wealth is the life-blood of the joint. Buying champagne, buying newspapers, ordering drinks for the house, giving handouts to the Salvation Army, to the boy out of a job, to the unfortunate prostitute, he keeps the people of the play going, but, being detached from the life of action, he is powerless to save them from Blick. This is left for one of their own numbers, the old trapper (God the Son), who shoots the interfering moralist as calmly as if he did it every day, and regretfully throws his beautiful pearl-handled revolver into San Francisco Bay. When Joe sees that everything

is straightened out, and that the two main characters are ready to start life on their own, he goes home, and the understanding is that he will not be back tomorrow.

There is no point in commenting on this intellectual structure, for it is not an intellectual structure at all, but a kind of finger-exercise in philosophy. Whenever it makes itself explicit, its juvenility is embarrassing; when it is allowed to lie somewhere behind the lines, it gives the play a certain strangeness, another dimension that is sensed but not seen. The real living elements of the play, however, owe nothing to philosophy. . . . Saroyan is still drawing on the street-life of his adolescence; it is inevitable, therefore, that his plays should belong to the theatre of that street-life, that is, to vaudeville. *The Time of Your Life* is full of vaudeville; indeed, almost every incident and character in it can be translated back into one of the old time acts. Kit Carson, the trapper, is W. C. Fields; the pinball machine that plays "America" and waves a flag when the jackpot is hit is out of Joe Cook; the toys Joe buys are a visual reminder of the juggling turn, and his money, deriving from nowhere and ostentatiously displayed, makes you think of the magic act; the young man who keeps telephoning his girl is the comic monologist; Harry the hoofer is Jimmy Durante; the boy out of a job is the stooge; and Joe (or God) . . . has that slim, weary, sardonic, city-slicker look that was the very essence of the vaudeville artist. Even the serious part of the play, the soul-searing drama involving Kitty, the beautiful prostitute, and the boy who wants to marry her, and Blick, takes you back to those short problem melodramas starring a passée actress that were occasionally interspersed with the regular acts. And *The Time of Your Life,* like an evening of vaudeville, is good when it engages the fancy and bad when it engages the feelings. (pp. 48-50)

Saroyan is in love with America, and very insistent about it. Just as a girl in his plays will be an ordinary girl and at the same time "the most beautiful girl in the world," because Saroyan is young and feeling good when he looks at her, so America is an ordinary place and at the same time "the most wonderful country in the world." This excessive, rather bumptious patriotism has created a certain amount of alarm; it has been suspected that Saroyan has joined the propagandists of the second crusade for democracy. The alarm is, I think, unjustified. Actually, the second statement is no more realistic than the first; it is not the literal fact but the state of mind that the reader is asked to believe in. And there is a kind of pathos about both statements that arises from the discrepancy that must exist between the thing described and the description of it. How far, in the second case, the pathos is intentional it is impossible to tell, but the contrasts in Saroyan's work show that he is at least partly aware of it.

In each of these plays there is a character that, more than the "gentle people" he talks so much about, represents the America he loves. This national type, exemplified by . . . the trapper in *The Time of Your Life,* is an elderly boaster who is both a fraud and not a fraud, an impostor and a kind of saint. . . . Kit Carson moves along through the plot telling one tall tale after another. At the end, after he has shot Blick offstage, he comes into the saloon and begins a narrative that sounds exactly like all the others: "Shot a man once. In San Francisco. In 1939, I think it was. In October. Fellow named Blick or Glick or something like that." This statement is a bombshell. It gives veracity to all the improbable stories that have preceded it, and at the same time the improbable stories cast a doubt on the veracity of this statement, which the audience nevertheless knows to be true. A boast becomes a form of modesty, and the braggart is maiden-shy.

This kind of character undoubtedly belongs to the tradition of American life and especially to the tradition of the West. It is Paul Bunyan and it is also the barker. But the tradition is dead now; it died when the frontier closed on the West Coast at some point in Saroyan's childhood. The type, if it exists at all outside of W. C. Fields, is now superannuated, for such anomalous human beings could only thrive under nomadic conditions of life. Today the barker has become an invisible radio announcer, and the genial, fraudulent, patent-medicine man has turned into a business house, with a public relations counsel. The America Saroyan loves is the old America, and the plays he weaves around it are not so much daring innovations as legends. (pp. 50-2)

Mary McCarthy, "Saroyan, an Innocent on Broadway," in her Sights and Spectacles: 1937-1956, *Farrar, Straus and Cudahy, 1956, pp. 46-52.*

HOWARD R. FLOAN

[*Portions of the essay excerpted below were originally published under the title "Saroyan and Cervantes' Knight" in* Thought, *Spring, 1958, and also in Spanish translation in* Atlántico, *1959.*]

The Time of Your Life is the best of Saroyan's plays because it expresses most completely his mind and art. In form it consists largely of incidental routines: a hoofer . . . dances and does comic monologues; a Negro improvises mood pieces on the piano; an Arab pours his sadness into the harmonica; a crusty old-timer tells tall tales of the early West. There are such miscellaneous items as a gum-chewing contest and a Salvation Army band, while in the background a young man struggles continuously with a pinball machine. The scene is water-front honky-tonk in San Francisco, "an American place," says the stage directions, and yet its cosmopolitan flavor is apparent. The proprietor is Nick, of Italian birth. At the bar is the silent Arab, with a Mohammedan tattoo on his left hand to indicate that he has been to Mecca. A Greek newsboy sings Irish songs. At the piano is Wesley, a Negro whose music, like that of the Arab, evokes a sense of suffering from long ago and far away. The native American environment, both past and present, is represented, too—the past as it is mythologized in the popular imagination; the present as reflected in economic, social, and moral conflicts.

An effective combining of past and present is achieved in Kitty Duval, who tells of her youth in a small Ohio town. She remembers the large house, the shade trees, and the big dog asleep on the doormat. But Kitty is a streetwalker, not a standard on-stage prostitute but one with such indubitable goodness of heart that one might think of her as a descendent of the bosomy, whisky-voiced habitué of the Western saloon, a type that has grown more pensive and fragile with the years. She reminds us of a world behind swinging doors in which the tart had status and even a kind of legal immunity. But earlier days are more specifically recalled by a crusty swaggerer who introduces himself as "an old trapper." Kit Carson, as he is called at Nick's, provides some lively comic interludes and turns out to be indispensable to the main drift of the play. He comes in asking a patron if he had ever fallen in love with a midget weighing thirty-nine pounds, and then Kit unlooses a glib, breezy string of anecdotes. In New Mexi-

co, he had bashed in a man's head with a brass cuspidor; in Texas, he had fought with a six-footer whose right hand was an iron claw; in Toledo, he had herded cattle on a bicycle: "Easiest thing in the world. Rode no hands. Had to, otherwise couldn't lasso the cows." Caught cheating in a poker game, he had been saved by a tornado—he was sure of it, for he remembered "sitting on the roof of a two-story house, floating northwest."

Kit Carson tells these yarns to Joe, a wistful, quiet-mannered fellow who regards Nick's place as a kind of microcosm and spends his waking hours sipping champagne. Joe is the first man ever to believe these stories. "Of course I believe you," Joe assures him. "Living is an art. It's not bookkeeping. It takes a lot of rehearsing for a man to get to be himself." Joe needs this mythologizing imagination, for it builds up an America he wants to know and accept. In this and in other ways, he is representative of his generation. He has come out of the depression having devised an economic system that goes on making money for him even as he has begun to see some of its less desirable consequences. In reaction against the vast impersonality of the new economics, he is no longer impressed by money alone and considers himself lucky not to know personally all those who have been hurt by his own rise to wealth. He now lives by a Christian conscience, he says, not by a social one. Hence he has a new-found respect for the little man and realizes that well-meaning people can make messes of their lives. He has saved the life of his dull but devoted *Johannes fac totum,* Tom, and he is eager to dispense kindness and charity wherever possible.

Joe provides the central reference point of the play, but the play is not about Joe, or about any other of its characters. It is about a state of mind, illusive but real, whose more readily recognizable components are, first, an awareness of America's youth—its undisciplined, swaggering, unregulated early life—and, secondly, a pervasive sense of America in crisis: an America of big-business, of labor strife, of depersonalized government, and, above all, of imminent war. Implicit is the suggestion that, if the nation survives, it will do so by reaffirming certain qualities of its youth and by solving the problems from below, through awareness and good will on the part of the little people. These notions are vague and never articulated, but they are there. In a theater that tends always to overconceptualize, Saroyan's willingness to understate, to rely on implication, and to use character and atmosphere for suggestive power only seemed to many like an evasion of his responsibility. Those who looked for a clearly defined theme and tightly constructed plot were disappointed by the apparent formlessness and the undeniable vagueness of the play. Like **My Heart's in the Highlands,** however, **The Time of Your Life** consists of a mood dramatized, an emotion conveyed directly. It has the power to move an audience, as its response clearly indicated.

The plot is melodramatic—a girl is saved from the clutches of a villainous wretch by a hero whose intentions, by axiom of course, are honorable—but its ironies are multiple: the heroine is a whore; the villain, a law officer; and the hero, inadequate in himself, needs the help of two other men. The innocent one who carries off the girl has no brains; the intelligent one who plans the rescue has no physical prowess; the dauntless one who takes care of the gunplay is an old man of the frontier who still has a pearl-handled revolver and judges shooting according to the self-reliant code of the vigilante. Nevertheless, the play has a hero—who rescues the girl and presumably takes her away to a life of innocence and joy. (She and the innocent one ride away in a truck to San Diego.) That she had become somewhat tainted increased the urgency for returning her to the pristine purity of American womanhood. Paradoxically, in this adaptation of old-time melodrama Saroyan provided a rather sophisticated means for his audiences to indulge their disenchantment with big-city ways and their nostalgia for a simple past.

The Romanticism of this latter-day horse-opera is made palatable to modern tastes not only by its nonchalance and its good-natured spoof of American myths, but also by its motley group of patrons at Nick's who bring variety and timeliness to the play. Presented in a desultory way, these characters help build up a believable, significant *mise en scène*. Though necessarily fragmented as individual portraits, they achieve a notable vitality and at times a sharp satiric edge. A wealthy couple, for example, has left a fashionable supper club to go slumming and has come to Nick's only to observe but cannot remain disengaged. The lady accepts one of Joe's cigars, biting off the tip and lighting up in the manner of Kit Carson, and the man surprises himself by putting in a word for Kitty when she is roughly questioned by the vice-squad officer. Their presence extends the world of the play and helps the theatergoer to take his chair at Nick's, too.

And Willy, who plays the pinball game throughout the entire action of the play, finally asserts his superiority over the machine as one of his marbles strikes home. With frenzied delight, he watches the dance of colored lights; and, as a mechanical arm raises an American flag, he comes to attention and salutes. "Boy, what a beautiful country," he shouts as he collects his six nickels. A more sardonic portrait is that of Dudley R. Bostwick, on whom life is playing a grim joke, for he has been taught that he has a chance in the world. His dignified name stands in amusing contrast to the complete mediocrity of his person. Over the public telephone at Nick's, he professes a great, desperate love for Elsie Mandelspiegel. But his connection is bad, and he pours out his heart to the wrong girl. His essential banality is pointed up further when Elsie finally comes in, for she turns out to be a nurse who has grown bitter through overexposure to sickness, disappointment, and death. In his shallowness and self-interest Dudley simply exploits her pathetic disillusionment. With unglamorous directness she suggests that they go to a cheap hotel together and dream that the world is beautiful.

The pervasive mood of the play is best reflected by Harry, an accomplished dancer who wants to be a comedian although he cannot make people laugh. To McCarthy, a hard-fighting longshoreman with a strike on his hands, Harry's lines are the funniest thing he has ever heard. But he does not laugh and cannot explain why. Actually, no one dares to respond to Harry's humor, for its source is too close to that of tears. It virtually identifies the anguish of the play, having much to do with poverty and the fear of armies. . . . (pp. 101-05)

The play has a five-act structure, with the first, third, and fifth acts devoted especially to the plot which I have described above; for the second and fourth acts are designed as supplementary mood pieces. Together they form [what Harold Clurman termed] a kind of "poetic harlequinade" in support of the preface: "in the time of your life, live." But they also produce a reverberating in the mind, suggesting many things. When Blick, the chief of the vice squad, walks in, the atmosphere immediately grows tense. Wesley cannot play, Harry cannot joke. Blick is the villain of melodrama; but in the fall

of 1939, when Hitler's armies had begun crushing helpless people, no audience could have missed the implications of authority dehumanized, grown corrupt and sadistic. And we must note that Blick is finally vanquished by a representative of the individualism of America, of a frontier contemptuous of authority and free of vice squads. Kit Carson is an anachronism, but he does what Joe cannot do. It was a brilliant, highly sophisticated touch for the playwright to bring in Kit Carson just before final curtain. "Killed a man once, in San Francisco, name of Glick or Blick or something." In drawling out these words he placed his action in the context of the tall tale, adding credibility to his earlier anecdotes as well as certain fantastic incredibility to what he has just done. Yet he has killed Blick, as the audience knows, and has thrown his pearl-handled revolver into the Bay. Thus the final effect is one of affirmation. The play expresses what its best people feel: it is a wonderful world, after all, as Krupp the Cop puts it, but in our weakness and fear we make a mess of things; sometimes we have to kill to preserve its goodness. (pp. 105-06)

Howard R. Floan, in his William Saroyan, *Twayne Publishers, Inc., 1966, 176 p.*

JAMES H. JUSTUS

> Zip! Walter Lippman wasn't brilliant today;
> Zip! Will Saroyan ever write a great play?
>   *—Pal Joey*

Lorenz Hart's question in 1940 contained its own implied answer: *no.* In the 60s, though the answer may still be the same, the Saroyanesque play as a unique amalgam of sentiment and fantasy deserves the attention of a new generation of readers. From the beginning, critics praised Saroyan for his freshness, irreverence, and promise, and from almost the same time condemned him for vagueness, egoism, and lack of discipline. . . . [Despite] the favorable reception of the two plays [*My Heart's in the Highlands* and *The Time of Your Life*] and the wider popular success of [his] stories, perhaps only Saroyan himself maintained a consistently favorable opinion of his contributions to American literature.

Like Steinbeck, Caldwell, Farrell, and the dramatists of social protest, Saroyan had a distinctive voice which spoke of and for the 30s. But where others were unremitting in their castigation of specific evils of American capitalism, Saroyan was merely occasional in his accusations. However deeply he felt about fascism and the abuses of political power, the literary treatment was usually generalized and moral. Placed against the programmatic social protest of Maxwell Anderson's *Winterset* (the moneyed classes pervert justice) and *High Tor* (the business world is ruthless in the name of economic progress), Paul Green's *Johnny Johnson* (the military and its mad supporters crush men of good will), John Howard Lawson's *Success Story* and Clifford Odets' *Golden Boy* (capitalism corrupts individual integrity), a play like *The Time of Your Life* seems mild indeed. Saroyan suggests, hints at, alludes to specific social wrongs, and then nearly always in comprehensive moral contexts (such as the deadening effects of materialism) which tend to dilute the anger with nostalgia and irony. A characteristic speech is the closing line of *My Heart's in the Highlands;* after their eviction, when Johnny and his penniless father take to the road, Johnny says: "I'm not mentioning any names, Pa, but something's wrong somewhere."

It was clear to The Committed that Saroyan was not effectively angry—he could not write *The Grapes of Wrath,* for instance. Neither was he interested in exploring the potential revolutionary spirit of the rural or urban dispossessed in the manner of *Studs Lonigan* or "Kneel to the Rising Sun." Most clearly, he was not interested in ideology—the determining motive behind *Awake and Sing!* or *One Third of a Nation.* Moreover, Saroyan was too bumptiously independent, he was too addicted to the vitality, rather than the privations, of children and immigrants, and he indulged himself too freely in a rhetoric that could only inspire fantasy and dreams. The Saroyan method, made clearer in the 1940s and after, is finally not frontal, but oblique; and the major mood it establishes is not anger, but poignancy.

Lack of money—and therefore food and shelter—is more the occasion for sorrow at The Way Things Are and indefinable longing than it is for a plea to correct those things. . . . Furthermore, the view is conservative when it is not merely comic; Cabot denies that he is unfortunate, proclaims his proud integrity, and boasts of being able to "shift for ourselves, the same as ever." Only in his best play, *The Time of Your Life,* does Saroyan resemble those dramatists who were choosing viably realistic situations which invited larger, symbolic readings. For all their differences, Harry Van of Robert Sherwood's *Idiot's Delight* and Gimpty of Sidney Kingsley's *Dead End* both anticipate Joe of *The Time of Your Life:* the little man of essential decency who understands the human predicament and who despite that gloomy knowledge idealistically clings to the hope of man's improvement. Entrapment, the common informing metaphor in the lives of those people herded together in a remote Italian lodge and the tenements along the East River in New York, fails to be the dominant metaphor for the habitués of Nick's San Francisco saloon simply because the hopes for escaping the trap are more stubbornly voiced.

Since the early 40s the familiar Saroyan stories have continued to flow, a few novels have appeared and been variously received; and plays both produced and unproduced, with seemingly tireless admonitory prefaces, have been published—all reminders that Saroyan is not only still around but that he is still the same old Saroyan. And, except for the tone of his non-dramatic work, which has grown increasingly solemn and self-conscious, and a few stories written in bile, Saroyan's is indeed the same voice heard in the 30s: there is grief aplenty, but man is a miracle, and merely living confirms life's miraculousness. That which seemed so distinctive to the spirit of the 30s no longer strikes us with the same relevant hopefulness, although such an observation may say more about our times than it does about Saroyan's themes, which were and still are largely prescriptions for ills which the author sees as endemic to no particular time. (pp. 211-13)

> *James H. Justus, "William Saroyan and the Theatre of Transformation," in* The Thirties: Fiction, Poetry, Drama, *edited by Warren French, Everett Edwards, Inc., 1967, pp. 211-19.*

CLIVE BARNES

[*The Time of Your Life*] is a play so warm-hearted that I could almost appreciate the excessive air-conditioning in the theater.

It has a quality of lovability that all those "most unforgetta-ble characters I've ever met" in the *Reader's Digest* can envy, and only Lassie surpass. There is nothing wrong about being lovable, but it can be taken to somewhat extreme degrees.

Mr. Saroyan is a poet of the ordinary—deeply concerned with rooting out the common or garden cliché at the heart of all human experience. In this play he succeeds.

It is often referred to as "a dramatic fugue" . . . [see revised excerpt by John Gassner above, 1954] and it does have something of the understated poetics, off-hand and suggestive, of Chekhov. In 1939, when it was first produced, I might well have gone to bat for it—but 30 years later it doesn't seem to have aged, just dated.

The quality of a fugue is basically governed by its theme. In the case of Chekhov it was the richness, the inpenetrability and the indestructibility of humanity. In Saroyan it is the eccentricity, the poisonously cyclamated sweetness of life. Believe it or not, he is a Ripley at heart. . . .

The hero Joe is worried about events in Europe. Because the time is 1939, Joe is disturbed. He drinks champagne all day and is civil to the whores. He says wise things, too. Wise, cute, quaint and poetic things. He has a gift.

Two years ago the Lincoln Center Repertory Company opened its season with an inferior Broadway revival—[Lillian Hellman's] *The Little Foxes*—superbly done. It has repeated the feat. . . .

But what is a nice company like that doing in a basically trivial and pretentious play like this?

> *Clive Barnes, "Saroyan Dated," in* The New York Times, *November 7, 1969, p. 37.*

WALTER KERR

[*The essay excerpted below was originally published in the* New York Times, *November 16, 1969.*]

Funny, how we remember it wrong. No, we don't even remember it wrong. We get it wrong in the first place.

What do we think of William Saroyan, author of that celebrated and now once again revived comedy *The Time of Your Life*? . . . Why, of course we think of him fondly, as though sometime or other we had forgiven him for something; we think of him with amusement because he has so often in his swarthy catlike laziness amused us; we think him rather a spoiled writer because nothing else was ever as good as those first stunning short stories; we think him a bit of a poseur perhaps; but above all—above all—we think him a sentimentalist.

We even know what he was sentimental about. Those beautiful people. Their goodness, their lostness, their dreaminess. How sweet Joe is, sitting in that barroom and dispensing all that money for free, ready to declare his love within minutes for the latest forlorn lady to occupy the next table, ready to take Kitty Duval, adorable whore that she is, out of her shabby quarters where sailors interrupt her weeping and her sleep and to install her grandly at a hotel reserved for ladies of quality. How kind they all are to one another, these bartenders and hoofers and piano players and idling cops, just so long as no alien principle of evil happens to move among them. When one does move among them, in the person of a particularly brutal fellow from the Vice Squad, his crime is quickly made plain: "He hurts little people." (pp. 163-64)

When Joe reminisced about just missing getting married and having all those imagined children ("My favorite was the third one"), the grin in the playhouse came up broad and warm. When a drunk offered a solemn toast to "reforestation" or Joe urged his runner to get rid of a gun by giving it to "some worthy holdup man," the laugh was quick, indulgent, genuine. . . . Inside its studied booziness the soft charms, the expected charms, lurked and worked.

Why, though, are these charms all we ever remember about the play and why do we persist in thinking of it as fundamentally cheerful, as fundamentally (and maybe spuriously) an act of faith? It's nothing of the sort, nothing at all. (pp. 164-65)

There isn't a shred of hope in *The Time of Your Life*. Central passage of the play, carried by a cop named Krupp:

> They're all guys who are trying to be happy; trying to make a living; support a family; bring up children; enjoy sleep. Go to a movie; take a drive on Sunday. They're all good guys, so out of nowhere comes trouble. . . . I been thinking everything over, Nick, and you know what I think? . . . I think we're all crazy. . . . We're crazy. We're nuts. We've got everything, but we always feel lousy and dissatisfied just the same. . . . There's no hope. I don't suppose it's right for an officer of the law to feel the way I feel but, by God, right or not right, that's how I feel. . . . We're no good any more.
>
> (p. 166)

Through this is threaded the one desolate line we *do* remember from the play, "No foundation—all the way down the line," repeatedly intoned by an Arab who sits alone at the bar. Somehow or other we seem to remember that line as funny, perhaps because it's a catch-phrase and is repeated so often. But in fact it's not funny: the bitterest explosion of the evening comes from this Arab when he is finally prodded into sustained speech.

And as we take a new look at the play now, attending to it as something less than affirmative, we're a bit surprised by what we see. Joe is, at his own evaluation, worthless: he detests money, he is certain that making money is invariably a matter of hurting people, he goes on making money. The one vigorous act he attempts to perform—shooting the Vice Squad man—he bungles. The girl at the table who has accepted the idea of Joe's love is a woman who should be happy. She has a husband and children and nothing in particular to be sad about. "Then why are you sad?" Joe wants to know. "I was always sad," she replies. "It's just that after I was married I was allowed to drink."

If Joe hates himself and the cop hates his job and the girl hates having grown up to drinking, no one else on the premises is really any better off. The dancing comedian cannot, by his own admission, get a laugh. The intelligent longshoreman cannot avoid becoming involved in a strike. The piano player is beat up, the society slummers are embarrassingly routed, Kit Carson is a fraud until he becomes something better than that, a murderer. Maybe there's some hope for the young innocent and his nice whore, running off to take a job driving a truck together. On the evidence offered, it would be a surprise if they survived the first turnpike.

Sounds almost like Artaud, doesn't it? It's not, naturally. An outline has no tone, whereas Saroyan's tone is omnipresent, and it is soft and friendly. In fact, you could say that if Saroyan is sentimental about the likeableness of people he is equally sentimental about the doom they are headed for. Even pessimism can be sentimental, since sentimentality is simply an excess of emotion in relation to the evidence offered. Pity can be too much as a pat on the head can be too much. Perhaps there's a shade too much of both here, for this slightly later and more ascetic age. (pp. 166-67)

Never mind. My point is that we think of Saroyan as incorruptibly sunny, whereas *The Time of Your Life* is really all about the day the last sun went down. There isn't any tomorrow in it for anybody—maybe the bartender, but will he have customers?—and instead of being a poem in praise of the green lawns of MGM and the high hopes of Mickey Rooney, it is much more nearly the matrix for all of the doomsday plays that have followed. (p. 167)

Walter Kerr, "Remembrance of Things Past," in his God on the Gymnasium Floor and Other Theatrical Adventures, *Simon and Schuster, 1971, pp. 161-87.*

HAROLD CLURMAN

I have written about William Saroyan's *The Time of Your Life* so many times that I would almost have preferred to note summarily that it is surely one of the best plays the American theatre has produced and to have that opinion stand by itself. But certain reactions to its [1969] revival . . . provoke me to say something more.

The Time of Your Life is not "dated"; it is a folk tale. It is not merely a play of the 1930s' depression, although its surface associations pin it down in time. It catches something permanently benevolent, gusty, zestful in the American ethos. It is as native to us as *Huckleberry Finn,* with greater contemporary relevance.

When in the fifties I spoke of the play I said that it was prebeatnick. Today I would say it is pre-hippie. What was and is salutary in these trends is their resistance to the fierce aggressiveness which springs from the very mechanism of our industrial civilization. Those who are strong and mature seek by active political and cultural means to lift the burden of evil attendant on our success-crazy society; the more innocent drift toward a passivity which consists chiefly of nonparticipation in the drive toward noisy achievement. Unconsciously, this withdrawal from the mad push is something like a religious phenomenon. It is the way of both the saintly and the pure in heart among humble folk.

A corresponding sentiment lies deeply rooted in our people ever since we have become *big*. Hence the fascination with the hobo; it is a sort of nostalgia, almost envy. Secretly we harbor an irrepressible affection for the person who invites his soul, dreams, laughs, talks with quiet compassion to his fellow man and hurts no one. There is a certain strength in this. Many among today's youth are in accord with this spirit. It is no less important and valuable for being deficient in "logic."

The tone of Saroyan's play is one of lyric anarchism. It is sentimental in a way that one should be ashamed not to be. Saroyan, it has never been sufficiently realized, writes beautifully, without any trace of affectation. His language is robust, juicy, colorful—true Americana with no vulgarity or recourse to current smart talk. It is lightened by warm laughter. It is loose but not limp. There is a wonderful freedom in it. It will for a long time remain representative of what is most attractive in us. In every respect *The Time of Your Life* rises head and shoulders above most of the new young dramatists whose work is too often imitative in style, petty in feeling, frivolously ambitious, shrilly pretentious.

The play has always been staged as if it were realism. It is real, but not "realistic." Its characters are painted in tender "clown" pigments; the world they float in is delicately inebriate, harmlessly "psychedelic." . . .

[Saroyan originally insisted] that the saloon in which the action takes place be literally rendered as a drab and crumby little joint. The play came to New York in that guise, . . . but with the other elements of production indifferent—the whole sufficient to carry the play's "message."

Saroyan may have been right. But I have always hoped to see the play done poetically, with its fancy made visible, and with more song in its total expression. Alas, no one has as yet had the imagination, courage and skill to do so.

> Harold Clurman, in a review of "The Time of Your Life," in The Nation, New York, Vol. 209, No. 18, November 24, 1969, p. 581.

JACK RICHARDSON

[Three] interesting examples of innocence . . . have appeared on the New York stage this season. . . . William Saroyan's *The Time of Your Life,* Tennessee Williams's *Camino Real,* and Thornton Wilder's *Our Town* are all, judged by the standards contemporary with their debuts, mavericks. Each created problems and confusions by playing with the accepted distance and decorum that were supposed to exist between the audience and the stage, each possessed an idiosyncratic notion of narrative and dramatic relevancy, and each attempted to make us aware of that old innocence and wonder in life before it is too late. . . . Not surprisingly, each of the plays fastens onto a very American symbol to bind all its fragments of life together: the saloon; the rural, *Saturday Evening Post* town of porches, main streets, and lifetime neighbors; Kilroy, the proper noun of American wandering and conquest during World War II—they are all very much national proclamations of our uniqueness and our near contradictory oneiric quest both for adventure and roots, experience and the joys of ingenuousness.

A good deal of time has passed since these plays first appeared—*Our Town* in 1938, *The Time of Your Life* in 1939, and *Camino Real* in 1953—and their stylistic peculiarities now seem quite mild-mannered and cautious compared with what has come out of the Theater of the Absurd, the Theater of Cruelty, Total Theater, and all the other momentary theoretical justifications for critical categories. It is much easier today to see their substance, and to assess both the dangers and strengths in this cultural tradition of innocence as a goal and a memory. (pp. 20, 22)

Saroyan's innocence is simply impregnable, and because he trusts it, because he does not make little winking *sotto voce* apologies to his audience on its behalf or festoon it with literary symbols, it has stood by him through the years; it has kept

[*The Time of Your Life*] from becoming merely a curio and has made it into a small, but sturdy, American classic. In this work, Saroyan puts all his enthusiasm for life into the sanctuary of a San Francisco bar—that is, into our country's traditional refuge from the assaults of workaday, petty actuality. Characters drop in and out with the apparent randomness of any group of saloon visitors, announcing themselves, their philosophies, and their problems; but in Saroyan's perfect bar they are at last listened to, and more, they discover that a propitious moral imperative exists in Nick's Pacific Street Saloon, Restaurant, and Entertainment Palace—namely, that the most broken-down piece of human circumstance will have a chance, indeed *must* have a chance if anything else in the world is to have human meaning.

It was not a good time for America when this play was written—we were just coming out of a depression, a world war was drifting toward us—and yet, unlike many of his contemporaries, Saroyan never fastened onto hysterical simplicities, never lost sight of what was important in the national life and the life of a writer's imagination. It is remarkable that although there is no mistaking the historical facts threaded through the play, there is so little of the time's facile styles present. Saroyan's humor and language make of particular American crises delightful dilemmas for all humanity simply because, like his central character, Joe, he takes nothing for granted and scrutinizes everything without prejudgment or artistic condescension. A two-dollar whore with a tender heart? A policeman yearning for beauty and tranquility? An intellectual longshoreman? A melodramatic blackguard from the vice squad? A hoofer who does comic routines about the dangers of *Realpolitik?* It would take a steel-like innocence not to have just a moment or two of sport at their expense, but Saroyan never falters. He gives them his complete artistic fealty and writes them deeply into our consciousness, as if they were the first and freshest objectifications of a deep, half-articulate myth about ourselves.

It is odd that *The Time of Your Life,* a play strung together by a gentle insistence on the goodness and possibilities of life, should end with a killing, but the way it has been arranged, it is really no more than American nostalgia having a glorious moment, a victory of the best notion of our history over the worst. Kit Carson, a garrulous old frontiersman with a dubious reminiscence to pay for each of the drinks that he can cadge, suddenly covers all his tall tales with the swagger of truth by doing in the play's villain, Blick, the detective from the vice squad who has gratuitously persecuted and humiliated the sweet prostitute, Kitty Duval. The play ends with his recounting this deed in the same pitchman's style as he has his other tales, giving our legend a second chance, and reminding us that high adventure and the innocent spirit need not be nothing more than sentimental bombast, that, in fact, they might be the most significant weapons we have still left to us.

I have no idea whether or not we are due for a recrudescence of interest in Saroyan's work, but I don't see how a generation that wants to revive old hopes about this country and the way to live in it could overlook such an ally. It would have to search very hard to find an artist skillful enough to make one believe that not only is it possible for evil and innocence to have a shoot-out in a significant work of art, but that it is even possible for innocence to win. And it might also learn from him what I did from seeing, on consecutive evenings, his and

Williams's and Wilder's plays: namely, that in art, innocence, like despair, cannot be undigested or unearned. (p. 24)

Jack Richardson, "Innocence Restaged," in Commentary, *Vol. 49, No. 3, March, 1970, pp. 20, 22, 24.*

CLIVE BARNES

Anyone incapable of changing his mind must run the risk of being suspected of not having a mind to change. However, it is always at best an embarrassing pleasure, and at worst an unpleasurable embarrassment, for a drama critic to admit he was wrong about a play. Not, I hasten to add, that right and wrong mean anything in the context of art—but usually a critic's reactions are consistent, at times perhaps dully so. Well, I have changed my mind over William Saroyan's *The Time of Your Life.*

When this play was last produced in 1969 I suggested it was sentimental claptrap [see excerpt above]. This was far too hasty and flip a judgment. I have now read it a number of times, studied it, and just seen it again. . . . The play is, I now think, everything its admirers claim for it. . . .

Saroyan's play is set in 1939 and is about 1939. It is also about a man called Joe, who had money and champagne to spare, it is a play about America, about Hitler, about frontier idealism, about the essential romanticism of that now almost completely lost American dream. Typically, it is set in a bar.

This is not O'Neill's realistic bar of *The Iceman Cometh,* this is a Hollywood dream factory bar where anything could happen but probably never would. . . .

Joe is the America that permitted peddled fantasies to become reality. Joe believes in the illusions of his friends—seeing everything very clearly through the drunkenly misty spectacles of a rich guilt that can only be washed away in a sea of champagne. Joe is the everhopeful morning-after of the American dream, and here, in 1939, with the world moving into new shadows, he is going out to face a new scene. It is the time of his life. It is a time when, as one of the bar-room denizens points out, there is: "No foundation. All the way down the line."

Nothing much happens. A man and a girl are possibly saved—another man, a brutal Vice Squad detective is certainly killed, and Joe seeing the scene moves on. It was 1939 and Joe had to be on the move. The champagne was over, the dreams of jackpots in the sky were fading.

Yes, it is a lovely play—full of sentiment, poignant with a sense of time and place, full of an immediacy all the more touching when seen in retrospect. It is—as I realize—a play easily got wrong.

Clive Barnes, "Saroyan Play Revived by Plumstead Troupe," in The New York Times, *February 25, 1972, p. 26.*

DOUGLAS WATT

The boozy aimless crowd with which William Saroyan populated his saloon play *The Time of Your Life* seemed a particularly dreary lot in last night's revival. . . .

A good deal of the fault is the author's, of course. Whether

viewed as realism, fantasy, parable or just another of Saroyan's countless attempts to fill an area with his "beautiful people," the play doesn't make much sense. The slangy talk is awkward, the people don't behave like people, and the sunny, sappy Joe, who is at the center of things, is as much a disturbing meddler as a good Samaritan. . . .

[The] main trouble, I'm afraid, is that Nick's bar has just about had it. Once a screwily entertaining hangout, it's become seedier and duller with the passing years as the regulars have gotten older. It happens to the best of bars.

Douglas Watt, "Off Night at Nick's," in Daily News, *New York, October 29, 1975.*

STANLEY KAUFFMANN

[*The essay excerpted below was originally published in slightly different form in the* New Republic, *November 22, 1969.*]

[In 1969], the year in which Samuel Beckett wins the Nobel Prize, [Saroyan's *The Time of Your Life* is revived]. . . . Surprisingly, it turns out to be a good idea: not because of any nostalgic contrast between a rosy past and a bleak present; not because Saroyan contends in a 1966 preface that (believe it or not) he was a predecessor of Beckett's in altering our view of the human condition, but because the passage of time lets us see that *The Time of Your Life* is not exactly the warm-hearted American vaudeville it has been called.

Saroyan's comedy is one of the last items in the two-decade era of the Well-Patched Play. For about a hundred years the stage had seen the Well-Made Play, which is not dead yet, but between the World Wars we got a spate of American plays that depended less on intricate plots with surprises and reversals and precisely spaced "big" scenes, and more on a parade of minor characters, each with a tiny "turn" of his own or a bit of subplot. Such an approach enabled an author to give his work a feeling of verism on the cheap (life was being sliced) and also freed him from certain demands of the Well-Made form. That form was not abandoned by any means, but the profligacy of the '20s induced the writer to fill it out with a series of vaudeville acts, rather than to dwell exclusively on his central characters, to develop them and his plot further. A prime exponent of this approach was the witty George S. Kaufman, any number of whose collaborations are samples. Of course this ragbag method . . . was tied to the prevailing economics of the theater: actors were cheaper then. But it was that current mode of show biz which Saroyan used and expanded in his poetically intended work. His play is a rather patently conceived Grand Music-Hall of Life.

The setting (except for one short inset scene) is a honky-tonk saloon in San Francisco, 1939. A consciously mysterious character named Joe sits there, drinking champagne, dispensing unexplained money, dispatching messengers, ordering and arranging the lives of people who pass through. There is a carefully balanced assortment of characters: . . . to complete the list would be almost to mock the play. But that would be misleading, because Saroyan has the ability to write sharp vignettes for many of them, which takes the curse off the arranged feeling and instead gives the play a comfy sprawl. Occasionally there is the oppressive feeling that we are being consciously shown America-1939, but most of the time the solos, duets, and trios are quite entertaining.

The play's theme—*In the time of your life, live*—is not new in the American canon. For instance, in almost exactly the same words, it's the advice that Strether gives Bilham in James's *The Ambassadors*. As Saroyan uses it, the theme combines a diluted descent from Thoreau with an augury of hippiedom—another American lunge at Edenic bliss. But contradictory things grow out of that free-living belief (as they do now in some hip films and novels). First, the world is made up of Good People and Bad People. There are more Goods than Bads, there is instant communion between the Goods, and there is instant hatred of the Goods by the Bads. *The Time of Your Life* has only one Bad, the vice-squad detective, Blick, and he really has to do yeoman service for his nasty cause. He is the only evil in the play and his part is small, so, as written and played, he has to cram an awful lot of badness into a little space. My heart went out to him as he sweated away to supply the necessary wicked contrast.

Then there is the character of Joe. He has a certain resemblance to Giraudoux's Madwoman of Chaillot. He sits in one place, more or less, the world comes to him, he rewards virtue and punishes vice (after deciding which is which), and dispenses largess as he talks about money like a minor Proudhon. The only difference between Joe and the villainous Blick is benevolence and malevolence—the despotism in them is exactly the same.

And the play ends with as prime a bit of lynch law as I have ever seen on stage. After we hear a couple of shots, the old hobo comes in and says that he has just killed Blick and has thrown away his gun. Then Joe gives the old man another revolver, presumably to carry on his good work.

The real fairy tale about this play is that it is a sentimental fairy tale. Underneath the boozy friendliness, its basic view is rigidly moralistic, with a view of Paradise as a place where everyone behaves in the way that the Good (self-appointed) order it, and where the Good have the right to kill the Bad but not vice versa. What makes the play specially interesting to see again is that this tension, between superficial humanism and underlying puritanism, is now more apparent than before. But also, to be sure, Saroyan's gift for cutting disrespectfully right to the core of every new situation is as humorous as ever, and some of his fancies still glisten untarnished. (pp. 111-13)

> *Stanley Kauffmann, " 'The Time of Your Life',"* in *his* Persons of the Drama: Theater Criticism and Comment, *Harper & Row, Publishers, 1976, pp. 111-14.*

JOHN A. MILLS

In the conclusion of his 1976 article entitled, "Joe as Christ-Type in Saroyan's *The Time of Your Life*" [see *CLC*, Vol. 10], Kenneth W. Rhoads suggested that "other interpretations of Joe may be validly advanced (although so far they seem not to have been)." Seven years of critical silence having followed the issuance of Rhoads's invitation, the time would seem to be ripe for an alternate reading of the character and the play, the more so since Saroyan's recent death is likely to have stirred up fresh interest in his work.

I should like to propose that Joe be viewed as an *"homme absurde,"* as defined by Camus in *The Myth of Sisyphus*, and that the play over which he presides be seen as an embodiment of the absurd sense of life, expressing in its structure and all its parts man's confrontation with nothingness, with "the unreasonable silence of the world."

To speak of a work by Saroyan in these terms is, in large measure, to fly in the face of received opinion. Saroyan's depiction of the human condition is usually thought of as sunny and positive, bordering on the sentimental. (p. 139)

Saroyan typically shows his characters coping with earthly existence with a light-heartedness which approaches the meretricious. There is an element of sweetness in his work which has no counterpart in the drama and fiction of Camus or Sartre, to say nothing of Dostoevsky or Beckett. But there is no fundamental incompatibility between an absurd view of the human enterprise and the adoption of an optimistic stance in the face of ultimate absurdity, pessimistic as most absurdist literature undoubtedly is. (p. 140)

One of the most conspicuous features of Joe's character is his immobility. Except for the move to Kitty's hotel room (about which more later) he scarcely stirs. Others come and go—indeed, the play is more than commonly replete with exits and entrances—but not Joe. He remains a still center amid the flux of quotidian activity, relying on the faithful Tom to do such fetching and carrying as he requires. At one point he hints that he is physically incapable of locomotion. "I don't dance," he tells Mary, and then goes on to say, "I can hardly walk." When she asks, "You mean you're tight?," he says "No. I mean *all* the time."

Saroyan comments revealingly on this exchange in *Here Comes There Goes:*

> Dance? I could hardly walk. Joe, in this same play I'm talking about, said it for me, precisely in those words. This didn't mean something was the matter with his feet and legs, though. It meant something else.

From the context in which this observation occurs it is clear what, for Saroyan, that "something else" is. He has been declaring his admiration for Bojangles and others he has seen who *can* dance and in the process the term is elevated to the metaphoric plane where it takes on the meaning of "to live, to know how to live, to be engaged, to have found a role, a purpose for living." Joe's physical immobilization may thus be seen as the external counterpart of an inner, psychic immobilization. Joe is stalled, incapable of movement, because, having glimpsed the absurd, he is unable to believe in the efficacy of human action, *any* human action.

This state of mind is manifested in many other ways, both explicitly and implicitly. As he can hardly walk, he can also hardly talk, can hardly summon up the will to verbally engage external reality. His typical utterances are terse, laconic, flat and monosyllabic. It is significant that he delivers himself of more than a single, simple declarative sentence almost exclusively on those occasions when he is goaded into explaining his inertia; paradoxically, he talks only to account for his failure to talk (or walk, or act). One such speech occurs when Tom finally musters the courage to ask where Joe gets his money. Joe looks at Tom *"sorrowfully, a little irritated"* and *"speaks clearly, slowly and solemnly":*

> Now don't be a fool, Tom. Listen carefully. If anybody's got any money—to hoard or to throw away—you can be sure he stole it from other people. Not from rich people who can spare it, but from poor people who can't. From their lives and

from their dreams. I'm no exception. I *earned* the money I throw away. I stole it like everybody else does. I hurt people to get it. Loafing around this way, I *still* earn money. The money itself earns more. I still hurt people. . . .

This much of the speech, if read in isolation from what follows immediately and in isolation from other materials in the play, might seem to make Joe a social rebel, a man who has withdrawn in protest from the capitalist system, who refuses to be party any longer to the social Darwinism which makes every man a predator of his fellow creatures. Indeed, there is no reason to deny Joe a social conscience. Undoubtedly it was a causative factor in his withdrawal from the world. But it was only a factor, and a relatively minor one. Joe's quarrel is with existence, with the human condition, *sub specie aeternitatis,* and not merely with the institutions of twentieth-century industrial society. This is revealed, in a negative way, in Joe's reluctance to condemn Blick, the play's chief representative of militant fascism. . . . (pp. 142-43)

Even when confronted with ocular proof of Blick's bullying ways, Joe is unable to take decisive action against him. He goes through the motions, points the gun and pulls the trigger, but nothing happens. He blames "dumb Tom" for having bought "a six-shooter that won't even shoot once," but, in fact, he had himself removed the cartridges not ten minutes earlier. Whether the attempted assassination of Blick is pure charade or Joe has actually forgotten about the cartridges (his mind dulled by drink?) is impossible to say. But if Saroyan manages the incident rather clumsily, his reason for including it seems nevertheless clear: he stays the hand of his protagonist because he recognizes that decisive action would run counter to the radically uncommitted nature of the character he has been at pains to depict in all that has gone before. Joe does not act because he lacks the necessary conviction, however much he may hide that fact from his own consciousness by conveniently "forgetting" that the weapon is unloaded, or however much he may hide it from others by blaming Tom.

That Joe cannot act, in the social sphere or any other sphere, he explains in the conclusion to his lengthy answer to Tom about the source of his income.

> . . . I don't do anything. I don't *want* to do anything any more. There isn't anything I can do that won't make me feel embarrassed. Because I can't do simple, good things. I haven't the patience. And I'm too smart. Money is the guiltiest thing in the world. It stinks. Now, don't ever bother me about it again.

Surely such remarks can be interpreted in a way that establishes a family resemblance between Joe and the alienated, disaffected, anti-heroes who people the world of modernist fiction and drama. In Camus's terms, Joe has come to regard all tasks as Sisyphean, as so much meaningless activity, activity which is "embarrassing" because it does not have, cannot have, intrinsic value or ultimate efficacy. Like Dostoevsky's Underground Man, Joe is cursed with "lucidity," that "full-fledged disease" which obviates action; he is "too smart." Like the Underground Man he envies those "spontaneous people and the men of action" who lack lucidity but he knows he can never again be one of them. He cannot "do simple things," cannot, like a Russian peasant, be a contented hewer of wood and drawer of water. Consciousness will not allow it. (pp. 144-45)

Joe's sporadic outbursts of self-analysis provide perhaps the most explicit evidence of his immersion in absurdity, but his state of mind manifests itself in other ways as well. In the play's opening sequence, after Joe has purchased a stack of newspapers, glanced at them and thrown them away in disgust, the Arab picks one up, reads the headline, and *"as if rejecting everything else a man might say about the world,"* intones for the first time a line which is to run through the play like a lyric refrain: "No foundation. All the way down the line." The incident establishes a spiritual nexus between the two characters; the Arab says what Joe thinks; they share a belief in the emptiness of all human endeavor; it has no foundation, no intrinsic value. Repeated and embellished throughout the play, the Arab's judgment upon the world carries the same thematic force as the cryptic pronouncement with which Estragon opens *Waiting for Godot:* "Nothing to be done."

The second time we hear from the Arab he develops his theme, his *sole* theme, at greater length:

> No foundation. All the way down the line. What. What-not. Nothing. I go walk and look at sky.

Krupp immediately turns to Joe for an explanation: "What? What-not? What's that mean?" It is significant that Krupp fails to comprehend because Krupp is a man who cannot live without absolutes, without direction. He has surrendered his freedom, put on a uniform, and follows orders, bashing heads at the command of his masters, secure in the conviction that they know what is to be done, even if he does not. It is also significant that Joe *does* understand and is ready with an explication, further revealing that he and the Arab are like-minded men, differing only in the beverages they choose as aids to lucidity:

> What? What-not? That means this side, that side. Inhale, exhale. What: birth. What-not: death. The inevitable, the astounding, the magnificent seed of growth and decay in all things. Beginning, and end. That man, in his own way, is a prophet. He is one who, with the help of *beer,* is able to reach that state of deep understanding in which what and what-not, the reasonable and the unreasonable, are one.

Once again, Saroyan shows himself to be Beckettian *avant la lettre;* that "inhale, exhale" reminds us of the later playwright's thirty-second dramatization of the human condition called *Breath,* and the evocation of "Beginning, and end" expresses the same sense of life as Hamm's "The end is in the beginning and yet you go on."

The Arab thus functions as a kind of choral character, articulating in a quasi-lyric mode that sense of estrangement, of being rudderless in [what Camus termed] "a universe suddenly divested of illusions and lights," which colors everything that Joe says and does. The Arab's presence in the play expands its reference, amplifies its resonance, by suggesting that Joe is not to be written off as a special case, an aberration, but is to be viewed as broadly representative. . . . [Both the Arab and Joe] have been stopped dead by their perception of the absurd. They have fetched up in "those waterless deserts where thought reaches its confines." For such men, Camus continues, "The real effort is to stay there . . . and to examine closely the odd vegetation of those distant regions." With the aid of champagne and beer, respectively, Joe and the Arab keep the absurd vividly present to consciousness, so as not to be seduced into "bad faith," into the delusion that "little stupid things" are important, into performing tasks which are "for nothing," as though they were "for something."

But stasis is not the only possible posture before the absurd. Camus points out that "on the one hand the absurd teaches that all experiences are unimportant, and on the other it urges toward the greatest quantity of experiences." This "quantitative ethic," this joyous acceptance and energetic use of freedom is exhibited in the play by Kit Carson ("real" name Murphy), a man who seems to know what Joe and the Arab know but who has gone on from there. Carson seems to know that in the absence of absolutes "everything is permitted," and so he has led a rootless, improvised, richly varied existence, reveling in a multiplicity of sensations in the brief time alloted before all sensation ceases. Of the four human types whom Camus describes as embodying most fully and clearly the quantitative ethic which absurdity leads to—Don Juan, the creative artist, the actor, and the conqueror—Carson most closely resembles the actor. He has herded cattle on a bicycle, passed himself off as a mining engineer, masqueraded as a woman and changed his name as casually as other men change their shirts. He calls himself Murphy now but Saroyan says *"he looks as if he might have been Kit Carson at one time,"* and that is the name the author assigns him throughout. (pp. 146-49)

Joe does not live as Carson lives but he immediately recognizes and approves of the ethic of experience which the latter has embraced. They are brothers in absurdity, fellow outsiders. "You're the first man I've ever met who believes me," says Carson.

That they are both alike and not alike is seen in their responses to the cruelty of Blick. Both deplore it but only Carson is able to turn his moral repugnance into effective action, striking down the oppressor moments after Joe's abortive attempt to do so. Though Carson has, by his own account, repeatedly run away from violence on occasions when only his personal safety was at stake, he feels constrained to stand and fight against the threat to the general good, to universal human nature, which Blick, the totalitarian idealogue, so chillingly embodies. In this, Carson resembles Cherea of Camus's *Caligula.* Though he agrees with Caligula, "to a point," that "all [actions] are on an equal footing," Cherea executes the tyrant, because, as he tells him, "you're pernicious, and you've got to go."

Joe, the Arab, and Kit Carson are perhaps the play's most vividly rendered exemplars of the absurd sensibility but others among the dramatis personae also bear witness in a variety of modes and degrees. Prominent among these secondary characters is Harry the Hoofer. Saroyan introduces him as a man who is *"out of place everywhere, embarrassed and encumbered by the contemporary costume, sick at heart, but determined to fit in somewhere."* In short, he is another character whose life has "no foundation"; he lacks a ground of being but manfully shoulders the task of improvising one, the existential task of "making himself." His primary medium is the dance and he thus embodies a variation on the dance metaphor which we have found Joe using. Harry's restless, ceaseless soft-shoe patterns and variations are the obverse of Joe's immobility; Harry constructs designs to fill the void left by nature, replacing one configuration with another in full awareness of the ultimate emptiness of all of them. (pp. 149-50)

Another familiar topos of absurdist literature occurs, if only

in a radically truncated form, in the behavior of The Lady, a socialite who has come to Nick's with her husband on a "slumming" expedition. When Joe passes cigars around, the Lady blithely takes one, bites the tip off, and accepts a light from Carson, to the distress of her straight-laced spouse: "The mother of five grown men, and she's still looking for *romance.* No. I forbid it." In thus flouting the arbitrary social code which proscribes cigar-smoking for a wife-and-mother, she opens herself up to experience, making a brave, if pathetic, little bid for that freedom which is a consequence of the acceptance of absurdity. Characteristically, Joe defends her against her serious-minded, law-giving husband: "What's the matter with you? Why don't you leave her alone? What are you always pushing your women around for?"

That we are to see the Lady's inchoate rebellion in existential terms is suggested not only by Joe's energetic support of it but also by the context in which it occurs. Joe distributes the cigars immediately after removing from his mouth the enormous wad of gum he has put there in his chewing contest with Tom and Carson. In the mock earnestness with which Joe engages in this competition, he parodies those struggles for achievement which characterize the serious world, the world of "aims," which he has repudiated. The incident has something of the flavor and point, though not the force, of the celebrated passage in Beckett's *Molloy,* where the eponymous hero is made to wrestle for five pages with the logistics involved in transferring sixteen pebbles, one by one, from his pockets to his mouth and back again. The gum-chewing match creates a climate of challenge to orthodox opinion about "allowable" adult behavior into which the "unseemly" conduct of the Lady fits very naturally. The point is underscored by the fact that Joe wraps his gum in a *Liberty* magazine, one of three publications (the others are *Time* and *Life*) which Joe had Tom purchase along with the gum and cigars. *Time* and *Life* echo, of course, the key terms of the play's title (as does Precious Time, one of the horses Joe bets on) and frequent use of such terms serves to remind us of the play's primary thematic thrust: the time of life is short and ends in death and time is therefore precious and must be savoured in the lucid acknowledgment of total liberty. (pp. 152-53)

The absurd sense of life is expressed not only in the statements and activities of the characters but in the very structure of the work. The play is conspicuously non-linear, palpably static, mirroring in its randomness and clutter that chaos which, in the absurdist view, characterizes life itself. The play lacks plot because life lacks plot. In life, as Camus says, "there is no scenario, but a successive and incoherent illustration." It is true, of course, that all of Saroyan's work, fiction as well as drama, is slack and disjointed, but the fact remains that on this occasion (whatever may be the case elsewhere) the looseness is thematically functional, operating in close congruence with the elements of thought and character which carry the essential import of the work. The harmony of feeling and form is much of the reason why **The Time of Your Life** is one of Saroyan's most aesthetically satisfying accomplishments. He once confessed that he wished to write "the way snow falls." The metaphor is strikingly apt. (p. 154)

But the play is not absolutely free of consequential action. In the relationship between Tom and Kitty Duval there is a boy-meets-girl plot, of sorts, presided over by Joe and by him propelled forward to a dramatically predictable denouement. Joe's involvement in this romance between a lovable stumble-bum and a whore-with-a-heart-of-gold represents his chief departure from non-alignment and, correspondingly, Saroyan's chief concession to conventional storytelling. As such, the whole episode seems out of key with the desultoriness which is otherwise pervasive; it represents an aesthetic lapse which is "given away," as it were, by the theatrically awkward shift of locale to Kitty's apartment in Act Three; the abrupt and short-lived excursion to a different physical world transports us to a different dramatic world, temporarily dissipating the emotional and spiritual ambience emanating from the honky-tonk. (p. 155)

Though the Tom-Kitty plot borders on sentimental cliché, Joe functions in it in a way that is not fundamentally alien to his nature as *homme absurde.* Though he succeeds in his match-making partly by providing material assistance to the lovers—a job for Tom, a new wardrobe and domicile for Kitty—his more important contribution is spiritual. Rhoads focuses on this point in developing his case for Joe as Christ-type. Tom becomes Lazarus, brought back from death by Joe prior to the action, and Kitty becomes the woman taken in adultery, treated with compassion by Joe and told to go and sin no more. These parallels are admittedly quite arresting, more so than some of the other scriptural analogues which Rhoads presents. Joe is indeed a kind of saviour. But if we are to think of him in such terms we would do well to associate him with the Christ of Dostoevsky's "Grand Inquisitor" vignette, rather than with the Messiah described by Matthew, Mark, Luke, and John. For, like Dostoevsky's Christ, Joe has no gospel to preach, no glad tidings to bring, except the gospel of existential freedom. He repeatedly refuses to be dogmatic. When Tom declares, with something like worshipful awe: "You're a different kind of a guy," Joe rebukes him: "Don't be silly. I don't understand things. I'm trying to understand them." Earlier, he has told Nick: "I study things," and when Tom asks him to explain why he has called his three hours in the automobile with him and Kitty "the most delightful, the most somber, and the most beautiful" he has ever known, Joe repeats the self-description with quiet emphasis:

> I'm a student. I study all things. All. All. And when my study reveals something of beauty in a place or in a person where by all rights only ugliness or death should be revealed, then I know how full of goodness this life is. And that's a very good thing to know. That's a truth I shall always seek to verify.

Hence, the only "word" he has to offer the lovers is that their lives are in their hands, that they are free to make, or remake themselves as they choose. There is no "way" except the way of choice. (pp. 155-56)

Joe's ministry to the "fallen" Kitty also stresses the paramount importance of freely-accepted, self-created values:

> I put her in that hotel, so she can have a chance to gather herself together again. She can't do that in the New York Hotel. You saw what happens there. There's nobody anywhere for her to talk to, except you. They all make her talk like a whore. After a while, she'll *believe* them. . . .

Understandably, Kitty reacts with fear and trembling to the freedom Joe offers her. Her first, very human, impulse is to assign irresistible power to the social and psychological forces which have cast her in the role of prostitute: "Too many things have happened to me. . . . I can't stand being alone. I'm no good. I tried very hard. . . . Everything *smells* different. I don't know how to feel, or what to think. . . . It's what

I've wanted all my life, but it's too late. . . ." Joe remains nondirective; the choice must be hers: "I don't know what to tell you, Kitty. . . . I can't *tell* you what to do. . . ."

But Blick precipitates a climax in Kitty's struggle for self-possession and self-determination. By forcing her to perform a strip-tease, he seeks to demonstrate, to her and to the world, that she *is* a slut, essentially and irrevocably. Only then does Joe take a hand. He stops the shameful proceedings and by sending her off across the country with Tom puts her feet, if only tenuously, on the first rung of the ladder of self-realization.

A few moments later, having failed to kill Blick and having learned that someone else has succeeded at that task, Joe says goodbye to the saloon, probably for good. . . . Where is he going? "I don't know," he says. "Nowhere." Rhoads finds "the aura of vagueness and mystery" which hangs over this departure appropriate to a Christ-figure, whose "ending, whether it be in death or mere disappearance" should be as obscure as his origins. His "ministry" here is finished, Rhoads concludes; "other Toms and Kittys in other places need him, and a new mission calls."

But Joe's mission has been a mission of self-discovery as much as anything else and it seems as reasonable to conclude that he now changes his base of operations in order to continue his "study"—of himself and the world and his place in it. He has, after all, some new material to work on; he has for the first time tried to act on an old desire: "I always wanted to kill somebody, but I never knew who it should be," he had announced as he took up the unloaded pistol. His action has brought with it both self-exposure and self-confrontation and we can imagine him wanting to withdraw in order to think further on these things. That something of the sort is on his mind is strongly suggested by the event which triggers his leave-taking. "Joe, you wanted to kill that guy," Nick says with surprise and admiration, and offers to buy him a bottle of champagne. Joe immediately goes for his hat and coat. "What's the matter?" Nick asks. "Nothing. Nothing."

Joe might be compared here to Scipio in *Caligula.* Invited by Cherea to join in the assassination of Caligula, Scipio cannot make that choice, though he understands and partly approves of Cherea's motives. Instead, he leaves, determined to "try to discover the meaning of it all."

At virtually every turn then, the dramatic materials which make up *The Time of Your Life* evoke comparisons with that spiritual topography familiar to us in the masterworks of modern existential literature. Saroyan's ability to translate his vision of the absurd into a wholly apposite and powerfully expressive symbolic form no doubt falls below that of his more illustrious forerunners and contemporaries. It is all too easy to read the play as an amiable, if somewhat eccentric slice-of-life, a mere chronicle of the quaint goings-on at a typically American waterfront saloon. On the surface, of course, the play *is* that, and it is as such that it has won an honored place among the classics of American realism. But its surface charm ought not to blind us to the weightier metaphysical import which lies just beneath. (pp. 157-59)

John A. Mills, " 'What. What Not.': Absurdity in Saroyan's 'The Time of Your Life'," in The Midwest Quarterly, *Vol. XXVI, No. 2, Winter, 1985, pp. 139-59.*

Arno (Otto) Schmidt

1914-1979

German novelist, short story writer, translator, essayist, critic, and biographer.

An influential figure in contemporary German literature who received relatively little recognition during his lifetime, Schmidt is renowned for scathingly satirical novels that present dystopian visions and feature bold innovations with prose structure and typography. His fiction is characterized by wordplay, scatological puns, parody, phonetic spelling, vivid metaphors, nonlinear narrative, and fragmentary representations of consciousness. Central to Schmidt's writing is his belief that individuals experience time not as a vast flow but in discrete details. Another element important to Schmidt's work is his Etym theory, which proposes that an author's vocabulary and imagery reveal suppressed sexual fixations. Throughout his writings, Schmidt explores the relationship between sex and creativity and the connection between fiction and reality. Most of Schmidt's novels take the form of diary entries composed by alienated intellectuals who seek salvation from what they view as an evil world but who dismiss all metaphysical conjecture as useless. Although he employed unconventional literary techniques, Schmidt nevertheless remained committed throughout his career to a realistic portrayal of human existence. Friedrich P. Ott commented: "If Arno Schmidt is going to prove—as he should—a seminal influence on modern writing, it will certainly be as an original 'visual' writer who has expanded the limits of his medium."

Born in Hamburg, Germany, Schmidt suffered a lonely and emotionally bereft childhood. Tormented by undiagnosed myopia and a father whom he perceived as authoritarian and uncultured, Schmidt took refuge from his despair through extensive and eclectic reading, thus forming an imagination influenced more by literature than by reality. In 1933, Schmidt entered Breslau University, where he studied mathematics and astrology, but he soon discontinued his education when the Nazi Party assumed power over the country. From 1940 to 1945, he reluctantly served as a soldier in the German artillery. While interned in a British prisoner-of-war camp, Schmidt learned the English language and became familiar with British and American literature, which profoundly affected his writing. After his release from the concentration camp, Schmidt and his wife lived in Cordingen, Germany, where he earned a meager living as an interpreter and free-lance writer. Critics generally maintain that these experiences contributed to the development of Schmidt's pessimistic temperament.

Schmidt's first book, *Leviathan* (1949), which won the Grand Literature Prize of the Mainz Academy, consists of three diaristic stories, one set in 1945 and two in antiquity, which relate oppressive experiences that inevitably result in death. The style and themes of *Leviathan* recur throughout the three novellas that comprise *Nobodaddy's Kinder: Trilogie* (1963). The first two works, *Brand's Haide* and *Schwarze Spiegel*, were published together in *Brand's Haide: Zwei Erzählungen* (1951). In *Brand's Haide,* a German prisoner of war named Schmidt returns to his ravaged homeland after World War II in hopes of living in isolation as a writer. He enjoys a brief

romance, but his mistress eventually leaves him for an American. *Schwarze Spiegel* (1951) relates the misanthropic thoughts of the sole survivor of an atomic war. The final volume of the trilogy, *Aus dem Leben eines Fauns: Kurzroman* (1953; *Scenes from the Life of a Faun*), is a bitterly satirical story of a civil servant's unsuccessful attempt to evade the fanaticism pervading Nazi Germany by immersing himself in books, nature, and a love affair. In these early works, Schmidt strives to recreate the disjointed quality of human consciousness through a similarly discontinuous narrative. To accomplish this, he writes in short paragraphs with italicized lead-in phrases, evoking a series of associations or memories with which the reader can identify.

In *Kosmas oder Vom Berge des Nordens* (1955), Schmidt creates parallels between late-Hellenistic Thrace, when belligerent, intolerant Christianity supplanted paganism, and contemporary Germany under the leadership of Christian Democrat Konrad Adenauer. Schmidt returns to the diary form in his next two novels, *Das steinerne Herz: Historischer Roman aus dem Jahre 1954* (1956) and *Die Gelehrtenrepublik: Kurzroman aus den Rossbreiten* (1957; *The Egghead Republic: A Short Novel from the Horse Latitudes*). *Das steinerne Herz* is a character study of the "collector" mentality as well as a portrait of the divided political nature of Germany. *The Egghead Republic,* Schmidt's first work to be translated into English, is set in 2008 after a nuclear war has annihilated most of the world's population and caused various mutations. The protagonist, an American journalist, travels to the International Republic of Artists and Scientists, an isolated community of geniuses established after the war by the United States and the Soviet Union to cultivate intellectual development. Expecting to find utopian cooperation, the journalist instead discovers that cold war attitudes prevail in The Egghead Republic. With *Kaff auch Mare Crisium* (1960), Schmidt's formal experimentation extends to dividing the text into two columns to relate activities in the "real" world of Kaff and in the imaginary world on the moon of Mare Crisium. The hero of this novel is consumed by obsessions he represses with his "mind game," which involves an American and Soviet lunar settlement established after an atomic war left earth uninhabitable.

Schmidt's works following *Kaff auch Mare Crisium* are strongly influenced by the writings of Sigmund Freud and James Joyce and demonstrate an increasing concern with the role of the subconscious in literary expression. This interest culminates in *Zettels Traum* (1970), which is often regarded by critics as Schmidt's masterpiece. An oversized book containing photocopied reproductions of illustrations, maps, and the author's corrections and marginalia, *Zettels Traum* is a complex, disjunctive novel divided into three columns of text. The center column concerns a day-long discussion about Edgar Allan Poe among a Schmidt alter ego and Poe expert, a married couple working on a German-language edition of Poe's works, and their daughter; the left column contains a study of Poe's life and writings in the context of psychoanalysis and Schmidt's Etym theory; and the right column consists of footnotes and miscellaneous statements on philosophical matters pertaining to the first two columns. In this book, Schmidt implies that sublime literature can originate from base instincts and that art must derive from the three Freudian divisions of the psyche as well as from a fourth category of ironic humor conceived by Schmidt. Some critics assess *Zettels Traum* as Schmidt's attempt to recreate Joyce's *Finnegans Wake.*

Schmidt's next two novels, *Die Schule der Atheisten: Novellen-Comödie in 6 Aufzügen* (1972) and *Abend mit Goldrand: Eine MärchenPosse. 55 Bilder aus der Lä/endlichkeit für Gönner der VerschreibKunst* (1975); *Evening Edged in Gold: A FairytalefArse. 55 Scenes from the Cou/untryside for Patrons of Erra/ota),* follow the form and linguistic inventiveness of *Zettels Traum.* A blend of drama and epic novel set in 2014 after an atomic war has left the United States and China as world powers, *Die Schule der Atheisten* is a farcical anti-utopian fantasy about two West German citizens and an East German Marxist professor who embark on a campaign for atheism. The professor eventually becomes stranded on a Pacific island with two American evangelists who convert him to Christianity and then exhibit him on a world tour. This novel, like such earlier works as *Leviathan* and *Nobodaddy's Kinder,* signifies the difficulty for intellectuals of maintaining religious belief in a seemingly malevolent world. *Evening Edged in Gold,* published as a facsimile of Schmidt's original manuscript, is composed in three columns of text, each of which centers on a trio of elderly men who represent different aspects of Schmidt's personality. These characters discuss literature, the problems of old age, and fantasies that help to combat their frustrations. A hedonistic group of hippies rejuvenates the lives of the aged characters by initiating

an orgy that recalls scenes from Hieronymus Bosch's painting *The Garden of Earthly Delights.*

In such collections as *Rosen and Porree* (1959), *Kühe in Halbtrauer* (1964), and *Trommler beim Zaren* (1966), Schmidt's strongly autobiographical stories, like his novels, are often concerned with the creative and sexual troubles of writers and their contradictory desires for isolation and camaraderie. In addition to his fiction, Schmidt published a substantial amount of literary criticism and biography. *Die Ritter vom Geist: Von vergessen Kollegen* (1965) provides accounts of six German-language writers whom he considers underappreciated, and *Der Triton mit dem Sonnenschirm: Grossbritannische Gemütsergetzungen* (1969) analyzes such authors as Joyce, Poe, and James Fenimore Cooper. Schmidt also wrote biographies of children's author Karl May and German Romantic writer Friedrich de la Motte Fouque, and he translated into German works of fiction by Joyce, William Faulkner, and Wilkie Collins. In 1973, Schmidt was awarded the prestigious Goethe Prize in recognition of his outstanding literary achievements.

(See also *Contemporary Authors,* Vol. 109 [obituary] and *Dictionary of Literary Biography,* Vol. 69.)

THE TIMES LITERARY SUPPLEMENT

Nobodaddy's Kinder is a collection of diary entries in three diverse hands—hands which are severally grafted on to Arno Schmidt's body. The fact that, whereas the entries run on chronologically, each successive diarist is younger than the previous one, also reveals intriguing facets of the author's technique.

The diarists' progressive rejuvenation is paralleled by a steady narrowing of focus. Whilst the wartime **Aus dem Leben eines Fauns** is densely—and the postwar **Brand's Haide** rather more sparsely—populated, the post-World War Three (!) **Schwarze Spiegel** is virtually a study in solipsism.

Decrease of breadth often involves increase in depth. This shift in emphasis can be all to the good if the recesses of the author's mind contain new metal-bearing strata. But, alas, Mr. Schmidt's workable seams all appear to trend vertically, so that, alike when mining open-cast and when drilling down to bedrock, he keeps on dredging up the same substance: atheist polemic, encyclopedic pyrotechnics, literary partisanship, and affirmation of sex—when stripped of its reproductive function.

The author's Malthusianism is motivated less by economic considerations than by hubris—he considers man in the mass so philistine as to have forfeited his right to continued existence. Thus the diary kept by ostensibly the last man on earth contains scant expressions of regret at the extinction of the human race; instead it abounds in disquisitions on carpentry, food-storing and ordnance-surveying which are so informative that **Schwarze Spiegel** intermittently reads like a manual for would-be atomic survivors.

Culture, of course, matters to Mr. Schmidt even more than carpentry. His post-nuclear diarist spends happy weeks looting archives, libraries and picture-galleries, and even when he temporarily teams up with the only female survivor we are assured that their tastes coincide both in the physical *and* the spiritual sphere. . . .

The best story in the collection is *Aus dem Leben eines Fauns*—the faun being a middle-aged civil servant joylessly enmeshed in domestic *ennui* and Nazi bureaucratic routine. The pressures bearing down on him have a leaden palpability, and his escape-reflexes (Herr Schmidt's panacea of Romantic literature, map-reading, blasphemy and extra-marital sex) here take on a bitter-sweet poignancy. Always adept at conveying the sombre moods of nature, the author in this story also startlingly evokes the human climate of Hitler Germany, with the mists of menticide shrouding the contours of the real world.

> *"Diaries of a Nobodaddy," in* The Times Literary Supplement, *No. 3215, October 11, 1963, p. 811.*

KURT OPITZ

The ten pieces in [*Kühe in Halbtrauer*], written consistently in first-person narrative of a strongly autobiographical flavor for its scenery of Lower Saxony and the aging artist's sensual and imaginative problems, prove that Schmidt's literary elective affinities extend to James Joyce and Lewis Carroll as much as to Kurt Tucholsky and Vladimir Nabokov, all of them in the last analysis bourgeois aesthetes *malgré eux*.

Schmidt is at his best where his reflective imagination stays just below the level of its own consciousness as, e.g., in **"Windmühlen,"** or where he forces his wit, as in **"Caliban,"** upon a prose full of puns and phonetic *double-entendre* which is as exhilarating as it is gratuitous. Because he knows his role of court jester to the bourgeoisie and is ready to capitalize on this situation, his voice rings a little hollow when he gets personal. It is all too easy to agree with his criticism, yet the questions he hides behind ridicule and scorn remain as pressing as ever. It is sad to see a good man being bribed by his own art.

> *Kurt Opitz, in a review of "Kühe in Halbtrauer," in* Books Abroad, *Vol. 39, No. 3, Summer, 1965, p. 321.*

HANS-BERNHARD MOELLER

Zettels Traum is an experimental, encyclopedic and ruthlessly cyclopic work in eight "parts," each one approaching novel length. (p. 25)

Schmidt's narrative structure is unique. Almost without exception, Schmidt's writings are distinguished by an unusual heteromorphous arrangement of the printed page, a mode of perception which seeks to follow the reactions of consciousness, and a brisk, leaping, and disjunctive narrative. The typographical arrangement of the printed page varies according to the specific prose form; one type runs the first lines of compositional units in italics; another employs two separated fields of texts; and two other types intershift text blocks. For the twentieth-century reader, who is visually oriented, Schmidt seeks to mobilize every means of expression known in the Gutenberg medium in order to clarify the modes of perception. The more intricate the cerebral developments, the more unconventional are the typography and prose form. However, Schmidt nearly always presents the world of fiction as the experience of a first-person narrator who lives among the characters of the novel. He relates, or more accurately he relives, the entire world in his imagination. This explains the archsolipsistic nature of Schmidt's heroes and of his oeuvre.

In his earliest prose, Schmidt makes use of the leaping and disjunctive narrative. This, too, underlies later prose forms, although it is then subordinated to still more unconventional arrangements of the text. For example, "Nummer 31," "Klopfen," and "Augen wie Bunsenbrenner" serve as introductions to three successive sections of *Das steinerne Herz* (1956), in which the first-person narrator becomes acquainted with his future home and his landlady. According to Schmidt's poetics such "Stationenprosa" corresponds to the functioning of human consciousness—a skipping, disjointed, discontinuous perception, a "perforated presence." As an early masterpiece of this first narrative style, **"Leviathan oder Die Beste der Welten"** (1949) is outstanding. It relates the story of an escape from the Eastern Front and examines to what extent cosmogonies can still be maintained in a chaos such as the collapse of Germany.

In his prose works, Schmidt always seeks to proceed on the basis of perception. This also applies to the "Längere Gedankenspiel" with its shifting text blocs. This form of prose represents daydream grown into an elaborate fantasy—the wish fulfillment. Besides the real world, then, a world of fiction exists for the dreamer. Schmidt therefore differentiates typographically between these worlds.

For example, in *Kaff auch Mare Crisium* (1960), Schmidt indents all terrestrial and real activities (*Kaff*) about ten spaces from the right margin; in a like manner he indents equally at the left margin any imagined activities which occur on the moon (*Mare Crisium*). (pp. 26-7)

Form with Schmidt is usually not the result of fiction, but its starting point. As early as 1955, he issued an original, programmatic blueprint for four forms of prose in **"Berechnungen I"** (Calculations I). The two forms which we described in detail belong to this group. In a third form Schmidt temporarily concerned himself with the linguistically and typographically correct portrayal of the act of recollecting (e.g., **"Die Umsiedler"**). The fourth form of prose he outlined at that time as "Traum" or "dream." Although only a perimeter of well-founded presumptions can be envisaged as yet, it may be assumed that this narrative type of "Traum" is in our hands with *Zettels Traum*. In any case, Schmidt again operates with a shifting typography. Indeed, he is now using three columns and, therefore, the reflected thought reactions and levels of consciousness are still more intricate than in *Kaff*. From left to right the three columns contain: 1. expert, quotation-loaded discussion concerning the life and works of Edgar Allan Poe; 2. action and interior monologue of the first-person narrator; 3. marginalia pertaining to columns 1 and 2, footnotes, source references, also comments pertaining to basic questions of life. The specific column which at a given moment contains the text, to some extent defines the topic under discussion. Sometimes, however, all three columns are filled at the same time, and very short texts may even be pushed in between. One realizes that this book is by no means just a historical novel about Poe, using the quasi-biographical method.

To summarize the plot of *Zettels Traum:* Some visitors and Pagenstecher, a quasi-Arno Schmidt in his mid-fifties, conduct a marathon private Poe symposium. The trio of visitors (like Schmidt and a colleague) have been working on a German-language edition of Poe. This is an opportune time for the Jakobis to renew their early friendship with host Pagenstecher, for this free-lance worker is the "Poeologist" among Poe enthusiasts. The quartet of characters, the action and details remind one of **"Die Wasserstrasse"** from *Kühe in Halbtrauer* (1964). Again the host is godfather of his friend's daughter Franziska, again he is captivated but still exercises self-restraint, again tension mounts between the friend and his wife, between mother and daughter, and again one walks through the heath. But this time the action lasts twenty-four hours and yet forms only the surface of a multilevel net of relations, which also includes the extensive Poe studies.

Compared to the earlier first-person narrators, the central male figure in *Zettels Traum* is in one dimension more passive, and in another more sovereign. Like his predecessor, Pagenstecher prefers the contemplative life. He criticizes, he imagines, and he observes with the ubiquitous field glasses. He has, however, newly acquired a sovereignty that is even more than an intellectual superiority. Pagenstecher has inherited this new trait from the bright, dominating voice of Schmidt's numerous radio dialogues. The radio listener hears, to use an overstatement but to grasp the formal qualities, "commercials" based on historical events in literature. The leading voice directs the "discussion" without fail in favor of the advertised "product." Here, too, Schmidt maintains and asserts his individuality and self—only carelessly veiled—and frequently recollects his own views. (Incidentally, "maintaining" and "recollecting" are words which are much too mild for expressing Schmidt's unmistakable habit of not concealing his own point of view and his merits.) All this is less irritating in a novel than in the radio essays, because, in the sphere of the unconscious in *Zettels Traum,* Pagenstecher/Schmidt seems to entertain himself, conducting a monologue and conversing with figures which emanate from him. "The dialogue among several partners" is considered by Schmidt in **"Berechnungen I"** as "ideal biography." Therefore Pagenstecher plays the role of a masterful spokesman who analyzes for the Jakobis the inner biography of Poe.

The more passive side of Pagenstecher's nature is rooted in the sexual realm. Schmidt's earlier first-person narrators made love, as in *Das steinerne Herz,* almost like sexual "pop supermen." To be sure, the first-person narrator in *Zettels Traum* continues to charm the females. Yet the comradely love affair which at times comforted the first-person narrator from *Leviathan* to *Kaff,* although it was insecure and subject to termination, has disappeared in *Zettel's Traum.* Pagenstecher must bitterly perceive himself as a resigned, impotent voyeur.

Schmidt's characters and most relationships in *Zettels Traum* exist on many levels. This multilevel quality is indicated in the relationship between Pagenstecher and Franziska. Is Franziska only the teenager of the 1960s? For Pagenstecher she may also have been a spiritual figure, a childlike mythical creation. At the same time she functions as an echo figure of Edgar Allan Poe's child bride Virginia, who was only thirteen years old at her wedding.

One recognizes that Schmidt not only casts a comprehensive, biographical light on Poe, but also enriches his own composition by drawing on Poe's life and works. To tell his story and to interpret Poe, Pagenstecher/Schmidt at times rigorously follows psychoanalytic thought patterns. As seen by Pagenstecher, Poe's nature denied him the normal conjugal relationship in marriage. Poe's sexual feelings obeyed the mecha-

nism of repression. This caused symptomatic aberrations (*Symptombildungen*) in Poe's writings. Visually, scenery has assumed the shape of slightly veiled parts of the body. Linguistically, sexual expressions in the preconscious and subconscious, have become masked. "Sodass also, anstât des eigntlichgedachtn: 'Phallus! Phallus!,' the pen dann . . . niederschreibt: 'palace-Pallas!' " In order to unmask such camouflage in Poe's text, Pagenstecher in his free-association method returns "palace" to "Phallus." On this level of *Zettels Traum,* the reader is immersed in a verbal jungle and witnesses a savage, spooky mixing of words. Here the irrational is the pattern. Furthermore, it is evident that literary psychoanalysis is meant to provide an additional element of fiction in *Zettels Traum.* In free association it is also possible to connect unrelated words and ideas and thereby expand the ambiguity of the text. The example of Joyce in *Finnegans Wake* and of Freud is continued.

The ambiguity of *Zettels Traum* is also evident in the title, which is worthy of some observations. "Zettel" is the name the Germans give to Bottom the Weaver in Shakespeare's *Midsummer Night's Dream.* From the same comedy, Schmidt chooses the motto for his novel, so as to be sure that the reader does not overlook the hidden sense and literary allusion. One is now prepared for a fabulous book, which, similar to Shakespeare's comedy, will weave fairies, magicians, and mythical aspects into an everyday group of persons. The word "Zettel" furthermore relates to the phrase "etwas anzetteln" (to scheme or contrive a plot; for instance: "Was habt Ihr àngeZettlt?"). Additionally, "Zettel's" as written by Schmidt is spelled contrary to German rules of grammar by separating the genitive *s,* thereby giving the word "Zettel" more independent emphasis. This is also a reference to Schmidt's working method. "Zettel" is German for an index card, and a "Zettelkasten" is a writer's index card file. Schmidt prepared for *Zettels Traum* with a collection of more than 100,000 index cards in his legendary card file. With "Zettel," the author conveys to the reading public his method of composition, and with "Traum" he indicates his theory of the fourth form of prose. Finally, the complete title also indicates a psychoanalytic aspect, for in 'dream of the bottom,' the English translation of his title, the author points to interwoven elementary needs and instincts. The title as well as indications in the chapter "Die Geste des Grossen Pun" suggest that Schmidt—in an intentionally humorous section of *Zettels Traum*—also molds the topography into the relevant anatomical structure. (pp. 27-9)

[One] would expect that Schmidt's impressive handling of language will serve as a model. This author even forms a single sentence in a typographically unconventional manner. Sentences have the ability to conceal themselves in brackets—the less conscious one may be of an impulse of feeling or thought, the more brackets are used. Punctuation carries the value of gestures: "-:-: ?-: !!!"—from anticipation to jubilation. Varying typefaces in one word can attune the writing to a workday timbre. Partially phonetic writing achieves special effects. For example, in "Ritt-mick" Schmidt has taught the word "Rhythmik" to ride horseback (in the German language). In "Roh-mann-Tick," he magically exposes the word "Romantik" (romanticism) to criticism: It is "roh" (raw), uncivilized; primitive man rises from the word. Furthermore, the literary movement is suddenly interwoven with a spleen. Schmidt makes us really see the cobblestone road in the country by calling it "the warty country road." He lets us discover that a bus "invitingly opens its gill covers." This author masters the idiom of typography, the language of punctuation, and all the methods of linguistic illustration. In his writings, the language seems to take the initiative and to stimulate further sensory perception. This language sounds strident yet refreshing, arrests the reading flow, is concentrated, but in its dry mass context is a treasure.

Readers and reviewers may feel more comfortable with Hemingway or Thomas Mann than with the linguistic experimenter of *Zettels Traum.* But Böll's earlier judgment of Schmidt is still valid today; he praised Schmidt's "passionate love for the German language which he is practicing with a writer's true and poetic fervor." (pp. 29-30)

> *Hans-Bernhard Moeller, "Perception, Word-Play, and the Printed Page: Arno Schmidt and his Poe Novel," in* Books Abroad, *Vol. 45, No. 1, Winter, 1971, pp. 25-30.*

THE TIMES LITERARY SUPPLEMENT

Die Schule der Atheisten deliberately recalls comedies of the seventeenth and eighteenth centuries and suggests, at the same time, one of the guiding themes of Schmidt's fiction since *Leviathan* and *Nobodaddy's Kinder:* the contradiction between being a thinking man and subscribing to any religious doctrine: the contradiction, above all, between what we see, hear, smell and know of the world around us and the very idea of a just and benevolent God. This is only the first of many links with Schmidt's earlier novels, short stories and essays. In fact, it would be hard to find any work, other than the much longer and much more difficult *Zettels Traum,* which affords so good an introduction to the world of this obsessed and fascinating writer.

The subtitle "Novellen-Comödie" prepares the reader for a mingling of the epic and the dramatic: a comfortable form which allows the author to construct an interestingly differentiated typographical picture and, at the same time, to play an intricate game with his narrative perspectives. Characters and topographies are introduced in elaborate stage-directions, inset towards the middle of the page; when the characters speak (and they are, for the most part, exceedingly communicative), their name appears, in capitals and underlined, on the left hand side of the page, and the speech that follows each such appearance is punctuated by further bracketed stage-directions and authorial comments. . . . Other comments, quotations, documents, even pictorial illustrations, appear at frequent intervals in the margins. This fusion of the epic and the dramatic recalls, at times, the experiments of Arno Holz and Johannes Schlaf in the early days of German Naturalism; as does also Schmidt's effort to reproduce the nuances of spoken language (with its regional inflections, hummings and hawings, omissions and repetitions) and his fascinated dwelling on details not usually mentioned in polite literature.

The scene is laid in Tellingstedt, "story-town". The very name prepares us for fantasy—the kind of fantasy Schmidt has called "sustained mental games", *Längeres Gedankenspiel,* a deliberate exploitation of day-dreaming which challenges the intelligent reader to reconstruct for himself the "reality" that induces men to have recourse to such fancies. However, like Gottfried Keller's Seldwyla, this dreamt-up little town, whose very name labels it fiction, is given an exact geographical location: on the river Eider, within a North German townscape and landscape whose features are evoked with an economy and a precision that would do credit to any nineteenth-century realist. Schmidt prides himself on his exactitude. . . . (p. 843)

As in *Schwarze Spiegel* and as in *Die Gelehrtenrepublik,* the main action of *Die Schule der Atheisten* takes place in a future divided from our own time by an atomic war. The year is 2014; only two superpowers, the United States and China, are left to confront each other, with a few protectorates and "reservations" in between. One of these reservations, deliberately preserved as a tourist attraction, is Tellingstedt and its surrounding countryside—a North German setting which is to Arno Schmidt's fiction what Wessex is to Hardy's. A good deal of the action takes place in and around a house attractively crammed with old books and prints which belongs to a man of seventy-five called William T. Kolderup. Kolderup's attitudes and ideas, of which we learn a good deal, are all but indistinguishable from those put forward or implied, from time to time, in stage-directions and incidental comments. His perspective therefore becomes that of the reader—though he is also reflected, and not always in a favourable light, in the consciousness of the other characters.

Like most of the central reflectors in Schmidt's novels, Kolderup is a *Sonderling,* a man apart, divided from those around him by his age, his intellectual interests, his collector's instincts (not as maniacal here as in *Das steinerne Herz* !), and his partly Danish ancestry. He is also a man of very decided views and prejudices (against "popular" art, against any kind of idealization of countryfolk, against the principle of collective authorship, against Christianity, against Marxism . . .) which he shares with most of the positive characters in Schmidt's earlier fiction, with the raisonneurs of his radio-essays, and with whatever persona Schmidt has constructed to articulate his literary views and criticisms. Unlike the earlier characters, however, Kolderup is a man of some consequence in his region: a man of substance, a Justice of the Peace of almost Solomonic wisdom (or rather, "a Daniel come to judgment", a further development of Daniel Pagenstecher, the hero of *Zettels Traum*), and, when need arises, a politician who can deal effectively with the foreign ministers of the super-powers.

Behind this fantasy, this *Längeres Gedankenspiel,* the reader is clearly invited to surmise the impotence of such intellectuals as Kolderup in the *real* society of contemporary Germany. Kolderup lives with his granddaughter Suse, who is in love with a young journalist and druggist (APOtheker—a wry grimace at a younger generation) and who has taken under her wing a much put-upon young woman always known as "Nipperchen". Into their idyll irrupts a party from the United States, headed by the formidable ISIS, a female Foreign Secretary; it includes also her hardly less formidable female bodyguards, her "court-poet" Cosmo Schweighäuser, and one Tim Hackensack, who has the unenviable task of assuaging, on demand, the Foreign Secretary's apparently limitless sexual needs. No sooner has this party arrived in Tellingstedt than it is joined by a similar delegation from China—all males this time except for one subordinate of indeterminate sex (the only pronoun which can effectively cope is *es*). There have been, it appears, some alarming landings from other planets, and it is advisable for the two earthly superpowers to sign a Treaty of Mutual Toleration.

From then onwards a number of plot-strands are skilfully and intricately intertwined: an intrigue to allow Cosmo and

Nipperchen, who have fallen in love, to live together despite laws forbidding intermarriage between United States citizens and inmates of the reservations; a plot to relieve Tim Hackensack of his burdensome duties by substituting a rustic whose sexual equipment and prowess are matched only by his stupidity; a judicial comedy centring on a drunken sea-captain and identical female twins (both of whom he is, in the end, allowed to marry); a sea-journey to the island of Fanö, where Kolderup retrieves from his old home a number of curios of great interest to the visiting dignitaries from the superpowers—and, incidentally, some copies of *Zettels Traum,* which seems to be as hard to get hold of in 2014 as it is in 1972. During this sea-voyage Kolderup begins to tell of an earlier one, supposed to have taken place in 1969, and continues his story in snatches and at intervals until the end of the book, so that two time-schemes and two sets of adventures become subtly entwined.

The earlier sea-voyage brought together three professed atheists: Kolderup himself (then a young man), a Marxist professor from East Germany, and Cosmo's father Gottfehd Schweighäuser. When their ship runs into difficulties, they find themselves thrown on to an inhospitable desert island in the company of a missionary, who rejoices in the name of Chadband, and who has brought along his delectable wife—a fact, it turns out, of great interest to the visiting Foreign Secretary from the United States, for Mrs Chadband was later to become her mother. On the desert island hunger, hallucinations and deliberate mystifications test the atheists' steadfastness. The Marxist fails his test miserably (if you can believe *that* doctrine, you can believe anything), but Kolderup emerges a wiser as well as a sadder man, ready to grow into the sage sceptic who tells the story in 2014. In good *Comödie* fashion—the archaic spelling is, of course, deliberate and pointed—*Die Schule der Atheisten* ends with the conclusion of a treaty, with rewards, decorations and titles handed out all round, and with a triple wedding.

This is a strange amalgam indeed: deliberate reminiscences of older comedies, from Shakespeare and Fletcher to Ferdinand Raimund, merge with pungent critiques of social and cultural phenomena of our own time and an immensely detailed presentation of the thoughts, sensations and apprehensions of a modern intellectual. The mixture works, however, and makes—for the most part—delightful reading. Arno Schmidt has here given us a refreshingly funny book, whose high and low comedy derives from many sources. The reader finds himself constantly challenged to hold Schmidt's fantastic elaborations against the literary originals they derive from and parody—Shakespeare's *Tempest,* Schnabel's *Insel Felsenburg,* Jules Verne, Poe and many others provide grist for Schmidt's fast-grinding mill.

We are asked to recognize, in the fantastic world of the future, heightenings of our own present and immediate past. Schmidt turns a jaundiced eye on Women's Lib and American Matriarchy—and, hey presto! the United States of 2014 is entirely dominated by women (her President, we learn with little surprise is one Joan Cunnydy); American men are reduced to a subjection whose ludicrous and scabrous details are unsparingly unfolded. Male-dominated literature has, of course, to be re-written—there is a hilarious account of Goethe's *Faust* in which all the characters have changed their sex while retaining their function in the plot. Modern journalism, advertising and tourist industries also have been projected into the future and now look twice as large as life and just as

horrible—the whole population in Kolderup's "reservation", under the direction of a professional Guide, racks such brains as it has to invent ever-new "archaic" customs, superstitions and saws for the delectation of tourists from the superpowers.

These anti-utopian fantasies are deliberately played against what we are to take as more positively utopian *Denkspiele.* Within the "reservation", the churches are disestablished; the right to vote depends on an educational test; and effective power is wielded by precisely the kind of intellectual whom earlier stories (notably the powerful and justly famous **"Caliban über Setebos"**) had presented as impotent and covertly snarling outsiders. Much amusement may be derived too from Schmidt's juxtaposition of incompatibles: brilliantly caricatured television programmes from East and West Germany unrolling themselves in one typed column while a parallel column gives us Kolderup's spoken and unspoken comments; or allusions to pastoral idyll while we are invited to watch some particularly unappetizing and grotesque aspect of rural life.

Many of Schmidt's finest comic effects inhere, as will have been realized, in the way he structures his tale: in the counterpointing and interlacing of different narrative timesequences; in different apprehensions of the same phenomenon presented side by side in parallel columns or divided horizontally like a mathematical fraction; in familiar works of literature prefiguring the action of the book or peeping out beneath parody and contrafacture; in fantasies designed to conjure up in the reader's mind an image of the reality that may have given rise to them.

No less important, however, is the texture of Schmidt's language. Following the lead of Joyce and Lewis Carroll . . . Schmidt abandons Duden rules of spelling and punctuation to produce typographical "estrangements" (*Verfremdungen*) capable of rendering regional peculiarities of speech and the inflections of the speaking voice with marvellous accuracy. They introduce, at the same time, a multitude of ulterior meanings through complex puns which involve, as the book progresses, all the major European languages. (pp. 843-44)

In the fantasy-world of *Die Schule der Atheisten,* Kolderup is given more of a chance to fulfil himself than other, similarly endowed and handicapped characters in Schmidt's writings; yet he too is made to reflect that his autobiography could have no title but ACCURSED TIMES: " 'VERFLUCHTE ZEITN!'—d's wär *Mein*—Titl! (Für Meine Selbst-Bio.))."

Not surprisingly, traces of the "accursed times" through which Arno Schmidt has himself passed are never far away. Ovens, in this imaginary world of the future, are known as "Eichmanns". Only Kolderup remembers why, and the macabre jest whose origin has been forgotten twists the knife once more. What is the foul and prurient *Furchenalmanach für 2015* but another crest of that wave of pornography that swept over the permissive 1970s? Kolderup's own dwelling on the details of the sexual act is anti-pornographic; like many of Schmidt's heroes he is obsessed with the pathos of the aging body and the black comedy of the struggles between the mind's high aspirations and the body's earthy desires. And that world made uninhabitable by atomic radiation which we must imagine not too far from the reservation of which Tellingstedt forms part—what is it but the consequence of the policies and events of our own world, the 1969 of Kolderup's flashback narrative, the 1972 in which we are ourselves reading the book? Even in Tellingstedt, the "story-town" in which Kolderup makes his corner of sane living—even there everything he encounters in his progress from immobility to silence only confirms the necessity of atheism. Would it not lead to blackest despair if we thought that the world had actually been planned to turn out as it did by an all-wise, all-foreseeing God? . . .

A school for atheists? Perhaps—though at times it seems more a school of Manicheans, or for those who believe that some evil demiurge is amusing himself at man's expense. But in reading *Die Schule der Atheisten* we undoubtedly enter a school in which we may usefully learn to question accepted values and conceive some respect for lonely, odd, usually underpaid and socially powerless intellectuals of a literary turn of mind—a respect which may yet prove a not unwelcome antidote to the self-hatred and self-doubt that afflicts so many of us who answer, at least in part, to that description. We may learn rather more scatology than most of us would like (that does get rather tiresome at times); but as a school of often grotesque verbal wit and fancy *Die Schule der Atheisten* is so enjoyable that many of its alumni will inevitably be drawn to that higher academy represented by *Zettels Traum.* But even if they go no farther they will never forget the distinctive if sometimes irritating voice of the story-teller and raisonneur who has been their teacher—the voice of Arno Schmidt, whose combination of the provincial with the experimental (a "productive misalliance" rightly praised by Peter Demetz) is proving for many one of the pleasures they would least like to miss in the literature of postwar Germany. (p. 844)

"Scenes from Storytown," in The Times Literary Supplement, *No. 3673, July 21, 1972, pp. 843-44.*

DAVID HAYMAN

Zettels Traum is [Schmidt's] attempt to write a German *Finnegans Wake.* Patrick O'Neill gives a suggestive account of that book:

> The text on each page is positioned according to its nature in a fluid arrangement of three columns. A large centre column usually contains the narrative, that on the left usually references to Poe's works and often extensive extracts from it in English, while the right-hand column contains a variety of marginal reflections from the narrator. The main body of text can be in any column or in all at once. It is written in eccentric German, highly eccentrically spelled and punctuated, and frequently breaking into English, French, or otherwise. The typescript is McLuhanesque in impact, and incorporates very numerous blacked-out excisions and handwritten additions and corrections.
>
> Not only is traditional orthography abandoned in favour of an attempt to reproduce the sounds and rhythms of colloquial German, words are further tortured to reveal their inherent Etyms, as Schmidt calls them: EDDY-POE'S COMPLEX, or pussynäss ist pussynäss. In his essays on the Wake he has developed his theory of Etyms, Freudian "pre-words," embryonic word forms embedded by the conscious expression.

Most striking in *Zettels Traum,* apart from its enormous format and bulk, are the adaptations (rather than direct borrowings), the sort of tricks played by an author fully aware of Joyce's contribution but intent on doing something radically different. Schmidt's opus can best be described as a running transcript of an extended seminar, with marginal notes. The purpose of this seminar is to explore Poe's work in terms of the Etym theory. Much of the first section is devoted in large measure to Pagenstecher's exposition of the term and its implications and the countering and encountering of objections, a playful testing rich in allusive byplay (or should we say "foreplay," since so much of the Etym-sense is polymorphously sexual if not perverse?). The operation of the Etym is often a function of homonymy as well as of etymological roots. Indeed, the problem in this first part is to decide how the Etym principle functions across linguistic traditions as well as within them. The effect of all this is distinctly Germanic as opposed to Irish-English. But *Zettels Traum* is also a spoof on Germanic pedantry, falling frequently into irreverence, resorting to a sort of dramatic discourse quite different in tone and feeling from the traditional philosophical discourse on which it is otherwise patterned.

Unlike the *Wake,* there is a clearly developed argument but no visible story line. There are five recognizable characters whose five speech patterns are continuously juxtaposed. In the *Wake* we seldom, if ever, find more than two characterized voices in any passage. Further, where the *Wake* generates a commonplace reality out of the dream texture, in *Zettels Traum* the oneiric erotic texture is generated out of a commonplace reality. The pun texture and the style shifts of the *Wake* constitute prime obstacles to scanning, and constant sources of reader participation and delight. In Schmidt's text, which resembles nothing so much as an MS draft of passages from *Finnegans Wake,* the notation functions both as clarification and as obfuscation. We are overwhelmed by an array of punctuation, of whimsical spacing and spelling, of allusive devices: in short of editorial gesticulation. It is this notation which enables the text to record words and gestures of participants along with the asides of an implied editor. But paradoxically these words and gestures, replete with in-jokes and allusions, are an obstacle to full understanding and a challenge to the reader. Further, since the whole text is presented as though told by an outside observer, we are obliged to fill in blanks in the thought processes as we might in real conversation.

Like the *Wake,* the reading/text becomes an extraordinary lived experience, an encounter with language. Unlike the *Wake,* however, *Zettels Traum* insists upon explaining and examining its premises. Written in dialogue, it has its dramatic component, but the drama, so far as I can judge, is not expressive in the aesthetic sense of conveying an organically coherent emotional circumstance or development. The reader is asked to participate in an enormously attenuated human situation, which despite its psychological content, and because of its length and complexity, resembles the flat surface rediscovered earlier in this century by artists like Fernand Léger. Schmidt's book insists upon itself as a work-in-progress, a concept enforced by the mode of presentation of the "traumscript" (see the term Joyce coined to describe ALP's famous letter). By contrast, *Finnegans Wake* presents itself as a finished text and only gradually reveals to the reader how much of the making is still to be accomplished. Again, *Zettels Traum* alludes to many texts but draws its substance from texts by Poe and Schmidt himself, divagates upon them. Although *Finnegans Wake* alludes to many other texts, it proposes as its focus the emblematic and absent letter, whose manufacture and delivery constitute the tale of the text which is also the text of the tale—the letter being finally identical with the uttered *Wake*.

Then there is the emphasis on synchrony, at the expense of diachronic or linear development. The page is only one aspect of this. Its three columns function . . . to provide an interchange of elements, a yo-yo of parallels, a tension or flux of signifiers or blocks of signification that virtually destroys linearity or at least impedes movement through, as opposed to across and within, the text. . . . On another level we have the calculated redundancy in both works, the continual cross-referencing or crosscutting of materials. In the *Wake,* at any given moment all the components of a development are present; only the order and emphasis are subject to change. But their constant presence serves to complicate the game texture, placing the emphasis on the delights of a shifting linguistic field within an otherwise stable frame.

Another attribute is a quality I call nodality. . . . The nodes I refer to are nodes or knots of allusion or signification, clusters which constitute topics and serve as means of structuring the text rather than as integral parts of the argument. We may see, for example, a scattering of references to Ezra Pound or Oscar Wilde or Irish history on a page or two of the *Wake* without assuming that the passage in question is primarily about such matters. Such nodes occur nearer the surface of the post-*Wake* texts. In *Zettels Traum* we have what we might call digressive nodes which, without sacrificing the essentially "palimpcestuous" nature of the multilayered text, *occupy* the conversation, serve as a topic, a focus for our interest not unlike that provided by action in narrative. In general, these elements require decoding, as in a passage which toys with the syllable or Etym "pen" in order to labor the concept penis. The passage turns on a Freudian joke which identifies the pen as a procreative instrument. . . . Schmidt's joke is dressed out in a quantity of philological and pseudoscientific and even dramatic rags, but it retains its crucial nodal quality. (pp. 19-22)

Schmidt's jokes are less numerous and more pointed than Joyce's, but his dramatic effects, the shifts in voice and tone, the shock of attitudes, the text's fluid format, and the typography all contribute to a textual richness which makes the nodal structure analogous to that of the *Wake*. Thus, in the dialogue rebutting Wilma's view of the Etym "pen," we find the sentence:

> Auch in umwallten Etyms, à la 'indePENdent';
> oder Seinen Lei(ie)bWort 'perPENdicular'.: 'the
> PEN phalls powerless from shivering hand'—
> (wenn De noch 10 Minutn aus HEL+SD, wirrSDe
> einsehn, daB hier dem NachMaler wahrlich der
> Pe(e)ni(i)sl aus der zitternd'n Hand sinkn kann).

Here we note such devices as the misplaced capital letter, dialectical German mixed with funnier English ("phalls"), immured Etyms, syllabic doubling, split words ("De noch"), all leading up to the usual play on penis-pen-drooping phall-writerly impotence. What is perhaps more important, since this is a reported conversation, is that many of the gestures are visible only to the reader, and could not have taken place in the dialogue. Thus, as in Joyce, we have the double text, visible vs./plus audible. (Also note the use of German vs./plus English.) In Schmidt, however, there is an added tension derived from the explicit and even realistic base. The pages may dream, the characters do not. The passage points up another difference between Schmidt's enterprise and Joyce's, the relatively loose texture of his language. (p. 23)

Finally, Joyce's text conceals high seriousness beneath a comic surface and an irreverent play of textures. Schmidt uses the theory of the Etym to turn Poe's high seriousness into scatological farce. As such, it constitutes a parasite text unveiling its host. It refuses to take itself seriously and is generated largely out of the skeptical responses of the auditor-participants. An exegetical session, an event about which one should not expect to read, is deliberately inverted when, with the aid of the Etyms and Freud, Poe's writings are the occasion for a text which frequently rivals the *Wake* in subtlety and humor. (pp. 23-4)

> *David Hayman, "Some Writers in the Wake of the 'Wake'," in* In the Wake of the 'Wake', *edited by David Hayman and Elliot Anderson, The University of Wisconsin Press, 1978, pp. 3-38.*

PAUL WEST

Much of *The Egghead Republic* (1957) is sheer, complex fun, the book's time being the year 2008, when an American journalist, Winer, visits two secret regions of the globe: an Arizona desert reserve, complete with mutants and experimental hybrids (centaurs, for example, and spiders with human heads), and an island afloat in the Pacific which serves as a ghetto for intellectuals. In Arizona the flippant Winer, having fun while compiling his report, learns the arts of love from Thalia, a centauress with an ashblond mane who is "24 Gow-chromms" old and who gives him supplementary tuition in the aphrodisiac uses of stinging nettles. On the jet-propelled island he learns about brain transplants and the art of freezing geniuses, neither of which gives him half the kick of the centauress' huge tongue in his mouth ("tasted good and warm; of grass-seeds") or watching centaur calves crack eggs with their hooves.

The reader may sigh for a less convulsive, less telegraphic prose style (supposedly Winer's fault of course), and fewer entities so close to cartoon, as well as wishing the egghead island weren't routinely polarized between East and West; but there is enough snazzy stuff to keep you cheerful as you flash forward from paragraph to paragraph (each with its topic sentence or phrase in eye-catching italics), assimilating puns ("moronsters," "inconsolubly," "I wasn't Her Cules after all") while overhearing Winer report on centaur soccer, a boy in love with a butterfly, the island's being made from 123,000 steel chambers riveted together, novels written by a committee called "Cadre 8," the "brain-sized dollop" of mashed potato you get in the greasy spoon near the transplant clinic, and, the quaintest epiphany of all: "If a strapping 30-year-old had her brain transplanted into a young man she could spend one or two nights with her own other-brained body."

Perhaps the sprightliest (and least overtly exploited) jape is that Winer's ostensible report, done in 21st-century American, has been punitively translated by the authorities into German, by then a dead language, from which we now have a retranslation back into 21st-century American, based on the text known as "Specimen No. 5 (Valparaiso)." If the tenses bother you, tempting you to recast "has been" into "will have been," they should; this is a prophetic novel, spawned by insecurity and especially by nightmares of impermanence, such as the one in which 2008 and 2009 never come, except in fiction (though 1984 looks reasonably certain now).

Whereas **The Egghead Republic** is a textual freak, a forward anachronism, **Evening Edged in Gold** dramatizes the fluid phase in a text's history known as the Final Draft. Weighing 10 pounds, measuring 17 inches by 13, and hard to manage manually unless you have a piano to rest it on, **Evening** takes the form of a reproduced typescript, thus reminding you that it might never have been published at all (and in one sense it hasn't, not at a price beyond the pockets of most book-lovers). Presumably any paperback edition would also have to have the same format: wide, wide lines, which excitingly lead the eye much farther to the right than usual, pages divided into two or three columns to convey a slewed simultaneity and pose the mesmerizing choice of which column to tackle first, other pages designed to be read from bottom to top, while still others sport important or trivial information set off in the margins or in boxes. Deletions, maps, postage stamps, clippings from magazines, diagrams, quotations, doodles and asides drag at the eye all over the place, signs not of a book gone wrong but of a book going fabulously well, a book which reveals the author's mind in the fine frenzy of cooking things up, attempting different versions of one phrase, and most of all auditing a tumult of language which is the backdrop against which the novel's compound voice will finally come clear.

Such is the narcissistic side of an engrossing superbook, superbly and creatively translated, whose title page says, disarmingly enough, "Materials gathered: 1972-75," as if the whole thing were an idiosyncratic album of folk songs, nursery rhymes, graffiti, or curses: unique but unintruded into. In a sense that's true of [**Evening Edged in Gold**], in which Schmidt voluptuously spreads himself over a continuum of voices heard and overheard, misheard and unheard of, awash with lubricious puns and preposterous echoes that bring back all the dead folk behind the words in the dictionary. Fifty-five scenes in 20 acts over three consecutive days, it transforms humdrum material into golden garrulity. (pp. 5-6)

What is so wonderful and welcome in this masterwork is how the voices, the narrator-cum-stage-director's among them, transcend themselves nonstop; what the reader hears in the mind's ear, never mind from whom, is the human heart of all the ages lustily or dreamily talking loneliness and boredom to a standstill. Or, contrariwise, fixating on bodily pleasure, in which this book abounds, until the mind almost (but never quite) gives up. The passages I'd really like to quote are so radiantly blunt that no newspaper would print them; but they can be found, on great big creamy pages that turn like wafting sails and settle with a noise of canvas. Be careful not to sprain your wrist. (p. 6)

> Paul West, "Bawdy Romps with a German Clown Prince," in Book World—The Washington Post, August 17, 1980, pp. 5-6.

S. S. PRAWER

Schmidt collected the material for this elaborate work [**Evening Edged in Gold**] on thousands of bits of paper in the years 1972-75; he began the task of typing it all out in July, 1974, and was ready to send the typescript to the Fischer Verlag in February, 1975. The working title he had in mind during this period of gestation was . . .

> Evening Edged in Gold
> An Autumn Gift for Patrons of
> Etymystics.

This tells us many things. First, it stresses the importance not only of evening but also of the autumnal setting of the whole book. Scene 48 begins with speculations about "autumnal worlds in literature"; but long before that it will have become clear to every reader that evening and autumn are more than just diurnal and seasonal. The book is about the evening of a life, the constrictions of approaching old age, and the fantasies with which a writer may beguile that time. These fantasies, taking off from a small corner of provincial Germany, may encompass a large intellectual and spiritual world. They have been worked into the book that is being offered to the author's patrons—patrons of a special kind, patrons who welcome the game of liberated meanings which is here, ironically, called "etymystics".

"Etyms" have played an important part in Schmidt's previous works. They are words, or rather word-components, which say one thing to the conscious mind and whisper another to the unconscious. Schmidt seeks to bring their subliminal message into the open by abandoning the usual rules of spelling. The injunction "Y ought t read the 'Interpretation of Dreams' again, so that y kn always recocknize a phallus despite its disguys" exemplifies the method and points to one of its originators. Another is revealed in the warning: "Don't go dragging in your 'Ulysses' by the tale again"—though it seems to be *Finnegans Wake* rather than *Ulysses* which has fascinated Schmidt . . .

In August 1975, when the book appeared in Germany, it was found that while keeping his main title intact, the author had abandoned his working sub-title. References to "autumn" and "etyms" can now be found in the body of the book, but not on its cover. The unaltered main title, however, conveyed yet another message to those capable of receiving it. Readers of Schmidt have grown accustomed, over the years, to listening out for literary allusions in his titles . . . The title **Abend mit Goldrand** continues this tradition: it plays a variation on a phrase used by Jean Paul, with whom Schmidt feels himself to have a profound affinity and whose work has provided important thematic and structural models for **Evening Edged in Gold.**

To replace the abandoned subtitle Schmidt provided a new one which again opens avenues into the work itself:

> "eine MärchenPosse
> 55 Bilder aus der Lä/ Endlichkeit
> für
> Gönner des VerschreibKunst".

This alerts us, first of all, to specific kinds of fantasy characteristic of this book. Its recluse author is spinning fairytales, as did the German Romantics with whom he has so much in common—again and again his realistic-seeming narrative takes off into fantasy-land, where characters can grow small and enter a painting, or be transported to some island-dwelling in the clouds. . . . As in his other books Schmidt shows himself particularly fond of island utopias and various versions of cloud-cuckoo-land.

The word *Märchen* which prepares us for these fantastic elements is joined, in Schmidt's definitive subtitle, with another in a way that deliberately flouts the Duden rules of word combination: the noun *Posse,* which announces farcical elements associated, in this book, with hippies, tramps, peasants, television personalities, and frenzied sexual activities.

The *Märchenposse* or *Märchenkomödie* has a respectable ancestry that runs from Gozzi to the German Romantics, particularly Tieck, whom Schmidt admires greatly. Since Schmidt's fun is often scatological, however, John E. Woods is justified in rendering *eine MärchenPosse* as "A FairytalefArse"; and he is also right when he translates "55 Bilder" as "55 Scenes". The different sections into which Schmidt's book is divided do indeed, recall theatrical scenes, for they have a great deal of dialogue supplemented by what often reads like elaborate stage-directions; and since the word "scene" has also been used (especially by Henry James) to describe certain ways of presenting the incidents of a *novel,* its employment would seem particularly appropriate here.

Schmidt's scenic devices, however, go considerably beyond any used by Henry James, or indeed by Tieck in his *Märchenkomödien.* As in his other books, the text frequently divides into three parallel columns, the middle one presenting some frenzied action while the two side-columns chronicle the words and actions of observers who either comment on what is going on in the centre or are so absorbed in their own affairs that they ignore it. There are times, in *Evening Edged in Gold,* where we have to read successive columns alternately from top to bottom and from bottom to top, because the characters whose conversation is being recorded are walking up and down. Some scenes are syntactically telescoped by having parts of a sentence printed above, and other parts below, a series of horizontal dividing lines. And again and again we have to stop our consecutive reading, in ways seasoned Schmidt readers have long learnt to do, in order to take in side columns or side panels containing quotations from Schmidt's favourite authors which have some bearing on his plot or argument.

The main action of the book is set in a provincial corner well known, by now, from the author's other books. This Lüneburg Heath setting is suggested, in the subtitle, by the words "aus der Lä/Endlichkeit", which the translator renders as "from the Cou/untryside".

Well, yes, that does bring out a scatological meaning subliminally present in the original. "End" may suggest the human fundament; and Schmidt has, after all, devoted a whole book to demonstrating that Karl May's landscape descriptions can be shown, by the "etymystic" method of interpretation, to resolve themselves into anal fantasies. In *Evening Edged in Gold* he plays similar games with writers who include George Borrow and (alas) John Bunyan. In the German subtitle, however, whatever scatological elements there may be are overlaid by a suggestion which the translation fails to bring out. *Endlichkeit,* finitude, the finitude of human life and the earthly world, becomes a more and more significant theme in the course of *Evening Edged in Gold.* The book's most prominent characters are old men, one of whom is clearly dying of heart-disease; and the phrase "we'r living in the latter days", which occurs just over half way through, widens the "Endlichkeit" theme and connects it with a supplementary one: the infinity of space and the infinity of the human (especially the poetic) imagination. (p. 949)

Freud's reading technique is exemplified again and again in the course of *Evening Edged in Gold,* with or without acknowledgement to the master; and Freud's views on the structure of the personality and on religion are subjected to characteristic paraphrases and variations. "Let us put it this way", says the chief raisonneur of the book; "each level of the personality has its own religion: the id its animism, or polytheism; the super-ego is strictly monotheistic; the ego attempts t steer its way thru with reasonable agnosticism; (the 4th level sacrifices at the altar of Laughter)." That "fourth level" of the personality is Arno Schmidt's own contribution: it is the ironic attitude he tries to cultivate, the ability to look down on the other three levels with some detachment. The "cultural pessimists" with whom he identifies in his books all attempt to reach such detachment, though they are not always successful.

Schmidt's English publishers have usefully summarized the wisp of plot with which *Evening Edged in Gold* plays its fantastic elaboration- and variation-games. Since this summary is not included in the book, it may be useful to reprint it here:

> The fairytale and the farce deal with the Fohrbach family, consisting of three aging men, plus the wife and teenage step-daughter of one of them. In the village of Klappendorf on the edge of the Heath of Lüneburg they lead an idyllic life whose pleasures are reading, talking, backbiting and reading. One warm October afternoon this household is overrun by a roving band of hippies, who call themselves the Bussiliatic Horde and resemble nothing so much as a sexual circus. Their "dompteuse" is a twenty-year-old Luxemburger named Ann "Ev", a "goddess" of strange psychic capabilities; her lieutenants are Egg and the Bastard Marwenne, the latter a divinity as well, albeit a priapic one.
>
> The confrontation between the world of frustrated senescence and libertine youth erupts into both sexual abandon and the tenderest love. It encompasses and describes the same excesses and beauties which Hieronymus Bosch called into being in his triptych, *The Garden of Earthly Delights,* a work that supplies a visual functional metaphor for the book as a whole.

That is fine as far as it goes, though it leaves out a dastardly plot by two sex-crazed dames to rob the old men and burn their books; the coming together of two young lovers in good fairy-comedy style; and the already mentioned flights into imaginary cloud-islands or other utopian realms. It also fails to prepare us for three features of this memorable book which do most to account for the fascination it has exerted on all who have read the German original.

The first of these features is the constant presence and pressure of older literature which is now quoted directly, now parodied, now alluded to, now analysed. (pp. 949-50)

The second feature to which any reviewer worth his salt is bound to direct the potential reader's attention is the introduction, into *Evening Edged in Gold,* of a typescript attributed to one "Martin Schmidt"—a sketch entitled "PHAROS, or Concerning the Power of Poets" which is either the working-over of an unpublished manuscript by the young Arno Schmidt or a deliberate recreation of his own earlier manner. It is a remarkable piece of prose in its own right and reveals a surprising affinity with Beckett—the opening might almost be Clov's account of a conversation with Hamm before the two of them settled down to their Endgame. In the book this work by a youthful incarnation of the author is read aloud, and commented on, by an incarnation of the same author in his latter days. . . .

The world-view that emerges from Schmidt's writings is bleak and frighteningly misanthropic. Attacks on rebellious youth, women who demand their rights, men who wear beards, acultural farmers, workers who demand a shorter working week, constantly recur with all the signs of authorial approval; and affluent West Germans, on or off the television screen, are rejected with the same ferocity as that shown to " 'East German bloc-heads, circumUrald by soulessdarity". For all its aspirations towards a serene *vierte Instanz* with which to look down on Superego, Ego and Id alike, Schmidt's voice is that of a sick man who has received a deep hurt and has retired to country solitude where he spins fantasies to dull his pain.

It is not the least achievement of *Evening Edged in Gold* that it takes the reader into its author's confidence and reveals the deepest source of that spiritual injury in a terrifying autobiographical excursus. We have had glimpses in other books of Schmidt's experiences as an unwilling soldier in Hitler's armies on various battlefronts, his experiences as a prisoner of war, his years of poverty and struggle in an increasingly affluent post-war Germany. Never before, however, has Schmidt given us, through the mouth of one of his characters, as fully documented an autobiographical account as we find in A & O's long narration of his childhood in the final section of *Evening Edged in Gold.* This hell's eye view of growing up in a German policeman's family, where brutal bawdry forms the warp and sentimental Kitsch the woof, is the finest thing of its kind since K. P. Moritz's *Anton Reiser. . . .*

That, then, is the ultimate source of Schmidt's Extended Mind-Games and arabesques; but what seems to me the most frightening part of it all is that the hated father's coarseness, bawdry, hatred of nonconformity, hatred of socialist ideologies and activities, are reproduced in the bookish son who has at last escaped from his physical tutelage. "Go on", one of the characters encourages the narrator. "So that for once y kn unburden your heart/hate." This unburdening makes *Evening Edged in Gold* essential reading for anyone who wants to understand not only Arno Schmidt and his works but also the secret and private history of Germany after the First World War. (p. 950)

S. S. Prawer, "Etyms and Endgames," in The Times Literary Supplement, *No. 4040, September 5, 1980, pp. 949-50.*

ROBERT M. ADAMS

Schmidt isn't an easily approachable writer, and in the two novels so far translated [*The Egghead Republic* and *Evening Edged in Gold*], we have a low road and a high road to his work; though neither leads to a complete view, the outlines are broad. *The Egghead Republic* of 1957 is a short anti-Utopian novel, the action set in the year 2008, i.e., fifty years in the future.

The book purports to have been written in the Americanese of that day by a journalist accredited to the newspaper of Douglas, Michigan (at the mouth of the Kalamazoo river, population as of 1980 minuscule). His name is Charles Henry Winer; he is at the time of writing 30.8 years old, and his report, though subversive, has been translated into a dead language (German; after the great atomic war, only 124 Germans remain alive), so that it may be preserved safely in the archives of the Egghead Republic. The translator, whose work (as he tells us) was done in Argentina, is 67.3 years of age, splendidly learned in Old High German, with an erotic drive rating of 0.04 (compared with the author's splendid

8.1). Temperamentally, politically, artistically, and intellectually, he despises the author he is forced to translate, venting his anger mostly in indignant footnotes.

These are the layers of irony in the German text; the work of Schmidt's translators has therefore been to translate *The Egghead Republic* back into American from its supposed translation into German. This they have done very well, catching not only a certain exaggerated slanginess but also the nervous jerkiness of journalistic style, setting riddles for the reader in the shape of distorted and phonetic spellings, and maintaining the conventions of the new punctuation, which produces constellations like: "Heeeeeahh!!" /—:!:!!: and :?—:!//:??:!!!:. From this sort of thing the prose acquires a nubby surface that can be pleasant when one gets used to it.

As for the Egghead Republic itself, we don't get to it until nearly halfway through the book. In the world of 2008, and especially for anyone proposing to visit IRAS (the International Republic of Artists and Scientists: one visitor every twelve years, time of visit strictly limited to fifty hours), there are innumerable formalities, document registrations, sanitary inspections, and security clearances. . . .

Suspense is created by the obvious eagerness of the authorities to dispose of our hero, Winer, permanently. They direct him into the most dangerous districts of the Zone, fill his canteen with poisoned gin, are surprised and sorry to see him reappear. But reappear he does, though very reluctantly, having fallen in love with a pubescent and passionate centauress, musically named Thalia. . . .

By jet (rocket?) and ferry, we are off now to the Egghead Republic itself, a big symmetrical island/vessel, divided down the middle into a Soviet bloc and a Western or democratic bloc. . . . [The] eggheads turn out, on closer inspection, to be disgusting representatives of their kind. They do no work, leave the splendid library quite untouched, and spend most of their time sneering at the other faction, a task in which they are encouraged by agents of the secret police on both sides. The climactic discovery of our reporter is that both sides have developed a technique of brain transplantation, which enables them to kidnap the best brains of the opposition and either keep them in deep-freeze or transplant them into other bodies. Having uncovered this culminating horror, our reporter is hastily bustled off the island, his last fond thoughts at the end of his trip being, appropriately, for the sleek young centauress, Thalia.

The Egghead Republic is more heavily stuffed with textual plums than a review can suggest; there are idiot interpolations by the pompous "translator," artful allusions to a profusion of literary analogues, blurred and distorted references to be deciphered. . . .

The weakness of most sci-fi novels lies in the flat explanation of mechanical ingenuities. Schmidt avoids this by taking a very short perspective; his reporter is constantly blundering about, finding anomalies that neither he nor the reader understands, and letting the explanations emerge only belatedly and partially. For reasons like these, *The Egghead Republic* has more texture than *Brave New World* and most of its successors, and has an artistic interest apart from its social commentary. It's a satiric vaudeville, to be sure, and can be read as such; but behind the vaudeville lies a distinctive temper, a special vision. (p. 31)

[*Evening Edged in Gold*] is, to a degree exceeded only by *Finnegans Wake,* a resistant and entangling book. It has been translated by John E. Woods with a meticulous particularity and brutal accuracy which extend even to reproducing the blots and crossings-out of Schmidt's original manuscript.

The book can never fully satisfy even a devoted reader because the text includes numberless puns and double-entendres, verbal deformations and distortions, buried unidentified quotations, and multiple allusions, not only to the full range of European literature, but to folklore, ballads, the vulgar subcultures, and to the author's personal history. There are bits of archaic poetry, attributed, against all probability, to one of the characters; there are extended quotations from analogous literary works—sources sometimes indicated, sometimes not, quotations more accurate or less.

On occasion the narrative splits into three columns to follow the simultaneous words or actions of three groups of characters. . . . Like *Finnegans Wake,* Schmidt's novel gets an unsoundable oceanic effect out of torturing the phonemes; the experience of reading such language remains in the mind like a multitude of tiny bruises.

So much resistance, it's to be anticipated, will exasperate readers with flat and regular expectations—linear readers, so to speak, who insist on the shortest distance between two points. . . . The book is divided into three days, twenty acts, fifty-five scenes; its form is semidramatic. It isn't hard to pick up after being put down.

And what's it all about? As the phrase in *The Egghead Republic* indicated, *Evening Edged in Gold* is the coming of night and old age, the surrender of youth, freedom, and sexual vigor. The big novel couldn't be more explicit in setting up this conflict. In a house near Klappendorf on the Luneburg Heath (province of Hanover) live three old men and two women more or less of their age:

Eugen Fohrbach (fifty-seven) called "the major," a double amputee from the thighs down, with an uncontrollable passion for the literary works of Friedrich Wilhelm Hackländer (1816-1877);

Egon Olmers (seventy), brother-in-law of Eugen, a retired librarian and avid searcher-out of buried sexual innuendos (errata/erota) in any conceivable text on any conceivable topic;

Alexander Ottokar Gläser (sixty), called A&O; writer, translator, polymath, and heart-patient. An evident *porte-parole* for Arno Schmidt, his last name bringing to mind the "glass-blue evening" of *The Egghead Republic,* his transparency a redemptive gift.

The adult establishment is completed by:

Grete Olmers Fohrbach (forty-five), sister of Egon, wife of Eugen, domestic, religious, tyrannical, stupid;

Asta Reichelt (fifty-eight), housekeeper.

For the first part of the novel, these old people sit about, discussing books (which they know in paralyzing detail), bickering, reminiscing, and complaining about the bad behavior of the younger generation. They have bitter, spiteful tongues and foul imaginations—Grete rather more than the average, A&O rather less, but it's a high average indeed. The weight of all this spite, venom, and disapproval falls on two girls, one permanent, the other transient:

Martina Fohrbach (fifteen) is the daughter of Eugen and Grete; encyclopedic in the book-learning she has picked up from her elders, and occasionally owlish about reciting it; sexually innocent, but bumptiously eager to learn, especially from her schoolfellow Martin, who adores her silently from afar;

Ann'Ev' (twenty) is Martina's friend, a skinny blonde Luxembourg girl with interesting powers of divination, self-transmutation, and romantic insight. At the moment she is not living in the house, having antipathies to such close quarters, but in a commodious barrel outside it.

Ann'Ev' is in fact the leader of a cult group of hippies-gypsies-scroungers, lawless, ragged, and libidinous, who set up on a "hillahay" in back of the house. Their appearance leads to an orgy of multitudinous fornications, a wild tumult of perversions and obscene interlacings which language is dislocated and fiercely fractured to express. The vision is not simply of a jungle of wild copulations, but of filth, fecality, bestiality. Bosch and Breughel are surely the progenitors of these grotesque scenes; the Bastard Marwenne, the drunken, unctuous Egg, and the tiny eleven-year-old prostitute Babilonia seem like carryovers from the peasant wars, followers of the Drummer of Niklashausen, or anabaptist anarchists seeking the New Jerusalem through orgiastic rites of sexual purgation. This is the "fArse" promised by the book's subtitle; but a black sex-farce it is, a Walpurgisnacht deluge of unspeakable practices and unnatural acts which rushes over the old peoples' compound and submerges some of them.

How out of this devil's brew there rises, as in Hindemith's *Mathis der Maler,* a music of pure and transcendent joy, I think is best not to explain here. As the book moves toward its end, the promised element of "fairytale" comes to the fore, but it is the sophisticated and ironic kind of fairytale cultivated by German romantics like Tieck and Jean-Paul Richter, to whom Arno Schmidt was obviously devoted. Ann'Ev' is the agent of this transcendence, old A&O the beneficiary—gold shadings on the gathering dusk being touched into the story with surpassing delicacy.

The novel is symphonic in its range of tones and play of fact with fancy. Readers will want to invest different measures of personal reflection in diverse episodes, such as a fantastic excursion (by Ann'Ev', naturally) behind the surface of Bosch's *Garden of Earthly Delights,* an extended parable of imagination's struggle for existence against dark authority, not to mention the bibliographical high jinks of the three old codgers. No doubt the novel has its *longueurs;* its obstructive mannerisms may be at moments exasperating. But the lyric end is not to be appreciated unless one works one's way through the thick and rough of the middle passage; the experience of reading the book as one rearranges it in retrospect becomes nothing less than immense.

Robert M. Adams, "Devil's Brew," in The New York Review of Books, *Vol. XXVIII, No. 3, March 5, 1981, pp. 31-2.*

FRIEDRICH P. OTT

The two works [of Schmidt's] now available in English are representative of the two main phases of a career which spanned thirty years: *The Egghead Republic,* a diaristic negative utopia from 1957, and his swan song, *Evening Edged in Gold,* a hybrid, an encyclopedic, dialogized "scenic fairy-tale farce" from 1975. They will serve to flesh out the following, necessarily sketchy, portrait of Arno Schmidt in his significance as a "visual" and an autobiographical artist.

Like all great humorists Schmidt was a pessimist. His world view, forged under the impact of a deprived childhood, was honed under the further abrasion of studying Schopenhauer and of personal experience: Nazi reprisals, the hunger and want of refugee existence which proved especially wretched and prolonged for the fledgling writer. This pessimism gives the *oeuvre* its unity. The protagonists typically are middle-aged or older men, the abandoned offspring of the "Leviathan" or "Nobodaddy's Children," as Schmidt titled two trilogies, the latter in deference to William Blake's hostile world demon. They are isolated men, alienated from the world and, in another sense, from themselves. They reject as futile metaphysical speculation and hope. One had better stick to one's own resources: reason and senses; they at least are certain, if limited. Thus positivism, close realistic observation, empirical data and psychological materialism (as a function of the inescapably forceful reality of instinct and sexuality) form the kaleidoscopic elements of works shunning the grand vision in favor of the collage. To Schmidt, statistics, lists of names, maps, and photos represent a concentrate of dormant reality; they are the germs for "Mind Games," blossoming forth into a new, metamorphosed reality via the writer's imagination.

In his earlier, pointillistic novels Schmidt gave those portraits of the time which he demanded of every writer. Of course, for Germans, this realist (and didactic) *desideratum* has had a special moral dimension, and Schmidt was indeed among the first to capture, in vivid snapshots, the evil banality of life under Nazism. He has equally focused on the German division, while his pessimistic (and unpopular) view of the fifties, especially of German restorative tendencies and the Cold War, resulted in a number of negative, post-atomic-war utopias that seem no less timely now than they were then. Such works are indeed captivating and challenging enough for their content alone, but they are more! Schmidt's significance lies primarily in his deep concern with the structural and linguistic capabilities of his medium, a concern that dominates in particular those late hybrid works for which language is equally medium and message.

If "formalism" is a dirty word, Schmidt's example may serve to remove the stigma, for his emphasis on form results in greater realism. . . . If Arno Schmidt is going to prove—as he should—a seminal influence on modern writing, it will certainly be as an original "visual" writer who has expanded the limits of his medium. This the German author/critic Martin Walser had in mind when he compared Schmidt to Paul Klee: where the painter tends to the graphic, the writer strives to be visual; both, however, are true artists in that they *evoke* where others merely describe. Schmidt is indeed famous for his evocative power, for endowing words with a maximum of expressive force, through concentration, striking metaphor, and phonetic spelling. His "erotic" relationship with nature has expressed itself in unforgettable, timeless depictions of trees, clouds, and especially the Moon, in all her phases. Still more significant is his technique of making "conformal reproductions" of reality "through external structure." It is, simply, the application to literary technique of modern insights into processes of mentation: through carefully "calculated" typographic arrangement, Schmidt reproduces, for the reader to follow, the mechanics and dynamics of internal processes, taking up, as it were, where the Joyceans left off.

The *Egghead Republic* is one of these formal experiments. The typography of such works may seem willful at first glance. In actuality, the "dissociative" structure of such diaristic novels is the formal consequence of our memory's function as a "merciful sieve." Typographic arrangement visually plots our discontinuous experience of time. Schmidt also spoke of recollection proceeding not as an epic stream, but as a cataract. It cascades from paragraph to paragraph, italicized lead-in phrases indicating the ledge which disperses the fall, jogging the memory into an associative epiphany which pointillistically unfolds as iridescent word spray. It is a vivid and suggestive method of great flexibility, one which evokes with equal effectiveness the lightning flashes of momentary association and the drawn-out boredom of, say, bureaucratic routine.

Economy as a function of this evocative style is Schmidt's trademark. It is most evident in ***KAFF auch MARE CRISIUM*** (1960), a formal experiment designed to reproduce the present or immediate past. Paradoxically evident, one may say, considering that the resulting typographic "sieve," text *cum* leading, is, of course, less porous than the memory of older events. . . . In *KAFF* Schmidt was attempting to give as complete a mind-portrait of a person as possible, given his own precondition of the porousness of time (different from Joyce's *Ulysses*). The work occurs in the mind and words of a Schmidt-like protagonist trying to enlighten and entertain his girl by inventing a story. This story within a story is set off typographically in that both strains of action appear as separate-but-intermeshing columns of print; it depicts the fact that one level of reality determines the other. For we have here a sort of "Portrait of the Narrative I as a Middle-Aged Man," a visual reproduction of the creative process, of the way in which a literary realist à la Schmidt associatively absorbs, reproduces, and metamorphoses reality into "Mind Games," into literature.

Schmidt's creative and critical preoccupations range widely: they include not only the mechanics of cognition, memory, dreams, and other mind games, but also biography, the way in which the subconscious manipulates language, the pathological basis of artistic creativity, and homage to precursors in structural experiment. A rich spectrum, but clearly one with a common denominator: an introverted, self-centered mind for whom "self" is not a given, not an evident starting point, but something elusive, problematic; something that gains artistic significance only as it is experienced through conflict, contrast, opposition (behind all the positivistic gesturing Schmidt was an arch-Romantic). The self-portrait in *KAFF* is not unique. All of Schmidt's works bear an unmistakably personal imprint. He speaks through his *personae,* masks which are congruent, though not identical, images of their creator. Typically, they pose as Ego, reasoning, defensive, self-assuring; minds looking equally typically with casual curiosity at what their appended physique, emotions, and instinctual reactions are up to. This autobiographically motivated concern with the multi-dimensionality of what we simplistically call "person" or "self" became predominant. In the *Egghead Republic,* H-bomb radiation had revealed and absolutized the more hidden facets of the human animal, in mutants such as the "Never-Nevers" and the "Flying Masks" (bestial and sexual libido), and the centaurs reminiscent of Swift's wise and noble Houyhnhnms. (pp. 68-71)

Among Schmidt's first literary efforts had been—not surprisingly—a biography, of one of his childhood heroes, the Romantic poet Friedrich Fouqué of *Undine* fame. Later on, Schmidt focused on other literary figures he felt an affinity for: he wrote dramatized radio essays (some of which are being translated), based on his conclusion that in its ideal form biography would consist of "discussion among several partners." This Jamesian definition certainly also applies to *Evening Edged in Gold*. If *Zettels Traum,* his *magnum opus,* had been, among other things, a gigantic essay on the interdependence between the life and the work of Edgar Allan Poe (another childhood voice), Schmidt now focused on himself, with one significant difference: synthesis takes the place of analysis. The analytical method (foreshadowed in *Egghead Republic*) had grown into the Freudian-Joycean "Etym Theory," according to which the "inspiration" of the literary artist is primarily manipulation by the Subconscious. In *Zettels Traum* the theory had served to analyze the poet's obsessions, encoded in "etyms", i.e. recurrent words, morphemes and set-pieces. (It should be clearly understood that Schmidt, from an awareness of his own pathological condition, was out to demonstrate the extent of humanly possible achievement, in the tension between ignoble impulse and artistic greatness.)

In *Evening Edged in Gold* the theory functions as creative method, as a last—and successful—attempt at resolution and integration. Schmidt presents himself here as one of those artists who finally manage to control *both* of the tyrannical Freudian categories: 1) with creative accomplishment comes autonomy over the Superego. Its tyranny Schmidt's alienated protagonists had combated all along, attacking State and Church. Now, in his swan song, the auctorial *persona* steps forward *sans* mask, settling accounts with his authoritarian father whom he saw as the centrally negative figure overshadowing his childhood. 2) As for the other tyrant, the Subconscious, its power wanes with the onset of senile impotence; thus it can no longer dictate language, and the literary artist—resigned, disabused, but free—can turn the tables on it, with that new voice, mocking it in conscious, scatological punning. The heavy sexual word-gaming in *Evening Edged in Gold* strongly suggests that the deposed tyrant in its heyday must have proved a cruelly efficient slave-driver.

This last-completed work thus traces the etiology of a literary *oeuvre* in its themes and preoccupations back to the isolation of an emotionally and sensorially deprived (extreme myopia that went undiagnosed) childhood and lonely youth. His compensatory efforts, voracious and eclectic reading, Schmidt blames for an acceleration of Ego development, along with that of an imagination feeding almost exclusively on a rarefied diet, on literature rather than reality! Young Schmidt removed himself to "cerebral worlds," the writer does the same, especially in his late phase: neurotic necessity has been converted into creative method, via the "synthetic" imagination of a mind seeking inspiration more selectively now, more from literature and pictures than from reality. (*Evening Edged in Gold* has been shown to be, among other things, the release into dramatic action of the characters visually frozen into Bosch's *Garden of Earthly Delights*—in a sort of dialectic reversal of the writer's visual emphasis, one might add.) If there is an element of wish-fulfillment in all this, it is due to this synthesizing esthetic effort. Schmidt, whose works are in some way the "Mind Games" occasioned by his reading experiences, in this last work takes stock of a life spent more in literature than in life. It is no mere subjectivism. Like any

true artist Schmidt goes beyond egocentricity to representativeness. In the book the facets of his early Hamburg childhood, for example, have objective value as a sociological document of life in the lowest middle-class European suburb, during the hunger years of World War I and after. Indeed, Schmidt wishes this and other works to be regarded as psychological autopsy. (pp. 72-3)

Schmidt's significance lies not so much in original psychological insight, but in applying it to literary form. The typographical and structural plotting of the experience of time and personality is more than formalism. Unlike topographical maps which function as visual replicas of statal realities, Schmidt's texts are not simply blueprints from a literary design bureau. They are both score *and* performance at once. They are artistically successful, convincing experiments which reproduce the mechanics of recollecting, for example, closely enough to result in a maximum of realistic suggestion, in a "déjà vu" recognition by the reader, for whom the fictive reminiscences and experiences thus become his own! To paraphrase the words of one observer: Schmidt's method in its concentration and economy is like a meat extract which may yet flavor many a literary "broth." (p. 74)

Friedrich P. Ott, "Arno Schmidt: 1914-1979," in
Partisan Review, *Vol. XLIX, No. 1, 1982, pp. 68-74.*

PATRICK PARRINDER

[*The Egghead Republic*'s] disjointed paragraphs relate the disconcerting experiences of Charles Henry Winer, a journalist who in the year 2008 travels across the Hominid Zone, a post-nuclear wasteland in the western United States, to visit IRAS (the International Republic of Artists and Scientists), a closed colony of geniuses selected from all parts of the world to live on an artificial floating island in the Pacific. Winer's progress is at once funny, bizarre, and predictably disillusioning. The Egghead Republic, he discovers, has split into two hostile camps occupying the 'left' and 'right' sides of the (elliptical) island. The Free World artists have gone to the island to be pampered and idle, while the Communists have been put in uniform and dragooned into novel-writing collectives. The scientists on each side are developing new means of filching each other's geniuses, and of artificially breeding the geniuses of the future. Our hero escapes just as peaceful coexistence finally breaks down, and jets back to Kalamazoo, Michigan, where his original MS is translated into German (publication in a 'dead' language being the preferred alternative to total suppression), while a suitably doctored version is put out for public consumption.

The hard-boiled and quick-witted Winer is not exactly a modern Candide, but, like Candide, he is allowed his brief vision of the realms of gold. The Hominid Zone which he must cross to reach IRAS is a radioactive corridor populated by grotesque new species, among them the centaurs with whom he briefly enjoys sex and companionship. Though its landscape is that of a wild and dangerous cactus desert, the Zone has much the same mythopoeic significance as Orwell's Golden Country and Voltaire's Eldorado. Winer's sojourn there is overshadowed by his impatience to reach IRAS, a macabre place which bears no resemblance to the Elysian Fields portrayed in the official propaganda; nor is there any going back. The Egghead Republic is by no means without literary precedents, but the most obvious parallels are with German, and global, political realities; here is a 'United Nations' administration in nominal control of a divided city and a divided state. It should be noted that Schmidt's tale of a playful utopia and a grimly topical anti-utopia could probably only be held together by a surrealistic narrative method such as he employs: and any initial doubts as to the method's success are swept away as the book proceeds. For all its inventiveness, *The Egghead Republic* can give the reader only a very partial view of the scope of its author's powers. Suffice it to say that it challenges comparison with the works of Zamyatin, Capek, Stanislaw Lem, and the brothers Arkady and Boris Strugatsky, in the front rank of modern European science fiction and fantasy. (pp. 152-53)

> *Patrick Parrinder, in a review of "The Egghead Republic: A Short Novel from the Horse Latitudes," in* Journal of Beckett Studies, *Vol. 68, No. 7, Spring, 1982, pp. 151-53.*

S. S. PRAWER

The central consciousness of *Scenes from the Life of a Faun*—an early novel which first appeared in 1953—is one Heinrich Düring, a head clerk in a provincial government office just before, and during, the Second World War. Though he likes some of his office colleagues, he despises most of them, along with their clients and most of the people he encounters at home. Even his own wife and children are seen, not without reason, through very jaundiced eyes. In his early fifties, he is drawn to a solidly built young woman in her teens whom he first encounters when she is still at school, and with whom he has a passionate sexual relationship. When the hated *Landrat,* who is his department-chief and with whom he plays some wonderful power games while acting the perfectly obedient and subservient German employee, selects him to make a historical and topographical survey of the rural district he administers, Düring discovers, in some rural archives, documents relating to a French deserter during the Napoleonic Wars. With the help of these documents he finds that deserter's forest hide-out, which he adopts as his own and where he becomes, in his own mind, the "faun" of the title. Such hide-outs in the forest are illegal, however. Tracked down and in imminent danger of discovery, Düring decides to set fire to his wooden refuge. Before he can carry out his intention, however, the French deserter's hut serves him one more time: it shelters him and his young beloved when an air raid sets off tremendous explosions in a local munitions factory and its underground stores. After witnessing scenes of terrible carnage, the ill-matched lovers reach the forest hut, spend a passionate night together after tending their—happily minor—injuries, and then, in one last symbolic action, abandon and destroy the "faun" 's hide-out.

Scenes from the Life of a Faun is written in a form that Arno Schmidt has likened, in various theoretical writings, to a snapshot album and a necklace of pearls. A flash of observation or memory, often interspersed with, or followed by, reflection, forms a single "snapshot" or constitutes a single "pearl" which is immediately followed by another. The flash, or the particle around which the pearl coagulates, is marked typographically by italics. . . . Schmidt plays a multitude of variations on this simple pattern—a pattern that proves most effective for the portrayal of a world apprehended by a strongly marked personality with a powerful inner life. . . .

The world which this central consciousness apprehends is one made hideous by the Nazis. Düring is as outwardly con-

forming as any of his fellow-citizens; he has experienced a pogrom, he hears of concentration-camp cruelties from a party-member who has taken part in them (no "we didn't know" alibis for Arno Schmidt), but his only outwardly visible act of dissent is his refusal to join the SA or another such party-organization. His dissent and his rage are bottled up inside, where they mingle with amused contempt for all those who have been fooled by "charismatic" leaders throughout history. The hide-out in the forest and its voluntary destruction before authority has sniffed it out becomes a potent symbol, paralleling the catastrophe described in the most violent passages Arno Schmidt was ever to write: that caused by the blowing up of vast underground munition stores, a miniature image of the catastrophe caused by the Third Reich and impotently foreseen by the narrator.

Düring's interior voice says many harsh things about his fellow-Germans; but Schmidt leaves us in no doubt of his narrator's own essential and ineradicable Germanness. The combination of a rich inner life with an outer life dictated by conscientious *Pflichterfüllung;* loving apprehension of a rural landscape that has few dramatic attractions, but is all the more dear for that; a host of literary allusions, quotations and reminiscences—these and other features remind, and are meant to remind, Schmidt's readers of German traditions that reach from *Aufklärung* and Romanticism to Biedermeier and Poetic Realism. The German Expressionists, outlawed by the Nazis whose bards and painters Düring despises as much as he loves older German forms of pictorial and verbal art, become particularly important. The book is full of allusions to Expressionist painting, and it deliberately employs the techniques pioneered by Expressionist writers, ranging from August Stramm to the younger Döblin, as one possible means of repairing the damage the Third Reich had done to the German language and of building a bridge between post-war German literature and respectable Modernist traditions. . . .

Alongside the often obscure German writers who form Heinrich Düring's literary pantheon many English and American writers surface again and again. They include Fenimore Cooper, Poe and Sir Walter Scott. The most potent presence of all, however, is that of Jonathan Swift: his disgust with Yahoo humanity, the physical nausea of some of the Brobdingnab scenes, seem appropriate responses to a Germany in which one's very act of greeting a neighbour or a colleague is distorted into hailing (or *heil*ing) a misleader of his people, whose nauseating speech and presence could only be removed by a catastrophic defeat—the approach of which we sense constantly, though *Scenes from the Life of a Faun* ends before Germany's final capitulation.

> *S. S. Prawer, "A Hide-Out in the Forest," in* The Times Literary Supplement, *No. 4175, April 8, 1983, p. 346.*

ERNST PAWEL

Like Heinrich Düring, the antihero of *Scenes From the Life of a Faun,* Schmidt spent the Hitler years in inner exile. Harboring no illusions about the state of his demented nation, he practiced his own form of resistance by withdrawing into recondite researches that took him far—and often far afield—in the natural sciences, literature and philology. During World War II he had the good fortune to be taken prisoner; he made the most of his stay in a British prisoner of war camp and returned to Germany after the war with a sound knowledge of English and an impressive familiarity with both English and American literature.

His arcane interests show up throughout his work, often with mixed results. Even *Scenes From the Life of a Faun,* for all its cogency, suffers from necrotic patches of pedantry. But Schmidt's wayward scholarship was itself merely the obverse of a fierce contempt for the mass mind. The stiff-necked individualism and manifest lack of faith in God as well as in humanity that made him a brilliant satirist also kept him from identifying with any party, faction or fad, Eastern or Western, that promised new kinds of final solutions. (p. 11)

The bruising prose that marked his debut in 1949 in the novella *Leviathan* seemed revolutionary to a public still recovering from a steady diet of blood-and-soil epics. Actually, the ideas behind his avant-garde fiction—simultaneity of action and fragmentation of consciousness as reflected in nonlinear narrative—were rather old hat even then. Schmidt may have reinvented the wheel; more likely, given his background, he was familiar not only with Joyce, Beckett and Céline but also with German precursors such as Kafka, Brecht and Alfred Döblin. Either way, he was among the first to restore the link between German literature and the 20th century.

His provocative avant-gardism, however, tended to obscure his more substantial achievements, those of a poet writing prose, using language with a slashing power as both a weapon and a tool. *Scenes From the Life of a Faun* is essentially a cluster of one-paragraph prose poems, as loosely linked as thoughts in free association but ultimately coalescing in a pattern of doom, disaster and redemption.

The focal consciousness is that of an acerbic county clerk who is smitten with sanity in a world gone mad but is shrewd enough not to be obvious about it. His wife won't sleep with him, but she worships Hitler; their only son wants a regulation Hitler Youth dagger for Christmas; his superiors prance about like little Führers; and his colleagues greedily lap up whatever swill the Ministry of Propaganda dishes out. We are not actually told any of this but rather made to watch as the dyspeptic underground man disgorges three clotted lumps of time—February 1939, May to August 1939 and August to September 1944, checkpoints on the road to hell.

With an economy of means uncanny in its effect, Schmidt evokes the very sound and texture of these convulsive moments, from the eve of the war to the Götterdämmerung. He can capture the essence of the era in a Nazi slogan. In struggling to contain his own lyrical streak, he often resorts to the forced stridency of early Expressionism: "*Moon. Me.* We stared at each other, until old stoney-face up there had had enough and with the help of the wind swindled himself a shade of blue, two against one, smeared the road's surface with pasty white light. . . ." But the people trapped in his beam reveal themselves in all their life-like monstrosity, and his terse, almost laconic description of the final inferno, the air raid that wipes out the clerk's secret sanctuary along with the entire town, is a vision of both past and future that is stunning in its impact.

Language of such evocative density tends to defy even the best of translations; this one goes slack all too often, missing the punch and power of the original. Two other books by Schmidt—*The Egghead Republic* and *Evening Edged in Gold*—have previously appeared in English, but his technique in this one imposes a handicap those did not. In his day the clang and clatter of the Nazi phrases in this book triggered instant recall in any German survivor; in English and at this remove, they often verge on comic-strip balloons.

And yet bringing out *Scenes From the Life of a Faun* some 30 years late and in defiance of all these obstacles strikes me as the sort of quixotic venture Schmidt himself would have appreciated. He is a writer well worth getting to know, even if in this instance it takes some work and imagination on the reader's part. (p. 31)

Ernst Pawel, "German Provocateur," in The New York Times Book Review, *May 8, 1983, pp. 11,31.*

KEITH BULLIVANT

As far as the theory of writing is concerned, Schmidt stands firmly in a German tradition of highly reflective prose writing that goes back into the eighteenth century (especially Wieland), but which has been very much to the fore in the twentieth. His ideas on prose and the consequences these have had in literary practice place him in a line that extends from Arno Holz, via Döblin, Broch and Brecht, to Dieter Wellershoff, Peter Weiss and Helmut Heißenbüttel. He sees the most common prose styles as having their origins in the eighteenth century and corresponding to prevailing social conditions (with the novel reflecting social discourse and the diary being "the first step toward mastering internal processes." While he does not reject such now traditional forms as totally outdated, he feels it essential "for describing and illuminating the world via the word (as the first premise for any sort of domination" to take account of a changed relationship of the writer to language since 1900 and to develop new, appropriate prose forms to reflect modern modes of experience and self-awareness.

In tension with this modernist thrust of Schmidt's views on writing, there exists, however, a more conventional concept of the role of the writer, one that seems more in keeping with nineteenth-century realism. The task of the "Dichter" (itself an old-fashioned term) "as observer and topographer of all sorts of characters and situations would consist, among other things, of describing them as they really are." His task is "the faithful depiction of a period in its typical and its most subtle traits"—a position not far removed at all from Auerbach's notion of the mimetic nature of the realist novel. At times, as we shall see, Schmidt's theoretical pronouncements get very close in their thinking to those of scientific naturalism, but it would be wrong to ascribe this to a regression to outdated literary debates. The concern with scientific thinking can be traced directly to his broad study at university, especially of astronomy, and his later interest in mathematics, physics and astrophysics, which in their turn led to the predominance, in his writing up to about 1960, of an optimistic belief in progress by means of human rationality (note above the term *domination*).

In Schmidt, then, we have a fusion of the striving for scientific thinking with a commitment to modernist writing; for him the founding father of his art is not Zola but Lewis Carroll. (pp. 86-7)

The fullest explanation by Schmidt himself of his literary theories is to be found in the **"Berechnungen,"** where he builds on his perhaps best-known statement, namely that his life is "not a continuum" but rather "a tray full of glistening snapshots." Given the lack of continuity in modern existence, narrative marked by epic flow is today impossible. Life is a "string of insignificance strung with small beads of meaning, of internal and external experiences"; correspondingly, modern writing has to replace conventional narrative with "a prose structure, lean but trim, which would conform more closely to the actual way in which we experience reality," such as Schmidt attempts to achieve in the *Nobodaddy's Kinder* trilogy (*Brand's Haide, Aus dem Leben eines Fauns, Schwarze Spiegel*). The text is constantly broken up, is full of "jump-cuts," goes off on tangents, but slowly builds up a mosaic, in much the same way as has been achieved in later years by the more sophisticated type of movie and TV drama.

The second category of writing, which is an intensification of the first, is characterized by the use of the "Extended Mind Game" (EG). The important thing, as with the first type of writing ("Recollecting"), is that the writer incorporates both types of reality (Foto/E I and Text/E II) into the text, the clear aim being "to render faithfully the everyday harmonies and confusions of a person. . . . To present precisely and without reservation—in other words: TRUTHFULLY!—how much of reality is taken over into the respective soap bubble world." Here we see a clear link from Arno Schmidt back through Alfred Döblin to Arno Holz, the most radical and reflective of naturalist theorists. Whereas, however, Holz sought to represent Schmidt's E II through free indirect speech and Döblin, in *Berlin Alexanderplatz,* through a mixture of FIS, collages and montages, with the result in both cases of difficulties at times in identifying which is objective and which is subjective reality, Schmidt strives for formal clarity. The earlier texts are divided up in various ways, but the structure is always clear; with the EG, Schmidt feels the need to go further "in order to produce a formally complete work of art, an EG in the sense of the theory discussed here, i.e., the complete portrait of a person within a given period of time *x*, E I and E II would have to appear alongside each other!" It was to take time and, presumably, the indulgence of his publishers to enable him to achieve this, but this is the formal principle at the heart of the last three books.

We can thus see the path that Schmidt takes from his earliest postwar writings (*Leviathan,* 1949) to the last ones; this does not, however, help us to understand the enthusiasm of younger writers and readers for the earlier work. Werner Riegel, in his survey of Schmidt's writing up to 1955, gives us, however, a strong clue: "They are notations of processes and opinions, which have no place in the epic endeavors of any of the present-day authors who are too preoccupied with an 'official' representation of this time." Many writers in West Germany in the 1940s and 1950s dealt with the Third Reich, the war and its aftermath and the restoration of society in metaphorical and metaphysical terms, having recourse to a poetic, more-or-less timeless language that seemed to stress cultural continuity rather than a critical concern with the issues of the day. Schmidt, however, whose radical anticlericalism and suspicion of ideology and state power lead one to ascribe to him a predominance of his third E II moods—the querulous—was a striking exception to this. His portrayal of life in the Third Reich in *Aus dem Leben eines Fauns,* of the plight of refugees in the first part of *Brand's Haide* and **"Die Umsiedler"**—which contrast the misery of the little outsiders with the already fat cats of a ruthlessly materialist society—his quizzical look at the emergent economic miracle and sober analysis of life in a divided Germany (*Das steinerne Herz*), his expression of fear that, in the wake of German rearmament, a nuclear catastrophe had come that much closer (*Die Gelehrtenrepublik*): these are undoubtedly the aspects of his work that led to his being "discovered" by a generation shaped by the student rebellion of 1968. To this must be added the impact of the graphic qualities of Schmidt's mimetic skills in which he is undoubtedly the heir of the so-called "consequential naturalists" who sought for photographic and phonographic accuracy in their portrayal of reality (this can be seen clearly in his depiction of his first type of writing, "Recollecting"). Above all, his imitation of the language of the ordinary people of the time, from all walks of life and all parts of Germany, provides us with a vibrant word picture of the early Federal Republic of Germany. At a time, though, when a peculiarly German tradition of antirealism was more acceptable in a state anxious to take its full place in the Western alliance, which led to a more or less unisonal rejection of realist writing by leading critics and academics (realism = Socialist Realism!), Schmidt was an uncomfortable outsider. Alfred Andersch was absolutely right when he said of Schmidt's early work: "What he does with language is something unique and indeed inimitable in today's Germany; and it will be decades before it will have a general effect on our language and literature."

Most critics are agreed that a crucial turning point in Schmidt's writing comes in 1960 with the publication of *Kaff auch Mare Crisium,* the last of his works with a significant realist element; some claim, indeed, that the transition from querulent to solipsist is accomplished in this book. It would be wrong, though, to push the idea of change too far: we have tried to show the link from earlier ideas about formal aspects of writing to the later works, and we should, therefore, see the greater concern with form as an extension or intensification of earlier aspects of his work. (pp. 87-9)

There is much to support the reading of Schmidt, . . . that the Schmidt protagonists belong to a very German tradition, a highly conservative one that is in contrast with the modernist, formal aspects of his prose. In Hegel's aesthetic writings, which are then taken up and intensified in crucial aspects by Vischer and Ludwig, the major theorists of the so-called "poetic realism" of the nineteenth century, the outer world is seen as prosaic and cold; poetic ideals have to be rescued by an intensified inner life, by their retreating from an increasingly philistine and materialist outer world into a timeless autonomous world of the spirit in which artistic values can be kept alive. This is very much the worldview of a major strand of the German novel, on up to Hesse's *Das Glasperlenspiel,* and it is one we find echoed by Schmidt as early as *Brand's Haide:* "What is boring to you: Schopenhauer, Wieland, [Jean Paul's] Campanerthal, Orpheus: is to me natural happiness; what you find madly interesting: swing, movies, Hemingway, politics: it stinks, as far as I'm concerned." This is a view which increasingly asserts itself, finding its fullest expression in the works of the 1970s. Put in this general way, though, such an interpretation ignores Schmidt's idiosyncrasies and the elements of play and irony, which are important constituent parts of his work. More particularly, Schmidt reminds us of Wilhelm Raabe, whose last novels are also peopled by odd loners clinging to cultural values sensed as outmoded by an alien outer world. Like Schmidt, Raabe is acutely aware of the idiosyncratic nature of withdrawal into solipsism and of the growing gulf between objective reality (= E I) and the subjective world (= E II); like Schmidt, he reflects the former awareness in humor and irony, the latter situation, through formal means, using the "reminiscence technique" to break up the narrative flow and thereby producing texts that are an uncanny anticipation of Schmidt pre-1960.

Schmidt is, however, far more than merely the last in a line of German writers of an essentially earlier age, more than someone who provides a literary Cook's tour through Adenauer's Germany. The enthusiasm of younger writers for Schmidt . . . indicates a sense of affinity in his work with contemporary literary practice, and, in a number of perhaps not always obvious ways, we would claim this to be so, and moreover maintain that this is the truly significant context in which to see Arno Schmidt today. For those writers who, having read their Brecht and Bloch, Barthes and Adorno, recognize the impossibility of merely continuing to narrate in the manner of the nineteenth-century novel, yet cling to the same epistemological intent as any realist writer (as expressed in Schmidt's terms: "domination" and "transillumination of the world via the word"), Schmidt was more or less the only postwar German model to whom they could turn. The most obvious example, where the debt is fully and openly acknowledged, is Walter Kempowski, whose whole range of novels (providing, in effect, a social history of Germany in this century through the medium of a family chronicle) is based on Schmidtian principles of structure. While it is not possible in every case to show an acknowledged sense of debt, it is difficult to conceive of a major strand of experimental prose writing in West Germany in the 1960s and 1970s—as represented by Helmut Heißenbüttel, Jürgen Becker, Alexander Kluge, Ror Wolf and Wolf Wondratschek—without the influence of some sort of Schmidt's early writing; common to so many of these texts is the abandonment of linear narrative and epic patterns, the breaking up of material into blocks along the lines of Schmidt's "Recollecting," the integration of the consciously subjective into the evocation of objective reality. From such texts it is but a short step to a particular sort of documentary novel in montage style; obvious examples are Kluge's *Schlachtbeschreibung* (1964), Manfred Franke's *Mordverläufe* (1973) and Uwe Timm's *Morenga* (1978). In all of these cases, as in Schmidt's early prose, E I (here documentary material from various sources) is intercut with E II (the subjective input, either as a structuring principle and/or in the form of authorial comment, analysis and speculation). The opening up of the text, the making clear—both in formal and perspectival terms—that we are not dealing with experience as self-evidently interpretable, but that an increasingly atomized world allows for a whole range of subjective responses should be seen as close to the intent and style of the early Schmidt, at the very least. (pp. 90-1)

Keith Bullivant, "Arno Schmidt: The German Contest," in The Review of Contemporary Fiction, *Vol. VIII, No. 1, Spring, 1988, pp. 86-92.*

Carolyn Slaughter

1946-

Indian-born English novelist.

In her fiction, Slaughter depicts complex relationships between family members, lovers, and friends while often exploring the effects of the past upon the present. Through detailed evocations of place and character, Slaughter dramatizes the lasting significance of childhood incidents and associations as well as the power of natural forces to influence emotion and behavior. Slaughter was born in India and educated in Botswana, and her experiences as a British citizen living abroad have contributed to the settings and subject matter of several of her novels. Jim Crace observed: "Slaughter has a well-earned reputation as a passionate and accomplished novelist. . . . [She] is a sentimentalist, but an uncomplacent one, with a rare and penetrating comprehension of sex and romance."

Slaughter's first novel, *The Story of the Weasel* (1976; published in the United States as *Relations*), examines the intricacies of sexuality and British society. Narrated through a private journal that the female protagonist begins as a means to escape her unhappy marriage, this work focuses on her incestuous childhood relationship with her brother. Although some reviewers regarded this narrative as awkward and archaic, others commended Slaughter's reserved treatment of a sensitive topic. *Magdalene* (1978) is an unconventional account of the life of Mary Magdalene, the biblical figure traditionally portrayed as a former prostitute who becomes a close follower of Jesus Christ and a witness to his resurrection. In this work, Slaughter demythologizes Mary by presenting her as a tragic woman beset by loss and death. Faulted by some critics as derivative, *Magdalene* nevertheless drew praise as a lushly detailed character study.

Slaughter's next two novels, *Dreams of the Kalahari* (1981) and *Heart of the River* (1982), are set in Africa. *Dreams of the Kalahari* is a semi-autobiographical work that chronicles experiences in the life of a British official's neglected daughter. This novel begins with her childhood in Botswana, where she develops a strong identification with the country's native people, and relates her unhappy years in England and return to the Kalahari Desert. Critics lauded Slaughter's acute evocation of childhood emotions as well as her unsentimental depiction of colonial life in decline. *Heart of the River* relates the story of a woman who returns to Botswana to confront memories of her former lover and forms a new emotional bond with an Afrikaner cattleman.

Slaughter's following novels, *The Banquet* (1983) and *A Perfect Woman* (1984), elicited mixed reviews. *The Banquet* examines a wealthy London professional's obsession for a working-class shop girl, while *A Perfect Woman* exposes the destructive interrelationships between a man, his wife, and his mistress. Although several commentators faulted these works as predictable, others applauded Slaughter for her observations of psychological dependencies and for skillfully rendering the complexities of contemporary life. Slaughter returns to an African setting in *The Innocents* (1986). This novel focuses on a white South African woman in conflict

with her family and the black woman who has become her closest friend as apartheid threatens to destroy her secure life on a remote farm. Critics commended Slaughter's vivid description of the African landscape as well as her effective dramatization of the effects of racism. Dennis Drabelle commented: "*The Innocents* is a well-wrought novel that presses beyond headlines and the figures who make them to provide glimpses into ordinary lives distorted by the arbitrary horror of apartheid."

(See also *Contemporary Authors*, Vols. 85-88.)

SYLVIA CLAYTON

Carolyn Slaughter, in a very assured first novel [*The Story of the Weasel*] describes the growth of an incestuous relationship between Catherine and her brother Christopher, children of an unhappy Victorian household. Catherine, who has a loyally obstinate nature, thinks of herself as a mole and of her secretive, independent brother as a weasel. Together they share a private world in which their drunken, sometimes violent father, their capricious mother and their surly elder brother have no part. The intensity and sensuality of their childhood feelings are recalled by Catherine when, as a woman of thirty, trapped in a boring marriage, she tries to exorcize her early experiences by keeping a journal.

The device of the journal is not wholly successful, for although the pastiche of mannered Victorian prose is precise, occasionally to the point of archness, Catherine as a narrator is not perfectly in focus. She is supposed to be writing in 1900 of events that happened twenty years earlier, but her frank analysis of her sexual feelings suggests a literary landscape shaped by D. H. Lawrence rather than the Brownings, whom she mentions. . . .

The author is at her best in dramatic rather than reflective writing. There is a fine scene in which Catherine confronts the deranged, suicidal wife of her cruel elder brother, which in its economy and sense of tragedy recalls Jean Rhys's *Wide Sargasso Sea*. But the constraint of writing in period costume often makes the novel seem chilly and contrived. Catherine's unhappiness is understood, but it is remote and leaves one unmoved.

Sylvia Clayton, "Brotherly Love," in The Times Literary Supplement, No. 3865, April 9, 1976, p. 413.

RONA JAFFE

[*Relations*] is a strange and powerful novel about incest between brother and sister, written in the form of a journal. It is 1900 in England. Catherine, an intelligent and strong-minded woman of 30, is trapped in a marriage to a man she does not love and cannot bear to be touched by, her emotions frozen. . . . Her past haunts her, and so she begins this secret journal about her passionate childhood love affair with her brother Christopher.

To have set the novel in Victorian times is a device that works well. Cathy and Christopher do not know anything, and yet they know everything, in the perceptive manner of young children who still listen to their intuitions. The dark side of Victorian sexuality is all around them: their mother's suitor, who is attracted only to prepubescent girls; the apothecary the family uses for a doctor, who calls the menses "the wound of the womb" and wishes all little girls would die before they can grow up to be disgusting; their cruel and impotent older brother, who drives his wife to insanity.

Cathy and Christopher adore each other. They are their only companions, able to communicate without words, but also voluble and honest with each other. One day, alone in the attic, Christopher and Cathy find a locked trunk their late, unlamented father brought back from a trip; it is filled with pornographic pictures. It seems natural to the two children to lie on the attic floor and re-create what they have seen.

Thereafter their lovemaking becomes more passionate. It is not just physical pleasure, but an expression of their consuming love for each other. She has no idea that it is "evil," yet they intuitively keep it a secret.

The Victorian novelistic use of nature as a powerful force that reflects and influences the characters' feelings is used to good effect here. The descriptions of the lush English countryside, the wild seashore, the changing seasons, are an integral part of the narrative.

The long love affair between sister and brother naturally must

end in tragedy. I wished it hadn't; I wished they had run away together and pretended to be married. No one would have found out; in the 1890's it was easier to disappear. My reaction to their forbidden love affair shows just how effective a writer Carolyn Slaughter is. (pp. 20, 22)

Rona Jaffe, in a review of "Relations," in The New York Times Book Review, September 25, 1977, pp. 20, 22.

ANTHONY THWAITE

Carolyn Slaughter is a risk-taker whom one has to admire even in her failure. Her first novel, *The Story of the Weasel,* established her theme—thwarted love—with a powerful, delicate story of brother/sister passion, set at the turn of the century and written in a kind of muted Brontésque. In *Columba* the setting was modern, but the style, rapt and exalted in its simplicity, looked more self-conscious. Now, in *Magdalene,* she's taken on the almost impossible job of writing a first-person narrative for Mary Magdalene, that shadowy but much venerated follower of Jesus. . . .

Carolyn Slaughter has rejected the tempting notion of giving us the true confessions of a big-hearted whore, which no doubt would have made a more sensational product. Her Magdalene is a passionate woman who has loved and lost, not in the brothels but through independence of mind; and Jesus, her chief thwarted love, addressed directly in vocative passages throughout the book, is not a narrated or circumstantial 'character'—this is the function of Mattathias, for whom she rejects her family, and Samuel, the carpenter she marries and who dies, as does her son.

The main difficulty in *Magdalene* isn't the events or their relationship to the original tenuous story but a stylistic one. It's a book which proceeds very slowly, dignified, studied, in a manner of plain prose-poetry: the sensuous details—food, clothes, flowers, bodies—have the artificiality of some types of French high prose, and indeed I kept on thinking the whole thing would sound much better in French. 'You wanted to vault me to heaven. I wanted to marry you,' Mary says to her memory of Jesus—but the physicality is rarified and thinned out by the labours of composition. It's a book to respect, but not one readily to warm to.

Anthony Thwaite, "Treasure in Heaven," in The Observer, August 20, 1978, p. 22.

ANTHONY BURGESS

Carolyn Slaughter considers herself to have a free hand in the imaginative labour of giving Mary Magdalene an identity, a character and a biography [in *Magdalene*]. There is no reason, she says in a prefatory note, "to suppose that she was the unnamed whore in St Luke 7". True, but there remains the myth, the weeper and her portable and compendious oceans, Magdalene becoming maudlin, with that pejorative semantic change as the best possible attestation to the true saltiness of the tears. It requires great imaginative authority to attempt to supplant a two thousand year legend with even so thoughtful and cogent a fictional creation as we are given here. But there is something so generic about Ms Slaughter's unhappy lady of Magdala that we are unlikely to find our mythic image much modified. She is there on the dust-cover, filling it up, great-eyed, generous-mouthed, pan-Mediterranean, sad but brave, finding nothing for tears. . . .

Christ is in Ms Slaughter's book, unnamed like the whore of Luke, no tiger, apostrophized as a kind of dead lover, dead like the dead flowers that are scattered all over the narrative:

> Far above me; my lips could brush your feet—shall I kiss them? How cruelly they are folded, spiked, so much blood, so much. I am afraid to lift my eyes. Your flesh, that body that I know, it has become singular, quite strange to me. It is as though you have entered a private domain, like a woman giving birth. Your torture fills me with awe—that you must suffer it alone. The muscles in your thin legs quiver purply through the skin; the hip bones butt out of the soft linen around your loins. . . . You are suffocating—O I know it—your mouth opens, gasping for air, your ribs are distorted, heaving.

Is it unfair to expect Mary the narrator to be able to modify her soft, anthoid, narcissistic prose in the direction of muscular outrage? As she speaks here, so she speaks always. Her life is full of outrages, but the brass and drums never intrude on the flutes. She marries a man in disobedience to her father's wishes, and her brothers find her husband and castrate him. Being already a bluestocking, what with her knowledge of Homer and Sophocles as well as the Scriptures, she is equipped to become Eloise when her Abelard goes off to join the Dead Sea sect, but instead she turns herself into Jane Eyre. She does not find a Mr Rochester in the household where she teaches but she marries a gentle son of the family given to woodcraft. She cannot produce a child, and this makes her accursed of the village.

She produces a child but loses her second husband. The villagers believe her responsible for his death and they burn down her house and kill her son. She gets away and lives with an Epicurean in Tiberias. And all the time the flower petals drift and fall, and it is hard to distinguish between the crushing of a stamen and the crunching of a bone.

If only the prose would occasionally accommodate a sonic brutality, a wisp of humour, a rasp of irony. If only Mary were not so joylessly concerned with the beauty of her hair and breasts and the swish of her skirt. Am I right in supposing that women novelists take more easily to narcissism than do men? And to masochism? Some nasty things happen in this novel, apart from that ultimate nastiness on Golgotha, and they are scored for muted strings. A woman, childless like Mary, steals a child and, when the women of the village come searching, drops it in hot water and puts the lid on. They find the child and make her eat it. Then she cuts her own throat. Did the Jews really behave in this way? And did they, for that matter, serve cheese at the same table as roast beef? And, while we're at it, could a woman of Magdala *c* 30 AD really use a term like "sublimation" when talking of Christ's impatience with his body?

These are captious grumbles. There is much good in the novel, some fine evocations of nature, some admirable sustentions of mood, especially the hopeless sadness that is mostly Mary's lot and almost justifies that pejorative semantic change. But there is no point in coming to it as if it were a historical novel, an attempt to put flesh on the bones of the evangelists. Nobody outside Mary is at all fleshy, even her Epicurean. The men are particularly wraith-like, and the Jesus would not even be substantial enough for *Godspell*.

Magdalene is about suffering woman, any place any time, and, by Jehovah, how she suffers.

Anthony Burgess, "The Story of the Weeper," in The Times Literary Supplement, *No. 3986, August 25, 1978, p. 945.*

HERMIONE LEE

In *Dreams of the Kalahari,* her fourth novel, Ms Slaughter's preoccupation with neglected children, and her own memories of growing up in the Kalahari desert, are fed into the childhood of Emily Jones, solitary and furious, alien to her horrible colonial parents and to the native life. She sees the panic of the English exiles, 'rejected' by the land, and hears in her father's servants 'the laugh of people biding their time.'

Sent to a convent school, she acquires discipline from her opposition to the nuns' 'delicate malice,' and falls in love with a schoolfriend. At a farm on the veld she has her first reckless sexual adventure; exiled to England, she begins to understand Africa, and returns to work in a village clinic and refugee camp in Botswana, learning arduously to cure herself of rage and isolation through 'kinship with others.'

The novel does not force any sentimental parallels between this self-education and a better political future for South Africa, but it is intelligently aware of the relation between domestic, emotional and political life: the unhappy family at the tail-end of the colonial era is particularly well done. I found the convent and first-love parts over-heated, and the debts to Olive Schreiner and Doris Lessing (and to *Jane Eyre* and *Frost in May*) very plain. Still, it is a rich, ambitious novel, lucid, and feelingly written.

Hermione Lee, "A Passage from India," in The Observer, *May 3, 1981, p. 32.*

WILLIAM BOYD

The prime dreamer in Carolyn Slaughter's fourth novel [*Dreams of the Kalahari*] is . . . one Emily Jones. We follow her life from the age of eleven over a period of some ten or fifteen years. Emily lives in Bechuanaland on the edge of the Kalahari. She is a strange withdrawn child, tearful, uneasy with her parents and entranced by her environment. People notice her precocity and her piercingly adult gaze.

Life in this remote colonial outpost is tellingly and accurately observed. Emily's father is an embittered minor official; her mother is a flirt and a snob, unable to provide her daughter with the love she craves. Unhappy at home, Emily mixes easily and unselfconsciously with the Africans around her and also with the le Rouxs, a family with whom she sometimes spends her holidays. It is while she is with the le Rouxs that she experiences the first stirrings of sexuality when she meets a young farmer named Patrick who, teasingly, tells her to come back and see him when she's sixteen.

Emily goes to a convent school in Rhodesia where her potent libido (astonishing for an eleven year old) is stimulated first by a nun and then by an older girl called Virginia. The novel picks up pace at this point and we move through the five years of education with little fuss. Leaving school she returns to the le Roux household and seeks out Patrick. A torrid affair ensues and the two fall rapidly in love. But Patrick is renowned as the local libertine and his affections are not to be trusted.

Emily's emotional problems are solved only by her parents' announcement that the family are returning to England.

In England Emily pines for the Kalahari and her confusions and dissatisfactions lead her on a predictably depressing route. . . . Rapidly approaching nervous breakdown, Emily is again saved by a twist of fate. She sees an announcement in a newspaper which provides her with Virginia's address and the two are reunited.

Virginia, now married, is heavily involved with the anti-apartheid movement and Emily plunges fervently into politics. She meets a radical South African called Reuben and they fall in love. Reuben gets her to return to Bechuanaland (now Botswana) to work in a refugee camp, while he pursues insurrectionary and fifth-column activities in the Republic. After much effort, heart-searching and danger, the novel ends with Emily and Reuben reunited, resigned to the difficulty of their struggle with apartheid but happy and content to have found a cause that fulfils them.

Dreams of the Kalahari covers familiar ground—notably that mapped out by Doris Lessing in *Martha Quest* and the *Children of Violence* sequence—but with less success. The major problem with the book is that it is soft-centred. Carolyn Slaughter's novels up until now have been highly praised and have been characterized by an unflinching and at times cruel candour. It's all the more strange, then, to find this sort of romantic cliché and convention so prevalent. . . .

The book positively throbs with sincerity and one feels that the passionate convictions behind it must temporarily have robbed Carolyn Slaughter of her normally well-functioning judgment. Happily, this last quality is strongly prevalent in the opening sections of the novel, which not only convey Emily's childhood obsessions with a vividness and force recalling *The Story of the Weasel* but also recreate with appalling clarity the sweaty tensions of remote colonial life. The ending too, though a trifle elegaic and creaking with a kind of weatherbeaten integrity, does round off the dream motif neatly. It recalls the modest but dignified ambitions of Conrad's Captain MacWhirr in *Typhoon*—"Facing it, always facing it"—and goes on a long way towards redeeming the novel and providing Emily's curious life with a genuine sense of development and significance.

William Boyd, *"Heart-Searching," in* The Times Literary Supplement, *No. 4078, May 29, 1981, p. 596.*

JIM CRACE

Carolyn Slaughter has a well-earned reputation as a passionate and accomplished novelist. Her first and best work, **The Story of the Weasel** (a deft description of incestuous love) won the 1977 Geoffrey Faber Memorial Prize. Since then Slaughter has produced three more engaging if workmanlike novels; she is a sentimentalist, but an uncomplacent one, with a rare and penetrating comprehension of sex and romance. Though there was much to admire in all four books, it was only in the first that Slaughter's standing as a stylist seemed anything but precarious. More recently she has allowed careless prose to undermine the emotional intensity of her narratives.

Now, sadly, in her fifth novel, **Heart of the River,** we encounter a collapse. The prose destroys the plot. Lazy adverbs ("suddenly" is the most abused) labour to energize spiritless sentences. Inept similes ("A solitary hawk was suspended in the sky like a truffle in aspic") and mannered phrases—"their eyes collided", for example, a Slaughter favourite—occur with insistent frequency. And the vocabulary has become cloyingly simplistic: "a well of sadness", "a soft ache", "a sad ache", "a crippling sadness seized her", "a great aching seized them both". What in the earlier novels were occasional but irritating aberrations have here established themselves as Slaughterisms. Here is a talent in premature decline.

But it is a decline which, on the evidence of this book, cannot be halted simply by tinkering with syntax or spicing vocabulary. The prose in **The Story of the Weasel** succeeds because the architecture of the whole novel is sound. The one invigorates the other. The prose in **Heart of the River** is weak and undernourished because the fictional scheme is ill-judged and carelessly conceived. Carolyn Slaughter has misappropriated promising material for social satire, and produced a solemn and sentimental debate: This Book Believes that "love can't be promised, it's an emotion, not a thing."

The plot is plain and familiar. Constance Martineau is newly divorced, emotionally marooned, and vulnerable. She visits Aunt Cynthia in "Africa" where, seventeen years previously, she had fallen for an impulsive white hunter/farmer but, intimidated by her own passions, had abandoned him. Now she prepares to lay his ghost and, thus, rediscover and revivify her blunted sensibilities. Her saviour is a stringy South African called Laurens de Villiers.

The repetitive manipulations, the countless lyrical love scenes . . . deaden the readers' sympathies for both Constance and "Africa". Where in Africa? Slaughter will not say, though there are tiny clues thinly littered throughout the book—a dozen words, at most—to indicate that she has one specific setting on her mind. Old Africa hands will recognize *pula, dumela* and "Gabs" as respectively the currency, the greeting word, and the affectionate, abbreviated nickname of the capital of Botswana. But for the general reader this is just "Africa", skimpily evoked in brochure English.

The characters, too, lack definition: Afrikaaners parade the occasional "Ja", "Ag" and "Bleddy Hell", European expatriates are crudely dismissive of Afs and Kaffirs; the Botswanans themselves are mechanical extras ("some carrying heavy loads on their heads"). Even the principals are lacking in idiomatic singularity. Constance and Aunt Cynthia banter in the same cheerless voice, sharing Slaughter's own narrative manner; Constance and Laurens worship each other in identically reverential tones.

Jacob, the "houseboy" who whines incessantly for Constance's heart and body, is the only character of any resonance. . . . He alone in **Heart of the River** is no talking-head. He is a touching and dramatic paradigm of hopeless affection. With Jacob, Carolyn Slaughter's old skills briefly reassert themselves, and a magical short story unfolds. But, too soon, Jacob is seen off with a bullet in his thigh from Laurens's gun.

Jim Crace, *"African Collisions," in* The Times Literary Supplement, *No. 4159, December 17, 1982, p. 1398.*

MARY KATHLEEN BENET

Food must be the most widely used literary metaphor. Raw or cooked, reward and punishment and love-substitute—hard to imagine a novel without it. Never, though, has the metaphor been carried so far as in [*The Banquet*]. . . .

Gourmet cook Harold spots delicious Blossom working in the food hall of Marks and Spencer in High Street Kensington. He watches and waits, admiring her peachy complexion, her cherry lips. . . . But though Harold may be a bit creepy, he doesn't want to hurt her like a Ripper or imprison her like a Collector. He just wants to eat her up.

For Blossom is a truly edible woman. "Her mouth like a cake warm from the oven . . . She had nipples like oatmeal biscuits with small pink tips. Her skin seemed to be dusted with icing sugar, it smelt of marzipan . . .". This and a lot more is lovely fun; but though the book is crafted with dandyish care, the dénouement slowly and skilfully teased out, it is no heartless black comedy.

The premonitions of disaster are there from the start. Blossom is tempted into Harold's perfect mews house where they consume many perfect meals together, make love, find happiness. But, we are told, a love so perfect and all-consuming is doomed. When will the axe fall? And why? It gradually emerges that Harold's adored mother went mad and left the family when he was six, and that his father retreated into religious mania. Harold has been left with an aching emotional void that no love can fill; Blossom feels herself being engulfed by his need; it is this that frightens the girl and precipitates the tragedy.

Carolyn Slaughter has covered some exotic fictional terrain, from the Kalahari Desert of her childhood to the life of Mary Magdalene to a tale of Victorian incest. Throughout her work, though, especially in the haunting *Columba,* the painful loss of parental love is the emotional charge. Here, it is so powerful it almost shakes the book apart. Harold's reminiscences are far more heart-rending than anything that happens between him and Blossom. . . .

Harold's work as an architect is vaguely sketched in; Blossom is placed among her mates at the store. There is a neat implication that the repressed professional classes, having failed each other emotionally, renew their strength with vigorous proletarian blood. Affluent Harold, never short of a bottle of champagne or a bunch of orchids but desolate within, is contrasted with Blossom's unemployed father, destitute but buoyed up by East End family feeling.

For all its precision of detail, the book has a claustrophobic quality. Harold's and Blossom's fate seems to have been ordained long before they came on the scene. It squeezes the juice out of them as characters; they never have that entirely spurious but entirely necessary air of being people with a certain measure of free will. They are caught up in an obsession all right, but it seems to be the author's.

Mary Kathleen Benet, "Blossoming Anew," in The Times Literary Supplement, No. 4182, May 27, 1983, p. 553.

ANITA BROOKNER

[The wilder shores of love are] investigated by Carolyn Slaughter in *The Banquet.* . . . Harold Moreton is a solemn young bachelor of refined habits. He has all the appurtenances of a successful life: the mews cottage, the antiques, the architectural practice. He is plausible without being convincing, which is a pity, because he intrudes into the third-person narrative with a few first-person chapters of his own. Harold, who shops at the Kensington branch of Marks and Spencer, falls in love with an assistant in the Food Hall, a girl called Blossom, who is slavishly described and compared with various edibles in the high-quality range: indeed, food plays a considerable part in Harold's sensorium, as does the noble house of Marks and Spencer. For a while all is King Cophetua and the Beggar Maid. But the Beggar Maid, in this instance, is sharp-witted enough to become uneasy when confronted with the full blast of Harold's adoration. What she does not know is that a specific kind of loss has consumed Harold's past and threatens his entire future. Blossom ends up dead, and the manner of her going is unclear, but by this stage the reader is caught in the mood of the story, which for all its brand names and secular particularities is really a mourning ritual of some intensity—unsatisfactory, but, like all Carolyn Slaughter's work, impressive. (p. 20)

Anita Brookner, "Good Girls and Bad Girls," in London Review of Books, Vol. 5, No. 10, June 2 to 15, 1983, pp. 20-1.

JONATHAN LOAKE

[Carolyn Slaughter] believes sex, love and marriage have more to do with food than bicycles. Beth, Humphrey's wife, "made you feel she loved you by feeding you". Sylvie, Humphrey's mistress, "slapped a plate of salami and French bread in front of you but he loved her just the same". And Humphrey? He runs an enormously successful business selling frozen gourmet meals to restaurants and hotels. The eternal triangle once again, and it's pretty obvious who's to blame for busting up the marriage. Frozen food, however tasty, is still a form of deception. . . .

[*A Perfect Woman* has little] detachment. Carolyn Slaughter writes as though every nerve and membrane (at least in her women characters) throbs with sensitivity. Beth seems to draw a physical response not only from her family and friends but from the carefully chosen contents of her perfect home. The troubles of the two women are expressed in symbolic physical acts, in a fascination with each other's material things as well as their emotions.

We are set up for the fall with great skill. The apparent perfection of Beth's traditional womanliness is warmly seductive. But perfection, in Carolyn Slaughter's vocabulary, has perjorative connotations. It is no substitute for passion. When passion breaks, she is more than equal to it. Her work is deeply felt and deeply female.

Jonathan Loake, "Sex, Love and Marriage," in Books and Bookmen, No. 345, June, 1984, p. 25.

JOANNA MOTION

Perfect woman billing, in Carolyn Slaughter's [*A Perfect Woman*], goes to Beth: such a performer as wife, mother, cook, company director, friend to punks and stabilizing force in the universe that it's hard to list her attributes in any hierarchy. Naturally she's married to a pretty perfect man. Humphrey is a bit of a shit, of course, but all the manlier for that.

He glistens with energy, and if he makes his pile in the dubious area of gourmet frozen foods, he atones through commitment to his vegetable garden and talent at his white grand piano.

Coming into focus behind Humphrey is the inevitable other woman, also a contender in the perfect female stakes. Motherless Sylvie is a successful builder. . . . She may be mannish by vocation and temperament, and incompetent with the spiced beef, but Sylvie asserts her femininity *via* her gratifyingly large breasts, lurking under the dungarees. With a star of a woman at either hand, Humphrey has a wonderful time, believing he can love them both to satiety. But as one woman gets ill and the other pregnant, the sharp, mature characters of Beth and Sylvie blur at the edges, Humphrey grows uneasy at their changing shapes and all their security tilts into chaos.

A Perfect Woman reads like a dismally familiar book. Ghosts of thoroughly chronicled middle class adulteries queue up behind the pages. . . . And the characters' histories are as packaged as Humphrey's briskly-selling products ("finally her father's hunter had gone too").

This stock naturalism is bracketed by a hefty symbolic pattern of apple trees and dreams of women who laugh hysterically as their curls go up in flames. In fact, the only two unexpected elements in the novel's 200 pages are that Humphrey doesn't just keep Sylvie content with promises for the future but actually marries her bigamously; and that neither of the women seems to have discovered the duvet. . . .

It's a shame. Carolyn Slaughter is sympathetic and acute in her perception of the seesaw of family life and the unpredictable weight that jealousy adds to it. She has a good ear for characteristic slabs of jargon. But she starts the novel with an overworked idea which she cannot agitate into revival. When she seeks to complicate the book at its halfway point, the narrative, which has been uninterestingly straightforward so far, fails to redeem itself in an uncertain obscurity. The short sections which conclude the novel seem tacked on one to another, zigzagging to a dénouement which is willed rather than achieved. *A Perfect Woman* gives off a disappointing sense of talent straining in a pointless direction.

Joanna Motion, "Two Little Beauties," in The Times Literary Supplement, *No. 4241, July 13, 1984, p. 790.*

LUCIE PRINZ

This contemporary morality tale [*A Perfect Woman*], set in an upscale Eden, reminds us once again that greed is a world-class transgression and that hell hath no fury like a woman scorned—especially if she can enlist her rival to do the bounder in. Humphrey, whose blessings include a charming house, prosperous business, three spunky daughters and Beth, the perfect wife, wants more. . . . [At] 44 it has come to him that he might one day die. This realization stirs an urge for change—he falls in love with Sylvie. Of course, he will continue to love Beth. By the time he decides that what he is doing is the "ultimate in selfishness," he can't stop. By contrast, the competent, successful Sylvie and the beautiful, passionate Beth possess between them most of the female virtues. From the outset this darkly delicious book celebrates the power of woman. Humphrey's two loves, drawn to one another by mutual anger, forge a bond that eventually makes sisters out of rivals. He is inextricably trapped by one. The

other causes his carefully tended paradise to come crashing down. Carolyn Slaughter has brought to this ancient story the trappings of modern life. Her touch is deft throughout and although the book occasionally demands too strenuous a suspension of disbelief, *A Perfect Woman* has a satisfying bite and the sweet tang of just desserts.

Lucie Prinz, in a review of "A Perfect Woman," in The New York Times Book Review, *April 21, 1985, p. 24.*

CHERI FEIN

As long as the atrocities taking place in South Africa continue, the devastation of racial separation there cannot be overdone by writers. The challenge is to make social and political issues into art. Carolyn Slaughter's latest novel [*The Innocents*] manages the transformation with grace and passion. This is a multilevel story of how personal and public acts affect each other. Zelda de Valera, a powerful farmer, shares her house with her childhood friend Hannah. But Hannah is black, so it is illegal for her to be living under Zelda's roof. This is not an undisturbed union, but rather one gnarled by a bitter history that includes Zelda's brother Dawie, a gentle man who has vanished or perhaps been banished. Also living with Zelda is her troubled teen-age niece, Ruth, who despises her coldhearted aunt. Ruth desperately wants to find out what happened to her parents, a story no one will tell her. Were they really killed in a car accident, as Zelda claims? Could her father still be alive? Although it's not hard to solve the puzzle, which verges on melodrama in its neatly wrapped ending, *The Innocents* unfolds like a good, tense mystery that is counterbalanced and broadened by the racial violence that erupts ever closer to the remote de Valera farm. Ms. Slaughter's ability to reveal the ultimate damage of suppression gives her novel its force. Only Willie, a spirited young black man, can rise above the flames.

Cheri Fein, in a review of "The Innocents," in The New York Times Book Review, *July 13, 1986, p. 18.*

LINDSAY DUGUID

The Innocents is an attempt to fuse—if not to reconcile—two visions of Africa: not simply the white view and the black view, but the opposition of old Africa, in which the benevolent *baas* was free to rule his men, and a new Africa without liberty and with the barest promise of hope. In the novel the old Africa, mostly seen through a child's eyes, is heat and emptiness, a land of shimmering horizons, dotted with native villages, orchards and *dorps*. . . . The new Africa is seen in the munitions factories, the ugly brick huts built to house black workers, and in the burnt-out buildings and corpse-strewn roads.

The focus is clearer on the old Edenic realm. Carolyn Slaughter tells a tale, set against a background of a feudal farm in a time not unlike the present, of family disintegration, prejudice and repressed passion. The account of the white twins Dawie and Zelda, growing up on the farm with the local black girl, Hannah, whom they treat as their equal, involves thwarted love, orphans, squandered inheritances and murdered lovers. It is partly told through Zelda and Hannah's evocations of the past and partly re-enacted through Dawie and Hannah's child Ruth, a character whose adolescent intensity makes her convincing as both victim and agent of the future, a fitting symbol for modern Africa. As each element in the family history is uncovered, the influence of the past on the present becomes clear and the cleverly mapped plot produces a series of minor revelations, detonated at intervals.

Slaughter is clearly at home in nostalgic re-creations of childhood, and her heavily cadenced monologues, with their jagged Afrikaans interjections, lend an intensity to the first two parts of her novel, which are concerned with the past. The third, in which the story moves to the riot-torn city, takes in the later career of Dawie, now a white liberal lawyer married to a vindictive but faithless wife, and attempts to describe the present reality of life in Cape Town and Port Elizabeth, is less convincing; one particularly notices the absence of the vivid descriptive writing of the earlier part of the book. Towards the end we return to the country, and as the local police chief makes sure that the black workers are turned off the farm and the rioting turns to bombing in the cities, there is a suggestion of a happy ending, a hint that, in the return of Dawie and the birth of Ruth's (black) son, there is a faint hope for the future.

In such a novel as this, history as well as geography is a backdrop to the action; Carolyn Slaughter uses impending disaster to heighten tension and, although she makes discreet use of symbols, she succeeds in conveying the passionate intensity of her characters. The vagueness and diffidence of the finale, however, in which several possible outcomes are suggested before the rather idealized ending, is a disappointment. There remains a sense of doomsday deferred.

Lindsay Duguid, "Doomsday Deferred," in The Times Literary Supplement, *No. 4348, August 1, 1986, p. 844.*

Sharon Thesen
1946-

Canadian poet and critic.

In her poetry, Thesen satirizes and celebrates elements of contemporary life by combining scatological imagery and intertextual associations in a lyric verse style. Asserting that the female poet must transcend her traditional role as passive muse, Thesen uses bold and startling syntax to examine the changing status of women in social and personal relationships. Judy Robinson stated: "Sharon Thesen's gutsy approach to language is a challenge to experience the unexpected and frightening roles that may well be the future of man's interpersonal relations."

In her first two collections of verse, *Artemis Hates Romance* (1980) and *Holding the Pose* (1983), Thesen concentrates upon the subject of communication in social relationships, particularly examining how male-dominated language contributes to exploitation of women. While occasionally faulting her poems as overwritten, critics generally praised Thesen's interpretation of romantic lyricism, comparing her style to the writings of such poets as Robert Creeley and William Butler Yeats. In *Confabulations: Poems for Malcolm Lowry* (1984), Thesen blends her own voice with that of novelist Malcolm Lowry to explore myths surrounding the troubled author's life and career. Reviewers commended Thesen's objective portrait of her subject and her imaginative recreation of Lowry's narrative technique. Sherrill Grace commented: "Thesen has attempted to meet Lowry on his own ground, and because she has succeeded in creating, capturing, and echoing his heteroglossia she has added to the story, continued the dialogue, contributed to the confabulating."

The Beginning of the Long Dash (1987), which takes its title from the National Research time signal that is broadcast daily on Canadian radio, examines the influence of time and human desire upon language. Emphasizing her acute observation and satirical wit, critics lauded Thesen's innovative use of the lyric form. Mary di Michele observed: "[Thesen] writes exquisitely in the lyric mode and manages to deflate it at the same time, like releasing a balloon she's blown up to bursting, for the effect, the rude sound it makes as it releases its load of stale breath."

to experience the unexpected and frightening roles that may well be the future of man's interpersonal relations.

Judy Robinson, in a review of "Artemis Hates Romance," in Quill and Quire, *Vol. 46, No. 12, December, 1980, p. 34.*

JUDY ROBINSON

[This book, by a western Canadian, attempts] to shatter the barriers in man's interpersonal communication. In *Artemis Hates Romance,* Sharon Thesen unlocks man's central anger, fear and frustration by stripping away romantic idealism. She personifies Eros in common objects such as steering wheels, streetlights and even stones. In **"Jack and Jill"** "Jack fell down the hill / breaking his head on the stones / of the earth / The stones of the earth / are the petrified heads of women / mouths agape." . . .

Sharon Thesen's gutsy approach to language is a challenge

BERT ALMON

Sharon Thesen's second book [*Holding the Pose*], like its predecessor *Artemis Hates Romance,* shows talent beset by some damaging mannerisms. Thesen often impresses me with the intensity of her attitudes—bitterness, passion, anger, boredom (in Baudelaire's sense). But the tone sometimes arises from verbal tricks that become tiresome and flippant: snappy colloquialisms, arch interjections (hey, oh, eh) and patronizing phrases.

The third poem in the collection, **"Spiritual,"** is a good example. It deals elegantly with silver imported cars, an inconsequential subject, and we are told that they "sleep / the night away, oh they sleep / that bad old night away." The poem is undercut by its own archness. The opposite extreme comes when Thesen assumes an intensity of mood that nothing in the poem quite justifies, as in **"Libretto,"** which ends:

One goes mad with it.
The cat dragging in birds, etc.
This absolutely black

mood a song for
graceless singers.

I won't linger on the "etc.," a flippancy that shows up in two other poems. The body of the poem hints that the black mood arises from a hangover or a cheating heart. We need to know which. But the poem holds out on us.

The poets Thesen echoes most often in her new book are Robert Creeley and William Butler Yeats, two highly mannered stylists. One important influence on Thesen's style seems to be Creeley's restrained, even choked lyricism. Like Creeley, Thesen writes in short lines that tend to hold back utterance as much as they release it. . . . Once in a while Thesen achieves Creeley's blend of diminished music and aphoristic statement, as in **"Discourse"**:

A quiet night, they all are.
My kid asleep
my husband out screwing around
the cat also. Even spring
is false, crocuses sprout purple
into January sunlight,
poor little things.

Outside, at a glance
headlights dance in the alleyway
mercury vapor night entranced.

Women laughing somewhere
dogs barking. Susie splitting up
with Tom at Bino's Pancake House.

And finally there's not
all that much
you can say.

The small vocabulary
of love needs its own
thin blue dictionary.

The witty juxtaposition of the cat and the husband redeems the archness of "poor little things," and the conclusion has a fine generalizing ring that doesn't sound pretentious because it makes a modest claim. I like poems such as **"The Plenitude"** where short lines are counterpointed with long, sinuous sentences. But this poet seems trapped inside a constraining style. Several poems display her knowledge of linguistics and contemporary criticism. She must be aware of possibilities for opening up the language of poetry to make it more daring, and more generous.

One way Thesen does extend herself is through the poetic sequence. There are two in this book. Neither is as interesting as **"Parts of Speech"** in *Artemis Hates Romance*. **"Radio New France Radio"** has an important subject: life in Quebec on the eve of the referendum. While the poet does create a tense atmosphere, the political and social issues don't emerge very clearly. Instead the situation is dealt with in a personal way and without a strong narrative line. One other poem in *Holding the Pose*, **"X,"** shows a desire to comment on public issues—this time the use of political torture. But it too is a purely personal response. . . . The other sequence is **"Long Distance: an Octave,"** which is close in style and content to **"Parts of Speech."** It doesn't arouse the expectations that the Quebec sequence disappoints, but deals wittily with love, separated lovers, and language.

I suspect that this will be a very successful book. Thesen writes well and in a fashionable style. I could linger over her skill at ending poems or single out some of her fine images. But I would rather invoke Yeats, a writer who could transcend his own success, widen his technique and subject matter, and find terms for dealing with public issues. Holding the pose is exactly what Thesen should not do. (pp. 39-40)

Bert Almon, "Thesen's Pose," in The Canadian Forum, *Vol. LXIV, No. 746, February, 1985, pp. 39-40.*

KATHLEEN MOORE

The Combined gifts of actress, analyst, and anecdotalist are essential to create convincing biography. Add to these the eventful language demanded of a poem, the compression, the crystallized insight, and the task may approach heroic dimensions. Dramatic identification with a morbid genius such as Malcolm Lowry was, must be especially difficult to achieve; no less the sustaining compassion from which a sensitive portrait must arise. . . .

That Lowry's talent for transmitting his mordant vision has been internationally celebrated with cannibalistic fervour, suggests to me the decayed spiritual health of the scatological voyeurs who rejoice in and feast upon his misery rather than weep that such personal horror is intellectually titillating and commercially viable. Thus, the historical and literary contexts in which Thesen has to struggle for a re-vision of this man, themselves demand perceptive analysis and comment.

Confabulations defeats dramatic development by uncritically shifting viewpoint from omnipotent narrator to first-person in the voice of Lowry. This creates a nebulous perspective. Clichés abound, and too many participles drain the cycle's potential energy, negating the subterranean tensions that must account for the volcano's gradual incandescence and eruption. Emotional identification is absent, and thus the sympathy is formal rather than special. Criticism of society's response to the man, and its part in creating him is virtually unattempted.

Thesen's painting of Lowry must, finally, compete with his own 10-year laboured image of himself: the language of *Under the Volcano;* the dramatic texture. So considered then, Thesen may not be entirely to blame if her treatment of one of the century's most complex and self-destructive personalities falls short of revelation.

Kathleen Moore, in a review of "Confabulations: Poems for Malcolm Lowry," in Books in Canada, *Vol. 14, No. 2, March, 1985, p. 25.*

PAMELA BANTING

Sharon Thesen's second book of poems, *Holding the Pose,* displays on its cover three identical snapshots of the author, herself holding the pose. Traditionally, it is the artist's model or the woman who plays the role of the muse who holds the pose. Sharon poses as her own muse. She is split: as woman she is a muse. But as a woman writer she is not amused. In her first book, *Artemis Hates Romance,* she talked back:

To "honeybunch," you stupid fucker, you never
thought I'd do it did ya, you slimy hogstool, I hope
you rot in hell you no good bum with your big

mouth and your endless threats about breaking both my thumbs. What a joke, it was just a lousy way of shutting me up and you knew it.

But of course, even the sass and backtalk trade to a large extent in masculine cliché and thus point to the female writer's aporia of discourse. She can only speak out against him in masculine terms, in masculine language. In the cover photographs for **Holding the Pose,** Thesen, as a woman, poses as the stereotype of the represented or the representable, the muse figure. As a woman writer, a "lady poet" (she has said that to be a lady poet is to perform a spectacle of the ridiculous in public life), she is a mimic, and the very act of speaking her own desire simultaneously alienates or distances that desire behind a barrier of language not her own.

Thesen presents the cover girl, she whose image is used by the dominant culture to maintain and promote women's marginalization, as radical subversive. Thesen's deliberate and wholly conscious holding of the pose . . . subverts the operation of the pose.

In her latest book, **Confabulations,** which was nominated for the Governor General's Award for 1984, Thesen strikes another pose and takes on another voice, that of the writer Malcolm Lowry, in a series of poems she calls "confabulations." A confabulation is a conversation, a familiar talk, a chat. To confabulate is also to devise imaginary experiences after the loss of memory, to fill in those gaps by free fabrication. In the acknowledgements to **Confabulations,** Thesen credits various reference sources, stating that "images and situations, however, have been lifted, spliced, and grafted where they were not just out-and-out invented." In the title and the credits, she invokes the play between truth and the imaginary and sets this play within the context of discourse, written and spoken. (p. 54)

All this dialogical play creates a fascinating weave of voices in the text. Some of the sections are written in the first person as Malcolm Lowry himself speaking. Some sections in the first person are in Thesen's voice. Others also written in the first person are indeterminate. The voice might be either Lowry's or Thesen's. In the following section, the voice, which until this point in the book had been speaking almost uniformly in the third person, shifts to first person as Thesen openly addresses Lowry—writer to writer:

> Should I say
> Malcolm, your name
> is the sound
> of clam-tracks,
> the knock of kelp
> on rock? Or Clarence,
> wooden matches hissing
> at nightfall?
>
> There you would be
> sitting on the clam-hole beach
> in the noonday sun
> & two seconds later
> your house is in flames.
> Again. Manuscripts
> & bottles of Bols gin
> snatched from the hellfire
> always at your heels
> panting & fanged.
>
> Correspondences
> too creepy to ignore.
> Or maybe just bad

> ventilation, rotten
> luck. You were right
> about a lot of things—
> *this world*
> scissored your mind,
> bone-dry shreds of ecstasy
> & terror igniting
> your fragile nests.

The voice shifts again for the next poem. It is written in Lowry's voice, or perhaps I should say in Thesen's imitation of Lowry's voice.

This is followed by a poem written technically in the third person, but the language creates such a degree of ambiguity that it is really impossible to tell whose voice this is, or whether it is a strange hybrid of Lowry's and Thesen's voices:

> On the third boozeless day he rose,
> virtue restored. Publishers
> written to. A long, less
> wibberley wobberley walk
> along the beach rocks.
> The delicate white haze
> outside now, flattened zinc
> coin of sea & sun a platinum
> wavering disc.
> Wharf creaking in the wake
> of a tug, ferns
> soaking up stones. The world
> his oyster.
> *"Welcome home," my wife*
> *smiles, greeting me.*
> *"Ah yes, my darling, it really is*
> *home now. I love those curtains*
> *you made."*

The parody in the first two lines suggests to the reader that despite the third-person pronoun this section of the poem may be an excerpt from Lowry's own ironic inner dialogue. Indeed the tone is similar to that in the famous epitaph Lowry wrote for himself, quoted as one of the epigraphs to Thesen's book. "Publishers / written to" suggests a mental checking off of items on a personal list, a list which seems to include, in the italicized lines, acting the role of husband to his apparently patient wife. Thesen also extends the ambiguousness of the speaker in her play with the distinction between inside and outside in the lines: "The delicate white haze / outside now." In these two lines, the absence of a pronoun (outside him, outside me?) and a verb further underlines the sense that this must be Lowry's voice. By the time the reader reaches "The world / his oyster," the word "his" itself seems inconclusive. It ought to name Thesen as the speaker, but it still could as easily be Lowry. Both possibilities are equally valid. These lines are followed by the italicized lines which are quoted from one of the documentary sources on Lowry's life. Lowry's spoken voice has become his written voice, in the context of a book written by a third writer. The next section of this long poem suitably begins:

> So why not a visit to our old friend
> the bootlegger
> on so fine an afternoon?

To whom does the "our" refer? Lowry, ostensibly, but it is capable of incorporating Thesen too.

The first stanza of the book as a whole is totally indeterminate as to point of view. In fact, the stanza itself is about the act of viewing. A film, a life, one's own life or another's? Where does the difference lie? What we have is Thesen's fiction- and poetry-making voice in dialogue with fragments of Lowry's voice also fictionalizing and constructing his life. (pp. 54-5)

Admist all this blending of voices, Thesen as writer situates herself as simply another voice in the text. A reader like you or me, she positions herself simultaneously both inside and outside the text. She engages her subject in conversation. She dialogues with language itself, variously the language of Lowry's own fictions, his letters, his biography, and even with her own words. (p. 55)

If the exigencies of patriarchal culture force the female writer to write in male language and within the old boys' network of canonized tradition, then it is in the process of her engagement with this language and this tradition that she begins to dismantle its codes and structures. In interweaving her own voice with that of Lowry, Thesen challenges traditional notions of the relationship of the writer to her documentary material. She does not write out of a self-reflexive identification with her subject, nor does she subject him to her "objective" gaze. Thesen is not the writer as "espider." Rather, she approaches Lowry through his own discourse, through confabulations. The voice we as readers hear is the throaty voice of the canny gypsy fortune-teller gazing into her crystal ball, confabulating, filling in gaps. (p. 56)

Pamela Banting, "Shifting Voices," in Brick: A Journal of Reviews, *No. 27, Spring, 1986, pp. 54-6.*

FRED WAH

Sharon Thesen writes lyric poetry. Along with writers like Gerry Gilbert and Barry McKinnon, she has written some of the finest lyric poetry in the west in recent years. While her output has not been large—*Artemis Hates Romance* (1980), *Radio New France Radio* (1981)—the sophistication of her writing indicates a major presence in the lyric. Her poems exude "feeling," and she has a well-trained and discriminating sense of language. The most useful approach I have found in evaluating her poetry is to try to clarify the notion of "lyric" through the use of a statement which Charles Olson pursued in his seminars in Buffalo in 1965: "the subjective as objective requires correct processing."

I have never been absolutely sure what Olson meant by that statement, but it has always intrigued me. I think it refers to the "private as public" and the "one and the many." In Thesen's poetry certain aspects of the statement start to make sense. The "subjective" is feeling, personal and private emotion, sensation, interior, physiology, and proprioception. The "objective" in this case is the public poem, the song, the lyric. Feeling gets registered in the body by the stomach, pulse, heart, breath, etc. and these sensations are notated in the lyric poem as "cadence," the "correct processing" through language.

Lyric distinguishes itself from narrative as being primarily cadential. Cadence is the movement of rhythm and harmony towards a close. . . . The poem itself can be felt as one large cadence. Shorter phrases, stanzas, and cadences can be determined within the poem. So as well as the elements of the syllable and the line important in all poetry, the lyric objectifies emotion into the basic relationship of the phrase or cadence. Sharon Thesen has been very successful in achieving a substantial voice in this mode.

How do you feel about "place": where you are, where you

were, where you want to be? The "locus," at least in western Canadian poetry, is a real concern and provides the impetus for a major portion of the writing there. Thesen's poetry is full of this sense of place. . . . *Radio New France Radio* is a collection of pieces written while Thesen lived in Montreal for a year. Her loneliness in the foreign city and her distance from her home city, Vancouver, are primary movers for this sequence. The actual city geography informs the poems which are responses to streets, laundromats, weather, politics, and her own aloneness. The book even ends with an abstract poem entitled **"The City of the End of Things."** The feelings which generate these poems arise from the poet's subjective reaction to a geographical and personal situation.

What makes a poem a lyric is the way in which the feelings are voiced by the cadence. Without going into the linguistic phenomena which signal cadence, I want to point out how the cadences generally operate in the poem beginning **"At the typewriter."** It is a direct response to being alone in the city.

> At the typewriter
> thinking something up
> while the Saturday night cabs
> honk & sidle up & down
> the snowy streets.
>
> I should probably be in one
> all dolled up
> in a midnight blue sequined gown
> but Christ, the air in this place
> so crackling & dry—
> too many more sparks
> & this whole town
> could go up in flames.

The movement of the poem feels shaped into three cadences, each one closing where the voice comes to a major natural rest. The first stanza with a high point on "Saturday night cabs" comes to a close on "the snowy streets." The next phrase ends on "gown," a rest not signalled by punctuation but certainly by syntax. The last section is perhaps two but definitely one cadence ending on "flames." These cadences are determined by the poet's recognition of internal motion. The feelings are signalled in the same way that any statement determined by feeling is then actualized by significant breaks and junctures in the syntax. The result is a phrasing or shaping of the language by the "voice," a physical response to an emotional impulse. There is other physiolinguistic evidence in the poem, such as line, pitch, and onset, but I think what is so impressive about Thesen's writing is the clarity of the larger phrase or cadence. The poem is successful because it so cleanly juxtaposes the movement of feeling and the movement of voice.

Thesen's perception of the place is overlaid with her feelings about being in it, and the place becomes imbued with images and sensations from inside the poet. She balances the geography out there with heartography within. **"Japanese Movies,"** the first poem in *Artemis Hates Romance,* illustrates how Thesen uses this balance in her play with phrasing. The poem is "for Prince George" and begins with an aloof descriptive language.

> The dreamy-eyed
> heading somewhere
> with their load of sticks
> for fire—
>
> the wholly seminal life—

unless we lead it
leads us
toward what dark wood
where cold Snow Lady waits
with blackened teeth
to cure you
of the fear of life—

The quotation shows Thesen using the close of the third cadence, "leads us," as a double, with the line also pivoting syntactically on the following phrase. This is a nice change from the prior phrases which are strongly signalled out by the spacing and punctuation. The aloof "we" in this section of the poem shifts in the second half to a closer "you," and the poet's feelings about the place are given a harsher and more striking definition. The second section also pivots very nicely on a repetition (shadows of the double space above).

    o, the fear of life
    stinks—

    dirty snow in the dogshit early spring
    & a life craved someplace else
    not here—

    the long hard kiss of death
    beauty gives
    unless she loves you

    her treachery then doubled
    & you don't wise up to it
    until you trust her

    & the snow blows away her footprints

I find the lyricism of this writing engaging. Thesen intensifies feelings by punctuating the longer cadences with shorter ones. There is movement in this variation, and the strong monosyllabic rhythm is stronger because of the clarity of the larger phrases in which it is enclosed.

Outside place is important to the lyric poet, to Thesen, because it provides a way of making some sense of the inside. The subjective place is a wave of nebulous impulses and sensations which can sometimes be articulated by zeroing in on the visual world. In a recent poem called **"Evocation,"** Thesen outlines her sense of the connections between things out there and the feelings they elicit.

    Among the many
    & many things
    there is a place
    for you & you & you.
    Among the many melodies
    the dustcloth plays upon
    piano keys there is
    Heart of My Heart

The poem continues naming qualities and things ("sunbeams," "windowpanes," "painful yellow tulips") and then settles on a metaphysical place.

    This pulsing thought
    that thinks of things,
    how yellow petals of the sun
    are metonymy for roses
    the bees devour.
    That certitude lies
    in the never-never place
    where no things dwell
    among the many things.

It is the "pulsing thought" that is the connection between the

subjective and the objective. Pulse and flow, from inside to outside to inside, rhythm, dance, and finally the poem's own pace of word-picture, line, syllable, cadence.

And how do you feel about being lost? Lost in yourself, lost in the world, lost in love? Such questions are a major kind of cadence which the lyricist can work with. The base from which questions can be asked dwells in the personal conception of being lost or confused. Thesen has a lovely poem which says much of this. It's called **"Being Lost, As Usual."** . . . The poem is based on a simple question and answer structure, but the way in which Thesen uses the shift from question to answer is very powerful and shows a strong ear for the shape and the shaping of the language. "Listen, I've never been lost / in the geography, / only in the map" is an intriguing statement and is given a lot of its strength by the way it is highlighted in the poem. It is one of those statements around which one can imagine writing a poem.

I think it is indicative of Thesen's prowess as a poet, however, that most of her poetry does not rely overmuch on the question-answer structure but moves more towards statement. One particularly unsettling piece which lightly circles around question and answer is **"Mean Drunk Poem."** It is generated not so much by questions as by anger and confusion at a sense of woman's "impotence." The poem moves through a series of arguments and metaphors and ends on a particularly harsh and cutting note.

    Sing Om as you take the sausage rolls out of the
      oven.
    The Gap is real & there is no such thing as
    female intelligence. We're dumber than hell.

Most of Thesen's poems end on such strong cadence because she pays attention to the overall phrasing of the poem, usually statement-focused, to develop an interplay of the larger and smaller rhythmical units, seen by the intelligence as the invisible plan.

In other words, the heave of the feeling should get registered in the poem as a heave (shape) in the language. Stomach and heart, pulse, if paid attention to, provide a plan for the movements in the words. The most easily described aspect of this projection is the line. Thesen's use of the line is conventionally (in terms of the past thirty years) accurate in its register as a unit of breath-rhythm. Her lines are usually short (four to six words) and in accordance with the syntax (as opposed to being in dissonance with the syntax). Read **"Jack & Jill,"** for example:

    Your heart
    aching in your head
    I did not care about that
    A monstrosity of boredom.
    Jack went up the hill
    & Jack fell down the hill
    breaking his head on the stones
    of the earth.

Such lines exhibit careful, polished registration of the movement of language as it is shaped by proprioception, body feeling. Thesen's ability to articulate the movement is an ability to perceive the close relationship between utterance and feeling in the lyric. The poem is more than a heart aching in the head. It is the linear control which can highlight the feeling. It is the particularization of the language by the ear hearing the heave of the heart.

As I pointed out in reference to **"Mean Drunk Poem,"** Thesen's accurate notation of feeling and language extends to larger cadences. In **"Jack & Jill,"** the line "A monstrosity of boredom" takes on the same weight of cadence as the following four lines all together. As we read the poem, each shift of Thesen's awareness and intelligence informs each step of the composition. One line leads to the next, one syntax leads to another: "The stones" to "the earth" to "The moon" to "The not caring." And "mouth," "heart," "head," and "elbow" generate one another as small and large steps (stops) of the cadential progression of the poem. . . . The whole poem is itself, finally, one utterance, one larger shape which the smaller phrases flesh out.

I have tried to show how Thesen's poetry is lyrical by describing it as a successful processing of the subjective as objective. The poetry is grounded in feeling. It is proprioceptive. This is not unusual. As Steve McCaffrey has pointed out in a useful statement on the French critic Julia Kristeva, this "interface where the linguistic sign meets the unconscious and its instinctual drives" is relevant to all contemporary writing. I believe it is important, however, to see the use of the cadence as being the concrete evidence and notation of the lyrical sublanguage, the urge for the song. Thesen's use of the cadence feels precise, and her poems are exemplary of the contemporary lyric. (pp. 114-21)

Fred Wah, "Subjective as Objective: The Lyric Poetry of Sharon Thesen," in Essays on Canadian Writing, No. 32, Summer, 1986, pp. 114-21.

RONALD BINNS

This slender, handsomely-produced volume [*Confabulations*] consists of a sequence of twenty-seven poems, none longer than a page, which uses Lowry's life and writings as a springboard from which to sketch images of a visionary artist at bay. Some are written from the point of view of Lowry's own troubled psyche, others take a more detached view and look at Lowry from the outside. Some imperceptibly merge scenes from *Under the Volcano* and *Hear Us O Lord from Heaven Thy Dwelling Place* with episodes from the novelist's life recorded in Lowry's own correspondence and Douglas Day's biography.

This method proves surprisingly effective. The eleventh poem in the volume, for example, reads:

> So why not a visit to our old friend
> the bootlegger
> on so fine an afternoon?
>
> The dripping path grows
> pitch black. Some dogs howl
> at an absent moon, no drunk
> tells time. A flashlight
> beam from the dead
> of night finds him sprawled
> on the forest floor
> gobbling ferns—
>
> spitting spores
> around the names
> of constellations
> crawling the sky.

Here, Sharon Thesen begins with a scene from Lowry's story "Gin and Goldenrod." The light conversational tone of the first stanza mimics the easygoing lyrical start to the story. But

Lowry's story—as its title indicates—is about opposites. Hell and darkness, signified by gin and alcoholism, lurk within Lowry's protagonist, constantly threatening to engulf the fragile paradise of Eridanus symbolized by the golden flower. . . . "Gin and Goldenrod," about a return visit to a bootlegger to pay off a debt, raises the spectre of the hero's alcoholism: "Where, actually, had he spent that night? Had he slept on the ground? drunk the bottle? where had he fallen?" The story, which ends on a note of hope and reconciliation, does not answer these questions. Sharon Thesen's second stanza gives us one possible answer in its picture of Lowry sprawled on the ground. Thesen gives us the dark underside of Lowry's Canada: the "dripping path" not only refers to "Gin and Goldenrod" but also evokes "The Forest Path to the Spring." The preponderance of monosyllabic words makes the stanza echo with the rhythms of a thumping sinister drum beat. This threatening world of mysterious howling dogs and unexplained flashlight beams has an oddly dislocated quality about it.

In part Thesen's poem owes something to an anecdote about Lowry's last days in Canada which his biographer has interpreted as a significant anticipation of the writer's subsequent semi-suicide:

> Lowry, crying with shame, threw himself onto the floor of the forest beside the path, rolled over on to his back, and stretched out his arms above his head. He was lying in a bed of tall ferns and when he grasped some of their leaves, he stripped them of their bitter spores, which he thrust into his mouth with both hands, chewing and swallowing compulsively. A very paradigm of compulsive orality— and ominously prophetic of the manner in which, one evening three-and-a-half years later, he clapped handfuls of sodium amytal tablets into his mouth.

But if the second stanza alludes both to Lowry's real and imaginary Canada it also draws on his nightmarish vision of Mexico. Thesen's evocative dark forest brings to mind Chapter Eleven of *Under the Volcano,* and the path in the rain to Parián. The figure of Lowry the future suicide "spitting spores / around the names / of constellations / crawling the sky" merges with that of his fictional creation Yvonne, who as she lies dying on the forest floor also sees the constellations wheeling in the sky and dreams of the destruction of her imaginary Canadian paradise.

Thesen's technique of blending the biographical with the fictional works well and parallels the often opaque transaction's in Lowry's own writing between his fictional protagonists and his legend. As a short economical poem of fifteen lines **"So why not a visit . . ."** exists successfully in its own right as a dramatization of a brief episode in Lowry's life. At the same time it is enormously enriched by the complex of factual and creative material it both incorporates and subliminally echoes.

What most attracts Thesen in her representation of Lowry the visionary writer are the final years of his life. The first poem in the volume seems to describe Lowry on his last trip to New York and begins on "A dove-grey morning / soon to turn blue." It takes us inside Lowry's confused and tormented mind, his "mouth talking" but the sense missing. The volume ends with a mirror image of Lowry at the very end of his life (perhaps on his last night alive), "all things for the mouth / shattered." This emphasis on Lowry's mouth neatly draws together the anecdote about Lowry swallowing the spores of ferns, Lowry gulping down a lethal overdose of sodium amytal tablets, and the novelist's compulsive fascination with what comes out of the mouth—words. The book ends on a moment of stasis and ironic lyricism. . . . (pp. 85-6)

Confabulations moves full circle from the "dove-grey morning" of the first verse to the morning which appears at the end of the twenty-seventh one. The wheel turns full circle, and this, too, seems appropriate given the cyclic structure of much of Lowry's writing. (p. 86)

In between these two mornings we encounter poems of Mexico, Canada, and England which take us into Lowry's prolonged dark night of the soul. Thesen's version of Lowry clearly owes much to Douglas Day's biography, but in acknowledging her sources she emphasizes that "Images and situations . . . have been lifted, spliced, and grafted where they were not just out-and-out invented. This, then, is not intended to be a factual account of Malcolm Lowry's life." This approach is a sensible one, given the labyrinthine complexity and manifold ambiguities of the Lowry myth. When Thesen lists the traumas of Lowry's childhood—"the nanny who tried to smother me / one day on the cliff, / the Syphilis Museum / on Paradise Road, / my diseased eyes"—they are, in strict biographical terms, probably untrue. . . . The doubtfulness of these "facts" is of little consequence, however: the important thing is that they were real for Lowry as he constructed a romantic edifice around his relatively quiet and conventional childhood. It is however careless of Thesen to identify Paradise Street as Paradise *Road,* a mistake Lowry would never have made, and in her brief account of Lowry's death at the beginning of the book she wrongly describes him as being 46 when he died.

In taking us inside Lowry's mind and ironically describing his "immense / imagination" Thesen seems wryly to acknowledge the fabulist in Lowry. (pp. 86-7)

Thesen's title, ***Confabulations,*** is beautifully appropriate, since it means both "to devise imaginary experiences after loss of memory" and to converse or chat. Many of these poems do have an elastic, conversational quality, without ever becoming prosaic and flat. Thesen's virtues as a poet are her spare, thoughtful use of words and her sense of rhythm. The words dance across and down the page, enlivened by striking metaphors. . . .

At its best Thesen's poetry is reminiscent of the later work of John Berryman, as in her superb evocation of Lowry at work in his shack at Dollarton, B.C. . . . In giving us an image of Lowry *the writer,* someone who takes "up to a whole afternoon / to find the word / I need." Thesen valuably reminds us that no matter how colourful and compelling the Lowry myth may be, it is the writing rather than the life that matters. ***Confabulations*** both enriches and is enriched by Lowry's work, and this is a striking achievement. (p. 87)

Ronald Binns, "Lowry's Mouths," in Canadian Literature, No. 112, Spring, 1987, pp. 85-7.

MARY DI MICHELE

Sharon Thesen hates romance: "the barren reach / of modern desire." Yoking romantic diction and lyric form with fragments of pop lyrics and culture, she subjects our world of "broken discourse" to an acerbic scrutiny [in ***The Beginning***

of the Long Dash]. As a poet, she's a brilliant lyricist who is always aware of the limits of that form:

> While the strictures of the lyric
> huddle in the aether
> fumbling with matches, trying
> to do something with language.
>
> **("Eclipse Calypso")**

You can light no fires in the aether. Thesen brings in oxygen, fresh air, satirical energy. She writes exquisitely in the lyric mode and manages to deflate it at the same time, like releasing a balloon she's blown up to bursting, for the effect, the rude sound it makes as it releases its load of stale breath. It's no accident that my analogy refers to breaking wind. Like all satirists, Thesen is often scatological in her imagery and language. If there's a bed of flowers, she'll have a dog trot in who "gilds the landlord's tiger lilies." Two pages before **"The Landlord's Flower Beds,"** "gild" was used in another poem, **"The Stone,"** to describe monks illuminating female figures in those parchments that preserved our culture through the Dark Ages. Thesen is one of the cleverest satirists I've read; she celebrates and smears at the same time. The activities of the monks and the dog are linguistically linked, and a contextual irony is achieved.

Thesen's work is essentially a poetry of linguistic impulse. She is constantly exploring where the language is taking her and the reader. She manipulates verbal associations and responses. In **"Being Adults"** she sets up, with the phrase "The doctor's BMW / etherized in the alley," the appearance of "old Prufrock" later on in the poem. It is not the logic of narrative that causes Prufrock's appearance but the concatenation of verbal association. In other words, the development of the poem is linguistically generated: "Our language careers / us around the bend" or "language breakdances / the invisible."

This is an intelligent and extremely selfconscious kind of writing. The "writer as satyr / in the front seat of a taxi aroused / & full of intent." The play of syntax and meaning is ingenious. How is a taxi aroused? When it is a satire or satyr of the poet, of course, the poet who is writing, ah, *driving* the taxi. (pp. 36-7)

Mary di Michele, "Breakdancing the Invisible," in Books in Canada, Vol. 17, No. 2, March, 1988, pp. 36-7.

PHYLLIS WEBB

This isn't exactly a garland for Sharon Thesen. After all, she has Malcolm Lowry, in ***Confabulations,*** saying, "I am murdered by the pistils / of mauve orchids in a white vase." There's also a "Nosebleed like an opened tap / pouring into my hands, tossed / like roses at the cheering crowd." Yet her flowers, the subject of this little piece, she calls "imaginations companion, compadre / Without Blame." The lack of the possessive apostrophe could possibly indicate that one cannot own or claim *"natura naturans";* it also pluralizes "imagination" so that one is tempted to speculate on the existence of different kinds of imaginations. For Thesen's flowers operate in various ways in her wry lyricism. These virginal (until the bees devour them), contingent beauties are there to be talked to, walked with, observed, aesthetically enjoyed, caught in their dollar value, neighbour's pruning shears, their pain. For, yes, they seem to suffer, as the poet does. . . . (p. 83)

I don't know what *The Secret Life of Plants* did to Ruskin's pathetic fallacy, but Thesen's consciousness is entirely twentieth century, despite her defense of a vocabulary that includes words like "soul," "beauty," and "spirit." In **"Postscript to Duncan McNaughton,"** where the idea of perfection the tulips convey is most accurately observed and precisely stated, the word "perfect," in one form or another, occurs three times in a twelve-line poem, the third climactic entry in a sensuous description of their seductive colouration: "—And the color, yellow creasing the edges / of that perfect blushy red." Gorgeous stuff, followed by the lyrical abstraction I dare to quote again:

> O *natura naturans*
> imaginations companion, compadre
> Without Blame
> **("Postscript to Duncan McNaughton,"** *Artemis Hates Romance*)

Without Blame? I slant over to the *I Ching;* I open it at random, chance is chance, after all, to hexagram number 62, "Preponderance of the small," in which the phrase "no blame" occurs twice in the interpretation of the lines. The commentary says that "No blame" means that one is in position to correct one's mistakes in the right way. If we amend mistakes by a return to the right path, no blame remains. We are in the territory of Thesen's own moral imperatives. Her tulips are without blame not because they have mistakes to amend, but because we do; they are our guiding stars, emblematic of our own lost innocence, gone beauty, fallen grace, our cracked ideal forms.

The flowers appearing in her first three books, *Artemis Hates Romance, Holding the Pose,* and *Confabulations, Poems for Malcolm Lowry,* occur repeatedly, though not, I think, all that consciously, mainly in two ways: either besmirched by men, falsified and degraded, or as blooming talismans of perfection, goodness, love, aesthetic delight, and as symbols of the creative lyric impulse.

> The defoliated
> imagination is the end
> of all lyric. The rose deformed
> & the daisy impotent
> & the poet dance
> to no sound but
> the sound stolen from God.
> **("Day Dream,"** *Artemis Hates Romance*)

In our time "defoliation" has sinister overtones of Agent Orange, Vietnam, and the local highways department. Poetry and imaginations must struggle for survival. Each flowery appearance intensifies the sense of compadre, companion: *an associate, comrade; a person paid to live or travel with another; one of a pair or set.* The companion shares jeopardy and violence, springs up to ward off the Evil Eye, or just plain evil. . . . Or their virginal innocence is defiled:

> The gray-faced neighbour
> clears his
> phlegmy throat
> before stooping
> into the car,
> spits
> into the lilac bush.
> **("Ladies Advice,"** *Malahat* #72)

That gratuitous insult is like a slap in the face or worse. Flowers are usually seen as female and sexual, and in women's poetry their presence might seem dangerously self-reflexive. There's an interesting absence of carnivorous blooms, e.g. the Venus flytrap, in the poetry of Sharon Thesen, though she comes close with those murderous "pistils of mauve orchids" that so scared Malcolm Lowry. Or their absence might reflect geographical exactitude—the west coast doesn't produce an abundance of floral carnivores, except in greenhouses where sexy orchids also grow. The female imagination prefers to image her companions as spontaneous perfect form and colour, unselfconscious, pure as the lilies of the field. Or she relates them to the airiness and movement of nonsyntactic music. . . . But Thesen never promised us a rose garden, and in **"Turquoise Carnations"** she considers the intrusive mentation, warped aesthetics, and sick fancy that can skewer the talismanic ideal of *"natura naturans."* . . . (pp. 84-6)

If, on the whole, her flowers are radiant bystanders to the events of news and history, they virtually disappear in a poem of personal displacement and alienation called **"Radio New France Radio."** It's about her time in Montreal, that city where "the Saturday night cabs / honk & sidle up & down / the snowy streets." There is only one reference to flowers in its dozen pages close to the end when un-named walkers are "bitten" by unnamed blossoms "extravagant & common." A street clown's spastic act, beige hills, a dry cleaner in another language, displaced flamenco dancers, late night bad TV, a sky yellow & greasy are all depressed presences in the depressed atmosphere of the poem. Thesen's natural landscape seems to be the west coast where the preponderance of the small rectifying moments of being are enough in evidence through all four seasons to offer hope, hope that is nevertheless so minimal, perhaps illusory, it can only be caught in unguarded moments. The resulting lyricism is usually undercut and given that Thesenesque bitter, sardonic twist:

> Crimson gladiolus
> in a shop window
> nearly brings me to tears—
> call the poet
> a love poet
> then watch her hands—
> you'd be surprised
> what she does
> with the roses.
> **("Lecture Noir,"** *Holding the Pose*)

This undercutting is characteristic of Artemis who hates romance. Of course, Artemis *really* loves romance, or would love *a* romance, a corsage for the prom, etc., but she knows only too well that the phlegmy neighbour will probably spit in the lovely lilac face. Hence Thesen's valuing of "strife" in a poem. "By strife," she says in **"A Few Notes on Poetry,"** "I mean the awareness, during the act of writing, of the field that we are in: the apparent 'tradition'; the forces of repression both inside and outside; the freshly-prepared ground of the contemporary (innovation, influence, pleasures, displeasures), and the tone of the culture generally—and these are just for starters." Her constant yet un-nervous awareness in her own poem-making allows this strife to keep the poem in motion, up in the air, falling on its face and getting up again. It's a dangerous and hard won freedom she continually seeks, unbounded, broken through to, achieved, like the painful yellow tulips, by opening and opening and opening.

In *Confabulations* strife dominates the life of the poems, the mystery of redemption is left unsolved, the last lines of the last poem telling us "a mockingbird / pipes the morning in." And even in Wordsworth country the daffodils for Lowry are merely background to "oh bleak / bleak days of separation / from self & catastrophic states of mind." Thesen's use of a shifting "I"—first person voice of Lowry and / or the poet (*companionate, one of a pair or set*)—in this her most objective work, allows us to read that single, solitary line, italicized in the text, *"where I am it is dark"* as either Lowry's condition or hers. Sharon Thesen did not choose her subject casually. Lowry, larger than life, is also one of her imaginations' companions—not Without Blame but to whom one must attend, artist, writer ("you no wrider / you an espider"), *compadre*:

> Alone in the garden
> after a violent night
> he kisses the bright pink faces
> of peonies along the fence
> tasting bees & the hereafter.

> (*Confabulations*)
> (pp. 86-8)

Phyllis Webb, "Imagination's Companion," in The Malahat Review, *No. 83, June, 1988, pp. 83-8.*

STEPHEN SCOBIE

Writers all across Canada, hearing the title *The Beginning of the Long Dash,* reacted with a delight that was not unmixed with envy: why didn't *I* think of that first?! The phrase is instantly recognisable; we hear it every morning on the CBC, the National Research Council Time Signal. "At the beginning of the long dash, following ten seconds of silence, it will be precisely 10 o'clock, Pacific Standard Time." Thus it carries with it the complex intertext of Canadian nationality: of transcontinental time zones (half an hour earlier in Newfoundland), of our country's vast distances and fragile unity. Yet its use as a title shows that the phrase is also purely *detachable:* quotable, citable, re-citable. On its own, it takes on a life of its own. Its multiple suggestions move back to its radio origins and forward into the poems that follow, across the intermediate intertexts (frames, parerga) of the book's epigraphs, of the poems' titles. In doing so, they disrupt the notion of "beginning" and engage the reader in the pauses, the silences, the intermittence of desire.

A dash is itself an intermittence, defined only in relation to the moments of its absence. It interrupts the silence, or the silence interrupts it. A "long" dash is a paradox, almost a contradiction in terms; it too is defined differentially, being perceived as "long" only in relation to the *short* dashes which come before and after it. Similarly, the *beginning* of the long dash exists as a beginning only because it is preceded by something else, by (on the CBC) the ten seconds of silence, dead air, before it begins. So the moment of "beginning" is not an absolute one; inscribed in the differential traces of language, it is involved ("always already") in its own pre-beginnings and post-intermittences. (pp. 89-90)

The first poem in *The Beginning of the Long Dash* is entitled "Poem in Memory of an Earlier Poem." While the later reference to Malcolm Lowry might possibly suggest that the "earlier poem" is *Confabulations,* nothing in the text necessitates this reading; rather, the reader is free to understand it as a kind of generic title. *All* poems exist "in memory of " ear-

lier poems: this is the general condition of intertextuality. The "earlier poem," unnamed, is an absent origin, a displaced source, to which this poem defers. The beginning (of the book, of the long dash) is always deferred, back to something which precedes it. The title ("in memory of ") suggests an Elegy, a poem written *for* the dead, for the inaccessible objects of desire. "A moment ago," the poem begins (the "moment" of desire), "the light was perfect." Perfection is displaced into the past, so that the "poem itself " is, can only be, "a perfect memory" whose "occasion" is "another" light. The poem yearns for a perfection "so sudden I was there / without getting there," but this ideal can only be evoked indirectly, like the shadows in Blake's poem ["Visions of the Daughters of Albion"], through the moment / movement of "getting there." "A moment ago" is the movement until.

Struggling inside his own "moment of desire," Malcolm Lowry "always wrote standing up / his soul wanting to avoid / being fixed." The linebreak here suggests its own, very Lowry-esque, variation: "his soul wanting to < < wards > > a void." Lowry wanted always towards the void, the abyss, the barranca of *Under the Volcano.* The avid void is again that silence, that pause, that ten second intermittence which creates "the beginning of the long dash." Its images proliferate throughout the book. . . . Insofar as it is (as it was for Lowry) an *object* of desire, even the void is not attainable: his soul wants towards it, but does not reach it. Though unattainable, the void is not invisible; indeed, it manifests "all over the place," it leaves its traces behind, especially in *writing.* (pp. 91-2)

Void and margin interact as the site in which the moment of desire takes place, and they are joined in the intertextual pun on "reach." **"The Landlord's Tiger Lilies"** satirises "the barren reach / of modern desire." Rilke calls out to his angels, "If I thought you would answer me" (if, the conjunction which defers closure), and is answered only by the banal propriety of the last three lines. "Modern desire," it seems, is a contradiction in terms. But the "reach" is still there, reaching out like Lowry, "wanting to a < < > > void." "Reach" is also a noun meaning area, expanse, a stretch of a river, a headland, a bay—a space at the edge of water, between land and sea, a marsh, a marge, a margin. (p. 92)

Another image of marginality, again enfolded amongst intertextual echoes, occurs in **"Byzantium,"** in the image of the lobby to a hotel.

> I am not
> the whole
> hotel. I am a lobby
> with red armchairs
> at one in the morning . . .

The lobby is margin (frame, parergon), an undecidable space between the private and the public, the inside and the outside. The image insists on the openness of this space (the hotel lobby as the gap of desire, the site of assignations), and on the fragmentation of the speaker who is that space (I am not the whole). Yet the inevitable pun resists this loss (I am not the hole). Hole + not = hotel. A few lines earlier, the "tourist of late Romanticism" is seen as "falling back against history / with everything open": all wholes holed, and on hold. This tourist has perhaps been reading Leonard Cohen ("I Am a Hotel"); she has certainly been reading Yeats—less perhaps the poem actually called **"Byzantium"** than the earlier "Sailing To Byzantium," less the achieved destination than the process of the journey towards.

The ubiquity of intertextual deferral (Yeats, Cohen, "late Romanticism," **"Poem in Memory of an Earlier Poem"**) speaks to the continual *inscription* of desire. The title poem asks "What does the body of the polar bear / inscribe on the ice in the cave / of her winter residence?" Perhaps she inscribes that God who resides between the lines; perhaps she inscribes "the goddess language . . . stretching among the remains"; the point is that she does inscribe. In **"Making a Break"** (itself a suggestive title, fragmentation as creative), in the first section of the sequence **"Being Adults,"** a household cat repeats the bear's gesture:

> An open space signals
> where the cat
> does his business
> in a far corner
> of the yard . . .

The inscription is doubled here: the cat leaves behind his mark, his trace, his remainder, and the "open space" in turn signals his signalling, re-marks his marking. One sign defers to another, as in the metonymic chain of desire . . . The intertext is continually reinscribed: as confusion, as substitution. Each term defers to the next in an endless recession or drift. But "I never did get the drift, / the allegory of the cave." The Platonic allegory does presuppose a world *outside* the cave, the realm of Ideas, where there would be neither deferral nor desire; but we, who never did "get" this idea, we live *in* the cave, creating amorous images out of its shadows like the "youth" in Blake, or, like the bear, inscribing the walls of the cave with the trace of our bodies.

Inscription is the gesture of writing, of poetry. Poems have their occasions: they are "occasional," in the generic sense, and also in the sense of intermittent (like the short dashes before the beginning of the long dash, or like "The intermittent sun" in the poem called **"The Occasions"**). **"The Occasions"** begins with a syntactic run-over of the title into the first line, across the gap of an epigraph (from Heraclitus). "THE OCCASIONS . . . Are dim. Are a missing / of the mark." Again the linebreak offers a double reading. The occasions of poetry *are* "a missing": something missing, a gap, a pause, the silence before the beginning of the long dash. The occasion for poetry is the opening of desire. And then, a missing of *the mark:* of the sign, of the writing, of the trace; but also a missing *of* the mark, a missing that *belongs to* the mark, is its property, the lack within the sign (an empty signifier, its meaning deferred) which marks the occasion of the (always already previous) poem.

The occasions are not only occasional (intermittent) but also momentary: "*Moments musicaux* < <which> > scatter / like mercury." If the poem provides, in the image of roses, a momentary understanding of perfection, it is immediately

displaced into an unrecoverable past: "Moments later amnesia." The moment of amnesia is "The moment of desire!"

The fourth and final section of **"The Occasions"** opens with these lines:

> Speaking English
> we go over & over
> the things that happen,
> but I would rather have you
> in my arms than in this conversation.
>
> Desire and ineptitude
> commit themselves to memory . . .

Language then is repetition, citing and reciting, siding and residing. The missing mark must be re-marked. We go "over & over" the occasions, events or causes, "the things that happen." Desire desires to break through to the real, to "have you / in my arms" rather than in language: but even this desire is immediately, compulsively, remarked in language (in the convention of the poetic "you," the absent addressee, the linguistic shifter). The object of desire is never "in my arms" but always "in this conversation," because desire and ineptitude can only "commit themselves to memory." That is, they memorise themselves, they exist in their own memory rather than that of the desiring subject. Also, they pledge a commitment (of themselves) *to* memory. Desire exists in (the) memory of that previous poem, in which

> A moment ago
> the light was perfect
>
> the poem itself
> a perfect memory—its occasion
>
> another light . . .
> **("Poem in Memory of an Earlier Poem")**

But memory itself is subject, "Moments later," to the split of amnesia. Desire commits itself to memory in the form of forgetting. We wait always in that gap, silence, or intermittence, before the beginning of the long dash, for desire to be fulfilled—

—or if not for that, at least for the shrimp boats to come in. The intertextual echo (Peggy Lee) is of the moment of song: "So why don't you / hurry home." But the question is closed; its mark is missing. Why indeed should we hurry. There is no ending to this beginning, only lingering until, in the moment of desire, writing. (pp. 92-5)

Stephen Scobie, "The Barren Reach of Modern Desire: Intertextuality in Sharon Thesen's 'The Beginning of the Long Dash'," in The Malahat Review, *No. 83, June, 1988, pp. 89-97.*

C(harles) K(enneth) Williams

1936-

American poet.

Williams is considered an original stylist whose verse is characterized by bleak descriptions of people and situations in American life. His poems project a hostile universe and are frequently filled with a sense of anguish, powerlessness, and despair. Some critics contend that Williams develops discordant images for their shock value and, as a result, renders his spare poetic vision less forceful than intended. Others, however, insist that Williams's wrathful observations create a sense of urgency.

In *Lies* (1969), his first collection, Williams lashes out at the alienation and deception that he sees as central to contemporary life. These poems are written in short, elliptical lines that jump from image to image. The final poem, "A Day for Anne Frank," with its epigram, "God Hates You!," sums up Williams's early philosophy of life. *I Am the Bitter Name* (1972) covers many of the same topics as *Lies.* Many critics regard this volume as a period piece, since Williams's anger is expressed in a series of protest poems focusing on the political and social turmoil of the late 1960s. "A Poem for Governments" rages against American involvement in Vietnam, and "In the Heart of the Beast" concludes with the statement, "May 1970: Cambodia, Kent State, Jackson State."

With Ignorance (1977) marks an important change of direction in Williams's work. Instead of using the short line form of his earlier volumes, Williams employs long, prose-like lines and emphasizes characterization and dramatic development. Critics note that these poems about capricious human behavior have more universal appeal than his earlier works due to their sympathetic portrayals of believable characters. In *Tar* (1983), Williams continues to use long lines to create scenes from urban life, but he also returns to topical issues. For example, the title poem concerns the threat of nuclear warfare. Although several critics faulted the long concluding piece, "One of the Muses," as intangible, *Tar* is generally regarded as an accomplished work.

Flesh and Blood (1987), Williams's fifth collection of verse, won the National Book Critics Circle Award. Comprised solely of eight-line poems and arranged in three sections, the work illuminates humanity's vulnerability, moving from fleeting perusals of daily life to complex themes addressing such concerns as Alzheimer's disease and death. Rather than becoming redundant, Williams's strict octave style unifies each poem into what Linda Gregerson described as "an impassioned essay on the moral life of urban humanity." The poems in *Flesh and Blood* are set in New York City and Paris, and the rapid pace of urban life is reflected in Williams's brisk verse, which, like *With Ignorance* and *Tar,* frequently explores personal relationships and individual eccentricities. The volume's final section, "Le petit salvié," has received significant critical attention. A tribute to Paul Zweig, Williams's friend and fellow poet who died in 1984, this long poem blends a sense of loss with feelings of empathy and respect in an evocative elegy for Zweig.

(See also *CLC,* Vol. 33; *Contemporary Authors,* Vols. 37-40, rev. ed.; and *Dictionary of Literary Biography,* Vol. 5.)

DON BOGEN

When Allen Ginsberg jokingly compared poetry to Henry Ford's mass-produced automobiles . . . he hit on a real problem for American poets. The temptation to crank out verse on an assembly-line pattern strikes many of our writers, particularly in middle age. The result, predictably, is increased productivity, but we can find ourselves yearning for a little more quality control as the texts pile up. Robert Lowell's five books of blank sonnets, Richard Hugo's interminable poetic letters, even a form as lively and multifaceted as John Berryman's dream songs, can seem vapid after the first hundred or so. Constructing a replicating verse machine of this sort might be partially a response to classic midlife doubts, the poetic equivalent of an executive taking up jogging. As a form of self-imitation, it meets publishers' and some readers' demands for a fairly uniform product every two or three years. But the poem machine holds out a still more seductive promise: the idea that a particular structure can transform any experience into art. No longer needing to find a form but merely to reconstruct one, the poet is free to take on practically any subject. It's not surprising that poets become rapidly prolific in their chosen form and that their attention often turns to the ephemeral—what I saw today, what I'm reading, what just occurred to me. These are the kinds of quick glimpses a machine working in high gear can best turn out.

C. K. Williams's new book of poetry, *Flesh and Blood,* has several of these glimpses in it. It starts with a clear reminder of the transitory, diseased elms being cut down:

> All morning the tree men have been taking down
>   the stricken elms skirting the broad sidewalks.
>
> The pitiless electric chain saws whine tirelessly up
>   and down their piercing, operatic scales
> and the diesel choppers in the street shredding the
>   debris chug feverishly, incessantly,
> packing truckload after truckload with the feath-
>   ery, homogenized, inert remains of heartwood,
> twig and leaf and soon the block is stripped

("Elms")

This is wonderful reporting. Williams's eye for detail and ingenious word choices—the debris "feathery" and "homogenized," the saws doing "operatic scales"—and his subtly appropriate music—those harsh *k*'s in the opening line or the unyielding rhythm that asserts itself at the end of the passage—sharpen this relatively common scene till the moment seems not only vividly present but entirely new. But how often can this be done? This opening poem of eight long lines is followed by almost one hundred more pieces in exactly the same form in Part I of *Flesh and Blood.* Part II contains thirty-three more eight-line poems arranged in five sequences; and the last section, an elegy for Williams's friend and fellow poet Paul Zweig, is made up of eighteen of these eight-line units. Williams's machine is definitely in gear, and there's no denying a certain deadening effect caused by the sheer uniformity of the shapes it produces. . . . If Williams's early work had a great deal of the angry young man behind it, *Flesh and Blood* is a middle-aged book: calm, outward-looking, comfortable in its habits and a bit long-winded.

The book's limitations are most noticeable in its first section. Here the brevity of format can result in some thin writing: a surface glimpse of tourists in Paris, a kindly nod to a friend—work that doesn't get beyond the immediate moment. Other poems tend to harp on the same basic points. Instead of one really striking vision of awkward young love, for instance, Williams provides several nostalgic, fairly predictable pieces. It's not that the ninety-six poems in Part I do the same thing over and over. Williams has a wide array of strategies for the form: abstract argument (some of the strongest poems are in this mode), narration, evocative description, even dialogue. But the format generally allows only one of these strategies per poem, and the result can seem constricting, especially after the rich complexity of the longer poems in Williams's previous work.

The individual line, rather than the stanza or the shape of the poem as a whole, has been the ordering principle of Williams's work since the mid-1970s. . . . Rhythmically varied yet regular in length, it gives him a controlled flexibility which fits the probing, speculative energy of his voice. Williams is a poet who needs to change approaches frequently, to find new perspectives and follow out ramifications. The

best poems in *Flesh and Blood* draw strength from that shifting, as in this description of a blackbird attacking a cube of cheese:

> Then a glister of licentious leering, a conspiratorial
>   gleam, the cocked brow of common avarice:
> he works his yellow scissors deeper in, daring
>   doubt, a politician with his finger in the till,
> a weapon maker's finger in the politician, the slob-
>   ber and the licking and the champ and click.
> It is a lovely day, it always is; the innocent daylight
>   fades into its dying, it always does.
> The bird looks up, death-face beside the curded
>   white, its foot, its fist of dying, daintily raised.

("Greed")

The bird is set vividly before us, but so are the allegory, the grotesque chain of corruption and the different levels of irony, from the creature's silly leer to the "innocence" of the daylight. When Williams gets a chance to worry his subject like this, his poems gain a startling mixture of immediacy and depth.

Isolated glimpses are not all *Flesh and Blood* has to offer. Part I includes a handful of poems in pairs about Williams's wife, his teen-age daughter and his parents-in-law that capture the lives of the young, the old and those in between with perceptive sympathy. In the second section poems are grouped around larger issues like suicide, motherhood and love. Using the eight-line units here as components—points in an argument, examples, stages in a progression—Williams builds intriguing meditations on some basic human concerns. The love poems (not expressions but studies of it) are wonderfully observant in their attention to small gestures: the posture of lovers at tables in cafes, the angles of their glances, the different ways new or more familiar couples might touch each other's hair. The opening series on reading has the same careful specificity. This group is full of delightful surprises: the weightlifter with a paperback Hume in his locker, the heavily armed rookie cop studying a pamphlet, the man changing a tire in sub-zero weather who stops to read a scrap of newspaper in his trunk. In considering one thing that people of all sorts do, Williams brings out the rich quirkiness of individual lives and the delicious solitude that envelops a reader even in the most public places.

With its New York and Paris settings, *Flesh and Blood* is a refreshingly urban book. There are no backyard epiphanies or dreamy beach scenes here, no mystic visions of nature. Instead, Williams is drawn to public environments—city parks, construction sites, concert halls, restaurants—not for the crowds per se but for singular actions within the social web. He builds some of his most revealing poems from observations in subways. In **"Reading: The Subway"** a civil servant takes a break from *Successful Investing* to look up at a mindless advertisement "as though to decathect a moment." **"Hooks"** defines the intricate conventions involved in watching fellow passengers but still managing "not to be noticed noticing." . . . (pp. 734-35)

Williams's skill at tracing shifting currents serves him well in the elegy for Paul Zweig that concludes *Flesh and Blood.* In these stanzas he weaves memories, self-doubt, description and metaphysical speculation into an exquisitely paced tribute and farewell. Grief and resolution do not appear in simple textbook stages here but rather circle around each other, obsessive and self-triggering, with the awkward indeterminacy of real experience. In this early passage on guilt, for example, Williams conveys both the endless reappraisals of the living and the dying man's more intimate response to his condition:

> We didn't know how ill you were . . . we knew
>   how ill but hid it . . . we didn't know how ill you
>   were . . .
> Those first days when your fever rose . . . if we'd
>   only made you go into the hospital in Brive . . .
> Perhaps you could have had another year . . . but
>   the way you'd let death touch your life so little,
> the way you'd learned to hold your own mortality
>   before you like an unfamiliar, complex
>   flower . . .
>
>   ("Le Petit Salvié")

Here and elsewhere the struggle for emotional clarity, for understanding rather than mere relief, comes to the fore. Resisting the temptation to lionize his friendship with Zweig, Williams notes the competitiveness and sublimated envy each poet felt. Despite the loving specificity of detail—Zweig's "dumb French farmer's hat," the "storm-split plum tree" in his yard, the canvas chairs behind the house where the two men sat discussing their work—the memories Williams recalls are not tinted with nostalgia. In one of the strongest sections of the poem, he confronts his own harsh needs as a survivor and elegist: "I seem to have to make you dead, dead again, to hold you in my mind so I can clearly have you." Elsewhere he enters into the suffering of Zweig's other friends, his daughter and the dying man himself, rendering the helplessness that everyone shares. By turns evocative, mournful, sympathetic and critical, the elegy shows Williams's powers at their fullest.

There is a restless intelligence behind all of C. K. Williams's work. His poems need a certain amount of elbow room, and the eight-line unit of *Flesh and Blood* doesn't always provide it. But if his new book is not a technical advance over his earlier work, the range of his concerns and the depth of his emotional insight give it value. Williams's poems, whatever their shape, remind us how much other poets leave out. (pp. 735-36)

> Don Bogen, "The Poem Machine," in The Nation, *New York, Vol. 244, No. 21, May 30, 1987, pp. 734-36.*

EDWARD HIRSCH

For his fifth collection of poems, *Flesh and Blood,* C. K. Williams has taken the flexible, rangy and capacious long line he first discovered in *With Ignorance* (1977) and then perfected in *Tar* (1983), and adapted it to a group of eight-line poems. The extensive book which resulted has the feeling of a contemporary sonnet sequence. . . . Mr. Williams's short poems are shapely and yet open-ended and self-generative, loosely improvisational though with an underlying formal necessity. Individually, they lack the narrative scope and sheer relentless force of Mr. Williams's longer poems, but together they have a strong cumulative energy and effectiveness. By continually applying his long lines to the same form, he has gone another step in developing a unique and inclusive poetry of consciousness.

There is a rapid, notational, ethnographic quality to the poems in *Flesh and Blood,* as if the poet had moved through the urban landscape with a notepad in hand. Mr. Williams

has a keen eye and an uncompromising sense of daily life. Many of his poems present single extended moments intently observed: a girl with an artificial hand stepping onto the subway or a bum scribbling into a battered notebook in the public library. Others are like miniature short stories, sudden fictions. In one, a man slips out of his house to telephone his lover, in another a couple unexpectedly confront each other on vacation. Still others take meditative jabs at our ideas of "nostalgia" or "the past" or "failure." All of these poems present people in situations where they are vulnerable, exposed, on the edge.

There is an immense amount of data in Mr. Williams's poems. They have a thick naturalistic surface and a fast narrative current. But a philosopher lurks behind the sociologist. The poems in the second section, for example, are small urban parables. They take a general idea—"reading" or "love" or "the good mother"—and yoke it to a specific story. . . . In these poems the general is exemplified by the particular and the individual story aspires to the archetypal.

In the 18-part elegy that closes the book, Mr. Williams not only describes the loss of his close friend, Paul Zweig, but also tracks the sorrows of a diligent consciousness holding onto that friend even as he lets him go. **"Le Petit Salvié"** is the masterful culmination of the book's method. The poems in *Flesh and Blood* jump-cut from radical scene to scene even as they describe the workings of a mind observing and meditating on itself. Mr. Williams is simultaneously one of the most documentary and one of the most thoughtful poets working today.

> Edward Hirsch, "Heroes and Villanelles," in The *New York Times Book Review, August 23, 1987, p. 20.*

ROBERT McDOWELL

When I reviewed C. K. Williams' last book of poetry, *Tar,* in these pages in 1984, I praised the poet's ability to tell his story without authorial intrusion. Acknowledging the visual monotony of his long, long lines, I nevertheless insisted on their virtuosity, their accurate depiction of dialogue's intimate hesitations.

What I must say about *Flesh and Blood,* his new volume, is quite different. This book consists of one hundred-thirty (and the last is a sequence of eighteen parts) poems of eight lines each, situated two on a page. For some, the visual monotony will be as bad as ever, but now the syntax, vocabulary, and stories do not redeem the poems.

What is fascinating is this poet's fascination with self-destruction. It is as if he decided to take the longest line in contemporary poetry and see how much of a minimalist he could become with it. If that was his goal, he has succeeded. The stories of *Tar* have given way in this book to abstract meditations and occasional scenes that, at best, suggest stories the poet will not tell. Perhaps the most revealing lines in the book conclude **"Kin."**

> What next? Nothing next. Next the wretched histo-
>   ry of the world. The history of the heart.
> The theory next that all we are are stories, handed
>   down, that all we are are parts of speech.
> All that limits and defines us: our ancient natures,
>   love and death and terror and original sin.

> And the weary breath, the weary going to and fro,
> the weary always knowing what comes next.

The impulse to turn away from story is expressed here, and so is the world-weariness that prompts the poet to turn inward to abstraction (love, death, terror, original sin). Since Williams opts for evasion rather than telling his stories well, his method requires nothing more than the construction of lists. As poem after poem piles up, or piles on, the reader begins to feel like an observer of a series of hit-and-run accidents.

When subject disappears from poems, the spotlight beats down on the language itself and here, too, these poems suffer. Assertions become tiring. In **"Cowboys,"** for example, the poet tells us that the structure of a science fiction movie is like that of a western. Don't all of us know this by now? Most of the poems are shackled by laborious adjectives, and almost as many are married by clichés. In one poem, lovers are "bruised and swollen"; in another, a skewered pig has an "angry wound." In too many the poet succumbs to the current fashionable temptation to make the most of the shock value of sex.

C. K. Williams can be, and has been, a better poet than this book suggests, but now he must resolve this argument with himself regarding story and renew his narrative strengths. In this book he sounds like many other poets, and that is depressing. (pp. 680-81)

> *Robert McDowell, in a review of "Flesh and Blood,"
> in* The Hudson Review, *Vol. XL, No. 4, Winter,
> 1988, pp. 680-81.*

REGINALD GIBBONS

The measure of C. K. Williams's last three books has been on a scale most poets do not often approach. To invent or discover or renew a distinct kind of poetic line is not easy in our time, but he has done that, as well as shaped a distinct sort of form with his lanky long lines and dramatic structures; and he has roamed readily and gracefully over great expanses of ground—that is, of feeling, serious preoccupation and responsibilities. And while he arrives at profound perceptions and potent feelings, and these are themselves worthy goals, they are for him the ground on which he builds a larger project—more ambitious, riskier of failure, and also exhilarating: he produces a profound sense of what we could call our lives-in-language.

The dramatic mechanism of this is his implied portrait of a general cultural craziness and savagery, by sketching precisely certain small moments of defeat and triumph within it. This is most apparent in the new collection, *Flesh and Blood,* which, using the same poetic format for every poem, reminds one a little of [Robert] Lowell's *Notebooks.* But if Lowell, while attempting the same thing, doesn't seem finally to have been scrupulous enough about either his choice of materials or the finish of the individual poems, Williams has managed his smaller form with great responsiveness to incident and idea, and has produced poems of greater finish and at the same time less strain—poems of a greater poetic exuberance.

Part of Williams's success must lie in the care with which he has chosen what Thomas McGrath calls the "representative moments" around which the poems are built. And while Williams's characteristically long line goes about extending the *process* of our thinking, noticing and feeling as we read, his short form is compressing and eliding all the materials at hand, so that we must, as readers, be agile enough to leap to the heart of the matter when each poem bids us to. Nuances build in the silence surrounding each chosen episode of flesh and blood, and the poems begin to echo each other down their hall the way the great sonnet-sequences do. This collection is at once a wholly natural record of generous and humane responsiveness to life, and also a deliberated artistic shaping of that responsiveness into poems that we are meant to see as intensely *formed.* And that combination of blood and flesh is rare, wonderful and welcome. (pp. 224-25)

> *Reginald Gibbons, in a review of "Flesh and Blood,"
> in* TriQuarterly 71, *No. 71, Winter, 1988, pp. 224-
> 25.*

LINDA GREGERSON

For three books now, C. K. Williams has been working in the long, commodious, flexible lines that have come to be his trademark. Even the byways of typography are part of the face by which his readers know him: not even the exaggerated proportions of an oversize book (Houghton Mifflin tried one in 1977) can keep these lines from extending to wraparound. Lines-and-a-quarter or lines-and-a-third produce the rhythm we see on the page: some prodigal, loquacious overspill that is rather a kind of second wind than the syncopated part-lines of enjambment. Williams has restricted his line to octaves in the new book, and what other eight-line poems in the language would prompt one to praise their orchestration? The term sounds oxymoronic in context. But orchestration is the genius of this book: multivocal, richly textured, finely scored.

The capaciousness of the line is matched by a capaciousness of spirit in *Flesh and Blood.* The poems are didactic fables, documentaries, confessions, indictments, portraits, billets-doux: and the list of exemplary instances would virtually reproduce the table of contents. One might have expected the eight-line restriction to produce a kind of semantic and perceptual uniformity after a while, especially in poems so committed to process (here must be the rising action, here the discovery). But the poems gain latitude from their very numbers and proximity; the cumulative pressures of interrogation and scrutiny free some poems for the simpler tasks of lyric description and vignette, though simplicity is always relative in a poetry this fertile. And page by page, the poems cease to be mere integers: together they constitute a strenuous, changeable, divided, and impassioned essay on the moral life of urban humanity.

One of the ethical tests to which Williams submits himself and his readers with some regularity is the test of flagrant disclosure. He will not turn his eyes away (or not soon enough) from the beautiful woman's artificial hand, from the young boy's deformed legs, from the car-struck dog and its frenzy of pain, from the manifold, mutable, resourceful means human beings have devised for visiting harm upon one another. He will make us flinch and make us behold our own flinching. He is especially uncompromising on the species of cruelty we direct toward children . . . and the radical critiques of adulthood that may be read in the play of children (see **"Artemis," "War," "The Park"**). He renders the vulnerabilities of the aged in such a manner that all of us may know just how far our love for them falls short and may know what we ourselves are in for (**"The Lens"**). (pp. 431-32)

Linda Gregerson, in a review of "Flesh and Blood,"
in Poetry, *Vol. CLI, No. 5, February, 1988, pp. 431-
33.*

MORRIS DICKSTEIN

The first thing we notice about **Flesh and Blood,** C. K. Williams' fifth book of poetry, is the sheer abundance: two poems to a page, over 80 pages; whole groups of poems that bounce around a single subject; reading, suicide, love. Astonishingly long lines that carom over the right margin and land effortlessly on the line below. Perhaps the longest verse lines we've seen in English since Kit Smart or Walt Whitman or some of Allen Ginsberg!

The next thing we're likely to notice is the voice, which has nothing to do with that special form of speech—"poetic diction," Wordsworth called it mockingly—which sometimes makes us feel that the life we lead, and the poems we read or ignore, have nothing in common. This is not the voice of a cerebral, donnish, smart-assed with putting clever words together, that are finally just words; this voice is always colloquial, always the sound and inflection of a figure of flesh and blood. It can be breathless, or patiently attentive; whimsical, or keenly emotional.

It's an introspective voice which is also endlessly curious about other people. Not as subjects for poems—mere occasions for the poet to practice his craft—but as precious specimens of the human comedy. In these novelistic vignettes, all just eight lines long. Williams can make adolescence, rhinos, in-laws, spouses, even babies, come alive as richly observed characters. These poems form a kind of sketchbook or diary in verse, like Robert Lowell's *Notebook,* or John Berryman's *Dream Songs,* which are also sequences in which a richly expansive temperament works in short takes against and within the constraints of a tightly knit form.

Williams plays his eight-line form with all the dexterity of an Elizabethan sonneteer, bearing his syntax and rhythm amazingly from line to line and poem to poem, playing off one quatrain against another, exploring all the sinuous possibilities of the complex English sentence, without drawing the least attention to these subtle effects.

In his final sequence, **"Le Petit Salvié,"** Williams does all this and a great deal more. He turns his form into a continuous elegy and meditation on the life and death of another poet, Paul Zweig, whose own book on Walt Whitman was nominated for this very prize, in biography, just three years ago. In this deeply moving work, to which several of the judges drew special attention, Williams risks comparison with "Lycidas" and "Adonais," yet writes something entirely in his own voice, ruminating, empathetic, generous and self-questioning.

It's with great pleasure that I present this award to C. K. Williams for **Flesh and Blood.** (pp. 3-4)

Morris Dickstein, in an introductory speech in The
National Book Critics Circle Journal, *Vol. 14, No.
4, May 15, 1988, pp. 3-4.*

C. K. WILLIAMS

I'm honored and pleased beyond measure, and I have so many people to thank that I don't even know where to start,

really. Catherine, my wife, and Jon Galassi and my family, and so many friends. Poets these days need friends.

I find that whenever I have the chance to speak to an audience that isn't the specialized audience of poets or extreme poetry lovers, who I love deeply, I end up making a plea for poetry. And this time, instead of trying to make a plea for poetry, I thought I would just read a poem. And if not convince you of the class "poetry," at least expose you to a particular. And I picked a poem that has to do with reading, since I presume all of us in this room do, from time to time at least, read. It's called **"Reading Early Sorrow."**

> The father has given his year-old son *Le Monde*
> to play with in his stroller and the baby does
>
> just what you'd expect: grabs it, holds it out in
> front of him, stares importantly at it,
>
> makes emphatic and dramatic sounds of declamation, great pronouncements of analytic probity,
>
> then tears it, pulls a page in half, pulls the half
> in quarters, shoves a hearty shred into his mouth—
>
> a delicious editorial on unemployment and recession, a tasty jeu de mots on government ineptitude.
>
> He startles in amazement when the father takes
> the paper back from him: What in heaven's name?
>
> Indignation, impotence, frustration, outrage,
> petulance, rebellion, realism, resignation.
>
> Slumping back, disgusted . . . *hypocrite lecteur,
> semblable* . . . Just wait he's muttering, just
> wait . . .

Thank you.

C. K. Williams, in an acceptance speech in The National Book Critics Circle Journal, *Vol. 14, No. 4,
May 15, 1988, p. 4.*

MICHAEL HOFMANN

The American poet C. K. Williams is now practically synonymous with the very long poetic line of his devising, the line in which he has written his most recent book, **Flesh and Blood,** and the two books that preceded it, **Tar** and **With Ignorance** . . . I will talk about the line later, but suffice it to say for the moment that the poetry Williams has written using it has as much scope and truthfulness as any American poetry since Lowell and Berryman. . . .

Whether or not Williams felt himself caught in the toils of the short-story-as-poem, he has given it the slip most elegantly and cleverly in his most recent and best volume to date, **Flesh and Blood.** This, too, is composed in the long line, now curling unerringly for up to a line and a half (a full line, justified at both ends; and a part of one, indented, beneath), for twenty or twenty-five syllables, or, say, a hundred microns: but now each poem may contain only eight of them; and there are two on a page, as with Lowell's sonnets, or Berryman's Dreamsongs in his *Selected.* The effect is an extraordinary combination of disciplined compression, and Williams's now fully assured, luxuriant exfoliation. The mind is flattered by matter and urgency, while the eye is soothed by space. The form is perhaps more spacious than the couplet, and it makes a far more interesting impression on the page. The poems are beautifully punctuated, with most of the lines end-stopped; and many of the lines are so managed that they seem to end twice: "She answers the bothersome telephone, takes the message, forgets the mes- / sage, forgets who called / /". Scrupulous rhetorical control is demanded for such a form, and Williams seems to bring it off quite effortlessly, without the little strainings and paddings ("born and born", "sorrow and sorrow") in the earlier books. A poem may be one sentence (**"Repression"**), or it may be seven (**"Love: Petulance"**), but in either case it will be for a reason, and it will be well managed, clear and easy to follow.

The subjects are the by-now familiar gallery of hobos and winos, children and old people, lovers and invalids; the settings, typically, public places, on holiday, in parks, on pavements and metro-stations. Little sequences have been put together—I particularly like the one on **"Reading"**—and also a set of metaphor-essays, entitled **"Vehicles"**, on abstractions such as **"Conscience"** and **"Forgetting".** These last, extended similes in a Rilkean manner, benefit especially from the dissolution of the earlier, baggier forms of *Tar* and *With Ignorance:* they are no longer outperformed by narrative. Finally, there is a sequence of eighteen of these eight-liners in memory of Williams's friend, the poet and biographer of Whitman,

Paul Zweig. Every aspect of Williams's writing is represented here, sincerity of feeling, plasticity of recollection, ardour of thought, all sifted and qualified in the tides of the long lines.

Clearly C. K. Williams is an important poet. For over a dozen years he has written like himself, he has matter and a manner, and has refined them both. One might see a Williams poem happening on the street, and there are not many poets of whom that could be said. If some of his earlier long-lined pieces had a somewhat posturing ("my friend Dave") garrulousness about them, and had arguments with himself that—Yeats to the contrary—remained firmly arguments with himself, he has come through that to sound, in *Flesh and Blood,* likeable, mature and even-tempered. The only defects he has are those of his virtues: his determined ordinariness, an unwillingness to let something go, a certain predictability. A word is rarely stretched in a C. K. Williams poem, rarely finds itself in an unaccustomed context, is rarely memorable. But then—unlike the generation preceding his, the Lowell and Berryman generation—he doesn't write as though nothing mattered beyond words.

Michael Hofmann, "A Long Line of Discovery," in The Times Literary Supplement, *No. 4477, January 20-26, 1989, p. 59.*

David (Keith) Williamson

1942-

Australian dramatist and scriptwriter.

One of Australia's most popular and critically acclaimed dramatists, Williamson composes satirical yet naturalistic plays featuring the interaction of urban, middle-class individuals in social situations. He comically undermines such stereotypical Australian characteristics as aggressiveness, male chauvinism, and verbal crudity to expose the latent sexual anxieties and moral failings of his protagonists. Peter Fitzpatrick asserted: "[No dramatist] has crafted images of Australians' social behaviour as skilfully and influentially as Williamson, or with his consistent intelligence of observation." While Williamson has continued to address such topical issues as sexual permissiveness and governmental corruption, several of his later plays feature psychologically complex characters whose personal conflicts often augment the sociological observations that dominate his earlier work.

During the early 1970s, Williamson was associated with the Australian Performing Group, an organization of dramatists and directors who rejected the naturalism of the established theater in favor of absurdism, stereotypes, and aggressive dialogue which, they argued, more accurately represented Australian society. Williamson's first major play, *The Coming of Stork* (1970), reflects the influence of the Australian Performing Group. This farce, which focuses upon an obnoxious Maoist gardener who disrupts the tense relationships between three recent university graduates involved with the same woman, garnered praise for its perceptive parody of the bravado concealing youthful male anxieties. *Don's Party* (1971) involves a group of former student radicals who gather on election night in 1969 to celebrate the expected victory of the liberal Labor party. As the evening progresses, tensions surface over the various characters' personal and moral shortcomings, and the gathering's superficial gaiety is ultimately destroyed by arguments and fights. Critics lauded Williamson's acerbic parody of social games in which coarse language and shallow wit are substituted for meaningful communication.

Williamson's best-known play, *The Removalists* (1971), examines the relationship between violence, authority, and repressed sexuality. While helping a battered wife move from her home, Ross, a naive police recruit, and Simmonds, his callous sergeant, develop a comical yet disturbing relationship with Kenny, the woman's estranged husband. Though initially harassed by both men, Kenny eagerly joins Simmonds in verbally and physically abusing Ross, long the victim of his superior's indiscriminate brutality. Growing increasingly hysterical, Ross attacks Kenny and beats him to death. Finally, Ross and Simmonds assault one another, hoping to create the illusion that Kenny died while resisting arrest. Most critics praised Williamson's deliberate stereotyping of characters and situations to highlight the brutality that underlies acceptable Australian masculine roles. Brian Kiernan observed: "While not being a literal representative of the actual, a direct slice of life, *The Removalists* . . . presents with compelling, if irrational, dramatic logic a metaphor of

a world in which relationships are predatory, cruel and vicious beneath the humdrum surface."

With *Jugglers Three* (1972), Williamson began to shift from creating the grotesque characters typical of the Australian Performing Group to more realistic, psychologically complex protagonists. While retaining the farcical antics of Williamson's previous plays, *Jugglers Three* presents an intricately developed portrait of Graham, the husband of a promiscuous woman who conspires with his wife's lovers to send her to America. Williamson's subsequent plays focus more closely upon the personal consequences of social and financial success, a concern which many critics regard as autobiographical. In *What If You Died Tomorrow* (1973), the demands of children, parents, agent, and mistress overwhelm a bestselling novelist living apart from his wife, while *A Handful of Friends* (1976) centers on underlying hostilities and attractions that surface between friends at a weekend gathering. Noting the commercial success of these plays, some critics contended that Williamson had compromised the experimental vitality of his earlier productions. Other reviewers, however, praised his amusing and detached portrayal of upper middle-class anxieties.

In the plays that succeed *What If You Died Tomorrow,* Williamson's examination of social dynamics extends to conflicts between ethics and personal gain in public institutions. *The Department* (1974), set during a staff meeting at a small technical college, focuses not on academic issues but upon the political manipulations of its department head. *The Club* (1977; produced in the United States as *Players*), one of Williamson's most popular plays, examines the growing dissension within a professional Australian football club as management and coach clash over administrative issues. *Sons of Cain* (1985) is based on a mid-1980s political scandal in Australia in which high-ranking government officials were accused of drug trafficking. This play focuses upon a newspaper editor's investigation of the incident and the opposition he encounters from his superiors. In his review of *Players*, Brendan Gill commented: "[Williamson] writes like a near-contemporary of Ibsen, taking care that the neatly turned cabinetwork of his plot should open up steadily . . . until at last one has penetrated to its very heart—to that inmost drawer which, on being opened, reveals not a pinch of any quality higher than self-interest."

The incompatibility of idealism and reality figure prominently in Williamson's dramas concerning personal relationships. Described by Wayne Fairhead as "a serene, passionate and touching play," *Travelling North* (1979) focuses upon Frank and Francis, an unmarried couple who leave their disapproving adult children in wintry Melbourne to pursue an idyllic lifestyle on the balmy Queensland coast. The protagonists must reevaluate the reasons for abandoning their families, however, when the discovery of Frank's terminal illness exposes their inadequacies as parents and lovers. *The Perfectionist* (1982) features a couple whose attempt to improve their marriage based on two psychologists' theories of sexual and emotional openness ends in disaster. *Emerald City* (1988) revolves around a critically acclaimed yet little-known screenwriter whose lucrative alliance with an amoral business executive jeopardizes his artistic integrity and his marriage to a talented editor. John Simon commented: "*Emerald City* portrays human rivalry with maximum comic and dramatic effect because it is as humorous as it is witty. Wit is diagnostic, humor is analytical. David Williamson is both."

In addition to his success as a dramatist, Williamson is also considered one of Australia's foremost scriptwriters. He is best known in this genre for his adaptation of C. J. Koch's novel *The Year of Living Dangerously* (1983), on which he collaborated with Koch and director Peter Weir. His original screenplays include the World War I drama *Gallipoli* (1981) and *Phar Lap* (1984), the story of a thoroughbred race horse that became a national symbol in Depression-era Australia. His television play *A Dangerous Life* (1989) chronicles from the narrative perspective of an American journalist the expulsion of Philippine dictator Ferdinand Marcos. Williamson has also adapted several of his plays for film.

(See also *Contemporary Authors,* Vol. 103.)

BRIAN KIERNAN

Graeme Blundell's phrase "quasi-naturalistic with absurdist overtones" . . . captured succinctly the dominant style of the "new wave" of Australian drama. It expressed characteristics that were common to many of the plays by young writers emerging in the "alternative" theatre: their delighted exploi-

tation of the vernacular and critical employment of local customs and attitudes in pieces that were unrestricted by the conventional structures prevailing in the "legitimate" theatre. A detailed history of the developments of the later sixties and early seventies has yet to be written, but it is clear that the largest group of writers sharing these characteristics were those associated with the Australian Performing Group. . . . More than a style, or a set of conventions, they had in common an opposition to the established theatre, both in itself and as an organ of the social establishment. For some of them, the development of an alternative theatre was a step towards the development of an alternative society—as the communal organization of the Group and its street performances during the Vietnam moratoria and visits to factories would suggest. Experimentation with various styles, even by individual playwrights, was the rule but the vein of social satiric reference in their work gave Blundell's phrase its aptness. However, although he carefully qualified it, the term "naturalism" has caused confusion in the reception of the work by new playwrights, not least that of David Williamson.

"Naturalism" provides one of the key terms of theatre reviewers in Australia; the other is "anti-naturalism". The survival of the late nineteenth- and early twentieth-century classics of this movement in the repertoire of local companies, the prevalence of well-made slices of life (dubbed naturalistic) amongst modern English and American plays produced here in the post-war decades, and of course, the success of [Raymond Lawler's *Summer of the Seventeenth Doll*] perhaps explain the preoccupation with naturalism as establishing a norm for discussing departures from it—some of which, like Patrick White's expressionism, are almost as old as the naturalism they had developed out of in the late nineteenth century. Critics, recognizing a strong mimetic element in the work of the writers produced by the A.P.G., and with an eye for movements and influences, reached instinctively for their portmanteau term, which contrary to the historical realities had become redefined as excluding experimentation, symbolism and poetic expression. The critics overlooked the fact that although these writers were concerned to represent their society (because they were critically concerned with it), they did so in a way that was free of theatrical conventions, the conventions that is of "bourgeois" theatre. This was an anti-theatrical and anti-literary movement. (pp. 315-16)

All this by way of background because David Williamson has been seen not only as the most "naturalistic" of the writers associated with the A.P.G. in the early seventies, but has also insisted himself many times on the naturalism of his own plays. His understanding of this term, however, may very well differ from that of his critics. **The Removalists** and **Don's Party,** both of which were produced for the first time in 1971 (within weeks of each other), move with such confidence that critics must be forgiven for imagining that their author had a long and close familiarity with the "legitimate" theatre and its traditions. The theatre that Williamson had first-hand experience of, through writing university revue sketches, was that of "rough" satiric farce. His earliest play to be published, **The Coming of Stork** (first performed at La Mama in 1970) shows this. Structurally, it would seem to take its lead from Hibberd's *White with Wire Wheels:* three young men flatting together are involved with the one girl. But the "narrative" development of this situation (which, as in Hibberd's play, allows the presentation of stereotyped interactions) is less important than the disruptive farcical antics of Stork, the randy, hypochondriac Maoist landscape gardener with the Honours

Maths degree. The nine scenes are individually built on gags and linked together as permutations on a situation calculated to appeal to the original audience—the pressure of adult demands confronting a group of still rather adolescent young graduates. Stork's insensitivity in communicating with others and his social ineptness provide the links between such gags as *"Eight and a Half"*, "Alaska" and "Smoked Oyster". In this prentice piece a number of characteristics of Williamson's developed style are apparent. The most important legacy of his revue experience would seem to be the "close" writing that later is to go together with his development of extended situation. Usually a number of situations or relationships are developing simultaneously; something is always happening. The dialogue is distributed over more characters than in the plays of his contemporaries at the A.P.G.—even the gags are presented by a number of characters. There are virtually no speeches, only interchanges, and the vernacular is not so much exploited for its own comic potentiality as subordinated to the interaction of the characters in a situation fraught with social and sexual tensions. (pp. 317-18)

The presentation (and preservation) of the self in everyday life, social ritual and destructive game-playing are some of the patterns of interaction revealed in *Don's Party.* When at the end of the evening, the social "masks" of Don and Mal are removed, their "true" selves revealed, and we see them as they were in their undergraduate days, they are as stereotyped, as conditioned by the roles they observed then, as they are in those they have adopted later. According to the tenets of psychological realism this may be superficial characterization, but what the play reveals about the self's need to interact adequately at this "superficial" level is perhaps more original than yet another "three-dimensional" portrait might be. In other ways also, *Don's Party* is no more naturalistic than *Stork:* indeed it is almost a farcical parody of a naturalistic play focused on a social issue. The potentially serious issue of the election (and presumably the future of the country) is all but ignored by the characters (and its result known to the audience anyhow). It is certainly a realistic play—realism could scarcely go further than incorporating into the text transcripts of the election results actually broadcast on the night chosen to set the action. The observation of social behaviour is acute, but the stylistic qualities are not limitedly realistic. The pace, variety, and "close" writing that keeps a number of characters interacting, and a number of situations developing, at every moment produce a more complex tonal quality.

After the establishment of the relationships between the various early-middle-aged, professional couples, the play proceeds to vary (rather than "develop") these in an elaborate game of sexual politics—a game whose aim is to try and take your partner's piece without losing your own. The theatrical formality of farce (formal even if unpredictable) becomes as important to the play's development as the accuracy of its social observation. As in *Stork,* the entrance of a zany disrupts the delicate ritualistic maintenance of norms amongst the others; in this piece it is Cooley, with Susan, his girl-friend, who has the "liberated" sexual attitudes of a younger generation. However, in contrast with the earlier play, the stylistic integration of stand-up gags, frenetic farce and the presentation of prevailing mores under threat from sexual tensions finds its own appropriate form. The rise to bacchanalian euphoria and fall to crapulous depression over two acts subtly relates the course of the party to the waxing and waning of the guests' political hopes chartered by the television broadcasts. The characters' responses to the possibilities of some correspondence between the promise of a "new life" politically, the realization of their youthful idealism, and the hope of some personal sexual liberation is left implicit. There is no direct positing of an analogy between the sexual and the political—the most overt association is made at the end of the play when Jody, who has become increasingly "liberated" during the evening, announces she is thinking of voting Labor next time.

The issue of "naturalism" as determining the appropriate style of production, and criteria for criticism, has arisen most sharply with *The Removalists,* the best play to have come out of the "new wave" and the "alternative" theatre in Australia. The Currency edition of the revised text . . . and John Bell's production notes, which refer to the play's "unfashionably strong naturalism" and unstereotyped men but stereotyped women, presents *The Removalists* as a quite different play from the one produced first at La Mama in 1971 (with the author representing Aussie Removalists). This was a brisk, two scene one-acter, a realistic farce that turned into black comedy. It had a purely theatrical exploitation of situation, reversing the audience's expectations in a brilliant sequence of moves and bewildering them as to what was real and disturbing, and what was, with comic relief, recognized as bluff and dissembling. In later productions . . . the play's realism was extended with gory sensationalism to bring out the "naturalistic" social implications at the expense of its inbuilt dimension of theatricality—the rituals the characters act out.

A sensational emphasis on violence (I cannot remember any blood in the original production) would be counter to the play's tone as comedy showing the games people play, and linking all the characters (not merely the police) in a struggle for dominance and ego-satisfaction. This comedy of games-playing and the "sub-text" of real motives that underlie social rituals is introduced in the opening scene of Ross reporting to Simmonds for his first day of duty, and Simmonds acting "as if he were auditioning him for a crucial role in some play". Simmonds's authoritarian, even sadistic, impulses to dominate Ross are disguised (not very convincingly for the audience) as a paternal, personal interest in the new recruit. He determinedly sets about breaking down Ross's idealistic conception of his new role as a policeman by posing as an anti-authoritarian. . . . As Ross tries to ingratiate himself, he is given the "wrong" cues by Simmonds. Ross answers in terms of the expectations of the policeman's role he has had reinforced by his training, only to be put straight by the contemptuous Simmonds. We feel, however, that Simmonds's moves could equally well be reversed: that if Ross tried to anticipate what the "right" answer would be Simmonds would revert to the rule book (as, in fact, he does at the climax when Ross tries to have him assume his share of responsibility for Kenny's presumed, then actual, death). In the opening scene, Simmonds's persistence and cunning in forcing Ross to reveal details of his father's occupation shows his need to dominate, humiliate and expose others. When, with reluctance and obvious shame Ross reveals that he is a carpenter and then, pressed further, a coffin-maker, Simmonds "rewards" him by his fatuous observations that "Christ was a carpenter" and

(*trying to suppress his laughter*) Coffin maker, eh? What's bloody wrong with that? I mean where would we be without coffin makers? Building a box to die in is every bit as important to the community as building a box to live in, in my estimation.

Then, having broken Ross down he similarly, with Kate as his accomplice, interrogates, humiliates, and almost literally, exposes Fiona.

The association of authority, violence and repressed sexuality suggested in the first act (and pointed in the story of Ross's predecessor who had assaulted the bikies accused of rape) are strengthened in the scene between Fiona and Kenny which opens the second act—a scene not in the original production. With the sexual frustration that underlies his aggressiveness and his censoriousness towards Kate, Kenny is Simmonds's counterpart, and in the ensuing action it is significant that both refer to blows they have given as "love pats". Later, they get on well together, having struck the bargain over the call girls, and join forces to turn on Ross. There had been an element of "game playing", of ritual taunts and vaunts in a comparatively controlled display of aggression, until Simmonds "goes beserk" at Kenny's account of Fiona's responses in bed the night before. Kenny, however, could claim this as his move. Simmonds's outburst reveals, to the other characters' dismay, his curious motivation—the sexual frustration that lies behind his vicious kneeing of Kenny in the groin after it has become clear that he is not to be "in like Flynn" with Kate or Fiona. At this point there is a sense of relief that Simmonds's outrageous abuse of power has run its course; the underlying psychological pattern has been revealed, and the other characters have departed, together with most of the props. The complicity of the reluctant Ross and the departed characters, the detached figure of the removalist with his farcical entries and exits, and his exercising of authority over Ross, and even Simmonds (who loses his tussle for dominance over what should be taken next) lend the action a grimly comic and absurd tone. The high frequency of simultaneous interaction is more farcical than realistic. (pp. 318-22)

The pivotal point, at which the play turns against the audience's expectations, is when Ross, goaded beyond endurance by all the humiliations inflicted upon him, beserkly bashes Kenny (offstage). In their ensuing, panic-stricken exchange until they notice Kenny sitting behind them, the near-hysterical Ross dominates and alarms Simmonds. Then, after Simmonds seems to have regained control and he and Kenny establish their essential similarity through discussing the call-girl bribe, the play even more unexpectedly reverts to the menacing as Kenny collapses. The shift into the coda, with the more panic-stricken recapitulation of the previous struggle between Simmonds and Ross, terminating in the absurd logic of their pummelling each other (now there is no one else left to pummel) brings out the play's symbolic pattern of interaction in a rhythmically satisfying way—and by essentially dramatic means.

While not being a literal representative of the actual, a direct slice of life, *The Removalists* (and the quiet irony of the title captures a lot of its black comedy) presents with compelling, if irrational, dramatic logic a metaphor of a world in which relationships are predatory, cruel and vicious beneath the humdrum surface. The calculated stereotyping of the characters—when Simmonds's official mask slips his "real" self proves to be *homo suburbiensis*—and the tangled web of authoritarianism-sexuality-insecurity-violence that enmeshes the characters produce a play which is only "quasi-naturalistic" and with very definite "absurdist overtones". In production, the pacing and the final fight, which is intended to take on "almost . . . the air of a frenzied ritual of exorcism" would be crucial to the establishment of these over-

tones. Too slow a pace (to fill out an evening's entertainment, with intervals), too strenuous an effort to flesh out the characters and give them naturalistic individuality, or allow a "star" performance, too insistent a determination to hammer home the play's immediacy, relevance and social significance—too heavy an emphasis in any of these ways and the play's original, satisfying achievement, the dramatic logic with which the situation is developed and turned, reversed and then turned again, in a movement that needs no explicatory dialogue to show Simmonds trapped in the violence he has initiated, would be obscured by misdirected production "business". (pp. 322-23)

[*Jugglers Three*] is a more "mature" *Stork*—though more mature only in that the three male characters involved with the *femme fatale* are older than Tony, West and Clyde in the earlier play. Again a zany intrudes to disrupt the tense pattern of their relationships, this time with the police in pursuit, and provides a (possible) farcical resolution of the sexual imbroglio. However, the ending with its engaging business of Graham and Karen playing table tennis and arguing as the lights go down, leaves open the final resolution of their conflict. The "quasi-naturalistic" strain and the "absurdist overtones" that blend so well in the styles of the two preceding plays are at odds here; and Williamson seems uncertain as to the level he is writing on. There are potentially real issues which are consistent with those in his other plays: Graham's war service in Vietnam, his menacing games with Neville, and his story of shooting the American general; the marital tensions that affect most of the characters (even the zany) and which are focused in Elizabeth, the pregnant deserted wife who feels the pressures to appear tolerant and "understanding" in a situation she finds bewildering. The essentially farcical action does not allow engagement with these issues, however. (pp. 324-25)

[*What If You Died Tomorrow*] is better integrated structurally; it is more conventionally structured than any of the earlier plays and the developments it shows are in the direction of "naturalism" understood as the well-made slice of life. The characters are located in a very specific milieu (an artists' colony on the outskirts of Melbourne; the world of publishing), some of them seem to invite identification with well known personalities outside the play, and there is an expository probing of past relationships (especially between the mother and the father) that is almost a guaranteed means of ensuring "deeper" characterization. *What If* is an autobiographical play, and a pièce à clef which does not so much present an imaginative world, as *The Removalists* does, as mirror a real one. I'd suspect, from a number of comments he has made in interviews, that one sense that Williamson had in mind in referring to his work as "naturalistic" is that it draws on personal experience and direct observation. However, as the plays of Dorothy Hewett show, the autobiographical does not in itself demand a naturalistic style, and *What If* is less a naturalistic autobiographical play (as Peter Kenna's *A Hard God* is) than a drawing-room comedy—or a mud-brick, exposed beam, family living-room comedy.

Andrew, the doctor who has become a successful novelist and a darling of the media, especially the women's magazines, we can take as being in some way a self-portrait executed with detachment, amusement, and accuracy (if one recalls some of the articles written about Williamson). Kirsty's statement that "There's an awful lot of women who aren't stereotypes and it's about time he started writing about them" picks up one of the most frequent criticisms of the earlier plays, especially *The Removalists.* References to Andrew's rival, Freddie Hubbard, and the figure of Harry Bustle, the literary hustler, provide not only some literary satiric comedy but also indications of Williamson's awareness of the pressures success brings. Bustle, the clown of the piece, is incensed by the literary agent's charge that he had "fucked up" the previous manuscript (*Jugglers Three?* or *The Removalists* in commercial production?)

> Fucked it up? The biggest success the local industry's ever had. Film sale within two months of publication. I wish I had someone to fuck things up like that for me, and as far as quality is concerned, O'Hearn, remember this. You can sell the public shit and you can sell the public quality, but the one thing you can't sell the public is boring shit or boring quality.

Longer speeches such as this represent a change of style from the usual more dramatically integrated exchanges of the early plays, and can become a means of padding out with purely entertaining gagging, as in Harry's story about Marcus mounting the horse. The demented entries and exits of Gunter show another familiar element in Williamson's theatrical style pointlessly developed in isolation from the rest. When they first appear with Gunter, Andrew's parents, very much stereotypes in a familiar Barry Humphries pattern, threaten to overpopulate the play with clowns and weigh it heavily on the side of farce; however, something more subtle and structurally satisfying develops.

Ken and Irene, who maintain the values and sexual attitudes of an earlier generation, are the figures from outside who introduce a different set of norms into the play. In their relationships with the other characters, especially Andrew, Williamson's interest in the histrionic games that people play in their interactions reasserts itself and shapes the play as both farce and existential drama. More important than any other structural principle is the awareness of how individuals respond to each other in terms of the roles of "parent", "adult" and "child", and shift from one to the other. As the chief character, Andrew of course provides the best example. When the play opens he is playing parent to Kirsty's children, when he comes downstairs he is adult in response to her being adult, when Ken and Irene appear he is a child to them—but insists on being adult and can play parent to his mother's role as child, and (as a doctor) to his father's also. Later he and Carmel wilfully play naughty childish games. His playing with the building set (again an engaging piece of stage business, with more symbolic point than the table tennis of the previous play) suggests both his regression under these pressures and his defiant building of his own life. What emerges finally is the sense that, despite all the conflicting demands made upon him, Andrew must make his own choice and structure his own life. He may, like his structure, appear chaotic but it is not randomly so; and it has a vitality that asserts itself against the entropy of his parents' lives. I suspect that behind the glossy sensationalism of the film *Petersen* is a similar existential attitude (delivered at one stage from the pulpit). To recognize, to understand, the conflict of attitudes, norms and personalities rather than to judge or impose his own values is Williamson's implicit, and essentially comic, stand. (pp. 325-27)

[*The Department*] shows a similar concern to present patterns of interaction with comic detachment, and understand-

ing. These interactions take place within an institution, and Williamson has drawn on his experience as a lecturer in the Mechanical Engineering Department at Swinburne College of Technology for many of his authenticating details. The situation is a staff meeting, and the focus is as much on the pattern of relationships that is revealed, the range of typical responses, the analysis of the leadership offered and the power struggle that develops within the ritual procedures as on the characters as individuals and the substance of their discussion. Williamson himself does not become involved with the personalities or the issues. His concern is to reveal the comedy of how institutions function, and with Robby, the department's head, to present an archetypal bureaucrat, rather than a reprehensible mini-Nixon. Principles and ideals are the first casualties in the battle to maintain or increase power; they become merely particular moves in the game of dominating one's challengers at any cost. By allowing the underlying pattern to emerge clearly instead of pursuing the particular substance of the discussion, the farcical possibilities inherent in the situation are brought nicely into balance with the realistic details, and implicitly allow extension to other institutions and other issues. The essential mimesis is not so much that this play imitates an actual staff meeting as that such meetings anywhere imitate plays, their scenarios have already been scripted, consciously or not, by the authority figure. Robby's script is quite obvious—the comedy springs from the difficulties he has in persuading his actors to play their roles. (pp. 327-28)

Williamson does not present Robby as a target for easy satire or judgement. As the discussion of the incident at the last Founder's Day ceremony shows, Robby's pragmatism can counter Myra's ideological purity with human sympathy—or is it that he uses sympathy for Miss Milton to justify not bucking the system? Ideals and practicability, principles and practice, ends and means become hopelessly confused in a way that is both realistic and absurd. By not allowing specifically educational issues to be pursued, Williamson can suggest a more general case: how any institution can (in the manner analysed by Weber) lose sight of its goals and direct its resources to maintaining and expanding itself, even in ways contrary to its ostensible function. This institution's absurd remoteness from reality is expressed by uncertainty whether the towing tank would burst if filled (and more comically by Robby's inability to build a model boat that will float). Robby's rival for authority is the fellow realist Gordon, the comic figure of this play, whose opening of the valves is the act of a true pragmatist. The sense of institutional entropy, of a futile loss of energy, that comes from Robby's converting this discovery into a future move in his battles with Fletcher brings out the underlying absurdity of these games. Meanwhile, outside Milton—as we know from Owen's telephone enquiries—the real world is renewing itself.

The Department is a better integrated play than the previous two Williamson has written for the established theatre. It is more consistent in its style, more even, if flatly realistic, in tone. Less flamboyantly farcical, its overtones are still absurdist. Like the best of his early plays, it is, in its implications, about more than its manifest content—which one cannot say confidently of *Jugglers Three* or *What If.* Like *The Removalists,* and perhaps most of the best plays that have come out of the "alternative" theatre, it is essentially a one-acter. There is some inflation: the attempts to give some realistic "depth" to the characters outside of their institutional roles at the beginning of Part Two degenerates into gagging (there is also the appalling Calwell gag in Part One); Myra is too obviously introduced to represent an alternative educational world. However, these are not excessive faults, and Williamson seems confidently in control overall, blending farce and "naturalism" in a dramatically coherent and meaningful way. Unlike many of the other writers associated with the "new wave", he has not shown any interest in experimenting outside his characteristic mode. In the first plays written outside his original theatrical ambience he seems to have confused the development of his "naturalism" (his writing from experience and direct observation) with the need to write well made conventionally structured entertainments. In these his style tended to fragment, to break down into its component elements. *The Department* moves back towards the structural and stylistic strengths of *Don's Party* and *The Removalists,* even if it lacks their exuberant, driving vitality, and promises interesting developments in the plays that, hopefully, will follow it. (pp. 328-29)

> Brian Kiernan, *"The Games People Play: The Development of David Williamson,"* in Southerly, *Vol. 35, No. 4, December, 1975, pp. 315-29.*

JOHN SIMON

Occasionally in the first act, and quite often in the second, there is genuine humor [in *Players*]. It is vulgar humor, though not without sophisticated undertones, and if you do not ask for more than light entertainment from the theater, you could do worse than this.

Actually, *Players* could have been more than what it ends up being. Williamson, as I have found also in another work of his, *Don's Party* (which is even funnier and also more vulgar), has difficulties with his exposition: It takes him rather too long to set the scene and get his characters established. Then, in this case at least, he does not quite have the courage of his convictions. A play that is clearly destined to be an utterly cynical dissection of the dirty doings in the boardroom of a professional football club—where players and coaches are ruthlessly bought and sold, and where fellow board members smile and lie and stab one another in the back—changes its course near the end, and becomes heartwarming and positively hopeful. Suddenly, there is sympathy for everyone (except one arch fool and one double-dyed villain) as natural opponents join hands, and I could as soon read the complete works of Henry Handel Richardson as believe that.

Well, of course, *Players* does not ask to be believed in, merely to be laughed at, and at that level it is passably successful. (p. 147)

> John Simon, *"Short of the Mark,"* in New York Magazine, *Vol. 11, No. 39, September 25, 1978, pp. 147-48.*

PHILIP PARSONS

At the end of David Williamson's *What If You Died Tomorrow* Andrew, the successful novelist, has survived another day's assaults on his family life, his professional life, his peace of mind. As the lights fade he is left alone with the structure he has been putting together throughout the play from the children's building blocks. *It is chaotic but not randomly so,* read the stage directions. He adds a couple of finishing touches and goes off to bed. *The structure remains in the dim light.*

It is quite aesthetically pleasing. The metaphor extends beyond the ordering of Andrew's life to the play itself; the writer's ordering of his work is equally a refuge from the chaos of experience, coming at him from all sides, and a means of making something of it.

This emphasis on structuring experience is fundamental to David Williamson's idea of the theatre. We are reminded that he came to play writing as a graduate in mechanical engineering who had extended his interests to psychology. The elements of experience are to be brought together, juxtaposed to suggest pattern, relationship, meaning; while the audience, he hopes, will 'compare and test their own reaction to situations against those of the stage characters'. And just as the point of Andrew's exercise is not to design new building blocks but to make something of them, so Williamson's characters and situations solicit our attention, not for their realistic execution, but for the structure of meaning of which they are components. To dwell on the conventional reticence of his naturalistic surface, as academic criticism has tended to do, is to be assured of missing the point.

Not building a structure, but drawing the threads of his life together, is the image used by old Frank, the retired engineer at the centre of *Travelling North,* in an explicit and final demand for meaning. Perhaps for this reason Williamson's writing in this play has the lovely athletic clarity of a thing stripped to essentials. The texture remains naturalistic, but the form is anatomised as unified time and place are dissected into a succession of scenes—a technique tried and abandoned after his earliest full-length play, *The Coming of Stork,* but returned to now with a sophistication far removed from the simple narrative sequence of the earlier work. On a stage that fluctuates between sub-tropical Tweed Heads and wintry Melbourne, an insistent fragmentation of the action signals that each scene—perhaps no more than a few lines—is to be inspected and registered as in some sense exemplary. Scenes are to be compared, connected, slotted together in a growing structure that will be complete only with the last scene of all. No form could more perfectly express the search for meaning in a life shortly to end, which is the theme of *Travelling North.*

At curtain rise, when the audience is most receptive, dramatists are inclined to introduce leading ideas. The first scene in *Travelling North* brings into sharp focus two contrasting, complementary temperaments. . . . Frank, the rational creature, Frances, the feeling creature. While Frances talks about their relationship and the pleasure of being together, Frank is working with a slide rule, pencil and notebook, calculating the unsatisfactory mileage per gallon of their campervan, and inveighing against dishonest salesmen. . . . Detail by detail the contrast is built up—yet not to the point of making Frank a monster or Frances a saint; on the contrary, Frank seems an attractive fellow in his shrewd, Jack Blunt way, and Frances simply gentle and reticent.

The angle of vision changes as the conversation moves on to the reactions of their respective children to the coming together of their elderly parents outside marriage. Frances is distressed that her daughters are shocked; Frank simply warns her of their exploitative nature—they will be reluctant to part with their mother's services as a baby-sitter. At the same time, Frances' obvious love for her daughters is contrasted with Frank's testy rejection of his own son. . . . (pp. 121-22)

The remarkable elegance and economy of the opening scene are achieved by the precise juxtaposition of its elements. The component scenes of the following action are similarly precise. In a sequence of five scenes all set in Melbourne, the relationships of Frank and Frances with their children are elaborated. . . . Finally, in an edgy teacup confrontation, the family lines are crossed as [Frances's daughter] Helen calls on Frank to let him know her feelings. Under the polite forms of suburban decorum each goes for the jugular. We have seen all we need know of life in Melbourne; with a burst of Vivaldi and a flood of golden green light the play moves to Tweed Heads and a new life.

It is the masterly juxtaposition of these scenes that most commands admiration. While their content is lucidly instructive, the audience learns most by looking at each in the light of the last and putting two and two together. The more sympathetically we look at domestic pressures which Frances and Frank need to leave behind them, the more they seem to be of their own making. Unlike Frank, Frances is sensitive to her daughters' unhappiness and blames herself for it. Her refusal to settle, to define herself, has kept her own spirit open to life but at the expense of her daughters' inner security. Travelling north, Frances needs to escape from her sense of guilt. Frank, untroubled by guilt, feels he needs to get away from the pressure of people to examine his life for its meaning. They both have a lot to do.

It will not be by avoiding people but through them that Frank will find himself. In the manner of this play, the people he meets in his philosophic retreat are exemplary. First, at the moment of congratulating themselves on their total isolation, Frank and Frances discover a neighbour in Freddie, common man, decent sort, RSL clubman, whose company is as unattractive to Frank as his views on Vietnam. Yet, reluctantly, Frank finds himself accepting Freddie's help in settling in. 'We mightn't see eye to eye on everything,' says Freddie, 'but I think you'll find I'm a good neighbour.' Frank's commitment to reason and principle are important (and, after all, Vietnam was wrong) but he will need good neighbourliness and affection before long. And he will need Saul, doctor and disabused European intellectual, who is content to take people as they come while he awaits his own death with cynical calm. Freddie and Saul will walk beside Frank to the end of the play, the believer and the unbeliever, common decency and fellow feeling.

For it is the shocking revelation of infirmity in his vigorous old age that will force Frank to realise his dependence on other human beings and their rights in him. At first he simply resists his illnesses with all the resource of an informed and determined mind. . . . But as his losing battle comes to occupy his whole attention, his temper and progressive withdrawal are making it impossible for Frances to live with him. . . . It is only when Frances is moved to tell him, 'You're a rude, arrogant, despotic old bully', and returns to Melbourne, that he is shocked into the realisation that principle, reason and an iron will are inadequate to his need. The only way to save one's life is to live it, and the only way to live it is through human beings. (pp. 123-24)

Frances, meanwhile, has had her own painful illumination. Forced to watch her daughters heading for catastrophe, she has come to realise as rationally as would Frank that they are responsible for their own lives. She can at last leave guilt behind as she returns north. She and Frank alike have entered now into a larger freedom of the spirit, where the union of marriage, which Frances has longed for and Frank denied, has become possible and necessary.

The play rises to their wedding, or rather fertility rite, in a last splendid access of comic energy. Descending on Sydney, they brush aside the ineffectual marriage celebrant and crash, with buccaneering vitality, the Brett Whiteley erotic exhibition, exhausting themselves afterwards in their motel bedroom. Back in Tweed Heads Frank dies with a sense of fulfilment.

If that carefully calculated structure described so far has suggested the engineer and the psychologist, it will also have emerged as the structure of a poet. The action moves steadily between wintry Melbourne and the perpetual spring of the sub-tropics. Winter, literally, is killing Frank and the constricting pressures of family have withered Frances. As Frank says, 'It's time you started enjoying life.' The whole current of the play runs from unrealised life to fullness of living. To this extent it looks like a seasonal celebration somewhat in the manner of *The Winter's Tale;* but the opposition of winter and spring is not simply that of death and life. Williamson's Melbourne is very noticably full of babies and clucky mothers, while death haunts the paradisal imagery of the tropic north. If Melbourne is associated with the diminished life of winter, it is because the whole world it represents—the world of business, of buying and selling, of marrying and giving in marriage, of babies and the daily domestic round—is to be seen as less than fully vital. In the midst of life we are in Melbourne. And if the paradisal north is associated with renewed and heightened life, it also means dying. To move from Melbourne to the tropics means to pass from one dimension to another.

The meaning of these seasonal polarities embraces politics and even religion. Here too we have the image of renewal. The end of the play, when Frank returns with Frances from voting for Whitlam, announcing 'the tide that is going to sweep in a new era', may at first seem a bitter irony in the light of the subsequent historical events. Yet not so. This moment has been carefully anticipated by Frank's wistful memory of his Communist hopes betrayed by Stalin. . . . Tempered, through thirty years' experience of Communism, Frank's political hopes are no longer naive. Whitlam may or may not bring in the brave new world. The point is that we must leave disillusion and defeat behind us and travel on. (pp. 124-25)

The end of the play is more ritual than realism. There occurs a series of incidents which deny death and affirm Frank's personality and enlargement into life. After his unremarked death we find him sitting in his chair in the final scene while Saul reads a letter full of Frank's authentic irony. He is launched into the next world with a magnum of champagne. The abrupt movement of his mechanical footrest almost brings him back to life, to the sardonic alarm of Saul. And Frances is specifically directed to bring Freddie and Saul out into the sunlight with their champagne glasses while the radio plays a Brandenburg concerto, the vigorous music of mathematics for an engineer. As Frances remarks that she believes she will continue travelling north, the author directs that Frank will rise from his chair and join the others at the front of the stage to acknowledge the audience applause. Wherever death may be in this play, it is not here. That is what it means to travel north. *Travelling North* is the most religious play that Williamson has ever written. (pp. 125-26)

Philip Parsons, "This World and the Next," in London Magazine, n.s. Vol. 20, Nos. 8 & 9, November & December, 1980, pp. 121-26.

DAVID DENBY

Gallipoli, a celebration of Australian innocence and courage in World War I, has the simplicity and fervent, bright colors of an old ballad. Peter Weir's film, written by Australian playwright David Williamson, is lyrical and anecdotal rather than dramatic. It doesn't give you the political background of that disastrous campaign of 1915 in which the British dreamed of gaining control of the Dardanelles, a folly in which thousands of Australian and New Zealand (as well as British and French) troops died without dislodging the Turks. The theme of *Gallipoli* is familiar (in a sense, it's the only World War I theme): the needless slaughter of valiant youth. The two heroes from western Australia, both fleet-footed sprinters who meet their destiny running, are likable, uncomplicated boys who haven't tasted much of life before they sign up for war. Golden-haired Archy is a stalwart eighteen-year-old who thinks that war is a great and glorious adventure; Frank, a harmless rascal, not so brave as Archy but more appealing, drifts into battle without feeling much of anything. They may be heroes out of a boys' adventure book, but this boys' book ends in horror—a pointless charge across an open field into Turkish machine guns. . . .

A good case can be made that the British made cynical use of the Australians at Gallipoli, and that the Australians were naïve and subservient. There's a suggestion of this in the movie, but only a suggestion. Weir and Williamson don't fall into the trap of mocking the patriotic sentiments of the past, though they show the innocent, dumb pathos of it—the country track meets in Australia that turn into rah-rah recruiting sessions; the high sentiment of soldiers sailing away to war; the clownishly inadequate training sessions in the Egyptian desert near the pyramids.

Like the American platoon movies of World War II, *Gallipoli* is devoted to the rituals of male camaraderie—rivalries and partings and exuberant reconciliations. The movie has a few too many "typical" incidents, and it's slightly impersonal—we don't know any more about those boys at the end than we did at the beginning. I wish the filmmakers had cleared up some key points: Was the senseless charge against the Turkish lines the result (as the film suggests) of simple errors and poor communication, or was there some more sinister design behind the Australian disaster? Why weren't the Australians equipped with mortars, so they could take out the Turkish machine-gunners? The movie's point of view is unformed and a little timid, and what we're likely to take away from it are individual sequences of great beauty—a night landing, with soldiers in longboats silently rowing toward shore while fires burn on the hill above the beach; a group of men, in a daredevil stunt, shucking their clothes and swimming naked underwater as shells explode on top of them (one man, grinning broadly, surfaces with a bloodied arm). [*Gallipoli* is] an essentially undramatic film of great pictorial beauty. (p. 52)

David Denby, "Boys at War," in New York Magazine, Vol. 14, No. 34, August 31, 1981, pp. 52-3.

STANLEY KAUFFMANN

Gallipoli is a Young Person's Guide to Grimness. This Australian film, which deals with the bloodily disastrous Allied expedition on the Turkish peninsula in 1915-16—at least, that's where it ends—is so thin that at times I felt that I was looking through the stretched film at the naked screen. The script was written by David Williamson, whose football play *The Club* was produced in New York a few years ago and was similarly thin. (p. 22)

Two young Australians, both runners, compete in a race in 1915, join the army because they have heard about their countrymen at Gallipoli, are assigned to different regiments but are reunited while training in Egypt, and are sent to Gallipoli together. We are not given much chance to miss the Bitterness of It All. The result of their shining youthful enthusiasm is that they are callously fed into a meat grinder. The officer's pistol shot that sends Youth One over the top to certain death reminds us of the starter's pistol in the races back home. As the boy charges through the machine-gun hail, he repeats his coach's instructions about running. (But he carries no weapon. What did he expect if he reached the Turkish trenches, a medal?) And Youth Two, who is running through the bombarded trenches with an order from the high command that would have saved his friend's life, is too late—he hears the "starter's" pistol before he can get back to his own trench.

Add to all this the *Journey's End* touches—the officer who, the night before the attack, celebrates his wedding anniversary by drinking champagne and listening to Bizet on the gramophone while his soldiers stand respectfully in the doorway, this same officer who next day utters that imperishable line, "I can't ask my men to do what I won't do," and leads them over the top—and you have a film perfectly geared to early high school ironies. *Gallipoli* has a few hints in it of resentment of the British high command's possible use of Australian troops as decoys to draw fire away from British troops. This theme might have given the picture some bite, but it's not developed. (pp. 22-3)

Stanley Kauffmann, "Innocents Abroad," in The New Republic, Vol. 185, No. 18, November 4, 1981, pp. 22-3.

DAVID DENBY

[In *The Year of Living Dangerously,* director Peter Weir] and his screenwriter, David Williamson (adapting a novel by the Australian writer C. J. Koch), have tried for the old Warner Bros. mix of romance and politics, but they can't seem to pull the different elements of the picture together. What is this movie about? A journalist's soul? The chagrin of being intellectual and a dwarf? (You heard me.) The moral squalor of Westerners in Asia? Love in the tropics? Whither Indonesia? . . .

Guy Hamilton [is] a young, untested Australian radio-TV journalist assigned to Jakarta. Hamilton is brash, a bit of a bumbler, but energetic and likable—the standard, uncomplicated movie hero of 50 years ago. Arriving in the capital . . . , he's dismayed by the impoverished people pressing in on all sides, and turned off by the other Western journalists, a besotted, cynical lot hanging out at the bar of an air-conditioned hotel. Instinctively decent but raw and unformed, Guy becomes the protégé of Billy Kwan, a Chinese-Australian dwarf of indeterminate age who acts as a cameraman for the Australians. . . .

Billy is a philosophical, despondent type who quotes Tolstoy at the drop of a hat and listens to Richard Strauss's elegiac *Four Last Songs* in his bungalow. He's meant to be a kind of diarist of the soul, a novelist without novels who tries to play God—he intones his "sensitive" observations of Guy and the other Western characters on the soundtrack. Billy, who brings money to a starving family living on a canal, represents the only strain of charity and humanity in the violent flux of Indonesian politics. He gets Guy to broadcast news about the Indonesian poor, and he introduces him to another protégé, swank Gillian Bryant, who works for the British Embassy as a military aide of some sort. As bamboos bend and groan in the wind, Jill and Guy begin a steamy affair. Meanwhile, in the film's impossibly shadowy background, the left and the right slug it out for political power (moviegoers unfamiliar with Indonesian politics, i.e., nearly all of us, are going to be baffled). . . .

Suddenly, out of nowhere, Guy's office assistant, a dour Indonesian Communist named Kumar, becomes a major character. Kumar solemnly leads Guy to some sort of retreat in the mountains, where he speaks of social reform in a slightly sinister way, causing Guy to have a sweaty nightmare. As critics in the screening room turned to one another in wonder ("*Now* what?"), the movie shifted to a consideration of Guy's integrity and honor as a journalist—something we hadn't thought to question before. . . . [Meanwhile, a] little boy [Billy] has been supporting dies, and Billy goes crazy, denounces his friends, and launches a suicidal protest against the corrupt Sukarno. (p. 62)

The filmmakers don't seem to realize that Billy is essentially a highminded voyeur: He brings people together, takes pictures of them, keeps notes on their moral character, and feels betrayed when they don't live up to his ideals. A nice guy, perhaps, but a bit creepy. . . .

The movie is dripping with highly moral sentiments, but despite its dislike of drunken Westerners and its grieving over poverty, *The Year of Living Dangerously* betrays nothing so indiscreet as a political point of view. "We will win because we believe in something," says the Communist, Kumar, at the end. The line pops out of nowhere. Kumar sounds like Paul Henreid in an anti-fascist movie, though as prophecy this is bizarrely inept, since the Indonesian Communists did not win in 1965 but were slaughtered by the thousands. . . . Are we meant to take the line as a portent of events in Vietnam and Cambodia? If so, the director and the screenwriter might have asked what happens to "belief" when the believers take power—a good subject for a movie. . . . (p. 63)

David Denby, "Java Jive," in New York *Magazine, Vol. 16, No. 4, January 24, 1983, pp. 62-3.*

JOHN SIMON

Based on a novel by C. J. Koch, who collaborated on the screenplay with [director Peter Weir] and the gifted David Williamson, [*The Year of Living Dangerously*] concerns the year in Sukarno's Indonesia when an abortive Communist coup resulted not only in large-scale slaughter, but also in the beginning of Sukarno's downfall. Guy Hamilton is a young Australian journalist who gets his first big chance in Djakarta, where he is taken under the wing of Billy Kwan, a photographer of Chinese-Australian parentage, and a midget to boot. Billy is an idealist who hopes against hope as well as

available evidence that Sukarno can lead his country out of poverty and away from being a political football. He aids the natives in every way he can and helps Guy, who likewise seems decent and concerned, to get good stories for which he, Billy, supplies the photographs. (p. 336)

Billy is hopelessly in love with the tall and beautiful young Englishwoman Jill Bryant, an aide at the British embassy, and possibly involved in some sort of espionage. . . . Billy is Jill's best friend, has promoted her previous love affair, and now, with vicarious satisfaction, steers Guy and Jill together. He also keeps elaborate pictorial and verbal files on the people who interest him, and altogether tries to be the puppet who'll pull the puppeteer's strings: the imp, not of the ridiculous, but of the sublime.

The Year of Living Dangerously (as Sukarno, grandiosely, dubbed the year 1965, and the film, typically, fails to explain) has some positive aspects. The location shooting in the Philippines succeeds (I am told) in plausibly evoking Djakarta and environs; the contrast between diplomatic affluence and immunity and native poverty and nonimmunity to deadly diseases is vividly enough conveyed; and the sodden, cynical Graham Greeneland of foreign correspondents working in frenzied spurts and as little as possible, while drinking and wenching (or, to coin a word, ladding) as much as conditions allow—and they allow plenty—is captured with slick but efficient nastiness.

Yet what is all this against the film's many thundering failures? Both Indonesia's bloody mess and the greater disaster of Vietnam looming in the background serve merely as a picturesque and allegedly suspenseful setting for a foolish love story involving Guy, Jill, and, indirectly, Billy. We get, for example, the lovers on their first night together, joy-riding through a military curfew blockade, and treating the gunfire riddling their car as if it were so much rice pelting newlyweds. When two of Guy's employees, secret Communists, abduct our hero so he cannot stand in the way of the putsch, he is taken to an exotic, secluded villa where he watches a stunning young woman do some sexy diving and has suitably erotic dreams. When Guy must catch the last plane out of Djakarta, on which Jill awaits him, he drives and marches (though seriously wounded) through revolution and counterrevolution (colorful mass executions by the roadside), bureaucratic red tape, and hundreds ahead of him trying to make that plane, triumphantly trots up into it and Jill's outspread arms at the last second, and blissfully flies off to haven and heaven.

Even that may not be the very worst. After Billy's idealistic, heroic, and quite unbelievable death, Guy and Jill are sadly going through the files in the dead dwarf's house in the woods. Soldiers are closing in on them; Guy bravely dispatches Jill in the car while bracing himself for the onslaught. The next scene takes place much later, and we never find out what happened. Still, I suppose, the audience should not know more than the [filmmakers]. (pp. 336-37)

John Simon, "Sweet and Sour," in National Review, *New York, Vol. XXXV, March 18, 1983, pp. 335-37.*

PETER LEWIS

Because 'comic' is so often debased to being no more than an antonym of 'serious', the comic dramatist today suffers from the suspicion that he is a lightweight entertainer, a purveyor of easy laughter. The commercial theatre and television have encouraged such a conception of comedy, one that would not have recommended itself to Jonson, Molière, and Congreve in the seventeenth century or to Wilde and Shaw nearer our own time. Indeed, for the great tradition of comic writers going back to Aristophanes, comedy is a way of being serious, and it is in this context that Williamson deserves to be approached as a comic dramatist. His last but one play, *Celluloid Heroes,* may have moved in the direction of farce, but his characteristic blend of the naturalistic and the comic is normally very different from farce. Like other writers of his generation who question the received pieties and liberal orthodoxies of the past twenty-five years, Williamson has found that comedy is not only an essential weapon but an altogether more satisfactory way of being serious than humourless solemnity. Furthermore, laughter in Williamson's plays can easily slide into pathos; jokes conceal pain; wit can be a means of holding anguish at bay. (pp. 70-1)

The Perfectionist recalls several earlier Williamson plays in its searching analysis of both marriage and the upper-middle-class Australian intelligentsia, but in this case the focus is on one couple, Stuart and Barbara Gunn, the only other participants being Stuart's parents, Jack and Shirley Gunn, and a handsome Danish Marxist called Erik, whom they employ as a childminder during a six-month academic visit to Denmark and who later visits Australia. (p. 71)

The play opens with Barbara functioning as narrator, a rôle she adopts intermittently, to explain to the audience that what they are about to see is her disastrous attempt to remake her marriage on 'open' lines according to the permissive gospel of George and Nena O'Neill in such influential books of American pop psychology as *Open Marriage.* While in Denmark at the opening of the play, Barbara is prepared to make all the usual female sacrifices so that her academic economist husband can advance his career by completing what he believes to be a world-shaking PhD, which has occupied him for nearly ten years. At the outset, Stuart is the perfectionist of the title, someone whose commitment to academic excellence is almost obsessional and who is totally convinced that he has a major contribution to make. He is blind to much else in his life, especially himself. Without lapsing into farce or caricature, Williamson wrings a great deal of wry humour from this situation, especially from Stuart's unwitting revelations of male chauvinism while believing himself to be far from 'piggish'. Erik's fashionably Marcusian rhetoric and jargon is another source of humour, although Williamson is careful not to belittle this character, who exerts a powerful influence on Barbara.

When the Gunns return to Australia with Stuart's magnum opus still incomplete, the long-suffering Barbara turns the tables on her husband by insisting on time to complete her PhD and pursue her career. Barbara, too, proves to be a perfectionist of a kind in her pursuit of an ideal relationship based on the O'Neills' conception of open marriage devoid of jealousy and possessiveness. According to the theory, independence and liberation from closed ideas should lead to mutual growth, greater enrichment and happiness, but this turns out to be as much of an illusion as Stuart's belief in his intellectual brilliance and superiority. Stuart's universe comes crashing down when he discovers that he has not only been scooped by another researcher but that his theory was in any case based on faulty assumptions.

Dropping the myth of his virtual genius, which has been nourished by his overbearing father, a successful and wealthy barrister, Stuart is persuaded by Barbara to devote himself to everything he has neglected for his work. He is now supposed to become a fuller, more liberated person capable of 'meaningful human relationships' and 'empathy', to employ two vogue terms of recent years. The spectacle is both hilarious and sad, as Stuart's own vulnerability becomes increasingly obvious. In Williamson's hands, the doctrine of open marriage as expounded by the O'Neills is exposed as more destructive than creative because it is based on such an optimistically naive and sentimental conception of human nature. Stuart is unable to discard all those traditional attitudes of jealousy and possessiveness that 'liberated' and 'beautiful' people are supposed to shed as they grow into fulfilling openness. At the end of the play, after Barbara has had an affair with Erik, Stuart and Barbara are left with their illusions crumbling and their marriage in danger of total collapse. Only by rejecting the utopian fantasy world of pop psychology, shedding layers of self-deception, and returning to reality, with all its contradictions and limitations, will they rescue themselves and their marriage. (pp. 71-3)

The Perfectionist is clearly a play about an issue that currently occupies plenty of space in newspapers and magazines: the institution of marriage and its (possible) future. But through this theme and the related issues of feminism and sexism, Williamson is also exploring the dangers inherent in idealism, the aspiration to create perfection in the realm of the human. Stuart is committed to one kind of perfection and fails. Barbara attempts to create an ideal relationship and fails. Erik, the ideological purist and social drop-out, is devoted to the perfectibility of society in Denmark, but is much more uncertain several years later while visiting Australia. The fate of perfectionists, Williamson is saying, is disillusionment. Nevertheless, if *The Perfectionist* is at heart a deeply serious play presenting an essentially pessimistic view of human yearnings and limitations, it does so with a wealth of verbal wit and comic invention. Indeed, the play is so amusing and jokey that the wider implications might easily be overlooked and engulfed in laughter. Williamson certainly walks an artistic tightrope throughout *The Perfectionist* but manages to keep a delicate balance between realism and caricature, seriousness and comedy. One of his most important achievements during the last ten or so years is to have rehabilitated comedy as a serious form for the Australian theatre, much as that very different playwright Tom Stoppard has done for the English theatre during a slightly longer period. (pp. 73-4)

Peter Lewis, "After 'The Perfectionist': An Interview with David Williamson," in London Magazine, *n.s. Vol. 23, Nos. 5 & 6, August & September, 1983, pp. 70-82.*

BENEDICT NIGHTINGALE

David Williamson is best remembered, at least in the filing-cabinet I carry on my shoulders, for his hilarious studies of antipodean macho in action. *Sons of Cain,* however, is on a more particular subject, investigative journalists versus corrupt politicians in 'a capital city of Australia'; and it turns out to be one that has stimulated its author's creative imagination rather less. At any rate, the play sometimes substitutes mere stereotype for the energetic grotesquerie of *The Removalists* and *Don's Party* and becomes pedestrian and plodding in its fictional reconstruction of a real-life scandal that does (let's face it) seem remote from the stance of north-west Europe, small and insular when compared with happenings in Washington in the early Seventies. Williamson could have opted for the gaudy ebullience of *Pravda;* he could have preferred the authenticity of Stephen Wakelam's *Deadlines.* As it is, his contribution to the theatre's intensifying debate on newspapers and newspeople falls between the two. It lacks both fun and documentary authority.

To be more specific, Max Cullen is the shambling, boozy but good-hearted editor hired to bring spirit to an ailing weekly review. With the help of three women reporters—each with her own personal or ideological axe heavily to grind—he's soon on the trail of those at the top who have been quietly benefitting from the dope trade. Inevitably, there are counter-pressures, from affronted politicians, libel lawyers, the newspaper's advertising people, and its nervous owner, who finds himself losing popularity on the old-school-tie circuit; but almost as inevitably, they're overcome by determination and graft and the editor's bloodyminded honesty. The play has its thoughtful moments. It is, let's also agree, refreshingly optimistic after *Pravda* and *Deadlines,* both of which suggested that truth invariably gets warped somewhere between the event and the page or TV screen. If only one could fully believe it, or feel it hugely mattered. (pp. 30-1)

> Benedict Nightingale, "Child's Play," in New Statesman, Vol. 111, No. 2879, May 30, 1986, pp. 30-1.

DAVID WILLIAMSON [INTERVIEW WITH PAUL KAVANAGH AND PETER KUCH]

[Kavanagh]: You have said that you don't see yourself as a catalyst for social or political change. Has this view of yourself changed in the last few years?

[Williamson]: Well, I suppose I didn't want to take on myself the claim that in some ways my plays could lead to social change. In the case of *Sons of Cain* something about society at that time did anger me. This was the blatant evidence of massive high-level corruption revealed by *The Age/National Times* tapes and the inactivity of the Government in investigating what was on those tapes. . . . A specific anger about society or something that was happening in society certainly sparked that play. In some other plays, such as *The Perfectionist,* I wanted to investigate the changing nature of the male-female roles in marriage. I suppose, because that problem was affecting me and my immediate friends, it could be said that a personal worry motivated that play. (p. 131)

[Kuch]: Once you have begun to write, are you more interested in exploring problems than in discovering solutions?

In *Sons of Cain* I was more concerned with exploring the complexity of the situation. The play may seem deceptively simple on the surface, but the central problem defies an easy solution. The fact is that the crusading journalist Kevin may in fact be an unwitting tool of the Right Wing. Whether he is or he isn't can't be resolved finally in the play. He is certainly accused of being that by one of the other journalists, Nicole, who tells him: "Well, I hope you take some responsibility for the Right Wing Government that will replace this one when you bring it down." He says, "Well, I will be just as tough on them." She replies, "Belconnen [the media proprietor] won't let you." So maybe it is true that investigative journalism is only let loose by conservative proprietors when there is a Labor Government in power. And the complexities

of that play, about what was morally right and morally wrong, are quite profound and disturbing under the surface of the play. The play is really a straight narrative tale about disclosing corruption—but what do you do when you discover that a government that has brought in a lot of needed social reforms is found to be corrupt in certain areas. I think that question leads to question leads to question, and the further you go into the issues the more you realize that there are no easy solutions.

[Kavanagh]: You once said about **The Removalists** *that you took the logic of the central situation to its end-point. I see a difference between what you did in that play and the plays that you are now writing where the problems are harder to solve. In* **The Removalists** *you resolved the problem dramatically.*

Yes, ***The Removalists*** is resolved dramatically. The two policemen start beating each other to try to set up a situation where they can say that they only acted the way they did because they were being beaten up by Kenny. This is described in the play itself as an exorcism; and it gave me a strong closing image—a neat dramatic ending. But what I was faced with in ***Sons of Cain*** was no possibility of an ending, which is a massive structural problem for a writer. ***Sons of Cain*** is a very pessimistic play. It says that real investigative journalism is a very rare creature in this country because the press is owned by three men who, as Kevin says, are not very interested in investigation. So, at root, it is a pessimistic play. All I can offer at the end of ***Sons of Cain*** is that the editor, Kevin, will keep fighting. I can't even offer the definite conclusion that his fighting is for the general good because it may actually lead to a worse government.

I suppose that earlier plays were more traditional in that they ended with some sort of closure—a happy ending or a tragic ending or something like that. It is much the same with ***The Perfectionist.*** A lot of hard-line feminists would have liked the wife to beat the husband savagely around the head, walk out, and start a new and independent life. But I refuse to bow to that sort of pressure. I want to pose the reality, and the reality that I know, and a lot of other married couples know, is that the cost of breaking up is worse than the cost of staying for both parties. (pp. 131-33)

[Kavanagh]: And the benefits of breaking up, as represented by the handsome young man, are often delusory.

The Perfectionist is in a sense a critique of that also, of that seventies me-generation idea. If a relationship has problems you bail out and find a new one and everyone, including the children, is better off. Well there is a lot of research coming in now to say that that is egotistical nonsense. . . .

[Kavanagh]: In the Preface to **The Perfectionist** *your director says that the last scene was not properly focussed when he put the play into rehearsal—and the process of rehearsal brought it up to completion. Would you tell us what happened?*

I have always had a good relationship with Rodney [the director], and what he got was a sense from the cast, who were a highly intelligent cast, that something was wrong with the end of the play. Now Rodney couldn't put his finger on it, and neither could the cast; they just knew that something was wrong structurally. In the original ending I had the Dane walk out on Barbara, the wife. I think I was venting my feelings of distaste for the Dane at the expense of the structure of the play. I had to let Barbara discover that the problems would be exactly the same if she took up with a controlling male who wanted her to bear children and do certain things. So she was exchanging an older model for a newer model who would manifest the same problems. But that realization had to come to her, and in the initial draft it didn't, and so there was no growth in her character. She was just rejected by the Dane. The cast were right in feeling that this ending was wrong. (p. 133)

In *Sons of Cain* I had the cast with me all the time, as I directed that play myself. We did a lot of reshaping, but not any great structural reshaping—just moment to moment reshaping of the texture.

[Kavanagh]: In the production of **The Perfectionist** *that I saw, I felt that even so we had been let off—but then I can't think of an alternative.*

Perhaps a greater time lag. Perhaps she doesn't come back the next day. Perhaps she really does want to go away and think things through, and find out what it is like to live by herself for a little bit longer. That could have been an alternative. Then, when she finds out what it is like away from the children and away from the emotional support, she may have been able to make a more rational decision. But prolonging the action would have caused structural problems because the audience would have said to themselves: "Oh, yes she is going away and she is going to find out that it is not all roses and she is going to come back"—which is dramatically dead. For once I suppose I was just pushing, just nudging her along too fast; right for structure, but probably wrong for psychology.

[Kuch]: As for the Dane—did you have a specific person in mind as you wrote, or did you think in terms of a type?

I usually start with an image of someone specific. We actually did live in a community with "the Dane" for a while. (p. 134)

[Kavanagh]: Is it true to say that your plays are often about a conflict, which may not be simple, between pragmatism and idealism?

Yes, I think the tension between idealism and pragmatism is one of the fundamental themes in my work. One of the fundamental queries below my writing is this: what kind of creatures are we? I suppose every writer has to face that eventually. When I was going through the tertiary education system in the 60s, it was thought that just about all our attitudes were conditioned and we were infinitely malleable as human beings. After I did Engineering, I did a full Psych course, and what I have just described was the sort of thing that I was taught. Social conditioning was the thing that shaped us and made us what we were. It was a very optimistic view of the world. All those deep rooted things like racism, patriotism, tribalism, even sexual jealousy were thought to be merely the things that we learn as we grow up, and a little bit of the right sort of enlightened liberal humanist conditioning would stamp them out and the world would be wonderful. Well, we still see rampant racism; we still see tribalism with soccer hooligans letting loose; we still see xenophobia; and we still see sexual jealousy. I have slowly come to the view, a fairly pessimistic view, that these deep-rooted instincts are going to be with us for a long time. (pp. 134-35)

Of course, concentration on the personal has its own dangers. . . . I would like to think that there is a compassionate impulse that is biological, somewhere deep in the organism, that occasionally makes us look out beyond ourselves.

[Kuch]: Is that what you would like audiences to go away with—that sense of looking beyond themselves?

I would hope so. But I would always hope to have the moral debate—the moral debate of realism—that most people are pretty selfish, that they look after their own ends, that they don't spend their time righting the injustices of the world. Not that I think that can be changed. In fact, there is some character in most of my plays that always says just that. In *Sons of Cain,* it is the cold character. She is realistic. She says: corruption goes on, but nobody wants to know. She is right. She is speaking the awful truth that nobody really does want to know. All they want to do is live in the breakfast-food world of happy kids on summer mornings. They don't want to know about injustice, intolerance. (pp. 135-36)

[Kuch]: Your plays suggest that Australians seem to like to be taken to a satirical edge. The walk to the edge is necessary for them to feel purged; yet one senses that if the satire threatened to take the audience too far, they might refuse to take even that first step. Do you ever draw back for fear of alienating an audience?

No, I don't consciously—maybe I do unconsciously feel that—but I don't draw back. I push it as hard as I'm feeling the issue at the moment, and as far as my perception of the situation can carry it. In terms of satire, I do think a lot of the humour in the plays is due to the audience recognizing that some deeply self-interested person is using his rational mind to create a smoke-screen as to why he is doing all this for other people's benefit. The capacity for self-deception is immense in the human species, and it can happen at two levels: it can be self-deception (the guy is actually believing that what he is doing is for the common good), or it can be deliberate manipulation, a front. Both can operate and both can be very funny to an audience. When it's deliberate, it's Machiavellian, and Machiavellian characters tend to become very thin when prolonged; so can a self-deception when we recognize that we know we do it.

[Kuch]: The main situation in many of your plays involves conflict between an institution and an individual. To what extent do Australians project their own self-deceptions on to institutions?

Well, a lot of our sense of what we are is bound up with the institution we work in, and I think we adopt institutional attitudes very readily. And it is very easy to rationalize our own needs by claiming that they are important for the common good. One of my plays, called *The Department,* has got that central theme running through it. The staff members of the Department are supposed to be running an institution that caters for the needs of students, but they are in fact running an institution which they have arranged to cater for their own needs. Institutions can indulge in self-deception too. They can believe that they are serving a community, when in actual fact they have been organized to serve the interests of those people who are employed by the institution.

[Kavanagh]: Given that you often begin with a situation or an idea for a character, how does the elaborate forward and backward referring texture of your plays develop?

I do a lot of drafts. I tend to do a very rough draft at first, and then I try to find those legitimate connections that will hopefully make the play resonant. I like to make and to discover structural tie-ups. Somebody once told me that structure is about logical surprises. That may be over-simplifying things. But bad structure is totally predictable. The audience knows from the very minute the play starts how it is going to evolve and how it is going to end. I suppose I consciously try to avoid that, try to create a structure in which there are tie-backs and tie-ins and logical surprises.

[Kuch]: Do you map out your plots, or do you rehearse and revise as you go along?

I've never been very good at doing plot lines or story lines or things like that. For some plays I have had a rough story line and I have had an end point that I am going to. But I usually prefer to start with an amorphous mass, which is a very hastily scribbled first draft, and then try to shape it. It is the organic muddle of starting with a situation and seeing where it leads—that is certainly what happened with *The Removalists.* I then usually try to get the structure working, although that can sometimes happen fairly rapidly. I think I only did two drafts (or perhaps three) of *The Removalists.* (pp. 136-37)

[Kavanagh]: In your plays you seem to be trying to work out a way of reconciling us with our society, in particular with our parents. I notice in your later plays you are using parents as sympathetic, if ambiguous, figures.

It is actually there in an earlier play of mine . . . called *What If You Died Tomorrow,* which was regarded at the time as just being a writer writing autobiographical stuff—which indeed it was! But I think that play does pose the problem very acutely, the problem of finding something admirable about parents who despite massive personal and sexual problems stayed loyally together through a forty-five-year-old marriage; whereas when the young protagonist gets into a bit of trouble, or when he gets bored, he skips out of the marriage and starts something new and exciting. The play contrasts the parents' generation with the younger generation, and by the end the audience hopefully have come to have some admiration for the apparently stultifying life that the parents have led. You have seen some courage and some commitment to making life good for the very son (one of the main reasons the parents stayed together was to provide the best for the son) who then blithely turns around and says all those values of commitment and loyalty are just stupid.

[Kuch]: You often see positive benefits coming from what would usually be thought of as negative emotions: for example, some of the benefits that flow from resentment. A lot of Kevin's drive in Sons of Cain, *for example, derives from his feelings of resentment.*

Yes, Kevin is anything but pure. Philip Adams wrote an article that attacked me and said that I had done a cheap job of hero worship of Brian Toohey and had been nasty to Neville Wran. That was his interpretation of the play. Well, I find the Kevin character a lot more complex than that. His prime motivation perhaps is not to uncover the main springs of corruption—he is not an idealist at base—but he is a boy from a Catholic parish school who really resents the Anglo-Saxon, or the Melbourne Grammar, set. Part of his basic motivation is to pull the bastards down for no other reason than for resentment and aggravation. I am sure there is some idealism in there somewhere, but his prime motivation is social resentment. That of course doesn't necessarily invalidate what he is doing; what he is doing may be invalid for other reasons.

[Kuch]: Do you feel that you treat your characters even-handedly?

I always try and put myself emotionally in the shoes of the character I am writing at the moment. When I am writing Nicole I really try and put her arguments with full force. I don't distance myself and say: this is a horrible character, I will put some arguments that I don't really believe in her mouth. I try and empathize with her position and give her full weight, give her arguments that are equal to Kevin's opposing arguments, or to Bronwen's opposing arguments. I find it very hard to take a moral line in most of my plays. I think I do successfully empathize with the range of characters. For example, in *The Removalists* I don't think I was saying that Simmonds was completely evil. I think what I was saying was that his restricted, awful background, and the sense of constriction that Australian society had imposed on all the characters he came into contact with, meant that he and they had a very narrow view of themselves and their potential. I'm a big man if I am a good fucker and a good fighter was about the only way that Kenny knew of gaining self-esteem. There are many other self-images that a much broader society than the Australian society of that time might have inculcated. So, right from the early days, I wasn't trying to say that some people are hideous human beings, although I have moral shades of grey. I think that what a lot of the plays are doing, particularly in my own mind as I am writing them, is weighing all the characters in the moral balance and saying, "Is he good, bad, or indifferent? What are the shades of grey? What are the good aspects of this character? What are the bad?" For me part of the act of writing a play is forming a moral evaluation of all the characters, while retaining an ambiguity in my own mind about them. I don't think I have ever written a character that I'm prepared to say is a real bad guy or a real good guy. I suppose the nearest I came to a good guy was in *The Club* with the coach, but even so, when the wily administrator says, "Look, would you be prepared to toss out Danny if you can get X?", his self-interest takes over.

[Kavanagh]: What about the Australian language? Is there anything one still can't say in Australian?

I wouldn't think so in terms of profanity. I think that battle has been won.

[Kavanagh]: No, I don't mean in terms of censorship. I mean as a medium of expression.

I'm pushing towards a fuller self-expression in the characters. I have felt a need for that because the communication between the males in my early plays, a communication I felt to be true to my observations of Australian society at that time, tended to be a communication that limited itself to negatives. Communication amongst males about their personal problems seemed to me to be almost non-existent. So writing heart-felt scenes where males bared their souls to each other just didn't seem plausible, correct, or indeed truthful. I suppose as I grow older and as I observe meaningful communication more frequently, a greater intimacy will reveal itself in the plays. But I do think the stereotype is true—that greater intimacy of communication does still take place between women. Circles in which confidences are expressed are a very typical female phenomenon in our society, while males still tend to be competitive loners. (pp. 138-40)

Paul Kavanagh and Peter Kuch, "What Are the Shades of Grey?" in Southerly, *Vol. 47, No. 2, June, 1986, pp. 131-41.*

MEL GUSSOW

Pragmatic self-interest is the key to success in David Williamson's new comedy, *Emerald City.* With sharp satiric thrusts, the playwright skewers opportunism in the movies and, tangentially, in publishing. In this new play . . . the Emerald City is Sydney, the heartbeat of Oz, or Australia. Sydney is, we are told, with all acerbity intended, "New York without the intellect." The view is from Down Under, but the angle is wide and global.

Moving to Sydney from the less competitive environment of Melbourne is Australia's most admired screenwriter. In Australia today, the character's rank is actually held by Mr. Williamson. . . . In other words, *Emerald City* is very much an insider's retort against an industry that feeds him.

Not so secretly hungering for power and money, the protagonist learns to keep all options open, even if it means collaborating with a North Sydney huckster of no discernible talent and king-sized chutzpah. As [Colin] knows, in show business "today's joke is tomorrow's genius." For [Mike], as joke-into-genius, everything is negotiable, beginning with principles. . . .

The new team, uniting art and commerce, turns [Colin's] pet project, an uplifting story about wartime patriotism, into a television mini-series. Though doomed to a low rating, the project gives [Mike] credibility and clout, and before he can say "global village," he is flooded with offers and has become a bicontinental tycoon. . . .

Shady and crass but with a rough-hewn charm, [Mike] has the soul of a dingo and the hide of a hippopotamus. Against him is poised [Colin], a nice guy about to finish last unless he can master the art of adapting himself to the changes in rules. These two characters . . . are at the crossroads of *Emerald City*. . . .

The play is short on plot; and it has its facile comic moments. The relationship between the screenwriter and his wife [Kate], a rising book editor, is less interesting than that between him and [Mike]. But *Emerald City* is impertinent on several levels, and, when applicable, Mr. Williamson names names. Not only is the author malicious about scoundrels in positions of power, he also is candid about an artist's own culpability in his soul-selling. When the characters speak their minds in asides to the audience, it is in jarring contradiction to their actions. . . .

The background is Sydney itself, in which everyone apparently aspires to an office or a home with a harbor view. . . . Prime among the aspirants is the screenwriter's wife, who speaks a socially conscious line until she finds a percentage of profits within her reach. Manipulating on the sidelines are a moneyman and a crusty agent, who warns her clients: "Don't blame the City. The demons are in us." Hype and hypocrisy amusingly help to speed the plow on the road to *Emerald City.*

> Mel Gussow, "Skewering the Movies with Australia as Oz," in The New York Times, *November 30, 1988, p. C20.*

JOHN SIMON

Unfortunately for David Williamson, Australia's leading playwright-scenarist, his fine play *The Club* opened here during a newspaper strike. His equally satisfying screenplay (from his own stage work) for Bruce Beresford's movie *Don's Party* was overlooked by critics and audiences, whose minds must have been on strike. Now comes an incisive, grimly graceful, painfully funny play, *Emerald City*—so let us not be three-time losers. Vastly more relevant to our lives than *The Year of Living Dangerously* (Williamson's biggest hit in America), this examination of how the noble ambition for fame deteriorates into lust for money and power, and how relationships of every kind subsist on deception, deserves our delightedly undivided attention.

Williamson's unabashedly autobiographical hero, Colin, is Australia's premier screenwriter, beloved of critics but often ignored by the public (*there's* a switch for you). He can't understand why such recognition is not tantamount to success, and so packs up his wife and children and moves from staid Melbourne to swinging Sydney, where the prime status symbol is how good your home or office view of the harbor is. Pretending not to harbor such arrant *arrivisme,* Colin nevertheless taunts his wife, Kate, a lowly book editor, for her socialist views, which include titanic efforts to get a protest novel by an aboriginal woman published over the boss's veto. Meanwhile, Colin has problems getting his agent, Elaine, behind his projected patriotic script about Australia's lonely, heroic World War II Coastwatchers, and he finally teams up with Mike, an opportunistic pragmatist whose piddling talent is wagged by an enormous and unsavory social and business savvy.

Mike deserves a berth among the theater's unforgettable comic creations, a larger-than-life pismire whose Machiavellian wheeling and dealing does not exclude a certain ingenuous charm. . . . Colin accepts Mike's suggestion that they turn *The Coastwatchers* into a TV mini-series, to which Mike's contribution is scarcely more than typing. Although the show ends up as a critically acclaimed flop, Mike mendaciously turns it into a major instrument of his rise to the top as scriptwriter and henchman to an omnipotent media dreadnought, and damn the occasional torpedoes. Colin, though not exactly a failure, remains a Prometheus chained to his halfway-up plateau.

Meanwhile, Kate, with the despised Mike's anonymous help, gets the protest novel published and acclaimed. Long restive in her husband's shadow, she climbs to a publishing position of, shall we say, harboreal heights, with a commanding office view of the harbor and an ex officio change of social and sexual philosophy. Whereas Colin's lust for Helen, Mike's sexy mistress, ends in a hilarious fiasco, Kate . . . but no more plot! What makes the play so impressive is its sneakily sweeping forward movement, marvelously propelled by intelligent dialogue in which characters often stop in mid-speech to reveal to us their interior—often contradictory—monologues while the interlocutor holds his pose. It is a time-honored device to which few authors have brought, or carried away from, more lustrous new honors. . . .

Emerald City portrays human rivalry with maximum comic and dramatic effect because it is as humorous as it is witty. Wit is diagnostic, humor is analytical; David Williamson is both. (p. 110)

> John Simon, "Boomerang Town," in New York Magazine, *Vol. 21, No. 49, December 12, 1988, pp. 110-11.*

MIMI KRAMER

Emerald City sounded promising, both as a window on contemporary Australia and as a comedy of ideas. Unfortunately, it sounds better than it plays. This is partly because the basic point Williamson is making about Australia—that it apes the West culturally—is not very interesting. (His one other insight into upper-middle-class Australian life has to do with the horrors of a twenty-four-hour Qantas flight.) Oddly, the play shows signs of the very sense of inferiority and cultural jet lag that are its main targets. It wants us to laugh with Colin at the dated trendiness of "Chardonnay socialists." But Red-bashing is itself passé: Tom Stoppard did it in *The Real Thing,* five seasons ago.

In fact, *Emerald City* often seems like an Australian *hommage* to *The Real Thing*—but written in the manner of Michael Frayn's *Benefactors.* Like Stoppard's play, Williamson's is about a successful writer driven by the idiocies of an uncomprehending world to question the merits of what he writes; like Frayn's play, it relies on characters' stepping momentarily out of the action and addressing the audience. But Frayn used the device of shifting points of view to weave labyrinthine complexities of irony and motivation. The ironies in Williamson's play are all linear: they're reversals of fortune rather than of perception. And the play is very repetitive. There are too many cocktail-party scenes, too many references to oceanfront property and harbor views, too many instances of Colin sounding off to his wife. We get not one but two Qantas jokes, not one but two comic tirades from the hero about how immensely rich and powerful he wants to become. There are lines that jangle ("You're about as ruthless as a toothless old pussycat"), and lines that take too long to arrive at a simple thought ("Mike is so insensitive he'd be hard put to spot the irritation on the face of a charging tiger"), and lines we feel we don't need to hear ("Prime-time television in America is to art what McDonald's is to cooking"). Given the way Williamson's hero carries on about artistic freedom, it's ironic that what *Emerald City* needs most is an editor. (p. 83)

Mimi Kramer, "Theatre from Down Under," in The New Yorker, *Vol. LXIV, No. 44, December 19, 1988, pp. 82-3.*

□ Contemporary Literary Criticism

Indexes

Literary Criticism Series
   Cumulative Author Index
Cumulative Nationality Index
Title Index, Volume 56

This Index Includes References to Entries in These Gale Series

Contemporary Literary Criticism

Presents excerpts of criticism on the works of novelists, poets, dramatists, short story writers, scriptwriters, and other creative writers who are now living or who have died since 1960. Cumulative indexes to authors and nationalities are included, as well as an index to titles discussed in the individual volume. Volumes 1-56 are in print.

Twentieth-Century Literary Criticism

Contains critical excerpts by the most significant commentators on poets, novelists, short story writers, dramatists, and philosophers who died between 1900 and 1960. Cumulative indexes to authors, nationalities, and titles discussed are included in each new volume. Volumes 1-33 are in print.

Nineteenth-Century Literature Criticism

Offers significant passages from criticism on authors who died between 1800 and 1899. Cumulative indexes to authors, nationalities, and titles discussed are included in each new volume. Volumes 1-23 are in print.

Literature Criticism from 1400 to 1800

Compiles significant passages from the most noteworthy criticism on authors of the fifteenth through eighteenth centuries. Cumulative indexes to authors, nationalities, and titles discussed are included in each new volume. Volumes 1-11 are in print.

Classical and Medieval Literature Criticism

Offers excerpts of criticism on the works of world authors from classical antiquity through the fourteenth century. Cumulative indexes to authors, titles, and critics are included in each volume. Volumes 1-3 are in print.

Short Story Criticism

Compiles excerpts of criticism on short fiction by writers of all eras and nationalities. Cumulative indexes to authors, nationalities, and titles discussed are included in each new volume. Volumes 1-3 are in print.

Children's Literature Review

Includes excerpts from reviews, criticism, and commentary on works of authors and illustrators who create books for children. Cumulative indexes to authors, nationalities, and titles discussed are included in each new volume. Volumes 1-18 are in print.

Contemporary Authors Series

Encompasses five related series. *Contemporary Authors* provides biographical and bibliographical information on more than 92,000 writers of fiction, nonfiction, poetry, journalism, drama, motion pictures, and other fields. Each new volume contains sketches on authors not previously covered in the series. Volumes 1-127 are in print. *Contemporary Authors New Revision Series* provides completely updated information on active authors covered in previously published volumes of *CA*. Only entries requiring significant change are revised for *CA New Revision Series*. Volumes 1-27 are in print. *Contemporary Authors Permanent Series* consists of updated listings for deceased and inactive authors removed from the original volumes 9-36 when these volumes were revised. Volumes 1-2 are in print. *Contemporary Authors Autobiography Series* presents specially commissioned autobiographies by leading contemporary writers. Volumes 1-9 are in print. *Contemporary Authors Bibliographical Series* contains primary and secondary bibliographies as well as analytical bibliographical essays by authorities on major modern authors. Volumes 1-2 are in print.

Dictionary of Literary Biography

Encompasses three related series. *Dictionary of Literary Biography* furnishes illustrated overviews of authors' lives and works and places them in the larger perspective of literary history. Volumes 1-84 are in print. *Dictionary of Literary Biography Documentary Series* illuminates the careers of major figures through a selection of literary documents, including letters, notebook and diary entries, interviews, book reviews, and photographs. Volumes 1-6 are in print. *Dictionary of Literary Biography Yearbook* summarizes the past year's literary activity with articles on genres, major prizes, conferences, and other timely subjects and includes updated and new entries on individual authors. Yearbooks for 1980-1988 are in print. A cumulative index to authors and articles is included in each new volume.

Concise Dictionary of American Literary Biography

A six-volume series that collects revised and updated sketches on major American authors that were originally presented in *Dictionary of Literary Biography*. Volumes 1-3 are in print.

Something about the Author Series

Encompasses two related series. *Something about the Author* contains heavily illustrated biographical sketches on juvenile and young adult authors and illustrators from all eras. Volumes 1-56 are in print. *Something about the Author Autobiography Series* presents specially commissioned autobiographies by prominent authors and illustrators of books for children and young adults. Volumes 1-8 are in print.

Yesterday's Authors of Books for Children

Contains heavily illustrated entries on children's writers who died before 1961. Complete in two volumes. Volumes 1-2 are in print.

Literary Criticism Series
Cumulative Author Index

This index lists all author entries in the Gale Literary Criticism Series and includes cross-references to other Gale sources. References in the index are identified as follows:

Author Index

CONTEMPORARY LITERARY CRITICISM, Vol. 56

Doctorow, E(dgar) L(aurence)
1931- . . . . CLC 6, 11, 15, 18, 37, 44
See also CANR 2; CA 45-48; DLB 2, 28;
DLB-Y 80

Dodgson, Charles Lutwidge 1832-1898
See Carroll, Lewis
See also YABC 2

Doeblin, Alfred 1878-1957 . . . . TCLC 13
See also CA 110

Doerr, Harriet 1910- . . . . CLC 34
See also CA 117, 122

Donaldson, Stephen R. 1947- . . . . . . CLC 46
See also CANR 13; CA 89-92

Donleavy, J(ames) P(atrick)
1926- . . . . CLC 1, 4, 6, 10, 45
See also CA 9-12R; DLB 6

Donnadieu, Marguerite 1914-
See Duras, Marguerite

Donne, John 1572?1631 . . . . LC 10

Donnell, David 1939? . . . . CLC 34

Donoso, Jose 1924- . . . . CLC 4, 8, 11, 32
See also CA 81-84

Donovan, John 1928- . . . . CLC 35
See also CLR 3; CA 97-100; SATA 29

Doolittle, Hilda 1886-1961
See H(ilda) D(oolittle)
See also CA 97-100; DLB 4, 45

Dorfman, Ariel 1942- . . . . CLC 48

Dorn, Ed(ward Merton) 1929- . . . CLC 10, 18
See also CA 93-96; DLB 5

Dos Passos, John (Roderigo)
1896-1970 . . . CLC 1, 4, 8, 11, 15, 25, 34
See also CANR 3; CA 1-4R;
obituary CA 29-32R; DLB 4, 9;
DLB-DS 1

Dostoevski, Fedor Mikhailovich
1821-1881 . . . . NCLC 2, 7, 21; SSC 2

Doughty, Charles (Montagu)
1843-1926 . . . . TCLC 27
See also CA 115; DLB 19, 57

Douglas, George 1869-1902 . . . . TCLC 28

Douglass, Frederick 1817-1895 . . . . NCLC 7
See also SATA 29; DLB 1, 43, 50;
CDALB 1640-1865

Dourado, (Waldomiro Freitas) Autran
1926- . . . . CLC 23
See also CA 25-28R

Dove, Rita 1952- . . . . CLC 50
See also CA 109

Dowson, Ernest (Christopher)
1867-1900 . . . . TCLC 4
See also CA 105; DLB 19

Doyle, (Sir) Arthur Conan
1859-1930 . . . . TCLC 7, 26
See also CA 104, 122; SATA 24; DLB 18,
70

Dr. A 1933-
See Silverstein, Alvin and Virginia B(arbara
Opshelor) Silverstein

Drabble, Margaret
1939- . . . . CLC 2, 3, 5, 8, 10, 22, 53
See also CANR 18; CA 13-16R; SATA 48;
DLB 14

Drayton, Michael 1563-1631 . . . . LC 8

Dreiser, Theodore (Herman Albert)
1871-1945 . . . . TCLC 10, 18
See also CA 106; SATA 48; DLB 9, 12;
DLB-DS 1; CDALB 1865-1917

Drexler, Rosalyn 1926- . . . . CLC 2, 6
See also CA 81-84

Dreyer, Carl Theodor 1889-1968. . . . CLC 16
See also obituary CA 116

Drieu La Rochelle, Pierre
1893-1945 . . . . TCLC 21
See also CA 117; DLB 72

Droste-Hulshoff, Annette Freiin von
1797-1848 . . . . NCLC 3

Drummond, William Henry
1854-1907 . . . . TCLC 25

Drummond de Andrade, Carlos 1902-
See Andrade, Carlos Drummond de

Drury, Allen (Stuart) 1918- . . . . CLC 37
See also CANR 18; CA 57-60

Dryden, John 1631-1700 . . . . LC 3

Duberman, Martin 1930- . . . . CLC 8
See also CANR 2; CA 1-4R

Dubie, Norman (Evans, Jr.) 1945- . . CLC 36
See also CANR 12; CA 69-72

Du Bois, W(illiam) E(dward) B(urghardt)
1868-1963 . . . . CLC 1, 2, 13
See also CA 85-88; SATA 42; DLB 47, 50;
CDALB 1865-1917

Dubus, Andre 1936- . . . . CLC 13, 36
See also CANR 17; CA 21-24R

Ducasse, Isidore Lucien 1846-1870
See Lautreamont, Comte de

Duclos, Charles Pinot 1704-1772 . . . . . LC 1

Dudek, Louis 1918- . . . . CLC 11, 19
See also CANR 1; CA 45-48

Dudevant, Amandine Aurore Lucile Dupin
1804-1876
See Sand, George

Duerrenmatt, Friedrich 1921-
See also CA 17-20R

Duffy, Bruce 19?? . . . . CLC 50

Duffy, Maureen 1933- . . . . CLC 37
See also CA 25-28R; DLB 14

Dugan, Alan 1923- . . . . CLC 2, 6
See also CA 81-84; DLB 5

Duhamel, Georges 1884-1966 . . . . CLC 8
See also CA 81-84; obituary CA 25-28R

Dujardin, Edouard (Emile Louis)
1861-1949 . . . . TCLC 13
See also CA 109

Duke, Raoul 1939-
See Thompson, Hunter S(tockton)

Dumas, Alexandre (Davy de la Pailleterie)
(pere) 1802-1870 . . . . NCLC 11
See also SATA 18

Dumas, Alexandre (fils)
1824-1895 . . . . NCLC 9

Dumas, Henry (L.) 1934-1968 . . . . . . CLC 6
See also CA 85-88; DLB 41

Du Maurier, Daphne 1907- . . . . . . CLC 6, 11
See also CANR 6; CA 5-8R; SATA 27

Dunbar, Paul Laurence
1872-1906 . . . . TCLC 2, 12
See also CA 104; SATA 34; DLB 50, 54;
CDALB 1865-1917

Duncan (Steinmetz Arquette), Lois
1934- . . . . CLC 26
See also Arquette, Lois S(teinmetz)
See also CANR 2; CA 1-4R; SAAS 2;
SATA 1, 36

Duncan, Robert (Edward)
1919-1988 . . . . CLC 1, 2, 4, 7, 15, 41, 55
See also CA 9-12R; obituary CA 124;
DLB 5, 16

Dunlap, William 1766-1839 . . . . NCLC 2
See also DLB 30, 37

Dunn, Douglas (Eaglesham)
1942- . . . . CLC 6, 40
See also CANR 2; CA 45-48; DLB 40

Dunn, Elsie 1893-1963
See Scott, Evelyn

Dunn, Stephen 1939- . . . . CLC 36
See also CANR 12; CA 33-36R

Dunne, Finley Peter 1867-1936. . . . TCLC 28
See also CA 108; DLB 11, 23

Dunne, John Gregory 1932- . . . . CLC 28
See also CANR 14; CA 25-28R; DLB-Y 80

Dunsany, Lord (Edward John Moreton Drax
Plunkett) 1878-1957. . . . . TCLC 2
See also CA 104; DLB 10

Durang, Christopher (Ferdinand)
1949- . . . . CLC 27, 38
See also CA 105

Duras, Marguerite
1914- . . . . CLC 3, 6, 11, 20, 34, 40
See also CA 25-28R

Durban, Pam 1947- . . . . CLC 39

Durcan, Paul 1944- . . . . CLC 43

Durrell, Lawrence (George)
1912- . . . . CLC 1, 4, 6, 8, 13, 27, 41
See also CA 9-12R; DLB 15, 27

Durrenmatt, Friedrich
1921- . . . . CLC 1, 4, 8, 11, 15, 43
See also Duerrenmatt, Friedrich
See also DLB 69

Dwight, Timothy 1752-1817 . . . . . . NCLC 13
See also DLB 37

Dworkin, Andrea 1946- . . . . CLC 43
See also CANR 16; CA 77-80

Dylan, Bob 1941- . . . . CLC 3, 4, 6, 12
See also CA 41-44R; DLB 16

East, Michael 1916-
See West, Morris L.

Eastlake, William (Derry) 1917- . . . . . CLC 8
See also CAAS 1; CANR 5; CA 5-8R;
DLB 6

Eberhart, Richard 1904- . . . CLC 3, 11, 19, 56
See also CANR 2; CA 1-4R; DLB 48;
CDALB 1941-1968

Eberstadt, Fernanda 1960- . . . . CLC 39

Echegaray (y Eizaguirre), Jose (Maria Waldo)
1832-1916 . . . . TCLC 4
See also CA 104

Echeverria, (Jose) Esteban (Antonino)
1805-1851 . . . . NCLC 18

Author Index

Author Index

     CONTEMPORARY LITERARY CRITICISM, Vol. 56

Author Index

Richardson, Ethel   1870-1946
See Richardson, Henry Handel
See also CA 105

Richardson, Henry Handel
1870-1946 .... **TCLC 4**
See also Richardson, Ethel

Richardson, Samuel   1689-1761 .... **LC 1**
See also DLB 39

Richler, Mordecai
1931- .... **CLC 3, 5, 9, 13, 18, 46**
See also CA 65-68; SATA 27, 44; DLB 53

Richter, Conrad (Michael)
1890-1968 .... **CLC 30**
See also CA 5-8R; obituary CA 25-28R;
SATA 3; DLB 9

Richter, Johann Paul Friedrich   1763-1825
See Jean Paul

Riding, Laura   1901- .... **CLC 3, 7**
See also Jackson, Laura (Riding)

Riefenstahl, Berta Helene Amalia   1902-
See Riefenstahl, Leni
See also CA 108

Riefenstahl, Leni   1902- .... **CLC 16**
See also Riefenstahl, Berta Helene Amalia

Rilke, Rainer Maria
1875-1926 .... **TCLC 1, 6, 19**
See also CA 104

Rimbaud, (Jean Nicolas) Arthur
1854-1891 .... **NCLC 4**

Ringwood, Gwen(dolyn Margaret) Pharis
1910-1984 .... **CLC 48**
See also obituary CA 112

Rio, Michel   19?? .... **CLC 43**

Ritsos, Yannis   1909- .... **CLC 6, 13, 31**
See also CA 77-80

Ritter, Erika   1948? .... **CLC 52**

Rivers, Conrad Kent   1933-1968 ...... **CLC 1**
See also CA 85-88; DLB 41

Roa Bastos, Augusto   1917- .... **CLC 45**

Robbe-Grillet, Alain
1922- ...... **CLC 1, 2, 4, 6, 8, 10, 14, 43**
See also CA 9-12R

Robbins, Harold   1916- .... **CLC 5**
See also CA 73-76

Robbins, Thomas Eugene   1936-
See Robbins, Tom
See also CA 81-84

Robbins, Tom   1936- .... **CLC 9, 32**
See also Robbins, Thomas Eugene
See also DLB-Y 80

Robbins, Trina   1938- .... **CLC 21**

Roberts, (Sir) Charles G(eorge) D(ouglas)
1860-1943 .... **TCLC 8**
See also CA 105; SATA 29

Roberts, Kate   1891-1985 .... **CLC 15**
See also CA 107; obituary CA 116

Roberts, Keith (John Kingston)
1935- .... **CLC 14**
See also CA 25-28R

Roberts, Kenneth   1885-1957 ..... **TCLC 23**
See also CA 109; DLB 9

Roberts, Michele (B.)   1949- .... **CLC 48**
See also CA 115

Robinson, Edwin Arlington
1869-1935 .... **TCLC 5**
See also CA 104; DLB 54;
CDALB 1865-1917

Robinson, Henry Crabb
1775-1867 .... **NCLC 15**

Robinson, Jill   1936- .... **CLC 10**
See also CA 102

Robinson, Kim Stanley   19?? .... **CLC 34**

Robinson, Marilynne   1944- .... **CLC 25**
See also CA 116

Robinson, Smokey   1940- .... **CLC 21**

Robinson, William   1940-
See Robinson, Smokey
See also CA 116

Robison, Mary   1949- .... **CLC 42**
See also CA 113, 116

Roddenberry, Gene   1921- .... **CLC 17**

Rodgers, Mary   1931- .... **CLC 12**
See also CANR 8; CA 49-52; SATA 8

Rodgers, W(illiam) R(obert)
1909-1969 .... **CLC 7**
See also CA 85-88; DLB 20

Rodriguez, Claudio   1934- .... **CLC 10**

Roethke, Theodore (Huebner)
1908-1963 ...... **CLC 1, 3, 8, 11, 19, 46**
See also CA 81-84; CABS 2; SAAS 1;
DLB 5; CDALB 1941-1968

Rogers, Sam   1943-
See Shepard, Sam

Rogers, Will(iam Penn Adair)
1879-1935 .... **TCLC 8**
See also CA 105; DLB 11

Rogin, Gilbert   1929- .... **CLC 18**
See also CANR 15; CA 65-68

Rohan, Koda   1867-1947 .... **TCLC 22**

Rohmer, Eric   1920- .... **CLC 16**
See also Scherer, Jean-Marie Maurice

Rohmer, Sax   1883-1959 .... **TCLC 28**
See also Ward, Arthur Henry Sarsfield
See also DLB 70

Roiphe, Anne (Richardson)
1935- .... **CLC 3, 9**
See also CA 89-92; DLB-Y 80

Rolfe, Frederick (William Serafino Austin
Lewis Mary)   1860-1913 ...... **TCLC 12**
See also CA 107; DLB 34

Rolland, Romain   1866-1944 ...... **TCLC 23**
See also CA 118

Rolvaag, O(le) E(dvart)
1876-1931 .... **TCLC 17**
See also CA 117; DLB 9

Romains, Jules   1885-1972 .... **CLC 7**
See also CA 85-88

Romero, Jose Ruben   1890-1952 ... **TCLC 14**
See also CA 114

Ronsard, Pierre de   1524-1585 .... **LC 6**

Rooke, Leon   1934- .... **CLC 25, 34**
See also CA 25-28R

Roper, William   1498-1578 .... **LC 10**

Rosa, Joao Guimaraes   1908-1967 ... **CLC 23**
See also obituary CA 89-92

Rosen, Richard (Dean)   1949- .... **CLC 39**
See also CA 77-80

Rosenberg, Isaac   1890-1918 ...... **TCLC 12**
See also CA 107; DLB 20

Rosenblatt, Joe   1933- .... **CLC 15**
See also Rosenblatt, Joseph

Rosenblatt, Joseph   1933-
See Rosenblatt, Joe
See also CA 89-92

Rosenfeld, Samuel   1896-1963
See Tzara, Tristan
See also obituary CA 89-92

Rosenthal, M(acha) L(ouis)   1917- ... **CLC 28**
See also CAAS 6; CANR 4; CA 1-4R;
DLB 5

Ross, (James) Sinclair   1908- .... **CLC 13**
See also CA 73-76

Rossetti, Christina Georgina
1830-1894 .... **NCLC 2**
See also SATA 20; DLB 35

Rossetti, Dante Gabriel
1828-1882 .... **NCLC 4**
See also DLB 35

Rossetti, Gabriel Charles Dante   1828-1882
See Rossetti, Dante Gabriel

Rossner, Judith (Perelman)
1935- .... **CLC 6, 9, 29**
See also CANR 18; CA 17-20R; DLB 6

Rostand, Edmond (Eugene Alexis)
1868-1918 .... **TCLC 6**
See also CA 104

Roth, Henry   1906- .... **CLC 2, 6, 11**
See also CAP 1; CA 11-12; DLB 28

Roth, Joseph   1894-1939 .... **TCLC 33**

Roth, Philip (Milton)
1933- ...... **CLC 1, 2, 3, 4, 6, 9, 15, 22,
31, 47**
See also CANR 1, 22; CA 1-4R; DLB 2, 28;
DLB-Y 82

Rothenberg, Jerome   1931- .... **CLC 6**
See also CANR 1; CA 45-48; DLB 5

Roumain, Jacques   1907-1944 ..... **TCLC 19**
See also CA 117

Rourke, Constance (Mayfield)
1885-1941 .... **TCLC 12**
See also YABC 1; CA 107

Rousseau, Jean-Baptiste   1671-1741 ... **LC 9**

Roussel, Raymond   1877-1933 ..... **TCLC 20**
See also CA 117

Rovit, Earl (Herbert)   1927- .... **CLC 7**
See also CANR 12; CA 5-8R

Rowe, Nicholas   1674-1718 .... **LC 8**

Rowson, Susanna Haswell
1762-1824 .... **NCLC 5**
See also DLB 37

Roy, Gabrielle   1909-1983 .... **CLC 10, 14**
See also CANR 5; CA 53-56;
obituary CA 110

Rozewicz, Tadeusz   1921- .... **CLC 9, 23**
See also CA 108

Ruark, Gibbons   1941- .... **CLC 3**
See also CANR 14; CA 33-36R

Rubens, Bernice   192? .... **CLC 19, 31**
See also CA 25-28R; DLB 14

     CONTEMPORARY LITERARY CRITICISM, Vol. 56

CONTEMPORARY LITERARY CRITICISM, Vol. 56

CLC Cumulative Nationality Index

Nationality Index

Nationality Index

Nationality Index

CLC-56 Title Index

Title Index